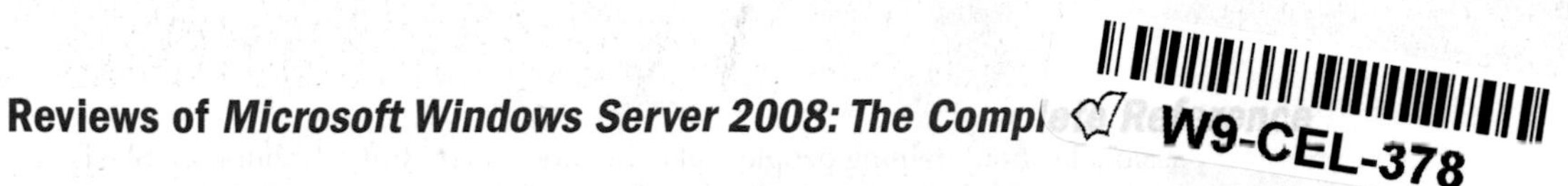

Reviews of *Microsoft Windows Server 2008: The Complete Reference*

"I've had the pleasure of working with Danielle and Nelson on other projects and enjoyed their previous books. When I heard they were working on a new book called *Microsoft Windows Server 2008: The Complete Reference*, I was very much looking forward to picking it up. I am impressed with Danielle's and Nelson's approach of showing Windows Server 2008 running in and on a virtualized Datacenter and distributing the resources to applications and servers as required. I am a firm believer of the power of virtualization and how businesses of all sizes can leverage it to more efficiently run their business. If you think virtualization is not for you and lives in the realm of test and development—think again. "The Complete Reference" is well worth the read."

—Rick Claus,
IT Pro Advisor, Microsoft Canada, blog: http://blogs.technet.com/canitpro

"I have no hesitation in saying this is a 'MUST have' book for any serious Windows Server 2008 implementer. It is equally useful to the managerial cadre planning a Windows Server 2008 deployment as well as the system administrator working to do the actual deployment and the people maintaining the network once the deployment is complete."

—Dilip Naik,
Microsoft File Systems/Storage MVP, author of *Inside Windows Storage*

"Build your network the right way with expert advice! This book provides real-world help in implementing Windows Server 2008 with attention to the use of Virtualization solutions covering all you need to know in one well-written guide to success."

—Bob Kelly,
AppDeploy.com & Technical Reviewer

"*Microsoft Windows Server 2008: The Complete Reference* is a one-stop-shop for learning all the essential steps for setting up Window Server 2008—but also a great guide on how to take advantage of Hyper-V virtualization to transform your IT infrastructure into a dynamic computing environment."

—David Greschler,
Director, Integrated Virtualization Strategy, Microsoft

About the Authors

Danielle Ruest is passionate about helping people make the most of computer technology. She is a senior enterprise workflow architect and consultant with over 20 years' experience in project implementations. Her customers include governments and private enterprises of all sizes. Throughout her career, she has led change-management processes, developed and delivered training, provided technical writing services, and managed communications programs during complex technology implementation projects. More recently, Danielle has been involved in the design and support of test, development, and production infrastructures based on virtualization technologies. She is familiar with most components of the Microsoft Windows Server System as well as security implementations, Active Directory Domain Services, Exchange Server, interoperability, manageability and virtualization. In addition, one of her best talents is communications through illustration, portraying complex concepts graphically and therefore, facilitating the understanding of these concepts. She is a Microsoft Most Valuable Professional for the Virtual Machine product line.

Nelson Ruest is passionate about doing things *right* with Microsoft technologies. He is a senior enterprise IT architect with over 25 years' experience in migration planning and network, PC, server, and overall solution design. He was one of Canada's first Microsoft Certified Systems Engineers (MCSEs) and Microsoft Certified Trainers. In his IT career, he has been computer operator, systems administrator, trainer, Help desk operator, support engineer, IT manager, project manager, and now, IT architect. He has also taken part in numerous migration projects, where he was responsible for everything from project to systems design in both the private and public sectors. He is familiar with all versions of Microsoft Windows and the Windows Server System, as well as security, Active Directory Domain Services, Exchange Server, systems management, intra- and extranet configurations, collaboration technologies, office automation, and interoperability solutions. He is a Microsoft Most Valuable Professional for the Windows Server product line.

In 2007, Danielle and Nelson released a free eBook: *The Definitive Guide to Vista Migration* (www.realtime-nexus.com/dgvm.htm). They also completed an Microsoft Press Training Kit: *MCITP Self-Paced Training Kit (Exam 70-238) Deploying Messaging Solutions with Microsoft Exchange Server 2007* and wrote the second half of the *Deploying and Administrating Windows Vista Bible* for Wiley, as well as the *MCTS Self-Paced Training Kit (Exam 70-640): Configuring Windows Server® 2008 Active Directory* for Microsoft Press. Nelson and Danielle are delivering a multi-city tour on Virtualization: Controlling Server Sprawl (http://events.techtarget.com/virtualization2008) which is designed to help organizations move to a virtual infrastructure.

Both are also co-authors of *Preparing for .NET Enterprise Technologies* (www.Reso-Net.com/EMF), which, despite its name, focuses on implementing and managing locked-down desktops, *Windows Server 2003: Best Practices for Enterprise Deployments* (www.Reso-Net.com/WindowsServer), a step-by-step guide for the implementation of an enterprise network, and *Windows Server 2003 Pocket Administrator* (www.Reso-Net.com/PocketAdmin), a guide for managing a network on a day-to-day basis. Both are involved as freelance writers for several IT publications, as well as producing white papers for various vendors (www.reso-net.com/articles.asp?m=8) and delivering Webcasts and conferences (www.reso-net.com/presentation.asp?m=7).

Nelson and Danielle work for Resolutions Enterprises, a consulting firm focused on IT infrastructure design. Resolutions Enterprises can be found at www.Reso-Net.com.

About the Technical Editor

Bob Kelly has worked in the IT field for over 18 years and has become well known as an expert on the subject of Windows desktop management. He has performed consulting services for a host of government and commercial customers, implementing various systems management solutions, and customizing them to meet their needs. Bob has authored many books and articles on the topics of scripting and desktop management, but is most well known as the founder of the online resource AppDeploy.com (www.appdeploy.com), a thriving community focused on application deployment. He is also author of a scripting column at *MCP Magazine* (http://mcpmag.com/columns/columnist.asp?ColumnistsID=24). Bob is president and co-founder of iTripoli, Inc. who brings you the Admin Script Editor (www.adminscripteditor.com), a unique and full-featured scripting environment specifically designed for Windows administrators. For more on Bob, visit www.bkelly.com.

Microsoft® Windows Server® 2008: The Complete Reference

Danielle Ruest
Nelson Ruest

New York Chicago San Francisco
Lisbon London Madrid Mexico City
Milan New Delhi San Juan
Seoul Singapore Sydney Toronto

The McGraw-Hill Companies

Library of Congress Cataloging-in-Publication Data

Ruest, Danielle.
Microsoft Windows server 2008 : the complete reference / Danielle Ruest & Nelson Ruest. — 1st ed.
p. cm.
ISBN 978-0-07-226365-7 (alk. paper)
1. Microsoft Windows server. 2. Operating systems (Computers) I. Ruest, Nelson. II. Title.
QA76.76.O63R865 2008
005.4'476—dc22

2008002847

McGraw-Hill books are available at special quantity discounts to use as premiums and sales promotions, or for use in corporate training programs. To contact a representative, please visit the Contact Us pages at www.mhprofessional.com.

Microsoft® Windows Server® 2008: The Complete Reference

1234567890 DOC DOC 0198

ISBN 978-0-07-226265-7
MHID 0-07-226365-2

Sponsoring Editor
Jane K. Brownlow

Editorial Supervisor
Patty Mon

Project Management
Madhu Bhardwaj, International Typesetting and Composition

Acquisitions Coordinator
Jennifer Housh

Technical Editor
Bob Kelly

Copy Editor
Lisa McCoy

Proofreader
Nigel O'Brien

Indexer
Kevin Broccoli

Production Supervisor
Jim Kussow

Composition
International Typesetting and Composition

Illustration
Danielle Ruest, Resolutions Enterprises Ltd.

International Typesetting and Composition

Art Director, Cover
Jeff Weeks

This book is dedicated to all of our readers.
We do hope you make the most of it and follow the advice it contains.
This has been many years in the making, but you'll find the content
is solid and chock-full of advice on all facets of network implementation.
Good luck with your deployment!

Contents at a Glance

Contents

Foreword

The first time I met Danielle and Nelson Ruest, they drew me a picture of a bullseye and said this was the future of software management. They explained that each circle represented a different part of the computing stack. At the center was the application. In the ring around the center was data, and within the outside ring was the operating system. If we could isolate each of these layers using virtualization, they described, it would make managing software dramatically easier. All the pieces could be put together without the testing and configuration that everyone had come to assume was part of the process. Instead, your management system would know what operating system, data and apps each person needed, and it would shoot out the right bullseye to the right person in real time. We agreed this was an excellent vision for virtualization, but one that would take a number of years to come true.

With the arrival of Windows Server 2008, this dream is one step closer to reality. Windows Server 2008 represents substantial advances around Web and security, but it also includes a brand-new feature: virtualization. Called Hyper-V, this feature means virtualization will be a standard part of using Windows servers. All the benefits of today's server virtualization—consolidation, power and space savings, and accelerated workload provisioning and business continuity—will now become an integral part of the way companies manage their Windows Server infrastructure.

But this is just the beginning. As more and more servers become virtualized with Hyper-V, the Ruests' "bullseye" vision for software management will get closer to reality as companies transform their server farms into "hypervisor farms"—pools of computing power defined by the total compute power of all physical servers that have been virtualized. This is the vision of the dynamic datacenter, where workloads are provisioned in real time and moved based on load and priorities, resulting in a more agile IT environment that can respond much faster to a business' needs. However, virtualization alone will not be enough to make this vision come true. It also requires management.

With virtualization, the role of systems management goes from important to *essential.* Management shows you where your virtualized resources reside (since they're no longer installed in one location) and, even more importantly, it enables the real-time allocation of resources—which is one of the core principles of a dynamic datacenter. At Microsoft, we have designed the System Center management suite (made up of Virtual Machine Manager, Operations Manager, Configuration Manager, and Data Protection Manager) to build the foundation for a dynamic datacenter by providing the provisioning, monitoring, and backup tools for both virtual and physical environments, both desktops and servers, both operating system and applications, and across multiple hypervisors—all from a single management console.

Today, in 2008, industry analysts estimate that less than 10 percent of servers worldwide are virtualized. One of the great things about making virtualization a key feature of Windows Server is that if a company's IT staff is already trained in Windows, adding virtualization is a natural extension of their skills. This should dramatically accelerate the percentage of servers that will be virtualized over the next few years. And that's where Danielle and Nelson's excellent book plays a critical role.

Microsoft Windows Server 2008: The Complete Reference is a one-stop-shop for learning all the essential steps for setting up Window Server 2008—but it's also a great guide on how to take advantage of Hyper-V virtualization to transform your IT infrastructure into a dynamic computing environment. Danielle and Nelson have infused their bullseye vision into the book, explaining not only the tactical uses for this technology, but also how to think strategically about virtualization with Windows Server 2008.

—David Greschler
Director, Integrated Virtualization Strategy, Microsoft Corporation

Acknowledgments

Thank you to our customers for helping us work with them to learn how best to create fully functional networks with Windows Server technologies. Also, thank you to the organizations who participated with us to flesh out the administrative tasks listed in Chapter 13. This list of tasks has been used as the basis of a training course for over four years. Thank you to the course attendees for their insight and helpful comments.

Together, we created a book that should help you, once and for all, gain control of the unruly Windows environments that seem to populate the world.

Thank you to Bob Kelly for his diligent efforts in proofing our book and making sure that its technical content was as right as could be.

Thank you to David Greschler for taking time out of his busy schedule to review and comment on this work.

Thank you to the editorial and preparation team, especially Lisa McCoy for her eagle eye in editing, Madhu Bhardwaj and Patty Mon for a wonderful preparation experience, and Jane Brownlow and McGraw-Hill for giving us the opportunity to help IT professionals everywhere by writing this book.

Introduction

Picture a breathtaking alpine setting, a small village nestled among the Pacific coastal mountains. Two chairs run from the base of the mountains—one to Blackcomb, one to Whistler—both offering some of the best skiing in Western Canada and a lonesome pub located at the base of both mountains, the Longhorn Saloon. Here, skiers come to rest after a full day's run and here is the setting where the software you are preparing to deploy, Windows Server 2008, formerly code-named "Longhorn" Server, first came into being.

Microsoft has parlayed its Windows operating system (OS) into the most popular operating system on the planet, despite the best efforts of its competitors. This applies as much to the desktop as to the server operating system. Now, with the release of a new version of its flagship server OS, Windows Server 2008 (WS08), Microsoft hopes to introduce a new benchmark in ease of use, integrated management capabilities, complete security, and simplicity of deployment, as well as interaction with other operating systems such as UNIX and Linux. Make no mistake. Microsoft has invested heavily in WS08 and has delivered a rock-solid foundation for any network.

WS08 builds on Windows 2000, Windows Server 2003 (WS03), and Windows Server 2003 R2 to provide a complete set of functions and functionalities for both wired and wireless networks of all sizes. Most of you should already be using a version of one of the aforementioned operating systems, so many of the concepts in this book—concepts such as Active Directory, Group Policy, Microsoft Management Console (MMC), and other management technologies of modern Windows server operating systems—will be familiar to you. If, for some unknown reason, you are still working with Windows NT, you will still find this book highly useful, as it includes several chapters reviewing critical information such as Active Directory design and the usefulness of Group Policy.

Since WS08 is a *server* operating system, this book is structured around the strategy you would use to build a network from the ground up, relying on the latest and greatest features offered by the new OS. As such, it is divided into seven parts, each focused on one aspect of the implementation of a new server OS. They include:

- **Part I: Tour Windows Server 2008**, which covers the new feature set of Windows Server 2008 as well as the interface changes built into the OS.
- **Part II: Plan and Prepare**, which helps you plan your network migration and begin the server preparation process through a description of the new imaging and staging capabilities in WS08.

- **Part III: Design Server Roles**, which provides guidelines for the elaboration of network services such as Active Directory, Internet, and remote connectivity, as well as outlining how you put these core services in place.
- **Part IV: Manage Objects with Windows Server 2008**, which outlines the management strategies you should use with WS08 to maintain and offer services to computers, users, and services within your network.
- **Part V: Secure Windows Server 2008,** which focuses on the critical security elements each network must put in place to protect the assets it contains. Even though this section deals specifically with security, standard network security concepts are used throughout the book.
- **Part VI: Migrate to Windows Server 2008**, which focuses on how to migrate existing network components to a WS08-based infrastructure.
- **Part VII: Administer Windows Server 2008**, which provides a comprehensive set of tasks for daily, weekly, and monthly administration of a WS08-based network.

Preparing a network is a complex process—even more so now that Windows is in its third post-NT edition. With Windows NT, decisions were relatively simple because the choices were limited. But with Windows Server 2008, this is no longer the case. It's not surprising, since the network has evolved today from being a loosely coupled series of servers and computers to being an integrated infrastructure providing and supporting the organization's mission. This evolutionary process is not unlike that of the telephone. At first, telephone systems were loosely coupled. Today, worldwide telecommunications systems have converged with Internet-based systems and are now much more complex and complete.

Similarly, networks are now mission-critical. The new organizational network has become a secure, stable, redundant infrastructure that is completely oriented toward the delivery of information technology services to its client base. These services can range from simple file and print systems to complex authentication systems, collaboration environments, or application services. In addition, these services can be made available to two differing communities of users: internal users, over whom you have complete control of the PC, and external users, over whom you have little or no control.

That's why moving or migrating to Windows Server 2008 is much more of a network infrastructure design project than one dealing simply with upgrading to a new technology. Each time you change a technology that is as critical as the OS of your network, it is important, if not essential, to use a complete process, one that includes the following steps:

1. Begin by reviewing organizational needs and requirements. Have they changed since the original network was designed? Are there new requirements defined by changing business rules or business environments? Have emerging technologies affected how your organization functions? The answers to these core questions will serve as the initial input into your new and updated network design.
2. Next, review the features and capabilities of the new OS. Windows Server 2008 sports hundreds of new features and functionalities over its predecessors, but inevitably, they cannot all apply to your situation. During this review, you need to identify which features are—first of all—applicable to organizations and—second—applicable to a network the size of yours. You don't want to waste your time on features that will simply never be used in a corporate network because they target home users.

3. Once you fully understand what you will use from the new OS, move to the design of a comprehensive architecture of the new services you want to take advantage of. WS08 offers many new features that will change the way you work—features such as full IPv6 support, redesigned TCP/IP stack, and improved Terminal Services will have an impact on the way you do things today. Make sure your architecture merges your existing capabilities with those you will add from this new OS.
4. Next, create a proof-of-concept network, one that is designed with the new architecture in mind. Test, test, and test again to make sure that you fully understand how new features will affect the way you do things today.
5. Once you're familiar with the way your new architecture will work, move to the creation of an implementation plan. This plan outlines how you want to deploy the new technologies into your network. Take baby steps and focus on "low-hanging fruit," or features that cost little to implement but provide some immediate returns on investments.
6. Make sure your implementation plan includes a proper deployment strategy, relying on pilot projects first, then moving to full deployment. Pilot projects will help iron out any deficiencies in deployment planning, so don't skip this important step.
7. Finally, make sure your implementation plan includes lots of time for system administrator, Help desk, and operator training. These people are the ones who will make your migration a success or a failure, so don't skimp on the efforts to support them during the migration.

Aligning a project of this magnitude with the business strategies of the organization will make the transition more easily accepted and more profitable for the organization as a whole. Too many organizations cannot fully profit from the benefits of a structured network because they have never taken the time to perform each of these steps. As a result, they don't benefit from the maximum potential or performance of their network.

In fact, planning and preparing for the implementation of Windows Server 2008 should be 80 percent planning, preparing, and testing, and 20 percent implementation. We use this rule to emphasize just how important it is to prepare and test before you implement. We guarantee it. If you use the 80/20 processes outlined in this book, your network will just run. It's as simple as that. This applies to you whether your organization has one or one million users. If your organization is an organization of one, you'll still want to take the time to prepare properly, but you probably won't take the time to invest in automating procedures; you'll still want standard operating procedures, but you probably won't involve a series of technicians and architects to validate them; and, you'll still want to design based on architectural models, but you won't take the time to create them yourself.

Building a network with Windows Server 2008 consists of designing the network architecture and its implementation procedure while identifying opportunities for and relying on standard operating procedures. The network infrastructure is divided into specific service delivery areas that must be supported by a structure for network administration and management. For each aspect of this infrastructure, it is essential to have a complete understanding of the features that WS08 offers in this area. It is also important to identify which of these features offer the best cost/benefit scenario for the enterprise.

For example, in our opinion, very few organizations today can live without Active Directory. For organizations of all sizes, it is always better to take the time to centralize all authentication and authorization services than to keep them distributed through the use of workgroups, because if a change is required, you only have to make it in one central place. Thus, the organization that requires a business-level network infrastructure will not invest in workgroups; they will invest directly in Active Directory, bypassing workgroups altogether. This business-level approach is the one that will be used throughout this book in an effort to facilitate your implementation of Windows Server 2008.

Use a Parallel Network

Building a network based on a server operating system is no small task. Worse, it seems you have to start over every time the server operating system changes. This book provides a structured approach that lets you create a brand-new network that fits your organization's size and needs, and that is built on the best features of Microsoft's new Windows Server 2008 operating system. Ideally, this network will be built in a parallel environment that does not affect your current production network. But if you cannot afford the additional hardware required to build the core set of features into the parallel network, it also outlines how to integrate new features into existing environments without disrupting production environments. We strongly recommend the use of the parallel network approach for several reasons:

- First, when you move to a new operating system, especially a new server operating system, you need to make sure that you do not carry over any legacy components on the servers because they may affect their proper operation. This is why new installations are recommended, even though Microsoft has endeavored to finally make the upgrade process work properly.
- Second, as server operating systems evolve, the manufacturer often discovers new ways of doing things, replacing the old way with a brand-new technology—a technology that often works in a completely different manner. A good example is the comparison of home directories, which are a legacy from the Windows NT days, with the use of folder redirection, which was introduced with Group Policy in Windows Server 2003. Using a parallel network, you can move to the new feature and have no carry-over from the old feature in the new network.
- Third, preparing the new network in parallel lets you ensure that everything is working as expected before loading it up with users. In addition, if problems arise, you can simply tear down the new systems and replace them completely—a luxury you simply do not have when integrating new systems into an existing network.

Then, when you're ready to make the migration, this book outlines how to take security principals, documents, data, and applications and move them from your legacy network to the new, parallel environment. This way, you can immediately begin to profit from the best of this powerful OS. Finally, this book outlines how to administer the network once it is in place.

TIP *Microsoft itself admits that most of their customers tend to migrate to a new network rather than perform an in-place upgrade. As such, this book is the only one on the market that provides you with a fully planned and detailed implementation based on the parallel network.*

To achieve this goal, the book is divided into seven parts, each building on the concepts of the previous parts to finally cover all of the elements required to build your new network. The core concept of this book is its focus on business features—only those features that are relevant to a business environment. Windows Server 2008 is not intended for the home, but if you want to rely on this powerful operating system to build a home network, look for the recommendations for small business networks that are outlined throughout the book. Similarly, medium and large organizations will find recommendations for implementations that fit their needs.

Windows Server 2008 Editions

Ever since the release of Windows NT, Microsoft has been publishing its server operating systems in editions. In Windows Server 2003, there were at first four (then more) editions. Today, WS03 includes Web, Standard, Enterprise, and Datacenter editions, as it did from the very beginning, but it also includes new editions, such as Windows Storage Server 2003, Windows Small Business Server 2003, and Windows Compute Cluster Server 2003—all specialized editions of the server OS that are designed to play specific roles in organizations of various sizes.

Windows Server 2008 will continue this tradition and will also include several different editions. Note that this book focuses on the core editions of Windows Server 2008 only and does not cover editions such as Small Business or Compute Cluster. This book covers the following WS08 editions:

- Windows Server 2008, Standard edition
- Windows Server 2008, Enterprise edition
- Windows Server 2008, Datacenter edition
- Windows Server 2008, Web edition
- Windows Server 2008 for Itanium-Based Systems
- Windows Server 2008 Standard without Hyper-V
- Windows Server 2008 Enterprise without Hyper-V
- Windows Server 2008 Datacenter without Hyper-V

Note that each version that includes Hyper-V is designed to run on 64-bit infrastructures. Most of these systems run on x64 processor architectures, not Itanium, though there is an Itanium version as well. Microsoft has already announced that the next release of Windows Server 2008, release 2 (R2) will only run on 64-bit processors and will no longer be available for 32-bit systems.

NOTE *This book does not cover the Itanium-based edition for obvious reasons. Our testing facility cannot host an Itanium server, but if you do intend to use this version, you'll find that it has a lot of similarity with the x64 editions of Windows Server.*

Each version includes specific feature sets, which are described as follows:

- Windows Server 2008, Standard edition, is designed for most networking tasks. It is aimed at file and printer sharing, Internet connectivity, small-scale application deployment, and collaboration scenarios. It is designed to provide low-cost networking services, where a single machine can operate independently of others. It is often used as a domain controller in an Active Directory deployment, as a standalone file and print server in branch offices or in small to medium organizations, as the basis for collaboration services through Windows SharePoint Services (WSS), and as the front end to any application environment.
- Windows Server 2008, Enterprise edition, provides more robust support for service scenarios that require continuous availability. The Enterprise edition also supports the Microsoft Cluster Service, which lets you connect up to eight systems together to provide high availability for specific services. The Enterprise edition is aimed at infrastructure support, as well as application and Web services support, and is often used to protect systems such as Microsoft Exchange Server or Microsoft SQL Server.
- Windows Server 2008, Datacenter edition, is usually provided by original equipment manufacturers, though it is available as a software OS as well, and is aimed at very large organizations that require constant operation of their most mission-critical applications. It is aimed at business-critical and mission-critical applications demanding the highest level of scalability and availability.
- Windows Server 2008, Web edition, is specifically focused on providing a trimmed-down and secure Web server supporting ASP.NET. This edition does include the Network Load Balancing (NLB) service, so it can be used to provide protection for front-end systems in a high-availability scenario.

New to Windows Server 2008 is the Server Core. This toned-down edition of Windows Server is most famous for its complete lack of graphical interface. Server Core provides the same functionality as the full installation, but does not support all of its scenarios. Server Core includes support for nine server roles. It does include many of the core security features inherent in WS08, such as BitLocker full drive encryption, and will also support the read-only domain controller (RODC). Server Core is a low-maintenance version of Windows that can provide good functionality in key situations. When launched, Server Core only provides access to a command shell window. Scripters and command-line aficionados will delight in this version.

32- and 64-bit Versions

Several editions of Windows Server 2008 support both 32- and 64-bit processors. In fact, these editions will support both x64 and IA64 processors. This book covers both 32-bit, which are called x86, and 64-bit, or x64 processors. IA64 is based on the Itanium microchip from Intel—Itanium is a 64-bit reduced instruction set computer (RISC) processor—and while it is in use in very large organizations, has a very small following. As such, it is not covered in this book, although, since it basically offers the same capabilities as other versions of WS08, the guidance in this book still applies to this version of Windows Server.

x64, on the other hand, offers the most important evolution in computing since the release of 32-bit processors. Because of the exponential nature of microchip technology,

64 bits actually offer significantly more processing power than simply doubling the capability of 32 bits. According to Bill Gates, the coming of 64-bit computing will break all the barriers we face today. That may be true. One thing is certain: x64 machines provide a lot more horsepower than x86 machines. x64 systems run a series of different processors from the two microprocessor manufacturers: from AMD, the Opteron or the Athlon 64; and from Intel, the 64-Bit Xeon or the Pentium with EM64T. What's exciting about these processors is that they are a lot more affordable than the I64 systems. In addition, you have a much larger variety of operating systems to choose from: Windows Vista 64-bit edition, as well as Windows Server 2008 Standard, Enterprise, and Datacenter editions.

There are two ways to work with an x64 system: run native 64-bit software, or run software that is compatible but runs in 32-bit mode. You might think that because the x64 versions of Windows Server and Windows Vista have only been out for a little while that there might not be a lot of applications available for this version of the OS. But that's not the case. According to the Microsoft Web site (see the Windows Server Catalog of Tested Products at www.windowsservercatalog.com), there are hundreds of applications that run in native x64 mode and more are coming. In addition, several more can run in 32-bit compatible mode.

So how does x64 measure up? The first thing you'll notice is that everything—yes, everything—runs faster. That is as you would expect, but it is surprising to see that even applications that aren't designed for the x64 system run faster. Just like the 32-bit version of the operating system, x64 runs a special Windows on Windows (WOW) session that lets 32-bit applications run inside the 64-bit operating system. WOW32 sessions provide better performance than even native 32-bit systems. Why is that? Because of the limitations that x64 finally breaks.

Previously, with a 32-bit system, you needed to use at least Windows Server 2003 Enterprise edition to gain access to more than 4 gigabytes (GB) of random access memory (RAM), then add the /PAE (physical address expansion switch) to the Boot.INI file that controls how the operating system is launched. Although this gave you access to more than 4 GB of RAM, it only fools the system, because a 32-bit machine is limited to a 4-GB address space in the first place. With x64, this limitation changes to 32 GB for Windows Vista and the Standard edition of Window Server, but jumps to 1 terabyte (TB) when running the more advanced editions of the Windows Server operating system. In addition, there is less reliance on the page file for virtual memory expansion in a 64-bit system. This means less disk activity for memory-intensive applications.

These are not the only benefits of x64. It also provides faster input and output (I/O) because it can take advantage of larger data blocks. It provides higher data transfer rates because it can run more concurrent processes. More client connections can be set for a given server, breaking the limits of Transmission Control Protocol/Internet Protocol (TCP/IP) on 32-bit. In fact, Microsoft states that it has been able to vastly reduce the number of servers running Microsoft Update, the Web site providing patch downloads, because each 64-bit server can manage vastly more connections per server. But these file system changes have an impact. For example, your 32-bit third-party backup and restore tool will not work with a 64-bit machine because the file I/O driver is completely different from the 32-bit version.

Not everything works on x64 machines today, while some applications only run on x64 platforms. One good example is Microsoft Exchange Server 2007; it only runs in 64-bit mode.

This is exactly the way it was when 32-bit machines were introduced. One thing is certain: What does work on 64-bits will always work faster. Our advice: If you need speed and you know that your core applications are ready to run on x64, take the plunge. Costs are not that far off from 32-bit systems, and the advantages are far-reaching. If you're buying hardware today and you want to make it last, buy x64 machines.

The Perfect Client: Windows Vista

Microsoft Windows Server 2008 is based on the same code that built Windows Vista. In fact, the code is so similar that Microsoft's releases of this software uses the single-instance store principle—only one copy of a file if it is the same in two or more sources—to giving them the ability to put Vista and Windows Sever 2008 on the same DVD. Therefore, it goes without saying that they are designed to work together better than any other versions of Windows. Of course, you can continue to rely on Windows Server 2003, especially the R2 edition, and on Windows XP with Service Pack 2 or later to run your network. But if you are building a new network based on the feature set that Windows Server 2008 can provide, you should consider upgrading all clients to Windows Vista as well. If you do so, you will gain the following benefits:

- A simplified maintenance model, because both the server and the client use the same mechanism for service packs and updates.
- Central monitoring and reporting, because Vista clients can monitor specific events and report them to a central WS08 server.
- Increase the ease of operating system deployment through Windows Deployment Services (WDS) on WS08. Note that WDS will also run on WS03 with the proper update.
- Increase network protection through the integration of Network Access Protection (NAP) in Windows Server 2008 to ensure that Vista clients are compliant with all security policies and updates before they can access network resources.
- Clients will also have improved performance through the capability of rendering print jobs locally and then sending them on to the server for impression.
- In addition, Vista can cache server resources locally, so the client always stays working, whether the server resource is available or not. Then, once connectivity is restored, the resources update automatically.
- Both Vista and WS08 can take advantage of the new New Technology File System (NTFS) Transactional File System (TFS) to increase disk storage reliability and provide rollback in the event of a failure to write in either the file system or the registry.
- Clients and servers can rely on Quality of Service (QoS) policies to ensure that critical applications benefit from prioritized bandwidth.
- Search is integrated between the client and the server to improve users' ability to locate server resources.
- IPv6 is integrated with both the client and the server, and both use the newly rewritten TCP/IP stack, ensuring better network communications scalability.
- The new Server Message Block (SMB) version 2.0 will provide better performance between Vista and WS08, as well as mutual authentication.

- Terminal Services running on Windows Server 2008 can provide Vista clients with access to applications through the Hypertext Transfer Protocol (HTTP) gateway. In addition, remote applications will operate seamlessly, letting users believe they are actually using local applications.

These are only a few of the features and benefits users of both WS08 and Vista will gain. In addition, there are increased Group Policy settings that are only available between the two updated versions of Windows. Finally, both use the same new interface and rely on the same access to resources through integrated search capabilities. If you want the most of your new WS08 network, you should seriously consider working with Vista as the client.

TIP *For more information on migrating to Windows Vista, look up the free eBook, The Definitive Guide to Vista Migration, by Ruest and Ruest at www.realtime-nexus.com/dgvm.htm.*

TIP *For more information on Windows Server 2008, rely on the Windows Server 2008 Documentation Survival Guide on Microsoft TechNet at http://technet2.microsoft.com/windowsserver2008/en/library/6c504a47-4a82-459f-8755-fe59630f4c1d1033.mspx.*

Build the Dynamic Datacenter

In addition, this book is focused on building the dynamic datacenter. A dynamic datacenter is one where all resources are divided into two categories:

- **Resource Pools** consist of the hardware resources in your datacenter. These hardware resources are made up of the server hardware, the network switches, and the power and cooling systems that make the hardware run.
- **Virtual Service Offerings** consist of the workloads that each hardware resource supports. Workloads are virtual machines that run on top of a hypervisor—a code component that exposes hardware resources to virtualized instances of operating systems.

In this datacenter, the hardware resources in the resource pool are *host systems* that can run between 10 and 20 *guest virtual machines* that make up the virtual service offerings.

This approach addresses resource fragmentation. Today, many datacenters that are not running virtual machines will most often have a utilization that can range from 5 to perhaps 15 percent of their actual resources. This means that each physical instance of a server is wasting more than 80 percent of its resources while still consuming power, generating heat, and taking up space. In today's green datacenters, you can no longer afford to take this approach. Each server you remove from your datacenter will save up to 650,000 kilowatt-hours per year. By turning your hardware resources into host systems, you can now recover those wasted resources and move to 65 to 85 percent utilization. In addition, the dynamic datacenter will provide you with the following benefits:

- **High availability** Virtual workloads can be moved from one physical host to another when needed, ensuring that the virtual service offering is always available to end users.

- **Resource optimization** By working with virtual workloads, you can ensure that you make the most of the hardware resources in your datacenter. If one virtual offering does not have sufficient resources, fire up another hardware host and move it to that host, providing the required resources when the workload demands it.
- **Scalability** Virtualization provides a new model for scalability. When your workloads increase, you can add the required physical resources and control growth in an entirely new manner.
- **Serviceability** Because of built-in virtualization features, your hosts can move one virtual workload from one host to another with little or no disruption to end users. This provides new serviceability models where you can manage and maintain systems without having to cause service disruptions.
- **Cost savings** By moving to virtualization, you will earn savings in hardware reductions, power reductions, and license cost reductions.

The result is less hardware to manage and a leaner, greener datacenter.

Run Physical or Virtual Machines

With the coming of Windows Server 2008 and its embedded virtualization technology, or hypervisor, you need to rethink the way you provide resources and build the datacenter. With the advent of powerful new 64-bit servers running either WS08 Enterprise or Datacenter edition, it has now become possible to virtualize almost every server type, with little or no difference in performance, especially if you base your host server builds on Server Core. Users do not see any difference in operation, whether they are on a virtual or physical machine. And with the advent of the new hypervisor built into WS08, the virtual-versus-physical process becomes completely transparent. That's because unlike previous Microsoft virtualization technologies, which actually resided over the top of the operating system, the new hypervisor resides below the operating system level (see Figure 1).

In addition, the WS08 hypervisor has a very small footprint and does not need an additional operating system to run. When you install the WS08 Hyper-V role with Server Core, the hypervisor is installed directory on top of the hardware. An advantage this model gives you is that all system drivers reside in the virtual machine itself, not in the hypervisor.

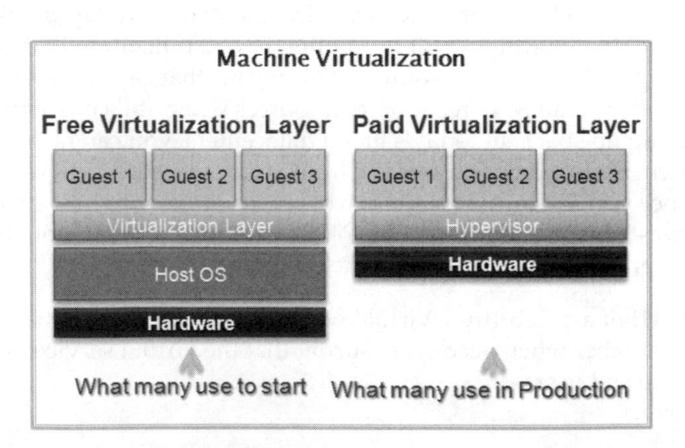

FIGURE 1 Free versus paid hypervisor virtual machine engines

All the hypervisor does is expose hardware resources to the virtual machine (VM). The VM then loads the appropriate drivers to work with these hardware resources. VMs have better access to the host system's resources and run with better performance because there are fewer translation layers between them and the actual hardware.

To further support the move to the dynamic datacenter, Microsoft has changed the licensing mode for virtual instances of Windows Server. This change was first initiated with WS03 R2. In WS03 R2, running an Enterprise edition version on the host system automatically grants four free virtual machine licenses of WS03 R2 Enterprise edition (EE). Add another WS03 R2 EE license, and you can build four more VMs. On average, organizations will run up to 16 virtual machines on a host server, requiring only four actual licenses of WS03 R2 EE.

Microsoft carries over this licensing model with WS08. The first Enterprise edition license grants one license for the host and four licenses for VMs. Each other license grants four more licenses for VMs. If you purchase the WS08 Datacenter edition, you can run an unlimited number of VMs on that host. Remember also that the licenses for VMs support any version of Windows Server. This means you can run Windows NT, Windows 2000, or Windows Server 2003, as well as WS08.

Virtualization provides great savings and decreases general server provisioning timelines, as well as reducing management overhead. For example, one system administrator can manage well over 100 virtualized servers, as well as the hosts required to run them.

TIP *For more information on the benefits of server consolidation and optimization, download a presentation called "Consolidation Roadmap—Improving Your Infrastructure" from www.reso-net.com/presentation.asp?m=7. Microsoft also offers planning and design guidance on virtualization, especially how to decide which Windows technologies to virtualize at http://technet.microsoft.com/en-us/library/bb969099.aspx.*

Push the Virtualization Envelope

WS08 is designed from the ground up to support virtualization. This means that you have the opportunity to change the way you manage servers and services. With the WS08 hypervisor, Hyper-V, there is little difference between a machine running physically on a system and a machine running in a virtual instance. That's because the hypervisor does the same thing as a physical installation would by *exposing* hardware to VMs. The real difference between a physical installation and a VM running on the hypervisor is access to system resources. That's why we propose the following:

- The only installation that should be physical is the hypervisor or the Windows Server Hyper-V role. Everything else should be virtualized.
- Instead of debating whether service offerings—the services that interact with end users—should be physical versus virtual installations, make all of these installations virtual.
- The only installation that is not a VM is the host server installation. It is easy to keep track of this one installation being different.
- It takes about 20 minutes to provision a VM-based new server installation, which is much shorter than that of a physical installation.

- Creating a source VM is easier than creating a source physical installation because you only have to copy the files that make up the VM.
- The difference between a traditional "physical" installation and a virtual installation is the amount of resources you provide the VM running on top of the hypervisor.
- All backups are the same—each machine is just a collection of files, after all. In addition, you can take advantage of the Volume Shadow Copy Service to protect each VM.
- All service-offering operations are the same because each machine is a VM.
- Because all machines are virtual, they are transportable and can easily be moved from one host to another.
- Because VMs are based on a set of files, you can replicate them to other servers, providing a quick and easy means of recovery in the event of a disaster. More on this will be covered in Chapter 11.
- You can segregate the physical and virtual environments, giving them different security contexts and making sure they are protected at all times.
- You can monitor each instance of your "physical" installations, and if you see that it is not using all of the resources you've allocated to it, you can quickly recalibrate it and make better use of your physical resources.
- Every single new feature can be tested in VMs in a lab before it is put into production. If the quality assurance process is detailed enough, you can even move the lab's VM into production instead of rebuilding the service altogether.
- You are running the ultimate virtual datacenter, because all systems are virtual and host systems are nothing but resource pools.

With this in mind, this book divides the tasks of preparing your new network into resource pool and virtual service offering tasks. To facilitate this, the inside front cover includes a Resource Pool table of contents that lets you move directly to the content that will help you prepare hardware resources. This facilitates your move to the dynamic datacenter.

TIP *Microsoft offers the Microsoft Assessment and Planning Solution (MAPS) which will automatically scan your network to propose migration and virtualization strategies. Look for MAPS on www.microsoft.com/downloads.*

Manage as a Project

Migrating to a new server OS is not a task that should be taken lightly—ever. Compare this to a renovation in a house. Depending on the scope of the renovation, you will need to align the appropriate resources, make sure they are available in the right sequential order, and make sure they complete their assigned activities on time and on budget; otherwise, you will never be able to complete the project on time. In addition, if you renovate a house at the same time as you are working, you'll find that if the project is not managed properly, it will affect your ability to continue to generate income—income that is, of course, required to pay for the project. Similarly, when you want to implement a new operating system, you still have to make sure that current operations continue to function smoothly and that they do not overwhelm you and take you away from the new implementation.

This is why you should run this implementation as a project and make sure your project team includes all of the right players. These should focus on at least two groups: one that will work on the elaboration of the network architecture and one that will focus on the preparation of installation procedures and perform the installation itself. The technical project team should include architects, system administrators, installers, user representatives, support personnel, developers, and project managers, or at least personnel whose role is to wear these hats in the organization. You should make sure you involve your current administrative and operational staff in this project. This will help you recover the best of the existing network and help them learn more about the new operating system they will soon be using. Depending on the size of your organization, you may consider hiring replacement staff to free up your existing personnel to work on this project.

In addition, you need to make sure that you involve the right stakeholders. Not having the right stakeholders can be as disastrous as not making the right technical decisions.

Finally, managing a project of this magnitude can be complex and can give you the impression it is never-ending, unless you structure it properly. To facilitate the process, each chapter has been designed to help you structure the technical activities needed to perform the migration. This does not mean that every chapter needs to be addressed in a sequential order. Though this is possible, and even appropriate in some cases, in very large organizations, it would improperly stretch the project timeline. Some chapters require the participation of your entire technical project team, but others do not because they are focused on specific areas of technical expertise.

Figure 2 illustrates a sample timeline distribution for the activities required to migrate to this OS. It lets you divide the technical project team in appropriate subgroups to shorten the overall project timeline while still achieving your goal: doing the best implementation you

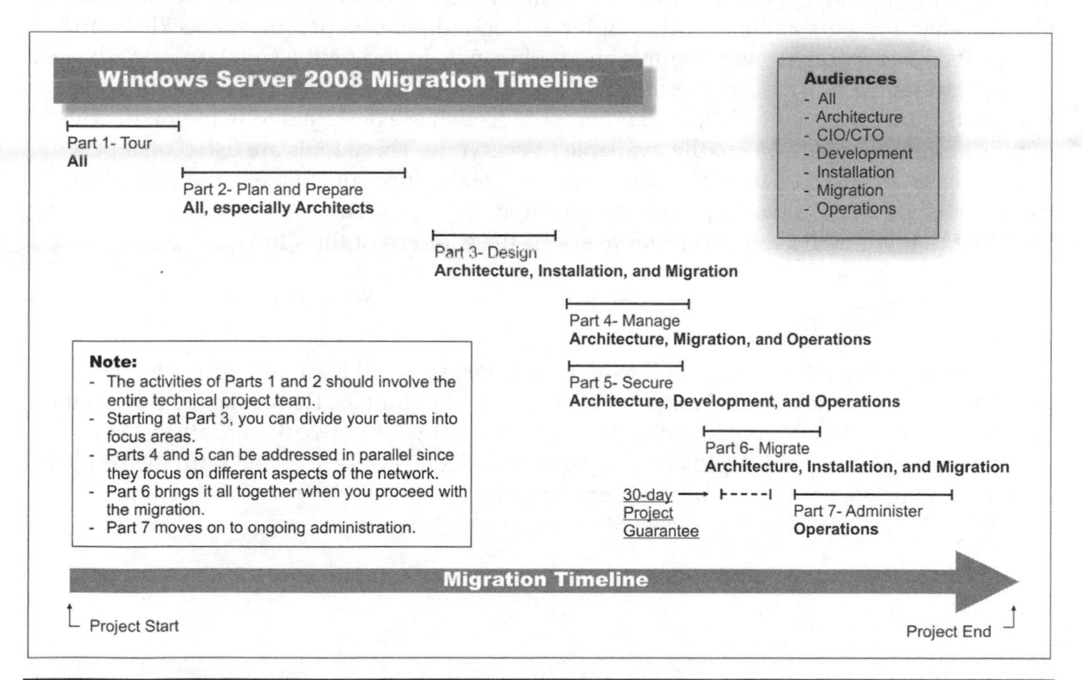

Figure 2 The Windows Server 2008 migration timeline

can so that all can profit from an improved networking environment. More on this timeline will be discussed in appropriate portions of this book. Note that this timeline is focused on virtual service offerings or the services your end users will interact with.

You will also need to test each new service you deploy. Because you are moving to the dynamic datacenter, you will be able to facilitate the testing process. Use the following strategy:

- Begin by building a core set of hardware resources. Rely on the Resource Pool table of contents to do so.
- Use this core set of resources as the basis of your testing lab, and begin to create the virtual service offerings you require on top of this core resource pool.
- If you make mistakes, either rely on the snapshot feature of Windows Server Hyper-V to undo the changes you made to virtual machines or simply scrap the VM and return to the beginning.
- When you feel you have it right, move the VM hosting the new service to the new production network. In most cases, you will be able to simply move the VM instead of having to re-create it.

You'll soon become familiar with the concept of working with resource pools and virtual service offerings, and once you do, you'll never go back.

The Companion Web Site

Throughout the book, you'll find that each chapter includes both discussion points and step-by-step implementations. Each chapter is chock-full of best practices, checklists, and processes. In addition, relevant figures and tools can be found on the Companion Web site (www.reso-net.com/livre.asp?p=main&b=WS08). It lists dozens of job aids, forms, checklists, blueprints, spreadsheets, and other tools that are designed to help you in your network migration. All are readily available to everyone. These tools are listed on a per-chapter basis to help you locate them more easily. Make sure you connect and download these items; they will definitely simplify your migration project.

Note that you will need to register to access the contents of the site.

Move On

Let the journey begin! As you read through this book, you will learn not only what makes WS08 tick, but also how to make the very most of its capabilities. Remember to rely on the processes outlined in this book and to make the most of your network migration. Do it right. Test everything and deploy only when you are completely satisfied with the results. You're on your way to the creation of a great network!

PART I

Tour Windows Server 2008

This section serves to prepare system administrators for Windows Server 2008. You will learn what to expect from this new version of Windows Server. It also addresses the core structure of the book: a division according to the size of organization you are in and a division according to the process of deploying new network service offerings based on Windows Server 2008. This section helps you to identify which features best meet the needs of your organization.

CHAPTER 1

The Windows Server 2008 Delta

Microsoft made some major inroads with the release of Windows Server 2003. This version of Windows Server became the flagship version, since it proved to be stable and reliable, and was available in a number of different configurations. It became even more reliable when Microsoft released version R2.

Now, with the release of Windows Server 2008 (WS08), Microsoft is making more inroads, as this version provides much more robust and integrated capabilities. Built with a foundation on Windows Vista, WS08 includes many of the features that made this client operating system the best of breed in the marketplace. But, WS08 is a *server* operating system; as such, its market is not the home user, but businesses and organizations everywhere. This is why the primary audience for this book is the system administrator, whether you are a generalist who is responsible for all system administration tasks in your organization or whether you are a member of a system administration team within a large enterprise.

Our advice to you is *pay attention to the structure of this book*! It covers both migrations for existing networks and new network installations. With our previous books, we have developed a proven methodology for server system implementations as well as system administration. This methodology relies on careful planning and selection of feature sets, comprehensive preparation, and testing and then, finally, deployment of the selected feature sets. When you use this approach, you will have a better-than-average chance of having a flawless implementation that will run smoothly and that will operate as expected. Too many operators rush into installations and implementations without proper planning and then need to rely on troubleshooting books to try and repair or patch the systems they implemented without proper guidance. *This is not that type of book!* This book outlines detailed explanations of each new feature in Windows Server 2008, and then it provides guidance on how to implement them. Because we do not work for Microsoft, we do not need to provide information for every possible installation situation. Instead, we provide known recipes—recipes that are proven to work when you want to use a specific feature set. If you use the recommended approaches we outline, then you will meet some very specific goals that will provide some very compelling benefits.

We've gathered feedback on our approaches through the delivery of multiple courses and conferences over the past few years as well as through direct interaction with customers.

This feedback proves that when system administrators rely on our administration practices, they finally gain control over their schedule and don't work in reactive mode all the time. In many cases, they only work overtime for very special situations, not on a regular basis, like many administrators do today. Isn't that a worthwhile goal?

Resource Pools vs. Virtual Service Offerings

In addition, this book outlines a new approach to the delivery of IT service offerings. This approach is based on virtualization, now that virtualization—the ability to run a "guest" operating system (OS) or a virtual machine inside a "host" OS—is a core element of the new datacenter. This approach was popularized by manufacturers such as VMware, Citrix, and Virtual Iron, as well as Microsoft themselves through the delivery of a series of different products aimed at supporting the ability to run virtual machines. In this approach, service offerings, or the services your end users interact with, are delivered inside virtual machines. Hardware systems are only used to run the virtualization services, or hypervisor, that expose resources to the virtual service offerings. As you will see, this approach liberates the service offerings from their dependency on hardware and provides the foundation for a dynamic datacenter—a datacenter where you can allocate resources as needed to meet the demand of the moment. In addition, using virtualized service offerings will enable almost any datacenter to have a simplified disaster recovery and business continuity strategy. This approach revolutionizes the way IT administrators have managed service offerings in the past and lets them look to the future, with a greater breadth of possibilities.

NOTE *Hyper-V, the new integrated virtualization engine in Windows server, is not included in the original release of WS08. Instead, it has been marked for availability after the market version has been released. You will need to download the virtualization components from the Microsoft web site at http://downloads.microsoft.com.*

New Feature Listings

OK. Now that we have laid down our approach, let's get to it. The very first thing you need to do when examining a new operating system is to understand its new feature set. Next, you need to wade through the sometimes hundreds of new features in order to identify which ones apply to organizations of your size and structure. Once this is done, you need to identify which of these features you want to implement, when you want to implement them, and how you will proceed. This is the structure of this book. In this chapter, we begin by laying out the general categories of the new WS08 feature set and then go on to examine each new feature in depth, identifying who it applies to—small, medium, or large organizations—as well as laying out a recommended timeframe for implementation of this feature. Each feature is laid out in a grid that covers core elements. This chapter is also available online on the companion web site (www.reso-net.com/livre.asp?p=main&b=WS08) so that you can integrate it into your own technical architecture documents—documents you will create in support of your planned WS08 migration or implementation. We recommend that you read this chapter carefully, mark those features you think apply to your organization, download our document, and remove or at least indicate which features do not apply to your organization. This will greatly facilitate your implementation and set you well onto the path for migration or new network design.

NOTE *Actually, the very first step you should address when changing server operating system is to review your business objectives to make sure that the selections you make will be in line with your business needs. How to do this is beyond the scope of this book, but we have written a series of articles on the subject of developing an enterprise architecture and identifying business requirements. You can find these articles at www.reso-net.com/articles.asp?m=8 under the "Architectures" heading. This should greatly assist you in outlining what you need to gather in terms of information about the business before you proceed.*

Build the Windows Server 2008 Network

Networks of all sizes require specific features and functionalities to provide support for the organizations that use them. As mentioned earlier, this book addresses the needs of organizations of all sizes—small, medium, and large—in terms of the networking functionality you can draw from Windows Server 2008. But to do so, it is important to begin with the establishment of some core principles. Two principles in particular are essential at this point:

- A common definition of the meaning of small, medium, and large in terms of networking and network functionality
- A common definition of the various functions any network requires and an identification of where WS08 adds new or enhances existing functionality

The latter will help you understand where you can see gains with the addition of Windows Server 2008 to your existing network. If you're building a brand-new network, you'll find that WS08 can support almost any networking function and provides an excellent means to support team productivity for any size of organization.

Organization Size Definitions

WS08 has been designed to respond to the needs of organizations of all sizes, whether you are a company of one working in a basement somewhere or whether your organization spans the globe, with offices in every continent. Obviously, there is a slight difference in scale between the two extremes, but for the purposes of this book, it is important to provide a definition of what is meant when we address the needs of small, medium, and large organizations. Each of these is defined as follows:

- Small organizations are organizations that include only a single site. They may have several dozens of workers, but given that they are located in a single site, their networking needs are fairly basic.
- Medium organizations are organizations that have more than one site but less than ten. The complexities of having a network with more than one site address the networking needs of medium organizations.
- Large organizations are organizations that have ten sites or more. In this case, organizations need more complex networks and will often rely on services that are not required at all by the two previous organization sizes.

Small organizations have all of the requirements of a basic network and will normally implement a series of technologies, including directory services, e-mail services, file and printer sharing, database services, and collaboration services. Even if the organization includes a very small number of people, these services will often be at the core of any networked productivity system. For this reason, it is often best for this type of organization to use Windows Small Business Server 2008 (SBS08), because it is less expensive and it includes more comprehensive applications for e-mail and database services. Nevertheless, some organizations opt for Windows Server 2008 anyway, because they are not comfortable with the limitations Microsoft has imposed on the Small Business Server edition. For example, it is always best and simpler to have at least two domain controllers running the directory service because they become automatic backups of each other. SBS08 can only have a single server in the network and therefore cannot offer this level of protection for the directory service. This is one reason why some small organizations opt for Windows Server 2008 even if it is more costly at first. However, realizing this business need, Microsoft is releasing Windows Essential Business Server 2008 (WEBS) as a multi-component server offering for these organizations. WEBS is made up of three server installations:

- **Windows Essential Business Server Management Server** To manage the WEBS network as well as worker collaboration and network services centrally.
- **Windows Essential Business Server Security Server** To manage security, Internet access, and remote-worker connectivity.
- **Windows Essential Business Server Messaging Server** To provide messaging capabilities.

Medium organizations face the challenge of having to interconnect more than one office. While small organizations have the protection of being in a single location, medium organizations often need to bridge the Internet to connect sites together. This introduces an additional level of complexity.

NOTE *Secondary sites may or may not have administrative personnel on site. This adds to the complexity of working with and managing remote sites.*

Large organizations have much more complex networks that provide both internal and external services. In addition, they may need to interoperate in several languages and will often have internally developed applications to manage. Large organizations may also have remote sites connected at varying levels of speed and reliability: Integrated Services Digital Network (ISDN) or dial-up. From a Windows standpoint, this necessitates a planned replication and possibly an architecture based on the Distributed File System (DFS). For this reason, they include many more service types than small or medium organizations.

This book addresses the needs of each organization type. When core networking features are addressed, they will apply to all levels of organizations, since best practices for network service implementations should be used no matter which organization size you have. Interconnection issues will address the complexities of medium and large networks, and finally, advanced network functionalities will address the needs of very large organizations. If you find that your organization does not quite fit this trend, rely on the information provided for the other organization types to supplement your networking configuration requirements.

Common Networking Functions

WS08 includes features and functionalities that support almost every conceivable networking service. But not all of these functionalities are new or updated in Windows Server 2008. It is, therefore, important to first establish a common vocabulary on standard networking services and then identify where WS08 brings new features and functionalities to help draw a graphical map of the new WS08 features. This will provide you with a simple graphical layout of the new Windows Server 2008 feature set.

Small organizations or networks that include only a single site will often include a basic set of networking services. These services tend to focus on the following:

- **Domain Services** Using Active Directory to centrally store and manage all user accounts makes sense in organizations of all sizes. The alternative—using workgroup practices—means having to manage multiple security account databases, one on each server or workstation, in fact. Active Directory is so simple to use that it simply does not make sense to use anything else.

NOTE *Active Directory Domain Services (ADDS) relies on the Domain Name System (DNS) to operate. Therefore, any installation of ADDS will require at least one server running the DNS service. Note that in small-scale ADDS installations, you are automatically prompted to perform a simple DNS installation.*

- **File and Printer Sharing** Storing documents centrally has always made sense because you only have to protect one single location. Every organization has a use for central file and printer management, even if new collaboration features offer a better way to manage documents and have teams interact.
- **Collaboration Services** With Windows SharePoint Services (WSS), organizations can have teams interact with each other through a Web-based team structure. Since almost all organizational activity takes the form of a project, using team sites and collaboration services only makes sense, especially since WSS is so easy to install and manage.
- **Database Services** Windows SharePoint Services relies on a database—in this case, the Windows Internal Database, which is, in fact, a version of SQL Server Embedded edition.
- **E-mail Services** Most organizations also rely on e-mail services. Though Windows Server 2008 does provide the simple message transfer protocol (SMTP) service, organizations usually opt for a professional e-mail service, such as that provided by Microsoft Exchange Server.
- **Backup and Restore Services** All organizations will want to partake of Windows Backup to protect their systems, both at the data and the operating system level. The new Backup tool in Windows Server 2008 provides protection for both.

These often form the basic services that most organizations require. Optionally, even small organizations will also rely on the following services:

- **Firewall Services** Any organization that has a connection to the external world through the Internet will want to make sure they are completely protected. The only way to do so is to implement an advanced firewall service.

- **Fax Services** Windows Server 2008 can provide integrated fax services, freeing organizations from needing a conventional fax machine.
- **Terminal Services** Terminal Services (TS) provides the ability to run applications on a server instead of on the user's workstation. The advantage of this is that organizations need to manage applications only in one central location. In addition, with Windows Server 2008, the use of TS applications is completely transparent to end users, since it appears as if they are working off the local machine.

CAUTION *Terminal Service applications are not appropriate for mobile or disconnected users because they do not offer any kind of offline caching. Therefore, when a user is disconnected, they do not have access to TS applications.*

- **Hyper-V** This is a core service of the new datacenter. It supports the virtualization of all other service offerings. This service is installed on all hardware, and all other services are installed within virtual machines.
- **Network Access Services (NAS)** With the proliferation of home offices, more and more organizations are relying on network access services, such as virtual private networks (VPNs), to let home workers access the corporate network over common home-based Internet connections.
- **Deployment Services** With the advent of new Windows Deployment Services in Windows Server 2008, many organizations will want to take advantage of this feature to automate the installation and deployment of Windows XP and Windows Vista machines. Larger organizations will definitely want to use these services to deploy servers as well as workstations.
- **Windows Server Update Services** With the proliferation of attacks on systems of all types, organizations of all sizes will want to make sure they implement a system for keeping all of their computers—workstations and servers—up to date at all times. Windows Server Update Services (WSUS) is not part of WS08, but is free and can be obtained at www.microsoft.com/windowsserversystem/updateservices/downloads/WSUS.mspx. Registration is required to obtain the download.

In addition, any organization that includes more than one site will need to ensure that the services they provide at one site are available at any other. This is done through a series of different features, which rely mostly on either a duplication of the base services in remote sites or the use of a replication mechanism to copy data from one location to the other. The implementation of these systems is more complex than single-site structures.

Larger organizations will add more services to their network just because of the nature of their organization. These will include:

- **Certificate Services** Anyone who wants to control identity and ensure that users are who they claim they are at all times will want to take advantage of Active Directory Certificate Services, a public key infrastructure system that provides electronic certificates to users and machines in order to clearly identify who they are.

NOTE *For more information on public key infrastructures (PKI), see the "Advanced Public Key Infrastructures" section at www.reso-net.com/articles.asp?m=8.*

- **Rights Management Services** Organizations concerned about the protection of their intellectual data will want to implement Active Directory Rights Management Services (ADRMS). ADRMS can protect electronic documents from tampering through the inclusion of protection mechanisms directly within the documents.
- **Advanced Storage** Organizations maintaining large deposits of information will want to take advantage of advanced storage systems, such as storage area networks (SANs). Windows Server 2008 provides new ways to access and manage SANs.
- **Clustering Services and Load Balancing** Organizations running N-tier applications applications that are distributed among different server roles—will want to protect their availability through the use of the Windows Clustering Service (WCS)—a service that provides availability through a failover capacity to another server running the same service—and/or Network Load Balancing (NLB)—a service that provides availability through the use of multiple servers running identical configurations.
- **Database Services** Organizations relying on large data structures will want to run more than the Windows Internal Database and will rely on other versions of SQL Server to protect their databases.
- **Web Applications** Organizations providing custom services, both internally and externally, will need to rely on Internet Information Services (IIS) to deliver a consistent Web experience to end users.
- **Middleware Services** Organizations running N-tier applications will want to support them with middleware, such as the Microsoft .NET Framework, COM+, and other third-party components. These run on middleware servers.
- **Key Management Services** Organizations that take advantage of Microsoft Software Assurance and Volume Licensing will want to implement this new WS08 role. Key Management Services (KMS) controls the activation of Microsoft volume-licensed software from both clients and servers from within your firewall.

Figure 1-1 provides a graphical legend for each of the aforementioned service. This legend will be used through the book.

Figure 1-2 illustrates the basic structure of a network located in a single site. These services are illustrated as being at the central location. Medium-sized organizations will need to duplicate some core services to remote sites. This is illustrated as the remote site connection. In addition, both small and medium organizations may want to implement services that are not part of the core but that simplify systems management and support enhanced productivity. These are illustrated as optional services.

Large organizations will add more functionality to their network. This is illustrated as enterprise services. Organizations having more than two sites will simply duplicate the services found in the remote site. Finally, this illustration demonstrates where Windows Server 2008 provides new and updated functionalities. Use it as a guide for the identification of what you would want to add to your network in terms of modern, secure services.

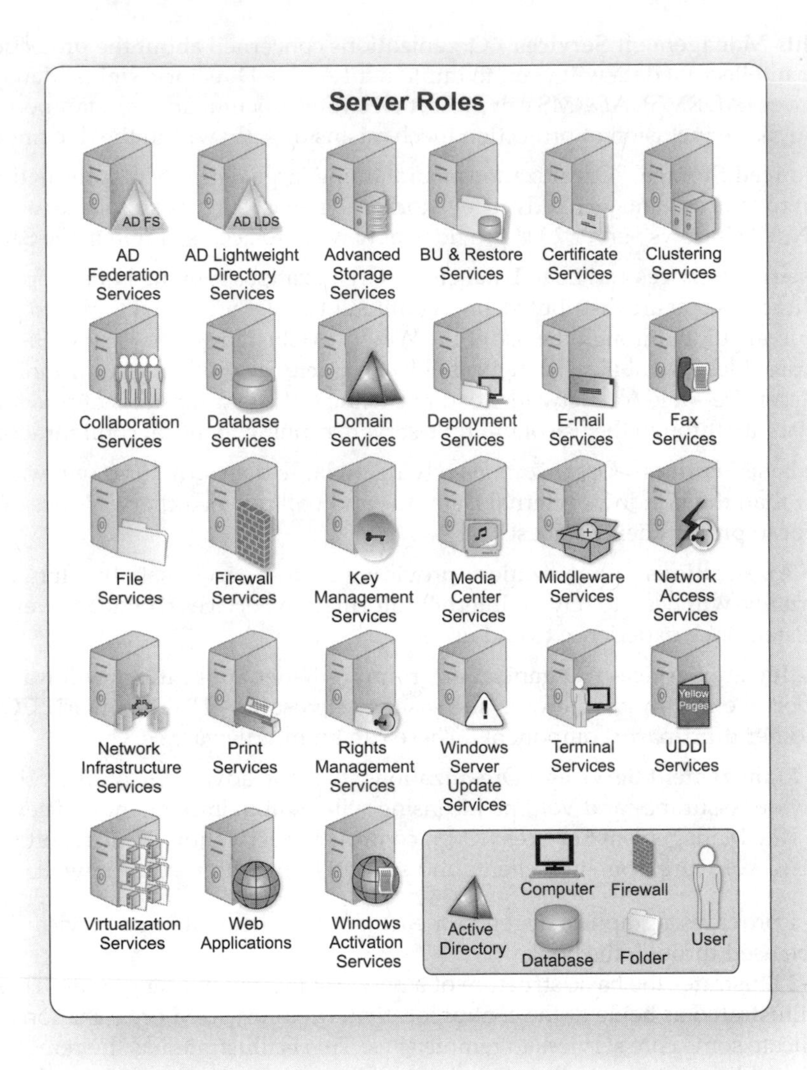

Figure 1-1 Graphical legend for network server types

Caution *Figure 1-2 is a simplistic representation of a complex network. More advanced features of each service will be covered as we proceed through the general configuration of network services throughout the book. In addition, each service represented here is illustrated with the image of a server for graphical purposes; this does not mean that you need to have the same number of actual hosts for each of these services. Several of these functions can be combined on the same host to reduce service management costs and overhead. Finally, both Terminal Services and Key Management Services have been singled out as new in this graphic. While they are not actually new, their new features are significant enough to call them out as such.*

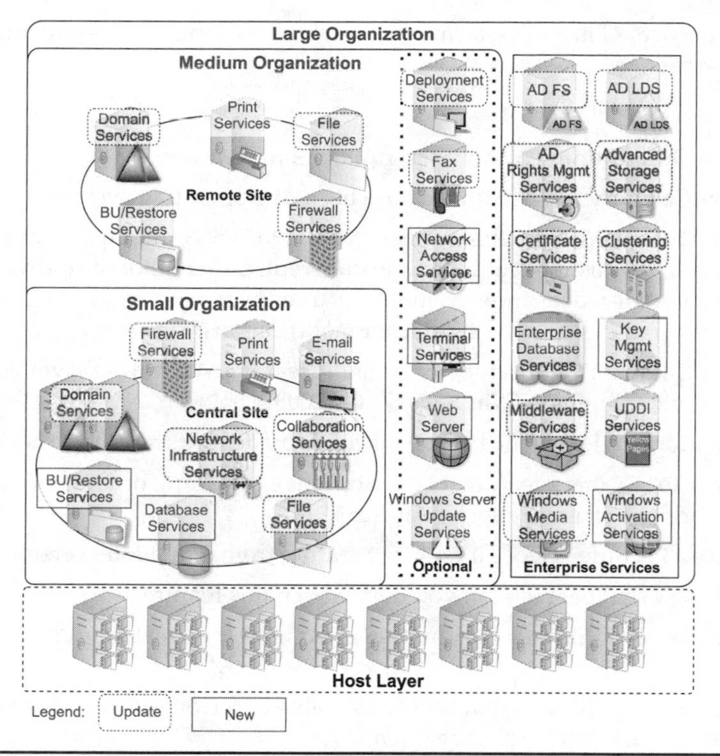

Figure 1-2 New and updated functionality for Windows Server 2008 in any network.

New Features in Windows Server 2008

Windows Server 2008 has a foundation in several different editions of Windows—Windows Server 2003, WS03 Service Packs, Windows Server 2003 R2, and Windows Vista—each of which had extensive feature sets of their own. Several of the most powerful features of Windows Server 2003, and especially Windows Server 2003 R2, have made their way into the WS08 feature set. This is why we will include information about these features in this chapter. This will act as a refresher and help you understand the complete WS08 feature set.

This feature set falls within the following categories:

- Improvements to operating system fundamentals
- Usability
- Networking infrastructure
- Deployment infrastructure
- Application infrastructure
- Security infrastructure
- Disk and file subsystem

Each functional section contains details of the specific features that make it up. Overall, they provide a compelling story for an upgrade or migration to WS08.

Features are covered in a table format—one table for each feature—including the following information:

- **Feature Name**
- **Feature Description** A short description of the feature.
- **Feature Category** Where the feature fits in the operating system.
- **Feature Type** Whether this is a new feature to WS08, an improvement, or an upgrade to an existing feature or a feature replacement. Both improvements and upgrades are listed, as improvements focus on tweaking an existing feature, whereas upgrades provide significant modifications.
- **Feature Source** What is the source of the feature: Windows Server 2008, Windows Vista, or older builds of Windows Server 2003?
- **Installation** When is the feature installed, by default or through additions?
- **Applies To** Is this a feature focused on small, medium, or large organizations, or does it apply to organizations of all sizes?
- **Replaced Features** Does it replace a feature from a previous version?
- **Benefits** What benefits can you derive from this feature?
- **Functions** If additional information is required for a feature, it is provided in this section.
- **Related Links** This section is only available in the online version of this chapter, since such links tend to change often.

This format provides a complete description of the feature in a concise design.

CAUTION *The features and functions described here address the most common editions of Windows Server 2008. However, the Itanium version of WS08 does not support all of them, as it runs a subset of WS08 roles and features. To find out the different functions the Itanium version of WS08 supports, go to http://technet2.microsoft.com/windowsserver2008/en/library/f6857978-ae92-4123-a87b-aa36cb30f3551033.mspx?mfr=true.*

Improvements to Operating System Fundamentals

Microsoft has endeavored to add several functionalities to Windows Server 2008 at the core operating system level. Building on Windows Server 2003, Microsoft has added several new features to this category. They include:

- **Server Core** A new version of Windows Server that does not include a graphical interface.
- **Windows Backup** A brand-new backup application that relies on the Volume Shadow Copy service to provide consistent backup images.
- **Microsoft Management Console version 3.0** A more complete console, which provides ready access to functions related to the feature being managed.
- **Performance Self-Tuning and Hardware Diagnostics** A new capability that automatically tunes Windows for better performance and addresses potential hardware issues before they occur.

- **Performance and Diagnostics Console** A new console that centralizes all performance and diagnostics activities.
- **Key Management Services** A new in-house licensing system for volume licenses of Microsoft products.
- **Hyper-V** A service that is designed to expose hardware resources to multiple instances of virtualized service offerings.

Each feature is fully described as follows.

Feature	**Server Core**
Description:	Installs Windows Server 2008 with only core server functionality and no graphical user interface. Server Core supports a limited number of roles, such as Dynamic Host Configuration Protocol (DHCP) Server, Domain Naming Service (DNS) Server, File Server, Print Server, Lightweight Directory Services, Hyper-V, Internet Information Services 7 (IIS), Domain Controller, and Windows Media Services.
Category:	*Operating System Fundamentals*
Feature:	☑ New ☐ Improvement ☐ Update ☐ Replacement
Feature Source:	☑ WS08 ☐ Vista ☐ WS03 R2 ☐ WS03 Service Packs
Installation:	☐ By Default ☐ Add-on Through Server Manager ☑ Custom
Applies to:	☐ Small ☐ Medium ☑ Large Organizations

Replaced Feature

- None

Benefits

- Improved security because of reduced attack surface.
- Reduced management overhead.
- Reduced software maintenance.
- Uses only about 1 gigabyte (GB) of disk space for installation.

Functions

- The installation option installs only a subset of the executable files and supporting dynamic link libraries (DLLs).
- The default user interface is the command prompt. One command window is opened by default.
- Server Core only supports a clean installation. It should be installed using an unattended installation.
- IIS 7 offers limited functionality on Server Core, since it does not include the .NET Framework and cannot run ASP.NET. It will, however, run static Web content, classic Active Server Pages(ASP), and Hypertext Preprocessor (PHP).

Optional Features

- Server Core also supports the following capabilities:
  - Failover clustering
  - Network Load Balancing
  - Subsystem for UNIX-based applications
  - Backup
  - Multipath I/O
  - Removable storage management
  - BitLocker drive encryption
  - Simple Network Management Protocol (SNMP)
  - Windows Internet Naming Services (WINS)
  - Telnet client

Feature	Windows Backup
Description:	The backup feature provides a more comprehensive backup and recovery solution for WS08.
Category:	*Operating System Fundamentals*
Feature:	☐ New ☐ Improvement ☐ Update ☑ Replacement
Feature Source:	☐ WS08 ☑ Vista ☐ WS03 R2 ☐ WS03 Service Packs
Installation:	☐ By Default ☑ Add-on Through Server Manager ☐ Custom
Applies to:	☑ Small ☑ Medium ☑ Large Organizations

Replaced Features

- The previous backup feature with earlier versions of the Windows operating system
- Backup no longer supports tape drives

Benefits

- Automatic backup of data.
- Image-based backup of servers.
- Access to previous versions of user files.

Functions

- More comprehensive backup technology. Relies on Volume Shadow Copy Service (VSS) and block-level technology to back up volumes.
- Back up to CD, DVD, internal or external disk, or network file share. Tape backup is no longer supported.
- Wizard-based backup and recovery. Recovery is performed from a single image; Backup will find the files in the incremental backup copies.
- Recovery of servers can be done to the same or different hardware.
- Automatically monitors backup disk usage.
- Uses restore points to protect previous versions of data files.
- Can use System Restore to restore server to operational state.

Feature	Microsoft Management Console 3.0
Description:	Microsoft Management Console (MMC) has been improved to provide task-based information to administrators. MMC v3 now includes multiple panes to properly display management information based on a selected context.
Category:	*Operating System Fundamentals*
Feature:	☐ New ☐ Improvement ☑ Update ☐ Replacement
Feature Source:	☐ WS08 ☐ Vista ☑ WS03 R2 ☐ WS03 Service Packs
Installation:	☑ By Default ☐ Add-on Through Server Manager ☐ Custom
Applies to:	☑ Small ☑ Medium ☑ Large Organizations

Replaced Feature

- The previous MMC version (previous to WS03 R2, that is)

Benefits

- Task-based administration support.
- Contextual information based on current focus.
- Extensible model for added functionality.

(Continued)

Feature	Microsoft Management Console 3.0 *(Continued)*

Functions

- New three-pane look provides more information to administrators.
- Uses tree pane to identify installed features and components.
- Uses central pane to list details of selected feature.
- Uses right pane to provide task-based information related to the selected feature.
- Extensible model lets independent software vendors (ISVs) add functionality.

Feature	Performance Self-Tuning and Hardware Diagnostics

Description: WS08 boasts several performance-enhancing technologies, notably, Windows SuperFetch, ReadyBoost, and ReadyDrive, which can increase server performance. In addition, it now has the ability to automatically adjust its performance parameters based on detected system behavior.

Category: *Operating System Fundamentals*

Feature: ☐ New ☐ Improvement ☑ Update ☐ Replacement

Feature Source: ☐ WS08 ☑ Vista ☐ WS03 R2 ☐ WS03 Service Packs

Installation: ☑ By Default ☐ Add-on Through Server Manager ☐ Custom

Applies to: ☑ Small ☑ Medium ☑ Large Organizations

Replaced Features	Benefit
• Not applicable	• Improves system performance without necessarily requiring new hardware.

Functions

- Windows SuperFetch can monitor memory usage and ensure that applications have priority over background system tasks. If a system task runs when the system has available time, it is replaced in random access memory (RAM) with user applications as soon as it is complete.
- SuperFetch can also monitor for the most-used applications and provide quicker access to them by preloading them into memory at system startup.
- ReadyBoost can rely on external Universal Serial Bus (USB) memory sticks to enhance operation by treating this memory space as additional RAM. Data is encrypted on the device to protect it. Performance returns to normal levels when the USB device is removed.
- ReadyDrive can rely on new hybrid drives that include on-board Flash memory to have faster access to disk-based data.
- WS08 also uses low-priority input/output (I/O) to reduce the competition for input and output resources between applications and background tasks.
- Background disk defragmentation will also improve system responsiveness, as it takes advantage of low-priority I/O. Defragmentation is automatically scheduled at installation.
- Automatic performance monitors track system events and can perform automatic analysis when performance degrades. These reports are written to the event log to help administrators better understand performance issues.
- Relies on the new Windows Diagnostic Infrastructure (WDI) to monitor and control the way Windows behaves. WDI scenarios include protection from hardware failures, networking problems, resource exhaustion, and power transition problems.

Feature	Performance and Diagnostics Console
Description:	A console that provides centralized access to monitor and assess system performance and reliability.
Category:	*Operating System Fundamentals*
Feature:	☐ New ☑ Improvement ☐ Update ☐ Replacement
Feature Source:	☑ WS08 ☐ Vista ☐ WS03 R2 ☐ WS03 Service Packs
Installation:	☐ By Default ☐ Add-on Through Server Manager ☑ Custom
Applies to:	☐ Small ☑ Medium ☑ Large Organizations

Replaced Features

- Performance Logs and Alerts
- Server Performance Advisor
- System Monitor

Benefits

- Provides a single interface to both troubleshoot and identify performance issues.
- Automates performance data collection.

Functions

- Provides a graphical interface to customize performance data collection and event trace sessions.
- Includes Reliability Monitor, an MMC snap-in that tracks changes to the system and compares them to changes in system stability.
- Supports data collector sets, which group data collectors into reusable elements for use with different performance-monitoring scenarios.
- Includes wizards and templates for creating logs.
- Provides a Resource View, which gives a real-time graphical overview of central processing unit (CPU), disk, network, and memory usage.
- Includes Reliability Monitor, which calculates a system stability index to help identify reliability issues.
- Supports unified property configuration for all data collections, including scheduling.
- Includes user-friendly diagnostic reports.

Feature	Key Management Services
Description:	A centralized key management service (KMS), which controls the activation of Windows operating systems without requiring individual machines to connect to a Microsoft web site. KMS can run on either Vista or Windows Server 2008.
Category:	*Operating System Fundamentals*
Feature:	☑ New ☐ Improvement ☐ Update ☐ Replacement
Feature Source:	☐ WS08 ☑ Vista ☐ WS03 R2 ☐ WS03 Service Packs
Installation:	☐ By Default ☐ Add-on Through Server Manager ☑ Custom
Applies to:	☐ Small ☑ Medium ☑ Large Organizations

(Continued)

Feature	**Key Management Services** *(Continued)*

Replaced Feature	**Benefits**
• Volume licensing keys	• Ensures that all software is genuine and properly licensed. • Enables organizations to manage licenses more accurately.

Functions

- Enables Vista and Windows Server 2008 to be activated without requiring external access to a Microsoft validation web site.
- Requires at least 25 machines running Vista or 5 WS08 servers consistently connected to an organization's network to operate—virtual instances of operating systems do not count.
- Can support the activation of hundreds of thousands of machines from one single KMS device. Organizations should have at least two KMS devices in the network: one main device and a backup system.
- Clients must renew activation by connecting to the KMS device at least once every 180 days. New, unactivated clients will try to contact the KMS every two hours (configurable) and once activated, will attempt to renew their activation every seven days (configurable) to renew their 180-day lifespan.
- If the copy of Windows Vista or WS08 becomes deactivated for some reason, the following features will no longer work:
  - The Windows Aero user interface will no longer operate.
  - Windows Defender will no longer remove non-critical threats.
  - Windows ReadyBoost will no longer operate.
  - The Windows Update web site will no longer provide downloads.
  - Windows will provide persistent notifications that this copy is unlicensed.
- Location of KMS devices can be performed through auto-discovery, relying on the DNS service, or through direct connections, entering the machine name and port number for the connection.
- Unactivated or deactivated machines have a 30-day grace period before requiring reactivation.
- Copies of Windows that go beyond the grace period enter Reduced Functionality Mode (RFM). In addition to the reduced functionalities listed previously, a machine in RFM mode will display the following behaviors.
  - A default Web browser will be started when the user opens a session.
  - The session will have no Start menu, no desktop icons, and a black desktop background.
  - Users will be logged out after an hour without warning.

Optional Feature

- Organizations requiring multiple activations, but with fewer than 25 systems, can rely on Multiple Activation Keys (MAKs). MAKs are special activation keys that will support individual machine activation with no time limits, or you can go through a MAK proxy to activate several keys at once.

Feature	**Hyper-V**
Description:	A core feature of the operating system, which is designed to support the operation of "virtual machines" and transforms hardware into a pool of resources that can be shared by virtual instances of service offerings.
Category:	*Operating System Fundamentals*
Feature:	☑ New ☐ Improvement ☐ Update ☐ Replacement
Feature Source:	☑ WS08 ☐ Vista ☐ WS03 R2 ☐ WS03 Service Packs

(Continued)

Feature	Hyper-V *(Continued)*
Installation: ☐ By Default ☐ Add-on Through Server Manager ☑ Custom	
Applies to: ☑ Small ☑ Medium ☑ Large Organizations	
Replaced Feature • Microsoft Virtual Server	**Benefits** • Liberates hardware resources for better utilization. • Allows better assignment of resources on an as-needed basis for all service offerings. • Provides simplified business continuity.
Functions • Interacts directly with the hardware-based virtualization capabilities of advanced processors from AMD and Intel. • Provides support for both 32-bit and 64-bit virtual machines. • Also integrates with the Server Core installation of WS08. • Supports more than 32 GB of RAM per virtual machine. • Integrates with the Microsoft Cluster Service for either local or geographically dispersed clusters, as well as letting virtual machines work in a cluster. • Integrates with VSS for protection of both the virtual machines and the service offerings provided by the virtual machines. • Integrates with virtual Small Computer System Interface (SCSI), letting virtual machines link up to more than 256 virtual hard disks per virtual storage adapter and two virtual storage adapters per machine, meaning up to 512 virtual hard disks per machine. • Integrates with Network Load Balancing, letting you create an N-tier architecture for the virtualized service offerings hosted by this service. • Virtualization extensions to the core OS are part of most editions of WS08, letting service offerings that are virtualized work better when sharing resources.	

Usability

With the release of Windows Vista, Microsoft has developed comprehensive enhancements in Windows' usability. Many of these enhancements are now available in Windows Server 2008. Use those that seem most appropriate, as WS08 machines are servers and do not necessarily need to have the same interface as client workstations. You may want to ensure that these enhancements are available on all your servers in order to simplify the user transition from Windows Vista to WS08.

CAUTION *Windows Vista includes a myriad of new features. Not all are covered here, even though many have made it to the Windows Server 2008 code. This is because many of the new Windows Vista features are not aimed at a network operating system and are, therefore, irrelevant in WS08.*

New features in this category include:

- **Windows Aero User Interface** A new interface that provides an enhanced Windows visual experience.
- **Instant Search** An integrated indexing feature that simplifies finding the location of anything on Windows.

- **XPS Document Support** A new portable document format.
- **Server Manager** A unified MMC console that provides single access to all server functions and features.

Each is described in the following tables.

Feature	**Windows Aero User Interface**
Description:	The Windows Aero user interface takes advantage of new graphics capabilities to provide a clear and precise image to users.
Category:	*Usability*
Feature:	☑ New ☐ Improvement ☐ Update ☐ Replacement
Feature Source:	☐ WS08 ☑ Vista ☐ WS03 R2 ☐ WS03 Service Packs
Installation:	☐ By Default ☑ Add-on Through Server Manager ☐ Custom
Applies to:	☑ Small ☑ Medium ☑ Large Organizations
Replaced Features • The classical interface from Windows 2000 • The enhanced interface from Windows XP	**Benefits** • Provides a clear picture on the screen. • Includes enhanced functionalities for system management and interaction. • Interacts with the latest graphics card capabilities (requires custom hardware).
Functions • Includes Glass, a graphical rendering mechanism that provides as clear a picture as possible on a computer screen using a transparent glass design and smooth window transitions. • Windows Flip and Flip 3D provide live views of actual window contents, as well as advanced interaction with multiple windows open on the desktop at the same time. • Live taskbar thumbnails provide previews of actual window contents when hovering over the taskbar. • Relies on Windows Driver Display Model (WDDM) to provide improved desktop transitions, taking advantage of advanced graphics card capabilities.	

Feature	**Instant Search**
Description:	Search and indexing are a core part of the operating system. Access to all files and tools is controlled by the new search utility. Search is contextual and will modify its behavior depending on user activity.
Category:	*Usability*
Feature:	☑ New ☐ Improvement ☐ Update ☐ Replacement
Feature Source:	☐ WS08 ☑ Vista ☐ WS03 R2 ☐ WS03 Service Packs

(Continued)

Feature	Instant Search *(Continued)*
Installation:	☑ By Default ☐ Add-on Through Server Manager ☐ Custom
Applies to:	☑ Small ☑ Medium ☑ Large Organizations

Replaced Feature

- Previous indexing functions provided by Index Server

Benefits

- All user information is automatically indexed.
- Searches can be performed from the desktop on the desktop, as well as on network shares and collaboration sites.

Functions

- Integrated part of the Windows desktop. All activity is based on search, even the Start menu.
- Provides fast-as-you-type performance when searching.
- Integrated in all aspects of Windows: Documents Explorer, Music Explorer, Search Explorer, and more.
- Includes the Advanced Filter Pane, which lets you create searches with multiple criteria.
- Searches are integrated with Windows security, so users only see results to which they have been granted access.
- Search covers other computers, offline folders, redirected folders, SharePoint sites, and removable hard drives.
- Developers can produce iFilters to integrate their products with Instant Search.
- Provides the same level of search as Windows XP on legacy file shares that do not support the new distributed search engine.

Feature	XPS Document Support
Description:	Used to transform any on-screen content to a portable document format that supports viewing, printing, and indexing, and can be integrated to rights management for content protection.
Category:	*Usability*
Feature:	☑ New ☐ Improvement ☐ Update ☐ Replacement
Feature Source:	☐ WS08 ☑ Vista ☐ WS03 R2 ☐ WS03 Service Packs
Installation:	☑ By Default ☐ Add-on Through Server Manager ☐ Custom
Applies to:	☑ Small ☑ Medium ☑ Large Organizations

Replaced Feature

- None

Benefit

- Provides document portability without the need for third-party add-ons.

Functions

- Integrated XML Paper Specification (XPS) printer driver lets users print any on-screen content to XPS format for portability.
- Documents can be viewed in Internet Explorer or any other browser that supports the XPS format plug-in.
- Creates a standard paginated experience for unpaginated content, such as web pages.
- Supports automated document creation for custom programs.
- Generates high-fidelity vector-based graphics to provide accurate rendering of graphic images.
- Integrates with ADRMS to provide complete content protection.

Feature	Server Manager
Description:	Provides a single interface for server management, displaying system information and configuration details. Also used to manage server roles and add features.
Category:	*Usability*
Feature:	☑ New ☐ Improvement ☐ Update ☑ Replacement ☐ Custom ☐ Built-in
Feature Source:	☑ WS08 ☐ Vista ☐ WS03 R2 ☐ WS03 Service Packs
Installation:	☑ By Default ☐ Add-on Through Server Manager ☐ Custom
Applies to:	☑ Small ☑ Medium ☑ Large Organizations

Replaced Features

- Replaces the following Windows Server 2003 interfaces:
  - Manage Your Server
  - Configure Your Server
  - Add or Remove Windows Components

Benefits

- Server roles are configured with recommended security settings by default.
- Server roles are ready to deploy as soon as they are installed and properly configured.
- One single interface for server management.

Functions

- Centrally control the operational lifecycle of the server and any role installed on it.
- Quickly identify server status and critical events, as well as analyze and troubleshoot configuration issues or failures.
- Includes all of the different interfaces you need to manage any server activity.
- Relies on MMC version 3.0 to provide a rich user experience. Also includes:
  - Add or Remove Roles Wizard
  - Add or Remove Role Services Wizard
  - Add or Remove Features Wizard
- Supports multiple functions as well as server roles.
- Enables integration of additional roles and features that are available on the Microsoft download center and the Windows Update web sites as optional updates to WS08. For example, Windows Server Update Services which are not part of Windows server can be added through the Server Manager console. Windows SharePoint Services which supports team and personal web site creation to provide document management and collaboration, is also added to Server Manager in this manner.

Supports the Following Server Roles

- **Active Directory Certificate Services (ADCS)** Creates and manages digital certificates as part of a PKI.
- **Active Directory Domain Services (ADDS)** Provides traditional authentication and domain security services.
- **Active Directory Federation Services (ADFS)** Provides encrypted identity federation and single sign-on based on the Hypertext Transfer Protocol (HTTP) protocol.
- **Active Directory Lightweight Directory Service (ADLDS)** Stores application-specific data in Lightweight Directory Application Protocol (LDAP) format.
- **Active Directory Rights Management Services (ADRMS)** Protects documents from unauthorized use through digital signatures.
- **Application Server** Hosts and manages high-performance distributed business applications.

(Continued)

Feature **Server Manager** *(Continued)*

- **Dynamic Host Configuration Protocol (DHCP) Server** Provides central provisioning, configuration, and management of temporary IP addresses and related information on client computers.
- **Domain Name System (DNS) Server** Translates domain and computer DNS names to IP addresses.
- **Fax Server** Sends and receives faxes, and supports the management of fax resources.
- **File Services** Provides technologies for storage management, file replication, distributed namespace management, file searching, and streamlined client access to files.
- **Hyper-V Services** Provides support for the operation of virtual instances of operating systems. Hyper-V is a hypervisor—a small piece of code whose purpose is to expose physical resources to virtual machines—and is a role that should not be shared with any others as much as possible. Note that Hyper-V is not included in the original market release of WS08.
- **Network Policy and Access Services (NAS)** Supports local area network (LAN) and wide area network (WAN) network traffic routing and network access policy creation and enforcement, as well as virtual private network (VPN) or dial-up connection access to network resources.
- **Print Services** Manages and provides access to network printers and printer drivers.
- **Terminal Services (TS)** Enables access to a server running Windows-based applications or to the full Windows desktop.
- **Universal Description, Discovery, and Integration Services (UDDI)** Organizes and catalogs Web services and other programmatic resources in white or yellow page-like directories.
- **Web Server (IIS)** Provides a Web application infrastructure through IIS version 7.0.
- **Windows Deployment Services (WDS)** Provides hands-free remote deployment of Windows operating systems through network-based installation.

Networking Infrastructure

In addition to the many other feature improvements found in Windows Server 2008, Microsoft has endeavored to improve the basic communications infrastructure in Windows to further support a worldwide communications marketplace. The most important new features in this category include:

- **IPv6** A full integration of the new version 6 protocol for TCP/IP.
- **Refined TCP/IP** A full reworking of the Windows TCP/IP stack to increase the throughput that Ethernet networks provide with this protocol.

CAUTION *Only routers and switches that fully support all of the Internet standards outlined by the Internet Engineering Task Force (IETF) will be able to function with the refined TCP/IP protocol. Ensure that your network devices are fully IETF-compliant before implementing this feature.*

- **Domain Name System (DNS)** New improvements in the Windows DNS service provide support for all of the new networking features in Windows Server 2008.

Feature	IPV6
Description:	IPv6 is the long-term replacement for IPv4. IPv6 offers a significantly larger number of addresses than IPv4 and will be used going forward as a complete replacement of the older protocol. Emerging nations will focus on IPv6, as most IPv4 public addresses have already been assigned throughout the world.
Category:	*Networking Infrastructure*
Feature:	☐ New ☑ Improvement ☐ Update ☐ Replacement
Feature Source:	☐ WS08 ☑ Vista ☐ WS03 R2 ☐ WS03 Service Packs
Installation:	☑ By Default ☐ Add-on through Server Manager ☐ Custom
Applies to:	☑ Small ☑ Medium ☑ Large Organizations

Replaced Feature

- Will eventually completely replace IPv4

Benefits

- Vast number of additional addresses.
- Includes several built-in functionalities that were previously add-ons to IPv4.
- Each connection has a private address that is unique in the world.

Functions

- Installed and enabled by default.
- Includes the ability to operate with Intra-Site Automatic Tunnel Addressing Protocol (ISATAP) which is a transition technology that allows IPv6 to interact with IPv4.
- Many applications in WS08 directly support IPv6. Relies on Teredo for applications that are not IPv6 enabled.
- Includes Teredo, a transition technology that allows IPv6 and IPv4 connections that are separated by network address translations (NAT) to use end to end communications with IPv6 addresses.
- Teredo now functions with domain member computers as well as domain controllers. It was disabled by default in Windows XP and Windows Server 2003 when a computer became member of a domain.
- Teredo is not enabled by default and must be activated for networks that do not provide complete IPv6 support.
- Includes Multicast Listener Discovery version 2 (MDLv2) for source-specific multicast traffic. Corresponds to Internet Group Management Protocol (IGMP) version 3 in IPv4.
- Local Linking Multicast Name Resolution (LLMNR) lets IPv6 systems located on a single subnet but without a DNS server to resolve each other's names. This is useful for ad hoc networks.
- Dynamic Host Configuration Protocol (DHCP) version 6 client lets Windows Server 2008 systems obtain dynamic IPv6 addresses.
- Full support for Quality of Service is now provided through the new IPv6 protocol in WS08.

Feature	Refined TCP/IP
Description:	Includes the 'Next Generation TCP/IP' stack which is a complete redesign of the TCP/IP functionality in Windows.
Category:	*Networking Infrastructure*
Feature:	☐ New ☑ Improvement ☐ Update ☐ Replacement
Feature Source:	☐ WS08 ☑ Vista ☐ WS03 R2 ☐ WS03 Service Packs
Installation:	☑ By Default ☐ Add-on Through Server Manager ☐ Custom
Applies to:	☑ Small ☑ Medium ☑ Large Organizations

Replaced Feature

- All TCP/IP stacks from previous versions of Windows

Benefits

- Vastly improved networking speeds.
- Complete interoperability between IPv4 and IPv6.
- Compliant with all IETF standards.

Functions

- **Receive Window Auto-Tuning** Automatically adjusts the receive window size or the maximum amount a host can receive through a TCP/IP connection to improve reception speed.
- **Compound TCP** Automatically adjusts or increases the amount of data sent over a TCP connection based on a calculation of the bandwidth versus the sensed delay on the connection.
- **Throughput Optimization** In environments where there is high loss through the use of new algorithms.
- **Neighbor Unreachability Detection** Is automatic in IPv6. The new TCP/IP stack adds this functionality to IPv4.
- **Dead Gateway Detection** Is now constant. Connections are automatically redirected as soon as the dead gateway is up again.
- **PTMU Black Hole Router Detection** Allows TCP/IP to identify path maximum transmission unit (PTMU) routers or intermediate routers that drop either Internet Control Message Protocol (ICMP) or messages that cannot be fragmented so that messages are no longer terminated because of firewall rules in routers.
- **Routing Compartments** Are interfaces that include a logon session. Using compartments, TCP/IP can prevent unwanted forwarding or packets between interfaces such as VPN, Terminal Services, or multiuser logon configurations.
- **Network Diagnostics Framework** Now supports intuitive prompting, and even automatic correction, when network issues are detected to help administrators more easily correct the problem on their own. When the problem is one that cannot be solved automatically or manually, guidance with specific details about the problem is displayed.
- **Extended Statistics (ESTATS) Support** Allows TCP/IP to provide additional extended statistics on network transfers.
- **Windows Filtering Platform (WFP)** Provides a new architecture for linking third-party hooks into IP filtering.
- **IPv6 enhancements** Are also included in this new stack, providing comprehensive support for this next-version protocol.

Feature	Domain Name System (DNS)
Description:	The DNS service has been improved to work with new Active Directory features as well as IPv6.
Category:	*Networking Infrastructure*
Feature:	☐ New ☐ Improvement ☑ Update ☐ Replacement
Feature Source:	☐ WS08 ☑ Vista ☐ WS03 R2 ☐ WS03 Service Packs
Installation:	☑ By Default ☐ Add-on Through Server Manager ☐ Custom
Applies to:	☑ Small ☑ Medium ☑ Large Organizations
Replaced Feature • DNS from previous versions of Windows Server	**Benefits** • Support for IPv6. • Compliant with all IETF standards. • Complete integration with Active Directory.
Functions • Background zone loading allows DNS to start more rapidly when loading very large zones from the ADDS database. • Support for IPv6 addresses lets DNS store addresses that are 128 bits long, compared to the IPv4 addresses, which were only 32-bit. • New Primary Read-Only Zones (PROZ) lets DNS support the read-only DC (RODC) ADDS server role. • New GlobalNames Zones (GBZs), which are, by default, replicated to the entire Active Directory forest. Provides support for single-label names similar to the NetBIOS names supported by the Windows Internet Naming Service (WINS). GBZs can now be used to completely replace WINS servers and remove this role from the network.	

Deployment Infrastructure

Every time there is a new version of Windows, you have to deploy it. Microsoft has endeavored to make Windows deployment easier with each new version of Windows. Windows Vista in particular aims to ease deployment as much as possible. For this, Microsoft has developed two core technologies: a deployment engine and a new file-based disk image format. These deployment mechanisms support both Windows Vista and Windows Server 2008. In addition, the entire setup process has been modified in WS08 to move all of the decision-making to the end of setup process.

Deployment infrastructure features include:

- **Windows Deployment Services** A new version of the operating system deployment server tool, which allows you to stream system images to multiple end points through multicast in one single datastream.
- **Windows Image Format** A new file-based disk image format for installing Windows.
- **Initial Configuration Tasks** A new startup screen that combines questions previously asked during setup.

Feature	Windows Deployment Services
Description:	Windows Deployment Services provides server-based operating system deployment tools. Supports remote boot of bare-metal machines and the downloading of new operating systems to them.
Category:	*Deployment Infrastructure*
Feature:	☐ New ☑ Improvement ☐ Update ☐ Replacement
Feature Source:	☑ WS08 ☐ Vista ☐ WS03 R2 ☐ WS03 Service Packs
Installation:	☐ By Default ☑ Add-on Through Server Manager ☐ Custom
Applies to:	☐ Small ☑ Medium ☑ Large Organizations

Replaced Features

- Remote Installation Services (RIS)
- Automated Deployment Services (ADS)

Benefits

- Supports network-based installation of Windows Vista and Windows Server 2008, as well as Windows XP and Windows Server 2003.
- Reduces total cost of ownership (TCO) through integrated deployment technologies.

Functions

- Deploys Windows operating systems to bare-metal machines (no OS installed).
- Works as an add-on to Windows Server 2003 or as a server role in WS08.
- Built on integrated Windows setup technologies, including Windows Pre-Execution (Windows PE), Windows Image Format (WIM), and Image-Based Setup (IBS).
- Supports Pre-Execution Boot (PXE)-enabled network cards for 32-bit systems and Extensible Firmware Interface (EFI) for 64-bit systems.
- Uses Windows PE as native boot for OS installation.
- Multicast management tasks in both the graphical and command-line version of WDS.
- Client user interface indicating multicast transmission.
- Real-time client transmission view, plus discreet control over which clients should or shouldn't receive a transmission.
- Progress monitoring on transmissions.
- Reporting and logging of installation status via Event Log.
- Support for installation of a stand-alone WDS multicast server with management console and command-line tool support.
- Datastream management, letting clients request the multicast or join midstream and still get a full installation.
- Based on new multicast protocol, including congestion and flow control, as well as bandwidth control.
- Supports ImageX deployments without requiring WDS or Active Directory.
- Command-line multicast client for Windows PE.

Feature	**Windows Image Format**
Description:	Provides a hardware-agnostic image file format that captures entire disk images of Windows installations for redeployment. All installations of Windows, even new installation DVDs from Microsoft, rely on this image format.
Category:	*Deployment Infrastructure*
Feature:	☑ New ☐ Improvement ☐ Update ☐ Replacement
Feature Source:	☐ WS08 ☑ Vista ☐ WS03 R2 ☐ WS03 Service Packs
Installation:	☑ By Default ☐ Add-on Through Server Manager ☐ Custom
Applies to:	☑ Small ☑ Medium ☑ Large Organizations
Replaced Feature • None	**Benefits** • Supports both new installations and upgrades from previous versions of Windows (XP SP2 for Windows Vista and WS03 SP1 for WS08).
Functions	• Single image file can now work for computers using different Hardware Abstraction Layer (HAL) drivers. • Single image file can support worldwide deployments in multiple languages. • Relies on XML unattend installation files. One single unattend can support both new installations and installations prepared through the System Preparation (SysPrep) tool. • Non-destructive imaging can support in-place upgrades, retaining both user settings and application settings while wiping out and replacing all OS components. • Supports the Single Instance Store (SIS), letting organizations include multiple editions of Windows Vista, even Windows Server 2008, in the same distribution DVD. • Includes a total of 36 language packs in support of worldwide deployments. • Supports offline servicing, allowing system administrators to patch and upgrade images without having to rebuild a reference computer. • Relies on System Image Manager (SIM) to manage unattend files through a graphical interface. • Integrates with Windows PE for initial booting during the installation process. • Supports the new IBS for Windows installations. All installations, even commercial DVDs from Microsoft, rely on IBS for installations.

Feature	**Initial Configuration Tasks**
Description:	Window that opens automatically after the operating system installation process is complete. This window allows administrators to finish the setup and the initial configuration of a new server.
Category:	*Deployment Infrastructure*
Feature:	☑ New ☐ Improvement ☐ Update ☐ Replacement
Installation:	☑ By Default ☐ Add-on Through Server Manager ☐ Custom

(Continued)

Feature	Initial Configuration Tasks *(Continued)*
Applies to: ☑ Small ☑ Medium ☑ Large Organizations	
Replaced Features • Previous Windows setup process	**Benefit** • A single source to finish setup and configure a new server, making sure that administrators do not forget any aspect of setup.
Functions • Set the administrator password. • Set the server IP address and join it to a domain. • Configure Windows Update and Windows Firewall. • Add roles and features to the server immediately after installation. • Opt in or out to provide anonymous feedback to Microsoft.	
Default Settings • **Administrator Password** Forced change at first logon • **Computer Name** Randomly assigned during installation and can be modified at this stage • **Domain Membership** Not joined to a domain; joined to a workgroup called WORKGROUP • **Windows Updates** Turned off • **Network Connections** All connections are set to obtain IP addresses automatically by using Dynamic Host Configuration Protocol (DHCP) • **Windows Firewall** Turned on • **Roles Installed** No roles	

Application Infrastructure

Windows Server made its name in the industry through its integrated application support capabilities. Whereas other network operating systems only provided file and print services, Windows would also support the ability to run applications. WS08 is no slouch in this matter either. It includes vastly improved application support through the following features:

- **Windows System Resource Manager (WSRM)** Which was first released as an add-on to Windows Server 2003 and provides the ability to completely control the assignation of resources to applications through defined policies.
- **Terminal Services** Has been improved through the addition of a new Terminal Services Gateway, which lets Terminal Services run over the HTTP protocol; RemoteApp, which simply publishes an application to an end user, making the Terminal Services experience completely transparent; and TS Web Access, which lets users access Terminal Services through a browser interface.
- **IIS 7.0** Is a vastly revamped version of Microsoft's flagship Web server.
- **The Application Server Role** Has been enhanced to support all of the new functionality available in .NET Framework versions 2.0 and 3.0, as well as other application changes.
- **Internet Explorer 7** Provides a more protected browser with the ability to better control the Web experience.
- **Failover Clustering** Has been enhanced to eliminate dependence on a local quorum or on the disk that maintained consistency between cluster nodes.

- **Windows SharePoint Services** Is a team-based collaboration environment that is now an add-on to the WS08 code.
- **Windows Activation Service** Is a new service that manages application pool and worker processes in IIS 7.0.
- **Fax Server** Is a new integrated facsimile system.

Each of these features is described in detail in the following tables.

Feature	Windows System Resource Manager
Description:	Application that lets you control resource allocation (CPU and RAM) to applications running on a server.
Category:	*Application Infrastructure*
Feature:	☐ New ☑ Improvement ☐ Update ☐ Replacement
Feature Source:	☑ WS08 ☐ Vista ☐ WS03 R2 ☐ WS03 Service Packs
Installation:	☐ By Default ☑ Add-on Through Server Manager ☐ Custom
Applies to:	☑ Small ☑ Medium ☑ Large Organizations
Replaced Feature • Upgrade from previous version	**Benefits** • Improves system performance and reduces potential application conflicts for resources. • Creates more predictable user experience because the application is guaranteed access to the resources it has been allocated.
Functions • Policy-based resource allocation to applications. • Controls application management as well as user management on Terminal Services servers. • Can rely on conditional policies to make the best use of hot-add hardware in stand-alone or clustered environments. • Integrates with Web pools through the application pools in IIS. • Can be used to capture resource usage statistics and store them in SQL Server. Can include data from multiple servers into a single reporting database. • Available in all editions of WS08.	

Feature	Terminal Services Core Features
Description:	The Terminal Server role provides the ability to open remote sessions on other computers and servers. It includes new functionality in Windows Server 2008 as well as new server roles.
Category:	*Application Infrastructure*
Feature:	☐ New ☐ Improvement ☑ Update ☐ Replacement
Feature Source:	☑ WS08 ☐ Vista ☐ WS03 R2 ☐ WS03 Service Packs

(Continued)

Feature	**Terminal Services Core Features** *(Continued)*
Installation: ☐ By Default ☑ Add-on Through Server Manager ☐ Custom	
Applies to: ☑ Small ☑ Medium ☑ Large Organizations	
Replaced Feature • None	**Benefits** • Allows authorized users to connect to Terminal Services or Remote Desktop connections from their desktops.
Functions • Supports the Remote Desktop Connection version 6.x. • Provides Plug and Play redirection for media players and digital cameras. • Provides support for the redirection of Windows Embedded for Point of Service devices. • Display resolutions with Terminal Services now support display ratios of 16:9 or 16:10 and resolutions of 1680 × 1050 or 1920 × 1200. The maximum resolution is 4096 × 2048. Resolutions can span several monitors. In addition, resolution will automatically address the graphical theme from the user's desktop, eliminating the need to modify the interface on the Terminal Server. • Can also redirect devices that use Microsoft Point of Service (POS) for .NET 1.11. • Can provide Aero interface features to end users. • Can also install the TS license server to manage all client access licenses.	

Feature	**Terminal Services Printing**
Description: New Terminal Server feature that reduces TS print management overhead.	
Category: *Application Infrastructure*	
Feature: ☐ New ☑ Improvement ☐ Update ☐ Replacement	
Feature Source: ☑ WS08 ☐ Vista ☐ WS03 R2 ☐ WS03 Service Packs	
Installation: ☐ By Default ☐ Add-on Through Server Manager ☑ Custom	
Applies to: ☑ Small ☑ Medium ☑ Large Organizations	
Replaced Feature • None	**Benefits** • Eliminates error messages related to print connection configuration when opening a TS session. • Simplifies TS printing for users.
Functions • Relies on new Group Policy setting that lets you redirect only the default client printer. • Uses the TS Easy Print driver to enable users to print from a remote application to the correct printer on their client system. • Requires Remote Desktop Connection version 6.1 and .NET Framework 3.0 SP 1 on the client system. • No need to install client printer drivers on the TS server.	

Feature	Terminal Services Gateway
Description:	New Terminal Services server role that allows remote users to connect to remote sessions from any Internet-connected device through firewalls and network address translation (NAT) devices.
Category:	*Application Infrastructure*
Feature:	☑ New ☐ Improvement ☐ Update ☐ Replacement
Feature Source:	☑ WS08 ☐ Vista ☐ WS03 R2 ☐ WS03 Service Packs
Installation:	☐ By Default ☐ Add-on Through Server Manager ☑ Custom
Applies to:	☑ Small ☑ Medium ☑ Large Organizations
Replaced Feature • None	**Benefits** • Allows authorized users to connect to Terminal Services or Remote Desktop connections from anywhere on the Internet. • Eliminates the need for VPN connections to access applications remotely.
Functions • Can connect to the corporate network from the Internet over an encrypted HTTPS connection without the need to configure VPN connections by redirecting all remote desktop protocol (RDP) connections that normally run on port 3389 to port 443 using an HTTP Secure Sockets Layer (SSL) tunnel. This means that a PKI certificate is required for the server. • Excellent for home-based employees because it removes the need for VPN connections. • Gives IT complete access to and control over specific resources on the network. • Supports policy-based definition of the conditions that must be met for users to connect to resources on the network through connection authorization policies (CAP—access to TS) and resource authorization policies (RAP—access to remote desktops). Links to Network Access Protection (NAP) features in WS08. • Provides complete event monitoring for TS Gateway. • The console lets administrators view details about active user connections, set maximum connection limits, and perform other actions to control access to network resources through the TS Gateway server. • Works in conjunction with NAP to isolate computers that attempt connections but that do not meet corporate security guidelines. To do so requires the use of a Network Policy Server (NPS), not a TS Gateway.	

Feature	Terminal Services RemoteApp
Description:	Enables organizations to provide access to standard Windows programs from virtually any location to users of any Windows Vista-based computer or Windows XP systems that have the new Remote Desktop Connection client installed, using either the Internet or the intranet.
Category:	*Application Infrastructure*
Feature:	☑ New ☐ Improvement ☐ Update ☐ Replacement
Feature Source:	☑ WS08 ☐ Vista ☐ WS03 R2 ☐ WS03 Service Packs
Installation:	☐ By Default ☑ Add-on Through Server Manager ☐ Custom

(Continued)

Feature	Terminal Services RemoteApp *(Continued)*
Applies to:	☐ Small ☑ Medium ☑ Large Organizations

Replaced Feature
- None

Benefit
- Provides seamless access to applications running on Terminal Services.

Functions
- Programs that are accessed remotely through Terminal Services appear as if they are running on the end user's local computer.
- Supports Windows Vista clients and Windows XP SP2 with the addition of the new Remote Desktop Connection client version 6.0.
- Supports centralized application management while keeping the user experience the same as if the application was installed locally.
- Users do not need to open a Remote Desktop session first; they access applications directly.
- Simplifies application deployment through the simple deployment of a Remote Desktop Connection (.rdp) file.
- Administrators can view and manage all connections to remote applications.

Feature	Terminal Services Web Access
Description:	A Terminal Services role that allows users to connect to TS sessions from a Web browser.
Category:	*Application Infrastructure*
Feature:	☐ New ☐ Improvement ☑ Update ☐ Replacement
Feature Source:	☑ WS08 ☐ Vista ☐ WS03 R2 ☐ WS03 Service Packs
Installation:	☐ By Default ☐ Add-on Through Server Manager ☑ Custom
Applies to:	☐ Small ☑ Medium ☑ Large Organizations

Replaced Feature
- None

Benefits
- Removes the need to deploy either RemoteApps or Remote Desktop connections to Terminal Servers.
- Provides easy Web interface to applications and programs.

Functions
- Easily deploy TS RemoteApps over the Web internally or externally.
- List of TS RemoteApps is dynamically updated on the web page.
- Includes the Terminal Services RemoteApps Web part to add to a WSS Team Site page.
- Supports Vista, XP, WS03, and WS08 clients.
- Integrates Terminal Services sessions if users access more than one program from the same Terminal Server.
- Web pages listing programs can be customized for different users, showing them only the programs they have access to.
- ActiveX component is already contained within the RDC client version 6, so no additional download is required.
- Users can specify if they are using public or private computers; credentials are not saved on public computers.

Feature	Terminal Services Session Broker
Description:	New Terminal Server role service that allows remote users to reconnect to a TS session in a load-balanced server farm.
Category:	*Application Infrastructure*
Feature:	☐ New ☑ Improvement ☐ Update ☐ Replacement
Feature Source:	☑ WS08 ☐ Vista ☐ WS03 R2 ☐ WS03 Service Packs
Installation:	☐ By Default ☐ Add-on Through Server Manager ☑ Custom
Applies to:	☑ Small ☑ Medium ☑ Large Organizations
Replaced Feature • None	**Benefits** • Provides continuous session experience to end user when they need to reconnect to a session on a server farm. • Can now load-balance this feature.
Functions • TS Session Broker load balancing will provide continuity for the session broker service. • Works with the DNS service instead of the Network Load Balancing service. • Configure multiple TS Session Broker IP addresses in the same DNS entry, and the connection will be made to the first available IP address.	

Feature	Internet Information Services (IIS) 7.0
Description:	IIS provides a unified platform for Web publishing that includes ASP.NET and Windows Communication Foundation (WCF).
Category:	*Application Infrastructure*
Feature:	☐ New ☑ Improvement ☐ Update ☐ Replacement
Feature Source:	☑ WS08 ☐ Vista ☐ WS03 R2 ☐ WS03 Service Packs
Installation:	☐ By Default ☑ Add-on Through Server Manager ☐ Custom
Applies to:	☑ Small ☑ Medium ☑ Large Organizations
Replaced Features • All previous versions of IIS • Internet Server Application Programming Interface (ISAPI) filters and extensions	**Benefits** • Improved administration tools, with better support for delegation. • Improved security and reduced attack surface through modular component implementation.

(Continued)

Feature	Internet Information Services (IIS) 7.0 *(Continued)*

Functions

- IIS 7.0 has been completely rewritten to provide a more secure Web platform by default and to fully integrate ASP.NET with the base IIS Web functions.
- A new management interface provides better diagnostics and the ability to fully delegate management of IIS components.
- IIS installation is componentized into 40 different feature modules so that you can install only what you need. This simplifies management, since you do not need to patch what you do not install. It also improves security, since you can choose which components to run.
- The IIS configuration is based on the existing .NET Framework configuration store, which enables IIS settings to be stored alongside ASP.NET configurations in Web.config files. This provides one configuration store for all Web platform configuration settings.
- Administration tools include a new graphical mode console as well as the APPCMD.EXE command-line tool. Settings can be edited directly while applications are running.
- Delegated administrative tasks include individual sites and application configurations.
- The rewrite of IIS is such that you can now rely on ASP.NET authentication modules, such as Forms-based authentication or Uniform Resource Locator (URL) authorization. In addition, IIS now functions with a new core server module. Additional core server modules can be developed and replace the former ISAPI filters and extensions from previous versions of IIS.
- The integration with ASP.NET lets developers use managed code in all instances and for all Web functionality.

Feature	Application Server

Description: The Application Server role is an environment for building, deploying, and executing applications and Web services. It is made up of several components, including IIS, .NET Framework versions 2.0 and 3.0, ASP.NET, message queuing, COM+, and Web services. Because of its built-in components, this role supports rapid application development (RAD).

Category: *Application Infrastructure*

Feature: ☐ New ☑ Improvement ☐ Update ☐ Replacement

Feature Source: ☐ WS08 ☑ Vista ☐ WS03 R2 ☐ WS03 Service Packs

Installation: ☐ By Default ☐ Add-on Through Server Manager ☑ Custom

Applies to: ☑ Small ☑ Medium ☑ Large Organizations

Replaced Feature	Benefits
• Previous versions of this role	• Reduces attack surfaces because all code produced with the .NET Framework is managed code, making it rely on the integrated Code Access Security. • Reduces development time because many of the functions developers need in their applications are already integrated with the components of this role.

(Continued)

Feature	Application Server *(Continued)*

Functions

- Includes .NET Framework versions 2.0 and 3.0 functionality, along with new features such as Windows Communication Foundation (WCF), Windows Presentation Foundation (WPF), Windows Workflow Foundation (WFF) and the new Windows Color System (WCS).
- WCF provides support for building and running connected systems. It unifies a series of different technologies into one single platform, including transport mechanisms, security systems, messaging patterns, encoding, network topologies, and hosting models.
- WPF relies on Windows Vista's new graphical features to blend together the user interface, documents, and media content. It includes support for Tablet PCs, a better imaging and printing pipeline, accessibility and user interface automation, data-driven visualization, and integration points for enhancing application experiences through the Windows shell.
- WFF provides a platform for coding and running workflow-based applications. It includes support for both system and human workflows, as well as workflows for line-of-business applications, document-centric workflows, composite workflows for service-oriented applications, business rule-driven workflows, and, finally, system management workflows.
- WCS provides better fidelity for color at all levels of the system, including screen-to-print matching, better color appearance, and support for higher-fidelity printing.
- This role is easily installed through Server Manager.

Feature	Internet Explorer 7
Description:	Microsoft's flagship Internet browser now provides a streamlined look and feel, using tabbed pages to let you more easily browse multiple sites at the same time. Internet Explorer (IE) 7 now provides a much more secure platform for Internet browsing.

Category: *Application Infrastructure*

Feature: ☐ New ☑ Improvement ☐ Update ☐ Replacement

Feature Source: ☐ WS08 ☑ Vista ☐ WS03 R2 ☐ WS03 Service Packs

Installation: ☑ By Default ☐ Add-on Through Server Manager ☐ Custom

Applies to: ☑ Small ☑ Medium ☑ Large Organizations

Replaced Feature	Benefit
• All previous versions of Internet Explorer	• Provides an easier and more secure Web experience.

Functions

- IE 7 includes a completely new look that is easier to work with. Tabbed views let you view several different pages in the same browsing session and display thumbnails of all of the open tabs.
- IE 7 includes the ability to properly print any web page or Web content.
- You can include Really Simple Syndication (RSS) feeds into your Web browsing experience, enabling you to receive new pages or content in the background and viewing them when you are ready.
- New search technology lets you choose from a variety of providers, although Windows Live is the default search tool.
- New anti-phishing and malicious code control features provide a safer browsing environment by providing clear interface exposure to suspicious or malicious sites.

Feature	**Failover Clustering**
Description:	Failover clustering offers the ability to link servers together to provide high availability of networked resources, such as database or e-mail applications. Failover clustering focuses on applications known as back-end services.
Category:	*Application Infrastructure*
Feature:	☐ New ☑ Improvement ☐ Update ☐ Replacement
Feature Source:	☑ WS08 ☐ Vista ☐ WS03 R2 ☐ WS03 Service Packs
Installation:	☐ By Default ☐ Add-on Through Server Manager ☑ Custom
Applies to:	☐ Small ☑ Medium ☑ Large Organizations
Replaced Feature • Microsoft Cluster Service	**Benefit** • Provides high availability for mission-critical applications.

Functions

- Includes a new validation feature to let you know if the resources you intend to cluster are ready for failover clustering. Supported tests include nodes, network, and storage.
- Improves cluster setup and migration to simplify the upgrade to WS08.
- The interface has been improved to allow administrators to focus on applications, not the clusters themselves.
- The quorum resource—the resource that tells the cluster the status of its configuration—is no longer a single point of failure, as it can now be distributed geographically and does not need to be directly attached to the cluster nodes.
- Cluster configuration files can now be used to generate new clusters.
- Administrators now have a private view of clustered file shares, telling them which are clustered and where they are located.
- Administrators can now "hot-add" storage resources to a cluster while it is running. In addition, WS08 clusters now support Globally Unique Identifier (GUID) partition tables (GPT), which, unlike master boot record (MBR) disks, can span over 2 terabytes (TB).

Feature	**Windows SharePoint Services**
Description:	Windows SharePoint Services (WSS) 3.0 provides team-based collaboration services that allow users access to workspaces and shared documents through a browser interface.
Category:	*Application Infrastructure*
Feature:	☐ New ☑ Improvement ☐ Update ☐ Replacement
Feature Source:	☑ WS08 ☐ Vista ☐ WS03 R2 ☐ WS03 Service Packs
Installation:	☐ By Default ☑ Add-on Through Server Manager ☐ Custom
Applies to:	☐ Small ☑ Medium ☑ Large Organizations
Replaced Feature • Previous versions of WSS	**Benefit** • Improves productivity by providing a richer collaboration environment than simple file shares (WSS is an add-on to WS08).

(Continued)

Feature	**Windows SharePoint Services** *(Continued)*

Functions

- Improved administration tools centralize all management and administrative tasks. WSS also supports delegation of administrative tasks.
- New compliance features also improve management. For example, policies can now be configured for Web applications based on domain or server authentication zones. This allows administrators to create different policies for intranet and extranet zones.
- Better access controls allow users, even administrators, to view only the content they have access to, reducing web page clutter.
- Migrations from previous versions can be performed gradually, making it easier to upgrade complex sites without stopping critical business processes.
- New features allow you to rename both Web and database servers, as well as change the service accounts WSS relies on from one single administrative location and have the change take place immediately across an entire Web farm.

Feature	**Windows Process Activation Services**
Description:	This service is tied to IIS 7.0 and is designed to manage application pools and worker processes instead of the World Wide Web (WWW) Service.
Category:	*Application Infrastructure*
Feature:	☑ New ☐ Improvement ☐ Update ☐ Replacement
Feature Source:	☑ WS08 ☐ Vista ☐ WS03 R2 ☐ WS03 Service Packs
Installation:	☐ By Default ☐ Add-on Through Server Manager ☑ Custom
Applies to:	☐ Small ☐ Medium ☑ Large Organizations

Replaced Feature

- Some functions of the WWW Service

Benefits

- Supports the use of the same configuration and process model for HTTP and non-HTTP sites.
- Reduces attack surface because it supports IIS componentization.

Functions

- Windows Process Activation Service (WPAS) is focused on specific listeners in Indigo. For example, if an application is designed to listen on NET.TCP instead of HTTP.SYS, you do not need to load HTTP.SYS and only require NET.TCP.
- WPAS can include the following configuration information:
  - Global configuration information.
  - Protocol configuration information for both HTTP and non-HTTP protocols.
  - Application pool configuration, for example, the process account information.
  - Site configuration, for example, bindings and applications.
  - Application configurations, for example, application pools and so on.
- WPAS reads information from the ApplicationHost.config file that holds the IIS configuration settings.
- WPAS supports the inclusion of both HTTP and non-HTTP applications in the same application pool.

Feature	Fax Server
Description:	Single-purpose workload that manages the reception and sending of facsimiles electronically.
Category:	*Application Infrastructure*
Feature:	☑ New ☐ Improvement ☐ Update ☐ Replacement
Feature Source:	☑ WS08 ☐ Vista ☐ WS03 R2 ☐ WS03 Service Packs
Installation:	☐ By Default ☑ Add-on Through Server Manager ☐ Custom
Applies to:	☑ Small ☑ Medium ☐ Large Organizations
Replaced Feature • Previous fax utilities	**Benefit** • Provides centralized electronic facsimile services.
Functions • Send and receive faxes from users' desktops. • Integrate electronic faxing to all aspects of productivity. • Simplify faxing by having it directly available from any application.	

Security Infrastructure

With the release of Windows Server 2003, Microsoft endeavored for the first time to produce secure code for a server release. They succeeded to a certain degree, since it took several months before the first security bug was found in WS03. With WS08, Microsoft wants to up the ante and is relying on some major security improvements from previous versions to bolster WS08 security. They include:

- **Security Configuration Wizard** This was from Service Pack 1 of Windows Server 2003 and is now an integral part of Server Manager.
- **Windows Firewall with Advanced Security** This provides comprehensive inbound and outbound protection to networks of all sizes.
- **Active Directory Federation Services** This lets users rely on the credentials from their own domain to access partner Web Services.
- **Active Directory Domain Services** This includes new features for the creation of identity management systems and for the auditing of all changes to the directory. New fine-grained password policies let you set different password policies for different groups of users in your organization.
- **Active Directory Certificate Services** This controls the use of PKI certificates in your organization.
- **Active Directory Rights Management Services** This controls the protection of intellectual property.

- **Windows Defender** This can help protect systems by stopping and removing spyware.
- **Network Access Protection** This serves as a quarantine network to protect against systems that do not meet your security policies.
- **Pluggable Logon Authentication Architecture** This provides a new means of integrating custom login tools, such as two-factor authentication, with Windows.
- **Read-Only DCs** These let you provide this valuable service even in areas where the server is not protected physically.
- **Secure Socket Tunneling Protocol (SSTP)** This provides an alternate means of creating a VPN link in situations where environments do not allow Internet Protocol Security (IPSec) traffic to cross the firewall.

Feature	**Security Configuration Wizard**
Description:	The Security Configuration Wizard is an attack-surface reduction mechanism for Windows servers. It guides administrators through a series of steps to increase the hardening of servers in any role.
Category:	*Security Infrastructure*
Feature:	☑ New ☐ Improvement ☐ Update ☐ Replacement
Feature Source:	☐ WS08 ☐ Vista ☐ WS03 R2 ☑ WS03 Service Packs
Installation:	☑ By Default ☐ Add-on Through Server Manager ☐ Custom
Applies to:	☑ Small ☑ Medium ☑ Large Organizations
Replaced Feature • Security Configuration and Analysis	**Benefits** • Improves security through server hardening at several levels. • Provides scriptable output that can be used to apply role-based security models to all servers.
Functions • This feature is now integrated with the Server Manager interface and is applied by default when a new server role is activated. • Supports the creation of role-based policies that secure servers at all levels, including services, feature sets, the registry, networking, TCP ports, and the file system. • Provides support for policy testing as well as rollback in the event of errors. • Provides the best explanation ever as to why components should be turned off or removed from the system. • Uses XML format to output policies for application on other servers. Supports the inclusion of scripts that can be applied at system construction to ensure that all server roles are secured from the ground up.	

Feature	Windows Firewall with Advanced Security
Description:	Provides a stateful host-based firewall that allows or blocks traffic according to user configurations to help protect users from malicious code and hackers.
Category:	*Security Infrastructure*
Feature:	☑ New ☐ Improvement ☐ Update ☐ Replacement
Feature Source:	☐ WS08 ☐ Vista ☐ WS03 R2 ☑ WS03 Service Packs
Installation:	☑ By Default ☐ Add-on Through Server Manager ☐ Custom
Applies to:	☑ Small ☑ Medium ☑ Large Organizations

Replaced Features

- Previous versions of Windows Firewall
- Previous IPSec Security Policies
- Previous IPSec Security Monitor

Benefits

- Provides host-level protection from malicious intent.
- Interacts with hardware-based firewalls to provide complete server-level protection.

Functions

- Supports rule definitions for both incoming and outgoing traffic. For example, all inbound traffic can be blocked, except if it is solicited.
- Includes a new MMC 3.0 interface for improved manageability.
- Integrates firewall policies with IPSec settings.
- Complete support for Group Policy Object (GPO)—based configuration of all settings.
- Provides two interfaces for administration: the Windows Firewall applet in Control Panel and Windows Firewall with Advanced Security in Administrative Tools.
- Provides discreet exception rule creation, including support for IP port numbers, source or destination IP addresses, Transmission Control Protocol (TCP) or User Datagram Protocol (UPD) ports, types of interfaces—Network Interface Card (NIC), FireWire, or wireless, for example—types of traffic (such as IPv4 or IPv6), or even services.

Feature	Active Directory Federation Services
Description:	Active Directory Federation Services (ADFS) provides a means to support federated identity across the Internet through the use of Web Service architectures without having to open critical ports on the firewall.
Category:	*Security Infrastructure*
Feature:	☑ New ☐ Improvement ☐ Update ☐ Replacement
Feature Source:	☐ WS08 ☐ Vista ☑ WS03 R2 ☐ WS03 Service Packs
Installation:	☐ By Default ☑ Add-on Through Server Manager ☐ Custom
Applies to:	☑ Small ☑ Medium ☑ Large Organizations

(Continued)

Feature	**Active Directory Federation Services** *(Continued)*
Replaced Feature • None, though it removes the need to expose Active Directory to the Internet	**Benefits** • Provides a foundation for integrated identity management across boundaries. • Lets organizations use their own Active Directories to access both internal and external partner resources.
Functions • Extends Active Directory to the Internet by letting you rely on the internal directory to access partner resources. This helps reduce the number of security stores to manage. • Provides a means to use Windows-based Authentication in Web applications on the Internet. • Through the use of the Web Service foundation, ADFS provides interoperability with non-Windows environments that support the same foundation. • Supports passive clients, such as Web browsers. Provides the foundation for Simple Object Access Protocol (SOAP)—based smart clients, such as cell phones, personal digital assistants (PDAs), and desktop and server applications.	

Feature	**Active Directory Domain Services**
Description:	Active Directory Domain Services (ADDS) provides a means to create comprehensive identity management systems that serve to authenticate users, computers, and services in your network.
Category:	*Security Infrastructure*
Feature:	☐ New ☐ Improvement ☑ Update ☐ Replacement
Feature Source:	☑ WS08 ☐ Vista ☐ WS03 R2 ☐ WS03 Service Packs
Installation:	☐ By Default ☑ Add on Through Server Manager ☐ Custom
Applies to:	☑ Small ☑ Medium ☑ Large Organizations
Replaced Feature • Active Directory from previous versions of Windows Server	**Benefits** • Provides a foundation for integrated identity management within your network. • Provides a central location for all identity management.
Functions • The ADDS installation wizard (which can also be invoked using the DCPROMO.EXE command) has been reconfigured to provide better choices during setup. For example, administrators can select the options they need during installation, identify the site the server should belong to, determine forest and domain functional levels, and create DNS delegations directly in the wizard during installation. In addition, the wizard supports a completely unattended install in order to support the new Server Core, which provides no graphical interface at all. • Active Directory Sites and Services includes new features that let administrators find domain controllers more easily, as well as work with read-only DCs and identify their password policy, also seeing which passwords have been sent to the RODC and which are currently stored in them.	

(Continued)

Feature	Active Directory Domain Services *(Continued)*

- ADDS can also be restarted. This means that you can shut down the ADDS service on a domain controller (DC) to perform offline operations, such as database defragmentation and compression, without having to shut down and reboot the DC. ADDS services are not available from this server during this operation; this is one more reason for having more than one DC at all times.
- The Directory Services Restore Mode has not changed in WS08. This means that to restore objects to the NTDS.DIT database, you must still restart the domain controller in this protected offline mode.
- A new Directory Services audit policy can be set to capture all value changes in the directory. This lets administrators track the changes made to the directory at all times and makes it easier to roll back these changes.
- Fine-grained password policies let you set different password and account lockout policies for different groups of users in a domain.
- A new Snapshot Viewer lets you view objects that have been previously deleted from the directory. It functions much like the Previous Versions' client with file shares. Once you have identified which snapshot to restore from, you can perform the correction in your Active Directory.

Feature	Active Directory Certificate Services

Description: Active Directory Certificate Services (ADCS) provides a means to create and manage PKI certificates for users, computers, and services within your organization.

Category: *Security Infrastructure*

Feature: ☐ New ☐ Improvement ☐ Update ☑ Replacement

Feature Source: ☑ WS08 ☐ Vista ☐ WS03 R2 ☐ WS03 Service Packs

Installation: ☐ By Default ☑ Add-on Through Server Manager ☐ Custom

Applies to: ☐ Small ☐ Medium ☑ Large Organizations

Replaced Feature	Benefit
• PKI services from previous versions of Windows Server	• Provides a foundation for integrated certificate management within your network.

Functions

- A new console snap-in, Enterprise PKI or PKIView, now lets you view the health status of all of the enterprise certificate authorities (CAs) within your network. It also supports Unicode, allowing you to view certificate status in any language supported by Windows.
- Supports the Microsoft Simple Certificate Enrollment Protocol (MSCEP), which allows network devices such as routers and switches to enroll in the CA and obtain certificates of their own. This extends the chain of trust to these devices.
- Supports Online Certificate Status Protocol (OCSP), which, in some cases, can be used to eliminate the need for Certificate Revocation Lists (CRLs) and lets WS08 automatically distribute and update certificate revocation status information. OCSP provides information only about the single certificate at hand, as opposed to having to download and read an entire CRL. This speeds up the validation process.

Feature	Active Directory Rights Management Services
Description:	Active Directory Rights Management Services (ADRMS) provides information protection to help ensure that electronic information is secured from unauthorized use.
Category:	*Security Infrastructure*
Feature:	☑ New ☐ Improvement ☐ Update ☐ Replacement
Feature Source:	☑ WS08 ☐ Vista ☐ WS03 R2 ☐ WS03 Service Packs
Installation:	☐ By Default ☑ Add-on Through Server Manager ☐ Custom
Applies to:	☑ Small ☑ Medium ☑ Large Organizations
Replaced Feature • Windows Rights Management Server	**Benefit** • Protect all organizational data from tampering and illegal use.
Functions • Protects electronic information both inside and outside the firewall. • Protects information both online and offline. • Compliant with the Federal Information Processing Standards (FIPS). • Supports two-factor authentication. • Simple interface; easy deployment and configuration for persistent protection.	

Feature	Windows Defender
Description:	Microsoft's flagship anti-spyware tool, Windows Defender, provides protection from spyware and other malicious code.
Category:	*Security Infrastructure*
Feature:	☑ New ☐ Improvement ☐ Update ☐ Replacement
Feature Source:	☐ WS08 ☑ Vista ☐ WS03 R2 ☐ WS03 Service Packs
Installation:	☑ By Default ☐ Add-on Through Server Manager ☐ Custom
Applies to:	☑ Small ☑ Medium ☑ Large Organizations
Replaced Feature • None	**Benefit** • Helps protect servers from unwanted or malicious code installation through real-time protection and updated file definitions.
Functions • Provides real-time protection from unwanted or malicious code. • Supported by regularly updated definition files and the Microsoft Anti-spyware Research Center. • Can help remove and report suspected malicious or unwanted code.	

Feature	Network Access Protection (NAP)
Description:	Provides a framework that allows administrators to establish health requirements for device connections to the network and to prevent computers that do not meet these requirements from communicating with the network.
Category:	*Security Infrastructure*
Feature:	☑ New ☐ Improvement ☐ Update ☐ Replacement
Feature Source:	☑ WS08 ☐ Vista ☐ WS03 R2 ☐ WS03 Service Packs
Installation:	☐ By Default ☑ Add-on Through Server Manager ☐ Custom
Applies to:	☐ Small ☑ Medium ☑ Large Organizations
Replaced Feature • Network Policy Server replaces the Internet Authentication Service (IAS)	**Benefits** • Helps ensure the security of the network by making sure all clients that connect to it comply with the policies you set. • Will assist client systems in the update process during the quarantine.
Functions • Checks the health of a system before allowing it to connect to network resources. If systems are deemed not healthy, they are placed in quarantine and given the opportunity to meet compliance by installing missing components. Once a healthy state has been achieved, the systems are taken out of quarantine and allowed access to resources. • Checks the health and status of roaming laptops and ensures the health of internal desktop computers. • Can help determine the health of visiting laptops before they connect to network resources. • Can also verify the health and policy compliance of unmanaged home computers. • Relies on the Network Policy Server (NPS) to monitor health policies for all clients, including Vista, XP SP2, and Windows Server 2008.	

Feature	Pluggable Logon Authentication Architecture
Description:	Windows Server 2008 and Windows Vista rely on Credential Security Service Providers (CredSSP) to pass logon authentication data from the client to the server.
Category:	*Security Infrastructure*
Feature:	☑ New ☐ Improvement ☐ Update ☐ Replacement
Feature Source:	☐ WS08 ☑ Vista ☐ WS03 R2 ☐ WS03 Service Packs
Installation:	☑ By Default ☐ Add-on Through Server Manager ☐ Custom
Applies to:	☑ Small ☑ Medium ☑ Large Organizations
Replaced Feature • Graphical Interface for Networked Authentication (GINA)	**Benefit** • Simplifies use of multiple logon technologies, such as two-factor authentication methods, on Windows systems.

(Continued)

Feature	**Pluggable Logon Authentication Architecture** *(Continued)*
Functions • Provides a simpler mechanism for integrating multiple logon technologies, for example, smart cards or fingerprint authentication, to the Windows model. • CredSSP was formerly used with Terminal Services and Web Services to provide single sign-on (SSO); it has now been fully integrated with Windows. • Provides a simpler model for storing multiple identities, such as username and passwords for different applications. • Makes it easier for third parties to integrate additional logon technologies with Windows, because it is based on the .NET Framework environment.	

Feature	**Read-Only Domain Controllers (RODCs)**
Description:	A new type of domain controller that makes it possible for organizations to deploy a domain controller in locations where physical security cannot be guaranteed. The RODC hosts a read-only replica of the ADDS database for a given domain.
Category:	*Security Infrastructure*
Feature:	☐ New ☐ Improvement ☑ Update ☐ Replacement
Feature Source:	☑ WS08 ☐ Vista ☐ WS03 R2 ☐ WS03 Service Packs
Installation:	☐ By Default ☐ Add-on Through Server Manager ☑ Custom
Applies to:	☐ Small ☑ Medium ☑ Large Organizations
Replaced Feature • Backup Domain Controller in Windows NT	**Benefit** • Helps protect critical data on servers that you cannot physically secure.
Functions • Maintains a read-only copy of the Active Directory database through unidirectional replication. • Automatically uses Universal Group Membership Caching (UGMC) to replace the need for Global Catalog Servers. • Relies on a Primary Domain Controller (PDC) Emulator running on Windows Server 2008 to function. • Must run in a forest running a forest functional mode of WS03 or later. • Relies on the RODC DNS service using new PROZs. • Users can be granted administrative delegation to RODCs without receiving any access rights to any other DC in the forest. This allows them to log on locally and perform maintenance tasks without risk.	

Feature	**Secure Sockets Tunneling Protocol (SSTP)**
Description:	A remote access tunneling protocol that is used to create VPN links that rely on the SSL instead of on IPSec. SSL VPNs pass through port 443.
Category:	*Security Infrastructure*
Feature:	☑ New ☐ Improvement ☐ Update ☐ Replacement
Feature Source:	☑ WS08 ☐ Vista ☐ WS03 R2 ☐ WS03 Service Packs

(Continued)

Feature	Secure Sockets Tunneling Protocol (SSTP) *(Continued)*
Installation: ☐ By Default ☑ Add-on Through Server Manager ☐ Custom	
Applies to: ☑ Small ☑ Medium ☑ Large Organizations	
Replaced Feature • None	**Benefit** • Creates simpler VPN tunnels because they rely on SSL instead of IPSec.
Functions • Creates a link using port 443, which most firewalls keep open. • Does not require any custom settings to pass through NAT links, Web proxies, or firewall transversals. • Simpler to set up and maintain than any other VPN link. • Powerful VPN model that can be used by businesses of all sizes.	

TIP *For more information on SSL VPNs, read the white paper entitled "The Case for SSL Virtual Private Networks" at http://redmondmag.com/techlibrary/resources.asp?id=170.*

Disk and File Subsystem

The final category of new features focuses on the disk and file subsystem, because this is a critical component of Windows Server. Since all operations require some access to disk resources, this component is one of the most important in the entire OS. Some special features at this level include:

- **DFS Namespace and Replication** The Distributed File System (DFS) was vastly improved with the R2 release of WS03, especially in terms of replication.
- **Common Log File System** A system that ensures that all log files are compatible with each other, letting you collect and manage them in one interface.
- **File Server Quotas** Quotas that are assigned at the file share level instead of at the entire disk volume level, as with previous versions of Windows Server.
- **Storage Management for SANs** A common interface and driver to access SANs from any manufacturer.
- **Windows ReadyDrive** A technology that relies on new hybrid disks—disks that include RAM—to speed access to disk-based resources.
- **BitLocker Drive Encryption** A new encryption mechanism that can encrypt the entire disk drive, not only user files.
- **Automatic Disk Defragmentation** A system that ensures that all file components are located in the same sectors of the hard disk drive for speedier access.
- **Self-Healing NTFS** A transactional file system that writes all transactions to logs before committing them to the file system itself.
- **Symbolic Linking** A tool that allows you to use a file system object to point to another file system object.

Each of these makes for a cleaner, faster Windows Server 2008.

Feature	DFS Namespace and Replication
Description:	The Distributed File System (DFS) is a system for managing shared file resources across a network and make it easier for users to access these resources. DFS is typically a replacement for mapped network drives.
Category:	*Disk and File Subsystem*
Feature:	☐ New ☑ Improvement ☐ Update ☐ Replacement
Feature Source:	☐ WS08 ☐ Vista ☑ WS03 R2 ☐ WS03 Service Packs
Installation:	☐ By Default ☑ Add-on Through Server Manager ☐ Custom
Applies to:	☐ Small ☑ Medium ☑ Large Organizations

Replaced Features

- Previous versions of DFS in Windows 2000 and Windows Server 2003
- File Replication Service (FRS) for DFS

Benefits

- Gives users access to file shares using common naming practices, eliminating the need for mapped network drives.
- When linked with replication, gives users access to the same data in different locations across the WAN.

Functions

- DFS is now divided into two components: namespaces and replication. Namespaces let you designate a virtual name or alias for file shares across the network. Actual file shares are then linked to the new namespace. Replication lets you copy content from one file share to another by using a byte-level replication mechanism that only replicates changes to files, not entire files.
- Namespaces can create virtual folder trees that make more sense to end users. The actual file shares that are linked to this folder tree can be located on any server in the organization. Accessing files in the shares is performed through the virtual tree and is completely transparent to users. Namespaces can be used with or without replication. Domain-based namespaces are replicated in ADDS so that they are available to users wherever they are in the network.
- DFS Replication (DFSR) not only supports DFS, but can also replicate files from any server to any other server in the organization. It relies on the Remote Differential Compression (RDC) algorithm, which replicates only the changes to files and not the entire files themselves—after the source and the target have been synchronized at least once. Changes are monitored at the byte level, and through bandwidth throttling and replication scheduling, make more efficient use of WAN links. DFSR also supports a multimaster model, so changes can originate from any system in the namespace. Collision detection algorithms round this out to make sure that only the right changes are replicated.

Feature	Common Log File System
Description:	The Common Log File System (CLFS) provides a general-purpose log file subsystem in Windows Server 2008 that is exposed to both kernel and user mode applications. It supports consolidation and integration of logs from diverse applications.
Category:	*Disk and File Subsystem*
Feature:	☑ New ☐ Improvement ☐ Update ☐ Replacement
Feature Source:	☐ WS08 ☐ Vista ☑ WS03 R2 ☐ WS03 Service Packs

(Continued)

Feature	Common Log File System *(Continued)*
Installation: ☑ By Default ☐ Add-on Through Server Manager ☐ Custom	
Applies to: ☑ Small ☑ Medium ☑ Large Organizations	
Replaced Feature • Previous logging file systems	**Benefit** • Provides a single integrated way to log events in Windows and streamline event management.
Functions • CLFS provides a set of application programming interfaces (APIs) that lets developers log information about their applications without having to write reams of custom code. • Supports applications or middleware that rely on writing or reading sequential data. Applications in this category include replication agents, auditing agents, databases, and transactional resource managers. New applications such as DFSR rely on this subsystem to write the events related to their operation. • Relying on CLFS lets WS08 log information about a vast number of events that were not monitored in previous editions of Windows Server.	

Feature	File Server Quotas
Description:	Lets administrators control the space usage on file shares to keep users within limits and conserve disk space.
Category:	*Disk and File Subsystem*
Feature:	☑ New ☐ Improvement ☐ Update ☐ Replacement
Feature Source:	☐ WS08 ☐ Vista ☑ WS03 R2 ☐ WS03 Service Packs
Installation:	☐ By Default ☐ Add-on Through Server Manager ☑ Custom
Applies to:	☐ Small ☑ Medium ☑ Large Organizations
Replaced Feature • Volume quotas	**Benefit** • File server quotas are assigned at the folder level, giving administrators better control over file share usage.
Functions • Quotas can now be assigned either at the volume level, as in previous versions of Windows Server, or at the folder level, giving administrators more granular control. Templates can be created and automatically assigned at the creation of any new file share.	

Feature	Storage Management for SANs
Description:	Storage Management for SANs is a new console that lets administrators create and manage logical unit numbers (LUNs) on fibre channel and Internet Small Computer Systems Interface (iSCSI) disk drive subsystems in a storage area network (SAN).
Category:	*Disk and File Subsystem*
Feature:	☑ New ☐ Improvement ☐ Update ☐ Replacement

(Continued)

Feature	**Storage Management for SANs** *(Continued)*
Feature Source: ☐ WS08 ☐ Vista ☑ WS03 R2 ☐ WS03 Service Packs	
Installation: ☐ By Default ☐ Add-on Through Server Manager ☑ Custom	
Applies to: ☐ Small ☑ Medium ☑ Large Organizations	
Replaced Feature • None	**Benefits** • Provides a single view of SAN structures from within Windows. • Facilitates SAN LUN management.
Functions • Can be used on any SAN that supports Virtual Disk Server (VDS). • Can be used to create and assign LUNs, modify or change connections between LUNs and the servers attached to a SAN, or set security properties for iSCSI storage subsystems. • Eliminates need for proprietary disk managers.	

Feature	**Windows ReadyDrive**
Description:	Feature that takes advantage of hybrid hard disks or hard disks that include non-volatile Flash memory as well as the actual disk drive.
Category: *Disk and File Subsystem*	
Feature: ☑ New ☐ Improvement ☐ Update ☐ Replacement	
Feature Source: ☐ WS08 ☑ Vista ☐ WS03 R2 ☐ WS03 Service Packs	
Installation: ☑ By Default ☐ Add-on Through Server Manager ☐ Custom	
Applies to: ☑ Small ☑ Medium ☑ Large Organizations	
Replaced Feature • None	**Benefit** • Systems equipped with the appropriate hybrid hard disks will perform much faster than traditional systems.
Functions • Relies on Flash memory to boot faster, resume from hibernation in less time, preserve battery power, and improve the reliability of your disks. • While hybrid disks are mostly intended for mobile computers to help preserve battery power, they can also work with WS08.	

Feature	**BitLocker Drive Encryption**
Description:	Provides protection by encrypting the entire hard disk.
Category: *Disk and File Subsystem*	
Feature: ☑ New ☐ Improvement ☐ Update ☐ Replacement	

(Continued)

Feature	BitLocker Drive Encryption *(Continued)*
Feature Source: ☐ WS08 ☑ Vista ☐ WS03 R2 ☐ WS03 Service Packs	
Installation: ☐ By Default ☐ Add-on Through Server Manager ☑ Custom	
Applies to: ☑ Small ☑ Medium ☑ Large Organizations	
Replaced Feature • None	**Benefit** • Protects server systems by encrypting the entire hard disk drive, securing the data from loss or theft.
Functions • BitLocker encrypts the entire Windows system volume and protects from schemes like NTFS for DOS, which lets users bypass the security features of the hard disk drive. • BitLocker can rely on Trusted Protection Module (TPM) version 1.2—a hardware-based encryption key storage chip—or rely on an external USB Flash disk to store the encryption keys. Relying on TPM chips will greatly enhance security, since they are built into the system and will no longer work if tampered with. • BitLocker is an ideal companion to the RODC role, since it is often used in areas where servers cannot be physically protected.	

Feature	Automatic Disk Defragmentation
Description: Windows Server 2008 includes automatic built-in disk defragmentation that is turned on by default at installation.	
Category: *Disk and File Subsystem*	
Feature: ☑ New ☐ Improvement ☐ Update ☐ Replacement	
Feature Source: ☐ WS08 ☑ Vista ☐ WS03 R2 ☐ WS03 Service Packs	
Installation: ☑ By Default ☐ Add-on Through Server Manager ☐ Custom	
Applies to: ☑ Small ☑ Medium ☑ Large Organizations	
Replaced Feature • Older defragmentation tool	**Benefit** • Maintains hard disks at peak performance by ensuring that all files are stored contiguously on the disk.
Functions • Automatically defragments drives and volumes after the initial installation is complete. Schedule is set to once per week by default, but can be modified. • Defragmentation occurs in the background and does not affect system performance, since it is given a low-priority code, which stops the operation when other, higher-priority tasks are run.	

Feature	Self-Healing and Transactional NTFS
Description:	A disk formatting system that ensures disks are maintained at their optimal level when in use.
Category:	*Disk and File Subsystem*
Feature:	☑ New ☐ Improvement ☐ Update ☐ Replacement
Feature Source:	☑ WS08 ☐ Vista ☐ WS03 R2 ☐ WS03 Service Packs
Installation:	☑ By Default ☐ Add-on Through Server Manager ☐ Custom
Applies to:	☑ Small ☑ Medium ☑ Large Organizations
Replaced Feature • Previous versions of NTFS	**Benefit** • Ensures that data is properly committed on disks as they are in use and helps protect data recovery from hard drives.

Functions

- The move to a transacted file system ensures that transactions are properly committed to the hard disk. This is valuable for transactions that affect the Windows registry, protecting it from corruption. In the event of a shutdown before transactions are committed, they are committed at startup to ensure that the hard drive or volume has integrated the latest changes.
- Transacted file systems are also useful for multiple writes to the same volume, updates to multiple files on different volumes, or updates to files on remote volumes.
- Self-healing NTFS works in conjunction with the transactional file system to protect data that is stored on hard drives or volumes. When issues are discovered, NTFS initiates repairs of the damage automatically without having to run the CHKDSK.EXE utility.

Feature	Symbolic Linking
Description:	Used to point from one location to another in the file system.
Category:	*Disk and File Subsystem*
Feature:	☑ New ☐ Improvement ☐ Update ☐ Replacement
Feature Source:	☑ WS08 ☐ Vista ☐ WS03 R2 ☐ WS03 Service Packs
Installation:	☑ By Default ☐ Add-on Through Server Manager ☐ Custom
Applies to:	☑ Small ☑ Medium ☑ Large Organizations
Replaced Feature • None	**Benefit** • Lets you make better use of file system resources.

Functions

- You can transparently share data across volumes without complex reformats or disk extensions.
- Works with both local and shared network resources.
- Provides an additional way besides variables to point from one location to the other on the file system.
- Links can be permanent or volatile.

TIP *You can get an updated copy of all of these new features online at www.reso-net.com/livre.asp?p=main&b=WS08. A one-time registration is required, but once you're done, you can modify this text and set it up as part of your own migration documentation.*

The Next Step

The next step for you now is to collect all of these new features, put them together in a list that makes sense to you and your organization, and prepare for the migration. There is one more chapter in this part of the book. Chapter 2 will give you a tour of the new Windows Server 2008 interface and show you how things will be done from now on. After that, you'll be ready to move on to preparing for the migration itself. We will guide you through this process to make it as simple to upgrade or migrate as possible and to help you make the most of this powerful operating system.

CHAPTER 2

Interact with Windows Server 2008

If you believe Microsoft, the release of Windows Vista and, correspondingly, Windows Server 2008 (WS08), brings in a new era in user productivity. We've all heard it before, and we know that each time a new operating system (OS) comes out, especially when it is coupled with a new version of a productivity suite as Vista was with Microsoft Office 2007, we get these promises, and lo, most of us haven't seen this increase in productivity. Well, Vista has been out for a while, and now you know as well as we do that it does indeed improve user productivity.

That's because over the past decade, we've all been very good at producing information—tons of information, in fact—and storing it in digital format. What does that lead to? The impossibility of finding anything. The fact that the basic user interface in Vista and WS08 has integrated search has seriously improved the productivity of all end users. According to some industry analysts, users have been able to shave off three to nine hours a week because of this feature. This is an improvement. It is also a boon to administrators, since search also works for IT tools.

And because of this feature, we as IT professionals no longer have to worry about installing or deploying third-party search tools—tools that may or may not respect the security descriptors we apply to data within our networks. With Vista, search is how you access all information. The Start menu sports a search tool and provides constant search, the Explorer has an integrated search tool, Internet Explorer (IE) includes a search tool—search is everywhere. Vista's search indexes everything it has access to: personal folders, system tools, legacy shared folders, removable drives, collaboration spaces, and so on—all driven by the capability of the PC to index content. Now that Windows Server 2008 is available, you can integrate the desktop search with server-based indices and take a load off of the local PC. This should increase the power of Vista even more and add to users' productivity enhancements.

Tip *For full details on what is indexed by the Vista client, go to www.realtime-vista.com/administration/2006/12/vista_indexing_options.htm.*

Search is only one element of Vista that has been included in WS08. There are several more. The WS08 user interface (UI) is entirely based on the Vista interface, so if you have been working with Vista, you'll already be familiar with it; but if you haven't, you'll have to learn some new tricks. This is what this chapter is all about: bringing you up to speed on the interface changes you'll find in WS08. That's why this chapter covers:

- The user interface itself
- The Initial Configuration Tasks (ICT) interface
- Server Manager
- Remote Desktop modifications
- The command prompt
- Windows PowerShell
- Help and Support

Each of these will affect how you work with WS08 and Vista. To make it easier for you to locate new commands and new ways to do things, the chapter concludes with a table that outlines commands in older versions of Windows versus the corresponding commands in WS08.

The User Interface

By default, WS08 presents the traditional UI à la Windows 2000. If you're comfortable working with an interface that is more than seven years old, go ahead—talk about the ability of IT personnel to deal with change. Personally, we think you should transform this interface into Vista Aero Glass. Sure, your servers might not have the graphics cards required to run the Aero graphics, but at least you will have an interface that is similar to what you are working with on the desktop.

If you want to use this interface, you need to turn on the Themes service, which is off by default. Here's how:

1. Launch Server Manager, if it isn't already up, or, if you're more familiar with Computer Management, launch it instead.
2. In Server Manager, use the local server home page to click Add Features in the details pane.
3. In the Add Features Wizard, check the Desktop Experience feature.
4. Add the Desktop Experience, and restart the server to finish the installation process.
5. Then click Close on the Post-Reboot Configuration Wizard, return to Server Manager, expand Configuration in the tree pane, and click Services.
6. Find the Themes service in the list in the details pane. This service is disabled by default because it uses system resources.
7. Set the startup properties for the service to Automatic, click Apply, and start the service. Click OK to close the properties dialog box.
8. Next, minimize the Console, right-click the desktop, and choose Personalize.
9. In the Personalize window, select Theme.
10. In the Theme drop-down list, select Windows Vista, and click OK.

There you are. You now have the Vista theme on your server. To make sure that all users have access to this theme, you should update the default user on the server image before it is deployed. This will be discussed in future chapters. Now, isn't that more pleasant?

Now that you're working with the Vista interface, let's look at what has changed.

The Desktop

The desktop itself is mostly unchanged. It does sport a new Start button and a new Start menu. The Quick Launch area is still as useful as it has ever been. What's more, Microsoft finally added "Add to Quick Launch" to the context menu of any shortcut. This makes using the Quick Launch area even easier. Now there's no reason for clutter on the desktop.

That's good as well, since you will now need your desktop real estate to include items such as gadgets, the new small utilities Microsoft set up in the Vista Sidebar. Gadgets can include a whole series of items, one of which is cool for administrators, since it reports the uptime for a server. Many more gadgets are available. You'll find the Sidebar is quite useful, too, when you populate it right.

TIP *Several gadgets are available for administration. For a good list of gadgets, go to the Windows Live Gallery at http://gallery.live.com.*

You'll also want to work extensively with the Start menu. Mostly, you'll find that with the Sidebar properly populated, with the Quick Launch area and the ability to search directly from the Start menu, you won't really need anything else on the desktop to access your favorite administration tools. Note that in terms of content, there is little difference between the Start menu in the Vista theme or in Windows 2000 (Classic) mode. It just looks so much better in Vista mode (see Figure 2-1).

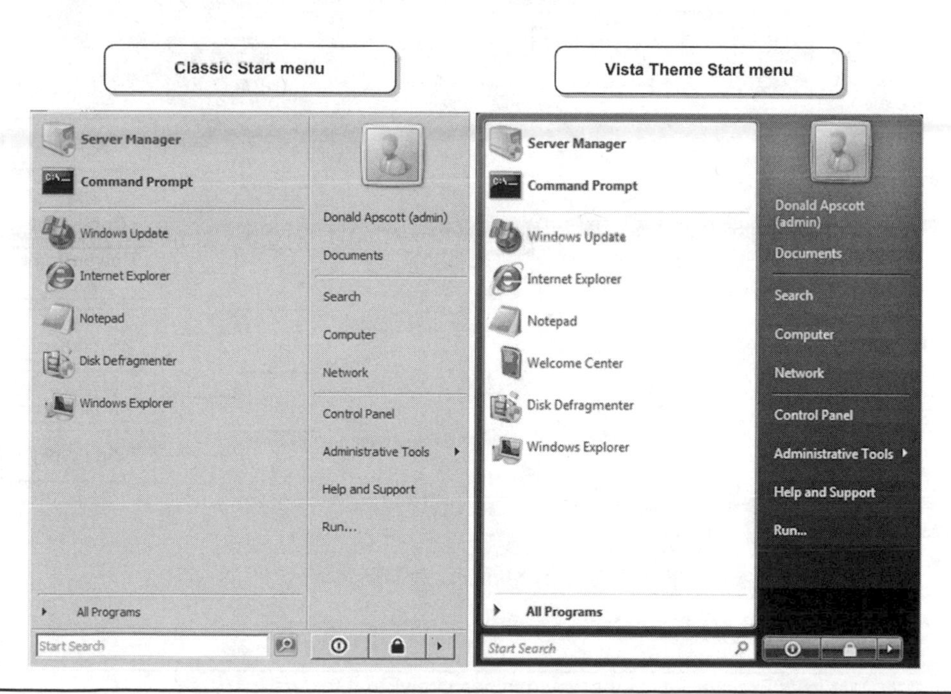

FIGURE 2-1 The Start menu in both the Classic theme and the Vista theme

The Windows Explorer

Windows Explorer has also had a bit of a facelift. Search is such an integral part of the Windows system today that Windows Explorer now boasts new search folders—folders that are virtual representations of data based on search criteria. It's not WinFS—Microsoft's flagship file system due to replace NTFS—but it works and works really well. Need to keep track of a special project? All you have to do is create a virtual or search folder based on a selection of keywords, and you will always have access to the data so long as you have the proper permissions and you have a connection to it.

Creating virtual folders is really simple: Just perform the search, click **Save Search**, and give the folder a meaningful name. Saved searches are dynamic, so any time new content is added, be it on an indexed network, local, or even removable drive, it will automatically be linked to your virtual or search folder. Figure 2-2 shows how saved search folders work. It also lays out the new Windows Explorer window. Note that this window includes a breadcrumb access bar. Breadcrumbs are at the heart of navigation in WS08. Make use of them often, and you will see just how useful they can be.

In addition to having access to indexed content, you have full control over the way you view and organize data in Windows Explorer. New buttons sort information in new ways, new views show extensive previews of document contents, and new filters let you structure information just the way you like it. Even better, you can restore a previous version of any document so long as it existed before the last shadow copy was taken—that's right, shadow copies are now available everywhere by default, even the PC. With Windows Server 2008 and Vista, there should be no reason why anyone would ever lose a document again.

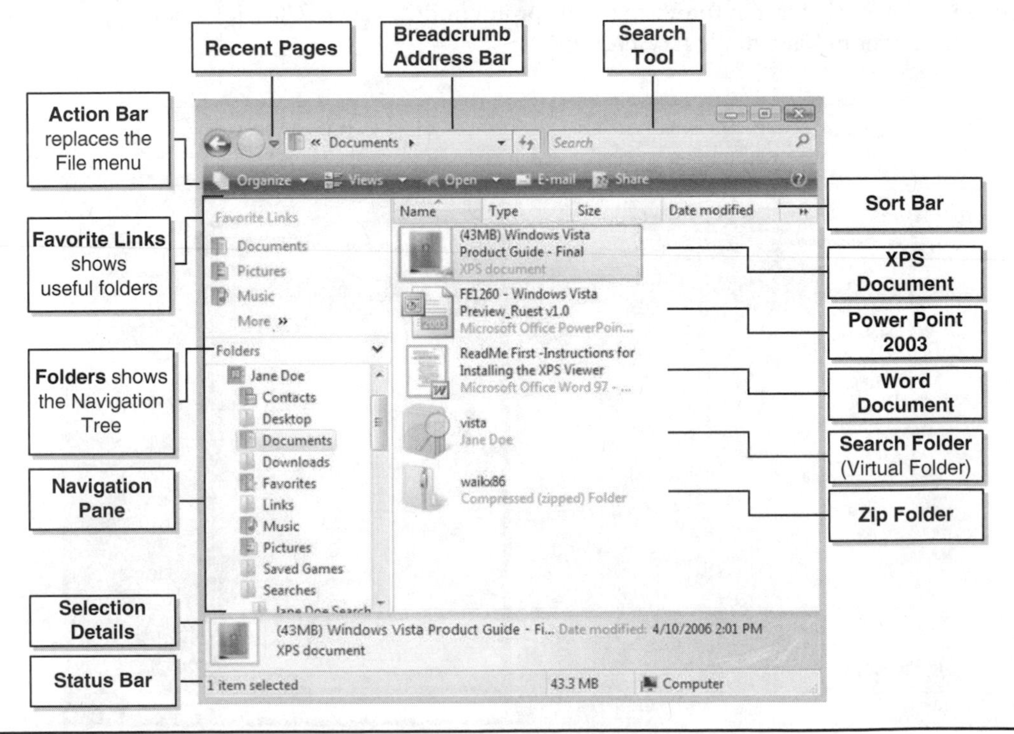

FIGURE 2-2 Windows Explorer lets you save searches into virtual folders.

Windows Server 2008 also includes many new features that were originally designed to speed up Vista. This includes:

- SuperFetch learns from your work habits and preloads your most common applications into memory before you call on them. When you actually do call on them, they will launch from random access memory (RAM) and not from disk.
- ReadyBoost relies on Flash memory to extend the reach of normal RAM and reduce hard disk access times. Several manufacturers have released special drives (Universal Serial Bus—USB—and Flash) to address this new need. Ideally, you will use an external drive that has up to four times the amount of memory available in the system's RAM. Imagine that you need to upgrade RAM on a server: Just pop in a Flash drive, and away you go. Ideally, this would be a temporary solution, but it is still valid. Keep in mind that if your servers support it, WS08 supports hot memory additions, or the ability to add RAM while the server is running.

With the exception of ReadyBoost, most performance improvements are completely transparent. Other speed enhancements include self-tuning performance and diagnostics that will detect and attempt to self-correct any performance-related issue. Like Vista, WS08 offers several improvements in speed. Our advice: Run Windows Server 2008 on a 64-bit system as much as possible, especially a multicore system. Servers gain a ton of capacity when running on 64-bit hardware.

User Account Control

If you've worked with Vista at all, you'll already be familiar with User Account Control (UAC). With UAC, Windows Server 2008 allows administrators to execute most processes in the context of a standard user and only elevate privileges by consent. This means that whether you have a standard user or an administrator account, your actions will be protected, since you will have to authorize any administrative task.

OUR ADVICE *Continue to use a standard user account for everyday work, then use the Run as Administrator command to perform administrative tasks. The major difference between a standard user account and an administrative account in UAC is that with a standard user account, you also need to give both the username and password to grant permission for an action. You might find it annoying at first, but you'll quickly get used to it.*

CAUTION *Because of UAC, WS08 and Vista no longer support command-line run-as commands. In XP and WS03, we were able to create run-as shortcuts that would call on a command file that would pass the proper credentials to the run-as command. However, since UAC restricts all elevation requests, you'll find that any run-as shortcuts of this type won't work. That is because the command-line form of run-as does not include an elevation switch. You'll have to use the graphical version of Run as Administrator from now on.*

UAC prompts are impossible to miss, because the entire desktop is dimmed when UAC is activated and only the UAC dialog box is displayed clearly (see Figure 2-3). UAC will require significant adaptation, since it is a completely new way to work as a standard user.

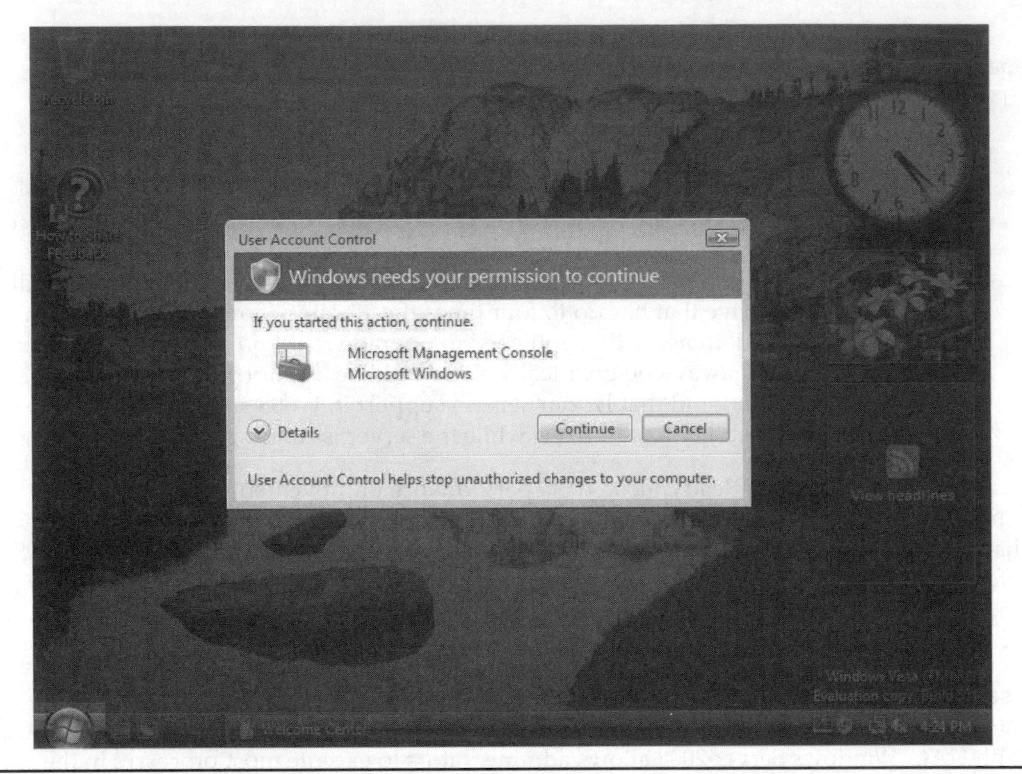

FIGURE 2-3 Using an application requiring UAC elevation

In addition to UAC, Windows Server 2008 supports Fast User Switching, even in a domain. If you want or need to use a computer that is already in use, there is no need to log off the current user—just switch users, perform your tasks, and then log off. The existing user's session will still be live, and the user may not even know someone else used the server.

Internet Explorer 7

WS08 also includes Internet Explorer (IE) version 7, which has several improvements in terms of ease of use—tabbed browsing, Really Simple Syndication (RSS) feed integration, and improved web page printing—but its major improvements are in secure Web browsing. You should already be familiar with IE7's features:

- Phishing web site identification and reporting tools
- A clearer way to determine whether you are connected to a web site using either the Secure Sockets Layer (SSL) or Transport Layer Security (TLS)
- ActiveX opt-in, which lets you determine which ActiveX controls are safe to use
- Single-click deletion of all browsing history
- Automatic protection from domain name spoofing
- Control of Uniform Resource Locator (URL) processing to avoid URL parsing exploits
- Protected mode, isolating itself from other applications running in the OS

As you can see, if you have experience with Vista, WS08 should be easy to master. If not, you'll have to get used to a few interface changes, but they're not major. Other changes have more impact. These are the changes we examine next.

Control Panel

Another significant change from Windows Server 2003 is the way Control Panel works and how it is used to access configuration changes on a system. You'll notice that as soon as you open Control Panel, it opens the classic view by default. To set it to the Vista view, click Control Panel Home in the left pane.

By default, Control Panel is divided into ten sections:

- **System and Maintenance** lets you control how the system works and is configured.
- **Security** gives you access to the new Vista-like Security Center.
- **Network and Internet** gives you access to the new Network and Sharing Center, a one-stop connectivity control center.
- **Hardware and Sound** let you control printers, mouse, sound devices, and any new device added to your system.
- **Programs** replaces the old Add or Remove Programs and lets you control applications and startup programs in one location.
- **User Accounts** controls accounts on member servers and other account details, such as pictures and passwords for domain accounts.
- **Appearance and Personalization** lets you control the look and feel of your interface.
- **Clock, Language, and Region** control the time zone and language you use in your server interface.
- **Ease of Access** is used to simplify the way you access the system.
- **Additional Options** is a kind of catch-all that includes everything else. In most cases, this option is empty.

The items that have changed the most are the Security Center, the Network and Sharing Center (see Figure 2-4), and Appearance and Personalization.

You may also find that it is more difficult to locate regularly used items, such as System Properties and so on. All you have to do is remember that Control Panel includes a task list in the left pane. Keep an eye on this list, as you will find several of your favorite property sheets are located here.

Initial Configuration Tasks

If you've worked with Windows Vista, you know that after a new installation, Vista opens with the Welcome Center—an interface that provides a single point of interaction for finalizing the PC configuration. In WS08, the Welcome Center is replaced with the Initial Configuration Tasks (ICT) interface (see Figure 2-5).

ICT is used to complete the configuration of a server installation. As with the installation of Vista, the installation of WS08 no longer requests information during the installation process. Once you have input the product ID key, the system is installed with defaults—blank administrator password that requests an immediate change at first logon,

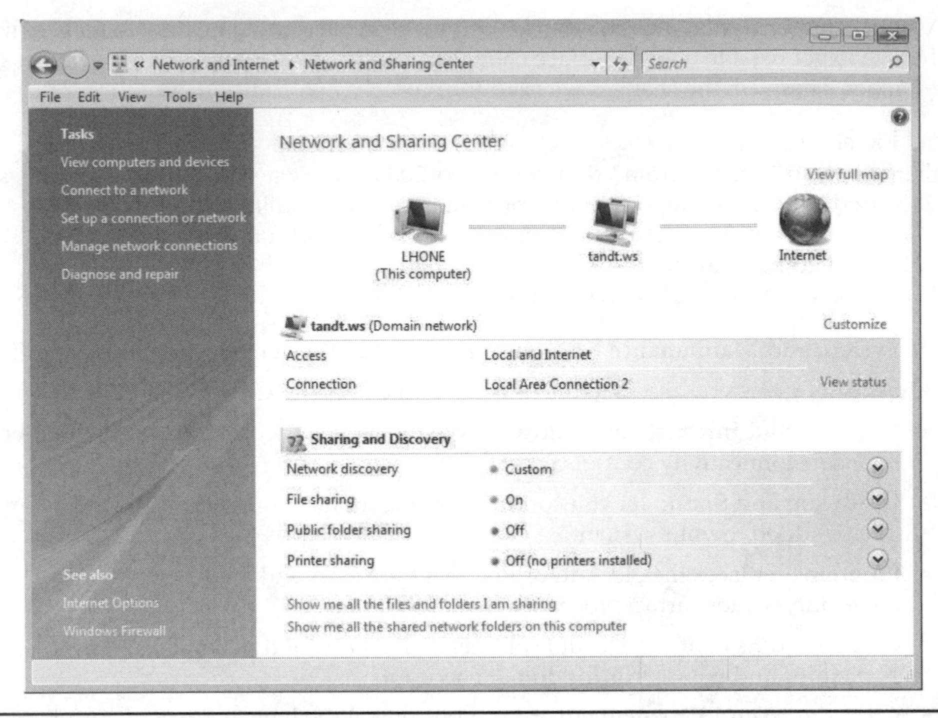

Figure 2-4 The Network and Sharing Center provides quick access to connectivity.

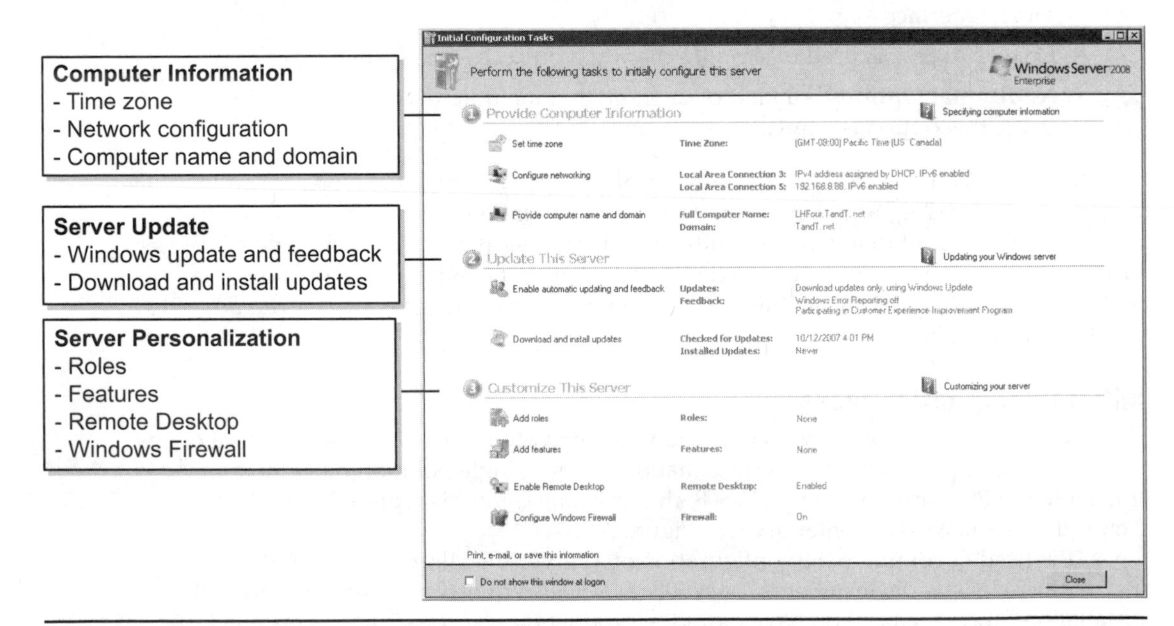

Figure 2-5 The Initial Configuration Tasks interface

IP addresses provided by Dynamic Host Configuration Protocol (DHCP), default computer name, and so on. ICT is designed to provide you with a single interface to modify each and every one of these settings.

ICT is divided into three parts:

- **Provide Computer Information** includes time zone configuration, networking configuration, and computer name and domain or workgroup membership.
- **Update this server** includes update configuration and installation.
- **Customize this server** lets you add roles and features, turn on Remote Desktop, and configure the Windows Firewall.

Using ICT is as easy as 1-2-3. Just follow the prompts. Change the IP address and then the computer name, and join the server to a domain when you need to. Then make sure updates are assigned to the server according to your corporate policy and make sure it is up to date. Finally, you can add roles and features, but let's keep that for a bit later. Turn on the Remote Desktop, and make sure the Windows Firewall is turned on with, at the very least, default settings. Much more on security will be covered in future chapters. After all, you can't put any WS08 server into place without configuring at least a set of baseline security settings.

Roles and features are discussed in the next section because they are easier to configure and add in Server Manager.

NOTE *You can configure all of the settings in the ICT through unattended Extensible Markup Language (XML) files that are applied during setup. This is by far the best way to configure this, especially if you have more than one server to prepare. Using an Unattend.XML file to script the installation automates it and also ensures that the installation is the same each time you run it. More on Unattend.XML files will be covered in Chapter 4 when server installations are covered in detail.*

Server Manager

For server management, Microsoft has introduced a completely new interface: the Server Manager console (SM). SM. provides a single source to manage a server's roles and system information, display server status, and identify server role configuration problems. SM replaces many of the common consoles administrators may be used to. For example, many are familiar with the Computer Management Console; this is replaced by Server Manager (see Figure 2-6).

Server Manager is such an integral part of WS08 that its shortcut is included in the Quick Launch area by default.

TIP *Server Manager has a corresponding command-line equivalent—ServerManagerCmd.exe—which can be used to script the addition of roles and features to the server. These scripts can be combined with Unattend.XML files to build a server and assign its roles and features automatically. For more information on this command, type* **`ServerManagerCmd /?`** *at the command line.*

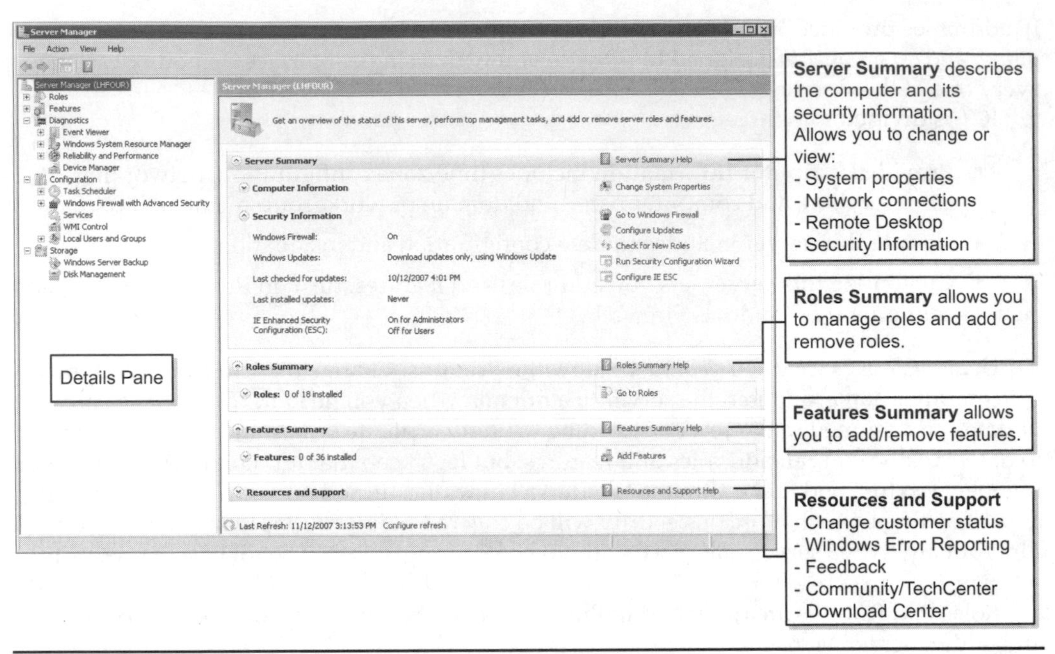

Server Summary describes the computer and its security information. Allows you to change or view:
- System properties
- Network connections
- Remote Desktop
- Security Information
Roles Summary allows you to manage roles and add or remove roles.
Features Summary allows you to add/remove features.
Resources and Support
- Change customer status
- Windows Error Reporting
- Feedback
- Community/TechCenter
- Download Center
Details Pane

FIGURE 2-6 The Server Manager console provides one-stop server administration.

When launched, SM. opens on the local server page. This page lists the settings for this particular server—name, domain or workgroup, IP address, Remote Desktop settings, and product ID. It also provides a security summary, much like the Initial Configuration Tasks window, and then goes on to list the server's installed roles and features. You can use this interface to add new roles and/or features to the server's configuration. Finally, the bottom of the local server page lists additional resources and support information.

Because it is based on Microsoft Management Console (MMC) version 3, SM is divided into several panes. The left pane is a tree structure that gives you access to the main functions of SM. console. This includes the local server page, roles, features, diagnostics, configuration, and storage. Each expands to include more information. It may take some getting used to, as many of the items are organized in a different manner than Computer Management. You'll need to learn that the Diagnostics area is where you'll find the Event Viewer, Windows System Resource Manager, Reliability and Performance analysis tools, and Device Manager. The Configuration area is where you find the Task Scheduler, Windows Firewall with Advanced Security—not to be confused with the Windows Firewall found in Control Panel—Services, and Windows Management Instrumentation (WMI) Control, as well as Local Users and Groups (for member servers only). Finally, the Storage area is where you locate the Windows Server Backup tool—yes, including all the great features of Vista's backup tool—and Disk Management.

You'll get used to it after a while, and you'll certainly find how useful it is to have everything in one location. But you'll also find that the part of the console you use the most is the Roles section.

Manage Roles and Features

Server Manager is the tool of choice in WS08 for any server-related configuration change. You no longer add roles or features through the Configure Your Server interface. Manage Your Server is also gone. Now, all server roles are centered into the SM. Server Manager provides a much smarter interface for adding roles and features. Remember that roles affect what a server does in a network, while features affect specific subcomponents that are installed on a server. For example, Active Directory Domain Services is a role, whereas BitLocker Drive Encryption is a feature. Refer to Chapter 1 for the different roles available in SM. console. Table 2-1 outlines all of the different features you can install on WS08.

Feature Name	Feature Description and Sub-features
.NET Framework 3.0	Programming engine for managed code, including: .NET Framework 3.0 XPS Viewer Windows Communication Foundation (WCF) activation: HTTP Activation Non-HTTP Activation
BitLocker Drive Encryption	Full drive encryption; requires at least two partitions
BITS Server Extensions	Background Intelligent Transfer Service
Connection Manager Administration Kit (CMAK)	Generates Connection Manager profiles
Desktop Experience	Turns on the ability to use the Vista theme, as well as photo management and Windows Media Player
Failover Clustering	High-availability services—two- to eight-node clusters
Group Policy Management	To deploy, manage, and troubleshoot Group Policy using the MMC
Internet Printing Client	To connect to and use printers that are on Web print servers using HTTP connection; enables connection for users and printers that are not in the same site or network
Internet Storage Name Server	Manages Internet Small Computer Systems Interface (iSCSI) device queries
LPR Port Monitor	Transmission Control Protocol/Internet Protocol (TCP/IP) print monitor
Message Queuing	Microsoft Message Queuing (MSMQ): MSMQ Services: MSMQ Server Directory Service Integration Message Queuing Triggers HTTP Support Multicasting Support Routing Service Windows 2000 Client Support Messaging queuing Distributed Component Object Model (DCOM) proxy
Multipath I/O	Works with the Microsoft Device Specific Module (DSM) or a third party to support the use of multiple data paths to a storage device on Windows

TABLE 2-1 Available Features in WS08

Feature Name	Feature Description and Sub-features
Network Load Balancing	Load balancing on multiple servers
Peer Name Resolution Protocol	Allows applications to register on and resolve names from the computer without using Domain Name Service (DNS)
Quality Windows Audio Video Experience	qWave is a networking platform for audio and video streaming applications on IP networks
Remote Assistance	Remote Help desk assistance
Remote Differential Compression	To support content replication between two servers in a network. Will compute the differences between two objects, compress the changes and replicate them to the other networked server.
Remote Server Administration Tools	To remotely manage roles, role services, and features of WS03 and WS08 from a system running WS08 (replaces the AdminPak from WS03) Role Administration Tools: Active Directory Certificate Services (ADCS) Tools: Certification Authority tools Online Responder Tools Active Directory Domain Services (ADDS) Tools: Active Directory Domain Controller Tools Server for Network Information System (NIS) Tools Active Directory Lightweight Directory Services (ADLDS) Tools Active Directory Rights Management Services (ADRMS) Tools DHCP Server Tools DNS Server Tools Fax Server Tools File services: Distributed File System (DFS) Tools File Server Resource Manager Tools Services for Network File Systems Tools Network Policy and Access Services Tools: Print Services Tools Terminal Services (TS) Tools: Terminal Server Tools TS Gateway Tools TS Licensing Tools UDDI Services Tools Web Server (Internet Information Server, or IIS) Tools Windows Deployment Services Tools Feature Administration Tools: BitLocker Drive Encryption Tools BITS Server Extensions Tools Failover Clustering Tools Network Load Balancing Tools Simple Mail Transfer Protocol (SMTP) Server Tools WINS Server Tools

TABLE 2-1 Available Features in WS08 (*continued*)

Feature Name	Feature Description and Sub-features
Removable Storage Manager	Manager for hierarchical storage devices
RPC over HTTP Proxy	Remote Procedure Call over Hypertext Transfer Protocol
Simple TCP/IP Services	Additional support for other TCP/IP services, such as echo, daytime, and quote of the day
SMTP Server	E-mail server
SNMP Server	Simple Network Management Protocol for both the service and its WMI extensions SNMP Service SNMP WMI Provider
Storage Manager for SANs	Unified storage area network (SAN) interface
Subsystem for UNIX-based Applications	Support for UNIX applications
Telnet Client	Acts as a client to connect to remote servers
Telnet Server	Acts as a server for telnet connections
TFTP Client	Trivial File Transfer Protocol
Windows Internal Database	Relational data store that can be used only by: Universal Description, Discovery, and Integration (UDDI) Services ADRMS Windows SharePoint Services (WSS) Windows Server Updates Services (WSUS) Windows System Resource Manager (WSRM)
Windows PowerShell	A command-line tool that can be used to manage the system and that includes more than 130 standard commands
Windows Process Activation Service (WPAS)	A service tied to IIS 7.0 designed to manage application pools and worker processes: Process model .NET environment Configuration application programming interfaces (APIs)
Windows Server Backup Features	Full system and incremental backups: Windows Server Backup Command-line Tools
Windows System Resource Manager (WSRM)	Manage workloads on servers equitably
WINS Server	Windows Internet Naming Services; should be unnecessary in most WS08 networks
Wireless LAN Service	Configures wireless connections and local area network (LAN) profiles

TABLE 2-1 Available Features in WS08 (*continued*)

Each time a new role or feature is added to a server, it is automatically populated in the SM console. Then, when you click a specific role, the console displays a summary of the status of the services supporting the role, as well as a summary of the potential services the role can include. Each role summary view also includes a Resources and Support section that outlines next steps and recommendations for role configuration.

Much more will be covered on SM as each role and feature is discussed in detail in the remainder of the book.

NOTE *Server Manager is for a local server only. It cannot connect to remote servers, unlike the Computer Management Console. For this reason, you must rely on a local or remote connection to a server to use Server Manager.*

The Super MMC

While Server Manager provides information that does not appear in other consoles, you might find that the Computer Management Console is still useful. In fact, you might be interested into turning this console into an all-encompassing tool. You can create a "super" management console that will include all the snap-ins you require in a single MMC. Remember that you will need to install the Remote Server Administration Tools before you build this console. In addition to all of the features of the Computer Management Console, this console can, and should, include the following snap-ins.

- All of the Active Directory snap-ins
- Active Directory Services Interface (ADSI) Edit
- Authorization Manager
- Backup
- Certification authority (you must specify the server to manage)
- Component Services
- Computer Management
- Enterprise public key infrastructure (PKI)
- Failover clusters
- Group Policy management
- Network Access Protection (NAP) Client configuration (you must specify the server to manage)
- Network Policy server
- Reliability and Performance
- Reliability Monitor
- Remote Desktops
- Resultant Set of Policy
- Terminal Services Configuration (you must specify the server to manage)
- Terminal Services Manager (you must specify the server to manage)
- Windows Firewall with Advanced Security (you must specify the server to manage)
- WMI Control (you must specify the server to manage)

You can also add any other item, such as DNS, IPSec management, and more. Add whatever you think you might need.

As you can see, this creates a powerful console indeed. What is nice is that since it is a custom MMC, you can link to any server in your network without having to open a Remote Desktop session. Create this console using the following instructions.

NOTE *To create the console on a PC, you need Windows Vista SP1 and the Remote Server Administration Tools (RSAT). Search for RSAT on www.microsoft.com/downloads.*

To create this console:

1. Use Start | Run to execute the following command:

```
mmc %SystemRoot%\system32\compmgmt.msc /a
```

2. Accept the UAC prompt if you are not logged on with the default administrator account.
3. This launches the Computer Management console in editing mode. Begin by using File | Save As to save the console as Super MMC.msc under the C:\Toolkit folder (you will have to create the folder).
4. Then use File | Add/Remove Snap-in to open the snap-ins dialog box.
5. Double-click each of the snap-ins listed earlier. Click OK when done.
6. Click File | Options, name the console Super MMC Console, make sure it is set to User mode—full access and 'uncheck' Do not save changes to this console. Click OK when done.
7. Use File | Save to save your changes.

There are several uses to this console, as you will see, but it is basically the most common tool you will use to manage your network of servers. You can copy it to any other system as long as the prerequisites—mostly the presence of the Administration Tools—are met. In addition, you can use this console to connect to any system in your network. You'll also find that the Remote Desktops snap-in is most useful, as it allows you to create automatic remote connections to each of your servers. From then on, you can establish a remote connection with just one click.

Make sure that you secure this console thoroughly, since it is powerful. The best way to do this is to store it in your profile, as all profile contents are secured from others by default.

Other Ways to Do Things

WS08 continues to provide some of the most common interfaces you are used to. Tools like the Remote Desktop, the Command Line Shell, and Help & Support are still very much the same—some with improvements. Microsoft also now includes Windows PowerShell as a new and much more powerful command shell. You need to understand how each will affect your ability to interact with WS08.

The Remote Desktop

The Remote Desktop Protocol (RDP) continues to be one of the best ways to manage remote servers. Just as in all other versions of Windows Server, WS08 also includes two free Terminal Services licenses for administration purposes. And, since Server Manager does not let you connect to another server, Remote Desktop may be the best way to access it.

Before you can work with the Remote Desktop on any server, you need to make sure that the Remote Desktop service has been activated on the server and that it is ready to accept remote connections. Remote Desktop activation is one of the items that is found on the Initial Configuration Tasks window. Make sure you turn it on.

Then, when you're ready to make a remote connection, use the Remote Desktop client on your system to connect to the server of your choice using either the server name or its IP address. You can also use the Remote Desktop snap-in in the Microsoft Management Console to create a list of connections to each system. Then you can easily manage connections to multiple systems in one single interface.

TIP *For instructions on how to build a Remote Desktop Console, go to http://searchwincomputing.techtarget.com/originalContent/0,289142,sid68_gci1243095,00.html.*

CAUTION *You need to have the RDP client version 6.x to connect to a WS08 server. This was delivered through Windows updates in December 2006, so it should be on any system you need to use. If not, you can download it at http://support.microsoft.com/default.aspx/kb/925876.*

As discussed in Chapter 1, Terminal Services has been enhanced in WS08. It now includes support for RemoteApp. Remote applications execute on the server, but without the need to open a full desktop session on the remote device. Since Server Manager cannot connect to another device, it might be best to bring it to you through a remote applications. Just configure Terminal Services RemoteApp on your servers, and then publish Server Manager as a remote applications. This way, you can access any server and obtain its information without needing to have a complete remote connection to the server. The procedure for the configuration of Server Manager as a remote program will be outlined later as we discuss application management.

The Command Prompt

The command prompt remains unchanged in WS08, but individual commands have been added to make it more powerful. The major advantage of the command prompt is that it provides a character-based interface for performing server operations. This means that you can capture each of these commands into a script or batch file that provides consistent experiences because it always repeats the same actions. In addition, the command prompt supports piping the results of a command into a text file. This means that when a command runs, its results are stored in a text file that you can review at a later date.

This is useful, because you can use it to run deferred commands and then review the results at a later time. Administrators can use this to create a series of different batch or command files—with the .cmd or .bat file extension—and schedule them to run through the Windows Task Scheduler. The results are piped into text files that can even be stored in one single location. For example, if you want to know the status of your servers, you can use the following command:

```
systeminfo /s computername >filename.txt
```

where *computername* references the name of the server you want to investigate. If omitted, it lists information about the local server. Use *filename.txt* to identify the name and path of the file you want to send the information to. You can put a series of these commands in a single command file and schedule them to automatically generate the output files every day. This helps you quickly identify the state of all services in your network.

NOTE *This is the approach that is used in Chapter 13 as we discuss the automation of most of the more than 150 administrative tasks you need to perform to maintain a WS08 environment.*

WS08 includes several new commands for server administration. Many will be covered as we deal with the actual task, but if you want a complete list, check out Table 2-2.

Command	Description
auditpol	Modifies audit policies
bcdedit	Boot configuration data editor
change	Sets special terminal server modes for logons, COM port mappings, and software installations
chglogon	Controls session logins
chgport	Controls COM port mappings for DOS application compatibility
chgusr	Changes application installation mode
choice	Lets you select one item from a list of choices and returns the result
clip	Used to redirect output from the command line to the Clipboard
cmdkey	Controls stored usernames and passwords
diskraid	Used to access the Diskraid command window
dispdiag	Displays diagnostics
forfiles	Used to select a file or files to execute a command on it; used mostly in batch jobs
icacls	Controls access control lists (ACLs) on files
iscsicli	Initiates iSCSI
mklink	Creates symbolic links and hard links
muiunattend	Control Multiple User Interface (MUI) unattend actions
netcfg	Network installer for Windows PE (WinPE)
ocsetup	Windows optional component setup; useful for Server Core
pkgmgr	Windows Package Manager
pnpunattend	Unattended online driver installation
pnputil	Microsoft Plug and Play (PnP) utility
quser	Displays information about users logged on to the system
robocopy	Robust file copy for Windows; formerly in the Resource Kit

TABLE 2-2 New Command-Line Tools in WS08

Command	Description
rpcping	Pings a server using remote procedure call (RPC)
setx	Controls environmental variables in the user or system environment
servermanagercmd	Provides command-line support for all the Server Manager Console functionalities
sxstrace	Windows side-by-side (WinSxS) tracing tool
takeown	Controls file ownership
timeout	Controls wait times in batch files
tracerpt	Used to generate trace reports
waitfor	Used to send, or wait for, a signal on a system: Use /S to send the signal to a specified system Omit /S to send the signal to all systems in a domain
wbadmin	Controls backups and restores
wceutil	Controls the Windows Event Collector
wevtutil	Controls Windows events
where	Used to display the location of files matching a given search
whoami	Gets username and group information, along with security identifiers (SIDs), privileges, and logon identifier (logon ID) for the current user (access token) on the local system
winrm	Controls Windows remote management
winrs	Launches the Windows remote shell
winsat	Launches the Windows system assessment tool

TABLE 2-2 New Command-Line Tools in WS08 (*continued*)

Windows PowerShell

You can continue to work with the command shell, and in many cases, you will need to continue to do so, but the most powerful command language in any Windows system today is the Windows PowerShell. The command prompt hasn't been updated since the first release of Windows NT, so it is high time that a new shell environment was made available. Windows PowerShell must be added as a feature, and then it can be launched through a shortcut in the Start menu. Windows PowerShell provides a complete command environment replete with automated command completion, instant help, and many forms of administrative assistance.

Windows PowerShell is based on the .NET Framework and requires it to run. This means a few things. First, it does not run on Server Core, the bare-bones edition of Windows Server 2008, since Server Core does not include a graphical interface and the .NET Framework has UI dependencies, though Microsoft is working on fixing this. You will need to continue using the traditional command shell if you deploy Server Core in your network, as this is the only interface available locally on these servers. Second, Windows PowerShell is not a replacement for all the other administrative tools available in WS08. It is a tool that is designed to assist in the automation of repetitive tasks. As such, it is very powerful.

Another nice aspect of Windows PowerShell is that it supports the concept of an alias for a command, and the Windows PowerShell team has created and included aliases for all of the existing command-shell commands. In fact, to use Windows PowerShell, you don't actually need to learn anything so long as you are familiar with the existing command prompt. But if you want to unleash the power of Windows PowerShell, you'll make a point of learning all of its commands—called cmdlets—and avoid using the outdated aliases.

It's easy to learn any command in Windows PowerShell. All you need is to know two things. The first is that when you type a command in Windows PowerShell, you can use the TAB key to automatically complete it and cycle through all of its potential options. The second is to know the cmdlet Get-. Get- is used to obtain information from Windows PowerShell. For example, Get-Help will provide you with help on Windows PowerShell. So if you type **Get-** in the cmdlet and then press the TAB key, Windows PowerShell will cycle through all of the available commands. This should provide you with an extensive amount of information on the other cmdlets you can run. Remember to include the trailing hyphen, as the command is not recognized without it.

NOTE *You'll be able to recognize the Windows PowerShell from the default command shell by its leading "PS" in front of the command prompt.*

TIP *You might be familiar with a useful Windows power toy called "Command Prompt Here." It automatically opens a command prompt at the right location when you right-click a folder and use the power toy. It saves you from having to type long and convoluted folder names. Windows PowerShell also has this power toy. You can get the "PowerShell Prompt Here" power toy from www.hanselman.com/blog/IntroducingPowerShellPromptHere.aspx.*

More on Windows PowerShell will be covered as we describe the administrative commands you need to rely on to maintain your server infrastructure.

NOTE *To learn more about Windows PowerShell, examine the documents in the PowerShell Documents folder (in the Start menu), or go to www.microsoft.com/windowsserver2003/technologies/management/powershell/default.mspx. There is a handy little four-fold sheet named "QuadFold.rtf" in the Documents folder that lists all Windows PowerShell shortcuts and syntax.*

Help and Support in WS08

Another useful tool to newcomers in WS08 is the Help & Support Center (HSC). This center is designed to demystify all of the features and interactions you will have with WS08. The home page of the Help & Support Center leads you directly to what you want to know. Because of this, you should keep in mind the most important key in any Windows environment, the F1 key. Pressing F1 at any time, or even on a empty desktop, will automatically open HSC. Of course, you can launch HSC from the Start menu, but F1 is often faster and easier.

Help content is regularly updated with patches and updates, but it is also directly linked to online content, so it should always up to date. Of course, isolated server environments will not have this luxury, but you can always use another system to get the information.

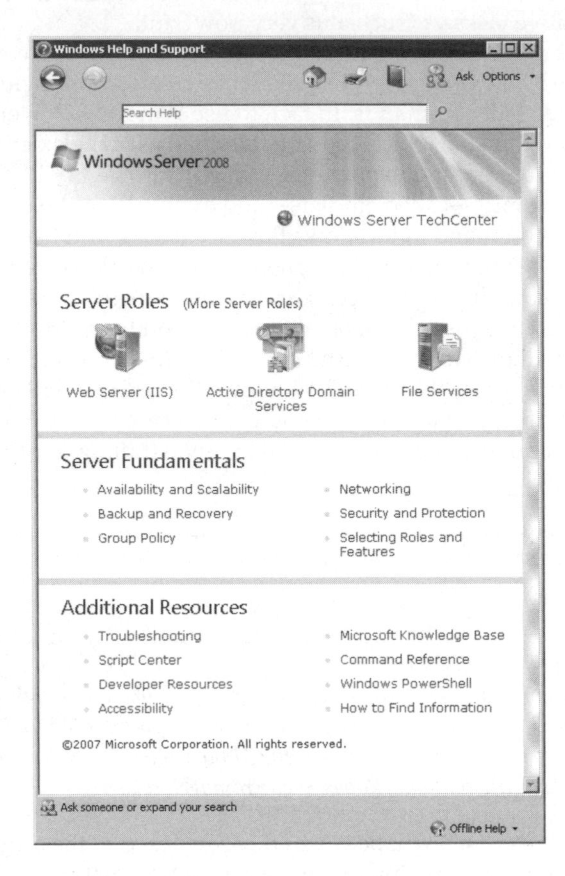

HSC is really useful when you first start working with an operating system, so make sure you browse through it and take the time to understand its structure and content as it evolves with time.

New Ways to Do Things in WS08

As you can see, there are several interface changes in WS08 compared to WS03, and even more if you haven't had a chance to run at least Windows Server 2003. Table 2-3 lists some of the new ways you'll need to work when you administer servers running WS08.

There—now you've explored more about WS08. You are ready to move on to the construction of your servers and the services they will offer in your network.

Action	Windows Server 2003	Windows Server 2008
Search	Limited search if Index Server turned on	Start menu Windows Explorer Internet Explorer Virtual Folders
Standard/ Administrative account	Run as shortcuts	Standard user use Run as Administrator Administrator approve UAC prompts Fast User Switching now supported in domains
Control Panel	System Network and Internet Connections Security Center Sounds, Speech, and Audio Devices Add or Remove Programs User Accounts Appearance and Themes Date, Time, Language, and Regional Options Accessibility Options	System and Maintenance Network and Internet Security Hardware and Sound Programs User Accounts Appearance and Personalization Clock, Language, and Region Ease of Access Additional Options Includes a task list in the left pane
To complete the configuration of a server installation	Manage Your Server	Initial Configuration Tasks Provide Computer Information Update this server Customize this server
Management tasks	Manage Your Server Computer Management Configure Your Server Security Configuration Add or Remove Windows Components Command shell PowerShell (add-on)	Server Manager Command shell Windows PowerShell (built-in, but not on Server Core)
Activation	Microsoft web site	Key Management Services Microsoft web site for Multiple Activation Keys (MAKs) and others
Performance	Performance Logs and Alerts Server Performance Advisor System Monitor	Performance and Diagnostics Console

TABLE 2-3 New Ways to Do Things in WS08

Action	Windows Server 2003	Windows Server 2008
Deployment	Remote Installation Services (RIS) Automated Deployment Services (ADS)	Windows Deployment Services Windows Image Format
Access applications remotely	VPN connections	Terminal Services Gateway Terminal Services RemoteApps
Cluster	Microsoft Cluster Service	Failover Clustering in Server Manager | Add Roles
Fax Management	Fax utilities	Fax Server
Security	Security Wizard Windows Firewall PKI Services Windows Rights Management Server Internet Authentication Service Backup Domain Controller in NT Active Directory Active Directory in Application Mode	Security Configuration Wizard Windows Firewall with Advanced Security in the Server Manager Windows Firewall in Control Panel Active Directory Certificate Services Active Directory Rights Management Services Windows Defender Network Policy Server Read-Only Domain Controllers Active Directory Domain Services Active Directory Lightweight Directory Services BitLocker Full Drive Encryption
Disk and File	Windows Backup	Windows Server Backup

TABLE 2-3 New Ways to Do Things in WS08 *(continued)*

PART II

Plan and Prepare

Preparing for a migration to Windows Server 2008 (WS08) requires planning and forethought. In Part I, you discovered what makes WS08 tick. Now, you need to prepare the services you want to deliver based on this new operating system. This section walks you through some key concepts and then shows you how to build the labs you need to prepare your deployment. It will cover how WS08 installations are performed and then look at how you should proceed to perform the migration.

3

CHAPTER

Plan for Windows Server 2008

Today's enterprise networks, whether for small, medium, or large organizations, need to respond to a variety of requirements, as illustrated in Chapter 1. Because the network is the core of every service offering IT provides to the business, it must be planned and tested before it is implemented. After all, the last thing you want is to introduce new services that either do not meet requirements or fail in critical business situations.

Enterprise networks have evolved from being a loosely coupled series of servers and computers to being an integrated infrastructure providing and supporting the organization's mission. This evolutionary process is not unlike that of the telephone. At first, telephone systems were loosely coupled. Today, worldwide telecommunications systems are much more complex and complete. And with new convergence trends, the separation between telecommunications and the IP network is quickly disappearing. This is one reason why networks are even more mission-critical than ever. Whatever its size, the enterprise network must be a secure, stable, redundant infrastructure that is completely oriented towards the delivery of IT service offerings to the business. These service offerings can range from simple file and print systems to complex authentication systems, storage area networks (SANs), or Web applications. In addition, these service offerings can be made available to two differing communities of users—internal users over whom you have complete control of the PC and external users over whom you have little or no control.

The move to WS08 should also involve a major change in your infrastructure strategy. In fact, the datacenter of the 21st century is now divided into two clear sets of services:

- **Service offerings** Services that are designed to provide given functionalities to end users.
- **Resource pools** Hardware resources—processors, memory, disk, and network resources—that are teamed together as a pool to support the proper operation of the service offerings.

Service offerings are virtualized instances of the operating system—instances that are designed to interact with end users and support them in the performance of their daily duties. Service offerings are, therefore, *outward-facing*. Hardware, on the other hand, is viewed as a pool of components whose function is to provide resources in support of the service offerings. Therefore, hardware runs only virtualization software, or a hypervisor—a special component that exposes hardware resources to virtualized operating systems. This is provided by the Hyper-V role. Because they are managed by a team of operators that interact only with the operators and administrators of the service offerings, and never need to deal with end users directly, resource pools are deemed to be *inward-facing*.

As you migrate your current service offerings—which are most likely running directly on the hardware in your datacenter—to WS08, you will also transform them into virtual machines (VMs). This will mean rethinking both operations and standard practices to make the most of the benefits and advantages server virtualization offers.

That's why moving or migrating to Windows Server 2008 is much more of a network infrastructure and datacenter design project than one dealing simply with upgrading to a new technology. Each time you change a technology that is as critical as the operating system (OS) of your network, it is important, if not essential, to perform the following tasks:

- Review corporate needs and requirements.
- Review the features and capabilities of the new OS—a task which Chapter 1 helped you perform.
- Design a comprehensive architecture and implementation plan—relying on proven processes such as lifecycles, system construction models, and standard operating procedures.
- Test all aspects of the implementation to ensure its quality.
- Move to the actual implementation.

Aligning a project of this magnitude with the business strategies of the organization will make the transition more easily accepted and more profitable for everyone involved. Too many organizations cannot fully profit from the benefits of an enterprise network because they have never taken the time to perform each of these steps. As a result, they don't benefit from the maximum potential or performance of their network.

NOTE *Of course, if you took the time to properly prepare your network when you migrated to Windows Server 2003, then integrating WS08 will be a less arduous process. You should still review the content of this chapter in order to ensure that you are using best-practice recommendations in all aspects of the network and that you are taking full advantage of virtualization.*

Planning and preparing for the implementation of Windows Server 2008, or any network operating system, should be 80 percent planning, preparing, and testing and 20 percent implementing. If your enterprise is an enterprise of one, you'll still want to take the time to prepare properly, but you probably won't take the time to invest in automating procedures, though you'll see that automating activities with WS08 is much easier than it ever has been before; you'll still want standard operating procedures, but you probably won't involve a series of technicians and architects to validate them; and you'll still want to design based on architectural models, but you won't take the time to design these models yourself. Guidance for each step is included in this chapter.

Build the Foundation of the Network

Building an enterprise network with Windows Server 2008 consists of designing the network architecture and its implementation procedure while identifying opportunities for the use of standard operating procedures (SOPs). The enterprise network infrastructure is divided into specific service delivery areas that must be supported by a structure for network administration and management. For each aspect of this infrastructure, it is essential to have a complete understanding of the features that Windows Server 2008 offers in this area. It is also important to identify which of these features offer the best cost/benefit scenarios for the enterprise.

For example, very few enterprises today can live without Active Directory Domain Services (ADDS). For organizations of all sizes, it is always better to take the time to centralize all authentication and authorization services than to keep them distributed through the use of workgroups, because if a change is required, you only have to make it in one central place. The organization that requires an enterprise-level network infrastructure will not invest in workgroups; they will invest directly into ADDS, bypassing workgroups altogether, except, of course, for special circumstances. This enterprise-level approach is the one that will be used throughout the elaboration of the enterprise architecture for Windows Server 2008.

The server operating system is the core of the enterprise network. When looking to replace this operating system, it is important to ensure that every aspect of the services that the network will provide has been covered. The best way to do this is to use the "lifecycle" approach. Two lifecycles are important here:

- **The server lifecycle** The cycle an individual server undergoes when it is introduced into the network until its retirement
- **The service-offering lifecycle** The cycle services must undergo from the moment they are first introduced into the network until their retirement

The server lifecycle, especially, will let you design the basic structure of all servers, whether physical or virtual. This will form the basis for the server construction model. And, once you have identified the different service offerings required within your network, you can then focus on network stability. Rely on to help determine which service offerings are required for a network the size of yours.

Also, since many operations within the network are performed by a variety of personnel, network stability is greatly enhanced by the use of SOPs throughout each aspect of the implementation and administration process. SOPs ensure that best practices are always used to perform operations, and will greatly simplify support.

Three more tools will help in the construction of the new or upgraded network:

- **A system construction and management model** A model for the design of all computer systems in your network
- **Standard operating procedures** Not to direct all operations, but to ensure some form of quality control over how each member of your team performs administrative, implementation, and operational activities.
- **The networking stack** Since WS08 is designed to build and maintain networked service offerings, it is important to understand the networking stack it offers.

Once you have all of these tools in hand, you will be able to move forward with the construction of your new network.

The Server Lifecycle

As mentioned earlier, building a network should be 80 percent planning and preparation and 20 percent implementation. The process of building servers is the same. Servers are designed to meet specific requirements within a network. More will be discussed on this topic throughout the book, but for now, it is sufficient to say that like all network components, servers have a specific lifecycle within the enterprise network—one that begins with the purchasing or requirements process and then moves on to the IT management process, to end with its retirement from service.

For physical servers, the purchasing process covers purchase planning, requisition, and procurement. In this process, the organization should focus on several factors, such as volume purchasing of servers (if possible), requests for proposal, minimum requirements for server hardware, hardware provider add-ons, and growth strategy. These processes can be supported by functionality and reliability testing of hardware and applications in the network environment. For this process to be a success, the purchasing department and IT must cooperate and work closely together.

One of the driving factors of this process is the volume-buying approach. Servers like PCs should always be bought in lots. They should never be bought piecemeal. The main objective of this process in an enterprise network is to reduce diversity as much as possible. When servers are bought in lots, you can expect the manufacturer to ship machines that are configured as identically as possible. In this way, you can simplify and standardize the server building and maintenance process. More and more organizations are even moving to specific partnerships with server manufacturers to further decrease diversity within their server hardware families. Even if you can't purchase servers in lots, and maybe especially if you can't, you should endeavor to form this kind of partnership, as it will go a long way towards the reduction of diversity.

One good and simple way to achieve server standardization is to rely on blade servers. Blade servers must be installed in enclosures—housing units that can take from 10 to 16 servers, depending on the manufacturer. Even if you don't buy all of the blades when you obtain an enclosure, you know that each of the blades you will acquire when you need them will, perforce, be standard because they will need to work with the enclosure. Most manufacturers today guarantee that blade servers will remain available and compatible with their enclosures for a number of years. In addition, blades can reduce cabling requirements by up to 80 percent, heat generation by up to 50 percent, and power consumption by 20 percent or more. Because of this, blade servers are a great choice for any modern datacenter.

For virtual servers, the purchasing process turns into a requirements analysis process. Since virtual server instances include reduced licensing costs, provisioning a virtual instance of an OS is simpler and easier than a physical instance. Here, you need to focus on system requirements—number of processor cores, random access memory (RAM), disk space, and network interfaces—before you create the instance of the OS.

Once the purchasing or requirements process is complete, the server lifecycle moves on to the IT management process. Here, IT personnel become responsible for and take ownership of the server itself until its retirement. The process begins with the reception of the server and its entry into the corporate configuration management database (CMDB). For physical servers, this should include information such as purchase date, receipt date, purchase lot, warranty, and service contracts, among other items. For virtual servers, this should include requestor, purpose, configuration, expected requirement duration, and so on. Next begins the server construction process. Here servers go through the staging process. At this stage, only generic software elements are loaded onto the server. Once again, this process differs slightly between physical servers and virtual servers. For physical servers, this would include a minimalistic core OS, antivirus software, management software, and a hypervisor in support of virtualization. For virtual servers, this would include the operating system,

Select Server Hardware with Virtualization in Mind

Server purchases today should take virtualization into consideration. One of the key roles of WS08 is the support of virtualization through a "hypervisor," or a level of abstraction that exposes and shares physical server components with multiple virtual machines without performance degradations.

In addition, Microsoft has modified its server licensing scheme to support virtualization. Licenses of WS08 Enterprise edition include the host along with four free virtualized editions, including any down-level version of Windows from NT on, and licenses of Datacenter edition include the host and an *unlimited* number of virtualized instances. This makes a compelling case for server virtualization in any organization. To calculate the number of licenses you need to run VMs, go to the Windows Server Virtualization Calculators at www.microsoft.com/windowsserver2003/howtobuy/licensing/calculator.mspx.

Therefore, when selecting server hardware, you should consider virtualization as the core role this system will play. The ideal virtualization system will run on 64-bit hardware, breaking all memory limitations, and provide the platform for extended performance by supporting multiple server roles on one single physical box.

You shouldn't consider buying any other hardware than 64-bit systems, because WS08 is Microsoft's last 32-bit server OS. With the release of WS08 R2 in 2009, Microsoft will no longer offer 32-bit server operating systems, except for down-level versions of Windows. That's right—WS08 R2 will be available in 64-bit versions only.

antivirus software, management software, and resource kit tools—everything that is either completely generic or that includes an enterprise license and thus does not entail additional costs. Both of these form their respective server kernels.

Next, the server is configured. This stage covers the application of the software that will support the server's specific role within the organization.

The final preparation stage is server testing. This should include stress testing as well as configuration acceptance testing. Once this phase is complete, the server is ready for production.

Putting the server in production often means recovering information, including security settings from another server, and migrating it to the new model, unless, of course, the server is designed to offer a new role within the network. Once this step is performed, the server officially enters its production cycle. IT management for the server becomes focused on routine administrative tasks, software updates, and service pack application, as well as performance and capacity monitoring. All are performed on a scheduled basis. This phase will also include physical server repairs or expansion, if required. Though most every task will aim for remote operation, some repairs may require shutdown and physical access to the server. For example, it is hard to upgrade server memory remotely. Administrators that have worked with Windows Server 2003 will know that all shutdowns must be documented and justified through a verbose shutdown dialog box, the Shutdown Event Tracker. While this was less than useful in WS03, it has now become the core of the Reliability Monitor in WS08. The Reliability Monitor tracks the server's reliability level from the moment it is introduced into the network to the moment it is retired, providing continuous data about the server's status. The Reliability Monitor can be found within the Server Manager.

NOTE *Migration of every aspect of the network will be covered in Chapter 12.*

Finally, after its lifecycle is complete, the server reaches obsolescence and must be retired from the network. It is then replaced by new servers that have, in turn, begun a new lifecycle within the enterprise network (see Figures 3-1 and 3-2). This cycle affects physical as well as virtual servers, as either instance will have a lifecycle of its own. Note the four major phases of this process:

- The planning phase
- Preparation and deployment
- Production
- Retirement

These four phases will reappear as the service lifecycle is discussed.

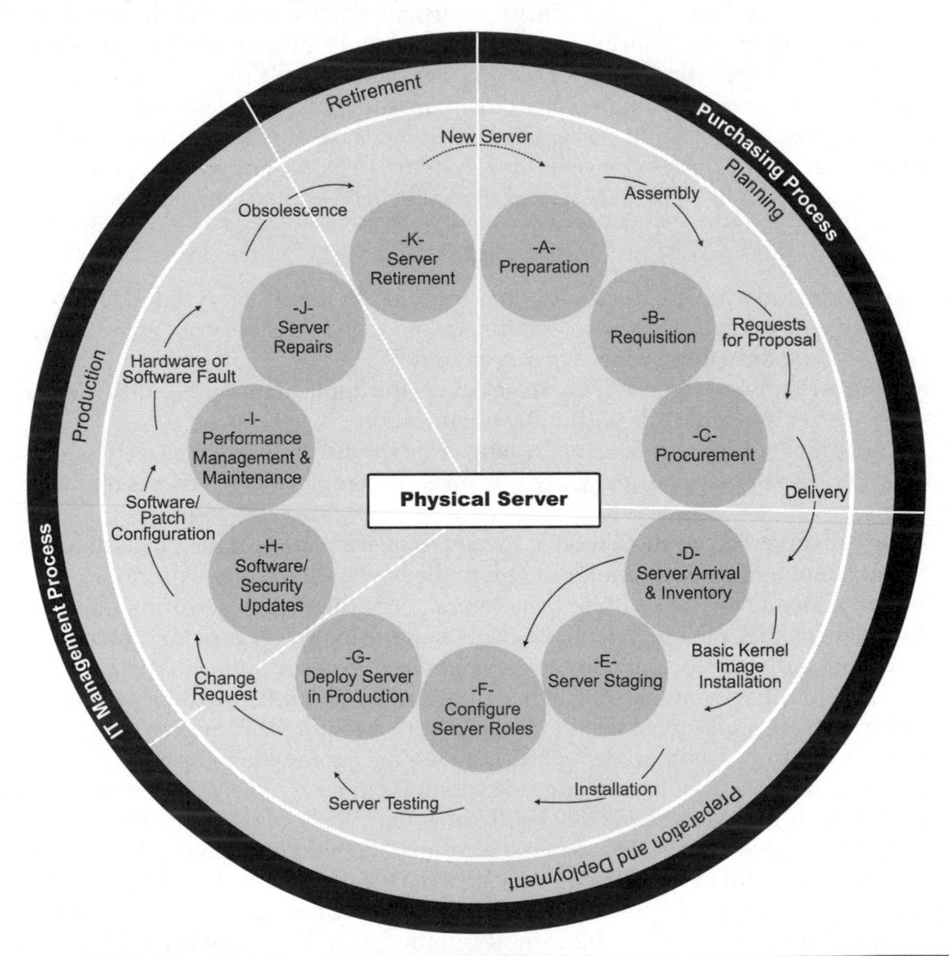

FIGURE 3-1 The physical server lifecycle covers every aspect of its existence within the enterprise network.

Upgrade	New Installation

❑ Select appropriate Windows OS
  ❑ 2 CPUs — Standard edition
  ❑ 3 or more CPUs — Enterprise or Datacenter edition
❑ Check upgrade compatibility
❑ Apply all system updates
❑ Read release notes
❑ Review server hardware manufacturer's recommendations for upgrade
❑ Perform server sizing exercise
❑ Review the order of the server upgrades:
  ❑ *Domain Controller first:*
    ❑ Provides all the new features of ADDS
    ❑ Requires a schema upgrade on the Schema Master
      ✓ adprep /forestprep
      ✓ adprep /rodcprep
    ❑ On the Infrastructure Master(s)
      ✓ adprep /domainprep /gpprep
  ❑ *Member servers first:*
    ❑ Provides new server roles
    ❑ Does not provide new features of ADDS
❑ Ensure all partitions use NTFS
❑ Disable anti-virus
❑ Check the system log for errors
❑ Install the operating system
❑ Perform post-installation review
	❑ Select appropriate Windows OS
	  ❑ 32-bit — Standard or Enterprise edition
	  ❑ 64-bit — Standard/Enterprise/Datacenter edition
	  ❑ Hosts — 64-bit Server Core only
	  ❑ Server Core or Full Install?
	❑ Read release notes
	❑ Review server hardware manufacturer's recommendations for installation
	❑ Perform server sizing exercise
	❑ One or multiple OS *(single OS recommended)*
	❑ Use NTFS for all volumes
	❑ Decide on partition:
	  ❑ System — Minimum 40 GB
	  ❑ Data — The rest
	  ❑ Logs — Only if required
	❑ If you already have a OS on a server:
	  ❑ Back up data files
	  ❑ Check the system log for errors
	❑ Install the operating system
	❑ Perform post-installation review

FIGURE 3-2 The virtual server lifecycle

The Service-Offering Lifecycle

Like the server lifecycle, the service-offering lifecycle is based on four phases, but because it is focused on a service offering, the contents of each of the four phases differ slightly. The four phases are focused on:

- **Planning** Identifying and preparing solutions for deployment
- **Deployment** Acquiring, packaging, configuring, installing, and testing deployment strategies
- **Production** Problem, change, optimization, and administration management within the production network
- **Retirement** Replacement/upgrade planning and removal of obsolete technologies and processes

This lifecycle model (see Figure 3-3) includes refinements that were added to reflect how modern networks have evolved. For example, the process of rationalization was added to the initial planning process in order to help organizations control costs through the reduction of diversity and through server consolidation. Rationalization affects not only server hardware and server instances through server consolidation practices, but also the applications and utilities that run on these servers. Too many organizations will accept multiple applications or utilities that offer the same function within a given network. No one can afford to work with applications that duplicate functionality or, even worse, applications or server utilities that are not compatible with each other. The administrative workload is heavy enough that you don't need to make work by relying on tools that cannot integrate with one another.

NOTE *This service-offering lifecycle was originally presented in* Windows Server 2003: Best Practices for Enterprises Deployments *by Danielle Ruest and Nelson Ruest (McGraw-Hill Osborne, 2003). The model was derived from an original model presented by Microsoft in a white paper entitled "Planning, Deploying, and Managing Highly Available Solutions" released in May 1999. The original Microsoft IT service lifecycle model can be found at www.microsoft.com/technet/archive/ittasks/plan/sysplan/availsol.mspx?mfr=true.*

Rationalization is an important aspect of service-offering preparation, and there is no better time to perform it than when you are migrating to a new server operating system. Each time a new operating system is released, new functionalities are included—functionalities that often replace third-party software products that were previously required to fulfill critical functions. For example, WS08 includes a vast number of features that replace the need for

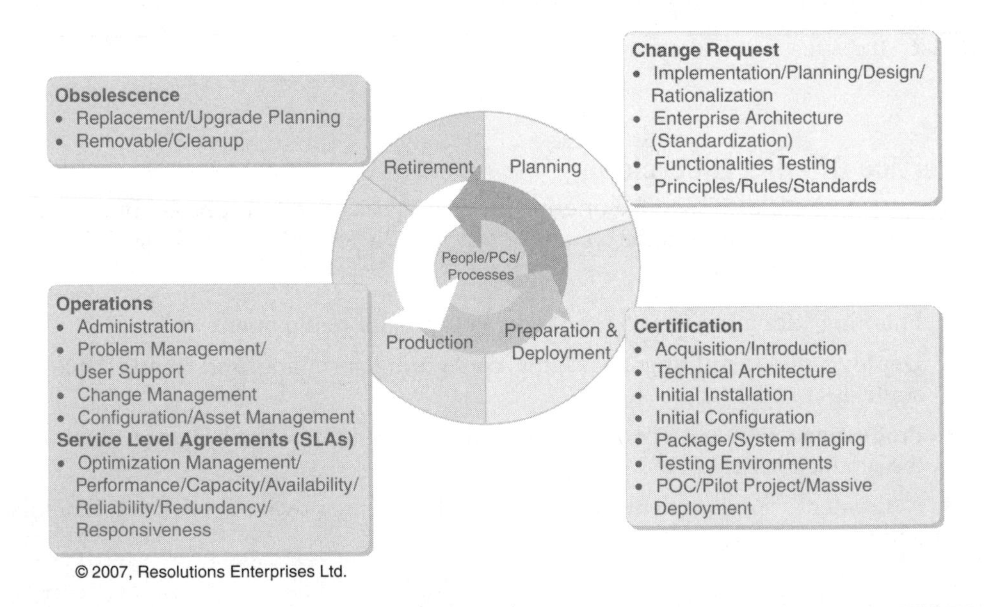

FIGURE 3-3 The service lifecycle demonstrates the four phases of the lifecycle of a service: planning, preparation and deployment, production and retirement.

third-party products. Examples include BitLocker Full Drive Encryption and Windows Defender, Microsoft's anti-spyware engine. Since these features are in the OS, there is little need to include third-party utilities that provide these functions in your deployment, unless there is a compelling reason to do so.

Rationalization is always necessary and is applied in varying degrees. It all depends on the starting point of your migration. Organizations that migrate from Windows NT will have to review most of their utilities. Organizations that migrate from Windows 2000 or 2003 will have a lower rationalization workload, because they will already have removed some obsolete utilities and applications from their network in their previous migration projects.

Beyond rationalization, you will also need to focus on standardization. This is the main purpose of the enterprise architecture design process. You want to standardize all operations to minimize administrative efforts and to reduce support issues. You'll also want to perform functionality testing through proofs of concept. This means testing the concepts that emerge from the enterprise architecture to ensure that they are valid and will provide all of the value the architecture expects.

In addition, you'll also want to perform application compatibility testing—testing existing applications to see if they will operate with the new service and the new OS. Remember that WS08 is based on Windows Vista code, and since Vista modified the way applications work, especially through its User Account Control (UAC) feature, you'll want to make sure each and every server application will run properly. The outcome of these tests should be a complete impact report on affected products. This report should include upgrade procedures or replacement recommendations.

TIP *For more information on Vista application compatibility, download "Chapter 6: Preparing Applications" of the* Definitive Guide for Vista Migration *at www.realtime-nexus.com/dgvm.htm.*

The focus of the enterprise architecture is the analysis of the needs and requirements of the organization; the features the new service will offer; and the elaboration of the principles, rules and standards that will be applied to its use within the organization.

TIP *For more information on enterprise architectures and the principles that drive them, see the "Architectures" section on the "Articles" page of the Resolutions web site at www.reso-net.com/articles.asp?m=8.*

The preparation and deployment phase focuses on the technical architecture process, which follows or can occur at the same time as the acquisition process. The technical architecture provides the specific technical parameters that will be applied to the service offering during its installation and during the rest of its lifecycle within the network. It is based on the orientations outlined in the enterprise architecture and simply details the specifics of the implementation.

The lifecycle then moves on to installation and initial configuration and packaging/staging. Packaging is used if the service offering relies on a software product or an addition to the current network. Staging is used if the service relies on a feature of the new operating system. With Windows Server 2008, you will need to rely on both packaging and staging, since you will have a tendency to begin with initial installation or staging of your servers and then follow with the application of the specific function or role the server will play in your network. Packaging is often used to automate the software or service-offering installation process.

Testing is the next stage, and it is vital because it ensures the stability of any new service offering introduced into your production network. There are several different levels of testing:

- Unit testing validates that the service offering operates in a stand-alone environment and helps technicians discover the intricacies of a feature.
- Functional testing begins the automation process for service-offering installation. It also includes a peer review to ensure that the service offering operates as expected.
- Integration testing validates the service offering's coexistence with other offerings on the same machine or in the same network.
- Staging testing is the final technical-only test and validates that the implementation process is flawless and will always operate as expected.
- Acceptance testing is part of the staging testing process and gives final users the right to approve the offering as it is packaged and prepared.

Finally, the service offering is ready for deployment. This deployment can be done in several stages. Another proof of concept (POC) can be used to perform a final validation of the service offering in operation. The target audience for this POC usually consists of the project team and some of its closest associates. This is followed by a pilot project that tests all aspects of the deployment methodology, including both technical and administrative procedures. Massive deployment follows a successful pilot project.

Not all service offerings must undergo a second proof of concept. This second POC is only applied if the target population for the offering is extremely large (1,000 or more users) and the organization requires a second validation. However, whatever the size of the target populations, you will always need to proceed with a pilot project before deployment. Pilot projects let you test the deployment solution with a small percentage of your client population. This test lets you validate the proper operation of each part of your solution. If you do not perform pilot projects, you'll find that your support costs will go up, since you are bound to discover issues once the offering is in production, issues you would normally have captured in the pilot.

Once the service offering is deployed, it enters the production phase of its lifecycle. Here, you manage and maintain a complete inventory of the service, control changes, deal with problems, and support its users. You must implement and manage service level agreements (SLAs) for each service offering you deploy. SLAs focus on performance and capacity analysis, redundancy planning (backup, clustering, failsafe, and recovery procedures), availability, reliability, and responsiveness of the service.

The final phase of the IT service-offering lifecycle is retirement. When the service reaches a certain degree of obsolescence, it must be retired from the network, because its operation costs often outweigh its benefits.

Of special note is the security element, which surrounds the entire service-offering lifecycle. Security has a special position in this lifecycle because it encompasses much more than just software and hardware. Security is a process in and of itself, and must be addressed at all times.

Both the server and the service-offering lifecycles will be used throughout this book. The server lifecycle will help with the construction and delivery of the servers you build.

The service-offering lifecycle will apply more specifically to the roles or configurations you give to your virtual servers as you prepare them for deployment. To simplify both delivery processes, you will need another model: the server construction and management model.

Benefit from a Server Construction and Management Model

The use of an architectural model can greatly simplify the design process for the construction and management of servers (and PCs) in your network. Such a model should outline the service offerings required in the network and should divide these offerings into appropriate categories or layers to group them by type. In addition, to properly reflect the security nature of these groupings, and to outline that they are designed to provide access to resources within the network, the model should be named in a manner that reflects its purpose. This is why we rely on a model called the "Point of Access to Secure Services (PASS)" model.

NOTE *This model was first outlined in* Preparing for .NET Enterprise Technologies *by Nelson Ruest and Danielle Ruest (Pearson Education, 2001) and was originally called the "Service Point of Access or SPA Object Model." It has been rebaptized as the PASS model here to better reflect its nature.*

The PASS model is based on an existing and well-known service model: the International Standards Organization's Open Systems Interconnection (OSI) networking reference model. The OSI model is a good source model because it is based on several principles and is well known in the industry. It describes networking between clients and servers through a series of layers, with each layer having its own set of functional services. Interactions between layers are based on common interactions and are limited to the layers immediately adjacent to each other.

The PASS model reflects these same principles. Each layer has a specific function, which offers a given set of services to the other adjacent layers. This layered model can be applied to either PCs or servers, either physical or virtual. Though it is similar to the OSI model, the content of the PASS model is divided into nine layers (see Figure 3-4):

- Physical
- Operating system
- Network
- Storage
- Security
- Communications
- Commercial applications
- Presentation
- Corporate applications

Graphically, the PASS model represents a design that is very similar to the OSI reference model with the addition of the two extra layers. This model demonstrates how you can construct and present IT technologies in understandable ways to both technical and non-technical audiences. But much about these technologies is not represented in this type of diagram. A separation of all the services into layers leads the reader to imagine that each layer can be independent with its own management model and its own approaches to service delivery. This is not the case.

In fact, even though all of the layers are related to each other in specific ways, some have a stronger relationship than others. By examining the content of each layer, you can see that some layers need to be implemented on every server, while others aim at specific server roles. This "common" versus "specific" components approach must influence the construction of the nine-layer model. To provide a clear construction model, the nine layers must be regrouped into specific sections that are meant for every single server and others that are meant for groups of servers that will play specific roles within the network.

For this, the model must be restructured into six sections. This new diagram can now serve as a map for server design and deployment. This is the PASS model. Its sections include:

- **Physical** Standard physical components
- **PASS system kernel** All components common to all servers

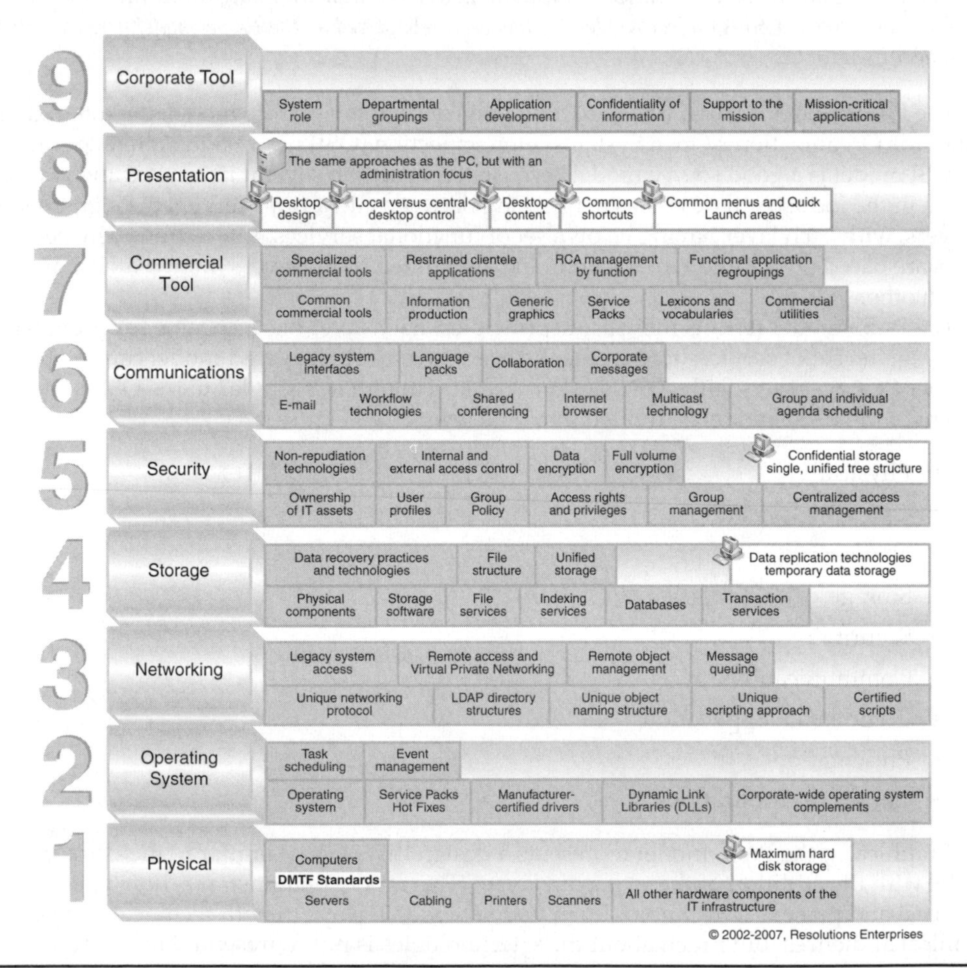

FIGURE 3-4 The nine layers of the PASS model apply to both PCs and servers.

- **Role-based commercial applications** Components that are installed on a server and are available to all users of the server
- **Ad hoc commercial applications** Commercial components that are installed on few servers, regardless of their role
- **Role-based corporate applications** Components that are installed on a server, but whose access is restricted to specific and authorized users
- **Ad hoc corporate applications** Corporate components that are installed on few servers, regardless of their role

At the core of this model is the concept of standardization, specifically within the physical and server kernel sections—the kernel being the component that you install as the core for every server. Standardization does not mean reduction in quality; it simply means doing everything in a single, unified manner. This alone can vastly reduce costs in the IT enterprise. The PASS model clearly displays the mechanisms that can be used to construct servers, so long as standards are available to support all of the processes that it identifies (see Figure 3-5).

The Benefits of the PASS Model

Using a single model for the outline of technical services provided by both PCs and servers has several major advantages. First, by using specific sections and purposely including a presentation section, it forms the framework for user and technology interactions within a

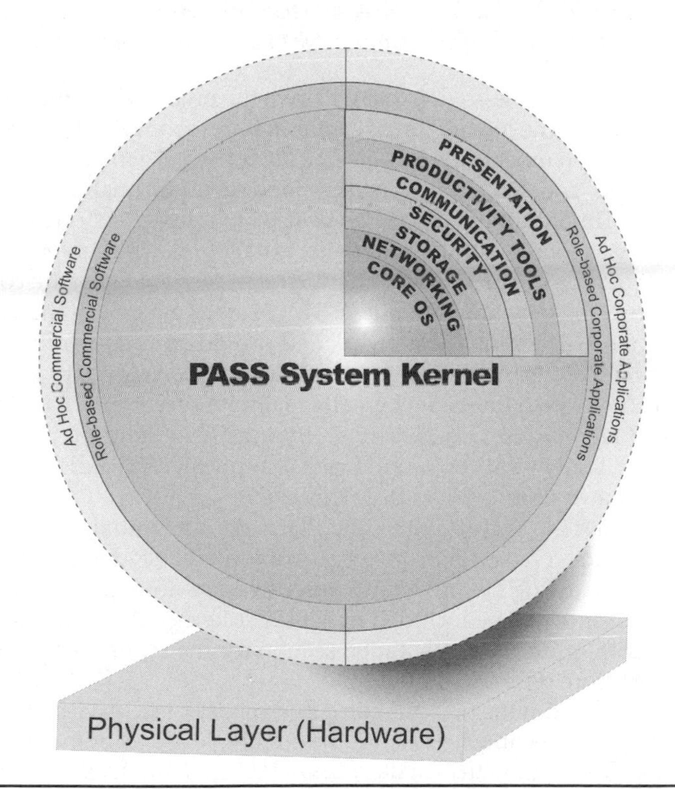

FIGURE 3-5 The point of access to secure services, or PASS, model

Windows-based distributed environment. Second, it outlines that there should be no difference in the approaches used to manage and maintain PASS objects (PCs or servers). Third, it describes how to construct both servers and PCs. Fourth, it uses a framework that will allow the systems—either physical or virtual—to evolve with time through structured management approaches. In addition, each of the six major sections of this model provides specific benefits.

Standardizing the physical section ensures that the organization has modern tools to perform its IT tasks. It also ensures the control of obsolescence within the organization. In addition, reducing the diversity of hardware within the organization reduces costs, since fewer device drivers need to be maintained for each type of peripheral. With Windows Server 2008, you'll even want to aim for the inclusion of peripherals that can all be certified: i.e., that come with and include device drivers that are digitally signed by the manufacturer, guaranteeing their stability. In fact, for 64-bit systems, all drivers have to be certified; as a result, it is good practice to apply the rule to all server models if you can. When stability is the top priority, reducing the number of potential problem sources is critical. The physical section should always be based on industry standards, such as those outlined by the Desktop Management Task Force (DMTF). More information on the DMTF and the standards they promote can be found at www.dmtf.org.

NOTE *If you opt to move to a virtualized datacenter, then all server hardware will be 64-bit and all server components will be certified. This will ensure that the virtual instances of the OS you run on top of these physical boxes will not suffer failures due to non-standard and uncertified components.*

The PASS system kernel is the section that will save the organization the most, because it provides the framework for the integration of common PASS services into a single unit. This means that the organization must begin by devising the technical content of each of the kernel's sub-layers, the rules and guidelines governing them and their personalization or interaction with other sub-layers. This information can then be used to interactively create reference systems that will serve as sources for the automated installation of all servers in the network.

Using new system imaging or Windows deployment technologies, the complete kernel can be captured into a single installation phase. This system image can then be deployed to every single physical server within the network and provide a single unified standard. This is in direct correlation with the new imaged-based setup (IBS) WS08 and Vista support. In addition, having a core system image will greatly facilitate server provisioning and server restoration in case of failures. For virtual server offerings, this standard image is much more easily captured, since it only requires you to make a duplicate of the disk files that make up the server and then spawn other servers from this copy.

But automation is not the only requirement. Planning is essential, since the new system will be made available to all users. Here the organization will need to identify the specific content of each sub-layer using the guidelines described previously. Only organization-wide software components will be included in the sever kernel. At this stage, it will also be vital to properly preconfigure the presentation section for the reference system that serves as the source device before reproduction.

The system kernel includes the presentation sub-layer. If IT is a service, then this is the most important section of the entire kernel. It is the one single aspect of the system that users and administrators will interact with on a daily basis. Presentation does not stop at the desktop. Every element users can see on a system should be standardized. The organization saves through clear reductions in training, since the interface of each system is exactly the same. If all hard disks, all desktops, all menus, and all display features are standardized on all servers, end users—even administrators and technicians—will always be able to quickly perform work on any given server or PC within the network. For newcomers, the organization can train them on how to use their own corporate systems, not in how to use basic Windows.

The role-based commercial software section contains all commercial applications that do not have a mission-critical role and that must be installed on a server, based on its role in the network. This layer benefits from the rationalization process and provides single applications for any given IT task. This section, especially the special commercial application sub-section, can save time and money, since applications are grouped as functional families of products that provide specialized services. Thus, deployment of these applications can be performed through the assignment of the family of applications to specific groups of servers—or server roles—within the organization.

Here, it will be important that the presentation of all applications be similar—that all menu shortcuts be coherently stored in appropriate locations, that extraneous shortcuts be removed, that all programs are stored within a unified disk structure, and that all saving procedures use the same default folder. These items form the standards for this section.

Ad hoc commercial applications are applications that must be installed on servers, regardless of the role they play. For example, a special monitoring application may need to be installed when you are facing issues with a particular server, but it would be removed once the problem is solved. Therefore, it is an ad hoc application. Because these applications traverse server roles, they are required only on specific servers.

The role-based corporate application layer focuses on mission-critical business roles. Once again, it is the guidelines of the presentation sub-layer that tie this application section to the entire system. Here, application deployment costs are considerably reduced, because families of applications can be deployed to specific servers within the network. Since applications are deployed as a group, the cost deployment is much lower than deploying applications one by one. The major difference between this section and the commercial software layer is restricted access. Users of corporate applications must be authorized, since they can have access to confidential information through these applications, whereas users of commercial applications do not need the same level of authorization, since commercial applications are most often licensed on the server and not by user.

Ad hoc corporate applications, like the ad hoc commercial applications, are installed regardless of server role, but unlike commercial applications, they are secured on a per-user basis. Because of this licensing distinction—commercial applications licensed on a per-PC/server basis and corporate applications controlled on a per-user basis—the commercial application layers are deemed horizontal and the corporate layers are deemed vertical. Horizontal layers can be accessed by all users or administrators in the organization, but vertical layers are tightly controlled because of the sensitive information they give access to. Keep this distinction in mind when designing your own version of the PASS model. All installation and administration approaches for the deployment of Windows Server 2008—physical or virtual—should make use of the PASS model and rely on its principles. To do so, you'll need to concentrate on two elements:

- The server kernel or all of the elements that will be common to all servers.
- Server roles or configurations—all of the applications or functions that can be consolidated onto similar groups of servers.

Design the Server Kernel—Resource Pools vs. Virtual Service Offerings

The server kernel is designed to deliver all of the services that are common to all servers. The decision to include a component is based on organizational need as well as licensing mode. If your organization owns a corporate license for a server component, it should be included in the kernel. If your corporation requires a specific function on all servers, the technology supporting it should be included in the kernel. Kernel contents also include the default server configuration. Finalizing the configuration elements of the server kernel and capturing them in a system image can greatly simplify the deployment process. This configuration should also include the preparation of the presentation sub-layer. Making sure that all new user environments created on the server have immediate access to server management tools and server utilities simplifies the server management process as well (see Table 3-1). You'll also note that there are significant differences between kernel contents for physical and virtual servers.

Sub-layer	Suggested Contents	
	Physical Resource Server	**Virtual Service Offering**
Operating System	Provides basic OS services, including: Windows Server 2008 Core either Enterprise or Datacenter edition Service packs and/or hot fixes, if applicable Certified drivers (video, power management, and so on) Task scheduling/event management configurations	Provides basic OS services, including: Windows Server 2008 (most suitable edition) Service packs and/or hot fixes, if applicable Certified drivers (video, power management, printing, and so on) DLLs (Visual Studio DLLs, .NET Framework editions, others) Standard typefaces Task scheduling/event management configurations
Networking	In order to apply network standards: IPv4, IPv6, or both Server identification (host name, NetBIOS name, machine name) Domain or workgroup membership	In order to apply network standards: IPv4, IPv6, or both Server identification (host name, NetBIOS name) Domain or workgroup membership Startup, shutdown, logon, and logoff scripts Virtual private network/routing and remote access components Message queuing components **Note:** This can also be a third-party hypervisor.

Table 3-1 Suggested Content for the Server Kernel

Sub-layer	Suggested Contents	
	Physical Resource Server	**Virtual Service Offering**
Storage	In order to standardize the way information is presented: Shared physical drives—network-attached storage, storage area network—for the OS and data Identical logical disks Local tree—software, current, and legacy Local tree—data Network tree (Distributed File System or DFS) Replication parameters (DFS replication) OS and data protection mechanisms	In order to standardize the way information is presented: Identical physical drives—OS, data, and logs (if required) Identical logical disks Local tree—software, current, and legacy Local tree—data Network tree (Distributed File System or DFS) Replication parameters (DFS replication) Database requirements OS and data protection mechanisms
Security	To standardize access control: System owner Local group policies Local (New Technology File System or NTFS) and network access rights and permissions Central access control management Group Policy management Antivirus software Intrusion detection and auditing tools OS encryption (mostly for remote sites) Data encryption Transport encryption	To standardize access control: System owner User profiles and local group policies Local (NTFS or New Technology File System) and network access rights and permissions Central access control management Group Policy management Antivirus software Intrusion detection and auditing tools OS encryption Data encryption Transport encryption
Communications	Both tools and procedures: Language packs	Both tools and procedures: Browsers (home page, internal corporate favorites, protected modes, anti-phishing, proxy/firewall controls) Communication tools to users (message from management, from IT, and so on) Data collection tools Workgroup/collaboration technologies Default profiles Language packs

TABLE 3-1 Suggested Content for the Server Kernel (*continued*)

Sub-layer	Suggested Contents	
	Physical Resource Server	**Virtual Service Offering**
Generic Tools	Including basic administrative tools: Hypervisor (Virtualization role) Monitoring and performance management Appropriate service packs	Including basic administrative tools: Administrative tools Support tools Resource kit tools Monitoring and performance management Appropriate service packs
Presentation	Controls generic functionalities: Common scripts Virtualization parent	Controls the desktop appearance and generic functionalities: Desktop components Menus and Quick Launch area shortcuts Default user profile and presentation Print queues

Table 3-1 Suggested Content for the Server Kernel (*continued*)

Once you've configured your system image, you will need to implement an update management process to make sure it is kept up to date. The best schedule is a quarterly schedule, where each quarter you generate a new version of the image. In the meantime, you apply patches to the image by deploying the image and then applying the patches once the image is deployed. Practice will help you determine which is the best schedule for you.

In addition, you should use a naming strategy for images. Use whole numbers for each major version, and use point numbers for each update/patch you apply. For example, image 1.02 would be the first image you create with two levels of patches, and image 2.00 would be the first complete rebuild of an image.

Manage Virtual Server Images

Virtual server "images" are easier to manage, since they are nothing but copies of the files that make up the virtual hard drives for the system. This means that you can always keep the reference computer around. On a physical installation, it is difficult to keep the reference computer around, because you need the hardware to work with it. This means you need to rebuild the reference computer each time you want to update it.

But on virtual machines, you can build the reference computer, copy the files that make it up while keeping the original reference computer as is, depersonalize the copy, and use it to seed new system installations. Then, each month, as patches are released, you can update the original reference computer and repeat the process. The process is longer for physical installations because of the fact that you cannot keep the reference computer around as easily as with virtual installations.

Configure Server Roles

Now that you have created your system kernel, you can proceed to the identification of server roles or functions. This is done by grouping service types by service affinity. Certain types of services or functions do not belong together, while others naturally tend to fit in the same category. As a result, you will have roles that are defined by the type of software servers run and the type of service they deliver. Eight main categories emerge (see Figure 3-6):

- **Network infrastructure and physical servers** These servers provide core networking functions, such as IP addressing or name resolution, including support for legacy systems. They also provide virtual private network (VPN) and routing and remote access services. And, because they are a base level service, they run the virtualization role on physical machines.
- **Identity management servers** These servers are the core identity managers for the network. They contain and maintain the entire corporate identity database for all users and user access. For WS08, these would be servers running ADDS. This function should not be shared with any other as much as possible, unless it is a core networking function, such as name resolution.
- **File and print servers** These servers focus on the provision of storage and structured document services to the network. As you will see, these functions are greatly expanded in WS08 and form the basis of information sharing within this technology.
- **Application servers** These servers provide application services to the user community. WS08 examples would be Exchange Server, SQL server, and so on; in fact, any service from the Windows Server system.
- **Terminal servers** These servers provide a central application execution environment to users. Users need only have a minimal infrastructure to access these servers, because their entire execution environment resides on the server itself.
- **Dedicated Web servers** These servers focus on the provision of Web services to user communities. The WS08 Web edition is specifically designed to meet these needs.

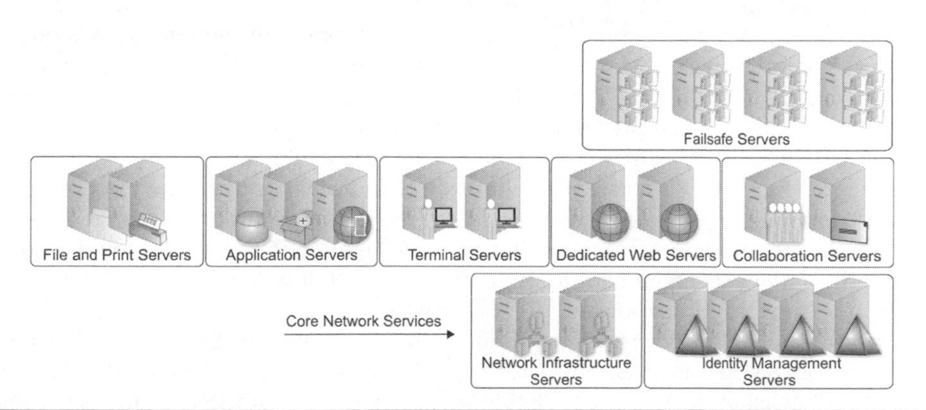

Figure 3-6 The eight server roles

- **Collaboration servers** These servers provide the infrastructure for collaboration within the enterprise. Their services include Windows SharePoint Services (WSS), streaming media services, and real-time communications.
- **Failsafe servers** This eighth role focuses on redundancy and provides business continuity by having identical images of production servers in stand-by mode. When a production server fails, the failsafe version automatically comes on line. The most important aspect of this server construction is replication technologies, ensuring that failsafe servers are always up to date and that no data is lost. This category is now extremely easy to create, since virtual servers are nothing but files that need to be replicated in another location. Physical servers are also easy to reproduce, since they run only a single role.

In addition, server placement comes into play. Placement refers to the architectural proximity or position of the server in an end-to-end distributed system. Three positions are possible:

- Inside the intranet
- In the security perimeter—often referred to as the demilitarized zone (DMZ), though for large organizations, the perimeter often includes more than just the DMZ
- Outside the enterprise

Each of these elements must be taken into consideration during the elaboration of the solution you design with Windows Server 2008. With the coming of virtualization, server placement tends to blur, as virtual machines on a physical host may be in one zone while others on the same host are in another. Make sure you keep server placement in mind when you position the virtual servers for each zone in your network.

Design the Network Architecture

As you can see, moving to Windows Server 2008 is not necessarily complicated, but it is a significant project. The scope of the project will vary, depending on the size of your network, the number of servers it holds, and the number of users it serves. But in all cases, you will consider it a significant project requiring a significant investment. This is one reason why it should not be taken lightly. Of course, everyone involved in an operating system upgrade project will do their utmost to deliver a great product (the new network), but not everyone will necessarily be ready to invest themselves fully into the new operating system or into this project, as there may be some resistance to this change.

This is why one of the first activities you should undertake is to define your project vision. A vision will help you identify the goals of the implementation. It will help delineate the scope of the change you want to implement and the direction you need to take. And, along with the change management tools described earlier, it will help focus the project so that everyone is on the same footing.

Microsoft, through the Microsoft Solutions Framework, uses the SMART approach for vision definition. SMART is an acronym for Specific, Measurable, Attainable, Result-oriented, and Timing. The vision statement you define should include all of these elements—it should specify what you want to do in measurable and attainable steps, be results-oriented, and specify the time it will take to make the change. It should also include information about service delivery, usually to users. For example, a vision for a WS08 implementation might be:

> *"Design and deploy a structured and standardized network based on the inherent capabilities of Windows Server 2008 to improve our capacity to meet business and user needs through the implementation of a dynamic datacenter, and complete the project within the next year."*

This vision includes all of the elements described previously. In addition, it is short, easy to understand, and easy to remember.

Why the vision? To ensure that the implementation project aims for the right objectives. One of the great failings of technological projects is that they don't always take full advantage of the technology's capabilities. For example, in Chapter 1, we outlined the features of WS08, and because of this new feature set, it is clear that Windows Vista is the client of choice for WS08. Of course, WS08 works with down-level clients, but if you want to take full advantage of its capabilities in your upgraded network, you should make sure that you deploy or use Windows Vista on your client PCs.

In short, the vision is there to ensure that you don't forget that you're implementing a new technology—a technology that surpasses the one you're replacing and that often provides lots of new ways to do things. The worst thing that can happen to your network is that you don't keep this in mind and continue to use old methods when newer, more efficient ones are available—all simply because you don't know or don't want to know that they exist. Don't let this happen to your project! Don't adapt the new technology to your old methods; adapt your old methods to the new technology.

In addition, make sure that you use a structured approach to perform the design of your new network of services. One of the best ways to do this is to introduce the concept of standard operating procedures (SOPs), if you don't already use them.

A Structured Approach: Use Standard Operating Procedures

SOPs help reduce costs and improve network stability because they ensure everyone is using the same process for any given procedure. Documented SOPs, even for interactive or manual procedures, can vastly reduce the margin of error when performing any procedure, especially on a server. A well-designed SOP will also supply a contact point for reference if something goes wrong during its operation, letting your staff intermix their skills and rely on each other when issues arise.

But technical staff are not well known for documenting and standardizing procedures and operations. Often, technicians find it easier to simply keep everything in mind and to know who to refer to if a specific problem arises. While this approach works and has given proven results, its major drawback lies with the availability of key personnel—when this personnel is no longer available, the knowledge disappears from the enterprise. On the other hand, it is often difficult for organizations to budget for SOP documentation. It is a time-consuming process whose benefits are not always immediately apparent to management.

Because of their proven value, SOPs will be used here as much as possible. Whenever a procedure must be outlined, it will be done through a standard operating procedure. Thus, you can save considerable time and effort by simply adapting the enterprise-ready standard operating procedures within this book to the conditions of your particular situation.

A standard operating procedure is a *documented set of instructions to be followed to complete a given procedure*. It focuses on maximizing efficiency during operational and production requirements. Once implemented, SOPs can help support guaranteed service levels and become the basis for the elaboration of service level agreements.

When well defined, SOPs allow an organization to measure the time it takes to perform a given task. SOPs are also used to simplify problem troubleshooting, since every process is the same everywhere. Finally, SOPs provide redundancy and reduced costs in administration, since all network technicians and administrators use the same processes wherever they are located and no retraining is required. Thus, the SOPs you write will also become the core of any technical training program you provide to administrative staff in your enterprise.

SOP Best Practices

There are several concepts to keep in mind when writing or adapting SOPs:

- Incorporate safety and environmental variables into the traditional how-to steps you write.
- All SOPs must meet the definition of an SOP (see the previous paragraphs).
- The actual SOP should include no more than 6 to 12 steps to be effective. If an SOP goes beyond 10 steps, consider these solutions:
  - Break the long SOP into several logical sub-job SOPs.
  - Prepare the longer comprehensive training SOP first to get a picture of what training is required. Then decide how to break it into shorter sub-job SOPs.
  - Make the long-form SOP a training document or manual to supplement the shorter sub-job SOPs.
  - If you write shortcut SOPs, explain the reason behind certain steps to provide understanding of the importance of following all the steps in the proper order.
- Write SOPs for people who perform under different interpersonal circumstances:
  - For people who work alone
  - For two or more people who work together as a team
  - For people who will supervise other people doing a job
  - For people who are not familiar with rules generally understood by your employees
- Consider the age, education, knowledge, skill, experience and training, and work culture of the individuals who will be performing the SOP steps.
- Forecast future effects and steps at certain points in the SOP to tell readers things they should know in advance (upcoming steps that require caution, precision, timing, and personal attention).
- Once the SOP is completed, have several coworkers test it and give you feedback.
- Review the effectiveness of SOPs after a few weeks, and make necessary changes if in-the-field practice suggests that descriptions should be improved:
  a. Review and update SOPs when processes and equipment are changed.
  b. When new equipment is installed, take the opportunity to write a new SOP, incorporating the good from the old, and adding what is necessary to satisfy the new equipment.
- Keep SOPs short as much as possible. This will ensure that they are followed.

- Rely on the expertise of your staff to create and test the SOPs. You can, of course, supplement this expertise with external help.
- Ensure that all SOPs have a designated owner and operator.
- Illustrate the steps in an SOP as much as possible. It is always easier to follow a diagram than written instructions.

There, now you have the organizational tools required to begin your new network design process. The structure of an SOP is illustrated in Figure 3-7.

To assist in the process of designing the new network, a sample SOP is described in the following section. It serves two purposes. First, it demonstrates how an SOP should be put together. Second, it outlines the steps to follow to design the logical architecture you'll need to upgrade to the new operating system.

The Logical Architectural Design Process

Every network infrastructure project must begin with the design of the logical architecture. This is where you make the architectural decisions that will affect how you will make use of the technology you are moving to. There are a lot of elements to consider and decisions to make before you perform your first production installation of WS08.

Designing a network architecture is a process that must begin by looking at the organization itself to identify the business needs that drive the type of services your network has to deliver. In fact, the process must follow some specific steps before the installation is ready to deploy. Every aspect of the network will have to be considered, and every need must be addressed. The blueprint in Figure 3-8 outlines the process to use for the design of a network architecture. It is concentrated on three basic steps:

- Identify business requirements.
- Identify technical requirements.
- Design the solution.

It is also important to remember that the logical network architecture is a product and should be treated as such. This means it must be iterative. Like in any development project,

FIGURE 3-7
A structured SOP

1- Review installation preparation checklist
2- Select the Windows version
3- Fill out the server data sheet
4- Use the post-installation checklist
5- Document configuration and customization requirements

For Reference Server Only:

6- Install Windows AIK on management system
7- Back up the reference server
8- Prepare the answer file
9- Create a .wim image (if required)
10- Test the deployment method

Analysis
Solution Design
1
2
3
Business Requirements
Technical Requirements
Enterprise Network Architecture
1- Business Model
Organization model
Organization goals
Products/services
Geographic scope
Organization processes
2- Organization Structure
Management model
Organization structure
Vendors/partner/ customer relationships
Acquisition plans (Business)
3- Organization Strategies
Business priorities
Projected growth and strategy
Legal implications
Tolerance for risk
TCO objectives
4- IT Management
Centralized/ decentralized management
Funding model
Outsourcing/ in-house?
Decision-making process
Change management process
1- Existing/Planned IT Environment
Organization size
Number of users
Resources location
Network geographic distribution and links
Available bandwidth
H/S performance requirements
Data patterns
Network roles and responsibilities
Security issues
2- Impact of Enterprise Network
Existing systems and applications
Planned upgrades/tollouts
IP infrastructure
Technology support structure
Current planned network & system management
Authentication services
3- Client/PC Desktop Management
End user requirements
Technology support for end users
Required client environment
Internal/external client base
1- Planning
Review requirements
Review new products features
Create initial architecture
Prepare for the installation
2- Installation
Preparation
Initial installation
Automating installations
Server staging
3- AD Infrastructure
AD design
AD installation
AD management
4- IP Infrastructure
Network settings
Connection management
IP addressing
Name resolution
5- PC Management Strategy
Managing objects with Group Policy
Software installation
Environment management
6- User Support Infrastructure
User management (accounts, groups, authentication)
User environment management
7- Shared Resources & Internetworking
Sharing folders
Sharing printers
Sharing applications
Auditing resources
Internet Information Server
IP routing
Remote access
8- Security Infrastructure
Security policy design
Security resources
IIS security
Public Key Infrastructure (PKI)
9- Resilience Management
Disaster recovery
Troubleshooting strategy
Redundancy planning
10- Network Administration
Administration design
Remote administration
Routine tasks
Performance management
Directory management

FIGURE 3-8 The blueprint for the design of a logical network architecture

it is a good idea to use versioning techniques when building this architecture. This way, you can aim for smaller steps as you build and prepare your environment. Don't try to do everything at once!

The design of the solution must cover the following elements:

- Plan the logical network design.
- Prepare and proceed to server installations.

- Design and implement the Active Directory Domain Services infrastructure.
- Design and implement the IP infrastructure.
- Design and implement the user support infrastructure.
- Design and implement the Group Policy strategy.
- Design and implement the resource sharing and internetworking strategy.
- Design and implement the security strategy.
- Prepare for network administration.
- Prepare for risk management.

Using the lifecycles outlined in Figures 3-1, 3-2, and 3-3, this book will focus on three of the four lifecycle phases: planning, preparation and deployment, and production. Some coverage and discussion of the retirement phase is included here, but it obviously will not deal with the solution that you design for WS08; it will focus on retiring and removing the older Windows or other operating system you currently have in place.

This blueprint has been used in a number of different enterprise network implementation projects with surprisingly good results. The first two phases of this blueprint, the analysis components, apply just as well to network design as to Active Directory Domain Services design, as you'll see in future chapters.

The blueprint shows that the design of the solution begins with the planning activity. This activity leads to the initial logical architecture. Since the architecture is crucial to the project (there's nothing to implement if you don't have an architecture), it becomes valuable for the organization to introduce its first standard operating procedure: the architectural design process. In this sample SOP, some SOP elements have been omitted, since they vary from organization to organization.

Sample SOP: Designing a Network Architecture

SOP Title Network Architecture Design

Category Planning and design

Purpose This procedure forms the basic outcome of the planning and design phase of the introduction of a new service into the organizational network. It is intended for architects, planners, and system administrators.

Two types of architectures are required when implementing a new technology: the enterprise or logical architecture, which is focused on orientations, rules, and standards for the service, and the technical architecture, which is focused on the technical details of the service implementation. Both can rely on this procedure, with small variations.

Task Coverage The procedure covers the design of an architecture. It begins with the review of the existing situation and a review of existing and updated inventories. If inventories are up to date, this procedure is greatly facilitated, since it can concentrate on its objective instead of getting sidetracked into actually performing inventory collection. The situation review should also list existing problems and issues that can be addressed by the new service being introduced. Make sure the review also focuses on the positive elements of the existing situation. This ensures that what is being done well continues to be so.

Tools Required

Equipment	• A personal computer • A technological laboratory able to reproduce the environment to be replaced • Evaluation or testing copies of the technology supporting the new service
Reference materials	• The new technology's Help files • Reference documents on the new technology • Internet access
Training requirements	Enterprise architects should take introductory training on the new technology. This can be in the form of external training or self-study.
General materials	• Information on the organization, its goals, and objectives • Inventory data in electronic format
Timing	• The logical architecture must be performed at the very beginning of the project. • The technological architecture must be performed as soon as the logical architecture is complete and the project go-ahead is authorized.

Steps to Perform The steps to perform are the following (see Figure 3-9):

1. **Current situation review** The architectural design process begins with a review of the current situation. What is wrong? Why do we need to change the current situation? What are our business objectives? Which problems do we intend to solve? These are the questions that need to be answered at this stage. Also, don't forget to project into the future. If some of the information you gather in this phase is likely to change in the near future, make sure you include it in your report.

Figure 3-9 Sample SOP steps to perform

2. **Update and review inventories** In order to answer some of the questions listed in step 1, you need to make sure that your inventories are up to date and review them. Make sure the inventories are as detailed as you need them to be so that you will have access to all of the information you require.
3. **Identify business needs** Use the results from the previous two steps to identify and prioritize the business needs of your enterprise. Concentrate on those that are specifically addressed by the service you wish to implement.
4. **Review market trends** Review the industry and market trends in this field. Categorize them as short-term and long-term. Identify those that affect your situation. Select the appropriate technology to support the service you wish to implement.
5. **Review product features** If the solution is to be based on a specific product, review and learn about the product's features. Now that you know what you will use to support your solution, you need to identify the specific features that it will be based on. You also need to be sure you understand the philosophy behind the features so that you can use them to the best advantage. If the solution will be based on the upgrade of an existing product, concentrate on new features and improvements.
6. **Use applicable best practices** Review best practices from both the industry and the manufacturer of the technology you expect to implement. Retain only applicable best practices.
7. **Customize to business requirements** Customize the solution to meet your current business requirements. Make sure all of the requirements on the list you produced in step 3 are met. If some are not met, explain why.
8. **Project to support future business requirements** Make sure your solution can evolve with time and, especially, with growing business requirements and future business trends. You don't want to implement a solution that cannot change with time.
9. **Rationalize hardware and software** Rationalize hardware and software as much as possible during your solution design. If your inventory tells you that you have more than one type of object that performs the same operations, reduce it to only one type. This will simplify the management and administration of the service you wish to implement.
10. **Deal with obsolescence** If your equipment, either hardware or software, is obsolete, replace it as much as you can, even if it still has a little life in it. It doesn't make sense to install something new on a piece of equipment that will be replaced within the next six months.
11. **Solve existing issues** Make sure your solution will specifically solve existing issues that were identified in steps 1 and 3. If your current environment has problems of any type (technical, situational, physical, or even human issues), ensure that your solution will deal with them appropriately.
12. **Test through proofs of concept** Test everything thoroughly. Perform proofs of concept if you're not sure of something. It is always easier to test first, then document.

13. **Standardize and certify your solution** Standardize within the solution. If there are procedures to document, ensure that they are outlined through standard operating procedures. Also make sure that every process you recommend is tried and tested. If you are using software that can be certified to work by its manufacturer, ensure that certification is part of your solution.

Additional Comments Don't forget the objective of the architecture: to solve problems, improve service levels, and stay within budget. Make sure you involve other groups, especially the groups targeted by the solution, into your solution design process.

Perform a Situation Review and Needs Analysis

As you can see, the starting point of any change situation is the current situation and the best place to start a review of the current situation is with inventories. As illustrated in the blueprint in Figure 3-8, an analysis begins with the identification of business-related information and then moves on to the details of the technical environment for which you will need to design the solution.

For the WS08 logical network architecture, your analysis will need to focus more specifically on two additional areas:

- If you intend to perform a migration from an existing environment, you will need to perform an extensive server inventory in order to identify which servers can be rationalized, which can be retired and replaced, and which services will require entirely new servers. You will also need a detailed inventory of the services and functions each existing server performs. This will mean detailing the actual users on each server, information stored on the server, security parameters for that information, and so on.
- If you are implementing a new network, you will need to clearly identify the business requirements in order to properly scale the servers you will deploy.

Don't hold back on this activity, because it is the driving force for the solution you design.

TIP *Since you will be moving to a virtual or dynamic datacenter, you may want to take advantage of the possibilities of physical-to-virtual migrations. For example, Microsoft System Center Virtual Machine Manager (SCVMM at www.microsoft.com/systemcenter/scvmm/default.mspx) has the ability to capture physical machine images and convert them to virtual machines. This is quite useful for both testing and preparing for your new virtual service offerings (VSO) environment. If you rely on a non-Microsoft hypervisor, such as that provided by VMware or Citrix, you can use other migration tools. VMware offers the free VMware Converter (www.vmware.com/products/converter); Citrix can actually rely on SCVMM, since it supports the same virtual machine format as Microsoft does.*

Change in Role of Servers

One of the major objectives of each new version of Windows Microsoft releases is to support new hardware and advances in hardware technology. In terms of servers, these advances are considerable, especially with the advent of 64-bit technology. Today, basic hardware performance for a server is no longer a limit or an issue. Most servers today are multiprocessing servers—servers that can be scaled through the addition of more central processing units (CPUs) or even more CPU cores. Servers today also support the "hot-add" features, such as RAM, hard disks, and even CPUs, without having to stop the server. In addition, storage technologies have evolved into storage area networks (SAN) or network access solutions (NAS), which are easy to scale transparently. In fact, your dynamic datacenter should rely on 64-bit blade servers tied to central and shared storage as much as possible to reduce server footprints and keep your datacenter as green as possible, reducing heat generation and power consumption.

Microsoft has helped considerably with the release of Windows Vista and especially Windows Sever 2008. More and more reboot situations are eliminated with each edition of Windows. Vista introduced Reboot Manager, an application that will stop and restart services instead of rebooting the server, eliminating even more reboot scenarios. Network modifications no longer require reboots, and the addition of a powerful Plug and Play engine mean adding some types of hardware no longer requires a reboot.

WS08 should run on 64-bit hardware, which breaks several performance barriers present in the 32-bit world. All of the versions of WS08 support the new "headless" server concept—servers without direct physical links to monitors or input devices. Server Core is an excellent example of this and should be the version running on all physical machines. WS08 is designed to take advantage of these new capabilities, since all versions of Windows Server 2008 have multiprocessing capabilities to some degree. In fact, Microsoft and chip manufacturers Intel and AMD continuously work hand in hand to develop the guidelines for server creation with each new generation of Windows. Both chip vendors have enabled virtualization extensions in their processors, extensions which Hyper-V can take full advantage of. Before you make your server decisions, you should definitely read the latest news on this collaborative effort. Microsoft publishes this information on their web site at www.microsoft.com/whdc/default.mspx.

Consolidate Servers with Windows Server 2008 Through Resource Pools

A server today provides a function. It is not a product. Many organizations have taken to single-instance servers when working with older versions of Windows. This approach started with Windows NT. Though NT itself was a solid product, many of the operations or applications organizations performed with it made it unstable. Often, the best way to deal with this instability was to dedicate the server to one specific role. Another reason for this approach was project-based hardware acquisitions—each time a new project required a server, it would acquire its own and add one or more new single-purpose servers into the network. Unfortunately, the single-purpose server approach serves to increase the number of servers in the organization to the point of proliferation. Many existing Windows servers are never used to their full capacity. In many cases, the server rarely exceeds *15 percent utilization*! The coming of Windows Server 2008, and especially the introduction of server virtualization technologies, allows organizations to review traditional server approaches and aim for increased server consolidation—up to 80 percent or more in most cases.

Consolidation involves fewer, fatter servers. Fewer servers mean simpler management. You can improve service levels because it is easier to maintain the operation of a few centralized servers than it is for several distributed servers. There is less downtime, since servers tend to be centralized and provide easier physical access. Applications can be deployed more rapidly because most of the code resides on the server itself. It is easier to standardize because fewer physical elements are involved. And, with virtual servers, you can easily move one virtual instance of a server from one physical host to another, providing dynamic responses to increased business needs.

There are four justifications for consolidation:

- **Centralization** Relocating existing servers to fewer sites
- **Physical consolidation** Many smaller servers are replaced with fewer, more powerful servers
- **Data integration** Several distributed databases are consolidated into a single data repository
- **Application integration** Multiple applications are migrated to fewer, more powerful servers. Applications must have a certain degree of affinity before this integration can occur.

Through the use of technologies such as WS08's hypervisor—the thin executive layer that virtualizes all physical hardware—or VMware's ESX Server or Virtual Infrastructure, you will be able to take better advantage of a single server's hardware by installing multiple instances of WS08 inside virtual machines. If you are among those who have servers performing at no more than 15 percent capacity, virtualization will help boost resource utilization. On average, you will be able to run between 10 to 20 virtual machines per physical host, depending, of course, on the configuration of the physical host.

Finally, Microsoft WS08 offers improved clustering functionality over older versions of Windows Server. Clustering services are now a role you add to the system you configure. When you activate or modify clustering services with WS08, you no longer need to restart the servers in the cluster. In addition, WS08 cluster services are Active Directory–aware; that is, they are published within Active Directory and are made available to all users in the same way that non-clustered services are. They are also more resilient, no longer having a single point of failure in the shared Quorum resource because they rely on a File Share Witness.

Clustering and server consolidation should be one of the objectives you keep in mind when designing your WS08 logical network architecture. To do so, you need to group servers by function to see which logical groupings are available to you for consolidation purposes. This is another reason for using the PASS model illustrated in Figure 3-5.

TIP *Simply moving all of your existing servers to virtualization will not accomplish your server consolidation goals. Think about it: If all of your existing servers are virtualized, you will actually have* more *servers than you did before because you have to add the new physical host servers. Think* consolidation *each time you virtualize a role. Is it possible to perform this same role with fewer machines? If so, rely on the new features of WS08 to reduce the number of virtual servers you run.*

Migration Considerations

In addition, it will be important to identify the migration path you will use to move from your existing network to the WS08 enterprise network. Several techniques can be used to migrate from one network operating system to another, but there are also guidelines that must be taken into consideration. Of course, if you're implementing a new network based on WS08, migration considerations are not your primary concern.

Migrating from an existing operating system could be easy to do if you could do it while everyone is on holidays or during an annual "shutdown" of operations. Unfortunately, most of you will be performing migrations during normal business operations. In addition, you'll have to make the migration process transparent to users and to the business process. Quite a challenge!

In fact, migrations must take several factors into consideration:

- You have to ensure that you provide, at the very least, exactly the same service levels users are currently experiencing in your network. Of course, your major goal will be to improve the user network experience, but you should ensure that whatever happens, you will not reduce service levels. This is one of the reasons why you must include user representatives in your network design project. They will help keep you focused. After all, the network is there as a service to them.
- You also have to ensure that you provide comprehensive training programs at all levels of your organization. If you're moving from Windows NT to WS08, you'll find that the major training task is technical, not user-oriented. While users do experience new features, such as interface improvements, it is mostly in manageability and reliability that WS08 improvements abound. Technical staff will have to undergo extensive training. They will have to be prepared well before you implement the new network. In addition, you'll probably want to ensure that the user training program you deliver occurs at the same time as you migrate. In fact, the best migration results occur when user training is synchronized with the migration program. If your users are already running Windows Vista, training will be reduced, since they will already be used to the interface.
- You'll also want to ensure that all of your applications run properly in WS08. If you're running Windows NT, or even Windows 2000, you'll need to test applications thoroughly to ensure that they operate properly under the new operating system. One of the major reasons for this is the new security model in WS08. Users are much more restricted in WS08 than they ever were in any previous versions because of the new UAC introduced with Windows Vista; thus, applications that run under older versions do not necessarily run properly under WS08. But there are other advantages in using WS08. WS08 offers an application compatibility mode that is the same as the one offered by Windows Vista. This is something that wasn't available in Windows 2000. Applications should run better in WS08 than in Windows 2000, and even in WS03, but nevertheless, you will discover that several of your applications will need to be upgraded or otherwise modified to run properly. Rationalization is a great help here because it means less upgrades. Both rationalization and extensive application compatibility testing should be part of your project.
- You'll want to determine if you need to upgrade your systems or if you perform clean installations. The decision will depend on a lot of factors, but the most valuable approach is the new installation. New installations simply offer better stability and reliability, since they give you the opportunity to "clean up" your existing systems.
- You'll also need to consider how to migrate your directory and authentication services. WS08 includes an improved tool for Active Directory migration. This tool allows for migration of user accounts and passwords from Windows NT and Windows 2000-2003. It is a good tool for domain consolidation and migration. More on this topic will be discussed in future chapters.

These aren't the only considerations you'll have to take into account when migrating, but they are a good starting point.

Network with Windows Server 2008

The basis of any network is the concept of communication. The competitive advantage an information technology network gives to an organization is one that no one can afford to be without today. Despite its detractors, the Transmission Control Protocol/Internet Protocol (TCP/IP) protocol has become the de facto standard for all network communications. And with the advent of version 6 of this protocol, it will become even more entrenched than ever before.

The principle behind TCP/IP is simple: Each network component is given a specific identifier. In version 4 (IPv4), this identifier is in the format of a 32-bit number: four sections of eight binary values each. This addressing scheme generates a total of more than four billion IP addresses. Given the number of addresses, you would think that IPv4 could serve the Internet requirements of the entire world, but this is not the case. This is due to the very structure of IPv4 addressing. Since every address is subdivided into a class, and organizations are given the opportunity to acquire classes for private use, even if they don't actually require all of the addresses within this class, the potential four billion addresses have been appropriated quickly and now turn out to be insufficient. Because of this, the networking world has had to come up with innovative ways to use IPv4 to fulfill the networking needs and requirements of a wired world.

One of these solutions is the use of network address translation (NAT). NAT is a great tool, since it allows an organization to use an internal address scheme that is different from the external address scheme it exposes to the outside world. Three address ranges have been reserved for internal use:

- Class A—10.0.0.0 to 10.255.255.255 (Mask 255.0.0.0)
- Class B—172.16.0.0 to 172.31.255.255 (Mask 255.255.0.0)
- Class C—192.168.0.0 to 192.168.255.255 (Mask 255.255.255.0)

Organizations choose the class that best fits their needs based on the number of hosts that are required inside the internal network. Class A supports over 16 million hosts per subnet, class B over 65,000, and class C only 254. When communicating on the Internet, NAT translates the internal address to an external address, one that is often provided by an Internet service provider (ISP). NAT uses TCP ports, polling from the 65,000 potential ports when more than one internal address needs translation, greatly multiplying the number of addresses organizations can use, even with the limitations of IPv4.

In addition, IPv4 cannot automatically assign host addresses without external help. If your internal network includes several thousand hosts, you'll definitely want to take advantage of automatic addressing mechanisms. In IPv4, this is done through the Dynamic Host Configuration Protocol (DHCP).

Even though all of the hosts on your network have a specific address, using this 32-bit number to communicate between hosts is not practical for human beings. Thus, we need to resolve these numbers to names—names we can more easily remember. The domain naming system (DNS) is the process we use to resolve an Internet address to a more manageable name. But if you use legacy technologies within your Windows network, you'll also require legacy name resolution. This is performed through the Windows Internet Naming System (WINS). With the advent of Windows Vista and WS08, there is little need for WINS. In fact, one of the new features WS08 offers for IPv4 is the possibility to use DNS to reproduce the type of service WINS offers. This is done through the inclusion of a new GlobalNames zone, which contains static, global records with single-label names, such as those provided through WINS. Organizations moving to WS08 should look to the use of this new zone type and remove WINS servers from their networks.

Despite these temporary solutions, IPv4 use is becoming increasing more difficult, especially in terms of routing. Internet routers using version 4 of TCP/IP are having more and more trouble storing routing tables, the path a host must use to reach a given destination. A permanent solution is needed if the entire world is to have access to the Internet, especially emerging nations.

The Internet Engineering Task Force (IETF) has been working for some time on a complete solution to the IPv4 situation. The solution is embedded into version 6 of the TCP/IP protocol: IPv6. Version 6 uses a 128-bit addressing scheme. This results in 340, 282, 366, 920, 938, 463, 463, 374, 607, 431, 768, 211, 456 unique entities on the Internet, quite enough for the time being. IPv6 can support true point-to-point communications between hosts and destinations without the use of schemes such as address translation. In addition, IPv6 includes numerous other improvements. For example, an IPv6 host does not necessarily require DHCP, since it can generate its own address from the unique number assigned to its network interface card, the media access control (MAC) number. If the host needs to communicate externally, its IPv6 address will be generated from both the MAC address and the address of the router it is connected to, greatly simplifying both addressing and communications, since the router address becomes part of the host's address. WS08 includes full support for IPv6. In fact, IPv6 is installed and enabled by default. Each host has its own automatic IPv6 address along with its IPv4 address. WS08 uses a technology called Teredo to map IPV4 to IPV6 addresses and vice versa.

Though all WS08 and Vista systems will be able to use IPv6 automatically, there are still issues with using it. For example, routers need to support IPv6 for the protocol to work. Most router manufacturers have implemented software solutions for IPv6 support for existing routers, and new routers include this support by default. Cisco systems and others have downloadable software revisions for their operating systems, which include IPv6 support. New router products have hardware solutions for IPv6 support. But router support is not the only requirement. Applications that are based on IPv4 today will not automatically function

TCP/IP Implementation

The Windows implementation of IPv6 provides an automatic link-local address. Link-local addresses are designed to communicate over the local area network (LAN) only. For you to be able to communicate over wide area networks (WANs), you will need to obtain a pool of addresses and assign them to your systems. This will be covered in future chapters as we discuss the implementation of your new network services.

More on the TCP/IP functionalities included in WS08 can be found in a Microsoft document entitled "Changes in Functionality from Windows Server 2003 with SP1 to Windows Server 2008," which can be found at www.microsoft.com/downloads/details.aspx?FamilyID=173E6E9B-4D3E-4FD4-A2CF-73684FA46B60&displaylang=en.

with IPv6, since the core operation of the TCP/IP protocol is different. In most cases, the translation technologies included in Vista and WS08 will make this transition seamless to these applications, but in all instances, it is best to convert applications for use with this new version of the protocol. Finally, you will need to make sure that your protection mechanisms—firewalls, intrusion detection systems, and so on—fully support IPv6 before you move to its implementation. Every organization that plans to move to IPv6 will have to carefully prepare their implementation before proceeding.

Prepare Network Communications

Most organizations using Windows networks already have a complex network addressing scheme in place to support the use of IPv4 within their internal networks. In many cases, these organizations will continue to use this scheme with Windows Server 2008. This addressing scheme includes the following elements:

- Centralized IP addressing, including both virtual and physical LAN planning
- Name resolution, both Internet and legacy
- Alert management
- Service load balancing
- Multicasting

But as you prepare to implement IPv6, you will benefit from a simplified addressing scheme, which will rely on updated centralized IP addressing systems such as DHCPv6 to automatically generate all IPv6 addresses. In addition, the U.S. government's Office of Management and Budget (OMB) has set a deadline of June 2008 for governmental agencies "…as the date by which all agencies' infrastructures…must be using IPv6…" This makes the timing for this move perfect for many organizations, not only in the United States, but worldwide.

NOTE *For more information on the OMB's memo, see www.whitehouse.gov/omb/memoranda/fy2005/m05-22.pdf#search=%22omb%20ipv6%22.*

Windows Server 2008 is completely based on the TCP/IP protocol. In fact, the entire functioning of the WS08 Active Directory, the core of the WS08 network, is based on TPC/IP addressing and name resolution. As such, the TCP/IP protocol in WS08 becomes a core component of any WS08 enterprise network. Because of this, future chapters will be entirely based on TCP/IP as the core protocol for the implementation of networked services.

The New TCP/IP Stack

Since WS08 relies so heavily on TCP/IP, Microsoft has enhanced the protocol and improved it over and above what was included in previous versions of Windows. These improvements include:

- Dual IP-layer architecture for IPv6
- Automatic configuration of stack settings based on networking environment
- Routing compartments
- Security and packet filtering application programming interfaces (APIs)

Each helps increase the speed of TCP/IP communications between computers running Vista and/or WS08.

Both the IPv4 and IPv6 protocol implementations in WS08 share common transport and framing layers through a dual IP-layer architecture. Because of this, both protocol implementations can run on the same device without interference, providing added functionality and simplifying the transition to IPv6 for organizations of all sizes.

With its ability to automatically configure its key performance settings, the WS08 TCP/IP stack will sense the network environment and provide optimum speeds through adjustments to the Receive window and other parameter tuning. This eliminates the need for manual configuration of these key protocol settings and will provide faster data transfer rates, better bandwidth usage, and fewer retransmissions. This helps speed up large file transfers and network backup operations.

Routing compartments are used to segregate traffic from different interfaces. For example, if a computer supports multiple connections, such as VPN, Terminal Services, and direct login connections, each login session can be separated so that IP routing tables and other connection settings are isolated from each other. This serves to limit the possible dangers of having a system bridge multiple connection types and linking potentially unsafe networks to your corporate environment.

The Windows Filtering Platform (WFP) can filter all layers of the TCP/IP stack, providing one single interface for links to TCP/IP security, the Windows Firewall, packet filter information storage, and local host traffic. This provides a more secure and integrated approach to content control and lets independent software vendors (ISVs) link more easily to this new security feature.

Tip *More information on WFP can be found at www.microsoft.com/whdc/device/network/WFP.mspx.*

The new TCP/IP stack also includes other features, such as the ability to modify network settings without having to restart the system, eliminating more reboot situations, as well as support for runtime diagnostics and enhanced event logging and tracing. Overall, this new stack vastly improves networked communications for both Vista and WS08, making this foundation component more flexible and stable. Anyone who has worked with Vista will already have experienced many of these improvements through increased speed and performance in any networked communication, even those with down-level operating systems.

Use the Technological Lab as a Testing Ground

The final activity for your WS08 network project is the preparation and implementation of a technological laboratory. Since application compatibility testing and proofs of concept are an integral part of the design and preparation process, the technological laboratory is crucial.

The laboratory should contain enough technologies to be able to properly reproduce the organization's existing IT infrastructure. It should include technologies that are as recent as possible. Most often, organizations use recovered equipment that is not the latest and greatest. This only limits the potential benefits of this lab, because its purpose is to work with new technologies. New technologies always require more powerful hardware. If you plan to purchase new equipment for your implementation project, it is a good idea to pre-purchase a few systems and use them for laboratory testing.

The lab must also include quick setup and recovery strategies. For example, if technicians are working on a case study that requires the staging of an Active Directory and WS08 infrastructure, you won't want them to have to rebuild it from scratch every time they return to the laboratory. One of the best ways to provide this capability is to rely on virtualization technologies. This allows each technical group to prepare and store their own working environments. It saves considerable time when they return. Using virtualization will require a powerful storage server because each environment must be stored independently for the duration of the tests.

In addition, the laboratory will require special stations that are disconnected from the laboratory network and connected to the internal network and the Internet. These stations serve for documentation, research, and software downloads. Ideally, these stations are positioned throughout the lab for ready access by technicians.

The most important aspect of the lab will be its activity coordination and resource sharing. Most organizations cannot invest as much as they would like into the laboratory; therefore, most must use timesharing strategies to ensure that technical staff have ready access to the resources they need for testing purposes. Good coordination and structured testing methods can only ensure better testing results.

Figure 3-10 illustrates a sample testing laboratory. This lab reproduces a typical internal network with a minimum of equipment. Internal TCP/IP addresses can be used since it does not connect to the external world. More servers can be added to test the migration strategy you will devise, but these can be older and more obsolete systems since you will not be performing performance testing with them.

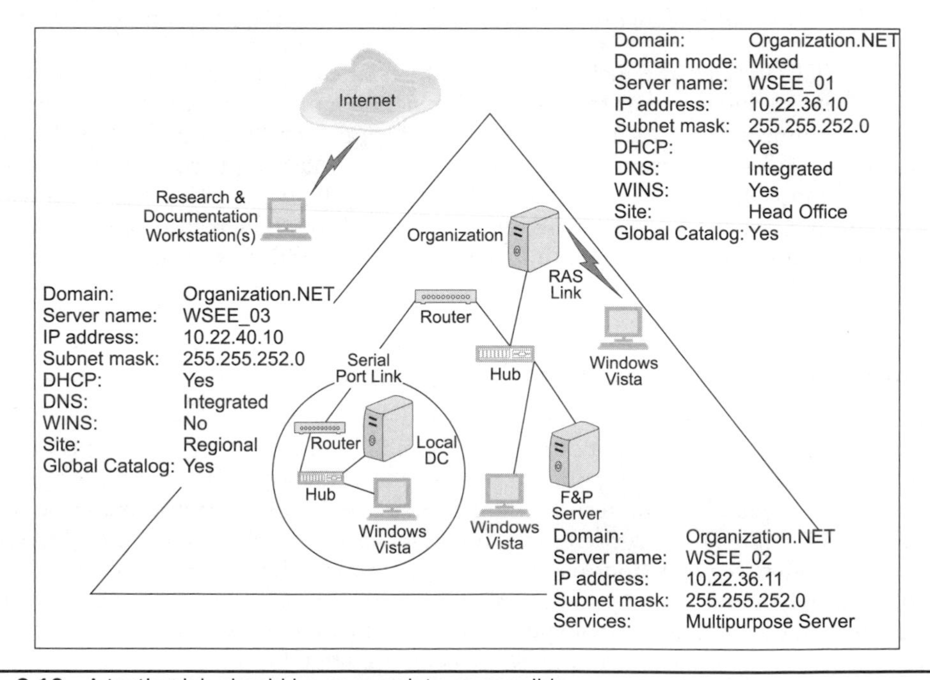

FIGURE 3-10 A testing lab should be as complete as possible.

Use a Structured Testing Strategy

Putting in place an enterprise network is 80 percent planning and preparation and 20 percent implementation. This means that the laboratory is one of the key elements of your future network. To ensure that your preparation phase goes well, you should use strict testing strategies. Most testing strategies include several different testing stages. Each focuses on a specific type of test. When building and preparing the enterprise network, you should use the following test types:

- **Unit Test** The first test is always an interactive discovery of a new technology. This phase lets you identify each of the elements of the technical architecture for the product. Once the first stages of discovery have been performed, you move to automation of an installation process. This second step focuses on evaluation of the automated procedure by itself.
- **Functional Test** Once some degree of automation has been performed, you need to validate that it operates as expected. One of the best ways to do this is to perform a peer review of the functionality.
- **Integration Test** The next stage is to integrate a given functionality with others it will have to coexist with. This should include deployment tests—focus on remote distribution of the functionality to ensure that it behaves as expected after remote installation. It should also include uninstallation tests—both interactive and remote—to ensure that it does not destabilize a system.
- **Staging Test** Finally, you move to an environment that duplicates the production network as much as possible. This will allow you to ensure that the processes tied to functionality will always operate as expected. In addition, you will want to perform acceptance testing—ensuring that intended clienteles approve of the functionality as designed and configured. Finally, you want to complete all quality assurance for the functionality. This involves the completion of all documentation and a final sign-off on all processes before final release of the product to the enterprise.
- **Pilot Testing** This final test is a pre-release into production to a select group of users. This test evaluates both technical and administrative processes tied to the deployment of a feature.

Each testing phase is important. If, for any reason, your product fails at any testing stage, it must be rolled back to the previous stage and corrections must be applied (see Figure 3-11). Following strict guidelines and rigorous testing procedures will only make your final product all the better. This is one of the definitions of enterprise-ready networking.

Build Your Resource Pool in Support of Virtual Laboratory Testing

Since the structure of your network will now focus on resource pools running virtual service offerings (VSOs), you will need to begin working with this structure as soon as possible. What better way to do this than with virtualized testing laboratories? You'll begin by building a few hardware-based host servers that will run the technologies you will need to test to build your VSO structure. Then, when you're ready, these host servers can form the initial resource pool you can use to begin your migration to WS08.

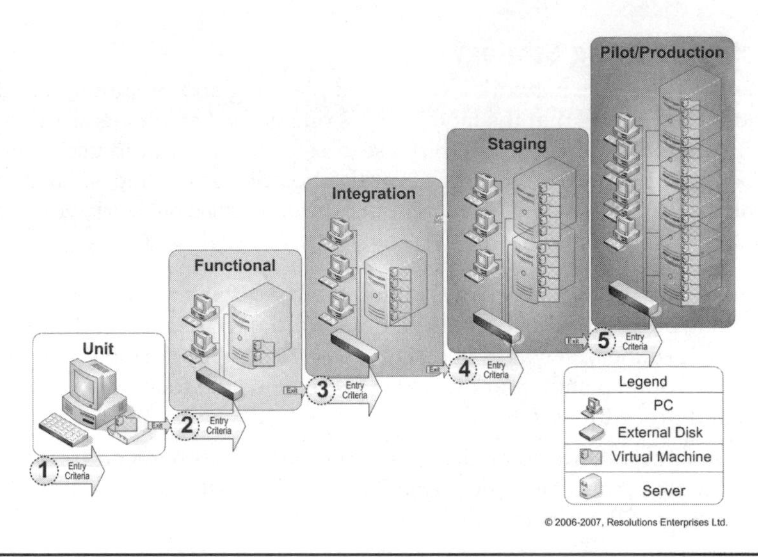

FIGURE 3-11 A graduated testing strategy

There are lots of reasons to use virtual laboratories. First, you can virtualize any of the server roles. In most of our tests, we've been able to run server roles with as little as 512 megabytes (MB) of RAM allocated to the virtual machine. Of course, you will have to increase the amount of RAM when you add roles to the server, but if you have the appropriate host—a host with enough firepower to run several virtual machines—you should easily be able to run any server role you need.

Working with both client PCs and servers through VMs will seriously cut down the cost of building the laboratory. As mentioned earlier, you can rely on virtual technology from either Microsoft or VMware, as both offer free copies of their tools. Both offer full support for running Windows servers or PCs. In addition, you may want to obtain tools for the conversion of physical machines to virtual instances. This saves a lot of time, as you simply point to the physical machine you want to capture and easily transform it into a virtual instance. Once again, both manufacturers offer these tools for free.

TIP *If you begin early and Hyper-V has not been released yet, you can still start working on the laboratory in a virtual environment. You can do so with either Microsoft Virtual Server (www.microsoft.com/windowsserversystem/virtualserver) or XenServer (www.citrixxenserver .com/Pages/default.aspx since the machines you create with each of these tools will be compatible with the machines you will run on Hyper-V.*

We suggest you buy some very large host machines to begin your resource pool. The ideal machine will be an x64 server running several multicore processors, lots of RAM, and lots of disk space. Use Windows Server 2008 x64 Enterprise Edition Server Core as the host OS for this server, since it includes four free licenses for virtual instances. The cost of a few servers with the right mix of firepower will outweigh the cost of running several lower-end machines and having to manage physical installations instead of virtual instances of servers, and it will prepare you properly for your new dynamic datacenter. In addition, you may even be able to take virtual machines you constructed in the testing lab and move them directly into production if you've done your homework right. This will provide immeasurable savings in time and costs during your deployment.

TIP *For a detailed description of the design and creation of a virtual testing lab, see "Chapter 3: Creating the Migration Test Bed" from* The Definitive Guide to Vista Migration *by Ruest and Ruest and published by Realtime Publishers at www.realtime-nexus.com/dgvm.htm.*

There, now you're ready to move on to the creation of your network architecture and the complete design of your solution. This is what the next chapters take you through.

CHAPTER 4

Explore Windows Server 2008 Installation Modes

Windows Server 2008 (WS08) offers several significant improvements in installation methods, compared to Windows 2000, 2003, and especially compared to Windows NT. Four installation methods are available with WS08:

- Manual or interactive installation
- Unattended installation through an answer file
- Disk imaging with the System Preparation Tool
- Remote installation through Windows Deployment Services (WDS)

All of these installation modes are really quite similar. Whereas in previous versions of Windows, each of these modes required different answer files and different preparation modes, WS08 now relies on an image-based setup (IBS) just like Vista does. This means that the installation media uses a .wim, or Windows Imaging, file as the installation source. IBS relies on this file-based system image to provide the input to any server setup. The actual edition that is installed is determined by the product key you enter during the setup process.

NOTE *Microsoft offers installation guidance in two formats. The first is in regards to installation automation. Microsoft Deployment guidance can be found at http://technet.microsoft.com/en-us/library/bb945074.aspx. The second is in regards to entire infrastructure design. Infrastructure Planning and Design can be found at www.microsoft.com/downloads/details.aspx?familyid=ad3921fb-8224-4681-9064-075fdf042b0c&displaylang=en.*

IBS offers the following features over traditional setup approaches:

- Instead of actually performing a setup, IBS captures the installation mode requested by the user—upgrade or clean installation—and then performs the installation by decompressing the INSTALL.WIM file to the hard disk and then applying it with the appropriate parameters.

- The .wim image format uses a single instance store (SIS) to store multiple editions of WS08 on the same DVD. SIS stores only one copy of each shared file for each edition, saving space and allowing Microsoft to include multiple editions on one DVD.
- Because IBS is file-based, it can perform a non-destructive upgrade of a previous version of Windows Server. You do, however, need at least 105 gigabytes (GB) of free space to support the decompression of the .wim file. More would be better.
- Because it is file-based, you can generate a .wim image on one system and then apply it to almost any other system, supporting the concept of a single worldwide image for your server setups. That is because .wim images are no longer dependent on the hardware abstraction layer (HAL) of the reference computer that was used to generate it. The only limitation is processor architecture. For example, a 32-bit image cannot be installed on a 64-bit server and vice versa.
- Because they are file-based, you can also mount and unmount .wim images as folders to add components such as drivers, patches, and other options to them.
- Answer files are in Extensible Markup Language (XML), and one single answer file—UNATTEND.XML—is used for each setup type.

NOTE *This is not quite true, as the same file has to be renamed to AUTOUNATTEND.XML when running an unattended setup by combining the installation media with a Universal Serial Bus (USB) memory stick or floppy disk drive.*

- All the tools used to manipulate file-based images are command-line tools, which makes it possible to string them together and place them into command files, simplifying the automation of the installation process.
- .wim files are language-agnostic, which means that the same image can be reused in any international location. All you need to do is apply the appropriate language pack to the image to customize it for any locale.

Despite the fact that one single answer file is used to set up WS08, you still have the choice of using one of the four installation methods outlined earlier. That's because each method is appropriate for specific situations; some can even be combined for improved effectiveness and efficiency. But, before you select the installation method, you need to determine which method you will use if you are migrating from an existing network. Once again, you need to make architectural decisions before you move on to the installation itself.

TIP *You'll need two different installation processes. The first will be for the servers hosting the Hyper-V role. This setup process should be identical for each server running this role. This will greatly simplify your hardware installations. The second will be for the virtualized service offerings. Once again, this will be simplified, since you will be able to rely on stored copies of the virtual hard drives that make up the virtual servers.*

The Installation Process

Even though four different installation modes are supported, you'll still need to begin with the very first, the interactive installation. That's because you need to discover how the installation actually occurs. You'll find that it is a lot simpler than any previous version of

Windows Server. In fact, if you've installed Windows Vista, you're already familiar with much of the process. The only difference is in the final configuration step. But first, you need to determine what the hardware requirements are for each edition of WS08 and then perform a server-sizing exercise to make sure that your servers will have a long life once they are installed.

Hardware Requirements

As with any other version of Windows, Windows Server 2008 requires a minimum hardware level. The minimum, recommended, and optimal hardware requirements for each version of WS08 are identified in Tables 4-1 and 4-2.

NOTE *Servers with multiple gigabytes of random access memory (RAM) will require more disk space for the paging file, hibernation, and dump files. Also, Server Core installations do not require complex graphics cards.*

Server Sizing for Resource Pools and Virtual Service Offerings

You won't install servers that meet minimum requirements. In fact, if you're planning on putting together an enterprise network, they won't be at Microsoft's recommended levels either. If you're wise, you'll either simply double Microsoft's recommendations and use that

Requirements	Minimum	Recommended	Optimal (Sever Core)	Optimal (Full Install)	Datacenter and Itanium Editions	Web and Standard Editions	Enterprise Edition
CPU Speed	1 GHz (x86) 1.4 GHz (x64)	2 GHz	3 GHz or more	3 GHz or more			
RAM	512 MB	1 GB	1 GB or more	2 GB or more			
Disk Space for Setup	8 GB		40 GB or more	80 GB or more			
Minimum Number of CPUs	1	2	2	2	8	1	1
Maximum Number of CPUs					64	4	8
Additional Drives	DVD-ROM	DVD-ROM	DVD-ROM	DVD-ROM	DVD-ROM	DVD-ROM	DVD-ROM
Video Mode: Minimum	SVGA or higher	SVGA or higher	SVGA or higher	SVGA or higher	SVGA or higher	SVGA or higher	SVGA or higher

TABLE 4-1 Minimum, Recommended, and Optimal Hardware Requirements for WS08

Requirements	32-bit Web and Standard Editions	32-bit Enterprise and Datacenter Editions	64-bit Web and Standard Editions	64-bit Enterprise, Datacenter, and Itanium Editions
Maximum RAM	4 GB	64 GB	32 GB	2 TB

Table 4-2 Maximum RAM Requirements for WS08

as a starting point or perform a formal server-sizing exercise. This exercise will help you determine the hardware and software configurations for each of your servers. It will tell you what size your server should be, where it is needed, and what it should deliver in terms of services.

TIP *The server-sizing exercise differs slightly for physical versus virtual servers. Both are designed to assign resources to the server. Obviously, you would want much more resources for the physical host and also make sure it has room to grow. In addition, keep in mind that version R2 of Windows Server 2008 will run only on 64-bit hardware. The same goes for virtual servers; but in this case, since they are virtual, you can add resources from the resource pool as you discover the need.*

When performing a server-sizing exercise, take the following items into consideration:

- **Identify server bases** Identify where your client groupings are. You will need to position your servers where you have a concentration of client systems or users.
- **Physical or virtual** This decision should be relatively easy. All physical servers should be host servers, and all service offerings should be virtual. When you decide to create a virtual instance of a server, you'll still need to run through the rest of the steps in this exercise, but some of the choices will differ because of the nature of virtual servers.
- **Physical host: number of guest operating systems per server** Identify a maximum number of guest operating systems per host server. To provide a given level of service, you need to ensure that there are never more than a specific number of guests, depending on this server's resources. On average, organizations run between 10 to 20 virtual machines per host.

TIP *Remember that all physical hosts must be 64-bit servers if you want to run Hyper-V on them. If you want to reuse 32-bit servers as hosts, you can do so, but you will need to run either Microsoft Virtual Server or VMware Server on top of a 32-bit version of WS08 to provide virtualization services.*

- **Guest operating system (OS): number of users per server** Identify a maximum number of users per server. To provide a given level of service, you need to ensure that there are never more than a specific number of users, depending on this server's services. On average, organizations set up one server per 250 users, depending, of course, on the server's function. But with the new trend towards consolidation, you might consider boosting this value up to 1,000 users.

- **Maximum acceptable server load** Determine the speed of response you want from a server when providing a given service. For host servers, this load must take into consideration the maximum central processing unit (CPU) usage. Usually, CPU and RAM are the bottlenecks. For guest operating systems, this will take into account the number of users as well. One good way to do this is to monitor CPU and input and output (I/O) performance on the server.
- **Server variance** The location of the server is also important to consider, because it often serves to determine the nature of the server. Most guest operating systems located in headquarters or large regional offices will tend to be single-purpose servers—they will either perform one role or another, but not mixed roles. In smaller regional offices, organizations often tend to use multipurpose servers to reduce the cost of hardware. But with the advent of virtual service offerings, you can now rely on several single-purpose virtual machines since the licensing costs are the same. Single-purpose machines are much simpler to recover and simpler to manage.

TIP *The virtual datacenter will run two host machines (if possible) in regions along with shared storage to provide fault tolerance for the resource pool and run the appropriate number of guest operating systems to meet demand.*

- **Minimum server capacity** Determine the minimum hardware capacity you want for your host servers. Remember that you don't want to change them for some time. The purpose of your network is to deliver high-quality services to your user base. Take this into consideration when you determine the minimum server capacity. Capacity planning should identify items such as number and size of the processors, amount of RAM, and disk size. Each item is influenced by the decisions you've made before: How many users will the server cover? Where will the server be located? Will it be single-purpose or multipurpose?
- **Multiprocessing and multicore** Most will use multiprocessing servers, servers that have more than a single processor, as well as multicore processors, processors that have more than one CPU core. You'll have to take care here, since there is a clear demarcation between operating system requirements. Make sure you keep Table 4-1 in mind as you select the number of cores and processors for your systems. This will have an impact on your server budget. Table 4-3 lists the basic recommendations for a host server.
- **RAM sizing** The rule is simple: The more RAM you have, the better your server will perform. Thus, RAM is not a place you should skimp on. It all depends on the function of any given server, but it is a good rule of thumb to double Microsoft's minimal recommended requirements and start all physical servers at 4 GB of RAM and then go up from there.

  Some server functions are RAM-intensive, such as Terminal Services servers, virtual machine hosts, or application servers. These will require more than the minimum

> **64-bit Servers**
>
> This is an excellent opportunity to move to 64-bit servers. 64-bit servers provide much more processing power than their 32-bit counterparts and will thus have a much longer lifespan. Traditionally, 32-bit processors are limited to 4 GB of address space, reserving 2 GB for kernel processes and allocating 2 GB to applications. You can use special boot switches, such as the /3GB switch to modify the system behavior, but this switch, in particular, will reduce kernel memory to 1 GB, which can prove disastrous when multiple kernel processes are required. Another switch, the /PAE—Physical Address Extension—switch extends memory addressing to 36-bit, allowing application code to swap from the address windowing extensions into the first 4 GB, but once back into the first 4 GB of space, applications are limited again.
>
> 64-bit servers remove all of these convolutions and limitations. 64-bit servers can address up to 32 GB of RAM and up to 16 terabytes (TB) of virtual memory, eliminating memory barriers for the time being. 64-bit systems can also rely on Data Execution Prevention (DEP) to prevent code from entering or being executed from reserved memory locations, ensuring that servers run more securely. Also, you don't need to run 64-bit applications to take advantage of these features, because native 32-bit applications will, for the first time, have access to a full 4 GB of RAM, as the system no longer needs to reserve space for the kernel. The end result: 32-bit applications actually run better and faster on 64-bit operating systems than on x86 operating systems.
>
> For example, all of your host systems will be 64-bit servers. In order to use a 32-bit server as a host, you will need to load WS08 on it and then install virtualization software, such as Microsoft Virtual Server or VMware Server. The Hyper-V role is only available for 64-bit systems, since it can provide so many more resources to virtual machines (VMs).

you set. In addition, RAM size affects the paging file. The best rule of thumb here is to start the paging file at double the size of your RAM and set its maximum size to four times the size of RAM. This rule changes when you're dealing with massive amounts of RAM, such as 16-GB configurations, but at first, it means that you'll need to reserve a minimum and maximum amount of disk space for the paging file.

TIP *When sizing RAM for virtual machines, you can usually cut the requirement in half—but never less than the minimum RAM requirement—because virtualization engines can maximize memory usage for virtual machines. Set your virtual machines to start at half the memory they may need and also set a maximum. Then let the virtualization engine do its magic and allocate resources as needed.*

- **Disk sizing** The size and number of disks you put into each server will depend on a number of factors. How many partitions do you want to make? How much space do you want to reserve for the operating system, programs, and special elements such as the paging file? How much space for data storage? Do you want to use direct-attached storage or remote storage? Whatever you choose, most servers will end up with three, perhaps more, partitions: one for the manufacturer's server utilities, one for the operating system and programs, and one for data. Windows Server 2008 uses only the last two partitions. The operating system partition should also store a paging file. Keep in mind that Windows Server 2008 offers better performance when it reads and writes to multiple disks. So you might want to reproduce the paging file on other disk drives. If that is the case, each drive will need to reserve the same amount of space for this file. System drives should be a minimum of 40 GB and should be more if you plan on having a lot of RAM in your server.

Data partitions should always be separate from system partitions and are often significantly larger. Keep in mind that if you are preparing a file server to store user data, you'll have to offer a valid storage size on a per-user basis. Many organizations don't have a consistent storage policy. They offer low amounts of storage space per user, often amounts that almost no one can live with today, and yet they insist that any data stored on the user's local PC is not protected by the organization. If you plan on storing user data centrally, you'll have to consider allocating at least 200 to 500 MB per user and expect that it may well grow to much more. It all depends on the types of activities your users perform. But worry not—disk space is a lot cheaper today and always getting more so.

For host servers, you should aim to use shared disks. Shared disks will allow you to run the OS as well as data drives. In addition, shared disks will let you implement high-availability strategies to make sure that your virtual service offerings are always available.

- **Hardware protection for host servers** All this data needs some level of protection. Local disk drives should be protected by a redundant array of inexpensive disks (RAID).

  Many people opt for a disk mirroring system (RAID 1) for the system drives and stripe sets, with parity (RAID 5) for data partitions. There are differing opinions, but with today's fast-paced advances in disk technology, it is quite acceptable to opt for a single RAID 5 system and partition it into system and data drives. Don't forget the RAID overhead: 50 percent more disk space is required for RAID 1, and a minimum of 20 percent is required for RAID 5, which jumps to 33 percent if you only have

Additional Disk Partitions

If you plan on using BitLocker drive encryption or the Windows Recovery Environment (WinRE), you'll need to create two primary partitions. On master boot record (MBR) disks, primary partitions are type 0x27, and on globally unique identifier (GUID) partition table (GPT) disks, they are type GUID: {DE94BBA4-06D1-4D40-A16A-BFD50179D6AC}.

For BitLocker, this separate partition is used to store the unencrypted boot partition, while the second stores the encrypted OS. For WinRE, the first partition stores the recovery environment and the second stores the OS. Using two partitions for WinRE lets you recover broken system disks. If you combine BitLocker and WinRE, then you will need to store WinRE on the same partition as the OS because it should be encrypted to protect the system. For both BitLocker and WinRE, the partitions they are stored on need to be set as active. WinRE partitions should also be set as hidden to protect them from accidental deletion.

Also, if you are creating database servers, or any server that will run a client-server database, you should create a special partition to store the log files separately from the data files.

three drives. Rely on your shared storage system to help you select the best possible configuration for the drives.

You should also use a random array of inexpensive network (RAIN) cards. They are similar to a RAID disk system in that they are composed of two network cards using the same resources. When one fails, the other automatically takes over using the same Media Access Control (MAC) address. Make sure the drivers for such cards are compatible with WS08.

- **Storage strategy** The hardware protection system you choose will also depend on your storage strategy. If you're building a multipurpose regional virtual server, you'll probably want to focus on local storage. But the host servers should share drives. Many manufacturers are delivering innovative all-in-one boxes that include two host servers with shared storage, all in a convenient cooling casing for regional networks. For central servers, you should implement shared storage based on your organizational needs. Small to medium organizations will often opt for Network Attached Storage (NAS) devices, whereas larger organizations will need Storage Area Networks (SANs). WS08 will work with several different types of shared storage; just make sure you select something that is on the hardware compatibility list (HCL) Microsoft publishes.
- **Physical location** The physical location, the actual physical space the server will occupy, will help you determine whether you will choose a rack-mounted or tower server configuration. In most cases, regional servers are tower servers and centralized servers are rack-mounted because they are concentrated in a single physical space. If you opt for rack-mounted servers, then consider the blade server. Blade servers offer much more compact footprints, often saving as much as 70 percent of rack space, 50 percent power consumption, 80 percent cabling, and 20 percent heat generation compared to other rack-mounted servers.

  Remember, your physical location should be lockable and offer temperature controls.
- **Backup method** Once again, the physical location of the server will help determine the backup method selected. Regional servers often used tape drives for backup, but this is no longer supported by WS08 by default. Depending on the speed and available bandwidth of your wide area network (WAN) connection, you might just back up all data to a central location. WS08 includes a delta-compression replication engine, which makes it really simple to create centralized backup strategies. This strategy can also be used to create offsite copies of data. You'll quickly learn that WS08's backup strategy is disk-oriented. It also has the ability to do backup snapshots—time-based images of the hard disk drives that are then used to create the backup, allowing the server to continue with other operations. More on this topic will be covered when discussing business continuity strategies.
- **Operating system** Are there any special requirements for the operating system this server will host? For Windows Server 2008, it's easy. Everything—hardware and software—has to be certified. Microsoft has made great advances in stability with its operating systems, but these advances depend on products that follow strict guidelines. In a high-quality network, only certified products are allowed. If you have existing hardware that is not certified, you'll have to weigh the risk of using it on a critical component, such as a server, against the cost of buying replacement parts.

If you're buying new hardware or software, make sure it is certified for WS08. Since your host systems will be running 64-bit processors, you should make sure each component is certified. Then, for guest operating systems, you won't have to worry so much, because they will be addressing virtualized hardware and will use the certified drivers Microsoft provides in WS08.

- **Growth potential** Finally, you don't want to be replacing this system six months after you put it in place, so make sure that it has a lot of capacity for growth. All systems should have the ability to add more processors, more memory, and more disk space. As such, you'll need to consider the server life expectancy—when the server was introduced by the manufacturer, when it will be retired, what its projected growth potential by the manufacturer is, and so on. If you plan carefully, you'll be able to implement servers that will have a rich lifecycle that meet your expectations. In some conditions, this lifecycle can last up to five years or more. Do this for host servers. Guest operating systems can be provided with more resources as they need them, so they are less of a concern.

TIP *In the past, AMD processor-based servers have offered excellent value, since AMD processors use the same footprint for dual- or quad-core processors. This means that you can add life to your servers by simply replacing the processor. If Intel hasn't yet moved to this model, then perhaps AMD-based servers continue to offer a longer lifespan because they do not need "upgrade kits" to replace the processor for a more powerful one.*

This exercise helps you identify the generic size of each server (see Figure 4-1). Special service offerings, such as domain controllers, Microsoft Exchange, or SQL Server, will require different sizing parameters. Microsoft offers sizing tools for most of its server family. All are available on the Microsoft Servers web site at www.microsoft.com/Servers. In addition, Compaq, Dell, HP, and IBM all offer sizing tools for their servers on their respective web sites.

Sizing Recommendations for Resource Pools

The most complicated configuration you will need to set up is for the host systems. You already know that these should be 64-bit systems using shared storage. They should also be blade servers, if possible, because blades can be implemented faster than other server types once the casing has been configured. They should include multiple network interface cards (NICs) so that they will provide sufficient throughput for the multiple virtual machines (VMs) they will run. The OS should be stored on the shared storage, as this will facilitate provisioning. Data—the storage space for the VMs—should also be on shared storage and should form the bulk of the disk space allocated to this server. Another smaller partition should be used to store the snapshots that will be required to back up the virtual machines.

Table 4-3 outlines hardware recommendations for host servers.

TIP *If you intend to run massive numbers of virtual machines on very large hosts, then use WS08 Datacenter edition, as it provides an unlimited number of licenses for Windows VMs. As mentioned in Chapter 3, rely on Windows Server Virtualization Calculators (www.microsoft.com/windowsserver2003/howtobuy/licensing/calculator.mspx) to determine which license best suits your needs.*

Plan Minimum Requirements

- ❑ Identify server bases
  - ❑ Concentration of client systems
  - ❑ Concentration of users
- ❑ Decide if physical or virtual server
  - ❑ Physical for the host servers
  - ❑ Virtual for all service offerings
- ❑ Determine minimum hardware capacity for the host servers
- ❑ Physical host — Identify number of guests per server
  - ❑ Maximum number of guest operating systems per host server
- ❑ Guest OS — Identify number of users per server
- ❑ Determine maximum acceptable server load
- ❑ Determine server variance
  - ❑ Single-purpose
  - ❑ Multipurpose
- ❑ Determine minimum server capacity
  - ❑ Server model
- ❑ Determine the number of:
  - ❑ Processors
  - ❑ Processor cores
- ❑ Determine the RAM sizing
- ❑ Determine the disk sizing
- ❑ Determine hardware protection for host servers
- ❑ Determine storage strategy
- ❑ Determine physical location
- ❑ Determine backup method
- ❑ Identify if there are any special requirements for the OS
- ❑ Determine the growth potential

FIGURE 4-1 The server-sizing exercise

Dual-Boot Considerations

Many organizations have a tendency to create multiple boot partitions on a server. While this is seen as a best practice for many, in reality, it only creates additional installation overhead with little benefit. You may argue that you can use a second bootable partition on a system for recovery purposes, and the concept had some validity: If your drives use only the New Technology File System (NTFS) file format, as they should in any serious network, then you need a second bootable partition in case your system drive crashes.

While this may have been a good practice with previous versions of Windows, it is not necessary with WS08. Instead, organizations should install the Windows Recovery Environment (WinRE). This console is new to Windows Vista and is specifically designed to support the recovery or repair of a system. It is based on the Windows Preinstallation

Component	Recommendation
CPU speed	3 GHz or more
CPU architecture	x64
Minimum number of dual- or quad-core CPUs	2
RAM	16 GB
OS	Windows Server 2008 x64 Enterprise
OS selection	Server Core
OS role	Hyper-V
OS location	Shared Storage
OS configuration	Clustered
Data disk configuration	Two volumes in shared storage; bulk for data and small partition for snapshot backups
Shared storage connection	iSCSI
NICs	Minimum 2, at least 1 Gbit speed
Server type	Blade

TABLE 4-3 Sizing Recommendations for Host Servers

Environment (WinPE) used in the installation of Windows Vista and WS08. It provides several features, two of which are:

- Automatic diagnosis and repair of boot problems with the Startup Repair tool
- A centralized platform for advanced recovery tools

A second bootable partition, on the other hand, will be difficult to manage because it is inactive when it isn't running. This means that to perform any updates or modifications to this partition, you must shut down your production system to reboot within this second partition, update the second partition, and then reboot into your production partition. Quite a convoluted operation, and since most organizations that have implemented this solution do not take the time to do this—servers, after all, are designed to run 24/7—they end up having outdated passwords and unpatched systems in these partitions. It is conceivable that these partitions could eventually damage data if they are not kept up to date while the main system evolves. At the very least, they provide a serious security flaw.

So use WinRE. And if you want to absolutely protect your systems, separate system and data drives. If your system drive does crash despite all of the precautions you take, you can reinstall it without affecting the data partition or losing any data.

TIP *WinRE is applicable to both hardware and virtual installations. After all, a server is a server, whether it is physical or not.*

Rely on Installation Documentation

Documenting installations means covering three specific processes:

- Installation preparation
- Server installation
- Post-installation verification

Each requires a specific type of documentation. This process applies to both physical and virtual installations.

The Installation Preparation Checklist

In any network, you want to ensure that everyone performs the same operations all the time. As such, you need to prepare specific checklists for operators to follow. Figure 4-2 outlines the recommended checklist for installation preparation. Note that it is impossible to upgrade from any version of Windows NT or Windows 2000 to WS08. Upgrades are only supported from Windows Server 2003. This checklist takes these considerations into account.

Documenting Server Installations

In addition, you'll need to document every server installation. The best way to do this is to use a standard Server Data Sheet. This sheet should include vital information, such as:

- System name
- System role

Upgrade

- ❑ Select appropriate Windows OS
  - ❑ 2 CPUs — Standard edition
  - ❑ 3 or more CPUs — Enterprise or Datacenter edition
- ❑ Check upgrade compatibility
- ❑ Apply all system updates
- ❑ Read release notes
- ❑ Review server hardware manufacturer's recommendations for upgrade
- ❑ Perform server sizing exercise
- ❑ Review the order of the server upgrades:
  - ❑ *Domain Controller first:*
    - ❑ Provides all the new features of ADDS
    - ❑ Requires a schema upgrade on the Schema Master
      - ✓ adprep/forestprep
      - ✓ adprep/rodcprep
    - ❑ On the Infrastructure Master(s)
      - ✓ adprep/domainprep/gpprep
  - ❑ *Member servers first:*
    - ❑ Provides new server roles
    - ❑ Does not provide new features of ADDS
- ❑ Ensure all partitions use NTFS
- ❑ Disable anti-virus
- ❑ Check the system log for errors
- ❑ Install the operating system
- ❑ Perform post-installation review

New Installation

- ❑ Select appropriate Windows OS
  - ❑ 32-bit — Standard or Enterprise edition
  - ❑ 64-bit — Standard/Enterprise/Datacenter edition
  - ❑ Hosts — 64-bit Server Core only
  - ❑ Server Core or Full Install?
- ❑ Read release notes
- ❑ Review server hardware manufacturer's recommendations for installation
- ❑ Perform server sizing exercise
- ❑ One or multiple OS *(single OS recommended)*
- ❑ Use NTFS for all volumes
- ❑ Decide on partition:
  - ❑ System — Minimum 40 GB
  - ❑ Data — The rest
  - ❑ Logs — Only if required
- ❑ If you already have a OS on a server:
  - ❑ Back up data files
  - ❑ Check the system log for errors
- ❑ Install the operating system
- ❑ Perform post-installation review

FIGURE 4-2 The installation preparation checklist

- System location
- Hardware specifications
- BIOS version
- Firmware version
- Drivers for integrated or connected hardware
- Disk partitions
- Kernel version (including operating system versions, service packs, and hot fixes)
- Disk folder structure
- Installed services
- Any additional comments or information required

The companion web site (www.reso-net.com/livre.asp?p=main&b=WS08) includes a Server Data Sheet. This sheet includes each one of the items described previously. It can be used either on paper or in electronic format. It can also be adapted to database format. Each Server Data Sheet should provide detailed and up-to-date information on the configuration of each server, host or guest, in your network.

TIP *Host servers will run either the Enterprise or the Datacenter edition of WS08. In addition, they will run Server Core installations only to minimize the overhead taken up by the OS. But guest servers will run any one of the most common WS08 editions—Web, Standard, Enterprise—but will most likely not run the Datacenter edition, as this edition is costly and is designed for actual hardware and not for virtualized instances. Guest operating systems will also run a selection of Server Core or the full installation, depending on their location and their role in the network.*

Physical to Virtual Transformations

As you move to the dynamic datacenter, you'll realize that you won't be running upgrades on the host servers. Each host server will most likely be a new installation. Then, the service offerings that will now be virtualized can undergo either upgrades or new installations. We would argue for new installations at all times, but that is obviously your choice. Remember that before you can perform an upgrade on an existing system, you will need to convert it from a physical to a virtual (P2V) installation. Both Microsoft and VMware offer P2V tools, among others. Microsoft's best P2V tool is found in System Center Virtual Machine Manager (VMM). Information on VMM can be found at www.microsoft.com/systemcenter/scvmm/default.mspx. VMware offers VMware Converter, a graphical tool that converts physical machines to virtual versions and also converts machines between virtual formats. Converter is free and can be found at www.vmware.com/products/converter/. Of course, if you own VMware's Virtual Infrastructure, you will already have the Enterprise version of Converter, which allows you to capture running machines and virtualize them. There are also third-party P2V tools, such as those offered by PlateSpin (www.platespin.com), that offer much more functionality.

The Post-Installation Checklist for Resource Pools and Virtual Service Offerings

Finally, when the installation is performed, you'll want to perform a post-installation customization and verification. Two checklists are required because of the nature of the dynamic datacenter. The first deals with host server installations (see Figure 4-3). This checklist can also be used for any Server Core installation you perform. The second is more traditional in approach and deals with service offerings (see Figure 4-4). Both list the activities you should include at this stage. Use these post-installation checklists to customize your systems and to perform a quality assurance verification of all systems. The activities outlined in these checklists are detailed further in this chapter.

Run Through the Installation

Now that you've reviewed installation prerequisites and put some thought into how systems should be selected and constructed, you're ready for the massive installation preparation process. Whether you install one server or several, you should at least learn how automated installations work to make sure that your server setups are always the same, with the same core components and the same basic configuration. They will be easier to support this way. You can also use the automated installation method you choose to recover failed machines, so it does become quite useful.

First, you need to understand how the basic interactive installation works. With Windows Vista, Microsoft simplified the installation process to ensure that there were no more blockers for the installations to complete. In previous versions of Windows, there were several instances

Resource Pool and/or Server Core

Post-Installation Checklist

- ❑ **Initial Configuration Tasks**
  - ❑ Set time zone (if required)
  - ❑ Configure networking
  - ❑ Provide computer name and domain
  - ❑ Enable updates
  - ❑ Download and install updates
  - ❑ Enable Remote Desktop
  - ❑ Configure Firewall
  - ❑ Add features
    - ❑ BitLocker Drive Encryption (optional)
    - ❑ SNMP services (optional)
- ❑ **Additional Tasks**
  - ❑ Activate the server
  - ❑ Rename administrator account
  - ❑ Create a Backup administrator account
  - ❑ Set OS time to 10 seconds
  - ❑ Set recovery options to 10 seconds
  - ❑ Configure page file and recovery settings
  - ❑ Install WinRE (optional)

FIGURE 4-3 The resource pool post-installation checklist

Virtual Service Offerings and/or Full Installation

Post-Installation Checklist Part 1

- ❑ **Initial Configuration Tasks Wizard**
  - ❑ Configure networking
  - ❑ Provide computer name and domain
  - ❑ Enable updates
  - ❑ Download and install updates
  - ❑ Add features
    - ❑ XPS Viewer
    - ❑ BitLocker Drive Encryption (optional)
    - ❑ Desktop experience
    - ❑ SNMP services (optional)
    - ❑ Windows Server Backup
  - ❑ Enable remote desktop
  - ❑ Configure Windows Firewall
  - ❑ Close and check: Do not show at logon
- ❑ **Additional Task**
  - ❑ Set administrator account name
- ❑ **Server Manager**
  - ❑ Diagnostics | Event Viewer | Windows Logs
    - ❑ To review/set the size for all logs
  - ❑ Diagnostics | Device Manager
    - ❑ To view/repair device configurations
  - ❑ Configuration | Services:
    - ❑ To enable the Theme service

Post-Installation Checklist Part 2

- ❑ **Desktop**
  - ❑ Personalize the desktop
- ❑ **Quick Launch Area**
  - ❑ Create shortcuts and double-size the taskbar
- ❑ **Server Manager**
  - ❑ Configuration | Local Users and Groups
    - ❑ Create a Backup administrator account
- ❑ **Control Panel**
  - ❑ System and Maintenance | System | Advanced Settings
    - ❑ Set OS time to 10 seconds
    - ❑ Set recovery options to 10 seconds
    - ❑ Refer to server sizing exercise to configure paging file
- ❑ **Microsoft website**
  - ❑ Install Administration pack and WinRE
- ❑ **Control Panel**
  - ❑ System and Maintenance | System | Advanced | Performance | User Profiles settings
    - ❑ Update default user settings

FIGURE 4-4 The virtual service offering post-installation checklist

during the installation where you had to provide input: CD keys, time zone, keyboard layout, regional settings, administrative password, and more. Now, Microsoft has modified the installation to collect all information at the very beginning of the process and then have you finalize the configuration once setup is complete. This means that you can start multiple interactive installations and do something else while they run, returning to them once they have completed. Since machines are set up in a locked-down state, you don't even need to worry about the setups being vulnerable when you're not there.

This is a good place for a standard operating procedure (SOP), since it is always the same, no matter which version of Windows you want to install. This SOP is documented in SOP 4-01 and is basically outlined as follows:

- Begin by choosing the Windows Server version to install
- Perform the initial installation to discover the process
- Document all configuration requirements (specifically)
- Choose the massive installation method
- Automate the installation
- Deploy the new OS

As mentioned earlier, Windows Server 2008 offers four installation methods:

- Interactive
- Unattended with an answer file

- System imaging with the System Preparation tool
- Remote OS installation through Windows Deployment Services

Only the last three apply for massive deployments.

Each of these has its benefits and disadvantages. None of these methods is really new to WS08, but what is new is the way they work. Since there is only one answer file, you generate it once and can then reuse it for any installation method. The method you choose then becomes based on what you want to use and how you want to deploy your servers. But everything begins with the initial installation and discovery of the installation process (see Figure 4-5). In addition, the installation methods for WS08 support three installation scenarios:

- **Upgrade**, which aims to replace the existing operating system without damaging data or installed applications

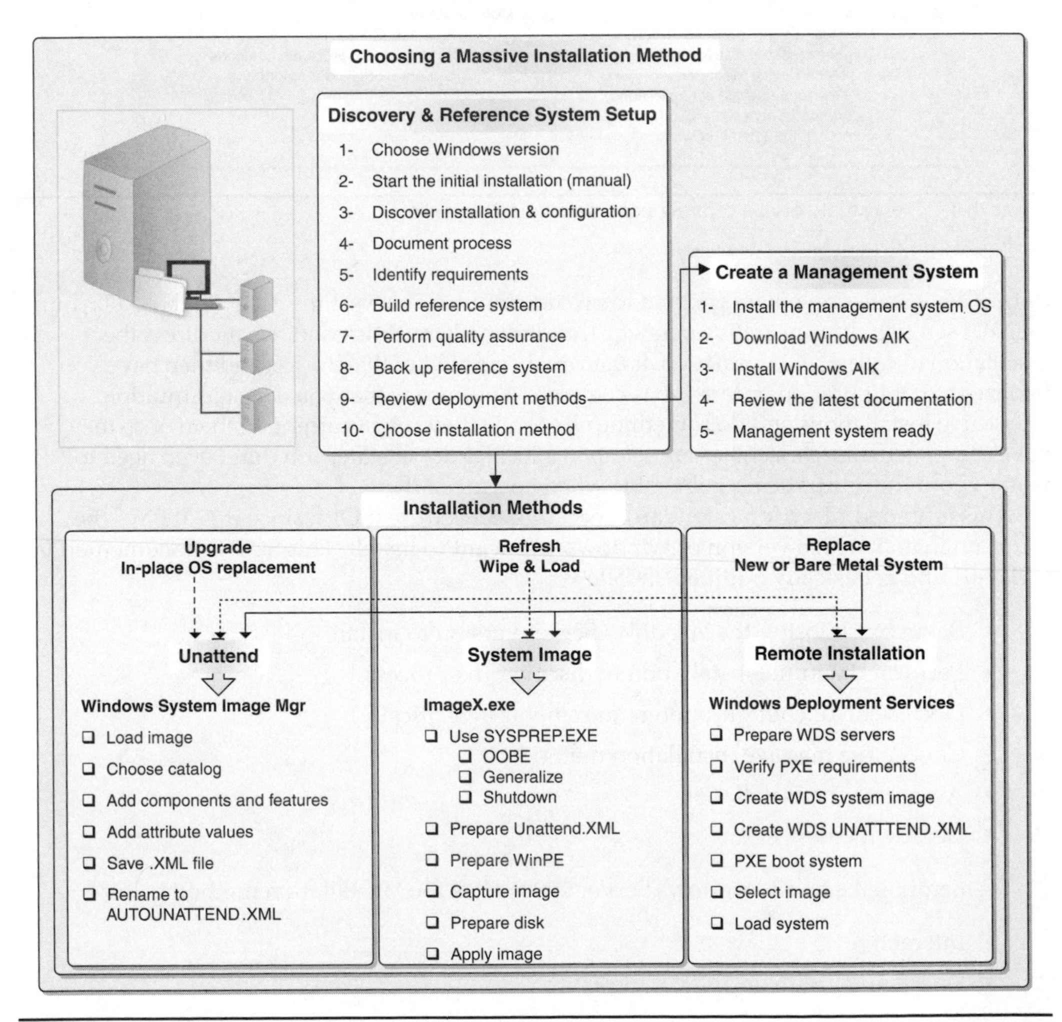

FIGURE 4-5 The massive installation method selection process

- **Refresh**, which is a wipe-and-load approach where the system disk is wiped out, reformatted, and a new operating system is installed
- **Replace**, where a brand-new or bare-metal system with no existing operating system is prepared and a new OS is installed

As you can see in Figure 4-5, each scenario is covered by a specific massive installation method.

These scenarios are for use with physical machine installations. In the dynamic datacenter, these scenarios will apply mostly to the host server installation and perhaps to those few service offerings that you can't virtualize for some reason. When you are running service offerings as guest operating systems, you will be able to take advantage of a different installation process because you do not need to capture images to run the installation. Instead, you can rely on copies of the files that make up the virtual hard disk drives for the machines and use them as you would normally use a disk image (see Figure 4-6). Of course, if you decide to proceed with the upgrade of your systems, you will also be able to run a basic unattended installation within the virtual machine.

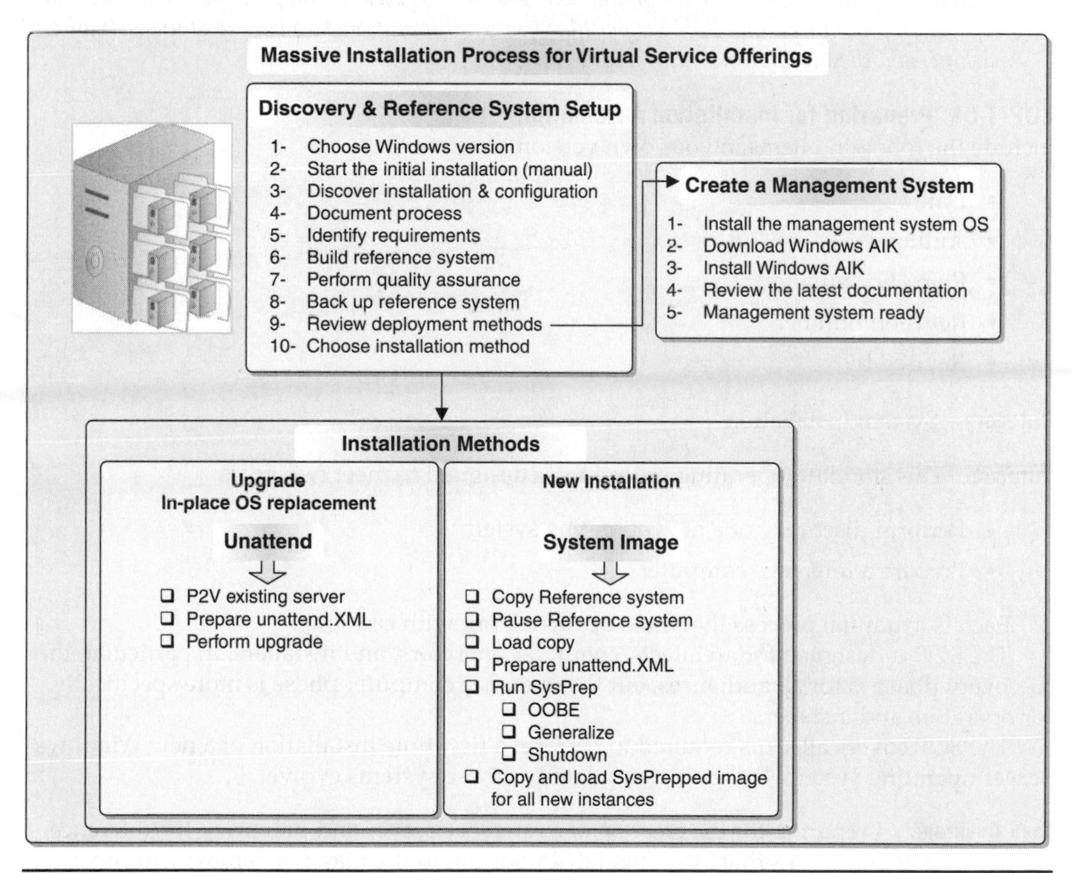

FIGURE 4-6 The massive installation process for virtual service offerings

Virtualize Service Offerings

There should be few reasons why you cannot virtualize a service offering. For example, you may decide to continue running some service offerings on older 32-bit hardware just because you're not ready to move off of those systems. But consider the advantages of running virtual machines. Because they are virtual, they can be loaded on any hardware system. In addition, they are easy to deploy and protect—just copy the disk files to another location.

Another reason for maintaining physical service offerings may be to use older 32-bit hardware in regions. Once again, you should run these as virtual instances as much as possible. If you do find that you need to maintain older hardware and run it in your datacenter, why not make them host systems anyway? It's true that the Hyper-V does not run on 32-bit platforms, but you can still rely on tools such as Microsoft Virtual Server or even System Center Virtual Machine Manager. Both will run on 32-bit systems, giving them more life as physical hosts instead of actually delivering service offerings to users. This way, all your physical machines—32 and 64-bit—are hosts and all your service offerings are virtualized.

Tip *Virtual machines are not only for production. You can use them in support of all your test and preparation procedures. Just P2V the machine you want to test, make a backup of the virtualized machine, and then test to your heart's content.*

SOP 4-01: Preparing for Installation Automation

Include the following items in your own version of this SOP:

- Date
- Author
- Reference number
- Revision number
- Revised by

Category System Installation

Purpose This standard operating procedure is designed to meet two goals:

- Perform discovery of a new operating system
- Prepare a reference computer

Each is a manual process that must be carried out with caution.

The SOP is designed for architects, computer operators, and installers. In particular, the discovery phase is for all audiences, but the reference computer phase is more specifically for operators and installers.

The SOP covers all steps required to perform a first-time installation of a new Windows Server operating system. It should be updated as these systems evolve.

Task Coverage Preparing for the creation of a reference server and preparing the reference server itself are two tasks that are extremely important in the massive deployment process because they are the starting point of the entire deployment. These steps should be performed with care and discipline if you do not want to discover problematic situations later on in your network. Use the 80/20 Rule for computer and server preparation.

Tools Required

Equipment	• Windows Server 2008 installation media • Server hardware • Testing lab
Reference materials	• Microsoft web site • Hardware manufacturer's web site • WS08 Help and Support
Training requirements	• Advanced installation for Windows NT, 2000, and/or 2003
General materials	• Online Help
Tools	• Installation preparation checklist • Server Data Sheet • Post-installation checklist • Windows Automated Installation Kit (WAIK)

Terms and Concepts Two key terms are used here:

- **Discovery process** The process of examining a new operating system installation to discover new features, new ways of doing things, default components and settings, and especially, modifications and customization settings.
- **Reference server preparation** The preparation of the source server that will serve as the image for all servers deployed within the organization.

Warnings! Make sure that you carefully document each step of the process. Reference servers are duplicated throughout the network. Any errors at this stage will require starting over the entire process. *You do not want to deploy an improperly prepared reference server.*

Figures Use this flowchart to step through the process (see Figure 4-7).

Steps to Perform

1. Use the installation preparation checklist to review the requirements for this installation.
2. Select the Windows version to install.
3. Fill out the Server Data Sheet during installation and during installation discovery. Modify the Server Data Sheet as required.
4. Use the post-installation checklist to perform discovery of the new operating system configuration process.
5. Document all configuration and customization requirements. Update the kernel data sheet as you proceed.

   For reference server preparation only:

6. Install the Windows Automated Installation Kit (Windows AIK). Obtain the latest version of this tool from the Microsoft web site.

1- Review installation preparation checklist
2- Select the Windows version
3- Fill out the server data sheet
4- Use the post-installation checklist
5- Document configuration and customization requirements

For Reference Server Only:

6- Install Windows AIK on management system
7- Back up the reference server
8- Prepare the answer file
9- Create a .wim image (if required)
10- Test the deployment method

Figure 4-7 The SOP flowchart

7. Create a backup of your reference server by using Windows Backup. This step can be repeated whenever you make a modification to the reference server. This backup image is used to reset the reference server in case of errors or misconfigurations.
8. Prepare an answer file. Use Computer System Image Manager (SIM) to generate the answer file based on the configuration settings you want to reproduce.
9. If you have selected either system imaging or Windows deployment as your deployment method, use ImageX to create a Windows Imaging Format (.wim) image of the server and store this image in a central repository.
10. Test and retest the automated installation you are preparing to deploy. Use quality assurance to ensure that everything is exactly as you expect on the deployed servers. If any problems occur, return to step 2.

The Initial Installation

Tip *Virtual machines are ideal for the installation discovery process, since it is easy to run through installations over and over again without having to erase a complete system.*

The discovery process is very important because this is where you'll find out what makes the Windows Server 2008 installation tick. Unlike previous versions, the WS08 installation is completely graphical. That is because it boots into the Windows Preinstallation Environment (Windows PE) if there is no operating system on the server; if there is, and the upgrade is supported, it will run in graphical mode anyway. The first splash screen will ask three questions:

- Language to install
- Time and currency format
- Keyboard or input method

These settings determine in which language the installation will proceed. Like Vista, WS08 uses a language-agnostic core installation that is then converted into whichever language you select during installation.

Next, you are presented with the Install Now screen. Note that this screen also includes two options in the lower-left corner:

- What to know before installing Windows
- Repair your computer

The first provides you with up-to-date information on system requirements and procedures for installing WS08. It is always a good idea to review this information, especially during the installation discovery process. The second is used to recover systems that may be damaged. It first lets you choose an existing system partition. Then, when you click Next, you are presented with a series of choices for system repair, including:

- Windows Complete PC Restore: Restores Windows from a backup image.
- Windows Memory Diagnostic Tool: Verifies the system's memory.
- Command Prompt: Launches a Windows PE session with an open command prompt.

But, since your goal is to discover how the installation works, click Install Now. This takes you to the next screen, where you need to input the product key to use for the installation. Like Vista, WS08 uses a single-instance store on the installation media and the version you install will be determined by the product key you enter. Note that the product key screen also includes an automatic activation check box. More on activation and license management will be discussed later, but if you are only exploring the installation and may repeat it several times, you will probably not want to activate this option. You can also proceed without inputting a product key. You will have 30 days before you need to input a product key and activate the installation. But, for discovery, no key is required because your installation will most likely be volatile at first.

The next screen is where you decide whether you will be installing Server Core or a full installation of WS08. If you want a server without any graphical interface that will support only key server roles, then use the Server Core installation. If not, use the regular version. Remember, Server Core will be used for all host servers. Accept the license agreement, click Next, and you are then moved to the installation type selection screen. Two main options are available:

- **Upgrade** Select this option if there is already a supported operating system on your server.
- **Custom (advanced)** Select this option if you are installing a new server or if the server you are upgrading is not running a supported operating system for upgrade.

NOTE *Just as in Windows Vista, the upgrade process in WS08 actually works! That's because every installation of WS08 uses an image to perform the installation. Remember IBS? Because of IBS, the upgrade removes all previous operating system components, protects all data and application settings as well as all installed applications, and then installs WS08 by decompressing the installation image and customizing it to the hardware you are installing it to. You should investigate this process if you intend to upgrade systems performing the service offering role.*

If you are installing on a bare-metal system or a bare-metal virtual machine, then select the second option. This will take you to a screen where you can select and create the disk partition that will run the OS. This screen also gives you access to partitioning and formatting tools, as well as giving you the ability to load new drivers. Examine each option and then proceed with the installation.

TIP ***BitLocker Partitions:*** *If you intend to run BitLocker and encrypt the system partition for this server, then you need to create two partitions. The first should be at least 2 GB in size, should be formatted as NTFS, and should be marked as active. This will be the boot partition once BitLocker is activated. The second should also be NTFS and should normally use the remaining space on the server's system disk.*

TIP ***WinRE Partitions Without BitLocker:*** *If you intend to install a recovery environment on the server, then you'll need the same kind of partition as you would for a BitLocker system. Remember that if you install both BitLocker and WinRE, then you need to install WinRE into the OS partition to protect the system from tampering through WinRE.*

Once the partition is created or selected, Windows begins the installation process. From this point on, there is nothing left to do until the installation is complete. It will copy the Windows installation files, expand them, install features, install updates, and then complete the installation. During this process, Windows will install and reboot then ask for a password change once the installation is finished.

The installation process also covers five steps; note that the system will restart several times during the installation:

- Copying Windows files
- Expanding files
- Installing features

Installing x64 Operating Systems

If you're installing an x64 version of WS08, you will run through the same process as for x86 versions, with minor differences. For example, the x64 OS will support a non-destructive upgrade from x86 operating systems—that is, replacing the existing OS and maintaining data on the system—but the end result will retain all data as well as application folders, except that applications will be non-functional and will need to be reinstalled because the installation is not an actual upgrade. The best way to perform this type of installation is to actually move the data off the system if there is data to protect, or at least ensure that data is not on the OS partition, then reformat the OS partition and install a fresh version of the x64 OS.

In addition, x64 versions of WS08 require digitally signed drivers and only digitally signed drivers. If your hardware provider does not offer signed drivers for its systems, then you might have to install an x86 version of WS08 on the system until such drivers are available.

- Installing updates
- Completing installation

There is no time-to-finish information display anymore; instead, it displays the percentage of each step. It takes about 40 minutes for an installation, depending on hardware and the options you select.

When the system reboots, it will request a password change at the first logon. The default password is blank. Change the password to something complex because it is for the default administrative account. The password should include at least eight characters and complex characters, such as numbers, uppercase and lowercase letters, as well as special characters. If you have difficulty remembering passwords, you can replace letters with special characters. For example, replace the "a" with "@", replace the "e" with "€", and so on. This makes passwords more difficult to crack. Even so, if a hacker or an attacker has access to the system, they can use password-cracking tools to display the text of the password. If this is an issue, you can use a combination of ALT plus a four- number Unicode key code to enter characters into your password (example, ALT 0149). The advantage of this method is that these characters often display as a blank square or rectangle (▯) when displayed as text by password-cracking software. If you're really concerned about password security, then either use more than 14 characters—password-cracking tools stop at 14—or implement a two-factor authentication system for IT administrators.

NOTE *You also have the opportunity to create a password reset disk at this point.*

Post-Setup Configuration Tasks for Full Installations

Post-setup configuration tasks are similar for full installations and for Server Core. On full installations, WS08 will reboot the system once the installation is complete and, after generating the initial profile, will display a wizard: the Initial Configuration Tasks (ICT) Wizard (see Figure 4-8). This screen includes three categories of post-installation tasks:

- Provide computer information
- Update this server
- Customize this server

Unlike previous versions of Windows, the WS08 setup reserves all of these configuration steps for the post-installation process.

As you can see, the ICT screen covers the first part of the post-installation tasks listed in the post-installation checklists (refer to Figures 4-3 and 4-4 presented earlier in this chapter). This makes it handy to perform these initial tasks. You'll also need to use other tools to finalize your discovery of the preparation process. Be sure to document all configuration modifications you retain. This will be important for when you prepare your reference computer for the massive deployment staging process. This documentation also forms the heart of the kernel for each server. This documentation must also be specific; i.e., it must specifically detail the steps you need to perform to complete the core system's configuration. This process should include all the steps in the appropriate post-installation checklist, but special attention should be paid to the following:

- Set the time zone (if required)
- Configure networking

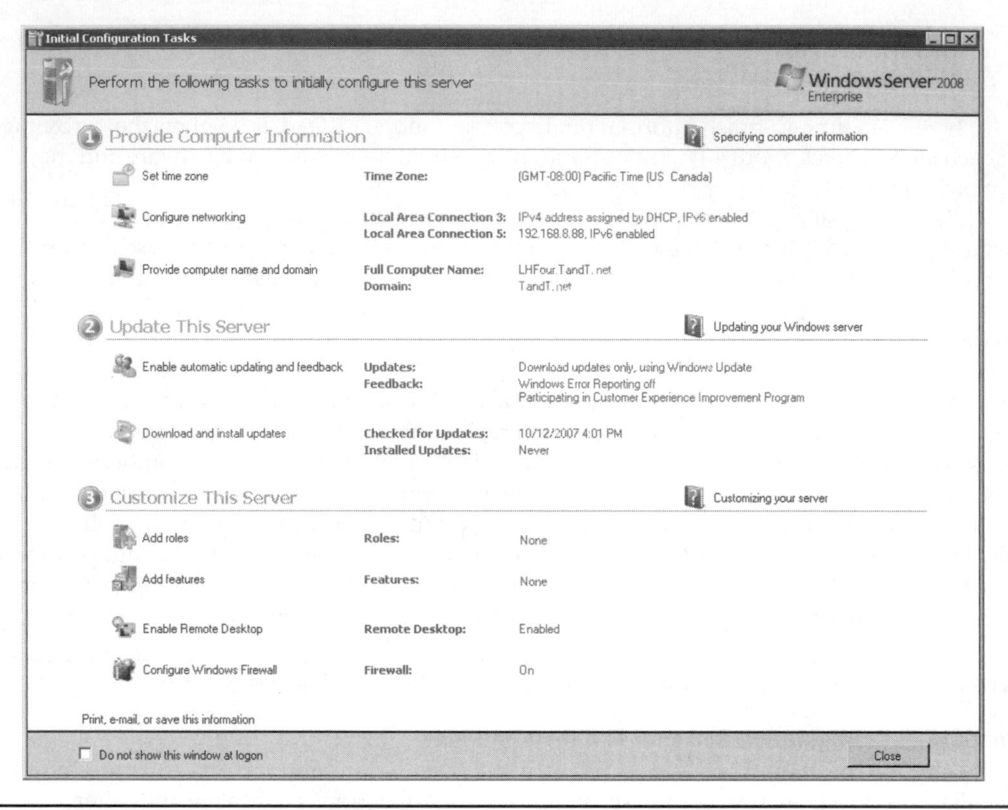

Figure 4-8 The Initial Configuration Tasks Wizard

- Provide the computer name and domain
- Enable updates and feedback
- Download and installing updates
- Add core system features
- Enable the Remote Desktop
- Configure the Windows Firewall
- Configure the Event Log
- Configure devices
- Rename the administrator account
- Create a backup administrator account
- Configure paging file and recovery settings
- Install administration, support and resource kit tools
- Install the Windows Recovery Environment

- And, for service offerings running the full installation:
  - Enable the Themes service and configuring the Windows Vista interface
  - Update default user settings

On full installations, begin with the tasks in the ICT.

Begin by setting the time zone if required and move on to configure networking. Once the Network Connections screen appears, either right-click a connection to select its properties or select the connection you want to modify and click the breadcrumb commands displayed under the menu bar. To modify the settings, choose the Change Settings of This Connection command. By default, WS08 installs and enables two versions of the TCP/IP protocol: IPv4 and IPv6. IPv4 is set to receive an automatic address from a server running the Dynamic Host Configuration Protocol (DHCP). IPv6 is set to a private local link address by default.

The Network Properties dialog box is the same as in Windows Server 2003, so it should be familiar to most administrators. Use your corporate guidelines to assign settings to both IPv4 and IPv6. One configuration parameter that may be different for the IPv4 configuration is the link to a Windows Internet Naming Service (WINS) server, since the Domain Name System (DNS) running in WS08 now supports a GlobalName feature. More on this topic will be covered during the design of the network infrastructure in Chapter 6, but if you can do it at all, you should get rid of WINS servers as much as possible, since they provide outdated services in today's networks. Modify the properties of each connection on the server. Close the Network Connections window when done.

NOTE ***Reference Computer:*** *The networking properties for the reference computer might best be left at default values, unless you have specific values you can use for default settings. Remember that whatever is configured in the reference computer will be retained in the system image you create from it.*

Next, you'll want to provide a computer name for the system. By default, the installation process generates a random computer name. Once again, this dialog box has not changed from previous versions. Click the Change button to rename the computer and join it to a domain. Use an appropriate naming convention for servers and locations in your network. You can choose to restart later, as you still have several options to modify.

You can also activate the Remote Desktop option here, since it is in the same dialog box. If your organization allows remote connections to servers for administrative purposes, then click the Remote tab and select the appropriate setting. The most secure setting uses network-level authentication, but requires connections from systems running the Remote Desktop Connections 6.0 client update. Make sure this update has been deployed in your network before you deploy either Vista or WS08 systems.

NOTE ***Reference Computer:*** *It is a good idea to name the reference computer, but keep it in a workgroup instead of joining it to a domain, since it will be depersonalized to generate a system image. Ideally, you can create a workgroup that uses the down-level or NetBIOS name for your domain so that it appears in the same groupings when viewing available networks. Then, you can join it to the domain during the setup process as you configure the image.*

You should also enable updates according to the settings in your organization. Select Manually Configure Settings in the Enable Windows Updates and Feedback dialog box, because choosing the automatic option will install updates automatically as well as send all feedback to Microsoft. Most organizations prefer different settings. In the Manually Configure Settings dialog box, use the Change Settings button to set Windows Updates to your corporate setting. If you do not use a corporate updates management tool, then set updates to be downloaded but allowing you to choose when to install them. This automatically downloads updates, but lets you choose to apply them during maintenance windows not affecting any users. In addition, choosing to download them automatically will save time when you apply them, since they will already be available on the server. Finally, select the Include Recommended Updates option so that it will also provide updates for device drivers and other optional software. Close the window when done. The other options in this section include error reporting and customer feedback. Modify these according to your organization's recommended settings. Error reporting, in particular, can be fed to a central error-reporting server within your network, allowing you to identify issues with your servers as they occur.

Now that updates are configured, you can download and install any available updates. Click the link in the ICT. This Windows Update screen is displayed. Before you check for updates, make sure you click the Get Updates For More Products link. This takes you to the Microsoft Update web site and installs the utility that will allow you to get updates for drivers and other software. Accept the terms of use and click the Install button. This will automatically get the server to check for updates. Install them if they are available. Close the windows and return to the ICT when done. This is a good time to restart the server.

TIP *If for some reason, you lose the ICT window, simply type 'oobe' in the Start Search box in the Start menu and press Enter to display it once again.*

Once the server is restarted, the next task in the ICT is to add roles. If you are performing a discovery with the intention of creating a reference computer, do not use this setting here. It is also available through Server Manager and should really be used once the baseline server is completely configured. You can, however, use the next option to add features. Here you should add the following to a full installation:

- XPS Viewer under .NET Framework 3.0 to view XML Paper Specification (XPS) documents on any server.
- BitLocker Drive Encryption, but only if this server is destined for a physically unprotected zone, though this feature can be enabled later so long as the system includes at least two NTFS partitions.
- Desktop Experience, since it will be necessary to enable the Windows Vista Theme service later on.
- Simple Network Management Protocol (SNMP) services if your organization enables the Simple Network Management Protocol on servers to monitor their status. Make sure you secure it properly.
- Windows Server Backup to protect both the operating system and data on the server.

All other features should be installed only when the server has been provisioned and needs to be assigned a specific role in the network.

Finally, verify the Windows Firewall settings. In any corporate network, firewall settings will be controlled centrally through Group Policy, so you only need a default level of protection on this server.

Before you close the ICT window, make sure you select the Do Not Show This Window At Logon check box in the lower-left corner, since the configuration options in this window are complete.

Restart the server, since you have several operations pending a restart to complete. Once the server has restarted, log in with the Administrator account. Once the session is open, launch Server Manager. An icon for it is found in the Quick Launch area beside the Start button. You will use it for several discovery steps. When Server Manager opens, you will see several of the options you configured in the ICT screen. First, review the settings for the Event Logs. Expand the Diagnostics section in the left tree pane, then Event Viewer, and then Windows Logs. Logs are used to register information about events on the system. Each log has a given size and is set to a rotation mechanism, usually overwriting older events when the log fills up. Your organization may have a different policy. By default, logs are set to:

- Application: 20 MB with oldest events overwritten
- Security: 20 MB with oldest events overwritten
- Setup: 1 MB with oldest events overwritten
- System: 20 MB with oldest events overwritten
- Forwarded Events: 20 MB with oldest events overwritten

NOTE *You use the oldest events overwritten setting because logs will stop your server when they fill up.*

Right-click the name of each log, and select Properties to set its file size and determine its looping mechanism. Don't forget that they are backed up every day—based on your organization's backup schedule—so you only need the size that will be convenient without having to resort to a backup. Note that you can't change the Forwarded Events log, since it stores events that are forwarded from other machines and none are available.

Next, move to the Device Manager. You can also find it under Diagnostics. Use it to view any potential hardware problems. Review any item that has either an exclamation mark or a stop sign. You might have to install new drivers or update existing ones. This is where the notes you acquired from your hardware manufacturer's web site will come in handy. Continue until there are either no conflicts or no critical conflicts left. A system where all the items are closed is what you're aiming for.

Add the Desktop Experience feature, then once the system has rebooted, move to the services node under Configuration to enable the Themes service. This service is disabled by default because it uses system resources. If you're up to date and are already using Windows Vista on your desktops, you'll want this service activated in order to have the same look and feel on servers and workstations. Otherwise, you'll always be moving from one interface to another. In fact, every server should have this service activated by default.

1. Find the Themes service in the Services list in the middle pane, right-click it, and select Properties. In the drop-down list on the General tab, select Automatic, then click Apply, and click Start. Click OK when done.
2. Next, minimize Server Manager, right-click the desktop, choose Personalize, and then select Theme.
3. Choose the Windows Vista theme, and click OK.

Now that you are using the Vista interface, customize the Quick Launch area. You want to do this to ensure that every administrator in your organization will have the same, or at least a very similar, experience whenever they access a server to perform activities on it. Begin by doubling the size of the taskbar. Do so by moving the mouse pointer to the top of the taskbar beside the Windows Start button until the pointer transforms into an up-down arrow. Drag upwards to expand the taskbar.

The taskbar includes running programs as well as the Quick Launch area. Each area is preceded by a row of four series of dots at the very left of it. Move the pointer on top of this row for the running programs list until it turns into a left-right arrow. Drag the running programs bar to the lower-left of the Start button. Now you should have running programs displayed below the Quick Launch area. Right-click the taskbar and select Lock The Taskbar.

Next, click the Start button, then click All Programs, and run through the default programs as well as the administrative tools to add the ones you will use the most to the Quick Launch area. To add each program shortcut, right-click it and select Add To Quick Launch. For example, you might consider adding the following items:

- Internet Explorer, customized according to your corporate standard
- Under Accessories:
  - Command Prompt
  - Notepad
  - Windows Explorer
- Under Accessories | System Tools:
  - System Information
- Under Administrative Tools:
  - Computer Management
  - Local Security Policy
  - Terminal Services | Remote Desktops
  - System Configuration

The resulting taskbar should include most of the tools anyone will need to use to administer this server or even remote servers. Arrange the tools in the order of most used from left to right (see Figure 4-9). Your interface is set.

FIGURE 4-9 A well-managed server taskbar

Now, rename the administrator account. To do this, return to Server Manager. Expand Server Manager | Configuration | Local Users and Groups and click Users. Right-click Administrator and select Rename. Type in the new name and press Enter. When done, log off and log back on because you need to open a new session with the new account name.

CAUTION *By default, the administrator account is set to have passwords expire based on the account policy of the server. Though it is not good practice, you may want to change this feature. To do so, right-click the account to choose Properties and check Password Never Expires on the General tab, click OK when done.*

Return to Server Manager to create a backup administrator account. This account may or may not be required according to your organization's security policy, but it is required, at least temporarily, to update the default user profile. Expand Configuration, then Local Users and Groups, then right-click Users and select New User. Name the account BUAdmin—or use your organizational standard—give it a full name of Backup Administrator, add a description, give it a strong password, and assign the Password Never Expires right. Click Create and then click Close. Next, right-click BUAdmin and select Properties. Move to the Member Of tab and select Add. Once the dialog box appears, click Advanced, then Find Now. Double-click Administrators and OK. Click OK to close the dialog box. Your account is ready.

Now, open Control Panel, make sure you are using Control Panel Home view, and click System and Maintenance. Select System, and in the left pane, select Advanced System Settings. Several modifications are required here. Begin by setting Startup and Recovery options. Use the following settings in this dialog box:

- Time to display list of operating systems: 10 seconds
- Time to display recovery options when needed: 10 seconds

Click OK to close the dialog box. Next, go to Performance and click the Advanced tab. Click Change to set the paging file. The size of the paging file depends on the amount of RAM on the server; refer to your server-sizing exercise to see how to set your paging file size. Close all dialog boxes when done. Next, use Server Manager to add the Remote Server Administration Tools feature.

Two more activities are required in the exploration of the installation process. The first is the installation of WinRE. You'll remember that WinRE is accessible from the installation media, but when things go wrong, it is more practical to have it installed directly on the server than to have to hunt for the installation media before you can repair a server. As mentioned in the server-sizing exercise, you'll need a second primary and active partition to install and run WinRE. But you also need to rely on the Windows Automated Installation Kit (Windows AIK) to perform this installation. Since the Windows AIK is also required to prepare for massive installation processes, the WinRE installation process is described as part of those processes later in this chapter.

The final operation in the discovery process is to update the default user profile. Whenever a new user logs on to a system for the first time, Windows generates a new profile for them by copying the contents of the default user profile. If you customize your environment and then update the default user profile from your customized environment, you can ensure that each time a new profile is generated it includes a core set of tools and interface enhancements. In an organization that wants to ensure that all of their administrators and technicians rely on standard operating procedures, updating the default user profile is absolutely essential.

WS08 does not allow you to copy an open user profile to another, because many of the open features are volatile and are, therefore, stored in RAM and not persisted until the user logs off. So to update your default user, you must use the backup administrative account created earlier. Use the following procedure:

1. Log off of the administrator account.
2. Log on using your backup administrator account. WS08 creates a new profile based on old settings.
3. Open Windows Explorer and set Folder Options to view hidden files.

4. In Server Manager, click Change System Properties in the Summary screen. This gives you quick access to the dialog box you need for the next operation.
5. Move to the Advanced tab, and click the Settings button under User Profiles. Select the Administrator profile, and click the Copy To button.
6. Use the Browse button to navigate to the Users folder on the C: drive and select Default profile, and then click OK.
7. Click Yes to replace existing files.
8. Close all dialog boxes and log off of the backup administrator account.
9. Log back in using the primary administrator account.
10. Launch Control Panel, select System and Maintenance | System | Advanced System Settings, and click the Settings button under User Profiles.
11. Select the backup administrator's profile and delete it. Confirm the deletion.
12. Close all dialog boxes, go to the Start button, and use the right arrow beside the lock to select Switch Users.
13. Log on using the backup administrator's account. This will test the default user profile. Note that you now have a copy of the Administrator profile. Log off of the BUAdmin account.
14. Return to the administrator profile.

You're done. The discovery process is complete. Now you should repeat the process to create a new reference computer. If you've documented each of these steps, you should be able to repeat this process without flaw. This reference computer will be the model you use for your massive installation method.

NOTE ***Windows Activation:*** *Do not activate the installation as you are performing discovery. You have 30 days to do so, which is ample time to perform the discovery. You can activate the reference computer, however, since it will be a machine you keep on a permanent basis.*

Post-Setup Configuration Tasks for Server Core (Resource Pools)

As mentioned previously, the post-setup configuration tasks for Server Core are similar to those of the full installation, yet because there is no graphical user interface (GUI), you need to perform each action through the command line (see Figure 4-10).

NOTE *You do not have to rely on the Hyper-V role to run your dynamic datacenter. Several manufacturers offer hypervisors, notably VMware, Citrix, Virtual Iron, and more. If you decide to rely on another hypervisor because it is more mature or includes features not found in the Hyper-V, then look to the following instructions as a means for configuring Server Core installations for other purposes than that of a host server. If you do choose the Hyper-V role, you will need to obtain and install the Hyper-V add-on. Search for the add-on at www.microsoft.com/downloads.*

After setup, Server Core will ask you to log on and await input. Click Other User, type in Administrator as the user name and use a blank password. The system will now ask you to change the password. Use a strong password. Once you are logged in, perform the following operations:

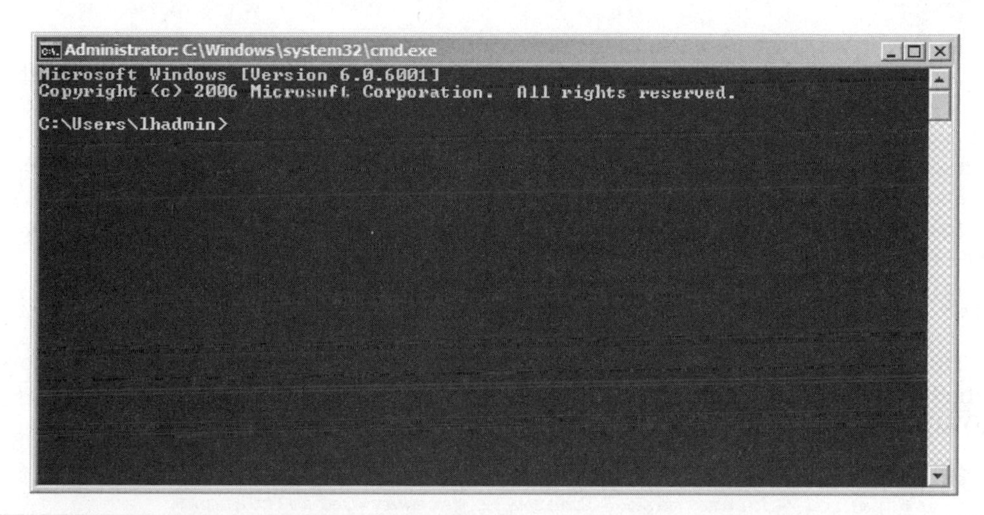

FIGURE 4-10 The Server Core interface or lack thereof

- Rename the administrator account
- Configure networking
- Provide the computer name and domain
- Change the time and date
- Enable updates
- Download and install updates
- Enable the Remote Desktop
- Configure the Windows Firewall
- Activate the server
- Add core system features
- Create a backup administrator account
- Configure the paging file and recovery settings
- Install the Windows Recovery Environment

Each requires the use of a different command-line script. Remember that Windows PowerShell does not work in Server Core because it relies on the .NET Framework and the latter cannot be installed on Server Core because it has GUI dependencies. The commands to perform each activity are listed as follows.

To rename the administrator account, type the following commands:

```
wmic UserAccount where Name="%username%" call Rename Name="NewName"
```

Where *%username%* is the variable that calls your account name, Administrator, and *NewName* is the name you want to assign to the account. If, for some reason, you need to change the password again, use:

```
net user NewName *
```

The star (*) character will cause the net user command to display a prompt for the password. Type the password, press ENTER, retype the password, and press ENTER. Log off and log back on to the computer to begin using the new credentials. The easiest way to do this is to press CTRL-ALT-DELETE and use the Log Off command. Do this even if you only changed the username. You need to reopen a session with the new credentials otherwise your security context will no longer work.

To configure networking, you need to use the netsh command. First, find out which network interfaces exist:

```
netsh interface ipv4 show interfaces
```

This will provide a list of the available interfaces running IPv4. Note the number shown in the IDX column for each interface. You will need it to configure the interface. Next, use the netsh command again to configure the interface.

```
netsh interface ipv4 set address name="ID" source=static
address=staticIPAddress mask=SubnetMask gateway=DefaultGateway
```

Where *ID* is the number discovered in the previous command and *staticIPAddress, SubnetMask*, and *DefaultGateway* are the values you need to assign for each. Then add the DNS server address for the interface:

```
netsh interface ipv4 add dnsserver name=ID address=DNSIPAddress index=1
```

Where *ID* is the number of the interface and *DNSIPAddress* is the IP address of the DNS server you are adding.

NOTE *If you want to add more than one DNS server, reuse the same command, but increment the index number value by one each time. This sets the order of the DNS servers on the interface.*

If you want to configure IPv6 addresses, use the same command. Begin by finding out the interface ID:

```
netsh interface ipv6 show interfaces
```

Make note of the IDs in the IDX column. Then use the following two commands to set the address and the DNS server(s):

```
netsh interface ipv6 set address interface="ID" address=IPv6Address
netsh interface ipv6 set dnsserver name="ID" source=static
address=DNSIPAddress register=both
```

Repeat for each interface you want to configure.

NOTE *By default, every installation of WS08 includes IPV6 with automatic addresses. If you only need local area network connectivity, you do not need to configure the IPv6 protocol.*

Next, set the computer name and the domain the computer should join:

```
netdom renamecomputer %computername% /newname:NewComputerName
```

Reboot the computer to make this change take effect. Use the following command:

```
shutdown /r /t 3
```

You use the /t switch to speed up the process; otherwise, you need to wait a full minute for the shutdown to take effect. Once the system is rebooted, join a domain:

```
netdom join %computername% /domain:DomainName /userD:AdministrativeAccount
/passwordD:Password
```

Where *DomainName* is the name of the domain you want to join, *AdministrativeAccount* is the name of an account with domain administrative privileges, and *Password* is the password for the account. Note the administrative account should be in user principal name format, for example: administrator@tandt.ws. Reboot the computer again once this is done; otherwise, your other commands will not work.

NOTE *Server Core installations for host systems should be part of a domain that is not part of your production service offerings domains for security reasons. But they should be part of a domain to gain centralized account management. More on this will be covered when we discuss security strategies for the dynamic datacenter.*

Now you can change the time and date, as well as time zone:

```
control timedate.cpl
```

This launches the time and date Control Panel applet where you set these values. To see the time and date on the command prompt, type:

```
prompt $p$s$b$s$t$s$b$s$d$g
```

Alternatively, you can use the time and date commands to set time and date in a batch file:

```
time hh:mm:ss
date mm-dd-yy
```

These commands let you automate this process.

Several commands cannot be performed through the command line only. This is why Server Core includes a custom script to help you perform some of the configuration tasks that you need to complete. This script will configure automatic updates and enable the Remote Desktop, among other things. This script is in the System32 folder of your installation. To find out how the script works, type:

```
cd \Windows\System32
cscript scregedit.wsf /?
```

To set both automatic updates and remote administration, type:

```
cscript scregedit.wsf /AU 4
cscript scregedit.wsf /AR 0
```

To view your changes, type:

```
cscript scregedit.wsf /AU /v
cscript scregedit.wsf /AR /v
```

Next configure Windows Firewall to make sure you can get into the system. Use the following command to enable remote administration of the system's firewall:

```
netsh firewall set service remoteadmin enable
```

Now you will be able to remotely manage this system.

To activate this server, type:

```
cscript slmgr.vbs -atp
```

System features are controlled through the operating system configuration commands. To view what is installed and what is available, type:

```
oclist
```

To get information on setting up OS roles and features (see Figure 4-11), type:

```
ocsetup /?
```

For example, to install the Windows Server Backup feature, type:

```
start /w ocsetup WindowsServerBackup
```

Using the /w switch will prevent the command prompt from returning until the command is completed. Otherwise, the only way to know if the command completed successfully is to run the OCLIST command again. Use the same structure for the other features and roles you want to install. For example, host servers should be running the Hyper-V role.

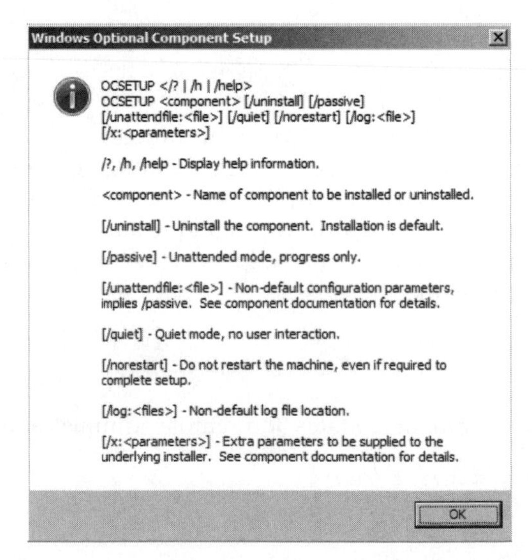

FIGURE 4-11 The OCSetup command options

NOTE *The Hyper-V role is not part of the default build of WS08. It is a role that is released after the final build of WS08 was released. You will need to download the update in order to install and run this role on your Server Core installation. Since the link was not available at press time, you'll have to search for "Hyper-V" in your favorite search engine to locate the download.*

Depending on your organizational security policies, you might want to create a backup administrative account on your Server Core installation to make sure you always have access to it. Use the following command:

```
net user username password /add
net localgroup administrators username /add
```

Where username and password are the values you want to assign to the backup account. The final setting you can make is for the paging file and recovery settings. Use the following commands:

```
wmic pagefileset where name="path/filename" set
InitialSize=initialsize,MaximumSize=maxsize
```

Refer to the server-sizing exercise covered earlier to determine which values you should set. Make sure you create a large enough system drive to hold the page file on host systems, since they will have large amounts of RAM. Note that the default page file is located at C:\PAGEFILE.SYS.

NOTE *To set recovery options with the WMIC command, follow the guidelines in Microsoft Knowledge Base article number 307973 at http://support.microsoft.com/kb/307973.*

One more item may be required. Since you are creating Server Core machines to run virtualized service offerings, you will need to add at least two more disks to the system. As mentioned earlier, these disks should be located in shared storage, as would the system disk be in an ideal scenario. But since you may not be sure of the details of these disks at this time, it might be easiest to set up your Server Core machine so that you can remotely manage disks and other components through the Computer Management console on a computer with a full installation of Windows. To do this, you need to run two more commands:

```
net start VDS
winrm quickconfig
```

The first command starts the virtual disk service (VDS) and lets you manage disks remotely, while the second enables the Windows Remote Shell (WinRS) on the system. This means you can now run commands remotely on this system with the WINRS command.

TIP *More information on installing and configuring Server Core can be found in the "Server Core Installation Option of Windows Server 2008 Step-By-Step Guide" at http://technet2.microsoft.com/windowsserver2008/en/library/47a23a74-e13c-46de-8d30-ad0afb1eaffc1033.mspx?mfr=true.*

The last item on the list is the installation of the WinRE environment. As mentioned earlier, it is covered later in this chapter. Now you can see why you would want to automate this process as much as possible. All of the operations listed here can be placed into a batch file that can be run at installation. In addition, you will want to make as many of these changes as possible on your base or reference installation of Server Core and capture this installation as a system image that can be reproduced on other systems in as simple a way as possible.

NOTE *Server Core installations do not support the Run Once command—a command that allows you to automate post-installation processes. Because of this, you need to use a special means of automating post-installation operations. Fortunately, the Windows Server installation process automatically runs a command file at the end of the installation, the SETUPCOMPLETE.CMD file. If you create a script and name it with this name, then put it in the %WINDIR%\SETUP\SCRIPTS\ folder, it will be executed before the first logon screen appears after the installation is complete. Use this script in combination with a system image to automate the builds of your Server Core hosts.*

NOTE *There are two ways to automate Server Core configurations. First you can create a command script that includes all of the required changes. Second, you can use an UNATTEND.XML file during setup. The latter option is discussed in the following section. For more information on Server Core configuration, see: http://technet2.microsoft.com/windowsserver2008/en/library/47a23a74-e13c-46de-8d30-ad0afb1eaffc1033.mspx?mfr=true.*

Automating Installations

Now that you have discovered the interactive setup and configuration process and know how to prepare reference computers, you're ready to move on to installation automation. For this, you will need a custom set of tools from the Microsoft web site. These tools include:

- The **Windows System Image Manager** (Windows SIM) will be used to build and customize automated installation answer files—files that provide installation and configuration settings as the installation is performed. Answer files are created on a management computer and then transferred to the reference computer before its system image is captured.
- **WinPE**, which is a 32-bit operating system that has only a 72-hour duration at any given time—it can only run for a maximum of 72 hours at a time, though it can be rebooted any number of times—and includes a limited set of services. WinPE is aimed at preinstallation and deployment of Windows Vista and WS08.
- **ImageX**, which is a command-line tool that supports the creation and manipulation of system images for installation and deployment.
- **Sysprep**, or the System Preparation Tool, which is used to depersonalize a system image for replication to multiple computers or servers.

Sysprep is installed with each version of Windows Vista or WS08 and is located in the %SYSTEMROOT%\SYSTEM32\SYSPREP folder. The other tools are contained in the Windows AIK, which can be obtained from the Microsoft download site at www.microsoft.com/downloads. Make sure you obtain the latest version of this kit before you begin to prepare for installation automation.

Preparation and Prerequisites

The tools from the Microsoft web site are not the only items you need to be able to facilitate the automation of a server installation. You'll also need additional components, which include:

- The **reference server** you've prepared. This can be running inside a virtual machine, since you'll only need it to create the automation system image.
- The **WS08 installation media** you want to create images for. Remember that installed versions are controlled by product key, so one installation DVD should be enough.
- You've already downloaded the **Windows AIK**.
- A **management system** where you will be installing the Windows AIK and working to create the system image. This can also be a virtual machine.
- Your **build environment** should also be able to simulate a deployment situation. This means a small network. Perhaps the ideal setup is to have a powerful workstation running with at least 4 GB of RAM and an external or separate hard disk drive with sufficient space to store multiple virtual machines, allocating at least 10 GB per machine. Install a virtualization product (whether from VMware at www.vmware.com or Microsoft at www.microsoft.com) and create virtual machines for each role. The separate disk drive will ensure that your physical machine will not be slowed down by the need to run virtual machines and an actual operating system from the same physical disk. Ideally, this computer will be running Windows Vista or WS08.
- You'll also need access to a **floppy disk drive** or a **Universal Flash Device** (UFD), such as a USB thumb drive.
- Your physical machine will need to include a **DVD writer**, and, of course, you'll need blank DVDs to store the new image you create.

Install the operating system on the host machine and install the virtualization software. If you choose to run WS08, then use the Hyper-V server role. Create your first virtual machine and install a guest operating system on it. This can be either Windows Vista or WS08. It might be best to install Vista, as this should really be a workstation. Ideally, you will add two disk drives to the system: one for the OS and one for data. The data drive will host all of the images you create. This will serve as your management system.

The Windows AIK is a CD/DVD image. If you are working on a physical machine, transform the image into a CD and then load it into the CD drive. If you are working with a virtual machine, simply link the ISO file to the CD/DVD drive of the machine and launch the VM.

NOTE *The Windows AIK is in .img format. If you do not have software that understands CD images in this format, rename the file using the .iso extension.*

When the CD launches, you will be presented with several choices. Select Windows AIK Setup. Once this setup is complete, your management system is ready.

Now you can begin the automation of your WS08 setups. Use the following order:

1. Create an automated response file.
2. Create system images.
3. Deploy the images

Each is covered in detail in the following sections.

Use Unattended Installations

In the case of WS08, the unattended installation using an answer file is best left to the upgrade of a system from Windows Server 2003. In fact, unattended installations are the only way to perform an automated upgrade because both of the other two massive installation methods replace the operating system.

The advantage of the upgrade is that there are no reinstallations required for existing and compatible software. This means that your server should be up and running immediately once you've finished the installation. Unattended installations present a couple of challenges because they do not reproduce an image of what is located on the hard disk of the reference system. This means you may need to script a number of post-installation operations. The best way to determine if this is required is to perform a post-installation validation. Make sure you fully test the configuration before deploying it.

Deployment can be performed through a number of methods. After all, the only thing you need to deploy is a command script running the SETUP.EXE command from the installation media. These upgrades can be delivered through machine scripts that are remotely executed or through a system deployment product, such as Microsoft System Center Configuration Manager. Use your lab to ensure that all installation and deployment methods work in all situations. You don't want to be found with a dead server on Monday morning when 250 users are logging into it.

If you decide to use unattended installations instead of the other methods for new systems, then make sure you buy servers in lots. This way, you can ask your dealer to provide a workable and well-documented UNATTEND.XML file including all the particularities that are specific to their system. This will save you a lot of hard work and make the unattended installation process much more practical. All you'll have to do is customize the provided unattended answer file.

In short, unattended installations are a lot of work. While they may be acceptable for small organizations where fewer servers are required, they do not tend to provide adequate return on investment for medium to large organizations. In these organizations, unattended installations are really only practical for the installation of reference systems. And even though the upgrade process actually works in WS08, many opt to use the refresh scenario instead of performing an upgrade. But you still need to know about the unattended installation process.

TIP *Ideally, you will use virtual machines for your reference systems, especially for the virtualized service offerings. This means you can build the reference system manually—with extreme care, as you don't want to deploy garbage into your network—and then just keep it around. Any other automation step you need to perform on this system can be done on a copy of the system, something that is difficult to do with physical reference systems.*

Create Automated Response Files

Creating answer files in WS08 and Vista is completely different from previous versions of Windows. With Windows NT, you could configure a system and then just capture its settings into an answer file. With Windows 2000, XP, and 2003, you used the Setup Manager to walk through the different options in the file and, when complete, a file was generated for you.

Now, you need to use the Windows System Image Manager to generate the answer file. Windows SIM is part of the Windows AIK and should now be installed on your management system.

In order to work with an answer file, you will need three elements:

- An **answer file**, which is an XML file that automatically provides answers to setup requests during the installation process. This automates the installation process so that it can run in unattended mode.
- A **Windows system image** (.wim), which is a compressed file containing all of the information required to support an installation of Windows Vista or WS08. The .wim image format uses a single-instance store, which allows it to contain multiple images within the same .wim file without the need to duplicate files that are common to each image.
- A **catalog file** (.clg), which is a binary file containing the state of the settings and any particular packages that were included in the system image when it was captured. The .clg file is required to indicate to Windows Setup which installation inside the system image you want to work from.

Use the following instructions to build your answer file:

1. Log on to the management system with an administrative account.
2. Create a new folder on the data drive. Call it D:\System_Images. Share the folder as System_Images with Everyone Change permissions. You will rely on NTFS permissions, so it is all right to give share permissions to Everyone.
3. Link to the WS08 installation media. Either insert the DVD or link the CD/DVD drive of the virtual machine to the proper ISO file.
4. Open the DVD drive and go to the \SOURCES folder. Locate the INSTALL.WIM file and copy it to the D:\System_Images folder.
5. Click Start | All Programs | Microsoft Windows AIK to open Windows System Image Manager.
6. Go to the File menu and click Select Windows Image. Open D:\System_Images\INSTALL.WIM.
7. In the Select An Image dialog box, choose the Server Enterprise image, and click OK. If you get an error message stating that you do not have a valid catalog file, click Yes to create it. The system will create it for you. Each version of Windows needs its own catalog file (.clg).

The image is open, and you are ready to proceed. You'll note that Windows SIM includes five window panes (see Figure 4-12). They include:

- **Distribution Share**, which is in the upper-left area and will include the network share you wish to use as a distribution point for your image.
- **Windows Image**, which is in the lower-left area and includes the actual image you just opened. The image includes the image name and two sub-entries: **Components** and **Packages**.
- **Answer File**, which is in the upper-middle area and will include the details of your answer file.

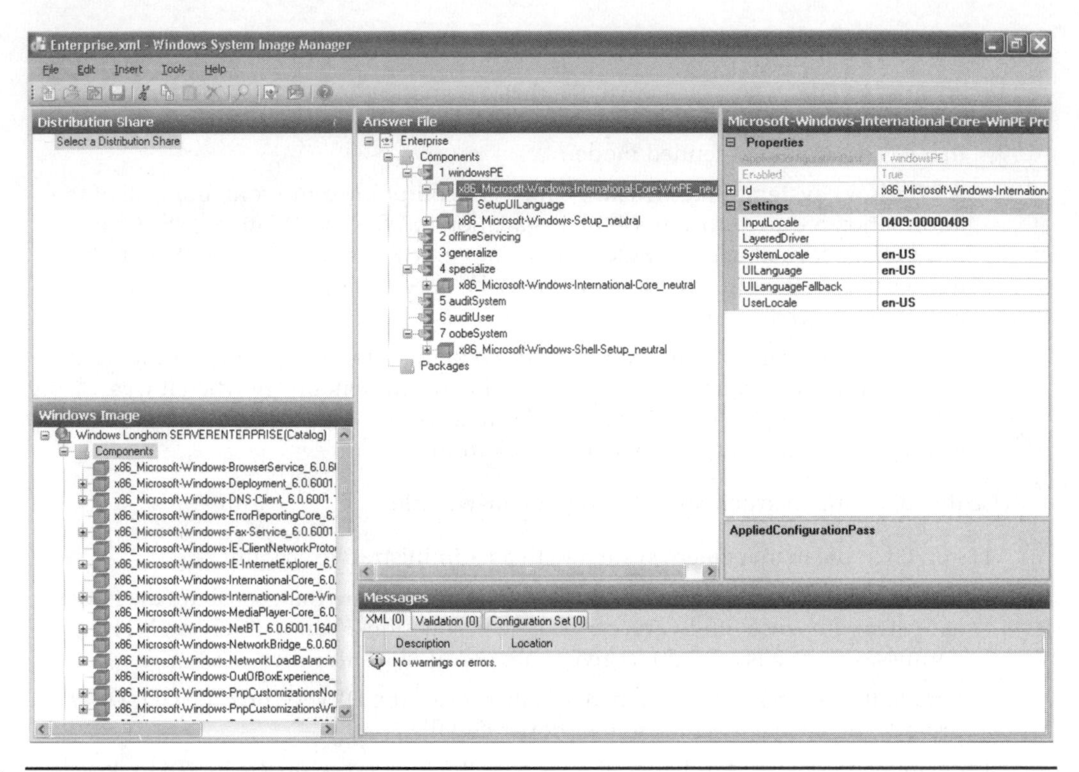

Figure 4-12 The Windows System Image Manager

- **Properties**, which is in the upper-right area and will detail the contents of the objects you select in the answer file.
- **Messages**, which is at the bottom and includes information about the settings you modify.

Now create and modify the answer file.

1. Move to the File menu, and choose New Answer File. This populates the Answer File pane with an untitled file.
2. Move to the File menu again, and choose Save Answer File. Name it appropriately. Since this is a file for the Enterprise edition, call it Enterprise. Click Save.

The Windows Image includes each of the activities that will be performed during setup. In order to automate these steps, you need to insert custom commands to the answer file. You do so by locating the appropriate command in the appropriate pass under the Windows Image pane and then modifying the setting under the answer file. For example, if you wanted to create a new disk partition and format it, then you need to tell Windows PE to perform these tasks before Windows Setup begins.

As you can see, there are hundreds of settings and features you can modify during setup. Ideally, you will keep these to a minimum and capture information from your reference

The Structure of an Answer File

Note that the answer file was automatically listed as a tree form including the Components and Packages items found in the Windows Image pane. The Components section is expanded, but the Packages section is empty. That is because you have not personalized anything yet.

The Components section is divided into the setup passes Windows performs as it installs. They include:

- WindowsPE
- OfflineServicing
- Generalize
- Specialize
- AuditSystem
- AuditUser
- OOBESystem

To automate steps in the setup, you need to add items to the appropriate pass.

computer as much as possible. More information is available in the Windows AIK Help file. Take the time to look it over and ensure that you understand its feature set before you deploy your systems. The best option is trial and error. Test each automated setting as much as possible to make sure you understand exactly what it does before you deploy the image.

The following example walks you through the changes you need to make in an answer file in order to create a basic server setup. This setup will perform the following:

- Create a setup for a 32-bit server
- Create a 40-GB partition for the OS and format it in NTFS
- Install WS08 on the partition
- Automatically provide the product key during installation

Use the following instructions to do so.

1. Go to the Windows Image pane, and expand the Component node.
2. In the Component node, locate the x86_Microsoft-International-Core node. (Note: The node name will be followed by numbers identifying the version of the OS.) Right-click the node name, and select the available Add command for Pass 4. All other components will only offer one Pass command. Select the one presented by default.
3. Repeat for the x86_Microsoft-International-Core-WinPE node.

4. Next, under the x86_Microsoft-Windows-Setup node, add the following items. Once again, expand each of the following items and right-click them to choose the available Add command. Each item will be added to the answer file.
   - DiskConfiguration | Disk | CreatePartitions | CreatePartition
   - DiskConfiguration | Disk | ModifyPartitions | ModifyPartition
   - ImageInstall | OSImage | InstallTo
   - UserData
5. Next, under x86_Microsoft-Windows-Shell-Setup add OOBE.
6. Now move to the Answer File pane, and add the following settings to each listed component. Unlisted components do not need settings, as they will use the default. To do so, click the component name in the Answer File pane, then move to the Properties pane, click the setting, and select the appropriate value from the drop-down arrow or write the value out.
   - Pass 1 — International Core WinPE
     - InputLocale: 0409:00000409
     - LayeredDriver: *none*
     - SystemLocale: en-US
     - UILanguage: en-US
     - UILanguageFallback: *none*
     - UserLocale: en-US
   - Pass 1 — International Core WinPE | SetupUILanguage
     - UILanguage: en-US
     - WillShowUI: OnError
   - Pass 1 — DiskConfiguration
     - WillShowUI: OnError
   - Pass 1 — DiskConfiguration | Disk
     - DiskID: 0
     - WillWipeDisk: True
   - Pass 1 — DiskConfiguration | Disk | CreatePartitions | CreatePartition
     - Order: 1
     - Size: 40000
     - Type: Primary
   - Pass 1 — DiskConfiguration | Disk | ModifyPartitions | ModifyPartition
     - Active: True
     - Extend: False
     - Format: NTFS
     - Label: SystemDisk

    - Letter: C
    - Order: 1
    - PartitionID: 1
- Pass 1 — ImageInstall | OSImage
    - WillShowUI: OnError
- Pass 1 — ImageInstall | OSImage | InstallTo
    - DiskID: 0
    - PartitionID: 1
- Pass 1 — UserData
    - AcceptEULA: True
    - FullName: *your organization's selected name* (e.g., Server Installer)
    - Organization: your organization's name
- Pass 1 — UserData | ProductKey
    - Key: *your product key*
    - WillShowUI: OnError
- Pass 4 — International Core
    - InputLocale: 0409:00000409
    - SystemLocale: en-US
    - UILanguage: en-US
    - UILanguageFallback: *none*
    - UserLocale: en-US

TIP *This installs WS08 in U.S. English using an English setup interface. WS08 supports quite a few languages. If English is not your language of preference, then change the values in the International Core settings. Search for "Supported Language Packs" on the Microsoft web site to locate the appropriate values for each supported language.*

- Pass 7 — OOBE
    - HideEULAPage: True
    - NetworkLocation: Work
    - ProtectYourPC: 3
    - SkipMachineOOBE: blank (the server setup does not have a machine out of box experience)
    - SkipUserOOBE: True

7. Save the answer file when done.
8. Now, validate the answer file to make sure it works. Go to the Tools menu, and select Validate Answer File. If your entries are correct, you should have no warnings or errors. If not, review the settings listed here and compare them to yours. If there are discrepancies, modify your settings. If you cannot modify your settings, delete

the component from the answer file by right-clicking it, and then add it again and reapply the settings.

9. Save the file again.

TIP You first save the file with the name of the edition you are configuring so that you can go back to that particular edition to make specific changes.

10. Now, save a new copy of the file. Name it AUTOUNATTEND.XML. This file will be used to automate your installation. Windows Setup automatically searches removable drives, such as floppy and USB drives, for a file named AUTOUNATTEND.XML during setup. If it locates it, it will use it to apply settings during installation. Close Windows SIM.
11. Complete the process by saving the file to a floppy or USB thumb drive.

Now you're ready to test your setup automation. Insert the installation media into the DVD drive (or attach the appropriate ISO file to a virtual machine), and insert the floppy or USB thumb drive. Boot or reboot the computer. Setup should perform the installation without any input from you.

---

*TIP **Using Floppy Disks:** If you decide to use floppy disks to store the AUTOUNATTEND.XML file, then you should make sure that the boot order for the server lists floppy drives last. Otherwise, the server will try to boot from the floppy and your automated setup will fail. You want to make sure the server boots from the DVD-ROM drive so that setup will launch automatically.*

---

*TIP **Creating More Complex Setups:** Microsoft provides extensive documentation on the Windows SIM. If you want to learn more through example, go to the Microsoft web site and search for "Windows AIK Customization Walkthroughs." These will take you step by step through a series of different customization scenarios for both servers and workstation installations. You can also look up more information in the Windows AIK Help file.*

In addition, if you want to install WinRE on your systems, search for "Build a Windows Recovery Solution" on the Microsoft web site. This provides you with extensive step-by-step instructions on how to create the WinRE image and automatically apply it to your servers during setup.

Use Unattended Setup Files for Upgrades

In the previous example, you used the unattended setup to install WS08 to a new server without an existing operating system. As mentioned previously, unattended files can also be used in support of upgrades. Upgrades are a bit trickier because they retain existing settings and applications. In the case of a server, these applications are, in fact, services that provide functionality to a series of users. Before you choose to perform an upgrade, you need to make sure that the applications or services on the server will continue to work properly once the upgrade is complete. One of the best ways to do this is to simply try it out. As you're working with virtual machines, you can use a physical-to-virtual transfer tool to capture a physical machine installation and transform it into a virtual machine. Then you can test the upgrade on the virtual version of the machine with no impact on the actual server.

TIP *If you choose to upgrade your current virtual service offerings, you will use the previously described process. Just P2V the system, then run the upgrade on the virtual instance. This lets you try it over and over again until you get it right. Make sure you back up the virtual hard drives before you test anything, though.*

When you work with upgrades, you name the answer file UNATTEND.XML and use command switches with the `SETUP.EXE` program to apply the answer file as you perform the upgrade. `SETUP.EXE` supports several different switches (see Figure 4-13). Use the ones that are most appropriate in your command line. Normally, you store the installation media on a server share in your network and apply the upgrade through a scripted command that is executed on the server to be upgraded.

Unattended Installations of Server Core (Resource Pools)

Unattended installations are a good choice for Server Core. Because Server Core does not provide a graphical interface, its installation and configuration lends itself ideally to scripting, as discussed previously. Everything is command-line–driven and anything related to the command line can be captured in a script. In addition, when the Server Core catalog is selected in Windows SIM, the list of components and features that can be added and controlled is reduced, listing only the items that Server Core supports.

Preparing an unattended installation for Server Core uses the same process as those for full installations of WS08. Make sure you fully discover the installation process, perform and document your configurations, and then determine just exactly how you want your base Server Core installation to look. Then, once you're ready, use Windows SIM to prepare the answer file, create a Server Core system image, and test your system deployment.

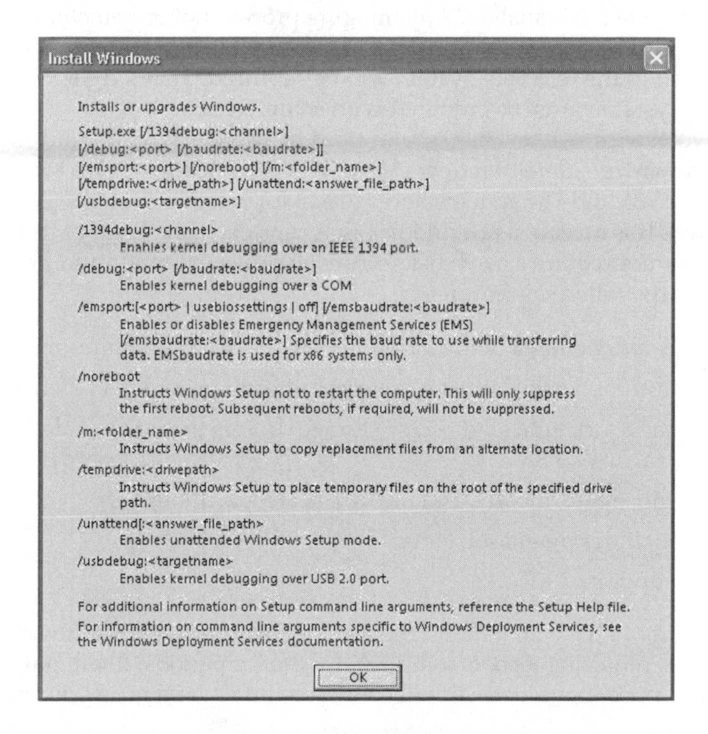

FIGURE 4-13 Switches supported by the SETUP.EXE command

Use Custom System Images

Disk image technologies have been around for ages, but they have mostly been focused on PCs in the past. Since the coming of Windows Server 2003, though, Microsoft has made it possible to support disk imaging of servers. Traditionally, disk-imaging technologies capture sector-based images, basically capturing an image of the disk hosting the operating system sector by sector. In addition, you had to go to a third-party vendor to obtain a tool that would allow you to create a disk image. But with the release of Windows Vista, Microsoft has entered into the system-imaging fray. System imaging, as opposed to disk imaging, is called that because it does not capture an exact copy of the disk; instead, it creates a file-based image that captures only the files that make up the operating system.

File-based images have advantages over disk-based images. For example, before capturing a disk image, you need to defragment the disk in order to make sure you capture a disk that is using an optimized structure. You don't need to worry about that with file-based images, since you're not copying the disk structure. In addition, file-based images can be mounted as if they were disk drives, letting you modify their contents without having to rebuild the reference system. In some conditions, this is more practical than modifying the reference system itself.

TIP *Virtual hard disk drives can also be mounted as disk drives. This means that you can update information in a virtual machine without actually having to open it, just the same way you would do it with a file-based system image. This is what you would do for a virtual service offering as opposed to a physical host. For the physical host, you'll have to work with the system image.*

The major advantage of system images is that they can capture much more than just the operating system installation. Any imaging process not only includes the operating system, but also customization, additional software installations, and much more; everything, in fact, you do to the reference system will be captured. That's right, everything. That's why reference systems must be prepared with so much care.

To work with system images, you need to also work with Windows PE. WinPE is a striped-down version of Windows Vista. It is designed to fit on a single CD. It takes about 120 MB for x86 and x64 systems and 220 MB for Itanium systems (custom 64-bit systems from Intel). It is a version of Windows that runs exclusively off of its own media, meaning that it does not require a hard disk. It runs in protected mode and provides a 32-bit console that offers the following features:

- It is independent of the hardware it runs on and requires minimum RAM.
- It automatically detects network cards and provides TCP/IP connectivity.
- It can work with all massive storage drivers that are enabled for Windows XP, 2003, Vista, or WS08.
- It can create, modify, and destroy NTFS partitions.
- It includes diagnostic tools.
- It supports PXE.

WinPE does have limitations, though. As mentioned earlier, it will only run for a period of 72 hours, requiring reboots if it is run for longer periods. It will only support a maximum of four network connections. It will connect to other servers on your network, but you cannot remotely connect to a computer running Windows PE. And it only supports standard Video Graphics Array (VGA) graphics.

Windows PE is designed to replace DOS. For system deployment, especially server deployment, it is a godsend, because it lets you boot a server with absolutely nothing on it and download a server image to load the operating system. Without Windows PE, using disk images for servers was difficult, if not impossible. Windows PE used to be reserved for special customers—customers who acquired volume-licensing deals with Microsoft—but since the release of Vista, it has been made available to all. As such, it is now included in the Windows AIK.

TIP *Two versions of Windows PE exist: 32-bit and 64-bit versions. You need to use the appropriate version to install either a 32-bit or 64-bit version of WS08.*

Prepare an Unattend.XML File

Now that you understand how to work with answer files and how to automate installations, you're ready for further customization. The unattended installation customizes and automates a default Windows installation. This might not be sufficient for all deployments. In some cases, you will want to add additional components to your installation image, customizing the INSTALL.WIM file by adding applications and drivers that are not included by default. For this, you need to work with two tools:

- **SYSPREP.EXE**, which is located in the %SYSTEMROOT%\SYSTEM32\SYSPREP folder
- **ImageX**, which allows you to generate a custom system image from the reference computer

Make sure you have completed the reference computer build before you begin this process. Also make sure the reference computer is up and running.

TIP *You can use unattended setup to help create the reference computer. During the reference computer preparation, you may find that you have to repeatedly re-create a fresh system to make sure its build is absolutely clean. Unattended setups can greatly help in this process.*

When you are using virtual machines, however, you can either use undoable disks to revert to a pristine version of the installation if you do something wrong, or, better yet, save a pristine copy of the installation and return to it each time you need to restart a process.

But before you can create a system image, you'll want to prepare and include an UNATTEND.XML file on the system. Windows Setup automatically scours the system for such a file, and if it finds it in the right spot, will automatically apply it during installation. Use the process described previously to prepare your UNATTEND.XML file and then, since you will be working with a system image, place it into the %WINDIR%\SYSTEM32\SYSPREP folder. Because it is located in this folder, it will automatically be applied when the system is deployed.

TIP *Remember you can mount both virtual disk drives and Windows system images as disk drives. You can use this feature to update this Unattend.xml file as needed as you rely on this image to deploy new systems.*

Work with Sysprep and the Windows Image Format

Now you're ready to capture the image. Make a complete backup from your reference computer. If you are using a virtual machine, make a copy of it before moving on. These backups are necessary because you will be using the Sysprep command to depersonalize the installation. This means that from that point on, the installation will become a source installation that can be used to generate multiple installations. Saving a backup copy lets you return to the reference system without having to run through the repersonalization of its installation. This is useful when you want to update the reference computer with patches, updates, new drivers, or additional components.

Once your reference server system is protected, use the Sysprep tool to depersonalize the installation.

1. Log in with administrative credentials.
2. Open Windows Explorer and go to %SYSTEMROOT%\SYSTEM32\SYSPREP.
3. Launch SYSPREP.EXE.
4. In the Sysprep dialog box, select the following options (see Figure 4-14):
   - System Cleanup Action: Enter System Out-of-Box Experience (OOBE)
   - Select the Generalize option
   - Shutdown Options: Shutdown
5. Click OK. Sysprep will depersonalize the system and shut it down.

Your reference system is ready for system image capture.

TIP *You can also use the following command-line string to run the Sysprep tool:*

```
C:\Windows\System32\Sysprep.exe /oobe /generalize /shutdown
```

Create a WinPE CD

To create the image from your reference system, you need to be able to boot into a separate partition. For this, you will need to work with WinPE. One of the actions this environment lets you complete is the capture of a system image from an installation into a reference computer. But WinPE does not include the capture software by default, so you need to customize it. To create your system image, you will need to perform the following actions:

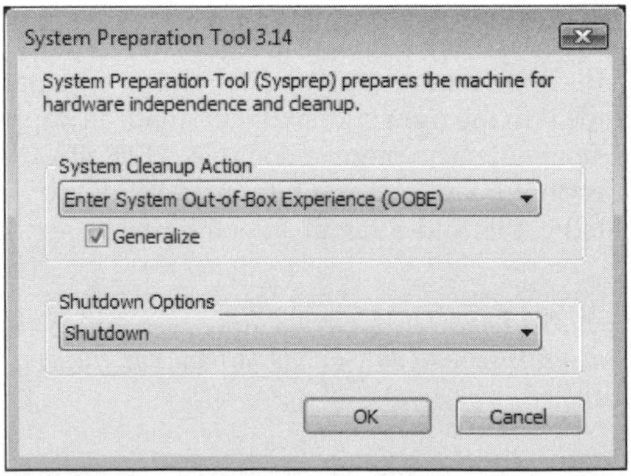

FIGURE 4-14 Using the graphical version of Sysprep

- Create a WinPE CD you can use to boot the system.
- Boot the reference server with WinPE.
- Capture the installation image using ImageX.
- Store the image on a network share.

Once this is complete, you will be able to use ImageX to deploy the image to other machines. For example, this is the process you would use to create an image of your Server Core installation for host servers.

TIP *On a virtual machine, you do not need to create a system image. The files that make up the machine's virtual hard disk drives* already make up *the image you can duplicate.*

Begin by creating the Windows PE bootable CD:

1. Log on with administrative credentials.
2. Go to Start | All Programs | Microsoft Windows AIK, and select Windows PE Tools Command Prompt.
3. In the new Command Prompt window, use the following command to create a Windows PE build folder:

```
Copype.cmd x86 d:\system_images\WinPE_x86
```

4. The structure of the command is *command architecture destination*, where architecture can be x86 for 32-bit systems, amd64 for 64-bit systems, or ia64 for Itanium systems.

NOTE *For Server Core host server installations, you will use the amd64 switch, since it only runs on 64-bit hardware. Change all references in this procedure from x86 to amd64.*

5. Once the command is complete, you need to copy the right version of ImageX into the build folder. In this case, launch Windows Explorer and go to C:\Program Files\Windows AIK\Tools\x86. Right-click `IMAGEX.EXE` and select Copy.
6. Now, go to D:\System_Images\WinPE_X86\ISO and create a new folder called x86.
7. Move to the x86 folder, and paste the ImageX.exe file.
8. Now you need to create a configuration file to run the ImageX tool. The best way to do this is to use Notepad. Launch Notepad and type the following:

```
[ExclusionList]
ntfs.log
hiberfil.sys
pagefile.sys
"System Volume Information"
RECYCLER
Windows\CSC
[CompressionExclusionList]
*.mp3
*.zip
*.cab
\WINDOWS\inf\*.pnf
```

9. Save the file into the new x86 folder and name it WIMSCRIPT.INI. Close Notepad.
10. You're almost done. Now create an ISO image file. To do this, return to the WinPE Command Prompt window and use the following commands:

```
cd..
cd PETools
oscdimg -n -bd:\system_images\winpe_x86\etfsboot.com
d:\system_images\winpe_x86\ISO d:\system_images\winpe_x86\winpe_x86.iso
```

11. Burn the WinPE_x86.ISO file onto a blank, bootable CD. Label the CD appropriately.

You are ready to create your image.

Capture the Image

Make sure the boot order of your reference computer starts with the DVD-ROM drive. This is necessary to ensure that you boot into WinPE instead of into WS08. Once this is done, you are ready to create your image file. Use the following procedure to do so:

1. Insert the WinPE CD and boot the server. The server should boot into Windows PE and automatically open a command prompt window.
2. Map a drive to your network share and provide the appropriate credentials to access this share:

```
net use s: \\servername\sharename /user:domainname\username *
```

   where *servername* is the name of your management system and *sharename* is the name of the share you assigned to the D:\System_Images folder you created earlier. In this case, it should be System_Images. *Domainname* should be the name of the domain or server your management system is in, and *username* is your account name, while the * will prompt you for a password.
3. Type your password to complete the net use command. It should be encrypted and not displayed.
4. Change to the x86 folder in WinPE by typing the following command:

```
D:
cd x86
```

5. By default, WinPE loads into RAM and creates an X: drive. In order to get to your ImageX command, you need to go back to the actual DVD-ROM drive, which in this instance is the D: drive.
6. Now use the ImageX command to create the image and store it on the network share:

```
Imagex.exe /compress fast /capture C: S:\x86_Server.wim "Custom x86
Server Install" /verify
```

7. This command will capture the C: drive, compress the image, name it X86_SERVER.WIM, and name the catalog Custom x86 Server Install, as well as verify the image during capture (see Figure 4-15).

Once the command completes, you are ready to proceed to image deployment. If you've done everything right, you'll be ready to use the image to deploy multiple 32-bit servers. But first, you need to test image deployment and verify that you get the anticipated results.

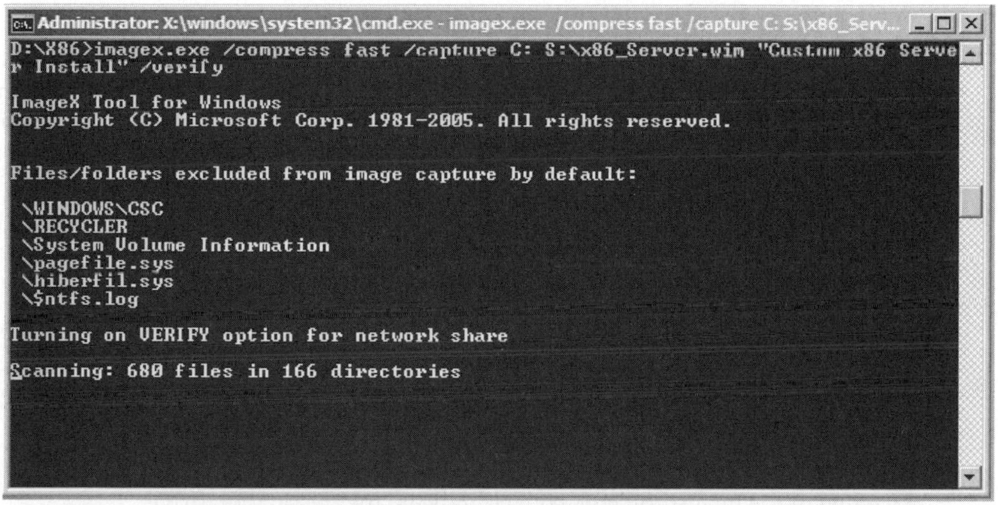

```
Administrator: X:\windows\system32\cmd.exe - imagex.exe /compress fast /capture C: S:\x86_Serv...
D:\X86>imagex.exe /compress fast /capture C: S:\x86_Server.wim "Custom x86 Serve
r Install" /verify

ImageX Tool for Windows
Copyright (C) Microsoft Corp. 1981-2005. All rights reserved.

Files/folders excluded from image capture by default:

 \WINDOWS\CSC
 \RECYCLER
 \System Volume Information
 \pagefile.sys
 \hiberfil.sys
 \$ntfs.log

Turning on VERIFY option for network share

Scanning: 680 files in 166 directories
```

FIGURE 4-15 Using the ImageX Command to Capture a System Image

Test Image Deployment

Use the same process to test the image, but in reverse. Boot a new machine into WinPE, prepare the environment, and then use ImageX to apply the image.

TIP *For virtual service offerings, all you need to do is copy the sysprepped virtual machine's files, rename them, add them to the host configuration, and boot the new machine.*

The process described here is manual and interactive, but it can be automated through scripts.

1. Prepare the system hardware or the virtual machine you intend to use. Make sure the boot order of the machine includes the DVD-ROM.
2. Insert the WinPE CD and boot the machine from that CD.
3. In WinPE, run the following commands to create the destination partition and format it in NTFS. You use the diskpart command to do this:

```
diskpart
select disk 0
clean
create partition primary size=40000 align=64
select partition 1
active
format label=diskname
exit
```

TIP *All of these commands can be stored in a script that will run automatically once WinPE is booted. You need to update the WinPE image to include this script and rebuild the WinPE CD before you can use it.*

4. Map a network drive to your installation share:

```
net use s: \\servername\sharename /user:domainname\username
```

where *servername* is the name of your management system and *sharename* is the name of the share you assigned to the D:\System_Images folder you created earlier. In this case, it should be System_Images. *Domainname* should be the name of the domain or server your management system is in, and *username* is your account name.

5. Type your password to complete the net use command. It should be encrypted and not displayed.
6. Change to the x86 folder in WinPE by typing the following command:

```
D:
cd x86
```

7. Apply the image to the new server:

```
Imagex.exe /apply S:\x86_Server.wim "Custom x86 Server Install" c:
```

8. When you use the apply command, you need to name the source .wim file, indicate the name of the image you created, and indicate the destination drive.
9. When the process is complete, remove the WinPE CD.
10. Reboot the server. It should launch into WS08.
11. Run through the server to test the installation and configuration, making sure it is the same as the reference server you created.

Your deployment process is complete. You now know how to work with the ImageX command to both create and deploy .wim system images.

Windows Deployment Services

The last part of the deployment process is to use a server role to remotely deploy system images. In WS08, this server role is Windows Deployment Services (WDS). WDS works in both WS08 and in Windows Server 2003, replacing a previous role WS03 included called Remote Installation Services (RIS).

Remote installation is the most promising automated installation method for medium to large organizations because it provides the ability to repair a system as well as install it and it combines the system image process with the ability to install it remotely. Windows Server 2008 supports not only the hosting of Windows Deployment Services, but also the installation of servers through WDS, but it requires and depends on PXE network cards—cards that can be used to boot the server when the F12 key is pressed. Conversely, you can change the boot order in the system parameters to start with PXE, but you will have to change it back once the server OS is loaded. If your servers include these cards as they should, then WDS is the tool to use.

NOTE *Remote installation is quite acceptable for small organizations as well, though there are more costs involved than with unattended or system image installations. Consider the benefits when you decide which model to use.*

Both RIS and WDS require a significant infrastructure to run. They need a working Active Directory Domain Services to provide authorization for the service in a domain,

Changes in Sysprep

In previous versions of Windows, the Sysprep tool captured the installed state of the machine and depersonalized the image without changing anything. In WS08 and Windows Vista, Sysprep goes a little beyond the changes it used to do. For example, if you renamed the default administrator account on the reference system and then used Sysprep to capture the image, Sysprep will automatically reset the account name to Administrator. It will, however, keep the password as you applied it. This means that you will need to rename the administrator account again once the image is deployed. You might consider putting together a post-installation script that would do this automatically.

In addition, Sysprep contains a bug. If you used a static IPv4 address on your reference server and then captured the image, Sysprep will keep the original address assigned to the interface, but the address will not appear in the graphical Properties page of the IPv4 settings for the interface. The address will only appear when you use the `ipconfig /all` command in a command prompt (see Figure 4-16). You must remove this address otherwise every system you generate from the Sysprep image will have an IP address conflict. To remove the address, use the following command:

```
netsh interface ipv4 show interfaces
```

This will provide a list of the available interfaces running IPv4. Note the number shown in the IDX column for each interface. Next, use the `netsh` command again to remove the duplicate address:

```
netsh interface ipv4 delete address name="ID" address=duplicateIPAddress
```

Another and easier way to remove this address is to avoid the issue altogether by using the Dynamic Host Configuration Protocol (DHCP) to assign an automatic IP address on the reference server. Since the address is automatic, there will be no duplication when you reuse the Sysprep image.

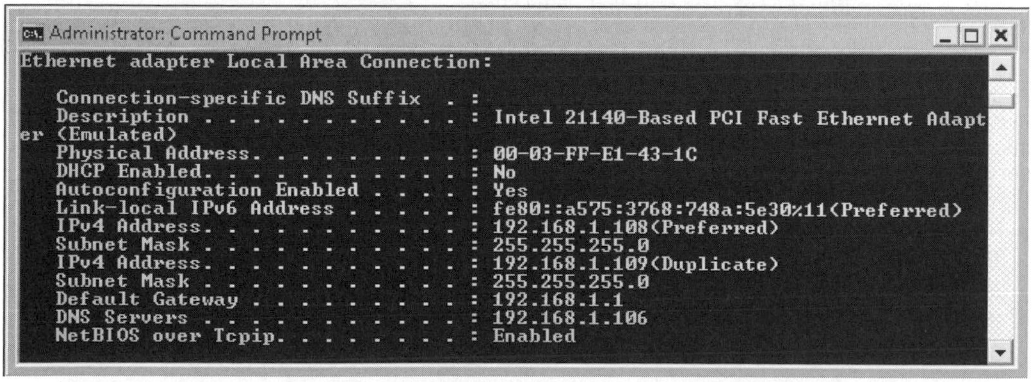

```
Administrator: Command Prompt
Ethernet adapter Local Area Connection:

   Connection-specific DNS Suffix  . :
   Description . . . . . . . . . . . : Intel 21140-Based PCI Fast Ethernet Adapt
er (Emulated)
   Physical Address. . . . . . . . . : 00-03-FF-E1-43-1C
   DHCP Enabled. . . . . . . . . . . : No
   Autoconfiguration Enabled . . . . : Yes
   Link-local IPv6 Address . . . . . : fe80::a575:3768:748a:5e30%11(Preferred)
   IPv4 Address. . . . . . . . . . . : 192.168.1.108(Preferred)
   Subnet Mask . . . . . . . . . . . : 255.255.255.0
   IPv4 Address. . . . . . . . . . . : 192.168.1.109(Duplicate)
   Subnet Mask . . . . . . . . . . . : 255.255.255.0
   Default Gateway . . . . . . . . . : 192.168.1.1
   DNS Servers . . . . . . . . . . . : 192.168.1.106
   NetBIOS over Tcpip. . . . . . . . : Enabled
```

FIGURE 4-16 Duplicate Addresses appear in systems generated by a Sysprep image

PART II

as well as a DHCP server to provide automatic IP addressing during the system installation process. Because these roles are comprehensive and require advanced skills to put in place, their installation and configuration is not covered here. Instead, ADDS is covered in Chapter 5 and DHCP is covered in Chapter 6. Once these two technologies have been described and deployed, you will be ready to make use of WDS. This is covered in Chapter 6. Once these services are in place, you can rely on the WDS process to deploy servers (see Figure 4-17).

The WDS process is made up of four major stages:

- Preparing the WDS server (Chapter 6)
- Preparing the system image on the WDS server
- Preparing the answer file to use (if required)
- Deploying the WDS system image

If you already have a WS03 network in place, you already have the required infrastructure for this service. In this case, look up how to upgrade your RIS servers to WDS on the Microsoft web site at http://technet2.microsoft.com/WindowsVista/en/library/9e197135-6711-4c20-bfad-fc80fc2151301033.mspx?mfr=true.

At that point, you will be able to support remote deployments of WS08 and Vista.

TIP *Microsoft has released guidance that helps you step through the server installation and deployment process. Look for this guidance on the Microsoft Windows Server 2008 web site at www.microsoft.com/windowsserver2008/default.mspx.*

NOTE *If you are moving to the dynamic datacenter and will be running host servers along with virtualized service offerings, you may not need a full-fledged WDS installation, mostly because it will apply only to the host server installations. You should not be mass-producing host servers, since one host should run more than ten virtual service offerings. Since hosts are more rarely required, using a system image without a central deployment system may be more than acceptable for your needs. Deployment of the virtual service offerings will not rely on WDS, so its services will not be necessary at that point.*

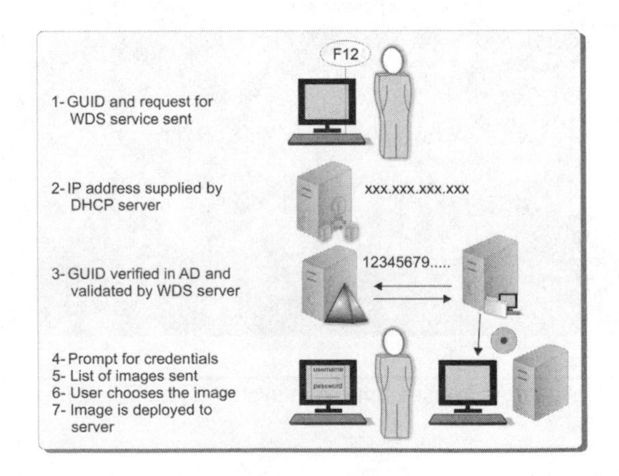

FIGURE 4-17 The remote installation of servers with WDS

Put the Server in Place

Special care and attention will be needed when you put staged servers in place. If you are putting a new server in place, you can take your time because no user is currently using it. But if you are replacing an existing server, you will need to ensure that you have a complete inventory of all network-related services and dependencies on that server before you proceed. Replacing each of these dependencies is at the core of the process for putting a server in place.

In addition, now that you have a server kernel in place, you will need to begin assigning roles and functions to your servers. These assignations and the processes that must be associated with them begin in Chapter 6.

PART

Design Server Roles

This section begins the network design process. It outlines how you go about creating networks running Windows Server 2008 (WS08). As such, it covers the design and implementation of Active Directory Domain Services and basic network connectivity, as well as Windows Deployment Services. Note that it covers these aspects for both the hardware resource pool and the virtualized service offerings.

5

CHAPTER

Prepare Your Identity Management

Active Directory (AD) is the branding name that Microsoft now uses to regroup all of its identity management solutions. As outlined in Chapter 1, the AD brand includes five components:

- **AD Domain Services** (ADDS), which was originally called Active Directory, providing authentication and authorization services in a network.
- **AD Lightweight Directory Services** (ADLDS), which was formerly known as Active Directory Application Mode (ADAM) and is aimed at providing a data store for environments that do not have access to a full ADDS service level.
- **AD Rights Management Services** (ADRMS), which helps control the appropriate use of documents and data your organization generates.
- **AD Certificate Services** (ADCS), which was formerly known as public key infrastructure (PKI) and is used to create and manage certification authorities.
- **AD Federation Services** (ADFS) which is used to provide simplified and secure identity federation as well as single sign-on services for Web applications.

Together, these roles form the identity management infrastructure Microsoft provides to organizations running networks. Each provides a specific identity management service, a service that is targeted to a specific part of the network.

- ADDS is the core of the Windows Server 2008 network. It is the central component that not only serves to provide authentication and authorization, but also administration, information sharing, and information availability. In fact, ADDS can be defined as follows: *"A secure virtual environment where users can interact either with each other or with network components, all according to the business rules of the enterprise."*
- ADLDS, on the other hand, has two main uses:
    - First, it is used to integrate applications to a directory service without having to modify the structure of the ADDS directory. In this case, ADLDS forms an extension of the core directory in your network, an extension that can be structured on a per-application basis. In addition, this extension becomes portable and can be applied to the application wherever it resides.

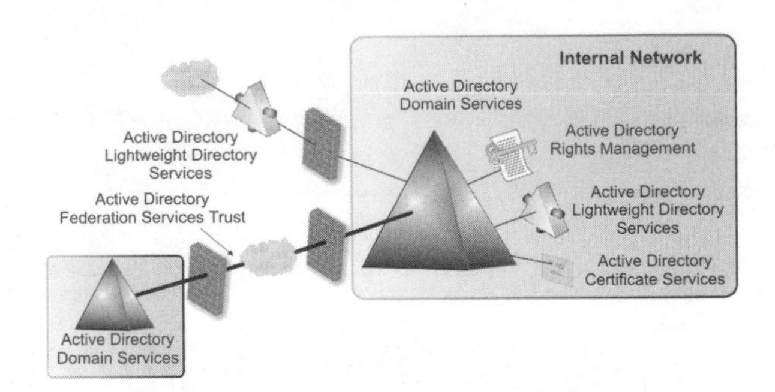

FIGURE 5-1 Each AD technology integrates with the others to form a complete identity management infrastructure.

- Second, ADLDS is used in demilitarized zone (DMZ) scenarios. Few organizations want to implement an ADDS structure in DMZs, and even fewer want to link their internal ADDS to external zones. This is where ADLDS comes in. It can serve as the source directory for applicative permissions without endangering any data that can be found in the internal ADDS structure.

- ADRMS is used internally to protect your intellectual property. It becomes an extension of the ADDS and forms the core of your data protection system.
- ADCS is also used mostly internally, as it is designed to provide PKI services to both users and computers. It can be used to digitally sign software and system drivers, integrate with smart card authentication, and generally provide nonrepudiation services to your internal community. It can also be used to provide these services to external communities, but in order to do so, it should be linked with an external, renowned certification authority that will prove to others you are who you say.

NOTE *For more information on PKI infrastructures and how to apply them in your organization, visit www.reso-net.com/articles.asp?m=8 and look for the "Advanced Public Key Infrastructures" section.*

- ADFS is aimed at extending your internal ADDS structure to the external world through common Transmission Control Protocol/Internet Protocol (TCP/IP) ports, such as 80 (Hypertext Transfer Protocol—HTTP) and 443 (Secure HTTP or HTTPS). Therefore, it normally resides in the DMZ and is used to create partnerships with other organizations.

As you can see, each AD technology plays an important role in providing a fully integrated identity management infrastructure in your organization (see Figure 5-1). But, as you can also see, nothing can begin until you have implemented your internal ADDS infrastructure. This is the focus of this chapter.

NOTE *For more information on the five Active Directory technologies, look up* MCTS Self-Paced Training Kit (Exam 70-640): Configuring Windows Server 2008 Active Directory, *by Holme, Ruest and Ruest* (Microsoft Press, 2008).

Introduce Active Directory Domain Services

Many organizations have already implemented the Active Directory Domain Services service offering. For them, this chapter is focused on reviewing the structure and design of their directory to make the most of the passage to WS08. For others, which may either have not implemented ADDS or who are creating new networks based on ADDS, this chapter is focused on a step-by-step process for the design of their directory structures.

NOTE *This chapter outlines how you should configure ADDS for your service offering—the service that will authenticate all of your end users. For the resource pool, you will also be using ADDS, but in a much simpler mode, since it is an authentication service that will only be used by administrators and system operators. This simpler ADDS structure will be described and implemented in Chapter 6. If you are not familiar with ADDS, take the time to review this chapter thoroughly, as it is the central core of any WS08 network.*

The first rule you must set for yourself when working to design or review your design of your Active Directory structure is "Use best practices everywhere!" Don't try to change the way ADDS is designed to work, no matter what you might think. It provides a wealth of opportunities that you will discover as you implement, use, and operate them. Changes that might make sense according to IT concepts today may well have a negative impact on the operation of your directory structure tomorrow.

Thus, the first step towards the implementation of your network—you could say the most significant step towards this implementation—is the design and implementation of your ADDS structure.

NOTE *The guidelines in this chapter have been in use for several years to help organizations structure their directory services. They are proven practices that will help ensure you build the most flexible directory solution—a solution that will help your organization meet its business needs through the services the network offers.*

Active Directory Domain Services are first and foremost based on a database, a hierarchical database, in fact (see Figure 5-2). As such, the directory database contains a *schema*—a database structure. This schema applies to every instance of ADDS. An instance is defined as an Active Directory *forest*. The forest is the largest single partition for any given database structure. Everyone who participates in the forest will share a given set of attributes and object types. That's not to say that the forest is the Active Directory global boundary. Forests can be grouped together to share certain information. Windows Server 2003 introduced the concept of *forest trusts*, which allow forests to share portions of their entire Active Directory database with others and vice versa. This concept is brought forward with WS08.

If you compare the WS08 forest to Windows NT, you can easily see that while NT also included an identity management database—the domain—its scope was seriously limited compared to ADDS. NT could basically store the user or computer name along with passwords and a few rules affecting all objects. The ADDS database includes over 200 object types and over 1,000 attributes by default. You can, of course, add more object types or attributes to this database. Software products that take advantage of the information stored in the ADDS directory may also extend its schema. Microsoft Exchange, for example, practically doubles the number of objects and attributes in the forest because of its integration with the directory.

PART III

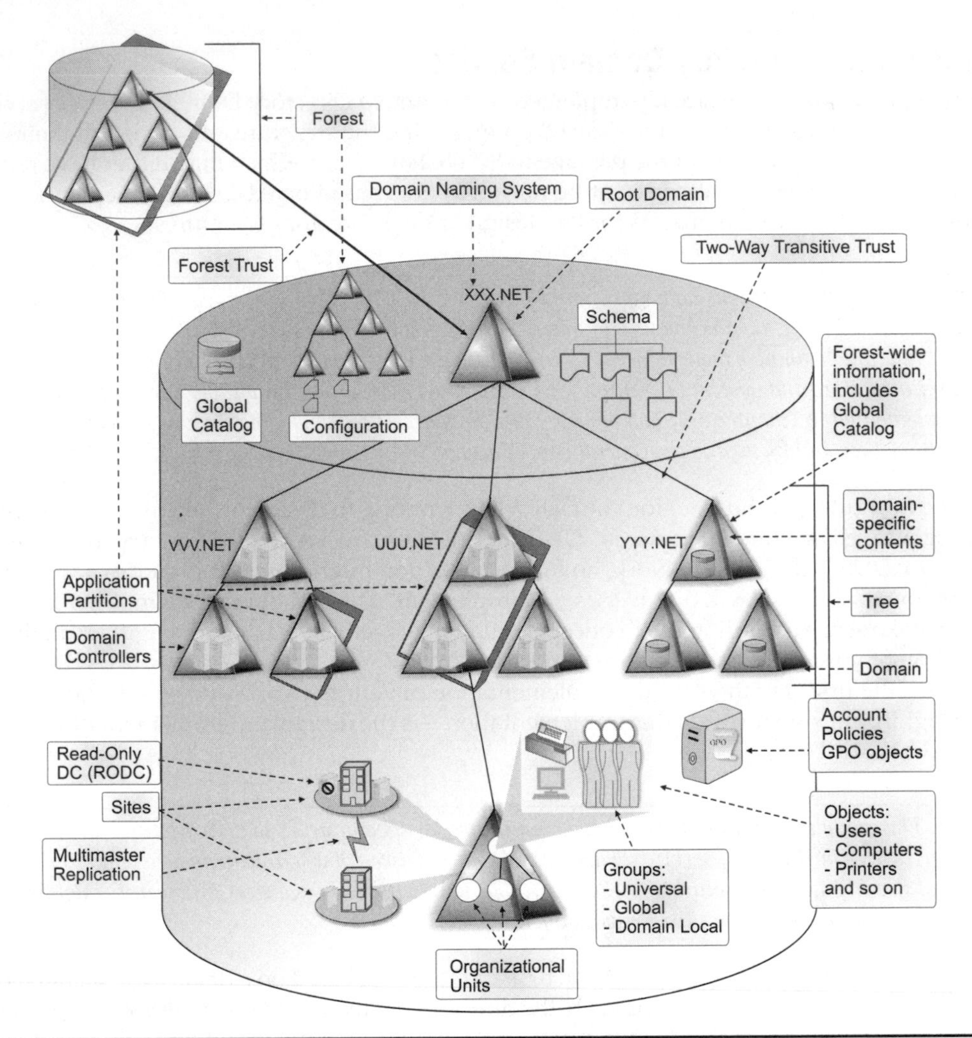

Figure 5-2 The Active Directory Domain Services database structure

Like any database, it categorizes these objects, but unlike relational databases, this database structure is hierarchical because it is based on the Domain Naming System's (DNS) structure. Anyone with experience with the World Wide Web will know that everything is hierarchical. Going to www.microsoft.com is arriving at the root of Microsoft's web site. Everything spans from this page. Moving to any other section—TechNet or MSDN, for example—sends you to special pages whose names are based on the microsoft.com root.

Forests act in the same way. Except that in a forest, the root point (analogous to the home page) is the root domain. Every ADDS forest must have at least one domain. Domains act as discrete object containers within the forest. Domains can be regrouped into *trees*. Trees are segregated from each other through their DNS name. Microsoft, for example, has a multitree forest. Its "namespace," the DNS element that defines the boundaries of the forest, is microsoft.com. As such, all domains within this tree have names similar to domain.microsoft.com. Microsoft created a second tree when it incorporated MSN.com within its forest. The MSN.com namespace automatically created a tree, and all domains under it are named domain.MSN.com.

Every forest will include at least one tree and one domain. The domain is both a security policy and administrative boundary within the forest. It is required to contain objects such as users, computers, servers, domain controllers (DCs), printers, file shares, applications, and much more. If you have more than one domain in the forest, they will automatically be linked to all others through an automatic transitive two-way trust. The domain is defined as a security boundary because it contains rules that apply to the objects it contains. These rules can be in the form of security policies or Group Policy Objects (GPOs). Security policies are global domain rules. GPOs tend to be more discrete and must be applied to specific container objects. While domains are discrete security boundaries, the forest will always remain the ultimate security boundary within an ADDS structure. The domain is termed an administrative boundary because, by default, the policies that apply to its objects do not cross the domain boundary.

Domain contents can be further categorized through grouping object types such as *organizational units* (OUs) or *groups*. Organizational units provide groupings that can be used for administrative or delegation purposes. Groups are used mainly for the application of security rights. WS08 groups include universal, which can span an entire forest; global, which can span domains; or domain local, which are contained within a single domain. OUs are usually used to segregate objects vertically, because objects such as users and computers can only reside inside a single OU, but groups can span OUs. Because of this, groups tend to contain horizontal collections of objects; an object such as a user can be included in several groups but only in one single OU.

Users also have it easier with Active Directory Domain Services. Working in a distributed forest composed of several different trees and sub-domains can become confusing to the user. ADDS supports the notion of *universal principal name* (UPN). The UPN is usually composed of the username along with the global forest root name. This root name can be the name of the forest or a special alias you assign. For example, in a forest named TandT.net, you might use *name.surname@tandt.com* as the UPN, making it simpler for your users by using your external DNS name for the UPN. Users can log on to any domain they are allowed to within the forest using their UPN. In their local domain, they can just use their username if they prefer.

Forests, trees, domains, organizational units, groups, users, and computers are all objects stored within the ADDS database. As such, they can be manipulated globally or discretely. One major difference between Active Directory and a standard database is that in addition to being hierarchical, it is completely decentralized.

Most Active Directory databases are also distributed geographically because they represent the true nature of an organization. Only very small organizations that have a single site will have a database that is wholly located in one location.

Managing a completely distributed database is considerably more challenging than managing a database that is located in a single area. To simplify distributed database issues, Active Directory Domain Services introduces the concept of *multimaster replication*. This means that even though the entire forest database is comprised of distributed deposits—deposits that, depending on their location within the logical hierarchy of the forest, may or may not contain the same information as others—database consistency will be maintained. Through the multimaster structure, ADDS can accept local changes and ensure consistency by relaying the information or the changes to all of the other deposits within the domain or the forest. This is one of the functions of the *domain controller* object in the directory. In addition to multimaster replication, ADDS supports the concept of a read-only domain controller (RODC). The RODC was introduced in WS08 to help protect directory data stored in remote and unsecured domain controllers. Despite this, you should always strive to protect DCs, any DC, to the utmost, because they are the engines that provide access to your network and all its objects.

The only deposits that have exactly the same information within the AD database are two domain controllers within the same domain. Each of these data deposits contains information about its own domain, as well as whatever information has been determined to be of forest-wide interest by forest administrators. At the forest level, you can determine the information to make available to the entire forest by selecting the objects and attributes from the database schema whose properties you want to share among all trees and domains. In addition, other forest-wide information includes the database schema itself and the forest *configuration*, or the location of all forest services. Published information is stored within the *Global Catalog* (GC). ADDS publishes some items by default, such as the contents of universal groups, but you can also add or subtract items to your taste. For example, you might decide to include your employees' pictures in the directory and make them available forest-wide.

NOTE *Not all items are unpublishable; some items are prerequisites for the proper operation of Active Directory Domain Services.*

Whatever is published within the Global Catalog is shared by all domain controllers who play this role in the forest. Whatever is not published remains within the domain. This data segregation controls the individuality of domains. Whatever is not published can contain discrete information that may be of the same nature, even use the same values, as what is contained in another domain. Properties that are published within the Global Catalog within a forest must be unique, just as in any other database. For example, you can have two John Smiths in a forest so long as they are both within different domains. Since the name of the object includes the name of its container (in this case, the domain), ADDS will see each John Smith as a different object. Of course, both John Smiths will not be able to use the same UPN.

The *directory store*, or NTDS.DIT database, is located on each domain controller. It includes several partitions that store all of the data that make up the domain (see Figure 5-3). Three items are in every directory store—the schema, the configuration, and the domain data—and two are optional—the Global Catalog and the *application partition*.

The Global Catalog, schema, and configuration each contain information that is replicated throughout the forest. Domain data is information that is replicated only within the domain. Replication over local and distant networks is controlled through regional database partitions. Organizations may decide to create these partitions based on a number of factors. Since the domain is a security policy boundary, authoritative organizations—organizations that span a number of geographic locations they control—may want to create

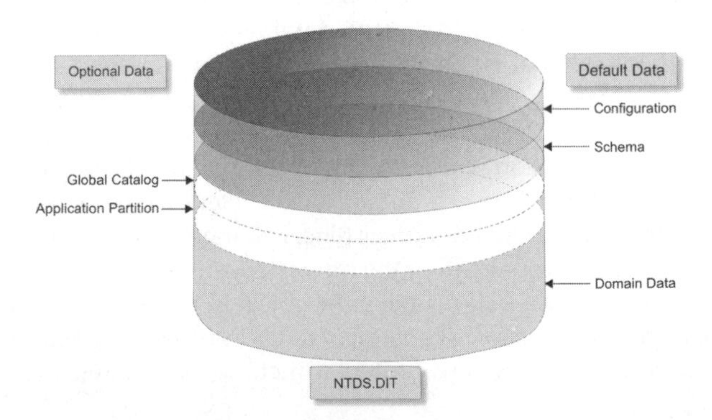

FIGURE 5-3 The structure of the directory store

a single domain that spans these locations. To segregate each region, and thus control the amount and timing of database replication between regions, the domain would be divided into *sites*. Sites are physical partitions that control replication by creating boundaries based on Internet Protocol (IP) addressing.

Organizations that are not authoritative, have independent administrations, do not control their regional locations, or have slow links between each location may want to further control replication through the creation of regional domains. Regional domains greatly reduce replication, since only forest-wide information is replicated from location to location. Forest-wide information rarely exceeds 20 percent of global forest data. In addition, organizations that only have the control of a portion of the forest namespace will be owners of the trees within the forest. Organizations that cannot guarantee a minimum level of consensus or authority between groups will always create separate forests.

There is one more replication partition within the ADDS database. This partition was introduced with Windows Server 2003. It is the application partition. This partition has several features, such as the ability to host several instances of the same application and COM+ components on the same physical machine, but for the purposes of replication, this partition can be defined as a specific group of domain controller IP addresses or DNS names. For example, WS08 automatically creates a forest-wide application partition for forest-wide DNS data, so this information will be available on all domain controllers within the forest. If they also host the DNS role, then each DC can make this information available to users.

That's it. That's the basis of Active Directory Domain Services. What's truly impressive about this database is that once it's in place, it can let you do some truly amazing things. You can manage an entire network from a central location. All management interfaces are the same throughout the forest, even across forests. Since everything is hierarchical, you can implement forest-wide standards for naming conventions, operations, database structure, and especially, security policy implementations. If you do it right, you can implement these standards automatically. This must be done before you create anything below the root domain. Though simple to understand, Active Directory Domain Services is indeed quite powerful.

New Features for Active Directory

Windows Server 2008 boasts several improvements in regards to Active Directory Domain Services. While this technology was introduced in Windows 2000, it has been refined and enhanced in Windows Server 2003 and even further in WS08. Table 5-1 lists the new features found in WS08 for Active Directory Domain Services since WS03. This table first identifies new features that can operate within a mixed WS03 and WS08 forest but running in a WS03 forest functional mode and then identifies features that can only operate in WS08 forest functional mode.

As you can see, WS08 supports several functional modes for Active Directory. You can run AD in Windows 2000 (W2K) native mode, which limits WS08 functionality to Windows 2000 AD capabilities; you can run it in WS03 forest functional mode, which enables several replication features; and finally, you can run it in WS08 forest functional mode. This last mode precludes the inclusion of any domain controllers other than WS08 within all domains. Remember also that before WS03, native or mixed modes were domain-specific, not forest-specific. A WS08 forest can still include domains that operate in any of the three mentioned modes. Table 5-2 identifies the differences between each functional mode. It serves to identify the limitations of older modes versus a full WS08 environment. To obtain WS08 forest functional mode, all domains must be native WS08 domains.

Feature	Description
ADDS Auditing	• Audit ADDS changes in the event log: Directory Service Changes • Record old and new values when changes are made
Undelete	• Ability to restore deleted objects from the directory
Read-only domain controller (RODC)	• Ability to create a domain controller that will only cache ADDS data • Can be used in unsecured environments to provide logon services while protecting ADDS data from tampering • Also supports a read-only DNS service
Restartable ADDS	• The ADDS service can be stopped and restarted without having to shut down the domain controller • When ADDS services are stopped, the DC no longer services ADDS requests
Installation improvements	• Changes in the ADDS installation wizard address bugs from previous versions of Windows, notably the ability to create DNS application partitions in the right ADDS location and the ability to create the proper DNS delegation when installing DNS services with the ADDS role • New forest functionality modes can be selected directly at installation
Management interface improvements	• The ADDS management console has been updated to manage new DC roles, such as the RODC • Search for DCs throughout the ADDS structure has been improved • Control of password policies for RODCs is now available
New Domain- and Forest-wide ADDS Features (in WS08 Forest Functional Mode)	
Distributed File Services Replication (DFSR)	• When in WS08 forest functional mode, the DCs now rely on DFSR's delta compression replication (DCR) engine
256-bit Advanced Encryption Services (AES) encryption	• Supports advanced encryption of the Kerberos authentication protocol
Multiple account policies	• Each domain can contain more than one account policy • Policies are assigned to either OUs or security groups

TABLE 5-1 New Active Directory Features

This new feature listing will be useful for the next step, designing your organization's Active Directory Domain Services structure.

The Nature of Active Directory Domain Services

One final key element to understand before you move on to the creation of your ADDS design is the nature of the directory. You already understand that a directory is a distributed database and, as such, must be viewed as distributed data deposits. But databases and data deposits include two basic components:

- **The database service** The engine that allows the database to operate
- **The data** The data contained within the database

Feature	W2K Mode	WS03 Mode	WS08 Mode
Number of objects within domain	1,000,000	Same as W2K	Same as W2K
Domain controller rename	Disabled	Enabled	Enabled
Update logon timestamp	Disabled	Enabled	Enabled
Kerberos KDC key version numbers	Disabled	Enabled	Enabled
User password on InetOrgPerson object	Disabled	Enabled	Enabled
Universal Groups	Enabled; supports security and distribution groups	Same as W2K	Same as W2K
Group Nesting	Enabled; allows full group nesting	Same as W2K	Same as W2K
Converting Groups	Enabled; allows conversion between security groups and distribution groups	Same as W2K	Same as W2K
SID History	Enabled; allows universal scope for security and distribution groups	Same as W2K	Same as W2K
Global Catalog replication tuning	Disabled	Enabled	Enabled
Defunct schema objects	Disabled	Enabled	Enabled
Forest trust	Disabled	Enabled	Enabled
Linked value replication	Disabled	Enabled	Enabled
Domain rename	Disabled	Enabled	Enabled
Improved replication	Disabled File Replication Service (FRS)	Enabled FRS	Delta compression replication
Dynamic auxiliary classes	Disabled	Enabled	Enabled
InetOrgPerson object class	Disabled	Enabled	Enabled
256-bit Advanced Encryption Services (AES) encryption	Disabled	Disabled	Enabled
Multiple account policies	Disabled	Disabled	Enabled

TABLE 5-2 Forest Functional Mode Features

The WS08 directory is the same as any other database. Active Directory Domain Services management is divided into two portions: service management and data management. ADDS management is comparable to intranet web site management. Technicians and technical staff are required to manage the service behind ADDS just like the Web service for the intranet site, but it is users and user departments that must be responsible for and administer the data contained within the ADDS as they would for information contained within the intranet pages.

For ADDS, the management of the data contained within the database can and should be delegated. Users should be responsible for their own information—telephone number, location, position within the organization—and departments should be responsible for information that is department-wide—organization structure, level of authority structure, and so on. Service management—management of domains, operation masters, domain controllers, directory configuration, and replication operations—must be maintained and operated by IT. This takes the pressure off IT staff and allows them to focus on IT-related operations within the directory (see Figure 5-4).

Active Directory Federation Services

ADDS forms the core of your internal network access controls, but AD Federation Services (ADFS) will be quite useful if you need to interact with partners or other organizations that are located outside your zone of influence. ADFS basically relies on your own internal directory to provide credentials to applications that are shared with partners. In fact, each partner relies on their own internal directory to gain access. Authorization requests are sent securely over common TCP/IP ports, ports which are usually open in most firewalls. Authorizations are based on business policies, including which other organizations and which users within these organizations are trusted, as well as privacy policies. Other features include:

- Web single sign-on (SSO) relying on Windows Integrated Authentication on web sites, even providing automated logon to users if it is within the policy.
- Interoperability because ADFS relies on a Web service (WS) that is called WS-Federation. This lets it interoperate with any other WS-Federation service and thus opens the solution to almost any service-oriented architecture (SOA) in the world.
- Passive or smart client support, letting partner organizations either use passive clients, such as a Web browser, or smart clients, such as Simple Object Access Protocol (SOAP)–based clients, such as servers, cell phones, personal digital assistants (PDAs), and desktop applications.

Overall, ADFS lets you use a simplified, encrypted identity management system, entirely based on internal ADDS structures. Once in place, the operation of ADFS is fairly

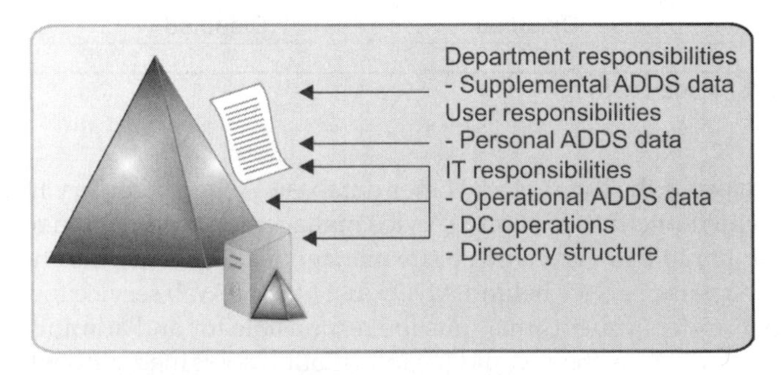

FIGURE 5-4 The separation of responsibilities in ADDS management

straight forward. ADFS works seamlessly for users, but requires the presence of an internal ADDS structure to work. Chapter 10 covers ADFS in more depth.

NOTE *More information on ADFS can be found at www.microsoft.com/windowsserver2003/techinfo/overview/adfsoverview.mspx.*

Design the Solution—Use the Active Directory Blueprint

Like the enterprise network blueprint presented in Chapter 3 (see Figure 3-8), the Active Directory Domain Services design blueprint emerges from the structure of the Microsoft Certification exam number 70-219, "Designing a Microsoft Windows 2000 Directory Services Infrastructure." It also includes the same prerequisites: business and technical requirements analyses. The advantage of using the same blueprint structure for both operations is that at this point in time, you should already have most of the prerequisite information in hand. If not, now's the time to complete it. Without this information, you can go no further. You simply cannot achieve a sound ADDS design without fully understanding your organization, its purpose, its objectives, its market, its growth potential, its upcoming challenges, and involving the right stakeholders.

TIP *For more information on the construction of an enterprise architecture and the identification of business requirements, see www.reso-net.com/articles.asp?m=8 and look for the "Architecture" section.*

Your ADDS design must be flexible and adaptive. It must be ready to respond to organizational situations that you haven't even anticipated yet. Remember, ADDS creates a virtual space where you will perform and manage networked operations. Being virtual, it is always adaptable at a later date, but if adaptability is what you're looking for, you need to take it into account at the very beginning of the design.

Once you have the information you need, you can proceed to the actual design. This will focus on three phases: partitioning, service positioning, and the implementation plan. This forms a blueprint for ADDS design (see Figure 5-5).

ADDS Partitioning

Partitioning is the art of determining the number of Active Directory Domain Services databases you want to manage and segregating objects within each one. This means you will need to determine the number of forests your organization will create remembering that each one is a separate database that will require maintenance and management resources. Within each forest, you will need to identify the number of trees, the number of domains within each tree and the organizational unit structure within each domain. Overall, you'll need to identify if your Active Directory database will need to share its information with other, non-ADDS network operating system (NOS) databases. This will be done either through integration of the two database structures (if the other database is compatible to the

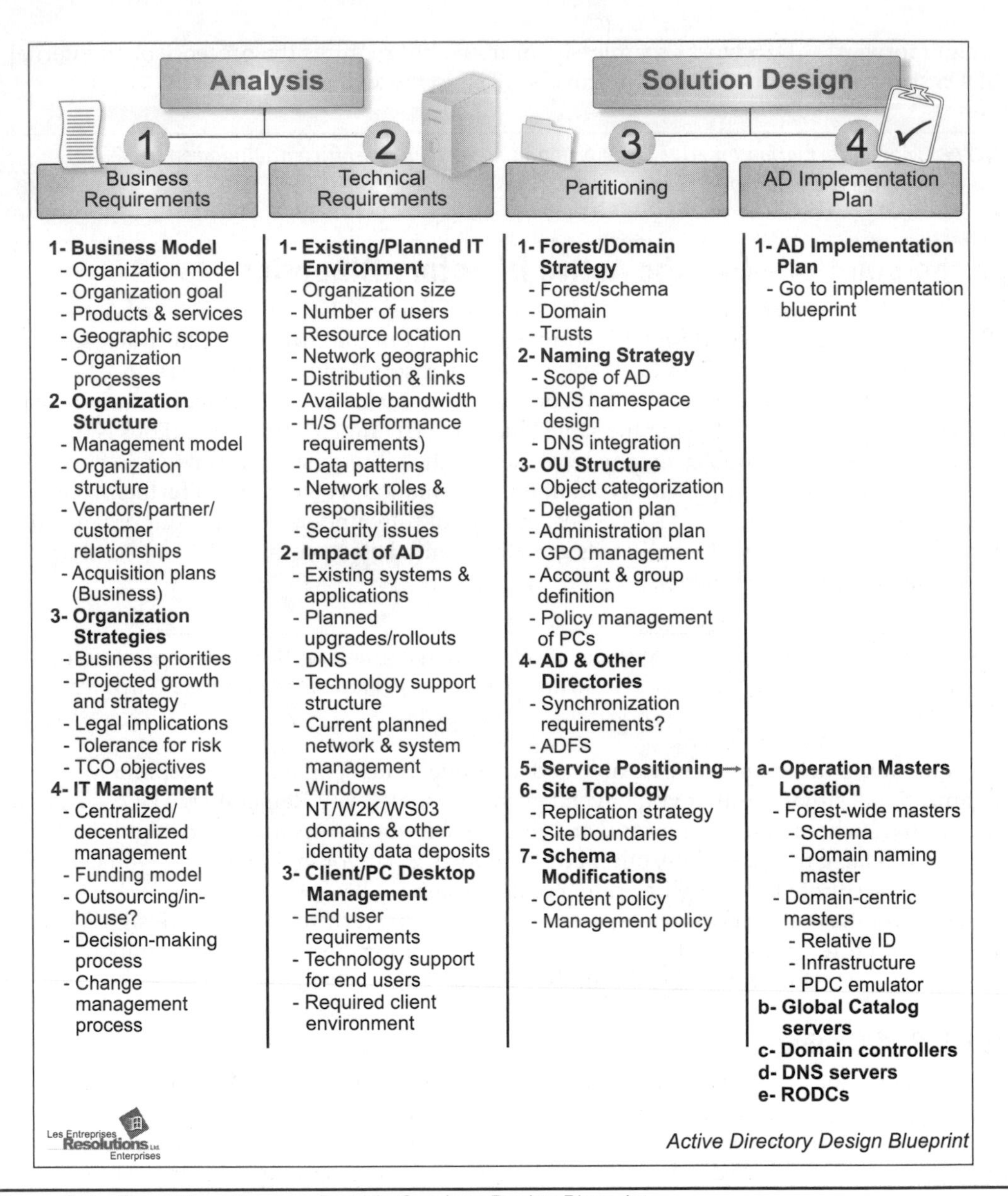

FIGURE 5-5 The Active Directory Domain Services Design Blueprint

Active Directory Domain Services format) or information sharing. In this case, you will need to identify the information sharing strategy to use.

To control data replication and minimize the impact on your bandwidth, you will identify and structure sites, design replication rules and identify replication methodologies. This is *site topology* design. Since you intend to fully exploit the ADDS database (after all why go through all this trouble if you're not going to fully use it?), you'll have to put in place a *schema modification strategy*. Since every schema modification is replicated to every domain controller in the forest, you'll want to ensure you maintain a tight control over them.

ADDS Service Positioning

Site topology design is closely related to *service positioning*. Each Active Directory domain controller performs important operations that support the proper functioning of the overall database. In fact, the objective of site topology design is to determine how each of these database containers will be linked to the others. Since ADDS is a distributed database, domain controllers can and should be positioned as close as possible to the user. These points of service should be convenient without becoming overabundant and increasing your administrative workload.

Flexible Single Master of Operations (FSMO) servers are special domain controllers that manage global forest or global domain operations. Global Catalog (GC) servers are domain controllers that maintain copies of forest-wide information, acting as the information locator for the forest. But since WS08 domain controllers can cache frequently requested global information, GC servers do not need to be as widely spread as domain controllers. Read-only domain controllers (RODCs) are DCs that include a read-only copy of the domain database, helping provide services while maintaining security. Finally, DNS servers are a must, since they provide namespace management functionality to the directory. Because of this integration with the directory service, DNS servers should be seen as subsidiary functions for directory support

Resource Pool versus Virtual Service Offering ADDS Designs

If you choose to rely on Microsoft's Hyper-V to run your resource pools, then you will need two different Active Directory Domain Services structures: one for the resource pool that manages all hardware resources and one for the virtual service offerings your end users will interact with. This will serve to segregate the security contexts of the two environments. Resource pools should *not* use the same directory service as the virtual service offerings. Using the same directory service at both levels can put your entire infrastructure at risk should any portion of your directory be compromised. Segregating these two infrastructures keeps them completely separate and can serve to protect the resource pool in the event of a compromise of the VSO directory.

VSO directories are at a higher risk by default because end users and therefore, potentially malicious users, interact directly with them. Resource pools, on the other hand, are less at risk because only administrators interact with them. Creating separate directories for each enhances the protection of the resource pool because there is no interaction between the two security contexts.

Of course, if you decide to use a different, non-Windows, hypervisor you will be segregating the security contexts of the resource pool and the VSOs automatically because non-Windows infrastructures do not participate in ADDS by default.

Therefore, you should endeavor to keep your resource pool ADDS structure as simple as possible since no end users can participate in it. The guidelines included in this implementation plan cover many aspects of the directory implementation you need to prepare for each environment, yet most of these aspects focus on VSO directories since this service will interact with users. Keep this in mind as you run through the details of this implementation plan.

and should be married to every domain controller. Proper positioning of each of these services can vastly improve directory performance.

Implementation Plan

The last step of the blueprint is the ADDS implementation plan—the actual procedure you will use to put your Active Directory Domain Services design in place. Indeed, this is where a parallel network strategy comes in handy or the ability to stage a new network while the original production network continues to function, and then migrate information from one network to the other, decommissioning the old production network once the process is complete. The parallel network gives you the freedom to implement a brand-new Active Directory Domain Services structure without any limitations due to legacy content. This directory can immediately operate in full forest functional mode, since it does not have to share database space with previous versions of the directory service. The limitations of older versions of Windows can be contained within specific domains or can even be excluded entirely from your Windows Server 2008 forest. In this way, you can obtain immediate benefits from the native functionality mode.

Put the Blueprint into Action

While the information collected for business requirements is the same as the information collected for the enterprise network blueprint, your view of the information collected for technical requirements has to be slightly different. In particular, the second section, the impact of the enterprise network, is modified to reflect the impact of Active Directory Domain Services. Here, you need to see how existing systems and applications will be affected by the arrival of a central database containing primary information such as usernames and user identity. You also need to see how these systems and applications can be integrated with this new central data repository so that you rely on one single authoritative source for all identities.

You need to review planned upgrades and rollouts to make sure that they will be compatible with ADDS and that these projects will not negatively affect the rollout of your ADDS structure. In terms of IP infrastructure, your focus needs to be the internal network DNS, since this function becomes integrated with the directory itself. You also need to identify how the technological support structure functions within your organization in order to determine who has authority over what. This will allow you to determine where your authoritative ADDS boundaries (forests, trees, and domains) will lie and where you will be able to perform delegation (through organizational units). You also need to review your system management structure, both current and planned, in order to see which functions you will want to delegate to or integrate with ADDS. Finally, you need to review your current identity management repositories, whether Windows NT, Windows 2000 or Windows Server 2003 domains, or other repositories, such as Novell eDirectory Services, or even UNIX systems, to see how they will be integrated or how they will interact with the WS08 directory.

Once this is complete, you can proceed to the third step of the blueprint, the *partitioning design*. The directory partitioning exercise allows you to determine the number and size, the naming strategy, the organizational unit strategy, the integration model, the position for core services, the topology, and the schema modification strategy for each forest in your enterprise.

Tip *Microsoft produced an excellent partitioning guide: "Best Practice Active Directory Design for Managing Windows Networks." It can be found at www.microsoft.com/technet/prodtechnol/windows2000serv/technologies/activedirectory/plan/bpaddsgn.mspx.*

Forest/Tree/Domain Strategy

The first place to start in the partitioning exercise is to determine the number of forests, the nature of the trees within each forest, and the nature of the domains within each of the trees your enterprise will require.

Forest Design

Forests are the partitions that contain:

- **The database schema** Only one database structure can be stored within a single forest. If someone in your organization needs to modify the schema for a given reason and does not want to share this modification with others in the organization, they should be placed within their own forest. Obviously, this would not be departments that share physical locations, but it could be a subsidiary or a partner organization.
- **The configuration data** The structure of the forest, the number of trees it contains, and the domains within each tree, as well as the structure of replication sites, make up the configuration data for the forest.
- **The Global Catalog** The Global Catalog includes all of the searchable objects for the forest. It contains the values and properties for all of the objects you deem important to users within the entire forest.
- **The trust relationships** Trust relationships between the domains in a forest are also forest-wide information. This is because of the transitive nature of Windows Server 2008 intra-forest or inter-domain trusts. Every domain in a forest will automatically be linked to its parent domain. Its parent domain will be linked to its parent and so on. Since all domains of a forest include two-way transitive trusts, all domains trust all other domains of the forest.
  In Windows NT, you needed to create specific trusts between each domain if you wanted domains in a group to trust each other. Trusts were not transitive. That means that Domain A would not trust Domain C even if they both trusted Domain B. For Domain A to trust Domain C, you had to create an explicit trust. You do not need to create direct trusts between domains within a forest with WS08. If Domain A and Domain C both trust Domain B in a forest, Domain A will automatically trust Domain C without an explicit trust. You can, however, create shortcut trusts if the hierarchical path between two domains that share a lot of information is too long or too complex (see Figure 5-6).

Forests can contain millions of objects. Because of this, most small, medium, and even large organizations will usually require a single production forest. The main reason for the creation of separate forests is to protect the database schema. Schema modifications are complex and must be tightly controlled if you want to minimize their impacts on production environments. In addition, schema modifications are permanent—additions cannot be removed, even though

PART III

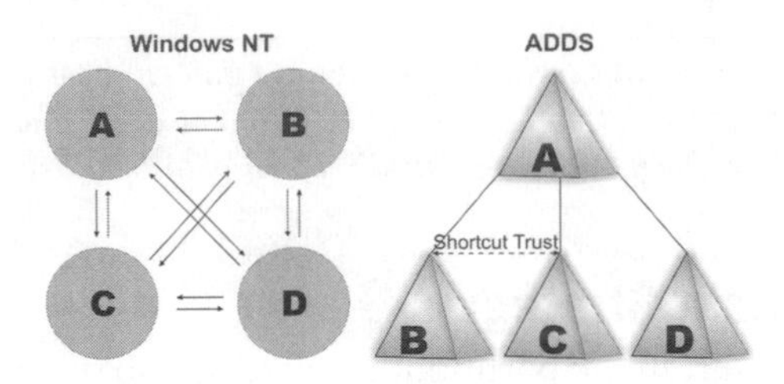

FIGURE 5-6 The nature of trusts

they may be renamed or deactivated. If you need to "play" or experiment with the schema, you need to create a forest that is separate from your production forest. Most medium to large organizations have *development* and *test* forests as well as at least one production forest.

A second reason for the segregation of forests is the level of authority of the central organization. You can only include organizations, divisions, or departments over which you have political and economic control within your forest. This is because of the hierarchical nature of the forest and the inheritance model that is derived from it. The organization at the root of the forest has influence and even authoritative control over all of the organizations or departments that are grouped into its trees and sub-domains. For example, the Ford Motor Company and Volvo would both have had separate forests before the acquisition of Volvo by Ford. But once Ford bought Volvo, it established financial authority over Volvo. In an Active Directory Domain Services structure, Volvo could then become a tree under the Ford production forest. Much depends on how well the Volvo and Ford IT staffs get along and if Ford imposes the joining even if the Volvo staff does not agree.

As you can see, no matter what the size of your production forest—whether it is in a small organization located within a single site or a multinational corporation spanning the entire world, the role of the forest owner is an important one. Forest owners manage forest-wide services. This means they are:

- **Forest-wide FSMO administrators** The forest owner is the administrator of the domain controllers that execute the Schema and Domain Naming FSMO roles and have the authority to affect the entire forest.
- **Root domain administrators** Every forest, even if it only has a single tree and a single domain, includes a root domain. The first domain in a forest is the root domain, because all other domains within the forest must be created as sub-domains of this domain. The operation of the root domain is critical if the forest is to run properly; therefore, forest owners are responsible for its maintenance.
- **Root domain data owner** Since the root domain is the basis of the forest, the forest owner is also the owner of the data contained within the root domain.
- **Schema and configuration container owner** Since the forest operation is based on the structure of its schema and configuration containers, the forest owner is responsible for their integrity.
- **Forest-wide security group owner** The forest owner is also responsible for forest-wide security groups. These groups should reside in the root domain. ADDS creates two management forest-wide groups: Enterprise Administrators and Schema Administrators. Membership in these groups is limited because they can affect the operation of the entire forest.

- **Root domain security group owner** In addition to the two universal administration groups, the root domain contains its own administrative group, Domain Administrators. The forest owner is also owner of this security group.

If there is more than one domain in the forest, the forest owner will have to communicate frequently with sub-domain owners to coordinate forest-wide efforts. In fact, determining the number of forests in your organization can be summarized as the identification of all forest owners. These will be the highest level of IT administration within the organization for any given network. Once this is done, you will be able to proceed to identifying forest content.

Forests share a lot of elements. Many are required elements; others are recommended elements based on common sense. Forests require the sharing of:

- **Security** Only include people you trust within a forest. This would include employees as well as IT administrative staff. Since a forest is made up of distributed database containers—domain controllers—you need to trust the people who will be responsible for all domain controllers, both inside and outside your main site.
- **Administration** Everyone who participates in a forest is willing to use the same schema and configuration.
- **Name resolution** Everyone who participates in a forest will use the same DNS to resolve names throughout the forest.

In addition to the required elements, you might decide to share the following:

- **Network** If all organizations in a forest trust each other, they may have put a private network in place. Though it is not impossible to separate forest sites with firewalls, it is recommended to minimize the exposure of your ADDS information to the outside world. If forest members must use public network links to transport replication traffic, they may opt for separate forests or, at the very least, use VPN links to secure all data transfers.
- **Collaboration** If you work with other organizations today and have implemented domain trusts with them, they may well be candidates for joining your new ADDS forest. If not, then consider using ADFS to link your resources together without linking your ADDS structures.
- **IT groups** If organizations share IT groups, then it is a good idea to create single forests to simplify network administration.

You must also keep in mind that creating more than one forest will have administrative impacts:

- Forests do not share transitive trusts. In WS08, these trusts must be created manually, but once created, will allow two entire forests to trust each other. If forests need to interact at a specific domain level, you can still use explicit domain trusts between the two specific domains, limiting the trust relationship between the forests.
- The Kerberos security protocol, the native Windows Server 2008 authorization protocol, will only work between forests that have implemented forest trusts.

Secure Your DCs

This point is extremely important. Even though you can secure domain controllers by locking down the system and placing servers in locked computer rooms, you should be absolutely sure that any DCs that will be in remote locations are under the responsibility of people in whom you have absolute trust. If you do not have this level of trust, then use a read-only domain controller.

Because of its multimaster replication model, ADDS will accept changes to its content and structure from any DC, except, of course, for RODCs. A rogue domain administrator who has physical access to a DC can do a lot of damage in a forest. For example, they can take the DC offline and edit the directory store in debug mode, adding special access rights for themselves. Once the DC is back online, these changes are replicated to all other DCs. There are ways to control this by securing the directory beyond the defaults, and they will be discussed in Chapter 11. For now, use the RODC role each time you feel the need to place a DC for increased service levels in a remote office but you cannot guarantee its absolute control.

- Using an e-mail-like logon name (name@domain) or a UPN will also only work if a forest trust is in place.
- Global Catalog replication is limited to a single forest, unless there is a forest trust in place.

Forest Design Example

Now that you're comfortable with the forest concept, you can identify the number of forests you need. Use the following examples to review the forest creation process.

NOTE *Medium to large organizations will use a multidomain forest as is illustrated in this example. Small organizations—organizations that are mostly located within a single site or that have fewer than 500 users—will most likely implement single domain forests. Because of this, all objects will be contained within the forest root domain. While it is always best to use multiple domains, it is good practice to use a single domain forest when the number of objects it contains is so small. You must however maintain proper management and security practices in regards to the ADDS forest.*

The first example focuses on a medium-sized organization with 5000 users. It is distributed geographically into ten regions, but each region is administered from a central location. The organization operates under a single public name and delivers the same services in each region. Because the organization has a "buy, don't build" policy, it tries to make use of commercial software whenever possible, but even with this policy, it still needs to create custom code or adapt existing applications. Because of this, it requires a separate development environment. In addition, it has had a lot of growing pains in the past because of friction between IT and Information Systems (IS). In fact, IS was seriously disappointed when IT created a single-master domain network with Windows NT.

In their forest design, this organization would create at least two, possibly three or more, permanent forests:

- A production forest that replaces the single-master Windows NT domain
- A staging forest to test, analyze and prepare new products for integration, especially those that may integrate with Active Directory and modify its basic database schema
- A development forest to allow the testing and development of corporate applications that take advantage of schema customizations or ADLDS implementations
- A separate forest may also be created for the extranet. Because this forest is exposed through the security perimeter of the network, it is separate from the production forest.

No trust would be established between three of these forests: production, staging, and development. In this model, the lack of trusts is represented by bold black lines separating each Active Directory database (see Figure 5-7). There may, however, be a trust established between the perimeter forest and the production forest, but since the nature of this trust (one-way, explicit, domain-to-domain) is not completely precise at this time, its boundary with the production forest is displayed as a dotted line.

Production Forest Design

Now that you have determined how many forests will exist, you can move on to the design of the production forest, since it will help determine the content of all other forests. Here you will determine the structure of the production forest, the forest you use to run your network. Once again, authority boundaries will determine the structure you create. Here you need to determine the number of trees and the number of domains your forest will contain.

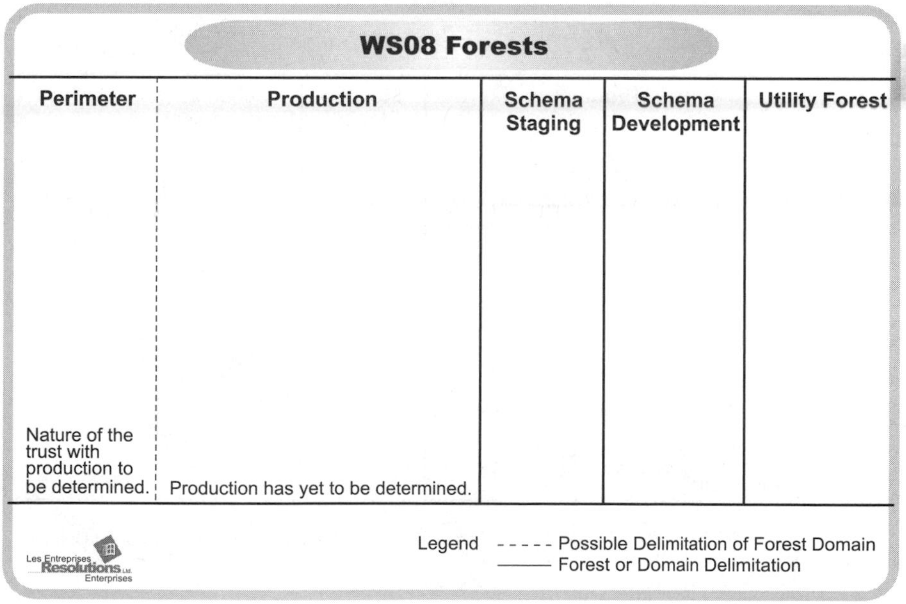

FIGURE 5-7 Determining the number of forests to create

Begin with the trees. Does your organization operate with a single public name? If not, these are good candidates for different trees. Even though the tree structure is completely internal and will rarely be exposed to the external world, its structure should reflect the names your organization uses publicly. Good candidates for trees are organizations that rely on others for service completion, organizations that form a partnership and want to collaborate closely, enterprises that merge with each other, and organizations who share IT management resources.

The second example covers a worldwide organization that has four subsidiaries. The organization is one single enterprise, but each of its business units is known under a different public name. It understands the complexity of interbusiness administration, but wants to implement operational and security standards throughout the corporation. IT budgets are controlled centrally, but most of the administrative work is performed by large IT groups from each of the business units.

After a series of discussions, the different IT groups decided on a single production forest with multiple trees. The forest owner identified and began ongoing discussions with each tree owner, and as a group they determined the level of integration for each tree and the level of authority the forest root domain would be allowed. This model allowed the organization to set standards while supporting regional diversity (see Figure 5-8).

Had the different IT groups not been able to agree, they would have created multiple production forests. In this case, the organization would not have met its goals for standardization. These goals could only have been obtained through political enforcement measures and not through the operational infrastructure of ADDS.

An organization can interact through multiple forests and thus gain benefits such as single sign-on and global interforest searches but cannot enforce standards through ADDS (see Figure 5-9).

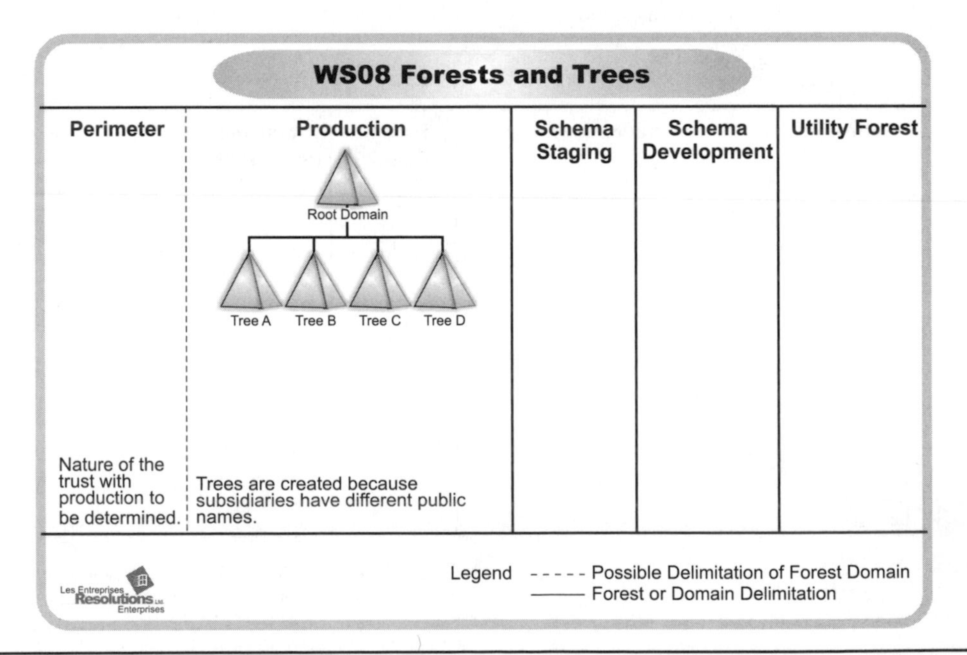

FIGURE 5-8 Designing a worldwide tree structure

In a multiple forest design, each forest must trust each of the others.

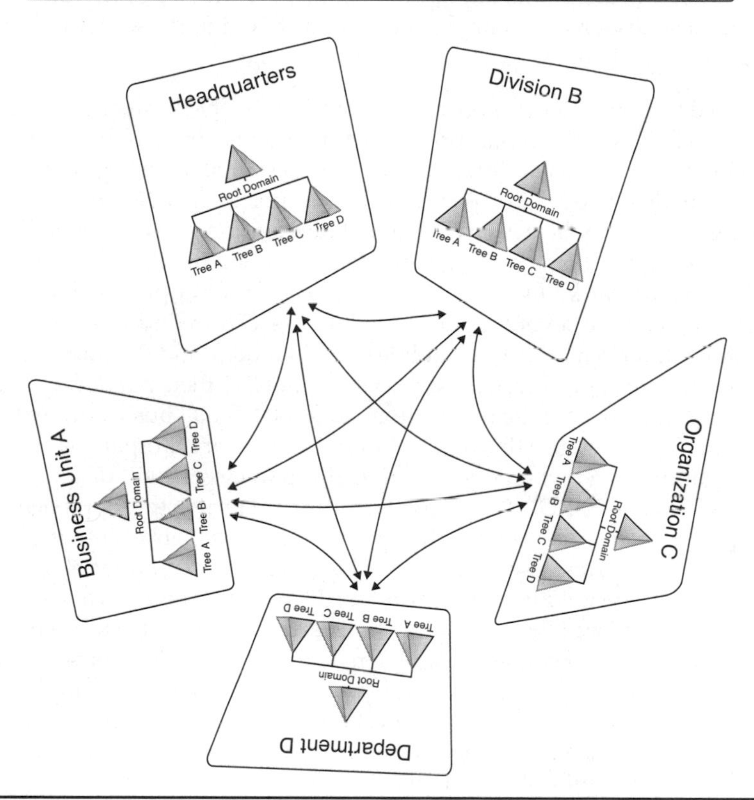

FIGURE 5-9 Separate forests must create forest trusts to interact with each other.

Domain Strategy

The first thing to remember when working with ADDS domains is that they are *not* like Windows NT domains. In Windows NT, the largest identity database boundary was the domain. If you wanted multiple domains to work with each other in either a master-master or a master-resource relationship, you had to enable trusts between each of the domains. In WS08, domain trusts in a forest are transitive. Here, the domain must be viewed as what it is—a security policy boundary that can contain:

- **Authentication rules** Domains form the boundary for the rules used to authenticate users and computers, since they are the container into which these objects must be created and stored. These rules are also called account policies.
- **Group Policies** Policies are limited by domain boundaries because they are objects that reside within the domain container.
- **Security policies for user accounts** Security policies applying to user accounts are stored within the domain. These can differ from one domain to another or even within domains.

- **Publication services for shared resources** All of the resources that can be shared within a domain are published through Active Directory Domain Services. By default, these resources—shared printers and shared folders—are published only to members of the domain.

Your domain design will depend on a number of factors: the number of users in a forest and the available bandwidth for replication from remote sites. Even though domains can contain one million objects each, it doesn't mean you need to fill them up. You might decide to create multiple domains to regroup objects into smaller portions. If, however, you find that you are applying the same policies to two different domains and it is not because you need to reduce the impact of replication, you've got one too many domains. In fact, you may consider upgrading wide area network links to eliminate the need for multiple domains.

In addition, you can use several domain models, just as in Windows NT. WS08 forests support the unique domain model, the multiple domain model, and the mixed model. Because of the hierarchical nature of the forest, these models are not like their Windows NT predecessors. Few organizations today opt for the unique domain model. Small businesses with less than 500 employees may decide to use this model, but it is rare in larger organizations.

Most organizations of a certain size—read medium to large—will decide to create a *protected forest root domain* (PFRD). There are several advantages to this approach. A protected forest root domain is often much smaller than production domains because it only contains forest management groups and users. As such, it has a minimum amount of data to replicate, which makes it easier to rebuild in case of disasters. It contains a small group of forest-wide administrators, which reduces the possibility of mistakes that may affect the entire forest. It is never retired, since it does not contain production data. Because other domains are created below the forest root domain, organizational restructuring is easier to accomplish. Because it is small and compact, it is easier to secure. And should transfer of ownership be required, it is easier to transfer a relatively empty domain than to transfer your entire production domain, which contains all of your multiple hundreds of users.

Production domains are created under the protected forest root domain. Any medium to large organization that was using a single-master domain in Windows NT should create a single global child domain (SGCD). This single global child domain has the same purpose as the single NT domain—regrouping all of the users of your network into a single production environment. The only users that are not within this child domain are the forest root domain user accounts.

CAUTION *The protected root domain is the most overlooked feature of an ADDS design, though it is becoming more and more common. If your organization has more than a few hundred users and you can afford the cost of the two domain controllers the PFRD requires—you should use virtual instances of WS08 for this—it is highly recommended that you implement a PFRD in your design. This will give you the greatest level of flexibility in your design and will stand the test of time.*

Now that you have a parent-and-child domain structure, you can expand forest contents to include other security boundaries. The main requirement of a single global child domain is that users be identifiable and that their actions be traceable within the network. As such, you will definitely want to exclude *generic* user accounts from the production domain. Generic accounts—accounts that are named according to function rather than individual—are used for three activities: testing, development, and training. You can use security boundaries—domains—to segregate these accounts from the production domain. In this manner, you can create other security containers where rules can either be more or less stringent than in the production domain to enclose testing, development, and training activities. In fact, not all tests or development will require schema modification. In most organizations, 95 percent of all tests and/or development will *not* require schema modifications. Using separate domains segregates these accounts from production, but does not add the workload another forest would. In addition, the creation of both testing (or, rather, staging) and development sub-domains becomes quite easy, since the parent-child structure is already in place (see Figure 5-10). The same would apply to a training domain. This is a *functional domain* design model. This model does not include multiple trees, but rather multiple child domains.

Domains can be required in other situations as well. For example, an organization whose operations span several different countries will often require multiple sub-domains because of the legal restrictions in some of those countries. If there are legal requirements that differ from country to country and that may even require contradicting account policy settings, it may be easier to create additional domain boundaries than to manage these policies in the same domain.

The final reason for domain segregation is WAN bandwidth. If your *available* bandwidth is inappropriate to support intradomain replication, you will need to create regional domains.

Keep in mind that every domain you create will require an administration team. Each new domain requires at least two domain controllers for redundancy and reliability. The administrative costs may become prohibitive if too many domains are created. In addition, each new domain means new trust relationships. While they are transitive and automatic, they still need to be monitored. Finally, the more domains you create, the more it is likely that you will need to move resources and objects between them.

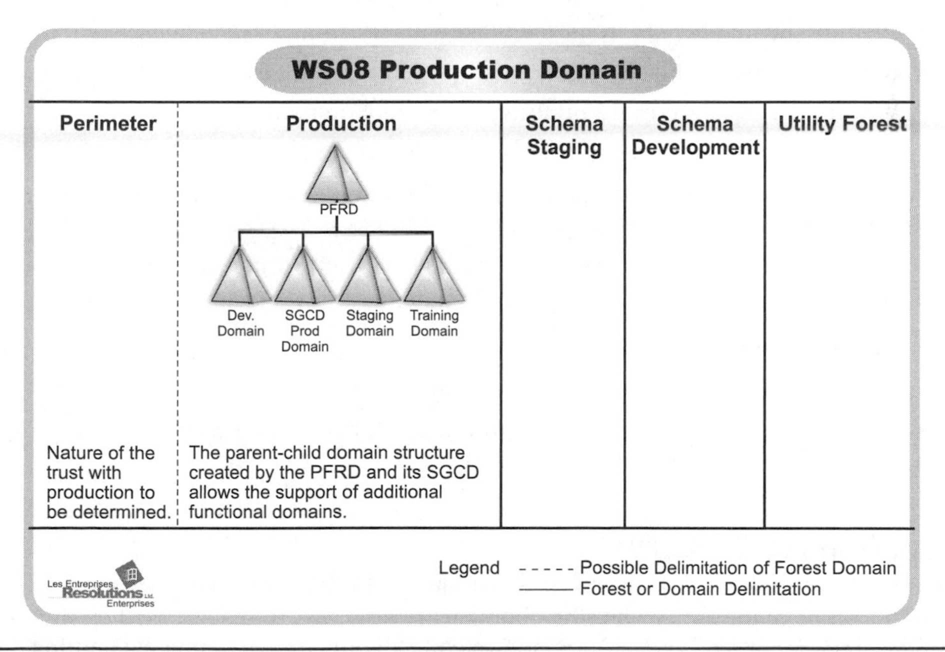

FIGURE 5-10 Spawning additional domains from an initial root/child relationship

Other Forest Domain Designs

Now that you have determined the domain structure to implement within your production forest, you can use it to derive the structure for the other forests you created. The staging forest is simple. It should represent the same structure as the production forest. As such, it requires a parent and a child domain. Since it is designed to represent only the production environment, it does not require additional domains for training, development, or other purposes.

The development and utilitarian forests require a single combined root and production domain, since schema development testing is not dependent on the parent-child naming structure found in the production forest. Finally, the perimeter forest is made of a single domain because this structure reduces the complexity of its management. Since it is exposed to the outside world (through a firewall, of course), its structure is also kept as simple as possible.

There you go! Your forest design is complete. Now you need to populate the domains and design their replication strategy.

TIP *Development forests are created when organizations want to integrate their applications to the ADDS they use to manage their network. Though this is discussed later in the blueprint, consider having your development teams rely on ADLDS instead of modifying the ADDS schema. This will help keep your production forest pristine and will make their applications more transportable, yet grant them every feature they would expect from ADDS integration.*

Forest Design Best Practices

The forest design process includes the following best practices:

- Identify the number of forests and write a justification for each one.
- Identify the number of trees and write a justification for each one.
- Wherever possible, create a protected forest root domain.
- Limit the number of trees as much as possible in your design.
- Wherever possible, create a single global child domain for production within each tree.
- Identify the number of additional domains required within each tree.
- Identify the scope and contents of each domain.
- Justify each domain.
- Choose the generic name for each domain.
- Once the domain structure for the production forest is complete, design the domain structure for the other forests you created.

Design the Naming Strategy

Once the forest is designed, the next step is defining the ADDS *namespace*. The namespace defines the scope of the Active Directory Domain Services structure. It is based on the hierarchical nature of the Domain Naming System. Not only does it define the naming boundaries of the ADDS database, it also defines the structure of the database and the relationships between its objects. The actual object naming convention for Active Directory Domain Services is not DNS. It is based on an X.500 naming scheme that identifies containers when naming objects. This supports the creation of duplicate objects, so long as they are located in different containers. For example, cn=Mike Smith,ou=IT,dc=root,dc=com means that Mike Smith's user account is contained within the IT organizational unit in the ROOT.COM domain.

As you can see, the X.500 naming scheme is not practical for everyday use. But most everyone is familiar today with the Domain Naming System; as a result, this is the naming scheme that is presented to users and administrators. For example, DNS names create trees within the forest. Because of its hierarchical nature, DNS is used to subdivide the forest into trees. This is done through the modification of the DNS root name. Remember, MSN.com is a root name change from Microsoft.com, creating a second tree within the Microsoft.com forest.

Since the domain name of your forest is a DNS name, you should use only publicly registered DNS names. When you register a name, you ensure that you have complete ownership over it. For example, if you use Microsoft.com as your external name, you might use Microsoft.net as your internal network name. By buying the rights to the Microsoft.net name, you ensure that no outside event will ever affect your internal network. You are also segregating your internal namespace from your external namespace. This allows you to identify the source of all traffic more easily and track intruders more effectively should anyone ever try to penetrate your network, because no one but your internal users would ever use the .net name root.

If, for some reason, you choose to use a name you do not own, ensure that you verify that it does not exist on the Internet before creating your first domain controller. A few organizations that did not perform this step often found themselves using an internal name that was used externally by a different organization. This will lead to problems, from having to rename your forest to being unable to reach the external domain from inside the network. Even though renaming an entire forest is possible with Windows Server 2008, it doesn't

Choose the Right Name

A lot of people use made-up internal domain names—for example, internal.local—for their ADDS structures. But consider this: You're building the core authentication engine for your network. Is it really wise to use a made-up name, a name that anyone else can decide to use for their own network? What if you're faced with a merger or acquisition in the future and both organizations have silly, made-up names in their network? You'll probably be faced with having to rename your ADDS structure. While it is possible, it is a lot of work that doesn't provide that many benefits. Why not get it right the first time and buy a proper name? Your organization, if it has done its homework properly, probably already owns every possible permutation of your public domain name. Why not use one of those instead? You're already paying for them; might as well put them to work.

Make sure that you continue to separate the internal from the external domain names. For example, if you are using Mycompany.com as your external domain name, use Mycompany.net as your internal name. It will reduce the potential issues you may face in the long run.

mean that you'll find it pleasant to have to change your internal name because someone outside your organization forces you to do so. Use a real DNS name with standard DNS naming conventions, with the .gov, .com, .org, .net, .edu, .biz, .info, .name, .cc, .tv, .ws, or .museum name, and register it. That way, you'll control your namespace.

CAUTION *One of our clients decided to use an .intra root for their production ADDS structure, but as the project progressed, someone decided to shorten it to .int. As it turns out, .int is owned by the United Nations and, of course, this organization had business dealings with the UN. The error was not discovered until the system was well into production when one user tried to look up a UN web site and couldn't. The customer eventually had to rename their entire internal ADDS structure just because they didn't follow the simple advice of buying a proper DNS name and using it internally.*

Never use the same forest name twice, even if the networks are not interconnected. If you know that your sister organization has named their development testing forest DEVTEST, name yours something else. Many organizations have a testing forest that is an exact duplicate of the production forest. While this may be practical, it is also dangerous. All you need is someone to make a mistake and link the two ADDS structures together—all it takes is plugging the wrong cable in the wrong socket—and disaster strikes. ADDS will not allow two Schema Operations Masters using the same name to run in the same network at the same time. One of them will fail immediately. Be prepared; don't *ever* use the same forest name twice.

You'll also have to worry about NetBIOS names. NetBIOS names are composed of 15 characters, with a reserved 16th character. They must be unique within a domain. The first part of the DNS name you choose should be the same as the NetBIOS name. Since DNS names can contain 255 characters—in fact, you have 254 characters to choose from; DNS places a final dot in the name, the 255th character—per fully qualified domain name (FQDN), you should limit the size of the DNS names you use. Use short, distinct, and meaningful names. Distinguish between domain and machine names. Therefore, when you browse the network, you will see meaningful names.

You should also identify your *object naming scheme* at this stage. All objects, such as servers and PCs, will have a distinct DNS name (or host name). This name, like the Universal Principal Name for users, will have a DNS structure and use the domain and forest root names to complete its own. You can use a structured naming scheme (see Figure 5-11). This example is based on T&T Corporation's network name. T&T uses TandT.com for their external name and TandT.net for the internal network. In their naming scheme, every object

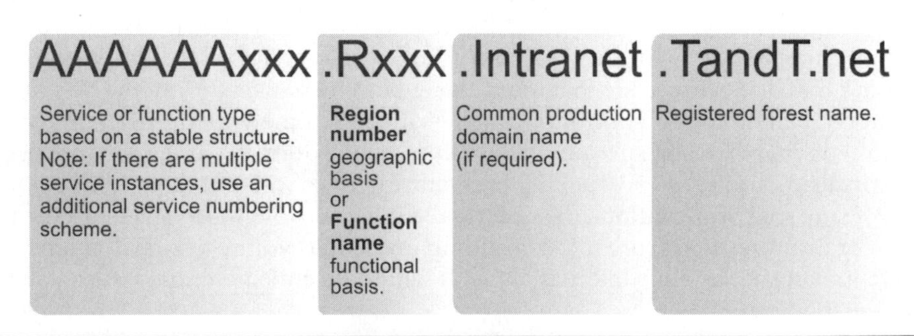

FIGURE 5-11 Using a structured object naming scheme

uses TantT.net, a registered DNS name, as a forest root. Next, it uses either a geographic naming scheme for child domains (single-letter code for region and three-digit number code for each region) or a functional scheme (function name, such as Intranet.TandT.net). Finally, servers and PCs can use up to five letters for the function code, along with three digits, to identify the number of machines offering this function. An example would be ADDSDC001 .Intranet.TandT.net for the Active Directory PDC Emulator in the Intranet child domain of the TandT.net forest.

Forest, tree, and domain names should be considered static. You should try to find a name you will not need to change, even if you know you can later. The domain and domain controller renaming process in Windows Server 2008 is complex and can cause service outages. Geographic names are often the best. In most cases, it takes a lot of momentum to change a geographic name, so they are considered quite stable. Don't use organizational structure to name domains, unless you are confident that it is and will remain stable.

Table 5-3 lists the types of objects that you could place within domains and the holding domain for each object. Each object will require a naming structure.

Objects	Production	Development	Training
Internal regular PCs	☒	☒	
Internal portables	☒	☒	
External PCs for development (outsourced)		☒	
Managed external PCs	☒	☒	
Unmanaged external PCs	☒	☒	
Multimedia PCs	☒	☒	
Member servers (Services: Terminal Services, Web, SQL Server, etc…)	☒	☒	
Domain controllers	☒	☒	☒
Quotas—shared folders	☒	☒	
Printers and printer queues	☒	☒	☒
Meeting rooms	☒		
Projectors, shared PCs	☒		
Service accounts	☒	☒	☒
User accounts	☒	☒	
Administrators	☒	☒	☒
Technicians/installers	☒	☒	
Groups	☒	☒	☒
Generic accounts		☒	☒
Organizational units	☒	☒	☒
Domain administrators	☒	☒	☒
Applications	☒	☒	☒

TABLE 5-3 Domain Objects

Naming Best Practices

Use the following best practices to name your ADDS forests:

- Use standard Internet characters. If they work on the Internet, they will definitely work in your network. Avoid accents and solely numeric names, even though the DNS namespace now supports Unicode characters. Keep it simple; this is always the best approach.
- Use 15 characters or less for each name.
- For the root name, use a simple, short name that is representative of the identity of the organization.
- Follow all DNS standards and make sure your internal name is different from your external name.
- Use different, but related names for the resource pool and the VSO directories. For example, your resource pool forest could be named TandT.ms (for Microsoft) while your VSO forest could be TandT.net.
- Finally, before proceeding, find out if the name is available and then buy it.

DNS is a cornerstone of Active Directory Domain Services. Since it is designed to manage the ADDS namespace, Microsoft has vastly enhanced the Windows DNS service. It can now be completely integrated with Active Directory Domain Services. In fact, it should be, because proper ADDS operation depends on DNS, since DNS is used to locate domain controllers at logon. In addition, when running the DNS service on domain controllers, the DNS data is incorporated into the ADDS database and replicated securely along with other ADDS data. Since the data is available to any DC, even RODCs, you should make sure the DNS service is available on the DC as well so that it can provide this information to users.

You should also avoid using third-party DNS servers with Windows, especially if they are non-Windows based. This is a hard sell, especially if your DNS namespace is managed by non-Windows administrators. At the very worst, make a deal: Anything Windows is managed by ADDS DNS, and everything else is not. WS08 brings several enhancements to the DNS service, so long as it is integrated with ADDS. With WS08, the DNS service has moved from being simply a network infrastructure service to an Active Directory Domain Services and Windows–based service. Therefore, both roles—DC and DNS—should always be married together as much as possible.

Your forest design can now be named. As mentioned earlier, the production forest belongs to the T&T Corporation. Their Internet name is TandT.com. They have researched and bought TandT.net. It will be the name for their forest root. Sub-domains are named after their function. The production domain is named with something more meaningful to users, such as Intranet.TandT.net. Development, training, and staging domains are named as such. The external forest found in the perimeter is named TandT.com. The staging forest is named TandT.Lab, and the development forest is named TandT.Dev. These forests do not require registered DNS names, since they are not production environments and are volatile in nature. The impact of recreating or renaming a staging or development forest is always much smaller than for the production forest. Volatile or utility forests can be named when needed. This model will be illustrated further in this chapter when more design components have been completed.

Design the Production Domain OU Structure

What's truly amazing with Active Directory Domain Services is how a simple database can be used to manage objects and events in the real world. That's right—the objective of ADDS is to manage the elements you store inside its database. But, to manage objects, you must first structure them. Forests, trees, and domains begin to provide structure by providing a rough positioning for objects throughout the ADDS database. This rough positioning needs to be vastly refined, especially when you know that a single domain can contain more than a million objects.

The tool you use to refine the structure of objects is the organizational unit (OU). An OU is a container that, like the domain, is designed as an object repository. OUs must be contained within a domain, however. But since they can act as object repositories, they can and should be used to identify your network administration structure. Remember also that OUs can store other OUs, so you can create an administrative structure that reflects reality.

A second advantage of an OU is the ability to delegate the management of its contents to someone else. This means that when you design the structure of the organizational units within the domains of your Active Directory Domain Services structure, you design the way the objects in your network will be managed and will interact with each other. In addition, you identify who will manage which components of your network.

You might, for example, decide that account information for the users in a given business unit are the responsibility of the business unit, delegating the management and administration of this group of user accounts to a local business unit administrator. In this way, the OU in ADDS is comparable to the domain in Windows NT. Whereas in Windows NT, you needed to give "Domain Administrator" rights to anyone responsible for groups of users, in Active Directory, you delegate ownership of an organizational unit, thus limiting these control or access rights to the contents of the OU and nothing else.

In short, the OU is designed to help support the data/service concept of ADDS. Since OUs contain ADDS objects and their properties, they contain data. By controlling access to OUs through security settings, in much the same way you would do so for a folder on an NTFS volume, you can give someone ownership of the data contained in the OU. This frees up domain administrators to focus on the services that drive ADDS. Making sure that all ADDS services are healthy and operating properly is the new role of the domain administrator. In a well-rounded Active Directory, you have a series of new interaction roles, such as the *OU administrator*, the *domain operator*, and the *service administrator*—roles that have significantly less authority in a domain than their Windows NT counterparts. You can now limit the Domain Administrator group to a small, select group of people in whom you have complete trust. Because it is so small, the activities of this group are now much easier to trace.

The OU Design Process

In this design process, administrators must create a custom OU structure that reflects the needs of their organization, identify administrative groups—from the data administrator that manages items such as addresses and job positions for user accounts to the technical role of populating user and computer accounts in the directory—and proceed to the delegation of the ADDS contents to respective administrative groups. The best place to start the design process is with the single global child domain. Since this is the production domain, it will be the domain with the most complex OU structure. Once this domain's structure is complete, it will be simple to design the structure for other domains, both within and outside the production forest, since their needs are derived from the production forest's own requirements.

There are four reasons to create an organizational unit:

- To regroup ADDS objects
- To administer ADDS objects
- To delegate the administration of ADDS objects
- To hide objects in ADDS

Because OUs can include objects, your first objective should be to categorize the objects your network contains. Once you do, you'll find that there are three basic object types: people, PCs, and services. These should form your first level of custom OUs. There are other categories of objects—printers, servers, file shares, Distributed File Service (DFS) namespaces, domain controllers, and more—but they are either contained within one of the three top-level object categories, must be managed on their own, and already have an existing container, or the objects they contain can only be classified and do not qualify for the other objectives of the OUs you create.

Your next goal should be to regroup objects for administrative purposes. Windows operating systems running any version of ADDS manage objects through the application of Group Policy Objects (GPOs). What is important to understand here is that the way you design your organizational unit structure will directly affect the way you apply GPOs.

WS08 applies two policies by default to each domain: the Default Domain Policy and the Default Domain Controller Policy. You should review the contents of these policies to ensure that they conform to your security requirements. You may wish to tighten these default policies with your own settings. WS08 also creates a number of default containers when it first generates a domain (see Figure 5-12). Containers are not all OUs. Some containers are system folders that do not follow OU rules. Two such containers are the Users and Computers containers. The icon representing them is different from a normal

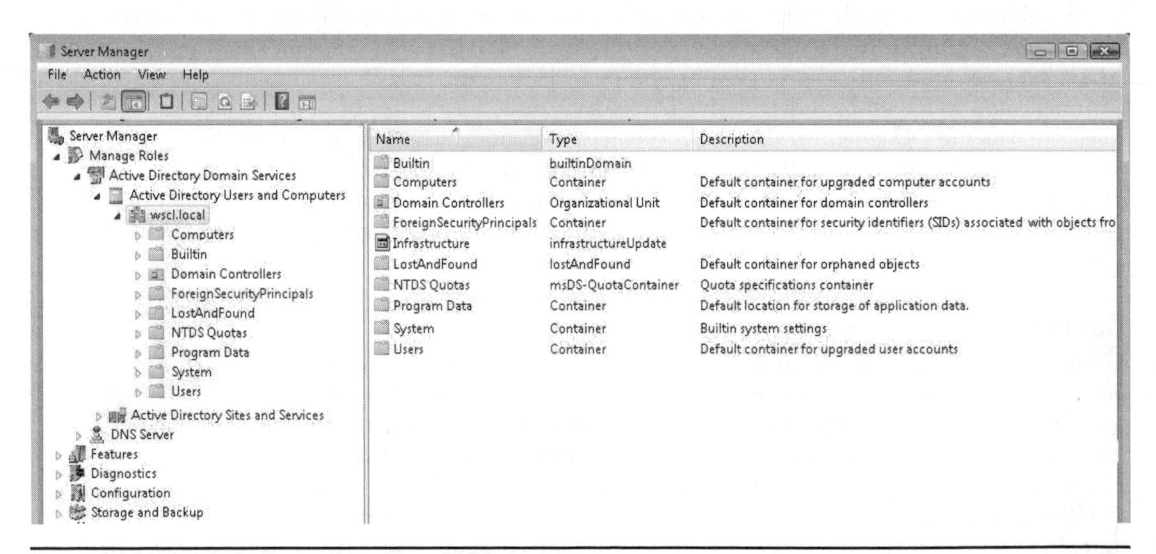

FIGURE 5-12 The default structure of an ADDS domain

OU icon because they will automatically contain objects of this type. When you create a user or computer account, if you haven't taken any other measures, these objects will be created in these containers by default. In addition, these containers do not process GPOs. The only way to apply GPOs to objects in these containers is to apply them to the domain itself, which would naturally apply the GPO to every object in the domain. GPO application is an art that must be learned through practice, but one thing is certain—applying all GPOs at the domain level is not the best practice. More on this will be covered in later chapters; for now, the rule to follow is to apply GPOs to categorized OUs as much as possible. Finally, you cannot create OUs within either the Users or the Computers containers. If you want to manage these object types, user and computer accounts, you need to create custom OUs to regroup these types of objects.

While you're planning your management strategy, think about the third reason for OU creation: delegation of administration. Delegation should be considered hand in hand with administration to create the secondary layers of OUs in this structure. For each type of OU, you must identify potential object subtypes and determine if they are significantly different. Each significantly different object, either at the administrative or delegation level, will require a separate OU. WS08 will support a hierarchy of over ten levels of OUs, but you should try for as flat an OU structure as you can. Objects buried within multiple layers of organizational units will be demanding to index and locate when you need to find them in the directory. Aim for a five-layer OU structure as a maximum; allow few, if any, exceptions. If you have control only on the top layers of the structure and you need to delegate the finalization of other sub-layers, you should leave at least two untapped layers for local departments to use.

The final reason you will create OUs is to hide objects. Since the directory is a searchable database, users can query for any object it contains. Some objects, such as administrative accounts, service accounts, and some security groups, are sensitive and, therefore, should be hidden from prying eyes. Because OUs contain access control lists, it is possible to hide sensitive objects within the directory. These objects are placed within special OUs that have access control lists that are under tight control. The objects contained in these OUs become "invisible" to nonadministrative users of the directory because their ability to read them has been denied.

The administration design process begins when you create the three different object type OUs—people, PCs, and services—and regroup objects under them. To do so, you need to identify every manageable object in your network and use a questioning process for each. For example, Table 5-4 lists a series of objects that require management within the directory. In addition, it defines a classification and expected contents for each object. Two questions need to be answered for each object: Do I need to manage this object? Will I ever delegate this object? Each "Yes" answer means that a custom OU needs to be created. A third question: Do I need to hide this object? should also always be on your mind during this process.

Though the OU design process begins with object categorization, it is not complete until you have also designed the following ADDS structural components:

- Group Policy Object management strategy (Chapter 7)
- PC management strategy (Chapter 7)
- Account and group definition and generation (Chapter 7)
- Service management strategy (Chapter 8)
- Security design (Chapter 10)

Objects	Classification	Contents	Delegation?	GPO?	Hidden?
Workstations	Resource OU	Local Administrators Standard users Multimedia PCs		☒	
Portables	Resource OU	Local Administrators Standard users		☒	
External PCs	Resource OU	PCs for development projects (managed)		☒	
External PCs	Resource OU	Consultant PCs (managed)		☒	
External PCs and Portables	Resource OU	Consultant PCs (unmanaged)			
Member Servers	Resource OU	Services: file server, SQL server, Exchange…	☒	☒	
Domain controllers	Service OU	Services: authentication, identity management, security		☒	
Quotas—shared folders	Resource OU	Information sharing		☒	
Printers	Service OU	Delegate printer queues	☒	☒	
Meeting rooms	Resource OU	Reservation system	☒		
Projectors, shared PCs	Resource OU	Reservation system	☒		
Service accounts	Service OU	System process tracking		☒	☒
Users	Data OU	Similar to the organizational structure	☒	☒	
Administrators	Data OU	Master OU in a delegated OU		☒	☒
Domain administrators	Service OU	Located in default OU		☒	☒
Technicians/ installers	Service OU	Global but limited delegation rights	☒	☒	☒
Searchable groups	Service OU	Global	☒	☒	
Technical groups	Service OU	universal, domain local	☒	☒	☒
Generic accounts	Data OU	Domains other than Production	☒	☒	
Applications	Service OU	COM+ objects, MSMQ	☒	☒	

TABLE 5-4 Manageable Objects Within ADDS

- Delegation plan (Chapters 7 and 8)
- Business continuity plan (Chapter 11)
- Administration plan (Chapter 13)

Though you begin the OU design here, this design will not be complete until you consider each of the elements in this list. Each will have an impact on the overall OU design. Don't make the mistake of creating your OU structure without taking each of these into consideration.

The PCs Object OU Structure

The first place to start is by categorizing PCs because it tends to be the simplest structure you'll create. Table 5-4 identifies six possible types of PCs within the organization. Most organizations have their own PCs as well as PCs from external sources, such as consultants or partners. This means PCs are first divided into two categories: internally owned and external PCs. The former are all managed PCs, but may still require further categorization. Portables have different policies from desktops—firewall and power settings, for example, should be different. Among the desktops, you'll find more basic PCs as well as multimedia and shared workstations. Among external PCs, you'll find managed and unmanaged systems. External PCs that are onsite for the development of code or long-term projects must be tightly controlled and must use the same image as internal PCs in order to ensure code quality. Other consulting PCs may be present for productivity purposes only. PCs that are used only to produce documentation should not and are not the organization's responsibility so long as they conform to a basic policy. This means they need to be segregated within the OU structure (see Figure 5-13). Of course, this structure assumes that PCs are managed centrally. If not, the PC OU structure will resemble the People OU structure outlined later.

The Virtual Service Offerings Object OU Structure

Next, organize the virtual service offerings in your network. This means creating OUs to delegate application servers, such as those from the Microsoft Server System family: SQL Server, Exchange, Host Integration Server, and so on. You'll also want to include more standard roles, such as file server, print server, virtual private network server, and so on. By placing the server objects within these OUs, you can delegate their management and administration without having to give global administrative rights. Each of these servers should be a member server. All of these server roles do not require domain controller status. You should always beware in WS08 when someone wants to install an application or any other service on a domain controller. Each of these services should be created within the Virtual Service Offerings root OU. This way, if you need to apply a policy to all member server objects, you can apply it at the root OU level.

NOTE *In the ADDS OU structure for the VSOs, you will create a service offerings OU that is called Virtual Service Offerings. In the resource pool ADDS, you should call this OU Host Service Offerings. You will not require either the PC or the People OUs in the Resource Pool since users do not interact with it.*

This OU should also include all of the *service accounts*—special administrative accounts that are used to run services in a Windows Server 2008 network. These accounts are all data objects of the same type, they are all sensitive accounts, and they should all use the same policy settings; because of this, they should be stored in a single container. Finally, sub-administrative groups—groups that do not have administrative rights but have higher rights than normal users—such as *support technicians* or *system installers* can be located in an Installer/Technician OU, making it easier to give them rights to other objects in the domain. In addition, a special OU should contain technical groups—groups that are used to provide services but that do not contain users, only other groups. These groups are deemed technical because their only function is to provide services and they do not contain information that is of interest to users. This OU should be named Technical Groups.

The additional advantage this Virtual Service Offerings OU grants is that all system-type objects or objects that are used to provide the IT service are all located within the same OU structure (see Figure 5-13).

The People Object OU Structure

The last OU structure to populate is the People OU. This OU structure will contain either user accounts and/or searchable groups or groups that contain data that is relevant to users. This is also the OU structure that will most resemble your *org chart*. In fact, the org chart is a good information source for regrouping people in your enterprise within the directory. Like the org chart, the People OU structure defines a hierarchy of distinctiveness. The difference is that the two are inversed. The org chart defines a hierarchy of authority (who controls whom), whereas the People OU structure defines the most common to the most distinctive. In the org chart, the employee mass is at the bottom. In the People OU structure, it is at the top.

CAUTION *Many organizations decide to create a separate structure for searchable groups. This has its merits, but it is really unnecessary. If you create your delegation strategy in the proper manner, the same person should be managing both the users and the groups in certain locations in your network. If both are in the same OU, you only have to create one. If not, not only do you have two OUs, but you also have two delegation rules. Avoid redundancy in your OU structure. Keep it as simple as possible.*

When you want to manage all of the People object types, you can do so by applying a Group Policy to the top OU level. The second level of this OU structure should reflect the business unit structure of the organization. This does not necessarily mean the organizational chart structure. Remember: No OU should be created if there is no need for it. While there may be excellent reasons for the creation of administrative units in the organization's administrative structure, it does not mean that these will be reflected in the OU structure. Many organizations only use lines of business at the second level of OUs for the People object.

This OU level may also have special team groupings—business teams whose purpose is to provide administrative support to business units across the organization. It will also contain regional groupings if your organization spans a large geographic territory. In this case, regional groupings are essential, since you must delegate ownership of regional objects to regional administrative representatives.

In most cases, you will generate three general levels of OUs within this OU structure:

- **Root level** Used to manage all People objects (user accounts and searchable groups). This level contains only other OUs and administrative groups supporting the structure.
- **Line-of-business level** Used to manage all user accounts that are within this line of business and located at headquarters or central offices, as well as all searchable

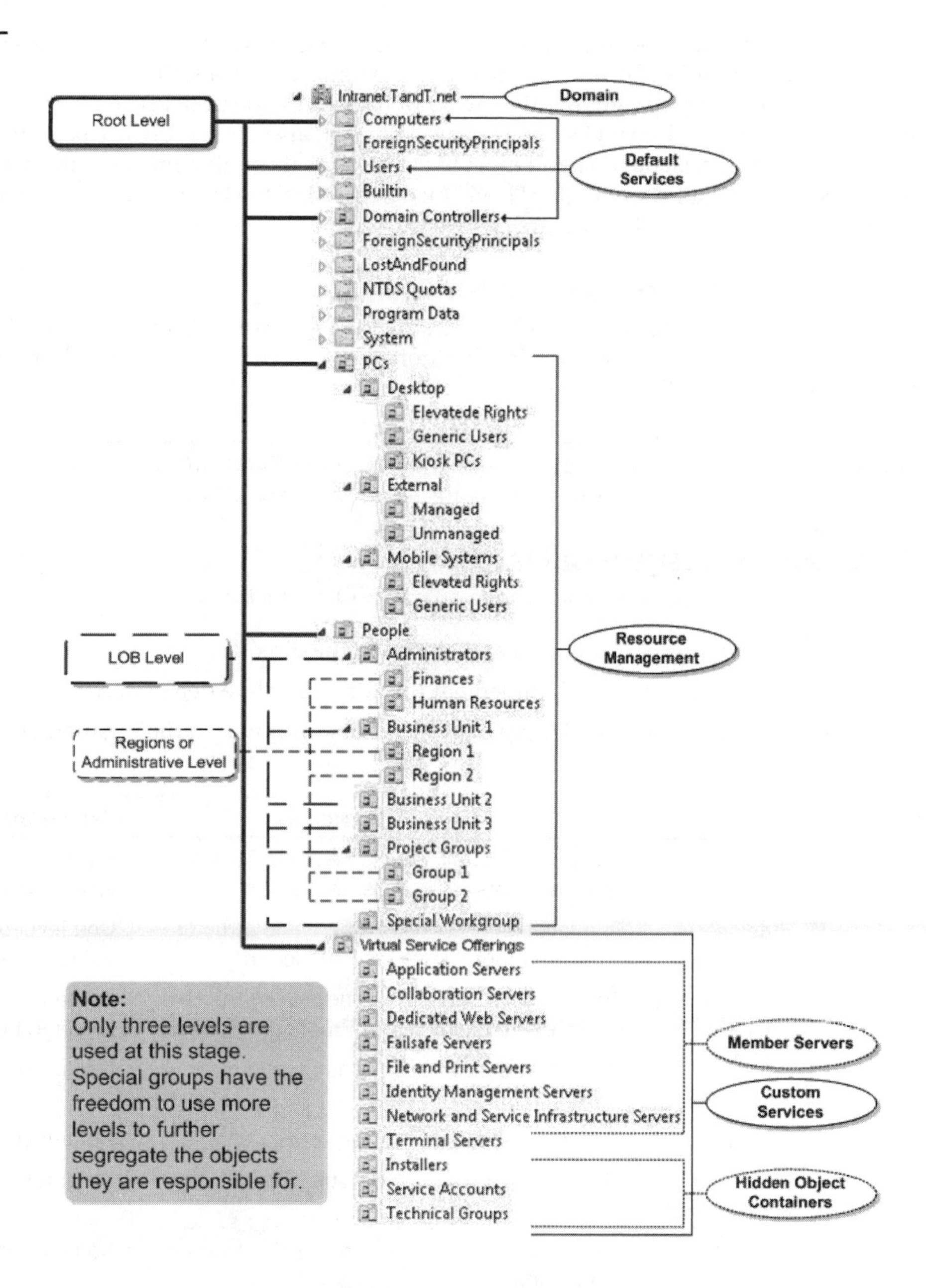

FIGURE 5-13 A complete production OU structure

groups for the entire line of business. The administrative groups to whom this level is delegated are all located within the Root OU.

- **Regional level** Used to manage regional offices. This includes user accounts for every line of business located within the regional office, as well as regional searchable groups. The parent OU for the regional OUs contains every regional administrative group.

The line-of-business level may also contain special groups or administrative services. For example, IT and IS will be found within the organization's administrative line of business, but you can be sure that they will not have the same policies and rights; thus, they are segregated at the third OU level. IT, especially, will also most probably be segregated into further sub-levels, but this will most likely be done through a process internal to the IT department. The final structure for IT will be delegated to the IT group.

This completes the OU structure (see Figure 5-13).

Replicate the OU Structure to Other Domains

Now that you have a solid and complete OU structure, you can replicate it to other domains. Table 5-5 identifies the OU structure in other domains. This completes the forest, tree, domains, and OU structure (see Figure 5-14).

NOTE *The development domain will include default OU structures only, unless the Production OU structure is required for testing. In this case, it will be replicated here.*

Production OU Design Best Practices

Keep the following rules in mind when you create OU structures:

- Think in terms of equipment and objects in the directory.
- Determine how you will implement the administrative delegation process.
- Identify standards for all administrative categories within the organization.

Forest	Domain	PC OU	Service OU	People OU
Production	Training	One level only; all objects in root	Same basic structure as Production	Same as first two levels in Production
	Staging	One level only; all objects in root	Same basic structure as Production	One level only; all objects in root
	Development	Same as first two levels in Production	Same basic structure as Production	Same as first two levels in Production
	Protected Forest Root	Default OUs only	Default OUs only	Default OUs only
Perimeter	Perimeter	Default OUs only	Default OUs only	Default OUs only
Staging	Protected Forest Root	Default OUs only	Default OUs only	Default OUs only
	Production	Same as Production	Same as Production	Same as Production
Development Testing	Forest Root	Default OUs only	Default OUs only	Default OUs only
Utility Forests	Forest Root	Defined as required	Defined as required	Defined as required

TABLE 5-5 OU Structure in Other Domains

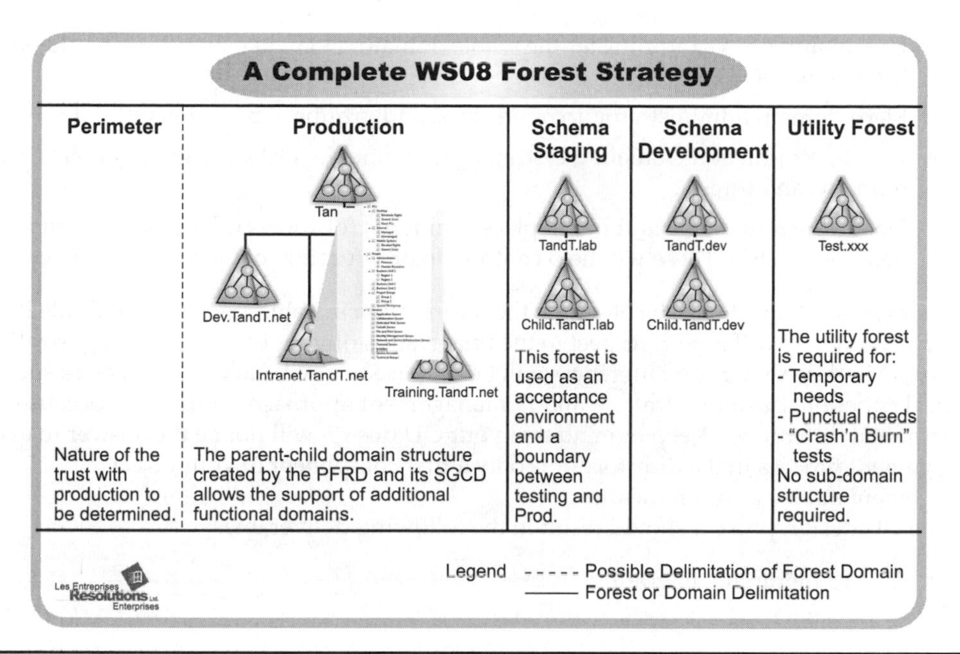

FIGURE 5-14 The complete forest, tree, domain, and OU design for T&T

- Use the administrative service or function or the line of business to name OUs. These tend to be more stable than the organizational structure.
- Choose stable OU names; you want to change OU names as little as possible.
- Limit your structure to five levels, three if you are not responsible for the finalization of the structure. Recommend a maximum of five levels, even though ten are possible. This gives you some breathing room and improves performance.
- Remember the four reasons for the creation of OUs: categorization, administration, delegation, and isolation.
- Each OU you create must add value to the system.
- Never create an OU that does not contain any objects.
- Never create an OU that does not have a specific purpose.
- If an OU reaches an empty state, consider removing it. This may not be necessary because it may only be temporarily empty. If not, remove it.
- Identify an OU owner for each one you create. If no owner can be identified, remove the OU.
- Justify all OUs you create.
- If you find that two OUs have the same purpose, merge them. This means that the combination of owner plus GPO plus delegation strategy is the same between two OUs.

- Use default OUs to administer the whole domain. Domain controllers should be kept in the DC OU.
- Place domain administrator accounts, PCs, and groups in a hidden OU.
- Use the Production Domain OU strategy to define the OU strategy for other domains and forests.
- Don't forget to define and put in place standards for the recurring creation and deletion of OUs. These will help control the proliferation of OUs in your directory.

Your OU strategy should be based on the information in Tables 5-4 and 5-5. While its categorization may differ with respect to the final results of your own object categorization exercise, it is clear that those differences will be minor. They will vary due to factors such as political situation, business strategy, and IT management approach, rather than because of fundamental differences. Keep in mind that your OU design will not be the answer to every management process in the directory. It is only a first component of your object management strategy within the directory.

The OU design process should result in the following deliverables:

- An OU hierarchy diagram
- A list of all OUs
- A description of the contents of each OU
- The purpose of each OU
- A list of groups that have control over each OU
- A list of the object types each group can control in each OU
- The rules for the creation and deletion of OUs within regular operations

ADDS and Other Directories

As you have seen so far, Active Directory Domain Services provides much more than a simple authentication and authorization system. ADDS provides a central identity management system. As such, it will interact with other systems on your network, some of which may already hold identity data. For example, since ADDS provides a central identity management system, other systems that can integrate with ADDS will not require identity management components. Microsoft Exchange is an excellent example of this level of integration. In version 5.5, Exchange required its own complete identity management infrastructure. In the 2000 and later versions, it integrates completely with Active Directory Domain Services and uses the functions of ADDS to manage all identity components.

In this manner, ADDS is comparable to Windows itself. When programmers prepare software for Windows, they do not need to be concerned with how the application will print or how it will interact with a display device; Windows manages all of these components. Thus, the developer only needs to make sure that the new code will work with Windows and concentrate on the functions to be built within the application itself. ADDS provides the same integration features to applications. Application developers no longer need to worry about identity and security management; ADDS provides all of these functions. They can now concentrate on richer product-specific features, and Exchange Server 2007 is an excellent example of this, providing unified messaging while relying on ADDS for system and service integration. In addition, developers can rely on Active Directory Lightweight Directory Services to integrate object extensions. For example, if you want to include a fingerprint hash in your authentication scheme but don't want to modify your ADDS directory structure, you can add this functionality to an ADLDS directory and link it to your ADDS directory. This avoids custom schema extensions that must be replicated through the entire organization and maintains the portability of the solution. If, later on, you want to move from fingerprint hashes to a retinal scan, then you just have to change your ADLDS application with no impact to the ADDS directory or the services it provides.

In addition, you may already have systems—human resource systems, custom corporate applications, enterprise resource planning (ERP) systems, third-party software—that may not integrate directly with ADDS. For each of these systems, you will need to determine which data repository, the original system or Active Directory Domain Services, will be the primary source for specific data records. For example, if ADDS can store the entire organizational structure through the information properties you can add to each user account (location, role, manager, and so on), shouldn't ADDS be the primary source for this information, since it is also the primary source for authentication?

These are the types of decisions you need to make when determining how ADDS will interact with other directories. Will it be the primary information source? If so, you need to ensure that information is fed into and maintained within the directory. This information feed must be part of your initial AD deployment process. You will also need to consider the changes you must make to your corporate systems so that they will obtain primary data from ADDS; otherwise, you will need to maintain several authoritative sources for the same data. If this is the case, you should consider using Microsoft Identity Lifecycle Manager (MILM).

Microsoft Identity Lifecycle Manager

MILM is a special application that is designed to overview multiple directory services and synchronize changes between them, as well as provide lifecycle management of public key infrastructure (PKI) certificates. This provides metadirectory, user provisioning, and certificate management services in one envelope. As a metadirectory, MILM oversees the operations of several directories to ensure data integrity. If you install MILM with ADDS and you identify ADDS as the primary source of information, MILM will automatically modify the values in other directory services when you modify values in ADDS and will ensure that all user data is consistent across directories. In its certificate management function, MILM can help simplify the management of two-factor authentication systems, such as smart cards.

NOTE *More information on Identity Lifecycle Manager can be found at www.microsoft.com/windowsserver/ilm2007/default.mspx.*

Microsoft also offers the Identity Integration Feature Pack (IIFP). The feature pack offers less functionality than MILM, but it does provide some features that are of use when trying to integrate several different directories. IIFP manages identities and coordinates user details across ADDS, ADLDS, and Microsoft Exchange Server (versions 2000 and later). IIFP provides a single logical view of all of a user's or resource's properties and automates the provisioning of identity data for these object types. As a feature pack, IIFP is free to owners of Windows Server licenses.

If your needs expand beyond the products IIFP supports, then focus on MILM, as it provides not only much more functionality, but will also manage data between heterogeneous repositories. MILM is more complex to deploy than IIFP, but both run on member servers and have a simple installation process. Because of the need to store integrated data values, both require a SQL Server database in support of the services they provide.

MILM or IIFP implementations are additional and separate from initial ADDS implementations. But the advantages are clear. If you need to integrate several directories, such as in-house databases, third-party software applications, and even other forests, MILM is the best way to ensure that data is populated from one information source to all others. It will also help you manage the employee move/add/change process, since it provides a single, integrated view of all employee data. Integrating ADDS, ADLDS, ADCS, and MILM or IIFP provides a clear set of functionality (see Figure 5-15).

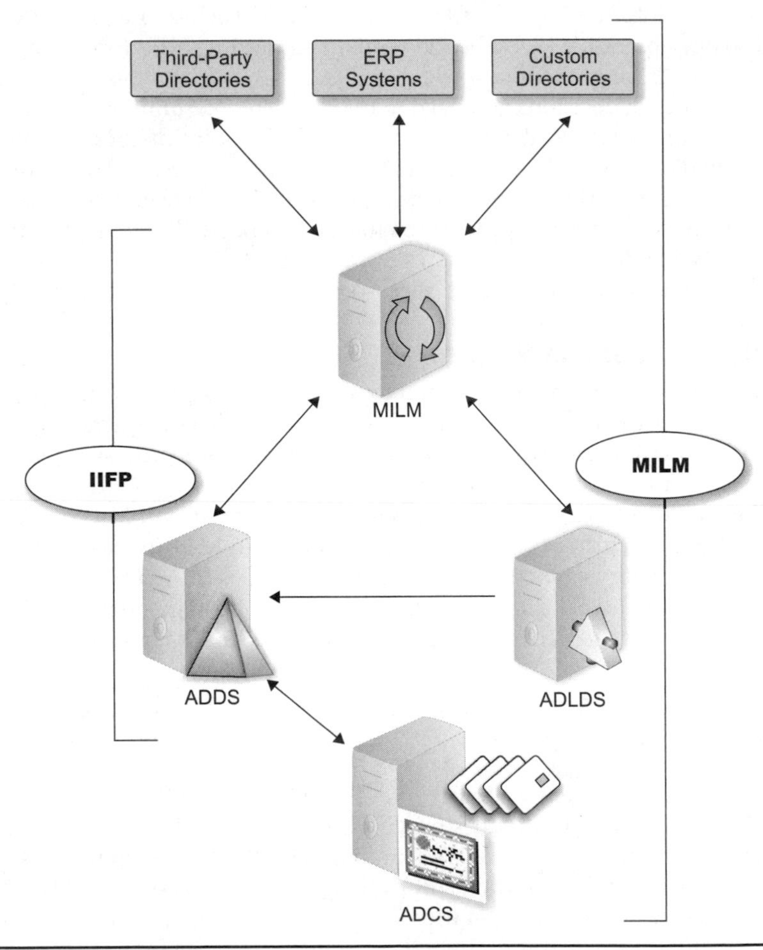

FIGURE 5-15 Integrating ADDS, ADLDS, ADCS, and other directories with IIFP or MILM

Integrated Applications for Network Operating System Directories

Microsoft introduced a new application certification program with Windows 2000: the Windows Logo program. This program continues with Windows Server 2008. Logo-approved applications will integrate with Active Directory to use its identity management and authentication capabilities, as well as to provide full support for all WS08 features. Today, several applications fall within this category. For a complete and up-to-date list of Logo-certified applications for Windows Server 2008, go to www.windowsservercatalog.com.

Integrating a few applications to the directory is inevitable, especially management or directory extension applications. A good example is the Windows Server System (WSS) family. Several of these integrate directly with Active Directory Domain Services, and through this integration, bring modifications or rather extensions to ADDS database schema. These extensions are necessary because each application adds functionality, which is not usually required within a basic ADDS structure. Some examples of applications from the WSS family that change the ADDS schema include:

- **Exchange Server** Exchange, in fact, doubles the size of the ADDS schema, adding twice the object classes and twice the properties.
- **Internet Security and Acceleration Server** ISA modifies the schema to add special ISA objects. This integration streamlines the security, authentication, and management processes for ISA.
- **Host Integration Server** If you require integrated access between a legacy environment and Windows Server 2008, you will require HIS. HIS also extends the ADDS schema to streamline HIS management and authentication.

The reason why it is important to identify how your ADDS structure will integrate with other applications or information sources is because of *schema extensions*. If this is your first implementation of an Active Directory Domain Services structure, you should add all schema modifications when you install your forest root domain. In this way, you will limit the amount of replication on your production network. That's right—every time you make a schema modification, it will be replicated to every domain controller in the forest. If you have regional domain controllers that replicate over WAN lines, massive modifications may incur service outages. Extending the schema within the forest root domain before installing child domains will contain replication and limit it to the installation process for each server.

WS08 supports the population of a domain controller from backup media at installation. This means that while you had to build all domain controllers while they were connected to a high-speed network with Windows 2000, in WS08, as in WS03, you can rebuild and repair DCs remotely so long as you have created an offline copy of the directory with the Windows Backup tool. Domain controllers should still be built in a staging area using a high-speed network during ADDS deployment if possible.

CAUTION *Another reason why it is so important to consider schema extensions so carefully is because they cannot be removed. Once you add a schema extension, you can modify it, but you can never delete it. So be careful what you add to your directory because it will be with you for a long time. The best rule of thumb is to only add necessary extensions. In most cases, the safest extensions to add are those provided by the NOS manufacturer—in this case, Microsoft. If you need to add schema extensions, you should always consider using Active Directory Lightweight Directory Services first.*

ADDS Integration Best Practices

Five activities need to be performed at the ADDS integration stage:

- Position the Active Directory Domain Services structure as the core directory service within the organization.
- Position the role of Active Directory Lightweight Directory Services, if required, in your organization.
- Position the relationship other corporate directories will have with ADDS.
- Identify the interaction model between directory services, and position the role the Identity Integration Feature Pack or Microsoft Identity Lifecycle Manager will play in your organization.
- Determine which operational applications will be integrated in your directory structure.

Use the following best practices during this process:

- Active Directory Domain Services should form the core directory service. ADDS can be modified through a graphical interface. You can also use scripts to perform massive modifications with ADDS. ADDS also supports a powerful delegation model. Finally, it supports PC management, something few directory services can perform.
- Use ADDS as your single point of interaction. ADDS structures provide a single point of interaction because they are based on distributed databases that use a multimaster replication process. Users can modify data in any regional office and have it automatically updated through the directory.
- If you need to maintain data integrity between multiple directories, use Microsoft Identity Lifecycle Manager, with ADDS as your primary data source.
- If you need to install NOS-related applications that modify the schema, add them to the forest root domain *before* creating the child domains.
- If you need to integrate in-house applications with the directory, use Active Directory Lightweight Directory Services. This will have no impact on the ADDS directory.
- Integrate NOS-related and other applications to ADDS only if it is absolutely required. Schema modifications can be retired and reused, but only through a complex process that will involve replication throughout your distributed ADDS directory.
- Maintain your ADDS structure as a NOS directory first and foremost. This will limit the amount of replication in the forest and will make it easier to upgrade to future versions of Windows Server operating systems.

Service Positioning

Now that you have identified the number of forests, trees, and domains in your Active Directory, designed your OU structure, and identified how the directory service will act within your organization, you can move on to service positioning. Service positioning relates to the position and role domain controllers will have within each forest and domain. Domain controllers are the core service providers for Active Directory Domain Services. They provide multimaster replication throughout the entire forest. Some types of information cannot be maintained in a multimaster format. To store and manage this information, some domain controllers have a special role, the Flexible Single Master of Operations (FSMO). Another special role is the Global Catalog; this server supports the research and indexing of forest-wide information. Core Active Directory Domain Services fall into three categories: Flexible Single Master of Operations, Global Catalogs, and generic domain controllers. A fourth category must also be considered if the Active Directory is to stay healthy: the DNS Server.

Flexible Single Masters of Operations Positioning

Flexible Single Masters of Operations (FSMOs) are ADDS systems that manage requests for specific information changes at either the forest or domain level. Without these systems, ADDS cannot operate. They fall into two groups: forest-wide FSMO roles and domain-centric FSMO roles. FSMO, or, as they are sometimes called, Operations Master, roles are called flexible roles, because even though only a single instance in the forest or the domain can exist, this instance is not rooted to a given server; it can be transferred from one domain controller to another. It is flexible and it is single because it must be unique within its scope of influence.

Forest-wide Operations Master roles are:

- **Schema Master** The master system that maintains the structure of the forest database and authorizes schema changes.
- **Domain Naming Master** The master system that controls and authorizes domain naming within the forest.

Only a single instance of each system can exist in the forest at a given time. Both systems can be located on the same domain controller if required. In large forests, these systems are distributed on two separate domain controllers.

In addition to forest-wide FSMO roles, there are domain-centric FSMO roles. If you only have one domain in your forest, you will have a single instance of each of these roles, but if you have more than one domain, every domain will have one instance of each of these systems. These include:

- **Relative ID (RID) Master** The master system that is responsible for the assignation of relative IDs to other domain controllers within the domain. Whenever a new object—user, computer, server, or group—is created within a domain, the domain controller that is performing the operation will assign a unique ID number. This number consists of a domain identification number, followed by a relative identification number, that is assigned at object creation. When a domain controller runs out of its pool of relative IDs, it requests an additional pool from the RID Master. The relative ID role is also the

PART III

placeholder for the domain. If you need to move objects between domains in the same forest, you need to initiate the move from the RID Master.

- **Primary Domain Controller (PDC) Emulator** The master service that provides backward compatibility to Windows NT. If there are Windows NT domain controllers or Windows NT network clients within the domain, this server acts as the primary domain controller for the domain. It manages all replication to backup domain controllers.

  If there are no legacy Windows (read pre-Windows 2000) clients or DCs in the forest structure, then the forest can operate in full functional mode. In this case, the PDC Emulator focuses on its two other roles: *time synchronization* on all DCs and *preferential account modification replication* to other DCs. All domain controllers in the domain will set their clock according to the PDC Emulator, as will all member servers and PCs. In addition, any account modification that is critical—password modification, account deactivation—will immediately be replicated to the PDC Emulator from the originating server. If a logon attempt fails on a given DC, the DC checks with the PDC Emulator before rejecting the attempt because it may not have received recent password changes. The PDC Emulator supports two authentication protocols: Kerberos V5 (Windows 2000 and later) and NTLM (Windows NT).

  The final role of the PDC Emulator is preferential Group Policy management. By default, all GPOs are stored first and foremost on the PDC Emulator. If it is not available, they will be stored on other servers.

- **Infrastructure Master** The master system that manages two critical tasks:
  - The update of references from objects in its domain to objects in other domains. This is how the forest knows to which domain an object belongs. The Infrastructure Master has a close relationship to the Global Catalog (GC). If it finds that some of its objects are out of date compared to the GC, it will request an update from the GC and send the updated information to other DCs within the domain.

CAUTION *The Global Catalog service and the Infrastructure Master system should not be stored on the same DC, unless there is only one server in the forest or the forest root domain is very small. Problems can arise if they are on the same computer, because the Infrastructure Master shares the same database as the Global Catalog. It will not be able to tell if it is out of date or not. Thus, it will never request updates. In a large forest, this can cause other DCs to be out of synch with GC contents.*

  - The second function it fulfills is the update and modification of group members within the domain. If a group includes objects from another domain and these objects are renamed or moved, the Infrastructure Master will maintain the consistency of the group and replicate it to all other domain controllers. This ensures that users maintain access rights, even though you perform maintenance operations on their accounts.

These domain-centric master roles should be separated, if possible. This depends, of course, on the size of each domain. Whatever its size, each domain should have at least two domain controllers for redundancy, load balancing, and availability.

Global Catalog Server Positioning

The Global Catalog is also a special domain controller role. Any domain controller can operate as a Global Catalog. The GC is the server that holds a copy of forest-wide database contents within each domain. By default, it includes about 20 percent of forest data—everything that has been marked within the forest database schema as having forest-wide interest.

The GC has three functions:

- **Find objects** The GC holds information about users and other objects in your domain. User queries about objects are automatically sent to TCP port number 3268 and routed to the GC server.
- **Allow UPN logons** Users can log on to other domains across the forest using their User Principal Name (UPN). If the domain controller validating the user does not know the user, it will refer to the Global Catalog. Because the GC holds information about every user in the forest, it will complete the logon process if it is allowed by the user's rights.
- **Support universal groups** All universal groups are stored within the Global Catalog so that they can be available forest-wide. If a GC is not available at logon, logon is denied because the user's universal groups cannot be enumerated. Since these groupings can include access denials, the logon is denied.

Native WS08 forests have enhanced GC functionality because they gain the features of a fully functional WS03 forest. For example, they can replicate only universal group modifications instead of the entire universal group when changes are made. In addition, native WS08 DCs can cache users' universal membership data, removing the need to constantly consult the GC, so the GC service does not need to be as widespread as in Windows 2000 networks.

The GC service should, however, be widely available. If your network spans several regions, you should place at least one GC DC per region. If it is not practical to place a GC locally, then you should enable Universal Group Membership (UGM) Caching for all DCs in the region. Placing the GC server in the region will ensure that universal group logon requests are not sent over the WAN. The WAN is required for the first logon attempt if no GC is present in the region, even if UGM Caching is enabled, because the logon DC must locate a GC server. Local GC servers are also useful for applications using port 3268 for authentication requests. Consider potential cross-domain logons when determining where to place GC servers.

Domain Controller Positioning

Positioning both FSMO roles and Global Catalogs is positioning domain controllers, because each of these services or systems will only operate on a domain controller. As mentioned before, in a single domain forest, all of the FSMO roles and the GC could run on a single DC. Even then, the best-practice rule is to always have two DCs. But in a medium to large network, these roles are usually distributed among several domain controllers.

In addition to performing these roles, domain controllers support authentication and multimaster replication. This means that the more users you have, the more DCs you will need if you want to keep your login time short. Large multiprocessing servers running the DC service can handle millions of requests a day. Regional servers, though, tend to have several additional functions, as they often become multipurpose servers. Regional servers also often tend to be smaller in capacity than centralized servers. If they are multipurpose servers as well, consider adding DCs whenever the user load exceeds 50 users per server.

If some of your regional sites have fewer than ten users, don't place a domain controller in the site. Instead, use Terminal Services to create terminal sessions for the users in the closest site containing a DC. All logons will be performed at the remote site. But if you can afford it, place a DC in each site that has more than ten users.

Use the read-only DC role whenever you cannot guarantee the physical security of the DC. RODCs do not participate in the multimaster replication scheme, since they only receive data and cannot be used to initiate a replication. This protects your directory from tampering.

The best way to determine how many DCs to position across your network is to evaluate network performance. In many cases, it is a matter of judgment. Define a rule of thumb based on your network performance and stick to it. You can also predict the number of DCs during the site topology exercise.

DNS Server Positioning

Network performance is exactly the reason why the DNS service is the fourth ADDS service that needs positioning for optimal directory operations. Since part of the ADDS structure is based on the Domain Naming System, and since all logons must resolve the name and location of a domain controller before being validated, the DNS service has become a core ADDS service. When positioning services for ADDS, you will quickly learn to marry the DNS service with the domain controller service.

In Windows Server 2008, as in Windows 2000 and 2003, every domain controller in every domain in every forest should also be a Domain Naming server. Why? Because ADDS uses DNS to locate objects in the network and because DNS data can be integrated with the directory. If DNS is configured to integrate with ADDS, it can become completely secured. You can ensure that only trusted network objects and sources will update information in the DNS partition of Active Directory Domain Services. Directory integration also means secure replication. Since DNS data is integrated to the directory, it is replicated with the directory to every domain controller.

DNS data can also be stored in application partitions, which are directory partitions that can designate which domain controllers are to store the information. For example, in a multidomain forest, WS08 automatically creates a forest root domain DNS data application partition that spans the entire forest. This means that since the data is replicated to every domain controller in the forest, root domain name resolution will always work everywhere.

ADDS brings many new concepts to the Domain Naming System. This is why DNS should change from a simple IP service to an integrated ADDS service.

TIP *In an initial ADDS design, one firm elected to have DCs located in every one of ten regional sites, but the DNS service was only made available within the DCs located in the two central sites. This means that at every logon, users needed to make a WAN connection to the central sites, despite the fact that the DNS data was locally available within their DC. Adding the DNS service to regional DCs saw a 75 percent decrease in logon times and a lot of happy users.*

Server Positioning Best Practices

Use the following rules to design your service positioning scenario:

- In large ADDS structures, place the forest-wide FSMO roles in a protected forest root domain.
- If your forest spans multiple sites, place the Schema Master in one site and the Domain Naming Master in another.
- Carefully protect access to the Schema Master role.
- In smaller ADDS structures, place the RID Master and the PDC Emulator roles on the same DC.
- Create a dedicated PDC Emulator role in domains that have more than 50,000 users.
- Separate Global Catalogs and Infrastructure Masters if you can.
- Place at least two domain controllers in each domain.
- If a small domain spans two sites, use at least two domain controllers—one for each site.
- Place a Global Catalog server in each geographic site that contains at least one domain controller.
- Enable Universal Group Membership Caching in each geographic site that does not include a local GC.
- Use read-only DCs wherever you apply UGM Caching.
- Use RODCs whenever you cannot guarantee the security of the DC, but absolutely need a local DC for performance reasons.
- Place a domain controller wherever there are more than ten users, unless the WAN link speed will adequately support remote logon attempts.
- Add a regional domain controller whenever there are more than 50 users per DC, especially if it is a multipurpose server.
- Install the Domain Naming Service on every domain controller.
- Use application partitions to designate DNS replication scopes.

Server Positioning Scenario

The best way to learn how to perform server positioning is to use scenarios. In this scenario, the T&T Corporation endeavors to create and populate its ADDS structure. It has more than 10,000 users. It has decided to use a multidomain production forest. Its headquarters are in a single city, but in separate buildings. Both buildings are linked together through a metropolitan area network (MAN) operating at high speed. In addition, it has 15 regional offices—some in other metropolitan areas that are of considerable size (see Figure 5-16). In these metropolitan areas, satellite offices use local links to "hop" into the wide area network.

T&T needs to position its domain controllers, Global Catalogs, DNS, and FSMO roles. Table 5-6 describes the position of each domain within each region.

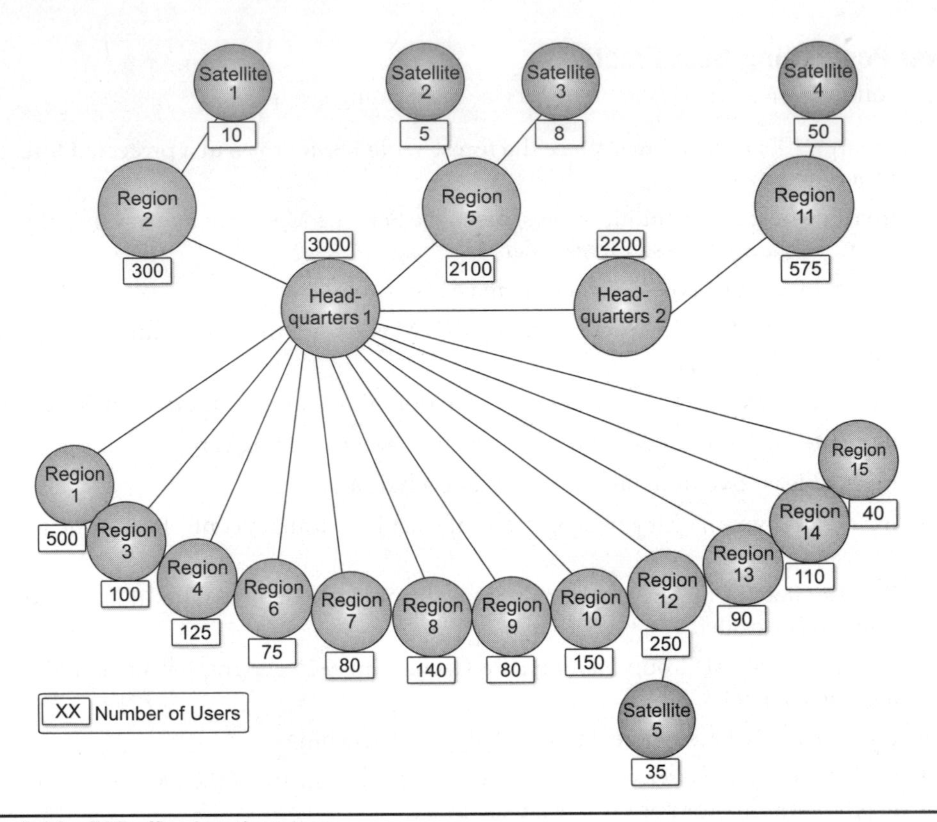

FIGURE 5-16 T&T office locations map

NOTE *In Table 5-6, development users include the developers themselves, as well as test accounts, while users in the training domain only represent generic accounts.*

As you can see, the first step for T&T in this phase is to identify the geographical layout of its offices. Once this is done, T&T can proceed to server positioning. Using the rules outlined previously, T&T will begin the positioning process. It needs to proceed systematically; as such, it will place servers in the following order:

1. The first servers to position are the forest-wide FSMO roles. These will be within the protected forest root domain (PFRD): Schema Master and Domain Naming Master.
2. Next will be the domain-centric FSMO roles of the PFRD: RID Master, PDC Emulator, and Infrastructure Master. These should be positioned according to the best practices outlined earlier.
3. The size (number of users) and location of the PFRD will help determine the number of domain controllers required to operate the PFRD.
4. If PFRD DCs are separated physically, the Global Catalog service should be added in each location that includes at least one DC.

	Region	Domain	Number of users
1)	HQ Main	Dedicated Root	7
2)	HQ Main	Production	3,000
3)	HQ Main	Development	200
4)	HQ Main	Training	300
5)	HQ Main	Staging	20
6)	HQ Site 2	Production	2,200
7)	HQ Site 2	Development	250
8)	HQ Site 2	Training	200
9)	Region 1	Production	500
10)	Region 2	Production	300
11)	Region 3	Production	100
12)	Region 4	Production	125
13)	Region 5	Production	2,100
14)	Region 6	Production	75
15)	Region 7	Production	80
16)	Region 8	Production	140
17)	Region 9	Production	80
18)	Region 10	Production	150
19)	Region 11	Production	575
20)	Region 12	Production	250
21)	Region 13	Production	90
22)	Region 14	Production	110
23)	Region 15	Production	40
24)	Satellite 1 (Region 2)	Production	10
25)	Satellite 2 (Region 5)	Production	5
26)	Satellite 3 (Region 5)	Production	8
27)	Satellite 4 (Region 11)	Production	50
28)	Satellite 5 (Region 12)	Production	35
Total			10,750

TABLE 5-6 Production Forest Server Positioning Scenario Information

5. Next are the child domain DCs. Begin with the production domain because it is the most complex. The first services to position are the domain-centric FSMO roles: RID Master, PDC Emulator, and Infrastructure Master.

PART III

6. Now that the core roles are positioned, position domain controllers. A DC should be positioned in each region with at least 50 users. Regions with more than 50 users should have more than one DC. Regions with less than 50 users should be gauged on an as-needed basis. Set a rule of thumb for DC positioning in large sites: one DC per 1000 users (remember, central DCs tend to be more powerful servers than regional DCs).

NOTE *You can use a downloadable tool from Microsoft, the AD Sizer, to calculate how many users a DC will handle. In fact, it will tell you that you can manage more than 40,000 users per DC. This may be overly optimistic, however, because DCs have other roles than simply managing user logons. Test performance and determine if the 1000-user rule is appropriate for your network.*

7. Each region that has at least one DC also hosts at least one Global Catalog, if possible. If not, use UGM Caching in the site. Also use read-only DCs in these sites.
8. Next, position FSMO roles, GCs, and DCs for the three other domains: development, training, and staging. Staging is easy, since it is located in a single geographical site; two servers are more than adequate. Training can also perform with two DCs: one in each HQ office. The positioning of development DCs will depend on the level of activity. It is not unusual for development DCs to be used for stress testing analysis. In such situations, the development DC needs to host as many users as the entire production domain.
9. The easiest is kept for last. Position the DNS service wherever there is a DC.
10. Use application partitions to determine how DNS information should be shared from domain to domain.
11. Also, it is safe to position the GC role with the Infrastructure role in the PFRD because the root domain holds very few objects and will not affect replication.
12. An interdomain application partition is used between the production and development domains. Users from the development domain often require information from the production domain. Because of the partition, this information is automatically made available to them.
13. A local domain application partition for DNS data is used in the development domain because queries from the development domain to other domains are rare. The same applies to the training and staging domains.

The result is described in Table 5-7. Keep in mind that the DNS strategy is described in more detail in Chapter 6.

As you can see, the server positioning stage requires the application of a given set of rules to the data you have collected on your organization to produce a working result. T&T Corporation, for example, will implement the servers and the roles identified in Table 5-7. They will have three server models: one for regions where servers are protected, one for regions where servers are not protected (RODC), and one for large offices [dedicated Domain Controllers (DCs)].

Region	Domain	Users	Servers	Role
HQ Main	Dedicated Root	7	1	First DC in the forest: • Forest FSMO: Schema Master • Domain FSMO: PDC and RID • Global Catalog • Integrated DNS—Forest-wide application partition
HQ Site 2	Dedicated Root	7	1	Second DC in the forest: • Forest FSMO: Domain Naming Master • Domain FSMO: Infrastructure • Global Catalog • Integrated DNS—Forest-wide application partition
HQ Main	Production	3,000	3	First domain DC: • Domain FSMO: PDC • Global Catalog • Integrated DNS—Interdomain application partition Second domain DC: • Domain FSMO: RID • Integrated DNS—Interdomain application partition Other DCs: • DC role only • Integrated DNS
HQ Site 2	Production	2,200	3	FSMO domain DC: • Domain FSMO: Infrastructure • Integrated DNS—Interdomain application partition GC domain DC: • Global Catalog • Integrated DNS—Interdomain application partition Other DCs: • DC role only • Integrated DNS

TABLE 5-7 T&T Server Positioning Results

Region	Domain	Users	Servers	Role
Region 1 Region 2 Region 3 Region 4 Region 5 Region 6 Region 7 Region 8 Region 9 Region 10 Region 11 Region 12 Region 13 Region 14 Region 15	Production	250 300 100 125 2,100 75 80 140 80 150 575 250 90 110 40	2 2 2 2 2 1 1 2 1 2 2 2 1 1 1	GC domain DC: • Global Catalog • Integrated DNS—Interdomain application partition Other DCs: • DC role only • Integrated DNS
Satellite 1 (Region 2) Satellite 2 (Region 5) Satellite 3 (Region 5)	Production	10 5 8	0	n/a
Satellite 4 (Region 11) Satellite 5 (Region 12)	Production	50 35	1 1	Read-only DC: • Universal Group Membership Caching • Integrated DNS
HQ Main	Development	200	1	First domain DC: • Domain FSMO: PDC and RID • Global Catalog • Integrated DNS—Local domain application partition
HQ Site 2	Development	250	1	Second domain DC: • Domain FSMO: Infrastructure • Global Catalog • Integrated DNS—Local domain application partition
HQ Main	Training	300	1	First domain DC: • Domain FSMO: PDC and RID • Global Catalog • Integrated DNS—Local domain application partition

TABLE 5-7 T&T Server Positioning Results (*continued*)

Region	Domain	Users	Servers	Role
HQ Site 2	Training	200	1	Second domain DC: • Domain FSMO: Infrastructure • Global Catalog • Integrated DNS—Local domain application partition
HQ Main	Staging	20	2	First domain DC: • Domain FSMO: PDC and RID • Global Catalog • Integrated DNS—Local domain application partition Second domain DC: • Domain FSMO: Infrastructure • Global Catalog • Integrated DNS—Local domain application partition
Total		10,750	40	

TABLE 5-7 T&T Server Positioning Results *(continued)*

NOTE *With the advent of virtual service offerings, your regional DCs can and should become virtual machines. In this case, you do not need to create multipurpose DCs since they are harder to manage. When using virtual machine, it does not cost any more to create a dedicated regional DC and then create another virtual machine to run the other roles that are normally shared on the multipurpose DC such as file or print services.*

T&T will also need to monitor performance on these servers to ensure that service response times run as expected. If not, they will need to refine their model. If that is the case, they will need to update Table 5-7 to ensure that it always reflects reality. The server positioning strategy for T&T Corporation is illustrated in Figure 5-17. For simplicity's sake, this figure only includes the root and production domains.

Another factor that will affect this evaluation is the network speeds at which each office is linked with others. Analyzing network speeds and adjusting directory replication is what the next stage, site topology design, is all about.

Site Topology

The Active Directory design is almost complete; only two further stages are required: site topology design and schema modification strategy. Site topology design relates to the analysis of the speed of all WAN links that bind the forest together and the identification of the forest replication strategy. A site is a physical replication partition. Replication is key to the proper operation of ADDS.

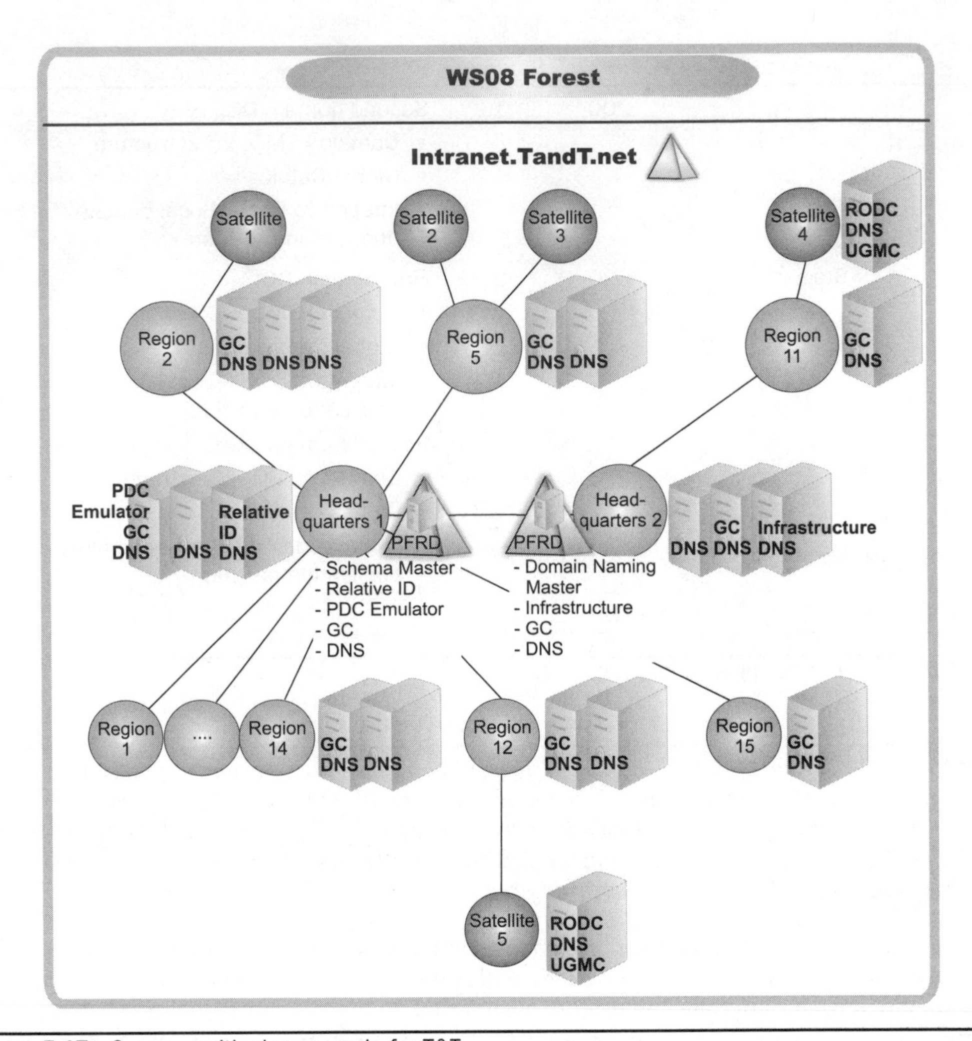

Figure 5-17 Server positioning scenario for T&T

Windows Server 2008 DCs replicate information on an ongoing basis because they are all authoritative for certain portions of forest information, except, of course, for the RODCs. This multimaster environment requires constant replication if the distributed forest DCs are to be kept up to date. WS08 can perform two types of replication: intrasite and intersite. Intrasite replication is at high speed because it uses the local area network. Local servers are also often on high-speed links to ensure faster information transfer between them. Intrasite replication occurs constantly because the link speed can support it. Because it is constant and because the link speed can support it, intrasite replication is not compressed.

Intersite replication occurs at lower speeds because it must cross a WAN link to other offices. Intersite replication must be scheduled and compressed; otherwise, it will use more than the available bandwidth. The process of creating ADDS sites is the process of identifying if replication between servers is intra- or intersite. A site is a physical regrouping of servers. A site is usually defined as a TCP/IP subnet. It can be a virtual local area network (VLAN)—a group of network nodes that are strung together in a single subnet within a geographic location—or a regional subnet. Intersite replication occurs at 15-minute intervals. Two transport modes are supported: Internet Protocol (IP) and Simple Mail Transfer Protocol (SMTP). *Never* consider SMTP for intradomain replication! It is more complicated to set up than IP, and it is an asynchronous replication method because changes are sent in discrete messages that may arrive out of order. Who hasn't sent a message to someone only to have it come back a week later telling you the person never received it? No wonder they didn't answer! You can't take the chance that this will happen with directory replication data. SMTP replication should only be considered in the most extreme situations, even for intersite replication.

IP uses Remote Procedure Calls (RPC) to send changes to other DCs. It uses the Knowledge Consistency Checker (KCC) to determine automatic routes between replication partners. For this to occur between sites, a site link must be created between each site that contains a domain controller. This site link includes costing information. The KCC can use this information when determining when to replicate, how to replicate, and the number of servers to replicate with. Special values, such as password changes or account deactivations, are replicated immediately to the PDC Emulator in the domain, despite site-specific schedules. Intersite replication data is also compressed. ADDS compresses replication data through a compression algorithm. Data is automatically compressed whenever it reaches a certain threshold. Usually, anything greater than 50 kilobytes (KB) will automatically be compressed when replicated between sites.

In a forest running in WS08 functional mode, you should enable linked value replication. This option greatly reduces replication by sending only the values that have changed for any multivalued attribute, such as groups. Whenever a change is made to a group member, such as a new member addition, only the changed value (the new member) is replicated instead of the entire group. In addition, this functional mode relies on DFS replication, replicating only the delta changes of any content.

Site Topology Design

To perform site topology design, you need the following elements:

- A map for all site localizations.
- The WAN topology and link speeds for each location. Router configuration is also important. In addition, the TCP/IP ports that are required for replication are often closed by default. These ports are identified in Chapter 6.
- The number of DCs in each site.

Site design is simple: It should follow the enterprise TCP/IP network design. Sites are IP subnets; thus, they have the same structure as that already in place for TCP/IP. Now you can proceed with the design. This will result in the creation of:

- Site boundaries for each geographic location
- Site replication links
- Backup replication links
- Costing scheme for each link

Sites are independent of the domain structure. This means that you could have multiple domains within a site and multiple sites within a domain, as well as multiple sites and multiple domains within a wide area network.

Forest replication is divided into three categories: forest-wide, application partition, and domain-centric replication. Both forest-wide and application partition replication span domains. Fortunately, the data replicated through these partitions is relatively small. This is not the same for domains. Production domains, especially, contain vast amounts of information. This is the core reason for site topology design: data availability between separate sites in the same domain.

Production domains should be split if they must replicate over link speeds of 56 kilobits (Kbit) per second or lower. Very large production domains require high-speed WAN links if they are to span regional offices, even though data is compressed and replication is scheduled. If vast amounts of data must be sent, the "pipeline" sending it must be big enough for the time allowed. In very large sites with low-speed links, it is possible to have a situation where replication never completes. The replication window opens at intervals that are smaller than the time it takes to replicate all changed data.

Site link routes should resemble the basic IP structure of your WAN. The cost of each link should reflect the link speed; the lower the cost, the higher the speed. Lower costs also mean faster replication. Keep in mind that costs are simply values you use to tell ADDS replication that one link is better than another. Table 5-8 identifies sample link costs for given bandwidths.

Create Site Link Bridges

In some cases, it is necessary to bridge replication. If you create site links that overlap, you should create a site link bridge (see Figure 5-18). This will allow the replication to use the bridging site to create a direct connection to the destination site. If you want to further control intersite replication within given sites, you can designate preferred bridgehead servers at the site. The bridgehead server manages all intersite replication within a site. All updates are received and sent through the bridgehead server. Thus, no other DCs in the site need dedicate resources to intersite replication. If you designate bridgehead servers, however the KCC will no longer be able to calculate replication routes automatically. You will have to monitor replication closely to ensure that all sites are up to date.

Available Bandwidth	Suggested Cost for Prime Link	Suggested Cost for Backup Link
56	Separate domain	n/a
64	750	1000
128	500	750
256	400	500
512	300	400
1024	150	300
T1	100	150

Table 5-8 Recommended Link Cost per Available Bandwidth

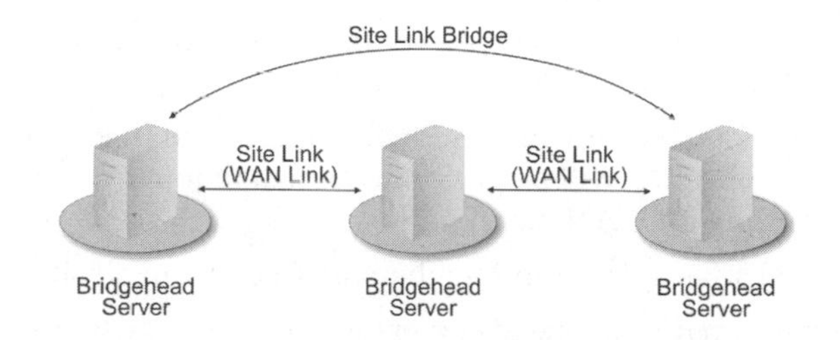

FIGURE 5-18 A site link bridge with bridgehead servers

It is a good idea to calculate replication latency—the time between a modification on a DC and the reception of the modification on all other DCs—in the site topology. This will allow you to identify what the longest possible replication delay can be within your network. Replication latency is calculated based on the replication interval—the time it can take to replicate data—and the number of hops required to perform replication. For example, if your site topology includes two hops, your replication interval is set at 180 minutes, and it takes 30 minutes to complete a replication change, your replication latency will be 420 minutes (180 times 2, plus 30 minutes times 2). Also, remember to base all your replication calculations on available bandwidth, not global bandwidth. If only 10 percent of bandwidth is available for ADDS replication, it will affect your calculations.

Finally, as mentioned before, the Universal Group Membership Caching option is assigned to sites within a native WS08 forest. This option should be set for all sites that do not have a GC. DCs in these sites will be able to cache requesting users' Universal Group Memberships, reducing the amount of communications with the server hosting the Global Catalog.

Best Practices for Site Topology Design

Use the following best practices to design your site topology:

- Use the default configuration for intersite replication.
- Do not disable the Knowledge Consistency Checker.
- Do not disable transitive trusts.
- Do not specify bridgehead servers.
- Calculate replication latency between sites.
- Create sites according to network topology; site links and WAN links should correspond.
- Make sure that no single site is connected to more than 20 other sites.
- Each site must house at least one DC.
- Do not use SMTP for domain-centric replication.
- Do not use SMTP replication if at all possible.
- Use 128 Kbps as the minimum WAN circuit for a site link.
- Associate every site with at least one subnet and one site link; otherwise, it will be unusable.
- Create backup site links for each site. Assign higher costs to backup site links.

- Create site link bridges wherever there are two or more hops between sites to reduce replication latency.
- If your available network bandwidth can afford it, ignore replication schedules in all sites. Replication will be performed when required with this option, but it will be demanding on WAN bandwidth.
- Enable Universal Group Membership Caching in all sites that do not host a GC.
- Use preferred bridgehead servers if replication must cross a firewall.
- Size your DCs accordingly, as replication affects performance.
- Monitor replication traffic once your forest is in place to determine the impact on your WAN links.

T&T Corporation's Site Topology Scenario

T&T's site topology (see Figure 5-19) is once again based on the information displayed previously in Figure 5-17, as well as on the WAN link speed for each site. Using this information, T&T produced the grid outlined in Table 5-9.

T&T used some global settings in their site topology design. These included:

- Open schedules for all sites.
- KCC on by default in all sites.
- All site link costs decrease as they get closer to HQ1, so HQ1 replication is prioritized.
- Replication is only performed with RPC over IP.
- Default schedules are enabled in all sites (replication every 180 minutes).
- High-priority replication can occur immediately.
- Every site has a backup replication route at a higher cost.
- Everything is based on calculated available bandwidth.

Of course, T&T will need to monitor AD replication performance during the operation of the directory to ensure that the values in this table are appropriate to meet service levels. If not, both the table and the site links will need to be updated.

NOTE *The perimeter forest is also included in Table 5-9 and Figure 5-19 in order to demonstrate the potential use of bridgehead servers. If you do not have a perimeter forest, then you will probably have no need of bridgehead servers. If you use ADFS, then you will not place DCs in the DMZ.*

Schema Modification Strategy

Now that your forest design is done, you can put it in place. The final process you need to complete is the outline of your schema modification strategy. Operating an Active Directory Domain Services structure is managing a distributed database. Modifying the structure of that database has an impact on every service provider in the forest. Adding object classes or object class attributes must be done with care and in a controlled manner. Adding components

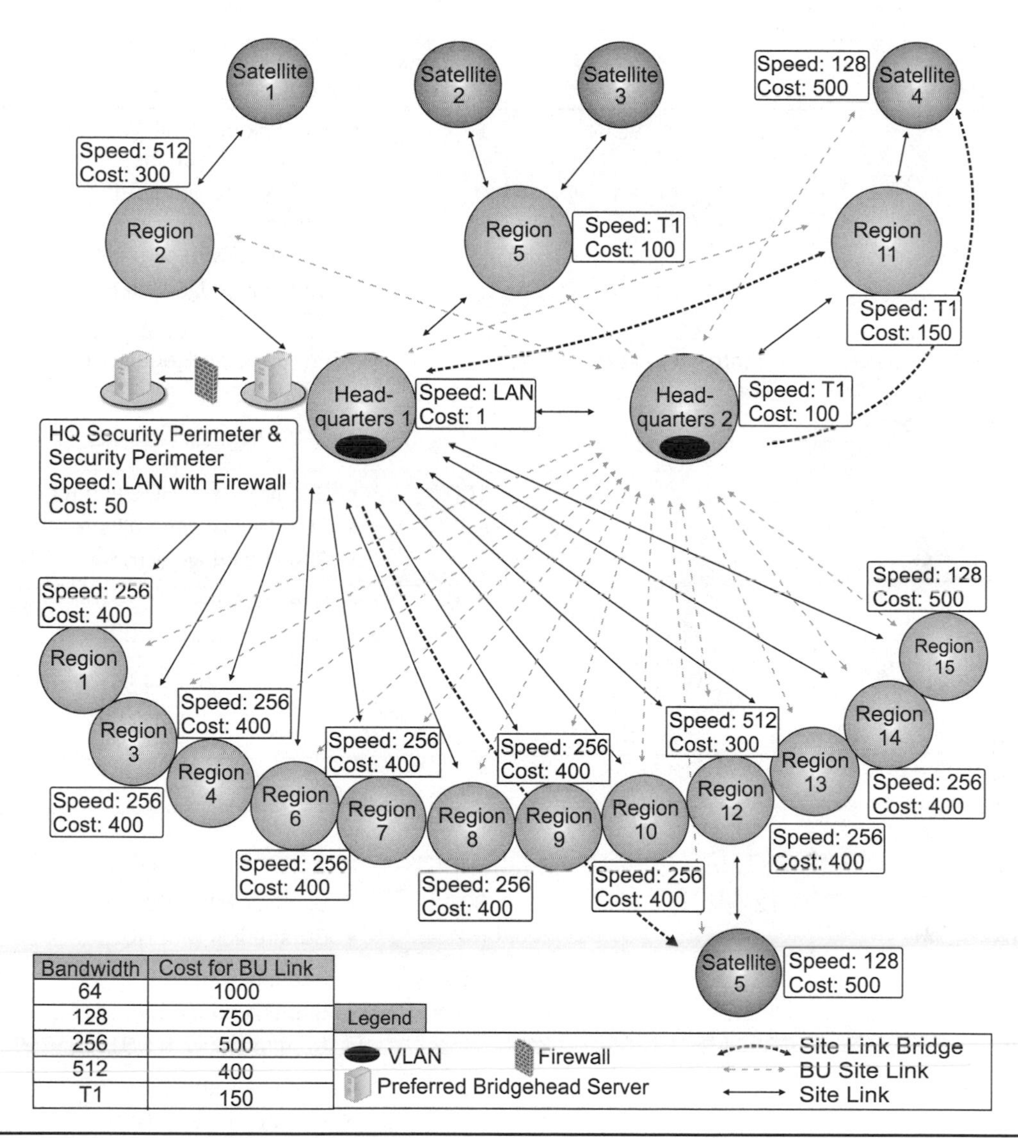

Bandwidth	Cost for BU Link
64	1000
128	750
256	500
512	400
T1	150

FIGURE 5-19 T&T's site topology design

always implies added replication at the time of the modification. It may also mean added replication on a recurring basis, depending on the contents of the addition. Retiring components also implies added replication at the time of modification. It may mean reduced ongoing replication because you are removing an item from replication. Forests operating in WS08 functional mode support the reuse of certain types of deactivated object classes or attributes. But this reuse can be tricky to implement. It's best to always be sure and proceed carefully when modifications are required.

Expect your ADDS database schema to be modified. Even simple tools, such as enterprise backup software, will sometimes modify the schema to create backup objects within

Site Link Name	Link Speed to HQ	Site Link Type	Site Link Cost	Options
HQ Main	LAN	VLAN	1	• Site link available (VLANs for server connections) • KCC on (default setting for all sites) • Site links with all sites • Site link bridge with S5 and R11
HQ Main to Security Perimeter Security Perimeter to HQ Main	LAN with Firewall	VLAN	50	• Preferred bridgehead server
HQ Site 2 Region 5	T1	VLAN	100	• Site links with HQ1 and R11 • BU site links with all sites • Site link bridge with S4
Region 1 Region 3 Region 4 Region 6 Region 7 Region 8 Region 9 Region 10 Region 13 Region 14	256	Regional	400	• Site link with HQ1 • BU site link with HQ2
Region 2 Region 12	512	Regional	300	• Site link with HQ1 • BU site link with HQ2
Region 11	T1	VLAN	150	• Site link with HQ2 • Site link bridge with HQ1 • BU site link with HQ1
Region 15	128	Regional	500	• Site link with HQ1 • BU site link with HQ2
Satellite 1 (Region 2) Satellite 2 (Region 5) Satellite 3 (Region 5)	64	n/a	n/a	n/a
Satellite 4 (Region 11) Satellite 5 (Region 12)	128	Regional	500	• Site link with R11 • One-way site link bridge with HQ2 • BU site link with HQ2

TABLE 5-9 T&T Site Topology

the directory. Without a doubt, some of the commercial server tools you acquire—be they only Microsoft Exchange—will modify your production ADDS schema.

In addition, you may want to take advantage of schema extensions for your own purposes. You will definitely shorten application development timelines if you choose to store frequently requested information in a directory. ADDS will automatically replicate information throughout your enterprise if it is part of the directory. Be careful what information you include in the directory. Because of their multimaster and hierarchical models, ADDS is not designed to provide immediate data consistency. There is always replication latency when more than a single DC is involved. Use the directory to store static information that is required in every site but that is unlikely to change often. You can also rely on Active Directory Lightweight Directory Services. As its name implies, ADLDS provides a lightweight means to use the functionality of a directory, including replication, but without the heaviness of modifying your ADDS schema.

However you decide to use your directory, one thing is sure: You should always be careful with schema modifications within the production directory. The best way to do so is to form a schema modification policy. This policy is upheld by a schema change policy holder (SCPH) to whom all schema changes are presented for approval. The policy will outline not only who holds the SCPH role, but also how schema modifications are to be tested, prepared, and deployed. Assigning the SCPH role to manage the schema ensures that modifications will not be performed on an ad hoc basis by groups that do not communicate with each other. Since all modifications must be approved by the SCPH first and foremost, the process is clear for everyone.

In addition, the X.500 structure of the AD database is based on an object numbering scheme that is globally unique. A central authority has the ability to generate object identifiers for new X.500 objects: the International Standards Organization (ISO). Numbers can also be obtained from the American National Standards Institute (ANSI). X.500 numbering can be obtained at www.iso.org or www.ansi.org. Microsoft also offers X.500 numbering in an object class tree it acquired for the purpose of supporting Active Directory Domain Services. You can receive object IDs from Microsoft by sending an e-mail to oids@microsoft.com. In your e-mail, include your organization's naming prefix and the following contact information: contact name, contact address, and contact telephone number.

Object identifiers are strings in a dot notation similar to IPv4 addresses. Issuing authorities can give an object identifier on a sub-level to other authorities. The ISO is the root authority. The ISO has a number of 1. When it assigns a number to another organization, that number is used to identify that organization. If it assigned T&T the number 488077, and T&T issued 1 to a developer, and that developer assigned 10 to an application, the number of the application would be 1.488077.1.10.

To create your schema modification strategy, you need to perform three steps:

- Identify the elements of the schema modification policy.
- Identify the owner and the charter for the schema change policy holder role.
- Identify the schema change management process.

The schema modification policy includes several elements:

- List of the members of the Universal Enterprise Administrators Group.
- Security and management strategy for the Universal Schema Administrators Group. This group should be kept empty at all times, with members only added when

modifications are required. These said members are removed as soon as the modification is complete.

- Creation of the SCPH role.
- Schema change management strategy documentation, including:
    - Change request supporting documentation preparation, with modification description and justification.
    - Impact analysis for the change. Short-term and long-term replication impacts. Costs for the requested change. Short-term and long-term benefits for the change.
    - Globally unique object identifier for the new class or attribute, obtained from a valid source.
    - Official class description, including class type and localization in the hierarchy.
    - System stability and security test results. Design standard set of tests for all modifications.
    - Modification recovery method. Ensure every modification proposal includes a rollback strategy.
- Modification authorization process; meeting structure for modification recommendation.
- Modification implementation process outlining when the change should be performed (off production hours), how it should be performed, and by whom.
- Modification report documentation. Did the modification reach all DCs? Is replication back to expected levels?

This process should be documented at the very beginning of your implementation to ensure the continuing integrity of your production schema. If this is done well, you will rarely find your staff performing midnight restores of the schema you had in production yesterday.

Use Active Directory Lightweight Directory Services

The purpose of ADLDS is to offer a pure Lightweight Directory Access Protocol (LDAP) directory service. It offers data storage and retrieval for directory-enabled applications without the dependencies or stringent preparation requirements an ADDS structure requires.

Directory-enabled applications rely on directories rather than on a standard database, flat file, or other data storage structure to hold its data. Because ADLDS relies on a hierarchical database structure, it offers significant performance improvements over relational databases for certain types of data lookups. LDAP directories are optimized for read processing, as opposed to the transactional processing relational databases are optimized for. This means that if you need to read access rights for a user for a given directory-enabled application, LDAP directories would return it faster than a relational database.

The advantage of working with ADLDS is that it is based on the same code base as ADDS, but without requiring the presence of domains or domain controllers. Despite this, ADLDS offers multimaster replication, Active Directory Services Interface (ADSI) programming, application directory partitions, and the ability to use the secure sockets layer (SSL) for secure communications. One main difference with ADDS is that ADLDS does not store Windows

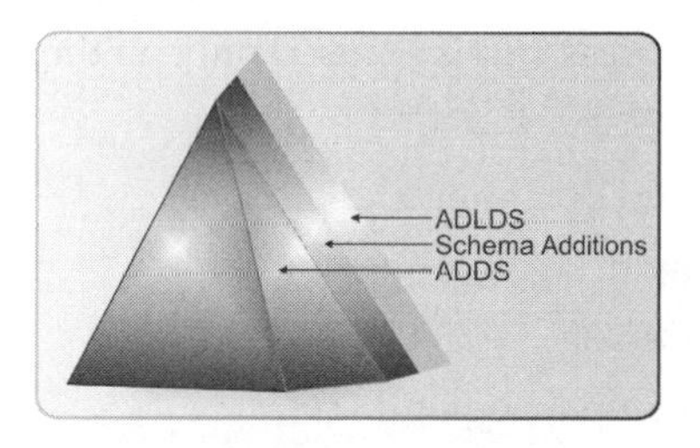

FIGURE 5-20 The different nature of schema modifications versus ADLDS directories

security principals. It can, however, call upon security principals that are stored within an ADDS directory, such as domain user accounts, for example, to control access to objects in the ADLDS directory. You can store user accounts in ADLDS, but they will not be able to interact with Windows, as Windows does not recognize the accounts ADLDS stores. These accounts can be useful for other applications, though. For example, a Web application in a DMZ would happily rely on an ADLDS directory. This would provide a much safer access structure than placing an ADDS directory in the DMZ and risking its compromise.

Always consider an ADLDS, even in the internal network, instead of making a custom schema modification. Schema modifications are permanent and actually expand the size of an ADDS directory, whereas ADLDS directories interact with, but do not affect, ADDS directory structures (see Figure 5-20).

Schema Modification Strategy Best Practices

Use the following schema modification best practices:

- Don't make your own modifications to the schema, unless they are absolutely necessary.
- Use ADDS primarily as a NOS directory.
- Use ADLDS to integrate applications with ADDS.
- Use the Identity Integration Feature Pack to link multiple ADDS and Exchange structures.
- Use Microsoft Identity Lifecycle Manager to link ADDS with third-party directories and to manage ADCS infrastructures.
- Make sure all commercial products that will modify the schema are Windows Logo-approved.
- Limit your initial modifications to modifications by commercial software.
- Create a Schema Change Policy Holder role early on in the ADDS implementation process.
- Document the schema modification policy and process.

ADDS Implementation Plan

The first stage of ADDS preparation is complete. You have designed your ADDS strategy. Now you need to implement the design. To do so, you require an ADDS implementation plan. This plan outlines the ADDS migration process. Basically, this plan identifies the same steps as the design process, but is focused only on those that deal with implementation. As such, it is reduced to four major steps:

- Forest, tree, and domain installation
- OU and group design
- Service positioning
- Site topology implementation

Once these four steps are complete, your ADDS will be in place. These four steps form the ADDS Implementation Blueprint (see Figure 5-21).

This blueprint is designed to cover all the major steps in a new ADDS implementation. It uses the parallel network concept outlined earlier to create a separate new network that can accept users as they are migrated from the existing production network. Because this process is closely related to the implementation of the IP network infrastructure, the implementation of a new Active Directory Domain Services structure and the implementation of the IP network infrastructure are covered in the next chapter. If, however, you already have an Active Directory structure in place, you are more likely to use an upgrade process. This upgrade process is also outlined in the next chapter.

New and Revised ADDS IT Roles

One final aspect of ADDS design is the creation of new IT roles. If you're migrating from Windows NT to Windows Server 2008, all these roles are completely new. If you're already using Active Directory, then you now know that all of these roles are necessary. The new IT roles are outlined in Table 5-10. Once again, depending on the size of your organization, you may combine roles. What is important here is that each *function* be identified within your IT group.

All of these roles will need to interact with each other during ongoing operations. A regular roundtable discussion is an excellent way for each of the people filling these roles to get to know each other and begin the communication process. The frequency of these meetings does not need to be especially high. Gauge the number of meetings you need per year according to the objectives you set for your directory. They could be as few as two per year.

The Ongoing ADDS Design Process

In summary, the ADDS design process is complex only because it includes a lot more stages than the Windows NT design process. One of the things you need to remember is that creating a production ADDS structure is creating a virtual space. Since it is virtual, you can manipulate and reshape it as your needs and comprehension of Active Directory Domain Services evolves. WS08 makes this even easier by supporting drag-and-drop functionality within the ADDS management consoles: Active Directory Users and Computers, Active Directory Domains and Trusts, and Active Directory Sites and Servers. WS08 also supports multiple object attribute changes—for example, if you need to change the same attribute on several objects.

To help simplify the ADDS design process for you, sample working tools are listed on the companion web site. One tool is a glossary of Active Directory terms. You can use it along with Figure 5-2 to ensure that everyone has a common understanding of each feature.

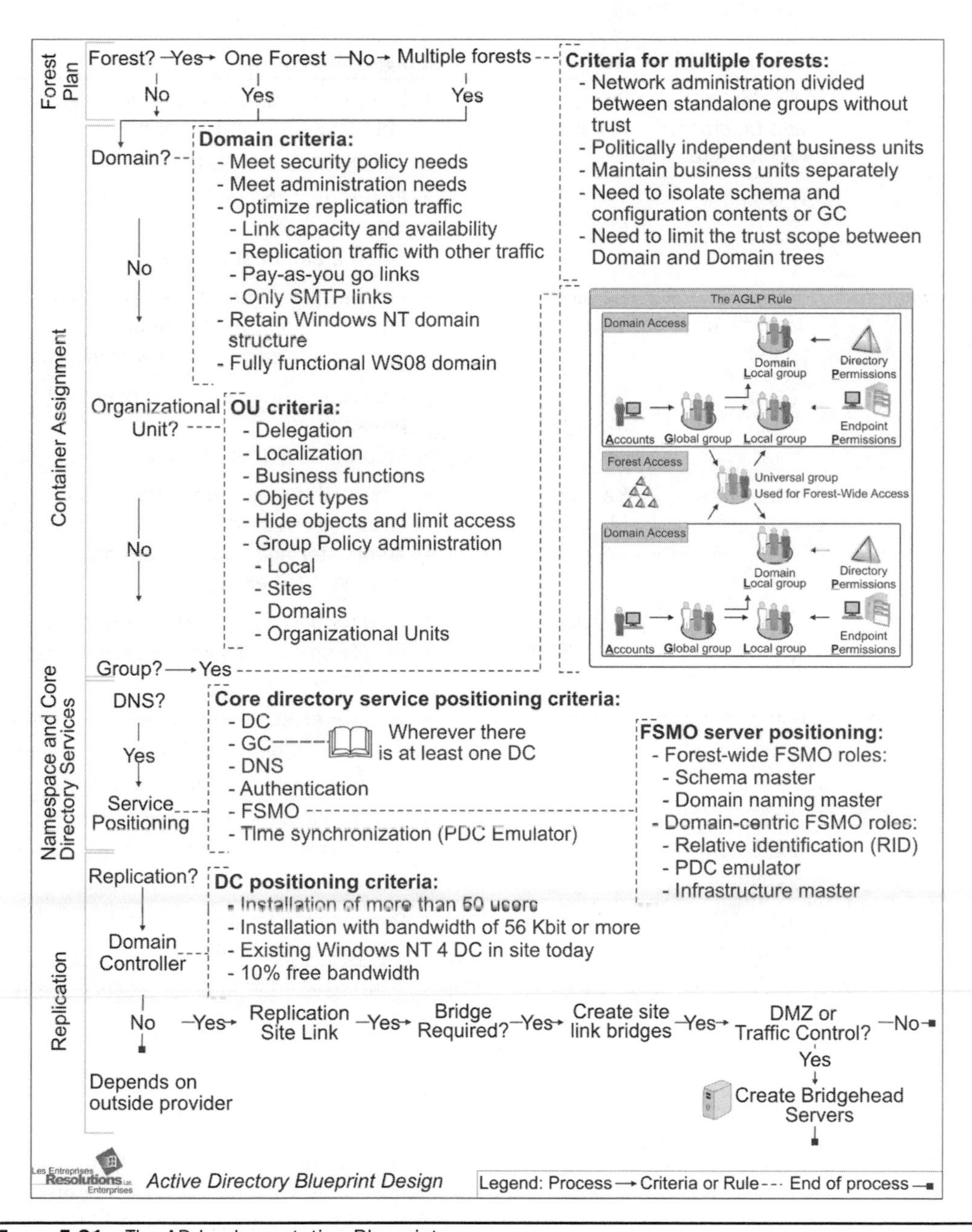

Figure 5-21 The AD Implementation Blueprint

Another outlines the ADDS Design Blueprint illustrated in Figure 5-5. It is a working process control form that lets you follow the ADDS design process stage by stage and check off completed tasks. Both will help you design the ADDS that best suits your organization's requirements.

Role	Department	Role Type	Responsibilities
Forest Owner	IT Planning and Enterprise Architecture	Service Management	• Ensure that all forest standards are maintained within the forest • Identify and document new standards
Forest Administrator	IT Group	Service Management	• Ensure that the forest is operating properly • Enforce all forest standards
Domain Owner	IT Group/ Training/IS	Service Management	• Ensure that all domain standards are maintained within the domain • Identify and document new standards
Domain Administrator	IT Group	Service Management	• Ensure that the domain is operating properly • Enforce all domain standards
DNS Administrator	IT Group	Service Management	• Ensure the proper operation of the forest namespace • Administer and manage internal/ external DNS exchanges
Site Topology Administrator	IT Group	Service Management	• Monitor and analyze forest replication • Modify site topology to improve forest replication
Schema Change Policy Holder	Entire Organization	Service Management	• Monitor all schema changes • Authorize schema changes after review • Control the schema change policy
Root Domain Owner	IT Planning and Enterprise Architecture	Data Ownership	• Responsible for Universal Administrative Groups • Placeholder for the entire forest
OU Owners	Entire Organization	Data Owner	• Responsible for all information delegated within the OU

TABLE 5-10 New AD IT Roles

NOTE *The companion web site can be found at www.reso-net.com/livre.asp?p=main&b=WS08.*

These tools can only *assist* you in the design process. The success or failure of the Active Directory Domain Services design process you complete will depend entirely on what your organization invests in it. Remember: ADDS is the core of your network. Its design must respond to organizational needs. The only way to ensure this is to gather all of the ADDS stakeholders and get them to participate in the design process. In other words, the quality of the team you gather to create your ADDS design will greatly influence the quality of the output you produce.

6

CHAPTER

Build the Windows Server 2008 Network Infrastructure

Now that you understand Active Directory, you're ready to begin the implementation of the services Windows Server 2008 (WS08) will provide in your network. Here, you can find yourself in one of three situations:

- You have an existing network and you want to migrate to a dynamic datacenter infrastructure.
- You do not have an existing network and you want to implement a new dynamic datacenter to provide services to a given organization.
- You have an existing datacenter and you simply want to upgrade its service offerings to WS08.

In each case, you'll need to determine how you're going to migrate the service offerings; but in the first two cases, you also need to prepare the resource pool that will enable you to create the virtual service offerings (VSOs) to provide functionalities to the organization. This means you need to think about how you will build the base infrastructure that will run host services. Then, once it is ready, consider the method you will use if you are migrating from an existing network to a VSO. If you're not using virtual service offerings, then you should go on to the second part of this chapter, which looks to service offerings design. In either case, you will need to make architectural decisions before you move on to the implementation itself.

Build Your Resource Pool Infrastructure

When you think about it, the architecture of the resource pool, while extremely important because it will support your entire service-oriented infrastructure, is relatively simple because of the fact that it never needs to interact with end users. This infrastructure, because of its very nature, will be entirely under the responsibility of the operations department of IT. Resource pools become similar to the networking infrastructure you use. End users profit from these devices, but it is the IT operations staff that interacts directly with these devices. The same goes for the resource pool.

In addition, because the resource pool is an infrastructure of its own, it will be contained inside an Active Directory Domain Services (ADDS) forest of its own that will be separate and independent of the forest structure you will use for your virtual service offerings. This "utility" forest will help provide a centralized authentication and authorization environment for virtual machine management, as well as provide a central platform for service administration through Group Policy. This will also secure the hardware platform and keep it separate from other systems.

Since this is a server infrastructure, you will want to implement a virtual local area network (VLAN) structure to provide high-speed communications between devices. Once again, this means the Internet Protocol (IP) infrastructure for the resource pool will be independent from that of the virtual service offerings. It may be a good idea to implement an IPv6 infrastructure for resource pools, since their communications could be more secure than other systems. These servers only communicate with each other and with administration consoles. So long as these consoles run Windows Vista, you can rely on IPv6 just as you could on IPv4.

Ideally, the resource pool will be constructed of diskless blade servers attached to back-end shared storage (see Figure 6-1). Blade configurations will vary with organizational needs, but if you intend to run the average of 16 virtual machines (VMs) per blade, you will want to have something along the lines of a typical configuration (see Table 6-1).

Chapter 4 covered how you could build and prepare system images for these machines. In fact, since they will be running from shared storage, it becomes really easy to provision these systems, since all you need to do is copy a logical storage unit (LUN) to generate another system disk. This will speed up the provisioning process even more. Each system should be running a centrally controlled antivirus program, as well as include other standard protection mechanisms.

NOTE *The resource pool will only be running WS08 Enterprise or Datacenter editions because these editions include multiple free licenses for virtualized versions of WS08. This will also simplify provisioning.*

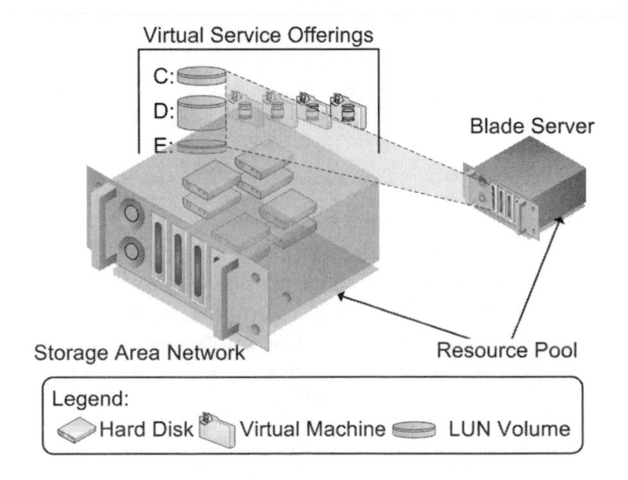

FIGURE 6-1 Resource pools using blade host servers with shared storage

Component	Description
Processors	Minimum: Two dual-core processors Recommended: Two quad-core processors or four dual-core processors
RAM	Minimum: 8 GB Recommended: 16 GB
Storage connectivity	Host bus adapter (HBA) for fiber optics or iSCSI
C: Volume	40 GB plus space for paging file (minimum two times RAM)
D: Volume	Allow an average of 50 to 100 GB for each virtual machine Example: 16 x 100 GB = 1.6 TB
E: Volume	20 GB for volume shadow copies
VM Volume structure	Expandable disks to make the best use of disk space
Networking Configuration	Minimum: 2 x 1 Gbit Ethernet Recommended: 4 x 1 Gbit Ethernet

Table 6-1 A Typical Host Server Blade Configuration

Because of the nature of the Hyper-V role, each host server will need to run a management partition (see Figure 6-2). As you can see, Hyper-V is based on a thin hypervisor layer that runs directly on top of hardware certified for Windows Server. Then the parent partition provides the interface to virtual machine management, while virtual machines use the virtual machine client extensions to interact with the virtual machine bus that is exposed

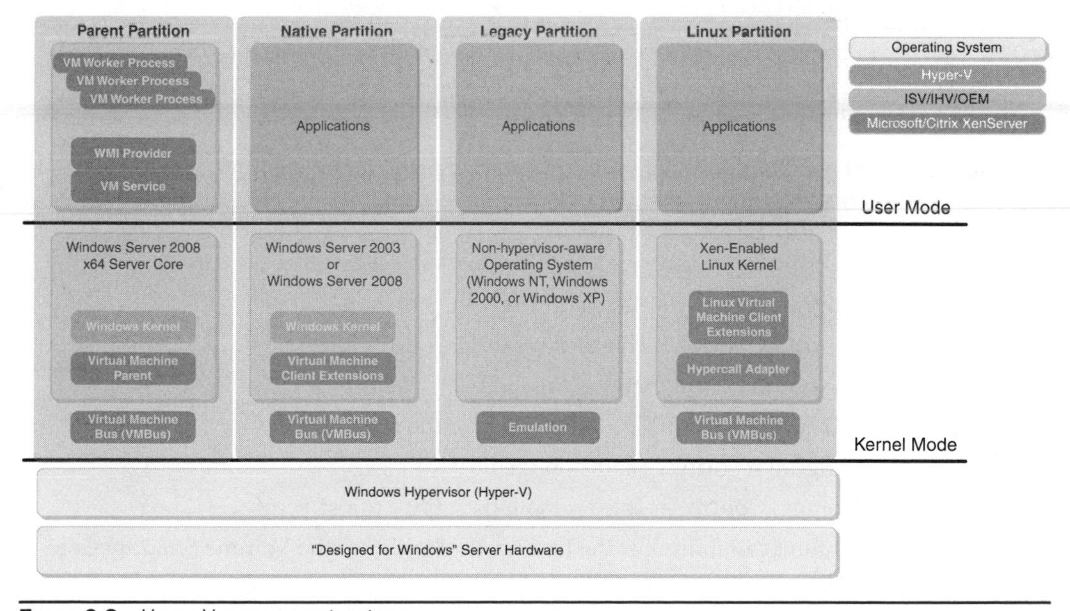

Figure 6-2 Hyper-V resource structure

through the hypervisor. These client extensions are built directly into WS08. This means that any virtualized instance of WS08 will be able to properly contend for physical resources and will be a "well-behaved" virtual client. And, because of Microsoft's partnership with Citrix, Xen-enabled Linux distributions can also take advantage of the VMBus through special client extensions of their own.

In addition to the parent partition, you will have to load the Domain Controller (DC) role on at least two host servers. These should be properly identified and configured appropriately, since they will be playing an additional role along with Hyper-V. Two domain controllers should be sufficient for this forest, since only utilities such as host servers will be connecting to this domain. In addition, you want to keep this number small because it adds overhead to the server, limiting the number of virtual machines it can host.

CAUTION *Do not make these domain controllers virtual machines. If you need to start the host machines and the domain controllers are stopped, you will have difficulty entering into the domain. The problem becomes compounded when the stopped domain controllers are on hosts that are also stopped. Run this role on actual, physical machines and make sure one of them is up at all times.*

These servers should be clustered as much as possible to provide high availability for the virtual service offerings they will support. They should also be running the Distributed File System (DFS) replication services to help protect the virtual machines they host. These high-availability configurations are covered in Chapter 11, since it discusses business continuity strategies. For immediate protection, you should configure the Volume Shadow Copy service to ensure that you have a local backup of each VM. For management purposes, you will need an appropriate number of consoles to administer each of the resource pool's nodes. Ideally, this will be performed from operator PCs running the Hyper-V administration role or running Microsoft System Center Virtual Machine Manager (SCVMM).

NOTE *SCVMM is an excellent addition to any dynamic datacenter running a virtual infrastructure. Information on SCVMM can be found at www.microsoft.com/systemcenter/scvmm/default.mspx.*

Therefore, you need to do the following when you prepare the resource pool:

1. Provision an initial host server.
2. Configure IP and other settings to personalize the server.
3. Install/configure security systems on the host.
4. Add the Domain Controller role and create the utility forest.
5. Provision a second host server.
6. Configure IP and other settings to personalize the server.
7. Install/configure security systems on the host.
8. Add the Domain Controller role and join the utility forest.
9. Configure high availability for the two hosts. Configure the Volume Shadow Copy Service (VSS).
10. Install consoles to begin managing the resource pool.

Then, once this is done, you can begin to add additional host servers and join them as member servers to the resource pool forest.

Create the Utility Forest

To create the centralized environment for resource pool authentication, you need to build two domain controllers. This forest will be a single-domain forest, since it is a utility forest that only IT will interact with. This is why you do not have the same considerations as you would with the virtual service offerings forest you will create later. In the latter, end users will interact with the directory. Because of this, you will want to create a child domain that removes access to the enterprise administrative roles found in the root domain of any forest.

Because this domain will be hosted on Server Core installations, you will be running the ADDS command-line utility—DCPROMO.EXE—in automated mode with an unattended answer file. Though it is a utility forest, it should still follow the guidelines outlined in Chapter 5 and be properly named and configured. For example, if you have remote sites that will be running servers from the resource pool, you will need to decide if you want to run the DC role on one of them to ensure authentication in the event the wide area network (WAN) links are down.

CAUTION *Do not install the read-only DC role (RODC) on these servers. RODCs do not store administrative credentials and need to make a WAN call to a read-write domain controller to log on administrators. The RODC role is only for virtual service offerings. You may, in fact, not need to have remote DCs for this forest. Logon and boot credentials are cached locally on member servers once they are retrieved from a DC, so WAN links are not always required. In addition, if you do not have administrative staff in these remote sites, you will need to have a WAN connection anyway to perform work on these systems. If you have a WAN connection to perform work, you have a WAN connection to the DC that will let you log on.*

The properties of this forest should be identified in the answer file. Buy a proper name for this forest, just as you would for any other. A good name is one ending in the .ws extension, since it could stand for Windows Server, but you should choose what makes the most sense to you. This is the example used here. It uses the T&T Corporation as the sample organization. Create an answer file with the following entries:

```
[DCINSTALL]
InstallDNS=yes
NewDomain=forest
NewDomainDNSName=TandT.WS
DomainNetBiosName=TANDTWS
ReplicaOrNewDomain=domain
ForestLevel=3
DomainLevel=3
RebootOnCompletion=yes
SafeModeAdminPassword=password
```

This will install a forest in WS08 forest and domain functional mode, name it TandT.WS, give it the TANDTWS NetBIOS name, install the Domain Name System (DNS) service, and make the server a Global Catalog. It will also install the databases and other ADDS folders in default locations. Since this domain only has two DCs and a few member servers, it does not require any special consideration in terms of the configuration aspects of the files that make up the directory.

To apply the role, use the following command line on your Server Core system:

```
dcpromo /unattend:pathtotheanswerfile
```

TIP *More information on unattended answer file settings can be found at http://technet2.microsoft.com/windowsserver2008/en/library/fb7bf6dd-6940-4744-9028-323fdc073ad71033.mspx?mfr=true.*

Use a similar file on both DCs. The second file, of course, must tell the DC to join the existing domain. The following should be used on this second installation:

```
[DCINSTALL]
InstallDNS=yes
ReplicaOrNewDomain=replica
ReplicationSourceDC=HostDCOne.TandT.WS
RebootOnCompletion=yes
SafeModeAdminPassword=password
```

As you can see, this second installation file is simpler because this domain controller is joining an existing domain. All other systems will be member servers that join this domain.

Now that the forest is created, you should transfer the Operation Master roles so that they can be shared between the two domain controllers. This is a best practice that was recommended in Chapter 5. Once again, you need to use the command line to perform this operation. You will transfer the Domain Naming Master and the Infrastructure Master to the second DC. To do this, log onto the second DC and type the following commands:

```
ntdsutil
roles
connections
connect to server servername
quit
transfer naming master
transfer infrastructure master
quit
quit
```

Where the *servername* is the DNS name of the second DC. The NTDSUTIL command is a command interface and lets you type commands as you need them. The DCs are now ready.

Configure the Volume Shadow Copy Service

One of the most exciting features that emerged from Windows Server 2003 is the Volume Shadow Copy Service (VSS). This service is also available with Server Core. What's most impressive with this feature is that it is really fast and easy to implement, and it provides an immediate solution to shared file protection. The VSS service automatically takes a "snapshot" of the files located in any shared folder where the service has been enabled. These snapshots include an image of the contents of the folder at a given point in time. Depending on the space you make available to it (each VSS snapshot is 100 megabytes, or MB, in size), you could have up to 512 different snapshots of a disk volume. And because Microsoft has made a client component of VSS, the Previous Versions client, available along with VSS, users and administrators can have access to these snapshots. While you had to deploy the Previous Versions client on Windows XP, it is built into Windows Vista and WS08.

On regular file servers, this means that once VSS is implemented, users can recover pretty well any lost file by themselves, at the privacy of their own desk, without having to bother anyone and without the embarrassment of having to tell someone they've lost a file once again. That's because the shadow copy service is designed to assist in the process of recovering previous versions of files without having to resort to backups. In this way, VSS is very much like a server "undelete." In terms of virtual machine management, this tool is extremely useful, because it protects the files that make up each virtual machine and gives you ready access to them should any untoward event occur.

By default, Windows Server 2008 creates shadow copies twice a day: at 7:00 A.M. and noon. This schedule can be changed if you find that it does not meet your requirements. *Shadow copies do not replace backups* because they are not backed up, so if a shadow copy is no longer available, it is no longer available. That's because shadow copies rely on a write-forward procedure. When the disk goes to write a new file, instead of replacing the existing file, the disk writes it to a new empty location. VSS creates a point to the original location, and so long as this original location is not overwritten, VSS can recover the original file. As you can see, VSS only works well if you have a lot of free space on your disks, but nevertheless, it is a good solution and requires very little overhead to run. Therefore, you should implement it as much as possible.

TIP *If you are using either a network attached storage (NAS) or a storage area network (SAN) to host shared storage for your resource pools, you may already have a snapshot feature directly within the shared storage environment. If so, rely on the built-in feature instead of VSS.*

Here's how you implement it. VSS will store the snapshots on the E: drive you configured for your system. When this drive fills up, it will simply overwrite older versions of the shadow copies.

1. Prepare your host server. The host server already has three different volumes on it. The first, C: drive, is reserved for the operating system and the paging file. The second, D: drive, is your data drive. It will host the virtual machine's hard disk drives and configuration files. The third, E: drive, is reserved to store the shadow copies. Use the DISKPART command to create and assign the two extra disks. DISKPART is a command interface. You begin by entering the interface and then type commands. Once you're done, you exit the command interface. Use the following commands. Make sure you attach the disks to this server in your shared storage technology first.

NOTE *You may have to reassign the drive letter for the DVD drive first to properly assign the D: drive to a disk. This is reflected in this script. It begins by selecting the DVD drive and reassigning its letter to Y: Then it goes on to prepare the other disks. This assumes that disk 2 is the D drive and disk 3 is the E drive. It does not assign sizes because the total disk size is formatted by default.*

PART III

```
diskpart
list volume
select volume 2
assign letter=Y
list disk
select disk 2
create partition primary align=64
assign letter=D
format quick label=VMdata
select disk 3
create partition primary align=64
assign letter=E
format quick label=VSSdata
list disk
exit
```

2. Enable the Volume Shadow Copy Service. VSS is a property of a disk volume in Windows Server. Since this is a Server Core installation, you will need the command line to enable it. You want to create shadow copies from the D: drive and store them on the E: drive. View which volumes exist first, assign the shadow copy, and then create your first shadow copy. Use the following commands:

   ```
   vssadmin list volumes
   vssadmin add shadowstorage /for=ForVolume /on=OnVolume
   ```

   Where *ForVolume* is the D: drive and *OnVolume* is the E: drive. The command line should look like this:

   ```
   vssadmin add shadwostorage /for=D: /on=E:
   vssadmin create shadow /for=D:
   ```

3. Manage shared folders. VSS is now enabled, but you do not need to share any folders to use it. That's because all servers have automatic shares for administrative purposes named *driveletter$*. For example, the administrative share of the D: drive is \\servername\D$. These shared folders will automatically be able to take advantage of the VSS service.
4. Use the Previous Versions client to access shadow copies. This is probably the easiest part of the process. To view previous versions of a file or folder, open Windows Explorer on a remote machine, connect to the administrative share, locate either the file or, if the file is gone, the folder in which it was stored, right-click it to select Properties, move to the Previous Versions tab, select the version you need, and click Restore. Close the Properties dialog box when done. You can also copy and compare files (see Figure 6-3).
5. Monitor VSS usage to determine if the default schedule is appropriate. Review how you make use of the VSS service on host servers to see if you need to modify the default schedule. Perhaps you want more than two copies per day. Gauge what you need and modify the schedule as appropriate.

That's it. You might want to add this to your remote console for host server management. Begin by installing the Hyper-V administrative tools on administrative PCs (ideally, they should be running Vista). Next, you can use the Computer Management console to remotely manage the Volume Shadow Copy Service on your host servers. You are ready to begin working with your virtual service offerings.

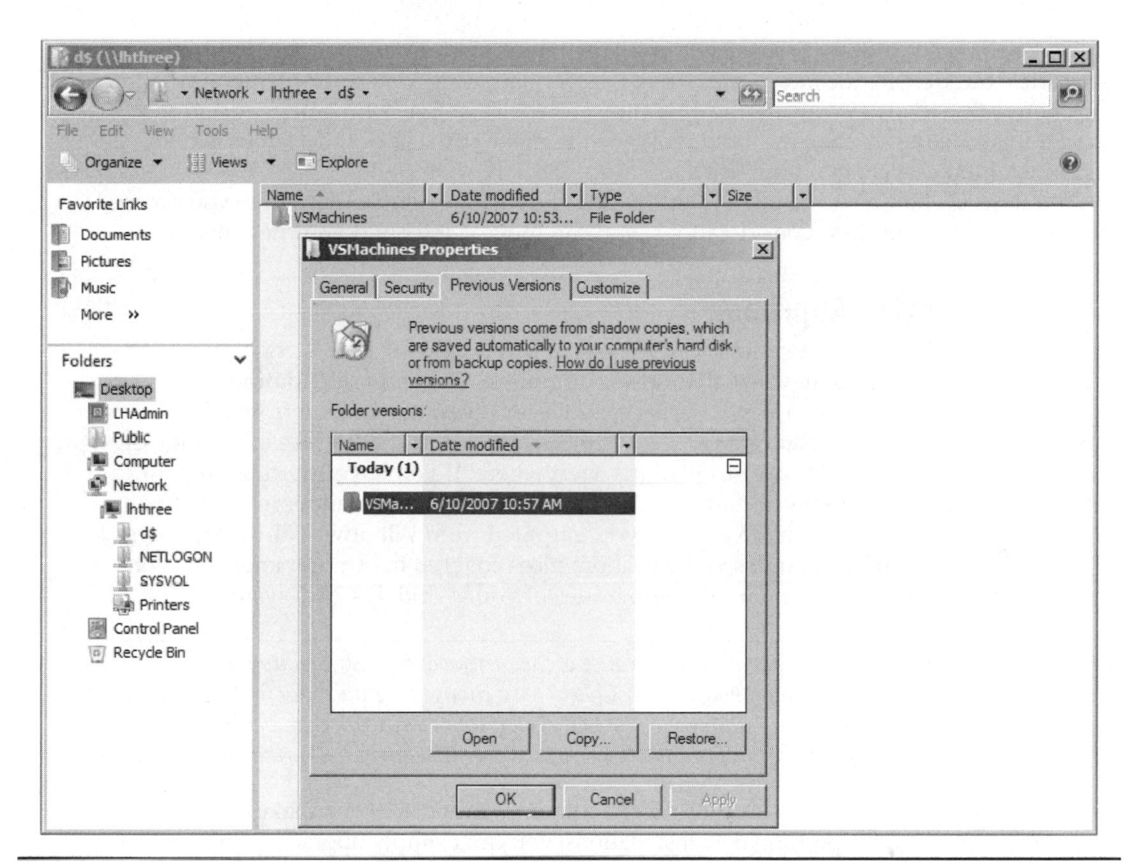

Figure 6-3 Accessing previous versions of virtual machines

Note *At this stage, you should build one or two management machines running the WS08 full installation with the Hyper-V role. These machines will assist in the management of the resource pool and the creation and configuration of the VSOs. This procedure is outlined in Chapter 13.*

Build Your Virtual Service Offerings

Now that your host server infrastructure is ready to receive the virtual service offerings, you can begin to work more extensively on the VSOs. When you move your VSOs to a network based on WS08, like any other Windows network, you'll need to work with three major categories of systems:

- **Identity management servers** These include domain controllers or the systems that contain and maintain the corporate identity database for users and other network objects.
- **Member servers** All other servers in the network fall into this category. These include application servers, file and print servers, Web servers, and so on.
- **Personal computers** These include all of your workstations, including portables.

In the case of Windows Server 2008, you'll be mostly concerned with the first two categories, but despite the fact that WS08 is a server operating system, implementing it in your network will also involve some operations on the PCs. Everything depends on the migration strategy you choose. In fact, you need to make some critical decisions *before* you begin installing servers into your VSO.

You need to choose how to migrate and, especially, what to migrate first before you proceed. Once you've covered these considerations, you can move on to build your new network.

Choose the Migration Approach

One of the most important decisions you will make before you migrate is *how* you want to migrate: Will you perform new installations or upgrades? Our recommendation: If you are moving from Windows NT to Windows Server 2008, or if you are moving from a Windows 2000/2003 network that was upgraded from Windows NT, you should take advantage of this opportunity to perform new installations everywhere. If you have anything in your network that you'd like to revise and re-order, then perform new installations. But, if you already performed new installations when you migrated from Windows NT to Windows 2000/2003—for example, if you used the best practices covered in our previous books on WS03—you can simply perform in-place upgrades of your Windows 2003 systems.

CAUTION *We recommend new installations because of the carryover from system upgrades. Servers that have been around for a long time will most likely have changed significantly from their baseline install. Building new servers is always the best bet, even if it is more work than performing an upgrade, because it lets you start fresh and will save lots of potential headaches further down the road.*

The answer to this first question will greatly influence the choices you make during your migration. If you need to perform new installations, you can't simply upgrade existing servers, because it will be difficult to design a migration approach that will not disrupt normal operations. There are, however, methods that could simplify the migration process. For example, you could stage a new server using a separate network, give it the name of an existing server in your network, and replace the old with the new. But this approach has some issues. Even though the new server has the same name, it will not be seen as the same machine within your network because WS08 does not use the machine name to communicate and identify a server. Rather, it uses the security identifier (SID), a random identity number that is generated at installation. This identifier will never be duplicated on a given network and will never be the same between two machines that were installed using one of the four supported installation methods. There are workarounds, and they will be considered as we proceed.

If you want to take advantage of WS08 to implement a new network, using new principles and a new architecture, you should consider the *parallel network* approach. This is the safest approach because it involves the least risk. It focuses on the implementation of a new, parallel network that does not touch or affect the existing environment. Ongoing operations are not affected because the existing network is not removed or modified. The parallel network approach is based on the creation of new virtual machines that are used to create a migration pool. This migration pool becomes the core of the new network. Then, as you put new systems in place to replace existing services, you recover machines from the existing or legacy network and change their role before adding them to the new network (see Figure 6-4). If the machine has sufficient resources, it can then become a virtual server host and be joined to the resource pool.

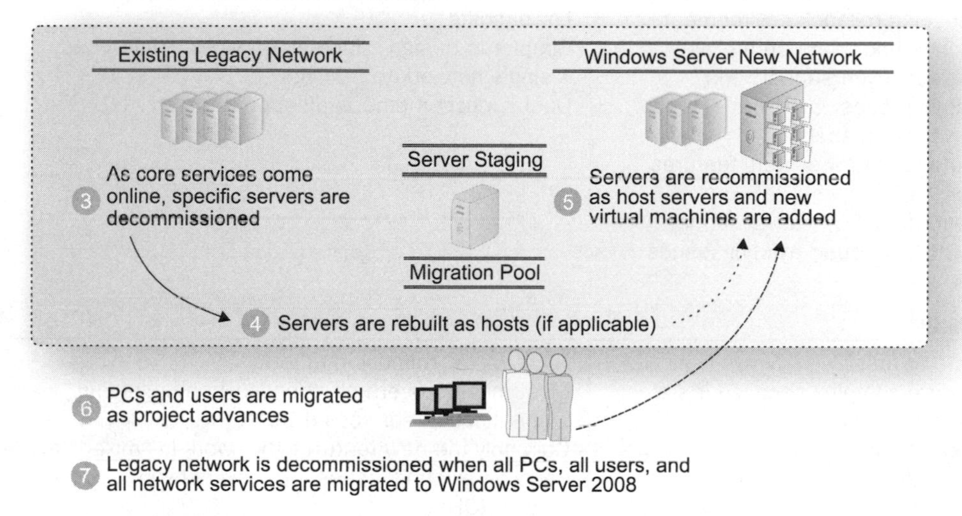
1 Core host servers are formed from new acquisitions
2 Core of new network is built with virtual machines
Core network services are activated
Existing Legacy Network
Windows Server New Network
Server Staging
3 As core services come online, specific servers are decommissioned
5 Servers are recommissioned as host servers and new virtual machines are added
Migration Pool
4 Servers are rebuilt as hosts (if applicable)
6 PCs and users are migrated as project advances
7 Legacy network is decommissioned when all PCs, all users, and all network services are migrated to Windows Server 2008

FIGURE 6-4 The Parallel Network Migration Approach

TIP ***Reusing older hardware.*** *Hyper-V only runs on x64 hardware. If you have older hardware that includes sufficient resources to run virtual machines, yet is only based on x86 hardware, you can still add them to the resource pool. To do so, install an appropriate copy of Windows Server 2008 on the new host then, instead of using Hyper-V, install Microsoft Virtual Server to run the virtual machines.*

The parallel network has several advantages. First, it provides an ongoing rollback environment. If, for some reason, the new network does not work properly, you can quickly return to the legacy environment because it is still up and running. Next, you can migrate groups of users and machines according to your own timetable. Since the existing network is still running, you can target specific groups without affecting others. Also, since the existing network is still running, you can take the time to completely master new technologies and services before putting them in place. And, since the new services are based on virtual machines, you can use trial and error until you get it exactly the way you like it.

It does have some disadvantages, though. It takes more time than doing an in-place upgrade. But if you want a better return on investment (ROI) at the end of your project, you will want to take the time to redesign your network to take full advantage of new WS08 features. The parallel network is a harder sell in a migration project, but its advantages far outweigh its disadvantages in most situations. Because you are migrating to VSOs, the parallel network makes sense because it lets you master the VSO concept before you put services in place.

Table 6-2 compares the upgrade to the parallel network. The parallel network implementation process is outlined in Chapter 12.

Parallel Network	Upgrade
Advantages	
Provides ongoing rollback environment Migrate groups and users on an "as needed" basis—even support and administrative groups Migrate at your own speed Take advantage of new system features immediately Implement features in "native" mode Can deal with and repair existing issues Faster ROI	Lower costs Simpler to design, since all services exist already A single network to manage Dual support methods disappear faster
Disadvantages	
Higher costs at first Design is more complex because it's a completely new network Two networks to manage Dual support methods last longer	No "simple" rollback method Must migrate users all at once when upgrading authentication services (PDC) Gain only the new features that work in "mixed" mode Carry on existing issues into new network Slower ROI

Table 6-2 Parallel Network Versus Upgrade

Choose What to Migrate First

Of course, if your existing network is based on Windows 2000/2003 and you have taken the time to perform a proper migration to this operating system, your migration path to WS08 will be much simpler than the parallel network. What you'll want to determine is which systems you will migrate first: identity servers, member servers, or PCs? For one category of systems, PCs, the answer is easy. If you're already using Windows XP Professional or Windows Vista, you won't have to touch PCs until you've migrated the servers the PCs are linked to. But the question still remains between identity and member servers: which to do first?

Since Windows Server 2008 supports multiple operating modes and is compatible with Windows NT, as well as with Windows 2000/2003, you could choose to migrate each category of server in any order. Figure 6-5 illustrates the migration "slide-rule." This concept shows that identity servers, member servers, and PCs can be migrated in any order. It also displays the relative migration timelines for each type of system, graphically demonstrating the duration of each migration process compared to the others. The slide-rule is used to demonstrate that each migration process can be moved from one place to another on the project timescale, allowing you to begin with the process that suits your organization best.

Identity Servers First

In Windows Server 2008, migrating identity servers means working with Active Directory Domain Services. If you're already running Windows 2000/2003, this step should be relatively easy to perform, since you can upgrade a Windows 2000/2003 domain controller and run a "mixed" environment of Windows 2000/2003 and WS08 domain controllers.

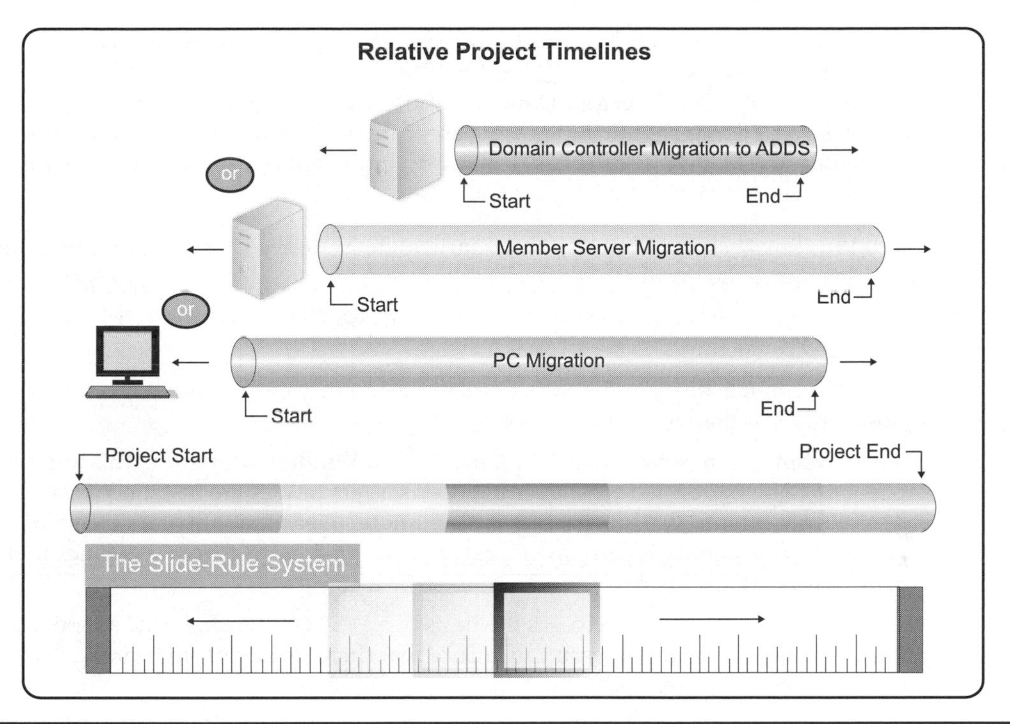

FIGURE 6-5 The migration slide-rule

Then, when all your servers are migrated to WS08, you can activate the full functional directory mode for this version of Windows. WS08 has four Active Directory modes:

- Mixed mode with 2000, 2003, and WS08, which is the Windows 2000 native mode
- Mixed mode domain with Windows Server 2003 and WS08, which is the domain functional mode for WS03
- Mixed mode forest with Windows Server 2003 and WS08, which is the forest functional mode for WS03
- WS08 functional forest mode

Switching to full functional mode is not something that is lightly done. You can only do so when you've verified that legacy domain controllers are either upgraded or decommissioned and that all other conditions are met. But if you have experience with Active Directory Domain Services, you'll also realize that while it isn't done lightly, switching functional modes is not a very complex operation.

If you're currently running a Windows NT network, migrating identity servers first will mean implementing Active Directory Domain Services. You'll have to make sure you're ready before taking this step. ADDS is to the Windows NT Security Accounts Manager (SAM) what a handheld computer is to a full-fledged notebook. You can do a lot of stuff with the handheld, but there is so much more you can do with a real computer. And if your experience is with a handheld, you'll need a bit of training before you discover everything you can do with the notebook.

The same applies to Active Directory Domain Services. If you're moving from NT to WS08, you'll need to undergo significant training and fully understand your needs before you can implement ADDS. But in either case, there are significant advantages for doing the identity servers first:

- Every Windows version from 98 on can participate in Active Directory, though older versions require the installation of a client pack.
- Member servers running Windows NT and Windows 2000/2003 also work in a WS08 ADDS structure.
- The number of machines required to operate the identity environment is often significantly less than for other purposes.
- Every machine from Windows NT 4 on must *join* a Windows network. This joining process must be performed whenever member servers or PCs are installed if they are to be controlled centrally. This process is also unique to each identity environment. If you migrate the identity environment first, you will only need to join machines to the new directory environment once.
- Active Directory Domain Services is the basis of a WS08 network. It makes sense to put it in place first. That way, you can ensure that there is little or no "garbage" in your directory database.

Each of these justifications should be considered before making your decision.

NOTE *Try to go for a fresh ADDS install as much as possible. Even though ADDS has been around for several years, many organizations have made a mess of it—Group Policies, organizational unit (OU) structures, duplicate or unused groups, even replication disasters—are common occurrences. Rebuilding the entire directory lets you put in place the latest best practices for ADDS design and lets you clean up all of the data contained within your directory.*

Member Servers First

If you're working with a Windows NT network, chances are that you have a lot more domain controllers than you need. Windows NT had serious limitations in terms of member services. You often had to install a server as a domain controller just to make it easier to manage or because applications required direct access to the domain security database. Member servers are significantly different in Windows Server 2008. Now you can make full use of the Member role and significantly reduce the number of identity servers in your network. In fact, one of the questions you'll have to ask yourself when replacing network services is "Should this be a member server only?"

So far, we have identified six categories of member servers: application servers, file and print servers, dedicated Web servers, collaboration servers, network infrastructure servers, and terminal servers. Each of these must take its own migration path to Windows Server 2008. Because of this, you would only migrate member servers first if you have a minimal network infrastructure in place and if you have already begun the migration process for server-based corporate applications. If, for example, you have very few existing member servers that have a minimal load, it might be appropriate to migrate them first and simply get both performance and stability improvements from Windows Server 2008. If your corporate applications are based on commercial software products that already have been designed for Windows Server 2008 Logo certification, you might decide to do these first as well. Or, if you initiated a corporate application redevelopment effort to adapt them to Windows Server 2008 and they are now ready, you might consider migrating application servers first. But these are the only conditions where you will want to migrate member servers first. In addition, you'll need to ensure that each server you migrate supports WS08. You might even want to take advantage of this opportunity to reassess server requirements such as random access memory (RAM), processors, or disk space.

NOTE *For more information on the WS08 Logo certifications, go to www.microsoft.com/whdc/winlogo/downloads.mspx.*

Even though it does not have the scale of an ADDS implementation project, the migration of member servers will also require time for reflection and consideration. For example, file and print servers are easier to migrate than application servers, but they still require significant preparation. Since both file and print services are controlled through access rights, you'll need to take a full inventory of all access rights if you are replacing an existing server with a new one. You might even decide that you want to take the time to redefine access rights to your file and print services—perform a cleanup—to ensure that your security levels are appropriate, especially with regards to confidential information.

Whatever you do, you'll have to rely on some migration tools to make the process go smoother. These migration tools let you stage a new file and/or print server, mirror information and data between an existing server and the new server, and then migrate users and PCs to the new server remotely so that you can decommission the old system.

NOTE *All of these migration considerations are covered in Chapter 12.*

Next, you'll want to consider migration approaches for application services. These services fall into two major categories: commercial and corporate application services. For commercial software, you'll need to identify if product updates are required and available. For corporate applications, you'll need to identify which portions need to be modified in order to properly operate on the WS08 platform. To improve stability, Microsoft modified the application execution infrastructure of Windows. Windows NT had several stability issues; one of the most important was that the application execution environment in Windows NT allowed applications to write to critical portions of the system's disk. In NT, applications were allowed to write to the WINNT and the WINNT\System32 and, of course, the Program Files folders. What's worse—users were given some access to the WINNT folder since their profiles were stored under it.

Microsoft changed the entire infrastructure with Windows 2000/2003. Windows Server 2008 continues to build on this new infrastructure and also includes improvements from Windows Vista. Applications do not write to any of these folders. Every file that needs to be modified while a user is making use of an application is now stored in the *user profile*.

This profile is now located in the Users folder. Application data is now in the ProgramData folder. In this way, anyone who damages their profile does not affect anyone else using the system. The Windows—WS08 installs to the Windows folder and not the WINNT folder—and Program Files folders are locked and in read-only mode to applications (see Figure 6-6). The same changes have been included in the registry. Only user sections are modified during application operation. If applications are not designed for WS08, users will be faced with User Account Control (UAC) prompts as the application tries to modify areas that are not under their control.

Commercial applications that are modified to use this new architecture are often also modified to support every aspect of the Microsoft Logo program. This means that they will provide an integrated installation mechanism based on the Windows Installer service and offer self-healing. User applications that have not been modified to work with this structure will simply not operate properly on Windows Server 2008 unless everyone is given an account with administrative privileges, something no network administrator should allow.

If you must run legacy applications on Windows Server 2008, you will need to run them in compatibility mode. WS08 includes the Program Compatibility Assistant, which is a wizard that watches applications that do not behave properly and provides input into the compatibility modes you should use for the application. Or, worse, you won't be able to run the application in compatible mode and you'll have to change registry and file access rights to let it run. While this may be acceptable for applications that are intended for users, it is totally unacceptable for applications that are designed to support your network environment. Products like third-party quota managers, backup, antivirus, and monitoring software should all be Logo-certified.

The best approach is to have user applications that are compatible with the security strategy in WS08, so you don't need to compromise security in any way. Whatever you do, you will need to sit down and test each of your applications to ensure that they work properly in the WS08 environment. You'll also have to ensure that each and every one is tested using an account with only standard user privileges. This will avoid any nasty surprises during deployment.

Since you need to test every application, you might consider repackaging their installations to be compatible with the Windows Installer service. This operation automatically gives self-healing capability to every application, not to mention that any application using the Windows Installer service can also be deployed through Active Directory. More on this will be covered in Chapter 7. Both commercial and corporate applications will need to be treated as sub-projects during your migration. Once again, you can use the parallel network to install new application servers and then migrate your member services to these new servers. You will need to carefully plan each service migration. Microsoft Exchange, for example, provides a

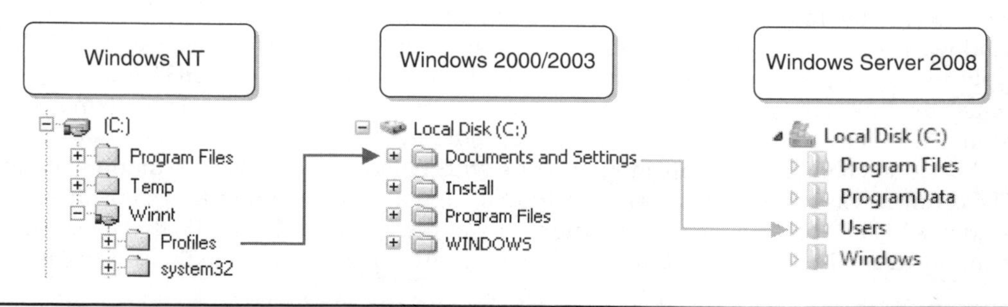

FIGURE 6-6 The WS08 application execution folder structure

centralized e-mail service that is not simple to migrate and that is difficult to address through a simple software upgrade. The same applies to line-of-business applications. The impact of migrating from one version of a widely used application to another is always significant and must be managed.

TIP *For information on how to manage migration projects and prepare applications for operation under the new Vista security model, read the "Definitive Guide to Vista Migration" by Ruest and Ruest, published through Realtime Publishers, and available for free at www.realtime-nexus .com/dgvm.htm.*

Given these considerations, it is most likely that you will not migrate member servers first. But if you do, you will want to use a member server migration timeline (see Figure 6-7). You can begin the migration of either type of server whenever you want to, but you will need a sub-project for each server type. You may decide to begin with corporate applications, since, as you can see, you will require time to convert existing applications before the migration can take place and to do so, you need to put development servers in place.

TIP *Our recommendation: Start with identity servers if you can. They are easy to integrate to either existing or new environments and form the very core of the network service.*

Prepare Detailed Inventories

Whichever you migrate first, identity servers or member servers; the first thing you'll need is a detailed inventory of everything that is on every server. Chapter 3 detailed the general inventories you need to build a logical network. One of these inventories relates to the servers themselves. Each one includes access control lists, files and folders, installed

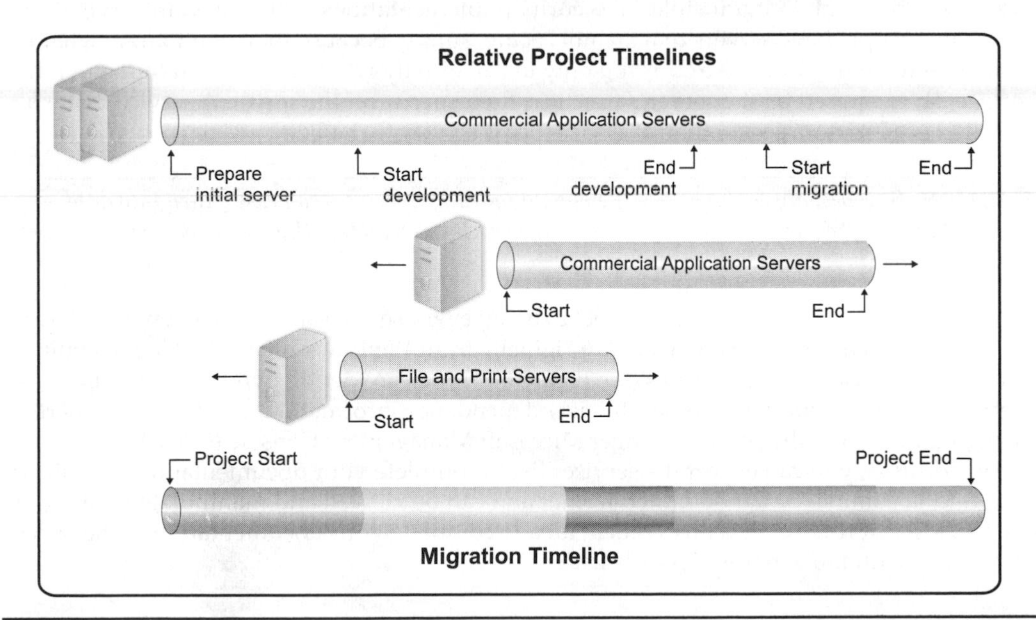

FIGURE 6-7 The member server migration timeline

PART III

applications, installed services, and which of these will be required in the new configuration. This inventory should be performed in two phases. The first should be at the beginning of the project. This inventory is less detailed. It is used to give you a general picture of the services and service points that are required in the new network.

The second is much more precise and should occur as close as possible to the moment you will migrate the server. Servers are complex environments that are constantly changing, especially if users are assigned to them. A good place to start is with server documentation. If you are already using standard documentation procedures for each of your servers, you'll probably want to update them to take into account modifications brought by Windows Server 2008. If you're not using standard server documentation approaches, now's a good time to start.

TIP *A complete Windows Server Data Sheet is available at www.reso-net.com/articles.asp?m=8 (search for "data sheet"). You can also learn how to work with this data sheet at http://searchwincomputing.techtarget.com/originalContent/0,289142,sid68_gci1245531,00.html. Use it to document both legacy and parallel network server construction.*

You'll also need to review other inventories during your project, especially the network service inventory. This last inventory will be essential for the building of a parallel network. Now you begin to see the value of maintaining ongoing inventories, because performing all of these inventories from scratch at the beginning of a migration project really slows you down. It's amazing how many companies are in exactly this situation every time they begin such a project.

Security Considerations

The Server Data Sheet will also be useful in the support of your efforts to build a secure network. One of the first principles of security implementations is "Know your servers!" Too many people have servers that are not secure, simply because they don't know what is installed on them. Also, make sure you only install exactly what you need on the server. If a service isn't required by the server's function, then keep it off the server. A service that isn't installed is a lot more secure than a service that is simply turned off.

CAUTION *Be especially cautious here. Removing unwanted services can easily turn into dead machines. Make sure you have carefully studied each service's function and dependencies before you remove it.*

Once again, use the Server Data Sheet to detail every service and its function. Windows Server 2008 offers a most useful feature (originally from Windows 2000/2003) in the ability to display a service's dependencies (see Figure 6-8). You can identify when a service is required simply to support another. To view dependency information, display the properties of any service using the Server Manager Microsoft Management Console (MMC).

In addition, you can export the services list to complete your documentation. This list is exported in comma- or tab-delimited format and can be viewed and manipulated with tools such as Microsoft Excel. It is an excellent idea to complete your documentation in the Server Data Sheet with the exported services list.

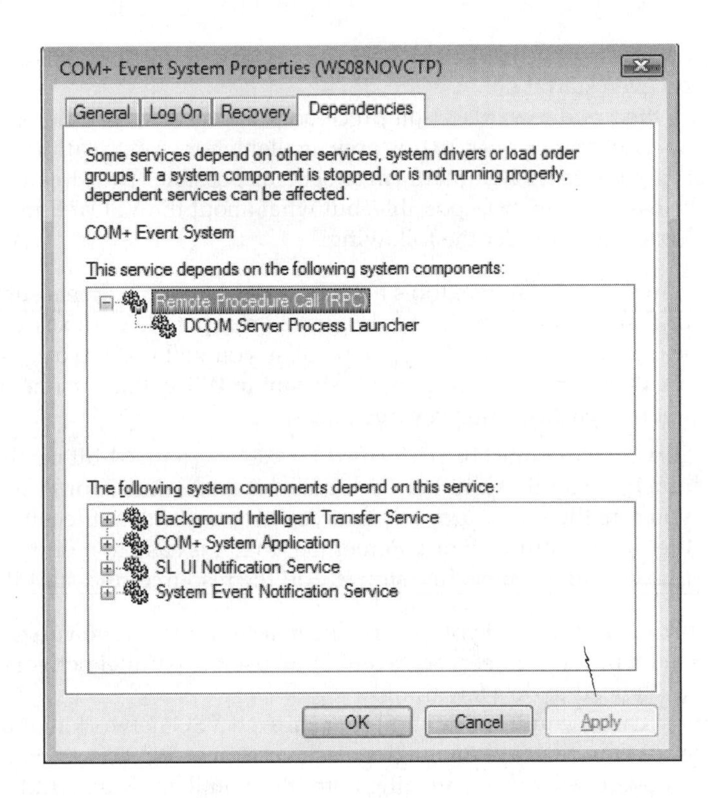

FIGURE 6-8 The COM+ Event System Properties dialog box

Licensing Considerations

As mentioned in previous chapters, the operating system you run on the host server will determine the number of licenses you have access to for your virtual service offerings. Each copy of Enterprise edition lets you run up to four VSOs with any version of Windows. Each copy of Datacenter edition lets you run an unlimited number of VSOs. Datacenter is licensed per processor, while Enterprise is licensed per server. If you want more than four VSOs running on top of Enterprise edition, buy another Enterprise edition license. In the end, you will rely on the host license that makes the most sense to you; then you should choose the appropriate edition of WS08, depending on the role the server will play and the number of users it will support. Rely on the server-sizing exercise in Chapter 4 to determine which version suits the role best.

You may also have to implement a key management server to manage licenses in your organization. It all depends on your size and the number of machines you run in your network. If you do, then you can add it as part of the network infrastructure services you implement in the new network.

Choose the Processor Architecture

The topic of 32-bit versus 64-bit processor architectures has been covered before, but it needs to be revisited at this stage. That's because you're just about to start building your new network and you need to make this decision now. WS08 is the very last server operating system Microsoft will release for the 32-bit platform. This means that if you decide to put your network in place while relying on 32-bit processor architectures, it is going to be obsolete before you even start it up.

Given the trend towards 64-bit processors, and given that Microsoft is moving in this direction—Exchange Server 2007 is only available for 64-bit platforms—you should consider moving to a 64-bit platform as soon as possible. You already know that hardware should be 64-bit as much as possible, but what about the VSOs? Should they be 32- or 64-bit? To decide, consider the following:

- Low-level file system tools must be x64-compatible. Items such as antivirus software or disk defragmentation tools must be compatible with x64 versions of WS08. This should not be a show stopper, because you will need to upgrade these components for WS08 anyway, since the file system in WS08, like the one in Windows Vista, is not compatible with previous releases.
- Server sizing must be performed for each system. 64-bit machines will give you a much longer lifespan than 32-bit machines. As such, you want to make sure that you size the server properly and you scope it with sufficient upgradability for its lifetime in your network. Remember that it is easy to modify the resources assigned to a virtual machine. Just stop it, add the resource, and start it again.

Unfortunately, most of you will not be in a situation where you can just build a new network with brand-new servers, even if you use the parallel network approach. This means you'll need to do a few things.

In most cases, you'll end up building a mixed VSO network that includes both x86 and x64 systems. Don't worry—managing each version of WS08 is similar, so you won't have additional overhead when managing both. But you'll have to identify which systems to keep on x86 platforms and which ones to move to x64. Table 6-3 lists some options in this regard by recommending which server roles best fit the x86 and x64 models.

Assign Resources to VSOs

In addition to determining the processor architecture, you will need to determine how many resources to assign to them. In some cases, roles require massive amounts of resources. This includes roles such as Terminal Services, Exchange Server 2007, and some application servers. This means you need to introduce a new VM role: the *single-VM host*. Table 6-4 lists recommendations for server role virtualization. Note the correspondence with Table 6-3; each role that is well suited to x64 processor architecture is also well suited to being the sole virtual machine on a system.

TIP *Monitor these "single-VM" hosts to determine resource utilization. If resources are available, then add new VSOs to this host.*

Okay, how do you apply the recommendations in Table 6-4? The best way is to look to the next steps. You are about to generate your new, parallel network. Each of the servers in this network will require physical, shared-, or single-VM assignments. Table 6-5 lists which should be which. It only covers domain controllers because they are the first servers you need to create. Other roles will be covered in similar tables in each of the following chapters. The data

Server Role	x86	x64	Comments
Network Infrastructure and Server Services	☒	☒	Network infrastructure servers are suitable to 32-bit workloads in most cases. Consider 64-bit servers only for virtual private network servers that must manage thousands of connections. Host servers should run 64-bit hardware because this role is resource-intensive.
Identity Management Servers	☒		Most identity servers (domain controllers) are quite well suited to 32-bit architectures because the very nature of ADDS is to add multiple servers for redundancy. If one server can't handle the load, another will. Consider 64-bit servers if the ADDS domain contains more than 50,000 objects.
File and Print Servers	☒		File loads are not processor-intensive, so 32-bit is satisfactory. If your clients are running Vista, then they are pre-processing all print jobs, reducing the print server workload and making it 32-bit compatible. Besides, it may be difficult to obtain 64-bit printer drivers.
Application Servers		☒	Application servers are ideally suited to 64-bit architectures because their workloads are memory- and processor-intensive.
Terminal Servers		☒	Terminal servers are ideally suited to 64-bit architectures because they require massive amounts of RAM and other resources.
Dedicated Web Servers	☒		Dedicated Web servers, because of their nature, are well suited to 32-bit architectures. If more resources are needed, just add another server. If, however, you have thousands of connections to your servers, then consider 64-bit hardware. Because they have access to more RAM, x64 servers can manage many more TCP/IP connections.
Collaboration Servers		☒	Collaboration servers are ideal for 64-bit hardware because they run memory-intensive processes.
Failsafe Servers	☒	☒	These servers need to match the architecture of the server they aim to replace.

TABLE 6-3 Comparison of 32- or 64-bit Hardware Considerations per Server Role

in Table 6-5 follows the recommendations for forest generation and server placement outlined in Chapter 5. Only enough servers to seed the network are identified here.

Since all machines are VMs, except for the hosts themselves, there is no need to indicate whether they are single- or shared-VM machines in their name. Remember, the server name will be seen by users, so use a standard nomenclature. You can, however, add the information in the server's description so that administrators will quickly know in which mode a machine is running.

Server Role	Physical	Shared-VM	Single-VM	Comments
Network Infrastructure and Server Services	☒			Server services servers, such as host servers, must be physical and should run on 64-bit hardware, but can run on 32-bit hardware with Microsoft Virtual Server.
		☒	☒	Network infrastructure servers, such as Dynamic Host Configuration Protocol (DHCP) servers, can run on shared-VMs. Consider single-VM servers only for virtual private network servers that must manage thousands of connections.
Identity Management Servers		☒	☒	Consider single-VM servers if the ADDS domain contains more than 50,000 objects. Run most DCs in shared-VM mode.
File and Print Servers		☒		File servers must be tied to virtualized storage. Print servers do not have a heavy load, since all rendering is on the Vista client. If you have legacy clients, consider a single-VM server.
Application Servers		☒	☒	Application servers will depend on their load. Begin with a single-VM server and monitor performance to see if you can move to shared-VM mode.
Terminal Servers			☒	Terminal servers are ideally suited to single-VM mode.
Dedicated Web Servers		☒		Dedicated Web servers, because of their nature, are well suited to shared-VM mode.
Collaboration Servers			☒	Collaboration servers should be single-VM, but should be monitored.
Failsafe Servers		☒		These servers are the first to consider for shared-VM because they are usually only required as failovers.

TABLE 6-4 Physical, Shared-, or Single-VM Recommendations

Forest and Domain	Server Role	Host	Shared-VM	Single-VM	Comments
Production Forest Root	First DC Second DC	Host01 Host02	☒ ☒		Host01 is in HQ1 site. Host02 is in HQ2 site.
Production Single Global Child Domain	First DC Second DC Third DC Fourth DC	Host01 Host02 Host03 Host04	☒ ☒ ☒ ☒		Host 03 is in HQ1, and Host 04 is in HQ2.
Staging Forest	All DCs	Host05	☒		All DCs are shared-VMs. A new host is created to separate this forest from production.
Training Forest	All DCs	Host05	☒		If sizing allows, this forest should share the same host as Staging.
Development Forest	All DCs	Host06	☒		These DCs should be in shared-VM mode, but should reside on a separate host.

TABLE 6-5 Shared- or Single-VM Recommendations for the Parallel Network

Implement the Parallel Network

The opportunities presented by the parallel network are quite bountiful and beneficial. For one thing, you get to re-create your production network from scratch using a design that capitalizes on the new operating system's core features. It's an ideal opportunity to revise every network concept and detail to see how it can be improved upon to further meet its basic objective: information service delivery and intraorganization communications support.

Of course, every part of the parallel network implementation process must be fully tested in a laboratory before being implemented in actual fact. The parallel network also gives you the opportunity to restructure domains if you feel that your Windows domain structure needs to be modified, especially in light of the information provided in Chapter 5 and in light of the Active Directory Domain Services implementation blueprint outlined in Figure 5-21. Restructuring can be done in three ways:

- Everything can be created from scratch. This means that there is nothing to be recovered from the existing network. All principals are re-created from scratch.
- The existing production network will be used as an information source for the new network. During this transfer process, administrators can perform additional data filtering to "clean up" information such as the identity database for the organization. If the existing domain is a Windows NT or Windows 2000/2003 domain, two options are available to recover information. The first involves integrating the existing Windows NT domain(s) into a Windows Server 2008 forest as a sub-domain, creating a new production domain in native WS08 mode, and then performing an intraforest

transfer. The MOVETREE command is used to perform this information transfer from domain to domain. MOVETREE can also be used at this time to filter information from one domain to the other. When emptied, the Windows NT domain is decommissioned and removed from the forest.

- The third mode is to perform an interforest transfer. This means that a new WS08 forest is created within the parallel network while the legacy domain structure remains as is. Interforest data migration tools are used to perform the transfer. This can be performed with the Active Directory Migration Tool (ADMT). ADMT can transfer data objects, such as user accounts, from the legacy domain to the WS08 forest, including passwords. Commercial data migration tools are also available. While ADMT offers limited filtering capabilities, commercial tools will offer sophisticated filtering and reporting tools as well as complete rollback capabilities. ADMT performs well for migrations of only a few thousand or less objects. But if you have tens of thousands of objects and dozens of Windows domains to consolidate, you would be well advised to obtain a commercial migration tool.

Of the three restructuring options, few are likely to perform the first, since it is extremely rare to find a network from which there is nothing to recover. The second limits the growth of the Windows Server 2008 network for the duration of the migration. Remember, a WS08 forest cannot operate in forest functional mode until all domains are in domain functional mode. Including a legacy domain into the forest will limit its growth potential until the migration is complete. Migrations take time—time that is evaluated in a proportional manner based on the number of users in the network and on the deployment strategy: parallel deployments (several deployments in several regions at the same time) or sequential deployments (one after the other).

The recommended migration strategy is the third one. It applies whether you are migrating from Windows NT or Windows 2000/2003 and you need to restructure the forest. Its great advantage is that the forest can immediately operate in full functional mode, profiting from this functionality level from day one. You can also filter all data input into the new forest. This means you can start your new WS08 network with a squeaky clean environment. In addition, it is an opportunity that is supported by the move to VSOs. Keeping the existing network separate gives you a clear rollback strategy in case you need it.

Implementing a parallel network and designing a new forest is based on the ADDS implementation blueprint (see Figure 5-21), but implementing this blueprint is a complex process that must be taken a step at a time. The first stages of this implementation are begun here, but the implementation will not be complete until the data migration process is complete. This will be done in all future chapters.

To implement the parallel network and perform the restructuring exercise, you must begin with the following activities:

- Prepare for the parallel network.
- Create the production Active Directory Domain Services.
- Connect the parallel network.

The details of each procedure are outlined in this chapter. They follow the steps outlined in the parallel network blueprint (see Figure 6-9). If, on the other hand, you simply need to

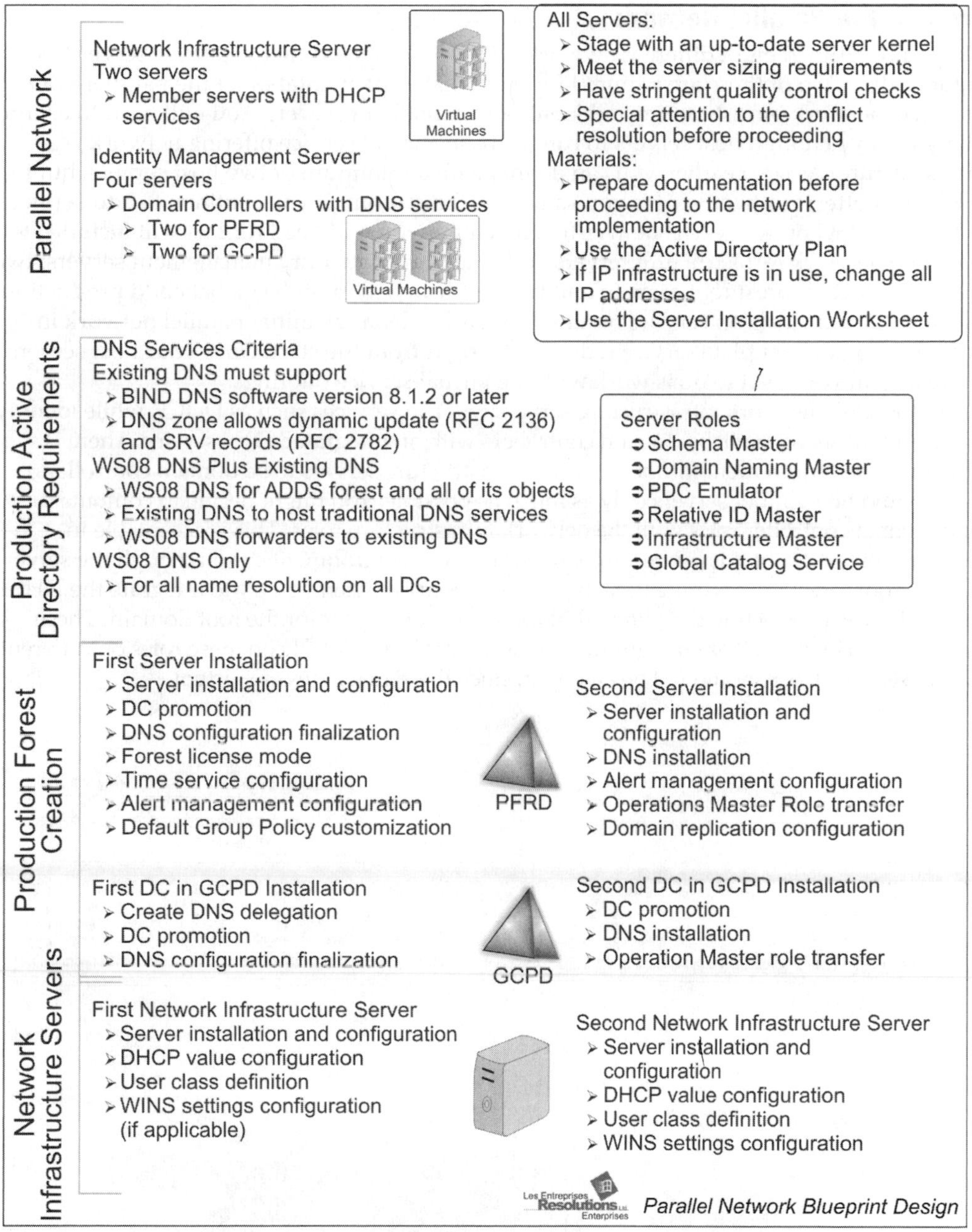

Parallel Network

Network Infrastructure Server
Two servers
- Member servers with DHCP services

Virtual Machines

Identity Management Server
Four servers
- Domain Controllers with DNS services
  - Two for PFRD
  - Two for GCPD

Virtual Machines

All Servers:
- Stage with an up-to-date server kernel
- Meet the server sizing requirements
- Have stringent quality control checks
- Special attention to the conflict resolution before proceeding

Materials:
- Prepare documentation before proceeding to the network implementation
- Use the Active Directory Plan
- If IP infrastructure is in use, change all IP addresses
- Use the Server Installation Worksheet

Production Active Directory Requirements

DNS Services Criteria
Existing DNS must support
- BIND DNS software version 8.1.2 or later
- DNS zone allows dynamic update (RFC 2136) and SRV records (RFC 2782)

WS08 DNS Plus Existing DNS
- WS08 DNS for ADDS forest and all of its objects
- Existing DNS to host traditional DNS services
- WS08 DNS forwarders to existing DNS

WS08 DNS Only
- For all name resolution on all DCs

Server Roles
- Schema Master
- Domain Naming Master
- PDC Emulator
- Relative ID Master
- Infrastructure Master
- Global Catalog Service

Production Forest Creation

First Server Installation
- Server installation and configuration
- DC promotion
- DNS configuration finalization
- Forest license mode
- Time service configuration
- Alert management configuration
- Default Group Policy customization

PFRD

Second Server Installation
- Server installation and configuration
- DNS installation
- Alert management configuration
- Operations Master Role transfer
- Domain replication configuration

First DC in GCPD Installation
- Create DNS delegation
- DC promotion
- DNS configuration finalization

GCPD

Second DC in GCPD Installation
- DC promotion
- DNS installation
- Operation Master role transfer

Network Infrastructure Servers

First Network Infrastructure Server
- Server installation and configuration
- DHCP value configuration
- User class definition
- WINS settings configuration (if applicable)

Second Network Infrastructure Server
- Server installation and configuration
- DHCP value configuration
- User class definition
- WINS settings configuration

Les Entreprises Resolutions Enterprises *Parallel Network Blueprint Design*

Figure 6-9 The parallel network blueprint

upgrade your existing Windows 2000/2003 forest to WS08, you can use the procedure at the end of this chapter. It is still a good idea, though, to review the contents of the parallel network creation process to ensure that your upgraded forest uses the latest WS08 concepts and features.

Prepare the Parallel Network

Chapter 3 outlined eight different network server roles, including the failsafe server (see Figure 6-10). Two of these are required for the initial implementation of the parallel VSO network: network infrastructure and identity management servers. You will need to ensure that you have enough host servers to run the basic virtual service offering network infrastructure. As seen earlier, you can do this with a minimum of two host servers, but four would be better, as it would give you some breathing room as you continue to add services to the new VSO network. The new virtual machines you will need for this will include at least two network infrastructure servers and at least four identity management servers: two for the protected forest root domain and two for the creation of the global child production domain (GCPD). Two servers are required for each role in the initial parallel network in order to provide complete service redundancy right from the start. Once your host servers are ready, all you need to do is work with the virtual service offerings.

In the VSO, network infrastructure servers will run services such as DHCP, while identity management servers will be domain controllers with an integrated DNS service. There is absolutely no requirement for the network infrastructure servers to be domain controllers; they should be member servers only as much as possible. You might decide to combine the root domain controller roles with the network infrastructure roles. This is acceptable in smaller networks, but it is not recommended in larger environments, even though the server load on root forest DCs is quite light. Several issues arise when you try to integrate the DHCP service for the production domain with the domain controllers for the root domain. These include security as well as configuration issues. If at all possible, keep these roles on different virtual servers. Cost should not be an object, since these machines are virtual.

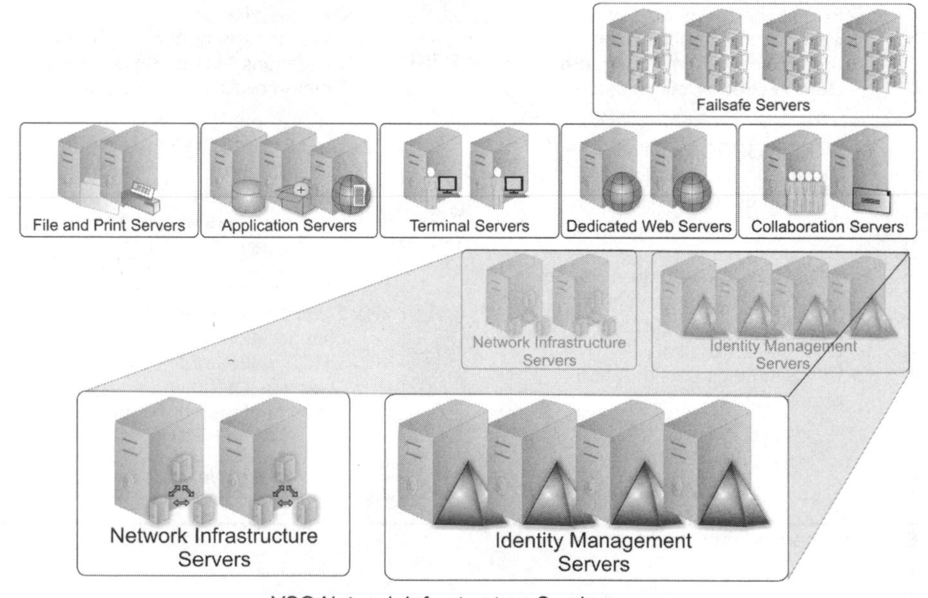

FIGURE 6-10 WS08 VSO network infrastructure server roles

NOTE *You don't want to proliferate machines, but these are significant roles in the network and should be dedicated to special servers.*

All parallel network servers should be staged with an up-to-date server kernel according to staging practices outlined in Chapter 4. Since they are virtual machines, this means copying the Sysprepped source and then personalizing it. Assign each machine to the appropriate host, as listed in Table 6-5. Start each server with a single processor and 512 MB of RAM. Monitor their progress and then adjust the RAM as required. Once it is prepared, each server should have stringent quality control checks to ensure that it is ready for production. These checks should ensure that everything on the server is running smoothly.

If you have several large sites within your organization, you'll most likely want to separate each double server role physically, putting a server for each role in each of two physical sites. This provides network redundancy and creates an automatic service backup in case of disasters. This is the approach used here. Since the machines are virtual, you will eventually be able to replicate their contents from one site to the other, letting you always keep a complete copy of the infrastructure within each site.

You'll also need prepared documentation before proceeding with the network implementation. Your existing IP infrastructure design will most likely be adequate for the implementation of the parallel network. You will, however, need to change all IP addresses, since the new network and the old network will need to coexist for some time. You will also need to implement IPv6 in this network. You should have this information in hand before proceeding with network creation.

In addition, you will also require your Active Directory Domain Services plan. For this, you must have performed the planning exercise outlined in Chapter 5. This plan will serve as a directory map for you to follow during the implementation of the WS08 Active Directory. With these documents in hand, you can prepare the parallel network. Remember, everything is done in a laboratory first. Here you can specifically document every single step that is required for the actual creation of the production enterprise network. The more documentation you have, the less likely you are to commit errors when creating the new network. This is not a time where errors are allowed.

TIP *Since the machines you create in the test lab are virtual, you can actually create your entire VSO in the lab and then copy it—or simply connect it—to production once you are ready to put it in place. In addition, because the machines are virtual, you can simply scrap any machine that is not pristine and start the process over again quite easily. Don't put the machines into production until you are completely happy with the results.*

Once your parallel network is up and running, you'll be able to create a trust relationship between the new production domain and your legacy domain(s). This trust relationship will last for the duration of the migration to provide cross-forest services to all users. Then you can migrate users, computers, and services at will using either ADMT or a commercial migration tool (see Figure 6-11). This will be your first step towards the VSO and simpler systems management.

Let's start with the first stage, implementing the production Active Directory.

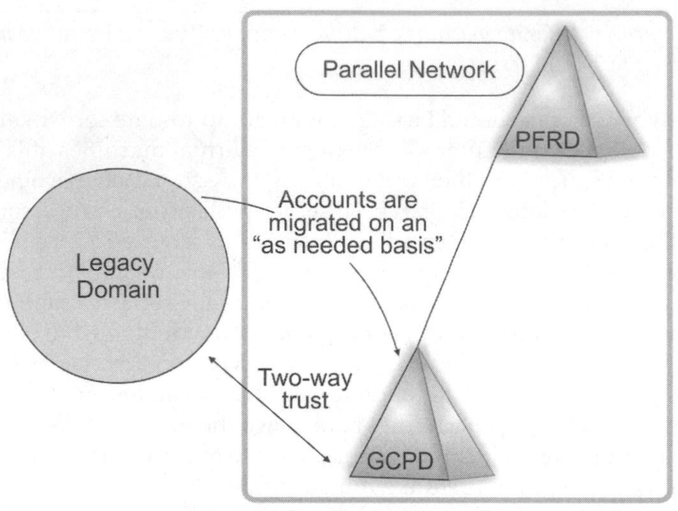

FIGURE 6-11 Using a parallel network to migrate data between forests

Create the Production Active Directory

Creating a brand-new Active Directory Domain Services structure is a straightforward process. It involves the creation of at least four domain controllers according to the server positioning strategy identified in Figure 5-16 in Chapter 5. Two of these domain controllers belong to the protected forest root domain. Each will host a forest-wide operations master role: Schema or Domain Naming Master. These two DCs will also host the domain-centric operations master roles: PDC Emulator, Relative ID, and Infrastructure Masters. In addition, these DCs will host the Global Catalog service.

TIP *The Infrastructure Master and Global Catalog can be hosted on the same DC in the forest root domain because, like the domain in the utility forest, the root domain contains so few objects. This will not be the case in the production domain.*

Additional tasks must be performed during the creation of these servers. Since the very first DC is the first server in the parallel network, it must host a few additional functions. These functions include:

- **Time service hosting** You may require that your entire network be synchronized with an external time source, such as an atomic clock. Whether you do so or not, you must ensure that time synchronization is implemented in your network. Time synchronization is essential, since Kerberos, the preferred authentication protocol in Windows Server 2008, is time-sensitive. In ADDS, all time synchronization is performed through each member system's link to the PDC Emulator of the domain they belong to. Linking the first PDC Emulator in the forest to a secure time source will automatically link all other PDC Emulators in child domains.

- **Alert management** If you rely on an alert management community for server administration, then it must be configured on this server as well.

  Name resolution will also be required. The first DC in a network requires a DNS server to function properly. You could use an existing DNS server for this purpose, but Windows Server 2008 has particular requirements for the DNS service. If you choose to use a DNS server other than the WS08 DNS server, this DNS server must support the following criteria:

  - Berkeley Internet Name Domain (BIND) DNS servers must be version 8.1.2 or later of the BIND software to meet the DNS requirements for Active Directory support.
  - The DNS zone must allow dynamic updates (RFC 2136).
  - The DNS server hosting that zone must support the Service Location (SRV) resource records (RFC 2782) to advertise the directory service.

- **Our recommendation** If there are issues (most often political) and you cannot move existing DNS services to WS08, then compromise. Use WS08 DNS for the AD forest and all of its objects and use the other DNS service to host traditional DNS services. Include forwarders in your WS08 DNS servers to perform name resolution of non-AD objects through your legacy DNS servers.

PART III

If there are no issues, political or otherwise, then use the WS08 DNS service for all name resolution. WS08 uses the directory for DNS operation, so DNS services are automatically available to every object that is part of the domain. For objects that are not part of the domain, just direct them to one or both of the forest root domain DNS servers. The WS08 DNS service includes additional features:

- **Background zone loading** DNS zones are loaded in the background when the server starts, letting it respond more quickly to requests.
- **IPv6 support** DNS supports the long address format of IPv6 as well as its original support for all things IPv4.
- **RODC support** DNS supports read-only primary zone transfers to read-only domain controllers.
- **Global single names** These single-label name zones eliminate the need for legacy services such as the Windows Internet Naming System (WINS).

These features provide additional justification for relying on the Windows DNS service for Windows networks.

You will also need to identify whether client resolution will be performed through root hints or through forwarders. This will define the name resolution mechanism for clients. By default, WS08 DNS servers include all root hints, so you should aim to keep the default and use root hints if possible.

One of the critical operations supported by DNS is the logon process. When a user logon is initiated from a Windows 2000/XP/Vista client, the NetLogon service collects the required logon information for the domain to which the user is attempting to log on and sends a DNS query to its configured DNS servers. This query includes the following characteristics:

- **Query type** SRV (Service locator resource record)
- **Query name** _ldap._tcp.domain_name

The DNS server responds with the name of the domain controller that is closest to the client based on the client's location within the ADDS site structure. The logon request is sent to the DC, and if the username and password are valid for that domain, the user is logged onto the domain (see Figure 6-12).

When WS08 stores DNS zones within Active Directory, it simplifies replication and ensures the security of these records. Security is important here, since Windows 2000/XP/2003/Vista systems using DHCP will also use the dynamic feature of the DNS service to update their own records within it. If your network includes non-Windows objects that require name resolution, you will need to enter static canonical names for these objects within your WS08 DNS server, unless, of course, their IP addresses are assigned through the Windows DHCP server. Finally, when the DNS service is integrated with the directory, WS08 no longer requires the use of secondary zones to provide information from one DNS domain to another. WS08 uses application data partitions as replication partitions that can span several domains to ensure that data is available to everyone within the forest in the right location in the forest structure. These partitions are automatically created when you integrate DNS with Active Directory.

For these reasons, the DNS service should be married to the DC service in Windows Server 2008. This ensures that the name resolution service is always available in the same place as the domain controller and logon service. It also ensures that all DNS zones are secured and replicated through the directory replication mechanism. This is the approach that is recommended and used throughout this book.

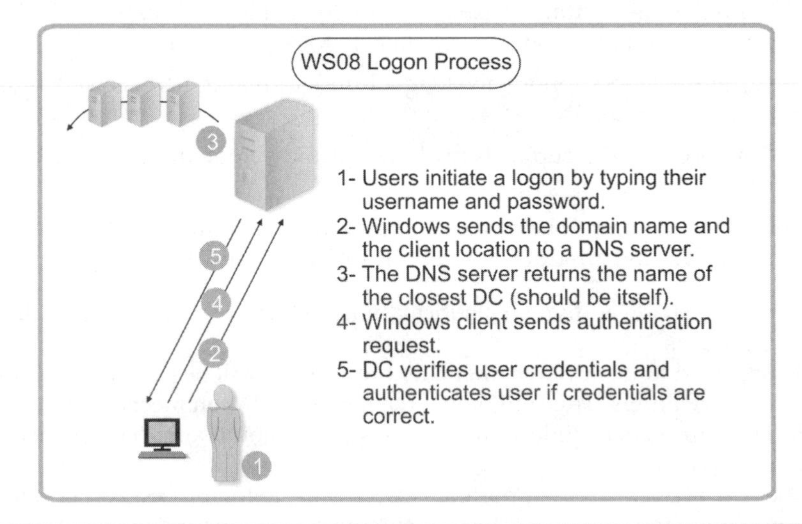

FIGURE 6-12 The WS08 logon process

Forest Staging Activities

Staging the new forest requires a given set of activities, each of which include several steps. These activities are listed in the production forest creation checklist (see Figure 6-13). As you can see, this checklist is divided into four primary activities: creation of the forest and root domain, creation of the production domain, creation of the IP infrastructure, and system finalization.

Active Directory Domain Services Checklist

1 Root Forest Creation

Install and name the 1st server in the network - Install this server in a workgroup at first

- ❑ Promote the first server to ADDS creating the forest root domain
- ❑ Configure DNS service
- ❑ Configure the time service for this server
- ❑ Configure alert management for this server and license management

Install and name the 2nd server for the forest root domain - This server can be a member of the forest root domain

- ❑ Promote the second server to ADDS within the forest root domain
- ❑ Install and configure the DNS service
- ❑ Transfer Operation Master roles to this server
- ❑ Verify that the domain is operating properly

2 Production Child Domain Creation

Install and name the 1st server for the Global Child Production Domain (GCPD) - Install this server in a workgroup at first

- ❑ Rely on DNS delegation
- ❑ Promote this server to ADDS creating the Global Child Production Domain
- ❑ Include the DNS service during this promotion
- ❑ Finalize the configuration of the DNS service

Install and name the three other servers for the core operation of the parallel network - Install each server as a member of the production domain

- ❑ Promote each one of the servers to ADDS within the production domain
- ❑ Install and configure the DNS service
- ❑ Update DNS delegation
- ❑ Transfer Operation Master roles as required

3 IP Infrastructure Creation

Proceed to the configuration of the network infrastructure servers

4 System Finalization

Move servers to their final site and then configure domain replication

- ❑ Verify that all domains are operating properly

5 Forest Finalization

Move servers to their final site and then configure domain replication

- ❑ Proceed to the creation of the other forests as needed

FIGURE 6-13 The production forest creation checklist

Install the First Server in a Forest

The first place to start is with the first server in the VSO forest. This server will have several characteristics: It will be a DC with integrated DNS service, it is the Schema Master for the forest, it is also the PDC Emulator and the RID Master for the forest root domain, it hosts the Global Catalog service, and it synchronizes time for the forest.

Server Installation and Configuration

Begin with the server kernel installation as per the procedures outlined in Chapter 4. Ideally, you will have built a custom virtual machine template that is Sysprepped and ready to be reused for the generation of servers. You use this seed virtual machine to generate all others by copying the files making up the source VM, renaming them, and booting it up.

Once the system is launched, configure the following elements, if they are not included in your Unattend.XML file:

- Computer name
- IPv4 address and configuration
- IPv6 address and configuration

In IPv4, for the client DNS configuration for this server, you should set the server to first point to itself. The second DNS server address should be one of the servers you intend to use as a forwarder, if forwarders are what you intend to use; otherwise, it should be the IPv4 address of the second DC you plan to install, even if it isn't installed yet. Ideally, you will rely on the default root hints that the WS08 DNS service relies on for name resolution requirements.

Finally, this server should belong to a workgroup that uses the same NetBIOS name you will use for your forest. For example, if you intend to use TandT.net as your VSO root forest name, your workgroup name should be TANDT. This will simplify the communication process between this server and the next server you create.

TIP *Remember the host forest is named TandT.ws and its down-level name is TANDTWS in order to avoid naming conflicts with this new production forest.*

Perform DC Promotion

The best way to perform this first DC promotion is through Server Manager. This tool is launched automatically at system startup. If not, you can start it with the Server Manager shortcut located in the Quick Launch area. Then use the following procedure to create your first forest domain controller.

1. Click Add Roles in the details pane. This will launch the Add roles Wizard. Click Next.
2. Windows Server 2008 will show the existing roles on the server.
3. Select Active Directory Domain Services (ADDS), and then click Next (see Figure 6-14).
4. Review role information and click Next.
5. Confirm your selection by clicking Install. This installs the ADDS binaries. Click Close when done.

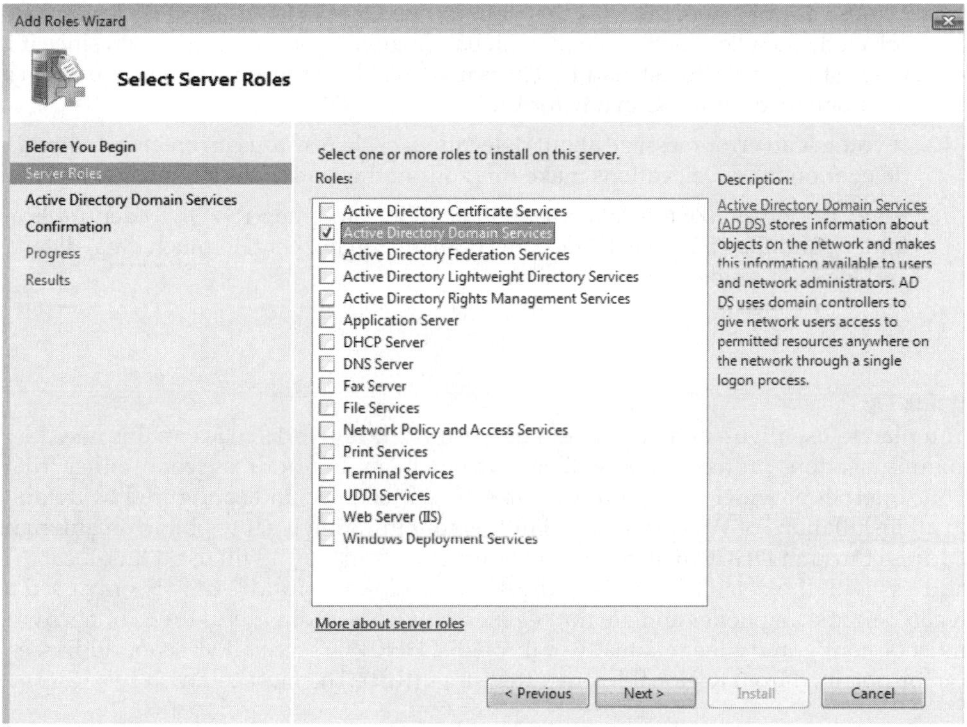

Figure 6-14 Adding the ADDS role

Tip *You do not need to access the installation media for WS08 in order to add any role or feature. WS08 automatically caches the binaries for all roles and features locally during installation. This facilitates the addition or removal of roles or features, even in disconnected mode. These binaries are automatically updated in the event of security updates or service packs.*

6. Next, click the new ADDS role in Server Manager. Note the information displayed in the top of the details pane. Click the provided link to begin the domain controller promotion. Alternatively, you could use the same procedure as with the utility forest earlier. This launches the Active Directory Installation Wizard. Make sure you select Advanced Mode and then click Next. This will make sure you get a chance to control all of the settings for this forest.
7. Select Create A New Domain In A New Forest, and then click Next.
8. Enter the full DNS name for the new forest root domain. Click Next.
9. The wizard will verify the NetBIOS name for the forest. Verify the NetBIOS name and click Next.
10. Choose the forest functional level—in this case, Windows Server 2008—and click Next. The system will then examine the DNS configuration.

11. Choose additional options for this domain controller. Make sure DNS Server is selected, and click Next. Note that Global Catalog is selected by default, since it is the first DC in the forest, and RODC is unavailable because you must start with at least one read-write DC in any forest.
12. If you get an error message about delegation, click Yes. You can create a manual delegation later. Delegations make this zone authoritative for the records it contains.
13. Select the location of the database and log folders and the SYSVOL folder (replication folder), and then click Next. Since this domain will not contain much data, database and logs can reside on the same disk.

Quick Tip

You plan to use IPv6—and you should because WS08 networks relies on this new communications protocol—you will need to obtain an IPv6 address scope, either from your Internet provider or for your own use. IPv6 is enabled and configured by default in all installations of Windows Vista. But this configuration is set to obtain an automatic address through DHCPv6. If no DHCPv6 server is available, it will use a link-local address with the default fe80::/64 address prefix. Link-local addresses are only used to reach neighboring nodes and are not registered in DNS. More useful IPv6 connectivity must be configured either manually or through a DHCPv6 server. IPv6 scope addresses can be obtained from Regional Internet Registries (RIR). The most common five RIRs are:

- American Registry for Internet Numbers (ARIN) for North America (www.arin.net)
- RIPE Network Coordination Centre (RIPE NCC) for Europe, the Middle East, and Central Asia (www.ripe.net)
- Asia-Pacific Network Information Centre (APNIC) for Asia and the Pacific region (www.apnic.net)
- Latin American and Caribbean Internet Address Registry (LACNIC) for Latin America and the Caribbean region (www.lacnic.net)
- African Network Information Centre (AfriNIC) for Africa (www.afrinic.net)

Once you obtain your scope, you can use it to configure your servers. Configuration of IPv6 settings is similar to that of IPv4. You need to configure the following settings:

- IPv6 unicast address
- Subnet prefix length—by default, this is 64
- Default gateway—again in IPv6 unicast format
- Preferred DNS—again, a unicast address
- Alternate DNS server

You can use the advanced settings to add either multiple IPv6 addresses or additional DNS servers. There are no WINS servers for IPv6 since it does not use NetBIOS names.

14. Set the directory service restore mode administrator password, and then click Next. This password is extremely important, since it is the password used to perform authoritative restores or restores that overwrite existing directory information during system recovery. Guard it carefully.
15. The DC promotion service will outline your choices. Review them carefully, and when ready to proceed, click Next. If you see errors in your choices, use the Back button to correct them. Clicking Next launches the Active Directory Installation Wizard. It will perform a series of tasks, including the reapplication of security parameters on the server's disks, and it will launch the DNS installation process. Select the Reboot On Completion check box. This will make sure the services are started and ready to operate once the system is back up.

The Active Directory installation process completes once the DNS server is installed. Proceed to the completion of the first server creation process as follows.

DNS Configuration Finalization

The ADDS DNS service installation prepares the DNS server to operate with Active Directory Domain Services, but it does not complete a full DNS configuration. Several elements are required to complete the configuration:

- Set aging/scavenging for all zones.
- Verify application partitions for DNS replication.
- Finalize reverse lookup name resolution configuration.

DNS server configuration is performed through Server Manager. Use the following procedure to configure your server.

1. Locate and expand the Roles item in the left pane of the console.
2. Locate and expand the DNS Server item in the left pane.
3. Expand the DNS item in the left pane. Then click the server name.
4. Begin with the aging and scavenging settings. To do so, right-click the server name and select Set Aging/Scavenging For All Zones from the context menu.
5. Select Scavenge Stale Resource Records to turn the feature on. Accept the default refresh interval (seven days) and click OK. This will ensure that your DNS database will not contain outdated records.
6. This will also give you the opportunity to set the scavenging mode for all future Active Directory–integrated zones. Make sure you select Apply These Settings To The Existing AD-Integrated Zones, and then click OK.
7. Next, verify the application partitions for the forest and the root domain DNS information. Windows Server 2008 separates forest DNS information from the root domain DNS information. It automatically sets the application partition scope for each set of DNS data. Application partitions are special replication partitions that can store any information that is not related to security principals. These partitions are composed of a set of IP addresses or DNS names defining the scope of the application partition. Using an application partition to store DNS information saves

you from having to create copies of DNS zones within child domains as read-only secondary DNS zones. This ensures that all DNS replication is secured and controlled through Active Directory Domain Services (see Figure 6-15).

8. To verify that appropriate application partitions have been created for DNS data, right-click each forward lookup zone name and select Properties from the context menu. WS08 includes a Replication section under the Type section of the General tab in zone properties. This Replication section controls the scope of the application partition. WS08 automatically sets the forest DNS data (_msdcs.*forestname*) to use a forest-wide application partition. It sets domain-specific data to use a domain-only application partition. Verify that this is the case, and close the dialog box when done.
9. Next, select the *Forestname* zone and verify that it is being replicated in the root domain only.
10. Finally, configure your reverse lookup zone. To do so, right-click the Reverse Lookup Zone item in the left pane, and select New Zone. This launches the New Zone Wizard. Click Next to begin the zone creation process.
11. Select the zone type—in this case, a primary zone—and make sure you select Store The Zone In Active Directory. Click Next.
12. Define the application partition for replication of zone data. Since this is information that is domain-specific, select To All DNS Servers In This Forest (see Figure 6-16). Click Next.
13. Select whether this is an IPv4 or IPv6 zone, and click Next.
14. Identify the parameters for the reverse lookup zone you want to create, and then click Next.

TIP *To have the New Zone Wizard automatically provide the name of the reverse zone, select Network ID and type the network address for the zone—for example: 192.168.1. The New Zone Wizard will automatically provide the value for the reverse lookup zone, even though it is not selected. To clear the Network ID box, select the Reverse Lookup Zone Name option.*

FIGURE 6-15 ADDS separates forest-wide DNS data from domain-specific data.

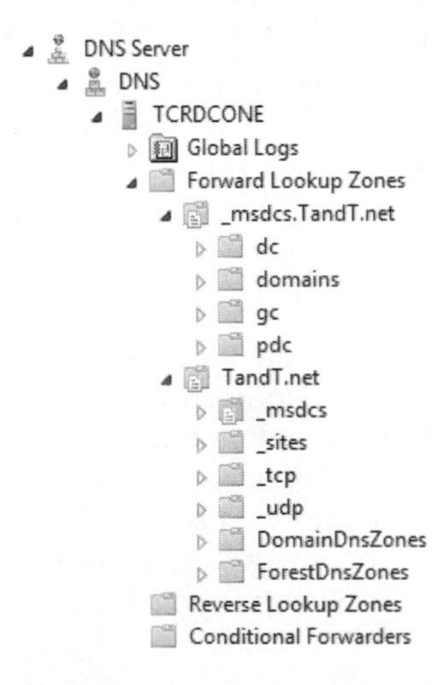

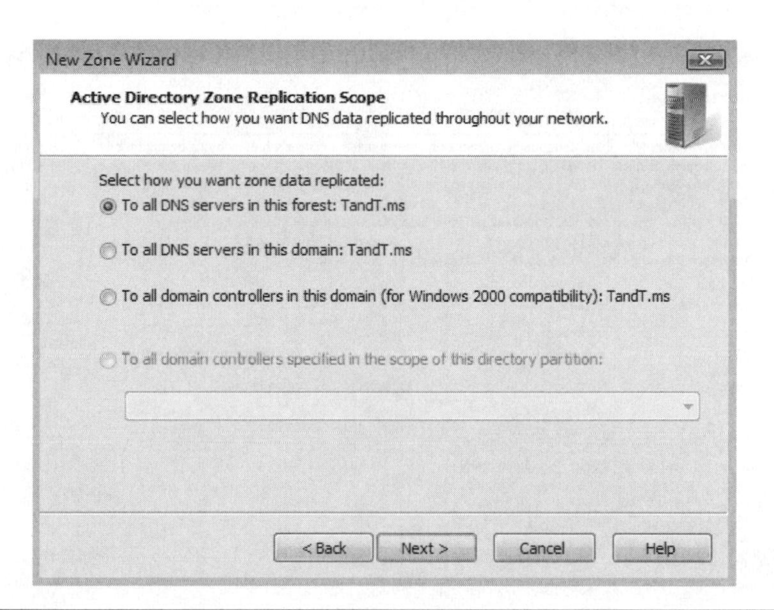

Figure 6-16 Active Directory zone replication scope

15. Next, select Allow Only Secure Dynamic Updates, and then click Next. Click Finish to create the zone.

That's it; your DNS server is ready. You can move on to the next stage.

Note *Like Windows Vista, WS08 also supports Peer Name Resolution Protocol (PNRP). This is a feature you can add to your DNS servers. For more information, go to: http://technet.microsoft.com/en-ca/library/bb726971.aspx.*

Time Service Configuration

Networks are very sensitive to time synchronization. That's why WS08 includes a built-in time synchronization system. In a WS08 forest, the Windows Time service configures itself automatically, taking advantage of the time service that is available on domain controllers. A special domain controller, the PDC Emulator, serves as the authoritative source for time within a domain. In a forest, PDC Emulators synchronize with time sources in parent domains. Ultimately, only one server needs manual time synchronization. This is usually the first domain controller in the forest.

You need to decide if you are willing to synchronize your AD forest with an external time source, whether you want to use an internal time source, or whether you want to let the forest synchronize on this server, even though its time setting may not be accurate. Each one has its own issues. Not setting the time source will create ID 12 events in the System Event Log (see Figure 6-17).

You can synchronize with any of several sources. For example, Microsoft provides a time source at time.windows.com. If you don't want to use Microsoft's source, you can find a list of several accurate time sources provided by the U.S. Naval Observatory Master

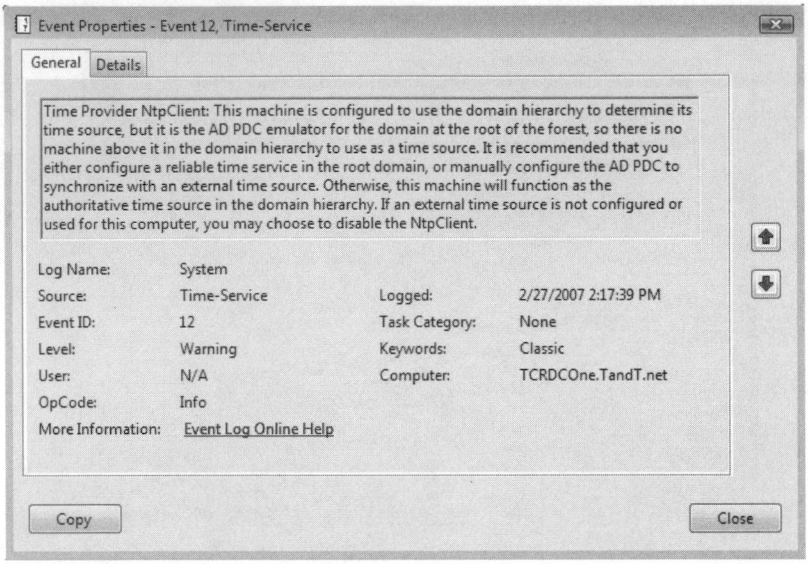

Figure 6-17 Event ID number 12

Clocks at http://tycho.usno.navy.mil. Use the appropriate setting according to the time zone your source server belongs to.

To set a time source server, use the w32tm command-line tool. For example, the command to use to set your clock with the Windows time service would be:

```
w32tm /config /manualpeerlist:"time.windows.com" /update
```

This will set the first DC to synchronize time with the source system listed. Remember, to do this, you will have to open the outgoing User Datagram Protocol (UDP) port (123) in your firewall to allow Simple Network Time Protocol (SNTP) traffic.

Caution *You need to reset this value each time you move the PDC Emulator role from this DC to another.*

Alert Management Configuration

Most enterprise networks use a system-wide alert management tool. This is performed through the Simple Network Management Protocol (SNMP). This feature must be installed on all servers and computers if the alert management system is to work. Because there are security risks in running this service without a rigid configuration, its configuration must be customized. Verify that SNMP services are installed. If not, use the Add Features Wizard to install them, and then proceed to its security configuration.

1. To do so, you need to expand Configuration | Services in the left pane.
2. Then find the SNMP Services item in the details pane. Double-click it when you locate it.

3. Three items need configuration here: Agent Information, Trap Destinations, and SNMP Security Properties. Select the Agent tab, and type the operator's name and physical location.
4. Select the Trap tab, and identify the community name and valid trap destinations. The destinations should normally be your two root forest servers or other servers if you have management servers.
5. Finally, select the Security tab and set the accepted community names. Add your organization's community in read-only mode. Click Add. Your community name should be complex and not easy to guess. Select Accept SNMP Packets From These Hosts, and add the valid hostnames. Click OK when done.

There you are. The first server in your network is almost ready. One final operation needs to be performed.

Set Up the Key Management Server

Organizations with volume-license agreements with Microsoft will find they will need to implement a central key management service (KMS) to activate and maintain Vista PC and WS08 activation in their network. Anyone using volume activation keys (VAKs) will need both activation and reactivation in order to maintain a proper level of user experience with their systems. This protects volume activation keys in ways that have never been possible before. Organizations using multiple activation keys (MAKs) can also rely on KMS to provide activation services. The major difference between the MAK and the VAK is that the MAK requires a one-time activation only. The VAK requires constant reactivation (every 180 days). In addition, the MAK requires a communication with Microsoft, at least through the proxy service, if not from each machine using a MAK, whereas VAKs never require access to Microsoft's activation web site.

If you are using MAKs, then you do not need a KMS server. If you are using VAKs, then you need to install a KMS server.

NOTE *Download KMS at www.microsoft.com/downloads/details.aspx?FamilyID=81d1cb89-13bd-4250-b624-2f8c57a1ae7b&DisplayLang=en.*

If you decide to use KMS servers, then set it up on this server. For instructions on how to set up the KMS server, go to http://technet.microsoft.com/en-us/windowsvista/bb335280.aspx. For more information on volume activation in general, go to www.microsoft.com/licensing/resources/vol/default.mspx.

Default Group Policy and Security Customization

The first DC in a forest includes two default Group Policy Objects (GPOs): the Default Domain Policy and the Default Domain Controller Policy. While there is no such thing as recurring Group Policy inheritance between the domains in a forest, there is a one-time GPO inheritance process during domain controller installation. This means that every subsequent domain controller you create in any part of the forest will inherit the settings for these two GPOs. This is an excellent opportunity to ensure that a given set of standards is implemented within your forest. To do so, you must customize both of these default GPOs.

You might want to change settings, such as forcing the renaming of the administrator account, enforcing strong passwords throughout the forest, strengthening domain controller security settings, and much more. The suggested parameters for both of these policies are outlined in Chapter 10, which covers security. Ensure that you review these settings and modify the ones you deem appropriate for your environment.

Once this is complete, your first server is ready. Ensure that you verify every aspect of this server's configuration before moving on. You will then be ready to proceed to the creation of the second domain controller for the forest root domain.

Create the Second DC in the Forest Root Domain

The second domain controller in the forest root domain is much simpler to create than the first. You need to perform the installation of the server, install Active Directory with DNS, review the configuration of the DNS server, optionally install SNMP, and then migrate two of the Operations Master roles. Once this is complete, you will need to configure and verify the proper operation of the AD replication system. Then you'll be ready to move on to the creation of the global child production domain.

Server Installation and Configuration

Proceed with the standard virtual server installation process. Ensure that the server kernel is up to date, and perform a quality control check on the server. This server can be configured to be a member server of the TandT.net domain since it is destined to become a domain controller for this domain. If you decide to install it in a workgroup, ensure that, at the very least, it is part of the TANDT workgroup. This will facilitate the communication process with the TandT.net domain because it uses the same NetBIOS name.

Also, remember to configure Transmission Control Protocol/Internet Protocol (TCP/IP) client properties in the same way that you configured the first server in the network. There is one variation here, though: You can configure the DNS address to be itself as the first address and the first DC as the second address.

DC Promotion

Next, install the ADDS binaries and promote this server to a domain controller. Use the same procedure as with the first domain controller in the forest root domain, with the following variations:

1. In the first screen of the Active Directory Domain Services Installation Wizard, select Existing Forest and then Add A Domain Controller To An Existing Forest. Click Next.
2. Type the name of the root domain, select Alternate Credentials, and then click Set.
3. Type appropriate credentials to create the DC in the existing domain. This account must be a member of the Enterprise Administrators group. Click OK and then click Next.
4. Next, select the domain to join, and click Next.
5. Select a site for the new domain. Select the default first site name for now. Click Next.
6. If they are not already selected, select DNS Server and Global Catalog. Do not select RODC. Click Next. Click Yes in response to the delegation message.

7. Since you are on the same network, select Replicate Data Over The Network From An Existing DC, and click Next.
8. Select Any Writable DC and click Next.
9. Finally, locate the database and logs, as well as the system volume, in the same places as the first DC. Click Next.
10. Set your Restore mode password, click Next, review the summary, click Next, and select Reboot On Completion.

Use the AD consoles to verify the proper operation of the DC after it reboots.

NOTE *The summary dialog box lets you export this data to an answer file to support the automation of this process when you have a lot of servers to add as domain controllers.*

The interactive DC Promotion Wizard automatically installed the DNS service on the domain controller when it performed the installation of ADDS. You don't need to do anything to configure zones in DNS since they will be loaded from the directory. You should, however, take the time to review the DNS configuration and make sure everything is working properly.

Perform the same operations on this server as on the first DC to configure the SNMP service. Ensure that proper community names have been entered and that messages are received and sent to approved sources. This will ensure a secure SNMP and alert management configuration.

Operations Master Role Transfer

Next, transfer the appropriate Operations Master roles to this server. Transferring Operations Master roles is a delicate procedure. Some roles are extremely sensitive. The Schema Master, in particular, must be transferred with care, since only one Schema Master can exist per forest and the forest schema can be corrupted by the simultaneous existence of two Schema Masters. Operation Master role transfers occur in two situations: during the installation of a forest or domain and during service failures. You must be extremely careful in both cases.

Take, for example, the following situation. The Schema Master server fails. It is turned off for repairs. An administrator seizes the Schema Master role and applies it to another DC in the forest. The original server is repaired and reinserted in the network without removing its Schema Master role. The consequence: two Schema Masters in the forest and a corrupt schema. The ADDS database must be reloaded from backups. As you can see, you must be as careful with the Schema Master role as with the schema itself. Only stringent processes and procedures can help ensure the proper operation of the enterprise network.

Several different tools are required to migrate Operations Master roles:

- **Schema Master** Use the Active Directory Schema MMC
- **Domain Naming Master** Use the Active Directory Domains and Trusts MMC
- **PDC Emulator, RID Master, Infrastructure Master** Use the Active Directory Users and Computers section in Server Manager

Since you need to transfer both the Domain Naming and the Infrastructure Masters, you will need to use two consoles to perform the task. The operation can also be performed from the command line using the NTDSUTIL command. But since it only has to be done once, use the consoles. It is easier and will familiarize you with the contents of ADDS. Begin with the Domain Naming Master.

1. Open the Active Directory Domains and Trusts console on the second DC. It can be found in Administrative tools.
2. Right-click Active Directory Domains and Trusts, right above the domain name, and select Operations Master from the context menu.
3. Click Change to move the role to this server, and then click Yes. Click OK when the role transfer is complete. Click Close when done. Close this console.
4. Next, move to Active Directory Users and Computers in the Roles section of Server Manager, located under ADDS.
5. Right-click the name of the domain, and select Operations Master from the context menu.
6. Select the Infrastructure tab, and click Change to move the role to this DC.
7. Click Yes in response to the security warning. Click OK and click Close when the operation is complete.

It is okay to transfer this role to this Global Catalog because it is a small domain. The operation is complete. Your second DC has now been created and configured. Perform a quality check to ensure that everything is operating normally within both DCs. Once everything has passed quality control, proceed to the creation of the global child production domain.

Note *If you decided to use a KMS server, then set it up on this DC as well. This will provide a redundant service to the network. This is also a good time to create named administrator accounts.*

Create the First DC in the Global Child Domain Production Domain

The production domain DCs are slightly different from the forest root and other domain controllers because the production domain is where massive domain information will be stored. One of the configuration differences you should make is to create special disks on the server to store ADDS database logs. It is a standard database server practice to store transaction logs and databases on separate disks when database volume is high. This practice needs to be applied to domain controllers that will store massive amounts of data. This is the case for production domain controllers. This means that these virtual machines should have three disks: C, D, and E. Size the D and E partitions based on the number of users in your domain. In most cases, 30 GB is sufficient for the data drive and 10 GB is enough for the log drive. It is easy enough to expand virtual disks, so you can't make any major mistakes. Monitor disk size to make sure you don't run out of space once the domain is up and running.

Otherwise, the installation of this DC is similar to the installation of the preceding DCs. In fact, every operation is the same, except for the following:

- **Server TCP/IP configuration** The DNS servers should be set to this server, then one of the root domain servers.

- **DC promotion** This will be the first DC in a new domain. Also install the DNS service.
- **DNS configuration finalization** The DNS service configuration needs to be finalized.
- **Account creation** The Administrator account needs to be renamed. You'll also need a special account for the DHCP service to be installed later.

The following procedures will highlight these differences. It will still be necessary to apply all of the modifications normally required for server configurations.

Perform DC Promotion

On the first DC for the child domain, use the same procedure as with the first DC in the forest, with the following modifications:

1. Install the ADDS binaries and then launch the ADDS Installation Wizard. Make sure you select Advanced Features on the first screen.
2. In the first screen, select Existing Forest and then select Create A New Domain In An Existing Forest. Do not select Create A New Domain Tree since this domain will use the same name structure as the root domain.
3. Next, type the name of the forest root domain to join, and click Set to type appropriate credentials to create the DC in the existing forest. This account must be a member of the Enterprise Administrators group.
4. On the next screen, type the name of the forest root domain again and then the name of the new domain. This should be Intranet.
5. Next, verify the child domain NetBIOS name. After that, confirm that Default First Site Name is the site you want to place the domain controller in.
6. Assign the DNS Server and Global Catalog roles. After that, select Any Writable Domain Controller as the source of replication.
7. Locate the database and logs, as well as the system volume. Note that the AD database should be on D: and the logs should be on drive E:. The system volume should also be on the D: drive. Use the default folders to store each item.
8. Assign the restore password.
9. Verify the summary information. Note that this time a proper DNS delegation will be created.
10. Don't forget to select Reboot On Completion as it completes the operations.

Use the AD consoles to verify the proper operation of the DC after it reboots. You can proceed to the next operation: finalizing DNS configuration.

NOTE *DNS delegations are important at this stage, because having a delegation to this DC will automatically store the DNS information in an application partition that resides in this domain. Windows Server 2003 did not do this and, therefore, required the creation of manual delegations before you could perform this operation.*

Finalize the DNS Configuration

Since the DNS service is installed, all you need to do here is finalize its configuration. Perform the same steps outlined in the "DNS Configuration Finalization" section described earlier during the creation of the first DC in the forest. Once the DNS service configuration is complete, you can proceed to the modification of the Administrator account. You will also require an additional account in this domain. This account will be used as credentials for DHCP/DNS interaction. It should be a service account with domain administration privileges. Use a complex name and password, ensure that the user cannot change passwords, and that passwords never expire. Make note of this account because it will be required when configuring the DHCP service on member servers.

NOTE *You did not need to indicate the functionality level for this domain since you performed this action for the forest during the creation of the first DC. Native WS08 forests will only allow native WS08 child domains to be created. You are now ready to complete the child domain preparation.*

Create the Second DC in the Global Child Production Domain

This installation will be similar to the installation of the second DC in the forest root domain. The major difference is the migration of the domain's Operation Master roles. Since this is a child domain, it does not include any forest-wide Operation Master roles.

In addition, the remaining three servers—this DC and the two network infrastructure servers—will all belong to the production domain; therefore, all three can be staged at the same time and installed as member servers for this domain. Once these servers are staged, set the two network infrastructure servers aside for the time being while you complete the configuration of the second DC for this domain. This DC will be the same as the first DC in this domain, but with the following differences:

- **Client TCP/IP configuration** The DNS servers should be set to this server, then the other DC for this domain.
- **DC promotion** This will be an additional DC in an existing domain.
- **DNS installation and configuration** Once again, only the DNS service is required. AD will replicate zone information.
- **Operation Master role transfer** Migrate the Infrastructure Master role to this server.

Perform DC Promotion

Promote this server to a domain controller. Use the same procedure as with the first domain controller in the child domain, with the following variations:

1. Install the ADDS binaries and then launch the ADDS Installation Wizard. Make sure you select Advanced Features on the first screen.
2. In the first screen, select Existing Forest and then select Add A Domain Controller To An Existing Forest.
3. Next, type the name of the forest root domain to join, and click Set to type appropriate credentials to create the DC in the existing forest. This account must be a member of the Enterprise Administrators group.
4. On the next screen, select the Intranet domain.

5. Next, confirm the that the default first site name is the site you want to place the domain controller in.
6. Assign the DNS server, but do not select Global Catalog roles, because this server will host the Infrastructure Operation Master role. In the error screen, select Transfer The Infrastructure Master Role To This Domain Controller (see Figure 6-18).
7. In the next screen, ADDS will offer to update the DNS delegation to include this DC. Select Yes. This will make sure this server will also include the application partition that hosts DNS information for this domain.
8. After that, select An Existing Domain Controller as the source of replication and then Any Writable DC.
9. Locate the database and logs, as well as the system volume. Note that the AD database should be on D: and the logs should be on drive E:. The system volume should also be on the D: drive. Use the default folders to store each item.
10. Assign the restore password.
11. Verify the summary information.
12. Don't forget to select Reboot On Completion as it completes the operations.

You're ready to move on to other operations once the system has rebooted.

Other DC Creation Considerations

You do not need to move any other Operations Master roles at this time, but you may once this domain grows to its intended size. If you expect to have more than 50,000 users in your production domain, you will need to create a dedicated PDC Emulator. But this is not necessary at this time, since directory objects have not been created yet. And since you are performing a migration of objects from older Windows domains to the new WS08 forest, you will not require this until enough objects have been migrated.

Two strategies can be used for data migration:

- **Create all DCs first.** Deploy DCs once the parallel network is up and running, then migrate users and other objects. For this strategy to work, you need enough new virtual machines to create all of the DCs.

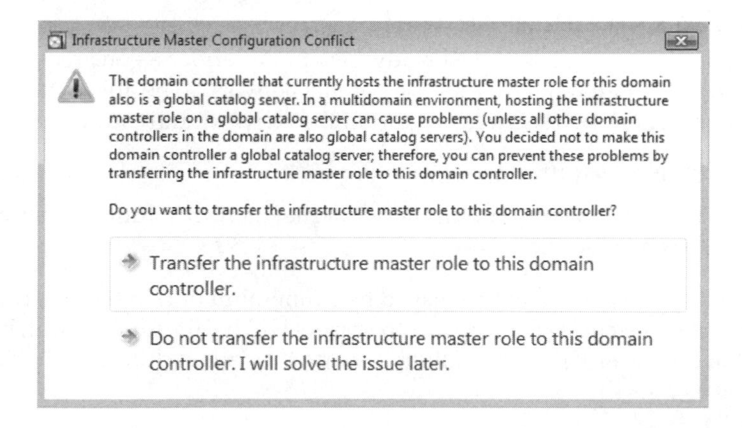

Figure 6-18 Automatically transferring the Infrastructure role to this DC

- **Migrate users and create DCs as you go.** In this case, use your judgment, but you might decide to add new DCs at every 500 users migrated (depending on whether it is a central or regional DC). Of course, you will need to add at least a DC in each remote region that has more than a given number of users (10 or more if you can afford the server hardware for host machines). Regional DCs are ideal candidates for the RODC role.

This second DC does not need to be a Global Catalog (GC) server, since you will be adding more DCs—which will also be GCs—to this domain as it grows. Thus, you can be guaranteed that the site that holds this DC will have at least one more that can act as the Global Catalog server for the site. In this manner, you will not be faced with potential problems that might occur from the cohabitation of a GC and the Infrastructure Master.

Finally, when you create massive numbers of domain controllers, you will most likely want to automate the process. As in the setup of the utility forest, DC promotion in this domain can be scripted with unattended text files. This scripted installation can also automatically install the DNS service. One of the best ways to do this is to perform one more DC installation with the wizard, and at the Summary page, capture the unattended installation answer file for the creation of all other DCs.

In addition, you can repair DCs and avoid network replication with WS08. To do so, you require an ADDS backup. This can be done to CD or DVD, or even to a network share (see Figure 6-19). Then, if you need to rebuild a remote DC, you can use the following command:

```
dcpromo /adv
```

This will display an additional data source screen, which lets you input AD data from the backup copy, reducing the amount of replication required. Once the DC is rebuilt, normal AD multimaster replication will take over and update this DC's contents. Even if you choose a network location for backup data, you can discard extra information and limit the data transfer to the new DC during its creation. Note that this method is impractical for DC staging, since most DCs will be staged in a central area with high-speed connections.

Now, you are ready to proceed to the preparation of the two network infrastructure servers.

Connect the Enterprise Network

Your parallel network is almost ready. Two more services—one required and one optional—need to be prepared in order for the parallel network to be able to accept client computers and users. These two services are part of the Network Infrastructure server role:

- Centralized IP addressing
- Legacy name resolution, since Internet name resolution is performed by the directory service

Both of these roles will be played by a minimum of two servers located in different sites, if possible. The configuration of both servers will be almost identical, but, of course, each will have some slight modifications because they are in different physical locations.

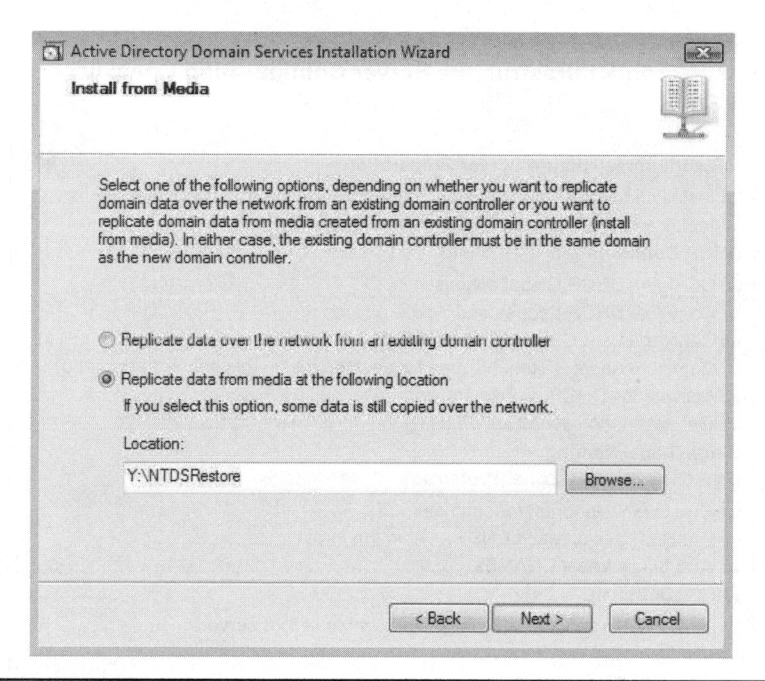

Figure 6-19 Using offline data to create a DC

Network Infrastructure Staging Activities

The activities that must be performed to install both network infrastructure servers are detailed in the network infrastructure server configuration checklist illustrated in Figure 6-20. They include four activities: server preparation, DHCP configuration, WINS configuration (optional), and system verification. The first three activities are repeated for each of the two servers.

Both of the network infrastructure servers should be member servers only. Both should belong to the production domain since this is where their services will be needed most. Few legacy operations will occur in the forest root domain, so legacy name resolution is rarely required. The forest root domain will also have very few objects, such as users and computers; therefore, it will not be necessary to dynamically assign IP addresses to these objects.

Both of these virtual machines use the basic server kernel and can be staged now. Also perform a quality control check on the servers themselves before proceeding to the next step.

Configure the First Network Infrastructure Server

Most of the improvements in DHCP lie with the integration of IPv6. Other changes that were brought out with Windows Server 2003 is the Alternate Client Configuration feature for clients using DHCP and an improved Backup and Restore function for the DHCP database. You can now back up and restore a DHCP database directly from the DHCP console.

Since Windows 2000, the DHCP service is closely integrated with the DNS service. The DHCP service can enable dynamic updates to the DNS namespace for any clients that support these updates. For clients that do not support the updates, DHCP can perform the update for them. In addition, the DHCP server must now be authorized in Active Directory, ensuring that only official DHCP servers can operate on any given enterprise network.

Network Infrastructure Server Configuration Checklist

Network Infrastructure Server Preparation
- ❑ Install and name the servers as member servers of the production domain
- ❑ Install and configure the DHCP service

DHCP Configuration
- ❑ Configure DHCP Global options
- ❑ Configure DHCP Scopes and Scope options
- ❑ Configure User Class IDs (if required)
- ❑ Configure Address Reservations for each scope on this server (if required)
- ❑ Activate the DHCP scopes and authorize the DHCP server
- ❑ Repeat on the second server using the 80/20 rule

Single Label Naming

DNS GlobalNames Zone (Preferred)
- ❑ Create GNZ in forest root domain
- ❑ Enable GNZs on each DNS server in the forest
- ❑ Add Single Label CNAMEs

WINS (Optional)
- ❑ Install WINS service on both network infrastructure servers
- ❑ Configure the WINS service
- ❑ Activate WINS backups
- ❑ Configure WINS replication

System Verification
- ❑ Verify the operation of both DHCP and Single Label Naming services in the network

FIGURE 6-20 The network infrastructure server configuration checklist

If you already have a DHCP and WINS strategy in place, there is probably no need to modify it, unless you feel you need to. Remember, a WS08 DHCP server can easily manage 1,000 scopes and 10,000 clients given the proper system resources.

NOTE *DHCP is disk-intensive. Because of this, DHCP servers should include more RAM. Paging files should also be set to maximum values.*

Some networks still rely on single label names, which were formerly provided by the WINS service. If you do not want to deploy WINS, then you can rely on the new GlobalNames zone (GNZ) available in WS08 DNS. Optionally, you can deploy WINS on the same servers as the DHCP service. If so, two WINS servers for redundancy are more than enough for your production network.

Service Installation and Configuration

Once again, you will use the Server Manager console to add the DHCP role to your server.

1. Build the server and join it to the Intranet domain. Log on with Domain Administrator credentials.

2. Launch Server Manager and move to the Roles section. Click Add New Role.
3. In the Select Server Roles page, select DHCP Server and then click Next.
4. Review your selections, and then click Next. Select the network cards you want to bind the service to, and click Next. WS08 will begin the DHCP service configuration process.
5. Select the parent domain (Intranet.TandT.net), but do not put in preferred DNS servers at this time. This page configures global DHCP settings and because you want users to connect to their local DNS server, you will add it in their specific address scope settings. Click Next.
6. If you decided to install WINS, then select WINS Is Required and add the addresses of the WINS servers. They do not need to be installed at this stage. If you are using a GlobalNames zone, select WINS Is Not Required. Click Next.
7. Do not add a scope at this time. Scopes will be created later. Click Next.
8. As you must also use DHCPv6, select it now. Click Next.
9. Select the parent domain (Intranet.TandT.net), but do not put in preferred DNS servers at this time. Click Next.
10. Select Use Current Credentials To Authorize This Server. Click Next.
11. Confirm your selections and click Install.
12. Click Close once the installation process is complete.

You can now move on to create DHCP values.

Configure DHCP Values

There are a number of steps required to configure DHCP properly. First, you begin by configuring global scope options. Global scope options include everything that is the same for every DHCP client. Local scope options are items that are specific to a particular scope. For example, local scope options will now include the DNS server, since DNS is now integrated with Active Directory and each client will most likely find a DNS server that is local to its network (especially in regions).

Global options often include:

- 003 Router
- 006 DNS Servers
- 015 DNS Domain Name
- 044 WINS/NBNS Servers (optional)
- 046 WINS/NBT Node Type (optional)

You configure DNS servers in global options—use the two DNS servers you created for the child domain—just in case other DNS servers are not available. Local scope options include:

- 006 DNS Servers

Local scopes also include all of the scope details, such as the address pool for the scope, the address leases in use, and reservations.

You'll also want to configure user class options if you need to use them. One example of a useful user class is a special user class for mobile users. This allows you to differentiate mobile users and set their lease duration to a shorter time period than those of the PC workstations in your network. Thus, when a mobile user goes from one site to another, addresses are automatically released when they leave the site.

Next, you configure DHCP scopes and scope-specific options. If you use the 80/20 rule for scope redundancy (creating a scope on two servers and enabling 80 percent of the scope on one and 20 percent on the other), you will need to create each scope and exclude the appropriate range on each server. Once all scopes are created, you must join them into a superscope. Superscopes are scope groupings that allow the DHCP server to service more than one subnet. They are required whenever multinetting is used; thus, they are required in an enterprise network. Use the superscope to include all of the scopes in a set of server ranges. Superscopes should be the same on both the servers you will create.

Each of the two servers you configure should also include the same address reservations, especially if these reservations are for servers such as domain controllers. In this way, the reservation will stand no matter which DHCP server responds to the DHCP request. Servers using dynamic address allocation should also have their alternate configuration set to the same values as the reservation.

In Windows Server 2008, DHCP services must be authorized and scopes must be activated. This is quite useful, since you can configure your server, review all scopes, and correct potential errors before putting the server into service. In addition, scope activation can act as a failsafe mechanism; where spare scopes are prepared before they are actually required and activated only as needed.

The best place to work with the DHCP services is the Server Manager console. You will need to configure both IPv4 and IPv6 scopes.

1. To begin configuring the DHCP server, launch the Server Manager console.
2. Locate the DHCP node and begin by setting the server properties. This is done by right-clicking IPv4 or IPv6 and selecting Properties. Move to the DNS tab, and set the DNS update settings you require. Since this is a parallel network that should only have updated Windows clients, the default settings are okay. If you must allow down-level clients, then choose to have the DHCP server update A and PTR records for them. Next, move to the Advanced tab, and click Credentials. This will allow you to input the account you created earlier to ensure that you can always track DHCP operations within DNS servers. Click OK when done.
3. This is now an ideal time to set up user classes if you wish to use them. They can then be assigned as server options. The procedure for creating and using user-defined classes is outlined in the next section.
4. Next, input your other server options. Right-click Server Options and choose Configure Options from the context menu.
5. Configure the following options as a minimum: Router, DNS Servers, and DNS Domain Name. Click OK when done. This will set the global options for all scopes on this server. DNS servers are set globally even though they will be overridden by local scope values. In this way, a DNS server is always available for all clients. If you do use WINS, then the WINS/NBT Node Type should be set to H-node. H-node resolution is best, even in wide area networks, because it greatly reduces the amount of broadcasting on each network.

6. Next, create your first DHCP scope. Right-click the IPv4 or IPv6 item, and select New Scope from the context menu. DHCP will launch the New Scope Wizard. This wizard allows you to input all of the values for the scope: scope name, starting address, end address, exclusions, and even scope-specific options. Even though the wizard displays options that are not required locally, such as WINS servers, simply skip these screens by clicking Next. You can choose to activate the scope or not at the end. It is best to skip activation at this stage. This lets you review all of your settings before activation.
7. Repeat step 6 for each scope you require. Remember to exclude 80 or 20 percent of the scope, depending on where you want the main portion of the scope to be hosted.

NOTE *Superscopes cannot be created until at least one scope has been created on a DHCP server.*

8. Once all scopes have been created, right-click IPv4 or IPv6 once again, and select New Superscope. This will launch the New Superscope Wizard. Click Next to proceed. Name the superscope, and then select the scopes that will be part of this superscope. Close the dialog box when done. Once a superscope is created, new scopes can be added to it in one of two ways: The scope can be created within the superscope by right-clicking the Superscope Name and selecting New Scope; or the scope can be created outside the superscope and added to the superscope once created. This is done by right-clicking the scope and selecting Add To Superscope.
9. If you need reservations, select the appropriate scope to create reservations within it. Once again, click Reservations in the left pane, then right-click Reservations, and choose New Reservation from the context menu. Fill in the reservation details. You will require the Media Access Control (MAC) address for each of the network cards for which you want to reserve an IP address. MAC addresses can be displayed by typing IPCONFIG /All at the command prompt of the system for which the reservation is required. Close the dialog box by clicking Add. Repeat as necessary.

   Reservations ensure that the network interface card whose MAC address you typed will always have the same IP address. They are similar to static IP addresses, but benefit from a central administration console.
10. Finally, after you have reviewed your DHCP settings, you can activate the scopes. One advantage of using superscopes is that you can activate the entire superscope in one fell swoop. Right-click the superscope name, and select Activate from the context menu.

Your first DHCP server is ready. You can move on to configuring the single label name service. As you'll see, this service is easy to configure. But first, define user classes.

Define User Classes

As mentioned previously, user classes are quite useful when you want to designate special DHCP assignments to specific classes of machines in your network. For example, you can use a user class to define mobile computers and, once defined, ensure that their lease duration is shorter than that of workstations. You can also ensure that whenever the mobile computer is shut down, it releases the IP address lease it was granted. This makes it more

PART III

effective for users who frequently move from one site to another. User classes are defined within DHCP.

1. Right-click IPv4 or IPv6 in Server Manager, and select Define User Classes.
2. Click Add in the User Class dialog box.
3. In the New Class dialog box, type the class display name and description, and then place your cursor directly below the word "ASCII." Type the class name. You will note that the New Class dialog box inputs the ASCII values as you type characters (see Figure 6-21). Do not modify these characters! Remember: Class names are case-sensitive. You'll need to make note of how you spelled the class name. Repeat the process for each class you need to add.
4. Ensure that your class(es) have been added, and then close the User Class dialog box.
5. Next, right-click the Global Server Options item, and select Configure Options. Move to the Advanced tab, and select Microsoft Windows 2000 Options as the Vendor Class and Mobile Users as the User Class. Set the value for number 02, Microsoft Release DHCP Lease on Shutdown Operating System, by selecting the relevant check box.
6. Next change Vendor Class to DHCP Standard Options to set option 51, Lease. The value is in the 0x*seconds*, where *seconds* is the number of seconds for lease duration. For example, 0x86400 means 24 hours. Close all dialog boxes.
7. Now you will need to set this user class on mobile systems. To do so, you need to use the IPCONFIG command on each computer. This setting can be performed during PC staging and could be within a system image. The command structure is as follows:

   ```
   ipconfig /setclassid adapter_name class_id
   ```

   For example, if your class ID is "TandTMobile," your command would be:

   ```
   ipconfig /setclassid Local Area Connection TandTMobile
   ```

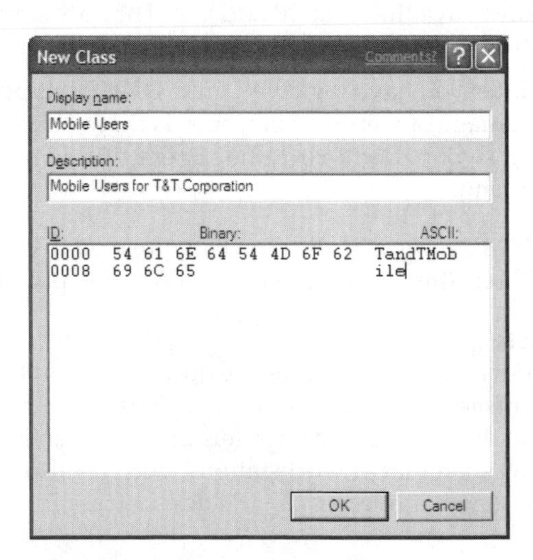

FIGURE 6-21 Creating a new user class

CAUTION *Remember: Class IDs are case-sensitive. You must type the exact class ID wording for it to work properly.*

TIP *User-defined class options can be assigned to either server or scope options, depending on whether they apply to systems in all scopes or only to systems in specific scopes.*

TIP *User-defined classes are also useful for the assignation of domain names to systems that are located in the same physical locations. For example, if you have users in the same physical location that use different domains, such as the Intranet and Development domains, you can use a user-defined class to ensure that systems register DNS values in the proper DNS domain controller. Ensure that you use the user-defined class for the smallest number of systems. This will make it easier to stage and manage the systems.*

Configure GlobalName Zones in DNS

A single GlobalName zone is required for the entire forest. This is done on each DNS server in the forest, and the GNZ is defined to replicate to all DNS servers in the forest. Basically, the process of creating this zone is straightforward. It requires five steps:

- Create the GlobalNames forward lookup zone.
- Set its replication scope to all DNS servers in the forest.
- Do not enable dynamic updates for this zone.
- Enable GNZ support on each DNS server.
- Add single label names to DNS.

As you can see, this is a pretty straightforward operation.

1. Log on to the first DC in the forest root domain.
2. Open Server Manager and go to the Roles section to expand DNS until you view the Forward Lookup Zones section. Click this section.
3. Now right-click this section to select New Zone from the context menu.
4. Choose a primary zone, and make sure you select the Store The Zone In Active Directory option.
5. In the next screen, select replication to occur to all DNS servers in this forest.
6. Use GlobalNames as the zone name.
7. Do not allow dynamic updates, and finish the configuration.
8. Next, enable GNZ support on this DNS server. You need to do this through the command line:

   ```
   dnscmd /config /EnableGlobalNamessupport 1
   ```

   This command needs to be run on each DNS server in the forest. You might want to make it part of your standard DNS server configuration. Put it in a command file, and run it each time you build a DC with the DNS service.

PART III

9. Restart the DNS service. Select the server name in the DNS tree, right-click it, go to All Tasks, and select Restart.
10. Now add single label names. Remember that like WINS names, they cannot have more than 15 characters—they actually use 16 characters, but the system reserves the last character. You can use the graphical interface's New Alias (CNAME) command in the GlobalNames zone (see Figure 6-22), or you can use the command line to do so:

    ```
    dnscmd dnsservername /recordadd GlobalNames singlelabelname CNAME
    correspondingDNSname
    ```

    Where *dnsservername* is the name of the DNS server that you are adding the name to, the *singlelabelname* is the 15-character name you want to add, and *correspondingDNSname* is the DNS name of the server whose GNZ name you are adding.

You might want to script this again if you have a lot of names to add. You're done!

Install WINS (Optional)

If, for some reason, you absolutely insist on installing WINS—you may have applications that absolutely require it—then use this procedure to do so. Do not configure GNZs with WINS, as they are redundant services. WINS hasn't changed at all since Windows 2003, and even then it didn't change much from previous versions. It can accept replication partners, though, giving you more control over replication sources. Two good features were also added in Windows 2000: persistent connections and record verification. Persistent connections ensure that a link is always open between push replication partners. This provides real-time replication capabilities for WINS servers. Record verification performs a

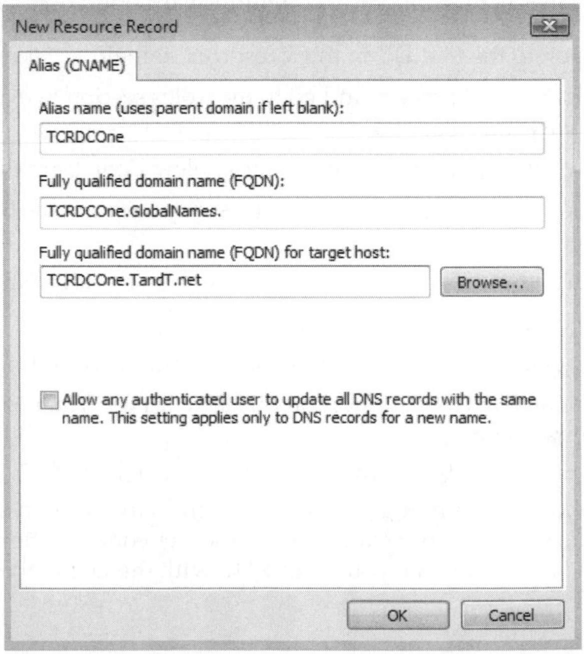

FIGURE 6-22
Adding a GNZ name. Do not allow updates!

consistency check on registered names, replicating only valid records from the database. Otherwise, the configuration you used with WINS in your current network should work with WINS in WS08.

WINS is not a server role, but a feature.

1. Begin by installing the feature. Open Server Manager and click Add Feature in the startup screen.
2. Select the WINS feature and install it. Once it is installed, you can configure it.
3. Use the Computer Management console to manage WINS. Launch Computer Management (it should be in the Quick Launch area), expand Services and Applications, and then click WINS. Right-click the WINS item, and select Properties from the context menu.
4. Review the WINS server properties and ensure they are modified, if required. To set automatic WINS backups, simply type the location of the backup file. You can also select the Back Up Database During Server Shutdown option. Close the dialog box when done.
5. Next, add a replication partner. This partner is the second server you will prepare next. Right-click Replication Partners and select New Replication Partner. Type the name of the other server. If it isn't available, you will get an error message. Type the server's IP address.
6. Now right-click Replication Partners to set replication properties. Ensure that the option to replicate only with partners is set under the General tab, and then move to the Push Replication tab. Select all the options on this tab. This will turn on real-time replication.
7. Configure pull replication settings on the appropriate tab, and then select the Enable Automatic Partner Configuration option in the Advanced tab. WINS uses multicasting to provide configuration parameters to its replication partners. This ensures consistent configurations. Close the dialog box.

That's it; your first network infrastructure server configuration is complete.

Configure the Second Network Infrastructure Server

The configuration of the second network infrastructure server is the same as the first, but in reverse. You need to install and configure DHCP and WINS (if you did on the first server). Create all of the DHCP scopes in the DHCP server, ensure that these scopes are the reverse of the 80/20 configuration you performed on the first server, activate all scopes, and authorize the DHCP server. Don't forget to set DHCP server credentials to ensure secure DNS updates.

If you decided to use WINS, configure WINS properties and create the WINS replication partner. Now that the first server exists, you should not face any error messages during this configuration. Refer to the server configuration worksheets for complete server configuration steps.

WINS Connectivity (Optional)

Depending on your migration strategy, you may need to temporarily configure your Windows Server 2008 WINS servers to share information with the legacy network you are replacing. If this is the case, create only one-way replication partnerships: from the WS08 network to the legacy network. You do not want your new WINS databases to fill up with objects that have nothing to do with your new network.

In addition, DNS can be linked to WINS for additional name resolution support. If you have done your homework and have convinced the organization to move to a complete Windows Vista and WS08 network, this connection should not be necessary. Even though many Microsoft networks still require NetBIOS name resolution to some degree, failures of DNS name resolutions, especially failures that could be solved with WINS, should be rare.

Move Servers and Configure Domain Replication

Now that all your servers are ready, you can move them to a new physical site. When you move DCs to another site, you need to ensure that ADDS replication operates properly. For this, you need to work with the Active Directory Domain Services Sites and Services console. Chances are that you'll also have to modify some of the properties of the DCs and network infrastructure server you move. Now that you will have DCs located in a different physical location, you need to configure domain replication. The activities you need to perform include the following:

- Create a new site in ADDS.
- Add subnet(s) to the site.
- Create a site link for the site.
- Create a backup site link for this site.
- Modify properties for each site link.
- Install or move DCs into the site.

As you can see, the first five steps are preparatory steps. It is only when you reach the sixth step, placing the DC in the site, that replication actually begins. To configure replication, you will require the Site Topology Report from the site topology planning exercise you performed during your Active Directory design exercise. An example of the contents of this report can be found in Table 5-9 in Chapter 5. You can configure site replication before moving the DCs physically into the site location, but if you do so, the Knowledge Consistency Checker (KCC) service will generate errors within the Directory Service portion of the Event Log. It is best to move the servers first and then configure replication.

Replication configuration is done through the Sites and Services section of Server Manager.

1. Expand Active Directory Sites and Services.
2. Right-click Sites and select New Site from the context menu.
3. Name the site and select a link for this site—in this case, IP.
4. Click OK to close the dialog box and create the site.
5. Next, add a subnet to the site. Right-click Subnets and select New Subnet from the context menu.
6. Type the IP prefix in either IPv4 or IPv6 format. Select the site to associate to this subnet. Click OK to create the subnet.
7. Next create the site link for this site. A site link always includes at least two sites. Move to Intersite Transports and right-click the IP transport. Select New Site Link from the context menu.

8. Name the site link and identify the two sites in the link. Click OK to create the site link.
9. Repeat the procedure to create the backup site link.
10. As you can see, WS08 automatically assigns a cost and a replication interval to each site link. The default cost is 100 (a value that is appropriate for T1 links). The default replication interval is 180 minutes. If your physical link is a T1, then you don't need to change the site link cost for your main replication link. If not, see Table 5-8 in Chapter 5 for the recommended values for site link costs. As you'll remember, you don't want to modify either the site replication interval or the site link schedule in order to let the KCC perform its work in optimal fashion.
11. You will, however, want to add a description for the main site link you just created. To do so, right-click the site link and select Properties. Type the description and change the site link cost, if you need to do so. Click OK when done.
12. Type a description and change the site cost for the backup link as well.
13. Now, you need to move the DCs into the new site. Move to the Default First Site Name, and right-click the server you want to move. Select Move from the context menu. Select the destination site, and click OK.

Your replication is now configured. Make sure you designated a Global Catalog server in the new site if you did not do so at DC promotion. The GC is a function of the NT Directory Service (NTDS) settings for the server you want to use as a GC. If you need to designate a GC manually, use Sites and Services again.

1. Expand the site information in the left pane until you see the server names in the site. Select the server you want to make a GC—in this case, the forest root domain server.
2. Right-click NTDS settings.
3. Select the Global Catalog Server check box, and click OK. Perform this at least once for each site you create.

TIP *You can also use Universal Group Membership Caching in some sites that have fewer users. This way, you do not need to replicate the entire contents of the GC to these sites.*

TIP *You might also consider configuring printer location tracking at this time, since it is done in this console and must be prepared on DCs. To do so, proceed to Chapter 7 and review the steps required to configure this option.*

You're all done. Now, you need to verify that replication works properly. To test intersite replication, perform some AD modifications in the AD Users and Computers console, and test them from the remote DC. You can use Terminal Services in Administrative mode to do so. Also verify the Directory Service portion of the Event Log to ensure there are no errors.

CAUTION *Your parallel network is now ready for prime time. The remaining chapters will show you how to populate this network and ensure its resiliency. Before moving on, though, ensure that you fully test every part of this network. It is the basis of your new enterprise network infrastructure. You want to ensure that everything is running smoothly. It is not too late at this stage to start over and repeat the parallel network creation process. It will be too late once you have begun populating this network.*

Work with Windows Deployment Services

Network infrastructure servers can also run the Windows Deployment Services role since it is also an infrastructure role. Windows Deployment Services (WDS) is a set of services that works in conjunction with the new image-based setup (IBS) Windows supports. These services let you capture system images and then deploy them remotely to end points, which are either PCs or servers. As you know, you don't really need WDS to deploy servers, since the only actual installations of WS08 on hardware you perform is for host servers. All other installations are based on virtual machines and, therefore, do not rely on WDS. But WDS can be useful for PC deployments, and because of this, you might need to deploy it. Use the following strategy to do so.

Install WDS

Because it is a network infrastructure service, WDS requires certain components to be present before it can be installed and configured. These include:

- Active Directory Domain Services, which is already installed
- DNS, which is part of the installation of each DC in your network
- DHCP, which is also already deployed
- New Technology File System (NTFS) partitions, which should be the only partition type you use on your servers

Like other roles, WDS is installed through Server Manager.

1. Add the Windows Deployment Services role.
2. In the next screen, select the services for the role. WDS includes two services: Deployment Server and Transport Server. Deployment Server includes the full functionality of WDS. Transport Server includes only a subset and is useful for large networks, where you need to transport data from a central location to remote offices. This service would be available in the remote office to support system image deployment across the WAN. Since this is the first server in the network, select both services.
3. Click Install to perform the installation.

You're ready to begin working with WDS. If you want redundant services, then configure them on the second network infrastructure server.

CAUTION *WDS servers host system images for deployment. These images are often multiple gigabytes in size. Make sure you create a D: drive for this server and assign sufficient space for the storage of these files.*

NOTE *For more information on deploying this role go to: http://go.microsoft.com/fwlink/?linkid=84628.*

Work with WDS

You can work with WDS in one of two ways: with the Windows Deployment Services Configuration Wizard or through the WDSUTIL command. When you configure WDS, you need to:

- Create a shared folder that contains the following files:
  - Files needed for Preboot Execution Environment (PXE) boot
  - Files for booting Windows PE into a RAM disk
  - Windows PE boot images
  - System images for Windows Vista or Windows Server 2008
- Upload system images of Windows Vista, Windows Server 2008, Windows Server 2003, or Windows XP in Windows Imaging Format (VIM) format.
- Configure the settings for the PXE listener to control how the server services incoming client boot requests.

Let's proceed.

1. Start by launching the WDS console. Choose Start | Administrative Tools | Windows Deployment Services.
2. Expand the nodes in the left pane once the console is open, and right-click the server name to select Configure Server from the context menu.
3. In the Remote Installation Folder Location page, type the path to the shared folder containing system images—for example, **D:\RemoteInstall**.
4. Since this is also a DHCP server, you must select the two options in the next screen: Do Not Listen On Port 67 and Configure DHCP Option Tag 60 To 'PXEClient'.
5. Next, configure your PXE listener options. Ideally, you will select Respond Only To Known Clients. This means you will need to pre-stage all computer accounts in ADDS before you can use WDS to deploy system images to them. Clear the Add Images option and click Finish.

Your server is ready. You can add images and learn to use WDS when you need to work with PC system image deployment. Your servers are ready for prime time!

Upgrade an Existing Active Directory to WS08

Upgrading to a native WS08 forest from an existing Active Directory is much less complex a process than migrating from Windows NT to WS08. The advantage of having AD is that everything is already in place. You may not need to plan for a new or parallel IP infrastructure.

PART III

You may not need to perform an AD design, though it is necessary to review the design in light of new WS08 features. Even though this review might indicate a forest restructure, it is a task that is much less complex than creating an entirely new WS08 forest.

CAUTION *Only perform a Windows 2000/2003 upgrade to Windows Server 2008 if you performed a clean installation of Windows when you migrated from Windows NT. If you performed an upgrade from NT to Windows 2000/2003, this might be the right time to review your needs and use the parallel network to move to a native WS08 enterprise network.*

Even if you feel you are ready for the upgrade, make sure you review the information presented previously in this chapter to enable new WS08 features in your forest.

Upgrading a production network to Windows Server 2008 is a major undertaking that will affect the entire network. This is why you should proceed with care. It is especially at this stage that you discover the usefulness of the testing and staging processes outlined in Chapter 3. Make sure you thoroughly test your upgrade procedure before you proceed.

The Upgrade Process

The recommended steps for an upgrade to WS08 are detailed in the forest staging activities checklist illustrated in Figure 6-23. It is divided into four stages:

- Preparing for the upgrade
- Performing the upgrade
- Post-upgrade tasks
- Ongoing forest management.

Several subtasks are derived from each stage. Make sure everything is tested and documented in the lab before proceeding with this operation in your production network.

Prepare for the Upgrade

The first thing to do to prepare for the upgrade is to perform a forest consistency check. This activity basically involves a review of the choices that were performed when planning your original Active Directory. Are they still valid in light of what you have learned from Active Directory Domain Services and in light of new Windows Server 2008 features? Don't make light of this step. There's never a better time than an infrastructure project to implement structural changes. Since you will be performing a system-wide upgrade, you may as well take the time to check how things are running and see if there are any possible improvements you could make.

The second step is to make sure your DCs are ready to upgrade to WS08. Use the recommended system settings to perform this verification. Make any required hardware modifications *before* you proceed.

TIP *If you will be moving to a dynamic datacenter, then you will probably want to perform physical-to-virtual (P2V) conversions of these systems. You'll find that it is much easier to upgrade disks and other resources on these DCs once they are virtualized.*

Forest Staging Activities Checklist

1 Prepare the Upgrade

- ❑ Perform a forest consistency check
- ❑ Check WS08 compatibility for each DC
- ❑ Perform required P2V conversions
- ❑ Prepare an upgrade task list
- ❑ Obtain authorization to modify the schema

2 Perform the Upgrade

- ❑ Prepare the forest
- ❑ Prepare domains
- ❑ Upgrade DCs
- ❑ Automate the upgrade

3 Post-Upgrade Tasks

- ❑ Verify WS08 functional forest compatibility
- ❑ Migrate domains to WS08 functional mode
- ❑ Migrate the forest to WS08 functional mode
- ❑ Update forest server roles
  - ❑ Modify DC role (add/delete from Global Catalog)
  - ❑ Modify Operation Master roles
- ❑ DNS strategy review
  - ❑ Add DNS service on all DCs
  - ❑ Create/modify application partitions
- ❑ Review Active Directory Domain Services replication
  - ❑ Replication within sites
  - ❑ Replication between sites
  - ❑ Create/modify ADDS site
  - ❑ Create/modify replication rules between DCs
- ❑ Restructure domains (If required)
  - ❑ Update domain structure (movetree command)
  - ❑ Create/modify OUs
  - ❑ Create/modify OU structure
- ❑ Implement forest trusts (if required)
  - ❑ Create/modify trust

4 Ongoing Forest Management

- ❑ Site coverage monitoring
- ❑ Directory replication
- ❑ Schema modifications
- ❑ AD operations follow-up and maintenance

Figure 6-23 Windows 2008 ADDS upgrade checklist

Three steps need to be performed before you can move on to the WS08 upgrade:

- Perform an Active Directory preparation for the forest.
- Perform an Active Directory preparation for every domain.
- In addition, if you used a server kernel concept, as described in Chapter 4, and you installed the Windows 2003 Administration Tools on every DC, you will need to remove them before proceeding.

This should bring your DCs to WS08-compatible levels. One last thing to check is free space. Depending on the size of your directory, you will require a minimum of 10 GB of free space on the disks hosting the database and SYSVOL shares on each DC to perform the upgrade.

It is also a good idea to prepare an upgrade task list. This list should detail every activity you need to perform to upgrade your Active Directory from Windows 2003 to Windows Server 2008 in a step-by-step format. Set it up as a checklist, and check off each item as you proceed with your upgrade. The basic steps in this list should include all of the steps in the list identified in Figure 6-23, but may also include some custom activities based on your organizational requirements.

The last step for preparation is to obtain authorization for a schema modification. Since you are using Active Directory, you have taken the time to put a schema change management structure in place. You should get authorization to perform both a forest and a domain preparation. This authorization should include a time window outlining when the upgrade will be possible.

CAUTION *Make sure the domain controllers you upgrade include lots of free disk space on the drives where the NTDS.DIT file resides. You should have at least enough free space to double the size of your NTDS.DIT file.*

Upgrade to WS08

You're ready to proceed. Remember, test and retest in a laboratory first. Use the following procedure. You will need the WS08 installation media to perform this operation.

1. Log on to the Schema Operations Master using an Enterprise Administrator account (this should also be a schema and domain administrator).
2. Load the installation DVD for WS08, and locate the \SOURCES\ADPREP folder. Copy its content to a folder on the Schema Master.
3. Open a command-line window, and navigate to the new \SOURCES\ADPREP folder you just created. Type the following command:
   ```
   adprep /forestprep
   ```
4. Consent to the upgrade by typing **C** and pressing ENTER. This will launch the forest preparation process. In fact, this process consists of importing a number of different objects to extend the forest's schema. This process is fairly quick, but by default, it doesn't give you a lot of feedback while executing. Have patience. Don't stop it in the middle because it seems to be "hung."
5. Next, prepare the forest for read-only DCs, but only if you think you will use them. Run the following command:
   ```
   adprep /rodcprep
   ```
6. Confirm your command and wait for the process to finish.
7. Once the preparation is complete, you need to wait until the changes have been replicated to the entire forest. If you performed a forest replication latency calculation during your migration to Active Directory, you will know exactly how long you need to wait, because replication latency is the longest possible time of completion for a forest-wide replication process.

Once the forest change is complete, you can perform the domain preparation on *each domain of the forest*. Use the following procedure:

1. Log on to the Infrastructure Master for each domain with Domain Administrator credentials (Enterprise Administrator in the root domain).
2. Load the installation DVD for WS08, and locate the \SOURCES\ADPREP folder. Copy its contents to a folder on the Infrastructure Master.
3. Open a command-line window, and navigate to the new \SOURCES\ADPREP folder you just copied. Type the following command:

   ```
   adprep /domainprep /gpprep
   ```
4. Confirm the command and wait for the process to finish. As before, you need to wait for domain replication to complete.

Now you can upgrade each DC to WS08. WS08 will automatically propose an upgrade when you connect the installation media to your server. The upgrade process is simple. The entire process can be automated, as was outlined in Chapter 4.

Post-Upgrade Tasks

Once all DCs have been upgraded, you can migrate your forest to WS08 forest functional mode. But before you do so, you need to verify that every domain in the forest supports this mode. Windows Server 2008 offers two functional modes: domain and forest. The functional domain mode requires that all domain controllers in the domain be running WS08. The forest functional mode requires every domain in the forest to be in WS08 functional mode. Use the following procedure:

1. Open the Active Directories Domains and Trusts console. Perform this operation for each domain in your forest, including the root domain. Make sure all DCs have been upgraded first.
2. Right-click the domain name.
3. From the context menu, select Raise Domain Functional Level. Select Windows Server 2008.
4. Click Raise. Agree to all the warning messages.
5. Wait for domain replication to occur. Repeat for each domain in the forest.
6. Once all domains are raised to WS08 functionality, proceed with the forest functional level.
7. Right-click the console root (Active Directory Domains and Trusts).
8. From the context menu, select Raise Forest Functional Level.
9. Select Windows Server 2008.
10. Click Raise. Agree to all the warning messages, and wait for replication to occur to all DCs within the forest before using WS08 native forest functions.

Other operations you might consider at this stage are updating forest server roles and performing a DNS strategy review. If you decide to modify DC roles, you'll find that operations are much the same as they were in Windows 2003. Operations you might perform at this stage are:

- Modify DC role (Add/Remove Global Catalog Service)
- Modify site structure (Enable Universal Group Membership Caching)
- Modify Operations Master roles

As far as DNS is considered, it should be on every DC. If it isn't, add the DNS service on all DCs. It doesn't generate a lot of overhead and it makes DC location a lot easier. Next you can create or modify application partitions to hold DNS data. The DNS Wizard will automatically create these partitions for you. These can be forest-wide or domain-centric. The advantage of application partitions in this case is that you no longer need to create secondary DNS zones anywhere in your network.

Your final migration tasks should cover a review of Active Directory replication. Ensure that all replication works properly. This should include replication within a site and replication between sites. You may need to create or modify AD sites or modify your replication rules to match WS08 best practices.

You may also be interested in restructuring domains. If you find that your original Windows 2003 forest and domain structure does not meet all your needs, you can restructure domains. WS08 offers several tools for this step. The MOVETREE command allows you to move computers and users from domain to domain. This command must be performed on the Infrastructure Master. You might also use the Active Directory Migration Tool. It can migrate users and passwords from one domain or forest to another. You can also use third-party migration tools. Remember that to restructure domains, you will first need to update your domain structure, then create or modify its OU structure, and then migrate users and computers.

The final upgrade operation is the implementation of forest trusts. Now that you have WS08 forests, you can decide to implement global forest trusts. These will link multiple forests together. Beware though! You can easily find the same difficulties in forest trusts that you found in Windows NT domains. Forests are designed to protect schemas. Unless there are significant requirements for forest trust implementations, you should avoid creating them.

Ongoing Forest Management

Ongoing forest management will not be much different with WS08 as it was with Windows 2000. You still use the same tools you used before: Active Directory Sites and Services, Active Directory Domains and Trusts, and Active Directory Users and Computers. But all have increased functionality. Each will be examined in turn as this book progresses through the WS08 implementation outlined in the logical network blueprint in Figure 3-8 in Chapter 3. In addition, administrative operations for directories will be examined in Chapter 13 as we look at common administrative tasks.

You're ready to move on! Now, you'll begin to work with the directory to manage objects and services in your VSO network.

PART IV

Manage Objects with Windows Server 2008

This section begins to look at how you manage end-user facing or virtual service offerings infrastructures with Windows Server 2008 (WS08). As such, it deals with PC management, user management, and server management. It covers the design of the infrastructure for management purposes, as well as the actual management operations to perform. This section is essential for anyone who needs to manage service delivery to end users.

7

CHAPTER

Prepare for Object Management

Chapter 6 described how to prepare your resource pool and put the virtual service offerings (VSO) parallel network in place. Eventually, this network will begin to offer structured services as you migrate users from your existing network to the new VSO infrastructure. But before you can begin this migration, you need to finalize the network infrastructure you have begun to put in place. Several different activities must be completed before you can claim that your new network is ready to accept users. One of these is the finalization of your organizational unit (OU) infrastructure.

Chapter 5 identified the three object types that should be managed through an OU infrastructure: PCs, People, and Service Offerings. This chapter begins the creation of the OU infrastructure with the PC and user containers, or the containers that are designed to interact directly with end users and the systems they work with. To do this, you must finalize three key PC-related elements and three user-related elements:

- The PC Group Policy management strategy
- The PC delegation strategy
- The PC management strategy
- The user and group management strategy
- The user delegation strategy
- The user Group Policy management strategy

The first of these activities is the design of a PC management infrastructure within the new directory. This begins the design of your overall management infrastructure for every object contained in Active Directory Domain Services (ADDS). This design should be complete by the end of Chapter 10 when you design your security strategy. Your VSO network will then be ready to host new objects of every type and offer a complete set of service offerings. Once the PC structure is designed, you will look at delegation strategies. After all, with the ability to host multiple object types and store additional information about those objects, ADDS brings a lot of control to the Windows network. But you can't manage every aspect of this network on your own. So you'll need to delegate administrative activities through a proper delegation of authority strategy, granting only those rights that are absolutely required to perform the administrative tasks you're delegating. Finally, you'll want to take a look at how you should manage PCs in an organization through the abilities inherent in ADDS.

Next, you'll move on to user object management. Once again, you'll need to create a core infrastructure for user management activities. Then you'll need to look at the delegation strategy for these objects—a strategy that is slightly more complex than with PCs because ADDS can contain additional user information, information that should be managed by end users, not administrators. Finally, you'll look at a structured user management strategy much like the one you use for PCs.

Once these strategies are defined and put in place, you'll then need to look at how you can massively migrate users and computers from your existing network to the parallel environment. This occurs in Chapter 12.

Manage Objects with Active Directory Domain Services

One of the main purposes of Active Directory Domain Services is to manage objects. ADDS provides a single infrastructure for the integration of the objects people interact with when using a Windows infrastructure. In addition, ADDS provides a centralized infrastructure for the management of these objects. This infrastructure is based on Group Policy and Group Policy Objects (GPOs). A GPO is a directory object that is designed to define the way a system—desktop or server—appears and behaves. This includes items such as the contents of the Start menu, icons on the desktop, the ability to modify the desktop, the ability to run various software products, and more. GPOs can be used to manage PCs, servers, and users. In Windows Server 2003 Service Pack 1, Microsoft included 1,671 different system settings you could manage and modify with Group Policy. WS08 now includes more than 2,450. This makes GPOs not only the most powerful management infrastructure for Windows systems, but also the engine of choice for object management, because it affects and touches any object that is part of a domain within an ADDS forest. For this reason, you should endeavor to work with and understand GPOs as much as possible.

Group Policy Concepts

GPOs were first introduced with Windows 2000 and were designed to replace the cumbersome system policies used in Windows NT. A GPO can manage the following elements:

- **User and computer settings** WS08 includes administrative templates that allow GPOs to write specific settings to user (HKEY_CURRENT_USER or HKCU) and computer (HKEY_LOCAL_MACHINE or HKLM) registry hives.
- **Scripts** Windows clients and Windows servers can run startup and shutdown scripts, as well as logon and logoff scripts. These are managed through GPOs.
- **Data management** WS08 can redirect user folders from the desktop to a central server location, allowing full availability of these folders from any PC as well as centralized backup of user information.
- **Software lifecycles** WS08 can deploy software to both desktops and servers so long as the software product is integrated with the Windows Installer service.
- **Security settings** WS08 can centrally manage security settings for PCs, servers, and users through GPOs. WS08 can also restrict access to software applications through software restriction policies.

Every computer running Windows XP, Windows Vista, or Windows Server includes a local GPO by default. The settings in this file are applied to each computer at every startup. Organizations that want to standardize certain elements of the desktop and other computer behavior should configure this policy object with default organizational settings and make sure that this file is part of the installation set for each computer. Since these GPOs are local, they can be different on each computer. To make the best of local GPOs, you should define a given set of parameters for each computer type (PCs, servers, and domain controllers) and change them as little as possible.

The local GPO is located in the %SYSTEMROOT%\SYSTEM32\GROUP POLICY folder. To view this folder, you must enable two settings in the Folder view options (Windows Explorer | Tools Menu | Folder Options | View tab):

- Show hidden files and folders
- Hide protected operating system files (Recommended)

Disabling the latter will generate a warning dialog box. The best practice in this regard is to enable the setting to capture a copy of the local GPO you want to deploy and then disable the setting afterward.

Computers running Windows NT, Me, or 9x versions of Windows do not contain local GPOs and will not be affected by global GPOs deployed by Active Directory Domain Services. For this reason, the VSO parallel network should include only up-to-date versions of Windows for all client systems. Ideally, this will be Windows Vista, since this operating system works best with WS08.

NOTE *Windows Vista and WS08 both support multiple local GPOs. This is done by assigning different security descriptors to each local GPO. This can be useful when you have kiosk systems that require tight security when users are logged on but that require less security when administrators are logged on. For step-by-step instructions on how to work with these local GPOs, go to http://technet2.microsoft.com/WindowsVista/en/library/5ae8da2a-878e-48db-a3c1-4be6ac7cf7631033.mspx?mfr=true.*

In addition, to local Group Policy objects, networks running Active Directory Domain Services will have centralized GPOs. Compared to local GPOs, centralized GPOs are management GPOs, because you can modify them in a central location and have them affect any group of objects. By default, every ADDS network includes two default policies:

- The default domain policy
- The default domain controller policy

A specific default domain policy is applied to every domain in a Windows Server 2008 network. In the case of the example used in Chapters 5 and 6, the TandT network will have several default domain policies since there are several domains in its production forest. In the case of your VSO parallel network, you will have two different versions of the policy since only the root and the production domains have been created at this point. The same applies for the default DC policy, except that instead of being applied at the domain level, this policy is applied specifically to the Domain Controllers organizational unit and, therefore, to each domain controller it contains.

Policies do not follow the hierarchical path of an ADDS forest because they do not traverse domain boundaries. If you design a new policy within the forest root domain, it will not automatically be applied to child domains that are below the root domain in the hierarchy. If you define a custom policy that you want to apply to every domain in your forest, you will have to copy it from domain to domain. There is one exception, as was mentioned in Chapter 6: At the creation of any child domain, ADDS automatically copies the contents of the two default policies from the parent domain. So, in the same manner that you would adjust the local GPO before deploying systems, you should adjust the default GPOs in the forest root domain before you create any of the child domains. This will ensure that a basic set of standards will be applied to both domains and DCs as soon as they are created. The recommended modifications for these two default policies are covered in Chapter 10, since it discusses security strategies.

CAUTION *You can link policies from domain to domain, but this is not a recommended approach because the client must traverse the interdomain trust to read it, which takes longer and can put a stress on your WAN communications.*

Group Policy Processing

Group Policies are applied in the following order:

- Computer settings are applied first.
- User settings are applied second.

It makes sense, since the computer starts before a user can log on. In a WS08 network, the computer has its own ADDS account and must negotiate a logon within the directory before it allows users to log on and open a session.

In addition, local and central GPOs have a specific order of precedence:

- The local GPO is applied at computer startup.
- If available, site GPOs are applied next.
- Domain GPOs are applied after site GPOs.
- Organizational unit GPOs are applied last. If the object (either computer or user) is located within a child OU and the child OU contains an additional GPO, this GPO is applied last.

This process is often called the L-S-D-OU process for the Local-Site-Domain-OU application order (see Figure 7-1). If conflicts arise between policies, the settings in the last policy override all others. For example, if you deny access to an item in the Start menu in the domain policy but it is allowed in an OU policy, the result will be that access will be allowed.

GPO Inheritance (and Blocking)

In addition to the application order, you can control the inheritance settings for GPOs. This means that if you assign a setting at the domain level or any other higher level, you can ensure that your setting is the one that is propagated to the object, whether or not there are conflicting settings lower down in the application hierarchy. This is done by forcing GPO inheritance.

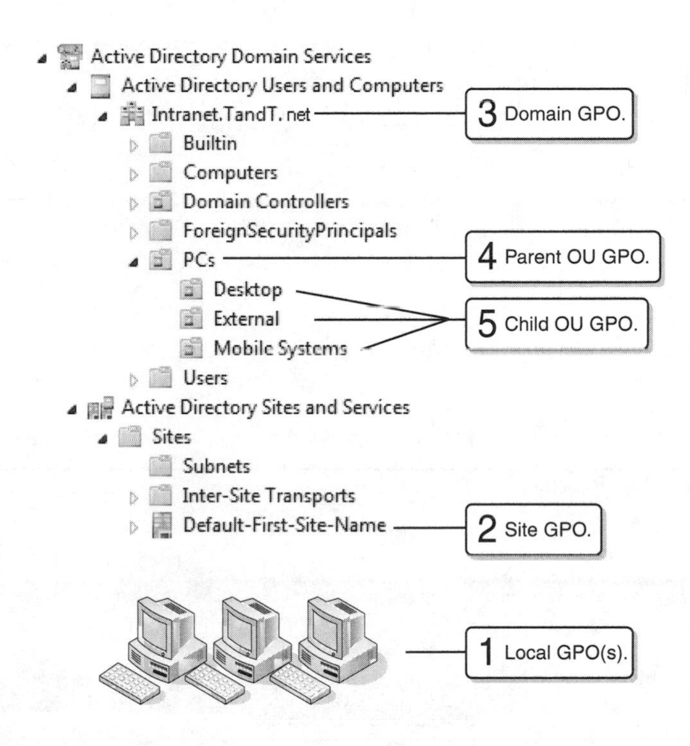

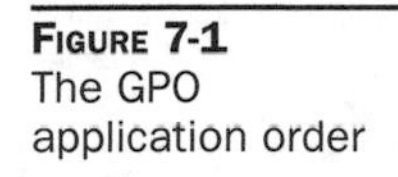
Figure 7-1 The GPO application order

Normally, GPOs are inherited automatically throughout the GPO application order. If a setting is enabled at the domain level and it is not configured at the OU level, the domain setting is applied. If a setting is not configured at the domain level and is disabled at the OU level, the OU setting is applied. If a setting is disabled at a parent OU and disabled at the child OU, the setting is not applied. To force GPO inheritance and make sure a top-level GPO setting is applied no matter what, you can assign the Enforced attribute to the GPO. This means that even if the settings are conflicting at the lower end of the hierarchy, the setting with the Enforced attribute will be applied.

GPOs are managed through the Group Policy Management Console (GPMC), which is a feature of WS08. Install this feature on servers you want to rely on to manage GPOs; preferably, this console will be installed on workstations—ideally Vista—since this operating system is the only client operating system that gives you access to the full gamut of WS08 GPOs. GPMC lets you view the entire domain structure and lets you control how you work with GPOs in either sites, domains, or OUs. The process is simple:

1. Begin by creating a GPO and naming it. This is best done in the Group Policy Objects container in GPMC (see Figure 7-2). Rely on the trusty right-click to get the appropriate context menu. This container lists only the GPOs that are available in the selected domain, since GPOs are restricted by domain boundaries.
2. Once the GPO is created, edit it by right-clicking it and selecting Edit. This opens the Group Policy Editor (GPEdit) and lets you view all of the settings you can control in the policy (see Figure 7-3). As you can see, each policy is divided into two sections. The first relates to computer-wide settings and applies to each affected computer.

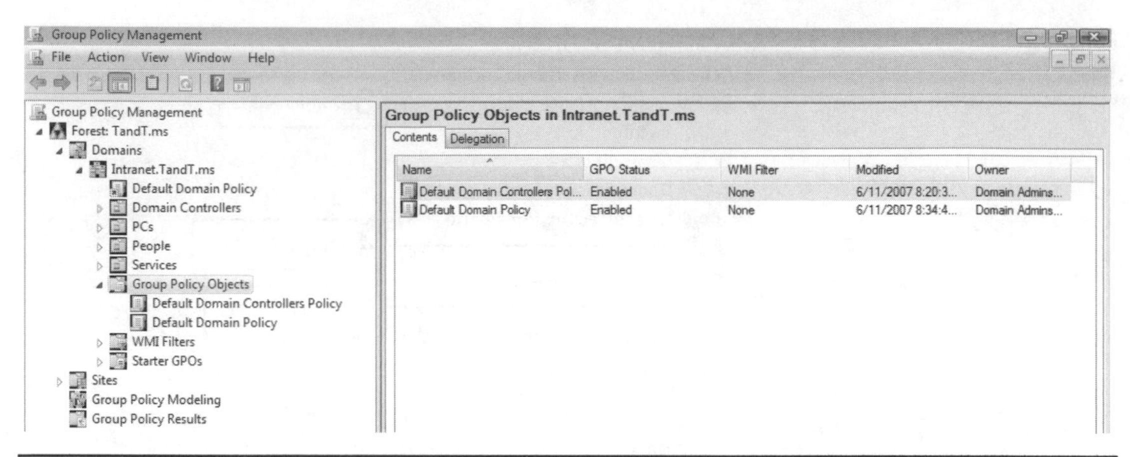

FIGURE 7-2 The GPMC interface

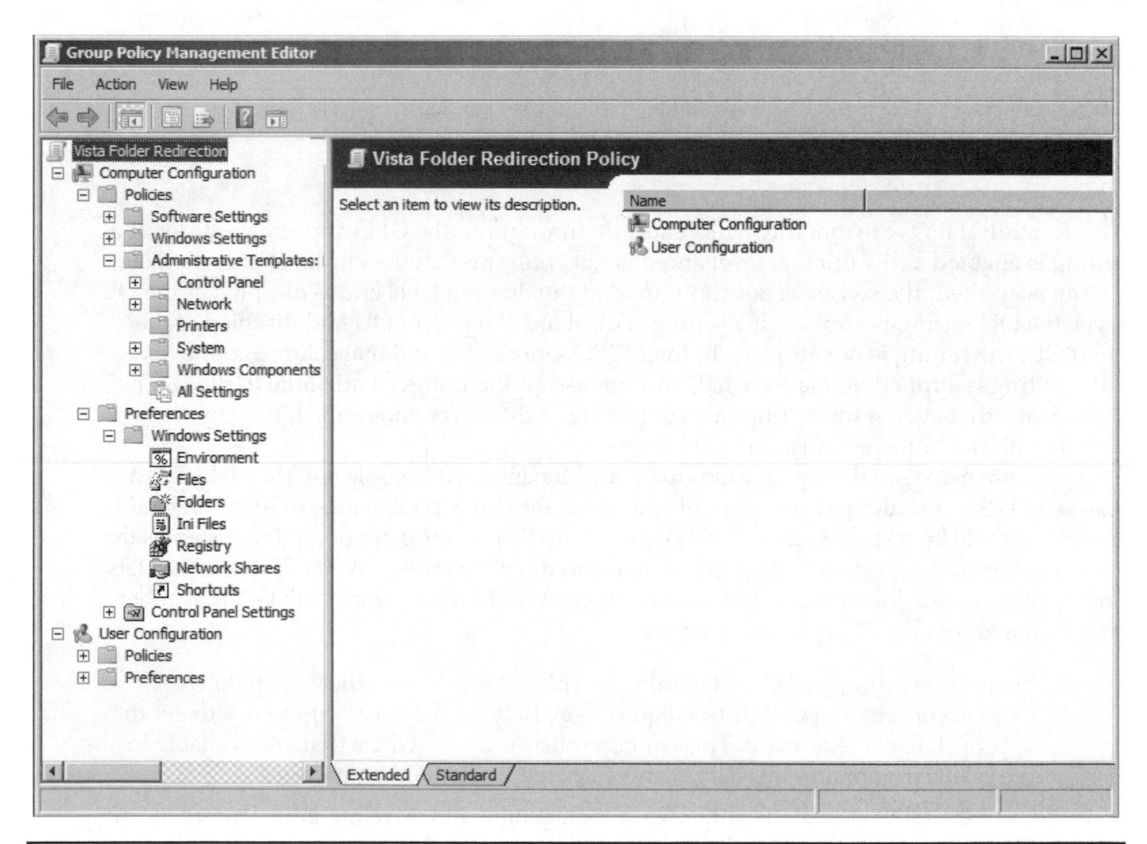

FIGURE 7-3 Editing a Group Policy Object

The second relates to user settings and will apply to affected users no matter which computer they log on to. When you are finished with the edits, you close the Group Policy Editor. Note that there is no Save option in this editor. Each setting you change is directly changed within the policy.

TIP *Since GPOs are split into computer and user settings, it is good practice to create GPOs either for users or computers alone and then disable the section that is not being used. This helps speed up GPO processing.*

In addition to the division between computers and users, each section of a Group Policy Object includes two subsections. The first, Policy, contains the actual policy contents. The second, Preferences, controls specific client-side settings and can be used to reduce post-installation configurations. Preferences includes two subsections: Windows Settings and Control Panel Settings. You use each to remotely configure system settings on any of Windows XP Service Pack 2, Windows Server 2003 Service Pack 1, Windows Vista and of course, Windows Server 2008. All but WS08 require updated client-side extensions to process the Preferences section of a GPO. The contents of the Preferences section are described in Table 7-1. The major differences between the Policies and the Preferences section of a GPO is that users can modify

Preferences Subsection	Setting	Application
Windows Settings	Applications	Lets you configure multiple application-specific settings through custom plug-ins. For example, plug-ins for Microsoft Office are available at (http://go.microsoft.com/fwlink/?LinkId=90745). A Group Policy development kit is available at (http://go.microsoft .com/fwlink/?LinkId=144).
	Drive Maps	Create, modify, delete or hide dynamic drive mappings either using the user's credentials or alternate credentials.
	Environment	Create, modify or delete user or system environment variables. Variables can also be used as conditions for other preference settings.
	Files	Copy, modify or delete a file on a system. Also modifies the attributes of a file.
	Folders	Copy, modify or delete a folder on a system. Can rely on conditions. For example, you can delete a folder only if it is empty.
	INI Files	Add, replace or delete settings in existing .ini or .inf files or even delete an entire .ini or .inf file.
	Network Shares	Create, modify or delete a file share on a system. Can also modify user limits, Access-based Enumeration settings or comments on a share.

TABLE 7-1 The contents of the Preferences section of a GPO

Preferences Subsection	Setting	Application
	Registry	Create, replace or delete entries in the registry. Can also copy multiple settings from one system and add them to other systems. Relies on a wizard to create multiple entries.
	Shortcuts	Create, modify or delete a shortcut.
Control Panel Settings	Data Sources	Create, modify or delete data sources.
	Devices	Enable or disable different device classes or specific hardware types on target systems. For example, can be used to control USB device classes.
	Folder Options	Configures folder options and file associations.
	Internet Settings (IE)	Configure IE settings. Supports IE 5, 6 and 7.
	Local Users and Groups	Control the contents of the local users and groups contained in member servers and PCs belonging to the domain.
	Network Options	Configure virtual private network (VPN) or dial-up networking connections.
	Power Options	Configure power settings on Windows XP or Windows Server 2003. To configure Power Options for Vista and WS08, use the Administrative Templates | System | Power Management section of either Computer or User Policy settings.
	Printers	Configure multiple printer connections for a system.
	Regional Options	Control regional options.
	Scheduled Tasks	Create, modify or delete scheduled tasks. Can be used to run commands as soon as GPOs refresh, automate recurring tasks, wake computers from sleep mode or even launch processes when users log on without requiring a script.
	Services	Modify the configuration of existing services.
	Start Menu	Control the structure and the options of the Start menu. Can also be used to add read-only sections of the Start menu while letting users control the read-write sections. Supports Start menu standardization.

TABLE 7-1 The contents of the Preferences section of a GPO (*continued*)

settings that have been applied through Preferences but they cannot modify settings applied through the Policies section. As its name implies, the Preferences section only applies administrative preferences and these are not necessarily absolute settings. However, using the Preferences section can often greatly reduce the need for logon scripts. Using the Preferences section is, after all, much easier than writing a Visual Basic or PowerShell script.

3. To apply the GPO, you need to link it to a container. This is performed through a drag-and-drop operation of the GPO to a destination folder, be it a site, a domain, or an OU. If the destination container is an OU and it does not exist, the GPMC will let you create it—once again, through the context menu.

TIP *GPOs are not "live"—i.e., they do not affect any objects, until they are linked to a destination container. This means that you can create GPOs in the Group Policy Objects container in the GPMC, edit it to your heart's content, and when you feel you have it right, link it to its final destination. This provides a form of change control over the GPOs you create.*

4. Both GPOs and GPO links have attributes. Each type of object is easily identifiable, since the link uses an icon in the form of a shortcut instead of the real object. If you want to make a change to the GPO's attributes that affects each container where the GPO is linked, then change the actual GPO's attributes. If you want to make a change that affects only one container the GPO is linked to, then change the attributes of the link itself. Changes include applying the Enforced attribute, disabling Computer or User sections of the GPO, and other control operations.
5. GPOs are not the only objects that can include Group Policy attributes. OUs can also include attributes that affect GPO application. For example, OU administrators can determine when they want to block inheritance. Blocking inheritance is useful when you want to store objects in your directory and you want to give them different settings from those that are set globally. For example, in the PC OU design illustrated in Figure 5-13 in Chapter 5, there is an External container at the second level. This container is designed to store computers that do not belong to your organization, such as consultants' PCs. In some cases, you want to manage some parameters on consultant systems, especially in the case of developers who are working on long-term projects and who will be creating code that will be deployed within your network. But there are other cases where you do not want to manage the external systems. This is why there are two OUs at the third level within the External OU: Managed and Unmanaged. The Unmanaged OU is an excellent example of where you would apply the Block Policy Inheritance setting. This, of course, would be done through the context menu of the OU in the GPMC.

As you can see, Group Policy management seems straightforward at first. But you have to be very careful with settings such as Enforced and Block Policy Inheritance. When the two are in contention, Enforced always wins, but if both are applied with abandon, you'll find it really hard to determine the final settings that have been applied to any given object. Fortunately, the GPMC lets you create resultant sets of policies (RSoPs), which will provide you with a list of the final GPO settings being applied to any object in your domain.

It is easily possible to apply any number of GPOs to objects. It is also easy to become confused with GPOs. The organizational unit structure has a direct impact on how GPOs are applied by default. The final result of GPO application is called the resultant set of policies (RSoP). The GPMC includes an RSoP tool that allows you to debug policy application so that you can identify the result of multiple policies on a specific object. There are also commercial tools that can provide much more comprehensive GPO management capabilities, such as complete change management, extended reporting, and GPO debugging, but most organizations will do well with the GPMC if they apply strict GPO management policies.

Policy application begins as soon as the computer is powered on. It uses a 10-step process (see Figure 7-4). This process relies on several technologies to complete: DNS, ping, the Lightweight Directory Access Protocol (LDAP), and Windows' Group Policy client-side extensions. Slow links can affect GPO processing; WS08 considers anything less than 500 kilobits per second (Kbps) as a slow link, although this setting can be changed through a policy. The process is also linked to the Group Policy Container (GPC), which is evident in the GPMC but which is hidden by default in Active Directory Users and Computers. To view the GPC in Active Directory Users and Computers, you need to enable the advanced features in the View menu. The GPC is used to identify the path to each of the Group Policy Templates (GPTs) that must be applied. These templates are located in the domain controller's SYSVOL share.

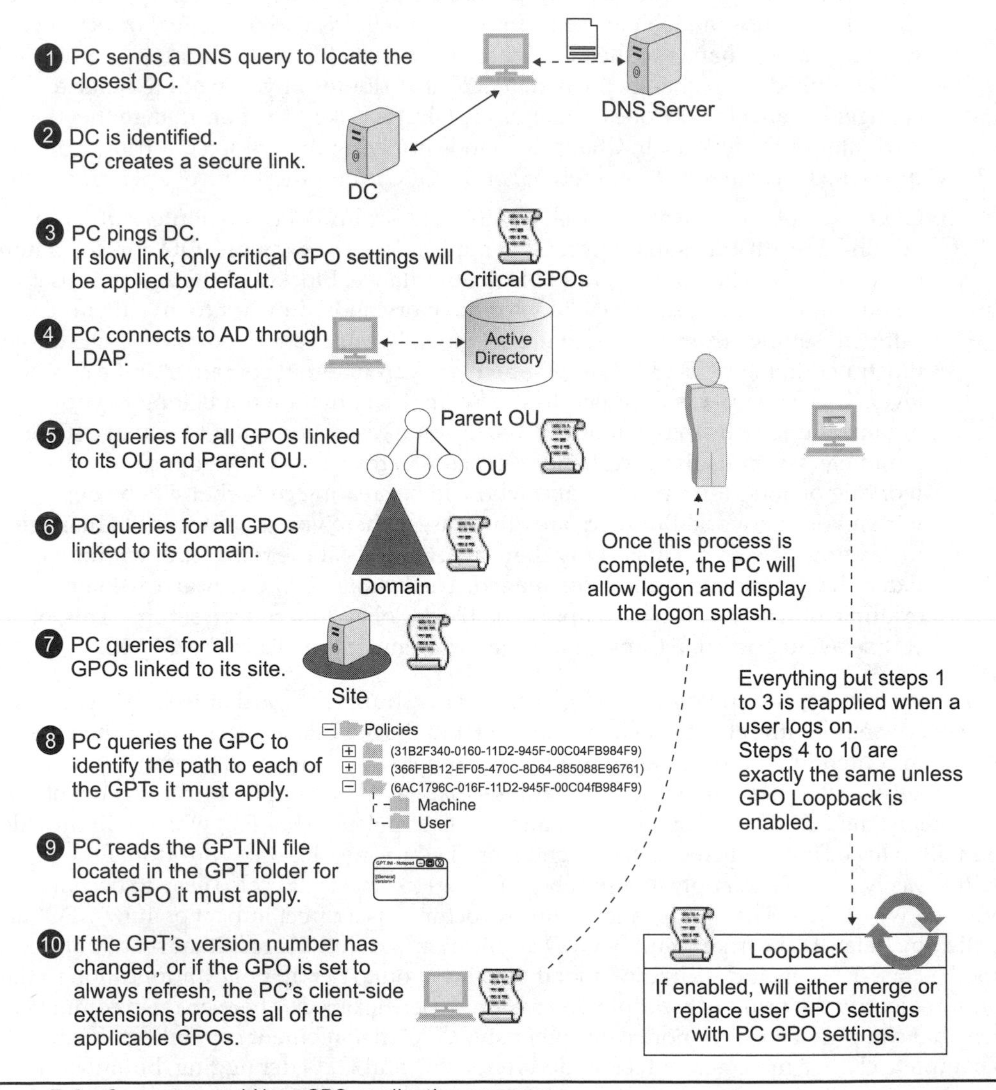
1 PC sends a DNS query to locate the closest DC.
DNS Server
2 DC is identified.
PC creates a secure link.
DC
3 PC pings DC.
If slow link, only critical GPO settings will be applied by default.
Critical GPOs
4 PC connects to AD through LDAP.
Active Directory
5 PC queries for all GPOs linked to its OU and Parent OU.
Parent OU
OU
6 PC queries for all GPOs linked to its domain.
Domain
7 PC queries for all GPOs linked to its site.
Site
8 PC queries the GPC to identify the path to each of the GPTs it must apply.
Policies
(31B2F340-0160-11D2-945F-00C04FB984F9)
(366FBB12-EF05-470C-8D64-885088E96761)
(6AC1796C-016F-11D2-945F-00C04fB984F9)
Machine
User
9 PC reads the GPT.INI file located in the GPT folder for each GPO it must apply.
10 If the GPT's version number has changed, or if the GPO is set to always refresh, the PC's client-side extensions process all of the applicable GPOs.
Once this process is complete, the PC will allow logon and display the logon splash.
Everything but steps 1 to 3 is reapplied when a user logs on.
Steps 4 to 10 are exactly the same unless GPO Loopback is enabled.
Loopback
If enabled, will either merge or replace user GPO settings with PC GPO settings.

Figure 7-4 Computer and User GPO application process

The GPO application process relies on the GPT.INI file located in the GPT folder for each GPO. This file lists the GPT's current version number, a number that is incremented each time the GPO is edited. By default, the number change forces a reapplication of the GPO. If the number has not changed, then the objects to not update the Group Policy when they process GPO application, though, once again, you can change this behavior through a GPO. Once the GPOs are applied, then any applicable scripts will run. Since these scripts run without a user interface, they are set to run a maximum amount of time—600 seconds by default—in case the script hangs while running. After the scripts run, the computer will allow logons and display the logon interface. Everything from steps 4 to 10 is reapplied when a user logs on.

Windows XP and Vista use an asynchronous policy application process, while versions of Windows Server use a synchronous process. This means that for servers, the computer session won't open until the entire list of GPOs is processed, including any scripts that are referenced in the GPO. On Windows client systems, though, GPO processing is delayed to speed up the session-opening process. This is called Fast Logon Optimization (FLO). This delay will have an impact on the way policies are applied to client systems. More on this subject will be covered later.

Policy Loopback

There is one more option for GPO application. Loopback can be used in special computer scenarios, such as for kiosks, schools, reception areas, or other zones where it is important that no matter who logs on, the computer settings must always remain in the same secured state. Since user settings are applied after computer settings in the application order, GPOs allow you to enable a Loopback setting to ensure that computer settings are reapplied instead of or along with user settings.

Loopback can be set to two modes:

- **Merge** This setting appends the computer settings to the end of the user settings during the application of GPOs at user logon. Thus, they are added to a user's settings. If the computer settings conflict with a user's settings, they override the latter.
- **Replace** This setting effectively replaces the user's settings in a GPO with the computer settings. Thus at logon, the computer settings are applied instead of the user's.

Loopback is set in the GPO under Computer Configuration | Policies | Administrative Templates | System | Group Policy. Double-clicking the policy setting allows you to configure it. Enabling the Loopback setting lets you to choose between the Merge or Replace option. Click Apply or OK. The advantage of using Apply is that if you have a lot of settings to change, you don't need to close the dialog box until you're done. You can use the Next or Previous button to move through all the settings without having to close the dialog box until you're finished.

If you do use the Loopback setting, make sure you create a special GPO and link it to a special OU that will be used to contain the computer accounts to which this GPO will be applied.

Policy Filtering

As mentioned before, the OU design is closely tied to the GPO strategy you intend to use. One of the factors you must remember at all times during this design stage is that objects can only be placed inside a single OU. In addition, you want to make sure that you keep your OU design as simple as possible. Therefore, you may find yourself in a situation where you must choose to create a complex OU design with too many OUs, just because you want to assign different GPOs to specific objects.

Don't. You will not have to, because Windows Server 2008 also includes the concept of policy filtering. Policy filtering means applying basic read and execute rights to the policy itself. By using filtering, you can apply any number of policies to a specific container and ensure that only the appropriate policy will affect the objects it is designed to manage. WS08 supports two types of policy filtering: security policy filtering and Windows Management Instrumentation (WMI) filtering.

Security Policy Filtering

Filtering through security settings is done by assigning access rights or permissions to a Group Policy object. To do so, you need to create security groups and assign the objects each policy is to manage, to the appropriate groups. Then you assign the policy object to the appropriate groups.

For example, if you have two groups of users within the same container—Common Users and Power Users—and you need to apply different policy objects to each group, you simply create two policy objects and set one to read and apply for the Common Users group and the other to read and apply to the Power Users group.

Applying security filtering to GPOs is fairly straightforward. Make sure you have already created the security groups in ADDS. Then, in the GPMC, go to the Group Policy Objects container and select the policy you want to modify. In the details pane, under the Scope tab, you will see the Security Filtering details. Click Add to select the appropriate groups. This automatically applies the Read and Apply Group Policy settings to the selected group. If Authenticated Users is listed in the Security Filtering section for this GPO, remove it. This will ensure that only the listed group(s) will be able to apply the policy.

Be careful how you use security policy filtering. Ideally, you won't need it and will rely on a proper OU structure instead.

WMI Filtering

Windows Management Instrumentation is a management infrastructure in Windows that allows the monitoring and controlling of system resources through a common set of interfaces and provides a logically organized, consistent model of Windows operation, configuration, and status. WMI is Microsoft's answer to the Desktop Management Task Force's (www.dmtf.org) Desktop Management Interface (DMI). The DMTF designed DMI to allow organizations to remotely manage computer system aspects such as system settings within the BIOS, BIOS replacement or upgrades, and system power on or off. But since no single standard management tool is available for all computer brands (each manufacturer tends to create their own tools to manage their own systems), a generic interface was required. Microsoft has attempted to provide this generic interface through WMI.

In the case of GPO filtering, WMI can be used to identify specific machine aspects before applying a GPO. In a way, this is similar to the user classes used in Dynamic Host Configuration Protocol (DHCP) because WMI filters can apply settings only to machines that meet the filter's conditions. Several example applications are available in the WS08 Help files. Take, for example, a system monitoring policy that should be applied only to systems that run Windows Server 2008. To do so, you can create the following filter:

```
Root\CimV2; Select * from Win32_OperatingSystem where Caption = "Microsoft
Windows Server 2008 Enterprise Edition"
```

Then you can apply this filter to the Group Policy object you create for the monitoring policy.

Another example is when you need to apply a policy to a specific set of computer systems. If you have a series of computer systems that do not have the capacity to host specific policies, you can create a WMI filter that identifies them and that denies policy application to this group of machines. For example, if the machines were Toshiba Satellite Pros, such a filter would include the following instructions:

```
Root\CimV2; Select * from Win32_ComputerSystem where manufacturer = "Toshiba"
and Model = "Satellite Pro 4200" OR Model = "Satellite Pro 4100"
```

WMI filters can also be saved to special files, making them easier to manage. WMI filters are basically text files that have a special structure and that use the MOF file extension.

Applying WMI filters is done in much the same way as security filters. In this case, you should create the filters first. Save them in a special folder, and name them with the MOF extension. Then import your filters into the GPMC by moving to the WMI Filters node and selecting Import from the context menu. Browse to the appropriate folder, and select the file(s) to import. You can also create the filters directly in the GPMC by using the New command. Once the filters are created or imported, you can select the policy you want to modify and once again go to its Scope tab. WMI Filtering is at the bottom of this tab. Simply select the appropriate filter from the drop-down list. Only one filter can be applied to any GPO.

CAUTION *Be careful how you use WMI policy filtering, and be especially careful when you delete WMI filters. Deleting a filter will not disassociate it from all of the GPOs it has been assigned to. You must disassociate the filter from each of the policies it has been applied to; otherwise, the policies will not be processed, since the filter no longer exists, but it is still a condition for application. Make sure you fully document all GPOs and all of their properties at all times.*

Fast Logon Optimization

As mentioned previously, modern Windows clients, such as XP and Vista, use Fast Logon Optimization to speed up the process of opening a user session. Fast Logon Optimization refers to a feature that supports the asynchronous application of some policy settings. These settings are related to three specific policy categories:

- Software installation
- Folder redirection
- Roaming user profiles

All other policy settings are applied synchronously. Remember also that GPOs are only applied if they have changed, unless otherwise specified in your Group Policy application settings. This also helps speed up the logon process.

FLO and Software Installation

Since it is impossible to install, or rather uninstall, software in an asynchronous manner, because the user may be using the application as the uninstall begins, it will take up to two logons before software that is delivered through the directory will install on Vista machines using Fast Logon Optimization. The first time a user logs on, the machine identifies that a software package is ready for delivery. It then sets a flag for software installation at next logon. This means that when the user logs on a second time, GPOs will be applied in a synchronous manner to allow the software installation to proceed. Once the software product is installed, GPOs are reset to asynchronous application.

FLO and Folder Redirection

Folder redirection refers to the redirection of user folders, such as Documents, Pictures, Start menu, and desktop. In Windows XP, five folders can be redirected. In Windows Vista, this has been increased to ten folders. Folder redirection is designed to replace the older home directory concept found in Windows NT networks. Folder redirection supports two modes: Basic and Advanced. Basic redirection sends everyone's folders to the same location and creates special subfolders for each user. Advanced allows you to set folder redirection paths for specific security groups.

It is obvious that if you redirect a user's Documents folder, you cannot do so while he or she is using it. If you use folder redirection, it can take up to three logons before the policy is applied, especially if you are using advanced settings. This is because advanced redirection is based on policy filtering. The first logon is required to update the user security group memberships. The second detects the change in the policy and sets the flag for synchronous GPO application at the next logon. The third applies the change and resets the GPO processing mode to asynchronous.

FLO and Roaming User Profiles

Fast Logon Optimization speeds up the logon process by caching all user logons. This means that if you make a change to a user's properties, such as changing their profile from local to roaming, it won't be applied until after two logons. The first is required to update the cached user object, and the second is required to apply the change. If a user has a roaming profile, Fast Logon Optimization is automatically disabled for that user.

Deactivate Fast Logon Optimization

Some administrators may decide to deactivate FLO because they are concerned that GPOs are not applied properly or that it may take a few logons for specific GPO settings to be applied. *It is not recommended to deactivate this feature.* Deactivate this feature only if you feel you absolutely must. Think about it. Deactivating this feature will make all logons take longer on all XP and Vista machines when, in fact, only two or three aspects of GPO are affected by it. Instead, follow these recommendations for FLO:

- If you do not use directory-enabled software installations, do not deactivate FLO.
- If you intend to redirect folders, make your users perform a double logon before beginning to work with their systems. This can be included in their training program or their migration activity sheet.
- If you use roaming profiles, FLO is deactivated automatically.

As you can see, there is little justification for deactivating Windows' default behavior.

Policy Design

The policy application process outlines a clear division between both computer and user settings. This is by design. Policies are correspondingly divided into two parts: computer configuration and user configuration. Since both portions are designed to address specific settings for either a machine or a user, you can and should disable unused portions of GPOs. You can use a GPO's properties to disable either the computer or the user portion. Once again, rely on the context menu to do so. You can also disable all settings. This has the effect of disabling the entire GPO.

Since policies have a natural separation between user and computer configurations, you can use them to define how you will manage both types of objects. There are, however, certain GPO settings that are applied at the domain level and that cannot be overridden by lower-level GPOs, such as those found in organizational units. Policies that should only be defined at the domain level focus on *account policies* and include:

- **Password Policy** Includes settings such as password history, maximum and minimum password age, minimum password length, and password complexity requirements, as well as reversible encryption for passwords.
- **Account Lockout Policy** Includes lockout duration, lockout threshold—the number of failed logon attempts before lockout—and the lockout reset timer.
- **Kerberos Policy** Includes enforcing user logon restrictions, such as account lockout, maximum lifetime for service and user tickets, maximum lifetime for user ticket renewal, and maximum tolerance for computer clock synchronization. Kerberos authentication functions through the issuing of access tickets to services and users. These tickets are time-based, so clock synchronization is very important within a domain.

There are other policies you might decide to set at the domain level in order to ensure that they are applied globally, but the three mentioned here should only be set at the domain level. The settings you should use for your domain-level policies are outlined in Chapter 10.

PART IV

Design a GPO Strategy

You can see that the application of policy or the management structure you want to apply within your production domain will affect the way you design your OU structure. Even though you can disable computer or user settings in a GPO, you still don't want a user object to read computer-related GPOs while logging on in order to speed up the logon and GPO application process. This is one reason for the OU strategy outlined in Chapter 5.

Computer-related GPOs will be applied in both the PCs and Virtual Service Offerings OUs, as well as in the Domain Controllers default OU. And user-related GPOs will be applied to the People OU. In addition, your GPO strategy should include domain- and site-level GPOs. You will most certainly use domain-level GPOs, but site-level GPOs are more unusual. They are useful in some circumstances, since a site can host more than one domain. If you want a default set of parameters to apply to objects within a site, even if they are from different domains, you can create a site-level GPO to enforce standards. This should be your basic GPO scoping strategy (see Figure 7-5).

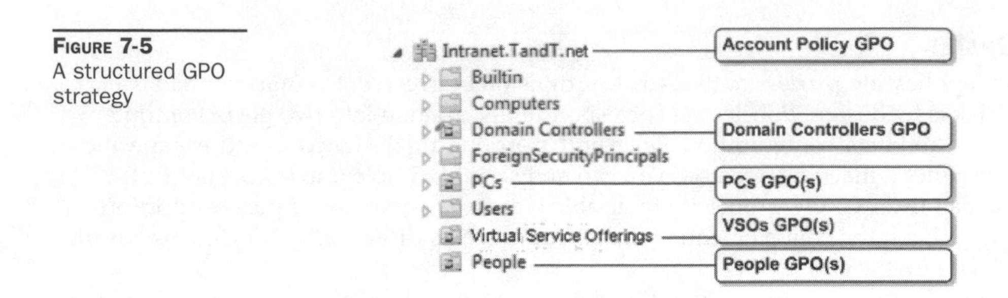

FIGURE 7-5 A structured GPO strategy

NOTE *Remember, the User and Computer default containers in ADDS are* not *organizational units and, therefore, do not support the application of Group Policy objects, except as objects within the domain.*

GPO Application and Processing Speed

Be careful how you design your GPO strategy. Many organizations choose to create regional OU designs. In such a design, each region is created as a top-level OU. Then, inside each region, two OUs are created: one for PCs and one for People. In some of the worst implementations, these containers are even called Users and Computers, like the default containers that are not OUs. The problem with this strategy is that when you need to apply a GPO to all PCs, you have to use one of three strategies (see Figure 7-6):

- Create the GPO and link it to each PC OU.
- Create a separate GPO for each PC OU.
- Create a global PC GPO, assign it to the domain, and filter it with a special PC security group.

The last option, applying the GPO at the domain level with filtering, is by far the easiest one to implement and especially to manage afterwards. But it does cause issues, since by assigning it at the domain level, every PC, server, DC, and user will attempt to read the GPO, even if it is only to discover that according to the access control list for the GPO, they are denied rights. If your domain includes several GPOs that every object must review, it will affect the speed of GPO processing on your systems.

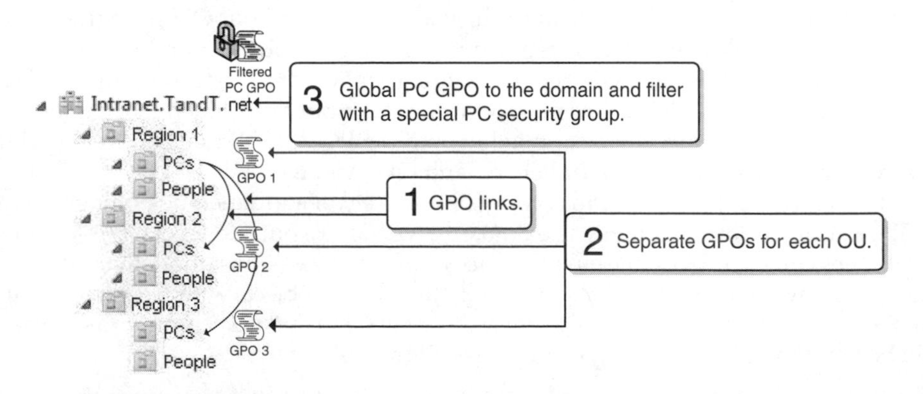

FIGURE 7-6 A regional OU design

TIP By creating object-type OUs at the top level, you can ensure that your GPOs are only applied to and read by the object type for which they are designed. Thus, PC GPOs are only read by PCs, user GPOs by user objects, DC GPOs by DCs, and server GPOs by servers. The only GPO that is read by all is the account GPO that is set at the domain level. This eases the GPO management and administration process, and it also speeds up the GPO application process at computer startup or user logon. After all, the problem you want to avoid at all costs is GPO proliferation—too many GPOs will make a mess of your management strategy.

NOTE Microsoft provides a Group Policy diagnostic best practice analyzer tool. Rely on it to validate your GPO strategy once it is in place. Obtain the tool at: //support.microsoft.com/Default.aspx?kbid=940122.

Create an OU Design for PC Management Purposes

Since user and computer management do not focus on the same activities, they are treated separately. Server management is outlined in Chapters 8 and 9, while domain controller management is outlined in Chapter 10, since they are considered part of the security strategy for the organization. Begin with PC management. It should include the configuration of GPOs for three different types of machines:

- Desktop PCs
- Portable computers
- External PCs

The OU design you use for these types of machines will depend on a lot of factors—size of the organization, number of PCs to manage, differentiation among your PCs, and especially, your administrative strategy: centralized or decentralized. Both strategies are examined in the following sections.

Centralized PC Administration

The PC OU design in Chapter 5 is an example of a centralized PC administration strategy. In this sample scenario, T&T Corporation has a decentralized user administration, but a centralized PC management strategy. If this is the case in your organization, it will greatly simplify your OU strategy for PCs.

Three levels of OUs were used in this scenario. Each is used to further segregate the PC object type. Level one is used to regroup all PCs. This is where global PC GPOs are applied. Level two begins object segregation. If a global GPO is required for all desktops or all portables, or even all external PCs, it is applied at this level. Finally, level three is used to apply GPOs to specific types of PCs within each grouping. For example, desktop PCs whose users have some local administrative rights still require some management, but a lighter management than PCs whose users are more generic. Because of this, you may require a special GPO for power users. No special GPO is required for normal users' PCs, because they should be covered by the general GPOs set at levels one and two (see Figure 7-7).

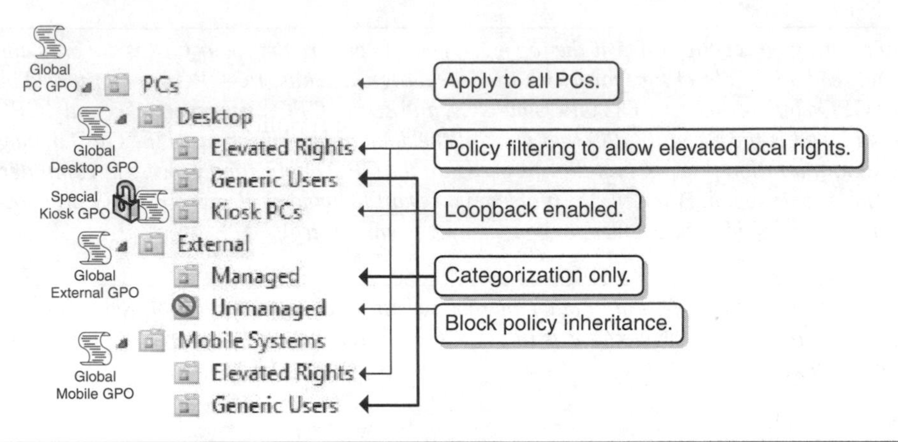

FIGURE 7-7 GPO application in a centrally managed PC OU structure

CAUTION *You should endeavor to remove administrative rights from as many users as you can in your network. In fact, each user should log on with a normal user account. If administrative rights are required, then they should use elevated rights through the Run As Administrator command. This way, if security issues arise, each user's security context has lower privileges and cannot damage systems as much as with the elevated privileges administrators are granted.*

CAUTION *When you create OUs in WS08 through the AD Users and Computers section of Server Manager, you can optionally protect the container from accidental deletion. This means that you will not normally be able to move or delete the object if you either make a mistake or want to restructure your directory. To remove this setting from a created object, you need to select Advanced Features from the View menu and then view the object's properties. The option is listed on the Object tab that appears in the property sheet when the Advanced Features feature is turned on.*

The Desktop OU

The segregation applied at the child level of the Desktop OU could have been performed directly at the Desktop OU itself using GPO filtering, but creating a child level also gives you the advantage of being able to categorize objects. This will make it easier for you to find each type of PC.

In addition, the desktop OU includes a special OU for kiosk PCs. These systems are placed in public zones and give people access to your network. You need to ensure that they are always highly secured. This is an ideal place to use the Loopback feature to ensure that no matter who logs on to these computers, the secure GPO you apply to these computers is always in effect. To manage these systems, you will need to be able to reopen the secure environment in order to perform updates and system fixes. This might be an ideal situation to use multiple local GPOs.

TIP *If you are running Vista on the PC, then the Desktop OU is also a good location for "green," or power management, policies. Green policies will help you lower power costs by putting computers "to sleep" whenever they are not in use.*

The Portable OU

The Portable OU is designed to help apply special GPOs for portable computers. For example, since portables are computer systems that often leave the secure network your organization provides, you will want to ensure that certain policies are always applied to these systems. These could include the enforcing of file encryption on the portable and the use of a personal firewall whenever the PC connects to any system through its modem, wireless network connection, network connection, or even the infrared port. These policies are applied directly to the Portable OU. If you are using Vista on the desktop, you could assign BitLocker system drive encryption settings through this GPO.

In addition, there is a second level of segregation for portables: common users and power users. The same types of policies applied to these child OUs in the desktop OU are applied here. This can be done through the use of a separate GPO object or through the linkage of the appropriate desktop GPOs to these OUs.

The External OU

An External OU is created to ensure that external PCs are always regrouped. Policies that apply specifically to all external PCs are applied at the top level of this OU. Once again, a child level is included to help categorize systems that are managed versus systems that are unmanaged. If the unmanaged systems are completely so, you can set the Unmanaged OU to block policy inheritance. If not, you can filter policies in this OU.

Managed external systems are often not quite the same as your own managed systems. The reason is that it is often very difficult for you to ensure that consultant systems are exactly the same as your own. Consulting firms often tend to buy clone systems that are less expensive than corporate systems and that do not fully support your managed systems environment. Because of this, some of the settings you apply to your own systems will be different from the settings you need to apply to this group of heterogeneous machines (especially if you have more than one consulting firm on site).

Managed systems tend to be mostly desktops, though, while unmanaged systems are often portables. This is because the consultants that use managed systems are often programmers and programmers prefer to have desktops because for the same price, you can get a lot more speed and power on the system. This gives you a natural segregation between desktops and portables in the external OU structure.

Table 7-2 outlines the use of each of the OUs in this PC administrative strategy.

NOTE *You may decide not to use block policy inheritance in the Unmanaged OU. You will have to determine and negotiate with consultants to define your own policy for unmanaged consultant PCs.*

Computer Policy Contents

As mentioned previously, Group Policy objects are composed of two categories of settings: computer and user configurations. Since the GPOs that you will be designing for the PCs OU structure are all related to computers, the first thing you should do when creating a GPO for this organizational unit structure is disable the User Configuration portion of the GPO. Remember this is a GPO attribute and is configured through the GPO's context menu.

OU	Level	Objective	GPO	Notes
PCs	One	Grouping of all PCs in the organization	Global PC GPO	Applies to all PCs
Desktops	Two	Grouping of all desktops in the organization	Global Desktop GPO	Includes differences from Global PC GPO only
Power Users	Three	Grouping of desktops whose users have local administrative rights		Policy filtering to allow local administrative rights
Generic Users	Three	Grouping of desktops with common user rights		Categorization only
Kiosks	Three	Grouping of special high-risk PCs	Special Kiosk GPO	Loopback-enabled Special exclusion group for repairs (deny read to Kiosk GPO)
Portables	Two	Grouping of all portables in the organization	Global Portable GPO	Includes differences from Global PC GPO only
Power Users	Three	Grouping of desktops whose users have local administrative rights		Policy filtering to allow local administrative rights
Generic Users	Three	Grouping of desktops with common user rights		Categorization only
External	Two	Grouping of all external PCs in the organization	Global External GPO	Includes differences from Global PC GPO only
Managed	Three	Grouping of all managed external PCs in the organization		Categorization only
Unmanaged	Three	Grouping of all unmanaged external PCs in the organization		Block policy inheritance

TABLE 7-2 A Centralized PC Administration OU Structure

Now that your GPO is structured only for computers, you can begin to examine the settings you can manage with this GPO. The Computer Configuration section is divided into several subcategories. Table 7-3 lists these categories and their possible application in your network.

NOTE *Different settings apply to different operating systems. Out of the 2,450 potential settings, more than 800 apply only to Vista. Make sure you review which operating system settings apply to before you assign them to your PCs. The system a setting applies to is displayed in the setting's explanation.*

GPO Section	Comment	Applicable
Software Settings	This section deals with software installations. If you want to assign a software product to a computer instead of a user through Windows Server 2008 software delivery, you set the parameters here.	See the PC management strategy later in this chapter
Windows Settings	This section deals with general Windows settings and includes elements such as scripts and security settings.	Partially
Scripts	Controls access to startup and shutdown scripts.	If required
Security Settings	Includes account policies, local policies, Event Logs, and more. For example, this is where you would configure Windows Firewall settings.	Partially
Account Policy	Controls all account policies.	Set at the domain level
Local Policies	Specific to each computer or to the domain. Includes audit policy, user rights assignments, and security options. Most user rights assignments are set at the domain level, but some, such as modify firmware environment values and perform volume maintenance tasks, should be assigned at the PC level to allow technical groups the rights required to maintain PCs.	Audit policy and some user rights
Event Log	Controls size of each Event Log.	Yes
Restricted Groups	Controls who belongs to high-security groups such as Domain Administrators. Set at the domain level for high-level administrative groups (Domain and Enterprise Administrators). Set at the PC level for local administrators such as technician groups.	Partially
System Services	Determines how given services will behave on a computer.	Yes
Registry	Allows you to set access rights to registry hives.	No
File System	Allows you to set access rights to files and folders.	No
Wired Network (IEEE 802.3) Policies	Controls secured access to networks and single sign-on settings.	Yes
Windows Firewall with Advanced Security	Controls inbound and outbound firewall rules. Controls the state of the firewall, both when connected to the internal network and when roaming outside the office.	Yes
Wireless Network (IEEE 802.11) Policies	Allows you to set policies for wireless network connections.	For portables
Public Key Policies	Controls all public key infrastructure (PKI) settings, including the Encrypting File System.	For portables
Software Restriction Policies	Allows you to determine which applications are allowed to run in your network.	At the domain level
Network Access Protection	Controls access to networks based on health status. Lets you set the enforcement clients, define user interface settings, and identify trusted server groups.	For portables or any roaming computer
IP Security Policy	Allows you to set the PC behavior when using Internet Protocol Security (IPSec).	For portables

TABLE 7-3 Computer Policy Categories and Contents

GPO Section	Comment	Applicable
Policy-based QoS	Defines Quality of Service (QoS) settings for video and audio streaming.	Yes
Administrative Templates	Administrative templates are scriptable GPO components that can be used to control a wide variety of settings, such as Control Panel items, Windows components, system, network, and Printers.	Yes
Control Panel	Controls regional and language options, as well as allows you to modify the default user logon pictures.	Set at the user level only
Network	Controls network-related settings, such as Background Intelligent Transfer Service (BITS), DNS Client, Link-Layer Topology Discovery, Microsoft Peer-to-Peer Networking, Offline Files, Network Connections, QoS Packet Scheduler, Simple Network Management Protocol (SNMP), Secure Sockets Layer (SSL) Configurations, and Windows Connect Now. Offline files settings should be set so that users cannot configure them for themselves. Network connections should be set so that wireless connections should use machine authentication. SNMP is not normally configured for PCs.	Yes
Printers	Mainly controls how printers are used with the Active Directory Domain Service. Supports the ability to publish printers through GPOs.	At the domain level
System	Controls system-wide settings, such as User Profiles, Scripts, Logon, Disk Quotas, Net Logon, Group Policy (Loopback, for example), Remote Assistance, System Restore, Error Reporting, Windows File Protection, Remote Procedure Call, Windows Time Service, and more. This section controls the behavior of each listed feature. The Scripts section, for example, determines the behavior for scripts, not the script names. Remote Assistance should be set to facilitate help desk tasks, especially, the Offer Remote Assistance setting. Error Reporting should be set for critical applications. This will enable them to send any error reports to a corporate share without telling users. It also controls device driver signing. This should be turned on for all deployed PCs. It also controls the behavior of user profiles on PCs. You should modify this behavior if you intend to work with roaming profiles and folder redirection. Use Device Installation to control whether or not users can plug in devices such as Universal Serial Bus (USB) drives. Use Local Services, which allow you to automatically change settings on PCs to match an employee's language settings. Power Management helps reduce the power consumption of PCs in the organization. Use User Account Control to have everyone run with a standard user token.	Yes Shared with the user level

TABLE 7-3 Computer Policy Categories and Contents (*continued*)

GPO Section	Comment	Applicable
Windows Components	Controls settings such as NetMeeting (for the Remote Desktop), Internet Explorer, Task Scheduler, Terminal Services, Windows Installer, Windows Messenger, and Windows Update. Several settings are of use here. Terminal Services (TS) determines how the TS session is established between the local and remote systems. Windows Update, in particular, allows you to assign an internal server location for update collection. Internet Explorer configurations are also controlled here. Also controls everything from Movie Maker to the Windows Sidebar.	Yes
All Settings	Lists all of the settings that are available under Administrative Templates. You can sort them through each of the headings in the details pane, giving you an easier access to each of these settings.	Yes

TABLE 7-3 Computer Policy Categories and Contents *(continued)*

NOTE *Registry keys and files and folder access rights should be set using the Secedit command with Security Templates. These can be applied through local Group Policy objects. More on this will be discussed in Chapter 10.*

The System and Windows Component sections of Administrative Templates include most of the settings you can control through GPOs. With Vista, this section was greatly enhanced. There is a significant amount of settings in these sections. Take the time to review all of them and determine which ones should be set. You should document all of the GPOs you create. You should also use a standard naming strategy for all GPOs and ensure you maintain a complete GPO registry.

TIP *Microsoft provides a useful Excel spreadsheet for GPO documentation at www.microsoft.com/downloads/details.aspx?familyid=7821C32F-DA15-438D-8E48-45915CD2BC14&displaylang=en. Microsoft also provides a good tool to inventory Group Policy, which can be found at www.microsoft.com/downloads/details.aspx?FamilyID=1d24563d-cac9-4017-af14-8dd686a96540&DisplayLang=en.*

TIP *For guidance on deploying Group Policy with Vista, go to http://technet2.microsoft.com/WindowsVista/en/library/5ae8da2a-878e-48db-a3c1-4be6ac7cf7631033.mspx?mfr=true.*

Administrative Templates in Vista

Administrative templates are, by far, the most powerful portion of Group Policy. They basically let you control any portion of the system registry by creating the appropriate text file and importing it into Group Policy. Prior to Windows Vista, all GPO definition templates used an ADM file format—pure text files that were organized in a structured manner. With Vista, Microsoft introduced the ADMX format—a format based on the Extended Markup Language (XML), which provides much richer content for GPO templates. ADMX templates are now language-independent, globalizing Group Policy settings. Each ADMX file is accompanied by one or more ADML file which includes language-specific content. Global organizations will want to include an ADML file for each language their administrators work in. In addition, ADMX files can be centrally stored, as opposed to the distributed approach used by ADM files—one on each domain controller in a particular ADDS domain. And, because of the increased number of policy settings in Vista, 143 ADMX files are included in the release version of WS08.

Because of the changes to Group Policy in Vista, the ADMX format is incompatible with the ADM format, meaning that environments managing a mix of Windows 2000 and/or XP with Vista will need to either translate their existing templates to ADMX format or create new ones. Organizations that manage a mix of Windows clients will need to put in place a strategy that will support the translation of ADM to ADMX and vice versa, but, of course, only for the settings that apply to any Windows version.

TIP *Obtain the AMD/ADMX Conversion Tool. Microsoft licensed an ADM-to-ADMX conversion tool from FullArmor Corporation. This free utility is available at www.fullarmor.com/ ADMX-download-options.htm.*

In previous versions of Windows, each time a new ADM template was created, it would be copied from the local system to the SYSVOL share on the domain controller. It would then be copied to every DC in the domain. With Vista, ADMX templates are referenced locally on the system they were generated from, but if you have several PC administrators working on these templates, you'll want to create a central storage container that everyone will reference when working on new or existing templates. To create the central store:

1. Log on to any connected system with domain administrative rights.
2. Locate the PDC Emulator domain controller in your network. The easiest way to do this is to open Active Directory Users and Computers in Server Manager, right-click the domain name to choose Operations Masters, then click the PDC tab to find the name of the DC. Then use Windows Explorer to navigate to its SYSVOL shared folder. You use the PDC Emulator because it is the engine that drives GPO changes in the network.
3. Navigate to the SYSVOL*DOMAINNAME*\POLICIES folder where *domainname* is the DNS name of your domain.
4. Create a new folder called PolicyDefinitions.
5. Copy the contents of the C:\WINDOWS\POLICYDEFINITIONS folder from any WS08 system to the new folder you created in step 4. Use WS08 because it has more ADMX files than the release version of Vista.
6. Include the appropriate ADML folders. For example, U.S. English systems would use the en-US folder.
7. Launch the Group Policy Editor. It will automatically reference the new central store, as will all editors on any Vista or WS08 system in your domain.

Do this once to make sure all templates are stored in a central location.

NOTE *There is no Group Policy interface for loading ADMX files into a GPO. If you want to add new settings based on an ADMX file, create the ADMX file and copy it to your central store. It will appear in the Group Policy Object as soon as you reopen the Group Policy Editor.*

Decentralized PC Administration

The OU structure defined previously is useful if all PC operations are centralized, even if your organization includes regional offices. But if your regional offices include a vast number of computer systems, you'll probably find that you need to be able to allow regional technicians to perform some degree of operations on the regional PCs. If this is the case, you'll need to be able to design an OU structure that will support delegation of administration. To do so, you need to be able to create geographic containers for all PCs.

Once again, it remains useful to segregate your object type at the first OU level. The difference lies in the second-level OU structure. Here, you will need to create a geographic structure to store PCs. Since you will most likely still have external PCs in this structure, you will need to create an External OU as well. Most organizations that hire consultants will do so in central or large offices. This means that your External OU does not necessarily need to be divided into regions. Your desktop and portable computers, however, will require regional distribution.

Even if you create regional units, you will still require some form of segregation for the two types of machines. Since you know that creating a regional structure followed by Desktop and Portable child OUs will only complicate the application of GPOs by either requiring individual GPOs for each container or having to link GPOs from one container to another, you'll need to use a different strategy. In this case, the best strategy is to use Group Policy filtering.

Create two principal OU levels, the PC, and then the regional child OUs. Then create global security groups for each type of PC: desktop and portable. Apply all Group Policy objects to the PC OU, and filter them through the use of your security groups. In this way, all PC objects will receive the GPOs, even the PCs located in the regional child OUs. Since GPO filtering is enabled, policies that apply to desktops will only apply to desktops and policies that apply to portables will only apply to portables.

In most cases, the PC OU will contain the following policies (see Figure 7-8):

- **Global PC Policy** Applicable to all PCs; no filtering applied
- **Global Desktop Policy** Filtered with the Desktop global security group

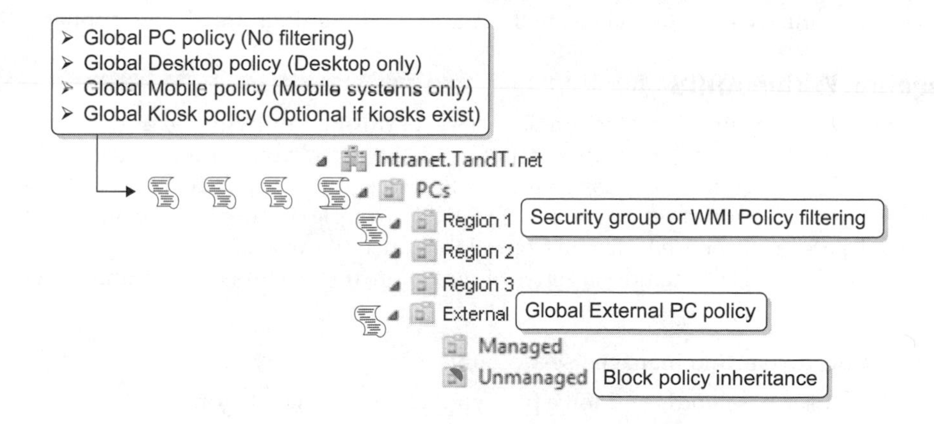

FIGURE 7-8 A decentralized PC OU strategy

- **Global Portable Policy** Filtered with the Portable global security group
- **Global Kiosk Policy** Filtered with a Kiosk global security group

This policy structure is a little more difficult to manage than the centralized PC management structure, since it must be managed through group memberships, but it allows you to design a strategy that maintains central control as well as allowing delegation to regional technicians.

Design for Delegation

The decentralized OU strategy outlines the need for delegation of administration. In this case, it means that regional technicians must be allowed to perform specific activities related to PC management and administration. These activities can range from simple user management, such as resetting user passwords, to much more comprehensive administrative tasks. Users of Windows NT will likely not be familiar with the concept of delegation, since in this operating system, to delegate authority, you basically had to give someone domain administration rights. There were, of course, third-party products that allowed some form of delegation within Windows NT, but they were costly and took time to implement.

This is not the case in Windows Server 2008. In fact, since Windows 2000, the concept of delegation is embedded into the operating system. ADDS offers delegation rights and permissions by default. This is because each object in the directory can hold security properties. You can assign user rights to any object, user, computer, site, domain, organizational units—any object. Delegation is inherent to an Active Directory Domain Services design.

In terms of Group Policy objects, you can delegate administration, creation, linkage, modification, and much more. You'll soon learn to be careful what you delegate in terms of GPOs, because the more you delegate, the more complex your GPO administration will become. For example, if all GPO creation and administration is centralized, there is never any requirement for the Enforced option to be applied to a GPO, since you are in control of everything and no one will try to block the application of a GPO or replace it with another. If you delegate GPO rights, then you'll most likely consider the use of the Enforced option, since you'll definitely want to make sure that global GPO settings are always applied.

Delegation Within ADDS

Delegation in Active Directory Domain Services is performed through the use of a wizard. The tool you use to perform delegation depends on the object you want to delegate. If it is a site, you need to use Active Directory Sites and Services. If it is a domain or an OU, use Active Directory Users and Computers. Delegation is simple: Right-click the object you want to delegate, and choose Delegate Control to launch the wizard.

Windows Server 2008 includes a series of preassigned tasks you can delegate. These include:

- Create, delete, and manage user accounts
- Reset user passwords and force password change at next logon
- Read all user information
- Create, delete, and manage groups

- Modify the membership of a group
- Manage Group Policy links
- Generate Resultant Set of Policy (Planning)
- Generate Resultant Set of Policy (Logging)
- Create, delete, and manage inetOrgPerson accounts
- Reset inetOrgPerson passwords and force password change at next logon
- Read inetOrgPerson user information

On the other hand, you may decide that you wish to delegate a specific operation that is not included in the default list. To do so, you need to choose Create A Custom Task To Delegate in the Tasks To Delegate window. This will lead you to a new window listing the custom tasks you can delegate.

There are more than 60 different objects or combinations of objects that you can choose to delegate under the Active Directory Objects To Delegate window. Finally, you can assign a variety of permissions to the custom objects. Everything from full control to read or write all objects can be assigned at the general, property-specific, and/or creation/deletion of specific child objects level.

Delegation Through Group Membership

In addition, some global delegation rights can be assigned in a more traditional manner: through group memberships. Special groups, such as the Group Policy Creator Owners, DnsAdmins, Print Operators, Server Operators, Backup Operators, and more, allow the delegation of certain tasks at the domain level, simply through their group memberships. You have to be more careful with this type of delegation, though, since it gives domain-wide delegation rights. This may grant more authority than what you originally intended.

Create Custom Microsoft Management Consoles

One of the impacts of delegation within Active Directory Domain Services is the need for custom consoles to allow access to delegated objects for groups with delegated rights and permissions. This means that you can create a custom version of a Microsoft Management Console (MMC) containing only the objects you have delegated access to and distribute this console to members of the group with delegation rights.

NOTE *You must install the Remote Server Administration Tools (RSAT) on the target machine before you can create these consoles.*

1. To create custom consoles, you need to start the console program in authoring mode. To do so, run the following command:

   ```
   mmc /a
   ```

2. This launches an empty MMC. You then need to add the appropriate snap-in to the console. To do so, move to the File menu, and select Add/Remove Snap-in. In the Snap-in dialog box, click the Add button. Select the snap-in you require—for example, Active Directory Users and Computers. Many snap-ins include extensions. You should view the extensions to see if they are required for the group to whom you intend to delegate this console. If not, clear all of the extensions that are not required.

PART IV

3. Click OK when done. Save your console and give it an appropriate name.
4. Once the snap-in is added, navigate to the OU you want to delegate.
5. Next, you need to create a Taskpad view for the console. This allows you to modify the way information is presented to console users. To do so, move to the Action menu and choose New Taskpad View. This launches the Taskpad Wizard. This will allow you to choose the presentation mode for the console. Good options include Horizontal list and InfoTips for item descriptions. Apply the Taskpad to the selected tree item. Name the Taskpad, and then, when the wizard finishes, make sure the Add New Tasks option is selected to add tasks to the Taskpad.
6. Add menu commands. Choose the node in the tree as the command source, and add commands such as New User, New Group, Properties and so on. Make sure you select the option to run the wizard again until you've finished adding tasks. If you miss it, use the Action | Edit TaskPad command and move to the Tasks tab to add more tasks.

NOTE *Make sure there are items in this OU; otherwise, you will not have access to all of the task commands you want to delegate.*

7. Next, you need to set the focus for this console. To do so, select the object you want to delegate—for example, an organizational unit. Right-click this object and select New Window From Here. This will create a new window that displays only the appropriate information for console users. Minimize it, close the other window, and then maximize the new window again.
8. Now you need to set the view options for this window. Since the console users will not require the ability to create consoles, you can remove a number of items, such as the console tree, standard menu, standard toolbar, etc. To do so, move to the View menu, and select Customize. Clear all of the items you do not deem necessary for console users. This dialog box is live: When you clear an item, you immediately see the result in the console behind the dialog box. Click OK when done.
9. Finally, you need to customize the console. Move to the File menu, and select Options. Here, you can type a console description, assign a new icon, and determine the console operation mode. There are four console operation modes:
   - Author mode
   - User mode, full access: The same as author mode, but users cannot add snap-ins, change options, and create Favorites or Taskpads.
   - User mode, limited access, multiple windows: Gives access only to the selected items when the console was saved. Users can create new windows, but cannot close any previously saved windows.
   - User mode, limited access, single window: Same as the previous mode, but users cannot create new windows.

   For single-purpose consoles, the last setting is appropriate.

NOTE *Make sure you select the Do Not Save Options For This Console option; otherwise, users will be prompted to save the console each time they use it.*

10. Save the console again when done. Test the console to ensure it operates as designed. To do so, close it and reopen it in operation mode (as opposed to authoring mode) by double-clicking its icon.

TIP *The %WINDIR%\System32\SHELL32.DLL file contains several icons that can be used to customize MMCs.*

You can save the console and distribute it to users through Group Policy using software distribution. To do so, you will need to package consoles, including any snap-ins that are required for them to operate. Remember that snap-ins must be registered on the target computer for the console to work. The best way to distribute consoles is to package them as Windows Installer executables. You can use a repackaging tool to do so.

Another way to distribute consoles is through Terminal Services. The advantage of using Terminal Services to distribute consoles is that only one installation of the snap-in is required—on the hosting server. In addition, since all users access the same console on the same computer, global modifications are simple: change one single console in a single place. Finally, distribution is simple: All you need to do is send the console icon to the users requiring it. More on Terminal Services is covered in Chapter 9. Custom consoles are an important part of any WS08 delegation strategy (see Figure 7-9).

Design a Delegation Strategy

The delegation strategy you require will have a direct impact on your organizational unit strategy. This design will also have to take into account the Group Policy object strategy you designed. When designing for delegation, you need to take several factors into account.

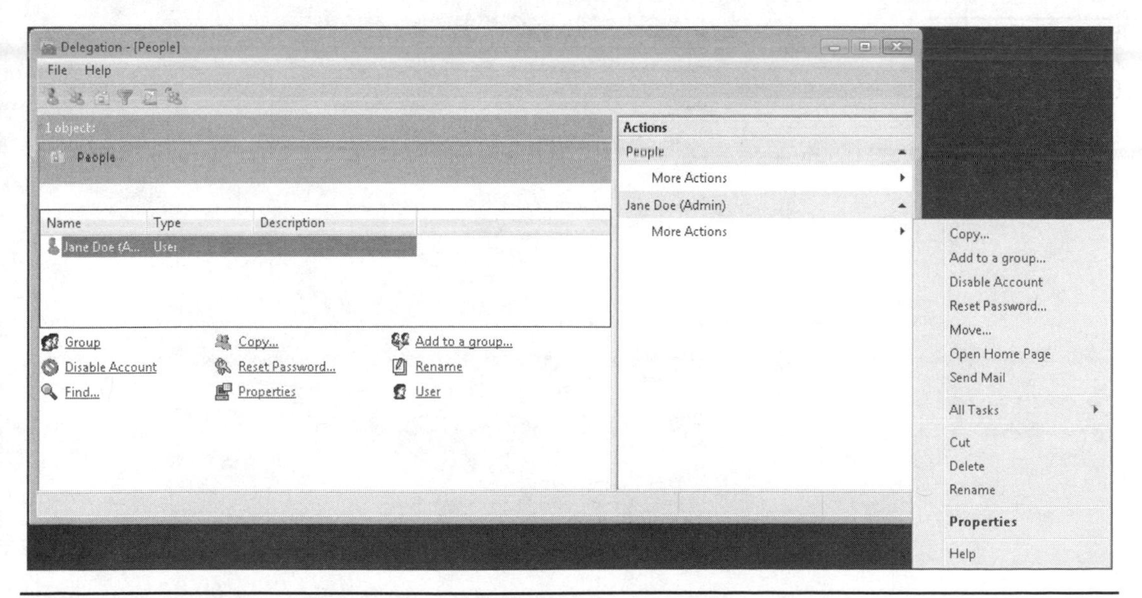

FIGURE 7-9 A custom Microsoft Management Console

Begin by identifying the business needs that influence delegation. Many of these will have been inventoried at the very beginning of your project. You also need to have a good understanding of your IT organizational structure. In addition, you need to review how you can change your administrative practices now that you have access to a technology that fully supports delegation. More on this is covered in Chapter 10.

If you decide to delegate, you will need to formalize the delegation process. This includes a series of activities such as:

- Identifying all delegated officers
- Identifying the role for each officer
- Identifying the responsibilities for each officer
- Identifying the name of the backup delegated officer for each officer
- Listing any special consoles you may have created for each delegation level
- Specifically identifying all rights and permissions that have been delegated
- Prepare and deliver a delegation training program to ensure that all delegated officers are completely familiar with their responsibilities

Another required aspect is the identification of object owners and the addition of object managers within the properties of each object in the directory (see Figure 7-10). This will allow you to use the directory to support the documentation of your delegation program.

NOTE *Figure 7-10 displays a generic user name. Chapter 5 outlined that generic account names are not allowed in the Production domain, and they shouldn't be. A generic name is used here for the purpose of illustrating the type of user you would identify as owner of an OU.*

FIGURE 7-10 Assigning OU ownership

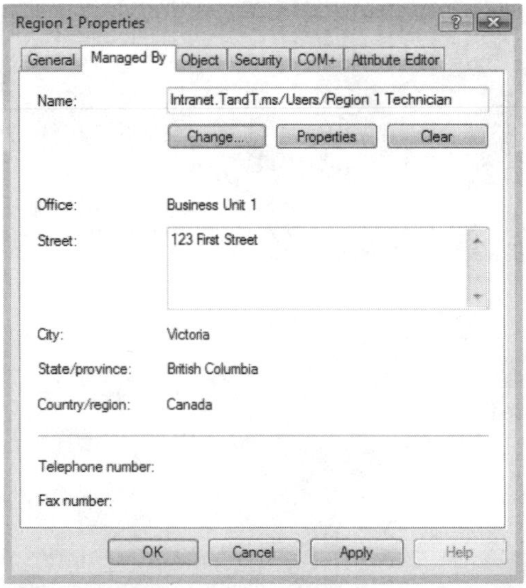

Finally, your delegation plan will most likely require the creation of a new position within your administrative activities: the delegation manager. This role concentrates all delegation activities within a centralized function. The delegation manager is responsible for overseeing all delegation and making sure that all information that is related to delegation is maintained and up to date.

PC Management

The last part of your organizational unit design strategy for PCs is the PC management strategy you intend to use. PC management in an organization deals with a lot of activities, which include but are not limited to:

- Hardware inventory
- Software inventory
- Remote control and Remote Assistance
- Software Lifecycle Management
- Software usage metering

By default, Windows Server 2008 offers several of these capabilities. In fact, both Remote Assistance and Software Lifecycle Management are features that are now built into Windows.

TIP *More information on PC management in general can be found in our free e-book:* The Definitive Guide to Vista Migration, *which can be downloaded from www.realtime-nexus.com/dgvm.htm. For information on deployment and PC administration, look up* Deploying and Administering Windows Vista Bible *by Cribbs, Ruest, Ruest, and Kelly published by Wiley.*

Software Installations with WS08

Windows Server 2008 includes a set of Group Policy Objects that can be used to deliver software to both users and computers. This GPO is closely tied to the Windows Installer service, which is available for both PCs and servers. Windows Installer is a service that has been designed to help take control of the software lifecycle. This does not only mean remote installation of software, but more specifically, it means software upgrades, patches, maintenance fixes, and something that is more often than not overlooked, software removal. The Windows Installer service manages several different aspects of the software lifecycle (see Figure 7-11).

Policy-based software installations will usually only work with installation files that are supported by Windows Installer. These files have MSI extensions. A Windows Installer executable is, in fact, an installation database that is copied to the computer system along with the program it installs. This is one reason why Windows Installer supports both software self-healing as well as clean software removal. Once a program is installed on a system, Windows Installer will perform a program consistency check every time the software program is launched. If there are inconsistencies between the actual program state and the contents of the installation database, Windows Installer will automatically launch a software repair phase.

During this repair phase, Windows Installer will connect to the original installation source of the software program by default and reinstall missing or damaged components. This means that if self-healing is to work, installation source files must be maintained on a permanent basis. This is a significant change from traditional approaches, which focused on

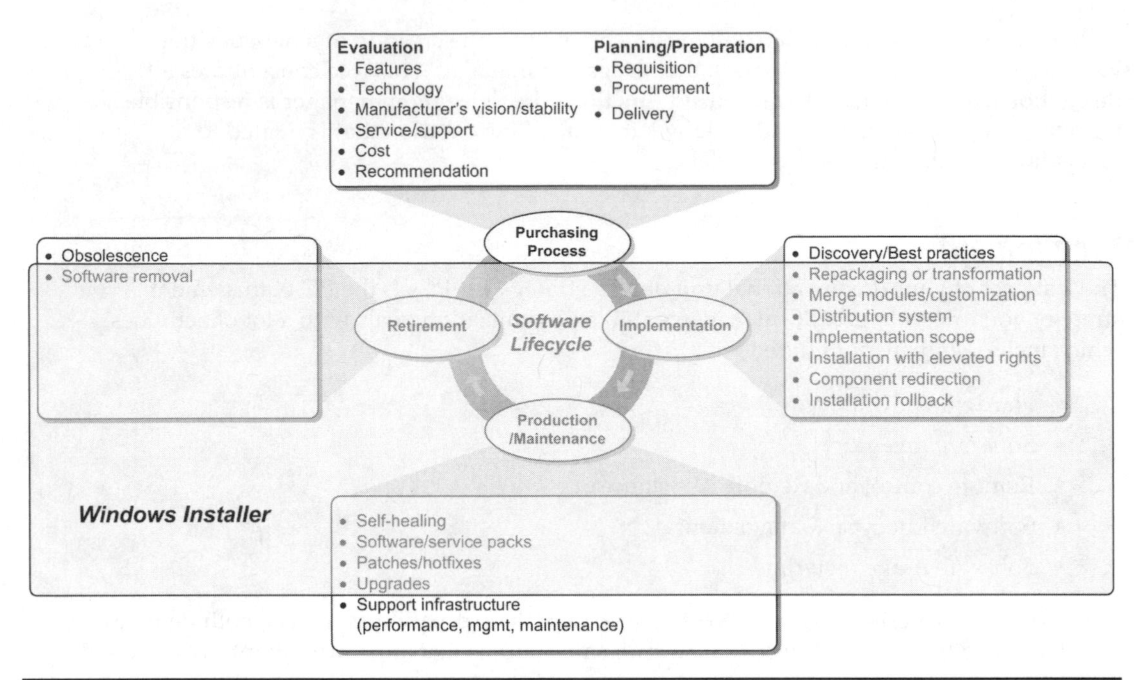

FIGURE 7-11 Software lifecycle management with Windows Installer

deploying software and then removing installation source files once deployment was complete. Organizations who want to use the self-healing capabilities of Windows Installer must maintain permanent software installation depots.

The Windows Installer consistency database is used to perform clean removals of software from a system. Anyone who has had any experience with software removal in versions of Windows previous to Windows 2000—or older systems that have the Windows Installer service installed—will know that for those systems, the concept of a clean install is nothing more than a myth. This is not the case with Windows Installer–enabled software. In fact, one of Windows Installer's main functions is to manage software conflicts and ensure that shared system components are not damaged by software installations. If conflicting components are added during a software product installation, Windows Installer will automatically ensure that these components are installed in a special directory called %SYSTEMROOT%\WINSXS or side by side to avoid potential conflicts. This is a simplistic definition of this function, but it is sufficient to help you understand that any application installed through Windows Installer will cleanly uninstall because its components are isolated by this service. Uninstalling software has little or no impact on the rest of a computer system when software is managed by the Windows Installer service.

Since the Windows Installer installation file is, in fact, a database, it can be modified at will for different installation types. These are called transform files and have the MST extension. For example, you can create a global MSI file that includes all of the Microsoft Office program files and use custom transform files to install only Access, or install only Word, Excel, PowerPoint, and Outlook, or install only FrontPage, or FrontPage and Access, and so on. Finally, MSI files also support patching. Patch files have an MSP extension and allow the application of hot fixes and service packs to installed software.

TIP *For a detailed overview of the Windows Installer service, download "Working with Windows Installer," a free white paper, from www.reso-net.com/articles.asp?m=8.*

Software Assets

Given that Windows Server 2008 software installations through Group Policy require Windows Installer–enabled programs, and given the major advantages you can gain from using these types of installations just by integrating them with the Windows Installer service, you should seriously consider migrating all of your software programs and applications to versions that are integrated with this service. Of course, most corporations will not be able to achieve this through upgrades for several reasons. First, some programs, especially internally developed programs, may not be so easily upgraded. Second, the average corporation (more than 1000 users) has about 300 different software applications within its network. Upgrading all of these products would be prohibitive and often unnecessary. Third, some applications simply do not offer upgrades. Fourth, some manufacturers, unfortunately, still do not integrate their software products with the Windows Installer service.

In most cases, you will have to consider repackaging software installations in order to take advantage of the many features of the Windows Installer service. Several tools are available on the market for this repackaging process. If you are serious about installation packaging, you should consider Wise Package Studio from Altiris (www.wise.com) or Macromedia AdminStudio (www.macromedia.com). Both are comprehensive packaging solutions. These aren't the only products on the market, as you'll find out when you search for Windows Installer repackaging on the Internet, but one of the prerequisites for a structured solution is a tool that will provide the same functionality for both repackaging commercial software and packaging corporate applications that you develop in-house. These two products provide this functionality.

TIP *An excellent resource on MSI packaging is the MSI resource page on AppDeploy.com at www.appdeploy.com/techhomes/windowsinstaller.asp.*

Most likely, your software assets will fall into several categories:

- **Native Windows Installer software** This software includes any product that bears the Designed for Windows logo. Part of the requirement for the Logo program is integration with the Windows Installer service. You will most likely upgrade a portion of your network's software to this level. This should include the most popular software on your network.
- **MSI-integrated corporate applications** New versions of your corporate applications should be integrated with the Windows Installer service.
- **Repackaged commercial software** All products that are not upgraded should be repackaged. In most organizations undertaking this repackaging process, 99 percent of software has been repackaged to take advantage of Windows Installer. Only products such as device drivers or applications that install device drivers will resist Windows Installer integration.
- **Repackaged corporate applications** Corporate applications that do not require recoding or upgrades can be repackaged in the same way as commercial software.

This undertaking will take considerable effort, but it is one of the migration processes that provides the best and most immediate return on investment.

TIP *Today, many organizations use application virtualization instead of integrating their tools with the Windows Installer service. Application virtualization provides a protection layer that sandboxes each software product when it is deployed to a system. The software still runs and interacts with the operating system, but it makes no changes in either the file system or the registry, unlike software that installs through Windows Installer. In fact, software is often only cached locally with all of the advantages that managing local caches grants you. Several manufacturers provide application virtualization tools. Perhaps the best source of information on this approach to software management can be found in Chapters 6 and 7 of the* Definitive Guide to Vista Migration *at www.realtime-nexus.com/dgvm.htm.*

Software Delivery in the Network

The collection of services formerly known as IntelliMirror included software installation services. But software installation in the organization requires much more than what Group Policy can provide. A comprehensive software installation program must include elements such as:

- **Delivery guarantee** To guarantee that a software installation has occurred before a given time. This is useful in corporate deployments when versions of software applications must match central data deposits.
- **Scheduling** To control delivery times for non-working hours.
- **Bandwidth control** To control bandwidth usage and compress data when sent over the wide area network (WAN).
- **Inventory** To ascertain that target systems have the required resources to install and operate the software and to keep abreast of where software has been installed.
- **Status** To be able to determine the status of a software delivery job across the WAN to multiple geographic locations.
- **Reporting** To be able to generate comprehensive activity reports.
- **Software metering** To be able to determine if users you send software to actually require it.

None of these features are available with policy-based software delivery.

TIP *None of these features are available by default with policy-based software delivery, but one manufacturer, Special Operations Software (www.specopssoft.com), offers Group Policy extensions that bring all of these features to software management in ADDS as well as complete inventory services. While these features are really hot on their own, and you should definitely investigate them if you choose to run installations on your systems, they also offer free Group Policy extensions. For example, one of their free downloads lets you wake up computers when they are asleep through the directory using the Wake-on-LAN features of your systems.*

Software Deployment Concepts

Since GPOs do not support these features, and since an organization will not want to use multiple software delivery procedures (remember the standard operating procedure rule from Chapter 3), you will have to integrate a comprehensive software management system with your Active Directory Domain Services. Network software delivery means being able to ensure that a process is repeatable and always gives the same result (see Figure 7-12). In a standard operating environment, the software delivery process includes the following steps:

1. New software packages are prepared and, once ready, are integrated into the software asset repository. This registry is the single-source listing of all authorized software. All files within the registry are in MSI format.
2. The software package is assigned to a group. This can be either users or computers. Most often, you will assign software to computers (especially if your organization promotes assigned PCs to users). Assigning software to users, especially in environments where users move from PC to PC, will constantly enable software installations and removals. If at all possible, assign software to users' primary systems.

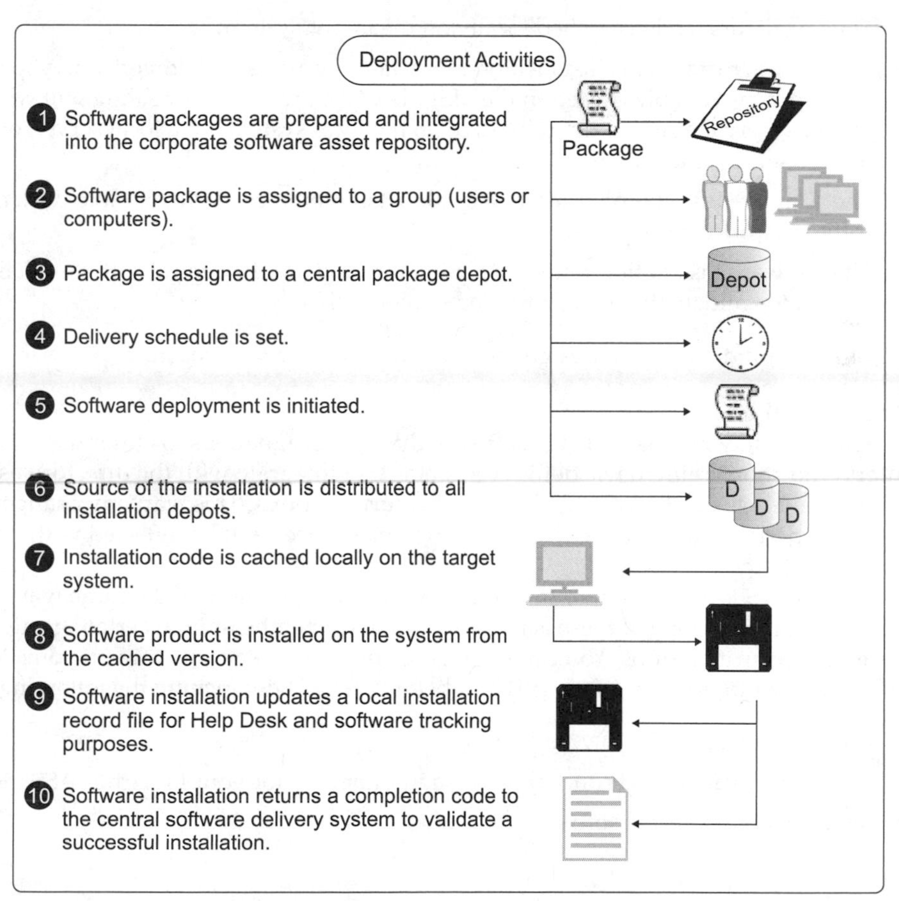

Deployment Activities
1 Software packages are prepared and integrated into the corporate software asset repository.
Package
Repository
2 Software package is assigned to a group (users or computers).
3 Package is assigned to a central package depot.
Depot
4 Delivery schedule is set.
5 Software deployment is initiated.
6 Source of the installation is distributed to all installation depots.
D
D
D
7 Installation code is cached locally on the target system.
8 Software product is installed on the system from the cached version.
9 Software installation updates a local installation record file for Help Desk and software tracking purposes.
10 Software installation returns a completion code to the central software delivery system to validate a successful installation.

Figure 7-12 The software delivery process

PART IV

TIP *Assigning PCs to Users: Windows today promotes the assignation of PCs to users much more than legacy Windows operating systems. This is because all versions now support the Remote Desktop. Making extensive use of the Remote Desktop greatly reduces the software deployment workload because you only need to install software on a user's principal machine. Then, if the user needs to use another system, instead of delivering the same software product to this system, you can enable Remote Desktop on the user's primary PC. Thus, the user can remotely connect to their primary system from the other system. Remote Desktop gives the user access to everything on their principal system, uses little bandwidth (since it is the same as Terminal Services), and greatly reduces the need for multiple installations of the same product.*

3. The package is assigned to a central package depot.
4. The delivery schedule is set.
5. Software deployment is initiated.
6. The source of the installation is distributed to all installation depots. This is a good place to use the Distributed File System (DFS), since it allows you to use a single alias for all deposits, wherever they are. More on this will be covered in Chapter 8.
7. The installation code is cached locally on the target system.
8. The software product is installed on the system from the cached version. A special environment variable is used in the MSI file to ensure that self-healing will work no matter where the source file is located: on the local system, on a local server, or on a remote server as a backup.
9. The software installation updates a local installation record file for Help desk and software tracking purposes.
10. The software installation returns a completion code to the central software delivery system to validate that it has installed successfully.

Keep this in mind when you design your software delivery approach.

Software Assignation

In any organization, you must manage software through assignations to either users or computers. You should aim to use delivery systems that integrate with the directory as much as possible, especially with ADDS' global security groups. This way, any changes to global groups performed in Active Directory Domain Services will be reflected within your software delivery tool.

In addition, WS08 allows you to treat machine accounts in many of the same ways you can treat user accounts. One of these is the assignation of membership in certain groups, notably, global security groups. You can use this feature to manage software on your PCs. To do so, you need to perform a few activities beforehand. These include the following:

- Inventory all software in your network.
- Use the software kernel concept outlined in Chapter 3 for your PCs (the PASS model).
- Identify all non-kernel software.

- Regroup non-kernel software into categories—groupings of software that are the same for given IT roles within the organization. For example, Web developers will always require FrontPage, Visio, Corel Draw, and Adobe Acrobat as well as the kernel. These four products would be included in a Web Developer category, but not in the PC kernel. Perform this for all IT roles within your organization.
- Create global security groups for each role within Active Directory Domain Services (the Production domain, of course).
- Assign principal machines to each user.
- Create an inventory tying together user, principal machine, and software category for each user.
- Assign the machines in Active Directory Domain Services to appropriate global groups.

Now you're ready to manage deliveries based on ADDS.

Another critical factor for this process to work is the deinstallation instructions within the software delivery package. This is vital. The purpose of this entire process is to ensure that you can maintain a legal status for all software you deploy. If you do not include deinstallation instructions in your software delivery packages, the software you deploy will not be automatically removed when a PC is removed from a group authorizing the installation and use of the software. See your systems management documentation for specific removal instructions. GPO-based delivery of software removes it by default when it falls out of the management scope.

Now you're almost ready. Make sure your delivery collections are linked to the global groups you created in ADDS. Ensure that they are dynamic collections, meaning that they will always refresh and reassign software to any new members of the collection. Then assign software installation packages to the appropriate collections. That's it. Your software management system is now ready. From now on, all you need to do to deliver the proper software to a system is ensure that it is a member of the appropriate group within ADDS. Then, if the PC's vocation changes, just change its group memberships. The system will automatically uninstall software that is no longer needed and install software belonging to the new vocation (see Figure 7-13).

Legality and Regional PC Assignments

This strategy is very useful, especially if you have remote offices. In many organizations, the management of PC assignations in remote offices is difficult because there is no official PC assignation process. For example, when a powerful new PC is delivered for use by an employee with little seniority, it often happens that this PC is "reassigned" by local staff to another staff member with more seniority. The employee to whom this PC was originally destined receives another PC that does not have appropriate software on it. While there are issues with this process, the major problem lies in the fact that neither PC has the appropriate software loaded on it. This is one of the reasons why organizations do not always conform to legal software usage guidelines.

The solution lies in the software management process outlined previously. Linked with the delegation process, this system will ensure that even if PC vocations are changed, the proper software will always remain on each PC. To solve this issue, you need to implement

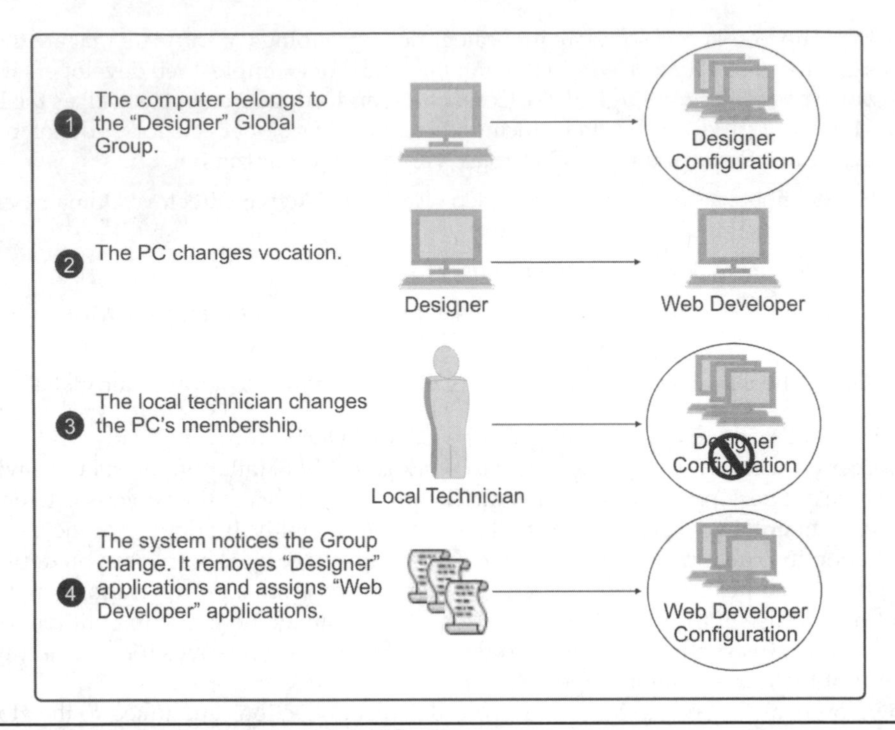

FIGURE 7-13 Using global groups to assign software

an official PC assignment process. It should include a number of different elements, but mostly it should include:

- The implementation of the software management process based on PC categorization groups.
- The creation of an OU structure that places regional PC objects within a regional organizational unit.
- The delegation of specific rights over PC objects to local technical staff. These rights should include the ability to modify a computer's group memberships.
- The documentation of the official PC assignation process.
- A formal training program for all regional technical staff.

Now that the process is official, there is no reason for copies of software products to be found on systems that have been reassigned.

Complete the OU Strategy

There. Now you're ready to complete your OU design for PC management and administration. You have reviewed the requirements for Group Policy application. You have reviewed the requirements for delegation within your organization. And you have reviewed the requirements for PC management and administration. You should have everything in hand to go ahead and finalize your OU design for PC management. Once it is finalized, you can implement it. The next section gives an example based on a centralized PC management strategy.

TIP *There are several free add-ons you can rely on to simplify PC administration. One good example is Specops Gpupdate which is a free add-on to Active Directory Users and Computers and allows you to restart, shutdown, and wake on LAN computer objects directly through this console. Obtain this tool from: www.specopssoft.com/products/specopsgpupdate.*

Put the PC OU Infrastructure in Place

T&T Corporation is ready to implement their PC organizational unit infrastructure. They have determined that they need to use a centralized management strategy with delegation only to central technicians for specific tasks, such as assigning PC group memberships for software delivery. They will, in fact, implement the PC OU design that is outlined in Figure 7-7 earlier in this chapter. To do this, they will need to perform the following activities:

- Create and document the entire OU/GPO/delegation/management strategy for PCs
- Create the OU structure using ADDS Users and Computers
- Create and document the appropriate GPOs for each container
- Assign the block policy inheritance property to appropriate OUs
- Delegate the proper level of authority to technical staff
- Create the groups required for software delivery

Once each of these tasks is complete, the infrastructure to receive new PCs within the parallel network will be in place.

For the first activity, you can use the information grids presented in Chapter 5. These will help you document your entire OU/GPO/delegation/management strategy for PCs. For your own network, do not proceed with the other steps until you have completed these grids. You should not begin to use any of these features until your strategy has been fully planned.

For the second activity, make sure you are within the Intranet.TandT.net domain and logged on with domain administration rights. Then proceed as follows:

1. Open Active Directory Users and Computers in Server Manager.
2. Place the cursor's focus on the domain. Then either right-click to create a new organizational unit from the context menu, or use the console toolbar to click the New Organizational Unit button. Both will display the New Organizational Unit dialog box.
3. Type the OU's name and click OK. Use the deletion protection option if you feel confident that your design is final.
4. The OUs you need to create are listed in Table 7-2 earlier in this chapter. Repeat the process until each OU has been created. Don't worry if you create an OU in the wrong place—all you need to do is drag it to the appropriate place, since WS08 supports drag-and-drop. Remember to use the OU's property sheet to deselect deletion protection if you need to move it and you turned it on at creation. The resulting OU structure is illustrated in Figure 7-14.

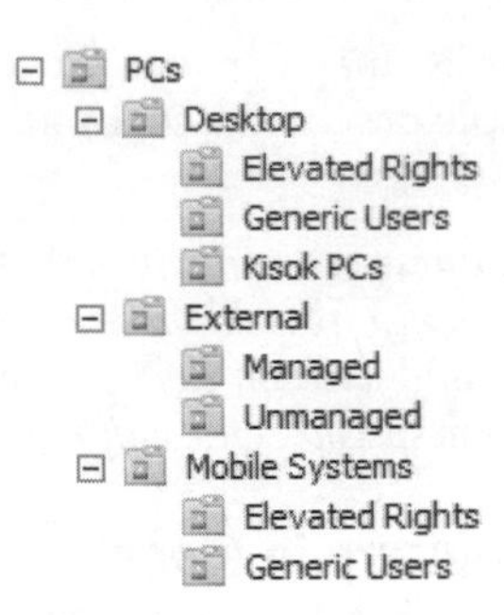

FIGURE 7-14
A PC management OU structure

Five PC-related GPOs are required for T&T Corporation. Here's how to create them:

1. Begin by downloading the GPO spreadsheet Microsoft provides on their web site.
2. Identify all of the settings you require for each GPO using the information in Table 7-3.
3. Fully document each GPO.
4. When ready, log on with domain administrator credentials, and launch the GPMC. Right-click the PCs OU, and select Create A GPO In This Domain, and Link It Here.
5. Name the policy, once again using the information in Table 7-2. This policy is named Global PC GPO. Click OK.
6. Click the link and click OK in response to the warning message. Move to the Details tab in the details pane, and change the GPO status to User Configuration Settings Disabled. Confirm your choice.
7. Right-click the GPO link to choose Edit. This launches the Group Policy Editor (GPEdit).
8. Use the * key on your keypad to expand all of the subsections of the Group Policy object. Return to the top, and move through the policy to modify appropriate settings. For example, in this GPO, you will want to set the Windows Update settings for all PCs. You could also set power management features. Close GPEdit when done.
9. Repeat this process for each GPO you need to create. This includes the Global Desktop GPO, the Global Portable GPO (mostly for security settings), the Global External GPO, and the Global Kiosk GPO (if required, add tighter security and enable Loopback).
10. Next, use the GPMC to select PC | External | Unmanaged OU. Right-click this OU and select Block Policy Inheritance. T&T has decided to leave all external unmanaged systems without any significant GPO assignment.

Two more tasks are required to complete the PC OU setup: delegating authority and creating software category groups. Both are relatively simple.

T&T has decided that the only task they will delegate to technicians is the ability to modify group memberships for PCs. This will ensure that they will be able to modify a PC's vocation when it is reassigned to a new user. Once again, this is done through Active Directory Users and Computers in Server Manager.

1. The first thing you need to do is create a group to which you can delegate authority. It doesn't matter if you don't know who will be in this group yet; all you need is the group with the proper delegation rights. You can assign members to the group later.

Create a global security group called PC Technicians (Local). Place this group in the top-level PCs OU for now. To do so, right-click the PCs OU and select New | Group. Make sure the Global option is selected (it is the default), ensure that Security is selected, and type the group name. Click OK to create the group.

2. Now, right-click the PCs OU and select Delegate Control from the context menu.
3. Follow the steps provided by the wizard. Add the PC Technicians (Local) group, and then click Next.
4. Delegate a custom task, and then click Next.
5. In the Active Directory Object Type window, select Only The Following Objects In This Folder, and select the Computer Objects check box, and then click Next.
6. Clear General and select Property-Specific. Then scroll down the list to select appropriate values. The technicians require the right to read most object properties and the right to write group memberships. Use your judgment to apply appropriate rights. For example, it will be useful for technicians to be able to write descriptions for computers that change vocation, but it will not be a good idea to let them change the computer name. Make a note of each security property you assign.
7. Click Next when done. Click Finish once you have reviewed the wizard's task list.

Delegation is now complete, but you still need to create a delegation console for the technicians. Use the instructions outlined previously for console creation, and ensure that you set the focus for the console on the PCs OU. Store the console in the PCs OU as well. Finally, use Terminal Services to distribute the console to technicians.

The final activity for the PC OU strategy is the creation of global security groups that correspond to the software categories in your organization. You can have several of these, but most organizations try to keep them to a bare minimum. If you have designed your PC kernel properly, then you should be able to satisfy a large clientele with it: all generic or common users, in fact. Then your software categories include only the systems that require additional software. This software should be grouped by common need. An organization that has over 3000 users, for example, only uses nine software categories over and above the kernel. Another with 12,500 users has 15 categories, mostly because they are distributed worldwide and special software products are required in different geographic regions. To create your software category groups, use the following procedure:

1. The first thing you need to do is create the groups. It doesn't matter if you don't know which machines will be in this group yet; all you need is the group itself. You can assign members to the group later. Create global security groups since they are the easiest to work with and support other features.
2. To do so, right-click the PCs OU object in the directory, and select New | Group. Make sure the Global and Security options are selected, and then type the group name. Use significant names for both names. Click OK to create the group.
3. Repeat as many times as required.

Your PC OU structure is now in place. Machine groups have been created directly in the PC OU so that they will be subject to machine policies.

Now, the only thing you need to do is ensure that machines are placed within the appropriate OU and the appropriate software category group when you integrate them into the parallel network.

Preparing the OU structure before integrating new machines into the network also ensures that they will be managed as soon as they join the network. Mistakes are minimized when you use this procedure, because everything is ready before PCs are integrated into the network. Next, you can begin to look at how you can use this same approach to prepare for user management within your network.

Manage User Objects with Active Directory Domain Services

User objects are special objects within the directory. After all, if it weren't for users, there wouldn't be much need for networks, would there? In traditional networks, such as Windows NT, user objects are mostly managed through the groups they belong to. Groups are also present in Active Directory Domain Services. In fact, it is essential to have a comprehensive group management strategy within your WS08 network if you want to be able to administer user-related events within it. But group management is not the only requirement anymore.

Like computers, users are also affected by Group Policy. The GPO strategy you design for users will complement the group membership strategy you intend to use. As with PCs, you will need to consider how and to whom you will delegate some administrative tasks, since user management is, by far, the heaviest workload in the directory. Each of these strategies serves as input for the design of your user organizational unit infrastructure.

As outlined in Chapter 5, a user object can only be contained within a single OU. And now, you also know how the location of an OU could affect the user object through the hierarchical application of Group Policy objects. You also know how GPOs can be filtered through the use of security groups. Though the user account can only be within a single OU, it can be included within a multitude of groups. Because of this, OUs are usually seen as a means to provide vertical user management, while groups provide horizontal management. Ideally, your user management strategy will take this cross-management structure into account (see Figure 7-15).

FIGURE 7-15 The cross-management relationship of OUs and groups

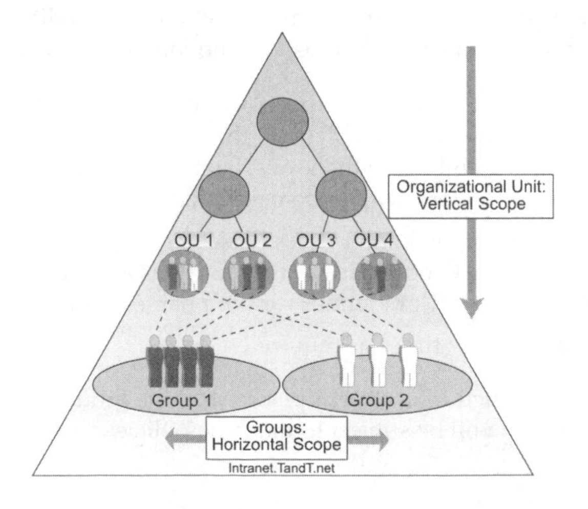

The Active Directory Domain Services User Object

The Windows Server 2008 user object is much the same as its Windows 2000 counterpart, but is it quite different from its Windows NT counterpart. This is because of the nature of a directory service. One of the basic functions of a directory service is to store information in order to make it available to users, administrators, and even applications. While the Windows NT user object basically stored the user's name, password, and account particularities, the WS08 user object can store more than 200 properties. Many of these are generated automatically. Nevertheless, there are almost 100 properties that can be set interactively for each user. These properties can then be used by users or applications to determine who someone is in your organization and what their role should be. You must determine which properties you will manage and who will be responsible for each of these properties within your network.

Fortunately, you will be able to delegate quite a few of these properties to other personnel. Since many of a user's properties have to do with their localization within the organization, it makes sense to let users manage many of their own properties within the directory. You'll also probably have a number of other administrative levels within your organization. System-related administrative levels will be covered in Chapters 8 and 9. User-related administrative levels are covered here. Administrative tasks will be covered in Chapter 13.

Tip *By default, users have access to several properties of their user object in the directory. The best way to find out which ones is to search the directory for your own account from your desktop and then see which properties you can change and which you can't. While in XP you search Active Directory through the general Search tool, in Vista, the Active Directory search engine is now located in the Network Center.*

User Versus InetOrgPerson

Active Directory Domain Services includes two user object classes: User and InetOrgPerson. The User class object is the traditional user object that organizations normally use when designing Windows network infrastructures. In the intranet portion of your network, the user object is the one you will focus on. If you migrate user objects from an existing Windows network to WS08, the user accounts will be created with the user object class.

InetOrgPerson is an object class found in standard Lightweight Directory Access Protocol (LDAP) implementations, and it has been added to ADDS to provide better compatibility with these implementations. In LDAP, it is used to represent people who are associated with an organization in some way. In WS08, it is almost exactly the same as the user class object because it is derived from this class. In fact, in the WS08 forest functional mode, the InetOrgPerson object becomes a complete security principal, enabling the object to be associated with a password in the same manner as a standard user object. InetOrgPerson is used in several third-party LDAP and X.500 directory implementations and is provided in WS08 to facilitate migrations from these directories to Active Directory Domain Services.

Windows Server 2008 implementations will tend to focus on the user object rather than the InetOrgPerson object. But if you need to integrate a directory application that requires use of this object, or if you intend to use Active Directory Domain Services within your extranet with partners hosting other directory services, you will find the addition of this class object quite useful.

CAUTION *In early implementations of Active Directory Domain Services with Windows 2000 or Windows Server 2003, people implemented ADDS in extranet or perimeter networks. With Windows Server 2008, you should rely on Active Directory Federated Services (ADFS) to give people access to extranets. ADFS uses common Internet ports to rely on each partner's internal directories for authentication. This is much more secure than implementing ADDS in a zone that could be compromised. ADFS is covered in Chapter 10.*

Both types of objects, user and InetOrgPerson, are created in the same way. Interactively, they can be created through use of either the New command in the context menu or the toolbar buttons within the Active Directory Users and Computers portion of Server Manager. Since both object classes are quite similar, we will focus on the user object class.

The Contact-Class Object

A third user-like object class exists within ADDS. It is the contact object class. This object is a sub-class of the user object. It is not, however, a security principal. It is mostly used as an e-mail address and can thus be used for communication purposes. The contact object includes fewer than half of the properties of the user object.

Contacts can be included within groups in the directory, but since they are not security principals, you cannot assign permissions or user rights to them. Creating contacts is the same as creating user or InetOrgPerson objects. The creation is performed within the Active Directory Users and Computers console, and is mostly done with a right-click and the New command.

Contacts are primarily used to store information about personnel outside your organization, since you require a means to contact them, but they do not require access to internal resources. More than 30 settings can be managed for each contact.

User Object Property Sheets

As mentioned previously, the WS08 user object includes more than 200 different properties, with about 100 that are manageable. One of the activities you will need to perform during the planning phase of your WS08 directory is to identify which of these properties you want to manage, who will be responsible for the administration of the values for each property, and how these properties will integrate with your other identity management databases within your organization. If you determine that ADDS will be the host database for some user-related primary data values within your organization, you will need to ensure that these values are always up to date and always protected and recoverable.

In fact, it is quite possible that you will decide that ADDS is the primary source for user data within the organization, since it is replicated on a constant basis and available to all members of the organization in all locations. Remember, though, that ADDS replication includes latency. This means that you shouldn't store data that is of a timely nature within the directory. For example, you can store a user's office phone number in the directory because chances are that other users within your network don't need it immediately if it changes. But you shouldn't store your company's price list in the directory, especially if your replication latency is significant, because it means that when you change a price, some users will have access to the old price (replication has not yet occurred) and some will have access to the new price (replication has occurred). At best, this would lead to unhappy customers. At worse, it could lead to potential losses for the company.

In addition, you will probably decide that the directory is the proper place to store employee business addresses and phone numbers, but not employee home addresses and other personal information, because users can search the directory. You yourself probably don't want other employees to phone you at home to bother you with office questions. On the other hand, your organization must have this information, but since it is of a private nature, it will most likely be stored within the human resources database. This latter database can have a link to ADDS to enable it to share information with the directory. Similarly, asset management databases would have a link to ADDS to share information on computer resources.

Table 7-4 provides a complete list of the default attributes that are provided for the user object. It also lists recommendations for attributes that should be considered as primary values within your organization. Three levels of responsibility are identified for attribute management:

- **User (U)** The user should be responsible for updating this information in the directory.
- **User Representative (UR)** A user representative should be assigned to update information for groups of users. In smaller sites, these values can be managed by an administrator.
- **Administrator (A)** The values managed at this level are part of normal system administration tasks.

Tab	Item	Field Type	Primary Value?	GPO Equivalent?	Responsibility	Additional Comments
General	First name	Free text	Yes		UR	
	Initials	Free text	Yes		UR	
	Last name	Free text	Yes		UR	
	Display name	Free text	Yes		UR	
	Description	Free text	Yes		UR	
	Office	Free text	Yes		U	
	Telephone number	Free text	Yes		U	More than one value possible
	E-mail	Free text	Yes		UR	
	Web page	Free text	Yes		UR	More than one value possible
Address	Street	Free text	Yes		U	
	P.O. Box	Free text	Yes		U	
	City	Free text	Yes		U	
	State/province	Free text	Yes		U	
	ZIP/postal code	Free text	Yes		U	
	Country/region	List box	Yes		U	
Account	User logon name	Free text	Yes		UR	Associated with the UPN suffix
	User logon name (pre-Windows 2000)	Automatic text (modifiable)	Yes		UR	Associated with the NetBIOS domain name
	Logon hours	Button			UR	Other dialog box
	Log on to	Button			UR	Other dialog box

TABLE 7-4 User Object Properties

Tab	Item	Field Type	Primary Value?	GPO Equivalent?	Responsibility	Additional Comments
	Account options: User must change password at next logon User cannot change password Password never expires Store password using reversible encryption Account is disabled Smart card is required for interactive logon Account is sensitive and cannot be delegated Use Kerberos DES encryption types for this account This account supports Kerberos AES 128-bit encryption This account supports Kerberos AES 256-bit encryption Do not require Kerberos preauthentication	List box			UR/A	Though all of the options have check boxes, some of these options are mutually exclusive
	Account expires: Never End of	Option			UR	Used to set the automatic end date for an account
Profile	User profile: Profile path Logon script	Free text		Yes	UR	Assigning a profile path automatically turns the user profile into a roaming profile

TABLE 7-4 User Object Properties (*continued*)

Tab	Item	Field Type	Primary Value?	GPO Equivalent?	Responsibility	Additional Comments
	Home folder: Local path Connect	Option and free text Option, list box, and free text		Yes	UR	Using the %username% value with the appropriate UNC will automatically create the home folder
Telephones	Telephone numbers: Home Pager Mobile Fax IP phone	Free text	Yes, but not for home		U	More than one value can be assigned for each attribute
	Notes	Free text			U	
Organization	Title	Free text	Yes		UR	
	Department	Free text	Yes		UR	
	Company	Free text	Yes		UR	
	Manager: Name Change Properties Clear	Other dialog box	Yes		UR	Used to build a virtual organization chart within the directory
	Direct reports	Automatic text	Yes		UR	Associated with manager
Environment	Starting program: Start the following program at logon Program file name Start in	Check box and free text		Yes	UR	Related to Terminal Services
	Client devices Connect client drives at logon Connect client printers at logon Default to main client printer	Check box		Yes	UR	
Sessions	End a disconnected session	List box		Yes	UR	Related to Terminal Services

TABLE 7-4 User Object Properties (*continued*)

Tab	Item	Field Type	Primary Value?	GPO Equivalent?	Responsibility	Additional Comments
	Active session limit	List box		Yes	UR	
	Idle session limit	List box		Yes	UR	
	When a session limit is reached or connection is broken Disconnect from session End session	Option		Yes	UR	
	Allow reconnection From any client From originating client only	Option		Yes	UR	
Remote control	Enable remote control	Check box		Yes	UR	Related to Terminal Services
	Require user's permission Level of control View the user's session Interact with the session	Check box		Yes	UR	
Terminal Services Profile	Terminal Services user profile Profile path	Free text		Yes	UR	Related to Terminal Services
	Terminal Services home folder Local path Connect	Option, free text, and list box		Yes	UR	
	Deny this user permissions to log on to Terminal Server	Check box		Yes	UR	
COM+	Partition set	List box			A	Related to COM+ partition

TABLE 7-4 User Object Properties (*continued*)

Tab	Item	Field Type	Primary Value?	GPO Equivalent?	Responsibility	Additional Comments
Published certificates	Issued to Issued by Intended purposes Expiration View certificate		Yes		A	Related to X509 certificates
	Add from store Add from file Remove Copy to file	Other dialog box			A	
Member of	Member of Add Remove	Automatic text and other dialog box			UR	Associated with the domain name or the forest
	Primary group Set primary group				UR	Related to Macintosh clients or POSIX-compliant applications
Dial-in	Network access permission Allow access Deny access Control access through NPS network policy	Option		Yes	A	Related to dial-in access and Network Access Protection; must be combined with the Network Access Policy
	Verify caller ID	Check box and free text		Yes	A	Requires special equipment
	Callback options No callback Set by caller (Routing and Remote Access Service only) Always callback to	Check box and free text		Yes	A	To ensure a more secure connection
	Assign a static IP Address Static IP addresses	Check box and other dialog box		Yes	A	Used if DHCP is not available for RAS

TABLE 7-4 User Object Properties *(continued)*

Tab	Item	Field Type	Primary Value?	GPO Equivalent?	Responsibility	Additional Comments
	Apply static routes Define routes to enable for this dial-in connection	Check box and other dialog box		Yes	A	
Object	Canonical name of object	Automatic text	Yes		NR	Associated with the domain
	Object class Created Modified Update Sequence Numbers (USNs) Current Original	Automatic text	Yes		NR	
	Protect object from accidental deletion	Check box				Sets a no-change policy on the object
Security	Group or user names Add Remove	List box and other dialog box			A	Controls the access permissions to this object
	Permissions for selected account Advanced	List box and other dialog box			A	Do not modify default options unless necessary
Password Replication	Read-only domain controllers Properties	List box and other dialog box			A	Lists the locations this user's password is cached in read-only domain controllers (RODC) if they exist in your directory
Attribute Editor	Edit Filter	List box and other dialog box			A	Used to edit any value that is tied to a user account but that does not have a graphical interface equivalent.

TABLE 7-4 User Object Properties (*continued*)

If attribute management is not required, either because it is managed automatically by the system or because it is not an important value to include in the directory, it is also indicated (marked as NR for not required).

Finally, many of the fields in the User dialog box come from Windows NT and are provided to help administrators make the migration to Windows Server 2008. Many of these are also designed to require specific modifications on a per-user basis. But in a network totaling several thousand users, per-user management of attributes such as User Profile Location or Terminal Services Options is cumbersome to say the least. This is why WS08 provides GPO settings to manage many of these fields. This table also identifies which values can be managed through GPOs instead of through the User Property sheet.

NOTE *To view each of the values listed in this table, you must enable the Advanced Features option in the View menu of the console.*

As you can see, several of the fields are in free-text format. When you allow users to update their own data, you will find that there is no quality control over data entry in ADDS. Users can enter phone numbers using dots, can forget to add their area code, can even enter more than one number in the field, and ADDS will accept the entry. Supporting this type of modification does not lead to the type of standardized information input required at your network.

One of the best ways to let users manage their own data is to provide them with an intranet web page that gives them the possibility to locate their name in ADDS and modify elements such as their address and phone number, additional phone numbers, and other personal information (see Figure 7-16). This web page can authenticate them as they arrive (using the single sign-on capabilities of WS08 and Internet Information Server), validate that the information they enter is in the appropriate format, and automatically update the directory when completed. Such a web page can easily be designed using the Active Directory Services Interface (ADSI) and simple content validation rules to ensure that all values are entered in a standard format. Note that the entire address portion can be further controlled through the use of drop-down lists, since the choices for each address can be preset and other fields, such as State/Province, Zip/Postal Code, and so on, can automatically be filled in when the street address is selected. This removes the possibility of errors when users update their own information.

Value and attribute management are part of the evolution of your network once your Active Directory Domain Services structure is completely operational.

TIP *Namescape offers a free community version of its rDirectory product, which lets you build self-service web pages like the one illustrated here. Download it from www.namescape.com.*

Create User Objects

Creating a user account is simple. Either use the New command in the context menu or use the New User icon in the Active Directory Users and Computers console toolbar. Once the wizard is activated, two main panels are displayed. The first deals with the account names. Here you set the user's full name, the user's display name, their logon name or their User Principal Name (UPN), and their down-level logon name.

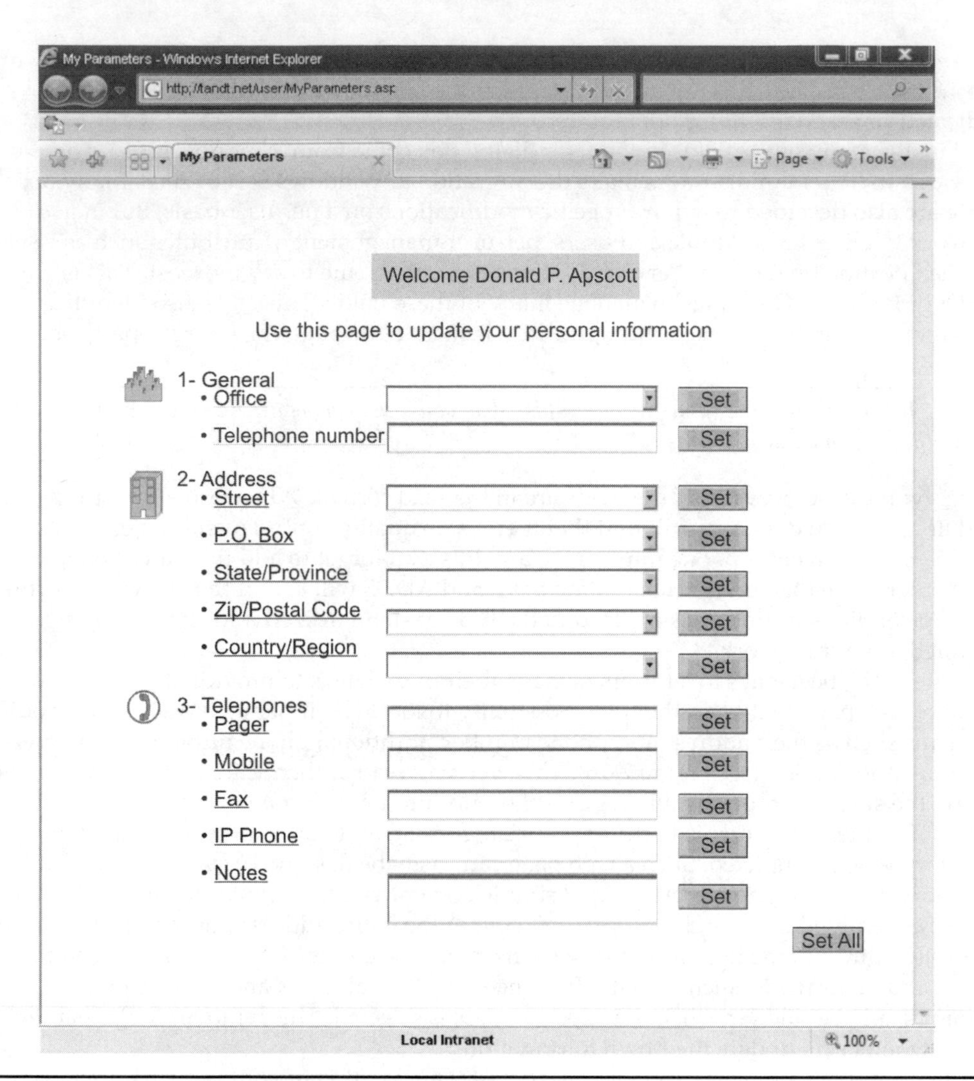

FIGURE 7-16 A user data management intranet page

NOTE *The UPN uses the same format as an e-mail address. The down-level logon name is also referred to as the "pre-Windows 2000" name. It is, in fact, the name used by the Security Accounts Manager in Windows Server 2008 and provides down-level or backward compatibility for operating systems before Windows 2000.*

The next screen deals with the password and account restrictions. Type the default user password and select the User Must Change Password At Next Logon check box. If the user is not ready to take immediate possession of the account, then you should also select the Account Is Disabled option. You can also set a password never to expire, as well as stating that the user cannot change the password. Both are usually set for non-user accounts—accounts that are designed to operate services or system accounts.

Windows Server 2008 supports two types of logon names: the UPN and the down-level logon name. The latter is related to the Windows NT logon name you gave your users. If you are migrating from a Windows NT environment, make sure you use the same down-level name strategy (unless there are compelling reasons to change this strategy). Users will be familiar with this strategy and will be able to continue using the logon name they are most familiar with. Down-level logon names are most often used within the same WS08 domain.

User Principal Names

If your users must navigate from domain to domain or from forest to forest, you should get them used to working with their User Principal Name. The UPN is usually composed of the user's name and a suffix composed of the domain or forest they log on to. Many organizations tend to use the user's e-mail address as the UPN. Of course, your internal directory will not be using the same name or extension as your external Web presence will. For example, you may have a forest name that is based on a NET extension and your external name may be based on a COM extension. If this is the case, you need to modify the default UPN suffix that is displayed when creating accounts so that you can match the external name in the internal network.

This is done through the Active Directory Domains and Trusts console.

1. Launch the Active Directory Domains and Trusts console. Use Start menu | Administrative Tools to do so.
2. Right-click Active Directory Domains and Trusts, and select Properties.
3. In the UPN Suffix tab, type the new suffix and click Add.
4. Type as many suffixes as required. One is usually all you need if your forest has only one tree. If you host more than one tree in your forest, you will require more suffixes. Click OK when done.
5. Close the Active Directory Domains and Trusts console.
6. The new suffix will now be displayed in the User Logon Name dialog box and can be assigned to users (see Figure 7-17).

FIGURE 7-17 Using other UPN suffixes

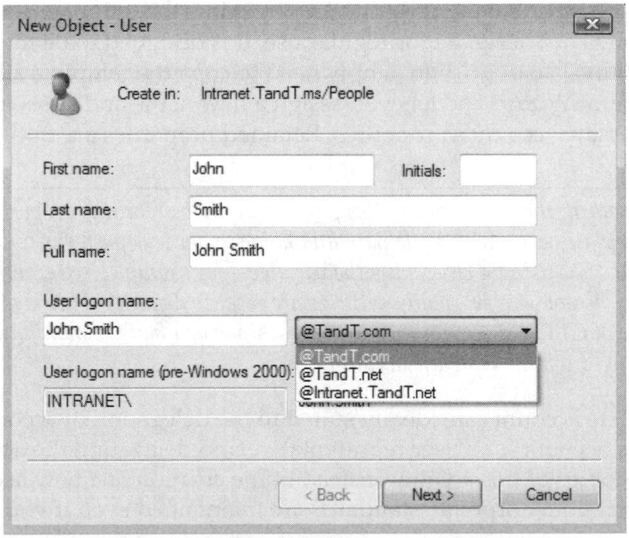

Be careful how you use UPN suffixes. Removing a UPN suffix that is in use will cause users to be unable to log in. But WS08 will give you a warning when you perform this operation.

Default WS08 Accounts

WS08 installs several default accounts when you create your first domain controller. These are similar to the default accounts created on either workstations or member servers, except for one account in particular. They include:

- **Administrator** This is the global administration account for the domain. It should be renamed through a GPO and locked. A strong password should be set on this account. All domain management activities should be performed through accounts that are copies of this main account. Other administration tasks should be performed through accounts that have specific permissions for the services they must manage.
- **Guest** This account is disabled by default and is not a part of the Authenticated Users group. It is designed to allow guest access to your network. Guest access is no longer popular, however. It is always best to create limited access accounts and enable them on an as-needed basis.
- **krbtgt** This account is the Key Distribution Center Service Account. It is disabled by default and is only used when you put a PKI in place within your domain.

These accounts are also found on local systems, except for the krbtgt account, since a Windows public key infrastructure requires a domain to function. Note that the built-in administrator account is disabled by default on Windows Vista.

These default accounts are located within the Users container in ADDS.

Use Template Accounts

The ideal way to create an account is to use a template. Template accounts have been supported in Microsoft networks since the very first versions of Windows NT and are supported in Windows Server 2008. There are some significant differences, though.

To create a template account, you use the standard user account process, but you assign different properties to the account. For one thing, the template account must always be disabled. It is not designed for regular use; it is designed to be the basis for the creation of other accounts. To do so, you simply need to copy the template account. WS08 launches the New Account Wizard and lets you assign a new name and password while retaining several of the template account's properties. Retained properties are outlined in Table 7-5.

NOTE *Items on the profile properties page will only be retained properly if the setting used to create the template account's profile path and home folder was performed with the %username% variable (i.e., using a UNC plus the variable—for example: \\server\sharename\%username%).*

Also, as you can see, many settings are reset to defaults. This is an excellent justification for the use of GPOs to control these settings, since you have to modify them each time a new account is created from the template account.

Template accounts are ideally suited to the delegation of account creation. Designing a template account for a user representative and delegating the account creation process based on copies of this account instead of the creation of a new account from scratch ensures that your corporate standards are maintained even if you delegate this activity.

User Property Dialog Box Tab	Retained Values
General	None
Address	Everything except the street address
Account	Logon hours Log on to… User must change password at next logon Account is disabled Password never expires User cannot modify password
Profile	Everything, but profile path and home folder are both changed to reflect the new user's name
Telephones	None
Organization	Everything except the title
Environment	None; the account is reset to default settings
Sessions	None; the account is reset to default settings
Remote Control	None; the account is reset to default settings
Terminal Services Profile	None; the account is reset to default settings
COM+	None
Published Certificates	None
Member Of	Everything
Dial-in	None; the account is reset to default settings
Security	Everything
Password Replication	None

TABLE 7-5 Template Account Attribute Retention

Massive User Management

Windows Server 2008 offers several enhancements in regards to the ability to manage several objects at once. For example, you can select multiple objects and drag-and-drop them from one location to the other within the directory because this functionality is supported in the ADDS consoles.

CAUTION *Always remember the protection from accidental deletion attribute. If you can't move an object, it is because it is protected.*

You can also select several objects and modify some of their properties at the same time. For example, you can select several user objects and modify their description in one step. You can use this procedure to move several accounts at once, enable or disable them, add them to a group, send mail to them, and use standard cut and paste functions.

But when you need to perform massive user management tasks—i.e., modify the settings on large numbers of users—you are better off using scripts. WS08 supports both the Windows Scripting Host (WSH) toolset and the PowerShell environment (except on Server Core). WSH includes the ability to create and run scripts in either Visual Basic Script (VBS) or Java Script. In addition, with the use of ADSI and WMI, you can create truly powerful jobs that will perform massive modifications for you. PowerShell also offers powerful scripting abilities, but it is simpler to use than WSH. More on scripting will be covered in Chapter 13, but for now, it is important to understand that for massive user administration tasks, you'll most likely want to use a scripting tool.

TIP *The TechNet Scripting Center provides useful information and code samples for generating scripts for a variety of purposes. For generating scripts with ADSI, it offers a free graphical interface for scripting, ADSI Scriptomatic, which can be found at www.microsoft.com/technet/scriptcenter/tools/admatic.mspx.*

When it comes to creating a vast number of users, you'll find that there are a number of different tools that can be used to help out in these situations. Some of the most important are:

- **ClonePrincipal** A series of VBS scripts that copy accounts from NT to WS08.
- **AddUser** A VBS script that adds users found in an Excel spreadsheet to the directory.
- **Active Directory Migration Tool (ADMT)** Migrates users from legacy Windows directories to WS08. Includes password migration.

There are also third-party tools that provide this functionality. Their advantage is that they provide full reporting capabilities while migrating or creating vast numbers of users.

Manage and Administer Groups

User objects are created within the directory for a variety of reasons. One of the most important is the assignation of permissions, both within the directory as well as permissions to access objects outside the directory, such as printer queues and file folders. Permissions are assigned through the use of groups. In fact, one of the first best practices you learn in any network environment is that you never assign permissions to individual users; you always assign them to groups.

It's simple; assigning permissions is a complex task. If you assign permissions to a user and the next day another user that requires the same permissions comes along, you have to start over from scratch because you can't copy the permissions from one user account to another. But if you assign permissions to a group, even if there is only one person within the group, and another user comes along requiring the same permissions, all you need to do is place the new user within the group.

On the other hand, this strategy works only if you have complete documentation about each of the groups you create in your directory. It's easy to include users into an existing group if you created the group yesterday and today someone requires the same rights. But if you created the group last year and someone requires the same rights today, chances are that you might not remember that the original group exists. This problem is compounded when group management is distributed. You might remember why you created a group, but other group administrators within your organization won't have a clue the group exists unless you find a way to tell them. In addition, it can lead to orphaned security IDs (SIDs) when users are deleted from ADDS and their tokens are still individually applied to security objects.

This usually leads to a proliferation of groups within the organization. Here's why: Admin 1 creates a group for a specific purpose. Admin 1 places users within the group. Admin 2 comes along a while later with another request for the same rights. Admin 2 does not know that the group Admin 1 created exists. So, just to be safe, Admin 2 creates a new group for the same purpose and so on. Most organizations that do not have a structured approach for group management will find that when they migrate to Windows Server 2008, they need to perform an extensive group rationalization—inventory all groups, find out who is responsible for the group, find out the group purpose, find out if it is still necessary, and so on. If answers cannot be found for these questions, then the group is a good candidate for rationalization.

The best way to avoid this type of situation is to document all groups at all times and to make sure that this documentation is communicated to all affected personnel. ADDS provides the ideal solution. Group management in ADDS is simplified since the group object supports several properties that assist in the group management process:

- **Description** This field was present in Windows NT, but was seldom used. Use it fully in Windows Server 2008.
- **Notes** This field is used to identify the full purpose of a group. This information will provide great help in long-term group management. Both Description and Notes are on the General tab of the Group Properties dialog box.
- **Managed By** This field is used to identify the group's manager. A group manager is not necessarily the group's administrator, as can be evidenced in the Manager Can Update Membership List check box. Select this box if you have delegation rules in place and your group manager is also your group administrator. This entire property page is devoted to ensuring that you know who is responsible for the group at all times.

Filling out these fields is essential in any group management strategy.

WS08 Groups Types and Group Scopes

Windows Server 2008 boasts two main group types:

- **Security** Groups that are considered security objects and that can be used to assign access rights and permissions. These groups can also be used as an e-mail address. E-mails sent to the group are received by each individual user that is a member of the group.
- **Distribution** Groups that are not security-enabled. They are mostly used in conjunction with e-mail applications, such as Microsoft Exchange, or software distribution applications.

Groups within fully functional WS08 forests can be converted from one type to another at any time.

In addition to group type, WS08 supports several different group scopes. Group scopes are determined by group location. If the group is located on a local computer, its scope will be local. This means that its members and the permissions you assign to it will affect only the computer on which the group is located. If the group is contained within a domain in a forest, it will have either a domain or a forest scope. Once again, the domain and forest modes have an impact on group functionality. In a fully functional WS08 forest, you will be able to work with the following group scopes (see Figure 7-18):

- **Domain Local** Members can include accounts (user and computer), other domain local groups, global groups, and universal groups
- **Global** Members can include accounts and other global groups from within the same domain
- **Universal** Members can include accounts, global groups, and universal groups from anywhere in the forest

Even if you can change group scope once your forest is fully functional, there are some restrictions:

- Global groups cannot become universal groups if they already belong to another global group.
- Universal groups cannot become global groups if they include another universal group.
- Universal groups can become domain local groups at any time because domain local groups can contain any type of group.
- Domain local groups cannot become universal groups if they contain another domain local group.
- All other group scope changes are allowed.

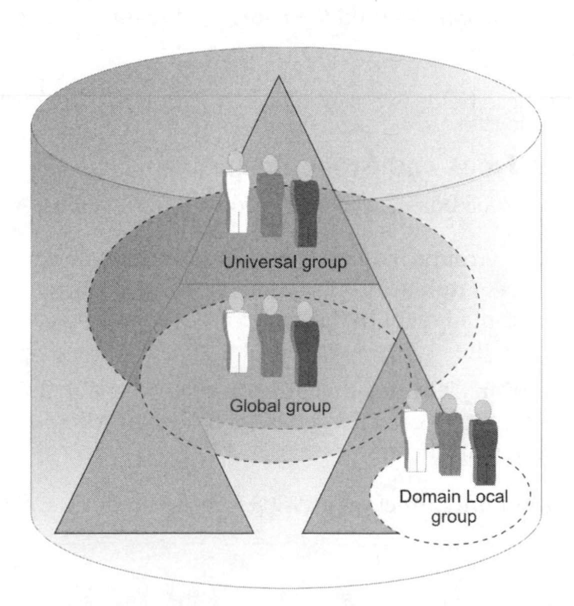

Figure 7-18 Group scopes within a forest

Groups can be nested in WS08. This means that a group can include other groups of the same scope. Thus, you can create "super" groups that are designed to contain other sub-groups of the same type. As you can see, without some basic guidelines, using groups in WS08 can become quite confusing. First, though, you need to understand how default groups have been defined within the directory.

Default Groups

WS08 includes two categories of default groups: local and domain or forest groups. For domain or forest groups, WS08 includes two other sub-categories: those that are considered built-in groups and those that are considered user groups. Table 7-6 outlines each of the default groups, whether they are found locally or within ADDS, their purpose, and their scope. It lists only

Group Name	Location	Scope	Purpose	Comments
Account Operators	ADDS: Built-in	DL	Can create accounts and groups anywhere in the domain except for the Built-in folder and the Domain Controllers OU.	This group does not have members by default. Account Operators cannot modify either the Administrator or the Domain Admins groups, nor can they modify the accounts of members of these groups. This is an excellent example of the delegation of the global account management task. This is a trusted role within the network.
Administrators	ADDS: Built-in Local	DL or L	Complete and unrestricted access to the domain or the computer, depending on scope.	This is the most powerful group on a computer; it must be managed carefully. If it is on the first DC in a domain, it becomes part of the Domain Admins group and is the most powerful account in the domain. This is a highly trusted role within the network and membership should be severely limited.

TABLE 7-6 Default Groups Within WS08

Group Name	Location	Scope	Purpose	Comments
Allowed RODC Password Replication Group	ADDS: Users	DL	Allows replication of passwords to read-only domain controllers.	If you use RODCs, then you should make sure that any user that may be in a location managed by an RODC should be a member of this group. You should include other groups here instead of individual users.
Authenticated Users	Special Group	n/a	Includes all users and computers that have been authenticated. Does not include Guest.	This group cannot be modified.
Backup Operators	ADDS: Built-in Local	DL or L	Can back up and restore files anywhere on a computer. Can log on locally and shut down a computer.	Includes no members by default. This is a trusted role within the network.
Batch	Special Group	n/a	Includes all users who log on through batch processes, such as task scheduler jobs.	This group cannot be modified.
Cert Publishers	ADDS: Users	DL	Used to publish certificates in ADDS.	Includes no members by default. This is not used without a PKI. This is a trusted role within the network.
Certificate Service DCOM Access	ADDS: Built-in	DL or L	Used to connect to certification authorities within the forest.	Includes no members by default. This is a trusted role within the network.
Creator Owner	Special Group	n/a	Includes any authenticated user who has created an object.	This group cannot be modified.
Creator Group	Special Group	n/a	Used to support permission inheritance.	This group cannot be modified.
Cryptographic Operators	ADDS: Built-in	DL	Used to perform cryptographic operations.	Includes no members by default. This is a trusted role within the network.

TABLE 7-6 Default Groups Within WS08 (*continued*)

Group Name	Location	Scope	Purpose	Comments
Denied RODC Password Replication Group	ADDS: Users	DL	Passwords are not cached in RODCs.	Includes most administrative groups by default. This protects the organization by ensuring that no administrative passwords are ever stored in the RODC cache and must always be obtained from secured read-write DCs.
Dial-up	Special Group	n/a	Includes all users who have logged on through remote access.	This group cannot be modified.
Distributed COM Users	ADDS: Built-in	DL or L	Used to run distributed COM objects on machines.	Includes no members by default.
DNS Admins	ADDS: Users	DL	Grants all rights to the DNS service.	Includes no members by default. This is a trusted role within the network.
DNSUpdateProxy	ADDS: Users	G	Grants rights to update DNS records on behalf of another entity.	This group is empty by default. Used only if you include machines running systems other than Windows 2000 or later in your network.
Domain Admins	ADDS: Users	G	Grants global rights to the entire domain.	Includes the administrators of the domain. This is a highly trusted role within the network and membership should be severely limited.
Domain Computers	ADDS: Users	G	Grants rights to operate within the domain.	Includes all workstations and servers that are joined to the domain.
Domain Controllers	ADDS: Users	G	Grants rights to manage system-level domain operations.	Includes all DCs in the domain.

TABLE 7-6 Default Groups Within WS08 (*continued*)

PART IV

Group Name	Location	Scope	Purpose	Comments
Domain Guests	ADDS: Users	G	Grants guest rights to the domain.	Includes all guest accounts. Of limited use today.
Domain Users	ADDS: Users	G	Grants common domain usage rights.	Includes every user account in the domain, even administrators.
Enterprise Admins	ADDS: Users	U	Grants global rights to the entire forest.	Includes the administrators of the root domain. This is a highly trusted role within the network and membership should be severely limited.
Enterprise Read-Only Domain Controllers	ADDS: Users	U	Grants the right to store passwords in a read-only cache.	Includes every RODC in the forest.
Event Log Readers	ADDS: Built-in	DL or L	Used to read event logs from machines.	Includes no users by default.
Everyone	Special Group	n/a	Includes Authenticated Users and Guests, but does not include Anonymous users.	This group cannot be modified.
Group Policy Creator Owners	ADDS: Users	G	Grants rights to create and modify GPOs.	Includes the administrator by default. This is a trusted role within the network.
Guests	ADDS: Built-in Local	DL or L	Contains the Guest account.	This group has limited use.
IIS_IUSRS	ADDS: Built-in	DL or L	Used by IIS.	Includes no members by default.
Incoming Forest Trust Builders	ADDS: Built-in	DL	Used to create forest trusts.	Includes no members by default. This is a trusted role in the network.
Interactive	Special Group	n/a	Includes all users that are logged on locally or through the Remote Desktop.	This group cannot be modified.
Network	Special Group	n/a	Includes all users that are logged on through the network.	This group cannot be modified.

Table 7-6 Default Groups Within WS08 (*continued*)

Group Name	Location	Scope	Purpose	Comments
Network Configuration Operators	ADDS: Built-in Local	DL or L	Grants client network configuration rights.	This is a special technical group that can be used to support client network troubleshooting activities.
Power Users	Local	L	Included for backward compatibility. Can create user accounts and modify and delete these accounts. Can create local groups and modify these groups. Can create shares and manage local printers.	This group is designed to give users more autonomy over their systems without having to grant them full administrative rights. Users can also run legacy applications. In this case, this group compares to the Users group in Windows NT.
Performance Log Users	ADDS: Built-in	DL	Used to track performance on systems.	Includes no members by default.
Performance Monitor Users	ADDS: Built-in	DL	Used to access performance data.	Includes no members by default.
Pre-Windows 2000 Compatible Access	ADDS: Built-in	DL	Grants read access to all users and groups in the domain.	Use only if Windows NT 4.0 machines are present in the domain.
Print Operators	ADDS: Built-in Local	DL or L	Can manage printers and print queues.	This group is used to delegate printer and print queue administration.
Remote Desktop Users	ADDS: Built-in Local	DL or L	Grants users the right to log on remotely on a computer.	Administrators do not need to be part of this group because they have this right inherently. Used to delegate remote support tasks.
RAS and IAS Servers	ADDS: Users	DL	Grants rights to access a user's remote access properties.	Contains only servers. Empty by default. Every server that will be used to provide either remote access or virtual private network access must be a member of this group.

Table 7-6 Default Groups Within WS08 *(continued)*

Group Name	Location	Scope	Purpose	Comments
Read-Only Domain Controllers	ADDS: Users	G	Grants the right to store passwords in a read-only cache.	Includes every RODC in the domain.
Replicator	ADDS: Built-in Local	DL or L	Supports directory replication.	This group should contain only service accounts or accounts that are designed to represent services and not actual users.
Schema Admins	ADDS: Users	U	Grants rights to modify the structure of the ADDS database.	Includes the administrators of the root domain. This is a highly trusted role within the network and membership should be severely limited.
Server Operators	ADDS: Built-in	DL	Can log on to servers, manage shares and services, back up and restore files, format the hard disk, and shut down the system.	This group is used to delegate server administration tasks. This is a trusted role within the network.
Service	Special Group	n/a	Includes all users that are logged on as a service.	This group cannot be modified. Controlled by the operating system.
Terminal Services License Servers	ADDS: Built-in	DL	Used to manage TS licenses in the network.	Includes no members by default.
Terminal Services Users	Special Group	n/a	Includes all users that are logged on to a Terminal Services server operating in TS4 compatibility mode.	This group cannot be modified.
Users	ADDS: Built-in Local	DL or L	Used to support common computer usage tasks. Can create local groups and modify these groups.	Includes Authenticated Users and members of the Interactive group. In a domain, also includes the Domain Users group. This is the most common group in your network.
Windows Authorization Access Group	ADDS: Built-in	DL	Used to access computed universal and global attribute tokens.	Includes enterprise domain controllers.

TABLE 7-6 Default Groups Within WS08 (*continued*)

local groups or groups found within a native WS08 forest. It also lists special groups that are part of the Windows operating system. Groups are identified as such: DL for domain local, L for local, G for global, and U for universal. Special groups are identified as non-applicable (n/a).

As you can see, WS08 provides a vast number of default groups. Several of these should be used for the delegation of administrative activities within the network. But as you examine these groups, you realize that there is a certain logic to the way groups are used. This logic forms the basis of your group management strategy.

Best Practices for Group Management/Creation

Group management practices can become quite complex. This is why a group management strategy is essential to the operation of a structured network. This strategy begins with best practice rules and guidelines. It is complemented by a strategic use of global groups or groups that are designed to contain users. Both of these elements are outlined in the following sections.

Best Practice: The AGLP Rule

The varying scopes of all of the groups within Active Directory Domain Services will not help your group management activities if you do not implement basic guidelines for group usage. Fortunately, there is a best-practice rule for using groups. It is the Account-Global Group-Local Group-Permissions rule, or AGLP rule. This rule outlines how groups are used.

It begins with the placement of accounts—either users or computers. All accounts are placed within global groups and only within global groups. Next, global groups are placed within local groups and mostly in local groups. Permissions are assigned to local groups and only local groups. When users need to access objects in other domains, their global group is included within the local group of the target domain. When users need to access objects located within the entire forest, their global group is inserted into a universal group (see Figure 7-19).

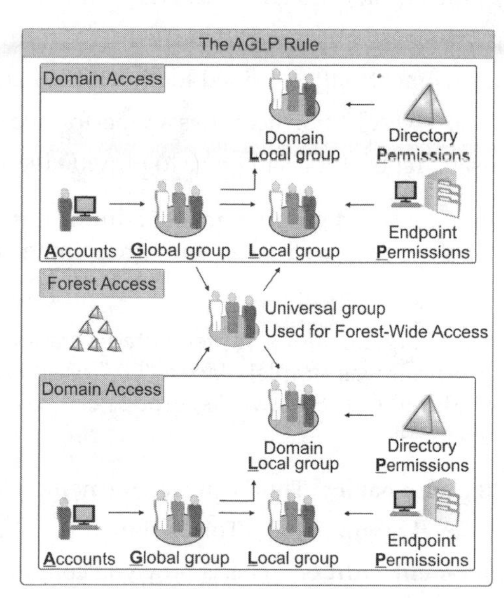

FIGURE 7-19 The AGLP rule

Domain Local Groups

Domain local groups should be used with alacrity because they populate the directory and have an impact on directory replication. They should only be used if the permissions you need to assign are ADDS permissions or permissions on ADDS objects. When targeting resources that are local to a computer or server, make sure you rely on the groups that are local to these systems when assigning resource permissions. This way, you can make use of the AGLP rule without proliferating domain local groups.

Many organizations have doubled the number of groups in their directory because each time they need to assign a permission, they create two groups: a global group and a domain local group. Yet, if the resource is local to a computer system, there is absolutely no reason to grant permissions to a group that would be contained in the directory instead of in the local security accounts manager (SAM) database that is located on the local server.

In short, this rule is summarized as follows:

- Global groups are the only groups that contain users.
- Domain local or local groups only contain other groups (global or universal).
- Permissions are only assigned to either domain local groups or local groups.
- Universal groups only contain global groups.

This rule is supported by the following additional guidelines:

- All group names are standardized.
- All groups include detailed descriptions.
- All groups include additional notes.
- All group managers are clearly identified.
- Group management staff is trained to understand and use these rules.
- Group purpose verification activities are performed on a regular basis.
- A group usage report tool is in place to provide regular group content updates.

Standard group names and group manager administration are two areas that require further discussion before you can finalize your group management strategy.

Standard Group Naming

In Windows NT, many organizations implemented a standard naming strategy for both global and local groups. It was simple; place a "G_" or an "L_" at the beginning of the name of each group type. But in ADDS networks, groups can have more complex names. In fact, groups have three names:

- **The WS08 group name** This is, in fact, the name you will use to manage the group.
- **The down-level group name** This is similar to the name you used in Windows NT.
- **The group e-mail address** This is how you communicate with members of a group.

Because of this, you should reconsider how you name groups to make better use of the directory. You should, in fact, take into consideration the possible delegation of group membership management. For example, if your public relations department wants you to create a special group for them that they will use to both assign file and folder permissions and communicate with all PR managers within the network, you might very well decide that once the group is created, you don't want to be burdened with the day-to-day administration of the contents of this group. As such, you could delegate group content management to someone in the PR department. This could be done for a vast number of groups in your organization.

And since only global groups should contain users, you only need to consider the delegation of global groups. Also, by retaining the management of local groups, you retain control over the permissions and rights you assign to any user in the organization.

In addition, remember that users can search the directory. In a structured network, you'll want to keep a tight rein on the creation and multiplication of groups. Your core strategy should focus on combining group functions as much as possible. For example, if you integrate Microsoft Exchange with your directory, you will need to manage many more distribution groups. But if your security group strategy is well defined, then several of your existing security groups will double as distribution groups. Therefore, you should have considerably fewer distribution groups than security groups. You may not even have to create any new distribution groups at all if you've done your homework.

TIP *Don't make the mistake of duplicating distribution and security groups. Group proliferation has a direct impact on network replication.*

If you think you will be delegating global group membership management, at least for some global groups, or if you think that you may one day need to have security groups, usually global security groups, double as distribution groups, you should reconsider your group naming strategy. Everyday users will not be comfortable with groups named G_PRMGR or L_DMNADM.

A solid group naming strategy should take into account the following guidelines:

- Global and universal groups should be named without identifying their scope. Scope identification is displayed automatically within the directory, so this is not an issue for administrators.
- Since they may be accessed by users for communication purposes or by user representatives for membership management purposes, global and universal groups should be named using common language.
- Universal groups should include the organization's name to identify that they are forest-wide groups.
- Down-level names should not include scope for global and universal groups because users can also access the down-level name.
- Domain local groups, if used, should be named including the "(Local)" identifier at the end of the name. This allows administrators to search for all domain local groups more easily.

- Down-level names for domain local groups should be preceded by an "L_" to make it simpler to identify them in the directory.
- All domain local groups should be contained within OUs that deny read rights to common users. This will ensure that user directory query results never include domain local groups and always only include groups to which they have access. Special groups such as Domain Admins, Enterprise Admins, Schema Admins, and Administrators should be moved to containers that deny user read rights so that users cannot locate these special security roles in your organization.
- Local groups can be named like domain local groups because they are on local machines and users do not have access to them.

Table 7-7 lists some sample names for different groups.

Using such a naming strategy will greatly reduce group management headaches. This naming strategy, along with the guidelines outlined previously, should produce the following results:

- Universal and domain local groups are the fewest in number. They are used only for very special purposes.
- Global security groups should be the most numerous group type in your forest. These groups perform double duty as both security and distribution groups.
- Global distribution groups should be less numerous than global security groups. Distribution groups should be used only if there is no security group that can fulfill the same purpose.

Keep to these rules. Group management requires tight controls, especially if it is a delegated task. Use a standard group creation process to simplify your group management activities (see Figure 7-20).

Group Scope	Name Example
Universal Group	T&T Public Relations Managers; T&T Technicians; T&T Administrative Assistants
Universal Group Down-Level Name	T&T PR Managers; T&T Technicians; T&T Admin Assistants
Global Group	Public Relations Managers; Region 1 Technicians; Region 1 Administrative Assistants
Global Group Down-Level Name	PR Managers; R1 Technicians; R1 Admin Assistants
Domain Local or Local Group	Public Relations Managers (Local); Region 1 Technicians (Local); Region 1 Admin Assistants (Local)
Domain Local or Local Group Down-Level Name	L_PR_MGR; L_R1_Techs; L_R1_AdmAss

TABLE 7-7 Group Name Examples

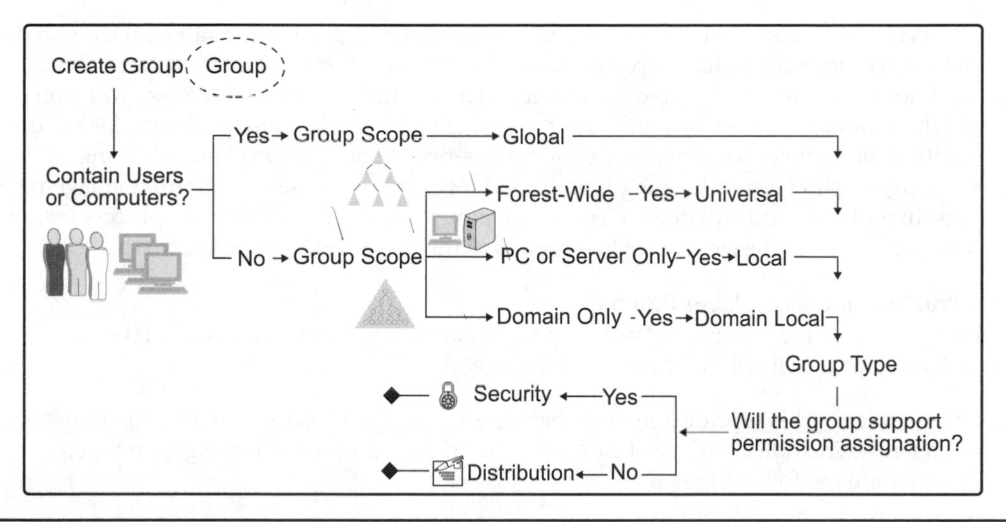

FIGURE 7-20 The group creation process flowchart

Group Ownership Management

One of the aspects of group management that is crucial to your strategy is the assignation of group managers. Group managers are individuals that are located within your directory. Thus, when you identify a group manager, you locate a user account in your directory and assign the manager's role to this user. When the manager changes, you must modify the ownership of each group. ADDS provides an automated way to do this.

While people work with the user on the basis of the account name, ADDS does not. It identifies all objects through special numbers: the Security Identifier (SID) or the Globally Unique Identifier (GUID). Security principals (user accounts) are identified through their SID. If, when a manager changes, you deactivate the former manager's account and create a new account, you will have to reassign all of the former account's permissions and user rights.

If, on the other hand, you treat user accounts as user roles within your organization instead of as individuals, you can take advantage of ADDS features to facilitate your work. To do so, you need to deactivate and rename accounts instead of re-creating them. For example, Ruth Becker, group manager for the PR global security group, leaves the company. Since you know that your organization will not operate without someone in Ruth's role, you do not delete her account; you only deactivate it. A few days later, John Purdy is hired to replace Ruth. Now you can reactivate Ruth's old account, rename it to John Purdy, reset the password, and force a password change at next logon. John automatically has all of Ruth's rights and permissions, or rather, all the rights and permissions that come with his new role within the organization.

This even applies if a person only changes positions within the organization. Once again, since people work with names and ADDS works with SIDs, using a new account or a renamed account is completely transparent to them. On the other hand, the advantages of renaming the account are great for the system administrator because you only have to perform a few tasks and you're done.

In some cases, security officers will be against this practice because they fear they will not be able to track user activity within the network. They are right in a way. Since ADDS tracks users through their SIDs, the SID is the only value that is guaranteed when you view audit reports. When you change a user's name, you are continually reusing the same SID. If you do not maintain strict records that help you track when the user name for a SID was modified, you will not be able to know who owned that SID before the current user. Worse, you won't know when the current user became owner of the SID. This could cause problems for the user, especially if the former owner performed some less-than-honest actions before leaving.

Once again, strict record keeping is an important part of any user and group management strategy. In addition, you will need to perform a group manager identification process before you can proceed with the creation of any groups within your VSO parallel network.

Best Practice: Manage Global Groups

Global groups are the groups that are used to contain users. In most networks, the global groups you create will fall into four specific categories:

- **IT roles** This type of role identifies a person's IT role within the organization. IT roles include a variety of different activities. Examples of these group types include the following:
  - Generic User
  - Information Worker
  - Management and Management Support
  - Professionals
  - End-User Developer
  - Web/Intranet Editor
  - System Developer
  - Systems or Security Administrator
  - Systems and User Support
  - And so on
- These IT roles allow you to create horizontal user groupings that span your organization and allow you to manage people who perform similar tasks, no matter where they are located, both within the organization and within your ADDS structure. These roles are related to the computer vocation roles identified earlier in the PC management strategy. Try to limit these roles to less than 20. For example, one organization that has more than 4000 users only has nine IT roles defined within its network.
- **Line-of-business groups** In most cases, you will also need to be able to manage users vertically. For example, if the Finance department wants to contact all of its members, a Finance global group will be required. Many of these groupings will have been created with the organization unit structure in your domain, but you cannot use an OU to send e-mail messages; you can only do so with a group. In addition, many departments will have personnel distributed in a vast number of OUs, especially if your organization includes regional offices and you need to delegate regional management activities. Try to keep these groupings to a minimum as well. In many organizations, the "Department minus 1" rule is all that is required. This means you follow the hierarchical structure of the company to one

level below departments. In the Finance department, you would find the Finance group, then Payables, Payroll, Purchasing, and so on. You may require a more detailed division for your groups within the IT department itself, though.

- **Project-based groups** Organizations are constantly running projects. Each project is made up of different people from different sections of the organization. Projects are volatile and last only for definite periods of time. Unlike the two previous group types, project-based groups are not permanent. Because of this, this group type is the one that gives you the most work. It is also because of this that this group type may involve the creation of other group scopes, not for the inclusion of users, but rather for the assignation of permissions to project resources. Once again, try to keep a tight rein on the number of groups you create.
- **Special administrative groups** The last global group type is the special administrative group type. Like the first two group types, this group type is more stable than project groups. It is required to support the application of special administrative rights to groups of users. For example, if you need to either filter Group Policy or assign specific Group Policy features through the use of security groups, you would do so through a special administrative group.

Whichever group type you create or manage, remember that the key to a successful group management strategy is documentation, both within and without the directory. Document your groups within the directory using the strategies outlined previously. And document your groups outside of the directory through external databases and other documentation methods.

Other Group Types

While there are four main categories for global groups, all other groups will fall into one single category: operational groups. This category includes domain local, universal, and local groups. These groups are named "operational" for two reasons. The first is that they are designed to contain only other groups. The second is that they are designed to provide access to resources.

Since these groups are operational, they will not be stored within the basic People OU structure. They should, in fact, be hidden from common users; i.e., users should not be able to find these groups when they search the directory. This means that you can use a more complex naming strategy for these groups, and it also means that you must store these groups within an OU structure that is normally hidden from users. This is the Virtual Service Offerings OU structure, which will be detailed in Chapters 8 and 9.

Create an OU Design for User Management Purposes

Now that you have a good understanding of groups and what you intend to do with them, you can proceed to the finalization of your OU design for user management. First, you need to review the People OU structure that was proposed in Chapter 5. A People OU is used here because the User container in ADDS is not an OU. Therefore, you cannot use it to create an OU sub-structure or to apply Group Policy to your people objects.

The People OU Structure

Chapter 5 outlined an OU structure for people objects. This structure is displayed in Figure 5-13, along with the two other main OU types: PCs and Virtual Service Offerings. The People OU structure is used to regroup people objects within a single OU structure. This OU structure must support both user-based Group Policy application as well as some user administrative task delegation. And, since Active Directory Domain Services relies on a database that should be as static as possible, you want to ensure that your People OU structure will be as stable as possible. Each time you perform massive changes to the OU structure, it is replicated to every domain controller within the production domain.

This is the reason why you do not want to include your organizational structure—as displayed in your organization chart—within the People OU structure. Many organizations tend to modify their hierarchical authority structure several times per year. Replicating this structure within your People OU design will only cause more work for you, since you will be constantly modifying your OU structure to reflect the changes your organization chart has undergone.

Your OU structure still needs to represent the structure of your organization to some degree. This is why the People OU structure is based primarily on three concepts:

- **Business units** By basing your OU structure on business units, you can ensure that you address the requirements of your user base through your organization's logical business structure. Business units are less volatile than organization charts. Organizations create new business units less often than they assign new responsibility centers.
- **Geographical distribution** If your organization is distributed and includes regional offices, chances are that you will need to delegate some administrative tasks to regional officers. The best way to support delegation is to create organizational units that regroup the objects you want to delegate.
- **Special interest groups** Your organization will most likely include groups of users that have special requirements, requirements that are not met by any other groups. Thus, you need to create OUs that will contain these special user groupings. For example, the IT department is an excellent example of a special interest group.

You'll also remember that the best OU structure does not extend beyond five sub-levels. This basic structure includes three major levels, but offers the possibility to delegate further sub-level creation to special interest groups. The final result of your People OU design aims to meet all user requirements. As such, chances are that you will need to perform some trial and error at first and refine the resulting OU structure within the first six months of its operation. The People OU structure proposed in Chapter 5 is reused, but now it has evolved to take into account a refined vision of your needs (see Figure 7-21).

A Group-Related OU Structure

Many organizations create a special OU structure to include groups in addition to the People OU structure. While the addition of such a structure has its merits, it will only lead to more work on your part if you do so. Remember that you will most likely want to delegate some of the group management or administration activities, perhaps not group creation, but certainly group membership management. To do so, you would need to implement delegation in two places: the People OU structure and the Group OU structure.

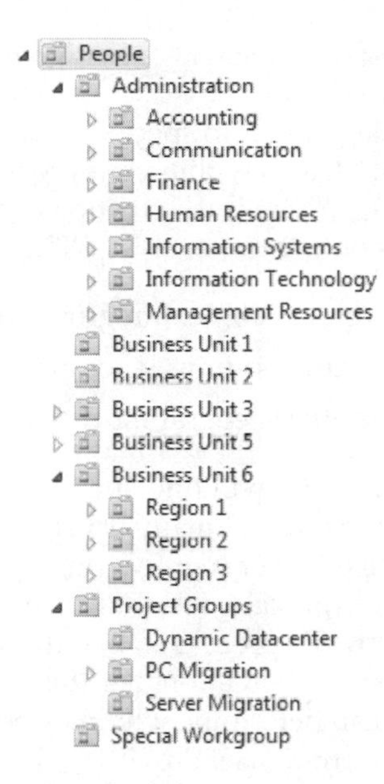

FIGURE 7-21 The proposed People OU structure

In the end, it is best to have the People OU structure perform double duty and include both groups and user objects.

Besides, the only group scope that needs to be included here is the group scope that actually includes user objects. This is the global group scope. This means that your People OU structure will house global groups, but that all other groups—domain local and universal—will be housed elsewhere. In fact, since these latter group scopes are of an operational nature—they provide either object access or forest access—they should be stored within the Virtual Service Offerings OU structure. As such, their read access can be controlled, making only global groups available to users for ADDS research purposes.

Delegation Within the People OU

There are two main categories of delegation required in a People OU. The first relates to user representatives. User representatives are responsible for basic user administration activities. These should include, at the very least, password resets and user group membership management and, at the most, user account creation based on template accounts. User representatives should not be allowed to create groups. You should have global account operators to provide this service.

Unlike the custom delegation used earlier for PC vocation management, the user representative delegation tasks are all standard delegation tasks that are included by default within Active Directory Domain Services. When you delegate control of a People sub-OU to a user representative (of course, this would be to the user representative group and not the individual), you can select the following standard delegation tasks:

- Create, delete, and manage user accounts
- Reset user passwords and force password change at next logon
- Read all user information
- Modify the membership of a group

Since these are standard delegation tasks, assigning delegation rights to user representative groups is a fairly simple activity.

The second type of delegation is to special interest groups. As mentioned before, these can include special "SWAT" teams within your organization or departments, such as IT itself. The task you want to delegate here is the creation of a sub-OU structure. The People OU illustrated earlier displays only three levels of OUs:

- The first is the OU type: People. It regroups all common users in the organization.
- The second covers business units, special interest groups, and Projects.
- The third regroups either geographic distribution or administrative services.

It is within the latter that you will find special interest groups that will require further OU segregation. Using a three-tiered main OU structure gives these groups two more levels they can use to perform this further segregation.

Delegation here refers to process delegation rather than actual task delegation within ADDS. You need to delegate the process so that these particular groups can identify their own needs in regards to sub-OU creation. For this, you will need to provide coaching to these groups so that they can determine why they need further segregation and decide what type of regroupings they want to use. Providing them with a preliminary coaching session can free you up to continue with other design tasks while they debate among themselves on the model they require. Then, once they have decided, you can ask them to present you with their OU sub-structure proposal and determine with them if their needs are met. Once you both agree on the design, you can implement it and provide them with the same type of delegated tasks you gave to user representatives.

Delegation in both of these situations will only work if you have previously identified who you will delegate to. Like the group manager identification process, OU delegation requires a comprehensive user representative identification process before you can begin the implementation of your People OU design within the VSO parallel network.

User-Related GPO Concepts

The PC management section of this chapter identified the general operation of Group Policy objects as well as their breadth of coverage. It also listed the computer GPO settings. Since the People OU structure will house user objects, it is now necessary to detail the user GPO settings.

In the PC OU structure, the user portions of the GPOs were deactivated. This time, the computer portions of GPOs must be deactivated, since only users are targeted in the People OU.

Table 7-8 details the user portion of a GPO and applicable settings for the network.

As you can see, there is a wide variety of configuration parameters available to you through user GPOs. Detailing each and every one is beyond the scope of this book, but some important items are outlined in the following sections. The settings you apply will mostly depend on the type of environment you want to create. Take the time to review and understand each setting. Then decide which you need to apply. Once again, comprehensive documentation is the only way you will be able to make sure you maintain a coherent user GPO strategy.

GPO Section	Comment	Applicable
Software Settings	This section deals with software installations. If you want to assign a software product to a user instead of a computer using WS08 software delivery, you set the parameters here.	No. If you use this for software delivery, send it to PCs.
Windows Settings	This section deals with general Windows settings and includes elements such as scripts and security settings.	Some
Remote Installation Services (RIS)	This policy is related to the RIS installation options you offer to users.	Some
Scripts	Controls access to logon and logoff scripts.	Required
Security Settings	Includes public key policies and software restrictions.	Some
Public Key Policies	Controls renewal policies for certificates (more in Chapter 10). Also controls enterprise trust for the inclusion of certificate trust lists.	Required for all users
Software Restriction Policies	Allows you to determine which applications are allowed to run in your network (more in Chapter 10).	Required for all common users
Folder Redirection	Allows you to redirect local folders to network locations. Replaces both the home directory and the roaming user profile. Supports data protection by locating user folders on central servers.	Required for most users
AppData (Roaming)	Includes two settings: Basic and Advanced. Basic redirects all folders to the same location. Advanced supports different redirection locations based on user groups.	Redirect for data protection
Desktop	Same as AppData	Redirect for data protection
Start Menu	Same as AppData	Redirect for data protection
Documents	Same as AppData Can include My Pictures folder.	Redirect for data protection
Pictures	Set to follow Documents	Redirect if your user policy allows it
Music	Set to follow Documents	Same as Pictures
Videos	Set to follow Documents	Same as Pictures
Favorites	Same as AppData	Redirect for data protection
Contacts	Do not protect	Users should rely on Outlook
Downloads	Do not protect	Files can be too large
Links	Same as AppData	Redirect for data protection
Searches	Same as AppData	Redirect for data protection
Saved Games	Do not protect	Not required
Policy-based QoS	Defines Quality of Service (QoS) settings for video and audio streaming.	For PCs only

TABLE 7-8 User Policy Categories and Contents

GPO Section	Comment	Applicable
Internet Explorer Maintenance	Controls browser user interface, connection, URLs, security, and programs. Controls IE settings for your organization (logos, home page, support URLs, etc.). Programs are derived from the settings on the desktop or server used to create the GPO. Many of these settings can replace the configuration in the Connection Manager Administration Kit.	Required for all users Can be personalized further at sub-levels
Administrative Templates	Administrative templates are scriptable GPO components that can be used to control a wide variety of settings, such as Windows components, Start menu and taskbar, desktop, Control Panel, shared folders, network, and system.	Yes
Control Panel	Controls regional and language options, as well as allowing you to modify the default user logon pictures.	In multilingual or corporate environments
Desktop	Controls the behavior of the desktop items	Yes
Network	Controls network-related settings, such as network connections, offline files, and Windows Connect Now.	Set at PC level only
Shared Folders	Controls the behavior of the Distributed File System. Covered in Chapter 8.	Yes
Start Menu and Taskbar	Controls the behavior of Start menu items.	Yes
System	Controls system-wide settings, such as CTRL-ALT-DEL options, driver installation, folder redirection, Group Policy, Internet communication management, local services, logon, performance, Control Panel, power management, removable storage access, scripts, user profiles, and Windows HotStart. This section controls the behavior of each listed feature. The Scripts section, for example, determines the behavior for scripts, not the script names. It also controls the behavior of user profiles on PCs. You should modify this behavior if you intend to work with roaming profiles and folder redirection. Use removable storage access to control whether or not users can plug in devices such as USB drives. Use locale services, which allow you to automatically change settings on PCs to match an employee's language settings. Power management should be set at the PC level.	Yes Shared with the PC level

TABLE 7-8 User Policy Categories and Contents (*continued*)

GPO Section	Comment	Applicable
Windows Components	Controls settings such as NetMeeting (for remote assistance), Internet Explorer behavior, Help and Support Center, Windows Explorer, Microsoft Management Console, Task Scheduler, Terminal Services, Windows Installer behavior, Windows Messenger, Windows Update, Windows Media Player, and much more. Several settings are of use here. Help and Support Center settings help limit the Internet information that is provided to your users. MMC helps support the custom MMCs you deliver to delegation officers. Terminal Services determines how the TS session is established between the local and the remote systems. This section should be used to avoid having to set these parameters for each user's account. Windows Update, in particular, allows you to control user access to this feature.	Yes
All Settings	Lists all of the settings that are available under Administrative Templates. You can sort them through each of the headings in the details pane, giving you an easier access to each of these settings.	Yes

TABLE 7-8 User Policy Categories and Contents (*continued*)

Manage User Data

If you're used to a legacy network, you'll have become quite adept at generating new user accounts that automatically manage all of a user's data deposits. Few administrators today don't use template accounts that automatically create a user's home directory or a user's roaming profile directory if roaming profiles are in use. For example, in NT, it is fairly simple to apply these settings to a template user account. Both are based on a universal naming convention (UNC) share structure coupled with the username variable (%username%). Since NT is based on the NetBIOS naming standard, everything needed to be in capital letters for the operation to work.

User data management is fairly straightforward in NT: Create a home directory, create a profile directory (if required), implement a quota management technology, and start backing up the data. If this is what you're used to, you'll find that while all of these operations work in Windows Server 2008, many of these concepts are no longer used.

With the introduction of IntelliMirror in Windows 2000, Microsoft has redefined user data management in the Windows platform. In WS08, home directories are no longer required. Much the same applies to the roaming profile. And in a parallel network, one where you endeavor to avoid the transfer of legacy procedures, you'll want to seriously rethink your user data management strategies if you want to make the most of your migration.

Originally, the home directory was designed to provide a simple way to map user shares on a network. In Windows NT, using the %username% variable automatically generated the folder and automatically applied the appropriate security settings, giving the user complete ownership over the folder. In addition, Windows NT Workstation automatically mapped the appropriate network drive at logon. Since the folder was on a network drive, you could easily back it up and protect every user's data. In Windows Server 2008 and Windows Vista, it is no longer necessary to use mapped drives. Windows Server 2008 offers a much more interesting technology, one based on the UNC concept, to manage all network shares. This is the Distributed File System (DFS). It is designed to provide a unified file share system that is transparent to users without the need for mapped drives. Of course, it may happen that you require some mapped drives, since you will most likely still be hosting some legacy applications, especially those that have been developed in-house. But for user folders, mapped drives are no longer necessary.

Since Windows 2000, Microsoft has focused on the use of the Documents folder as the home of all user documents. This folder is part of the security strategy for all Windows editions beyond Windows 2000. It is stored within a user's profile and is automatically protected from all other users. The same goes for all of a user's application settings. These are no longer stored within either the application or the system directory. Applications that are designed to support the Windows Logo program will all store their user-modifiable settings within the user's profile.

The folder redirection portion of a user's Group Policy can manage several critical folders and assign network shares for each. When redirection is activated through Group Policy, the system creates a special folder based on the user's name (just like in the older home directory process) and applies the appropriate security settings. Each of these folders is created within the user's parent folder. Data in these folders is redirected from the desktop PC to the network folders. Because of the Fast Logon Optimization process, it takes a user two logons before all of the data is redirected.

Replace the Home Directory

Folder redirection is completely transparent to the user. While they think they are using the Documents folder located on their desktop, they are actually using a folder that is located on the network. This way, you can ensure that all user data is protected.

TIP *Make sure your users are aware that they must store their data inside the Documents folder structure; otherwise, their data will not be protected.*

Using this folder redirection strategy rather than using a home directory simplifies the user data management process and lets you take advantage of the advanced features of the WS08 network. For example, even though data is stored on the network, it will be cached locally through Offline Files. Redirected folders are automatically cached through client-side caching when they are activated through a GPO, so long as the client computer is Windows XP and later (such as would be the case in the ideal parallel network). This means that the files in these folders will be cached locally and will be available to users, whether they are connected to the network or working offline. There are issues with client-side caching of files. These are covered in Chapter 8, since offline files are a feature of network shares rather than Group Policy.

Data in these folders can also be encrypted through the Encrypting File System (EFS). If the client is Windows XP or later, all offline files can be encrypted. But if you choose to continue to use a home directory structure and redirect documents to the home directory, you will not be able to activate data encryption on a user's files, since the user will not be able to decrypt data stored in the redirected folder; one more reason for avoiding the use of home directories. EFS is covered in Chapter 10.

Replace the Roaming Profile

Folder redirection is used to store a considerable portion of the user's profile; that is, all of a user's application-specific settings, the user's desktop contents, Favorites, the user's custom Start menu, and more. Redirecting these folders through Group Policy is very much the same as using a roaming user profile. The major difference is the time it takes to activate a profile.

When you use a roaming profile and you log on to a workstation, WS08 copies the entire contents of the roaming profile to the workstation. This can take a considerable amount of time. It is practical, though, since the user can find his or her own environment no matter which computer they log on to. In addition, when the user logs off, the entire profile is copied back to the server. Using roaming profiles has a considerable impact on network performance, since the entire contents of a user's profile is copied at logon and logoff.

Quotas are also difficult to enforce when user profiles are set to roam, since users will encounter errors when logging off because they are using more space in their profile than they are allowed on the network. In some cases, organizations using legacy networks and roaming profiles were forced to remove quotas to ensure the profiles worked all of the time. This led to users having profiles whose size was simply excessive. Imagine how long it would take to log on to a system with a profile in excess of 1 GB. Even in the best of networks, it is a great justification for an early morning coffee break while you wait for the logon process to complete.

Roaming profiles are no longer required in the WS08 network because of three major reasons:

- The core of a user's profile can be redirected through Group Policy, making it available to the user at all times.
- If profile backup is the justification for implementing roaming profiles, then local profiles can be backed up regularly through the User State Migration Tool (USMT). This tool can be used to create a recurring task that regularly copies all local user profiles to a central location that can then be backed up.
- Windows Vista and Windows Server 2008 both support the Remote Desktop. When properly managed, the Remote Desktop allows users to have access to their own local desktop from any location in the network. This virtually eliminates the need for roaming user profiles.

If you find you still need roaming user profiles, make sure you take the following restrictions into account:

- **Do not use client-side caching on roaming profile shares.** The roaming profile mechanism has its own caching system that will conflict with the offline files system.
- **Be wary of the quota size you set on users with roaming profiles.** If the disk quota is set too low, profile synchronization will fail at logoff.

The best thing to do is to begin to use the new network strategy and focus on folder redirection rather than either home directories or roaming profiles.

TIP *For a detailed strategy outlining how you can combine roaming profiles and folder redirection to get the best of both worlds, read Chapter 8 in* The Definitive Guide to Vista Migration, *a free download from www.realtime-nexus.com/dgvm.htm.*

Other Profile Types

A special profile type, the mandatory profile, was also in use within legacy networks. The mandatory profile is a locked profile that forces desktop settings on the system when a user logs on. Once again, while this profile type is supported in Windows Server 2008, it is no longer really required. Like the home directory and the roaming profile, the mandatory profile must be inscribed into the user's account properties. Having to inscribe specific settings on a per-user basis is less than practical. This is why Group Policy should be your favored approach. GPOs provide a central location for applying changes.

The PC management section of this chapter outlined how the Group Policy Loopback feature could be used to ensure that computers that were exposed to security risks, such as computers in a kiosk, could be protected. Loopback is a device that will protect computers that have generic roles. Temporary personnel that must be given a secure and controlled desktop environment should fall into this category. If you find that you need to create and maintain mandatory profiles, ask yourself first if you can secure the desktop through a kiosk-type computer configuration.

Logon and Logoff Scripts

Scripts are also managed through Group Policy and are no longer managed through user account properties. Windows NT compatibility is the only reason why it is still possible to type in a logon script as a property of a user account. Since Windows 2000, all Windows editions support startup, shutdown, logon, and logoff scripts. This means that while the script has become a much more popular and powerful tool within Windows, it is no longer applied on an individual user basis.

In addition, the logon script has also changed in nature. Many organizations used the logon script to map both network drives and network printers. Printers can now be assigned through Group Policy. Printer names are also now stored within ADDS and are directly searchable, making it much easier for users to find and use network printers. The same applies to network shares through the features of DFS. Enforcing mappings through a logon script is becoming a thing of the past.

It may be necessary to enable certain network drive mappings in order to provide support for legacy applications that have not yet been updated to take full advantage of features like DFS, but in most cases, this will be a temporary measure. If this is the case, you can assign logon scripts through the User Settings portion of Group Policy.

What is certain is that you will need to rethink your logon script strategy in order to ensure that you do not duplicate efforts that can be provided through Group Policy configuration. What is also certain is that when you configure and create user accounts, you will no longer require the use of the user account's Profile tab.

Scripts are now located in the SYSVOL share under the Group Policy object identifier in which they are activated.

Caution *Logon and logoff scripts are always run in a user's context. Keep this in mind when designing them. If you want scripts to perform administrative tasks on the PC—tasks for which the user will not have permissions to execute—you need to set them up as startup or shutdown scripts because these operate in an elevated context.*

Complete the People OU Structure

Now that you have a better understanding of the major changes within WS08 for user management and administration, you are ready to begin the completion of your people OU infrastructure. The easiest way to do so is to detail the requirements for each OU within a table, much like the one you used for the PC OU design.

Table 7-9 outlines a possible People OU structure for T&T Corporation. As mentioned before, T&T has several main offices where user creation is delegated to each business unit. In addition, T&T has several regional offices that have local security officers who perform

OU	Level	Objective	GPO	Notes
People	One	Grouping of all users in the organization	Global People GPO	Applies to all users Mostly a placeholder OU Includes all IT role global groups
Business Unit 1 to x	Two	Grouping of all users according to organizational business units	Possible, but not absolutely required Avoid if possible	Segregates users by business unit Includes only users for central offices Includes global groups for the business unit User creation (from template accounts) and group membership management is delegated to user representatives
Region 1 to x	Three	Grouping of all users within a region Created under the regional operations business unit	Possible, but not absolutely required Avoid if possible	User creation (from template accounts) and group membership management is delegated to user representatives Includes regional special administrative groups
Special Workgroup	Two	Grouping of all users, such as "SWAT" team	SIG GPO	GPO focuses on Terminal Services settings All users have access to their own Remote Desktop, as well as regional operations

Table 7-9 A People Administration OU Structure

OU	Level	Objective	GPO	Notes
Projects	Two	Grouping of all Project OUs		Categorization only Contains mostly other OUs Can contain an administration group if project-based OU administration and creation is delegated
Project 1 to x	Three	Grouping of all user groups that are related to any given project		Group membership management is delegated to project user representative
Administration	Two	Grouping of global groups and sub-OUs for the administration business unit		Group membership management is delegated to user representative
Human Resources, Material Resources, Finance, Communications, Accounting	Three	Grouping of all users according to organizational administrative service		Segregates users by service Includes only users for central offices Includes global groups for the service User creation (from template accounts) and group membership management is delegated to user representatives
IT and IS	Three	Grouping of all users according to organizational administrative service	Possible, but not required	Segregates users by service Includes only users for central offices Includes global groups for the service User creation (from template accounts) and group membership management is delegated to user representatives Sub-OU creation is also possible here and may be delegated

TABLE 7-9 A People Administration OU Structure (*continued*)

many of the user administration tasks. Since objects can only be contained within one OU, several users from different business units are located within the regional OUs. Thus, the actual business unit OU must contain both the users from central offices as well as the global groups that are used to regroup all users from the business unit, no matter where their user account is located within the directory. T&T also has special interest groups, notably a special "SWAT"-like team that is used to provide emergency replacement for personnel that are absent for one reason or another. Since the members of this group must be able to play any operational user role within the organization, they are regrouped in a special OU. Finally, T&T manages all operations through projects. Thus, its People OU structure must include project-based group management. These needs are taken into account, and the resulting OU structure is outlined in this table.

NOTE *Maintain a tight control over the sub-OU creation process, since you want to make sure that directory performance is not impacted by an OU structure that is too complex.*

Following the guidelines in this table gives you a complete People OU structure (see Figure 7-22).

Put the People OU Infrastructure in Place

You can proceed to the creation of this OU infrastructure since you have designed your People OU infrastructure matrix (see Table 7-9). This assumes that you have performed all of the identification activities listed earlier, such as preparing a group purpose matrix, identifying all group managers, and identifying all OU owners and user representatives.

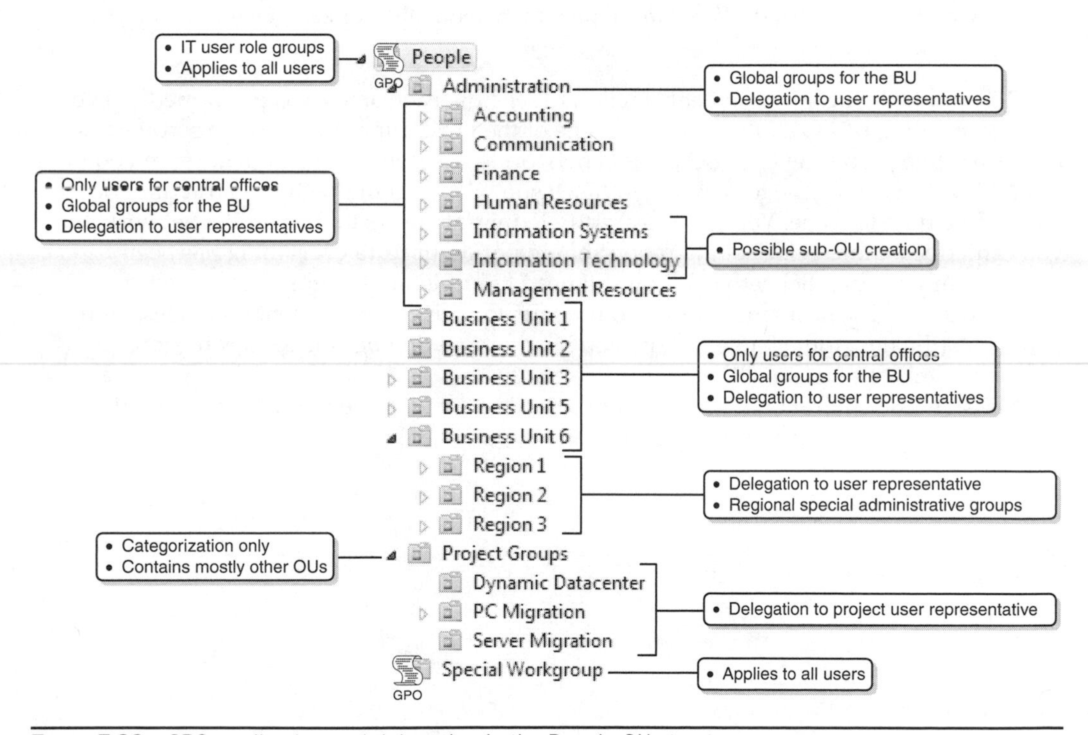

FIGURE 7-22 GPO application and delegation in the People OU structure

Once this is done, you can proceed to the creation of the infrastructure. The activities you need to perform to create this structure are:

- Create each OU.
- Create the Global People GPO and modify its settings (see Table 7-8).
- Create the group structure required to both assign rights and delegate management; these should include:
  - Global groups for each business unit (direction minus 1).
  - Project groups for each project OU.
  - Special administrative groups for both folder redirection and user representatives (for delegation purposes).
  - IT role global groups (should be stored in the People top-level OU).
  - Operational groups for rights assignation. These are not stored in the People OU infrastructure, but rather in the Virtual Service Offerings OU structure (see Chapter 8). For the time being, these groups can be stored in a temporary OU. They can then be moved to the Virtual Service Offerings OU when you are ready.
- All groups should be fully documented and each should have an assigned manager.
- Assign delegation rights to each OU.
- Create personalized Microsoft Management Consoles for each OU that includes delegation rights.

Return to the "PC Management" section to see how each activity is performed. As you will see, creating this OU infrastructure is one of the most intensive operations you have to perform while preparing the VSO parallel network. Take your time and make sure you do it right. Now is not the time to cut corners, since you will be living with this structure for quite some time to come. You're almost ready to migrate users to the parallel network, but you can't do so quite yet. User migration should not occur until everything has been prepared in your parallel network. You still need to implement your service structure, define structured security measures, and prepare your risk management strategies. Until you do so (the next four chapters show you how), you won't be able to start hosting massive numbers of users within your network.

Massive user migration will not occur until Chapter 12, since this activity is highly related to recurring user and group administrative activities.

8

CHAPTER

Build the Virtual Service Offerings Infrastructure: File and Print Servers

The very purpose of a network is the delivery of service offerings to a community of users. One of the most critical tasks you will undertake when designing the virtual service offerings (VSO) parallel network will be the implementation of the infrastructure that will support these offerings. Implementing this infrastructure will involve two major steps: creating the servers that will host each service offering type and creating the organizational unit (OU) infrastructure that will support service administration within the directory.

Chapter 3 identified eight server roles within the enterprise. Two of these have already been covered to some extent: identity management servers (domain controllers) and network infrastructure servers. Another, the failsafe server, is really a duplicate of existing servers, and with the virtualization of all service offerings, this role is one that focuses on duplication of the virtual machines that make up your VSOs. This role will be covered in part in this chapter as we discuss file replication technologies—the engine that allows the duplication of the files that make up a virtual machine.

This leaves five key roles to cover when designing your service infrastructure:

- **File and print servers** Servers that provide storage and structured document services to the network.
- **Application servers** Servers that provide application services based on either commercial applications, such as SQL Server, Commerce Server, and so on, or on custom corporate applications. This also includes applications based on the .NET Framework.
- **Terminal servers** Servers that provide a central application execution environment; the entire execution environment resides on the server itself.
- **Dedicated Web servers** Servers that provide Web services.
- **Collaboration servers** Servers that provide the infrastructure for collaboration within the enterprise. Their services include, among others, SharePoint Team

Services, streaming media services, electronic mail services, and real-time communications.

In addition, it will be important to complete the coverage of the network infrastructure servers, because only a few of their functions have been covered thus far.

NOTE *The dedicated Web server role will be covered in Chapter 9, along with the application server role.*

The structure for the coverage of each of these server roles includes:

- **Functional requirements** Discussions on how the service must be designed for the enterprise network and the rationale for the service.
- **Features** Features supporting the role or service offering within Windows Server 2008 (WS08), including new features.
- **Implementation instructions** How to proceed with the preparation of the server role within the parallel network environment.

Each server role will be based on the server construction model outlined in Chapter 3, the PASS model, and the basic server construction process detailed in Chapter 4, the design of the server kernel. In fact, here you only add functional roles to the core server design.

In addition, each time a role will affect the underlying resource pool, it will be described in detail. For example, the file service role affects resource pools because of the features that can be used to provide business continuity for the virtualized service offerings. Similarly, when business continuity is discussed, the features that offer redundancy for the host servers will be covered in detail. All, of course, with a focus on the Server Core installation that runs the virtualization engine that supports virtual service offerings.

All of the roles mentioned here are normally assigned to member servers. Domain controllers are reserved for one of two roles: identity management servers and multipurpose servers—servers that combine more than one role because of the size of the user base they support. Multipurpose servers are often found in smaller regional offices. These servers must be constructed with care because of the security risk involved in offering multiple user services on a domain controller.

CAUTION *With the advent of virtual service offerings, you may decide to forego the use of multipurpose servers because of the security risk and complexity of their configuration. Since you can now virtualize each server that offers a given service to users, it may be best to use a virtual machine for each service you need to offer to regions. While this will add to the total number of servers you need to manage, each server will be simpler to manage since its configuration will be more focused. In the end, you'll need to balance simplicity of administration with overall number of servers and the licenses each server will cost you. Of course, with the new license model for virtual servers, it becomes much easier to use a single license for multiple virtual machines.*

It will also be important to cover specific business continuity considerations for all server types, such as the network load balancing and failover clustering services. Both offer powerful redundancy features that minimize risk within the enterprise. These topics will be further discussed in Chapter 11. In addition, each chapter dealing with service offerings will include a table that outlines the resource requirements to build the server role. This will serve as a guide for server construction.

Finally, once the basis for enterprise services has been covered, it will be time to design the Virtual Service Offerings OU structure within the directory. As for the People and PCs OU structures, this design will include both Group Policy Object (GPO) and delegation principles, but it will also uniquely involve the design of a virtual service offerings administration plan. As with previous versions of Windows, WS08 offers the capability to focus specific administrative rights, based on the task the administrator is responsible for. This means you will no longer need to grant domain administration rights to one and all just to let them perform their work, as you did in Windows NT. This VSOs administration plan will be a key element of your security infrastructure for the network you are building.

The VSOs structure will be built up as each service is added to the network. It is at this point that OU contents will be identified. Once each service offering has been covered, the administrative, delegation, and Group Policy requirements for each will be covered in detail.

Prepare File and Print Servers

The most basic network server is the file and print server. Both services are one of the main reasons why groups of people tend to put networks in place. Central file storage provides the ability to share information as well as protect it, and provides a single location for backup and recovery operations. Print servers allow the reduction in hardware printer costs by sharing fewer printers among more users. In addition, central file storage servers can index content for all users, making it easier for everyone to reuse information.

Windows Server 2008 offers several features for the support of both operations. In fact, file and print sharing in WS08 has become quite sophisticated.

Share Files and Folders

One of the key aspects of any network is server standardization. When staging and preparing servers for file and folder sharing, you need to begin by identifying the purpose, or rather, the type of file sharing you intend to perform. After years of existence, file sharing has become concentrated on a few core file-sharing functions. The types of files most organizations need to share today are the following:

- **User data** The files that make up both personal user information and the user's profile. This is a private share.
- **Public data** Information that is made widely available to all corporate personnel, though with the advent of internal Web technologies, this file share is becoming less and less useful.
- **Departmental data** Information that is widely available to a department and to the services that are located within that department. Once again, this file share is becoming less used in favor of Web-based technologies.
- **Project data** Information that is shared between the members of a project.
- **Software applications** Applications that operate from a central location.
- **Installation sources** Source files for software installed on either servers or PCs.

- **System administration** Special system administration files used by technical and operational personnel.
- **Virtual machines** Host servers will often use shared folders to host virtual machines because of the redundancy advantages the file share offers. Without a file share, automatic backups and file replication features are not available. In many cases, the file share you can rely on for this service is the special administrative share that is automatically generated by Windows during installation. This special share takes the format of *drivename$* where the name of the share is the name of the drive—C, D, E, and so on—and the dollar sign ($) is added to hide it so that users cannot find it when browsing network environments.

As you can see, several of these shares are being replaced with Web technologies, especially Windows SharePoint Services. Most end users are comfortable with the traditional file share and continue to use it even though more innovative technologies are now available to replace this function.

File and folder sharing are supported by two core features: the file system itself and its capability for disk management and the Windows sharing sub-system. The first is the most important in terms of information storage.

About Disks and Volumes

All of the disks you work with, whether they are physical, logical, or virtual, should be formatted with the New Technology File System (NTFS) file system. This is the only file system you should use, because it is the only file system that allows complete control over disk features, especially security features. Since you're running an intelligent operating system, you need to rely on an intelligent file system.

Also, while Windows Server 2008, like its predecessors, supports the ability to manage disk protection mechanisms, such as the random array of independent disks (RAID), through the operating system (OS), you should rely on hardware components to manage disks at this level because using the OS to do so will decrease the performance of your servers.

In Windows, you will encounter several different terms for storage technologies. The most common are:

- **Disks** Disks are the actual hardware components that store data.
- **Volumes** Volumes are logical disk structures that delimit an area of storage on a hard disk.
- **Partitions** Partitions are portions of hard disks that function as though they were separate physical disks.
- **Basic disks** Basic disks are partitions that address only one physical disk. When using hardware-based RAID, the RAID structure can be viewed by Windows as a basic disk, even though it is made up of multiple physical disks.
- **Dynamic disks** Dynamic disks are created in Windows to allow the operating system to manage partitions that span more than one physical disk. Dynamic disks should only be used if you intend to manage disk redundancy through the Windows OS, which is not recommended.
- **Drive letters** Drive letters are used to address disk volumes through the Windows interface.

There are several other disk terms in use in Windows, but these are the terms you will address when working with both resource pools and virtual service offerings.

The one undeniable fact of file storage is that it always increases and rarely needs to shrink. Fortunately, disks are a low-cost commodity today. But since you know that you will probably be expanding the disk storage system at some point in time, it makes sense to use a disk sub-system that can easily accept physical expansions with little or no impact on logical partitions. This is why it is so important to use hardware-based RAID systems, because they free the operating system from low-level disk management tasks. RAID systems are available for both Small Computer System Interface (SCSI) and Serial Advanced Technology Attachment (SATA) disks today, so almost any organization can acquire the appropriate storage infrastructure and use its hardware capabilities to protect data at the disk level.

Structure Disk Volumes for Resource Pools

Whenever you talk file sharing, you need to talk about disk structures. And, with the coming of Hyper-V and the associated division of IT infrastructures into resource pools and virtual service offerings, the disk structure you build becomes more and more important. Resource pools will deal with physical disks since they act at the hardware level. But virtual service offerings will deal with virtual disk drives, which are files that reside on the physical disks used by the resource pool. This means that you need to begin by building and creating your resource pool of physical disks and then, once those are ready, you can build the virtual file servers they will host.

You've already begun this process, but a more in-depth discussion is necessary, one that will focus on the use of shared storage for the host servers. Shared storage is essential for resource pools if you want to build business continuity and high availability into your IT infrastructure. When host servers share disk resources, you can move workloads from one host to another, because both have access to the disk resource where the virtual disk drives making up the virtual machine reside. Of course, you also need to include the failover clustering feature to your host servers, but this will be covered in Chapter 11, where we discuss business continuity practices.

Shared storage means using either network attached storage (NAS) or storage area networks (SAN). Windows Server 2008 can connect to shared storage through SCSI, fiber channel, or Internet Small Computer Systems Interface (iSCSI) interfaces. Each requires its own hardware component to work. But once the shared storage is linked to the server, you begin to work with the disk units created and structured within your shared storage environment. These units will be able to take advantage of the redundancy features available in your shared storage infrastructure. Begin by preparing these structures, then move on to Windows to work with its disk management interfaces.

Since host servers run the Server Core implementation of WS08, you do not have access to the graphical interface enhancements WS08's full installation offers for shared storage management. Instead, you need to rely on command-line tools. One such tool is the `DISKPART.EXE` command. This command lets you control both direct-attached and shared storage. It lets you create initial disk configurations as well as expand disk volumes once they are created. It can either be used interactively, through its own command environment, or it can be scripted by first listing commands in a text file and then calling the text file when you run the command.

You should create a standard disk structure for all physical servers in the resource pool. This structure should include the following:

- **C: Drive** This is the system disk.
- **D: Drive** The shared data storage disk. This disk will host all of the virtual hard drives that make up the virtual service offerings.
- **E: Drive** A secondary shared disk that is used to provide backup services for the contents of the data drive.
- **Y: Drive** The DVD/CDRW server drive.

All of your host servers should use this disk structure. Since all disk volumes can be extended, no other drive letters should be required.

When working with the `DISKPART` command, you'll need to first select the disk, volume, or partition you want to work with, then apply the commands to the selected object. Since it is an execution environment, the best way to obtain help from this command is to first type `DISKPART` at the command prompt; then, once the execution environment is open, type `HELP`. Type `EXIT` to close the `DISKPART` execution environment and return to the command prompt.

Work with your storage manufacturer to determine how you should configure your storage and connect it to your Server Core installations.

NOTE *You should also store the C: drive in your shared disk infrastructure; this way, your blade servers can consist of nothing more than random access memory (RAM), processors, and network interfaces. Using shared-disk infrastructures to store boot drives makes it really easy to provision servers, since you can capture an installation, copy it through the shared disk infrastructure tools, run* `SYSPREP` *on it, and then use it to seed other installations, just like you would with a virtual hard disk drive. The major difference here is that you work with a storage partition inside your shared disk infrastructure, but you get all of the advantages disk abstraction provides when provisioning servers.*

Structure Disk Volumes for Virtual Service Offerings

You should also create a standard disk structure for each server in the VSO. It is similar to the one created for resource pools, but includes some minor differences. This structure should include the following:

- **C: Drive** This is the system disk.
- **D: Drive** The data storage disk.
- **E: Drive** An optional disk for servers hosting database applications as well as for file servers. In the Microsoft world, this includes servers hosting very large Active Directory Domain Services databases (domain controllers), SQL Server, and Exchange. For servers running database applications, this disk is used to store transaction journals. For file servers, this drive is used to support near-term backups.
- **Y: Drive** The DVD/CDRW server drive.

No matter how your server is constructed, it should use this structure for its logical appearance. Since all hard disk drives can be extended, even virtual hard drives, no other drive letters should be required.

On a file server, the disk that requires the most structure is the D: drive, since it is the disk that will store user and group shared data and documents. This disk should include a master folder for each of the different data types identified previously. In addition, it is a good idea to structure the disk folders according to content (see Figure 8-1).

Rely on the following principles when creating the folders in the D: drive:

- First, group information according to content. This means that three top-level folders are required: Data, Applications, and Administration. Each will be used to regroup subfolders that will store similar content.
- Second, use representative folder names. If a folder will be used to store user data, call it UserData.
- Third, use combined words. That is, do not include spaces or special characters between words. If your folder name is User Data, type it as UserData. Unfortunately, there are still some vestiges of NetBIOS in WS08. NetBIOS prefers word strings that do not use spaces or other special characters. Even Web-based technologies prefer folder names that do not include spaces. Spaces also complicate any file paths you may need to reference in scripts or command-line tools by requiring quote marks at the beginning and the end.
- Fourth, name your folders the way you will want to have your shares appear. A good example here is the use of the dollar sign ($) at the end of a folder name. Remember that when you share a folder with the dollar sign at the end, it becomes a "hidden" share; i.e., it cannot be seen through network browsing mechanisms.

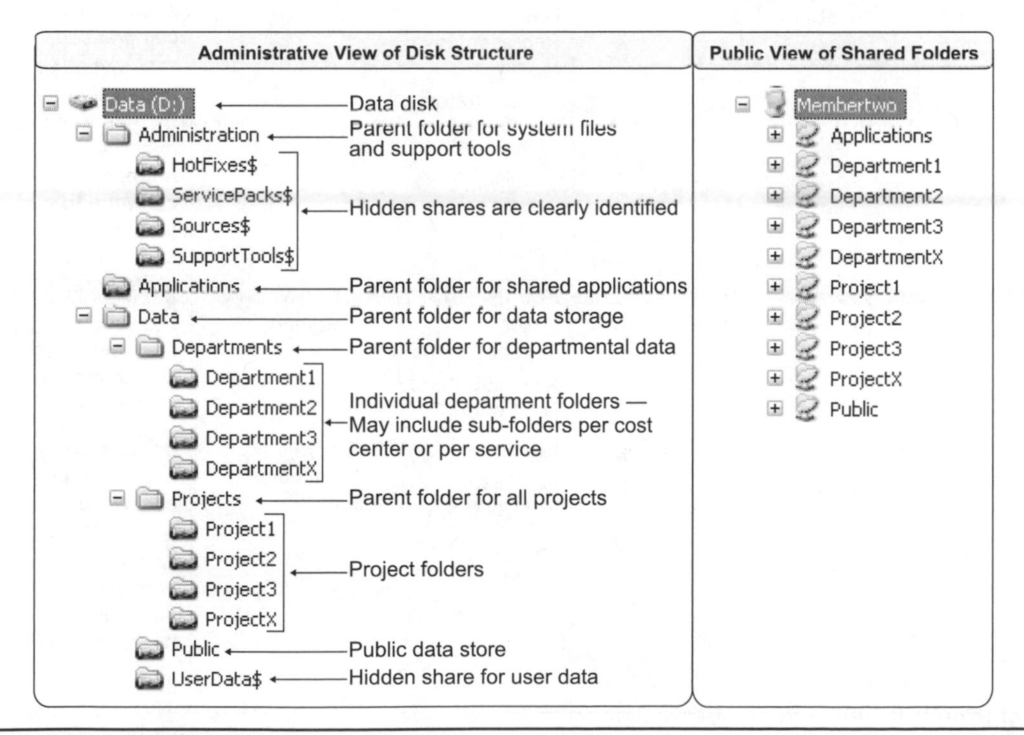

FIGURE 8-1 D: drive folder and share structure

- Fifth, create the same folder structure on all servers that have a file and print vocation, even though you will not share each of the folders on each server. This strategy allows you to quickly activate a folder share when a file server is down. Since each server has the same folder structure, activating a shared folder in an emergency is quick and easy.

Using these guidelines, folders should be created according to the details outlined in Table 8-1.

NTFS Permissions

Windows Server 2008 is similar to previous versions of Windows in that permissions on shared folders are based on a combination of NTFS and shared folder permissions. As such, the same rules apply. This means that since it is complex to manage both file and share

Folder Name	Share Name	Offline Settings	NTFS Permissions	Share Permissions	Comment
Applications	Applications	Automatically Available and Optimized For Performance	Users: Read plus Read and Execute Administrators: Full Control	Everyone: Reader	This folder shares centrally located applications.
Department *n*	Department *n*	User-selected	Department: Read User Representative: Modify Administrators: Full Control	Everyone: Contributor	Data can be encrypted, but should not be compressed. This folder is the main folder for the department; only user representatives can write to this folder and create subfolders.
Project *n*	Project *n*	User-selected	Project members: Modify Administrators: Full Control	Everyone: Contributor	Data can be encrypted, but should not be compressed.
Public	Public	No Caching	Everyone: Modify Administrators: Full Control	Everyone: Contributor	Data should not be either encrypted or compressed. Specific documents or subfolders can be set to read only for most users.

TABLE 8-1 Folder and Share Structure

Folder Name	Share Name	Offline Settings	NTFS Permissions	Share Permissions	Comment
UserData$	UserData$	Automatically Available and Optimized For Performance	Everyone: Modify Administrators: Full Control	Everyone: Contributor	Data can be encrypted, but should not be compressed. This folder will be used to support folder redirection for all users.
HotFixes$	HotFixes$	No caching	Everyone: Read plus Read and Execute Administrators: Full Control	Everyone: Read	Data should not be encrypted or compressed.
ServicePacks$	ServicePacks$	No caching	Everyone: Read plus Read and Execute Administrators: Full Control	Everyone: Read	Data should not be encrypted or compressed.
Sources$	Sources$	No caching	Everyone: Read plus Read and Execute Administrators: Full Control	Everyone: Read	Data should not be encrypted or compressed.
Tools$	Tools$	No caching	Everyone: Read plus Read and Execute Administrators: Full Control	Everyone: Read Administrators team: Contributor	Data should not be encrypted or compressed.

Table 8-1 Folder and Share Structure (*continued*)

PART IV

permissions, it becomes much easier to focus on NTFS permissions, since these are the last permissions applied when users access files through network shares (see Figure 8-2).

Combining shared folder permissions with NTFS permissions can become confusing and difficult to troubleshoot if you mix and match them. In order to simplify the process, you should use only NTFS permissions in most cases, because the most restrictive permissions are always applied.

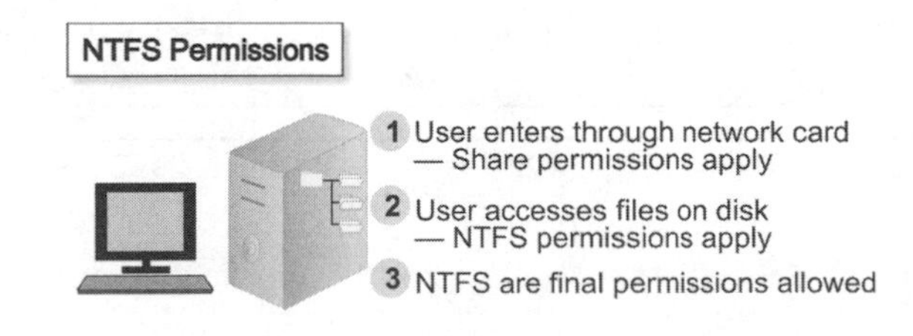
NTFS Permissions
1 User enters through network card — Share permissions apply
2 User accesses files on disk — NTFS permissions apply
3 NTFS are final permissions allowed

Figure 8-2 The file permission process

In Windows Server 2008, there are two primary ways to share a folder. The first is to right-click the folder and select Share. This command opens a File Sharing dialog box, which lists the creator of the folder as its owner. The drop-down list includes two items: Everyone and Find. In most cases, you can assign share rights to the Everyone group, since you will spend more time controlling access through the security or NTFS permissions of the folder. If you need to locate another group, select Find and type the name of the group to locate it in Active Directory Domain Services (ADDS). Once you've selected the right group, click the Add button. Windows Server 2008 automatically assigns the Reader role to the group you added. To change the role, click the drop-down menu to select another one (see Figure 8-3). You can assign the Contributor role, since you control permissions more tightly within the Security tab of the folder's properties. To complete the sharing process, click the Share button. A User Account Control (UAC) prompt will be displayed. Approve the change and click Done when you have completed the operation.

NOTE *Using the File Sharing dialog box does not allow you to change the name of the shared folder.*

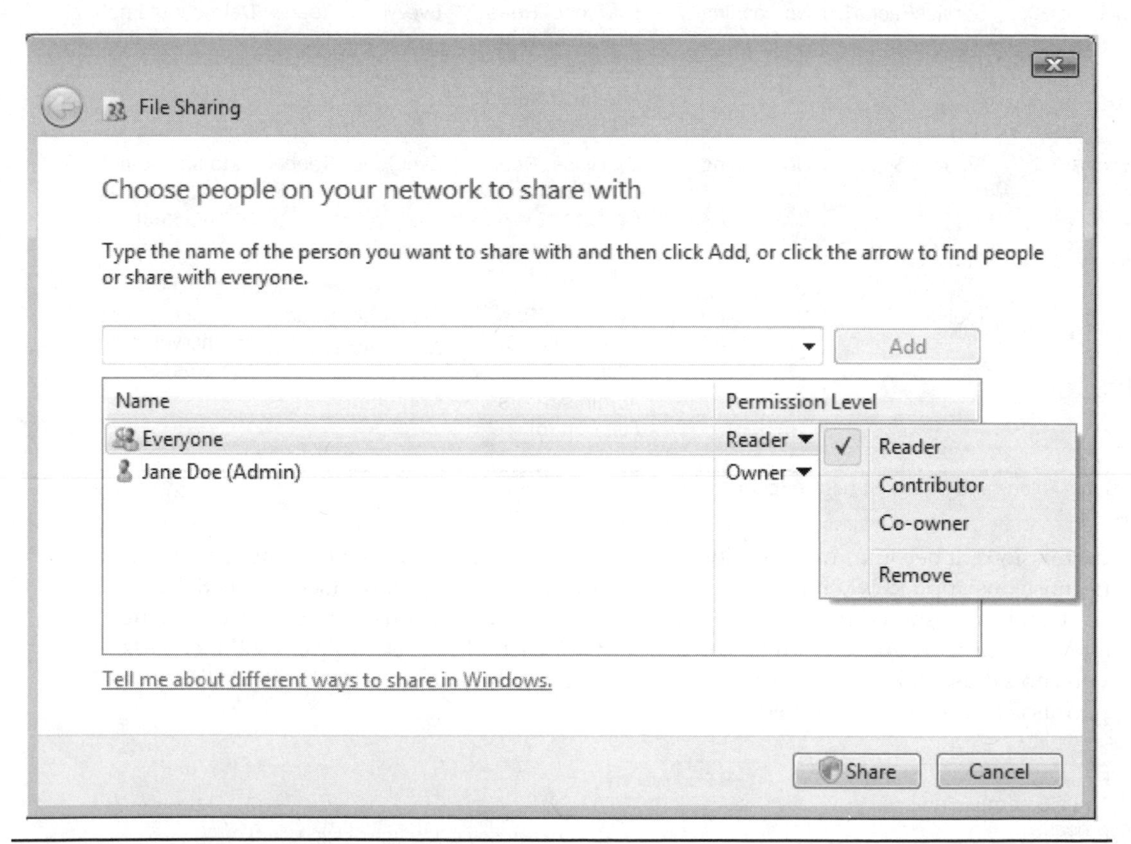

FIGURE 8-3 Assigning shared folder permissions

The second way to share a folder is to do it through the folder's Property dialog box. Right-click the folder and select Properties. Click the Sharing tab and then click Advanced Sharing. Approve the UAC prompt. This displays a new dialog box, which lets you control each of the features of the shared folder in one single location. Select the Share This Folder check box. Now you can change the name of the share, control permissions, and control caching settings. Note that when you share folders in this manner, Windows Server 2008 automatically assigns the same basic permissions to every new shared folder: Everyone Read. *This is different from all previous versions of Windows!* If users need to write to a shared folder, these permissions must be modified to Everyone Change. If not, the most restrictive permissions apply and no one is allowed to write to a shared folder.

CAUTION *It will be important for you to ensure that you take the time to verify shared folder permissions before finalizing the share. Otherwise, you will receive several support calls on non-functioning shares.*

It is quite all right to set share permissions on just about anything to Everyone Change (or Contributor) because NTFS permissions will apply, even though your share permissions are not restrictive. Microsoft set the default behavior of the shared folder process to read-only in order to provide better security for enterprises that did not prepare their NTFS settings beforehand. To be safe from prying users when you share your folders, you should always apply NTFS permissions *before* a share is enabled.

The best practice in terms of shared folder permissions is to set permissions according to the following:

- Set Everyone Read (or Reader) for all shared application folders, installation folders, support tool folders, and so on.
- Set Everyone Change (or Contributor) for all shared data folders, and set appropriate NTFS permissions on a per-folder basis.

There is rarely any need for the Everyone Full Control (or Co-Owner) shared folder permission setting.

CAUTION *It is important to set Everyone Change as the shared folder permissions for the shared folder hosting the redirection of user data. Otherwise, the automatic folder creation process that is enabled whenever the policy applies to a new user will be unable to automatically create the user's data folders.*

Disk Quotas

Another important factor in file sharing is disk quotas. Windows Server 2008 offers a true disk quota management process through the File Server Resource Manager (FSRM). WS08 quota usage is identified by file ownership. This means that you can track a user's total quota usage on a folder-by-folder basis. Quotas can be assigned on specific folders. They can either be definitive or relative. Definitive quotas, sometimes called hard quotas, automatically stop users from storing additional data once the limit has been reached. With a relative or soft quota, you as the administrator will receive a warning when the limit has been reached by the user, but the user will still have the ability to store data on the server.

You'll use the mode that best meets your needs, but since disk space is cheap and it is easy to expand virtual disks, you could aim for the relative quota approach, setting limits and then determining if you will increase this limit for users when warnings arrive.

You can also set automatic quotas, relying on a template to set a quota on a folder. When you do this, the quota template will automatically be applied to every subfolder you create. For example, automatic quotas are ideal for the UserData$ share since they are automatically applied whenever a subfolder for folder redirection is created for a user.

Quotas are values you need to monitor on an ongoing basis, so it is nice to know that WS08 will provide extensive reports on the file resources of your file servers. Not only will it monitor the shared folder usage, but it will also report on usage by user, as well as total available disk space, giving you lots of warning if or when you need to expand the disk used to store shared folder data. Several predefined reports are available: largest files, most used files, recently used files, files by owner, files by group, and much more. Reports can be run interactively or on a scheduled basis.

Quotas will also allow you to perform some form of file screening, making sure users store only acceptable file formats on your servers. For example, you probably prefer that your users not store executable files in their data folders. This can be done through file screening. Once again, this feature relies on templates that are assigned to the file server. As with quotas, you can use a hard or soft policy for file screening, completely blocking users from saving files to a share or simply getting a warning that an unauthorized file type was stored on your server. File screening is not a "be all, end all" system since it relies only on the file extension to work. Sophisticated users can easily rename the extensions of the files they want to store to circumvent the policy. You might consider the performance impact of having your file servers screen each and every file that is stored on them and opt for a written policy instead—a policy that you distribute to end users and that you support with FSRM's powerful reporting capabilities.

Shadow Copies

Windows Server 2008 includes a powerful feature for shared folder support: shadow copies. This feature automatically takes a snapshot of the files located in a shared folder at regular intervals. The shadow copy feature is designed to assist in the process of recovering previous versions of files without having to resort to backups. The shadow copy feature is very much like an "undelete" feature. It is useful for users who often require a return to either a previous version of a file or who accidentally destroy files they still need to use.

WS08 uses a default schedule for creating shadow copies: 7:00 A.M. and noon. If you find that this schedule does not meet your requirements, you can change it. For example, you might prefer to create shadow copies at noon and 5:30 P.M. if your staff tends to start early in the morning. But since you can create up to 512 shadow copies on a server, you can set just about any schedule you need. You should use a separate volume for shadow copies and set the maximum size for the shadow copies on this volume. Using a separate volume will increase the performance of the file server, since it will not need to perform the shadow copy write operation on the same disk as the file shares. Setting a maximum size will ensure that older shadow copies are overwritten when needed and that the disk used to store them will not fill up inadvertently.

Shadow copies are accessed through the Previous Versions tab of a file object's properties. A file object can be a file itself or a folder that stores the file. Users and administrators have access to previous versions so long as they have NTFS access rights to a file or folder.

Each shadow copy takes up 100 megabytes (MB). That's because a shadow copy is not a complete backup of a disk, but rather a copy of the file pointers that identify where a file is located on a disk. When a file is to be overwritten, WS08 uses a write forward process that writes the new version of the file in an empty area of the disk. Shadow copies can be retained as long as the disk has enough free space. Obviously, older versions of a file are eventually overwritten as the disk fills up. To size your shadow copy disk, you can calculate the number of shadow copies you hope to retain based on the schedule you set. For example, if you set a schedule to capture two copies a day for 30 days, you'll need 2 times 30 times 100 MB, or a total of 6 gigabytes (GB). You can usually get away with a 10-GB shadow copy disk.

Shadow copies do not replace backups. In addition, shadow copies are not backed up, so you cannot count on previous versions of a shadow copy. Finally, the shadow copy process is in fact a scheduled task. If you intend to delete the volume on which a shadow copy is performed, begin by deleting the shadow copy scheduled task. Otherwise, the shadow copy process will generate errors in the Event Log.

Shadow Copies for Resource Pools

Shadow copies can provide a first line of defense for host servers since they can let you quickly restore a failed virtual hard drive. Of course, you need to make sure your storage infrastructure works with the shadow copy service or that it doesn't include its own version of a shadow copy or snapshot feature. But if you want to set up shadow copies on the host servers, then you need to add a third partition or disk volume, as indicated earlier in the discussion on host server disk structures. And since host servers run Server Core only, you will need to configure shadow copies through the command line. Use the following commands to do so:

```
vssadmin add shadowstorage /for=D: /on=E: /maxsize=6000mb
vssadmin create shadow /for=D:
vssadmin list shadowstorage
vssadmin list shadows
```

The first command sets up the shadow copies according to the default schedule. The second creates the first shadow copy. The next two list the associations and then available shadow copies.

Shadow copy schedules are scheduled tasks. To control the scheduled task and modify its schedule, rely on the `SCHTASKS.EXE` command. Your shadow copies are ready.

Rely on the Search Service

One of the greatest features of Windows networks in terms of knowledge management is the ability to index data. WS08 can index all sorts of information and documents inside shared folders and on internal and external web sites. Windows Server 2008 relies on the search engine that is included in Windows Vista. PCs running Vista will now be able to rely on the indices generated by the server instead of having to perform all of the indexing on their own, as they did with networks running any previous version of Windows Server.

WS08 also includes the Windows Server 2003 Indexing service for backwards compatibility purposes, but you should always rely on the Search service instead, since it is much more powerful than the Indexing service will ever be.

You can install the Search service as you configure your file server. This service will index documents in the following formats:

- Text
- Hypertext Markup Language (HTML)
- Office 95 and later
- Internet Mail and News
- Any other document for which a filter is available

For example, Adobe Corporation provides an indexing filter for documents in the PDF format. This filter can be found at http://download.adobe.com/pub/adobe/acrobat/win/all/ifilter50.exe. Installing this filter will ensure that all PDF documents will be indexed and searchable. In addition, the Search service can index files for which it doesn't have specific filters. In this case, it will do the best it can, but performance will be slower.

In general, the default settings of the Search service are sufficient for shared folders storing data and documents. This is because even though all documents on a file server are indexed, users will only see the query results for which they have access rights. So even if you have five documents about system administration on a file share, but the user performing the query has access to only one of those, Search will respond with only one query result.

Offline File Caching

By default, each share that is created with Windows Server 2008 is set to allow the user to determine if they want to make the files available offline. Offline file caching allows users to transport files with them if they are using a portable computer or to continue working in the event of a network failure. Through offline files, users actually work on local copies of the files and the Windows Sync Center automatically synchronizes files between the server and the client. Sync Center includes a conflict resolution process, allowing even multiple users to work with offline files without fear of damaging information created by one or the other.

Offline files are part of Microsoft's original zero administration for Windows (ZAW) initiative. One of the basic principles of ZAW was to use processing power wherever it was available; therefore, storing information in a local cache and uploading it to a server when done makes sense. Caching options include:

- **Manual caching** Users specify which files to make available offline (this is the default setting).
- **Automatic caching** This supports either documents or applications and can be optimized for performance.
- **No caching** Offline files are turned off.

Offline files are a boon, especially for mobile users, because they offer local access to files while at the same time allowing central backup and protection of data.

Simple SAN

As outlined in the previous section discussing the implementation and preparation of the resource pool that will run the VSOs, network attached storage is becoming more and more important in organizations of all sizes, because it provides access to shared storage as well as storage virtualization—the abstraction of the physical disk drives from the logical storage structure viewed by your servers. Because of this, Microsoft has added a new feature to the file management infrastructure of Windows Server—it was actually added in Windows Server 2003 R2—a feature called Storage Manager for SANs (SMFS).

SMFS provides a graphical interface for SAN configuration and administration through Server Manager. When you add the File Server role to WS08, you can install this graphical component to provide a direct interface into your SAN's configuration, no matter who the manufacturer is. This provides a single way to maintain SAN environments. But since your hardware infrastructure—the actual infrastructure tied to the SAN—is running only Server Core, you will most likely not rely on SMFS to manage your disk volumes and logical storage units. SMFS does not work on Server Core except through the `DISKPART` and `DISKRAID` commands. Therefore, you should concentrate on these two commands to manage and modify your networked attached storage structures.

Create the File Server

Several processes are involved in the creation of a file server (see Figure 8-4). Each aspect of this installation process needs careful attention to detail.

The first place to start is with the creation of the server itself. Use the process outlined in Chapter 4 to create a basic member server. This server is based on the server kernel, but its primary role will be file sharing. As outlined previously, it will require three disk drives: the system, the data drive, and a drive for shadow copies. Next, you'll want to install the server role on top of the kernel.

FIGURE 8-4 The file server creation process

The File Server Creation Process

1. Install the file server role
2. Create folder structure
3. Apply NTFS permissions
4. Set share protocols
5. Enable quota policy
6. Enable file screen policy
7. Enable shadow copies
8. Enable Search services
9. Create shares through the File Server Resource Management console and Share a Folder wizard
10. Apply share permissions
11. Apply share caching options
12. Publish shares in Active Directory
13. Expose the shares to appropriate groups of users

NOTE *You can also rely on Server Core for this server role, but we think Server Core should really be reserved for the hardware-based Hyper-V role. That is because the full installation offers several advantages over Server Core. First, it provides access to Server Manager and the File Server Resource Manager, something Server Core does not have. Second, it provides access to PowerShell, which lets you automate almost every single task you need to perform. Third, you can secure the full installation as much as you want through the Security Configuration Wizard, which will be covered in Chapter 10. In short, there are few reasons for using Server Core in a virtual machine, especially for this role.*

Install the File Server Role

Once the member server is ready, you can move on to the installation of the File Services role. Once again, you rely on the Add Roles option in Server Manager to perform this task.

1. In the Add Roles Wizard, select the File Services role. Click Next.
2. Click Next again to move to the first configuration screen for the role.
3. In Role Services, select File Server, Distributed File System, and both subsections: File Server Resource Manager and Windows Search Service. If you need to integrate with non-Windows environments, then also select Services For Network File System. Each of these options will be covered later in the chapter. Note how the menu tree on the left of the wizard expands as you select options. Click Next.
4. In the next screen, select Create A Namespace Later Using The DFS Management snap-in In Server Manager. Click Next.
5. In Storage Monitoring, select drive D: and click the Options button (see Figure 8-5).
6. Select each of the monitoring thresholds you want to monitor. As you can see, several canned reports are available. The threshold is 85 percent. You can modify this if you think it is too high. Click OK, then click Next.
7. Under Report Options, store the reports on drive E:\StorageReports, select the Receive Reports By E-mail option, and enter the e-mail addresses to send to as well as the name of the Simple Mail Transfer Protocol (SMTP) server to use. Click Next.

CAUTION *If you use Microsoft Exchange Server as the SMTP server, make sure you include the name of this server in the allowed senders list under the SMTP Relay options.*

8. Under Volumes To Index, select drive D: and click Next.
9. Under Confirmation, review your choices and click Install. Use the Previous button if you need to modify your choices.
10. Click Close when the installation is complete.

Create the Folder Structure

The folder structure is not the same as the shared folder structure because shares are regrouped by content type (see Figure 8-1). You can create shares through the File Services node in Server Manager, but this process works only for one share at a time. Since you need to create a complete folder structure, use Windows Explorer. It will be much faster.

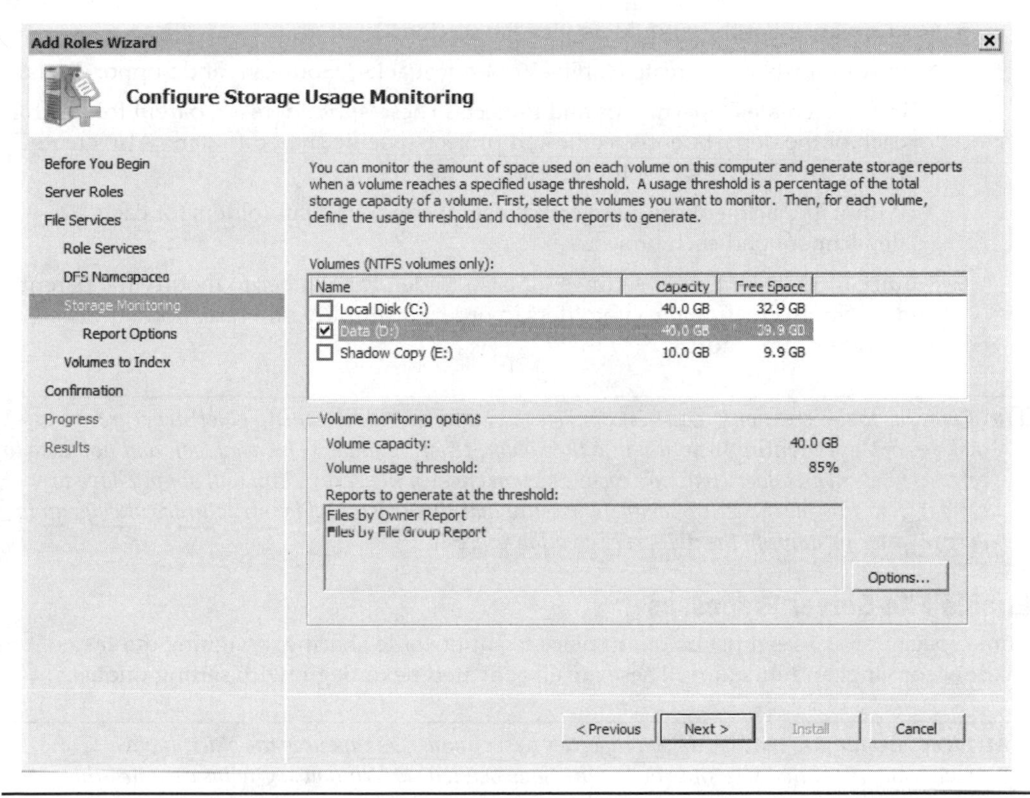

FIGURE 8-5 Configuring storage monitoring options

1. Launch Windows Explorer from the Quick Launch area.
2. In Windows Explorer, navigate to Computer | Data (D:).
3. Begin by creating the top-level folders. Right-click in the details pane, and select New | Folder from the context menu. Name the folder and press ENTER. Create three folders: Administration, Applications, and Data.
4. Next, apply NTFS security settings for each folder. Security settings are applied according to the details in Table 8-1. To do so, right-click each folder name and select Properties. Move to the Security tab. Add the appropriate groups, and assign appropriate security settings to each group. Also, modify the default security settings as per the requirements of Table 8-1. You modify security settings now because they are inherited whenever you create subfolders. Thus, you will only need to fine-tune subfolder security settings from now on instead of re-creating them all.

5. Next, create all of the subfolders for each section:
   - In Administration, create HotFixes$, ServicePacks$, Sources$, and SupportTools$.
   - In Data, create Departments and Projects. These subfolders are parent folders for each of the department-specific and project-specific shared folders. Also create Public and UserData$ at this level.
   - Within Departments and Projects, create the required subfolders for each department and each project.
6. Modify the NTFS security settings for each folder. Remember to modify the parent folders before creating the subfolders in order to simplify your creation process. Your folders are ready.

TIP *Once the folder creation process is complete, create a new folder called FolderStructure. Then make a copy of the entire structure into the FolderStructure folder. This way, you will not have to re-create the entire folder structure each time you create a file server. You will simply have to copy it from this file structure template. Ensure that this master folder structure is always up to date in order to simplify the file server creation process.*

Enable File Server Processes

Three special processes must be put in place to support file sharing: assigning quotas, shadow copying, and indexing. These are all activated next. Begin with setting quotas.

CAUTION *Do not use the disk drive properties to set quotas, as this uses the older quota management tool that was included in previous versions of Windows. Quotas assigned this way only affect the specific volume to which they are attached.*

1. Go to Server Manager and navigate to the Roles | File Services | Share and Storage Management | File Server Resource Management | Quota Management | Quotas node.
2. Right-click the D: drive in the details pane, and select Edit Quota Properties.
3. Since this is the first time you use quotas on this server, we recommend you begin with a soft quota. Under the Copy properties from the Quota Template drop-down list, select Monitor 200 GB Volume Usage, and click the Copy button. This assigns a monitor-only quota to the entire drive. Note the changes in the Notification Thresholds area of the dialog box.
4. Move to the Space Limit area, and change the limit to the actual size of your D: drive.
5. Click OK.

Quotas are assigned to the entire drive. You can remove quotas from specific folders by editing their properties. Move on to setting up shadow copies for this drive.

1. Move to Windows Explorer again, and right-click the D: drive to select Configure Shadow Copies.
2. Before enabling this feature, you must modify the drive that will store shadow copies. To do so, click the Settings button. In the new dialog box, use the drop-down list to

select the E: drive. Set the limit for the copy as appropriate—usually 6 GB is enough—and change the schedule if required. Click OK when done.

3. The default schedule is at 7:00 A.M. and noon, five days per week. If this schedule is not appropriate, click the Schedule button to modify it. This is a scheduled task. Its scheduling features are the same as with all scheduled tasks.
4. Click the Enable button to activate shadow copies.
5. WS08 will give you a warning about enabling this feature. Click Yes to close it. Click OK to close the Shadow Copy dialog box once the first shadow copy is created.

Shadow copies are ready for this volume. Next, set the indexing or search options.

1. Use the Start menu to open Control Panel. In Classic view, double-click the Indexing Options icon. In Vista view, navigate to System and Maintenance, and click Change How Windows Searches under Indexing Options.
2. If you want to change the indexed locations, click Modify. However, these should be fine, since you set them when installing the File Services role. To set indexing options, click the Advanced button. Accept the UAC prompt if it appears.
3. If you intend to encrypt user files, select the Index Encrypted Files option. Also, if there is a chance your users work in other languages, select the Treat Similar Words With Diacritics As Different Words option. This lets the Search tool know there are different languages in your data.
4. Next, click the Select New button to move the location of the index. It should be located on the E: drive under a new Search folder.

NOTE *You will have to stop and restart the Search service once you are done here to perform the actual move. Moving the index from the system drive will make it much more efficient.*

5. Next, move to the File Types tab. You can use this tab to add new file types to index. For example, you can add the PDF extension to index Adobe Acrobat files.
6. Type **PDF** into the bottom of the dialog box, click Index Properties and File Contents, and then click Add New Extension. Repeat the process to add other extensions—for example, CAD drawings. Click OK to close the Advanced dialog box and close the Indexing Options dialog box.
7. Now restart the service to move the index location. Return to Server Manager, and move to the Configuration | Services node. Locate the Windows Search service and restart it.

Now your server is ready to share folders.

Share Folders

The next stage involves creating the shares themselves, setting share permissions, and setting caching options for each share. Everything is performed through the Server Manager.

NOTE *You use the Server Manager console because it gives you access to every server management feature. The File Server Resource Management stand-alone console is mostly useful for file server management delegation purposes.*

1. Go to Server Manager and navigate to the Roles | File Services | Share and Storage Management node.
2. Click Provision Share in the actions pane.
3. In the Provision A Shared Folder Wizard, click drive D: and then click Browse.
4. This opens a dialog box that lists all of the hidden shares on the server. Click D$ and navigate to the folder you want to share—for example, Data\UserData$. Click OK and click Next.
5. You don't need to change NTFS settings, so click Next.
6. For Windows users, click SMB to share the folder. This enables server message block (SMB) shares, which is the Windows default. If you are using UserData$, you do not need to change the share name.
7. For non-Windows users, click NFS. This enables the Network File System (NFS), which lets UNIX and Macintosh users access your shares. If you are using UserData$, change the share name to UserData by removing the dollar sign at the end of the name.

NOTE *You cannot use the same share name twice.*

8. Click Next. Add a description to your share, and note its settings. There is no user limit by default, access-based enumeration or the enumeration of network shares based on user access rights is on by default, and offline settings are set to the default. In the case of UserData$, you need to change this last setting. Click Advanced.
9. Move to the Caching tab, and select All Files And Programs That Users Open From The Share Are Automatically Available Offline. Also make sure that Optimized For Performance is selected. Click OK and then click Next.
10. In the next page, select Full Control for administrators and Read Access and Write Access for all other users and groups. Click Next.
11. If you are sharing this folder for non-Windows users, you will have an NFS page displayed. Modify the access rights to grant read-write access to all machines. Click All Machines and click Edit. Make sure you are using the right encoding method, and click the drop-down list to select Read-Write. Click OK, and click Next.

CAUTION *Do not allow anonymous access, as it gives too much access to this share.*

12. On this page, you can apply a custom quota to this share if you need to. Otherwise, click Next.
13. Now you can apply a file screen if you need to. However, file screens are not recommended because they are easy to circumvent and they take up a lot of server resources. Click Next.

14. The next screen lets you publish this share into a Distributed File System (DFS) namespace. No namespaces have been set up yet, so click Next.
15. Review your settings and click Create to create the share. Click Close when done.

As you can see, this is a lot of work. Fortunately, there are a lot of ways to speed up this process.

You're almost done. Now, the only thing left is to make the shares available to users. This is done through Active Directory Domain Services (ADDS).

Publish Shares in Active Directory Domain Services

Shares are published in ADDS to simplify their access by users. Users can search the directory to locate the shares they require access to, reducing the requirement for mapping shares in logon scripts. You may still need to add share mapping in logon scripts for legacy purposes, but at least your users can start working with Windows' new features.

1. Move to a domain controller, and open the Active Directory Users and Computers console in Server Manager.
2. If it isn't already done, create a new organizational unit structure and name it Virtual Service Offerings (VSO). Under Virtual Service Offerings, create a new OU named File and Print (see Figure 8-6). Then create an OU under File and Print, and call it File Shares.

CAUTION *When you create an object in ADDS, you can protect it from accidental deletion. This locks the object! Once an object is locked, you cannot delete it, you cannot move it, and you cannot change it unless you open its properties first and clear the protection option on the Object tab. Note that you must use the Advanced Features in the View menu to see the Object tab in the object's properties.*

PART IV

FIGURE 8-6 Creating protected objects in ADDS

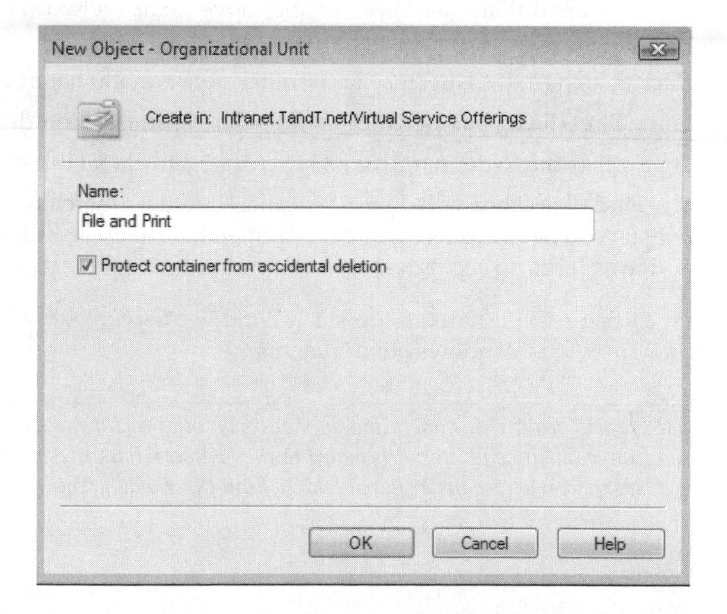

3. Within the File Shares OU, create new shares. To do so, move to the details pane and right-click to select New | Shared Folder from the context menu.
4. Type the name of the share and the path to the shared folder using the Universal Naming Convention (UNC) format. Click OK when done. Repeat for all the shares you need to publish.

CAUTION *Do not publish hidden shares because they will no longer be hidden. Any share that is published in Active Directory Domain Services (ADDS) will be visible to users.*

5. Once the shares are created, you will need to add a description and keywords to each. Folder descriptions are important, since they will serve to tell users the purpose of the shared folder. Keywords are also useful because users can search for shared folder by keyword instead of share name. To enter both, view the properties of each shared folder in ADDS.
6. Use this dialog box to add complete descriptions to each share and to identify its manager. To add keywords, click the Keywords button. Type the keyword and click Add. Click OK when done.
7. You should also assign a manager for each share. Do this through the Managed By tab. Assigning managers is a good practice, since they become responsible for the evolution and perhaps eventual removal of this share when it is no longer needed. Close the dialog box when done. Repeat for each share you publish in ADDS.

Your shares are now ready for access by users.

Find Shares in Active Directory Domain Services

Finding shares is performed through Windows Explorer's Search function.

1. To do so, open Windows Explorer and move to the Network node on either Windows Vista or WS08.
2. Click Search Active Directory in the quick access menu bar at the top of the window.
3. In the Find dialog box, select Shared Folders from the Find drop-down menu.
4. Type either the folder name or its keywords, and click Find Now.
5. The Find dialog box will display the shared folders matching the search criteria so long as you have access rights to it—remember the Access-Based Enumeration option you set. To access a shared folder, double-click its name.

As you can see, using shared folders in a Windows Server 2008 network is considerably easier than in previous Windows environments.

TIP *Your users will require this operation only once, because each time a new shared folder is accessed from a client computer, it is added to the Network Favorites portion of Windows Explorer. Users can access their shared folders from there when required.*

Manage Folder Availability

Though they are fully supported, mapped drives are no longer an orientation in Windows Server 2008. It is the UNC that is the favored method of rendering shared folder access. This method is based on a \\Servername\sharename naming structure. But there are features of mapped drives that cannot be rendered by a simple UNC name. For example, since a mapped drive is usually created through a logon script, it is easy for administrators to change the address or target of the mapped drive overnight, an operation that is completely transparent to users. As long as they are concerned, the K: drive remains the K: drive no matter where it connects.

Because of this, mapped drives support operational tasks, such as replacing servers and moving shared folders. They are not without problems, though. For example, ever since version 97, Microsoft Office tracks the UNC behind the mapped drive, making it difficult to use conventional drive mappings. If you change this UNC, then Office complains.

And with the advent of Windows Installer–compatible software, the UNC is becoming more and more important. For self-healing purposes, Windows Installer must remember the original installation source of a program. It prefers a UNC format to a mapped drive for this function, though you can control this by editing the Windows Installer package.

This is one reason why Microsoft has developed technologies that support fault tolerance for UNC shares. One main technology is DFS. It can be used to provide many of the same administrative advantages of mapped drives, but without their use.

Work with the Distributed File System

The preferred technology for fault tolerance of file shares is the distributed file system. DFS offers several enterprise features for the support and administration of file shares:

- DFS creates a file share *alias* that is unique and through which users can access files on a server. This means that you can change the target file share without affecting users because they access the alias and not the physical file server.
- The DFS alias does not only apply to file shares, it can also be applied to *Web server addresses*, allowing you to modify background Web servers without affecting use of your internal or external Web applications.
- DFS provides fault tolerance through its integration with Active Directory Domain Services. Since DFS *namespaces*, or aliases, are published in the directory, they are always available to users.
- DFS namespaces can be linked to any number of actual physical file shares. This is called *DFS namespace replication*. If a server must be shut down for any reason, users continue to work by being redirected by DFS to another physical server.
- DFS can provide load balancing by distributing file access to a number of physical locations, or *targets*.
- DFS provides transparent consolidation of distributed file shares. If files for a given department are distributed on several physical servers, then DFS can make it appear as if they are all located within a single *virtual DFS structure*.
- DFS is *site-aware*; that is, that it can identify ADDS sites and use them to redirect users to a file server located within their site. DFS is ideal for distributing file shares that span regions.

- DFR provides *block-level compressed delta replication*. It will synchronize the contents of different file share targets by replicating only the changed blocks within a file, not the entire file. By contrast, the File Replication Service (FRS) replicates entire files, even though only a byte of information has changed within them.
- Finally, DFS clients can cache *referrals* for DFS roots or links for a definable period of time, improving performance by accessing resources without having to perform an AD lookup.

The Distributed File System works in conjunction with DFS Replication system (DFSR) in Windows Server 2008 to provide fault tolerance and link-tracking features. DFS namespaces that are integrated with ADDS are named *domain DFS namespaces*.

DFS is extremely powerful. For example, if your developers need to work in different environments when preparing corporate applications, as discussed in Chapter 5, they can take advantage of DFS by creating a DFS root for development purposes in the development environment. When it is time to deploy the application into production, they do not have to modify paths within the code.

Another example is the source file for all installations and for the support of Windows Installer features, such as self-healing. By using DFS namespaces, you can have one single installation source path that is available in all sites and that automatically replicates all of the source files from site to site.

You can also work with stand-alone DFS namespaces. These namespaces do not profit from ADDS for redundancy. Because of this, you must run them on failover server clusters or groups of servers that run the same services and that can fail those services over from one to another to provide service continuity. Most organizations run domain-based namespaces since ADDS already exists and they are simpler to set up. Domain-based namespaces are also fault-tolerant at the site level. It is much more complicated to make stand-alone namespaces fault-tolerant at the site level. Use a decision tree to determine which type of namespace you need to work with (see Figure 8-7).

Install a Domain DFS Namespace

Begin by installing the domain DFS namespace. Perform this action on a server running the File Services role with DFS, DFS Namespaces, and DFS Replication. You need domain administrator credentials to create a domain DFS root, though you can delegate this management task to other groups through the action pane.

1. Launch the Server Manager, and go to the File Services | DFS Management node.
2. Click New Namespace in the actions pane.
3. In the New Namespace Wizard, enter the information found in Table 8-2.
4. Complete the wizard pages.

The DFS namespace root is ready. Now you can add root hosts as well as targets for the root.

CAUTION *Domain DFS roots should be hosted on member servers and not domains. If you host the DFS root on both member servers and DCs, clients will be directed to the domain controller if the names are the same. In addition, DFS roots are more secure on member servers.*

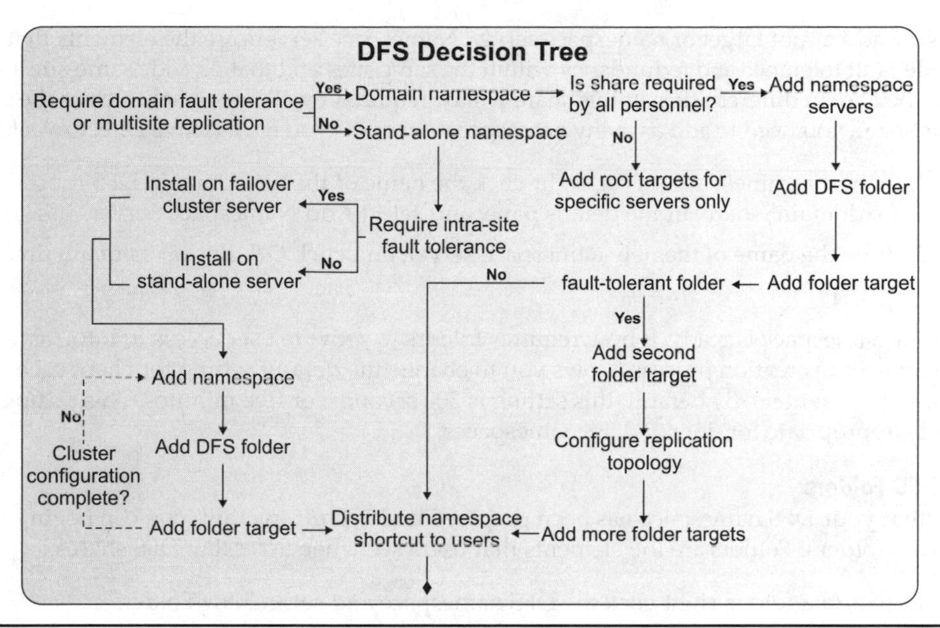

FIGURE 8-7 The DFS decision tree

Wizard Page	Entry
Namespace Server	Enter the name of the server to host the namespace. This server can be a domain controller (DC) or a member server. A member server is recommended. Use the file server you are creating to host the namespace.
Namespace Name and Settings	Name the namespace. Use a common name that will not be duplicated within the enterprise. For example, for the public share, use Public as the root name. Use the Edit Settings button to set share permissions (see Table 8-1) and point to the appropriate shared folder source. For example, for the public share, go to D:\Data\Public. You will get a warning that the existing share will be used. Click Yes to use the existing share with existing permissions.
Namespace Type	Assign a domain-based namespace because it provides the best and simplest fault tolerance, and enable WS08 mode to increase scalability and enable access-based enumeration.
Review Settings and Create Namespace	Review your settings and create the namespace. Close the wizard when done.

TABLE 8-2 New Namespace Wizard Entries

Now add a root target or namespace server. Namespace servers are the elements that provide fault tolerance and redundancy within the same sites and that provide same-site access when they are in different sites. If this share will be required by all personnel, such as the Public share, you need to add as many namespace servers as you have Active Directory sites.

1. To add a namespace server, right-click the name of the new domain DFS root (\\domain\share) in the details pane, and select Add Namespace Server.
2. Type the name of the new namespace server, and click OK. Repeat as many times as required.

Your namespace is ready. It now requires folders to provide user access to information. The namespace creation process allows you to change the default setting for client caching of namespace targets. By default, this setting is 300 seconds, or five minutes. This setting is usually appropriate for domain DFS namespaces.

Add DFS Folders

Now that your DFS namespace has been prepared and is fault-tolerant, you can begin to add DFS folders. Folders are the elements that users see when accessing DFS shares.

1. To add a folder, right-click the DFS namespace and select New Folder.
2. In the New Folder dialog box, type the name of the folder. The UNC path to the shared folder will be filled in automatically.
3. Since this is a fault-tolerant folder, you will need to add new folder targets to the initial folder. Targets make the shared folder redundant. To add a target, click the Add button in the New Folder dialog box.
4. Either type the UNC path to the shared folder or use the Browse button to locate the appropriate share. Click OK when done. Note that you can create a share from this dialog box if you need to.
5. Now add a second target for the folder. Repeat steps 3 and 4 to do so, but make sure you place it on another server. Click OK to close the New Folder dialog box.
6. Because you added at least two targets, DFS suggests that you configure a replication group for the shares within the folder. In the Replication message box, click Yes to launch the Replicate Folder Wizard. Use the values in Table 8-3 to fill out this wizard.

The folder creation process allows you to change the default setting for client caching of folder targets. By default, this setting is 1800 seconds, or 30 minutes. This setting is usually appropriate for DFS folders.

DFS Clients

Clients can view DFS shares in the same way they view standard shared folders: through network locations. But the best way to give access to domain DFS roots to clients is to send them a shortcut to the root. The advantage of the DFS alias is that it is not tied to a single server, but rather to the domain as a whole. The shortcut must point, not to a server UNC, but to a domain UNC. For example, in this case, the domain UNC would be: \\Intranet.TandT.net\Public.

The domain DFS root is listed as a component of the entire network.

Wizard Page	Entry
Replication Group and Replicated Folder Name	These entries should already be filled in by the wizard. You can change the name of the group if you wish to.
Replication Eligibility	Folder targets and eligibility should already be entered.
Primary Member	Select the server that contains the original data to be replicated. This will be the source server.
Topology Selection	Three topology choices are available (see Figure 8-8). Select Hub and Spoke if your servers are located in different sites and your wide area network (WAN) includes links at differing speeds. The T&T WAN example used in Chapter 5 is an example of a hub-and-spoke replication topology. You will need to identify the hub server if you select this replication topology. This should be the central server. You need three or more targets to be able to select this topology. Select Full Mesh if the servers staging the share are all in the same site and are connected with high-speed links or if your WAN links are all at the same speed. Do not select this topology it you have more than ten servers acting as targets. Select No Topology if you want to configure your own replication topology later.
Replication Group Schedule and Bandwidth	Two choices are available for replication scheduling. If you choose Continuous Replication, you have access to bandwidth controls. Choose the proper bandwidth setting based on the speed of the links that bind the targets together. If you do not want replication to occur continuously, then select specified days and times, and edit the schedule to suit your needs.
Review Settings and Create Replication Group	Review your settings. Use the Previous button to modify choices. Click Create when ready.
Confirmation	Close the wizard when done. You will get a Replication Delay message when you do so. This advises you that replication cannot begin until the configuration changes have been picked up by all group members.

Table 8-3 Entries for the Replicate Folder Wizard

The shortcut can be made available to users through the logon script. By double-clicking the shortcut, users have access to all of the published folders in the namespace, and this access is independent of the location of the user. In fact, the server they are connected to is completely transparent to users.

If you want your users to use the DFS links instead of standard shared folders, you should name all of your actual shared folders with a dollar sign (for example: Server$). This will hide your actual shares from being displayed on the network. Users will then only see DFS shares and not actual shares.

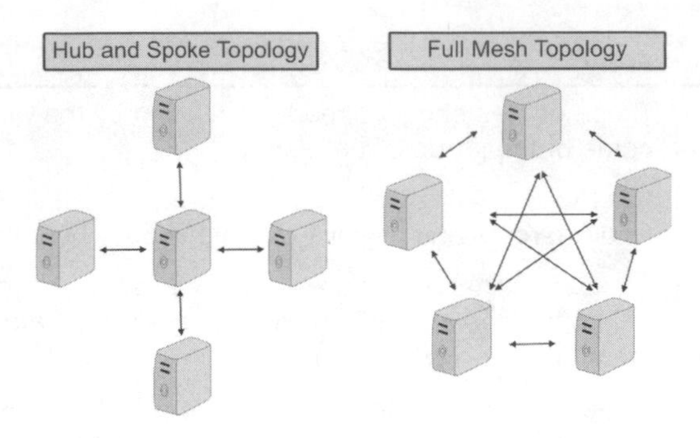

FIGURE 8-8 FRS replication topologies

TIP *For more information on DFS, go to the step-by-step guide for DFS on WS08 at http://technet2.microsoft.com/windowsserver2008/en/library/cf810bb7-51ed-4535-ab0d-86a7cd862e601033.mspx?mfr=true.*

Use DFS Replication for Resource Pools

As mentioned earlier, DFS replication (DFSR) is an ideal tool to provide fault tolerance for the VSOs supported by your resource pools. Since a VSO is nothing but a series of files on a server, you can rely on DFSR to provide a second line of defense for the protection of your virtual service offerings. DFSR can replicate the contents of the virtual hard disk drives that make up your VSOs. In the event of a failure at one site, you can simply use the copied VSO in the second site to restart the service and ensure your end users are up and running. More on this will be discussed in Chapter 11, but for now, it is important for you to understand how to set up DFSR on Server Core.

First, begin by installing the DFSR component on your server:

```
start /w ocsetup DFSR-Infrastructure-ServerEdition
```

This adds the required components to run DFSR. Make sure you install this component on each host server, both in the source site and in the target or disaster recovery site. Next, configure replication groups:

```
dfsradmin RG New /rgname:"ReplicationGroupName" /rgdesc:"Description"
dfsrAdmin RG Set Schedule full /RGName:"ReplicationGroupName"
dfsradmin member new /rgname:"ReplicationGroupName" /memname:FirstServerName
dfsradmin member new /rgname:"ReplicationGroupName" /memname:SecondServerName
dfsradmin conn new /rgname:"ReplicationGroupName" /SendMem:FirstServerName
/RecvMem:SecondServerName /ConnEnabled:true /ConnKeywords:"From First Server to
Second Server"
dfsradmin RF New /rgName:"ReplicationGroupName" /RfName:FolderName
dfsradmin Membership Set /RgName:"ReplicationGroupName" /RfName:FolderName
/MemName:FirstServerName /LocalPath:D:\vsmachines /MembershipEnabled:true
/StagingPath:E:\staging /StagingSize:1000 /CDSize:350 /IsPrimary:true
```

Where *ReplicationGroupName* is the name of your replication group and *FirstServer* and *SecondServer* are the names of the servers in the group. *FolderName* is the name of the folder to be replicated. For example, you could store all of your VSOs into a folder named D:\vsmachines.

The first command creates the replication group. The second adds the default schedule. The third and fourth add two servers to the group, and the fifth command creates the connection object from server one to server two. The sixth command identifies the folder to replicate. In this case, it could be VSMachines. The last command sets server one as the primary source for the replication.

TIP *For a short document describing the* `DFSRADMIN.EXE` *command, go to www.microsoft.com/downloads/details.aspx?familyid=49caf978-49e9-4eb6-9cc9-72b5dd160505&displaylang=en.*

To troubleshoot DFSR connections in Server Core, rely on the `DFSRDIAG.EXE` command. Repeat these commands on each host server you want to protect.

TIP *You do not need to match replication servers on a one-to-one basis. For example, you can have ten host servers protected by only five in the disaster recovery site. More on this will be covered in Chapter 11, but for now, it is important that you understand that disaster recovery sites do not need to have the same operating levels as production environments. Keep this in mind as you prepare your replication strategies.*

Folder Redirection and Offline File Settings

Folder redirection was discussed in Chapter 7. It lets you redirect folders for users so that all of their data is protected by being located on a server instead of on a PC. Up to ten folders can be redirected on WS08 and Windows Vista (see Table 8-4).

Rely on these recommended settings to prepare your folder redirection GPO. Folder redirection settings are found in the User Configuration | Policies | Windows Settings | Folder Redirection node of a Group Policy.

Enable Folder Redirection

There are special considerations when enabling folder redirection. First, you need to ensure that each user is redirected to the appropriate server. It wouldn't do to have a user in New York redirected to a server in Los Angeles. You must create special administrative groups that can be used to regroup users and ensure that each user is assigned to the appropriate server. You must also ensure that offline settings are appropriately configured to guarantee that users are working with the latest version of their offline files.

Redirecting folders through user groupings is, in fact, similar to creating regional, or rather, geographically based user groups. Since each server is, in fact, a physical location, you will need to create a user group for each server. Remember to create global groups to contain the users and assign the permissions. Begin by enumerating the location of each file server that will host user folders, then name each global and domain local group accordingly. Once the groups are created, you can begin the redirection process. Using groups allows you to limit the number of GPOs required for the People OU structure.

1. In your Global People GPO, move to User Configuration | Policies | Windows Settings | Folder Redirection.
2. Right-click the folder you want to redirect, and select Properties.
3. Under the Target tab, select Advanced - Specify Different Locations For Various User Groups, and then click Add.

Profile Type	Comments
AppData (Roaming)	This folder contains all roaming application data. Redirecting this folder will also support Windows XP clients with limitations.
Desktop	Users should not store data or any other items on their desktops; they should rely on the Quick Launch menu instead. This reduces the size of the folder to redirect. Include this in your communications to them. Redirecting this folder will also support Windows XP clients.
Start Menu	The contents of the Start menu are redirected. If you use application virtualization, then users will always have access to their applications on any PC, even if they are not installed. Redirecting this folder will also support Windows XP clients.
Documents	This contains all user data. Make sure your storage policy and quotas support today's large file sizes and give users enough room to breathe. Redirecting this folder will also support Windows XP clients. Applying this policy to pre-Vista operating systems will automatically configure the Pictures, Music, and Videos folders to follow the Documents folder, even if they are not configured.
Pictures	Determine if your organization wants to protect this folder. If you do, use the Follow The Documents Folder option or rely on the setting in Documents. Redirecting this folder will also support Windows XP clients.
Music	Determine if your organization wants to protect this folder. If you do, use the Follow The Documents Folder option or rely on the setting in Documents. Using this option will also support Windows XP clients.
Videos	Determine if your organization wants to protect this folder. If you do, use the Follow The Documents Folder option or rely on the setting in Documents. Using this option will also support Windows XP clients.
Favorites	Only applies to Vista.
Contacts	Only applies to Vista. If you are using Outlook, then this Contacts folder is not necessary.
Downloads	Only applies to Vista. You will need to determine if your organization wants to protect downloads users obtain from the Internet.
Links	Only applies to Vista.
Searches	Only applies to Vista.
Saved Games	Only applies to Vista. The contents of this folder are small and apply mostly to the games included in Vista. Your organization will need to determine if you want to spend network bandwidth and storage space on this content.

TABLE 8-4 Recommended Folder Redirection Settings

4. In the Specify Group and Location dialog box, type the group (using the down-level group name; i.e., domain\groupname) or click Browse to find the appropriate group.
5. Under Target Folder Location, select Create A Folder For Each User Under The Root Path.
6. Under Root Path, type the UNC path to the share name or click Browse to locate it.
7. Click OK to return to the Properties dialog box. Repeat for each group and server location you need to enter. Move to the Settings tab.
8. Under Policy Removal, select Return The Folder Back To The Local User Profile Location When Policy Is Removed. This will ensure that redirected folders return to original locations if, for some reason, the policy is removed.
9. You can also control how the settings will be applied. Note that the first two settings are selected by default. If you have down-level clients, then also select the Also Apply Redirection Policy setting. Click OK when done.
10. Perform the same operation for each of the other folders, and set them according to the recommendations of Table 8-4. Note that for the Documents folder, you have additional options and can set Pictures, Videos, and Music folders to automatically inherit the Documents settings.

Your folder redirection policy is set. Your file servers are ready to host user data. Rely on Chapter 12 to migrate this data.

Share Print Services

The Print server has greatly evolved with the latest editions of Windows Sever. WS08 now supports version 3 print drivers. Version 3 drivers are designed to integrate more properly with the operating system to provide better fault tolerance. One of the great advantages of version 3, or user-mode, print drivers is that when the printer driver fails, it does not require a server restart, but only a print spooler restart. In fact, WS08 can automatically restart the print spooler on a failure, making the failure transparent to the majority of the users connected to the printer.

Drivers can be either user-mode or kernel-mode. In Windows NT, drivers were moved to kernel mode because kernel-mode drivers provided better performance. Kernel-mode drivers are version 2 drivers. But a faulty kernel-mode driver can crash the entire kernel, or rather, the entire server. To provide better performance and reliability, WS08 drivers are now moved to user mode. In Windows Server 2008, a default Group Policy blocks the installation of version 2 drivers.

In addition, user-mode drivers allow users to set their own printing preferences, something that was an issue in Windows NT. Since the drivers operated in kernel mode, they did not provide the ability to separate user printing preferences from default driver configurations, causing a lot of frustration in the Windows NT user market. WS08, like Windows 2000, offers the ability to set printing defaults for the shared printer, as well as printing preferences for each user of the shared resource.

Printing preferences are separate from the printer properties, but are derived from the defaults you set. For example, if you use a double-sided printer and you set its default properties to double-sided output, the user's default preferences will be double-sided printing, but the user now has the choice to modify the setting for their own personal environment to single-sided without affecting general settings for other users. It is surprising how many organizations use double-sided printers but set the default print spooler setting to single-sided, forcing conscientious users to manually reset their preferences. One of the most important aspects of a shared printer implementation in any organization is the establishment of an enterprise-level shared printer policy. This policy should include elements such as default settings for all printers. A sample shared printer policy is outlined in the sections that follow.

TIP *With the greening of today's datacenters, every printer should print double-sided and all of your default printer configurations should make use of this paper-saving technique.*

WS08 Printer Drivers

WS08, like Windows 2000, uses three core printer drivers: the Unidriver, PostScript, and a Plotter driver. Each of these drivers provides the core printer protocol. Along with the core drivers, Windows Server 2008 calls upon a specific printer definition for each printer in your organization. This vastly simplifies the driver development process because all driver structures are standardized. These core drivers have been defined in conjunction with independent hardware vendors to ensure stability and robustness.

Another advantage of this shared development process is that drivers can be certified. A certified driver is a driver that conforms to the Microsoft "Designed for Windows" logo guidelines. Certified drivers are all version 3 drivers, which include a digital certificate that is used for code-signing purposes. Digitally signed drivers ensure their reliability. Your shared printer policy should be based on digitally signed and, therefore, certified drivers.

The Microsoft Hardware Compatibility List (HCL) web site lists all of the products that have been certified as designed for Windows. You should use this site when selecting new printers or other hardware components for your organization. If you want little trouble with your shared printer pool, only use printers that include "Designed for Windows" drivers. When you install printer drivers, Windows will indicate if the driver is digitally signed or not. The Add Printer Wizard dialog box even includes a link to the HCL web site. If you are running the 64-bit versions of WS08, you'll have to have certified drivers.

TIP *The Microsoft Hardware Compatibility List web site is at www.microsoft.com/whdc/hcl/default.mspx.*

But if your current printer pool includes a number of older printers, it is obvious that you will not be able to include only certified drivers in your shared printer policy. Try your best to use only certified drivers (updated versions are included in WS08 and may be available from your vendor), but if you can't, then consider a printer obsolescence strategy that will gradually replace older printers with new engines that include better support for the Windows operating system.

Integration with Active Directory Domain Services

Full support for the Windows operating system today also means integration with Active Directory Domain Services. Each shared printer is now published within the directory, much in the same way file and DFS shares are. Printers are published in the directory by default.

Their object names are stored in their parent domain. Users can use the directory to search for printers and automatically connect to the appropriate printing service.

ADDS stores information about printer features and locations. Locations are especially important, since it is one of the best ways for users to find printers within your network. Descriptions are also important, since these are also included in the elements users have access to when searching for printers in the directory.

Users now search for printers in much the same way as they search for file shares: through the Active Directory Search tool. They can search based on printer name, printer location, or model. They can also search based on features such as double-sided printing, stapling, color output, and resolution.

Windows Server 2008 supports Printer Location Tracking. This component is based on the Active Directory Domain Services site topology you designed in Chapter 5. One of the key elements of the site topology is the subnet. Each subnet includes a name and a description. It can also include location information. Location information is stored in the subnet properties under the Location tab. Location information is stored in hierarchical form. Each level is separated by a slash. You can use up to 256 levels in a location name, though the entire location name cannot be more than 260 characters. Each part of the name can include up to 32 characters. For example, a printer located in the northeast corner of the first floor of the headquarters building could be identified as HQ/First Floor/Northeast Corner.

To enable Printer Location Tracking in your domain, you need the following elements:

- Subnets and subnet locations entered into Active Directory Sites and Services
- A printer location naming convention
- The Location Tracking GPO must be enabled
- Location settings for all printers
- Location settings for all PCs and servers

Begin by making sure that your site structure is created and locations have been entered into each subnet; otherwise, the Browse button will not be populated in any of the dialog boxes you use for the other operations.

The Location Tracking GPO should be set at the domain level in order to have it apply to every object within the domain. In Chapter 5, you learned that you didn't want to modify default domain policies, since there is no rollback feature. Therefore, you need to create an *Intranet Domain Policy GPO*. This should be the GPO that includes the Printer Location Tracking setting. This setting can be found by selecting Computer Settings | Administrative Templates | Printers. To turn on Printer Location Tracking, you must enable the Pre-populate Printer Search Location Text setting. This setting enables the Browse button in the Location tab for printer and computer properties within the directory. It also enables this button in the Search Printers tool on servers and PCs.

TIP *Though you can choose to list printers in the directory when you share the printer, it doesn't appear automatically as an object. You can, however, find this object and, once found, place it into an OU for later manipulation. Use the Find tool in Active Directory Users and Computers to locate all printers, and select them from the Find window to move them into an OU. Create a Printers OU under the Service Offerings | File and Print OU.*

There are two ways to enter location information for printers. You can either enter it when you share the printer or enter it afterwards once the printer is shared. To enter location settings for printers once they are shared, locate all of the printers in your directory, and then open their Properties page. In the Attribute Editor tab, scroll to find the Location attribute, click it, and then select Edit. Enter the location using the notation format identified previously. You will usually want to be as specific as possible when identifying printer locations. For example, you can include more detail, such as room number, within the printer's location information. Perform this operation for each printer.

Perform the same operation on all computer objects in the directory. Open their Properties page, and use the Location tab to either enter the location or use the Browse button to select it. By entering locations for each object, you will make it easier for users to search for printers. Then, whenever users use the Search tool to locate a printer, printer location will automatically be entered in the Location field, enabling your user community to find printers near them without having to know your location naming strategy. Because of this, you may not need to include user printers in their logon script or through GPOs. You only need to show them how to locate printers close to them and how to connect to them during migration training (see Figure 8-9).

Printer drivers are automatically downloaded to user systems when a user connects to the printer, so long, of course, as the printer driver for their version of the OS has been loaded onto the server when you shared the printer. If you are using the parallel network, you will not require the installation of multiple client drivers on your print spoolers, especially if you are running Vista clients, but you will have to add drivers for 32-bit and 64-bit operating systems. If you're not using the parallel network, you will need to add other versions of printer drivers—one to support each client OS in your network. Keep in mind, though, that you do not need version 2 drivers for Windows NT clients. Windows NT clients can usually operate with version 3 drivers.

Manage Printer Permissions

Printer permissions are much the same in Windows Server as they are in Windows client systems. Print management is divided into printer queue and printer management. Print

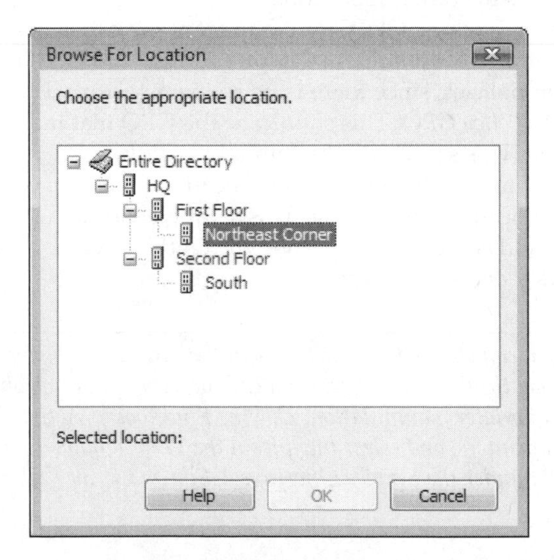

FIGURE 8-9 Browsing for printer or computer locations

operators are allowed to manage both the physical device and the logical queue. In addition, each user that prints a job has complete control over their own job. That is, they can delete the job, but cannot change its priority.

WS08 supports the segregation of printer and document management. Printer management allows operators to stop, pause, and restart the printer, but it does not give the operator control over the documents in a queue. Document management allows the operator to start, stop, pause, and reorder documents that are in a print queue. By default, print operators in WS08 have both these rights. If you need to segregate these rights within your organization, you will need to create the appropriate administrative groups and delegate the appropriate rights to each.

Establish a Shared Printer Policy

Now that you have a basic understanding of the printing support features in Windows Server, you can begin to establish your shared printer policy. This policy should be fully documented and distributed to all technicians. It should include:

- Printer selection criteria (based on "Designed for Windows"–certified printers)
- Minimum criteria for the addition of a shared printer
- Default printer setting standards
- Version 3 digitally signed drivers for all printers
- A standard printer naming convention
- A standard printer location naming convention in Printer Location Tracking format
- Standard description formats
- Printer Location Tracking activation
- Documented printer sharing procedures and processes
- Printer server construction principles

This list is not exclusive. Include in your printer policy anything you deem necessary. Keep in mind the following elements:

- Printing has a lower priority than file sharing, especially with the use of version 3 (user-mode) drivers. So if you have a region that requires high printing throughput, do not create combined file and print servers. Instead, create dedicated print and dedicated file servers.
- When you have more than one print server, create redundancy in your shared printer setups. That is, use the same approach for the design of print servers as you use for Dynamic Host Configuration Protocol (DHCP) servers. Create all of the printers on each server, then share only a portion (for example, half) of the printers on one server and the other portion on the other server. If one of your print servers goes down, you can quickly share and reactivate the lost printers on the other server. Each server acts as a standby server for the other.
- Most everything can be done with the Unidriver today. Acquire PostScript in your printers only if you absolutely require it (for example, if you have non-Windows clients or high-end graphical users). Instead, select additional features, such as duplex or stapling, to create multifunctional devices.

- Keep in mind that long jobs take a long time to spool when determining your default print setting standards. By default, WS08 printers begin printing as soon as the job begins spooling. But if you are spooling a 200-page document, other users would most likely have the time to print numerous 10-page documents before the job is done. If you set printing properties to spool and then print, small jobs will often clear much faster than long jobs.
- To speed up printing on a shared print and file server, move the spooling directory to a dedicated disk. This is done through Print Server Properties in the Printers Control Panel. Use the Advanced tab to redirect spooling to another disk (see Figure 8-10). This should be a folder you create on disk E:.
- Finally, use automatic detection when printing directly to network-enabled printers. This will automatically identify if the printer is shared on a Transmission Control Protocol/Internet Protocol (TCP/IP) printer port or as a Web services device. Both can indicate status errors, such as paper jams, low toner, and non-responding documents, as well as automatically configure clients connecting to them.

These are not the only considerations you will need to take into account for your shared printer policy, but they are often elements that are forgotten. Remember, printers are really there for users and should be designed in a way that facilitates the printing process for them.

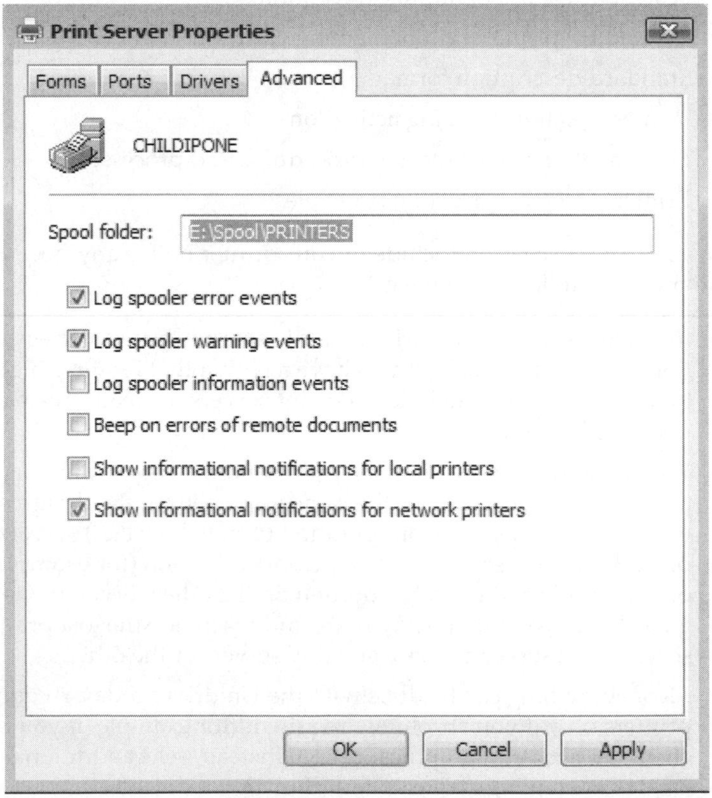

FIGURE 8-10 Moving the print spool location

Create the Print Server

Print servers are normally linked with file servers. Since your file servers have already been staged, you only need to add a print server function to these existing servers. Before you proceed, though, remember to prepare for the print server preparation process. This process includes several activities and is heavily based on your shared printer policy (see Figure 8-11):

- Identify all printers in your organization.
- Enable the Print Server role on print servers.
- Create your printer ports or set up Web services devices.
- Create the printers and install drivers.
- Identify locations for each printer.
- Set the spooling location for the print servers.
- Set spooling options for each printer.
- Ensure that the ADDS Printing GPOs are set.
- Ensure the printer is published in ADDS.
- Ensure clients can connect to printers.

Printers should have been identified in the inventory process outlined in Chapter 3. Use this inventory to create your print servers now. Then activate the Print Server role on your member server. Ensure that all printers are physically installed on the network and powered on.

TIP *You will probably want to rely on new printers that support Web services devices (WSD), since these devices provide automatic configuration and connections when they are plugged into your network.*

1. Start the Server Manager console, if it is closed (use the Quick Launch area icon).
2. Launch the Add A New Role Wizard. Select Print Services.
3. Follow the instructions in Table 8-5 to complete the wizard.

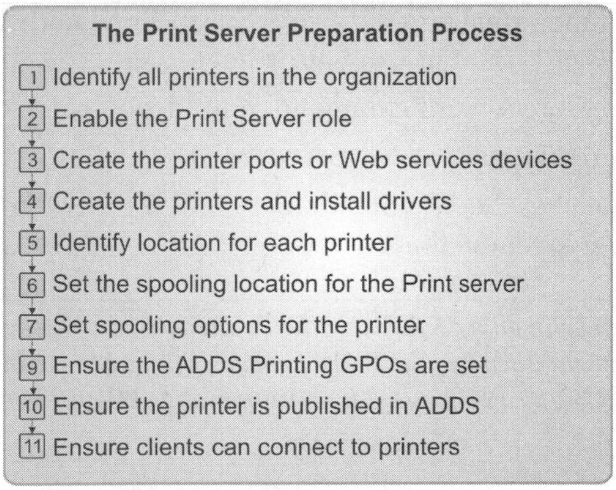

FIGURE 8-11 The print server preparation process

The Print Server Preparation Process

1 Identify all printers in the organization
2 Enable the Print Server role
3 Create the printer ports or Web services devices
4 Create the printers and install drivers
5 Identify location for each printer
6 Set the spooling location for the Print server
7 Set spooling options for the printer
9 Ensure the ADDS Printing GPOs are set
10 Ensure the printer is published in ADDS
11 Ensure clients can connect to printers

Print Services Wizard Page	Instructions
Server Roles	Select Print Services role.
Print Services	Review the information provided on the Print Services role.
Role Services	Select the options you want for this role. Select Print Server (the default), since it is the role you want to install. Select Line Printer Daemon (LDP) Service if you have users running UNIX editions that want to connect to the printers on this server. Select Internet Printing if you want to rely on the Internet Printing Protocol (IPP) to let clients connect to printers through a web site. **Note** You need to install Internet Information Services (IIS) and enable Internet Printing if you choose this option. The wizard will automatically suggest the installation of the appropriate components if you select this option.
Confirmation	Confirm your selections. Use Previous to modify selections. Click Install when ready.
Progress	Watch the progress of the installation.
Results	Click Close to complete the wizard.

TABLE 8-5 Adding the Print Services Role

Now that your printer role is installed, you can proceed to the creation of your printer pool. Begin with the creation of printer ports.

1. Launch the Print Management console. It can be found in Start Menu | Administrative Tools.

NOTE *Print management is unlike any other role added to Server Manager. Usually, all roles are managed in Server Manager directly, but with print management, you need a separate console. Print Services only lists the status of the service in Server Manager, as well as providing information on print management.*

2. Expand the Print Servers | *Servername* | Ports node in the tree pane, where *ServerName* is the name of your print server.
3. Use the More Actions command in the action pane to select Add Port.
4. In the Port Type list, select Standard TCP/IP Port. Then click New Port.
5. This launches the Add Standard TCP/IP Printer Port Wizard. Use the values in Table 8-6 to fill out this wizard.

NOTE *Ports can be in either RAW or Line Printer Remote (LPR) format. If the port is to be used by Windows devices, then use the RAW format. If the port is to be used by non-Windows devices, then use LPR. You can change this setting for any TCP/IP port by right-clicking it to select Configure Port.*

Repeat this operation for each port you need to create. Next, add your printers.

Add Standard TCP/IP Printer Port Wizard Page	Instructions
Add Port	Under Port Name or IP Address, type the Printer FQDN. The Fully Qualified Domain Name (FQDN) is preferred, since it will not change, whereas the IP address may, especially if you assign printer addresses through DHCP. Windows will automatically enter the port name as you type the printer name. Change this name only if you must.
Detecting TCP/IP Port	Windows tries to detect the port to identify the printer connected to it.
Additional Port Information	If Windows is successful, it will fill in the properties of the port. If not, it will request additional information. Identify the device type. If the device is unknown, select Generic Network Card.
Completing the Wizard	Click Finish when done. Use the Previous button to modify settings.

Table 8-6 Adding the Printer Ports

Tip *If you are already using version 3 drivers, and even if you're not, you can use the Microsoft Print Migrator (www.microsoft.com/WindowsServer2003/techinfo/overview/printmigrator3.1.mspx) to migrate printers from existing servers to the new servers. More on this task will be covered in Chapter 12.*

If you need to add new printers, use the following procedure.

1. In Print Management, expand the Print Servers | *Servername* | Printers node in the tree pane, where *ServerName* is the name of your print server.
2. Use the More Actions command in the action pane to select Add Printer.
3. Use the values in Table 8-7 to fill out this wizard.

Repeat this operation for each new printer you need to add. You should review each shared printer to ensure that it has the proper spooling settings and move the print spooler to the dedicated disk. You should also make sure that you move the printer to the Printers OU in ADDS.

Use the following procedure to change the print spooler disk.

1. In Print Management, expand the Print Servers | *Servername* node in the tree pane, where *ServerName* is the name of your print server.
2. Right-click the server name. Select Properties from the context menu.
3. In the Advanced tab, type the location for printer spooling. This should be E:\Spool\Printers. Click OK when done.
4. Next, move to the All Printers node under Custom Filters, right-click each printer, view its Properties, move to the Advanced tab, and set its spooling properties. Select Start Printing After Last Page Is Spooled and Print Spooled Documents First. Other settings can remain at the default selection.

Network Printer Installation Wizard	Instructions
Printer Installation	This dialog box can perform several tasks: It can search the network for available printers and add them to the console automatically. It can add a network (TCP/IP or Web services device) printer by IP address or host name. It can add a locally attached printer. It can create a port and add a printer at the same time. Select the default option since you created TCP/IP ports.
Printer Address	Use Autodetect to have Windows determine if it is a TCP/IP or WSD printer. Add the printer host name or IP address; the port name will be filled in automatically. Change the port name if you need to. Select Autodetect The Printer Driver To Use.
Printer Driver	If the printer driver is automatically detected, it will be listed. If not, select the proper printer driver from the list of devices, or add it using the disk provided by the manufacturer.
Printer Name and Sharing Settings	Change the printer name if required. Change the share name if required. Add the printer location. Include a comment. Publish the printer in the directory.
Printer Found	Review your choices and approve them. Use the Previous button to modify settings.
Completing Installation	Click Finish when done. You can print a test page from this page. You can also restart the wizard to add another printer.

TABLE 8-7 Adding Printers

5. Click Printer Defaults to set default printer settings, such as duplex printing, stapling, and paper type in each paper tray.
6. Next move to the Configuration tab, and ensure that the device is properly configured. Then move to Device Settings and apply proper settings for the printer.
7. Click OK when done. Perform this task for each printer.

You should now ensure that printing GPOs have been set (see Table 8-8). They should be set at the domain level, since they affect all computers and users. This means adding them to the Intranet Domain Policy GPO.

Location	Setting	Comment
Computer Configuration | Policies | Administrative Templates | Printers	Add Printer Wizard – Network scan page (Managed network)	This setting lists the number of printers that will be displayed on an Add Printer page when users try to locate printers in the directory. By default, this does not list any TCP/IP or WSD printers. Enable this setting to allow up to 50 printers of each type to be displayed.
	Add Printer Wizard – Network scan page (Unmanaged network)	By default, this setting lets users locate printers on unmanaged networks (networks that do not have ADDS).
	Allow print spooler to accept client connections	Determines if clients can connect to this print spooler. By default, printers need to be shared for this operation to succeed. Leave at default setting.
	Allow printers to be published	The default behavior is for printers to be published. Change this setting only if you want to disable the function on specific print servers.
	Allow pruning of published printers	Leave this setting as unconfigured. ADDS prunes a server's printers from the directory if the server is temporarily down, but republishes them when the server is restarted.
	Always render print jobs on the server	Windows Vista clients render the print job locally before sending it on to the print spooler. Keep the default setting.
	Automatically publish new printers in Active Directory	The default behavior is to publish printers. Change this setting only if you want to disable the function on specific print servers.
	Check published state	Should not be necessary. Enable only if you see that printers are removed from ADDS when they should still be there.
	Computer location	Used for Printer Location Tracking; enable only if you want to force a given printer for a specific set of computers.
	Custom support Universal Resource Locator (URL) in the Printers folder's left pane	Enable and set to an internal printing support web page.
	Directory pruning interval	Applies only to domain controllers; leave at default settings.
	Directory pruning priority	Applies only to domain controllers; leave at default settings.
	Directory pruning retry	Applies only to domain controllers; leave at default settings.

TABLE 8-8 Printing GPO Settings

PART IV

Location	Setting	Comment
	Disallow installation of printers using kernel-mode drivers	Enable this setting if you can. By default, kernel-mode printers are allowed on Windows XP Professional.
	Log directory pruning retry events	Leave at default settings.
	Pre-populate printer search location text	Enable in order to use Printer Location Tracking.
	Printer browsing	Not required wherever there is a domain controller because printers are published in ADDS.
	Prune printers that are not automatically republished	Required only if you have non-Windows Server print servers or if you publish printers across forests.
	Web-based printing	Required for IPP; only necessary if IIS is installed on the print server or if you want users to use a central web page to locate printers.
User Configuration | Policies | Administrative Templates | Control Panel | Printers	Browse a common web site to find printers	Used in conjunction with Web-based printing; can be used to redirect users to a common centralized web page to locate shared printers.
	Browse the network to find printers	Used to automatically list shared printers in the Network Printers dialog box of the Add Printers Wizard; not required when using ADDS to add printers.
	Default Active Directory path when searching for printers	Only required on very large networks to speed up directory searches.
	Only use Package Point and print	Forces clients to verify driver signatures when downloading them. Enable this setting. Use to let standard users install printers in managed networks.
	Package Point and print – Approved servers	Enable only if you want to restrict access to specific Package Point and print servers.
	Point and Print Restrictions	Enable only if you want to restrict access to specific Point and Print servers.
	Prevent addition of printers	Used only for highly restrictive accounts.
	Prevent deletion of printers	Used only for highly restrictive accounts.

Table 8-8 Printing GPO Settings (*continued*)

Finally, ensure that your printers are published within the directory. This is the default behavior, but it should be verified anyway. This can be done at the same time as the last activity: ensuring users have access to the printers. Return to your workstation and log on with your normal user account.

1. Open Network in Windows Explorer, and click the Search Active Directory button.
2. In the Find Printers dialog box, select Printers from the drop-down list.
3. The Location field should be filled in automatically if your Printer Location Tracking is activated. Click Find Now.
4. Windows will display all of the printers near you. Double-clicking any printer will connect you and install the driver.
5. Finally, move to Control Panel | Printers. Right-click the printer and select Printing Preferences. Your default printing preferences should be those set on the shared printer object. Modify them as you require. Click OK when done.

Your printing configuration is now done. You will need to perform this activity for each print server in your organization. Chapter 12 will also outline how you can migrate printers from existing networks if you have too many printers to create manually.

TIP *You may also need shared printers in the resource pool. It might be easiest to share printers on the virtual machines you build for management purposes, since you can then use the same process outlined here to prepare and share them in graphical mode.*

Share Files and Printers for Non-Windows Clients

Windows Server 2008 also supports printing and file sharing for non-Windows computers. These include the Macintosh as well as UNIX and Linux systems. Many networks contain either one or the other, or even both.

Windows NT has supported Macintosh connectivity since its earliest versions. Windows Server is no different. Macintosh connectivity used to be provided through Services for Macintosh, a service that included both File Services for Macintosh and Print Services for Macintosh and that had to be added to the file and print server. The service automatically added support for the AppleTalk protocol.

But with the advent of the newer Macintosh operating systems, Microsoft has deprecated this service because they no longer run custom Apple protocols since they run a version of UNIX. Rely on the UNIX connectivity tools in Windows Server to connect your Macintosh systems.

Windows Server supports UNIX integration at several levels. File and print integration was discussed earlier in the respective sections of this chapter. File services are enabled through the NFS protocol, and print services rely on LPR printers. Each is relatively easy to work with.

In terms of security, you can integrate Kerberos realms, including WS08 domains and UNIX networks, since Kerberos version 5 is a standard and is able to interoperate between the two environments. A Kerberos realm ensures that users can access files from both environments without having to use or remember two accounts and passwords. More on Kerberos is covered in Chapter 10.

Server Role	Processor Architecture	CPU	RAM	Drive D:	Drive E:	Network
File Server	x64	Low load	Required for Search service	Hosts shares	Hosts shadow copies and storage reports	Higher speeds or multiple cards required for file-sharing throughput
Print Server	x64	Medium load	Required for large print jobs	Not required	Hosts spool files	Multiple network interface cards (NICs) required for networked printers
Network Infrastructure Server (WDS role)	x64	High load	Required to support multiple system construction processes	Hosts WDS service and image files; use large, dedicated drives	Not required	High-speed network cards are required for better performance

TABLE 8-9 Resource Requirements per Server Role

Finally, if you need a higher level of interaction between UNIX and Windows Server networks, you can obtain Windows Services for UNIX (http://technet.microsoft.com/en-us/interopmigration/bb380242.aspx), a comprehensive set of tools that is designed to integrate UNIX and WS08 networks and even allow UNIX applications to run on WS08 servers.

Server Requirements by Role

Now that you have reviewed the creation process for several server roles, you have an idea of the hardware requirements to construct them (see Table 8-9). You'll need to review the central processing unit (CPU), RAM, disk volumes, and network capabilities required for the server roles seen thus far. Use these guidelines to prepare your servers when you stage the parallel network for VSOs. Other tables of this type will be presented as we examine other roles in future chapters.

Design the Virtual Service Offerings OU Structure

The final step of service preparation is the design of the Virtual Service Offerings OU structure and the application of proper delegation and Group Policy settings to each service (see Table 8-10). This OU structure is fairly flat, but it supports the ability to create sub-structures. While the Virtual Service Offerings OU structure was first introduced in Chapter 5, its purpose at that time was to identify the type of content you could expect in this OU structure. Now that you have had the opportunity to refine your understanding of the content for this OU structure, you will find that it is slightly different from the initial

OU	Level	Objective	GPO	Notes
Virtual Service Offerings	One	Grouping of all service offerings and utilitarian objects in the organization		Base Servers GPO for application of security settings; see Chapter 10 Also used for categorization
File and Print	Two	Regroups all file and print servers	Global File and Print GPO	This GPO controls all aspects of file sharing, DFS, and printing Delegated to file and print operators
File Shares	Three	Under File and Print to regroup all shares		Used to categorize all shares
Printers	Three	Under File and Print to regroup all printers		Used to categorize all printers
Network Infrastructure	Two	Regroups all operational servers	Global Infrastructure GPO	Contains settings for DHCP, Windows Internet Naming Service (WINS), and Remote Installation Service (RIS), as well as operational servers, such as Microsoft Operations Management, Systems Management Server, Internet Security and Acceleration Server, etc. Can be subdivided for further segregation Delegated to infrastructure server operators
Operational Accounts	Two	Regroups all special operational accounts, such as support technicians and installers		No delegation; managed by domain administrators
Service Accounts	Two	Regroups all special service accounts		No delegation; managed by domain administrators
Hidden Objects	Two	Regroups all special groups, including operational groups		Includes domain local and universal groups Includes special permissions to stop regular users from locating these groups when searching Active Directory

TABLE 8-10 Build the Service Offerings OU Structure

PART IV

presentation from Chapter 5. For example, while in Chapter 5, this OU structure presented the type of member server contained within the OU, in this chapter, it now presents the server role at the second level. This categorization allows further refinement. For example, if you find you need to further segregate collaboration servers because your policies for Exchange Server are not the same as those for SharePoint Portal Server (SPS), you can create a third level of OUs under collaboration servers and place Exchange and SPS servers in separate OUs.

For now, build out the OUs for the server roles already covered. Other roles will be covered in future chapters.

One of the key aspects of this OU design is the preparation of appropriate security groups for server operators. This is called the services administration plan. Since it is mostly the preparation of special groups with limited administrative security rights, this operation will be performed in Chapter 12.

As for the preparation of this OU structure, use the same operations outlined in Chapter 7 to create the OU structure and delegate the management of the content of each OU to appropriate operational groups.

CHAPTER 9

Build the Virtual Service Offerings Infrastructure: Application-Oriented Servers

Application-oriented servers are servers that provide specific application services to end users. Because of this, they are part of the virtual service offerings infrastructure. The servers in this category include:

- **Application servers** Servers that host applications that provide specific functionality to end users. These servers provide application services based on either commercial software, such as Exchange Server, SQL Server, Commerce Server, and so on, or on custom corporate applications. This also includes applications based on the .NET Framework. A good example of an application based on .NET Framework is PowerShell, since it requires .NET Framework to support its many cmdlets.
- **Dedicated Web servers** Servers that run Web application services in a single-purpose server model. This role is based on the Web edition of Windows Server 2008 (WS08). They are similar to the Application Server role, but only focus on Internet Information Services (IIS) or Web service applications.
- **Terminal servers** Servers that centrally host applications and provide access to them through a thin client model. The entire execution environment resides on the server itself.
- **Collaboration servers** Servers that host applications that are specifically designed to support collaboration efforts between end users. Examples of their services include, among others, Windows SharePoint Services (WSS) and Streaming Media Services.

NOTE *Streaming Media Services are also known as Windows Media Services and are not part of WS08 by default. You must download them at www.microsoft.com/windows/windowsmedia/forpros/server/server.aspx. In addition, WSS is now part of Server Manager's ability to integrate other roles and features from the Microsoft download center or the Windows Update Web site.*

These roles are the last server roles you need to set up before you can begin to move end users into the parallel network and provide them with a full complement of services.

Once again, the structure for the coverage of each of these server roles includes:

- **Functional requirements** Discussions on how the service must be designed for the enterprise network and the rationale for the service.
- **Features** Features supporting the role or service within WS08 (includes new features).
- **Implementation instructions** How to proceed with the preparation of the server role within the parallel virtual service offerings (VSO) network environment.

The roles mentioned here are normally assigned to member servers. As with the file and print server roles, it will also be important to cover specific considerations for all server types, such as the network load balancing and failover cluster services. Both offer powerful redundancy features that minimize risk within your organization. These topics will be further discussed in Chapter 11. As with Chapter 8, the table at the end of this chapter outlines the resource requirements to build each server role covered here. It serves as a guide for server role construction.

Finally, once the basis for network services has been covered, it will be time to continue the design of the Virtual Service Offerings organizational unit (OU) structure within the directory. As with the People and PC OU structures, this design includes both Group Policy Object (GPO) and delegation principles, but it will also involve the unique design of a services administration plan. WS08 offers the capability to assign specific administrative rights based on the task the administrator is responsible for. You no longer need to grant domain administration rights to one and all just to let them perform their work. This services administration plan will be a key element of your security infrastructure for the enterprise network. It is covered in Chapter 13.

The Virtual Service Offerings OU structure is built up as each service is added to the network. It is at this point that more OU contents will be identified. Once each additional service has been covered, the administrative, delegation, and Group Policy requirements for each will be covered in detail.

Build Application Servers

The Application server role is a multifunctional role because it is required to support commercial server software as well as corporate or in-house applications. Whether it is for software or applications, this server role, like all others, is based on the core server kernel installation for VSOs. Stage this server in the same way you stage all the other member servers in your VSO network. There are, however, some particularities, depending on the type of software or application the server will host. In addition, software products and/or custom applications often require a detailed architecture of their own before implementation.

For example, you could not install Microsoft Exchange Server without first determining its impact on your Active Directory Domain Services (ADDS) structure, on domain controllers, on the replication topology, and on other elements of the infrastructure you already have in place. Because of this, the Application server role is often one of the last server roles you implement.

Share Commercial and Corporate Applications

Most organizations will already have a vast number of software products and custom applications already in place. This is, after all, the basis of the client/server model. Organizations that are already using Windows networks will also know that both software products and applications hosted on these operating systems must conform to a specific set of guidelines in order to operate. This is outlined as the "Designed for Windows" set of specifications. Ideally, every application and software product you run will be upgraded to versions that are completely compatible with Windows Server 2008, but this is an improbable scenario.

NOTE *The specifications for Windows applications can be found at www.microsoft.com/winlogo.*

Few organizations will be able to afford the upgrade of all of their software products or the redesign of all of their custom applications during the migration to WS08. The best you can hope for is to upgrade a few core or critical software products and redesign a few core applications. For example, on the software side, if you're using anything previous to Microsoft Exchange 2003, it makes a lot of sense to upgrade to Exchange 2007 because it relies on features that are a core part of WS08. It also makes sense to upgrade other core software, such as the products found in the Microsoft Windows Server System, if you can. Finally, you should try to upgrade your mission-critical custom applications, if you can, because they will gain from the new capabilities of WS08.

TIP *Support lifecycles are also a good reason to upgrade your applications. Microsoft, for example, provides complete information on their application lifecycles at http://support.microsoft.com/gp/lifeselectindex. If your product is losing support, then it may be a good time to upgrade it. Sometimes, the cost of supporting an older product outweighs the cost of upgrading it.*

If you can't upgrade everything or redesign your applications, don't despair. Like Windows Vista, Windows Server 2008 now boasts a Compatibility Mode that can emulate almost any previous version of Windows, from 95 to XP Service Pack 1. In addition, WS08 includes a Program Compatibility Assistant that walks you through the assignment of compatibility parameters for legacy software or older applications. And finally, you can use the Application Compatibility Toolkit from Microsoft to create shims, or code snippets that will make your older applications work in WS08.

TIP *Application compatibility in Windows Server 2008 is the same as in Windows Vista because both use the same code base. For a comprehensive look at application compatibility and potential application issues in these versions of Windows, download Chapter 6: Preparing Applications from the free e-book,* The Definitive Guide to Vista Migration, *at www.realtime-nexus.com/dgvm.htm. You can also rely on the Microsoft Application Compatibility Toolkit, which is available at http://technet.microsoft.com/en-us/windowsvista/aa905072.aspx.*

One of the important aspects of application compatibility is security. Microsoft changed the security model for applications between Windows NT and Windows 2000, and continues to make it evolve in WS08. In NT, applications were allowed to write in critical areas of the system disk, such as the %SYSTEMROOT% and Program Files folders. This had the effect of potentially destabilizing the system. Now, neither users nor applications have the right to change or modify information in these critical folders. Therefore, if you have a legacy application that must run on Windows Server 2008, you must either modify security settings to allow users to modify specific files in critical folders or run the Program Compatibility Wizard to redirect program data to the user's profile area. You shouldn't, however, reset your server's security level from the defaults; that is, of course, if you want to keep it running. Rather, it is best to use the Program Compatibility Assistant to apply special settings to each program that requires it.

Application Development Support

If you choose to redesign your corporate applications, you'll find that Windows Server 2008 offers a wealth of new features focused on application support. These fall into several categories, such as scalability, availability, manageability, and enhancements to the programming model. They include:

- **Application pooling** With WS08, it is possible to create thread pools for Web applications and apply them to legacy applications that would normally operate in a single process. This gives the application more robustness, since it is no longer tied to a single process.
- **Application recycling** Some applications have a tendency to have degraded performance over time due to memory leaks and other programmatic issues. WS08 can recycle a process by gracefully shutting it down and restarting it on a regular basis. This can be done either administratively or through the COM+ software development kit. Administratively, apply it through the Component Services console by right-clicking a COM+ component, selecting Properties, and modifying the elements on the Pooling & Recycling tab (see Figure 9-1).

Tip *The Component Services console is no longer available by default in WS08 as it was in older versions of Windows Server. To access it, you must either install the Application Server role or create a new console and add the Component Services snap-in. Use Start Menu | Run, type* ***MMC****, and in the new console, use File | Add/Remove Snap-in. Scroll down the list until you see Component Services and click Add. Close the snap-in dialog box and save the console.*

- **Applications as NT services** Now, all COM+ applications can be configured as NT services, making applications load at boot time or on demand as required. Once again, this is performed through the application's properties on the Activation tab.
- **Low-memory activation gates** WS08 can check memory allocations before it starts a process, allowing it to shut down an application if it will exhaust memory resources. This allows other applications running on the server to continue operation while only the faulty application fails.

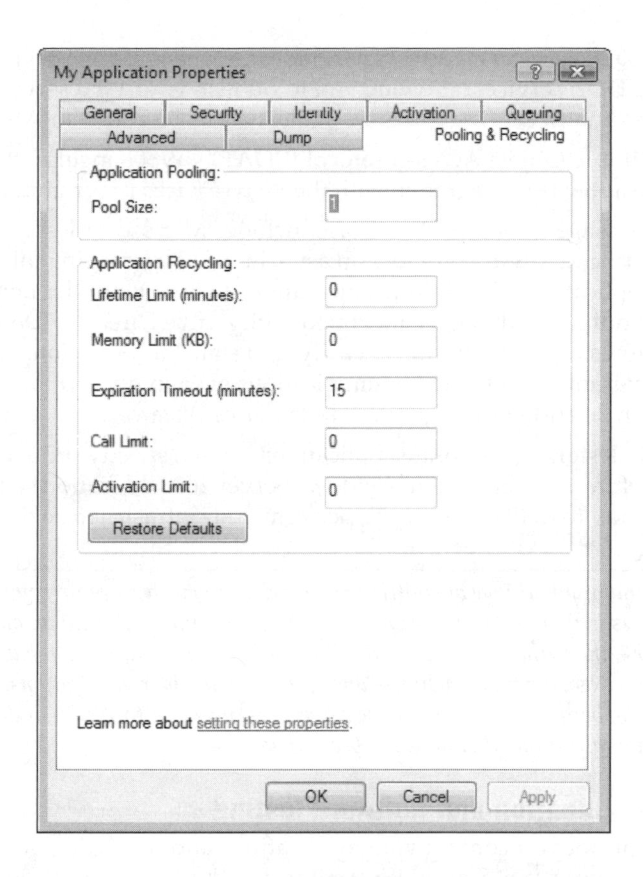

Figure 9-1 Changing application recycling properties

- **Web services** Any COM+ object can be treated as a Web service and any Web service can be treated as a COM+ object, greatly extending the remoting capabilities of your applications.
- **Application partitions** These were discussed in Chapters 5 and 6 when using Active Directory Domain Services. In terms of application support, these partitions allow you to host several instances of the same or different versions of COM+ objects on the same server. If, for example, you have 500 customers running a hosted application, you can create 500 partitions, one for each customer, segregating their operational environment from all of the others. Application partitions are created in Active Directory Users and Computers under System | ComPartitions and ComPartitionSets (Advanced Features in the View menu must be enabled). In addition, member servers must have partitions enabled. This is done through Component Services | Computer | Properties | Options tab.
- **.NET Framework** WS08 includes an integrated version of .NET Framework, version 2.0 by default. In addition, it includes an installable version of .NET Framework version 3.0 and 3.5. Therefore, you can program applications to make use of the Common Language Runtime and integrate them with Extensible Markup Language (XML) Web services to take advantage of this powerful new programming model.

- **UDDI services** WS08 also includes Universal Description, Discovery, and Integration (UDDI) services, allowing you to publish your Web services either internally or externally. UDDI services are a role that can be added to WS08 servers.
- **Simple Object Access Protocol (SOAP)** WS08 includes this XML-based protocol to allow full integration with the Web services programming model.
- **Message queuing** WS08 also includes Microsoft Message Queuing (MSMQ) services. MSMQ provides an asynchronous messaging infrastructure for applications. This allows applications to operate under non-constant networking conditions. MSMQ is integrated with Active Directory Domain Services, where it stores all configuration, security, and status information. MSMQ provides guaranteed network communications even in non-optimal networking conditions. It can be added through the Add Features Wizard.

  Redesigning corporate applications is not a speedy process. It must be planned well before you begin your Windows Server 2008 migration so that applications will be ready to deliver when you perform your infrastructure deployment.

TIP *The major advantage of splitting your environment between resource pools and virtual service offerings is that you can always build a VSO machine running an older version of Windows Server—the Windows Server 2008 Enterprise license supports the use of any older version of Windows as a virtual machine—and use it to run older applications. While this is not the ideal scenario, because you should have all servers migrated to WS08, it does work and it works well to run applications that have not been updated yet.*

Legacy Application and Software Testing

Whether or not you convert your applications and upgrade your software, one of the key elements of your WS08 migration will rest with your application testing strategy. Every existing server application and software product in your legacy network must be tested under your new network conditions in order to ensure that it behaves in the proper manner while running under Windows Server 2008. It is also a good idea to repackage legacy application installations to integrate them with the Windows Installer service (see Chapter 7). All software that boasts the "Designed for Windows" logo is integrated into this service. You should also ensure that all of the corporate applications you redesign for WS08 should be integrated with this service as well.

CAUTION *Even if you have existing applications running under previous versions of Windows Installer, you will need to upgrade them to run with Windows Installer version 4, which has been upgraded to work with the User Account Control features found in Vista and WS08. Once again, have a look at Chapter 6 of* The Definitive Guide to Vista Migration *at www.realtime-nexus.com/dgvm.htm for more information on application preparation.*

This will give all of your applications additional robustness and stability at little cost, since every software product or application must be configured to install automatically anyway. In addition, it will provide you with a single unified installation and deployment method for all software products.

TIP *Altiris, part of Symantec, offers Wise for Windows Installer and Wise Package Studio (www.wise.com) and Macrovision offers AdminStudio (www.installshield.com) to repackage software installations and integrate them with the Windows Installer service as well as to package new applications. Also, remember to test all of your software and application installations in* user mode *to ensure that they behave properly on WS08 with limited access rights.*

Use rigorous testing methods and ensure that expert users are part of your acceptance test group for each application or software product. This will help you guarantee that the software or application provides all the features they expect, since you can't be an expert on every aspect of every program in your network.

Application Server Types

There are two types of application servers:

- **Shared application servers** Servers that host an application or software product running in administrative mode.
- **Central application servers** Servers that run applications designed to run on a central machine, providing remote services to end users.

The first type of application server is really a file server more than anything else. In this case, you create a file share on a server, install the application to be shared—for example, Microsoft Office—perform an administrative installation, and then send the link to the shared application files to end users.

This type of application sharing is on its way out, as administrative installations of products like Microsoft Office are complex to manage and, especially, update in the long run. Windows Server offers so many more options for application sharing, especially the new RemoteApps feature of Terminal Services, that you should reconsider the use of the shared application server in your network, if you have any.

The second type of application server is much more popular, as it is the type of server that runs Windows Server System applications like BizTalk Server, Commerce Server, SQL Server, and so on. These implementations are designed to rely on the base features of Windows Server 2008 to provide centralized end-user services.

In addition, this server type includes running custom applications. For these applications, you need to install the components of the Application role in Server Manager. While some of these components run either COM+ or .NET applications, others include the ability to run Web applications. COM+ and .NET applications have already been discussed.

Explore Application Virtualization

Traditional application installation and delivery can be a lot of work. That's because traditional software products install on the server. Another option exists: application virtualization. Application virtualization tools isolate or abstract application components from the operating system and other applications, yet provide full capabilities for application and operating system interaction. Instead of installing an application, application virtualization captures its running state. Once that running state is captured, there is no need for an actual installation: You only need to copy the files that make up the captured running state to any machine that includes the virtualization agent and authorize the application for it to run.

In and of itself, application virtualization offers many benefits and may warrant an immediate implementation, but because of its nature, it requires redeployment of all of the applications you run in order to take full advantage of the virtualization capabilities. This is why it is ideal to adopt this technology during a migration project. Otherwise, you would have to replace all of the applications that are already deployed in your network—uninstalling the application and then redeploying it as a virtual application. This is why the best time to do this is when you are deploying a brand-new network, such as the parallel VSO network.

In addition, it is possible to use data streaming technologies, similar to those used for video and audio streaming, to send the applications to endpoints. This means that your application server now becomes more of a file server that copies these applications to other systems than one that serves applications to end users. Also, since the application is only copied to the system, it is extremely easy to remove it from a system when the application's lifetime ends.

Tip *To learn more on application virtualization, see the Application virtualization: Ending DLL hell once and for all webcast at www.bitpipe.com/detail/RES/1193672482_325.html.*

There are several different types of application virtualization technologies, but all of them basically produce a similar feature set:

- Altiris, part of Symantec, offers Software Virtualization Solution (SVS), which is a filter driver that is installed on the operating system (OS). The filter driver manages the virtualization process. More information on SVS can be found at www.altiris.com/Products/SoftwareVirtualizationSolution.aspx. SVS applications can be combined with AppStream's AppStream server to offer streaming capabilities. More information on AppStream and SVS can be found at www.appstream.com/products-application-virtualization.html.
- Citrix offers virtualization technologies within its Presentation Server. Citrix uses a principle similar to Microsoft's Application Virtualization and streams applications to desktops or servers. More information can be found at www.citrix.com/English/ps2/products/product.asp?contentID=186.
- Microsoft offers Microsoft Application Virtualization (MAV) as part of the Desktop Optimization Pack for Software Assurance (DOPSA). Microsoft acquired SoftGrid in mid-2006 and has reprogrammed the MAV client to get it to run with x86 and x64 versions of Windows Vista and WS08. More information on SoftGrid can be found at www.microsoft.com/windows/products/windowsvista/buyorupgrade/optimizeddesktop.mspx.
- Thinstall offers the Thinstall Virtualization Suite (ThinstallVS). Thinstall incorporates its virtualization engine directly into the software package it creates. As such, no pre-deployment preparation is required. More information on ThinstallVS can be found at www.thinstall.com.

  Each virtualization product is a third-party add-on to WS08. Pricing for each solution is relatively similar, as some require direct acquisition costs and others are subscription-based. Just as the dynamic network is divided into resource pools and virtual service offerings, so is the application operation model changed from an installation to a virtualization model. If you can add applications to your servers without actually installing them, be able to reset them with a click of a mouse button, and remove them at will, you will see tremendous benefits in your new network. Seriously consider application virtualization for anything you would normally host on a server and reduce your total cost of operations (TCO) on application management.

Prepare Web Servers (Dedicated or Application)

Web servers, whether they are dedicated or not, are based on Microsoft Internet Information Services (IIS). IIS has been seen as Windows' weakest point in the past. In older versions of Windows, it was installed by default and often not managed in the way that it should be, which lent it to abuse. This is no longer a problem with WS08, since no server role is installed by default. If you install a server role, you do it consciously and, therefore, you should be aware that it will require management to some degree. If any of you have had experience with IIS before, you will find that working with IIS version 7, the version built into WS08, is completely different.

Several characteristics of IIS have been modified in Windows Server 2008:

- IIS 7 has now been divided into modules that you install and activate as needed. For example, if you need Server Side Includes (SSI) on your Web server, then you must install the SSI component to make it run. IIS now includes more than 30 components you can install and configure as needed.
- IIS Manager, the IIS management console, has been completely revamped (see Figure 9-2). Each component is now clearly laid out and easier to access. It includes both a features and a content view. The content view provides an interface similar to previous versions of IIS. The features view gives you access to administrative interfaces for each of the installed components.

CAUTION *You cannot manage previous versions of IIS with the IIS 7 Manager. This is why WS08 includes the ability to install a compatible console for IIS 6 and lower versions.*

- The execution mode for IIS is completely different in WS08. Each application running in IIS 7 runs in its own execution environment or application pool and is completely isolated from other applications. If an application wants to perform illegal operations, it cannot affect other applications running on the same server. IIS can also automatically restart applications after crashing, limiting the damage a denial-of-service attack can have on each application. Application isolation occurs automatically in IIS 7 each time a new application is added to the Web server.
- The Web edition of WS08 includes only one role: Web Services (IIS) which is not installed by default. This edition of WS08 is a dedicated edition that is designed to provide a low-cost alternative to non-Windows Web servers. Use the same approaches as with IIS to manage and monitor servers running this edition.

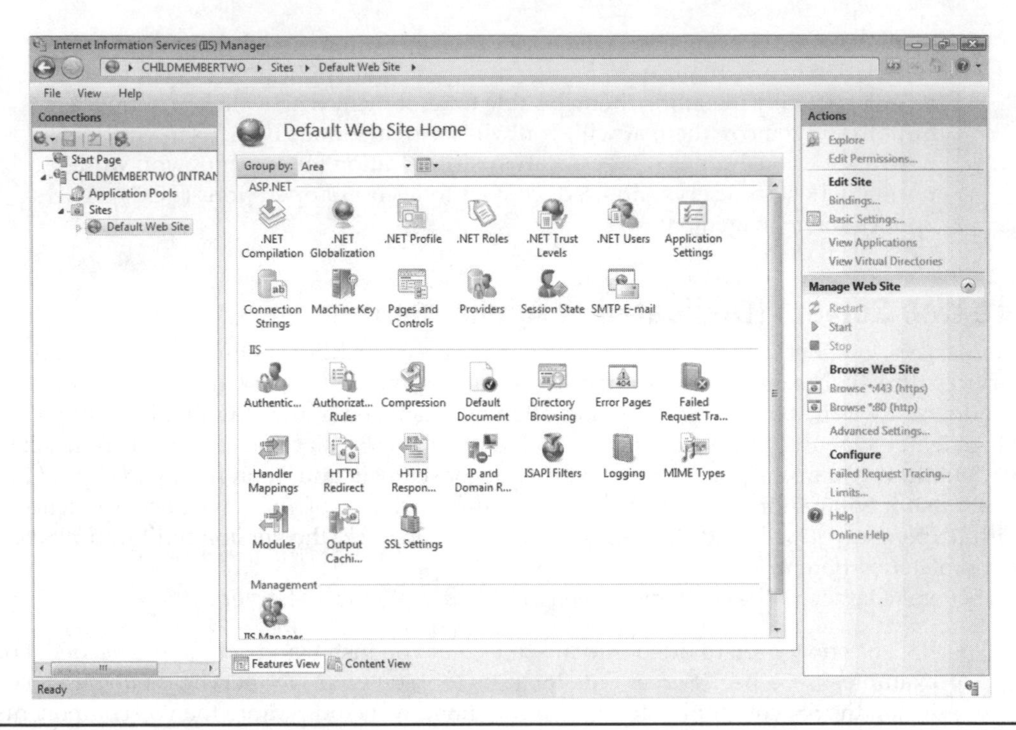

FIGURE 9-2 The IIS 7 management console

- IIS 7 is the most secure version of IIS to date. Before, IIS would install a whole series of components because its structure was monolithic. This increased its attack surface. Of course, you had control over whether components were enabled or not, but since they were installed, they could lend themselves to malicious use. Now, IIS 7 does not require component activation. If you choose to install the component, it is activated. If it isn't installed, then it can't be activated maliciously or inadvertently.

  These are the major new features for IIS security. Altogether, IIS is a much more secure and stable Web platform than it ever has been before.

Keep in mind, though, that IIS is no longer required on most of your servers. In addition, you should not place IIS on any of your domain controllers if at all possible. There may be some circumstances where you have no choice in this matter (for example, in the case of multipurpose servers).

The IIS 7 Feature Set

Table 9-1 describes all of the features that are installed by default. In addition, it outlines recommended features for modern web sites running IIS 7. Default features are installed automatically and are, therefore, recommended as well.

As you can see, IIS 7 is extremely modular—much more so than any previous version. Make sure you properly document each of the components you install. Also, if you find that you installed a component and are not using it, uninstall it. To do so, right-click the role in Server Manager and select Remove Role Services.

Feature Name	By Default	Recommended	Comments
Common HTTP Features			
Static Content	☑		
Default Document	☑		
Directory Browsing	☑		
HTTP Errors	☑		
HTTP Redirection	☑		
Application Development			
ASP.NET		☑	ASP.NET provides most of the power of the integration of IIS with the .NET Framework.
.NET Extensibility	☑		
ASP			
CGI			
ISAPI Extensions		☑	Most applications that fully integrate with IIS do so through the Internet Service Application Programming Interface (ISAPI).
ISAPI Filters		☑	
Server-Side Includes			
Health and Diagnostics			
HTTP Logging	☑		
Logging Tools	☑		
Request Monitor	☑		
Tracing	☑		
Custom Logging			Install only if it is built into your application.
ODBC Logging			Install only if you want to log to a database.
Security			
Basic Authentication			This is compatible with most browsers, but can be easily spoofed on the Internet because password encryption is very poor.
Windows Authentication		☑	Use for internal web sites, as it requires clients to have domain credentials to access a site.
Digest Authentication		☑	Provides better encryption of passwords. Use instead of Basic Authentication for external web sites.

TABLE 9-1 Installed Features for IIS 7

Feature Name	By Default	Recommended	Comments
Security			
Client Certificate Mapping Authentication		☑	Relies on public key infrastructure (PKI) certificates to authenticate users. Used internally with ADDS.
IIS Client Certificate Mapping Authentication		☑	Relies on PKI certificates to authenticate users. Used externally with no dependence on ADDS.
URL Authorization		☑	Controls access to portions of web sites based on authorization rules.
Request Filtering		☑	Used to filter out certain attack types by blocking malformed or overly long requests.
IP and Domain Restrictions		☑	Used to block either source Internet Protocol (IP) addresses or domain names from contacting your web sites.
Performance			
Static Content Compression	☑		
Dynamic Content Compression		☑	Compresses dynamic Web content for faster performance.
Management Tools			
IIS Management Console	☑		
IIS Management Scripts and Tools		☑	Lets you manage through scripts or command windows. Used to manage repetitive tasks on multiple Web servers.
Management Service		☑	Supports remote management of IIS 7 servers.
IIS 6.0 Management Compatibility			Use only if you need to manage older versions of IIS.
IIS Metabase Compatibility			Use only if you need to manage older versions of IIS.
IIS 6 WMI Compatibility			Use only if you need to manage older versions of IIS.
IIS 6 Scripting Tools			Use only if you need to manage older versions of IIS.
IIS 6 Management Console			Use only if you need to manage older versions of IIS.

TABLE 9-1 Installed Features for IIS 7 (*continued*)

Feature Name	By Default	Recommended	Comments
FTP Publishing Service			
FTP Server			
FTP Management Snap-in			
Windows Process Activation Service Features			
Process Model	☑		
.NET Environment		☑	Use to include managed code activation in the process model.
Configuration APIs		☑	Required for .NET applications to perform programmatic process activation.

TABLE 9-1 Installed Features for IIS 7 *(continued)*

Install the Application or Dedicated Web Server Role

The Application server role and the Dedicated Web server role are similar because both can rely on IIS to provide a platform for applications to run. The major difference is that the Dedicated Web server role is based on the Web edition of Windows Server 2008. The Application server role is based on the other three editions.

There are several tasks to perform when preparing IIS Web or Application servers:

- Everything begins with the addition of the role in Server Manager. Right-click Roles in Server Manager, and select Add Roles.
- In the Web edition, the role is called Web Server (IIS), and in the other three editions, you can select simply the Web Server (IIS) role or you can select the Application server role, which will let you include the Web server role. For the purposes of simplicity, the installation of the Application server role is covered here.
- Use the values in Table 9-2 to run through the Application—and, therefore, the Web—server role installation.

Once installed, you will manage IIS through the IIS management console. As mentioned earlier, this console includes two views: the features view and the content view. The features view is used to access the components that make IIS and web sites run. The content view is used to see the files that make up a web site. Administrators familiar with previous versions of IIS will be more comfortable in the content view, since it closely resembles previous versions of IIS Manager. You will, however, need to switch from one view to the other to be able to modify the settings of any component in the content view. But if you want to modify the Windows properties of the objects you select, you need to do so in the content view.

In addition, the previous metabase—the database that contained all of the settings for IIS in previous versions—is now completely gone. Instead, IIS takes its configuration structure from ASP.NET and now includes XML-based configuration files, just as ASP.NET web sites did in previous releases. Default configuration information is now contained within a file called `applicationHost.config`. This file contains server-level configuration settings.

PART IV

Add Application Server Role Wizard Page	Value
Select Server Role	Select Application Server. The Web Server (IIS) role will be available as you run through the options for the main server role. On the Web edition, select Web Server (IIS) role.
Add Roles Wizard Dialog Box	When you select the Application server role, Server Manager warns you of its dependencies. In this case, you also need the Windows Process Activation Service (see the features tables in Chapter 1), along with its three subcomponents.
Application Server	Review information about this role if required before you move on.
Role Services	Several services are available for this role: Application Server Foundation is selected by default. Select Web Server (IIS) Support to include the Web server installation in the application server. Required services and features will automatically be selected. Add the required role services. Note that this also includes.NET Framework version 3. Add COM+ network access to support remoting of COM+ or enterprise services applications. Add Transmission Control Protocol (TCP) port sharing to support application isolation, even if they share the same TCP port, for example, port 80. Under Windows Process Activation Service Support, note that HTTP Activation is selected by default. Add Message Queuing Activation, TCP Activation, and/or Named Pipes Activation based on the requirements of the applications you need to support. Your developers or the documentation of the application should indicate which activation service is required. Note that additional features will be required to support these activation methods. Add Distributed Transactions if your application will reside on multiple servers and interact with multiple information sources. Once again, your developers or the documentation of the application will indicate whether these components are required or not.

Table 9-2 Values for the Application Server Role Installation

Add Application Server Role Wizard Page	Value
Server Authentication Certificate	If you selected the WS-Atomic Transactions method to support Distributed Transactions, then Server Manager will want you to select and install a PKI certificate to authenticate this server to others. Three choices are available: Choose an existing certificate Create a self-signed certificate Choose a certificate later The first or third choice is recommended. If at all possible, you should select a certificate from an external certificate authority (CA) because it will automatically be trusted by the clients on your network. If you choose a self-signed certificate, you will need to install it manually on each client that interacts with this IIS server.
Web Server (IIS)	Review information about this role if required before you move on.
IIS Role Services	Use the information in Table 9-1 to select the options you need to install for this role. Select only the options you need. Remember that you can add or remove role services when required.
Confirm Installation Selections	Review your choices before proceeding. Use the Previous button to make corrections if required. Click Install when ready.
Installation Progress and Installation Results	Review the installation progress, and click Finish when done.

TABLE 9-2 Values for the Application Server Role Installation (*continued*)

Then, a hierarchy of `web.config` files is stored within each application's directory and provides further configuration settings for applications. In previous editions of Windows and IIS, you needed to manually configure settings in these `.config` files. In IIS 7, you configure settings through the modules in IIS Manager, and these modules make the required modifications in the `.config` files.

In addition, IIS 7 includes a command-line tool, `APPCMD.EXE`, that lets you script any activity on the server. IIS Manager also supports remote administration through normal Hypertext Transfer Protocol Secure (HTTPS) ports, such as 443. This is enabled by modifying the Management Service settings under the Management section of the details pane (see Figure 9-3):

1. Double-click the Management Service icon.
2. Click Enable Remote Connections.
3. Determine the authentication mode.

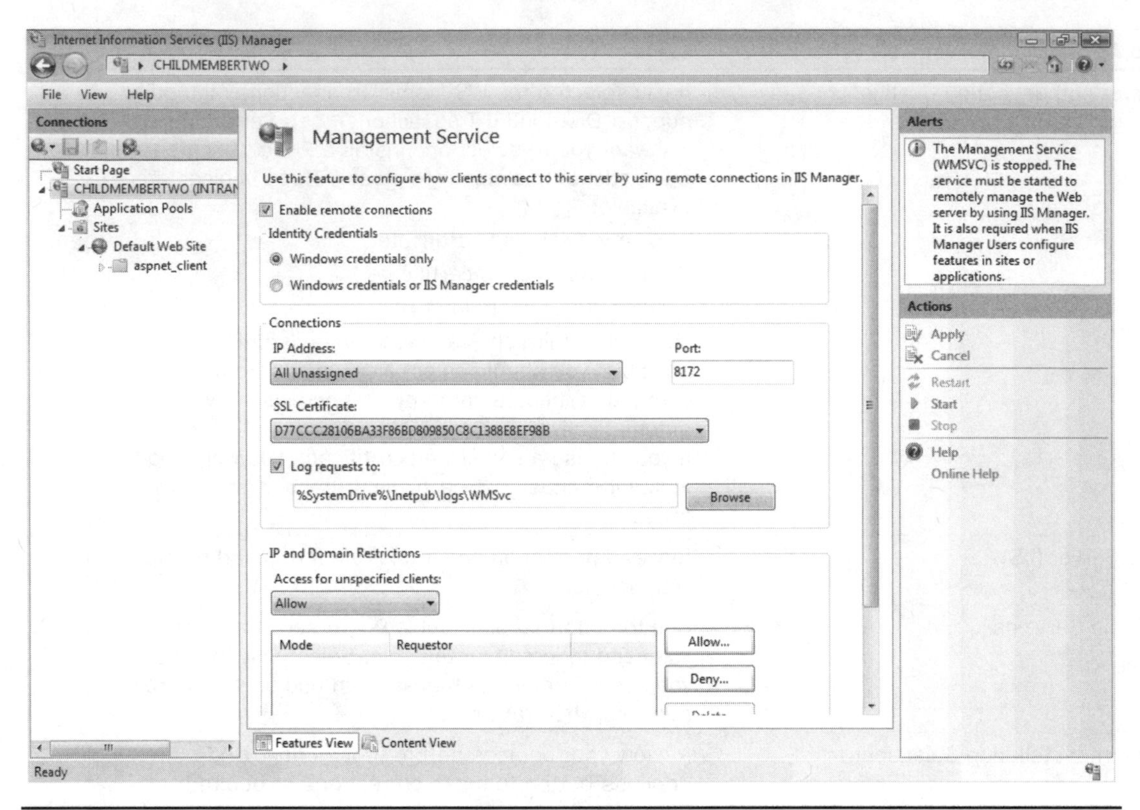

Figure 9-3 Enabling remote management in IIS 7

4. Move to the action pane, and click Start to start the service.
5. Then click Apply in the action pane to enable remote administration. Click the server name in the tree pane to return to the features view.

Finally, you can delegate any activity within the IIS 7 console. This is performed through the Feature Delegation icon in the Management section of the features view (see Figure 9-4). Each component of IIS can be delegated. Several settings are available in the action pane: Read/Write, Read Only, Not Delegated, and Reset to Inherited. By controlling each of these settings, you can create a fine-grained delegation strategy for IIS management. This is ideal to provide Web masters with the ability to manage their own sites, but without the ability to manage overall IIS Server settings.

Tip *More on IIS Manager can be found at www.iis.net/default.aspx?tabid=7&subtabid=73. More information on IIS 7 in general can be found at www.iis.net/default.aspx?tabid=1.*

Work with Application Support Services

In addition to its base application services, WS08 offers other support services that together provide a powerful application support platform. Two such services are Active Directory

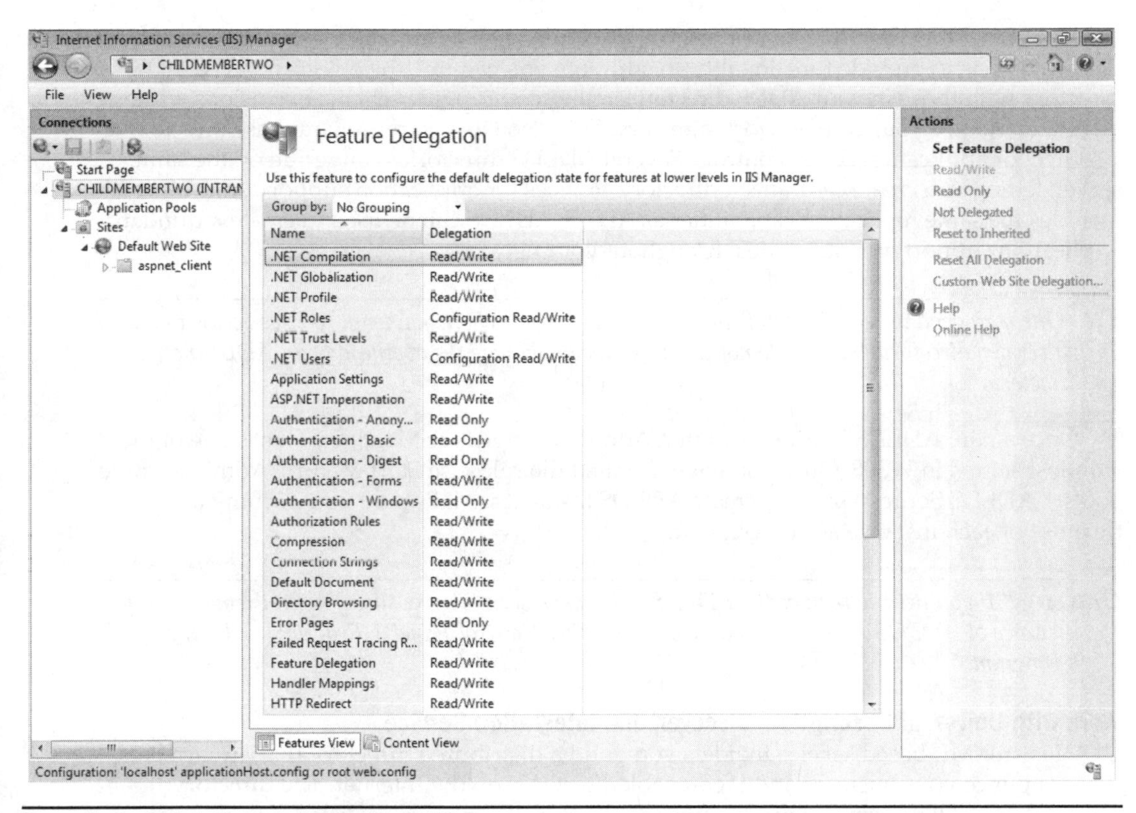

FIGURE 9-4 Delegating administration in IIS 7

Lightweight Directory Services (ADLDS) and the Universal Description, Discover, and Integration (UDDI) service. Both are directory services that provide complementary services to applications. ADLDS lets you have the power of a Lightweight Directory Application Protocol (LDAP) to provide authentication and user management services in support of your applications. UDDI provides a cataloging service that lets you easily locate Web service components.

When you work with complex enterprise-class applications, you will want to take advantage of these two services to extend the power of your applications.

Work with Active Directory Lightweight Directory Services

Directory-enabled applications profit from the power of a directory to store user and group objects. However, directory-enabled applications often require modifications to the directory schema in order to support custom application-specific objects. Since you know that you should minimize the modifications to the ADDS schema as much as possible because you cannot remove them, even though you can disable or reuse them, you need to rely on another directory service. This is where ADLDS comes in. Like the ADDS directory you use to manage your network, ADLDS provides a structured directory service, but one that does not support security principals.

You use ADLDS for directory-enabled applications that require user groupings and other custom objects to provide functionality. In addition, you can link the objects in an ADLDS directory with those in your ADDS directory, letting you provide schema extensions without having to modify your core network directory. This also lets you reuse your base directory as a source for application access controls. Several ADLDS directories can reside on the same server, letting you create centralized directory services for application support. And, since it includes the same replication capabilities as ADDS, ADLDS can be used to create redundant application support infrastructures throughout your network.

TIP *One very good use of ADLDS is in perimeter networks where you want to have access to the power of a directory, but you do not want to have to manage the overhead of an ADDS network directory.*

Once again, ADLDS is added through Add Roles in Server Manager. This is one of the simplest setups in WS08. Once you have installed the role, use Start Menu | Administrative Tools | ADLDS Setup Wizard to create ADLDS instances. Make sure you document the purpose of each instance as you create it.

CAUTION *If you need to remove the ADLDS role from a server, make sure you first remove every instance of ADLDS from the server. Do so by using Control Panel | Programs | Uninstall a Program.*

Work with Universal Description, Discover, and Integration Service

UDDI is an XML-based service that lets you build a distributed directory that, in turn, lets you announce your business and Web-enabled services on the Internet. The directory provided by UDDI is similar to a telephone directory. Businesses are listed by name, product, location, and Web service. Like a telephone directory, you can search by business name, Web service name, or even Web service type. This makes it easier to build distributed service-oriented architectures (SOAs), since it's simple and straightforward to discover Web services that complement the applications you build.

UDDI is also installed through Add Roles in Server Manager. When you install UDDI on the server, WS08 will install both the Discovery service and a services database to store service information. Installations can be on a single server, where each portion of the service is installed together, or in distributed mode, where the Discovery service is installed on one server and the database on another. The database portion of the server must run SQL Server and can rely on the Windows Internal Database to do so. In larger implementations, you should install a full version of SQL Server to provide enterprise-level support for this service.

Once installed, you configure UDDI services through the UDDI Services snap-in in Microsoft Management Console (MMC) version 3. Here you can modify UDDI users, integrate your UDDI directory with Active Directory Domain Services, control the encryption of UDDI data on your network, and modify database settings for the service, among other things.

TIP *More information on UDDI services in Windows Server 2008 can be found at http://technet2.microsoft.com/windowsserver2008/en/servermanager/uddiservices.mspx.*

Prepare Terminal Servers

One of the greatest features of Windows servers is the Terminal Service (TS). This service enables you to publish applications to remote computers, giving them full access to programs running in the Windows Server 2008 environment. The greatest advantage is in deployment and maintenance. Since the application operates on the terminal server, it is the only place it needs to be installed on, updated, and maintained. Also, since the application runs from the server, you only need to deploy shortcuts to users, nothing else, saving vast amounts of time. And this shortcut doesn't change, even though you may upgrade or otherwise modify the application.

The WS08 version of Terminal Services also provides a richer experience for users than previous versions. TS now includes several improvements. It supports several monitors on the client system and also provides a new, remote application mode, appropriately called RemoteApps, which lets you publish just the application itself instead of the entire desktop environment. This makes the use of Terminal Services much more seamless to end users.

TIP *As you know, Server Manager cannot manage a remote system. Therefore, you either have to log into the server itself to use Server Manager or, ideally, you simply publish Server Manager as a RemoteApp so that it can appear to run locally on your own workstation. Do this for each server you need to manage.*

Terminal Services runs in two different modes: Remote Administration and Application mode. The first lets you remotely administer servers and allows two remote connections at one time on a server. These remote connections can either be through RemoteApps or the Remote Desktop, which then gives you access to all of the features of the server because it displays the server's desktop on your system. Application mode is used when you want to publish applications to end users. This is also called Presentation Virtualization because it acts at the presentation layer of the network stack, providing users with a complete environment for application operation.

Thin client models are becoming more and more popular, especially with the proliferation of wireless Pocket PCs and the new Tablet PC device. Both have more limited resources, making server application hosting attractive to these user bases.

NOTE *Many organizations rely on centralized application sharing or presentation virtualization. But with the advent of application virtualization, many are also moving to this model, because application virtualization only requires file services to stream the applications to end-user systems, whereas Presentation Virtualization requires massive server configurations, with lots of random access memory (RAM) and network firepower, since the execution environment is the server itself. Nevertheless, the Presentation Virtualization option is still highly useful, since it allows you to share Server Manager for remote system management.*

Share Applications with Terminal Services

The Terminal Service is a core WS08 role. In fact, with WS08, Terminal Services can now automatically provide load balancing of terminal applications. For this feature to work, terminal servers must be clustered at the network level to work together to run a common set of applications and appear as a single system to clients and applications. To do this, they must be clustered through session broker load balancing. Once this is done, session directories can be used to transparently balance workloads between groups of terminal servers.

In addition, the WS08 version of Terminal Services supports roaming users. This means that users can open a session on a terminal server or terminal server cluster, disconnect from the server without closing the session, move to another computer, and reconnect to their existing TS session. This is a great advantage over previous TS capabilities. Finally, you can share TS applications through a new gateway service that lets users access these applications over common HTTP ports, such as 80 and 443, making it much easier for TS applications to cross the firewall.

Use the following process to prepare to use Terminal Services:

- Install and configure Terminal Services.
- Define your terminal server licensing model.
- Determine the application model for hosted applications.
- Install hosted applications.
- Define Terminal Services access policies.
- Define Terminal Services Group Policy objects.
- Determine how you will deploy shared applications.

Each of these steps requires care and forethought.

CAUTION *Do not install applications on servers prior to installing the Terminal Services server role! Terminal Services requires applications to be installed in a special sharing mode that can only be accomplished once the TS components have been installed on a system. If you install applications prior to TS, you will need to uninstall and reinstall them after TS has been installed.*

Install and Configure Terminal Services

The Terminal Server role is defined in the same way as all other server roles in the enterprise. It begins with the server-sizing exercise outlined in Chapter 4. Then it involves the basic server staging process, applying your customized kernel to the server, again as outlined in Chapter 4. Next, proceed as follows:

1. Use the Server Manager console to select Add Roles.
2. Select the Terminal Services role.
3. Use the values in Table 9-3 to run through the installation and configuration wizard.

The role is installed. Now you're ready to proceed to the next steps.

CAUTION *The TS Gateway role should be installed on a separate server because it may be in a perimeter network.*

Prepare Terminal Server Licensing

Terminal Services requires special CALs for each client that connects to the server. This is because each client connecting to Terminal Services in application mode—as opposed to administrative mode—is actually opening a Windows Server 2008 remote session. Even if

Add Terminal Services Role Wizard Page	Values
Terminal Services	Review the available information, if you need to, and move on to the next page.
Select Role Services	Several role services are available: Select Terminal Server since you want to share applications. TS Licensing is required if you want to use Terminal Services in Application mode. TS uses separate client access licenses (CALs) for sharing applications. If you are installing Terminal Services for administrative purposes, then TS Licensing is not required. Note that only a few TS Licensing servers are required in the network for redundancy. Do not install this on each TS server. TS Session Broker is used to provide connection continuity for users roaming from system to system. TS Gateway lets users connect to shared applications over common Internet ports. This service requires IIS, Network Policy and Access Services, and Windows Process Activation Service. Add required role services. TS Web Access lets users access shared applications through a Web portal. This service requires additional Application Development and Security components for IIS, as well as .NET support in the Windows Process Activation Service. Add required role services.
Application Compatibility	If applications are already installed on the server, you will need to uninstall and then reinstall them once the TS components are installed so that they can operate in multiuser mode.
Authentication Methods	Select Require Network Level Authentication. All clients will require the latest edition of the Remote Desktop client in order to use shared applications, but application connections will be more secure. Vista and WS08 systems already have this client.
Specify Licensing Mode	This lets you determine who needs a CAL, the user or the device. If users roam from system to system, using shared computers to access shared applications, then use Per User. If, however, your users have a principal PC that is assigned to them, then select Per Device. Make sure you select the proper TS CALs when you configure licensing later.
User Groups	Select the user groups that will be allowed to access these shared applications. If you intend to restrict application access to specific groups—for example, you are setting up a server to run financial applications and only want the financial group to access them— then select or create the appropriate group. Otherwise—and this is more common—select Domain Users to allow any user in your domain to access these applications.

TABLE 9-3 Install the Terminal Services Role

Add Terminal Services Role Wizard Page	Values
Configure Scope for TS Licensing	The scope of the TS licenses can cover either the entire forest or the domain you are in. If you followed the practices outlined in Chapter 5, you will only have a single global child domain; therefore, select This Domain. **Note** *In this case, only administrators will need access to shared applications throughout the forest—Server Manager, for example—and since they do not need a license for remote administration, you do not need to apply the licensing scope to the entire forest.*
Server Authentication Certificate	TS Gateway uses the Secure Sockets Layer (SSL) to secure communications between clients and servers. To do so, it requires a PKI certificate. Three choices are available: • Use an existing certificate • Create a self-signed certificate • Choose a certificate later The first or third choice is recommended. If at all possible, you should select a certificate from an external CA because it will automatically be trusted by the clients on your network. If you choose a self-signed certificate, you will need to install it manually on each client that interacts with this server.
Create Authorization Policies	Policies are required to allow Internet users to access TS Gateway applications. You can configure them later or configure them now. Select Now.
Select User Groups	Select the user groups that will be allowed to access shared applications through the gateway. If you intend to restrict application access to specific groups—for example, you are setting up a server to run remote applications and only want a select group of users to access them—then select or create the appropriate group. Otherwise, select Domain Users to allow any user in your domain to access these applications through the Internet.
Create a TS CAP	Connection authorization policies (CAPs) allow users to connect to the server when they meet specific conditions. CAPs can rely only on passwords, providing simple security, or on smart cards, relying on two-factor authentication. Two items are required, something you have, the card, and something you know, the password, to authenticate. Select Passwords for now. Chapter 10 will cover the use of smart cards.
Create a TS RAP	Resource authorization policies (RAPs) let you limit the internal resources Internet users can connect to inside your network. Users can connect to any computer or only specific computers. In this case, since you are creating a RAP for Terminal Services, make sure you create a custom security group in ADDS that includes the computer accounts of all of the servers that will run the TS role, and assign the RAP to this group.

Table 9-3 Install the Terminal Services Role (*continued*)

Add Terminal Services Role Wizard Page	Values
Network Policy and Access Services (NPAS)	NPAS servers are used to enforce both CAPs and RAPs. Review the information about this role before moving on. More on this topic is covered in Chapter 10.
NPAS Role Services	For NPAS support of the TS Gateway, only the Network Policy Server is required. Select only this role before you move on. **Note** *Only a few network policy servers are required in the network for redundancy. If this is not the first server you install for this role, then make sure you do not add this role to this server.*
Web Server (IIS)	Review information about this role, if required, before you move on.
Web Server Role Services	IIS is required for both the TS Gateway and TS Web Access. Accept the default selections and move on. **Note** *Only a few TS Gateways and TS Web Access servers are required for redundancy. Do not assign this role to every TS server in your network.*
Confirm Installation Selections	Review your choices before proceeding. Use the Previous button to make corrections if required. Click Install when ready.
Installation Progress and Installation Results	Review the installation progress, reboot the server, and then click Finish when the installation is complete.

TABLE 9-3 Install the Terminal Services Role (*continued*)

you have hardware that does not support Windows Vista, you can give users access to all of its features through remote terminal sessions on WS08 servers. If, on the other hand, you do have client hardware that supports Windows Vista, you gain a lot of advantages through Terminal Services. For example, there is no client component to deploy to have Terminal Sessions operate on a Windows Vista client because it already includes an updated Remote Desktop client. This means that you can focus on centralizing applications and the use of a simpler application deployment model.

CAUTION *It is important to install the Desktop Experience, activate the Themes service on WS08 TS servers, and enable the Windows Vista theme; otherwise, Windows Vista users will be faced with a Windows 2000–like interface when accessing remote applications in Terminal Services mode. This will most certainly lead to confusion (Windows Vista on the desktop and Windows 2000 on remote sessions) and increase support calls.*

Unlicensed servers will only allow clients to operate for 120 days, after which all sessions will end and the TS server will no longer respond to client requests. In order to license servers, you must install a Terminal Services license server. This server must be activated by Microsoft before it can begin to issue permanent licenses to your organization. Activation is the first step for this role.

1. Begin by moving to the Terminal Services node in Server Manager.
2. In the details pane, scroll down to the Advanced Tools section.

3. Click TS Licensing. This launches the TS Licensing Manager (TSLM). TSLM begins by scanning the network for TS licensing servers and then displays them once they are found.
4. To activate a server, right-click it and select Activate Server (see Figure 9-5).
5. This launches the Activation Wizard. Click Next.
6. Select the connection method. Automatic Connection is the best. Click Next.
7. Enter your personal information and click Next.
8. Provide contact information and click Next.
9. This will activate the server. Make sure the Start Install Licenses Wizard option is selected, and click Next.
10. Review the information and click Next. This locates the Microsoft Activation Server.
11. Select the appropriate license program based on the type of licenses you purchased, and click Next.
12. Type your license code(s), and click Add. Click Next when done to complete the Install License Wizard. The wizard then connects to the Microsoft Clearing House and installs the license key packs. Click Finish when done, and close the TS License Manager.

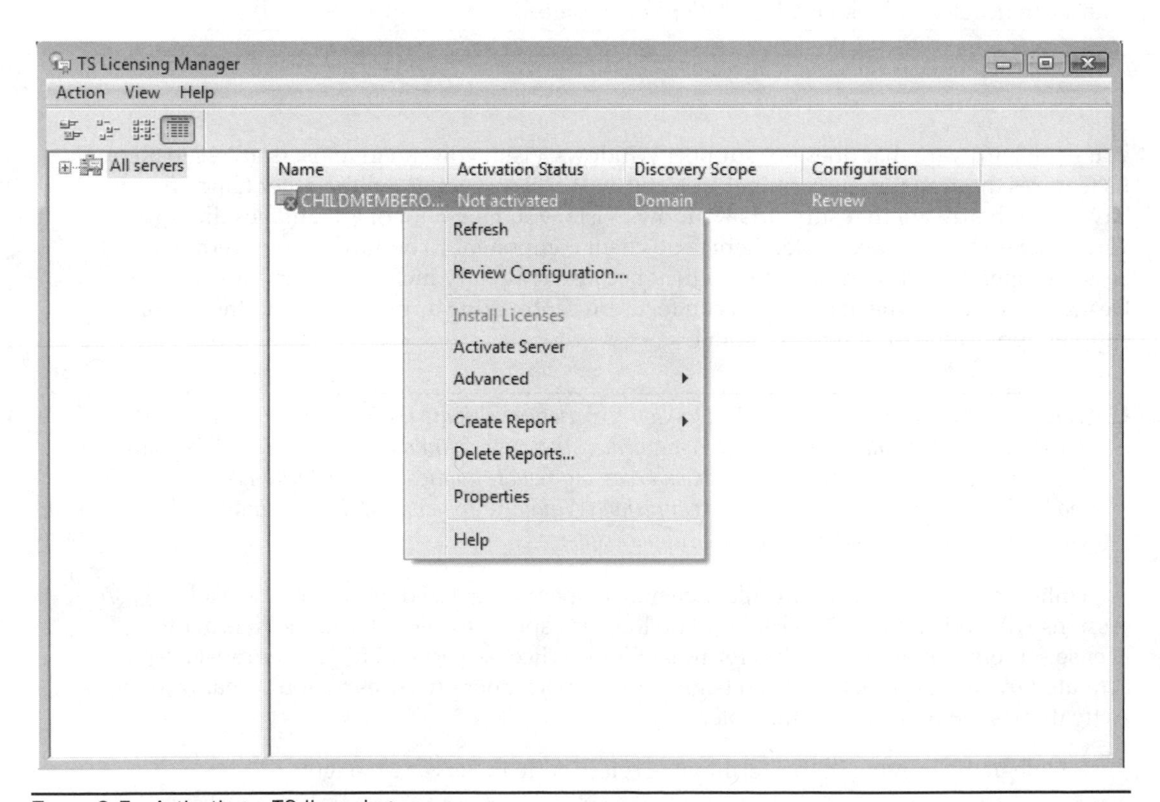

Figure 9-5 Activating a TS licensing server

Now you're ready to start issuing licenses to TS sessions. This is an area where you will want to apply Group Policy settings. By default, TS servers issue licenses to any server that requests one. By using the License Server Security Group GPO setting—under Computer Configuration | Policies | Administrative Templates | Windows Components | Terminal Services | TS Licensing—you can restrict TS sessions to authorized TS servers only. To do so, you will need to place the TS servers you want to grant licenses to in the Terminal Server Computers group on the TS licensing server. This will ensure that licenses are not wasted by being granted to servers running Terminal Services in remote administration mode.

Determine the Application Model and Install Applications

Terminal Services applications should be installed through Add or Remove Programs, because this component ensures that applications are installed in multiuser mode. If you prefer to install remotely or through the command line, you must use the `CHANGE USER` command. Use `CHANGE USER /INSTALL` to set the terminal server to installation mode, perform the installation, and then use the `CHANGE USER /EXECUTE` command to reset the server to execution mode.

Applications and software products should be installed before allowing users to connect to the server so that you can test their operation properly before users start activating them. In addition, you should take the following guidelines into consideration when deciding which applications should be installed on a terminal server:

- Do not run 16-bit applications, since they can reduce the number of concurrent users by up to 40 percent and require 50 percent more RAM per user. 16-bit applications will also not run in x64 installations of WS08.
- Do not run MS-DOS applications, since they can consume all of the central processing unit (CPU) resources of a server.
- Applications that run constant processes in the background (spell checking in Microsoft Word, for example) consume more resources.
- Applications that use high-quality graphics consume more bandwidth.

Your Terminal Services should be used to run applications that fall into the following categories:

- Applications that require complex installations. Placing these applications on TS servers reduces the number of installation points and thus the risks of having problems with the installation. You can also solve these problems through application virtualization, as discussed earlier.
- Applications that require frequent changes. Placing these applications on TS servers reduces the number of installation points and, therefore, the installation and deployment workload.
- Applications that are prohibitively expensive on a per-user basis so long as their licensing model allows TS sharing.
- Applications for users with low bandwidth access. This is ideal for wireless devices.
- Applications for users in sites where there are no local servers. If the number of users in a site (ten or fewer) does not warrant a local server, you can give these users access to the same service level by allowing them to use applications remotely.

The Terminal Services application operation model is slightly different from the standard WS08 model because of the multiuser environment. You should also check for compatibility scripts for the applications you install. These scripts modify standard installations to make them TS-compatible. They should be run after the application installation. Scripts are found in the `%SYSTEMROOT%\APPLICATION COMPATIBILITY SCRIPTS` folder.

Prepare GPOs for Terminal Services

There are 80 Group Policy Object settings for Terminal Services. They fall into several different categories that control many of the settings for users, PCs, and servers when connecting to remote applications.

As you can see, most every TS setting can be managed through GPOs. Like the user folder information outlined in file sharing services (see Chapter 8), user Terminal Service information is no longer entered in the user account properties (see Chapter 7) in ADDS because if you do it there, you must do it on a per-user basis. User parameters are now set through the user configuration of a GPO. Server and PC settings are set through the computer configuration of a GPO. Table 9-4 outlines the settings you should apply to each section.

TIP *If you use GPO settings to control the behavior of your TS sessions, you will not need to configure them in either the user account properties or in Terminal Server Configuration Manager. You will also ensure that all systems are configured in exactly the same manner.*

Location	Settings	Applied to...	Comments
Computer Configuration | Policies | Administrative Templates | Windows Components | Terminal Services | Remote Desktop Connection Client	Allow .rdp files from unknown publishers	PC	Disable to provide a more secure TS environment.
	Allow .rdp files from valid publishers and users' default .rdp settings	PC	Enable to provide a more secure TS environment.
	Configure server authentication for client	PC	Enable: Do not connect if authentication fails Ensures the TS server is the authorized.
	Do not allow passwords to be saved		Makes connections easier because passwords are stored in the .rdp file.
	Prompt for credentials on the client computer		Keep default setting.
	Specify Secure Hash Algorithm Version 1.0 (SHA1) thumbprints of certificates representing trusted .rdp publishers	PC	Enable and include certificate thumbprints if you enabled valid publishers previously.

TABLE 9-4 Terminal Services GPO Settings

Location	Settings	Applied to...	Comments
Computer Configuration | Policies | Administrative Templates | Windows Components | Terminal Services | Terminal Server | Connections	Allow reconnection from original client only	Server	Disable if you want to use Session Broker for fault tolerance.
	Allow remote restart of unlisted programs	Server	Disable if you want to control the programs users can run when linked to the Remote Desktop.
	Allow users to connect remotely using Terminal Services	PC	Enable to allow Remote Desktop.
	Automatic reconnection	PC	Enable.
	Configure keep-alive connection interval	Server	Enable to synchronize the client and the server connection state.
	Deny logoff of an administrator logged in to the console session		Keep default setting.
	Limit number of connections	Server	Could be used to monitor server loads.
	Restrict Terminal Services users to a single remote session	PC	Enable to control resource use on servers.
	Set rules for remote control of Terminal Services user sessions	Server	Enable full remote control with user's permissions.
Terminal Server | Device and Resource Redirection	Allow audio redirection	Server	Enable to limit bandwidth use.
	Allow time zone redirection	Server	If required in multiple time zones.
	Do not allow Clipboard redirection		Keep default setting.
	Do not allow COM port redirection		Keep default setting.
	Do not allow drive redirection		Keep default setting.

TABLE 9-4 Terminal Services GPO Settings (*continued*)

PART IV

Location	Settings	Applied to...	Comments
	Do not allow Local Printer Terminal (LPT) port redirection		Keep default setting.
	Do not allow smart card device redirection		Keep default setting.
	Do not allow supported Plug and Play device redirection		Keep default setting.
Terminal Server | Licensing	Hide notifications about TS licensing problems that affect the terminal server		Keep default setting.
	Set the Terminal Services licensing mode		Keep default setting.
	Use the specified Terminal Services license servers		Keep default setting.
Terminal Server | Printer Redirection	Do not allow client printer redirection		Keep default setting.
	Do not set default client printer to be default printer in a session		Keep default setting.
	Redirect only the default client printer	PC	Enable to avoid potential printer error messages on the server when print drivers are not available.
	Specify terminal server fallback printer driver behavior		Keep default setting.
	Use Terminal Services Easy Print driver first		Keep default setting.
Terminal Server | Profiles	Set path for TS roaming profiles	Server	Enable. Create a share for user profiles and home folders, and map it.
	Set TS user home directory	Server	Enable. Create a share for user profiles and home folders, and map it.

TABLE 9-4 Terminal Services GPO Settings (*continued*)

Location	Settings	Applied to…	Comments
	Use mandatory profiles on the terminal server	Server	Use only if you have a strict environment.
Terminal Server | Remote Session Environment	Always show desktop on connection		Keep default setting. Not required if you use RemoteApps.
	Enforce removal of Remote Desktop wallpaper		Keep default setting. Not required if you use RemoteApps.
	Limit maximum color depth		Keep default setting. Not required if you use RemoteApps.
	Remove Disconnect option from Shut Down dialog box		Keep default setting.
	Remove Windows Security item from Start menu		Keep default setting. Not required if you use RemoteApps.
	Start a program on connection		Keep default setting. Not required if you use RemoteApps.
Terminal Server | Security	Always prompt for password upon connection	Server	Use only if you have a highly secure environment or for protected applications.
	Do not allow local administrators to customize permissions		Keep default setting.
	Require secure Remote Procedure Call (RPC) communication	Server	Enable to secure communications.
	Require use of specific security layer for Remote Desktop Protocol (RDP) connections	Server	Enable. SSL (TLS 1.0) will provide the most secure connection.
	Require user authentication using RDP 6.0 for remote connections	Server	Enable only if all your clients use Vista.
	Server authentication certificate template	Server	Enable along with the SSL security layer in previous setting.

Table 9-4 Terminal Services GPO Settings (*continued*)

Location	Settings	Applied to…	Comments
	Set client connection encryption level	Server	Keep default setting. Encryption is set to high by default.
Terminal Server | Session Time Limits	Set a time limit for active but idle Terminal Services sessions	Server	Enable and set to 60 minutes. Long idle times can use server resources when no one is actually working.
	Set a time limit for active Terminal Services sessions		Keep default setting.
	Set a time limit for disconnected sessions	Server	Enable and set to 30 minutes. Long disconnected times can use server resources when no one is actually connected.
	Terminate session when time limits are reached		Keep default setting.
Terminal Server | Temporary Folders	Do not delete temp folder upon exit		Keep default setting.
	Do not use temporary folders per session		Keep default setting.
Terminal Server | TS Session Broker	Join TS Session Broker	Server	Enable to support high availability.
	TS Session Broker farm name	Server	Enable and list farm name.
	TS Session Broker load balancing	Server	Enable to make best resource usage of the TS farm.
	TS Session Broker Server	Server	Enable and list server name.
	Use IP address redirection		Keep default setting.
Computer Configuration | Policies | Administrative Templates | Windows Components | Terminal Services | TS Licensing	License server security group	Server	Enable. Create a security group containing all TS server computer accounts, and list it here. This ensures that licenses only go to authorized TS servers.

TABLE 9-4 Terminal Services GPO Settings (*continued*)

Location	Settings	Applied to...	Comments
	Prevent license upgrade		Keep default setting. Only required when you have a mix of server operating systems running TS.
User Configuration | Policies | Administrative Templates | Windows Components | Terminal Services | Remote Desktop Client	Allow .rdp files from unknown publishers		Set at the PC level.
	Allow .rdp files from valid publishers and users' default .rdp settings		Set at the PC level.
	Do not allow passwords to be saved		Set at the PC level.
	Specify SHA1 thumbprints of certificates representing trusted .rdp publishers		Set at the PC level.
User Configuration | Policies | Administrative Templates | Windows Components | Terminal Services | Terminal Server | Connections	Allow reconnection from original client only		Keep default setting if you have users roaming from PC to PC.
	Set rules for remote control of Terminal Services user sessions		Set at the PC level.
User Configuration | Policies | Administrative Templates | Windows Components | Terminal Services | Terminal Server | Device and Resource Redirection	Allow time zone redirection		Set at the PC level.
	Do not allow Clipboard redirection		Keep default setting, unless you are sharing a secure application with confidential data.
User Configuration | Policies | Administrative Templates | Windows Components | Terminal Services | Terminal Server | Printer Redirection	Redirect only the default client printer		Set at the PC level.

TABLE 9-4 Terminal Services GPO Settings (*continued*)

PART IV

Location	Settings	Applied to...	Comments
	Use Terminal Services Easy Print driver first		Keep default setting.
User Configuration | Policies | Administrative Templates | Windows Components | Terminal Services | Terminal Server | Remote Session Environment	Always show desktop on connection		Set at the PC level.
	Enforce removal of Remote Desktop wallpaper		Set at the PC level.
	Start a program on connection		Set at the PC level.
User Configuration | Policies | Administrative Templates | Windows Components | Terminal Services | Terminal Server | Session Time Limits	Set a time limit for active but idle Terminal Services sessions		Set at the PC level.
	Set a time limit for active Terminal Services sessions		Set at the PC level.
	Set a time limit for disconnected sessions		Set at the PC level.
	Terminate session when time limits are reached		Set at the PC level.
User Configuration | Policies | Administrative Templates | Windows Components | Terminal Services | TS Gateway	Enable connection through TS Gateway	User	Enable only for specific user groups that connect from external sessions.
	Set TS Gateway authentication method	User	Enable and use locally logged on credentials for single sign-on.
	Set TS Gateway server address	User	Enable and list TS Gateway server address.

TABLE 9-4 Terminal Services GPO Settings (*continued*)

NOTE *While many of the load-balancing settings for Terminal Services required at least the Enterprise edition of Windows Server 2003 to function, they only require the Standard edition in WS08. More on load balancing is discussed in Chapter 11.*

GPO settings for WS08 are set at three levels:

- Server
- PC
- User

The Server settings should be applied to a GPO that is targeted to the Virtual Service Offerings | Terminal Services Servers OU, which contains all of the computer accounts for your TS servers. The PC settings should be set to a global PC GPO that will affect all PCs. The User settings should be assigned to a special GPO that affects all users, but is filtered through a security group that contains users that access TS servers remotely.

CAUTION *Remember that Group Policy only affects users and PCs that are members of your domain. Keep this in mind, especially for the settings for the TS Gateway. If users connect to remote applications from public systems, these GPO settings will not affect them.*

Deploy Terminal Services Applications

Terminal Services can be set to operate in either remote application mode or in full desktop mode. Single applications are deployed to users already having access to full desktops. Full desktop mode should be reserved for users lacking the capability on their own system; this mode is mostly reserved for administration purposes now that WS08 supports RemoteApps.

In either case, you can deploy an application or a Remote Desktop through several means:

- You can use the delivery of a Terminal Services connection file or Remote Desktop Protocol that include the proper parameters for accessing the TS server.
- You can make a connection visible in TS Web Access.
- You can deploy a Windows Installer package. This last method only works for RemoteApps.

Each of these deployment methods is performed through Server Manager.

But, before you can deploy these files, you need to add RemoteApps.

Add RemoteApps

Adding RemoteApps is easy and straightforward. Begin by installing the application to be shared, as per the procedures outlined earlier. Then add them as RemoteApps:

1. Once the application is installed, move to Server Manager and navigate to Roles | Terminal Services | TS RemoteApp Manager.
2. Click Add RemoteApps in the action pane. This launches the RemoteApp Wizard. Click Next.

PART IV

3. Select the program to add to the RemoteApps list. This list displays all known installed applications. You can view its properties before moving on to the next page. Properties lets you control command-line arguments as well as icons and whether or not the application will be available in TS Web Access (see Figure 9-6). Click OK when done.
4. You can also add all of the applications at once in this page if you want to. Click Next.
5. Review your options and click Finish when ready. Use the Previous button to correct any settings that don't look right.

Repeat this operation for each product you want to make available remotely. You are now ready to deploy the application.

Deploy with RDP Files

RDP files contain all of the settings required to perform a remote connection. They are most useful for connections to entire Remote Desktops. They also work for RemoteApps, but the latter should really be deployed with Windows Installer packages.

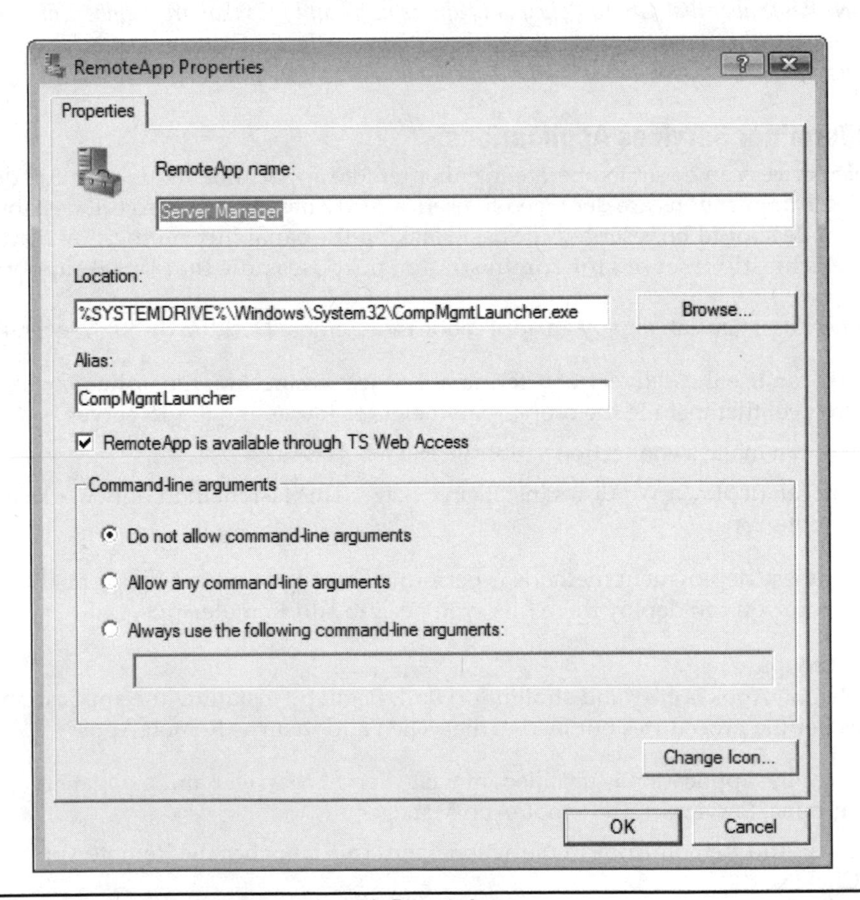

FIGURE 9-6 Deploying Server Manager through RemoteApps

To create RDP files, use the following procedure:

1. In Server Manager, navigate to Roles | Terminal Services | TS RemoteApp Manager.
2. In the TS RemoteApp Manager details pane, move to the RemoteApps list to select the application you want to deploy.
3. Next, select Create .rdp File under Other Distribution Options. This launches another RemoteApps Wizard. Click Next.
4. In the Specify Package Settings page (see Figure 9-7), review and modify the following settings:
   - Change the location to save packages to a drive that includes a shared folder, for example, D:\Administration\Packaged Programs. Share the folder as Package$ to hide it from end users. Terminal server settings will include the server name, the port it uses, and the authentication level to be used. By default, RDP connections use port 3389.
   - TS Gateway settings should be detected automatically if you set your GPOs properly.
   - Certificate settings are controlled by whether or not a certificate has been installed on the server. Remember, public certificates are best, since they will automatically be trusted by client PCs.

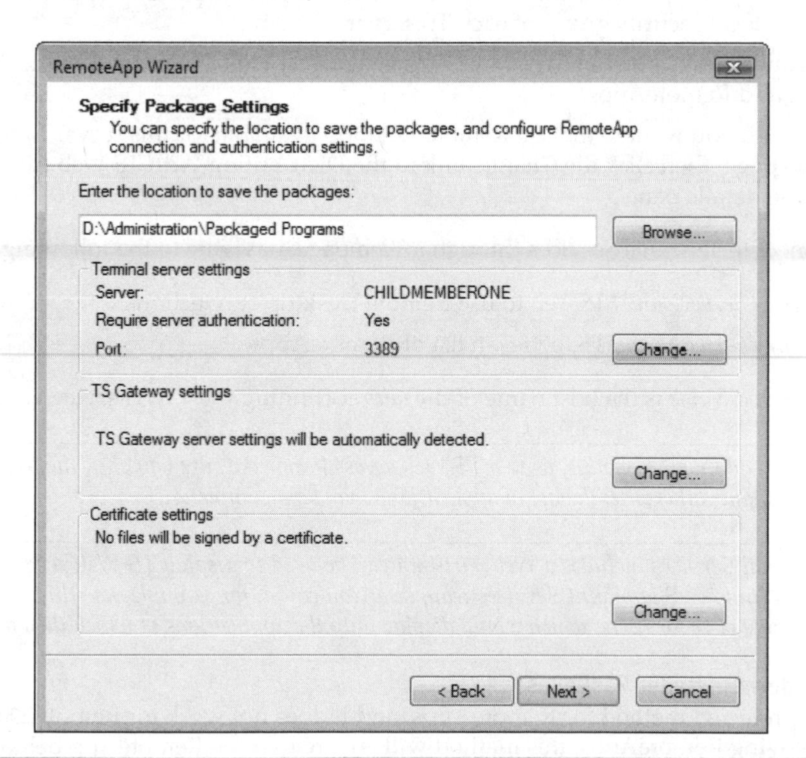

FIGURE 9-7 Configuring RDP settings

5. Click Next when done. Review your options and click Finish when ready. Use the Previous button to correct any settings that don't look right.
6. The wizard automatically names and saves the RDP file. Test the connection before deploying it to users.
7. Deploy the RDP file to users through a logon script or other deployment mechanism.

Users will now have access to your TS server RemoteApp.

Deploy Through TS Web Access

In addition, Windows Server 2008 supports Web access to both Remote Desktop connections and RemoteApps. The advantage of this model is that no deployment is required, since client access is located on an internal web page. WS08 includes a sample web page that can serve as a starting point for your Terminal Services Web access page.

Configuration of TS Web Access (TWA) content is controlled through the Server Manager | Terminal Services | TS RemoteApp Manager node. The details pane includes settings for each of the components that make this deployment mode operate. Three actions are required:

- First, if you have separated the TS Web Access and the TS server roles onto different servers, then make sure you add the computer account of the server running TS Web Access into the TS Web Access security group on each of the TS servers you want to access through the Web. Ideally, you will make a security group containing the computer accounts of all TWA servers in your network and include this account in the local security group of each TS server.
- Second, publish RemoteApps in TWA web pages. This is done automatically when you add RemoteApps.
- Third, if you want to make a Remote Desktop available for this server in the TWA web page, then click the Change link in the Distribution With TS Web Access section of the details pane.

To connect to Terminal Services through a Web page, navigate to the following pages:

- http://*ServerName*/TSWeb to use Remote Desktop connections
- http://*ServerName*/TS to view a list of RemoteApps

Where *ServerName* is the host name of the server running the TWA service.

TIP *When you add new RemoteApps to a TS Web access list, make sure you click the Refresh link in the details pane; otherwise, the list of applications may be incomplete.*

NOTE *Terminal Services includes a Web part that can be used to display TS Web access contents within a Windows SharePoint Services team site. You could, for example, use this to create a custom home page for users, which would display only the applications to which they have access.*

Deploy Windows Installer Packages

This is the preferred method for RemoteApps, and it does not work for Remote Desktops. When deploying RemoteApps, this method will ensure that the RemoteApp behaves as if it was part of the user's own desktop. This means that documents will be linked, shortcuts will appear in the Start menu, and so on. In addition, using Windows Installer packages will make the shortcut much easier to deploy, since you can deploy it using Group Policy Software Delivery with ADDS. Overall, this method greatly simplifies your work.

Deploy applications by using the following procedure:

1. In Server Manager, navigate to Roles | Terminal Services | TS RemoteApp Manager.
2. In the TS RemoteApp Manager details pane, move to the RemoteApps list to select the application you want to deploy.
3. Next, select Create Windows Installer Package under Other Distribution Options. This launches another RemoteApps Wizard. Click Next.
4. In the Specify Package Settings page, review and modify the following settings:
   - Change the location to save packages to a drive that includes a shared folder, for example, D:\Administration\Packaged Programs. Share the folder as Package$ to hide it from end users by removing it from the network browse list. Terminal server settings will include the server name, the port it uses, and the authentication level to be used. By default, RDP connections use port 3389.
   - TS Gateway settings should be detected automatically if you set your GPOs properly.
   - Certificate settings are controlled by whether or not a certificate has been installed on the server. Remember, public certificates are best, since they will automatically be trusted by client PCs.
5. Click Next when done. On the next page, you configure the way the application interacts with the user's desktop (see Figure 9-8). Place it in the Start menu into a custom program folder, for example, Central Applications. Also, make sure you select Associate Client Extensions For This Program With The RemoteApp, as this will let users run the RemoteApp by double-clicking the document formats it generates. Click Next.
6. Review your options and click Finish when ready. Use the Previous button to correct any settings that don't look right.
7. The wizard automatically names and saves the RDP file. Test the Microsoft Installer (MSI) before deploying it to users.
8. Deploy the MSI file to users through a GPO (see Chapter 7) or other distribution mechanism.

Users will now have seamless access to your TS server RemoteApp.

Create Highly Available Terminal Services

Windows Server 2008 includes the Terminal Services Session Broker Load Balancing (TS SBLB) feature to let you create highly available TS server infrastructures. TS SBLB is performed through an integration of the Domain Name Service (DNS) with the service. Basically, you create a single entry in DNS for the TS farm. Include the IP address of each TS server in the farm into this DNS entry. Also, as seen in Table 9-4, configure the TS SBLB feature through Group Policy.

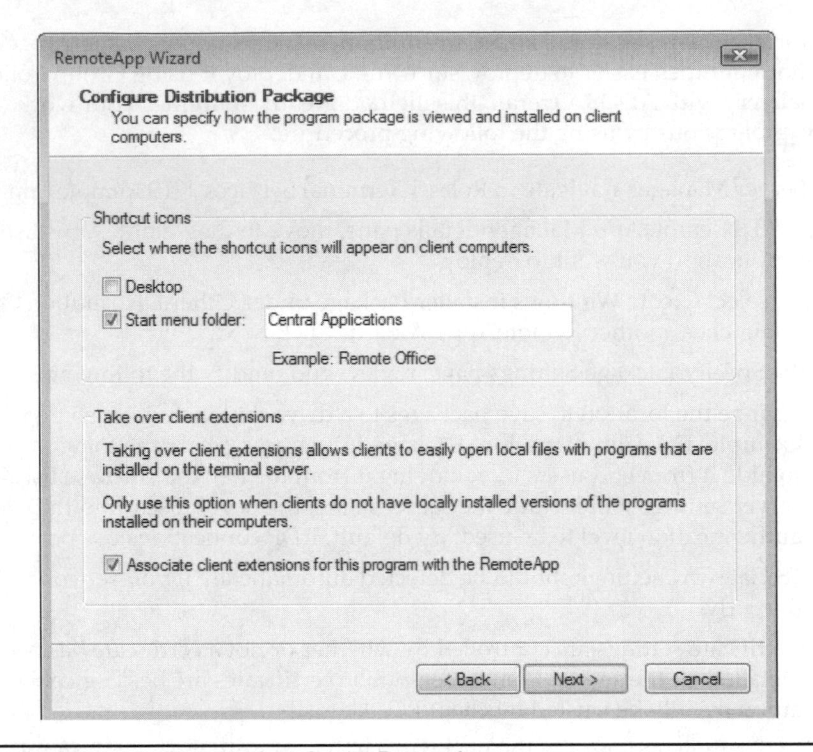

FIGURE 9-8 Configuring desktop settings for the RemoteApp

When users first connect to a TS session, the Session Broker will automatically connect them to the first IP address in the list, but then redirect them to a TS server with a lower workload. If the connection to the first IP address fails, the Session Broker will connect the user to the next IP address and so on.

This provides a more refined user experience and allows users to disconnect from a session and reconnect to the appropriate session in the farm. If you plan to make extensive use of Terminal Services in your network, especially if you plan to go beyond remote administration, then you should consider working with the Session Broker.

TIP *More information on the Session Broker is available at http://technet2.microsoft.com/windowsserver2008/en/library/9da3742f-699d-4476-b050-c50aa14aaf081033.mspx?mfr=true.*

Your Terminal Services environment is now ready for production. Ensure that you use a thorough testing policy before giving users access to the applications you host on your terminal servers.

The Remote Desktop Console: The Administrator's Best Friend

One of the greatest tools you'll find in Windows Server 2008 for remote administration is the Remote Desktops console (RDC). That's because this console lets you regroup all of the RDP connections you need to manage every server in your network in one single place, providing a central location for the administration of your entire network. And, what's even better, you can save the credentials you use to log onto each server within the console, making each server only one click away.

CAUTION *The RDC is a powerful tool since it stores passwords that provide access to servers. Make sure you store the console in your profile to secure it, and make sure you lock your computer any time you leave your desk.*

This console is present by default in Administrative Tools, but as you would expect, it is empty. If you want to use it to its fullest, then you need to populate it with your own list of shortcuts. This lets you build an ultimate RDC that provides a central interface and includes connections to every system you need to manage.

If you build it on a server, then you only need to add the shortcut connections. If you build it on a workstation, then you need to install the Windows Server 2008 Remote Administration Tools. Prepare your console as follows:

1. Begin by launching the console. It is located under Start Menu | Administrative Tools | Remote Desktops.
2. Save the console. By default, this console is stored within Administrative Tools, but since you will be saving your credentials with your connections to simplify server access, you should save this console in your Documents folder. This automatically secures it so that only you have access to it. To do so, use File | Save As, move to your Documents folder, name it Remote Desktops, and click Save.
3. Now you can begin to build the console. By default, this console includes one copy of the Remote Desktops snap-in. If you only have one environment to manage, that is fine. But if you build multiple environments for production, testing, and development, as discussed in Chapter 5, you should add one Remote Desktops snap-in for each environment you need to manage. Using multiple snap-ins makes it easier to differentiate between environments. For example, you can differentiate between the resource pools and virtual service offerings by using a different snap-in for each. This makes it clearer and easier to identify the servers of each environment.
4. Then use File | Add/Remove Snap-in to open the dialog box. Select the Remote Desktops snap-in under Available Snap-ins, and click the Add button (see Figure 9-9). Click the Add button as many times as you need the snap-in, once for each environment you manage. Click OK when you're done.
5. You're ready to add a connection with saved credentials for each server. Saving credentials allows you to make faster connections to the remote system. But you need to make sure the console is secure—all the more reason to put it under your Documents folder.
6. In the left pane, first select a Remote Desktops snap-in, and then right-click it to select Add New Connection (see Figure 9-10). Enter the following information:
   - The server name or the IP address
   - The connection name (give a logical name that represents what this connection links to)
   - Clear Connect To Console, since this only applies to Windows Server 2003 systems.
   - Select Allow Me To Save Credentials.

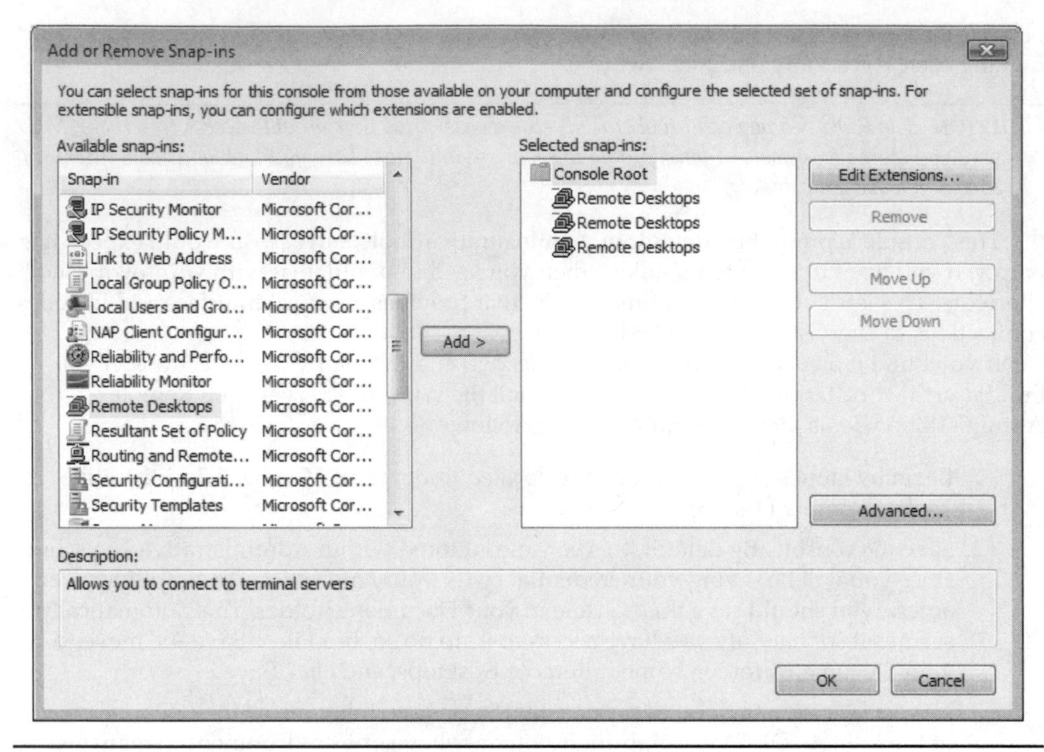

FIGURE 9-9 Add or Remove Snap-ins dialog box in Vista

FIGURE 9-10 Add New Connection dialog box

FIGURE 9-11 Add Credentials dialog box

7. Click OK to create the connection.
8. In order to save the credentials, you need to connect to the link. The credentials dialog box will appear (see Figure 9-11). Enter appropriate credentials, and make sure you select the Remember My Credentials check box. Click OK to connect to the server. Your credentials are now saved. If you return to the Properties dialog box, you'll see that it now includes your credentials (see Figure 9-12). Notice the Edit or Delete links that let you modify credentials for this connection.
9. Repeat the same steps for each connection you need in that environment. Move to a different snap-in for each different environment. Save the console again when you're done. Finally, you need to save the console settings to complete the creation of the console.

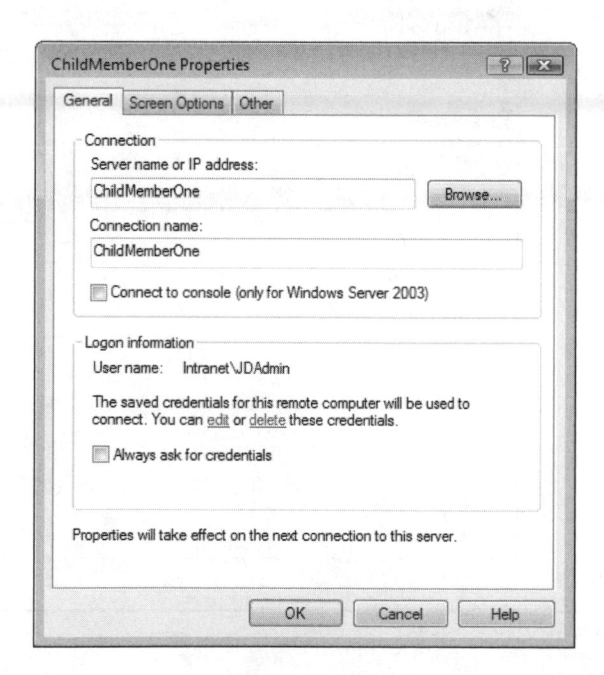

FIGURE 9-12 Connection Properties dialog box with saved credentials

10. Click File | Options and enter the name of your console. Make sure you set the console mode to User Mode - Full Access and that Do Not Save Changes To This Console is not selected. Also, make sure that Allow The User To Customize Views is selected. Click OK when you're done. Save the console again. Now you won't be prompted to save the console each time you close it.

You're done. Now you can use your console to manage your multiple physical servers or virtual machines in a single interface. For example, an ultimate RDC console could include as many different environments as you need (see Figure 9-13). Moving from machine to machine is as easy as clicking the machine name.

TIP *If the console or the connection becomes unresponsive, simply right-click the connection name and choose Disconnect. Right-click again to choose Connect, and you're right back in.*

The connections contained in this console are really nifty and can save you a lot of time. Here are some tips for its use:

- To use the console, just open it and click once on the link you want to connect to.
- To break a connection, either log off from the remote server or right-click Disconnect.

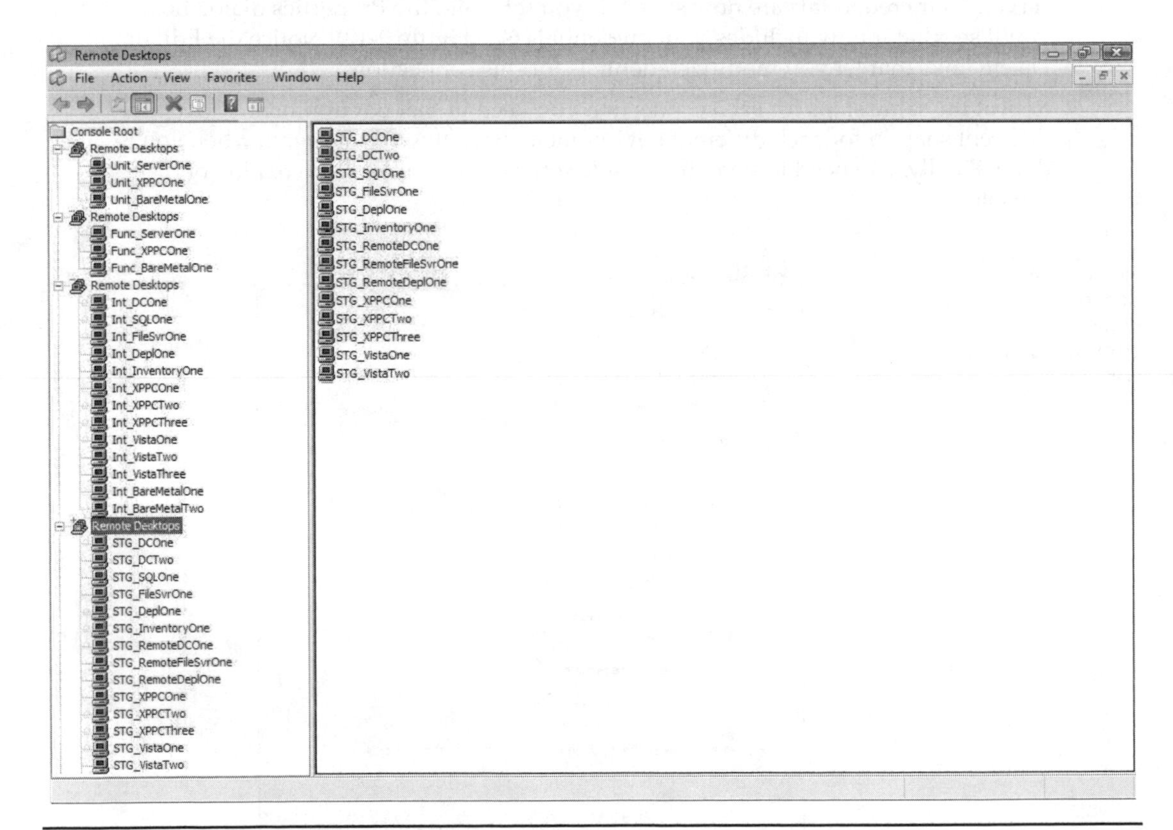

FIGURE 9-13 An ultimate RDC console

- If you have already connected to a link and you are disconnected, reconnect by right-clicking the link and selecting Connect.
- You'll want to keep connection names short and make sure the tree pane is as small as possible, because Remote Desktop connections will automatically fill the details pane. Maximize the console and maximize the console window to get as much screen real estate as possible for your connections.
- Once your connections are made, you can modify their properties, including such items as screen resolution, linking your local disk drives to the remote machine and more. To make these types of modifications permanent, you need to right-click the console and select Author. This will let you modify settings and save them for next time.
- Once the console is ready, place it in your Quick Launch area. That way, you'll only be one click away from any server you need to administer.

You'll soon find that this is the most valuable console in your administrative toolkit.

Collaboration Servers

Most users are used to the File Sharing service, and for them, this service is an effective way to collaborate with their peers. But for several years now, a new movement has been dawning in IT circles: the use of collaboration web sites that replace the need for file shares. This is the focus of Windows SharePoint Services (WSS).

WSS is based on the Internet Information Services Web infrastructure and is designed to provide a collection of integrated services to support collaboration. Its main capabilities include the ability to create team-based web sites that support the exchange of information as well as document sharing. WSS is also the base platform for Microsoft's flagship collaboration tool, Office SharePoint Portal Server. While the inclusion of SharePoint turns WSS into a comprehensive collaboration environment, the use of WSS on its own still provides several powerful features for working with peers.

For example, administrators can create a custom team site that hosts all of the tools they need to manage servers. This could include integration with Terminal Services in Remote administration mode to provide Web access to the Server Manager application on each of the servers you need to manage. If you need to manage a server, go to the team site, locate the TS Web Access Web part, find the link for the server you want to manage, and double-click it. Team sites are also great for integration of all administrative and operational documentation. Microsoft provides a host of team site templates that can be loaded, once WSS is deployed, to provide free starting points for collaboration environments of all types.

TIP *Free Windows SharePoint Services Templates can be found at www.microsoft.com/technet/windowsserver/sharepoint/wssapps/templates/default.mspx.*

In addition, WSS sites can be a boon to end users in every category in your network. But most importantly, because they are based on Web technologies, team sites can provide both structured and unstructured information to your end users, without the need for special system infrastructures, because everything runs through the Web browser.

CAUTION *WSS also provides workflow services, but in order for most of the features of these services to work, you need to e-mail–enable your server. Do so by installing the Simple Mail Transfer Protocol (SMTP) Server feature in Server Manager. Note that you will need to use the IIS 6 Management Console to manage and administer this service.*

Deploy Windows SharePoint Services

Because it is in its third iteration, WSS provides several enhancements over its predecessors:

- The administration model has been integrated into one central location, making it easier to control the various features of WSS.
- A better security model based on IIS 7 to provide more thorough compliance with regulations.
- Simpler network configurations.
- Simpler programming model for custom development.

The base structure of WSS is a two-tiered structure. The interface front end is provided by IIS 7 and is the main component users will interact with. The second part of the WSS infrastructure is the data persistence component. In simple deployments, this is provided by the Windows Internal Database (WID). In more complex deployments, you will need to rely on the installation of SQL Server.

NOTE *In order to locate WSS in the Add Roles Wizard, you need to update Server Manager with available add-ons. Use the Windows Update Web site to do so.*

Deployment is simple. Once again, you rely on the Add Roles Wizard in Server Manager.

1. Begin by launching the Add Roles Wizard.
2. Select the Windows SharePoint Services role.
3. Use the values in Table 9-5 to complete the entries in this wizard.

Once the role is installed, you will find two new additions to Administration Tools:

- SharePoint Central Administration
- SharePoint Products and Technologies Configuration Wizard

The first is used to centrally administer WSS. The second is used to perform mostly one-time configuration changes to your WSS installation.

The first thing you need to do to finalize the WSS installation is to launch the SharePoint Products and Technologies Configuration Wizard. This wizard will perform ten automated tasks to finalize the configuration of your server. Then, once it is finalized, you can use the Central Administration interface (see Figure 9-14). You'll have to provide your credentials for the connection. Make sure you sign on with local administrative access rights, and make sure you select Remember My Password in the credentials dialog box. Also, since you are using Internet Explorer (IE) with enhanced security, it will ask you to add the local host as a trusted site. Do so, and the Administration home page will appear.

Windows SharePoint Services Add Roles Wizard Page	Values
Select Server Role	Select the WSS role. This role is dependent on a wide series of different components. For example, it requires the IIS 6 Management Compatibility components, because it makes use of the IIS 6 Metabase, a component that is no longer used by pure IIS 7 sites. Add the required components.
Windows SharePoint Services	Review information about this role, if required, before you move on.
Configuration Type	Select Install Only On This Server if you are performing a simple installation of WSS. This will automatically use the WID to store WSS information. Select Install As Part Of A Server Farm (Advanced) if you intend to connect this server to a central database running SQL Server on another server.
Administration Language	Select the appropriate administration language.
E-mail Settings (for simple configurations)	Add the values for the Outbound E-mail Server as well as the To and From e-mail addresses. This is used by WSS to send status and system messages to users and administrators.
Web Server (IIS)	Review information about this role, if required, before you move on.
Role Services	Review required role services for IIS support of WSS, and proceed.
Confirm Installation Selections	Review your choices before proceeding. Use the Previous button to make corrections if required. Click Install when ready.
Installation Progress and Installation Results	Review the installation progress, and click Finish when done.

TABLE 9-5 Installing Windows SharePoint Services

Note the structure of the new Central Administration page. The home page is a summary page. Two additional tabs are displayed here: Operations and Application Management. Server administrators will mostly work with the Operations page. The home page lists administrator tasks you need to perform. As you can see, several tasks are required to finalize the configuration.

NOTE *If you have worked with Windows SharePoint Services version 3.0 or Microsoft Office SharePoint Portal Server before moving to WS08, you will be familiar with this interface already, since it hasn't changed.*

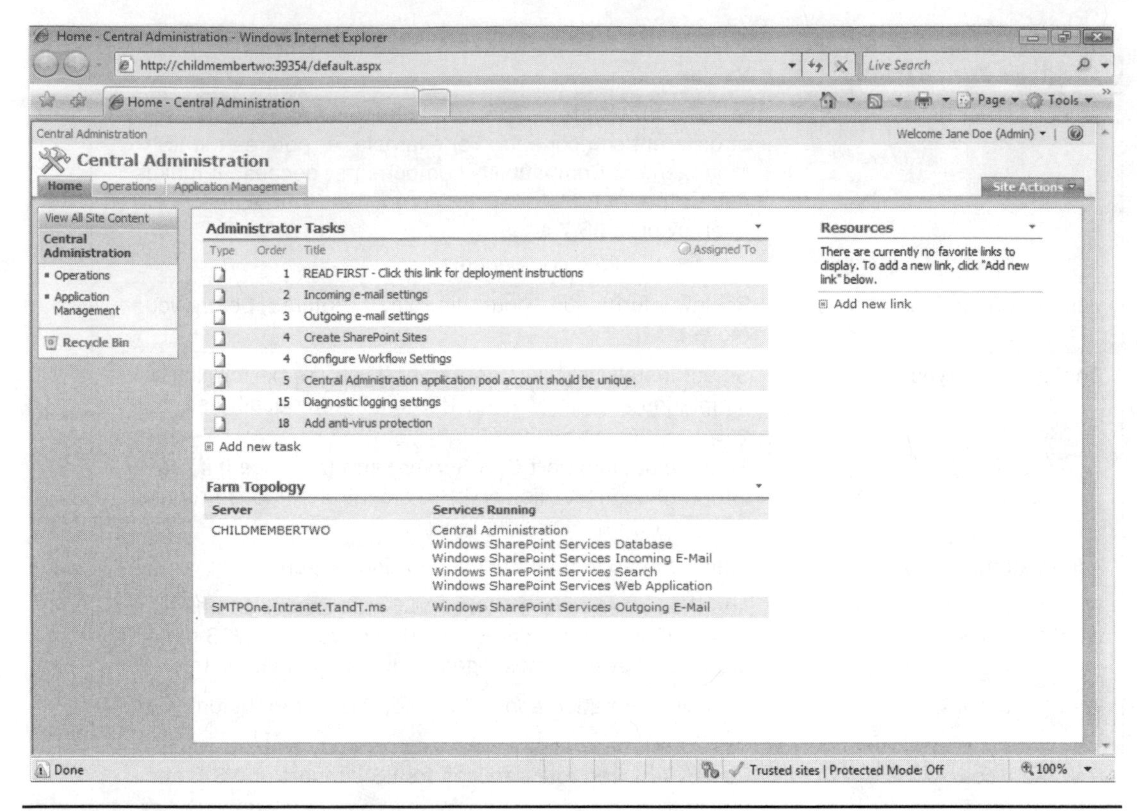

FIGURE 9-14 The SharePoint Central Administration webpage

Control Access to WSS Central Administration

The first thing you should do is make it easier for you to access the Central Administration web site. IE can automatically pass credentials to web sites through a single sign-on (SSO) operation. IE controls this through the different zones that connections fall into. In order to use SSO to get to the Central Administration web site, you need to add the connection to the Intranet zone.

1. To do this, move to the Tools | Internet Options menu in IE.
2. Click the Security tab.
3. Select Local Intranet and click Sites.
4. Add the server's address to this zone. You will get a warning message that it already exists in the Trusted Sites zone. Click Yes and click Close.
5. Click OK to close the Internet Options dialog box.

If you look at the lower-right area of your IE screen, you will see that this site is now in the Local Intranet zone. This means you will not be prompted for credentials next time you go to this site because IE will pass your current credentials to the site automatically.

Finalize WSS Configuration

Several tasks are listed for server finalization. They include:

- Read deployment instructions
- Incoming e-mail settings
- Outgoing e-mail settings
- Create SharePoint sites
- Configure workflow settings
- Change service accounts
- Configure diagnostic logging
- Add antivirus protection

To complete an item, click its link, perform the operation, and then click Edit Item. In the Editing window, change the status to Completed, and click OK. You can also delete the item if you want to, but marking it as Completed lets you track the changes you've made to the system.

TIP *Make sure you use an antivirus program that is designed for SharePoint Services. Find out from your antivirus manufacturer if this is the case before you configure it to work with WSS.*

You should enable sites to receive e-mail and configure them with appropriate settings. You can rely on the SharePoint Directory Management Service to integrate the groups in ADDS with your WSS implementation. Point to the appropriate OU in your production domain; this should be somewhere in your People OU structure. Use relative distinguished names to list the OU (for example, DC=net,DC=TandT,DC=Intranet,OU=People). This will let you manage group contents in one single location.

You should also use the predefined accounts to run the Central Administration web site. Normally, this should be NetworkService. You can also create a special service account, which will need local administration rights on this server. More on service accounts can be found in Chapter 10.

When you set antivirus properties, you should be able to scan documents on upload and attempt to clean infected documents. If the documents are cleaned on upload, then they don't really need to be cleaned on download.

Finally, create as many sites as you need. The process is simple and straightforward. Your WSS environment will be ready for use once done.

TIP *By default, WSS installs to the default web site on the target server. However, users find it easier to access a site with a more "Internet-sounding" name than with the server name. You can map the site to a proper DNS name. Create an alias (CName) within the production domain DNS zone, for example, Collaboration.Intranet.TandT.Net. You might also create a user GPO that changes the IE home page to this address so that they go to the Collaboration web site by default when they open IE. You can then add the new address in Central Administration | Operations | Global Configuration | Alternate Site Mappings. Select Add An Internal Mapping, and set the new name to Collaboration on port 80 or, if you want secure communications, port 443. You will also need to install a PKI certificate on the server to use port 443.*

Change WSS Administration Port Number

By default, SharePoint uses a random port to connect to the administration web site. This port is listed in the Connection link at the top of the Internet Explorer window. Ideally, you will want to standardize all of the administrative ports for each of your WSS installations. For example, you might standardize all systems running WSS to port 8088.

1. Open a command prompt.
2. Navigate to Program Files\Common Files\Microsoft Shared\Web Server Extensions\12\BIN.
3. Type:

   ```
   stsadm.exe -o setadminport -port 8088
   ```

   And then press ENTER.
4. Close the command prompt. This will automatically change all of the shortcuts that reference this administration site.

This will make it easier to manage each SharePoint site, since you only need to remember that to access Central Administration, you just type **http://*servername*:8088** in any Web browser.

NOTE *To validate your WSS deployment, download the SharePoint Best Practices Analyzer from: http://technet2.microsoft.com/windowsserver/WSS/en/library/ea5996c0-3ca4-427d-a1e5-71aa46ab64b71033.mspx?mfr=true. In addition, WSS books online are available at: http://technet2.microsoft.com/windowsserver/WSS/en/library/ea5996c0-3ca4-427d-a1e5-71aa46ab64b71033.mspx?mfr=true.*

Prepare Windows Streaming Media Servers

WS08 does not include the components for Windows Streaming Media (WSM) services. It does, however, include the capability to manage streaming media and, especially, multicast IP connections to provide a seamless streaming experience. This is the Quality Windows Audio Video Experience (qWave) engine that is available as a WS08 feature. qWave enhances audio and video streaming by providing Quality of Service (QoS) when streaming data. On your servers, this will ensure that rate-of-flow and prioritization services are enabled throughout the IP network when you stream data to end points.

WSM clients can take the form of a number of platforms:

- Computers or devices that play the content using a player, such as Windows Media Player.
- Computers running Windows Media Services (WMS) that are proxying, caching, or redistributing content.
- Custom applications that have been developed using the Windows Media Software Development Kit (SDK).

Beginning with Windows Server 2008, Windows Media Services contains a new, built-in cache/proxy plug-in that can be used to configure Windows Media servers, either as a cache/proxy server or a reverse-proxy server. Since WMS is not a part of WS08, most of the documentation pertaining to these configurations is available on the WMS web site.

TIP *Access the WMS Web site at www.microsoft.com/windows/windowsmedia/forpros/default.mspx.*

Install the required features by using Server Manager.

1. Move to Server Manager | Features, and right-click to Add Features.
2. Select Quality Windows Audio Video Experience. Click Next.
3. Click Install. Click Finish when done. A server restart is required to complete the operation.

Your server is now ready for Windows Media Services. Follow the instructions in the WMS documentation to perform the installation.

Server Requirements by Role

Now that you have reviewed the creation process for several more server roles, you have an idea of the resource requirements to construct them (see Table 9-6). You'll need to review the CPU, RAM, disk volumes, and network capabilities required for these server roles. Use these guidelines to prepare your servers when you stage the parallel network for VSOs.

Design the Virtual Service Offerings OU Structure

The final step of service preparation for these server roles is the design of the Virtual Service Offerings OU structure and the application of proper delegation and Group Policy settings to each service (see Table 9-7). This OU structure was begun in Chapter 8 and is coming close

Server Role	Processor Architecture	CPU	RAM	Drive D:	Drive E:	Network
Application Servers and Dedicated Web Servers	x64	Medium to high load	Required to increase processing speeds	Hosts data files	Hosts transaction logs	Required for large user bases
Terminal Servers	x64	High load (depends on the number of users)	Required for server processes as well as for each user (minimum 20 MB per user)	Hosts program and data files	Required only if the server hosts database applications	Required for better Remote Desktop Protocol throughput
Collaboration Servers	x64	High load	Required for collaboration services	Hosts data files	Hosts transaction logs	Required for better collaboration throughput

TABLE 9-6 Resource Requirements per Server Role

PART IV

OU	Level	Objective	GPO	Notes
Virtual Service Offerings	One	Grouping of all virtual service offerings and utilitarian objects in the organization		Base Servers GPO for application of security settings (see Chapter 10). Used for Categorization also
Application Servers and Dedicated Web Servers	Two	Regroups all application servers Also regroups all Web servers	Global Application Server GPO	This GPO controls database servers, general-purpose Web servers, .NET Framework, and corporate applications. Also controls all settings for IIS and Web services. Items can be sub-divided if further segregation is required. Delegated to application server operators.
TS Servers	Two	Contains all TS servers	Global TS Server GPO	Contains server-side Terminal Services settings. Delegated to terminal server operators.
Collaboration Servers	Two	Regroups all servers dedicated to collaboration services	Global Collaboration GPO	Contains general settings for Voice over IP (VOIP) communications services, Exchange Server, SharePoint Portal Server, and Streaming Media Services. Delegated to collaboration server operators.
SharePoint Servers	Three	Regroups all servers running SharePoint	Global SharePoint GPO	Contains settings that are particular to SharePoint servers. Delegated to SharePoint administrators and possibly Web masters.
Streaming Servers	Three	Regroups all servers running streaming services	Global Streaming GPO	Contains settings that pertain to streaming data. Delegated to data-streaming administrators.

Table 9-7 Build the Virtual Service Offerings OU Structure

to completion. Settings and structures for the servers you created in this chapter will be prepared here (see Figure 9-15). The structure will be completed in Chapter 10, when you finalize the security settings of your virtual service offerings. Build out the OUs for the server roles covered here.

- Intranet.TandT.ms
  - Virtual Service Offerings
    - File and Print (Global File and Print)
      - Printers
      - File Shares
    - Network Infrastructure (Global Infrastructure)
    - Operational Accounts
    - Service Accounts
    - Hidden Objects
    - Application/Dedicated Web Servers (Global Application Server)
    - Terminal Services Servers (Global TS Server)
    - Collaboration Servers (Global Collaboration)
      - SharePoint Servers (Global SharePoint)
      - Streaming Servers (Global Streaming)

FIGURE 9-15 The Virtual Service Offerings OU structure

Complete the OU structure using the same operations as those outlined in Chapter 7 to create an OU structure and delegate the management of the content of each OU to appropriate operational groups.

V

PART

Secure Windows Server 2008

This section deals with the implementation of secure practices to protect networks at all levels. It also includes methods for implementing disaster recovery and providing business continuity, both at the resource pool and at the virtual service offerings levels.

10

CHAPTER

Design Your Security Infrastructure

Security is *the* hot topic in IT. In most recent surveys, it always comes out in the top four major preoccupations for Chief Information Officers (CIOs). It's no wonder. In the past few years, there have been significant security threats to anyone using computers, especially with Windows operating systems. Whether it was through virus attacks, trojans, worms, root kits, or other malicious code on the PC or on the server, distributed denial of service (DDoS) attacks on Domain Name System (DNS) servers, password or identity theft, or simply through social engineering, everyone is at risk. One thing is certain: Organizations that do nothing about security or about business continuity are vulnerable and can possibly stand to lose everything, even their very existence. Security is a full-time occupation no matter the size of your organization. Whether you are an IT generalist running a small shop for your organization or a specialized technician working in a large organization, you have to pay attention to securing your resources. Malicious hackers on the Internet are after your wares. Worse, hacking is now moving into the mainstream and becoming profitable, as organizations try to find new ways to obtain and preserve information about you and what you do.

So protect yourself. Microsoft, as the manufacturer of Windows, provides you with tools and guidelines for securing your systems. One excellent example is the Windows Server 2008 Security Guide, as well as its sister publication, the Windows Vista Security Guide. Both offer a structured way for you to further protect your systems beyond the base protections enabled when you install Windows. But security has a lifecycle of its own. On the technical side, it begins with the installation of a computer system and lasts throughout the duration of its usefulness to you until its retirement. Security is not only a technical operation; it must also involve everyone in your organization. Even if you provide the most stringent technical levels of security on your systems, all of it can come crashing down if your users are not aware of their own responsibilities in the security lifecycle.

TIP *Look up the Windows Server 2008 Security Guide at www.microsoft.com/technet/security/prodtech/windowsserver2008/default.mspx and the Windows Vista Security Guide at www.microsoft.com/technet/windowsvista/security/guide.mspx.*

CAUTION *Windows Server 2008 is secure by default. Because of this, many applications, especially poorly designed applications, may not work properly on this operating system (OS). Keep in mind that each time you modify the OS to allow legacy applications to run on it, you decrease its level of security and, therefore, increase your level of exposure. You must balance the cost of upgrading applications with the cost of running a more exposed OS.*

It also seems that organizations that use Microsoft technology are especially at risk. In a way, it's true. Being the largest operating system supplier in the world has made Microsoft the number one target for malicious code. It always seems that one security flaw doesn't wait for another as far as Microsoft is concerned. But in actual fact, Microsoft technologies are no worse than others in terms of the security and other flaws found after release.

Microsoft's goal with Windows Server has been to change this situation. Their motto is "Secure by Design, Secure by Default, and Secure in Deployment." That means that they've raised the bar with Windows Server 2003 and continue to do so with Windows Server 2008 (WS08). In fact, Microsoft is so confident that WS08 is secure that it has submitted it for Common Criteria evaluation and certification. The Common Criteria is an internationally recognized method for certifying the security claims of information technology (IT) products and systems. They define security standards and procedures for evaluating technologies. The Common Criteria are designed to help consumers make informed security decisions and help vendors secure their products.

TIP *More information is available on the Common Criteria at www.commoncriteriaportal.org.*

The Common Criteria are not the only security standard on the marketplace. There are others. ISO 17799 (www.iso-17799.com) is a generic standard on best practices for information security. The Operationally Critical Threat, Asset, and Vulnerability Evaluation (OCTAVE, at www.cert.org/octave) is an IT security risk assessment method that is based on industry-accepted best practices. The Federal Information Technology Security Assessment Framework (FITSAF, at www.cio.gov/spci/spci/security/secfitsaf.htm) is a methodology that allows federal agencies to assess their IT security programs. While Microsoft does not necessarily embrace all of these standards, it is their goal to do away, as much as possible, with the common security threats people using their technology have faced in the past. As such, they have created an updated operating system that is, in fact, secure by default. This alone is the continuation of a new direction for Microsoft who, in the past, has been known for pushing features above all else. But with Windows Server 2008, Microsoft has created a blend of features and security that can make this the most secure Windows operating system ever. Its set of features and server roles that are not installed by default; IIS 7, which is divided into components that are only installed on an as-needed basis; and a powerful Security Configuration Wizard, which can lock down any server configuration, are only a few of the powerful new features that can make this OS secure from the ground up.

With commitments of this level, there is no doubt that Microsoft has designed this operating system to be chock full of security features. But like every other operating system, these security features will only protect your organization if they are properly implemented.

Security Basics

Security is an issue that is pervasive because it involves almost everything within your network. In fact, security has been discussed at every stage of the network creation process so far. The object of security is to protect information. To do so, you must put in place a layered protection system that will provide the ability to perform the following activities:

- Identify people as they enter your network.
- Identify appropriate clearance levels for people who work within your network, and provide them with appropriate access rights once identified.
- Identify that the person modifying the data is the person who is authorized to modify the data (irrevocability or non-repudiation).
- Guarantee the confidentiality of information once it is stored within your network.
- Guarantee the availability of information once it is stored within your network.
- Ensure the integrity of the data stored within your network.
- Monitor the activities within your network.
- Audit security events within the network, and securely store historical auditing data.
- Put in place the appropriate administrative activities to ensure that the network is secure at all times.

For each of these activities, there are various scopes of interaction:

- **Local** People interact with systems at the local level; these systems must be protected, whether or not they are attached to a network.
- **Intranet** People interact with remote systems. These systems must also be protected at all times, whether they are located on the local area network (LAN) or the wide area network (WAN).
- **Internet** Systems that are deemed public must also be protected from attacks of all types. These are in a worse situation, because they are exposed outside the boundaries of the internal network.
- **Extranet** These systems are often deemed internal, but are exposed to partners, suppliers, and/or clients. The major difference between extranet and Internet systems is authentication—while there may be identification on an Internet system, authentication is *always* required to access an extranet environment.

Whatever its scope, security is an activity (like all IT activities) that relies on three key elements: *people, PCs,* and *processes*:

- **People** are the executors of the security process. They are also its main users.
- **PCs** represent technology. They include a series of tools and components that support the security process.
- **Processes** are made up of workflow patterns, procedures, and standards for the application of security.

The integration of these three elements will help you design a security policy that is applicable to your entire organization.

Design a Security Policy

The design of a security policy is only one step in the security lifecycle, but, unfortunately, it is not always the first step. People often think of the security policy only after they have been victims of a security threat. Fortunately, since your implementation of WS08 is based on the design of a parallel virtual service offering network, it is an ideal opportunity to review your security policy, if it is already in place, or to design one, if it is not, and apply it as you build your new service infrastructure.

Like any other design process, you must begin by assessing your business model. Much of the information required at this level has already been collected through other design exercises you have already performed. In Chapter 3, you analyzed business and technical environments to begin the design of the network. You reviewed this information again in Chapter 5 when you created your Active Directory Domain Services design. This information will need to be reviewed a third time, but this time with a special focus on security aspects. This includes the identification and revision of current security policies, if they exist.

Next, you will need to identify which common security standards you wish to implement within your organization. These will involve both technical and non-technical policies and procedures. An example of a technical policy would be the security parameters you will set at the staging of each computer in your organization. A non-technical policy would deal with the habits users should develop to select complex passwords and protect them. Finally, you will need to identify the parameters for each policy you define.

The Castle Defense System

The best way to define a security policy is to use a model. The model we propose is the Castle Defense System (CDS). In medieval times, people needed to protect themselves and their belongings through the design of a defense system that was primarily based on cumulative barriers to entry, or as we would say today, defense in depth. A castle (see Figure 10-1) is used, because it is an illustration that is familiar to almost everyone, from users to technicians, as well as management. If you've ever visited a medieval castle or seen a movie with a medieval theme, or even just *The Lord of the Rings* movies, you'll remember that the first line of defense is often the *moat*. The moat is a barrier that is designed to stop people from reaching the castle wall. Moats often include dangerous creatures (alligators, piranhas) that will add a second level of protection within the same barrier. Next, you have the *castle walls*. These are designed to repel enemies. At the top of the walls, you will find crenellated edges, allowing archers to fire on the enemy while still being able to hide when fired upon. There are doors of various sizes within the walls, a gate, and a drawbridge for the moat. All entry points have guards posted. Once again, multiple levels of protection are applied within the same layer.

The third defense layer is the *courtyard* within the castle walls. This is designed as a "killing field" so that if enemies do manage to breach the castle walls, they will find themselves within an internal zone that offers no cover from attackers located either on the external castle walls or within the castle itself. The fourth layer of defense is the *castle* itself. This is the main building within which are found the crown jewels. It is designed to be defensible on its own; stairways are narrow, and rooms are arranged to confuse the enemy. The fifth and last layer of protection is the *vault* held within the heart of the castle. It is difficult to reach and highly guarded.

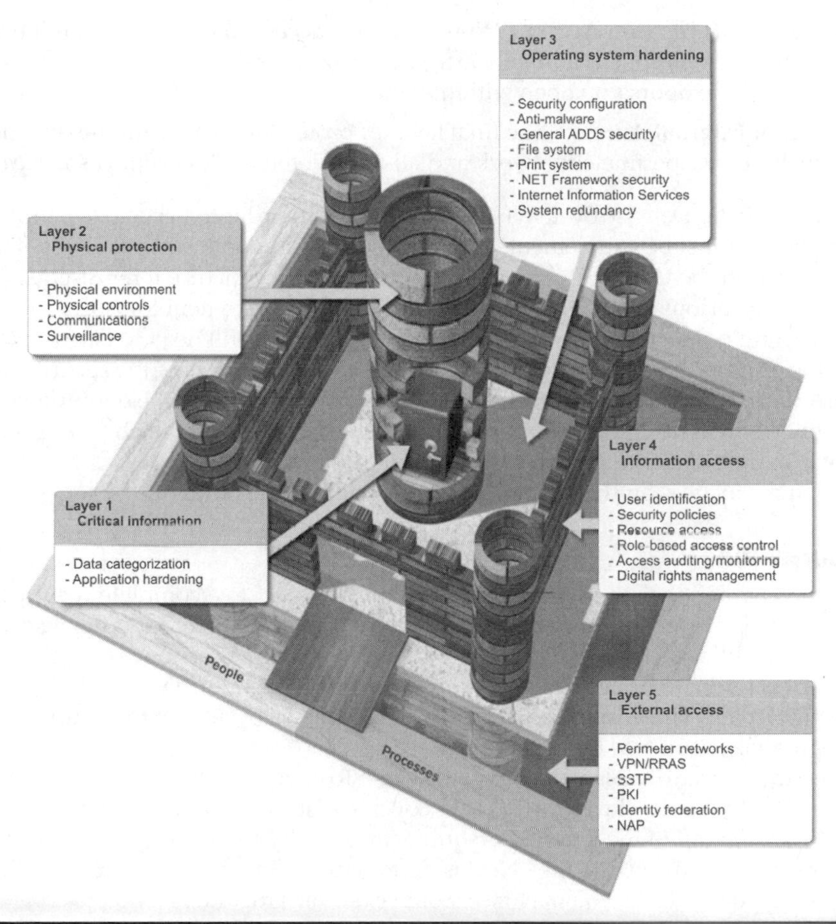

Figure 10-1 The Castle Defense System

This is, of course, a rudimentary description of the defenses included in a castle. Medieval engineers worked very hard to include multiple defense systems within each layer of protection. But it serves its purpose. An IT defense system should be designed in the same way as a CDS. Just like the CDS, the IT defense system requires layers of protection. In fact, five layers of protection seem appropriate. Starting from the inside, you'll find:

- **Layer 1: Critical Information** The heart of the system is the information you seek to protect. This is the information *vault*.
- **Layer 2: Physical Protection** Security measures should always begin with a level of physical protection for information systems. This compares to the *castle* itself.
- **Layer 3: Operating System Hardening** Once the physical defenses have been put in place, you need to "harden" each computer's operating system in order to limit the potential attack surface as much as possible. This is the *courtyard*.

- **Layer 4: Information Access** When you give access to your data, you'll need to ensure that everyone is authenticated, authorized, and audited. These are the *castle walls* and the doors you open within them.
- **Layer 5: External Access** The final layer of protection deals with the outside world. It includes the perimeter network and all of its defenses. It is your castle *moat*.

This is the Castle Defense System (see Figure 10-1). In order to become a complete security policy, it must be supplemented by two elements: people and processes. These two elements surround the CDS and complete the security policy picture it represents.

Defining the various layers of defense is not the only requirement for a security policy, but it is a starting point. There are several other activities you will need to perform to complete the definition of your security policy. These form the basis of the security blueprint (see Figure 10-2). This blueprint outlines a step-by-step approach for the definition of a security policy. It will need to be supported by additional activities, which focus on the way the policy is managed and administered once you put it in place.

This chapter focuses on the solution design portion of the blueprint.

The Security Plan

As mentioned earlier, the security policy is only the first step to a complete security plan. Once the policy has been issued, you need to design and implement your defenses, monitor them on an active basis, and regularly test and update them. These four security management activities—policy design, defense planning, monitoring, and testing—make up the security plan. These interact with the Castle Defense System to make up the practice of security management (see Figure 10-3).

The key to the security plan is in knowing what to cover and knowing why it needs to be covered. The first part—knowing what to cover—is outlined in the Castle Defense System. It identifies all of the areas that require coverage by the security policy and helps you be prepared for any eventuality. Next is defense planning; here, the first step lies in knowing the type of attacks you may face. Some examples include:

- **Accidental security breach** These attacks are usually caused accidentally by users or system operators. They stem from a lack of awareness of security issues. For example, users that do not protect their passwords because they are not aware of the consequences can be the cause of accidental attacks. Similarly, operators who place users in the wrong security groups and assign them the wrong privileges can also be the cause of a breach.
- **Internal attack** These are one of the major sources of attacks. In fact, they used to be the major source of attack, but with the proliferation of Internet-based attacks, their importance in proportion to all other attacks has diminished. They come from within the internal network. Their source can be the organization's personnel or other personnel that are allowed access to the internal network. These attacks are often the result of a lack of vigilance. Internal personnel often assume that since the internal network is protected from the outside, everyone that has access to it can be trusted.
- **Social engineering** Once again, these attacks stem from a lack of awareness. They are caused by external sources that impersonate internal personnel and cause users to divulge compromising information—for example, someone calling a user while

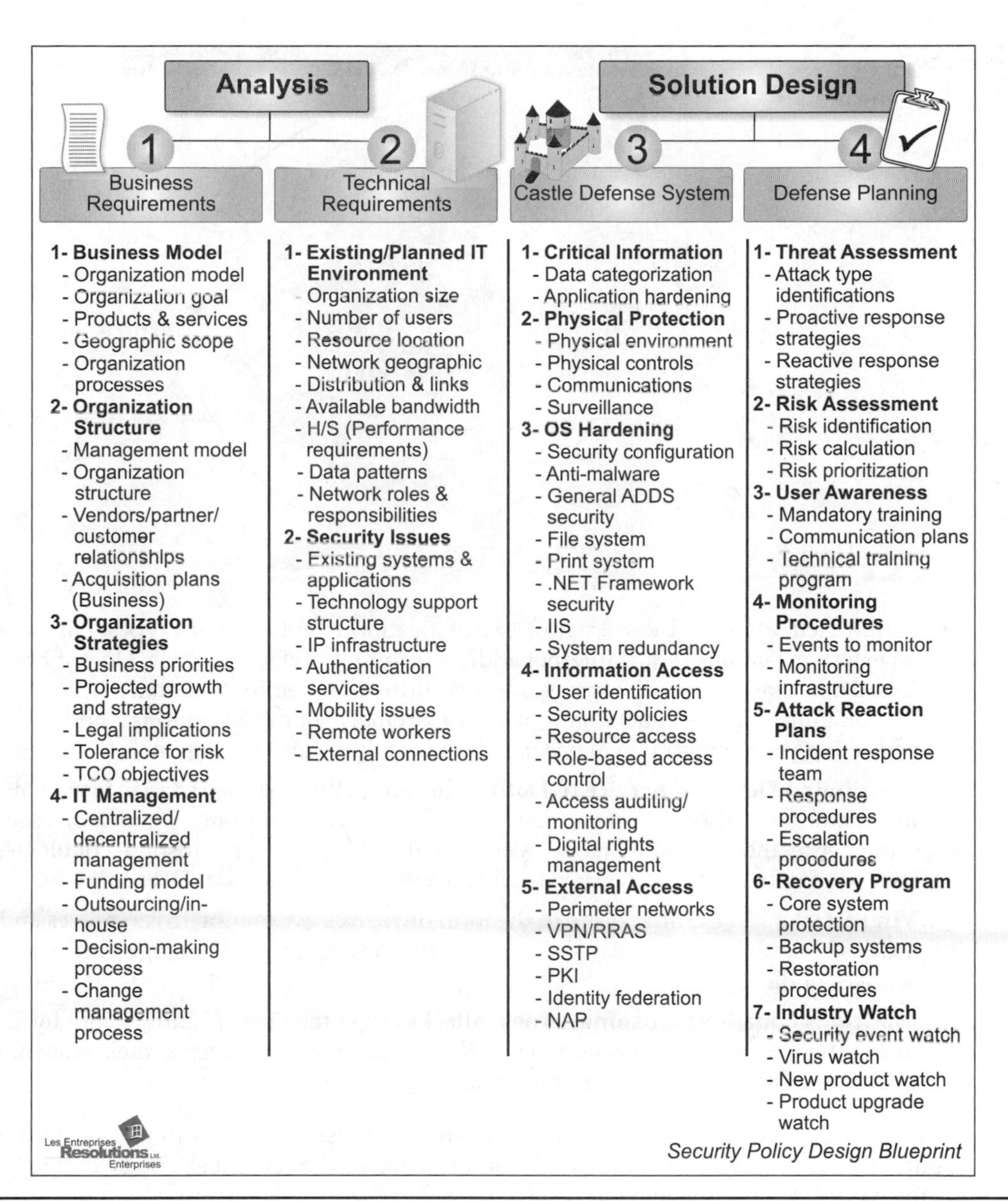

FIGURE 10-2 The security policy design blueprint

impersonating the Help desk and asking the user for his or her password. It is still common practice for Help desk personnel to ask users for their password. This behavior is completely unacceptable today. There is no reason for Help desk personnel to ever have access to a user's password.

- **Organizational attack** These attacks stem from competitive organizations who want to penetrate your organization and discover your trade secrets.

FIGURE 10-3 Security management activities

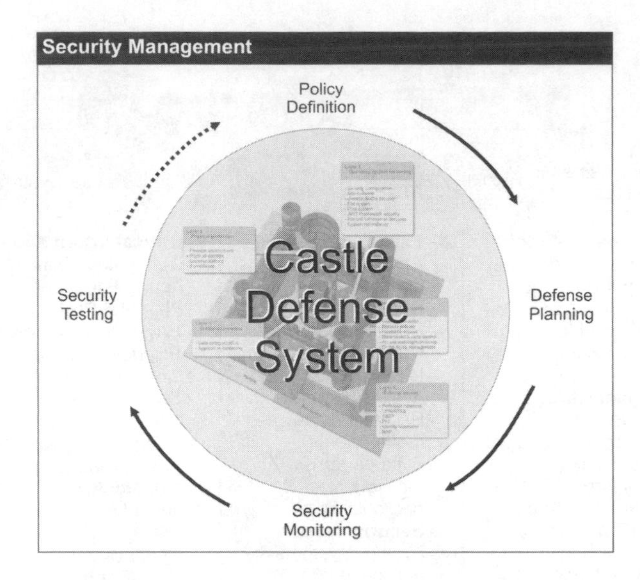

- **Automated attacks** These are now one of the most common attack types. Basically, an external computer scans Internet addresses until it finds a response. Once it has found a working address, it then scans this address to identify potential vulnerabilities. These attacks have become extremely sophisticated today, and protecting yourself from them has now become a full-time occupation.
- **Distributed Denial of Service (DDoS)** These attacks are designed to overwhelm the operation of a service on your network. They often stem from several sources at once; hence, the distributed name. Attacks that target generic Microsoft technologies instead of your organization specifically are excellent examples of DDoS attacks.
- **Viral attacks** These attacks are in the form of viruses, worms, or Trojan horses and are designed to infiltrate your systems to perform some form of damage to either services or data.
- **Malicious e-mails or phishing** These attacks target the unsuspecting victim by luring them to perform an action that will grant the attacker access to their system. Educating users is one of the best ways to prevent these attack types.

Each attack type requires a different defense strategy. Most are already in place with the CDS, but the processes that surround attacks and reactions to attacks must also be defined. This is the core of defense planning.

TIP *More information on attack types and defense strategies can be found at Microsoft Security Central at www.microsoft.com/security/default.mspx. Microsoft also publishes a Threats and Countermeasures document at www.microsoft.com/technet/security/guidance/serversecurity/tcg/tcgch00.mspx#EDD.*

The Microsoft WS08 Security Guide

As mentioned earlier, Microsoft has produced an excellent guideline for securing Windows 2008 technologies in the WS08 Security Guide. It uses an approach that is similar to the Castle Defense System, a defense-in-depth approach. The best part of this guide is that it includes a series of tools—specifically, Group Policy Templates generated through the GPO Accelerator tool included with the guide—that can be used to secure servers by role. To do so, it relies on an organizational unit structure, similar to the one you designed in Chapters 8 and 9. Each server type is located within a specific organizational unit (OU), and Group Policy Objects (GPOs) that include specific settings per server role are applied to the appropriate OU. This approach is also at the basis of the Castle Defense System, since it is the core approach for the Active Directory Domain Services (ADDS) design illustrated throughout this book. This ADDS design is conceived with the purpose of managing objects according to object type; you use the management approach whether you are managing object properties or you are applying security settings.

Rely on this guide and learn to use the tools it includes, but at the same time, review the contents of this chapter, as it guides you through complementary information. You can never know too much about security.

Windows Server 2008 Security

Windows Server 2008 is one of the key elements of Microsoft's Trusted Computing Initiative. As such, Microsoft has reviewed and improved the basic security features included in Windows 2000 and 2003. The previous Windows foundation was already a major improvement over the past; technologies such as Kerberos, Encrypting File System (EFS), public key infrastructure (PKI), smart card and biometric support, and especially Active Directory Domain Services, to name a few, are significant improvements over the basic security capabilities of older Windows versions, such as NT.

With WS08, Microsoft has enhanced and improved these features, as well as provided new security capabilities. The .NET Framework alone is a significant security improvement in and of itself because it brings with it the concept of managed code—code that fits within sandbox boundaries you define. It greatly enhances the capability to run secure code, because it provides the execution environment for software, limiting the possibility of errors in code you run. It also identifies if code is digitally signed by someone you trust, as well as its origin, ensuring a higher degree of trust within your execution environment.

In addition, WS08 offers several other new and improved features that help secure the system at all levels. Of course, the ideal level of protection you can obtain with WS08 will depend on the client you are running; there is no doubt that the most secure Windows platform you build will include both WS08 and Windows Vista. Nevertheless, the security features of WS08 include:

- **Software restriction policies** These policies can control which code is allowed to run within the network. This includes any type of code—corporate applications, commercial software, scripts, batch files—and can even be defined at the Dynamic Link Library (DLL) level. This is a great tool to prevent malicious scripts from even being able to run in your network.
- **Wireless LAN support** WS08 includes special policy objects designed to support secure wireless networking.

- **Remote access authentication** WS08 includes a policy-based structure to manage remote access and virtual private network connections through ADDS. This feature is focused on an improved Internet Authentication Server (IAS) and Remote Authentication Dial-in User Server (RADIUS).
- **Network Access Protection (NAP)** In addition to the improvements in remote access, WS08 can now enforce client health levels before they are allowed to connect to your network. NAP can even update the clients before they are given full network access.
- **Windows Server Firewall with Advanced Security** In order to facilitate the connections remote systems make with your servers, WS08 now provides an integrated interface for IP-level security (IPSec), with incoming and outgoing communications controls.
- **Multiforest operations** Chapter 5 outlined how WS08 Active Directory Domain Services forests can use forest trusts to extend the authentication capabilities of your directory with partner organizations. In addition, the use of Active Directory Lightweight Directory Services (ADLDS) allows you to create a central network operating system (NOS) directory and then the required number of application directories to support your corporate application needs. Finally, Active Directory Federation Services (ADFS) lets you work with partner organizations without building forest trusts, but rather, by relying on each other's own internal NOS directories.
- **Public key infrastructure** WS08 includes an improved PKI, Active Directory Certificate Services (ADCS), that supports auto-enrollment and automatic X.509 certificate renewal. It also supports the use of delta certificate revocation lists (CRLs), simplifying the CRL management process.
- **Web server security** Internet Information Services (IIS) version 7 is secure by default. It is not installed by default and, once installed, will only serve content based on installed components.
- **Temporary and offline file protection** WS08 supports the encryption of temporary and offline files, as well as protecting encrypted data while in transit, through the new Secure Sockets Tunneling Protocol (SSTP).
- **Credential management** The WS08 Credential Manager can securely store passwords and digital certificates (X.509). This supports seamless access to multiple security zones.
- **Kernel-mode encryption** WS08 supports Federal Information Processing Standard (FIPS)–approved cryptographic algorithms. This means that both governmental and non-governmental organizations can take advantage of this cryptography module to secure client/server communications. WS08 also implements the Suite B cryptographic algorithms defined by the U.S. government. This means it supports data encryption, digital signatures, and key exchanges, as well as hashing, letting third-party vendors rely on this infrastructure to create more comprehensive security solutions.

NOTE *More information on Suite B can be found at www.nsa.gov/ia/industry/crypto_suite_b.cfm.*

- **Digest Authentication Protocol (DAP)** WS08 includes a new digest security package that is supported by both IIS and Active Directory Domain Services.
- **Digitally-signed Windows Installer packages** WS08 supports the inclusion of digital signatures within Windows Installer packages so that administrators can ensure that only trusted packages are installed within the network, especially on servers.
- **Passport usage** WS08 no longer supports the mapping of Microsoft Passports to Active Directory Domain Services accounts. You must rely on ADFS instead.
- **Multiple password policies** ADDS supports the application of multiple password policies, letting you require highly complex passwords for administrators and less complex passwords for end users.
- **Role-based access control** WS08 includes the Authorization Manager, which supports the use of role-based access controls (RBACs) for applications. RBAC stores can be in either Extensible Markup Language (XML) or within Active Directory.
- **Authentication delegation** WS08 supports constrained delegation. This means that you can specify which servers can be trusted for user impersonation within the network. You can also identify for which services the server is trusted for delegation.
- **Permissions management and access-based enumeration** It is now possible to view effective permissions with WS08 through the Properties dialog box for file and folder objects. Also, users will only be able to view items they actually have access to, as opposed to previous versions, where users could see all of the contents of a share, even if they could not open the documents.
- **Limited Everyone membership** The Everyone group continues to include authenticated users and guests, but members of the Anonymous group are no longer part of the Everyone group.
- **Auditing** Auditing in WS08 is now operations-based. This means that it is more descriptive and offers the choice of which operations to audit for which users or groups. You can also audit ADDS changes and use the audit reports to reverse those changes if they were performed in error.
- **Reset defaults** It is now much simpler to use the Security Configuration Wizard (SCW) tool to reapply computer security settings from base templates.
- **Optional subsystems** Optional subsystems, such as POSIX (support for UNIX applications), are no longer installed by default.
- **Small footprint servers** Through the use of Server Core, you can deploy servers that provide a limited set of services and a smaller attack surface.
- **Read-only domain controllers (RODCs)** RODCs provide a more secure domain controller (DC) platform for branch offices or perimeter networks. RODCS are hard to compromise because they will only cache passwords based on the user policies you set. In addition, you can automatically reset any cached passwords in the event of a theft of an RODC.
- **Constrained roles and features** Each role or feature only installs components that are absolutely required to make it run. This lets you control exactly what is installed on your servers.

- **Service hardening** Services are now constrained and will only run within specific contexts. In addition, each service is only allowed to access components of the system that are related to it.
- **BitLocker drive encryption** You can now fully encrypt system drives on remote servers so that malicious users cannot access their contents.
- **User Account Control (UAC)** With UAC, administrators are constantly aware of when they actually make use of elevated credentials to perform tasks because prompts appear to request authorization. This provides a further level of protection. Of course, every administrator should run as a standard user and only use rights elevation when they need to perform an administrative task.
- **Information protection** With Active Directory Rights Management Protection (ADRMS), you can fully secure the contents of your intellectual property, making sure it cannot be tampered with.
- **Device control** Through device control, you can ensure that malicious users cannot connect rogue Universal Serial Bus (USB) devices to your servers, or even to your workstations, in order to steal the contents of your shared folders or collaboration environments.

This is not a comprehensive list of all the new security features of Windows Server 2008, but it is a list of the most important features for networks. These features, along with the basic features that stem from previous versions of Windows, will allow you to design your Castle Defense System.

Secure Resource Pools

With the arrival of resource pools and virtual service offerings (VSOs), you need to take a two-pronged approach to the design of your CDS. The first focuses on the resource pool itself. This pool must include very strict protection strategies, because it is so easy to walk away with an entire virtual machine. As such, the CDS for resource pools will require that particular attention be paid to the levels identified in Table 10-1.

Resource pools are a new concept in IT and, therefore, need a particular attention to detail when it comes to the implementation of their security settings. You need to make sure you understand the scope of protection you need to apply to this infrastructure (see Figure 10-4).

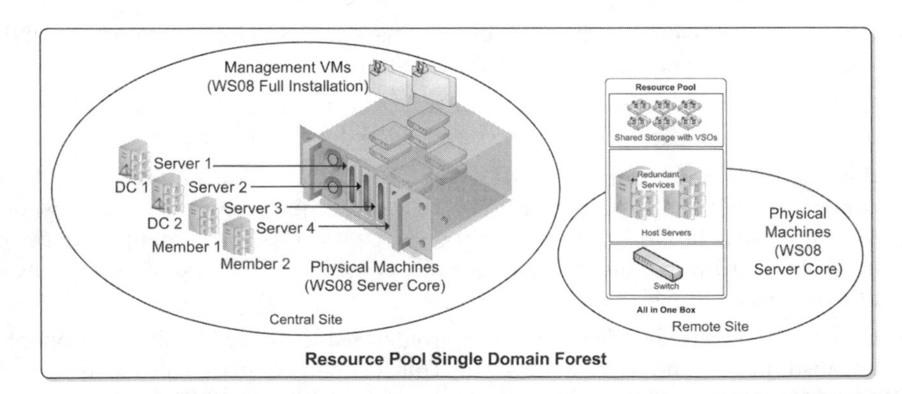

FIGURE 10-4 Scope of protection for resource pools

Layer	Contents	Comments
Layer 1 – Critical information	Data categorization	Pay special attention to the files that make up virtual machines.
	Application hardening	Secure the installations of Windows Server Hyper-V.
Layer 2 – Physical protection	Physical environment	Make sure datacenters have sufficient power and cooling resources. Remote offices should rely on server-in-a-box concept.
	Physical controls	Pay special attention to physical access to servers. All servers, especially remote servers, should be under lock and key.
	Communications	Make sure all resource pool administrators understand their responsibilities in terms of security practices.
	Surveillance	If possible, have sign-in and sign-out sheets for administrators accessing the datacenter.
Layer 3 – OS hardening	Security configuration	Pay special attention to the following: Server Core configuration Service hardening Security Configuration Wizard settings for host servers Limited role installations on each host; configuration of virtual management machines BitLocker Drive Encryption for servers-in-a-box systems in remote offices User Account Control (UAC) for all administrators Device Control to ensure that unauthorized USB disk drives cannot be connected to any physical server.
	Anti-malware	Implement Windows Defender along with proper antivirus technologies.
	General ADDS security	Implement very tight permissions management. Implement software restriction policies to ensure no malicious code is allowed to run in this domain.
	File system	Secure the file system to protect VSOs. Rely on digitally signed Windows Installer packages for all third-party or custom product installations.
	Print system	Not applicable, because only administrators have access to this network.
	.NET Framework security	Only applicable to the full installations used in the virtual management machines you create to administer the resource pool.
	Internet Information Services (IIS)	Implement tight Web server security if you need to rely on Microsoft Virtual Server to add life to 32-bit hardware.

TABLE 10-1 Applying the CDS to Resource Pools

Layer	Contents	Comments
	System redundancy	Rely on the principles in Chapter 11 to ensure business continuity of host servers.
Layer 4 – Information access	User identification	Rely on smart card or two-factor authentication for administrators in very secure environments.
	Security policies	Assign proper policies for the resource pool.
	Resource access	Only administrative accounts are required in this network.
	Role-based access control	Not applicable, because this infrastructure only runs virtualization services.
	Access auditing/ monitoring	Turn on auditing, as well as ADDS auditing, to track all changes.
	Digital rights management	Not applicable, since this infrastructure is not used to produce documentation.
Layer 5 – External access	Perimeter networks	There is no perimeter network in the resource pool, but you should still properly configure the Windows Server Firewall with Advanced Security to control access to host servers.
	Virtual private networks (VPNs)	Rely on VPN connections for all remote administration.
	Routing and Remote Access (RRAS)	Implement a remote access authentication service for administrators working remotely.
	Secure Sockets Tunneling Protocol (SSTP)	Ensure that all remote communications, as well as internal intraserver communications, are encrypted.
	Public key infrastructures (PKI)	Implement Active Directory Certificate Services (ADCS) in support of smart card deployment and software restrictions.
	Identity federation	Not applicable, since there is no need for federation in this infrastructure.
	Network Access Protection (NAP)	Implement NAP to ensure all machines that link to the resource pool have approved health status.

TABLE 10-1 Applying the CDS to Resource Pools (*continued*)

Secure Virtual Service Offerings

Similarly, virtual service offerings will also require a special application of the CDS. In this case, you need to focus on the elements identified in Table 10-2.

Virtual service offerings require more in terms of security settings because they are designed to interact with end users and, therefore, have more services built into the infrastructure. The scope of protection for VSOs will depend on the size of the organization (see Figure 10-5). Certain security technologies are reserved for resource pools, as some are reserved for virtual service offerings. For example, there is little need to run Server Core in your VSOs since they are virtual machines. It is more important to make sure that you apply the appropriate level

Layer	Contents	Comments
Layer 1 – Critical information	Data categorization	Follow the guidelines outlined later in this chapter, since the VSOs store the information that makes your organization run.
	Application hardening	Make sure your vendors and your internal developers create secure code.
Layer 2 – Physical protection	Physical environment	There is little physical access to virtual machines. The physical environment where host servers reside must be secured, though.
	Physical controls	Not applicable, since this is applied at the resource pool level.
	Communications	Make sure all users, including administrators, understand their responsibilities in terms of security practices.
	Surveillance	Be as vigilant as possible.
Layer 3 – OS hardening	Security configuration	Pay special attention to the following: Service hardening Security Configuration Wizard settings for virtual servers Limited role installations on each virtual machine with only required components for the service it delivers BitLocker Drive Encryption for servers playing critical roles User Account Control (UAC) for all administrators and all users Device Control to ensure that unauthorized USB disk drives cannot be connected to any access point, including any PC on the network BitLocker Drive Encryption for highly secure notebooks Wireless networking security
	Anti-malware	Implement Windows Defender along with proper antivirus technologies.
	General ADDS security	Implement very tight permissions management. Implement multiple password policies to require highly complex passwords for administrators. Tighten delegation-of-authority settings on your servers. Implement read-only domain controllers in remote offices. Implement software restriction policies to ensure that no malicious code is allowed to run in the production domain.
	File system	Secure the file system to protect VSOs. Implement access-based enumeration to further protect information. Rely on digitally signed Windows Installer packages for all third-party or custom product installations.
	Print system	Implement a full security strategy for all printers.

TABLE 10-2 Applying the CDS to Virtual Service Offerings

Layer	Contents	Comments
	.NET Framework security	Applicable to any machine that has an application role or any machine that includes PowerShell (in most cases, this will be every server in the VSO network).
	Internet Information Services (IIS)	Implement tight Web server security on all Web servers.
	System redundancy	Rely on the principles in Chapter 11 to ensure business continuity of key VSO servers.
Layer 4 – Information access	User identification	Rely on smart card or two-factor authentication for administrators in very secure environments. Highly secure environments will use two-factor authentication for all users.
	Security policies	Assign proper policies for the VSO network.
	Resource access	Tightly control all resource access. Implement EFS for mobile users. Rely on ADLDS for custom application resource access.
	Role-based access control	Implement in every application as much as possible.
	Access auditing/ monitoring	Turn on auditing, as well as ADDS auditing, to track all changes.
	Digital Rights Management (DRM)	Rely on ADRMS to apply DRM to all documentation that is copyrighted or sensitive in any other fashion.
Layer 5 – External access	Perimeter networks	Configure the Windows Server Firewall with Advanced Security to control access to all servers, especially those in the perimeter network. Apply the same tool to Vista PCs and mobile workstations.
	Virtual private networks (VPNs)	Rely on VPN connections for all remote access.
	Routing and Remote Access (RRAS)	Implement a remote access authentication service for users working remotely.
	Secure Sockets Tunneling Protocol (SSTP)	Ensure that all remote communications, as well as internal intraserver communications, are encrypted.
	Public key infrastructures (PKI)	Implement Active Directory Certificate Services (ADCS) in support of smart card deployment and software restrictions.
	Identity federation	Rely on ADFS for extranet access, if it is required.
	Network Access Protection (NAP)	Implement NAP to ensure all machines that link to the VSO network have approved health status.

TABLE 10-2 Applying the CDS to Virtual Service Offerings (*continued*)

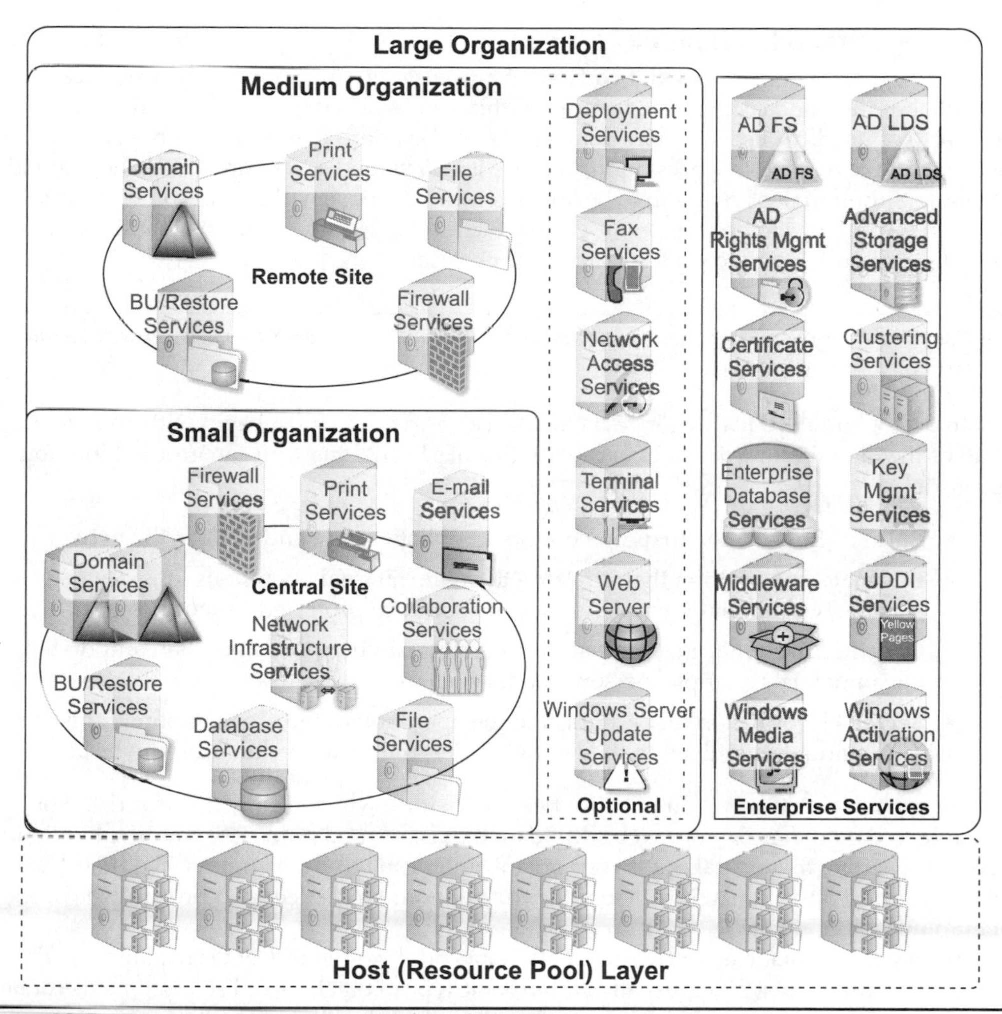

FIGURE 10-5 Scope of protection for virtual service offerings

of security on a full installation of WS08 than to deploy Server Core on virtual machines. In the long run, you'll appreciate the access to the graphical interface when it comes to long-term management practices of your VSOs.

The remainder of this chapter will use this separation of activities to help you understand when to apply it to either the resource pool or virtual service offerings or both.

Apply the Castle Defense System

Since you are designing a new parallel VSO network based on WS08, you have the opportunity to review your entire security infrastructure, and you should, especially since you now have two infrastructures to manage. Rely on the CDS to do this. Review each of its five layers, and determine if changes or modifications are required to your existing security approach, if it is already in place.

Layer 1 – Critical Information

The first place to start is with what you need to protect. Organizations have no choice: For collaboration and cooperation to work within a network, they must share data. They must also often allow users to store data locally on their hard drives. This is not so much an issue when the user has a workstation, because it is designed to remain within the internal network (although it is no reason to be lax in your policy design), but it becomes critical when the hard drive leaves the premises. It is the level of risk that must be identified so that the solutions you design to protect data are appropriate.

CAUTION *For resource pools, you must protect the virtual hard drives that make up each virtual machine in the VSO network.*

To do so, you need to categorize data. This categorization must begin with an inventory of all of the data within your network. Once this has been done, you can group it into four categories:

- **Public** Information that can be shared publicly inside and outside the network.
- **Internal** Information that is related to organizational operations. It is deemed as private, but not confidential. As such, it should be protected to some degree.
- **Confidential** Information that should not be divulged to other than authorized personnel. For example, personnel data such as salaries.
- **Secret** Information that is critical to the operation of the organization. If this information is divulged to the wrong parties, the organization itself can be at risk.

For each data category, you will also need to identify which elements are at risk. For example, if data that is on your web site—data that is deemed public—is modified without your knowledge, the reputation of your organization can be at risk. If payroll data is leaked within your organization, you will lose the trust of your employees and probably have a lot of employee discontent.

Information is made up of two elements: data and documents. Data is usually stored within structured tables and is usually within some type of database or list. Documents contain unstructured data and are within discrete objects, such as text files, presentations, images, or other document types. Both types of information require protection. Documents are protected through the capabilities of file storage systems or through database security, in the case of Windows SharePoint Services team sites. In the latter case, documents become data.

Data is protected at two levels. First, it is protected through the same mechanisms as documents, because databases store information in files just like documents. Second, it is protected through the features of the database system used to store it. For example, while Microsoft SQL Server stores databases in .mdb files, it also offers several security features for the data contained within these files. Because of this, organizations must also look to the hardening of applications, especially when it comes to data, if they want to absolutely protect their information. In this case, "hardening" means ensuring that security holes have been removed as much as possible within the applications the organization has either developed or purchased. It also means that the security features of the database engine have been implemented to protect the data it contains. Rows and columns that contain confidential and secure information should be secured at the database level, maybe even encrypted, and their access should be audited.

NOTE *You should also consider accessing Microsoft's Threat Analysis and Modeling Tool (http://go.microsoft.com/fwlink/?LinkId=86405). This tool lets you enter information about your organization to produce a rich list of the potential threats you may face. The results will let you better understand which aspects of the other four layers of the CDS you need to concentrate on.*

Layer 2 – Physical Protection

The second layer of security lies with physical protection of your computing systems. Physical protection deals with a variety of issues. A physical server that is located under a stairway in some regional office cannot be considered secure by any means. You should look to proper system casings, such as those provided by Kell Systems, for example (www.kellsystems.com).

CAUTION *As you will imagine, this layer mostly applies to resource pools, but it also extends to your PCs or any system that has the right to connect to your network, even if they only interact with VSOs.*

The elements that you need to cover at the physical protection layer include:

- **Geographical location** Is the physical location of your buildings within environmentally endangered locations? Is there the possibility of floods, avalanches, or cave-ins that may affect the buildings you do business in? Are they near roads where accidents may affect the building?
- **Social environment** Are your personnel aware that physical access to any computing equipment should be protected at all times? Are they aware that they should never divulge passwords under any circumstance?
- **Building security** Are your buildings secure? Are entries guarded, and are visitors identified at all locations? Are guests escorted at all times? Are rogue computing devices allowed within your buildings? Is the electrical input to the building protected; does it have a backup, especially for datacenters? Is the building's air control protected, and does it include a backup system? Is there a good fire protection plan in all buildings? Is the wiring inside and outside the building secure? Are wireless emissions secure?
- **Building construction** Is the building construction safe? Are the walls in your datacenters fireproof? Are datacenter doors firebreaks? Are floors covered in antistatic material? If there is a generator on the premises, is it in a safe and protected location? Does the computer room protect communication equipment as well as computer equipment? Does the building include security cameras to assist surveillance?
- **Server security** Are servers within locked rooms or locked cabinets in all locations? Is the access to server rooms monitored and protected? Are the servers themselves physically secured? Is physical server access controlled? Windows Server 2008 supports the use of smart cards for administrator accounts. In very secure environments, you should assign smart cards to all administrators. With new low-cost smart card options, especially USB smart cards, there are few reasons not to implement this policy.

- **BIOS security** All computing devices should have some form of protection at the Basic Input Output System (BIOS) level. For physical host servers, this should also include power-on passwords. For all systems, BIOS settings should be password-protected, and like all passwords, these should be highly protected and modified on a regular basis. New Desktop Management Interface (DMI) management tools allow the centralization of BIOS password management.
- **Staging security** Are all physical security policies extended to staging rooms where physical systems are installed? It doesn't do to have highly secure computer rooms when the staging facilities are wide open.
- **PC security** Are workstations and mobile devices secure? Are hardware identification systems, such as biometrics and smart cards, used for mobile devices? Is data on the mobile device secure when the device is in transit? Are external connections from the mobile devices to the internal network secure? Do you control the connection of rogue USB devices?
- **Network security** Are the network and its services secure? Is it possible for someone to introduce rogue Dynamic Host Configuration Protocol (DHCP) servers, for example? With Windows Server 2008, as with Windows 2000/2003, DHCP servers must be authorized to allocate addresses, but only if they are Windows-based DHCP servers. Is there a wireless network in place? Is it secure? Can rogue wireless users penetrate the network?
- **Redundancy** Are your critical systems redundant? This should include all systems—data systems, fire protection, Internet, and WAN connections, air conditioning, electrical, and so on.

All of the physical aspects of your installations must be maintained and documented. In addition, appropriate aspects of the physical protection plan must be communicated to employees at all levels. Finally, physical protection must be supplemented by a surveillance program. Once again, this is a part that can be played by personnel at all levels. Each employee must be aware that they can and should participate in the surveillance of any suspicious activity or the notification of any untoward event that may compromise your information systems.

Layer 3 – Operating System Hardening

The object of operating system hardening is to reduce the attack surface of your systems. To do so, you need to remove anything that is not required on a system. Windows Server 2008 does a good job of this right from the start because it installs only core components; you then add additional services when you add roles or features. In addition, IIS is not installed by default, which ensures that systems that do not require it do not have it.

But limiting the number of services is not the only activity you need to perform during system hardening. You also need to cover the following:

- System security configuration
- Anti-malware strategy
- Active Directory Domain Services security
- File system security
- Print system security

- .NET Framework security
- IIS security
- System redundancy

Each of these elements requires particular attention for both resource pools and virtual service offerings.

System Security Configuration

System security configuration involves the application of security parameters during the machine staging process. As mentioned in Chapter 4, when you install a machine, especially a server, you need to perform some modifications to the default installation to ensure that your machine is protected. These activities are performed on two levels:

- The first level focuses on performing some post-installation configuration modifications for security purposes.
- The second level involves the application of security templates to the server according to the server role. This second portion of the system configuration process relies on the Security Configuration Wizard to automatically apply security settings to your system.

Many of the items that are in your post-installation checklist can be automated through the application of security templates.

Post-Installation Security Checklist

Chapter 4 outlines the post-installation activities you should perform on a newly staged server. Chapter 6 outlines the minimum security configuration for a domain controller. On the security side, this should also include the following:

- Rename the administrator account. Although this has been mentioned in Chapter 4, it is essential to repeat it here. This is also an activity that can be performed through a security template because it is a Group Policy Object setting. Remember to use a complex account name and assign a complex password.

CAUTION *A complex password is your best defense system. In fact, a 15-character password—the Windows user interface supports up to 127 characters—that includes letters in both upper- and lowercase, numbers, and special characters is well-nigh impossible to crack. Well-known password-cracking tools can only work if the password has 14 characters or less. If there is one single feature that you implement to secure your servers, it should be complex passwords.*

- Copy the administrator account to create a backup account. Once again, use a complex account name and a complex password.
- Create a dummy administrator account and assign only guest access rights to it. Use a complex password for this account. Creating a dummy administrator account serves as a trap for users who want to try to access the real administrator account. Audit its access to see who is trying to penetrate your systems.
- Verify that the Guest account is disabled.

- Verify the list of running services, and make sure they are well documented. Use a server datasheet to do this. Shut down any service you deem unnecessary for this server role.
- Verify the list of open ports, and shut down the ports you deem unnecessary for this server role. You can identify the list of open ports by using the `NETSTAT` command. Use the following command:

  ```
  netstat -a -n -o
  ```

  The `a` switch asks for all ports, the `n` switch asks for numeric output for the ports, and the `o` switch asks for the process associated with the port.

That's about it for basic security. Everything else can be performed through the Security Configuration Wizard.

CAUTION *Though a complex password is your best defense system, it can also be your worst nightmare, because complex passwords are hard to remember. One of the things you can do is use real words or phrases, but replace letters with numbers and special characters, and mix up the cases, for example,* `Ad/\/\1n1$traT!on` *(Administration). You should also use different passwords for different locations. If you find that remembering complex passwords is too hard, you can use a password storage tool, like Password Keeper by Gregory Braun (www.gregorybraun.com/PassKeep.html). This handy tool stores all your passwords in an encrypted file on your desktop and requires another password to open. With such a tool, you only have to remember a single password.*

Rely on Security Templates

The security settings of Group Policy Objects are stored in three locations in Windows Server 2008. The first is in the GPO itself under Policies | Windows Settings | Security Settings in both Computer and User Configurations. The second is in a security template file. In many cases, it is best to store a setting in a security template file, because it automatically forms a backup file for the setting. The third option lets you create much more comprehensive security policies through the SCW. SCW security policies can even incorporate security template settings.

There are several ways to apply templates and security settings. The first is directly through a GPO by importing the template into it. This is done by selecting the Import Policy command from the context menu displayed when you right-click Security Settings in the Group Policy Editor. This displays a dialog box that lets you choose available templates. Imported templates can either be merged with or replace all of the security settings in the GPO. The difference is applied through the Clear This Database Before Importing option in the Import Policy dialog box. Selecting this option will automatically clear all security settings in the GPO and apply only those found in the template.

The second manner is through the Security Configuration Wizard. This tool lets you create a comprehensive security policy for your servers and then apply the settings in template format through Group Policy to all Windows servers.

Through security policies, you can configure the following security areas:

- **Account policies** Password, lockout, and Kerberos policies.
- **Local policies** Audit, user rights assignments, and security options.

- **Event Log** Settings for system, application, security, directory, file replication, and DNS service logs.
- **Restricted groups** Control group membership.
- **System services** Startup modes and access control for the services on each system.
- **Registry** Access control for registry keys.
- **File system** Access control for folders and files through New Technology File System (NTFS).
- **Wired network (IEEE 802.3) policies** Controls access to the network through smart cards and other secure devices. Implements single sign-on for the wired network.
- **Windows Firewall with Advanced Security** Controls server and client computer firewall settings.
- **Wireless network (IEEE 802.11) policies** Controls access to the network through smart cards and other secure devices. Implements single sign-on for the wireless network.
- **Public key policies** Regroups all policies related to PKI. For example, EFS, trusted root certificate authorities, automated certificate assignment, and more.
- **Software restriction policies** Controls which software is allowed to run on the network.
- **Network Access Protection** Controls the behavior and connection status of computers that do not meet health requirements.
- **IP Security policies on Active Directory** Controls secure communication settings between clients and servers.

The WS08 Help system offers comprehensive information about each of these security settings. Of these, only the first six are affected by templates, and three of them—system services, registry, and file system settings—are ideally suited to locally applied security templates because they control the access to specific object types. The application of access control rights to files, folders, the registry, and the configuration of system services can be quite time-consuming. Therefore, it is best to keep these settings in local security templates rather than setting them directly at the GPO level, because local security templates are applied manually (or automatically through schedules you control), while GPOs are constantly being reapplied on the systems in an Active Directory Domain Services domain.

NOTE *GPOs are refreshed every five minutes on DCs and every 90 minutes on servers and workstations.*

Make sure that your GPO strategy does not affect these three areas if you choose to set them through local security policies because of the application order for GPOs. Local security policies are set at computer startup, and they are always overridden by conflicting settings in Group Policy Objects.

Unlike previous versions of Windows Server, Windows Server 2008 does not include default templates with the system. There are, however, templates applied to certain system roles.

For example, DCs include a default DC template. Default templates, when available, are stored under `%SYSTEMROOT%\SECURITY\TEMPLATES`. Carefully review the settings in these templates before you apply them. You'll note that even Microsoft's own templates only apply to the three core settings: system services, file, and registry.

In addition, the Windows Server 2008 Security Guide includes role-based templates for member servers in general, domain controllers, application servers, file and print servers, network infrastructure servers, and Web servers running IIS. These are all based on a baseline template. Two baselines exist: one for member servers and one for domain controllers. In addition to the member server baseline, there are incremental templates for each member server role identified previously.

The WS08 Security Guide is not the only source of baseline security templates. The U.S. National Security Agency (NSA) offers templates for download, as well as complete security documentation on a number of Windows 2000 services and features (Windows Server 2008 will surely follow). These templates are available at www.nsa.gov/snac. The NSA documentation and templates are an excellent source for security recommendations.

The Center for Internet Security (CIS) is also an excellent source for security templates. Its templates are role-based and include the coverage of the basic operating system for both workstations and servers, as well as coverage of Internet Information Server. Its templates can be found at www.cisecurity.org.

Finally, templates can be acquired from commercial vendors, such as NetIQ, Symantec, Quest, and many others.

CAUTION *Careless application of security templates, especially templates you are not familiar with, may break running systems. Because security templates will modify default security settings on computer systems, it is essential that you apply them in a test environment before putting them on production systems. In fact, you should test every server and computer function before releasing a security template to production.*

Create Baseline Templates for Local Application

When you create templates for local application—during computer installation, for example—you will ideally start from a baseline template that you acquired from the NSA, CIS, or the Security Guide. As far as your servers are concerned, you will need a minimum of two baseline templates: one for domain controllers and one for member servers. These baseline templates should include only three types of settings: file system, registry, and system service settings. (Other security settings will be covered with templates for import into Group Policy Objects.)

Avoid multipurpose servers, especially mingling them with the DC role. Since your services are rendered by virtual machines, this is much easier to do than before. This will mean only one template for DCs.

You will need to identify which settings best fit your organization, but here are some recommendations for each of the three categories:

- The registry should be as secure as possible. First, make sure that access to the registry editor is controlled in your network. This is done by restricting access to both REGEDT32.EXE and REGEDIT.EXE through a GPO. (These settings can be found in User Configuration | Policies | Administrative Templates | System. Prevent access to registry editing tools.)

- Next, secure specific keys in the registry itself. The easiest way to secure registry keys and hives is to propagate inheritable permissions from the parent key to subkeys. But in some cases, this may not be possible.

CAUTION *The Windows Server 2008 registry is already tightly controlled, so you may not need to further secure its keys. Be careful when you decide to further block access to the registry, as it may have an impact on the operation of your software.*

- Also secure files and folders. Ideally, you will secure folders rather than files. Once again, propagation is preferable but not always applicable here.
- Be careful when securing files and folders that you do not modify security settings on objects that are automatically secured by WS08. For example, it is not a good idea to replace security settings on the Documents and Settings folder since WS08 must manage these settings every time a new user profile is created.
- Also, set system services to the appropriate start mode: Automatic for services that must start when the computer boots, Automatic (Delayed Start) for services that must start but are not required at boot, Manual when a user or process is allowed to start a service but it does not have to start automatically, and Disabled when the service is not required. You might consider removing services that are in a disabled state.

TIP *Windows Server 2008 includes service hardening, a feature that protects services by default. Each service uses reduced privileges to access resources and is designed to access only the specific resources it needs to run properly.*

- Finally, you can apply security to each service, limiting the access rights for starting, stopping, and otherwise controlling services. If you set security on services, be sure that you always include both the Administrators group and the System account; otherwise, you may encounter problems starting services. By default, three objects have access: Administrators, the System account, and the Interactive group.

CAUTION *Since Windows Server 2003, there are two "system" accounts: the NetworkService and the LocalSystem accounts. NetworkService has fewer privileges than LocalSystem and should be used to start services on high-risk servers. If someone manages to take control of a service and wants to use it to take control of a machine, they will not have the privileges to do so.*

Configure Security Templates

Once you have identified the registry keys, files, folders, and services you want to modify, you can move on to the creation or modification of your security templates. The first thing you need to do is create a Security Template and Configuration console, since none are available by default.

1. Move to the Start menu, select Run, type **MMC**, and then press ENTER.
2. In the MMC console, select File | Add/Remove Snap-in.

3. In the Add or Remove Snap-in dialog box, select Security Templates and click the Add button. Repeat the operation with the Security Configuration and Analysis snap-in. Click OK to return to the console. Move to File | Save, name the console Security Console, and click OK (see Figure 10-6).
4. You can add your own templates through this console. By default, new templates will be located in your `DOCUMENTS/SECURITY/TEMPLATES` folder. To create a new template, right-click your folder and select New Template. Give it a name and a description, and click OK to create it. Note that you're starting the template from scratch and will need to define all settings. Move to your new template, and modify its settings. Expand the template to view its components.
5. To set registry security, right-click Registry and select Add Key. In the Add Key dialog box, locate the key you want to secure, and click OK. Decide if you want to propagate permissions to subkeys, reset permissions on subkeys, or block permission replacement on this key. Use the Edit Security button to set the appropriate security rights, and click OK. Repeat for each key or subkey you want to secure.
6. To set file or folder security, right-click File System and select Add File. In the Add File dialog box, locate the file or folder you want to secure, and click OK. Set the appropriate security rights, and click OK. Decide if you want to propagate permissions to the file or folder, reset permissions on the file or folder, or block permission replacement on this file or folder. Repeat for each file or folder you want to secure.

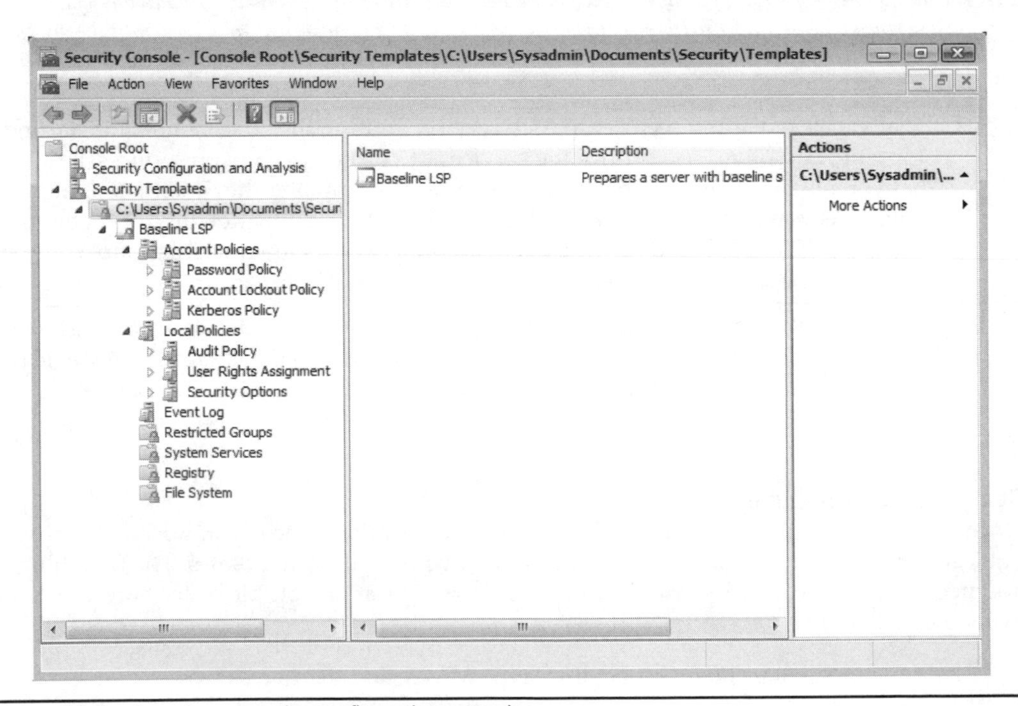

FIGURE 10-6 A custom security configuration console

7. To set security on system services, select System Services. Double-click the appropriate service in the right pane, select Define This Policy Setting In The Template, select the start mode, and, if required, click Edit Security to modify the security settings. Click OK when done. Repeat for each service you want to modify.

TIP *Make sure you right-click the template name and select Save before you exit the console.*

You can use this console to create your own templates or modify those you obtain from other sources. Make sure you fully test any templates you intend to deploy.

Use Local Security Templates

Local security templates can be applied in two manners: through a graphical tool called Security Configuration and Analysis or through a command-line tool called `SECEDIT`. Both have their uses. Both can be used to analyze and configure a system based on a security template.

Security Configuration and Analysis is an MMC snap-in that provides a graphical view to system configuration and analysis. This can be quite useful, since it relies on the same interface that you use to either create templates or modify Group Policy Objects. The snap-in has already been applied to your new Security console. This gives you a single tool to create, modify, apply, analyze, and import security policy settings.

To analyze a computer and compare it to a given security policy, use the following procedure:

1. Right-click Security Configuration and Analysis inside your security console, and select Open database.
2. In the Open Database dialog box, either locate the appropriate database or type a new database name, and then click OK. The default path setting is `DOCUMENTS\SECURITY\DATABASES`.
3. Next, you will need to select the security template you want to use for analysis. This must be a template that has been prepared in advance. Select the appropriate template and click OK.
4. To analyze your system, right-click Security Configuration and Analysis, and select Analyze Computer Now.
5. Since every analysis or configuration operation requires a log file, a dialog box appears to ask you the location of it. The default path setting is `DOCUMENTS\SECURITY\LOGS`, and the default name is the same as the database. Type the name of a new log file, use the Browse button to locate an existing file, or click OK to accept the default name.
6. The analysis begins. Once the analysis is complete, you can see the difference in settings between the template and the computer. Simply move to a setting you wish to view, and select it. Differences (if any) will be displayed in the right pane.
7. You can also view the log file. To do so, right-click Security Configuration and Analysis, and select View Log. The log file will be displayed in the right pane. To return to the database, simply clear View Log in the context menu.

8. You can modify database settings to conform to the values you want to apply by moving to the appropriate value and double-clicking it. Select Define This Policy In The Database, modify the setting, and click OK.
9. Use the right mouse button to display the Security Configuration and Analysis context menu, and select Save to save the modifications you make to the database.
10. To configure a computer with the settings in the database, select Configure Computer Now from the same context menu. Once again, you will need to specify the location and name of the log file.
11. Close the security console when done.

TIP *You can also use Security Configuration and Analysis to capture the settings from an existing machine. To do so, you need to modify all the settings you need on the model machine, create a new database, import a template, analyze the computer, verify that all settings are appropriate, and export the resulting database to a new template file. Export Template is once again found on the context menu of the Security Configuration and Analysis snap-in.*

You can also automate the application of templates to different machines through the use of the SECEDIT command. A typical command to do so would look like this:

```
secedit /configure /db filename.sdb /log filename.log
```

In addition, the use of the /verbose switch would create a log file that is highly detailed. If no log file is specified, SECEDIT will automatically log all information to the SCESRV.LOG file in the %WINDIR%\SECURITY\LOGS folder.

But since the local security template affects only the file system, the registry, and system services, you should ensure that the command you use applies only those portions of the template. To do so, use the following command:

```
secedit /configure /db filename.sdb /log filename.log /areas REGKEYS
FILESTORE SERVICES /quiet
```

This command will ensure that only the appropriate areas are applied, guaranteeing the application of your written security policy. In addition, the /quiet switch will ensure that no comments are output during the application of the template.

This SECEDIT command can be inserted in an automated system installation to ensure that computers are secured as soon as they are installed (through the Unattend.xml response file— see Chapter 4).

SECEDIT is also useful for regular security setting verification, since it also includes the /analyze switch. Both analysis and configuration can be automated through the Task Scheduler in Control Panel. The SECEDIT command must be captured in a script for automation to work.

These are not the only operations that can be performed through SECEDIT. You can find out more on this command through the WS08 Help system or simply by typing SECEDIT at the command prompt.

TIP *Perform these operations on a test server running inside a virtual machine. This will make it easier to correct mistakes.*

Security Template Best Practices

There are a few key points to remember when using security templates:

- Settings entered in a security template are not stored into the GPO until the security template has been imported into it.
- The security template can be reapplied on a regular basis to ensure that settings that may have been modified are reset to appropriate values.
- Applying a template through `SECEDIT` applies it only to the local policy. Any conflicting setting applied through Group Policy will override the local policy setting. For this reason, you should limit local settings to files, folders, the registry, and services.
- If you decide to use the Clear Database option when importing templates into GPOs, this means that you should never modify security settings in your GPOs directly, because these modifications will be overridden when you import a template.
- Always document your GPO changes, even if they are stored in a security template.

Security templates are useful, but Windows Server 2008 includes a much more powerful tool that can let you control many more security elements: the Security Configuration Wizard.

Move Beyond Security Templates with the Security Configuration Wizard

As you can tell, security templates only address a certain selection of the elements you need to control in order to create a complete security policy. The Security Configuration Wizard goes far beyond the security templates you can create. It can also import security templates to include their settings in anything you apply through the SCW. In addition, SCW lets you configure the following:

- Tighten service configurations through role-based configurations
- Tighten network security
- Tighten registry settings
- Implement an audit policy

These are the default controls you'll find in SCW. In addition, it lets you control IIS security, so long as you select the Web server role in the Server Roles page of the wizard. Perhaps the best part of the SCW is that it provides complete explanations for each of the settings it will modify. At last, you have a single place to determine what a particular security setting will modify and why it will modify it (see Figure 10-7).

In addition, SCW includes a corresponding command line, `SCWCMD.EXE`, which lets you mass-produce the application of security policies generated through the SCW graphical interface. SCW produces output in XML format, which is incompatible by default with GPOs. In order to convert SCW output into a readable format for inclusion into a GPO, you must use the following command line:

```
scwcmd transform /p:PolicyFile.xml /g:GPOName
```

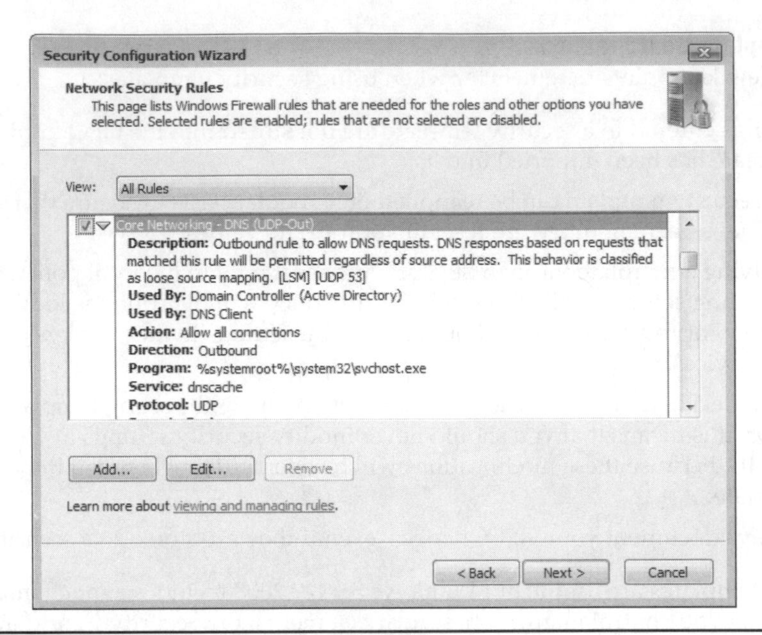

FIGURE 10-7 Working with the Security Configuration Wizard

This transforms the XML file into a new GPO, and must be run with domain administrator privileges. Policies are saved under the %SYSTEMROOT%\SECURITY\MSSCW\POLICIES folder. The resulting GPO will include the contents of the SCW XML file into various sections of the GPO. These settings will include content for security settings, IP Security policies, and Windows Firewall. SCW policies are much more powerful than any other single component for security application in Windows. This new GPO must then be linked to appropriate OUs to be applied.

CAUTION *IIS cannot be configured through Group Policy. IIS security configurations must be applied through* SCWCMD *or the SCW itself.*

You can use SCW to create new policies, edit existing policies, apply policies, and perhaps its best feature, roll back the assignation of a security policy. Security policies are generated from a base server configuration. Ideally, you will create base servers for each role you intend to deploy, create a baseline policy from each of these servers, and apply the policy each time you work with a new server for any given role.

TIP *More information on the Security Configuration Wizard can be found at http://technet2.microsoft.com/windowsserver/en/library/38f0693d-59eb-45ca-980d-31fe03eb54df1033.mspx?mfr=true.*

Secure Resources Through Device Control

Windows Vista introduced a new capability for the Windows OS: the ability to configure removable device controls through the use of Group Policy. This is done through the control of device installations. This lets you control which devices can be installed on a system. For example, it will prevent a malicious user from plugging in a removable disk drive and walking away with your confidential information.

Basically, you create an approved list of devices on your network and include it in your GPO. For example, you might let users install USB mice and keyboards, but prevent them from installing either Flash memory devices or external disk drives. Apple iPods, for example, are also in fact disk drives that can be used to transport very large amounts of information, especially the larger models. The same applies to Pocket PCs or smart phones. Since you can't prohibit the use of these device types on your network, you must control their use through a properly designed GPO.

Make sure you implement removable device controls in the resource pool so that no one can connect a USB drive to a server and use it to remove copies of your virtual machines. In addition, you should implement it on PCs linked to the VSO to ensure that no one can use a PC to connect a device and somehow traverse the VSO domain to the resource pool domain and steal virtual machines. The best protection is complete protection.

TIP *For more information on how to implement removable device controls for both the resource pool and VSO networks, go to http://technet2.microsoft.com/windowsserver2008/en/library/bab0f1a1-54aa-4cef-9164-139e8bcc44751033.mspx?mfr=true.*

Harden Systems with BitLocker Drive Encryption

With the release of Vista, Microsoft introduced BitLocker Full Drive Encryption. BitLocker lets you encrypt the contents of your operating system volume so that malicious attackers cannot access them. BitLocker is mostly used for mobile systems or systems that contain sensitive data and that leave your office premises.

BitLocker can also be used to protect server drives since WS08 fully supports its capabilities. You might, for example, apply BitLocker to all of your virtual machines so that even if someone steals the files that make it up, they won't be able to access any data that may reside inside them. This, however, is an extreme measure that would only be applied in very secure environments, because any encryption adds a certain amount of overhead to the operation of a server. A more likely scenario is the encryption of host server drives that are in remote offices. This way, if someone walks off with a physical server in a remote office, not only will they not have access to any of the virtual machines, but your host servers will also be protected.

In order to be able to use BitLocker, your system must meet the following specifications:

- Includes two NTFS partitions: a system volume and an OS volume. The system volume is the boot partition and only requires about 1.5 GB of space.
- Includes a USB flash drive and a BIOS that supports reading and writing to a USB Flash drive at startup.
- Ideally, includes a Trusted Protection Module (TPM) version 1.2 microchip.
- Ideally, includes a Trusted Computing Group (TCG)–compliant BIOS.

As you can see, BitLocker can be run through the use of an external USB Flash drive. This Flash drive will store the encryption key used to lock and unlock the OS partition. However, using a USB drive is a risk, since it can be lost or stolen. This is why it is ideal to use a server that has the full TPM components. In this case, the encryption key is stored securely within the TPM chip and cannot be stolen.

If the host servers you use for remote offices include these capabilities and you intend to encrypt their contents, then use the following procedure.

1. Begin by creating two partitions during installation. Both partitions must be primary partitions. In addition, the smaller partition should be set as active. Both partitions must be formatted with NTFS. You can use the installation media to create these partitions. Rely on the `DISKPART` commands listed in Chapter 4 to do so.
2. Install Server Core into the OS partition.
3. Once Server Core is installed, perform the post-installation configurations found in Chapter 4.
4. Next, install the BitLocker feature:

   ```
   start /w ocsetup BitLocker
   ```

   Restart the system once BitLocker is installed.
5. Once the system restarts, you'll be ready to configure BitLocker. Begin by getting BitLocker to list compatible drives. Make sure you go to the appropriate folder to do this.

   ```
   cd\windows\system32
   cscript manage-bde.wsf -status
   ```
6. Now, encrypt the system drive:

   ```
   cscript manage-bde.wsf -on C: -RecoveryPassword NumericalKey
   -RecoveryKey BitLockerDrive -StartupKey BitLockerDrive
   ```

   The *BitLockerDrive* is the drive letter you gave to the system partition. The *NumericalKey* is a 48-digit number, divided into eight groups of six digits, using hyphens to separate groups. Each group of six digits must be divisible by 11 but cannot be greater than 720,896.
7. You can repeat this command to encrypt any other drive on the host server.

There it is—a simple command with powerful results. Make sure you protect the encryption key, and make sure you save the recovery password.

CAUTION *Using BitLocker will impact server startup. Be careful which authentication mode you use because you may need to be physically present when you reboot servers. For example, this would impact your ability to remotely patch servers.*

TIP *More information on BitLocker can be found at www.microsoft.com/whdc/system/platform/hwsecurity/default.mspx.*

Install Anti-malware Tools

Another layer of security on all systems is the anti-malware (AM) engine. Implementing a complete security environment requires the use of a comprehensive antivirus, anti-spam, anti-spyware, and general malware removal solution. This is not a function of Windows Server 2008, but WS08 does offer special application programming interfaces (APIs) to support file and object scanning on a system. It also includes Windows Defender, Microsoft's free anti-spyware engine, but anti-spyware alone is not enough. This is why Microsoft has worked extensively with anti-malware manufacturers to ensure that their solutions work well under stress and reliably in any situation.

A complete anti-malware solution should include the following elements:

- Central management of both clients and servers
- Automatic installation and deployment to client and server machines
- A Microsoft Management Console (MMC) for management tasks
- Automatic download of new anti-malware signatures
- Variable download schedules to distribute the download workload
- Automatic deployment of signatures to all clients
- Automatic system scanning
- Central collection of all scanning results
- Alert generation on the discovery of malware
- Root-kit removal capabilities
- Integration and support for Server Core
- Central quarantine of detected malware and automatic machine clean-up
- Detection of unusual behavior to locate unknown malware
- Provide policy-based management
- Support for e-mail and database system inspection
- Support from the manufacturer for malware clean-up

One of the best solutions on the market today is Symantec Endpoint Security from Symantec Corporation (www.symantec.com/enterprise/products/category.jsp?pcid=2241). It is so simple to deploy that an administrator with no experience in the product can have it deployed and fully functional, including automatic update management, within one hour! Once it is deployed, there should be nothing else to do, because it automatically updates all systems and will install itself on any new system that joins the domain.

Whatever the solution you select, ensure that it is in place and fully functional *before* you provide any means to connect to the outside world in your parallel VSO network.

CAUTION *Make sure you implement your anti-malware solution in the resource pool before you implement another in the VSOs.*

Use Software Restriction Policies

Your anti-malware strategy cannot be complete without support from Windows Server 2008 and Group Policy. WS08 includes a special set of GPO settings that identify the code that is allowed to run and operate within a network. These are the software restriction policies (SRPs).

This set of GPO settings allows you to control unknown code in your network. Though the SRPs allow you to control over 38 file types—basically anything that is seen as code—there are two file types that you should absolutely control: scripts and macros. Most unknown threats come in the form of either one of these two file types. Since you control what occurs in your network, you should explicitly identify the scripts and macros that are authorized to run in your network.

The easiest way to do this is to digitally sign your scripts and macros. Signing places a PKI certificate within the code. You can then define SRPs that block all scripts and macros, except those that are signed with your certificate. SRPs are defined in Computer Configuration | Policies | Windows Settings | Security Settings | Software Restriction Policies. This section is empty by default. You must begin by selecting New Software Restriction Policies from the context menu. Then you must identify the extensions that you want to disallow, change the basic policy, and identify the certificate to trust. Make sure that you do not include the SRP within the default domain policy. That way, if you have to deactivate it for some reason, you will not deactivate your global domain security policy. You should also include Windows Installer files within this policy to ensure that only accepted code is installed in your networks.

For resource pools, assign this policy to the entire domain. This will affect all host servers. For VSOs, you might be satisfied with assigning this policy to PCs only. In that case, assign it through the Global PC GPO that is applied at the PC OU level.

General Active Directory Domain Services Security

Active Directory Domain Services is also an area that requires considerable security. In fact, the entire design of the directories that you have created to date has been done with security in mind. The resource pool relies on a single domain forest, which is secure because only administrators interact with it. The VSO network uses the concept of the protected forest root domain (PFRD) and of a child production domain, which secures forest-wide contents while letting users interact with the production domain. In addition, the concept of creating organizational units and delegating certain management activities to other people in your organization is an important part of the security foundation for ADDS. But no matter which security measures you put in place in your directories, you will always have one caveat: You must trust your administrators implicitly. Of course, ADDS allows you to limit the rights you grant to different levels of administrators, but nevertheless, the administrators you designate must be trustworthy; otherwise, everything you do to secure the directory will be useless.

A good place to start is by enforcing secure administrative habits. ADDS administrators, both at the domain and the member server level, should use limited access accounts for their everyday work and use the Run as Administrator command to perform administrative tasks. And, since WS08 supports the use of smart cards for administrators, it could be a good idea to implement them. This would mean two-factor authentication for all administrators in the network. WS08 fully supports this and eases the smart card administration burden because of the new features such as auto-enrollment and auto-update for public key certificates. Smart cards can, however, be expensive to implement, and they do add another layer of management to an already complex system. Because of this, you should consider their implementation only in more tightly controlled environments.

TIP *If you intend to work with smart cards in only one network, then assign them at the resource pool level. This helps secure this most important infrastructure first.*

To make sure that your ADDS directories are secure, you need to perform the following actions:

- Design the Active Directory Domain Services structure with security in mind (Chapter 5).
- Ensure that each domain contains at least two domain controllers to protect the data in the domain (Chapter 5).
- Run forests in fully functional mode to profit from the latest security features (Chapter 5).
- Position Operations Masters for maximum service efficiency (Chapters 5).
- Ensure that all services related to the directory use directory-integrated data storage, for example, DNS (Chapter 6).
- Ensure that you use a structured Group Policy strategy (Chapter 7).
- Create read-only custom consoles as much as possible (Chapter 7).
- Distribute consoles through Terminal Services and assign only read and execute permissions to them (Chapter 9).
- Ensure that all directory data is protected and can be modified only by the right people in your organization (Chapter 6).
- Manage groups effectively to assign permissions in the directory (Chapter 7).
- Make sure that sensitive information stored within the domain is hidden from prying eyes (Chapter 7).
- Ensure that your domain controllers are physically protected.
- Ensure that your domain controllers have specific local security policies applied to them.
- Configure the two default domain Group Policies *before* creating child domains to profit from policy propagation at domain creation.
- Manage your trusts properly to ensure rapid service response where required.
- Delegate only the administrative rights that are required and nothing else to both service and data administrators.
- Use the Read-Only Domain Controller role as appropriate.
- Tightly control the modify permissions and modify ownership permissions.
- Implement a strong global account policy within the directory for administrators and a strong one for users.
- Audit sensitive object access within the directory.
- Protect the directory restore password.
- Ensure that you have a comprehensive directory backup policy (Chapter 11).
- Verify directory replication regularly, and monitor system logs, especially the debug log (Chapter 13).

Many of these activities have been covered already. A few will also be covered in other chapters. The rest are covered both in this section and in the "Layer 4 – Information Access" section.

Security Within the Directory

Chapter 8 outlined how you could hide objects within the directory through the use of discretionary access control lists (DACLs) on directory objects. Chapter 7 used the same approach for OU delegation. These examples demonstrate how the Active Directory Domain Services uses DACLs to apply security on its principals. Each principal is automatically secured within the directory. Like Windows NTFS, the directory provides security inheritance. This means that all child objects inherit the parent object's security settings. What is particular to the directory is the way permissions are inherited.

Explicit permissions always override inherited permissions, even deny permissions. This means that it is possible to define a deny permission on a parent object and define an allow permission on its child object. For example, you can deny the List Contents permission on an OU and define an Allow List Contents permission on a child OU within the previous OU. The people who are denied access to the parent OU will never be able to see or modify its contents, nor will they be able to navigate the directory to the child OU, but they will be able to search the directory to locate contents within the child OU.

And, like NTFS, the directory offers two levels of permission assignment. The first regroups detailed permissions into categories such as Full Control, Read, Write, Execute, and so on. To view security settings for an object, you must right-click it and select Properties (within one of the ADDS consoles).

CAUTION *You need to enable Advanced Features in the View menu of the console in order to be able to view the Security tab in the object's Properties dialog box.*

Clicking the Advanced button of this dialog box leads to the detailed security permissions. Several types of information are available here. To begin, it gives you access to special security features, such as Permissions, Audit, Owner, and Effective Permissions.

Each tab outlines different information. The Permissions tab, for example, identifies if permissions are inherited and, if so, from which container or whether they are explicit. The Auditing tab identifies the audit policies that are applied to the object. The Owner tab lists the various owners of this object. And finally, Effective Permissions lets you identify the resultant permissions for a given security principal. Click Select to locate the user or group for which you want to view effective permissions.

If you want to view or assign specific permissions, return to the Permissions tab and click Add or Edit. This displays the Permissions Entry dialog box. Here you can assign specific permissions to users or groups.

CAUTION *It is* always *preferable to assign permissions to groups rather than users.*

This level of detail can make managing directory permissions quite complex. Always keep your directory permissions as simple as possible, and try to use inherited permissions as much as possible. Detail specific permissions when you delegate control of an OU.

Fine-Grained Password Policies

In the ideal environment, you would enforce very strong passwords for everyone who is granted the privilege of logging on to your network. Obviously, this could only occur in a perfect world. Humans being what they are, there will always be users who have difficulty working with highly complex passwords or who need to write down anything they use to access a system if it is more than a few characters.

In the past, this has meant that you needed to bring your password policy down to the lowest common denominator and make it as simple or as complex as your users can handle. That's because ADDS domains could only handle one single account and, therefore, password policy per domain. But in Windows Server 2008, this is no longer the case. That's because ADDS includes fine-grained password policies (FGPPs), the ability to specify multiple password policies within a single domain. Along with the password policies, you can assign different account lockout restrictions to different groups of users.

TIP *For a more comprehensive multiple-password policy tool, look to Special Operations' Password Policy at www.specopssoft.com/products/specopspasswordpolicy.*

Organizations who want to implement a tighter password policy for administrators while letting users work with a looser policy—since they do not have access to privileged content, at least not in the way administrators do—should rely on FGPP to create at least two different password policies.

NOTE *In order to use FGPPs, your domains must be in fully functional mode for WS08.*

Creating FGPPs is fairly straightforward. Begin by determining which users, groups, and OUs you intend to rely on to apply the FGPP. Then populate any new groups you need to create, define the password settings objects (PSOs) you need to apply the policies, and finally, apply them. You can create as many FGPPs as you need, but we recommend at least two: one for administrators and one for users. You can, of course, create many more, but remember that the more complex you make your environment, the more complex it will be to manage and the more likely it is that errors will occur.

TIP *More information on fine-grained password policies can be found at http://technet2.microsoft .com/windowsserver2008/en/library/056a73ef-5c9e-44d7-acc1-4f0bade6cd751033.mspx?mfr=true. Step-by-step instructions for implementing FGPPs can be found at http://technet2.microsoft.com/ windowsserver2008/en/library/2199dcf7-68fd-4315-87cc-ade35f8978ca1033.mspx?mfr=true. To obtain a graphical user interface for the implementation of FGPPs, go to http://powergui.org/entry .jspa?externalID=882&categoryID=46.*

PART V

ADDS Auditing

Windows Server supported the auditing of ADDS events since the first inception of Active Directory in Windows 2000. Audited events are stored in the Event Log by default, but these events left a lot to be desired, since they would only tell you that an object had been changed and nothing else. With WS08, Microsoft has improved the directory auditing capabilities. Now you can not only view exactly what has been changed, but also view previous values. In addition, you can even use these previous values to restore the settings back to what they were before the change.

Directories are finicky environments. With ADDS, Microsoft has implemented a powerful environment that supports both authentication and administration. In fact, many organizations relying on this directory service created highly complex directory structures and allowed several operators to control different components of the directory. In Windows 2000, there was no tracking or warning when an operator effected a change, for example, moving an OU from one location to the other inside the directory. Moving objects is a tricky proposition in ADDS, since it can greatly change the behavior of the system because assigned GPOs may no longer apply to them or worse—the wrong GPOs would be applied. This is why Microsoft added a warning in Windows Server 2003 each time operators moved an object. The problem with this warning, however, is that it provided operators with the ability to turn it off, bringing the system back to Windows 2000 settings (see Figure 10-8).

CAUTION *The warning with regards to moving objects is still available in WS08. Make sure your operators know not to turn it off so that they are always warned when objects are moved. Dragging-and-dropping is great, but it also makes it possible to make mistakes. Keeping the warning allows you to correct potential mistakes.*

In WS08, Microsoft went one step further—they added a new protection feature to objects created in ADDS. Each time an object is created, it is now protected from deletion by default. This means it is also protected from being moved. In order to move a protected object, you need to view its Object tab in the Properties dialog box (through the Advanced Features view) and clear its protection attribute. While this goes a long way toward protecting directory objects from wrongful operations, it is not enough. This is why you need to turn on ADDS auditing in your directories. This operation should be performed both on resource pools and virtual service offerings.

ADDS auditing, like all auditing, is a two-step process. First, you turn on auditing in the appropriate GPO; then you determine which objects need to be audited and for whom. Begin by turning on the audit policy. Since you want to audit directory contents, you can do this within the Default Domain Controllers Policy (DDCP).

1. Use Group Policy Management Console (GPMC) to launch the DDCP in Group Policy Editor.
2. Move to Computer Settings | Policies | Windows Settings | Security Settings | Local Policies | Audit Policy.
3. Locate the Audit Directory Service Access setting, double-click it, and configure it to identify successes, at the very least. You can also configure it to identify failures, but only if you suspect operators are trying to do things they are not allowed to. The goal of this policy is to view what has been changed and possibly have the ability to undo it.
4. Close the Group Policy Editor.

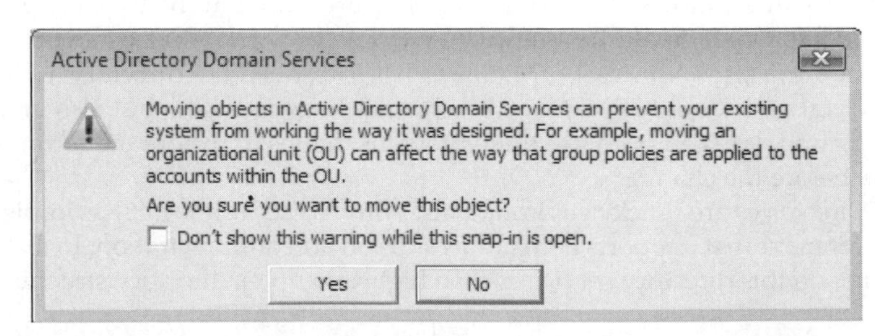

FIGURE 10-8 ADDS warning when moving objects

The audit policy is turned on. It will be updated on each DC within five minutes of your change.

Now you need to tell ADDS which objects you want to audit. For example, if you want to audit all changes to the People OU structure, including any changes to the objects it contains, use the following procedure:

1. Go to Server Manager | Roles | Active Directory Domain Services | Active Directory Users and Computers. Make sure Advanced Features is turned on in the View menu.
2. Expand your directory until you see the People OU. Right-click it to view the Properties dialog box.
3. Go to the Security tab, and click Advanced.
4. Go to the Auditing tab. Click Add.
5. Select Authenticated Users and click OK.
6. In the Auditing Entry for People dialog box, select Descendant User objects in the drop-down list (the last object in the list), select Write All Properties under Successful, and click OK to close the dialog box.
7. Close all other dialog boxes.

Now, each time you modify an object under People, an event ID number 4662 will be displayed in the Security Event Log. This is the behavior of all previous versions of Windows Server. In WS08, you can, however, go far beyond this to edit four more activities:

- Directory service access
- Directory service changes
- Directory service replication
- Detailed directory service replication

Unfortunately, these additional activities do not have a graphical interface to enable them. You must use a command line. For example, to audit changes in the directory—the activity that provides the most interesting information—you need to type the following command on any DC:

```
auditpol /set /subcategory:"Directory Service Changes" /success:enable
```

Make sure you open a command prompt with the Run as Administrator option.

Tip *Be careful which of the subcategories you enable because your Event Log will fill up quite rapidly with newly logged events.*

Now change any object under People. The system will log the change. To view the event, go to Server Manager | Diagnostics | Event Viewer | Windows Logs | Security. You should see normal ADDS events that have ID number 4662, but in addition, you should see a 5136 event (see Figure 10-9). In fact, ADDS auditing adds four new events to the log. These events are detailed in Table 10-3.

PART V

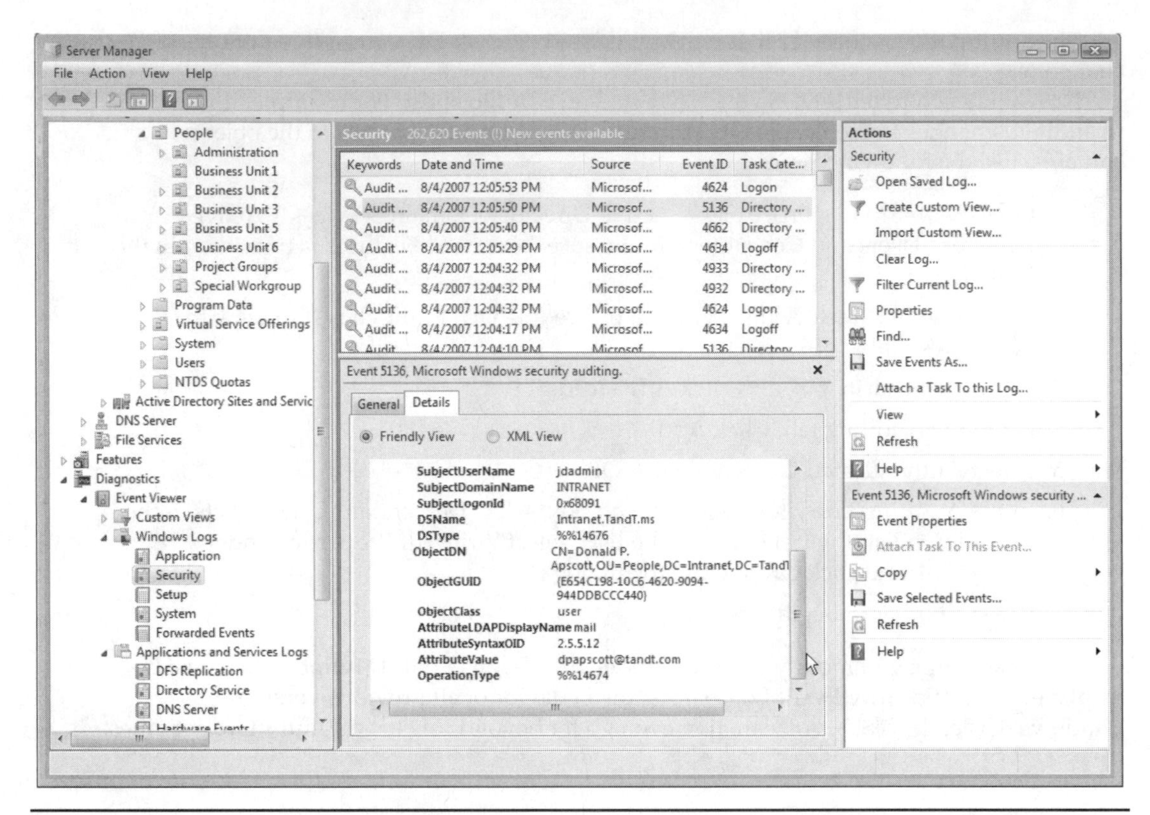

FIGURE 10-9 Viewing ADDS auditing events

As you can see, different audit settings apply to different event IDs. Ideally, you would audit as many activities as possible in your directory. You'll have to make sure you have a good strategy for backing up and otherwise protecting logs, since they store valuable information. This topic is covered in Chapter 13.

RODCs

Read-only domain controllers are not a throwback to Windows NT, despite their resemblance to backup DCs (BDCs). In NT, only the primary domain controller could write any properties to the directory—every other DC was in read-only mode. While the RODC does resemble the BDC, it offers significantly more protection than its predecessor.

Event ID	Description	Required Auditing Entry
5136	An attribute of the object has been modified.	Write property
5137	The object has been created.	Create all child objects
5138	The object has been undeleted.	Create all child objects
5139	The object has been moved within the domain.	Create all child objects

TABLE 10-3 New ADDS Auditing Events

RODCs are domain controllers that are provided with a special cache that can store user passwords. Remember that during the logon process, you must be able to contact a Global Catalog (GC) server in order to enumerate your Universal Group Memberships just in case there is a deny policy within one of them. If you cannot connect to a GC, then login is denied. The problem with contacting a GC is that it requires a WAN connection in remote offices. If you place a DC in the site but without a GC, then each time a user logs on, they need a WAN connection.

Previous versions of Windows Server included several features to assist in this process. For example, you could enable Universal Group Membership Caching (UGMC) in the site. This lets the user connect to the GC once and then stores the group memberships locally for a period of eight hours or the duration of the Kerberos ticket that is granted to the user. After eight hours, the GC must be contacted again to retrieve the memberships.

RODCs work in a similar way to UGMC, but instead of storing group memberships, they store user passwords inside a protected cache. This means users can rely on the RODC to log on to the domain, but the RODC is still a protected resource. In the event of the theft of an RODC, you can centrally cause all of the passwords that were stored within the RODC to be reset, making sure that even if the malicious attacker can hack the passwords, they will be of little use since they will all have been reset.

In addition, you can control which passwords can be stored in any RODC in your domains. Note that administrator passwords are never stored within RODCs by default because they provide access to too many resources. Password storage is both a property of the RODC and a property of user accounts. Within RODCs, you set the password replication policy (see Figure 10-10). User objects also include a Password Replication tab, which shows you which RODCs are currently caching their passwords.

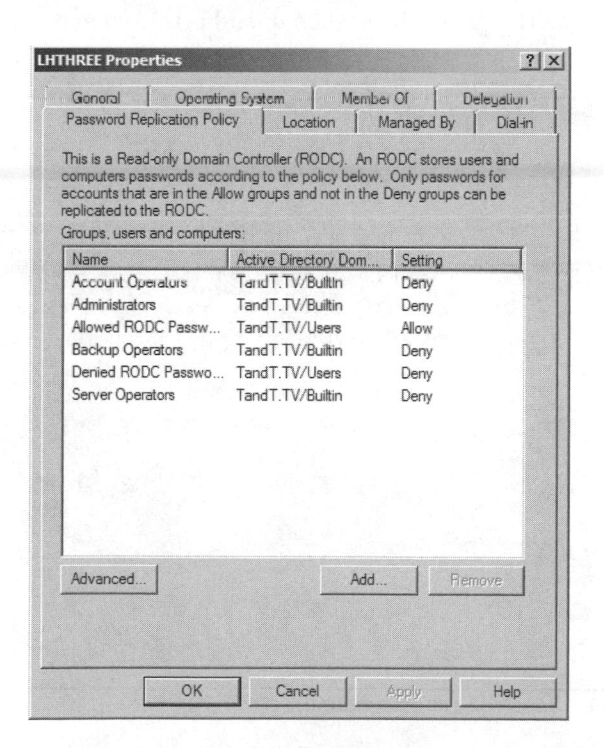

FIGURE 10-10 The password replication policy of an RODC

Unlike UGMC, RODCs can be pre-populated to cache passwords. For example, you can create regional groups of users and get their RODC to pre-populate all of their passwords. This is done through the Advanced button found in the Password Replication Policy tab of the RODC's Property dialog box.

Finally, you can automatically reset all the passwords that were stored in an RODC in the event of its theft. Simply delete the RODC account from the domain. Once you confirm deletion, you get the option to reset all of the passwords for the accounts stored in the stolen RODC (see Figure 10-11). You should take the time to export the list of users whose passwords you reset in order to send them a communication as to why their passwords were reset.

Use RODCs appropriately in your domain. Because they are read-only DCs, they are lacking several of the normal features found in a DC, such as replication capabilities (RODCs only have one-way replication), and so on.

TIP *For a full step-by-step procedure on building RODCs, go to http://technet2.microsoft.com/windowsserver2008/en/library/ea8d253e-0646-490c-93d3-b78c5e1d9db71033.mspx?mfr=true.*

File System Security

The file system is also a portion of operating system hardening that supports a secure environment. There is no doubt that despite its reported failings, NTFS is an absolute must and a pillar of the WS08 Castle Defense System. Chapter 8 covered NTFS and share permissions extensively. All of the advanced disk and file operations in WS08 are based on the use of the latest features supported by NTFS. The same applies to file encryption. Without NTFS, there is no encryption.

One of the important aspects of secure file management is the ability to log all file changes and alert organizations when unauthorized changes occur. This can be done in

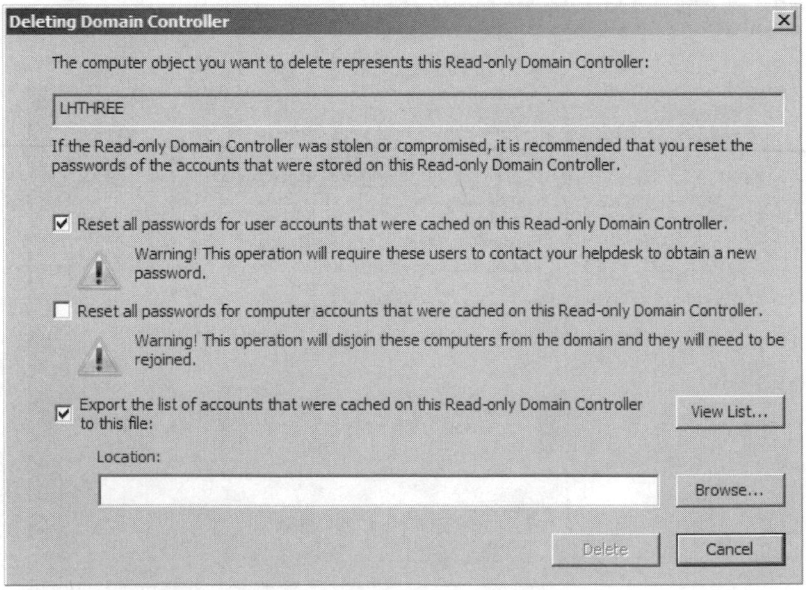

FIGURE 10-11 Resetting passwords from a stolen RODC

some form with file access auditing, but for critical data files, professional help is required. This help comes in the form of a utility such as Tripwire for Servers (www.tripwire.com/products/servers). Tripwire monitors all file changes, even down to the file's checksum properties. Therefore, it can alert administrators when core critical files have been modified by unauthorized personnel.

In addition, NTFS security has been considerably improved in Windows Server 2008. Like ADDS objects, it uses the concept of inheritance to apply access permissions. It also applies strong security settings to the User group for stability purposes. This means that users can no longer run legacy applications that modify files located in sensitive folders, such as Program Files and Windows. Administrators will need to take special measures to ensure that legacy applications will operate on Windows Server 2008 systems for normal users. WS08 also includes Windows Resource Protection, a feature that is designed to repair system files and registry entries when damaged by software installations or other untoward events. More information on these features is available in the WS08 Help system.

The Encrypting File System

The Encrypting File System (EFS) is a part of NTFS that also plays a significant role in the Castle Defense System. It is powerful because its operation is transparent to users once it is enabled. It also provides more file protection than permissions do, because if malicious attackers gain physical access to encrypted files, they will not be able to view their content. This is not necessarily the case with files that only include NTFS permissions. The ideal security level is one that uses both NTFS permissions and encryption.

TIP *Mixing EFS with BitLocker can give you a highly protected system. In most cases, if you use EFS, then you will not require BitLocker. Use BitLocker to provide complete system protection in highly secure environments. Use EFS to provide protection for sensitive data in environments where the OS does not need strict protection.*

Encryption is activated through the file or folder properties, just like permissions. It can also be performed with the `CIPHER` command. Encryption is a file property because of this, it cannot be applied if the file has also been compressed. These two properties are mutually exclusive. Files that are part of the operating system cannot be encrypted, nor can files found in the `%SYSTEMROOT%` folder. WS08 supports the encryption of data contained in folder shares. But data that is contained in encrypted files located on network shares is not necessarily encrypted when transported from the file share to the local computer. If full encryption, even to the communications level, is required, additional technologies, such as Internet Protocol Security (IPSec) or Secure Socket Tunneling Protocol (SSTP), must be used.

WS08 supports the encryption of offline files. This property can be set at the GPO level and applied along with folder redirection policies. Encrypted files will become decrypted if copied to non-NTFS volumes, so users should be warned of best practices for secure files. In addition, encryption does not prevent deletion of files; it only prevents unauthorized users from viewing their content. If users have permissions to a directory containing encrypted files, they will not be able to view their content, but they may be able to delete them. Encrypted files are displayed in a green color within Windows Explorer. This helps users quickly identify secure files. Once again, this information should be part of your user security communications program.

CAUTION *To avoid the possibility of deletion by other users, make sure you implement Access-based Enumeration (ABU) along with EFS. ABU should be enabled in any case, even if you do not use EFS.*

Encrypting a file is a simple process:

1. Open Windows Explorer.
2. Right-click the folder you want to encrypt, and select Properties.
3. Click the Advanced button on the General tab.
4. Click Encrypt Contents To Secure Data, and click OK.
5. Click OK to close the Properties dialog box.
6. EFS will ask you to confirm the setting you wish to apply. Select Apply Changes To These Folders, Subfolders, And Files, and click OK.
7. If folder tasks have not been turned on, EFS will ask you to turn them on. Click Yes. Folder tasks are part of the new Windows Themes interface.

Encrypted files will now appear in green in Windows Explorer. Using EFS is as simple as that, but there are guidelines:

- You should encrypt folders rather than individual files.
- You should ensure that offline files are encrypted.
- The entire Documents folder should be encrypted.
- Both `%TEMP%` and `%TMP%` should be encrypted to make sure that all temporary files are encrypted as well. Use a script based on the `CIPHER` command during system setup to set these folders as encrypted.
- You should encrypt the spool folder on print servers.
- You should combine EFS with IPSec or SSTP to ensure end-to-end data encryption.
- You should use Group Policy to control the behavior of EFS in your network.
- Protect the recovery agent, and limit the number of recovery agents in your network.
- Use a WS08 public key infrastructure (using ADCS) to manage EFS certificates and recovery agents.

EFS uses public and private keys (certificates) to manage the encryption and recovery process. The best way to manage these certificates is to use Windows' PKI features. In addition, to ensure the safety of encrypted files, you should remove recovery agent certificates to a diskette to ensure a two-factor process when recovering files. More on the Windows PKI features is provided in the following sections.

TIP *For a complete description of EFS and its integration with SSTP, look up "Working with the Encrypting File System" at http://redmondmag.com/techlibrary/resources.asp?id=101. For a detailed information protection strategy, look up Chapter 12 of* Deploying and Administering Windows Vista Bible *by Cribbs, Ruest, Ruest, and Kelly published by Wiley.*

Print System Security

Print system security is also important. As seen previously, if files are encrypted on user systems, they should also be encrypted in printer spooling shares. Security for the print system has already been covered in Chapter 8, but it is important to recall here that giving users management permissions to printer spoolers means that you trust them with sometimes confidential data. Use the data categorization that you performed while working with Layer 1 of the Castle Defense System to determine which printer spoolers must be protected and encrypted.

.NET Framework Security

The .NET Framework is another aspect of operating system hardening. First, it is included as a core element of the WS08 operating system, since version 2 of the Framework is installed by default in full installations and version 3 is available as a feature. Second, it provides core functionalities for Web services. As such, it provides the engine for both operation and execution of Web services. It is this engine's responsibility to determine if the code it is about to run can be trusted. The Common Language Runtime (CLR) applies security in two different manners; the first is for managed code and the second is for unmanaged code.

Managed code security is at the heart of the CLR. Two aspects of the code are evaluated by the CLR before allowing it to run: the safety of the code and the behavior of the code. For example, if the code uses a method that expects a four-byte value, the CLR will reject an attempt to return an eight-byte value. In other words, the CLR ensures that managed code is safe and well behaved.

The advantage of using this approach to security is that users need not worry if code is safe before they run it. If it is, the CLR will execute it. If it isn't, it simply won't run. But this applies only to managed code. Unmanaged code is allowed to run as well, but it does not benefit from these security measures. To run unmanaged code, the CLR must use a specific set of permissions—permissions that can be controlled but that must be declared globally.

The Evaluation Process for Managed Code

The CLR uses an eight-step evaluation process for managed code (see Figure 10-12). It uses the following steps:

1. When an assembly (a piece of managed code) calls upon another assembly, the CLR evaluates the permission level to apply to the new assembly.
2. The first thing the new assembly must do is provide evidence. This evidence is, in fact, a set of answers to questions posed by the CLR's security policy.
3. Three questions are asked about the source of the assembly:
   a. From which site was the assembly obtained? Assemblies are automatically downloaded to the client from a web site.
   b. From which Uniform Resource Locator (URL) did the assembly originate? A specific URL address must be provided by the assembly.
   c. From which zone was the assembly obtained? This applies to Internet Explorer zones such as Internet, Intranet, Local Machine, and so on. Some zones are more trusted than others.

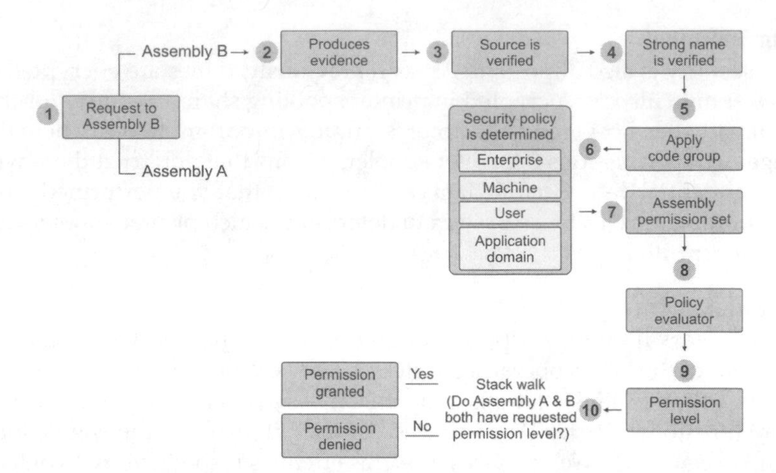

FIGURE 10-12 The .NET Framework security allocation process

4. The assembly must also provide a cryptographically strong identifier, called its strong name. This identifier is unique and must be provided by the author of the assembly. The identifier does not necessarily identify the author, but it does identify the assembly as unique.
5. Evidence is gathered from a series of different sources, including the CLR itself, the browser, ASP.NET, the shell, and so on. Once the evidence is provided, the CLR begins to determine the security policy to apply. First, it applies the evidence against standard code groups. These groups contain standard policies, depending on the zone from which the assembly originates. The .NET Framework includes basic code groups, but administrators can add their own or modify the default groups.
6. Once the code group is determined, the policy is defined. This policy can be defined at three levels and in this order: Enterprise, Machine, and User. A fourth level involves the application domain. This domain provides an isolated environment for the application to run in. An application contained within a domain cannot interfere with any other domain on the same machine.
7. Once the policy has been set, an initial set of permissions is created. The assembly can fine-tune this set of permissions in three ways:
   a. First, it can identify the minimum set of permissions it requires to run.
   b. Second, it can specify optional permissions. These are not absolutely required.
   c. Third, a well-behaved assembly can refuse permissions it doesn't require and deems too risky, actually reducing the permission set it is assigned by the CLR.
8. All of these factors are reviewed by the policy evaluator.
9. A final set of permissions is created for the assembly.
10. The final stage is the stack walk. The CLR compares the permission set to those of other assemblies that are involved in the original call for this assembly. If any one of these assemblies does not have permission to run with this permission set, the permission to execute is denied. If everything is okay, the permission to execute is granted.

Internet Information Server 7.0

As discussed in Chapter 9, IIS 7 is secure by default because it has been split into components that are only installed if you require them. The safest installation of IIS is, in fact, the one you'll find on Server Core because it only serves static web sites by default. In addition, Microsoft has improved upon the existing security models in earlier versions of IIS. For example, in previous versions, IIS and ASP.NET were separate entities. In IIS 7, both have been integrated into one model. While IIS still supports previous features, it now has a single integrated security model.

All web sites have an application pool, which is created automatically. This segregates the web site from all other sites or applications on the Web server. Application pools run under NetworkService by default, once again limiting the access rights they have on the server itself. In order to make sure your applications run under this context and only this context, you now have to install the Anonymous Authentication module and then make sure your `WEB.CONFIG` file for the application includes the following line:

```
<anonymousAuthentication enabled="true" username="" defaultLogonDomain="" />
```

By leaving the entries blank for both the domain name and the user name, you ensure that NetworkService is used to generate security contexts for the applications you run.

This is only one example of heightened security within IIS. The key point to remember when working with IIS at Layer 3 of the CDS is to install only those modules you actually require and then rely on the Security Configuration Wizard to help secure the base installation of IIS.

Final Operating System Hardening Activities

Two additional activities are required for you to finalize the hardening of your operating system: creating system redundancy and putting in place recurring security maintenance operations. System redundancy means building resilience into your servers and into the services they deliver. Resiliency was covered in detail in Chapter 8, especially through the use of the Distributed File System. More will be covered in Chapter 11 as you build additional resilience through cluster servers and backup operations.

Chapter 13 will cover security maintenance and the use of some of Microsoft's most powerful security verification tools. In addition, it will cover server and workstation patch management.

Layer 4 – Information Access

Layer 4 deals with user identification and the attribution of permissions allowing them to operate within your network. Much of this has been covered in Chapter 7 in the discussion on user and group management. Like Windows 2003, Windows Server 2008 includes a number of different security protocols for authentication and authorization. The most important of these for an internal network is Kerberos, even though NT LAN Manager (NTLM) is still supported. But in the parallel network, there is little need for NTLM, since all machines are using the latest operating systems and the forests are in fully functional mode.

A lot has been said on the Kerberos protocol. It has many advantages over NTLM. It is faster, more secure, more widely accepted, and simpler to use. One of its best features is the fact that once it has authenticated users, they do not need to return to the server for authorization. Whereas in NTLM, the user is constantly returning to the server for rights and permission validation, in Kerberos, the user caries rights and permissions within the access token that is granted by the Kerberos server. This access token is in the form of the Kerberos ticket that is granted to the user at logon. In addition, with Kerberos, the server authenticates to the client, making sure that it is authorized to grant user access within the domain. Finally, Kerberos also supports two-factor authentication. This can be in the form of a smart card or a biometric device, such as a fingerprinting device.

One of the key elements of a Kerberos realm—the Kerberos equivalent of a domain—is the timestamp. Time synchronization is essential in Kerberos because the authentication server matches the time of the client's request with its own internal clock. If the time differs by more than the allotted time—set within your account policies—the Kerberos server will not authenticate the user. This is one reason why Microsoft has integrated the time service into the PDC Emulator Operations Master role in Active Directory Domain Services, and it is the reason why the processes outlined in Chapter 6 for forest-wide time synchronization are so important.

Smart Card Authentication

One of the most important places for smart card authentication is with administrative accounts. Windows Server 2008 supports the use of two-factor authentication for administrators. If you want to design a highly secure infrastructure, you should take advantage of this feature for all accounts that are granted administrative authority. In addition, your administrators should have two accounts: a user-level account for everyday operations and an administrative account for administrative operations. They should be logged on as users and should perform their administrative activities through the Run as Administrator command, using their smart card to log on. Information related to the implementation of smart cards for administrators is outlined further in this chapter, since you need a public key infrastructure to assign certificates to the smart cards.

Another good way to proceed is to place administrative tools on a server and allow administrators to access these tools through Terminal Services, especially in RemoteApps mode. This way, you only have to manage administrative tools on a few servers, and you don't need to worry about creating special workstations for administrative purposes. Another advantage is that the administrator can use Run as Administrator to launch the administrative console on the terminal server. Use the instructions provided in Chapter 9 to create these consoles. Chapter 13 will outline the tools this server should include.

Secure User Identification

User identification happens on many levels within a WS08 network. The most obvious authentication is through the ADDS domain. For this, you need to set global account policies for the entire forest and refine them within each domain. In addition, authentication occurs in cross-forest scenarios. Remember, WS08 extends the notion of transitive trusts from inside the forest to multiple forests through forest trusts. For this, you need to establish trusts. Two other areas of authentication are found in WS08: Web server and Web service or .NET Framework authentication. Web server authentication is performed through IIS and uses a series of authentication techniques. .NET Framework authentication is role-based and can be specific to each application.

User Authentication in Active Directory Domain Services

In Windows networks, each security principal is identified by a unique number, the security ID or SID. Security principals include everything from computers to users to groups, and so on. The user SID is included in the access token for each user. When the information in the access token is used to determine if a user has access to an object, the user's SIDs are compared with the list of SIDs that make up the object's discretionary access control list (DACL) to identify the level of permission the user has to this object. In other words, every security principal in WS08 is identified as a number, not a name.

The impact of this is that ownership of objects is identified by SIDs. When you re-create an object, such as a user account, you assign it a different SID. When you create the parallel VSO network, you will transfer accounts from the originating domain to the new production domain, which means that all of your users will have new SIDs. When this occurs, your users will have access to their files and folders through their original SID. When they are transferred from originating file servers to the file servers in the parallel VSO network, you will also need to perform security translation to replace old SIDs with new ones. Chapter 12 outlines the procedures you use for this process. These are the keys to a successful implementation of a parallel VSO network.

TIP *A user will have several SIDs during a migration from one network to another. In this case, the user carries the SID from the original network as well as a new SID created for the user in the parallel VSO network. This is called SID history. This topic is covered in Chapter 12 as you perform the migration of security principals.*

Secure Layer 4 Through Group Policy Objects

The best way to manage authentication, authorization, and auditing is through Group Policy. Authorization has been covered to some extent in the discussion on operating system hardening, and especially in regards to access control of directory, file system, and registry objects. As you have seen, the latter two can be configured through security templates. Directory objects are secured as you create them. For example, the delegation procedures you use when creating your OU structure are part and parcel of directory object access management.

The best way to control authentication processes is to define their boundaries through Group Policy. So far, you have created several different GPOs for object management purposes. Now you can review these policies and see if they can be reused for security purposes. This will also allow you to identify if additional security policies are required. Table 10-4 outlines the GPOs created to date. Each GPO lists the OU it can be found in, its name, and its purpose. Four new GPOs are included here: the two default GPOs and two new ones—the Intranet Domain GPO, which is used to store global domain settings, and the Baseline Server GPO, which provides a first layer of security to all servers. New GPOs are listed in bold.

CAUTION *The Intranet Domain GPO is created to limit the modifications you make to the default domain policy. This will facilitate future upgrades and migrations by keeping the default policies as pristine as possible.*

In all, 18 GPOs are required to manage and secure the VSO network (see Figure 10-13). Two that are not listed here are the default policies of the forest root domain. Each policy contains both security and management information. You might consider creating a GPO for each purpose, but this will practically double the number of GPOs you need to manage for little reason. What is important is to fully document each GPO and use a structured change-management approach for modifications. Perform modifications in the appropriate

OU	GPO	Policy Type	Notes
Domain	Default Domain Policy	Computer	Contains global account policies
Domain	Intranet Domain GPO	Computer	Contains global settings for all systems, for example, Printer Location Tracking and software restriction policies
Domain Controllers	Default Domain Controllers Policy	Computer	Contains settings specific to DCs throughout each domain of the network
PCs	Global PC GPO	Computer	Applies to all PCs
Desktops	Global Desktop GPO	Computer	Includes specifications for desktop workstations
Kiosks	Special Kiosk GPO	Computer	Special features for kiosk computers
Mobile Devices	Global Mobile GPO	Computer	Includes specifications for mobile devices
External	Global External GPO	Computer	Includes basic settings for PCs not controlled by the organization
People	Global People GPO	User	Applies to all users
Special Workgroups	SWG GPO	User	Mostly designed to let special workgroup users have access to their own Remote Desktop
Virtual Service Offerings	Baseline Server GPO	Computer	Baseline security settings for all member servers
File and Print	Global File and Print GPO	Computer	Controls all aspects of file sharing, Distributed File System, and printing
Application Servers and Dedicated Web Servers	Global Application Server GPO	Computer	Controls database servers, general-purpose Web servers, .NET Framework, and corporate applications
Terminal Servers	Global Terminal Server GPO	Computer	Contains server-side Terminal Services settings
Collaboration Servers	Global Collaboration GPO	Computer	Contains settings for Windows SharePoint Services, Streaming Media Services, and other collaboration applications
Network Infrastructure	Global Infrastructure GPO	Computer	Contains settings for DHCP, Windows Internet Naming Service (WINS), and Remote Installation Service (RIS), as well as other operational server software

Table 10-4 Global Production Domain GPO List

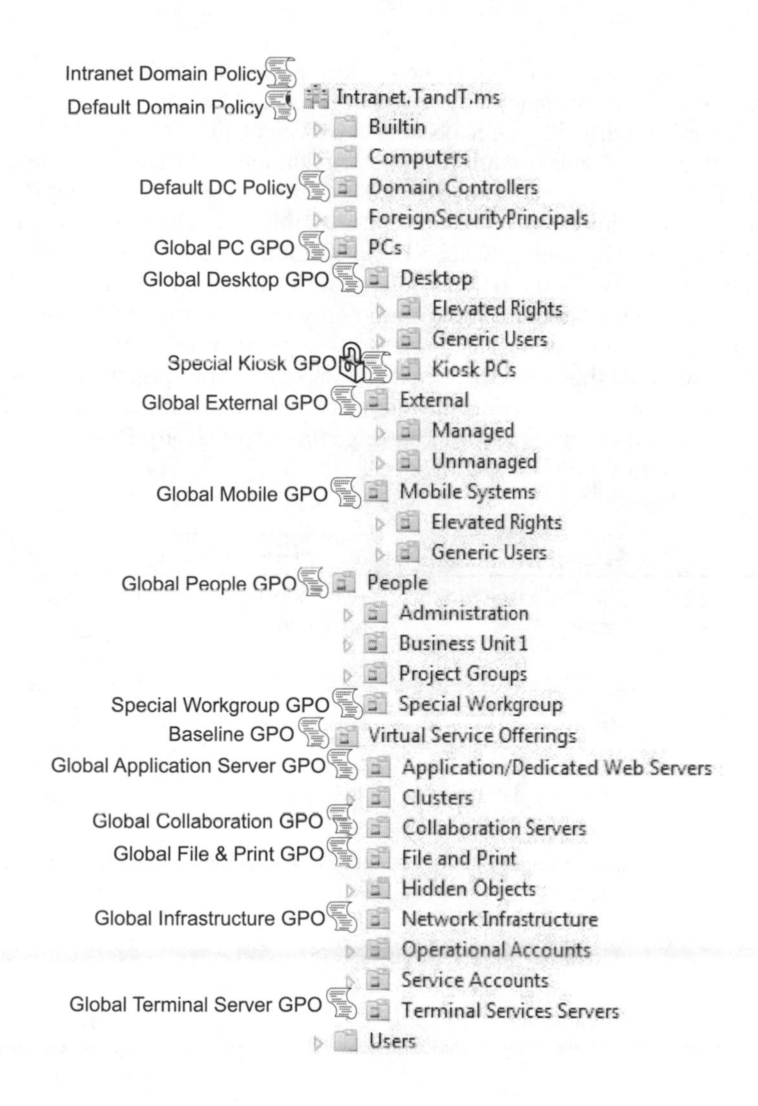

FIGURE 10-13 The Intranet Domain GPOs

GPO. For example, to encrypt offline files, assign the modification to the Global File and Print GPO, because it is the GPO that controls file management and this security modification is related to that area.

TIP *In WS08, you must use the* GPUPDATE *command to manually refresh GPO settings.*

Configure the Default Domain Policies

Chapters 5 and 6 outlined the importance of configuring the two default domain policies (default domain and default domain controllers) at the protected forest root domain. The reason for this is so that the content of these policies will propagate to child domains as soon as they are created. This means the default policies should be customized as soon as the forest root domain has been created.

The default domain policy is the account policy for the domain. Since only one policy can contain account information, this information should be defined in a single area. Be careful when working with this policy because it cannot be deactivated. If you make a mistake while editing this policy, you will affect the entire domain. This is one reason for a structured Group Policy change-management strategy. In fact, what you should do is define the policy in the root domain so that it is as complete as possible. This policy should correspond to the settings required by your global child production domain. It will propagate to child domains upon their creation. You can then make modifications as required in each child domain. (Remember, generic accounts are created only in development, training, and testing domains.) This is no reason for lax security in domains other than the production domain.

The elements that need to be covered in this account policy are outlined in Table 10-5. All of the elements outlined in this table are from the Computer Configuration | Policies | Windows Components | Security Settings branch of Group Policy. Once again, remember to document all of your GPO settings.

Section	Setting	Recommendation	Comments
Account Policies/ Password Policy	Enforce password history	Twenty-four passwords	At the rate of one password change per month, this setting remembers two years' worth of passwords.
	Maximum password age	Forty-two days	This is approximately a month and a half.
	Minimum password age	Two days	This stops users from changing their passwords too often.
	Minimum password length	Eight characters	This is the threshold where password crackers start taking longer to break passwords.
	Password must meet complexity requirements	Enabled	This ensures that passwords must contain both alphabetic and numeric characters, both upper- and lowercase, as well as special symbols.
	Store passwords using reversible encryption	Disabled	Enabling this setting is the same as storing plain-text passwords. This setting should never be enabled.
Account Policies/ Account Lockout Policy	Account lockout duration	Sixty minutes	This setting determines how long an account is locked after several bad logon attempts.
	Account lockout threshold	Three invalid logon attempts	After three bad logon tries, the account is locked out.
	Reset account lockout counter after	Sixty minutes	This must be equal to or greater than the account lockout duration.

TABLE 10-5 Account Policy Elements

Section	Setting	Recommendation	Comments
Account Policies/ Kerberos Policy	Enforce user logon restrictions	Enabled (default)	This ensures that users have the right to access either local or network resources before granting them a Kerberos ticket.
	Maximum lifetime for service ticket	Six hundred minutes (default)	This states the duration of the session ticket that is used to initiate a connection with a server. It must be renewed when it expires.
	Maximum lifetime for user ticket	Ten hours (default)	This must be greater than or equal to the previous setting. It must be renewed when it expires.
	Maximum lifetime for user ticket renewal	Seven days (default)	This details the duration of a user's ticket-granting ticket. The user must logon again once this ticket expires.
	Maximum tolerance for computer clock synchronization	Five minutes (default)	Kerberos uses time stamps to grant tickets. All computers within a domain are synchronized through the domain controllers.
Restricted Groups	*Domain*/Enterprise Admins	Individuals only	Select trusted individuals should be members of this group.
	Domain/Domain Admins	Individuals only	Select trusted individuals should be members of this group.
	Domain/ Administrators	Enterprise Admins Domain Admins	This group should contain only trusted groups.

Table 10-5 Account Policy Elements (*continued*)

Caution *The password and account lockout settings in this policy are the default settings. If you want to assign different settings to administrators, for example, use the instructions outlined in "Fine-Grained Password Policies" earlier in the chapter.*

Tip *All of the settings for Kerberos policy are set at the default Windows Server settings, but setting them explicitly assists your Group Policy operators in knowing what the default setting actually is.*

All of these settings are applied at the domain level to ensure that they affect every object within the domain. In fact, the account policy is a computer policy. This means that the user configuration portion of the GPO can be disabled.

TIP *It is important to ensure that you have a strong communications program to keep users aware of the importance of having a comprehensive account policy within your network. Also indicate to them the settings in your account policy. Finally, educate them on the protection of passwords and the need for immediate renewal of passwords that they think may be compromised. This will ensure that your account policy is supported by the very people who use it.*

The default domain controllers policy should also be modified; ideally, you will rely on the Security Configuration Wizard to do so. You can also review sample domain controller policies from the various sources and aim for as high a security setting as you can. It will be very important that all your domain controllers remain in the Domain Controllers organization unit; otherwise, they will not be affected by your default DC policy. This is one reason why directory service auditing is so important to implement.

Remember to fully document all changes you make to these GPOs.

Local Domain Controller Policies

Local policies have been covered extensively in this chapter. It is important, though, to mention that specific policies must be applied to domain controllers once they have been created. The DC promotion process will automatically secure different aspects of the local system and create the DC Security.inf template, but in most cases, additional local security is required. Once again, you can look to several sources of information for applicable security templates:

- The WS08 Security Guide for a baseline DC template
- The NSA DC security templates (see "Windows Server 2008 Security" earlier in this chapter)
- Commercial templates

Whatever template you use, make sure that you secure the following areas:

- Focus on Kerberos authentication rather than NTLM, even NTLM version 2
- Use data signing for Lightweight Directory Access Protocol (LDAP) queries
- Remove down-level client support
- Secure the NTDS.DIT storage file

Other security features are applied by the different templates listed here. Review them carefully and select those that are appropriate for your environment. Remember to apply the local policy to domain controllers once they are promoted.

All domain controllers should be located within the Domain Controller organizational unit in the Active Directory Users and Computers console. Member servers are addressed through the Virtual Service Offerings OU structure. Desktops and portables or mobile devices are addressed through the PCs OU structure. And users are addressed through the People OU structure. In an Active Directory Domain Services that is designed for object management, there is little justification in creating another OU for DCs. The creation of this OU would require you to link the default domain controller policy to this new OU to ensure that your DC strategy was the same on every DC. This is a process that is simply not necessary. What you need to do is ensure that all DCs are always placed in the Domain Controllers OU.

Here you can modify the default domain controllers policy to set security parameters that will not affect the three local policy areas (file system, registry, and services). One element that is useful in the DDCP is data transport encryption, or rather, using IPSec to communicate between servers. This is covered further in the following section. Once again, review the settings in the source templates mentioned previously, and select those that are appropriate for your DDCP.

The Member Server Baseline Policy

Another security policy that is global to a group of objects is the member server baseline policy. This policy includes a variety of settings that are applied to all servers. It is located in the Virtual Service Offerings OU, and because it is the parent OU for all member servers, is applied to all of them. Because of this, each specific server-role GPO includes only incremental security settings, as well as the settings it requires for its role to function properly. For example, in order to provide additional security, you can include the Prevent IIS Installation setting (from Computer Configuration | Policies | Administrative Templates | Windows Components | Internet Information Services) in this baseline template. This way, no one will be able to install IIS on any of your member servers. Then you can disable this setting in the incremental GPO that you apply to the Application Servers and Dedicated Web Servers OUs.

This concept originates with the WS08 Security Guide. Again, this is where you should look to identify the baseline security settings you want to include in your own baseline GPO. In addition, you should review each of the incremental templates found in the guide to identify the security settings required for your server roles.

Manage Trusts

Windows 2000 introduced the concept of automatic two-way transitive trusts within an Active Directory forest. Windows Server 2008 brings this concept even further with the addition of transitive trusts between forests, especially with the advent of Active Directory Lightweight Directory Services. But despite the fact that trusts are now mostly automatic, some degree of management is still required, because whenever a trust is created, you give access to your forests or domains to people and objects in other ADDS containers.

There are several types of trusts in Windows Server 2008. They are outlined in Table 10-6.

Trust Type	Directions and Nature	Comments
Parent and child	Two-way transitive	These are the automatic trusts that are established when a child domain is created.
Tree-root	Two-way transitive	These are the automatic trusts that are established when a new tree is created.
Forest	One- or two-way transitive	Extends the transitivity of trusts from one forest to another.
Shortcut	One- or two-way transitive	Creates a shortcut path for authentication between two domains. The domains can use this path for authentication instead of having to traverse the forest hierarchy.
Realm	One- or two-way transitive or non-transitive	Creates an authentication link between a domain and a non-Windows Kerberos realm (such as UNIX).
External	One- or two-way non-transitive	Creates an authentication link between a WS08 domain and a legacy domain.

TABLE 10-6 WS08 Trust Types

The trusts you will mostly use in your parallel VSO network will be forest, shortcut, and external. The latter is used to link your parallel VSO network to the legacy network. Shortcut trusts will be used to improve validation performance between child domains that require high levels of interaction. And forest trusts can be used primarily between your infrastructure forest and ADLDS directories.

Giving access to resources from other domains or forests through trusts is a two-step procedure. First, you must establish the trust. Second, you must insert user groups from one forest or domain into user groups in the other in order to give users access to resources. In fact, this means applying the Account-Global Group-Local Group-Permissions (AGLP) rule from Chapter 7. Trust implementations are outlined in Chapter 12.

Working with Active Directory security can be complex. But you will reduce the level of complexity if you keep a structured, well-documented approach to change management. Ensure you use standard operating procedures at all times, and ensure that these documented procedures are provided to all personnel who require them.

Web Server Access Control

Another area where authentication is required is at the Web server. IIS provides several different authentication types, from anonymous logon to full certificate-based authentication. Table 10-7 lists the authentication modes available in IIS 7.

Mode	Security	Limitations (If Any)	Client Support	Comments
Anonymous	None	No security	All	Works in any scenario.
Basic	Low	Clear-text password; use only with SSL	All	Works in any scenario.
Digest	Medium		IE 5 and higher	Works in any scenario.
ASP.NET Impersonation	High		All	Replaces NetworkService with either the user's context or a custom service account you create.
Windows Authentication	High		IE 5 on Windows in domain infrastructure	Works only in the intranet; DC needs to be accessible by the client.
Forms Authentication	Very high		All	Relies on internal application authentication methods rather than on those built into the OS. Works in any scenario.
ADDS Client Certificate Authentication	Very high	WS08 provides auto-enrollment and auto-update for certificates	All newer browsers	Works in any scenario.

Table 10-7 Authentication in IIS

Basically, you need to determine which authentication mode works best for you and for the Web server requirement. Internal and external solutions will be different, and there will also be differences between the solutions you implement on the Internet and in the extranet because you will most likely want more secure authentication in the latter.Table 10-8 outlines some recommendations in this regard.

IIS authentication is defined in the IIS console under the web site's home location in the authentication module. By default, only the anonymous authentication mode is enabled. Modify the settings for each authentication mode you need. Select and apply the appropriate authentication mode for each site.

.NET Framework Authentication

Since the .NET Framework uses Web services, authentication models rely heavily on IIS, but there are some core functionalities within the .NET Framework itself. It provides role-based security (RBS). The RBS in the .NET Framework can rely on three different types of authentication: Forms-based authentication (generates a cookie), IIS authentication, and Windows authentication. The first must be programmed within the Web service. The second and third methods are administered by network operations.

The easiest way to authenticate users and authorize access to Web resources within the intranet is to assign roles to them. Roles are groups that have different access levels within each application. These groups are application-specific, but they can be mapped to Active Directory Domain Services. Authorization stores must be created prior to group assignation. This can be done through the Authorization Manager console, which is launched by running the `AZMAN.MSC` command. Authorization Manager is also a snap-in that can be added to any custom MMC console. Developers must create the initial store and link it to an application,

Scenarios	Requirements	Recommendations
Intranet (parallel VSO network)	All clients have Windows accounts stored in your directory. All clients use Internet Explorer 6 or later. There is a strong level of password encryption.	Use Kerberos through Windows Authentication
Internet	You need to support multiple browser types and multiple versions. Most of the information on your servers is public. Some data or business logic may require a secure login. You do not have control over user computers, and you do not want to be intrusive. Some situations may require delegation.	Anonymous Basic over SSL Forms
Extranet	This requires a very secure solution. You might require mutual authentication. You may need a third party to manage the relationship between your server and the certificate holder. The operation should be seamless to the client.	Certificate Forms

TABLE 10-8 Web Server Authentication Recommendations

and then administrators can assign users and groups to it. The store can be located in Active Directory Domain Services, but the developer must have store creation rights within ADDS to do so. This is a security model that is very powerful and requires less management than former application authorization schemes. Ensure that your developers endeavor to use this approach when creating Web services for internal use.

Access Audition and Monitoring

The final aspect of Layer 4 is audition. It is important to track resource use and monitor log files to ensure that users have appropriate access rights and that no user tries to abuse their rights. As mentioned earlier, audition is a two-step process. First, you must enable the auditing policy for an event. Then, for given types of objects, you must turn on the auditing for the object you want to track and identify who you want to track. WS08 lets you audit several different types of events:

- Account logon events
- Account management
- Directory service access
- Logon events
- Object access
- Policy change
- Privilege use
- Process tracking
- System events

Audition of directory service events has already been discussed. Other events use a similar process. Enabling the audit policy can have significant impact in your network. Audited objects and events slow down the system, so it is important to audit only those events or objects you deem critical in your network.

To define the audit policy, move to the appropriate GPO and select Computer Configuration | Policies | Windows Settings | Security Settings | Audit Policy. Double-click the event you want to audit, and modify the policy. You can audit the success or the failure of an event or both. Audit failures only if you suspect malicious activity in your network. This will reduce the number of events generated by auditing.

If you want to audit object access, such as accessing a file on a server, you must then turn on auditing for that object and identify who you want to audit. To do so, you must view the object's security properties and use the Advanced button.

Information Rights Management

One other level of protection you can implement is information rights management. This is performed through Active Directory Rights Management Services (ADRMS). This protects the information you generate by linking PKI certificates into the document structure. An ADRMS infrastructure is based on the ADRMS server role, a database—in this case, the Windows internal database—and a client. It is a good idea to implement ADRMS along with Active Directory Certificate Services, since you must rely on certificates for ADRMS to work. Of course, you can also rely on external certificates for this purpose.

ADRMS will protect information in the following manner:

- It is designed to integrate into both custom and commercial applications, such as Microsoft Office. This level of protection lets you determine who can open, modify, print, forward, or otherwise handle information contained in document form. Documents can be presentations, e-mails, text, spreadsheets, and so on.
- ADRMS protection lasts because the protection is at the document level and persists even if the document is beyond the boundaries of your network.
- ADRMS is also extensible and can be integrated into other third-party document-protection mechanisms.
- ADRMS can be combined with Active Directory Federation Services to create a complete federated identity structure that also supports rights management.

Basically, ADRMS implements an infrastructure that allows you to issue licenses to users so that they may further protect the information they generate. It is a sound addition to any organization that requires full document protection at all times.

TIP *For a step-by-step guide on how to implement ADRMS, go to http://technet2.microsoft.com/windowsserver2008/en/library/437d3040-89f0-40ac-a2af-c288a48714c41033.mspx?mfr=true.*

Layer 5 - External Access

Layer 5 focuses on the perimeter network and the protection of your internal network from outside influences. In today's connected world, it is impossible to create internal networks that are completely disconnected from the external world. Because of this, you need to secure the internal network as much as possible, in fact, creating a barrier that must be crossed before anyone can enter. This barrier can take several different forms, but in the case of the parallel VSO network, it means the creation, or rather, the continued use of your perimeter environment. This environment is often called the demilitarized zone or DMZ.

Perimeter networks can contain any number of components. They can be limited to a series of firewalls that protects your internal network, or they can include and contain your Internet servers as well as your extranet services. If this is the case, this network will be fairly complex and will include defenses at every layer of the Castle Defense System. It is not the purpose of this chapter to review all of the features of a perimeter network.

TIP *Microsoft provides an extensive outline of a complex perimeter network through its Infrastructure Planning and Design. In fact, this guide is extremely complete and outlines how to design your perimeter network, and provides specific instructions for the implementation of the network for both Nortel and Cisco network devices. Find it at www.microsoft.com/downloads/details.aspx?familyid=ad3921fb-8224-4681-9064-075fdf042b0c&displaylang=en.*

In terms of resource pools and VSOs, you'll need to protect systems at the following levels:

- Resource pools do not have a perimeter network because they do not interact with users and do not provide any user-related services. They do, however, interact with remote administrators. For this level of interaction, you must work with either the SSTP or IPSec-based virtual private network connections. You will also need a public key infrastructure in support of SSTP and smart cards. You should also ensure that any remote site will use IPSec for server-to-server communications, especially when replicating virtual machine images. You may also determine that you need to implement Network Access Protection to ensure that any system that connects to the resource pool is always up to date in terms of security patches and anti-malware protection.

- Virtual service offerings do have a perimeter network and, therefore, need protection at multiple levels. Perimeter networks for VSOs can include a host of services, but most often they include:
  - Remote connections for mobile end users acting outside your premises
  - Federation services for partner organizations
  - Network Access Protection for any system that wants to connect to the network
  - Public key infrastructures to provide protection for the applications you make available in the perimeter as well as in support of smart card deployments

The level of implementation is more comprehensive in the VSOs than it is in the resource pool, since resource pools only interact with administrators.

CAUTION *Since the perimeter network is made up of virtual machines, you should rely on the internal settings of Windows Server Hyper-V or your hypervisor to create virtual LANs segregating the virtual machines that belong to each part of your VSO network. You might also consider placing perimeter machines on specific host servers and make sure they are never intermingled with machines from the Intranet zone.*

Secure Servers with the Windows Server Firewall with Advanced Security

One of the first tools you must work with within the perimeter—as with all servers in any zone of your network—is the Windows Server Firewall with Advanced Security (WSFAS). The Windows Firewall is now built into every edition of Windows and is installed by default. In fact, you'll remember that, by default, when you install WS08, the firewall is set to deny all remote access. Then, as you configure roles for your server, you modify the default firewall policy to open and control specific network ports.

The difference between the basic firewall and the WSFAS is that the latter combines a firewall with IPSec management into one tool to provide integrated secure communications management. This means that you use WSFAS to manage not only internal and external server communications, but also virtual private network connections.

A lot more can be said on the firewall, but basically, you should rely as much as possible on the Security Configuration Wizard to help you properly configure firewall rules based on server roles. This will go a long way to protecting your servers wherever they are in your network.

Note that in most perimeter networks, WSFAS is not enough on its own. Most organizations will also include either hardware-based protection technologies or software-based stateful inspection tools. It is also good practice to implement some form of intrusion detection in the perimeter.

TIP *For more information on Windows Firewall, go to www.microsoft.com/technet/network/wf/default.mspx. For a detailed information on configuring the Windows Firewall, look up Chapter 10 of* Deploying and Administering Windows Vista Bible *by Cribbs, Ruest, Ruest, and Kelly published by Wiley.*

Use Windows Server Secure Sockets Tunneling Protocol

Traditionally, virtual private network connections in Windows networks relied on the IPSec protocol, which provides an end-to-end connection at the networking layer. However, IPSec VPNs cannot work in every situation. For example, when you use network address translation devices or even Web proxy servers, your IPSec VPN connection will be blocked at the gate. In addition, IPSec VPNs are more complex to implement and require you to have some degree of control over the endpoint or client system making the connection from the external world. As you know, this is often not the case.

This is one reason why Microsoft has implemented the Secure Sockets Tunneling Protocol. SSTP relies on HTTP over Secure Sockets Layer (HTTPS) to create VPN connections over port 443. It supports Network Access Protection as well as IPv6. When you create an SSTP VPN, the client establishes a single connection to the internal server and all traffic travels over this connection. You cannot, however, use it to create site-to-site connections.

SSTP relies on PKI certificates to create connections. The servers hosting SSTP connections must have installed certificates that include the Server Authentication or the All-Purpose Enhanced Key Usage property in order to accept SSTP connections. This is one more reason why it is so important to build a proper PKI structure through ADCS in your network.

SSTP VPNs are part of the Network Policy and Access Services server role and must be managed through the Routing and Remote Access Services console node.

TIP *For a complete overview of SSL VPNS, see "The Case for SSL Virtual Private Networks" at www.reso-net.com/articles.asp?m=8#c under the Advanced PKI section.*

Rely on a Public Key Infrastructure

PKI implementations can be quite complex, especially if you need to use them to interact with clients and suppliers outside your internal network. The main issue at this level is one of authority: Are you who you say you are and can your certificates be trusted? When this is the case, you should rely on a third-party authority specializing in this area to vouch for you and indicate that your certificates can and should be trusted. Once again, WS08 can play a significant role in reducing PKI costs in these situations. Since it includes all the features required to implement a PKI service through Active Directory Certificate Services, all you need to do is acquire the root server certificate from an external source. This certificate will then be embedded into every certificate issued by your infrastructure. It will prove to your clients, partners, and suppliers that you are who you say you are, and you won't have to implement an expensive third-party PKI solution.

But you don't need this type of certificate for the purposes of the internal network, since you control all of the systems within the network and you don't need to prove yourself or your organization to them. The ADCS services support several types of security situations. You can use them to:

- Secure Web services, servers, and applications
- Secure and digitally sign e-mail

- Support EFS
- Sign code
- Support smart card logon
- Support virtual private networking
- Support remote access authentication
- Support the authentication of Active Directory Domain Services replication links over SMTP
- Support wireless network authentication

WS08 provides two types of certificate authorities (CAs): stand-alone and enterprise. The latter provides complete integration with ADDS. The advantage of enterprise CAs is that since their certificates are integrated with the directory, they can provide auto-enrollment and auto-renewal services. This is why the PKI service you implement in the internal network should be based on enterprise CAs.

PKI best practices require very high levels of physical protection for root certificate authorities. This is because the root CA is the core CA for the entire PKI hierarchy. If it becomes corrupted for some reason, your entire public key infrastructure will be corrupted. Therefore, it is important to remove the root CA from operation once its certificates have been issued. Since you will remove this server from operation, it makes sense to create it as a stand-alone CA (removing an enterprise CA from the network will cause errors in ADDS).

CAUTION *Root CAs should be removed from operation for their protection. This is why the ideal configuration for root CAs should be in virtual machines. Taking a virtual machine offline is much easier than a physical machine. In addition, the virtual machine can be placed in a suspended state indefinitely, making it easier and quicker to bring back online when it is needed.*

PKI best practices also require several levels of hierarchy. In fact, in PKI environments that must interact with the public, it makes sense to protect the first two levels of the infrastructure and remove both from the network. But in an internal PKI environment, especially one that will mostly be used for code signing, encryption, smart card logon, and VPN connections, two levels are sufficient. Subordinate CAs should be enterprise CAs so that they can be integrated with ADDS. In order to add further protection to the subordinate CA, do not install it on a domain controller. This will reduce the number of services on the server.

Even if your PKI environment will be internal, you should still focus on a proper PKI design. This means implementing a seven-step process:

1. Review WS08 PKI information and familiarize yourself with key concepts. An excellent place to start is online at http://technet2.microsoft.com/windowsserver2008/en/library/532ac164-da33-4369-bef0-8f019d5a18b81033.mspx?mfr=true.
2. Define your certificate requirements. Identify all the uses for internal certificates, list them, and define how they should be attributed.
3. Create your PKI architecture. How many levels of certificate authorities will you require? How will you manage offline CAs? How many CAs are required?
4. Create or modify the certificate types you require. Determine if you need to use templates. Templates are the preferred certificate attribution method.

5. Configure certificate duration. Duration affects the entire infrastructure. Root CAs should have certificates that last longer than subordinate CAs.
6. Identify how you will manage and distribute certificate revocation lists as well as which ADCS roles you want to include in your infrastructure. This can include Web enrollment and online responders in addition to CAs.
7. Identify your operations plan for the certificate infrastructure in your organization. Who will manage certificates? Who can provide them to users? If smart cards are in use, how are they attributed?

The result should provide the architecture you intend to use (see Figure 10-14).

Consider each step before deploying ADCS. This is not a place where you can make many mistakes. Thoroughly test every element of your ADCS architecture before proceeding to its implementation within your internal network. Finally, just as when you created your security policy to define how you secure your environment, you will need to create a certification policy and communicate it to your personnel.

TIP *For more information on PKI and the world of trust it supports, go to www.reso-net.com/articles.asp?m=8#c. For information on ADCS, go to http://technet2.microsoft.com/windowsserver2008/en/library/532ac164-da33-4369-bef0-8f019d5a18b81033.mspx?mfr=true.*

Active Directory Federation Services

Previously, when organizations wanted to interact with each other, they needed to share very sensitive information, often through the implementation of external ADDS directories. The problem with this is that any sensitive information store, such as a directory, that is exposed to external resources can be hacked if the malicious attacker is determined enough.

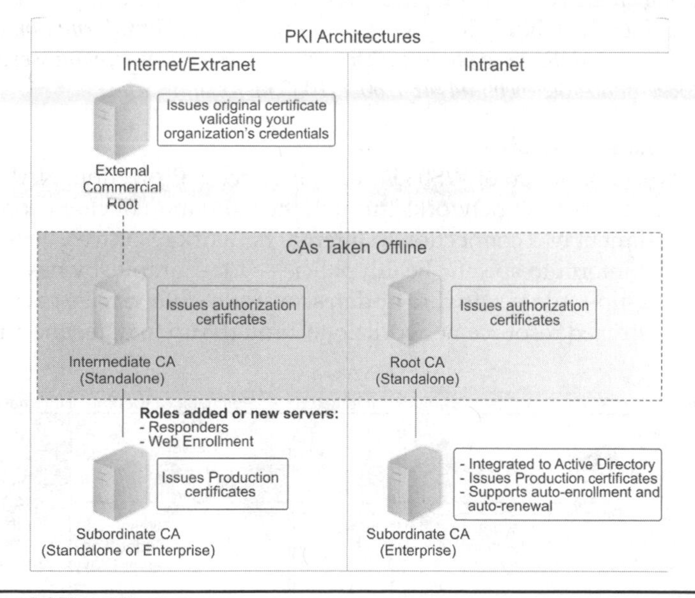

FIGURE 10-14 An ADCS architecture

Fortunately, WS08 includes a series of tools that avoid the need for the implementation of ADDS technologies in perimeter networks. For example, if you only intend to provide access to an external application, you can always rely on ADLDS to do so. ADLDS provides many of the features of ADDS without exposing highly sensitive information.

A better way to provide integration between organizations that want to share applications is through Active Directory Federation Services. ADFS provides a simple, encrypted identity federation process and supports Web single sign-on. In addition, ADFS can be integrated with ADRMS to provide extended information rights management services.

The ADFS process is simple (see Figure 10-15):

1. A client wants to access a Web application.
2. The Web server verifies with a Resource Federation Server (RFS) to see if the client is granted access. Because the request must traverse a firewall, the Web server first contacts a Resource Federation Proxy Server, who then contacts the actual RFS.
3. The RFS checks with an Account Federation Server (AFS), once again through a proxy, to see which access rights the user has. The AFS is directly linked to the organization's internal ADDS and obtains access rights from the directory.
4. The AFS responds to the Web server with the client's access rights.
5. The Web server grants access to the application.

The process is simple, but the implementation of ADFS is more complex. The advantage is that through ADFS, each partner organization can rely on their own internal ADDS directories to grant users access to external applications. This makes access management much simpler and straightforward.

Tip *For information on ADFS, go to http://technet2.microsoft.com/windowsserver2008/en/library/532ac164-da33-4369-bef0-8f019d5a18b81033.mspx?mfr=true. For information on how to integrate ADFS with ADRMS, go to http://technet2.microsoft.com/windowsserver2008/en/library/703206ee-638c-40c9-beb5-d474602b02af1033.mspx?mfr=true.*

Rely on Network Access Protection

Another very powerful function of WS08 is Network Access Protection. NAP regroups a series of technologies to protect networks through the validation of client configurations prior to the establishment of a connection to internal network resources. This means that clients who do not conform to specific health policies—for example, by having up-to-date antivirus signatures, up-to-date software updates, or up-to-date service packs—are quarantined in a restricted resource network zone, brought up to date, and then once they

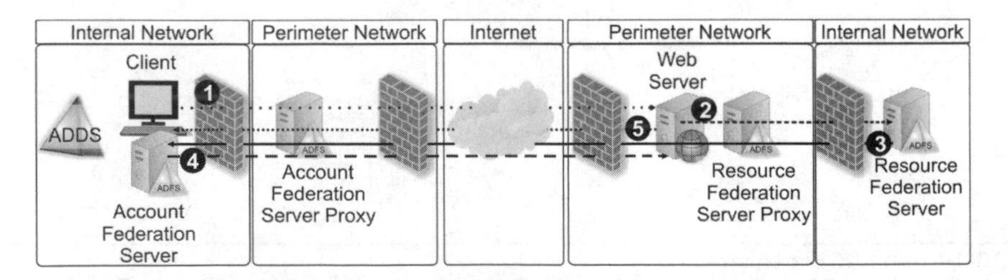

Figure 10-15 Relying on ADFS to establish partnerships

validate that they are up to date, are provided with a fully functional network connection. This level of protection is useful for both resource pools and VSOs.

NAP provides quarantines or limited access enforcement for the following technologies:

- IPSec connections
- Wired (IEEE 802.3) connections
- Wireless (IEEE 802.11) connections
- DHCP connections
- Virtual private networks
- Terminal Services connections
- Host Credential Authorization Protocol (HCAP) connections based on HTTP

NAP relies on a health validation server to determine the health status of devices requesting connections. NAP systems include remediation servers, enforcement servers, health servers, and policy management systems. Basically, any connection to the network can be protected, so long as the client supports this level of protection. By default, Vista clients include this level of support. When all the pieces are in place, you determine the level of protection you want to apply.

Once in place, your connection requests will always pass through the Network Policy Server (see Figure 10-16) and will work as follows:

1. The client will initiate a connection request using either a wired or wireless connection.
2. The connection provider (HTTP, DHCP, VPN, Switch, Router, or TS Gateway) will verify with the Network Policy to see what it should do with the connection request.
3. The Network Policy Servers will provide the provider with the appropriate policy. The policy should request a health validation of the client.

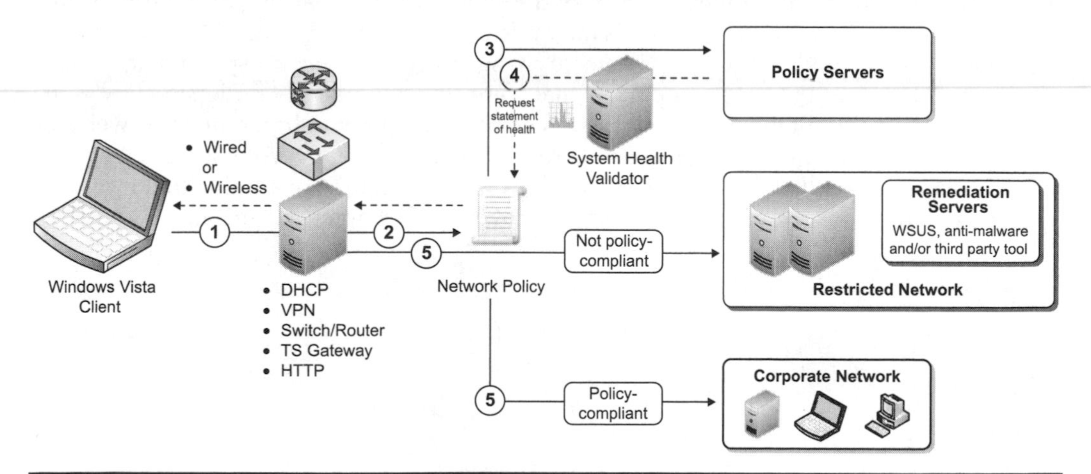

FIGURE 10-16 Using Network Access Protection

4. The System Health Validators will determine the health status of the client and return it to the provider by requesting a statement of health from the client.
5. Based on the health status of the client, one of two actions will occur:
    - If the client is not deemed healthy, then it will be directed to a restricted network. The restricted network will quarantine the system until it is brought to a healthy state. The restricted network will therefore include only access to remediation servers (Windows Server Update Services, Anti-malware and/or another configuration management tool). Once the client is updated, its health status is updated so that the provider can give it full access to the network.
    - If the client is deemed healthy or updated to a state where it is deemed healthy, it is allowed full access to the network.

Rely on NAP to protect resource pools from contamination at the hardware level. Rely on NAP to protect VSOs from contamination at the user services level.

TIP *For more information on NAP, go to www.microsoft.com/technet/network/nap/default.mspx.*

Manage the Security Policy

The Castle Defense System provides a structured approach to the design of a security policy. But it cannot stand alone to defend your critical resources. It must be supplemented by a defense plan, a plan that includes both reactive and proactive defense measures. This means additional defenses at several levels, especially in terms of system resilience (see Chapter 11 for more information).

There are also ongoing operations that must take place at regular intervals to ensure that your defense system is constantly monitored and that your reaction plans work properly. Simulations are good practice. You will see how you respond and also if your response plan is adequate. You do not want to find yourself in a situation where the only response is unplugging a system. One of the keys to a solid response plan is ensuring that everyone in the organization knows and understands their role in it. Windows Server 2008 and Active Directory Domain Services bring considerable change to your network, especially in terms of resource pools and VSOs. It is important that these changes are fully understood by your staff. It is also important that you identify each new role within your operations, as well as the modifications you must bring to existing roles. Finally, to support your security policy to its fullest, you need to limit the delegated rights you assign to both administrators and operators within your network. These items are covered in Chapters 12 and 13.

11

CHAPTER

Build for Business Continuity

A significant element of security is system resiliency: ensuring that your services will not fail, even in the event of a disaster or a security breach. Several elements of system resiliency have already been covered thus far:

- **Active Directory Domain Services** Resiliency here is created through the distribution of domain controllers throughout your network. It is also based on the multimaster replication system and the creation of an appropriate replication topology. This feature is described in Chapter 6.
- **DNS** By integrating the Domain Name Service (DNS) service with the directory, you ensure that your network name resolution service will always function because it has the same resiliency as the directory service. This feature is described in Chapter 6.
- **DHCP** Your address allocation infrastructure also has resilience built in because of the way you structured it with redundant scopes. In addition, if you place your Dynamic Host Configuration Protocol (DHCP) servers in different sites, you have a solution that would continue to work in the event of a disaster. This feature is described in Chapter 6.
- **Windows Internet Naming Service (WINS)** If you've decided to use them, your legacy name resolution servers are also redundant, since the service is offered by the same servers as the DHCP service.
- **Object management infrastructure** Your object management structure is also resilient, since it is based on the organizational unit (OU) structure in the directory and the directory service offers system resilience. This structure is discussed in Chapters 7, 8, and 9.
- **Domain Distributed File System (DFS) roots** Your file shares are resilient because they are distributed through the directory, making them available in multiple sites. They also include automatic failover—i.e., if the service fails in one site, it automatically fails user connections over to the other site. DFS replication ensures that DFS namespace targets are synchronized at all times. DFS strategies are described in Chapter 8.

- **Volume shadow copies** Your shared files, shared databases, Exchange stores, and other shared information repositories are also protected through the Volume Shadow Copy feature, taking system snapshots on a regular basis and even allowing users to recover files themselves. This feature is described in Chapter 8.
- **Terminal Services** The Terminal Services servers you deployed offer resilience through the Session Broker, which is, in turn, protected through Session Broker load balancing. This feature is described in Chapter 9.

Despite the fact that several of your systems are resilient, there remain areas that could have significant impact on your operations if they failed. Remember, one of the main reasons for hacker attacks is *Distributed Denial of Service* or DDoS. This type of attack can succeed for two reasons First, the server hosting the service is not protected, and second, the service is hosted by a *single* server, i.e., there is no failover service. Chapter 10 showed you how to protect your systems through the Castle Defense System. Now, you need to add additional resiliency to the network through two strategies: system redundancy and system recovery.

Plan for System Redundancy

System redundancy relies on the implementation of methods and measures that ensure that if a component fails, its function will immediately be taken over by another or, at the very least, the procedure to put the component back online is well documented and well known by system operators. Some of the most common administrator headaches are network security and disaster recovery. It's not surprising. We've all faced disasters, such as 9-11 and Hurricane Katrina, and we all know just how damaging these events can be to businesses of any size. In fact, a vast majority of businesses that do not have a business continuity plan in place and face a major disaster often go under since they cannot recover from such catastrophic events. These issues are at the very core of any network design. No matter what you do, you must ensure that your systems are protected at all times.

Once again, the Castle Defense System can help. Layer 1 helps you identify risk levels because it helps you determine the value of an information asset. Risk is determined by identifying value (the importance of an asset) and multiplying it by the risk factor that is associated with it. The formula looks like this:

```
Risk = asset value * risk factor
```

For example, an asset that is valued at $1 million with a risk factor of .2 has a risk value of $200,000. This means that you can invest up to $200,000 to protect that asset and reduce its risk factor.

While these calculations can be esoteric in nature, what remains important is to invest the most in the protection of your most valued assets. This is one reason why it is so important to know what you have. Figure 11-1 is a good reminder of this principle.

Protect the Resource Pool

By focusing on physical protection, or protection of the resource pool, Layer 2 also helps you plan for system redundancy. This is where some of the elements covered in the server-sizing exercise in Chapter 4 become important. Random arrays of inexpensive disks (RAID)

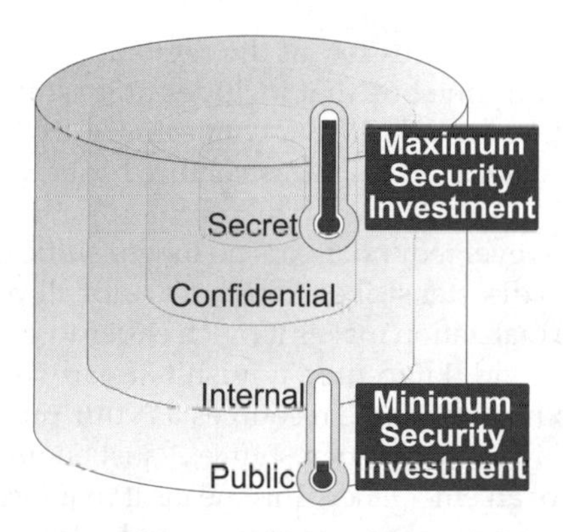

FIGURE 11-1 Information asset categories

and random arrays of inexpensive networks (RAIN), for example, provide direct, hardware-level protection for your systems. It is also important to include uninterrupted power supply (UPS) systems at this level. This can either be individual Universal Serial Bus (USB)-connected UPS devices (for regional servers) or centralized power management infrastructures that protect entire computer rooms (usually at central sites).

Resource pools also need redundancy. Each one of the physical servers playing host to a virtual service offering (VSO) must have some form of redundancy built in. If a host server is running 10 to 15 VSOs, it must be able to fail these VSOs over to another physical host in the event of a failure at the hardware level. This means the physical hosts must be clustered—sharing the VSO workload so that VSOs are available to users at all times. This is one reason why it is so important to host VSOs on shared storage. Because they are hosted on a storage structure that each host server has access to, VSOs can be moved from host to host with little impact on users. This provides site-level redundancy (see Figure 11-2).

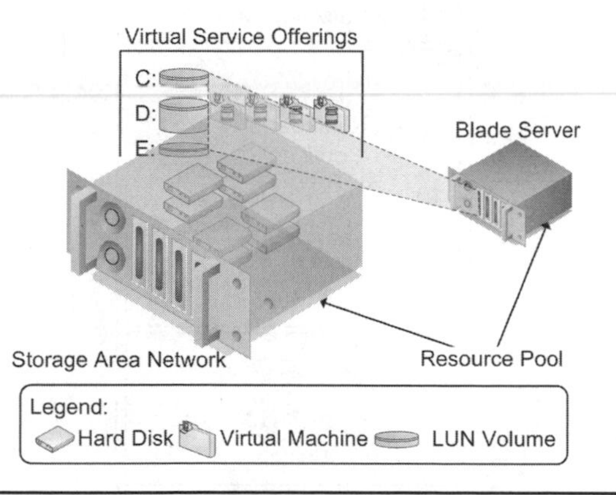

FIGURE 11-2 Rely on shared storage and connected hosts to provide site-level redundancy.

Site-level redundancy is also necessary at the regional level. This is why the ideal regional server will be an all-in-one box that includes at least two physical host servers, shared storage, and wide area network (WAN) connectivity. By including two host servers, you can make sure the regional VSOs this infrastructure hosts will always be available (see Figure 11-3).

As mentioned before, site-level redundancy is no longer sufficient. Too many organizations literally lose everything when disaster strikes. You don't want all your eggs in the same basket. Fortunately, the advent of virtualization makes it much easier to provide multisite redundancy. First, you need to build a second datacenter, if it isn't already available. This secondary datacenter does not need to host the same resources as your production environment (see Figure 11-4). It just needs a modicum of resources—just enough, in fact, to help you get back on your feet in the case of an emergency. This means it requires a few host servers attached to shared storage. It also needs central power protection devices and WAN connectivity.

Service level agreements (SLAs) for disaster recovery are not the same as those for normal production. This means you can run a reduced infrastructure in the disaster recovery site. You can rely on a formula to help you determine just how many physical resources your disaster recovery center will require. The formula looks like this:

```
Production Resources/Recovery Time=Disaster Recovery Resources
```

For example, if you are running your infrastructure on 15 physical hosts and you expect your recovery time to be three hours, then you can run the disaster recovery center with five physical hosts. The lower the recovery time, the more resources you will need to populate your recovery center.

Balance the number of physical resources in your recovery center with the need to reload critical services. In the event of a disaster, your recovery will require essential services

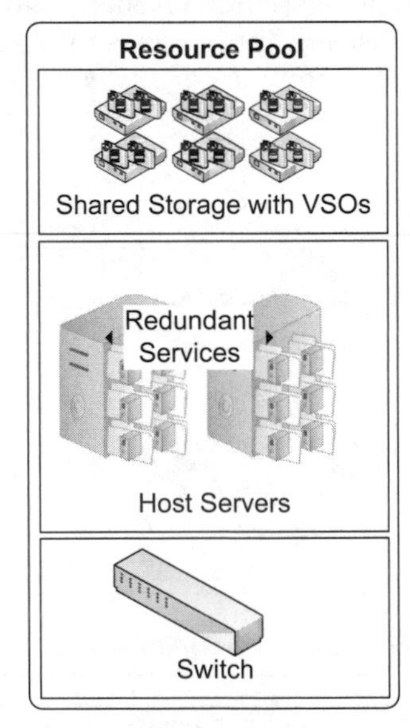

FIGURE 11-3 Use all-in-one boxes to provide regional site-level redundancy.

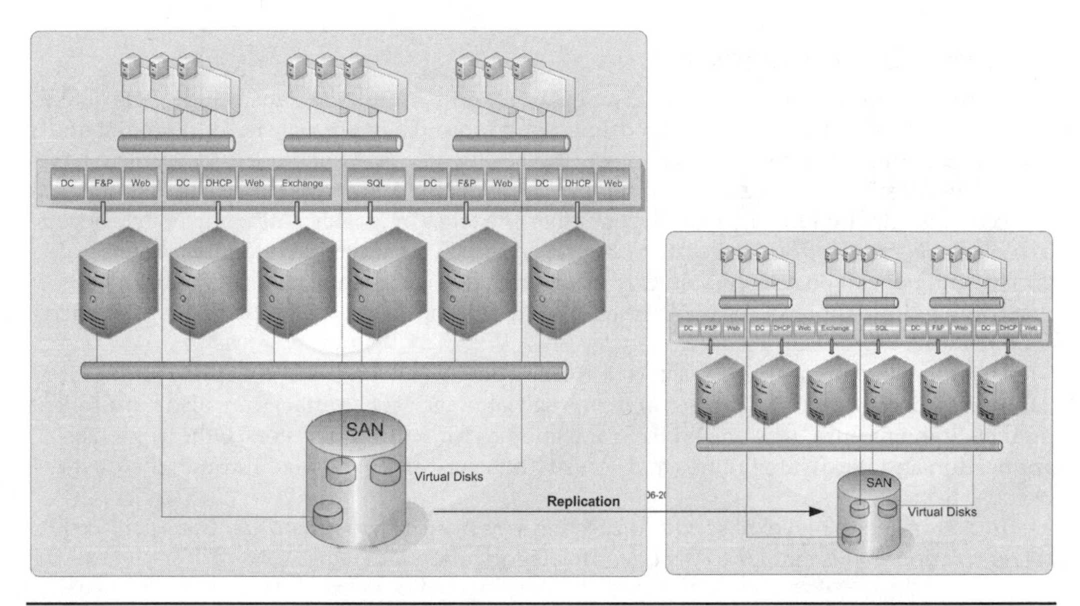

FIGURE 11-4 Providing multisite redundancy

first—for example, Active Directory Domain Services and DNS—then load secondary services, DHCP, file and print servers, and so on. Using a graduated approach for the reloading of services for users will let you bring everything back online in stages and will reduce the overhead cost of the secondary datacenter. In most cases, the recovery of your virtual service offerings can follow the structure of the implementation of VSOs in this book.

TIP *In many cases, you don't need to have your own recovery datacenter. Some vendors, such as Sungard (www.sungard.com), will offer hosting services for secondary datacenters. In many instances, it is much cheaper to use a hosted recovery center than to build your own.*

Protect the Virtual Service Offerings

The redundancy you build into your physical protection layer is only part of the solution. You'll need to ensure that you also have service redundancy. That can be accomplished through service clustering, either at the network level or the server level. Finally, you'll need to provide data redundancy. This is done through the elaboration and implementation of the backup and recovery systems. Here, it will be important to choose the right type of backup solution, since you need to protect data that is stored not only in the file system, but also within databases such as the Active Directory Domain Services.

Building redundancy in your systems is valuable only if you know it works. It's not enough to be prepared; you need to know that your preparation has value. To do so, you'll need to test and retest every single redundancy level you implement in your network. Too many organizations have made the fatal error of backing up data for years without testing the recovery process, only to find out that this recovery didn't work. This is not a myth. It actually happens. Don't let it happen to you. Test all your systems and document your procedures. In fact, this is an excellent opportunity for you to write standard operating procedures.

Prepare for Potential Disasters

There are two types of disasters: natural and man-made. Natural disasters include earthquakes, tornados, fires, floods, hurricanes, landslides, and more. They are very hard to predict and even harder, but not impossible, to prevent. The best way to prevent these disasters is to have redundant sites: Your core servers and services are available at more than one site. If your main datacenter is impaired for any reason, your other site takes over. This is also where the concept of the *failsafe server* introduced earlier comes into play. This server is a standby server that is dormant, but can be activated quickly if required. In the dynamic datacenter, this means providing redundant resource pool servers and saving copies of each of the VSOs you run in production.

There are also man-made disasters: terrorist attacks, power failures, application failures, hardware failures, security attacks, and internal sabotage. These attacks are also hard to predict. Some require the same type of protection as for natural disasters. Others, such as application and hardware failures and security attacks, can be avoided through the Castle Defense System.

To determine the level of service protection you need to apply, you can use a service categorization that is similar to the Layer 1 categorization for data:

- **Mission-critical systems** These are systems that require the most protection because interruption of service is unacceptable.
- **Mission-support systems** These require less protection than mission-critical systems, but interruptions should be minimized as much as possible.
- **Business-critical systems** These are systems where short service interruptions can be acceptable.
- **Extraneous systems** These are deemed non-critical and can have longer-lasting interruptions.

What most people seldom realize is that the basic network infrastructure for your network is, in many cases, part of the mission-critical level, because if it does not work, nothing works.

Use WS08 Clustering Services

One of the areas that can add service resiliency is service clustering. Clustering services are, in fact, one of the major improvement areas for Windows Server 2008 (WS08). Microsoft clustering services support three types of clusters:

- **Network Load Balancing (NLB)** This service provides high availability and scalability for Internet Protocol (IP) services—both Transmission Control Protocol (TCP) and User Datagram Protocol (UDP)—and applications by combining up to 32 servers in a single cluster. Clients access the NLB cluster by accessing a single IP address for the entire group. NLB services automatically redirect the client to a working server.
- **Component Load Balancing (CLB)** This service allows COM+ components to be distributed over as many as 12 servers. This service is not native to WS08; when needed, it can be provided by Microsoft Application Center Server.

- **Windows Server Failover Clusters (WSFC)** This service provides resilience through resource failover: If a resource fails, the client is automatically transferred to another resource in the cluster. Server clusters can be composed of between two to sixteen nodes.

These three clustering services work together to provide a complete service structure (see Figure 11-5).

Only two of these clustering technologies are available in WS08: network load balancing and failover clustering. Build your resiliency solutions based on these two technologies. Keep the following in mind:

- When protecting stateless systems or systems that provide read-only services, rely on network load balancing.
- When protecting stateful systems or systems that provide read-write services, rely on failover clustering.

It's a simple formula: Systems that do not persist data rely on NLB, and systems that persist data rely on failover clustering.

Cluster Services for Resource Pools

The host servers in the resource pool are designed to persist data by default. That's because they store the virtual hard drives (VHDs) that make up the VSOs. Since the VHDs are data files that are written to as the virtual machine operates, then it is imperative that the high-availability solution be designed to protect this data at all times. We've already discussed several ways this data can be protected, including volume shadow copies and DFS replication. Now you need to consider how the service that lets the VSOs run can be rendered highly available.

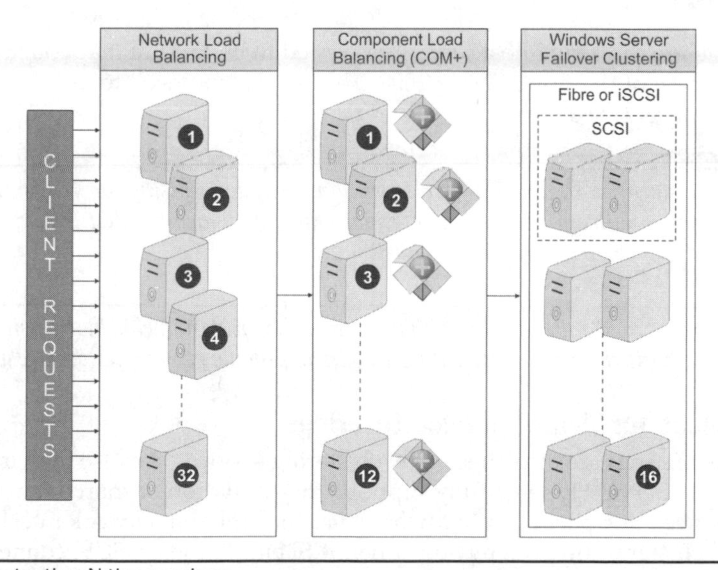

Figure 11-5 Protecting N-tier services

Since they persist data, host servers must run the Failover Clustering service to provide support for high availability of the VSOs. This means that when one host machine fails, the VSOs it runs are automatically failed over to another host server that is part of the cluster. For this, you must build your host servers accordingly. Take, for example, the following configuration.

- Host server 1 has 16 gigabytes (GB) of random access memory (RAM). It runs eight VSOs at 1 GB of RAM each.
- Host server 2 has 16 GB of RAM. It runs eight VSOs at 1 GB of RAM each.

In a clustered configuration, each of the host servers must reserve a spare portion of RAM in the event of a failover. When the failover occurs, the host that takes on the failed server's workload must have enough available RAM to run all of the services required for the failover to work.

Clustered server configurations must, therefore, be planned carefully because they will need to support each of the servers in the cluster configuration. Also, because the host servers are physical host servers, they will need special hardware components to connect to shared storage:

- Small Computer System Interface (SCSI) connectors will let two host servers connect to shared storage. They may be appropriate for regional office host server configurations because only two host servers are required.
- Fibre channel connectors through host bus adapters are appropriate for clusters of up to sixteen nodes.
- Internet Small Computer System Interface (iSCSI) connectors are appropriate for clusters of up to sixteen nodes. In fact, iSCSI connectors, because they are network connectors and are simpler to implement, are often the preferred connectors for clustered hosts.

Because you are clustering host servers, you need to make sure that you are using the appropriate version of Windows Server 2008. This means you need to use either the Enterprise or Datacenter edition.

NOTE *Both the Enterprise and the Datacenter editions include licensing for VSOs; therefore, you should be working with one of these two editions anyway. Remember that Enterprise is priced per server and Datacenter is priced per physical processor.*

TIP *Though you will not be using NLB with host servers, you should consider placing each of the members of an NLB cluster on different host nodes to provide even better service availability.*

Cluster Services for Virtual Service Offerings

Virtual service offerings are also affected by clustering services because the virtualization layer of Windows Server Hyper-V fully supports the emulation of shared hardware. NLB clusters do not need any particular hardware since they rely on network interface cards to work. Failover clusters, however, rely on either SCSI emulation or iSCSI connectors. As mentioned earlier, you can, therefore, create either two-node or up to sixteen-node clusters with these technologies. You'll find that clustering in VSOs will be more comprehensive than in resource pools.

Table 11-1 outlines the features and supported services for each clustering mode for VSOs. Since CLB clustering is not native to WS08, it is not covered in this table.

As you can see, NLB and failover clusters are rather complementary. In fact, it is *not* recommended to activate both services on the same server; that is, a failover cluster should not also be a member of an NLB cluster. In addition, NLB clusters are designed to support more static connections. This means that it is not designed to provide the same type of failover as a server cluster. In the latter, if a user is editing a file and the server stops responding, the failover component will automatically be activated and the user will continue to perform his or her work without being aware of the failure (there may be a slight delay in response time). This is because the server cluster is designed to provide a mirrored system to the user. But an NLB cluster will not provide the same type of user experience. Its main purpose is to redirect demand to available resources. As such, these resources must be static in nature, since NLB does not include any capability for mirroring information deposits.

Both clustering services offer the ability to support four service-offering requirements:

- **Availability** By providing service offerings through a cluster, it is possible to ensure that they are available during the time periods the organization has decreed they should be.
- **Reliability** With a cluster, it is possible to ensure that users can depend on the service offering, because if a component fails, it is automatically replaced by another working component.

Clustering Service	Network Load Balancing	Failover Clusters
WS08 edition	Web Standard Enterprise Datacenter	Enterprise Datacenter
Number of nodes	Up to 32	Up to 16
Resources	Minimum of two network adapters	SCSI or iSCSI disk connectors
Server Role	Application Servers (stateless) Dedicated Web Servers Collaboration Servers (front end)	Application Servers (stateful) File and Print Servers Collaboration Servers (storage) Network Infrastructure Servers
Application	Web Farms Internet Security and Acceleration Server (ISA) Virtual Private Network (VPN) Servers Streaming Media Servers Unified Communications Servers	SQL Servers Exchange Servers Message Queuing Servers

TABLE 11-1 WS08 Clustering Services for VSOs

- **Scalability** With a cluster, it is possible to increase the number of servers providing the service offering without affecting the service being delivered to users.
- **Maintenance** A cluster allows IT personnel to upgrade, modify, apply service packs, and otherwise maintain cluster components individually without affecting the service level of service offerings delivered by the cluster.

An advantage that failover clusters have over NLB clusters is the ability to share data. Failover cluster resources must be tied to the same data storage resource, ensuring the transparency of the failover process.

Clusters do have disadvantages. They are more complex to stage and manage than stand-alone servers, and services that are assigned to clusters must be cluster-aware in order to take advantage of the clustering feature.

Network Load Balancing

The basis of the NLB cluster is a virtual IP address: Client systems connect to the virtual IP address, and the NLB service redirects the client to a cluster member. If a cluster member fails or is taken offline, the NLB service automatically redirects requests to the other cluster members. When the member comes back online, it automatically rejoins the cluster and requests can be redirected to it. In most cases, the *failover* process—the process of redirecting clients to other cluster resources when a member fails—takes less than ten seconds.

NLB cluster members do not share components. They are independent servers that host the same applications and identical local copies of the data client systems access. This is why NLB is best suited to *stateless* applications—applications that provide access to data mostly in read-only mode. NLB servers normally use two network interface cards. The first is dedicated to cluster network traffic, and the second is for communications with clients and other normal network communications. Cluster network traffic from the member is mostly in the form of a heartbeat signal that is emitted every second and sent to the other members of the cluster. If a member does not send a heartbeat within a time span of five seconds, the other members automatically perform a convergence operation to remove the failed member from the cluster and eliminate it from client request redirections.

TIP *You can add more than one network interface card (NIC) for client access, but two are the minimum configuration you should run.*

NOTE *If you decide to build hardware-based service offerings for some reason, then consider this in the selection of the hardware configuration for the servers. Since each cluster member uses identical data, it is often useful to optimize the server hardware to support fast read operations. For this reason, many organizations planning to use hardware-based NLB clusters do not implement RAID disk subsystems because redundancy is provided by cluster members. Disk access is optimized because there is no RAID overhead during read operations. It is essential, however, to ensure that all systems are fully synchronized at all times. Whether or not you decide to construct NLB servers without RAID protection is a decision you will make when designing your NLB architecture. It will depend mostly on your data synchronization strategy, the type of service you intend to host on the server, and the number of servers you intend to place in your NLB cluster.*

Since the NLB servers are VSOs, you do not need to make any special hardware considerations, though you should create identical virtual machines to provide the service offering.

The core of the NLB service is the `wlbs.sys` driver. This is a driver that sits between the network interface card and network traffic. It filters all NLB communications and sets the member server to respond to requests if they have been directed to it.

NLB is similar to round-robin DNS, but it provides better fault tolerance. Round-robin DNS relies on multiple DNS entries for a service. When clients require a connection, the DNS service provides the first address, then the second, then the third, and so on. It cannot check to see if the address actually resolves. This is one reason why NLB is better. It always checks destination addresses to ensure the server is available when redirecting clients. And, since the NLB service is hosted by every cluster member, there is no single point of failure. There is also immediate and automatic failover of cluster members.

Multicast Versus Unicast Modes

NLB clusters operate in either multicast or unicast mode. The default mode is unicast. In this mode, the NLB cluster automatically reassigns the Media Access Control (MAC) address for each cluster member on the NIC that is enabled in cluster mode. If each member has only one NIC, member-to-member communications are not possible in this mode. This is one reason why it is best to install two NICs in each server.

When using the multicast mode, NLB assigns two multicast addresses to the cluster adapter. This mode ensures that all cluster members can automatically communicate with each other because there are no changes to the original MAC addresses. There are disadvantages to this mode, though, especially if you use Cisco routers. The address resolution protocol (ARP) response sent out by a cluster host is rejected by these routers. If you use multicast mode in an NLB cluster with Cisco routers, you must manually reconfigure the routers with ARP entries, mapping the cluster IP address to its MAC address.

Whether you use one mode or the other, you should use at least two NICs on each member. One advantage of doing so is that it allows you to configure one card to receive incoming traffic and the other to send outgoing traffic, making your cluster members even more responsive. You can also ensure that if your NLB cluster is only the front end of a complex cluster structure, such as the one illustrated in Figure 11-5, all back-end communications are handled by the non-clustered NIC.

Finally, if your NLB members are expected to handle extremely high traffic loads, you can add more NICs in each member and bind the NLB service to each one, improving the overall response time for each member.

Single Affinity Versus No Affinity

NLB clusters work in affinity modes. Each refers to the way NLB load-balances traffic. Single affinity refers to load balancing based on the source IP address of the incoming connection. It automatically redirects all requests from the same address to the same cluster member. No affinity refers to load balancing based on both the incoming IP address and its port number. Class C affinity is even more granular than single affinity. It ensures that clients using multiple proxy servers to communicate with the cluster are redirected to the same cluster member at all times. No affinity is useful when supporting calls from networks using network address translation (NAT) from IPv4 transmissions because these networks only present a single IP address to the cluster. If you use single affinity mode and you receive a lot of requests from NAT networks, these clients will not profit from the cluster experience, since all of their requests will be redirected to the same server. IPv6 connections can run in any affinity mode.

However, if you use an NLB cluster to provide VPN connections using either Layer 2 Tunneling Protocol/Internet Protocol Security (L2TP/IPSec) or Point to Point Tunneling Protocol (PPTP) sessions, you must configure your cluster in single affinity mode to ensure that client requests are always redirected to the same host. Single affinity should also be used for any application that uses sessions lasting over multiple Transmission Control Protocol (TCP) connections to ensure that the entire session is mapped to the same server. Finally, single affinity must be used if your client sessions use the Secure Sockets Layer (SSL) to connect to NLB servers.

Single affinity does not give the same load-balancing results as no affinity. Consider the type of requests your cluster will handle before deciding on your cluster architecture.

Install and Configure NLB Clusters

NLB cluster installation is fairly straightforward. Each member server should have enough disk space to host the application, and each should have at least two network interface cards. You will also need to have some information on hand before you begin the installation. This includes:

- The cluster's Internet name: the DNS name you intend to use for the cluster.
- The cluster's virtual IP address and the appropriate subnet mask: the address that will be linked to the DNS name.
- The IP mode you intend to use: IPv4, IPv6, or both.
- The current IP addresses and subnet masks for each cluster member.
- The cluster casting mode you want to use: unicast or multicast. If you use multicast, you will also want to use Internet Group Multicast Protocol (IGMP) Multicast to reduce the number of ports used to address cluster administration traffic and restrict it to the standard IPv4 class D range; that is, 224.0.0.0 to 239.255.255.255.
- The cluster affinity mode you want to use: single affinity, Class C, or no affinity.
- Whether or not you want to enable remote control of the cluster using the NLB.EXE application.

CAUTION *It is highly recommended not to enable this feature because it can cause a security risk. Any user with access to the NLB.EXE application can control a cluster. It is best to use the Network Load Balancing Manager console to administer your NLB clusters. Access to this console can be controlled better than access to NLB.EXE.*

- The unique IDs you want to assign to each cluster member.
- The TCP and UDP ports for which you want NLB to handle traffic.
- The load weight or handling priority you will apply to the cluster. Load weight is used when you filter traffic to multiple cluster members. Handling priority is used when traffic is filtered only to a single cluster member.

Now, you're ready to set up your NLB cluster. Keep in mind that you will always need to perform two tasks to create an NLB cluster:

- First, you need to add the NLB feature. You might even consider making this part of the Sysprepped virtual machine you use to seed NLB cluster members.
- Then you configure the NLB service on the cluster members.

Proceed as follows:

1. Use the Server Manager | Features node to select Add Feature in the action pane.
2. Select the Network Load Balancing feature. Click Next.
3. Click Install and then click Close once the feature is installed.

You're ready to build the first node of the cluster.

1. Launch the Network Load Balancing Manager. Move to the Start menu, select Administrative Tools, and click Network Load Balancing Manager.
2. This opens the NLB Manager Microsoft Management Console (MMC). To create a new cluster, right-click Network Load Balancing Clusters in the left pane, and select New Cluster.
3. Use the values in Table 11-2 to fill out this wizard.

New NLB Cluster Wizard Page	Settings
New Cluster: Connect	Enter the host name of the first member in the cluster, and click Connect. Select the interface to connect to.
New Cluster: Host Parameters	Select the priority for the host. You can select the default priority number. Select the dedicated IP address for the host. Select the default state for the host. Set it as Started. Select the Retain Suspended State After Computer Restarts option. This will ensure the system does not rejoin the cluster during maintenance operations.
New Cluster: Cluster IP Addresses	Add the IP address(es) for the cluster. Multiple IP addresses can be added here, but remember that a DNS entry will be required for each address you assign. Select an IPv4 or IPv6 address. Make sure you create the corresponding DNS entries.
New Cluster: Cluster Parameters	Add the DNS name for the cluster. Select Unicast with Unicast Interhost Communication, Multicast, or IGMP Multicast. If your network supports Multicast mode, then select IGMP Multicast. When you do so, WS08 gives you a warning message. Click OK to close it.
New Cluster: Port Rules	Define port rules for the cluster and the affinity mode for each rule. By default, all cluster members handle all TCP and UDP ports in single affinity mode. To modify this rule, click the Edit button. To add new rules, click the Add button.

TABLE 11-2 Settings for the NLB Cluster Creation Wizard

PART V

Now you can add cluster members. Right-click the cluster name to select Add Host To Cluster. Type the member's DNS name, and click Connect. Once again, use the values in Table 11-2 to prepare this host. When you complete this addition, the NLB service will perform a convergence to bring all the cluster members online.

You're done. From now on, you can manage the cluster—adding, deleting, and configuring members—through this console (see Figure 11-6). Note that this interface displays the cluster members in the tree pane, the status of each node in the details pane, and below, in the information pane, it lists the details of the NLB operation.

NLB clusters will be useful for load-balancing streaming media, unified communications, Web applications, and virtual private network servers within your network.

TIP *The companion web site offers a job aid for the preparation of NLB clusters at www.reso-net.com/livre.asp?p=main&b=WS08.*

NOTE *Many organizations decide to rely on hardware load balancers for this task. They provide exactly the same service as NLB, but they often also include WAN traffic acceleration capabilities. Vendors such as CAI Networks (www.cainetworks.com) and F5 Networks (www.f5.com) offer products in this category. These devices work well with VSOs.*

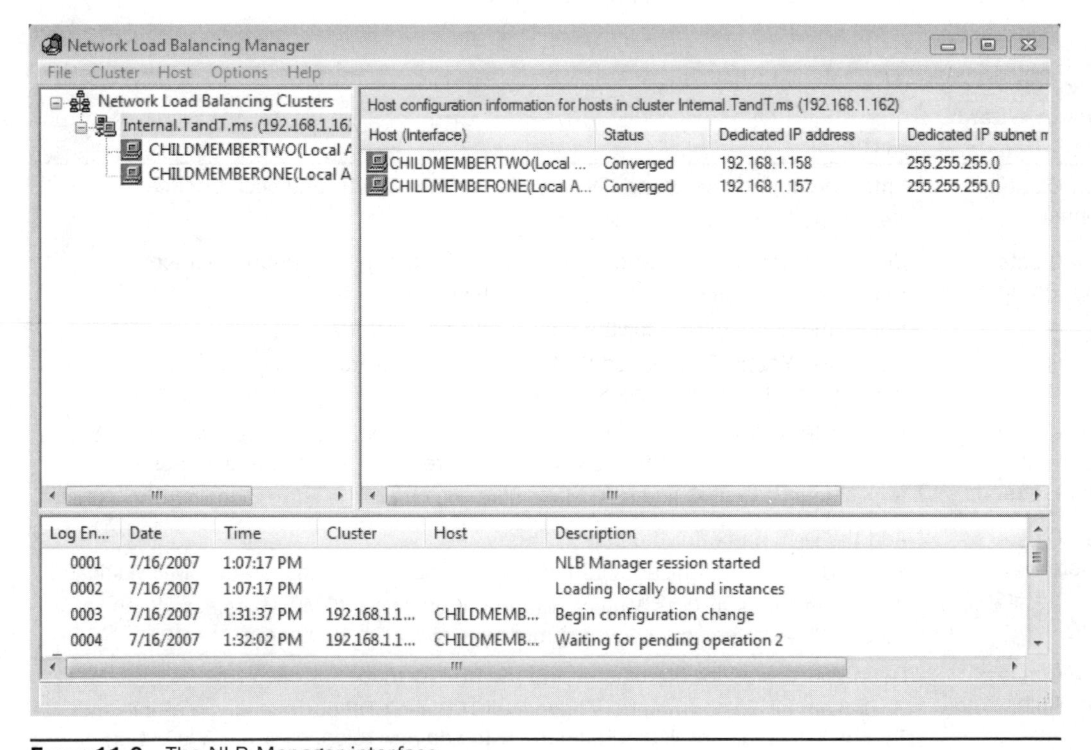

FIGURE 11-6 The NLB Manager interface

Windows Server Failover Clustering

WS08 failover clusters offer the same type of availability services as NLB clusters, but rely on a different model. Whereas in NLB clusters, server configurations do not have to be identical, it is the purpose of the server cluster to make identical servers redundant by allowing immediate failover of hosted applications or services. As illustrated in Figure 11-5, Windows Server 2008 supports up to sixteen node clusters.

WSFCs can include several configurations. You can design the cluster so that each node will perform different tasks, but will be ready to failover any of the other nodes' services and applications. Or you can design the cluster so that applications operate at the same time on each of the nodes. For example, you could design a four-node financial database cluster so that the first node managed order entry, the second order processing, the third payment services, and the fourth the other accounting activities. To do so, your application must be fully cluster-aware — completely compliant with all of the WSFC features. Not all applications or even WS08 services are fully cluster-aware.

Cluster Compatibility List

Even in Microsoft's own product offering, there are some particularities in terms of clustering compatibility. Cluster compatibility can fall into one of four categories:

- **WSFC-aware** is a product or internal WS08 service that can take full advantage of the cluster service. It can communicate with the cluster application programming interface (API) to receive status and notification from the server cluster. It can react to cluster events.
- **WSFC-independent** (or unaware) is a product or internal WS08 service that is not aware of the presence of the cluster but that can be installed on a cluster and will behave the same way as if it was on a single server. It responds only to the most basic cluster events.
- **WFSC-incompatible** is a product or internal WS08 service that does not behave well in the context of a cluster and should not be installed on a server cluster.
- **NLB-compatible** lists products that are well suited to NLB clusters. NLB and WSFC are often incompatible with each other.

Table 11-3 categorizes Microsoft's Windows Server System and WS08 functions in terms of cluster compatibility.

The information in Table 11-3 is subject to change as each of the products evolves, but it serves as a good starting point in determining how you can configure high availability for your services.

Server Cluster Concepts

The nodes in a server cluster can be configured in either active or passive mode. An *active* node is a node that is actively rendering services. A *passive* node is a node that is in standby mode, waiting to respond upon service failure. It goes without saying that like the eighth server role presented earlier, the failsafe server, the passive node is a more expensive solution in terms of resources, because the server hardware or the virtual machine is just

Product or Service	WSFC-Aware	WSFC-Independent	WSFC-Incompatible	NLB-Compatible	Comment
Active Directory Domain Services (ADDS)		X			Not recommended; availability is provided through multimaster replication.
Active Directory Lightweight Directory Services (ADLDS)		X			Not recommended; availability is provided through ADLDS replication.
BizTalk Server	X	X		X	BizTalk state server and message box are cluster-aware. Messaging and processing servers are cluster-independent. All other services should use a network load balancing cluster. BizTalk can also take advantage of a clustered SQL Server back-end.
COM +		X			Component load balancing clusters preferred.
Commerce Server			X		Component load balancing clusters preferred.
DFS	X				Stand-alone DFS namespaces only. Domain DFS namespaces use redundancy provided by ADDS.
DHCP-WINS	X				Fully compliant.
Distributed Transaction Coordinator	X				Fully compliant.

TABLE 11-3 Cluster Compatibility List

Product or Service	WSFC-Aware	WSFC-Independent	WSFC-Incompatible	NLB-Compatible	Comment
DNS		X			Redundancy provided by ADDS when integrated with the directory.
Exchange 2000 and later	X			X	Fully compliant. In Exchange 2007, different server roles can take advantage of different modes.
File sharing	X				Fully compliant.
IIS		X		X	NLB clusters are preferred
ISA Server			X	X	NLB clusters are preferred
Microsoft Identity Lifecycle Manager	X				Fully compliant.
Microsoft Message Queuing	X				Fully compliant.
Office Live Communications Server (LCS)			X	X	LCS is incompatible with WFSC. Use an NLB cluster for front-end servers. Use a WFSC for SQL Server back-ends.
Office Project Server	X				Only the SQL Server portion.
Office SharePoint Portal Server			X	X	Only the SQL Server portion. The IIS portion should use NLB.
Print services	X				Fully compliant.
SQL Server 2000 and later	X				Fully compliant.
System Center Configuration Manager	X				SQL Server back-ends can be clustered under special conditions.
System Center Operations Manager			X		Not supported.

TABLE 11-3 Cluster Compatibility List *(continued)*

PART V

Product or Service	WSFC-Aware	WSFC-Independent	WSFC-Incompatible	NLB-Compatible	Comment
Terminal Services		X			Terminal Services rely on Session Broker Load Balancing, a custom load-balancing feature.
Windows Deployment Services			X		Not supported.
Windows SharePoint Services			X	X	Only the SQL Server portion. The IIS portion should use NLB.
Windows Streaming Media			X	X	NLB clusters are preferred.

TABLE 11-3 Cluster Compatibility List (*continued*)

waiting for failures before it becomes useful. But if your risk calculations indicate that your critical business services require passive nodes, then you should implement them because they provide extremely high availability in certain scenarios.

Most organizations use the active-active cluster mode. In fact, the most popular implementation of WSFC is the two-node active-active cluster. This is called a cluster pack because the cluster nodes share data. This can be configured to either run exactly the same services at the same time—for example, Microsoft Exchange Server running on both nodes—or it can be configured to run different services on each node. In this configuration, each node is configured to run the same applications and services, but half are activated on the first node and half are activated on the other node. This way, if a service fails, the other node can provide immediate failover because it can run the service temporarily until the failed node can be repaired.

In active-active scenarios that run the same applications on all nodes, the applications must be fully cluster-aware. This means that they can run multiple instances of the application and share the same data. Many applications include their own internal capabilities for supporting this operating mode. Applications that are not fully compliant—that are only cluster-independent—should run in single instances; that is, on only one node.

Remember that the servers you choose to create your server cluster should be sized so that they can take on the additional load node failures will cause. You can use the server-sizing exercise outlined in Chapter 4 to help identify the components you require for your cluster nodes. Properly sizing servers is essential to support application failover (see Figure 11-7). It details how each node of a four-node cluster must be able to absorb the failure of each other node until a single node is left. This is, of course, a worst-case scenario, but it demonstrates that in a cluster, system resources must be reserved for failures; otherwise, the cluster will not be able to provide high availability.

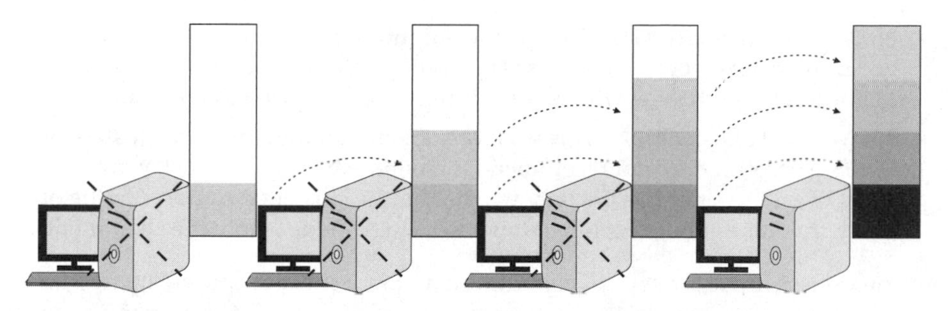

FIGURE 11-7 Node failover in a four-node cluster

You can configure your server clusters in many ways. In addition, on multiple node clusters, you can use a mix and match of multiple-instance services or applications with single-instance functions. If the application is mission-critical and cannot fail under any circumstances, you can configure it as a multiple instance on some nodes and host it in passive mode on other nodes to have the best possible availability for the application.

Finally, be careful with your failover policies. A two- to four-node cluster can easily use random failover policies—the failed service is randomly distributed to the other available nodes—because the possible combination of resources is relatively small. But if you have more than four nodes in the cluster, it is a good idea to specify failover policies, because the possible combination of resources will be too great and nodes may become overloaded during failover. The illustration in Figure 11-7 is an example of a random failover policy.

NOTE *Single-instance applications are best suited for two-node active-passive clusters, where one node runs the service and the other hosts the service in standby mode. That way, if the service fails on the running node, the second node can take it over.*

Cluster Configurations

In addition, your cluster configuration will require the ability to share information about itself between the nodes. This is performed through a quorum resource or a witness disk. By default, there is a single quorum resource per cluster. Each node of the cluster can access the quorum resource and know the state of the cluster because it contains a copy of the configuration of the cluster. The quorum helps the cluster determine if it should continue running when a certain number of nodes fail. WS08 supports four different quorum configurations:

- **Node Majority** When clusters have an odd number of nodes, use this configuration. For example, a cluster of one node would require a Node Majority quorum. An odd-numbered node configuration can then support the failure of half the nodes minus one. In a five-node cluster, for example, only two nodes can fail before the cluster fails.
- **Node and Disk Majority** This configuration is recommended when your cluster has an even number of nodes. It consists of a quorum disk plus node majorities. So long as the disk stays online, the cluster can fail up to half its nodes and continue running. If the disk fails as well, then the cluster will behave like a Node Majority configuration only, failing when half minus one nodes fail.

- **Node and File Share Majority** This configuration is normally recommended for geographically dispersed clusters. This configuration is the same as Node and Disk Majority, except that the witness disk is replaced by a witness file share.
- **No Majority: Disk Only** This was the standard configuration of clusters prior to WS08. Microsoft does not recommend it anymore because the disk provides a single point of failure since it is the only witness for the cluster operation. On the other hand, this configuration can fail down to a single node before the cluster fails.

As you can see, there are several configurations. Since most people create two node clusters, the Node and Disk Majority is the recommended configuration for the quorum. In a two-disk configuration, the cluster can run with only one node available so long as the witness disk is available.

NOTE *The Node and Disk Majority configuration is the same as the No Majority: Disk Only configuration when it comes to a two-node cluster. If the disk fails, the entire cluster fails. But it does provide better support for the cluster as you add new nodes.*

As mentioned earlier, WSFCs require a shared storage system. Shared storage systems can be connected through SCSI, fibre channels, or iSCSI. SCSI systems are only supported in two-node clustering. Arbitrated loop fibre channel is also only supported for two-node clustering, but provides better scalability than SCSI systems because it can host up to 126 devices. Note that WS08 does not support clustering through parallel SCSI interfaces.

Switched fabric fibre channel and iSCSI can be used for clusters that include up to sixteen nodes. Here, devices are connected in a many-to-many topology that supports the high availability and complex configuration requirements of multiple-node server clusters. Each service running in a multinode cluster will require access to its own protected shared storage area. This is because while running a service, the cluster node requires exclusive access to the storage area the service uses to persist data. When a failover is initiated, the storage connection is released by the failing node and picked up by the failover node and the service continues to work. This is called a shared nothing cluster service, because a node running a given service requires exclusive access to the storage linked to the service. This means that when you configure your clusters, you must configure a reserved storage area for each service you intend to run on it (see Figure 11-8). Each time a node is running a given service, it is considered an active node. Each time a node has reserved space for a service but is not running it, it is considered a passive node. Nodes can be active and yet reserve space in passive mode for other service failovers.

As in the NLB cluster, server cluster nodes should have at least two NICs: one for communication within the cluster and one for communication with client systems and other network resources.

Geographically Dispersed Clusters

Windows Server 2008 supports the dispersion of clusters over multiple physical sites. This means that in addition to application or service resiliency, you can add disaster recovery through the WSFC service. If an entire site fails for some unforeseen reason, the cluster will continue to provide services to its client base because failover will occur in the other site or sites that contain cluster nodes. Geographically dispersed clusters are more particular than

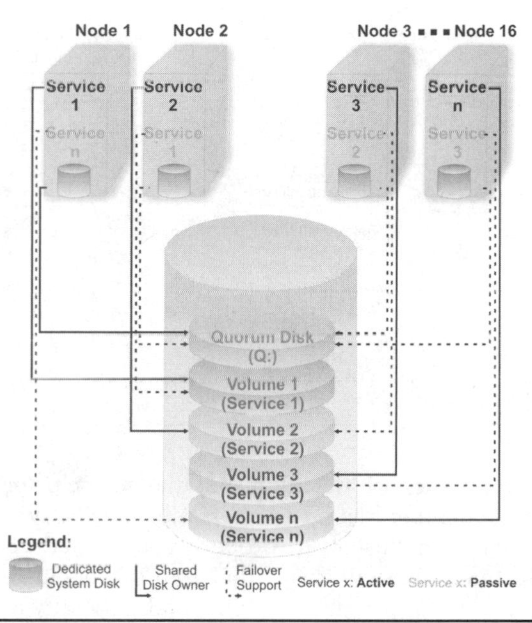

FIGURE 11-8 Assigning storage resources to clusters and relying on the Node and Disk majority quorum configuration

same-site clusters to configure because of the added difficulty of maintaining cluster consistency.

In fact, if you want to create a multisite cluster, you need to ensure that your WAN connection latency is as low as possible, though WS08 introduces the concept of the Witness File Share (WFS). A WFS is a separate file share that is often located in an independent site to provide an additional voting node during the failover process. During this process, each of the nodes wants to gain control of a service because it thinks the other node is not available. Through the WFS, the two nodes will be able to identify if the other has failed or not. Without the WFS, the nodes often both try to load the service, with sometimes catastrophic failures.

In addition, you need to configure a virtual local area network (VLAN) that regroups the multisite nodes, including the WFS. If you can't build low-latency WAN connections and you can't create a VLAN, including each site hosting a node, then you should not design multisite clusters.

When configuring multisite clusters, you need to use a new WS08 feature: majority node sets (MNS). Majority node sets are required because the multisite cluster cannot share data sets like the single-site cluster, since the nodes are not located in the same physical site. Therefore, the cluster service must be able to maintain and update cluster configuration data on each storage unit of the cluster. This is the function of the majority node set (see Figure 11-9).

Resource Pool Failover Cluster Considerations

Cluster server installation and deployment is not a simple task. It requires special hardware—hardware that is qualified to support Windows Server 2008 server clusters. For this reason, it will be essential for you to verify with the Windows Hardware Compatibility

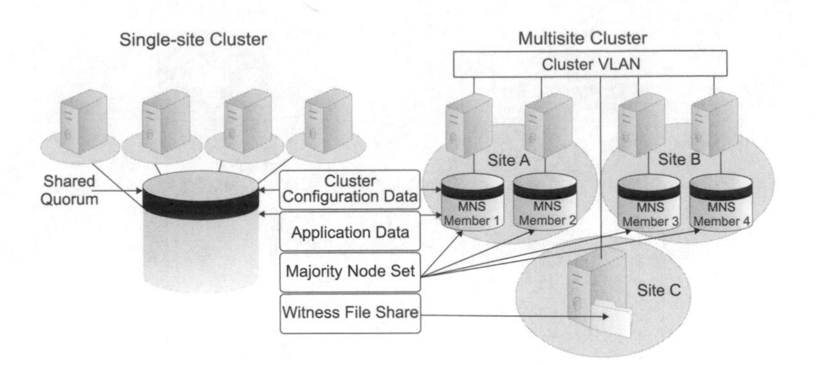

FIGURE 11-9 Single-versus multisite cluster configurations

List (www.microsoft.com/whdc/hcl/default.mspx) that your cluster hardware is fully compatible with WS08. Remember that host servers must be x64 systems. Then proceed with caution to ensure that your clusters are properly constructed. Ask for support from your hardware manufacturer. This will ensure that your server clusters take full advantage of both the hardware's and WS08's high-availability and reliability features.

In addition, you should take the following considerations into account:

- **Majority node clustering** WS08 supports only two-site majority node clustering. The WS08 majority node feature does not manage data replication for applications; this function must be available within the application itself. For example, Exchange 2007 includes the ability to run a geographic cluster. It is also important to note that majority node sets cannot survive for long periods of time with a single node; they need to have a majority of the nodes available to continue operating. Single quorum clusters can, on the other hand, survive with just one node because the quorum data is stored in a single location.
- **Clustering identity servers** It is not recommended to cluster domain controllers because of the nature of this service. For example, the Flexible Single Master of Operations roles cannot be failed over and may cause service outages if the hosting node fails. In addition, it is possible for the domain controller (DC) to become so busy that it will not respond to cluster requests. In this situation, the cluster will fail the DC because it will think it is no longer working. Do not cluster DCs.
- **Clustering resource pools** Resource pools can take advantage of both single quorum clusters and majority node sets. But since majority node sets are complicated to build and require highly specialized hardware, you may be best off running single quorum clusters to provide high availability for the VSOs running on the host servers. Then, if a total failure occurs at one site, you can bring up the secondary site's VSOs through a series of procedures or even automate it through scripts. Everything depends on your service level agreements for total site failures.

These are not the only considerations to take into account when creating and installing server clusters, but they provide a good reference and foundation before you begin. The best thing to do is to determine where failover clusters will help you most. Use the details in Tables 11-1 and 11-3 to help you make the appropriate clustering decisions.

The WS08 Failover Cluster Build Process

Like with the creation of NLB clusters, creating a WSFC must be performed in several steps. This process is the same for both resource pools and virtual service offerings.

1. Install the operating system (OS), secure it, and finalize the default setup process. Also join it to the domain.

NOTE *Cluster members must belong to an ADDS domain. Otherwise, you will not be able to build the cluster.*

2. Next, install the WSFC service and shut down the server. Do this for each of the cluster nodes.
3. Prepare the shared storage units.
4. Boot the first node to connect the shared storage and assign appropriate drive labels. Also configure the network interface cards. One card will link users to the cluster, and another will provide heartbeat traffic for the cluster. Configure each appropriately. You can also name them appropriately: "Public" for the public NIC and "Private" for the private NIC. Shut down the node.

TIP *Quorum or witness disks are often labeled as "Quorum," and data disks are often labeled as "SharedDisk" in two-node clusters. Correspondingly, the quorum drive is assigned letter Q:, and shared data disks are assigned letter S:. Use your judgment to properly name quorums and shared disks in your multinode clusters.*

5. Boot a second node, connect to shared storage, and assign appropriate drive labels. Repeat for any other node in your cluster. If you have more than two nodes, shut down each node after this operation.
6. Do not shut down the last node of your cluster. Instead, begin the construction of your cluster.

TIP *When building a cluster, you will need to assign a name and an IP address to it. The name should follow your standard server-naming convention, and the IP address should be a public static address in either IPv4 or IPv6 format.*

   Next, keep the first node of the cluster running, and boot another node. Use the cluster commands to add this node to the cluster. Repeat for each additional cluster node.

7. Configure services or applications on the cluster, and assign resources to them.

You need to follow this process closely; otherwise, your cluster will fail.

Build a WS08 Failover Cluster for Resource Pools

For resource pools, the activities required to install and create a WSFC are performed through the command line, since host servers run Server Core only. Use the steps provided earlier to build your WS08 failover cluster.

1. Begin by creating your Server Core installation. Use the procedures outlined in Chapter 4 to do so. Join the domain you created for your resource pool. Repeat for each node in the cluster.
2. Next, install the WSFC feature. Use the following command line to do so:

   ```
   start /w ocsetup FailoverCluster-Core
   ```

   You use the /w command to tell start to wait until the process is complete to return the prompt. Once the prompt is returned, you can verify if the feature is installed or not by using this command:

   ```
   oclist
   ```

   Shut down each node, and move on to the next task. Use the following command:

   ```
   shutdown /s /t 3
   ```

3. Prepare the storage units in your shared storage system. You will need to prepare at least three volumes in the storage unit. One small one, with about 1 gigabyte (GB) of space, is for the quorum or witness disk. The other will be a massive volume for storing virtual machine files. If you are going to host ten virtual service offerings on this unit, then allocate at least 200 GB per VSO—use the server-sizing exercise to determine exactly how much space you need. It is better to overallocate than to have to resize the volume right away. Next, prepare a third volume for the storage of volume shadow copies or storage snapshots. Repeat the creation of the last two volumes for each active node you intend to have in the cluster. Connect each volume to each node in the cluster.
4. Boot the first node of the cluster, and log on with domain administrator credentials.

CAUTION *Make sure the other nodes are shut off at this stage. Windows will try to contend for shared disks with other machines if the nodes are connected to each server while they are running.*

   a. Initialize the shared disks, format them, and assign appropriate drive letters. If you enabled the Virtual Disk Service (VDS), then you can perform this task remotely from a management machine; if not, use the following commands:

   ```
   diskpart
   list disk
   ```

   To identify the number of the disk to attach:

   ```
   select disk n
   clean
   create partition primary size=xxxxx align=64
   ```

Where *xxxxx* is the size in megabytes for the partition to create. For example, for a 200-GB disk, this value would be 200000. In addition, using the align parameter will ensure the disk is sector-aligned which should improve its performance by up to 20 percent.

```
select partition 1
active
format label=disklabel
```

Where *disklabel* is the label you want to assign to this disk.

```
assign letter=diskletter
```

Where *diskletter* is the drive letter you want to assign to the disk. The drive letter must not include a colon—for example, if you want to assign letter Q, simply type **Q**.

```
exit
```

Repeat for each volume you need to connect to.

b. Next, configure the network interface cards. Commands depend on whether you are using IPv4 or IPv6. Remember, one card will use a public address for user communications, and another will use a private address for internal cluster communications. For IPv4, use the same commands presented in Chapter 4. Begin by finding the ID of each interface and then assign appropriate addresses to them. Start with the public NIC:

```
netsh interface ipv4 show interfaces
netsh interface ipv4 set address name=ID source=static
address=staticIPAddress mask=SubnetMask gateway=DefaultGateway
netsh interface ipv4 add dnsserver name=ID address=FirstDNSIPAddres
s index=1
netsh interface ipv4 add dnsserver name=ID address=SecondDNSIPAddre
ss index=2
```

Next, configure the private NIC. Use the ID number discovered previously.

```
netsh interface ipv4 set address name=ID source=static
address=staticIPAddress mask=SubnetMask
```

NOTE *The private NIC does not use DNS servers or a gateway. Use an address from a private IPv4 range for this NIC.*

PART V

If you want to configure IPv6 addresses, use the same command. Begin by finding out the interface IDs and then assign addresses:

```
netsh interface ipv6 show interfaces
netsh interface ipv6 set address interface=ID address=IPv6Address
netsh interface ipv6 set dnsserver name=ID source=static
address=FirstDNSIPAddress register=both
netsh interface ipv6 set dnsserver name=ID source=static
address=SecondDNSIPAddress register=both
```

NOTE *Use an address from a private IPv6 range for the private NIC.*

Repeat for each public interface you want to configure.

c. Finally, shut down this server.

5. Boot the second node, and log on with domain administrator credentials.

a. Add the disks with appropriate drive letters. These should be the same as those assigned in the first node. Use the following commands:

```
diskpart
list disk
select disk n
select partition 1
assign letter=diskletter
exit
```

Repeat for each volume you need to add.

CAUTION *Do not format the disks again! If you reformat them, they will no longer work with the first node.*

b. Configure the NICs.

NOTE *If you have more nodes to add, shut down this node and repeat this operation for each node that is left. On the last node to add, leave the server running and proceed to the next step.*

6. Create the cluster on the last running node. This saves you at least one boot operation. Here, you need to create the cluster, name it, and assign its IP address, as well as select the quorum disk. Use the following command:

```
cluster /cluster:ClusterName /create /node:NodeName /ipaddr:IPAddress
```

Where *ClusterName* is the name of your cluster, *NodeName* is the name of the computer—usually in short notation format, for example, ServerOne—and *IPAddress* is the public IP address of the cluster in either IPv4 (xxx.xxx.xxx.xxx/yyy.yyy.yyy.yyy for the subnet) or IPv6 (xxxx:xxxx:xxxx:xxxx:xxxx:xxxx:xxxx:xxxx) format.

TIP *At this point, your cluster is created. You can continue to work with the command line to finalize the configuration of the cluster, but it is highly recommended that you move to your management virtual machine and finalize the operations from there. On the management machine, launch the Failover Cluster Management console, right-click Failover Cluster Management in the tree pane, and select Manage a Cluster. Type the name of your cluster, and then perform all of the final operations through this console.*

7. Add the other nodes. Boot each server in turn, and add them to the cluster. You do not need to log on to each server; simply add them through the console on the first server of the cluster. Go to the Nodes section of the tree pane, right-click, and select Add Node. Add each of the nodes in the cluster, and continue on through the wizard. You can choose to validate the configuration. Since you could not validate the configuration as easily through the command line, it might be a good idea to do it here.

8. Next, verify the quorum disk. If it is not right, change it. To do so, right-click the cluster name in the tree pane, and select More Actions | Configure Cluster Quorum Settings. The best selection is Node and Disk Majority, unless you are constructing a geographically dispersed cluster (see Figure 11-10). Run through the wizard, selecting your prepared quorum disk as the witness disk. Your cluster is ready for operation.
9. Now you can configure services or applications to run on the cluster. In this particular case, you want to run virtualization support. Right-click the Services and Applications node, and select Configure A Service Or Application. In this case, you need to use a generic script resource as well as physical disk resources. The generic script manages the shutdown and restart of the VSOs as they are moved from one node to the other. In fact, this script places the virtual machines in saved state and restores them on the other node. The physical disk resource hosts the VHDs that make up your VSOs.
10. Test failover for your new clustered service. To do so, right-click the generic script resource and select Failover. The script should run and the resources should be moved to another node in the cluster.

Your Server Core cluster is ready.

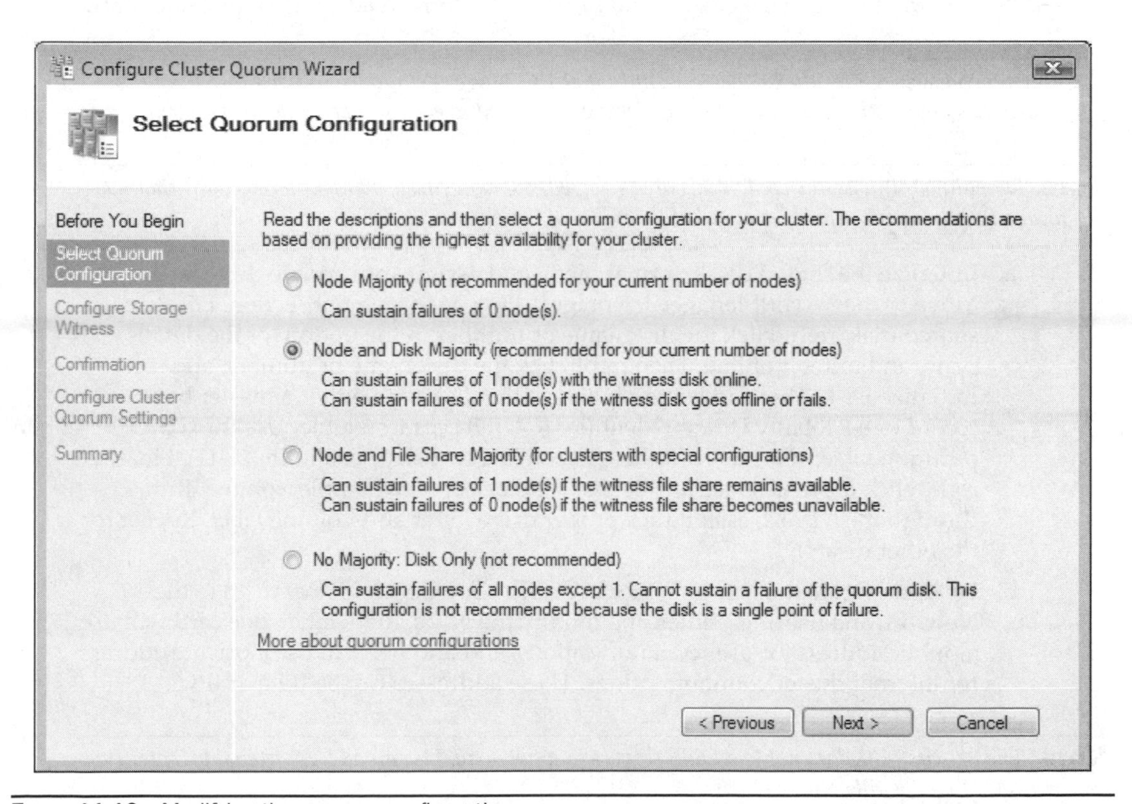

Figure 11-10 Modifying the quorum configuration

Build a WS08 Failover Cluster for Virtual Service Offerings

The advantage of working with VSOs is that you can rely on the graphical interface to build a failover cluster. As you'll see, it is easier and less prone to error.

1. Begin by creating your VSO installation. Remember, this should be based on the full installation of WS08. Use the procedures outlined in Chapter 4 to do so. Join the production VSO domain. Repeat for each node in the cluster. Next, install the WSFC feature. Use Add Feature command in the Server Manager | Features section. Once the operation is complete, verify that the feature is installed in the same section of Server Manager. Repeat for each node. Shut down each node when done.
2. Prepare the virtual disks that will be required for the cluster. You will need to prepare at least three volumes. One small one, with about 1 GB of space, is for the quorum or witness disk. The other will be a larger volume for storing data files. This should be the largest of the three disks. If you are going to run a service, such as file shares, print shares, or databases, then create a third disk to store log files or shadow copies. It is always better to overallocate than to have to resize the volumes right away. Repeat the creation of the last two volumes for each active node you intend to have in the cluster. Connect each volume to each node in the cluster.
3. Boot the first node of the cluster, and log on with domain administrator credentials.

CAUTION *Make sure the other nodes are shut off at this stage. Windows will try to contend for shared disks with other machines if the nodes are connected to each server while they are running.*

NOTE *Domain administrator credentials are preferred, but you can use any other account that has local administrative privileges on all of the nodes of the cluster.*

   a. Initialize the shared disks, format them, and assign appropriate drive letters. Move to the Server Manager | Storage | Disk Management section. Locate each shared disk, right-click the disk name or number in the bottom of the details pane, and bring it online. Then right-click the disk name or number, and select Initialize Disk. This will let you initialize the disk with either a master boot record or a Globally Unique Identifier (GUID) partition table. Use the GUID partition table, since it works better with larger disks (see Figure 11-11). Finally, right-click the disk space for the disk, and select New Simple Volume. Run through the wizard, assigning a proper drive letter and volume label. Repeat for the other disk(s).

   b. Next, configure the network interface cards. Use Control Panel to go to the Network and Sharing Center, and modify the NICs. Remember, one card will use a public address for user communications, and another will use a private address for internal cluster communications. These addresses can be IPv4 or IPv6.

NOTE *The private NIC does not use DNS servers or a gateway. Use an address from a private IPv4 or IPv6 range for this NIC.*

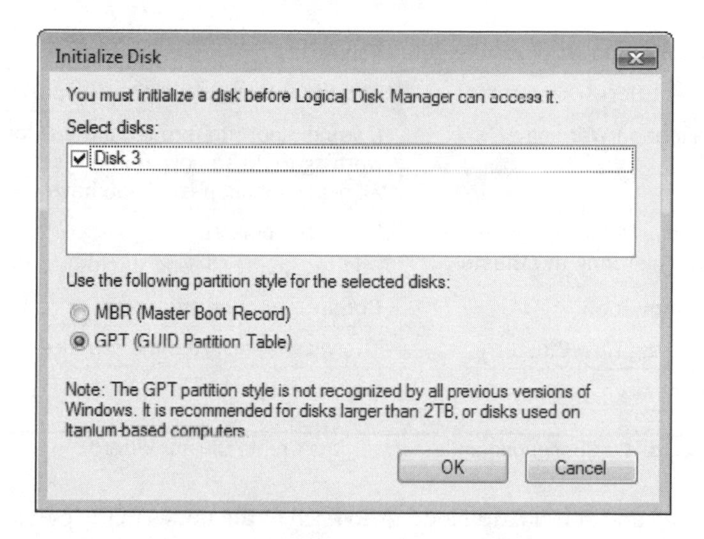
Initialize Disk
You must initialize a disk before Logical Disk Manager can access it.
Select disks:
Disk 3
Use the following partition style for the selected disks:
MBR (Master Boot Record)
GPT (GUID Partition Table)
Note: The GPT partition style is not recognized by all previous versions of Windows. It is recommended for disks larger than 2TB, or disks used on Itanium-based computers.
OK
Cancel

FIGURE 11-11 Initializing a disk with a GUID partition table

Only one private NIC is required, but you can run multiple public NICs in the cluster. If you do so, configure each one with a public address.

c. Shut down this server.

4. Boot the second node, and log on with domain administrator credentials.
   a. Add the disks with appropriate drive letters. These should be the same as those assigned in the first node. First bring the disk online; then use the Change Drive Letter And Path command to assign the appropriate letter. Repeat for each volume you need to configure.

CAUTION *Do not format the disks again! If you reformat them, they will no longer work with the first node.*

   b. Configure the NICs.

NOTE *If you have more nodes to add, shut down this node and repeat this operation for each node that is left. On the last node to add, leave the server running and proceed to the next step.*

5. Create the cluster on the last running node. This saves you at least one boot operation. Here you need to create the cluster, name it, and assign its IP address, as well as select the quorum disk.
   a. Use the Start menu | Administrative Tools | Failover Clusters Manager Console to do so.
   b. Click Create A Cluster in the details or action pane.
   c. Use the values in Table 11-4 to run through this wizard.
6. Next, add the other nodes. Boot each server in turn, and add them to the cluster. You do not need to log on to each server; simply add them through the console on the first server of the cluster. Go to the Nodes section of the tree pane, right-click,

Create Cluster Wizard Page	Value
Select Servers	Add the running server to this page.
Validation Warning	If you did not run through the Validation Wizard, you will get a warning to do so now. Run all tests and confirm your selection. All tests should pass if you have configured this node correctly.
Access Point for Administering the Cluster	Name the cluster. Add the cluster IP address(es) to the public network.
Confirmation	Confirm your choices.
Creating New Cluster	The wizard performs the creation operation.
Summary	View the report or click Finish.

TABLE 11-4 Configuring a Cluster with the Create Cluster Wizard

and select Add Node. Add each of the nodes in the cluster, and continue on through the wizard. You can choose to validate the configuration or not. If you already validated the first node's configuration and it passed and you performed all of the preparation activities properly, you can probably skip validation.

7. Next, verify the quorum disk. If it is not right, then change it. To do so, right-click the cluster name in the tree pane, and select More Actions | Configure Cluster Quorum Settings. The best selection is Node and Disk Majority, unless you are constructing a geographically dispersed cluster. Run through the wizard, selecting your prepared quorum disk as the witness disk.
8. Now you can configure services or applications to run on the cluster. All services and applications will require a physical disk resource. Services are configured through the Services and Applications section of the tree pane, through the Configure a Service or Application command. Applications such as Exchange or SQL Server usually require an actual installation onto cluster nodes once the cluster is configured. Use the appropriate approach to configure the service or application you want to run on this cluster.
9. Test failover for your new clustered service or application. To do so, right-click the service or application, and select Failover. The resources should be moved to another node in the cluster.
10. Make sure you document the configuration and purpose of this cluster, as you will most likely have several VSO clusters.

Your cluster is ready.

Further Server Consolidation

With its built-in virtualization capabilities for both hosts and guests, Windows Server 2008 offers some exceptional opportunities for server consolidation. This leads to fewer servers to manage and fewer resources to secure. These servers, though, have a more complex structure because they include more services than the single-purpose server model used in the NT world.

But server consolidation does not necessarily mean a more complex server structure; it can just mean more with less. For example, Microsoft has tested two-node server clusters that manage upwards of 3,000 printers. This means that you could greatly reduce the number of print servers in your organization, especially in large office situations, where network connections are high-speed and printer management can be centralized. And especially with Vista clients, where print rendering is performed locally before being sent to the server, server workloads are even lower.

The same goes for file servers. The same WS08 server can manage up to 5,000 domain DFS roots. A server cluster can manage up to 50,000 stand-alone DFS roots—another opportunity for massive server consolidation.

Internet Information Server (IIS) also offers great consolidation opportunities because of its architecture. Microsoft introduced Worker Process Isolation in IIS 6, meaning that any hosted web site could operate completely independently from all of the others. Though it was available, this isolation process—a process dependent on the use of special application pools for each service—was not very user-friendly. Now, with IIS 7, this process is automatic. When a new site is created in IIS 7, a corresponding application pool of the same name is created automatically. By default, each application pool will be isolated from all other application pools, letting you run many more web sites on the same IIS server than ever before.

This isolation allows the creation and operation of Web gardens, special affinity groups that can be assigned to specific server resources, such as central processing units (CPUs) and memory. The Web garden concept ensures that critical web sites get the resources they need even if they share server hardware. This again provides an excellent opportunity for consolidation.

This means that you can look to further server consolidation by sharing workloads on each of the VSOs you run. When thinking of creating a new server, first look to the possibility of sharing that workload on an existing server. This will greatly reduce the number of servers you need to manage in the long term.

Recovery Planning for Your Network

Even though you have done your best to ensure high availability for your servers and services, disasters can always happen and servers can always go down. This is why it is important to prepare for system recovery. No system is perfect, but the more protection levels you apply to your systems, the less chance you have of losing data and experiencing downtime. Therefore, you need to implement additional data protection strategies.

Backing up and restoring WS08 data is a complex process, but it has been greatly simplified by new WS08 features, such as the Volume Shadow Copy. In fact, the built-in Backup tool automatically initiates a shadow copy before taking a backup. Backups are an important part of the recovery operation, but they are not its only component. WS08 offers several different recovery strategies. Some of these will be familiar to you if you've worked with previous versions of Windows, but WS08 also includes new features that are specific to this operating system.

Recovering systems is never an easy task. The best way to avoid having to recover systems is by using a multilayered protection strategy. But if you do get to the stage where a recovery operation is required, you must have a detailed strategy to follow. Like every other operation in the VSO network, recoveries must be planned. Your recovery strategy must begin with an understanding of the operating system's own recovery capabilities. Next, once you're familiar with the tools the operating system offers to help you recover systems, you can outline or adjust your recovery strategy. Finally, you can integrate your troubleshooting strategy with the new or updated recovery strategy.

Recovery Strategies for Windows Server 2008

Recovery strategies for WS08 depend, of course, on the type of problem you encounter, but they include:

- **Driver rollback** If you install an unstable driver on your system, you can use the driver rollback feature to restore the previous version of a driver, so long as you can still log into your system. This is done by viewing the device properties in the Device Manager (Server Manager | Diagnostics | Device Manager), moving to the Driver tab, and selecting Roll Back Driver.
- **Disabling devices** You can also disable devices that are not operating properly. Once again, this is done by moving to the Device Manager, locating the device, right-clicking it, and selecting Disable from the context menu.
- **Last Known Good Configuration** Just like previous versions of Windows, WS08 includes a Last Known Good Configuration startup choice. This reverts to the last configuration saved in the registry before you applied changes. You can access this option by pressing the F8 key during system startup. This will also give you access to a number of different startup modes: Safe Mode, Safe Mode with Networking, and so on. These are also operation modes you can use to repair WS08 installations.
- **Windows Recovery Environment (WinRE)** In Chapter 4, you installed WinRE as part of your standard WS08 server staging process. This console allows you to perform recovery operations, such as disabling services, copying device drivers or other files to the system, and otherwise repairing an installation. Installing the console saves you from requiring the Windows Server 2008 original installation media to perform a repair because it is listed as an operating system in your startup choices.
- **Windows PE** Chapter 4 also outlined how to use Windows PE to create a bootable device that will boot into a character-based Windows environment. This is also an excellent recovery tool, because Windows PE will give you access to both network drives and local New Technology File System (NTFS) drives during your repair process.
- **Volume Shadow Copy** Users and administrators can restore any data file that is still available within the shadow copy store through the Previous Versions tab of the file's properties. Administrators can even use this feature to recover entire VSOs.
- **DFS replication** VSOs are especially easy to recover because they are replicated to other locations during their operation. If one fails, you simply launch the other copy.
- **Windows Server Backup (WSB)** Using the default backup tool included within Windows Server 2008, you can back up and restore data to removable medium or to spare disk drives. You can also back up entire systems to virtual hard drive images for complete system protection.
- **Third-party backup and restore tools** If you find that Windows Server Backup is not enough, there are a number of different third-party tools you can choose from.

When selecting a third-party product, there are three key elements you must consider: integration with the Volume Shadow Copy APIs to take advantage of this feature, complete system recovery from bootable media, and integration with Active Directory Domain Services.

Several of these strategies have already been covered. Recovery strategies are discussed in the sections that follow.

System Recovery Strategies

A recovery strategy is based on the following activities:

- Service interruption is detected.
- Interruption has been categorized through a standard troubleshooting strategy.
- Risk has been evaluated and has identified the required level of response.
- The recovery plan for this level of risk is put into action.
- There is always a "Plan B" in case the main recovery plan does not work for some reason.
- The results of recovery actions are fully tested to ensure everything is back to normal.
- Secondary recovery actions are performed; for example, broken servers that were taken offline are repaired, or users are notified that their files are back online.
- The incident is documented and procedures are updated, if required.

It is important to detail the actual recovery plan for each type of situation. This is one reason why risk evaluation is so important. You may not have time to document recovery processes for every single disaster situation, but if you have taken the time to evaluate risks, you can ensure that the most critical situations are documented. In the end, you will have multiple recovery plans that will "plug into" your recovery strategy. All of these should be standard operating procedures (SOPs).

In order to support your recovery plan, you'll also need:

- An offsite copy of the plan to protect the plan itself
- Spare hardware components onsite
- Reliable and tested data backups
- Distanced, offsite storage for rotated backup media
- Available resources to perform systems recovery

In addition, you need to have either the eighth server role—the failsafe server—or a hot site—a separate site that mirrors your production site and that can take over in the case of a disaster. As you know, with resource pools, this secondary site is really easy to set up.

Troubleshooting Techniques

The final element of the system recovery process is a sound troubleshooting strategy. This is the strategy your operations staff will use to identify the type of disaster they are facing. It is essential that this strategy be clear and be, once again, standard because it is critical to the recovery process. If the issue you are facing is wrongly identified, it may cause a worse disaster. This strategy applies to both resource pools and virtual service offerings.

In general, help requests and problem reports should be dealt with through an organized/scientific approach that treats system errors as always being causal; that is, problems don't just happen—they are deviations from a norm that have distinct, identifiable causes. The troubleshooting technician's job is to logically deduce causes of problems based on his or her knowledge of how the system works. The best way to do this is to use a standard procedure.

These steps outline a standard troubleshooting procedure:

1. Document appropriate information: for example, the time, date, machine, and user information.
2. Document all relevant information concerning the problem. Refer to baseline system operation information if necessary.
3. Create an itemized problem description. Answer these questions:
   a. Is the problem reliably reproducible or random?
   b. Is it related to the time of day?
   c. Is the problem user-specific?
   d. Is it platform-specific?
   e. Is it version-specific?
   f. Is it related to hard disk free space?
   g. Is it network traffic-related?
   h. What is it not?
4. Research similar occurrences in your internal troubleshooting databases. Review the Windows Server 2008 Help system, if it is available. Also, review external troubleshooting databases such as Microsoft TechNet (http://technet.microsoft.com) and the Microsoft Knowledge Base (http://support.microsoft.com). It is also a good idea to draw on the expertise of your coworkers.
5. Create a reasonable hypothesis based on all of the available information.
6. Test the hypothesis and document the results.
7. If the test successfully cures the problem, document and close the case. If unsuccessful, modify the hypothesis or, if necessary, create a new hypothesis. Repeat the hypothesize-then-test cycle until the issue is resolved.

Note that complex problems (more than one cause-effect relationship) may require several iterations of steps 2 through 7.

Categorize Issues for Resource Pools and VSOs

One of the important aspects of troubleshooting is problem classification. It is often helpful to categorize errors according to the circumstances surrounding the occurrence. Table 11-5 includes a non-exhaustive list of problem classes.

As you can see, your troubleshooting procedure is not only used in disasters. It can be used in all troubleshooting situations. But for disasters, the key to the troubleshooting and

Problem Classes	Key Characteristics
Resource Pools Only	
Peripherals	Keyboard, video display, hardware components, drivers
Network	Adapter configuration, traffic, cabling, transmission devices
Resource Pools and Virtual Service Offerings	
Installation	Procedure, media, hardware/software requirements, network errors
Bootstrap	Missing files, hardware failures, boot menu
Security	File encryption, access rights, permissions
Service Startup	Dependent services, configuration
Application	Application-specific errors
Virtual Service Offerings Only	
Logon	User accounts, validating server, registry configuration, network access
User Configuration	Redirected folders, user profiles, group memberships
Procedural	User education, control

TABLE 11-5 Sample Problem Classifications

recovery strategy is the quality of your backups. This is why the backup strategy is one of the most important elements of your system resiliency design.

Data Protection Strategies for Resource Pools

Backing up host servers means backing up three different types of objects:

- **Operating system** The partition that makes up drive C: and runs the host server.
- **Data partitions** The data drive that contains the virtual service offerings.
- **Virtual machine contents** The contents of the virtual service offerings must also be backed up. More on this is discussed in the next section.

Host servers are the simplest kind of server because they only run one major role: virtualization. If you set up your infrastructure right, backing these machines up will be relatively easy. As discussed previously, the ideal infrastructure for host servers is that of a blade server connected to shared storage. Ideally, each and every drive that makes up the server will be hosted within the shared storage infrastructure. This provides several levels of defense against data or system loss:

- Each partition can either rely on the Volume Shadow Copy service or the internal snapshot tool provided with the storage unit to provide a first line of defense.
- The second line of defense is provided by the volume shadow copy of the virtual machines located on the data drive.
- A third line of defense is provided through DFS replication of the files that make up each of the VSOs.

- A fourth line of defense is provided through failover clustering.
- The last line of defense is provided through backups of the disks that make up each host system.

CAUTION *You will need to add another disk partition to each host server or connect to a network drive in order to perform backups through Windows Server Backup. WSB does not support backup to tape.*

TIP *Our recommendation: Obtain a third-party backup tool, since you will want comprehensive backup support for the host servers. Good examples are Symantec BackupExec (www.symantec.com/backupexec/index.jsp), CommVault Galaxy (http://commvault.com/products/data_protection.asp), or Acronis True Image Echo (www.acronis.com/enterprise/products/ATIES/).*

Set up your schedules to protect systems on an ongoing basis. Though you can't do this with WSB, you should perform full backups once a week and then follow with differential backups every day, if your product supports them. Differential backups take up more space than incremental backups, but they are easier to recover from because they include all of the changes since the full backup. In a recovery situation, you only need the most recent full backup and the most recent differential to restore the system.

If you do decide to perform host system backups from WSB, then use the following command line. It performs a full system backup once a day at 6:00 P.M. to a disk partition.

```
wbadmin enable backup addtarget:DiskID schedule:18:00 user:Username password:Password
```

Where *DiskID* is the ID number of the disk to back up to; use the `DISKPART` command to identify the disk ID. *Username* and *Password* should belong to a service account with local administration rights on the host server.

NOTE *Destination drives should be reserved exclusively for backup purposes because all other data will be erased.*

System State Restores

In previous versions of Windows, you could perform a system state backup. This backup recorded only specific system components instead of a full disk image. In Windows Server 2008, you can no longer perform a system state backup, but you can perform a system state restore, repairing a broken server.

There are nine potential elements to a system state restore. Some are always backed up, and others depend on the type of server you are backing up. They are identified as follows:

- The system registry
- The COM+ class registry database
- Boot and system files
- Windows file protection system files
- Active Directory database (on domain controllers)
- SYSVOL directory (on DCs as well)

- Certificate services database (on certificate servers)
- Cluster service configuration information (on failover clusters)
- IIS metadirectory (on Web application servers)

System state data is always restored as a whole; it cannot be segregated. To perform a system state recovery from the command line, rely on the following command:

```
wbadmin start sysstaterecovery
```

Typing the command will provide you with available options. Most often, you will want to map a network drive previous to the restore in order to link to a working backup.

Data Protection Strategies for Virtual Service Offerings

Backing up your virtual service offerings will mean backing up several types of information: user data, corporate data, databases, documents, system state information for your servers, and Active Directory data. As mentioned earlier, you can use either WS08 Backup or a third-party backup tool to perform these backups. Whichever one you use, make sure that you will use a standard backup strategy, creating backup sets of specific data types—for example, creating only user data backups in one backup set and only system data in another. This will simplify the restoration process.

Data backups are rather straightforward; select the data drive and back it up. Remember that WS08 will automatically create a shadow copy before backing up the data. In fact, the backup set is created from shadow copy data. This avoids issues with open files. Shadow copy also has special APIs that enable it to work with databases such as SQL Server and Exchange Server, making the snapshots valid even for databases.

Basically, you should backup data and operating systems on a daily basis. Perform a full backup once a week and then rely on differentials.

NOTE *Windows Server Backup is not compatible with NTBackup, the backup tool from previous versions of Windows. If you have data stored in an NTBackup and you want to restore it to a WS08 server, then download NTBackup from Microsoft at http://go.microsoft.com/fwlink/?LinkId=82917.*

You need to support your backup strategy with both a remote storage solution and offsite media storage. Remember that you will need a third-party backup tool if you want to back up to tape. You will need to ensure that you have a safe offline storage space for media. You should rotate offsite media on a regular basis. For example, every second complete backup should be stored offsite in a controlled environment.

A common schedule relies on a four-week retention strategy. This means that you retain backup media for a period of four weeks. If you keep every second copy offsite, then you are always only a week away from complete disaster. In addition, your archiving schedule will outline which copies you should keep offsite on a permanent basis.

NOTE *If you are using DFSR to replicate all VSOs to a remote site, you may not need this particular policy, since you already have offsite copies of all of the virtual machines and Windows Server Hyper-V lets you mount VHDs in an offline mode, letting you recover any data file you need from the mounted virtual hard drive.*

Select a Third-Party Backup Tool

One of the most important aspects of the selection of a third-party backup tool is its awareness of the components that make a server operate. Many backup tools, especially backup tools that are designed to back up Windows data and store it on central, mainframe servers are "dump" backup tools; all they do is copy a file from the Windows server to a central location. When you choose a backup tool, make sure it is Windows Server–aware.

There are a number of third-party backup solutions on the market that are specifically designed for Windows Server 2008. They all meet specific criteria, which must include:

- Being aware of system state data
- Being integrated with the Volume Shadow Copy service, triggering a shadow copy before launching a backup operation
- Enabling complete system recovery from a simple process
- Being Active Directory–aware

Meeting these four basic criteria is essential. There are other criteria, of course, such as integrating with massive storage products that are supported by Windows, including special drivers for SQL Server and Exchange, and so on; but the four listed here are the core requirements for an intelligent, third-party backup solution.

Authoritative Active Directory Domain Services Restores

One of the most significant issues with WSB and WS08 in general in terms of backup, and especially restoration, is Active Directory Domain Services. ADDS is a complex database. Often, the best way to restore a downed domain controller is to rebuild the DC to a certain level and then let multimaster replication take over to bring the server up to date. The impact of this recovery strategy is that it taxes the network, especially if the DC is a regional server. It all depends on the level to which you rebuild the server and the obsolescence of the data it contains.

Fortunately, WS08 lets you stage DCs with offline media. This means that you can create an ADDS database backup on removable media and use it to stage or restore DCs. The more recent the media, the less replication is required. Recoveries of this type are not too complex. These recoveries assume that the data within the other replicas of the directory database is authoritative—it is valid data. It also means that there was no critical and unreplicated data within the downed DC.

Issues arise when there is critical data within a downed DC, data that is not within the other replicas, or when an error occurs and data within the directory is damaged and must be restored. In this case, you must perform an authoritative restore. This is where you begin to find the limitations of WSB.

Active Directory Domain Services manages directory replication through the update sequence number (USN). USNs can be thought of as change counters and represent the number of modifications on a domain controller since the last replication. Values for objects and properties that have the highest USN are replicated to other domain controllers and replace the values that are in the copies of the directory database located on the target DCs. USNs are also used to manage replication conflicts. If two domain controllers have the same USN, then a timestamp is used to determine the latest change. When you perform a normal ADDS restore, data that is restored from backup is updated according to the information in other domain controllers; in fact, it is overwritten if the USN for the data in other DCs is higher than the USN for the data in the restored DC.

When you need to restore data from a crashed DC that included critical data—data that is not found in the current version of the directory (for example, someone deleted an entire OU and it has been replicated to all DCs), you need to perform an authoritative restore. In this restore, the information you will recover from backup will take precedence over the information in the directory, even if the USNs are of a lower value.

To perform an authoritative restore, you must begin with a normal restore. Then, once the data is restored and the domain controller is still offline, you use the NTDSUTIL tool to make the restore authoritative. The authoritative restore can include all or just a portion of the restored Active Directory Domain Services data.

As you can see, restoring information that can be deleted from a simple operator error can be quite complex. This is one of the key reasons why you would consider using a comprehensive backup technology, a technology that is specifically designed to integrate and support all of Windows Server 2008's features.

TIP *When you delete an object in ADDS, it is moved to the tombstone container—a special system container that you cannot normally access. It is normally held in this space for the tombstone period, which can range from 60 days to much longer, depending on your configuration. Unfortunately, the default WS08 tools do not give you access to this tombstone data. You can, however, rely on free third-party utilities to open the tombstone container and restore the information it contains. This is much easier than performing a restore from backup, authoritative or not. Quest Software offers a free copy of Object Restore for Active Directory at www.quest.com/object-restore-for-active-directory. Use it. It is worth its weight in gold, and when combined with WS08's automatic object protection from deletion, can provide a powerful restoration strategy for ADDS.*

Physical to Virtual Conversions

Another important aspect of the dynamic datacenter is physical to virtual conversions (P2V). The key to moving to the dynamic datacenter is to perform these conversions, transforming all user-facing services to virtual service offerings. There are several ways to do this and as has been discussed throughout this book, converting an existing machine to a virtual instance and then migrating its services to a new installation of Windows Server 2008 is one of the best. But, as you consider your data protection strategies, you should also consider the benefits of integrating the backup tool you select with the ability to convert machines from one state to another.

Physical to virtual conversions are usually very straightforward: point to a physical server and transform it to a virtual machine. Of course, the tool you use to P2V must support the transformation of the drivers that were included in the physical installation of the operating system to those required for the virtual machine engine or hypervisor you are relying on. This is usually the most difficult aspect of a conversion.

Another important requirement for the dynamic datacenter is the ability to perform reverse conversions, instead of going from physical to virtual, you go from virtual to physical. While the need for these reverse conversions will disappear with time, it may still be a necessity in the early stages of your dynamic datacenter implementation. This is because some vendors may not be willing to support their applications on virtual machines and may require you to transform a virtual installation into a physical one when problems arise with the application. For example, Microsoft offers a support strategy for virtual workloads on a 'best effort basis' and in some situations may require you to convert a virtual instance of their OS into a physical instance to see if the problem or issue you are facing can be reproduced in the physical world.

NOTE *Microsoft's support policy is documented in Knowledge Base article number 897615 at http://support.microsoft.com/kb/897615.*

Because of this, you may need a tool that can not only perform P2V conversions, but also V2P conversions. Then, perhaps the best strategy you can use is to combine the requirements for backup and restore with the requirements for machine conversions. Ideally, you can use a tool that backs up any machine—physical or virtual—then stores this backup in a central location. In this case, disk image backups are often the best. When the time comes to restore the machine, then you can move the image from this central backup location to any potential target, once again physical or virtual. The key feature you need to identify is the ability to update OS drivers when the restoration process is run. Many such tools will be able to point to a central driver store to first obtain them, and then inject them into the image as it is being restored (see Figure 11-12). From then on, this tool will continue to support backups, restores and conversions from any machine whether it be in the resource pool or in the virtual service offerings.

Several tools on the market offer support for this. Look to disk imaging vendors such as Acronis who offers the True Image line of products or Symantec who offers the Ghost line of products to evaluate the best tool for your needs.

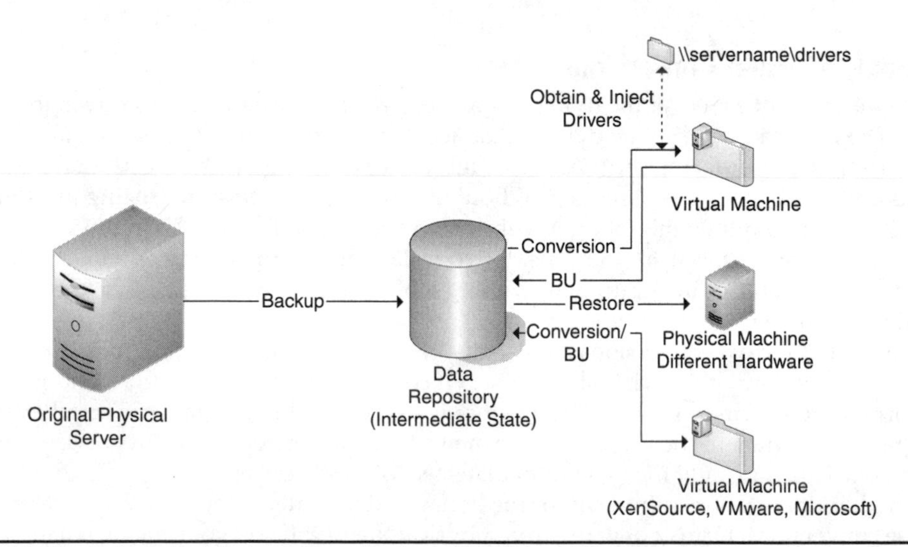

FIGURE 11-12 Using a tool that combines backup with P2V or V2P conversions

Finalize Your Resiliency Strategy

Choosing the right data protection technology is a core element of your resiliency strategy, but as you have seen here, it is not the only element. You need to design and implement the proper processes and ensure they are followed. This is an excellent opportunity for the design of standard operating procedures.

In addition, you must ensure that your data protection strategies complement your system redundancy strategies. One of the key elements of the former is integrated and regular testing: Your backup tapes or other media must be tested on a regular basis. Too many organizations have performed backups for extended periods of time and made the fatal mistake of never testing them or testing them only at the implementation phase of the solution and foregoing tests after that. Don't make this mistake!

Resiliency is at the core of any network. It is also the final preparation stage of the parallel network. Now your network is ready to provide complete services to your organization. Two key elements have yet to be covered before the parallel network is fully operational:

- The migration of both users and data into the parallel network, as well as the decommission of the legacy network.
- The modification of operational roles within your IT organization to cover new and sometimes integrated administrative activities for the new network.

Both elements are covered in the next chapter.

VI

PART

Migrate to Windows Server 2008

This section deals with moving to the new Windows Server 2008 infrastructure you prepared in the parallel network for virtual service offerings. All systems are go, and now you need to move all of the content from the legacy network to the new parallel network. This means performing the actual migration, as well as preparing your support and operational staff to work in the new environment.

CHAPTER 12

Put the VSO Network into Production

The final technical preparations for the parallel network for virtual service offerings (VSOs) are now done. It is almost ready to go online. Now you need to migrate all users, PCs, data, and services to the parallel network and decommission the legacy environment. It is at the end of this operation that you will have completed your migration to Windows Server 2008 (WS08). You will then move on to the operation of the new network. It is at this stage that you will discover that there are changes in the way you need to administer and operate a native WS08 network.

As you performed all of the operations outlined in the previous chapters, you noticed that several traditional IT tasks have been modified and that new tasks have been added to the operational roster. As you prepare to place the parallel network online and complete the user migration from the legacy network, you realize that there is one final activity you must perform. It is the review of administrative and operational roles within your enterprise network. Once this review is done, your network will be ready for prime time.

These changes will be discussed here. Chapter 13 will take a close look at the administration of Windows Server 2008 networks, outlining specific tasks and how you perform them. But before you get there, you need to populate your new VSO network.

Considerations for the Migration to the Parallel VSO Network

Remember that when you migrate services from your existing network to the parallel VSO network you must perform some form of server rotation. When you select a service to migrate, you should prepare the new virtual servers that will host this service first and ensure that you have a fallback solution in case of service failure. This is the advantage of the parallel VSO network: The legacy network is always available for service fallback if you need it. But if you've done your homework right, you won't. Throughout the process so far, you've carefully prepared native services in WS08 mode, running the latest and greatest features of this powerful operating system (OS). In addition, you've implemented business continuity solutions both for the resource pool and the virtual service offerings to make sure they are always running and always available.

In your considerations for the migration to the parallel VSO network, you'll want to think about the following:

- **The server rotation process** This process will be used to rotate and recover hardware as much as possible as you move to the new network.
- **The migration order** The order in which you will migrate services to the new network.

Both need to be addressed before you can move on.

The Server Rotation Process (Resource Pools)

Chapter 6 introduced the concept of server rotation during the migration of services to VSOs (see Figure 12-1). In the past, this process was relatively simple because you were moving from hardware server to hardware server, but in this case, it is different because hardware and services are now divided into two different infrastructures. Ideally, only 64-bit hardware will be reused and moved to the resource pool, but in most cases, organizations will not be using only 64-bit servers in their legacy network. This means that now is the ideal time to perform a serious server consolidation effort and rationalize as many of these devices as possible.

Keep the following in mind as you move through the server rotation process:

- Get rid of anything beige. Beige servers are usually stand-alone systems that use older hardware architectures, which use a lot of power and generate a ton of heat. If you can, get rid of them all.

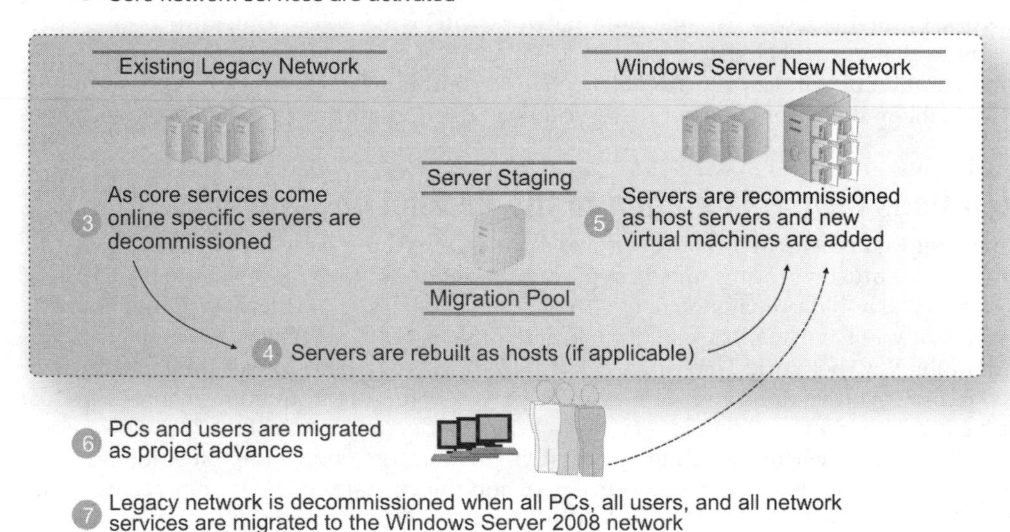
1 Core host servers are formed from new acquisitions
2 Core of new network is built with virtual machines
Core network services are activated
Existing Legacy Network
Windows Server New Network
Server Staging
3 As core services come online specific servers are decommissioned
5 Servers are recommissioned as host servers and new virtual machines are added
Migration Pool
4 Servers are rebuilt as hosts (if applicable)
6 PCs and users are migrated as project advances
7 Legacy network is decommissioned when all PCs, all users, and all network services are migrated to the Windows Server 2008 network

FIGURE 12-1 The server rotation process

- Recommission anything that is based on x64 hardware. Ideally, these will be rack-mounted or, even better, blade servers you can easily hook up to shared storage. The most important consideration for x64 server re-commissioning as host servers is the nature of the processor(s) it contains. In order to profit from x64 virtualization, the processors must be either Intel VT-enabled processors or AMD-V processors that offer integrated virtualization support.
- Recommission anything that is a recent acquisition. Even if you recommission some 32-bit systems, you can still run virtualization hosting services on them. You just have to run Microsoft Virtual Server (www.microsoft.com/windowsserversystem/virtualserver) instead of Windows Server Hyper-V. And you have to make sure you do so on a full installation of WS08, not Server Core, because Virtual Server requires components of Internet Information Services (IIS) that are not available on Server Core. Use these systems for lower-priority virtual workloads in production. Even better, move them to run testing or development environments in your laboratories. Note that if you deploy Virtual Server through System Center Virtual Machine Manager, you will not need IIS on the system.
- Acquire new hardware when possible. If you have a leasing program, perhaps you can exchange your 32-bit systems for new 64-bit systems, especially the server-in-a-box systems you will need for remote offices.

TIP *For example, cabinet manufacturer Kell Systems offers small-footprint portable server casings that are ideal for the server-in-a-box concept. Find out more at www.kellsystems.com.*

- Make sure you dispose of your unused servers in a proper manner. Several commercial organizations make a business of green server disposal. Look them up on the Internet.
- If you can, cannibalize systems that you will not be retaining for items such as random access memory (RAM) chips, network cards, and hard disk drives. Add them to your resource pool.
- Recommission some more powerful 32-bit servers as either development or administration workstations if you can.
- Make sure all hardware you retain will be part of the resource pool Active Directory Domain Services (ADDS) single-domain forest to ensure tighter security between resource pools and virtual service offerings.
- Make sure you completely wipe disks and all existing data from any systems you decommission. You don't want to have someone rebuild the data on a disk drive because it wasn't wiped properly.

TIP *There are some very good disk-wiping tools on the market. Just search for "disk wiping" on the Internet through your favorite search engine.*

This process will take some time, but you'll find that it is much more malleable and straightforward than resource management has ever been before.

As for the migration itself, we've discussed the preparation of the resource pool servers at length in Chapter 6; proceed with the steps outlined there to prepare enough host servers to start the migration of the VSOs.

TIP *Remember that if your host servers are blades and are connected to shared storage, you can actually rely on copies of the logical units making up the system partition to provision new host servers. This is faster and easier than using an actual deployment tool.*

The Migration Order (Virtual Service Offerings)

When you're ready to move to the new network, you'll have to put together a migration strategy. This strategy must cover four major activities:

- **Security principal migration** Migrating users and computers from the directory service in use in the legacy network to Active Directory Domain Services in the new network.
- **Member server migrations** Migrating all services found on member servers, including file, print, management, collaboration, and more. This also includes special products, such as Exchange, SQL Server, and other services that manage the back office.

TIP *To find out more about Microsoft Exchange Server migration, look up* MCITP Self-Paced Training Kit (Exam 70-238): Deploying Messaging Solutions with Microsoft® Exchange Server 2007, *by Ruest and Ruest, published by MS Press.*

- **PC migrations** Migrating PCs from obsolete operating systems to Windows Vista. This will also involve capturing and restoring user data and preferences or profiles. This portion of the migration may already be done.
- **Custom application migrations** This involves mostly conversions or redevelopment of both rich-client and Web-based in-house applications.

Each of the four stages is a mini-project of its own, and each will require its own resources. You should begin with the security principal migration. If you set up your environment the right way, you will be able to migrate user and computer accounts, as well as groups, at your own pace, giving yourself time to prepare the other aspects of the project. In addition, by using the parallel VSO network approach, you don't affect the current production environment so that users in either network will be able to share applications and services from both networks during the entire length of the migration project.

Next, you'll be able to move to member server migrations. Ideally, you will be able to migrate a service, stabilize the new virtual servers, and then proceed to the client migration. For client migration, you will ideally migrate their PCs to Windows Vista (if it isn't already done) in order to fully profit from the new services infrastructure. As you migrate PCs, you will need to move users to the new service and monitor service performance. It will usually take one to two months of operation before services are fully stabilized. Afterward, you will want to monitor services for growth potential. Meanwhile, you can have your development staff working on upgrades of your key applications, since these will take time and may not be ready until all other migration tasks have been performed.

TIP *If you need to migrate PCs, we strongly recommend you pick up the free e-book* The Definitive Guide to Vista Migration *at www.realtime-nexus.com/dgvm.htm. It provides a wealth of information that may also assist you in the migration of your servers.*

Keep the following considerations in mind as you prepare your migration:

- **Identity servers** You'll begin with the identity servers to perform the security principal migration. Domain controllers (DCs) and Active Directory Domain Services are absolutely essential for the new network to function. Prepare these servers first. Populate enough DCs in the virtual environment to provide a given level of service. If you are a small organization (SORG) with only one site, then you can begin the migration of other services once you have your base production forest infrastructure in place. In very small organizations (about 100 users or fewer), this will mean a single-domain forest and, therefore, two DCs for redundancy. In medium (MORG) to large organizations (LORG), which have at least two sites, you can usually begin the migration of some of your services once you have DCs located in at least two sites. Refer to the recommendations in Chapter 6 for the base requirements for the construction of these DCs.
- **Network infrastructure** Next, you can move to the migration of Dynamic Host Configuration Protocol (DHCP) and Windows Internet Naming Service (WINS)—if you haven't decided to use DNS GlobalNames Zones—because no special client is required for computers to use these services. They work with all versions of Windows. It may be easiest to use a new pool of addresses to do so, however, if you don't want to affect your production systems. Or another good way to perform this migration is to move up to IPv6 in the new network while the legacy network continues to offer IPv4 addresses. Make sure your applications are compatible with IPv6 before you decide to use this strategy. For example, verify network intrusion detection systems, antivirus systems, network analyzers, and so on. Next, create the Windows Deployment Services (WDS) servers because they are required to build PCs. Finally, create your systems management and operational servers so that your management infrastructure will be ready to manage new servers as they are added to the parallel network. The result should be a core network that is ready to deliver services both in a central office to meet the needs of SORGs, MORGs, and LORGs (see Figure 12-2) and remote offices to meet the needs of MORGs and LORGs (see Figure 12-3). And if you followed the advice in Chapter 11, you will already have your core business continuity strategy in place (see Figure 12-4).

TIP *Remember that because VSOs run on virtual machines, you don't really need a tool like WDS to provision them, since all you need to do is copy the files that make up source machines to create a new one. Also see the Application Virtualization: Ending DLL hell once and for all webcast at www.bitpipe.com/detail/RES/1193672482_325.html.*

- **Dedicated Web servers** If you're using single-purpose Web servers, then the dedicated Web servers can be next, since IIS 7 provides backward compatibility for Web applications. Be sure to thoroughly test all applications before putting them into production. There are serious modifications in IIS 7 that may affect application operation. As with network infrastructure servers, no special client is required to operate with IIS.

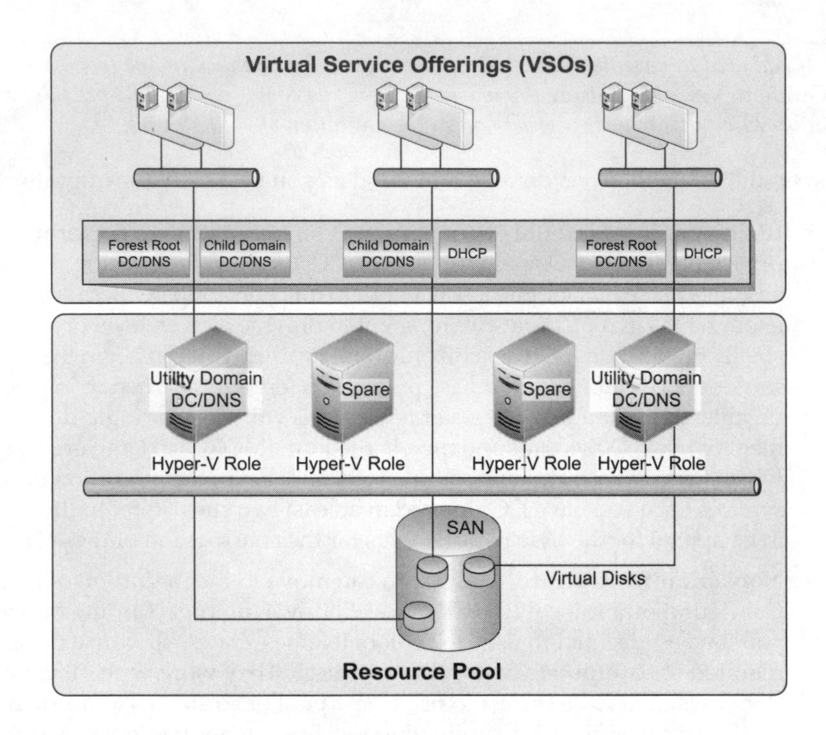

FIGURE 12-2
The core network for a central office

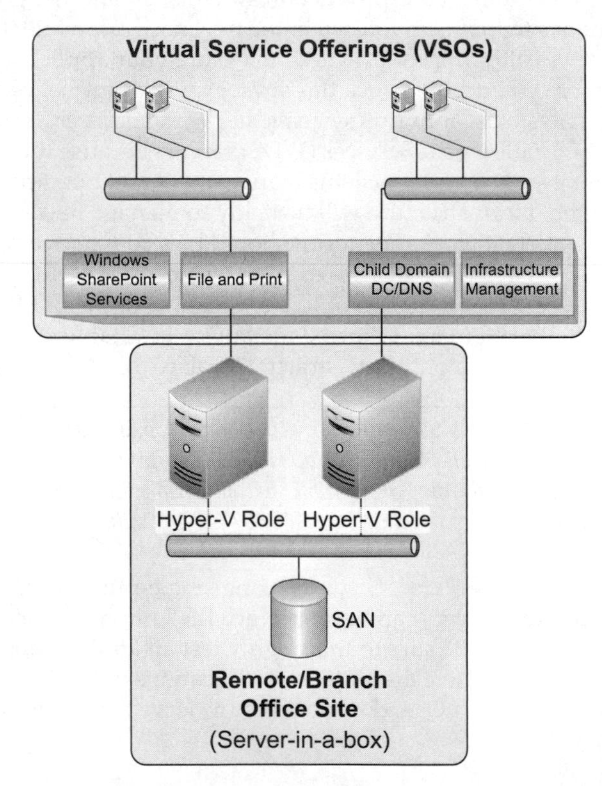

FIGURE 12-3
Using server-in-a-box for remote offices

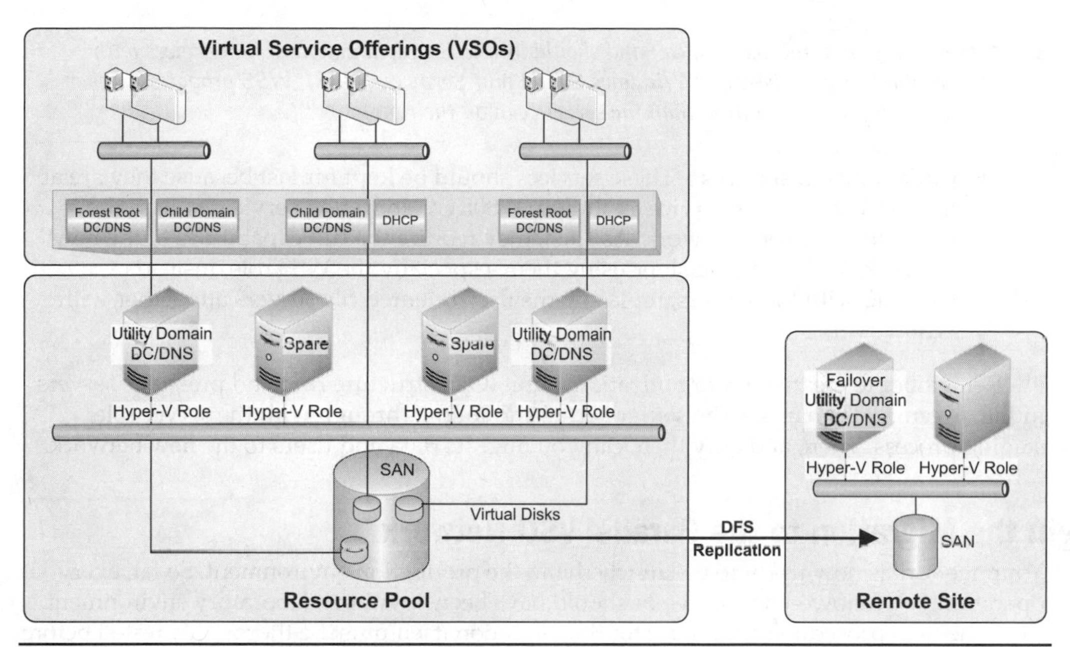

FIGURE 12-4 Business continuity from site to site

- **Application servers** General-purpose IIS servers can also be migrated at the same time as the dedicated Web servers for the same reason. Database servers can also be migrated since, once again, they will operate with existing clients. Corporate application servers can also be migrated since they will also operate with existing clients. Remember to test each component before releasing it to end users.
- **Terminal Services** WS08 Terminal Services (TS) servers can operate through Remote Desktop Web connections through TS Web Access. Clients need to be running the latest version of the Remote Desktop client (RDC). If you want to publish applications to take advantage of RemoteApps, and you want to make them available to existing PCs, then make sure you deploy the latest RDC to each PC.

TIP *You might not need to work with Terminal Services at all if you've decided to move to application virtualization. We strongly suggest you take a look at this operating model, since it is less expensive and more effective than running remote applications through Terminal Services. For more information, see Chapter 6 in* The Definitive Guide to Vista Migration *at www.realtime-nexus.com/dgvm.htm.*

- **File and print services** File services require transfers of large quantities of data to migrate. As such, they should be kept toward the end of your migration or, at the very least, they should be coordinated with PC migrations (servers first, then PCs). Special attention should be paid to file ownership and access rights when files are migrated from the legacy network to the new network. Print services can be moved at the same time. This will decrease the number of printer drivers you need to make available on your systems, since you will only have to deal with updated PC systems.

CAUTION *Keep in mind that you can and should look to the replacement of file services with collaboration services based on Windows SharePoint Services (WSS). WSS provides a richer environment for collaboration than file servers can on their own.*

- **Collaboration services** These services should be kept for last because they are at the basis of network service evolution. WS08 collaboration services extend the capabilities of your network. As such, they require the full capabilities of the new network. You might consider using them, especially the WSS role, instead of working with file servers, replacing the user-oriented file servers altogether with WSS servers.

Remember to create your organizational unit (OU) structure first and pre-stage servers in the directory. Then create the server kernel and follow through with the server role staging process. Then, and only then, can you migrate data and users to the new network.

Begin the Migration to the Parallel VSO Network

Your network is now ready to be launched into the production environment. So far, every operation you followed has been—or should have been—within a laboratory environment. Even the final procedures you'll use for the migration itself must be thoroughly tested before you move to the migration in the new production network. You'll begin by populating the directory in the new network.

Migrate Security Principals

Start by migrating user accounts, PC accounts, and data into the new directory. You'll need to perform the following steps.

- **Create trusts** The first step is to create a two-way trust relationship between the production domain and your legacy domain. This two-way trust serves to support the operation of both networks at the same time. It will need to remain in place until the migration is complete.
- **Nest groups** The second step is to nest the appropriate global groups into the local groups that are required to grant joint access to resources from both domains. For example, if you are migrating a select group of users and the migration cannot be completed all at once, you need to ensure that both sets of users—the ones located in the legacy network and the ones already migrated to the new network—have access to joint resources so that they can continue to work together for the duration of the migration. This approach will need to be extended to all users of shared folders because they must share resources for the duration of your migration.
- **User account migration** Next, you'll need to migrate user accounts from the legacy network to the new environment. Users should be given authority to modify their own personal information through the use of a user data modification web page, as discussed in Chapter 7, so that they can catch any errors in the data. The Active Directory Migration Tool (ADMT) available from Microsoft will provide great help here, since it migrates user accounts, passwords, groups and group memberships, service accounts, computer accounts, and more.

NOTE *This is an excellent opportunity to clean up your legacy directory database as it is imported into the new production domain.*

- **Service account migration** You shouldn't need to migrate service accounts since they have been re-created into the new network as new services have been activated.
- **User data migration** You can then proceed to migrate user data that is located on network shares, such as home directories, or, even better yet, through Folder Redirection Group Policy Objects (GPOs). This is where it is important to use the proper tool for user account migration because each account that is migrated is assigned a new security identifier (SID). This SID is different from the SID used to create the information in the legacy network. This means that it is possible for users to lose access to their data once it has been moved to a new network if you don't manage the migration properly. ADMT can either maintain a SID history when it migrates a user account, giving the account the ability to present a legacy SID when accessing data in the new network, or it can perform SID translation, replacing the legacy SID with the new SID on the object to avoid this problem.
- **PC account migration** Next, you'll need to migrate PCs. If PCs do not need to be restaged (they are already running Windows Vista or, at least, Windows XP), then you can use ADMT to migrate computer accounts and reset security descriptors on each system. If, on the other hand, they are not up to date and need to be staged, you will need to first recover all user data from the system, reinstall the system, join it to the new domain during reinstallation, and then restore user data to the system.

NOTE *Once again, look to* The Definitive Guide for Vista Migration *for more information.*

- **Decommission legacy network** The last step will consist of decommissioning the legacy network. This will be the step that identifies when the migration is complete.

Once these steps are complete, your migration will be finalized and you'll be ready to move on to the administration and optimization of your new network (see Figure 12-5).

NOTE *Using a commercial migration tool avoids many of the migration hassles because it takes all of these situations into account.*

Create Two-Way Trusts

The first step in the security principal migration is to create two-way trusts between the legacy and the new production domains. This is relatively straightforward, but it requires domain administration credentials in both domains. This means creating a trust between the new global child production domain (GCPD) and whichever legacy domain(s) that contain your user accounts.

CAUTION *Make sure your new virtual servers can communicate with the source legacy domains before you proceed with this operation. This may mean changing the properties of your Internet Protocol (IP) connections to include additional Domain Name System (DNS) servers. You should also ping the legacy domain before beginning this operation to make sure the names resolve properly.*

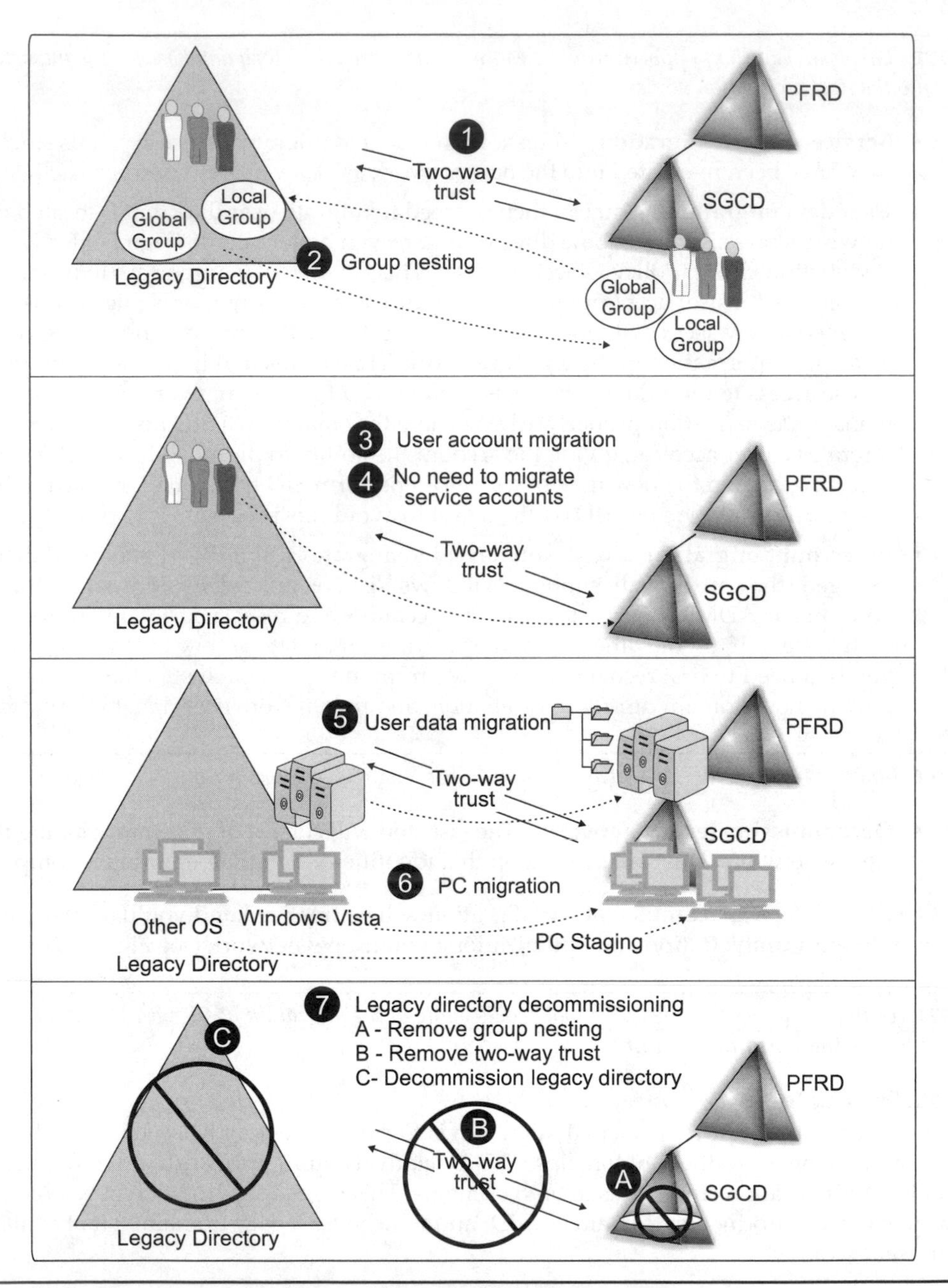

FIGURE 12-5 The user account, data, and PC account migration process

Trusts are created in the Active Directory Domains and Trusts console. Use the following steps:

1. Perform this operation from within the parallel network. Log on with domain administration credentials. Make sure you have the same level of credentials in the source domains.
2. Launch Start menu | Administrative Tools | Active Directory Domains and Trusts.
3. Expand the forest in the tree pane until you see the GCPD, and right-click the domain name to choose Properties.
4. Move to the Trusts tab.
5. Click New Trust.
6. In the New Trust Wizard, click Next.
7. You can create trusts between domains, forests, or Kerberos V5 realms (UNIX or Linux). In this case, you want a domain-to-domain trust. Type the name of the source domain, and click Next.
8. The system will search for the domain and then produce the appropriate trust creation page. Select Two-Way and click Next (see Figure 12-6).

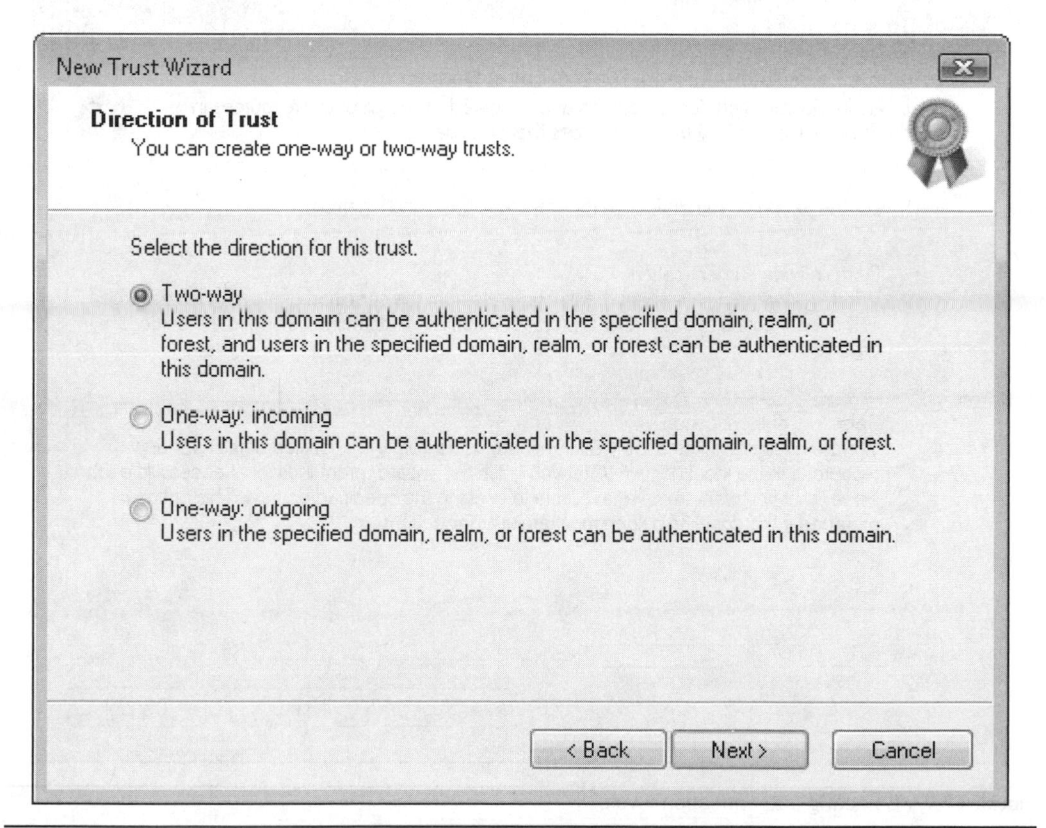

FIGURE 12-6 Creating a two-way trust

NOTE *You want to use a two-way trust to ensure that operations work for the duration of the migration and that users can access resources that have been migrated as well as those that have not.*

9. In the Sides of Trust dialog box, select Both This Domain And The Specified Domain to create both sides of the trust at once. Click Next.
10. Provide the credentials for the source domain. Remember to include the domain name in your credentials, either through a User Principal Name (UPN) or using domainname\username format. Click Next.
11. Next, specify the scope of authentication for users for the local domain. For a migration, it is best to use domain-wide authentication (see Figure 12-7). Click Next. Repeat for the source domain.
12. Review your selections and click Next to create the trust.
13. Once the trust is created, click Next to configure it.
14. Select Yes, confirm the outgoing trust, and click Next. Select Yes, confirm the incoming trust, and click Next.

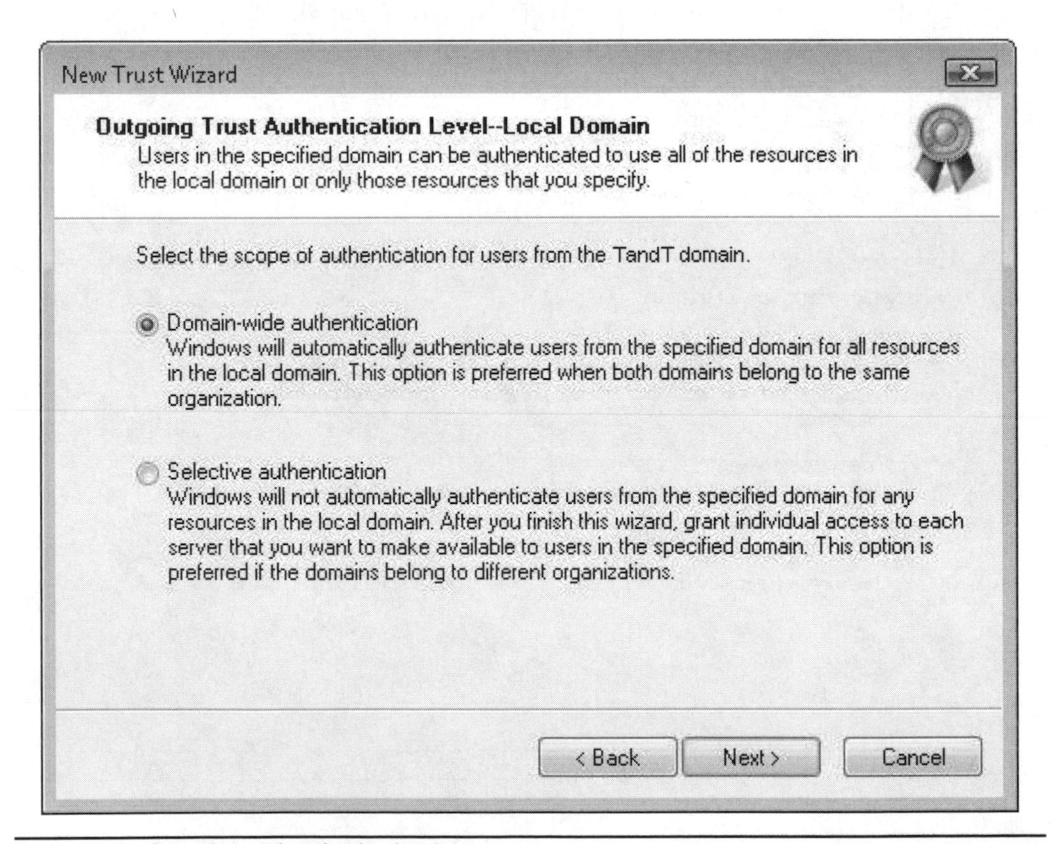

FIGURE 12-7 Selecting authentication levels

15. Click Finish upon confirmation of your trust relationship. A warning dialog box about enabling SID history will be displayed (see Figure 12-8). Click OK. Do not select the Do Not Show This Dialog Box Again check box, because it is useful to have a reminder about turning off SID history when you are done. Click OK again to close the domain Properties dialog box.

Repeat this operation for each source domain you need to link to. Make note of each trust you put in place, because you will need to remove them once you have completed the migration.

Nest Global Groups

The next step is to grant access rights to users in both domains. This will let users from the target domain access resources that are still in the source domain, and users in the source domain can access resources in the target domain; use Server Manager to do so.

You will need to create domain local groups to grant access to members of the source domain to target domain resources. Remember the Account-Global Group-Local Group-Permissions (AGLP) rule (see Figure 12-9); only domain local or local groups can contain objects from other domains in this case.

Keep this in mind as you assign access rights.

1. Go to Server Manager | Roles | Active Directory Domain Services | Active Directory Users and Computers.
2. Locate the container with the groups you want to target. For example, in your new domain, go to the People OU structure.
3. Create appropriate domain local groups.
4. Use the group's Properties dialog box to go to the Members tab, and click Add.
5. In the Select Users, Contacts, Computers, or Groups dialog box, click Locations.
6. Select the source domain, and click OK.
7. Search for the source group in the source domain, and click Add. Click OK when done.

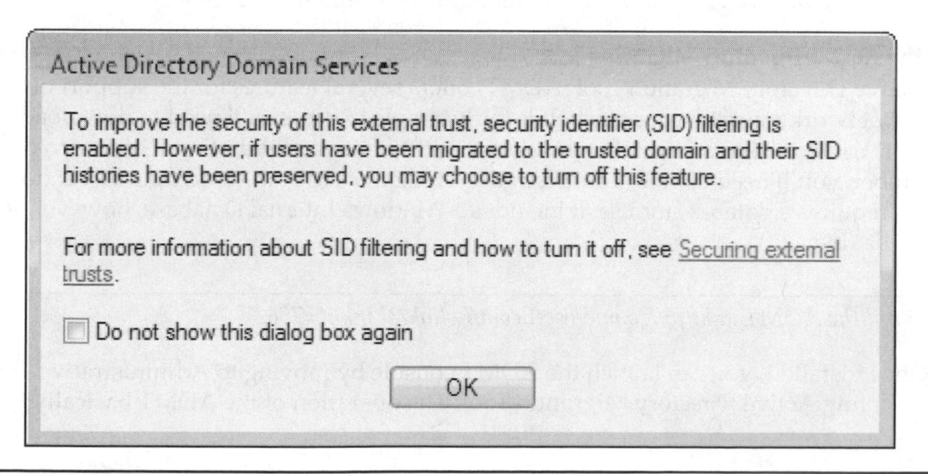

FIGURE 12-8 SID history warning

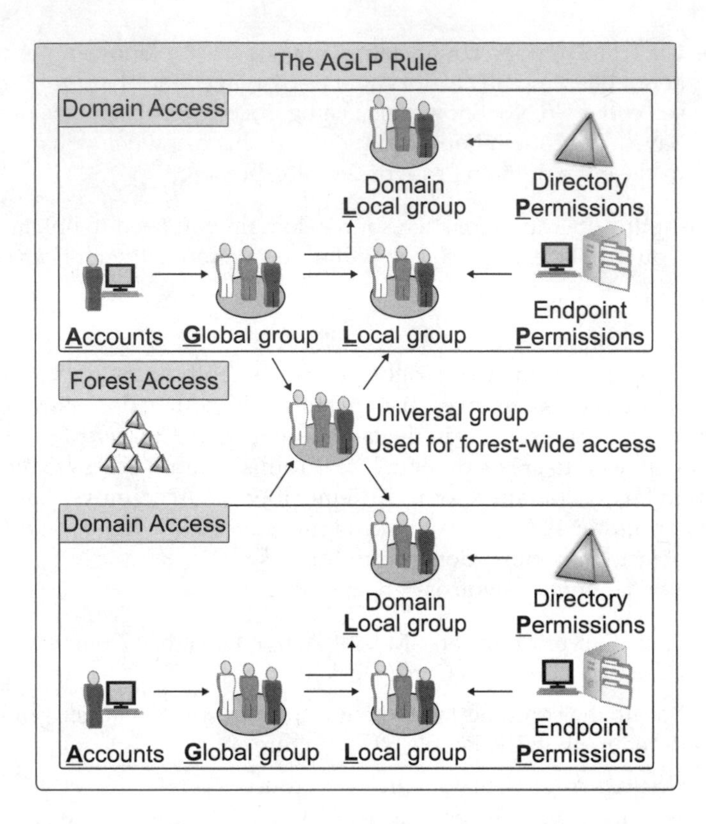

FIGURE 12-9
The AGLP rule

Repeat for each group you need to grant access to. You can also use the `DS` commands to perform this operation through a script. In this case, you'll need the `DSADD` and `DSMOD` commands.

For other resources, you'll need to use member server local groups to grant resource access. You're now ready to move contents from one domain to the other.

Use the Active Directory Migration Tool

The Active Directory Migration Tool (ADMT) offers several features for the support of the parallel network migration approach. It is fairly simple to use. You'll need to download and install it. You don't have to install it on a target server, but you might find it easiest to do so. Remember, you'll need domain administration credentials in both source and target domains. ADMT requires a database for use. It includes a Windows Internal Database, however, so you should be fine.

TIP *Find the ADMT at http://go.microsoft.com/fwlink/?LinkId=75627.*

Once installed, you can launch the ADMT console by moving to Administrative Tools and selecting Active Directory Migration Tool. The operation of the ADMT basically consists of using the right mouse button to click Active Directory Migration Tool, accessing the context menu, and selecting the appropriate wizard. ADMT offers several wizards:

- User Account Migration
- Group Account Migration
- Computer Migration
- Security Translation
- Reporting
- Service Account Migration
- Exchange Directory Migration
- Password Migration

The operation of the wizards is also straightforward. You need to identify the source domain, the target domain, the objects you want to migrate, the container you want to migrate them to, and then how you want to perform the migration. In addition to performing account or group migration, ADMT supports migration of Exchange objects, such as user mailboxes, distribution lists, and so on.

NOTE *The ADMT can be run in test mode. Choosing this mode allows you to test migration results before actually performing the operation. Simply select Test The Migration Settings And Migrate Later? when you use one of the wizards.*

The best way to use ADMT in the parallel network migration process is to migrate groups of users. When ADMT migrates a group, it can also migrate the users that are contained within it, making it easier for you to determine what to migrate. But before you can move users and computers from one network to another, you need to ensure that the data you will migrate will be filtered and that all obsolete records will be removed. You don't want to input obsolete data into your brand-new WS08 network!

Enable the Password Export Server

In order to migrate user accounts with their passwords, you must enable the Password Export Server (PES). Migrating user accounts with passwords is a lot easier on both users and administrators, because you do not need to provide users with temporary passwords and users do not need to reset their passwords before they log on. You can, however, get them to reset their passwords at first logon as part of a security policy for your new environment.

The PES must be installed on any domain controller in the *source* domain. This DC must support 128-bit encryption—this is supported by most versions of Windows Server from NT on. The tricky part of this installation is that you need to have an encryption key to perform the PES installation. This key must be generated with ADMT, but this time, it must be on the *target* domain.

Make sure you install ADMT on a DC in the target domain. Then generate the key with the following command:

```
admt key /option:create /sourcedomain:SourceDomain /keyfile:KeyFile
/keypassword:*
```

This will prompt you for a password that will not be displayed on the screen. Note that *SourceDomain* is the name of the source domain and *KeyFile* is the name of the file to generate. Place the file on either a very secure file share or a Universal Serial Bus (USB) device to secure it.

You should also create a service account in the target domain. This account needs domain administration rights. Make sure you grant this account local administration rights on the source DC. This account will be used to run the password migration service.

On the source DC, locate the PES installation file. It will be under `%SYSTEMROOT%\ADMT\PES` and is called `PWDMIG.MSI`. Double-click it to launch the installation. Specify the account to run the service under, point to your encryption key file, and provide the password to unlock it and complete the installation.

Once the service is installed, you need to start it. Go to the Services console, locate the Password Export Server service, and start it. It is a good idea to leave it on manual start because this way, you can start it only when you need it. Stop it again once you have performed the migration of the passwords.

Create Domain Data Reports

To filter data from your source domain, you need to use the ADMT Reporting Wizard. This reporting tool can support the creation of several different report types to summarize the results of your migration operations:

- Migrated Users and Groups
- Migrated Computers
- Expired Computers
- Account References
- Name Conflicts

The Expired Computers report lists the computers with expired passwords. The Name Conflicts report does the same with potential objects that will have the same name in the target domain. The Account References report lists the different accounts that have permissions to access resources on a specific computer.

You should try to identify obsolete contents of the original directory before you begin to migrate contents. You can perform this removal in several ways:

- You can remove the objects from the source domain and then migrate the accounts.
- You can create new groups that contain only valid objects in the source domain and migrate objects by using these groups.
- You can move the accounts to a specific OU in the target domain, clean them up, and then move them to their destination OUs.

NOTE *Reports must be generated before you can view them. Many reports are generated from information that is collected from computers throughout your network. This will affect their performance; therefore, you may decide to use dedicated servers for this function. Also, reports are not dynamic; they are point-in-time reports and must be regenerated to get an updated picture.*

The last approach may be your best bet, since the ADMT will allow you to control the way accounts are treated after the migration. In fact, you can ensure that no account is activated until you perform a cleanup operation on the newly migrated accounts.

NOTE *More information on ADMT can be found in the ADMT Migration Guide at www.microsoft.com/downloads/details.aspx?familyid=d99ef770-3bbb-4b9e-a8bc-01e9f7ef7342&displaylang=en.*

Special ADMT Considerations

There are a few items you must keep in mind when using the ADMT. The first is related to the security identifier (SID). As mentioned earlier, all of a user's data is associated with the SID that represents the user at the time the user object is created. All of a user's data will be associated with the user's *legacy* SID. When you transfer this data to the new network, you must use a special technique that will either carry over the user's legacy SID or translate the SID on the object to the user's new SID (the one generated by the new network).

The best way to do this is to ensure that the user's legacy SID is migrated to the new domain (using the appropriate check box in the Account Migration wizards) and then to use SID translation. The latter is performed through the use of the ADMT Security Translation Wizard. But in order for security translation to work properly, you *must make sure that all of a user's data has been migrated to the new network first*; otherwise, you will need to perform the SID translation again once this is done.

It is also important to note that for SID history migration to work, the Password Export Server is required. As mentioned earlier, the PES is installed on a domain controller in the legacy network. It is best to use a dedicated server for this operation because it is resource-intensive. Therefore, you should stage a new domain controller (a backup domain controller—BDC—in Windows NT or simply a DC in Windows 2000 or 2003) and dedicate it to this task. This could be a virtual machine and does not need to be a physical installation.

Your network also needs to meet the following conditions before you can perform password migration or SID translation:

- Auditing must be enabled on the source domain. If it isn't, ADMT will offer to turn it on during the migration.
- Your target domain must be in full functional mode, but this shouldn't be an issue, since it was set to this mode during its creation in Chapter 6.
- If you are migrating from Windows NT, you must also activate legacy access in the target domain by inserting the Everyone group into the Pre-Windows 2000–Compatible Access group.

CAUTION *It is recommended to activate legacy access only for the duration of a migration operation and to deactivate it as soon as the operation is complete because it is a potential security risk. This means that you activate it, perform a user or group migration, and then deactivate it. Do not activate it for the duration of the domain migration because this can last quite a while, depending on your migration strategy and the size of the legacy domain.*

There are other prerequisites you must take care of before performing a migration (such as the service pack level for the source domain machines). ADMT will also require some additional settings, but it can automatically perform the modifications during a migration operation.

You can use the ADMT to perform most of the operations identified previously to support your network migration, including:

- Create a source domain object report for filtering purposes.
- Migrate user accounts, groups, and computer accounts (if the systems are already running Windows Vista or, at the very least, Windows XP).
- Perform security translations to give users access to their data.

The only operation it does not handle is the migration of user data that is stored on network shares. As mentioned before, it is important to migrate user data before you perform security translations.

Use a Commercial Migration Tool

While ADMT offers some powerful features, you may find that it is cumbersome to work with if you have several thousand users to migrate. Several manufacturers have put together some more comprehensive commercial tools in support of migrations from one network environment to another. These tools do not only support directory migrations, but also file server and other migration scenarios.

A good source of information on these migration tools can be found in the article "Server Migration: Moving from Here to There": at http://mcpmag.com/Features/article.asp?EditorialsID=381. While this article is a bit dated and the industry has changed as firms performed mergers and acquisitions, the information itself is still quite valid. In addition, the tools themselves have greatly evolved, making migrations even easier.

Transfer Networked User Data

After the user accounts have been migrated to the new network, but before the security translation has been performed, you must migrate networked user data. This will involve the copying of data found on server shares within the legacy network. It should include public, group, project, and user data. User data should include home directory data, if it was in use within the legacy network.

This operation consists mostly of relocating shared data from one network to the other. In most cases, it will mean moving the data from a specific share on one server to the same share on another server. This may even give you the opportunity to consolidate server processes and regroup file shares on fewer servers. In addition, if you used the practices provided in Chapter 8, you will be now using Distributed File System (DFS) shares instead of mapped drives. You will have to ensure that your migration program includes a user information program showing them how to access the new shares. This user information program should also include the procedure to access personal user data, because this process is now different.

The parallel VSO network should no longer use the home directory concept. It should use redirected folders. There is a catch, though: Redirected user folders are not created until the user has logged on at least once. You cannot simply move the user's home folder files from one server to another, because the user's destination folder won't be created until later.

Because of this, you must devise a special personal user data migration strategy. There are three possibilities:

- First, you can ask all users to move all of their home directory files into their Documents folders on their desktop. Then, when they migrate to the new network and log on for the first time, the contents of their Documents folders will automatically be moved to the new shared folder thanks to the Folder Redirection Group Policy.
- Second, you can migrate data to a holding folder and, using a special one-time logon script, move the files to the user's newly created redirected folder once the user is logged on and the Group Policy has been applied.
- Third, if you need to stage PCs because they are not running Windows Vista, you can add an operation to the profile migration process, since it will be required on all systems. The operation you need to add is similar to the first approach: Script a process that takes all of a user's home directory data and copies it to the Documents folder before performing the profile migration. The data will automatically be redirected at each user's first logon to the new network, and the GPO is applied.

Of these three strategies, the first and third are the best. The first is relatively simple, but it has a flaw: You must rely on operations that are out of your control for the process to complete. It will not work unless you have a well-trained user base and you provide them with excellent instructions. The third works when users' PCs must be staged.

Finally, you may need to migrate roaming user profiles if they were in use in the legacy network. Remember that the new network does not use roaming profiles, but relies on folder redirection instead or, at the very least, uses a combination of both. To migrate roaming profiles, simply turn the feature off in the legacy network (only for users targeted for migration). The profile will return to the local machine. If the machine is already running Windows Vista, the profile will automatically be transformed to folder redirection when the machine is joined to the new domain and the user logs on, because the GPOs will activate folder redirection. If the machine needs to be staged, the profile will be captured through the staging process.

For the actual migration of files from the source domain to the target domain, refer to "Migrate File Servers," later in this chapter.

Tip *For detailed instructions on how to configure roaming profiles with folder redirection in the new VSO domain and use this strategy to migrate user data from the old to the new network, read Chapter 8 of* The Definitive Guide to Vista Migration *at www.realtime-nexus.com/dgvm.htm.*

Migrate Network Infrastructure Servers

Network infrastructure servers do not really require a migration. This category includes services such as DHCP, WINS, WDS, and Windows Server Update Services (WSUS).

It is possible to migrate the databases from previous versions of Windows Server running services such as DHCP and WINS if you have decided to use WINS in the new network. If you are completely happy with your existing DHCP service, you can simply move the DHCP database from the source server to new virtual servers running in the VSO network.

TIP *We strongly recommend that you move to DNS GlobalNames zones instead of using WINS, if it is at all possible in your network. These zones are simpler to work with and profit from all of the powerful features of DNS instead of relying on a legacy service such as WINS.*

However, you must keep in mind that there are several changes to DHCP in Windows Server 2008, changes that may not warrant the migration of your existing database. For example:

- Windows Server 2008 supports DHCPv6, which will work with IPv6 addresses. Your previous DHCP servers will not have this ability, and you will need to re-create the DHCP scopes for this data.
- Windows Server 2008 also changes the nature of the local scope because you need to assign DNS servers to each local scope that also includes a domain controller. DNS is now hosted on each domain controller; therefore, remote site users will rely on their local domain controller for DNS name resolution. Each recovered local scope will need to be updated with this information.
- You may want to update your scopes and begin using new features, such as superscopes, to make scope management simpler.

For these reasons, it may be easier to simply create new scopes in your new VSO network. But if you decide to recover existing scopes, you need to use the following procedure. Remember to rely on the 80-20 rule on your new servers.

1. Export the DHCP server configuration from the source servers.
2. Create an export file for each scope.
3. Import the scopes on the target server(s).
4. Disable the scopes on the source server.
5. Enable the scopes on the new servers.

Then you'll want to modify scopes to meet new requirements generated by the new VSO network.

Other content you can migrate in the network infrastructure server category is the images you use in Windows Deployment Services. Simply create new WDS servers, secure them appropriately, and then copy the images from the old servers to the new servers.

Finally, when it comes to Windows Server Update Services, the only thing you really need to recover is the list of approved updates. WSUS will automatically scan all PCs and servers to determine which updates have been applied to them, so recovering the inventory isn't really required. The best way to effect this migration is to simply install a new version of WSUS in the new VSO network, scan all systems, and make sure you've captured the approved list of updates from the legacy network.

Migrate Web Sites

Microsoft has also made it easier to migrate web sites from previous versions of Internet Information Services (IIS) to IIS version 7. The IIS Migration Tool is a command-line tool that will capture web site information and transfer it to an IIS 7 Web structure. This tool transfers configuration data, web site content, and application settings to the new server. It can also move only application settings if that is all you need.

This tool will also let you migrate web sites while they are in operation, letting you maintain 24/7 availability of the site as you perform the migration. Configuration data is translated from the metabase format used in previous versions to the new `.CONFIG` file format used in IIS 7. It will also migrate nested applications correctly, letting you migrate even complex web site structures. You can also perform site customizations, such as changing the IP address, port, or host headers of the sites you migrate as you migrate them.

Migrating web sites can be a complex operation, however. Make sure you fully test the web site once you have migrated it to guarantee that all of its functions operate properly on your new Web server infrastructure.

TIP *The IIS Migration Tool can be found at www.microsoft.com/downloads/details.aspx?FamilyID=2aefc3e4-ce97-4f25-ace6-127f933a6cd2&displaylang=en.*

Build Terminal Services Servers

Terminal Services servers do not really require migration, since they host applications that are run on a central platform. Most of the TS servers you will run in your new network, if you choose to run them and not replace them with desktop application virtualization, will be new server installations. They will, however, make it possible for users in both the legacy and the new VSO network to use the applications made available through Terminal Services, because client systems only need to have the updated Remote Desktop Connection client. This client is downloaded automatically to any Windows XP system that relies on software updates from Microsoft. It is also already installed on Windows Vista systems.

Perhaps the best way to make new TS applications available to users, whether they are migrated or not, is through the use of TS Web Access. This lets you place the remote application shortcuts on a web page—something everyone has access to—and provide them with immediate access to applications running on your new Windows Server 2008 infrastructure.

Because of this, you might consider moving these applications as soon as possible. Remember that you will need the cross-domain trusts in place to let users have logon access to the new network from the legacy network.

Migrate File Servers

By their very nature, Windows networks tend to be highly distributed. Somewhere, the industry got the feeling that if you needed more services from Windows, it was easier to simply add a new box to the network than to try to get multiple services to cohabitate on the same server. Well, Microsoft has gone a long way to help dispel this myth, not only by providing valuable information on how servers should scale up, but also by making Windows code faster and more robust. Today, Windows Server 2008 can easily run several thousand printers on one machine or store terabytes of information in a single cluster. That's why many organizations seriously consider server consolidation when it comes to the migration of both file and print services. Not to mention that the more boxes you have, the more complex they are to manage and, particularly, to patch.

The migration of distributed storage in legacy networks to a new disk and shared folder structure must support several activities (see Table 12-1). For example, it must automatically

File Server Migration Activity	Tool Requirements
File migration	Must be supported
Consolidation support	Migrate from many to one
Source operating systems	Any previous version of Windows Server
Target operating systems	Windows Server 2008
File usage analysis before migration	Evaluate different situations, such as duplicate files or unused files
File Re-ACL-ing	Change SID ownership of the files
Password-protected file support	Must support migration of files locked through tools such as Microsoft Office
Encrypting File System support	Required for secure environments
Map to DFS systems	Required to provide consolidation support
Parallel file server support	Provide access to both source and target servers through synchronization
User/PC setting migration	Modify settings on the local PC to remap file shares
Undo capability	Provide a back-out plan in case of failures
Delegation of migration task	Delegate task to other operators
Migration reporting	Report on analysis and task progression
Migration testing	Test a migration only before performing it
Database support	Store information in a database
Scripting or command-line support	Automate procedures

TABLE 12-1 File Server Migration Activities and Requirements

reassign proper security rights within the target network so that users can continue to access their data. Ideally, the file migration tool you use will either support parallel access to both the source and target servers until the migration is complete or provide a cut-off method to warn users that their files have been migrated. It should also support the verification and modification of access control lists (ACLs) in the target network to remove legacy permissions to the files. In the case of a migration, this means the tool will support SID history, since user accounts acquire new SIDs when moved from a legacy domain to a new directory. Once files are moved and permissions are updated, the migration tool must support the modification of user settings on local PCs. If at all possible, it will perform this task automatically or with little administrative effort. This migration tool must also support special file formats, such as files that include password protection, or, if migrating from more modern networks, files that have been protected with the Encrypting File System (EFS).

In the best migration scenarios, the tool you use should also support the migration of content from a standard file share system to a consolidated DFS system, since DFS has been designed to eliminate the need for mapped drives. Finally, it should help you move from outdated home directories to the more advanced folder redirection supported by Windows Server.

TIP *In the worst-case scenario, you can use NT Backup to back up the file services from your legacy servers and restore them to your new server, then use Microsoft's Security Migration Editor, which is free with Windows Server 2008, to perform SID regeneration on your files. Remember that NT Backup is not available on WS08 and must be downloaded (see Chapter 11).*

Change the Nature of Your File Servers

As mentioned earlier, the role of the file server is changing as organizations move toward better and more efficient collaboration tools. As such, you might find that it is much more practical for you to create SharePoint sites to host shared documents and other data rather than re-creating a very large number of file shares, as you had in your legacy network. If you decide to move to this model, you will not be migrating files from legacy file shares to new file servers, but rather, you will be moving files from legacy file shares to new SharePoint sites that are designed to host more comprehensive collaboration.

There is still room for the file server, however. Users have their own document space on their desktops—a document space that needs protection just as much as centralized file shares. This document space is stored in the user profile. Chapter 7 discussed the use of folder redirection, possibly linked to roaming profiles, to provide a more thorough protection policy for end-user data, as well as providing a better strategy for long-term profile management.

You may, therefore, find that the actual file server migrations you perform are focused more on user and perhaps administrative data than on shared data. If this is the case, then focus on the migration of data to Windows SharePoint Services instead of on file servers.

NOTE *Make sure you communicate the data protection policy to your users. In fact, it might be an excellent idea to use a WSS team site to provide an online users' manual to all end users. This way, they will know exactly what is going on in their new network.*

In fact, the migrations you perform should be mapped out to the new file services you deploy. Chapter 8 outlined how your file services should be structured (see Figure 12-10). These are the shared folders you need to focus on. Table 12-2 outlines how each type of file service should be migrated.

TIP *For instructions on how to create manual DFS shares for file migration, look up Knowledge Base article number 829885 at http://support.microsoft.com/default.aspx?scid=kb%3b%5bLN%5d%3b829885. Microsoft also offers a Solution Accelerator for the consolidation of file and print servers. Solution Accelerators are a set of documentation and tools to provide simpler operation of complex tasks. It can be found at http://go.microsoft.com/fwlink/?linkid=24719&clcid=0x409.*

You'll rarely have the occasion to migrate data when it isn't in use, unless you perform the migration during weekends or during times when your servers are shut down. Even then, it is difficult to find enough time to perform the migration. Most likely, you will be migrating data when users are online and need access to it. This is why running source file servers and target systems in parallel is the ideal situation. Make sure you communicate your plans to end users to limit the number of Help desk calls the migration may generate. If users are left with tasks to perform, then make sure these tasks are clearly outlined and detailed for them in your communications to them.

The first step in any file server migration is to run reports on your existing file shares, but unless you are running Windows Server 2003 R2 on the source servers, you won't have any

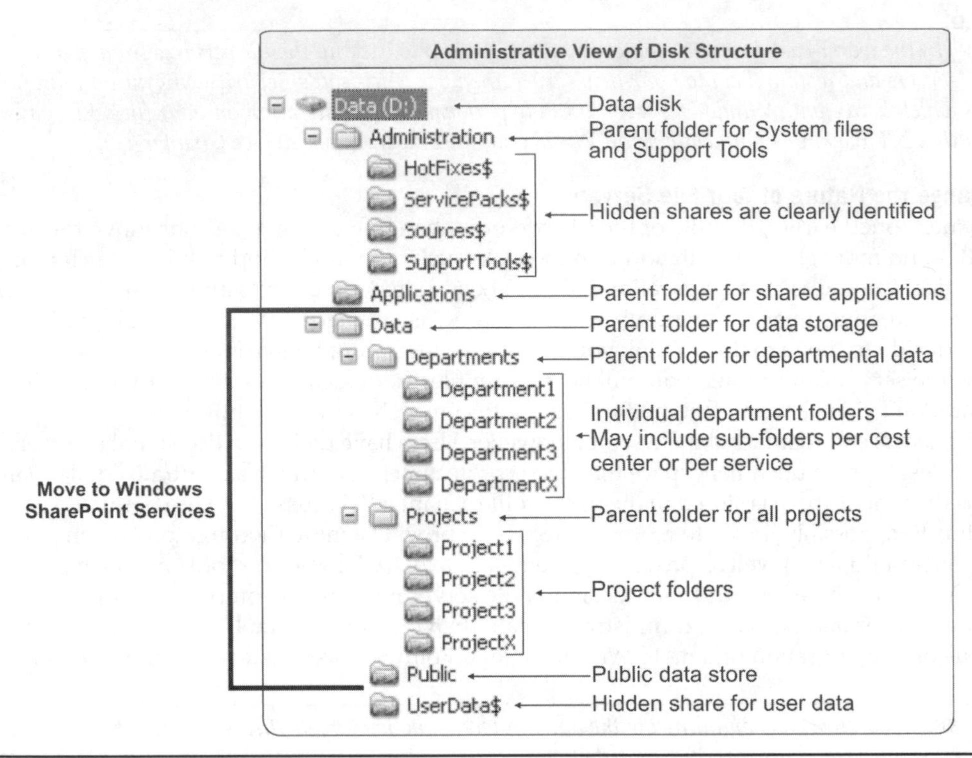

FIGURE 12-10 Mapping file server migrations to disk structures

built-in tools to create these reports. You'll have to manually check files as you migrate them. You can, however, migrate the files and once they are migrated, generate usage reports on the new servers through the File Server Resource Management Reporting feature.

TIP *You can generate reports with third-party file migration tools, or you can get a free or commercial inspection tool. For example, AdvexSoft offers both a free and a paid version of Disk Space Inspector at www.advexsoft.com/disk_space_inspector/disk_space_report.html?gclid=CMPVyoPnxY0CFRAkggod9BlfMQ.*

Once you have an idea of the space requirements—remember that it is always wiser to have more available space on your new servers than on the old ones—you can move to the migration of each file share service to its target technology.

NOTE *In previous versions of Windows Server, Microsoft provided the File Server Migration Toolkit. Unfortunately, this toolkit does not work on Windows Server 2008 and Microsoft has not seen fit to upgrade it for this version of the OS. This leaves you out in the cold as far as free migration tools are concerned. Rely on the migration paths outlined in Table 12-2 to simplify the process. It is unlikely, though, that medium to large organizations will be able to perform this operation without the purchase of migration tools. There are several very good tools on the market. We have worked with the tools from Quest and Metalogix, among others. These tools provide comprehensive features at reasonable cost.*

File Share	Migration Target	Comments
Administrative shares	Hidden shared folders	Move all data from legacy network to new VSO network. A simple copy should do, since there are no special permissions to migrate.
Application shares	File shares with same access rights or RemoteApps	Application shares are simple to migrate, since they rarely have custom permissions. If you choose to migrate them to new file shares, just copy the data and re-create the access control lists. If you choose to migrate them to RemoteApps, then apply new permissions.
Departmental shares, project shares, and public shares	Windows SharePoint Services	To migrate contents from a legacy share to WSS, you can use Windows Explorer to move the data from one location to another. But if you want to automate the process and apply complex access control lists, use a commercial migration tool. See the Migrate SharePoint Sites section in this chapter for more details.
User data	File shares with same access rights	The best way to migrate user data is to perform the migration through a combination of roaming profiles and folder redirection. Using this combination, you can move 100 percent of all user data through an automated process. See the Note in the "Transfer Networked User Data" section of this chapter for instructions on how to perform this operation.

TABLE 12-2 Mapping File Server Migrations

Migrate Print Servers

For printer migration, you must be able to migrate print queues, including printer drivers from one server to another, as well as redirect print queues on client computers. Since Windows Server prefers the use of user-mode drivers over kernel-mode drivers for increased server stability, your migration should convert the driver and block the installation of kernel-mode drivers. You should endeavor to remove any legacy printers requiring kernel-mode drivers from your network, since these can block and hang a print server, even a clustered print server. Finally, you need to publish printers in Active Directory Domain Services and implement Printer Location Tracking to facilitate printer searches in the directory. You will also have to change printer settings on user systems. This can be done either with the Printer Settings GPO or through logon scripts. If you use Printer Location Tracking, you might even be able to get users to change printers themselves.

You can use Microsoft's Print Migrator 3.1 to capture printer information from legacy servers and restore it to new Windows Server 2008 machines. What's nice about this tool is that it will automatically change Line Printer Remote (LPR) ports to the new Transmission Control Protocol/Internet Protocol (TCP/IP) standard port supported by Windows Server. In addition, it will automatically change printer drivers from kernel mode (version 2) to user mode (version 3) during the transfer. At the very least, you should use this tool to back up all your printer configurations, as it is one of its main functions. This way, you can restore them in the case of an emergency.

TIP *Microsoft Print Migrator can be found at www.microsoft.com/WindowsServer2003/techinfo/overview/printmigrator3.1.mspx.*

Print Migrator is easy to work with. Download the executable, and load it on any server. It doesn't actually require an installation, since the executable is self-contained. Use the following approach:

1. Double-click `PRINTMIG.EXE` to run the Print Migrator.
2. Accept the Run prompt that is presented.
3. Print Migrator automatically lists the printer configuration on the local system (see Figure 12-11).

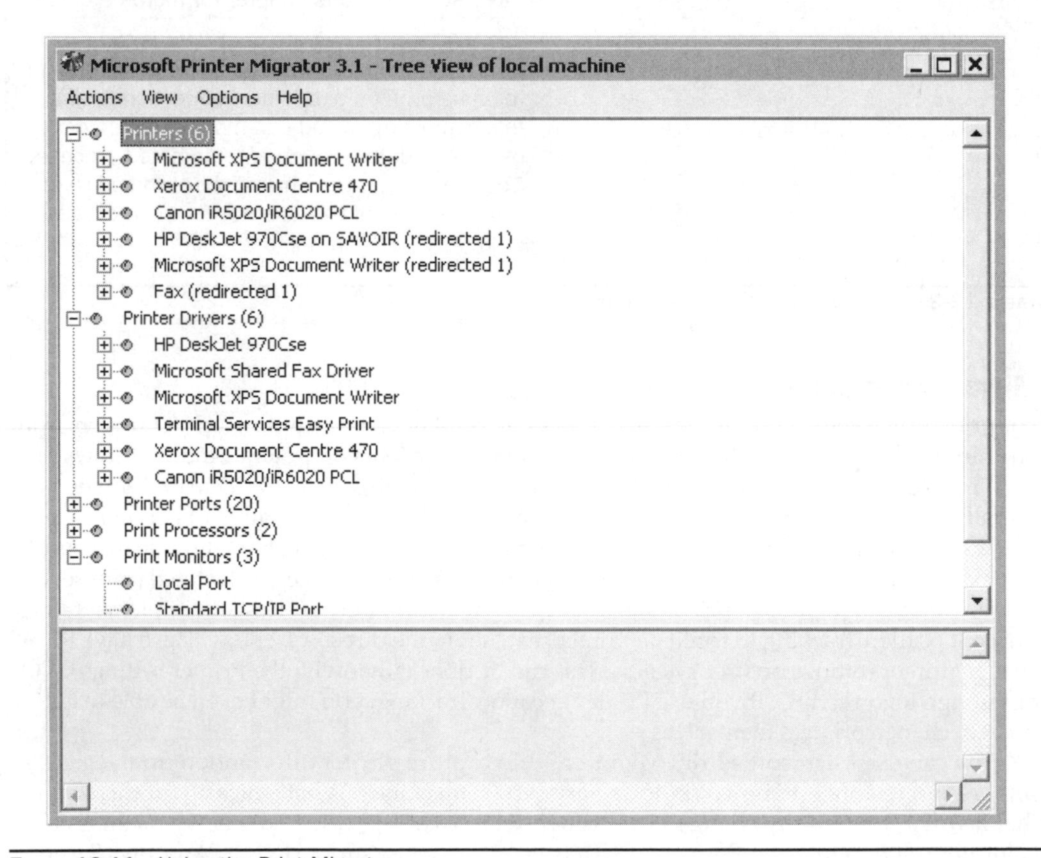

FIGURE 12-11 Using the Print Migrator

4. If you are running the tool on the source print server, move to the Actions menu, and select Backup. Identify the location where you want to save the CAB file—ideally a shared folder—and, optionally, identify the target server for the operation.
5. Click Save and then click OK to perform the backup.

To restore the settings on the target print server, repeat the operation with the Action | Restore command. Here you can select two options:

- Suppress warning popups. These will be captured into the log file even if they are not displayed to you as you run the restore.
- Attempt LPR to SPM conversion. If your old printers used LPR ports, try to convert them to Standard TCP/IP Port Monitor (SPM) for better performance.

Print Migrator can also connect to remote servers and capture their printer settings. Use the View | Target menu item to connect to remote servers.

Finally, printer migration can be automated, since the `PRINTMIG.EXE` program also runs from the command line. Use the following command to identify its options:

```
printmig /?
```

Repeat the operation for every print server in your legacy network. You can actually perform print migration at any time during the migration, since printers in legacy and new networks can run in parallel with no issues.

Migrate SharePoint Sites

Windows SharePoint Services is becoming more and more popular as Microsoft matures the collaboration engine it relies on. Many organizations will already have implemented SharePoint sites in one form or another. For the organizations already using SharePoint systems, the migration path is from one SharePoint system to another. For those who haven't implemented SharePoint systems yet but want to take advantage of this new collaboration paradigm, the migration will most likely be in the form of moving content from file shares to new SharePoint sites.

There are several ways to perform these migrations:

- Migrating an existing site could be as simple as performing a backup on one server and restoring the data on another.
- You can also upgrade database content from older versions of SharePoint to Windows SharePoint Services (WSS) version 3.
- Finally, you can move content from other repositories, such as file shares, to new SharePoint sites.

The tricky part of a migration for SharePoint sites is the back-end database. All SharePoint data is stored in a database. In addition, SharePoint can be run in two modes: stand-alone and server farm. If you run an older version of SharePoint in stand-alone mode, then you are running it with the Windows Microsoft SQL Server Desktop Engine (WMSDE). If you are running a farm, then you are running SQL Server.

If you are migrating from an older stand-alone version, then you will also be moving from WMSDE to the Windows Internal Database (WID). If you are migrating a farm, then it should be simpler, because you will be moving from SQL Server to SQL Server. These latter migrations are often best performed through commercial tools.

TIP *More information on Windows SharePoint Services can be found at the WSS TechCenter at www.microsoft.com/technet/windowsserver/sharepoint/default.mspx.*

Migrate from SharePoint to SharePoint

When you're migrating from SharePoint to SharePoint, you must first run the pre-upgrade scan tool (PUST). PUST will scan your existing site and map out potential upgrade or migration issues, including:

- **Customized content** PUST will scan your sites for any customized content, such as Web parts or site templates, and determine if they can be carried over in the upgrade.
- **Site components** PUST will identify if required components of the site to be migrated are missing from the target site.
- **Orphaned objects** Sites can sometimes have objects that have become orphaned and are no longer linked to the site. PUST will identify these objects and list them for you.

Once it has performed its scan, PUST will provide you with upgrade or migration recommendations and help you determine which migration approach to use.

TIP *Orphaned objects can be recovered before the migration. See Knowledge Base article number 918744 for more information at http://go.microsoft.com/fwlink/?linkid=69958&clcid=0x409.*

Once you have results from PUST, you can move to the migration itself. If you're moving from any version of SharePoint to stand-alone installations of WSS on WS08, then you must perform a WMSDE-to-WID migration since WID is only available on WS08. Basically, you need to perform the following steps:

1. Detach the databases from the WMSDE instance.
2. Copy the databases and attach them to SQL Server (WID).
3. Add the databases to the Web applications, re-creating sites.
4. Review the log files for any issues.

Repeat the operation for each database you need to migrate.

NOTE *Detailed steps for this operation can be found at http://technet2.microsoft.com/windowsserver/WSS/en/library/1f505e96-60e2-41ac-bf5d-9739105f047c1033.mspx?mfr=true.*

Migrate File Content to SharePoint Services

Migrating file content is simpler than migrating SharePoint sites. At its simplest, you can use Windows Explorer to open both the source file share and the target SharePoint site and drag-and-drop the files from one to the other. The problem with this approach is that the files will not include any metadata content, unless, of course, your users are disciplined and have already added it through the Microsoft Office interface.

The best way to migrate content from a file share to a SharePoint site is through a commercial migration tool. For example, Metalogix (www.metalogix.net) offers FileShare Migration Manager for SharePoint, which migrates any file share content to SharePoint. This product is reasonably priced (as are all Metalogix products) and works through a simple interface. In addition, it lets you analyze content prior to the migration, group content for migrations, and then, once you've begun the migration, you can tag metadata to each file as it is uploaded.

Tagging metadata is important in order to support better content searches when users are looking for information in SharePoint.

NOTE *Metalogix also makes tools to migrate content from Microsoft Content Management Server or other SharePoint Sites to WSS version 3. Check them out, as they provide a much better migration experience than the upgrade process described earlier.*

Decommission the Legacy Network

Once everything has been migrated from the legacy network to the new network, you can proceed with the decommissioning of the legacy network. This process involves the following tasks:

- Begin by removing embedded groups. You only need to do this in the new domain. Remove legacy global groups from your production domain local groups as well as from member server local groups.
- Next, turn off SID history. *You must make sure you have performed Security Translation with the ADMT beforehand!* SID history removal is discussed later in the chapter.
- Next, remove the trust relationships. Once again, you only need to remove trusts from the new production domain. Use the Active Directory Domains and Trusts console to perform this activity.
- Now you can move on to the decommissioning of the legacy domain itself. But before you do so, it is a good idea to perform full backups of the primary domain controller (PDC)—if it is a Windows NT network—or the DCs running Operations Master Roles—if it is Windows 2000 or 2003.
- When the backups are complete, store them in a safe place, then shut down the legacy domain's final domain controller (PDC or main DC).
- If you can recover this server as a new host, you can install Server Core or, if it is a 32-bit server, the Full Installation and join it to your new resource pool domain.

You might consider having a celebration at this stage, because you certainly deserve it! You and your migration team have done a lot of hard work preparing the new network and migrating every legacy resource to the new environment. Congratulations!

But, celebrations aside, it will also be a good idea for you to perform a post-migration review to ensure that you can reuse this process and improve upon it if you ever need it again.

Deactivate SID History

SID history is both a boon and a bane. It is a boon because it automatically provides additional SIDs when a user tries to access a resource from a legacy source. It is a bane because savvy malicious users can add additional SIDS to their own and use them to impersonate credentials they shouldn't have. Therefore, it is important to make sure you remove SID history and deactivate it as soon as you can after the migration and especially after security translation operations have been completed.

TIP *More information on SID history can be found at http://technet2.microsoft.com/windowsserver/en/library/01e5cf71-b317-4967-82a2-75b7b632b7461033.mspx?mfr=true.*

To deactivate SID history, use the following command with enterprise administrator credentials:

```
netdom trust TargetDomain /domain:SourceDomain /quarantine:No
/usero:UserName /password:Password
```

where *TargetDomain* is your new domain, *SourceDomain* is the legacy domain, and *UserName* and *Password* are the enterprise administrator credentials you are using.

CAUTION *Be careful when you perform this operation, as the password appears in plain text on the screen!*

Prepare Your New Support Structure

As you place the new network online, you will begin to realize that a review of administrative and operational roles is also required. In fact, this review of operational roles focuses on the third quadrant of the services lifecycle illustrated in Chapter 3—Production—since the activities of the first two quadrants are now complete (Planning and Preparation and Deployment). The operations outlined in the production quadrant require an updated organizational structure because many of them will be delegated to users with non-administrative privileges.

New and Revised ADDS IT Roles (VSO Network)

One of the areas where IT roles are modified the most is in terms of Active Directory Domain Services management, especially in the new VSO network. If you're migrating from Windows NT to Windows Server 2008, most of these roles are new. If you're already using Windows 2000 or 2003, then you now know that all of these roles are necessary (see Figure 12-12). The responsibilities of each role are outlined in Table 12-3. Once again, depending on the size of your organization, you may combine roles. What is important here is that each function be identified within your IT group. It will also be important to ensure that no unnecessary privileges are given to administrators and operators within ADDS.

All of these roles will need to interact with each other during ongoing operations. A regular roundtable discussion is an excellent way for each of the people filling these roles to get to know each other and begin the communication process. The frequency of these meetings does not need to be especially high. Gauge the number of meetings you need per year according to the objectives you set for your directory. There could be as few as two

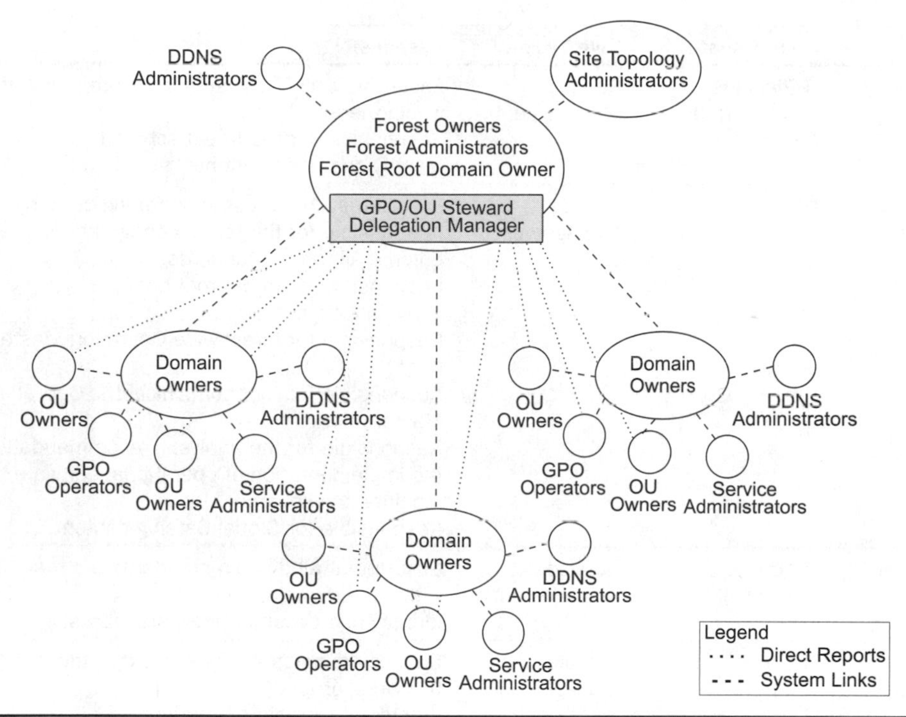

FIGURE 12-12 ADDS IT role relationships

meetings per year. Depending on the size of your organization, you might restructure your IT group to meet new demands (see Figure 12-13). Also, a shared team site within WSS is a great way to centrally store and protect data about system administration.

TIP *Microsoft offers a complete Active Directory Operations Guide. It is in two parts and is available at http://technet2.microsoft.com/windowsserver/en/library/9c6e4dd4-3877-4100-a8e2-5c60c5e19bb01033.mspx?mfr=true. It also outlines which role should perform which operation.*

New Resource Pool Roles

Since the network is now divided into two portions—resource pools and virtual service offerings—you will need a similar division in your IT roles. At the simplest, your resource pool administration team will consist of at least two people who focus only on resource pool management and administration, allocating appropriate resources on an as-needed basis. In more complex environments, the resource pool team will be divided into roles listed in Table 12-4.

Basically, the resource pool administration team is responsible for all hardware resources and their allocation to provide support for the virtual service offerings. This team is a high-powered team that focuses on Server Core and hardware-level operations. Because of this, they never interact with end users. Instead, they interact with either the Level 3 Help desk technicians from the VSO team or even VSO administrators (see Figure 12-14). It is the VSO Help desk, Levels 1 and 2, that interact with end users, since it is only the VSOs that interact with end users.

Role	Department	Role Type	Responsibilities
Forest Owner	IT Planning and Enterprise Architecture	Service Management	Ensure that all forest standards are maintained within the forest. Responsible for the forest schema. Identify and document new standards.
Forest Administrator	IT Group	Service Management	Ensure that the forest is operating properly. Responsible for the forest configuration. Enforce all forest standards. Responsible for forest root domain administration. Responsible for forest-wide Operation Master roles. Responsible for root domain-centric Operation Master roles. Responsible for the analysis/recommendation of the implementation of operational software that modifies the schema. Responsible for Global Catalog content.
Domain Owner	IT Group/ Training/IS	Service Management	Ensure that all domain standards are maintained within the domain. Identify and document new standards.
Domain Administrator	IT Group	Service Management	Service administrator ensures that the domain is operating properly. Enforce all domain standards. Ensure that all DCs within the domain are sized appropriately. Responsible for domain-centric Operation Master roles.
DDNS Administrator	IT Group	Service Management	Ensure the proper operation of the forest namespace. Administer and manage internal/external DNS exchanges.
Site Topology Administrator	IT Group	Service Management	Monitor and analyze forest replication. Modify site topology to improve forest replication.
Service Administrators	IT Group	Service Management	Responsible for a given service in the domain. Have limited rights in the domain (only to the service they manage).
GPO Operators	IT Group	Service Management	Design and test GPOs for use in production environments. Use the Group Policy Management Console to manage, debug, and modify GPOs. Report to the GPO/OU steward.
Root Domain Owner	IT Planning and Enterprise Architecture	Data Ownership	Responsible for universal administrative groups. Placeholder for the entire forest. Can be the same as the forest owner.

TABLE 12-3 ADDS IT Roles

Role	Department	Role Type	Responsibilities
GPO/OU Steward	IT Planning and Enterprise Architecture	Data Ownership	Responsible for the proper operation of all OUs within the production forest. Must ensure that all OUs are justified and that each has a designated owner. Must maintain the GPO registry (all GPO documentation). Must ensure that all GPOs conform to standards. Must manage the GPO production release process.
OU Owners	Entire Organization	Data Ownership	Responsible for all information delegated within the OU. Must report regularly to the GPO/OU steward.

TABLE 12-3 ADDS IT Roles (*continued*)

Design the Services Administration Plan

The management and administration of Active Directory Domain Services, especially a network operating system (NOS)-centric ADDS, is concentrated mostly on the delegation of specific administrative rights to both service operators and security officers. Chapter 7 identified the requirement for local or regional security officers. If you have decided to delegate specific IT operations related to both the management of PCs and the management of users, you will need to proceed with the delegation of appropriate rights to these officers, as outlined in Chapter 7. In terms of user management especially, you will also need to proceed with the identification of your group managers and give them appropriate rights for the management of their user groups, which was also outlined in Chapter 7.

NOTE *The procedures for creating custom Microsoft Management Console (MMC) consoles and delegating rights, as well as that for creating appropriate administrative groups, are outlined in Chapter 7.*

Finally, you will need to proceed with service management delegation, as outlined in Chapters 8 and 9. Service management activities must be closely related to the Virtual Service Offerings OU structure you designed during the preparation of the parallel VSO network's services. It is also closely tied to the seven core server roles identified in Chapter 3, but additional operations are also required, as you well know—system backup, performance monitoring, security management, problem management, user support, and so on. The core roles to cover here include:

- File and print operators
- Application server operators
- Terminal server operators
- Collaboration server operators
- Infrastructure server operators
- Dedicated Web server operators

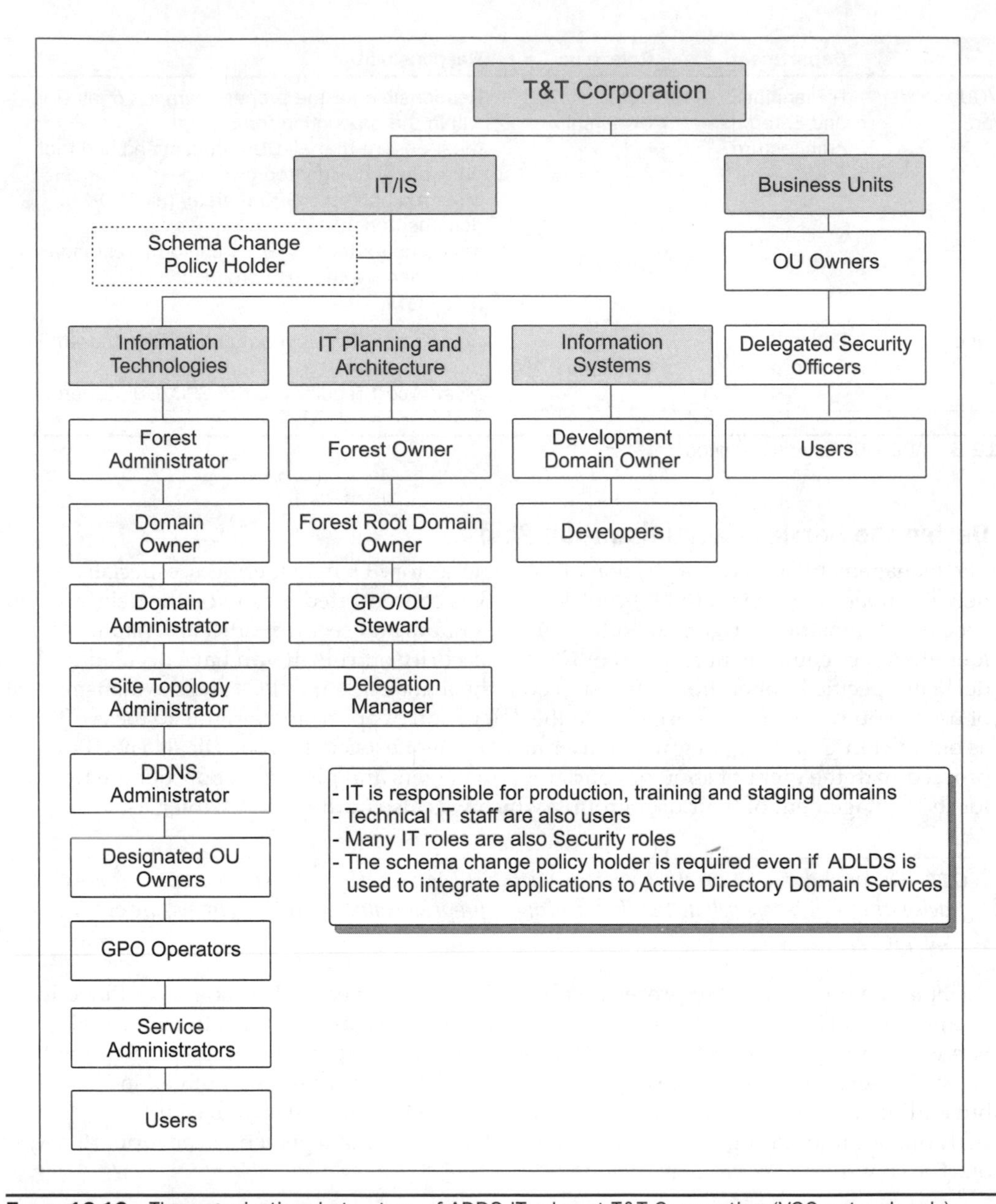

FIGURE 12-13 The organizational structure of ADDS IT roles at T&T Corporation (VSO network only)

These six operator groups require appropriate rights and delegation of the appropriate OUs. As with the Virtual Service Offerings OU structure, these operational groups may be subdivided into smaller, more focused groups that are responsible for specific technologies. Another role, identity management server operator, is your domain administrator and has already been identified earlier.

Role	Department	Role Type	Responsibilities
Forest Owner and Root Domain Owner	IT Planning and Enterprise Architecture	Service Management	Ensure that all forest standards are maintained within the forest. Responsible for the forest schema. Identify and document new standards. Responsible for universal administrative groups. Operational domain for the entire forest. May be divided roles for the resource pool and VSOs.
Forest Administrator	IT Group	Service Management	Ensure that the forest is operating properly. Responsible for the forest configuration. Enforce all forest standards. Responsible for forest root domain administration. Responsible for forest-wide Operation Master roles. Responsible for root domain-centric Operation Master roles. Responsible for the analysis/recommendation of the implementation of operational software that modifies the schema. Responsible for Global Catalog content. May be divided roles for the resource pool and VSOs.
DDNS Administrator	IT Group	Service Management	Ensure the proper operation of the forest namespace. Administer and manage internal DNS exchanges. Can also manage all resource-pool IP address allocations. May be divided roles for the resource pool and VSOs.
Site Topology Administrator	IT Group	Service Management	Monitor and analyze forest replication. Modify site topology to improve forest replication. Can also manage routing-level IP structure. May be divided roles for the resource pool and VSOs.
Virtual Service Administrators	IT Group	Service Management	Responsible for the virtualization service in the resource pool. Construct and deploy new virtual machines (or guest partitions). May be divided roles for the resource pool and VSOs.
GPO Operators	IT Group	Service Management	Design and test GPOs for use in production environments. Use the Group Policy Management Console to manage, debug, and modify GPOs. Report to the GPO/OU steward.
Resource Pool Administrator	IT Group	Service Management	Responsible for all hardware allocations. Responsible for all hardware staging. Build and run management virtual machines (or parent partitions). Can be the same as the Virtual Service Administrators.

TABLE 12-4 Resource Pool Administration Roles

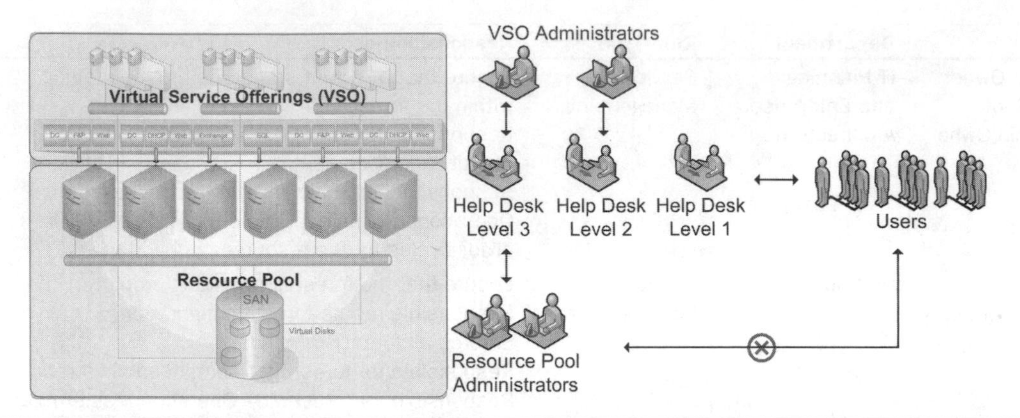

Figure 12-14 The interactions of resource pool administrators, Help desk technicians, virtual service administrators, and end users

Several of the management and administrative activities you need to cover will require special technologies. You need a tool to support application deployment, inventories, and software usage habit analysis. Another tool should support performance and alert management within the network, especially with critical services. But if you have a legacy network, you are most likely already using technologies of this type.

Rely on the WS08 Remote Server Administration Tools

Windows Server 2008 includes a whole series of new and improved management and administration tools. Several are located directly within the operating system and consist of command-line tools. WS08 includes several new command-line tools and over 200 command-line tools in general. In addition, Windows Server 2008 includes an integrated version of PowerShell, the most powerful scripting engine Microsoft has ever released. Both command-line tools and PowerShell are well documented in the WS08 Help Center. In addition, just like previous versions of Windows, WS08 includes the Remote Server Administration Tools (RSAT). These are useful to your administration team.

Chapter 3 outlined the importance of standard operating procedures (SOPs). In many cases, the best SOP is a script or command file because it ensures that the operation is always performed in the same manner. And since technical personnel often prefer not to write documentation, but to create automations and programs, the use of well-documented scripts (documented within the script itself) and a complete script inventory makes it easier to implement an SOP approach.

Tip *Microsoft provides excellent PowerShell scripting support in the TechNet Script Center at www.microsoft.com/technet/scriptcenter/hubs/msh.mspx.*

You should be careful who you give access to the RSAT. They are powerful tools that can cause a security risk if misused. One of the best ways to control their access is to store them on servers only and to use Terminal Services RemoteApps to give access to particular tools. An additional advantage of this approach is that you do not need to create and maintain administrative or operational workstations for your IT staff. Their workstations can be similar to other power users within your enterprise and focus on productivity tools. Then, when they need to perform an administrative task, they can launch the RemoteApps they need to access the appropriate tool.

This can also help increase security. Since the administrative tools are not on the operators' PCs, they can use their *user* account to perform their daily tasks. Then, when an administrative task is required, they can log in with their *administrative* account in the Terminal Services RemoteApps session. An additional layer of security can be added through the use of smart cards for administrative logons. Since WS08 supports the use of smart cards for administrators, you can ensure that two-factor authentication is required for the performance of all administrative tasks.

TIP *A good reference for administrators of Windows Server 2008 is the Windows Server 2008 Tech Center on Microsoft TechNet at http://technet.microsoft.com/en-us/windowsserver/default.aspx.*

Administration Tools for Resource Pools

As a resource pool administrator, you will be working extensively with the command line, since you will work mostly with Server Core. They will also be using some graphical tools through the use of management virtual machines—machines that are part of the resource pool domain but use the full installation in a virtual instance. This lets you use a graphical interface to manage the Server Core machines that make up your resource pool.

You might also obtain and work with System Center Virtual Machine Manager (SCVMM) because it is completely designed to work with and manage virtual machines, whether they run on Windows Server Hyper-V or through Microsoft Virtual Server. If you end up having a mix of hardware resources—both 32- and 64-bit—because you want to recover existing investments in hardware, SCVMM might just be the best tool to use.

TIP *More information on System Center Virtual Machine Manager can be found at www.microsoft.com/systemcenter/scvmm/default.mspx.*

Resource pool administrators may find themselves working with several additional tools, as listed in Table 12-5.

Administration Tools for Virtual Service Offerings

Like resource pool administrators, if you are a virtual service offerings administrator, you will be working extensively with Windows Server 2008. However, you will have the major advantage of having access to both PowerShell and the Server Manager graphical interface. This will give you a much more powerful management platform, since much more can be done with these tools than with the command line.

VSO administrators may find themselves working with several additional tools, as listed in Table 12-6.

Build a New Approach to Administration

Twenty years ago, when most computers were mainframes or minicomputers, operators and administrators had scheduled, specific tasks they needed to perform on an on-going basis. Each time a task was performed, they had to make note of the time and write their initials in a logbook to demonstrate when the task was performed and by whom.

Role/Feature	Tool	Command-Line
ADCS	Certificate Authority snap-in Certificates snap-in Certificate Templates snap-in Online Responder snap-in PKIView	CertUtil.exe CertReq.exe CertSrv.exe
ADDS	Server Manager | Active Directory Users and Computers Server Manager | Active Directory Sites and Services Active Directory Domains and Trusts	CSVDE Dsadd Dsmod Dsrm Dsmove Dsquery Dsget LDIFDE Ntdsutil
DNS Server	Server Manager | DNS Server	Nslookup
DHCP Server	Server Manager | DHCP Console	Netsh
File Services	Server Manager | DFS Management File Server Resource Manager Server Manager | Storage Reports Mgmt	Netstart, netstop (Macintosh) Dfsradmin.exe Dfsrdiag.exe Dirquota.exe FileScrn.exe StorRept.exe
PowerShell	PowerShell Interface on full installation or administrative workstation	No command
Print Services	Server Manager | Print Services Print MMC	Netstart, netstop (Macintosh) Lpg Lpr Print Prncnfg.vbs Prndrvr.vbs Prnjobs.vbs Prnport.vbs Prnqctl.vbs
Server Core	Local command-line Remote Custom MMC WS-Management and Windows Remote Shell (WinRS) Remote Desktop Remote PowerShell WMI Command (WMIC)	
Terminal Services	Server Manager | Terminal Services Terminal Services Manager Terminal Services Configuration Remote Desktops Console	Tsadmin.exe Tscc.msc Eventvwr.msc quser
Windows Server Hyper-V	Hyper-V Manager	

TABLE 12-5 Additional Administration Tools for Resource Pool Administrators

Role/Feature	Tool
ADCS	Certificate Authority
ADDS	Server Manager | Active Directory Users and Computers Server Manager | Active Directory Sites and Services Active Directory Domains and Trusts
ADFS	IIS Manager Active Directory Federation Services
ADLDS	Server Manager | Active Directory Users and Computers Server Manager | Active Directory Sites and Services Active Directory Domains and Trusts ADSI Edit Ldp.exe Schema management utilities
ADRMS	ADRMS MMC
Application Server	Server Manager | Component Services
DNS Server	Server Manager | DNS Server
DHCP Server	Server Manager | DHCP Console
Fax Server	Fax Service Manager
File Services	Server Manager | DFS Management File Server Resource Manager Server Manager | Quota Management Server Manager | File Screening Management Server Manager | Storage Reports Management
Network Access Protection	NPS MMC HRA MMC NPA Client Management MMC Routing and Remote Access MMC Wireless Network Policies Wired Network Policies
PowerShell	PowerShell Interface
Print Services	Server Manager | Print Services Print MMC
Terminal Services	Terminal Services Manager Server Manager | TS RemoteApp Manager Server Manager | TS Gateway Manager Terminal Services Configuration Terminal Licensing Manager Remote Desktops Terminal Web Access Administration

TABLE 12-6 Additional Administration Tools for VSO Administrators

Role/Feature	Tool
Web Server (IIS)	IIS 6.0 Manager IIS Manager
Windows Deployment Services	WDS Manager
Windows Server	Local command line WS-Management and Windows Remote Shell (WinRS) Remote Desktop PowerShell Server Manager WMI Command (WMIC)
Windows SharePoint Services	SharePoint 3.0 Central Administration SharePoint Products and Technologies Configuration Wizard

TABLE 12-6 Additional Administration Tools for VSO Administrators (*continued*)

Today, networks are made up of loosely coupled collections of servers and workstations that may or may not include either mainframes or minicomputers. Network or systems administration has become much more complex and covers many more tasks than in those days, but somehow, we've lost something in the transition. Today, most administrators don't keep logbooks any more. Most don't have fixed schedules for administrative activities. Many don't even perform the most basic administrative tasks.

We think it is time to go back to structured systems management. This is why Chapter 13 will provide an extensive list of administrative tasks and their scheduled occurrence based on our past experience. This chapter strives to be different by going straight to the heart of the matter. Each task outlined in the chapter is focused on the task itself. It does not usually include any extensive background information, because it assumes that when you need to perform the task, you do not need an explanation of how something works, but rather an explanation of how to do something because you're right in the middle of it and you want answers fast.

If possible, each task description covers at least three areas:

- The graphical interface
- The command line, if available
- A recommended script, if applicable

The first is how you would approach the task to perform it on one or two servers. In fact, the graphical approach is designed primarily for administrators of small networks that contain fewer than 25 servers. The second is how you would approach a task when you have to perform it on a series of servers. Unfortunately, even though Windows Server 2008 includes a host of new command-line tools, this type of tool is not always available for every task. The advantage of this approach is that it is easy to insert command lines into command files in either CMD or BAT format to run them automatically. Another advantage of the command file is that it can be piped into a text file for automatic record-keeping, making your task even simpler. A third advantage is that it runs on Server Core if the role is supported.

The third method is for extremely large networks, where there are hundreds of servers. Each time a script is applicable to a given task, it is referenced in the task.

The Administrative Task List

The core of Chapter 13 is the administrative task list. The list proposed here has been drawn from a series of different sources, including our own experience as well as our clients' real-life administrative environments. It has, in fact, been validated through discussion and demonstration with several system administrators, as well as several full-day administration courses delivered at Interop (www.interop.com). Much discussion and consultation produced the list you'll find in there.

In addition, the task list has been categorized according to recommended task frequency. Frequencies range from a daily, weekly, monthly, and ad hoc basis. The latter is a category that includes everything from biyearly, yearly, and basically any time because some tasks must be performed, but their timing cannot be predicted.

Wherever possible, tasks that pertain to resource pools and/or virtual service offerings are clearly identified and documented.

NOTE *If you find that the schedule or the task list don't fit your needs, send us a note. Let us know what suits you best, and we'll publish updated information on the companion web site. Write to us at Infos@reso-net.com.*

The System Administrator

As a system administrator, you'll use a variety of tools to perform the activities listed here. Some of the activities will be administrative, some technical. Some will always remain manual, while others will be automated. Some will use Windows Server 2008's graphical interface and others, the command line.

To perform this job, you'll have to be technician, administrator, manager, communicator, operator, user, negotiator, and sometimes, director. You'll also need a significant understanding of the environment you work in and of the technologies that support it. This is why it is so important for you to gain a sound understanding of Windows Server 2008.

Organize Your Task Schedule

The task frequency should help you organize and define an administrative schedule. You can use the Task Management feature in Microsoft Outlook to help manage your administration schedule, especially for weekly, monthly, and bi-annual tasks (see Figure 12-15). You should also include daily tasks in the schedule at first so that you can become familiar with them. It is also a good idea to review all the tasks that are listed as "ad hoc" tasks and determine when you want to perform them.

Basically, daily tasks are performed in the morning of each day. If you can automate them, then they consist mostly of verifying logs rather than actually performing the task. This saves considerable time. Weekly tasks are performed on Tuesday, Wednesday, and Thursday. If you manage your schedule right, you can perform most of these tasks in the mornings along with the daily tasks for those days. Spread out monthly tasks on Mondays and Fridays of each week. This leaves you a bit of time each day to perform ad hoc tasks as they come up.

November 07

Monday	Tuesday	Wednesday	Thursday	Friday	Saturday	Sunday
October 29	30	31	November 1	2	3	4
5	6	7	8	9	10	11
Daily Tasks	Daily Tasks	Daily Tasks	Daily Tasks	Daily Tasks		
Ad hoc	Weekly Tasks	Weekly Tasks	Weekly Tasks	Ad hoc		
Monthly Tasks	Ad hoc	Ad hoc	Ad hoc	Monthly Tasks		
12	13	14	15	16	17	18
Daily Tasks	Daily Tasks	Daily Tasks	Daily Tasks	Daily Tasks	Daily Tasks	Daily Tasks
Ad hoc	Weekly Tasks	Weekly Tasks	Weekly Tasks	Ad hoc		
Monthly Tasks	Ad hoc	Ad hoc	Ad hoc	Monthly Tasks		
19	20	21	22	23	24	25
Daily Tasks	Daily Tasks	Daily Tasks	Daily Tasks	Daily Tasks	Daily Tasks	Daily Tasks
Ad hoc	Weekly Tasks	Weekly Tasks	Weekly Tasks	Ad hoc		
Monthly Tasks	Ad hoc	Ad hoc	Ad hoc	Monthly Tasks		
26	27	28	29	30	December 1	2
Daily Tasks	Daily Tasks	Daily Tasks	Daily Tasks	Daily Tasks	Daily Tasks	Daily Tasks
Ad hoc	Weekly Tasks	Weekly Tasks	Weekly Tasks	Ad hoc		
Monthly Tasks	Ad hoc	Ad hoc	Ad hoc	Monthly Tasks		

FIGURE 12-15 A sample administrative task schedule

One objective of Chapter 13 is to help save you time. You might consider doing all daily tasks in the morning, then spending the afternoons of the middle of the week performing weekly tasks. Reserve two afternoons of each week for monthly tasks; this way you can spread them out over the course of the month. This should normally leave you time for other or ad hoc tasks. Start out with this type of schedule and refine it as you go.

Now that you've built a powerful new network and implemented the dynamic datacenter, you need to make sure it stays as pristine as when you first built it. That can only happen if you administer it in a structured manner. That is the goal of the task list found in Chapter 13—to help you maintain the network you built based on these first 12 chapters.

PART

Administer Windows Server 2008

This section deals with general administration tasks with Windows Server 2008. It covers both resource pool and virtual service offerings administration.

13

CHAPTER

Common Administration Tasks

Chapter 12 outlined how important it is to properly administer networks running Windows Server 2008 (WS08). The purpose of this chapter is to outline common administration tasks for each server category that was covered in the other parts of this book as you built and populated both your resource pool and the virtual service offerings it is designed to host. More than 150 tasks are listed here. If possible, each task description covers at least two areas:

- The graphical interface
- The command line, if available

In addition, since the PowerShell engine is available in Windows Server, you can generate scripts to perform most operations.

TIP *For a complete list of command-line tools, go to http://go.microsoft.com/fwlink/?linkid=81765.*

NOTE *You do not need to install the PowerShell engine on a server to run a script against it. You should install PowerShell on a Vista workstation and execute scripts remotely on your servers. Installing PowerShell on your servers increases risk, since it is one more component to manage.*

Tasks are divided by server role. The roles covered here are:

- **General server** Tasks that are common to all servers running WS08
- **File and print server** Tasks that are common to servers running the file and print role
- **Network infrastructure server** Tasks that are common to the network infrastructure role
- **Identity management server** Tasks that are common to the identity management role, including the Domain Controller (DC) role as well as the Domain Name System (DNS) role
- **Dedicated Web server and application server** Tasks that are common for Web and application servers, since these roles are so similar

- **Terminal Service server** Tasks that are common to servers running Terminal Services, both for remote administration and RemoteApps
- **Collaboration server** Tasks that are common for servers running the collaboration role

Tasks only cover common activities that are related to the base capabilities of WS08; add-on products from the Windows Server System or other sources are not covered.

NOTE *Task explanations are brief in this chapter, since the focus is on outlining what needs to be done. Background information for most tasks has already been identified in the previous 12 chapters of this book. For a corresponding list of tasks on Vista PCs, look up* Deploying and Administering Windows Vista Bible *by Shane Cribbs, Nelson Ruest, Danielle Ruest, and Bob Kelly (Wiley, 2008).*

Each section begins with a table that outlines the different tasks for this particular server role. The table lists each task by number, followed by the name and frequency of the task. In addition, the table lists whether the task applies to the resource pool, virtual service offerings, or both. The purpose of these tables is to help you both build a proper administrative schedule and identify which tasks need to be performed at which level on a system.

TIP *These tasks have borne the test of time. They are originally derived from* Windows Server 2003 Pocket Administrator *by Danielle Ruest and Nelson Ruest (McGraw-Hill, 2003). In addition, they have been tested through the delivery of full-day courses on Windows Server administration at Interop conferences (www.interop.com) in both Las Vegas and New York for the past several years. This course has been delivered to several thousand administrators, who all agree: Once you begin to work with the schedule outlined here, you will no longer have to work regular overtime to administer your network. Overtime mostly becomes a thing of the past! We urge you to follow this schedule and adapt it as your own.*

You will also need several tools to support each of these tasks. Throughout the implementation of your network, you installed several tools and discovered several ways to manage systems. Many administrators install administrative tools on their own PCs. This is fine to some degree, but some tools do not lend themselves to this type of installation. For example, Server Manager does not support remote computer connections; instead, you must publish Server Manager as a RemoteApp on each server and then link to the published application to remotely manage servers through this tool. This procedure is outlined in Chapter 9.

TIP *For additional information on tasks within Windows Server 2008, go to the WS08 TechCenter at http://technet.microsoft.com/en-us/windowsserver/2008/default.aspx.*

In addition, PowerShell does not run on Server Core, yet you can create a PowerShell command on a machine running the full installation of WS08 and execute it remotely on Server Core machines. This is why it is so important to have virtual machines that belong to the resource pool domain and that run the full installation just for the purpose of remote hardware resource management.

PowerShell is a command-line tool. This makes it a bit more complicated to work with for users who are not familiar with its commands. This is the reason why you should work through the PowerGUI, a free graphical interface for PowerShell that has been developed by Quest Software (www.quest.com). Quest has built a community of users that keeps adding functionality to the PowerGUI at http://powergui.org. For example, this community has provided a series of different add-ons and additional functionality in categories such as file system, Active Directory Domain Services, network management, and more (see Figure 13-1). There is no doubt that more and more will be added as administrators everywhere begin to work with PowerShell.

TIP *Microsoft also provides a lot of help on PowerShell. The main PowerShell page is at www.microsoft.com/windowsserver2003/technologies/management/powershell/default.mspx, and the TechNet Script Center offers many source scripts for PowerShell utilization at www.microsoft.com/technet/scriptcenter/hubs/msh.mspx.*

In addition, you can get help for PowerShell through the free PowerShell Help from Sapien Technologies. Sapien is the maker of PrimalScript, a powerful graphical scripting

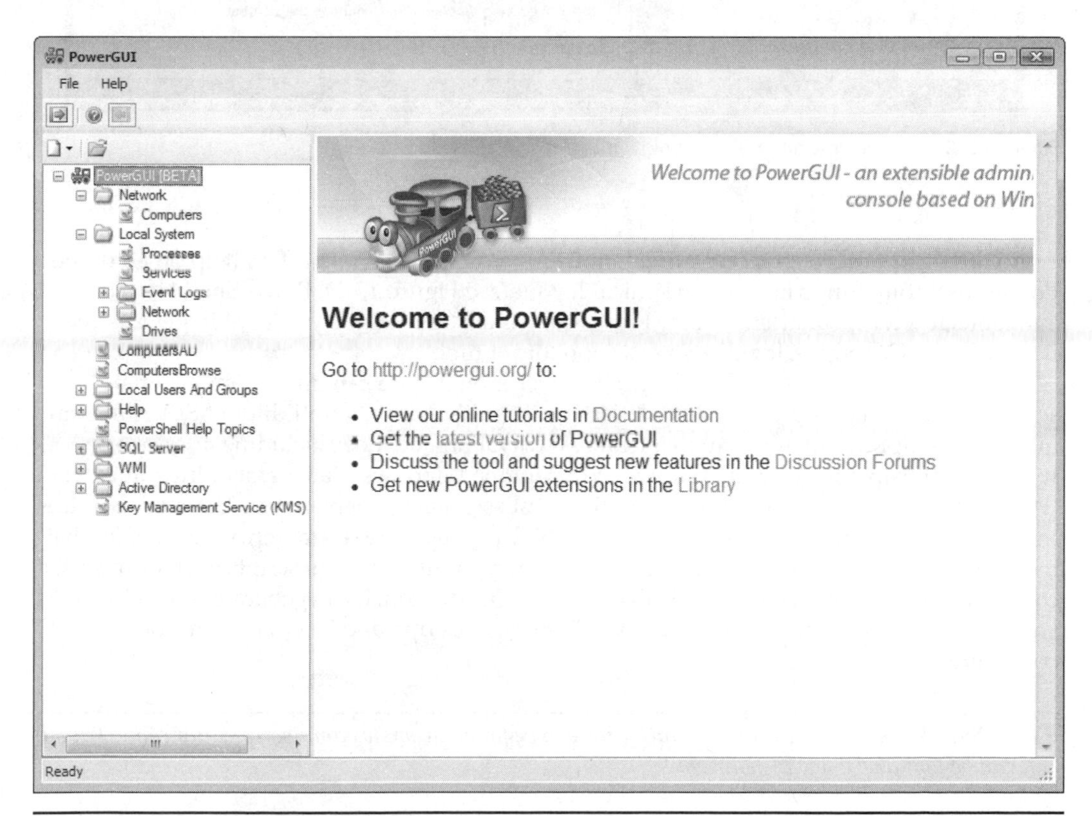

FIGURE 13-1 The PowerGUI interface with add-ons

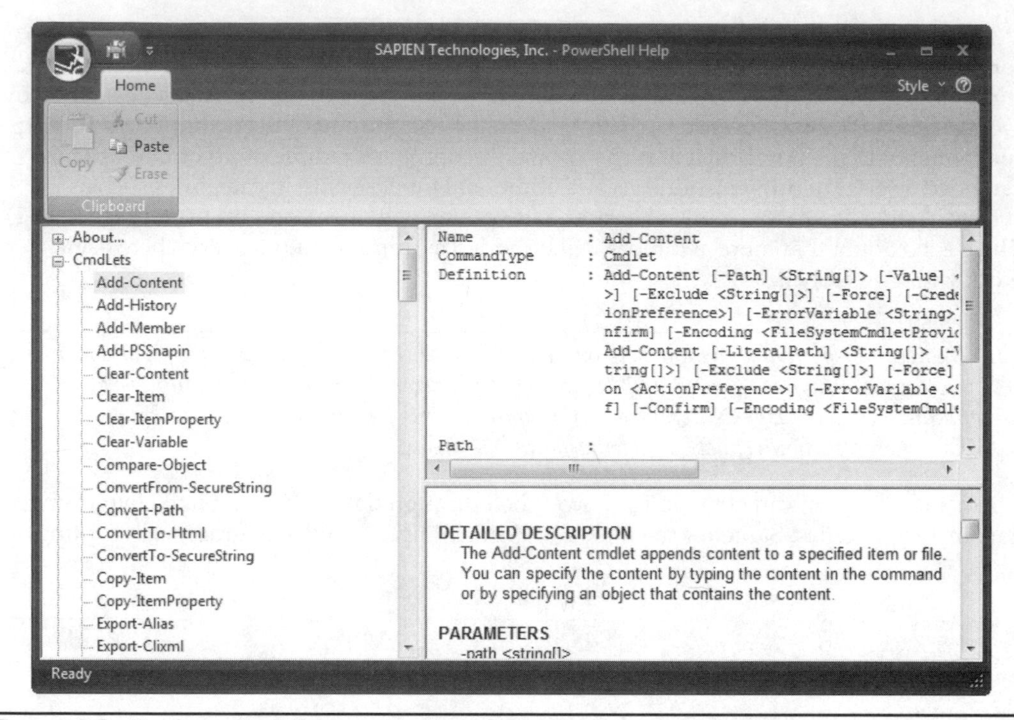

FIGURE 13-2 The PowerShell Help graphical interface

engine that supports several scripting languages. PowerShell Help offers help on all of the PowerShell commands in a nice graphical layout (see Figure 13-2). PowerShell Help is available at www.primalscript.com/Free_Tools/index.asp. While you're at it, get the free Logon Script Generator. It will also save you lots of time.

Finally, when all the help you can get just isn't enough, you can turn to professional scripting tools, such as Sapien's PrimalScript or iTripoli's AdminScriptEditor (ASE). ASE is an integrated scripting environment that features several unique tools, including a series of wizards that help you generate complex scripts for the Windows Management Instrumentation (WMI), Extensible Markup Language (XML), database management, Active Directory Services Interface (ADSI), and more (see Figure 13-3). ASE lets you create secure script executables that include encrypted administrator credentials, letting you run powerful scripts even in end-user contexts. For this alone, ASE is a valuable resource. In addition, it can generate scripts in a variety of languages, including PowerShell, KiXtart, VBScript, and just plain batch or command files.

TIP *More information on AdminScriptEditor can be found at www.adminscripteditor.com. iTripoli can be found at www.itripoli.com.*

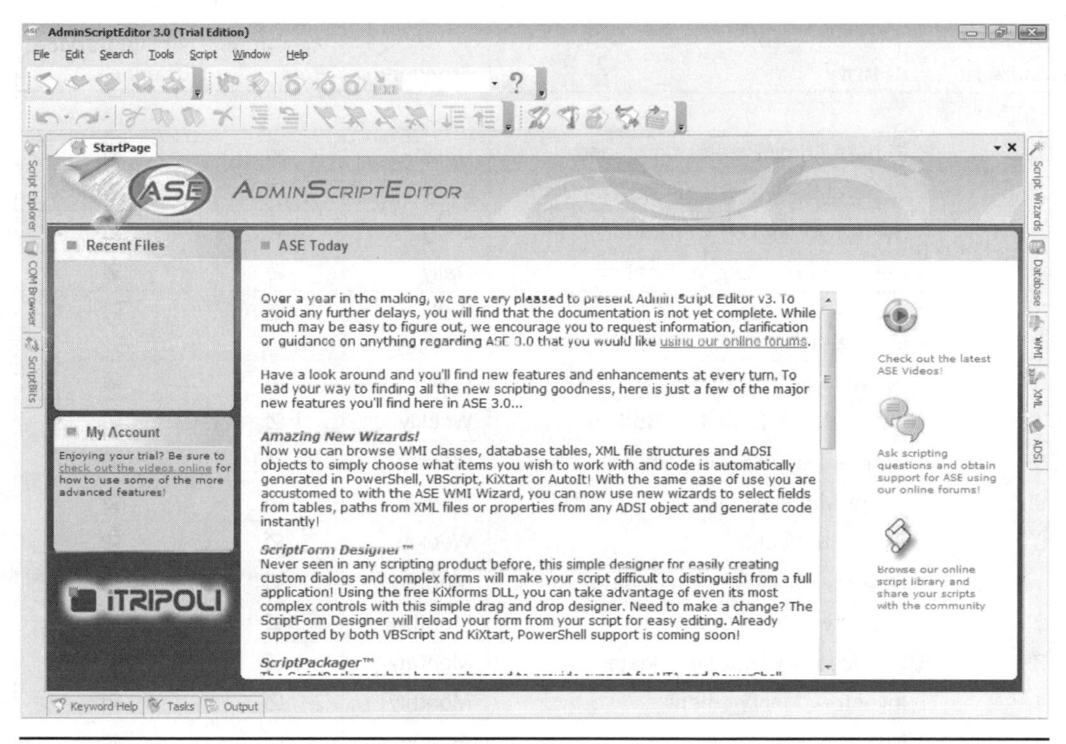

FIGURE 13-3 Working with AdminScriptEditor from iTripoli

General Server Administration

The general administration of Windows servers is divided into four administrative categories. These include general server, hardware, backup and restore, and remote administration. Table 13-1 outlines the administrative activities that you must perform on an ongoing basis to ensure proper operation of both the hardware resources you manage and the services you deliver to your user community. It also identifies the frequency of each task.

NOTE *Most of the activities in this section require local administrative rights.*

General Server Administration Activities

By their very nature, servers are designed to support multitudes of users in the performance of their daily work. It doesn't matter if the number of users in the organization is 4 or 4,000—a system administrator's job will always be to make sure the servers always work, that they are secure, and that they offer sufficient capabilities to continue providing a productive operation, now and in the future.

Several of the activities required to accomplish this goal apply to all servers. Many are related to the simple continued operation of the machine itself or the way you interact with the servers.

Procedure No.	Activity	Frequency	Resource Pool	Virtual Service Offerings
General Server				
GS-01	Run As Administrator Command	Daily	☑	☑
GS-02	General Service Status Verification	Daily	☑	☑
GS-03	System Event Log Verification	Daily	☑	☑
GS-04	Security Event Log Verification	Daily	☑	☑
GS-05	Service and Admin Account Management	Daily	☑	☑
GS-06	Activity Log Maintenance	Daily	☑	☑
GS-07	Anti-malware Definition Update	Weekly	☑	☑
GS-08	Uptime Report Management	Weekly	☑	☑
GS-09	Script Management	Weekly	☑	☑
GS-10	Server Reboot	Weekly	☑	☑
GS-11	Security Policy Review/Update	Monthly	☑	☑
GS-12	Security Patch Verification	Monthly	☑	☑
GS-13	Service Pack/Hot Fix Update	Monthly	☑	☑
GS-14	Inventory Management	Monthly	☑	☑
GS-15	New Software Evaluation	Ad hoc		☑
GS-16	Software Restriction Policies	Ad hoc	☑	☑
GS-17	Custom Microsoft Management Console (MMC) Creation	Ad hoc	☑	☑
GS-18	Resource Pool Management Console Creation	Ad hoc	☑	
GS-19	Server Staging	Ad hoc	☑	☑
GS-20	Automatic Antivirus Signature Reception	Ad hoc	☑	☑
GS-21	Scheduled Task Generation/ Verification	Ad hoc	☑	☑
GS-22	Security Template Creation/ Modification	Ad hoc	☑	☑
GS-23	Technical Environment Review	Ad hoc	☑	☑
GS-24	System and Network Documentation	Ad hoc	☑	☑
GS-25	Service Level Agreement Management	Ad hoc	☑	☑
GS-26	Troubleshooting Priority Management	Ad hoc	☑	☑
GS-27	Workload Review	Ad hoc	☑	☑

Table 13-1 General Server Administration Task List

Procedure No.	Activity	Frequency	Resource Pool	Virtual Service Offerings
Hardware				
HW-01	Network Hardware Checkup	Weekly	☑	
HW-02	Server Basic Input Output System (BIOS) Management	Monthly	☑	
HW-03	Firmware and Server Management Software Update Management	Monthly	☑	
HW-04	Device Management	Ad hoc	☑	☑
Backup and Restore				
BR-01	System Disk Backup Generation	Daily	☑	☑
BR-02	Backup Verification	Daily	☑	☑
BR-03	Offsite Backup Management	Weekly	☑	☑
BR-04	Disaster Recovery Strategy Testing	Monthly	☑	☑
BR-05	Restore Procedure Testing	Monthly	☑	☑
BR-06	Backup Strategy Review	Monthly	☑	☑
Remote Administration				
RA-01	Server Remote Desktop Connection (RDC) Management	Monthly	☑	☑
RA-02	PC RDC Management	Ad hoc		☑
RA-03	User Support Through Remote Assistance	Ad hoc		☑

TABLE 13-1 General Server Administration Task List (*continued*)

GS-01: Run As Administrator Command

Activity Frequency: Daily

Working with servers requires you to have administrative access rights to them. The access granted to Windows Server 2008 administrators is powerful, because it allows for complete control of a machine at the local level, a domain at the domain level, or a forest at the enterprise level. These rights must be used with care and consideration, especially because anything executing within an administrative context will automatically have all rights on a machine.

CAUTION *Because of the risk they pose to your organization, administrative accounts should both be renamed from the default and have strong complex passwords, usually of more than 15 characters. Ultimately, they should be linked to smart cards for additional security.*

A virus or a worm, for example, executing within an administrative context can cause a lot more damage than within a user context. This is the reason why the Run As Administrator command is so important. Because it supports the execution of a command or application within a different security context, this command lets you use administrative access more sparingly, working normally with a user-level account, but performing administrative activities with just the right amount of access and no more—and protecting corporate assets all the while.

NOTE *Any tool can be accessed through Run As Administrator. In Windows Server 2008, just right-click the tool and select Run As Administrator; give the appropriate credentials, and click OK to launch the tool.*

This activity is identified as a daily activity because you will be using this command on a daily basis as you perform administrative activities on every server in your organization.

Alternatively, you can use the Run As command through the command line. The problem with this, however, is that there is no way to circumvent User Account Control (UAC) through the command line. While you run command-line operations in different user contexts, the Run As command-line tool will never be able to elevate them to the appropriate administrative level. Therefore, it's best to rely on the graphical interface and use the Run As Administrator command. If you want to run command lines with administrative privileges, open a Command Prompt window with the Run As Administrator command.

TIP *There is no elevation command in Windows Vista so that your tools will run with administrative privileges by default. There is, however, a great little utility written by Michael Murgolo, a consultant with Microsoft Consulting Services, that does just that. Download it at www.microsoft.com/technet/technetmag/issues/2007/06/UtilitySpotlight/default.aspx.*

In addition, one of the most useful administrative utilities is the ability to launch a Command Prompt window through Windows Explorer in either normal or elevated mode. The only way to do this is to add a registry hack to your servers. For a list of the registry entries required to create command prompts in either normal or elevated modes, go to www.randyrants.com/2007/02/vista_tip_eleva.html. Save the entries into a file with the .reg extension, and double-click it to execute it on your servers. The result will be two "Command Prompt Here" commands (see Figure 13-4).

Finally, just like there is no default way to normally generate a Command Prompt window at the location you are in, there is no default way to do this with PowerShell either. This means you need to use a hack to do so. Use the utilities mentioned earlier for elevation

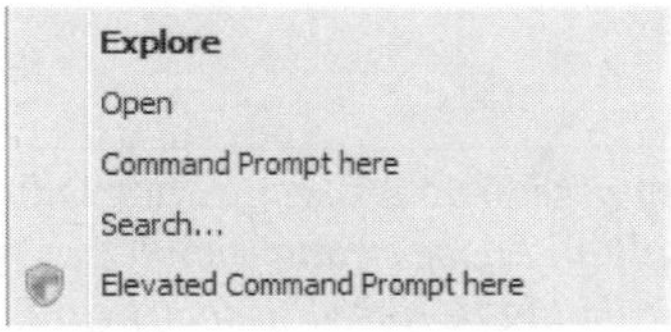

FIGURE 13-4 Using "Command Prompt Here" registry hacks

(by Michael Murgolo) to create similar entries in the context menu as those created for the command prompt earlier. Michael's files are not in REG format, but in INF format. This means that you must right-click the appropriate file and select Install to get it to run. Once installed, you will have appropriate prompts in the context menu of any folder through Windows Explorer.

GS-02: General Service Status Verification

Activity Frequency:	Daily

The very purpose of a server is to deliver services. It is deemed as functioning properly when all the services it is supposed to be delivering are up and running and in a fully functional state. This is why it is so important for you to properly document not only the specific role of each server in your network infrastructure, but also the actual services it has installed and the general state of each of these services.

NOTE *A detailed Server Data Sheet can be found at the companion Web site: www.Reso-Net.com/livre.asp?p=main&b=WS08. Use this sheet as the basis of your server documentation to identify installed services.*

To verify the status of services on the servers you work with:

1. Launch the Server Manager console for the appropriate server (Quick Launch area | Server Manager or other shortcut location).
2. Move to the Services window (Configuration | Services).
3. Sort the services according to status by clicking Status in the top of the Services window.
4. Verify against your records that all services are in the appropriate running and startup state. If some services use credentials other than Local System account, use Procedure GS-05 to make sure these credentials are entered properly.
5. Record and investigate any service that is not in its intended state. Verify all servers.

Alternatively, all services can be controlled through the `SC` or `NET` commands. For the latter, type `NET` at the command prompt to view the list of supported commands. Type `NET HELP COMMANDNAME` at the command prompt to get detailed information on each command. The only drawback of this command is that it cannot be run remotely. You have to open either local or remote sessions on the server you need to manage to use these commands.

The `SC` command, on the other hand, can run on any server you have access to. Its command structure is as follows:

```
sc \\servername query >filename.txt
```

Where *servername* is the name of the server you want to access—leave it blank for the local server—and `QUERY` provides the status of each service. Type `SC /?` for more information. Using the chevron character (>) along with a file name will automatically pipe the result of the command into a text file. You can put a series of these commands in a command file (using the .cmd extension) and use Procedure GS-21 to automatically generate the output files every day. This helps you quickly identify the state of all services in your network, because all you need to do is review the results of the text file to view the status of services on each server.

Finally, you can use a PowerShell script to perform the same action. PowerShell scripts have a .ps1 extension and must run on a system that has PowerShell installed. Use the following script to query service status:

```
get-service
```

GS-03: System Event Log Verification

Activity Frequency:	Daily

Another useful diagnostic tool is the System Event Log. It details information about general server health and operation. Each significant event is recorded, and an event description is entered. Events can be in one of three states:

- **Information** An event has occurred and it is significant enough to be recorded. These events usually record normal operation of the server.
- **Warning** A non-critical error has occurred and warrants a record in the Event Log. Watch these event types carefully, because they can quickly become errors.
- **Error** A critical error has occurred and should be investigated and repaired. All of these events must lead to investigation and repair. Windows Server 2008 will often list detailed information about avenues of investigation.

To verify the System Event Log on the servers you work with:

1. Launch the Server Manager console for the appropriate server (Quick Launch area | Server Manager or other shortcut location).
2. Move to the System Event Log (Diagnostics | Event Viewer | Windows Logs | System).
3. Identify any errors or warnings. Take appropriate action if either appears.

Make note of any corrective action you need to take. Use Procedure GS-06 to log the different events you investigate each day.

TIP *You can automatically view any critical event on each server by going to the Event Log home page, where a summary of the most important events will be displayed.*

You can also reset the size of each Windows Log. To do so, right-click the log name in the tree pane of the MMC, and select Properties. Set maximum log size and any other options that are relevant to your needs.

CAUTION *If you set the log file to lock (Do Not Overwrite Events) once it reaches maximum log size, Windows will automatically shut down the server until the log file is cleared.*

Use the WEVTUTIL command to create command scripts:

```
wevtutil qe system >filename.txt
```

Be careful, as this command will generate a ton of XML text.
A PowerShell script would consist of:

```
get-eventlog system | outfile filename.txt
```

This command will generate pure text as opposed to XML output.

GS-04: Security Event Log Verification

Activity Frequency:	Daily

If your organization has enabled access auditing, it will be important for you to verify the Security Windows Logs on a daily basis to ensure that there are no untoward events occurring in your network. Enabling auditing is discussed in Chapter 10.

TIP *By default, all audit events are turned on in Windows Server 2008; therefore, you only need to further refine and add to the objects you want to verify. In addition, the Security Windows Logs are defined at 132 megabytes (MB) and are overwritten as needed once the log is full.*

Follow Procedure GS-03 to review the Security Windows Logs. Change "System" for "Security" in all commands.
You can also use the AUDITPOL command to control the audit policies you set. Use AUDITPOL /? to get more information on this command.

TIP *For information on how to use the Event Log to its fullest measure, read the article series titled: "Manage Change in Windows Vista" at www.reso-net.com/download.asp?FIchier=A195.*

GS-05: Service and Admin Account Management

Activity Frequency:	Daily

Administrative accounts are high-priced commodities in every network. Gone are the days when they had to be handed out generally to almost anyone who complained loud enough. In today's Windows Server 2008 network, you can and should define just the right amount of access rights for each and every person who interacts with your system. Therefore, you should have very few administrative accounts at the domain or forest level and have many more specialty administrative accounts that focus on granting just the right amount of access to do a specific job. These accounts and the accesses they grant should be managed, or at least reviewed, on a daily basis.

Several procedures support the assignation of appropriate rights and permissions to administrative accounts. Some are assigned through the integration of built-in security groups, such as server or backup operators, while others are assigned through the association with user rights-assignment policies to the accounts, or rather, the groups that contain these accounts. Three tools support the assignation of appropriate rights:

- Use Active Directory Users and Computers to create the accounts and assign them to either built-in or custom administrative groups.
- Use Group Policy Management Console (GPMC) to locate and edit the appropriate Group Policy Object (GPO).
- Use Group Policy Editor to actually assign the user rights.

In addition, you might use Server Manager or the Computer Management console to assign local rights to domain groups and accounts.

To modify user rights, use Procedure DC-33 to edit the appropriate GPO, usually one that will affect all of the objects you want to modify. Locate the User Rights Assignment setting (Computer Configuration | Policies | Windows Settings | Security Settings | Local Policies | User Rights Assignment), and assign appropriate settings to administrative accounts. Remember, it is always easier to assign rights to a group than to individual objects. It is a good idea to regroup administrative accounts into administrative groups. Use Procedure DC-33 again to ensure proper use of these accounts.

In addition, in today's enterprise network, you must manage service accounts—accounts that are granted enough administrative privilege to support the operation of specific services in your network. For example, you might use service accounts to run antivirus engines or scheduled tasks (see Procedure GS-21). The advantage of using a service account to operate a given service or automated task is that you can also use the Security Event Log to review the proper operation of the service. A success event is written in this log each time the service uses its privileged access or logs on.

Service accounts, in particular, must have these specific settings and properties:

- Account must have a complex name
- Account must have a complex password at least 15 characters long
- Password never expires
- User cannot change password
- Act as part of the operating system right
- Log on as a service right

CAUTION *The last two settings should be applied with alacrity, especially Act As Part Of The Operating System, because they grant extremely high access levels to the service account.*

The last two settings must be set in a GPO or in the Local Security Policy (LSP) under the User Rights Assignment settings. Remember to regroup service accounts into service groups as well, if you can.

Service accounts present the additional operational overhead of requiring regular password changes. This cannot be limited to simply changing the password in Active Directory Users and Computers, because when service accounts are assigned to services, you must give them the account's password for the service to work properly. This means you also need to modify the password in the service's Properties dialog box. Use Procedure GS-02 to do so.

GS-06: Activity Log Maintenance

Activity Frequency:	Daily

Part of your job is also to record both what you do and what you need to do to maintain or repair the network on an ongoing basis. This is the reason why you should keep a daily activity log. Ideally, this log will be electronic and transportable so that you can make annotations whenever you need to. It can be stored in either a Tablet PC or a Pocket PC that you carry with you at all times. The Tablet PC is more useful, because it supports a fully working version of Windows and could allow you to run virtual machines to simulate problematic situations. In addition, Microsoft OneNote is ideally suited to logging daily activities.

If both devices are unattainable, you should at least use a paper logbook that you carry at all times. You can maintain this log as best suits you, but it is sometimes better to note activities as you perform them than to wait for a specific time of day.

NOTE *A sample daily activity log in Microsoft Excel format can be found on the companion Web site at www.Reso-Net.com/livre.asp?p=main&b=WS08.*

GS-07: Anti-malware Definition Update

Activity Frequency:	Daily

CAUTION *Virus and general malware protection is a key element of an integrated defense system. It is essential to make sure this tool is working properly on an ongoing basis.*

This is the first placeholder task. It is here because you need to perform this task on servers no matter what, but it isn't a core Windows Server 2008 task.

Three tasks are required on a daily basis for malware protection management:

- Check virus or malware management logs to make sure no viruses have been found in the last day.
- Check your virus or malware management console to determine that your signatures are up to date. Reconfigure the update schedule if it is not appropriate or if threats increase.
- Perform random protection scans on file shares, applications, and system drives to make sure they are not infected.

Use the virus or malware management console to set the appropriate settings. In some engines, most of these tasks can be automated and consoles can alert you if new malware is found.

GS-08: Uptime Report Management

Activity Frequency:	Weekly

Once a week, you'll need to produce an uptime report for all servers. This helps you track the status of various servers and identify which configurations are best in your environment. There are several tools you can use to produce these reports.

The SYSTEMINFO command gives you information on the server you are examining as well as how long it has been running. Another tool, UPTIME, is designed specifically to report on server uptime. This tool is available as a download only. Go to Knowledge Base article number 232243 to obtain it (http://support.microsoft.com/kb/232243).

Using the last tool and a little ingenuity, you can produce your uptime reports automatically:

1. Download and install UPTIME.EXE into the C:\TOOLKIT folder.

NOTE *Create a custom folder named Toolkit on the system drive of your servers so that administrators can share tools that you populate it with. Secure this folder with the appropriate permissions, for example, removing the Authenticated Users group and assigning access rights only to the Administrators' local group.*

2. Create a command file that contains the following code line, one for each server in your network:

   ```
   uptime \\servername
   ```

3. Save the command file when done.
4. Use Procedure GS-21 to assign the command file to a weekly scheduled task.
5. In the scheduled task, use the following command to assign output to a text file:

   ```
   commandfile.cmd >filename.txt
   ```

The uptime command will create the report for you every week. All you have to do is locate the output file and review the results.

CAUTION *Make sure the UPTIME.EXE tool is available to the scheduled task. Ideally, include the path to the command in the command file so that the scheduled task can find the command when it needs it.*

GS-09: Script Management

Activity Frequency: Weekly

Scripts are an essential part of Windows network administration. Windows Server supports several scripting engines: command files, PowerShell, and Visual Basic Scripts (VBScripts). Ideally, you will be using PowerShell scripts as much as possible, because it is a simpler scripting environment and is completely oriented towards system administration. But in many cases, you need to rely on VBScripts, for example, to create login scripts. VBScripts can be run in either graphic (intended for users) or character mode (administrative scripts). Running a script in either mode is controlled by the command you use to activate it:

```
wscript scriptname
cscript scriptname
```

Where WSCRIPT runs it in graphical mode and CSCRIPT runs it in character mode.

With the proliferation of script viruses and trojans, you should make sure the scripts you run are secure. The best way to do so is to sign your scripts with a digital certificate. First you'll need to obtain the certificate. This can be done from a third-party certificate authority, or it can be done by yourself if you decide to use your own certificate server (through Active Directory Certificate Services). Use Procedure DC-29 to do so.

NOTE *If you create all your scripts through Windows PowerShell, you won't have to sign them because all PowerShell scripts are digitally signed by default.*

Every script you create and sign should be fully documented. This documentation should include all pertinent information on the script and should be reviewed and kept up to date on a weekly basis.

In addition to a logon script, you may want to display a pre-logon message to your users. This helps make sure users are forewarned of the legal consequences of the misuse of IT equipment and information. Once again, this is done through a GPO. Use Procedure DC-33 to edit the appropriate GPO and modify the following settings to display a logon message:

- Computer Configuration | Policies | Windows Settings | Security Settings | Local Policies | Security Options | Interactive Logon: Message Title for users attempting to log on
- Computer Configuration | Policies | Windows Settings | Security Settings | Local Policies | Security Options | Interactive Logon: Message Text for users attempting to log on

GS-10: Server Reboot

Activity Frequency:	Weekly

CAUTION *If you choose to use this command on host servers, you will need to make sure that you do not perform it on both the active and passive nodes of your cluster at the same time. Perform it on one, wait about one hour, and then perform it on the other. Shutting down a node will automatically force the virtual machines running on that node to fail-over to the other so that they can continue to provide end-user services.*

Since the delivery of Windows NT by Microsoft, especially NT version 4 in 1996, most systems administrators have found it wise to regularly reboot servers running this operating system to clear out random access memory and to generally refresh the system. Since then, Microsoft has invested significant effort to limit and even completely avoid this procedure.

CAUTION *It is strongly recommended that you begin by examining how Windows Server 2008 operates within your network before you continue to use this practice. You will find that WS08 servers no longer require regular reboots. In fact, you will be surprised at the level of service you can achieve with this operating system. This will be in evidence in the uptime reports you produce in Procedure GS-08.*

If you feel you still need to perform this activity on a regular basis, you can use the `shutdown` command from the command line to remotely shut down and reboot servers. The following command shuts down and reboots a remote server:

```
shutdown -r -f -m \\servername
```

Where -R requests a reboot, -F forces running applications to close, and -M specifies the machine you want to shut down. As with all character-mode commands, you can create a command file that includes a command for each server you want to shut down. If you put the shutdown commands in a command file, you should also use the -C switch to add a shutdown comment to the command:

```
shutdown -r -f -m \\servername -c "Weekly Reboot Time"
```

Use Procedure GS-21 to assign the command file to a scheduled task.

NOTE *The shutdown command automatically bypasses the Shutdown Event Tracker—a dialog box you must normally complete when shutting down a server running Windows Server 2008. To track shutdown events, always add the -c switch to the command.*

The Shutdown Event Tracker is a tool Windows Server 2008 uses to log shutdown and reboot information. It stores its information in Event Logs and can be viewed through Server Manager | Diagnostics | Event Viewer | Windows Logs. It can be controlled through two GPO settings:

- Computer Configuration | Policies | Administrative Templates | System | Display Shutdown Event Tracker
- Computer Configuration | Policies | Administrative Templates | System | Activate Shutdown Event Tracker System State Data feature

Use Procedure DC-33 to modify the appropriate GPO. This GPO should affect all servers.

GS-11: Security Policy Review/Update

Activity Frequency:	Monthly

The security policy is the one tool that is at the core of your security program. It determines everything, including how you respond to security breaches and how you protect yourself from them. It serves to identify which common security standards you wish to implement within your organization. These involve both technical and non-technical policies and procedures. An example of a technical policy would be the security parameters you will set at the staging of each computer in your organization. A non-technical policy would deal with the habits users should develop to select complex passwords and protect them. Finally, you will need to identify the parameters for each policy you define.

Your monthly verification of the security policy should include a review of all of its items and answer questions such as:

- How effective is your user communications program? Should you enhance it?
- How effective are your security strategies? Should they be reinforced?
- Is your administrative staff following all security principles?
- Are there potential breaches that have not been identified?
- Is new technology secure? What is its impact on your global security strategy?

Document and communicate all changes you make during this review.

GS-12: Security Patch Verification

Activity Frequency: Monthly

Security patches are a factor of life in any computing environment. But if your operating systems are designed properly and your servers run only the services required to support their role, you can most likely limit your available security patch verification to a monthly review.

Microsoft offers several tools and techniques both within and without Windows to perform this activity. Microsoft offers e-mail notification for security bulletins. You can register for these and other Microsoft newsletters at www.microsoft.com/technet/security/secnews/default.mspx. You will require a Microsoft Passport to do so. If you don't have one, follow the instructions on the site to get one.

Microsoft isn't the only organization to send out security bulletins. An excellent source of this type of information is the SANS Institute. You can subscribe to SANS newsletters at www.sans.org/newsletters.

In addition, Windows Server 2008 includes automated updates. This means it can pre-download hot fixes and updates, and tell you when they are ready for installation. This feature can also be modified to tell all machines in your network to obtain patch information from a central intranet server. Once again, these are GPO settings. They are located in Computer Configuration | Policies | Administrative Templates | Windows Components | Windows Update, and include:

- **Configure Automatic Updates** In a corporate environment, you should use setting 4 to download and install updates according to a fixed monthly schedule.
- **Specify intranet Microsoft update service location** Name the server from which updates will be downloaded; use the server's full DNS name.
- **No auto-restart for scheduled Automatic Updates installations** Use this setting to stop servers from restarting after update installation. Servers can be restarted on a more regular basis with Procedure GS-10.

Use Procedure DC-33 to edit the appropriate GPO. This GPO should apply to servers only. Another GPO should be set similarly for workstations, but preferably using a different intranet source server. These settings should be used in conjunction with Windows Server Update Services (WSUS). Use the WSUS server to validate the security fixes and updates you require in your corporate environment. Document all your changes.

NOTE *To download and install WSUS, search for "Microsoft Server Update Services" at http://technet.microsoft.com/en-us/wsus/default.aspx.*

You can also use the Microsoft Baseline Security Analyzer (MBSA) to analyze the hot fix and service pack status of your systems. MBSA is available at www.microsoft.com/technet/security/tools/mbsahome.mspx.

Since the MBSA setup file is a Windows Installer file, you can install it interactively or you can use Procedure DC-15 to install it to several target systems. MBSA can be used to scan a single system or to scan a complete network. It will even scan network segments based on Internet Protocol (IP) address ranges. To scan a system:

1. Launch MBSA (Start menu | All Programs | Microsoft Baseline Security Analyzer).
2. Select Scan A Computer.
3. Use either the computer name or its IP address, and select the options you want to use in the scan. Click Start Scan (see Figure 13-5).
4. View the report in the MBSA details pane when the scan is complete. The report is automatically saved with the domain name, computer name, and date in the `\%USERPROFILE\SECURITY SCANS` folder directly under Users.

CAUTION *Store these reports carefully because they detail sensitive information about your systems.*

GS-13: Service Pack/Hot Fix Update

Activity Frequency: Monthly

TIP *Obtain the Microsoft Windows Server Update Services 3.0 Operations Guide at http://technet2.microsoft.com/windowsserver/en/library/9b65850d-17a0-440e-9cad-2eb881011f5f1033.mspx?mfr=true.*

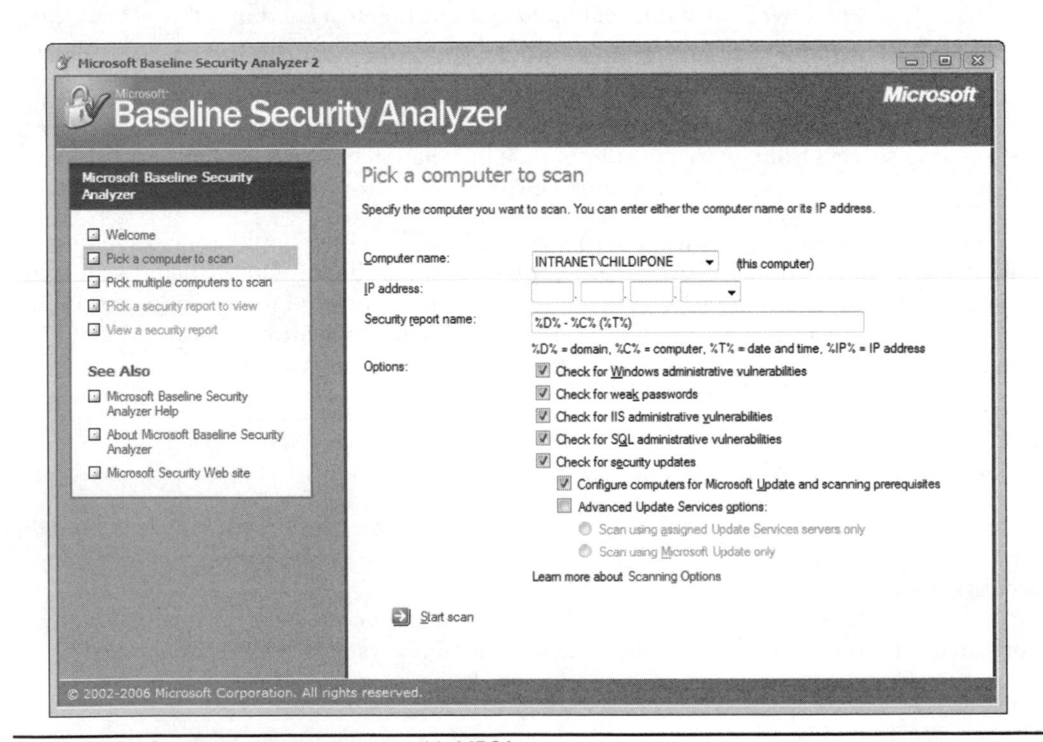

FIGURE 13-5 Running a computer scan with MBSA

The best way to manage updates is through a tool like Windows Server Update Services (WSUS) because once an update has been approved in WSUS, it will install automatically on all targeted systems if you have set your GPOs appropriately (see Procedure GS-12). The best way to run WSUS is to have two environments: the production environment and a test lab. Have a few test machines (PCs and servers) linked to the test lab server. Use the test lab to approve updates:

1. Launch the WSUS console on the test server by going to Start menu | Administrative Tools | Windows Server Update Services or through Server Manager.
2. Click Approve Updates to review available updates. Sort the updates based on status. Select the ones that apply to your environment.
3. Click the Approve button to apply each of the updates you selected. Wait until they are applied on your test machines, and reboot them if required.
4. Verify the proper operation of the test systems after application. If there is a problem, remove the updates one by one, until the problem is corrected, to identify the faulty update. Retry the remaining updates. Note the updates to approve.
5. Move to your production WSUS server, and approve updates for distribution to your production systems.

Hot fixes and updates install automatically through WSUS, but this is not the case for service packs. These tend to require more extensive deployment preparation for installation. Their preparation involves much more thorough testing than hot fixes because service packs affect so many areas of a server. Once a service pack is assessed and approved, use Procedure DC-08 to deploy it (unless you use a more robust deployment tool, which does not rely on Group Policy software installation).

GS-14: Inventory Management

Activity Frequency:	**Monthly**

One of the tasks you should perform on at least a monthly basis is inventory management. This includes both hardware and software inventories. You may or may not have a third-party inventory management tool in your network. If you do, great; your task is done. If you don't, you'll need to use other tools. Microsoft offers the Microsoft Inventory Analysis (MSIA) tool. It does not manage the inventory for all software, but at least it manages all Microsoft software. To download the MSIA, go to www.microsoft.com/resources/sam/msia.mspx.

MSIA is a wizard-based tool that lets you perform three tasks:

- Scan a local computer for Microsoft products.
- Prepare a command-line input file that includes all of the scan settings you want to use.
- Run a scan using a previously prepared command-line input file.

In addition, it lets you scan local systems, remote systems, or an entire network all at once. Installation is based on the Windows Installer service. You can install it interactively or use Procedure DC-15 to install it on target computers. To create a command-line input file:

1. Launch MSIA (Start menu | All Programs | Microsoft Software Inventory Analyzer). Click Next.

2. Select Scan Using Custom Settings and Create Custom Settings. Click Browse to select the output folder, and name the output file. It will have a .cli extension for command-line input. Click Save to create the file. Click Next to continue.
3. Select the scope of the scan: Local Computer, Network, or Report Consolidation. Click Next.

CAUTION *If you select Network, you will need to provide proper credentials to run the scan on all systems.*

4. In the Download Database Files dialog box, click Download. MSIA will go to the Microsoft Web site and download the latest data files for Microsoft products. You will be prompted to accept a Microsoft certificate for the installation of the database. Click Yes. Click OK when the download is complete. Click Next.
5. Select the products you want to scan for, and click Add. (You can use CTRL-click to select more than one product.) Select Save These Products As The Default, and then click Next.
6. Select the report format(s). Click Browse to select the report folder, and name the report file. Click Save to create the file. Click Next to continue.
7. You can choose to consolidate summary reports. These are useful for management. Click Next.
8. You can select to send the summary report by e-mail to someone (or you can send it later). If you need to send it to a group, create a distribution group and enter its e-mail address here.
9. Do not select Save Settings As Default because you are creating a command-line input file.
10. Click Finish to close the command-line input file.

To run an MSIA scan:

1. Launch MSIA (Start menu | All Programs | Microsoft Software Inventory Analyzer). Click Next.
2. Select Scan Using Custom Settings and Load Existing Custom Settings. If the file displayed is not the file you want to use, click Browse to select the folder and file you require. Click Open to load the file. Click Next to continue. MSIA scans the systems based on the file settings.
3. Select View Reports Now, and click Finish. This is a great tool for verifying the inventory of Microsoft software.

A second useful tool for free inventory management is the Microsoft Baseline Security Analyzer (MBSA) mentioned in Procedure GS-12. By default, you use MBSA to scan your networked systems for missing security patches, and reports are stored in files located on the system running MBSA. MBSA includes a powerful connector for Microsoft Visio. By linking MBSA with Visio through this connector, you will automatically generate a graphical inventory of your network. Click any items in this graphical view, and you'll see the details of the system and the software it runs. Of course, you need to have Visio, but which IT administrator doesn't need a powerful network drawing program like this? Obtain the connector at www.microsoft.com/technet/security/tools/mbsavisio.mspx.

GS-15: New Software Evaluation

Activity Frequency: Ad hoc

Once in a while, you should also take the time to review new administration software. The objective of this task is to see if you can reduce your workload by integrating a new operational product. A good example of a highly productive operational tool is System Center Operations Manager 2007 (SCOM). SCOM is highly effective because it monitors system events on servers and automatically corrects potentially damaging behavior as well as notifying you of the correction.

On the other hand, if your shop is of a size that does not warrant as sophisticated a tool as SCOM, you might prefer to search for another tool with similar capabilities. Many of the automated administrative tasks you perform can also be done through scripts, as you have already seen in a number of the tasks described previously. They can also be done with low-cost or public-domain tools. Two good sources of tool information are www.MyITForum.com and www.TechRepublic.com.

Make sure you do not acquire tools that are significantly different in usage from one another. This will help limit the number of tools or interfaces you and your fellow administrators will need to learn. Document any new addition to your network.

GS-16: Software Restriction Policies

Activity Frequency: Ad hoc

The best way to make sure that only signed scripts can run in your network is to use Software Restriction Policies (SRP). SRP provides script and program verification in one of four ways:

- Hash rules
- Certificate rules
- Path rules
- Network zone rules

The two safest and simplest to use are hash and certificate rules. Both can be applied to scripts and programs such as software installation packages (usually in the Windows Installer or .msi format). Here's how to apply or verify certificate-based SRP rules:

1. Use Procedure DC-33 to edit the appropriate GPO. It should apply to all targeted systems.
2. Right-click Software Restriction Policies (User Configuration | Policies | Windows Settings | Security Settings | Software Restriction Policies), and select New Software Restriction Policies from the context menu. This generates the SRP environment.
3. Double-click the Enforcement item in the details pane, and click Enforce Certificate Rules. Make sure that libraries (.dll) are not verified. Click OK. This will make sure your certificate rules are applied.

4. Make sure that Software Restriction Policies is expanded in the tree pane, then right-click Additional Rules, and select New Certificate Rule.
5. In the New Certificate Rule dialog box, click Browse to locate the certificate you use to sign both installation packages and scripts, select Unrestricted as the security level, and type a description. Click OK when done.
6. Move to Software Restriction Policies, and select Designated File Types from the details pane. You will note that both .wsc and .msi are already listed as restricted extensions. You can add any other extension here. Click OK to close the dialog box.
7. Select Trusted Publishers in the same location. Select Define These Policy Settings, and accept the default setting. Under Certificate Verification, select both items. Click OK when done.

CAUTION *You may decide to remove local administrators from being affected by this rule, but do so very carefully.*

Document all your changes. Place these settings in a GPO that affects all PCs and servers in your network.

GS-17: Custom MMC Creation

Activity Frequency: **Ad hoc**

Administration and management is performed through the Microsoft Management Console in Windows Server 2008 and mostly through the Server Manager console. However, you cannot perform two key tasks with this console:

- First, you can't delegate any Server Manager content without giving someone access to the entire Server Manager console.
- Second, you can't use Server Manager to connect to a remote computer.

The latter task is key, because it means that users will need some form of local login capability to run Server Manager. This also means that you cannot use Server Manager to manage any aspect of a Server Core installation.

You can, however, use a custom MMC to link to and manage Server Core components remotely. You can also use custom MMCs to delegate task management to administrators that are responsible for only one single aspect of your operations.

Begin by installing the Remote Server Administration Tools (RSAT). On WS08, add RSAT through Server Manager:

1. Right-click Features and select Add Features.
2. Check Remote Server Administration Tools. Click Add Required Role Services and click Next.
3. Click Next until you get to the Confirmation page and then click Install.

On Windows Vista, you must first ensure that Service Pack 1 has been installed. Then, installing RSAT is performed in two steps. The first installs an update on the client system and the second installs the actual tools themselves.

1. Begin by installing the update. The update for RSAT is available in Knowledge Base article number 941314 at http://support.microsoft.com/kb/941314. Download and install this update. Double-click on it to launch the installation process. This process requires elevated rights and is performed through the Windows Update Standalone Installer. Accept the license agreement to begin the installation. Once the installation is complete, the local Administration Tools will include a help topic for the Remote Server Administration Tools.
2. Next, once the update has been installed, you need to enable the new RSAT Windows feature. Move to Control Panel | Programs and select Turn Windows features on or off. Accept the UAC elevation prompt and scroll down to Remote Server Administration Tools. You'll note that the RSAT section is divided into two sub-sections: Feature Administration Tools and Role Administration Tools. Expand both and check all of the tools (see Figure 13-6).
3. Click OK to launch the addition of these tools.

Now you're ready to create the console. Use the same procedure on WS08 or Vista.

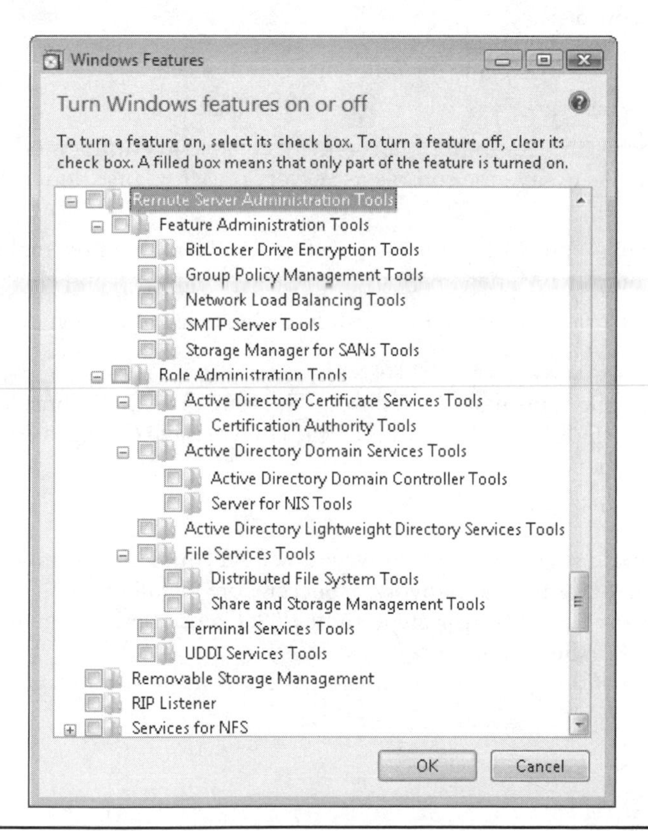

FIGURE 13-6 Choosing RSAT Tools

To create a console for Server Core management, start from the Computer Management console, which is a good general-purpose console. In addition to all the features of the Computer Management console, your custom console should include the following snap-ins:

- The three Active Directory Domain Services snap-ins
- Certification Authority (you must specify the server to manage)
- Distributed File System (DFS) Management
- DNS
- Failover Cluster Management
- File Service Resource Manager
- Group Policy Management
- Security Configuration and Analysis
- Security Templates
- Share and Storage Management
- Storage Explorer
- Terminal Services Configuration

To create this console:

1. Use Start | Run to execute the following command:
   ```
   mmc /a %SystemRoot%\system32\compmgmt.msc
   ```
2. This launches the Computer Management console in editing mode. Begin by using File | Save As to save the console as ServerCoreMMC.msc under the `C:\TOOLKIT` folder.
3. Then use File | Add/Remove Snap-in to open the dialog box, make sure you choose Computer Management under Selected Snap-ins, and click the Add button.
4. Double-click each of the snap-ins listed earlier. Click OK when done.
5. Click OK to return to the console.
6. Click File | Options, name the console "Server Core MMC Console," make sure it is set to User Mode - Full Access, and clear Do Not Save Changes To This Console. Click OK when done.
7. Use File | Save to save your changes.

There are several uses to this console, as you will see, but it is basically the most common tool you will use to manage your network of Server Core installations.

To connect to any Server Core system, right-click Computer Management (local) and select Connect To Another Computer.

Use a variation of this procedure to create custom consoles for delegation to other administrators.

GS-18: Resource Pool Management Console Creation

Activity Frequency:	Ad hoc

As you work with the resource pool, you'll soon realize that a graphical virtual machine management console is absolutely necessary. For this reason, it is a good idea to install two instances of Windows Server 2008 full installation x64 along with the Hyper-V role into your resource pool. These two machines should have the following characteristics:

- Install into virtual machines using the full installation process outlined in Chapter 4 and in procedure GS-19. Make sure you enable remote administration on each machine.
- Join the two machines to the resource pool or utility domain. Do not join these machines to the virtual service offerings domain. You can also use the console available in the RSAT on a Windows Vista machine, but like the two management machines, this Vista machine should not be part of the VSO domain.
- Install the required Hyper-V update; locate it at www.microsoft.com/downloads.
- Install the Hyper-V role through Server Manager (see Figure 13-7). Do not configure a Virtual Network on these systems since they will not host servers, but will be used to manage hosts only. You can also install only the console through the RSAT.

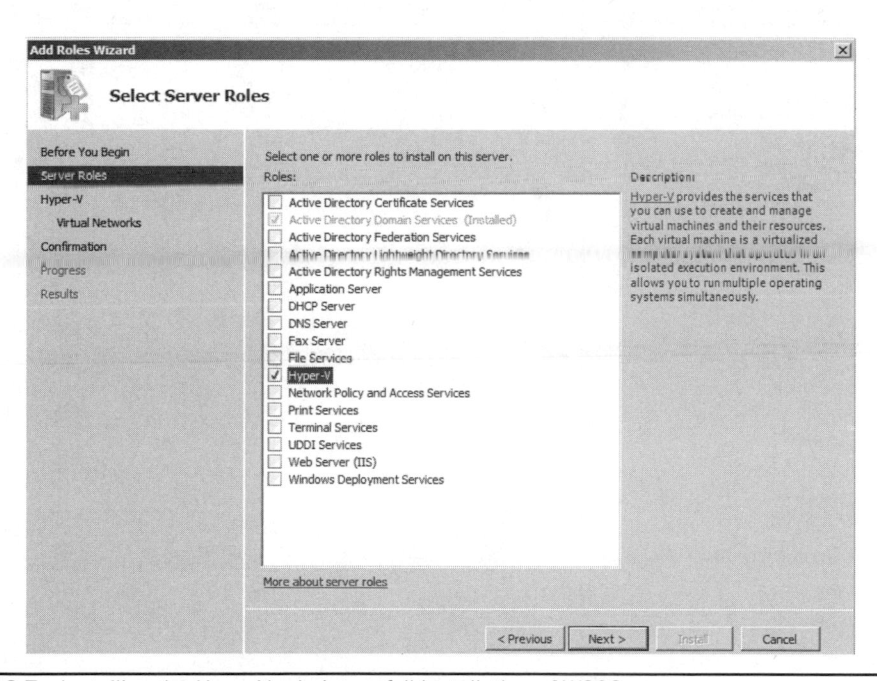

FIGURE 13-7 Installing the Hyper-V role into a full installation of WS08

- Once the role is installed and systems have been rebooted, launch the Hyper-V Manager (Start menu | Administrative Tools | Hyper-V Manager or you can also use Server Manager) and use the Connect to Server command in the Action pane to link to all of your host servers. Browse the directory to locate all your host servers.
- Finally, connect to each host and configure virtual machine storage defaults (see Figure 13-8). Use Virtualization Settings in the Action pane to do so. Remember that virtual machines and virtual hard drives should always be located in the D: drive.

From now on, use these two machines to manage your resource pool.

GS-19: Server Staging

Activity Frequency: Ad hoc

The size of the shop you are running and the number of servers within it will determine the frequency of this task. But in some shops, they stage servers on a regular basis, if only to rebuild aging servers and redesign their service structure.

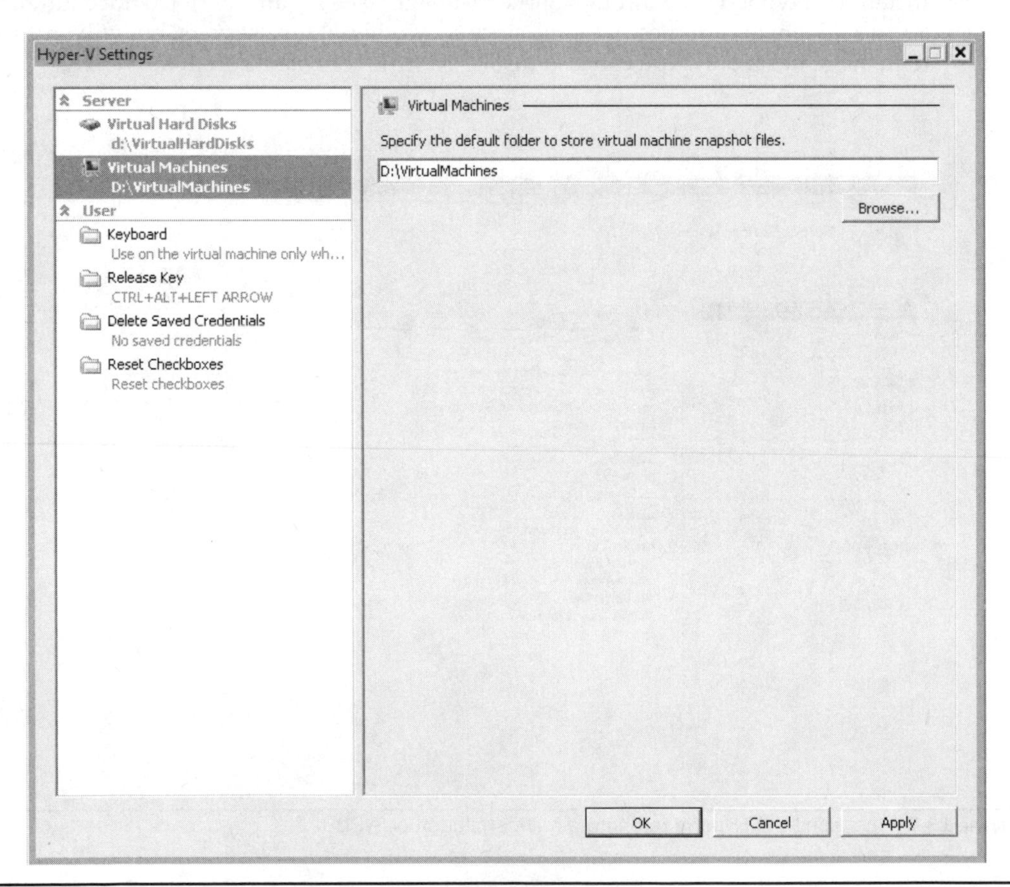

FIGURE 13-8 Changing virtual machine default location settings

Server staging involves a lot of different activities. As discussed in Chapter 4, Windows Server 2008 supports different server staging methods:

- **Manual or interactive staging** This method should be at least based on a thorough checklist.
- **Unattend response file** This method is based on a rigorous and complete response file and is mostly used for upgrades or to build a reference server.
- **Disk imaging with Sysprep** This method reproduces a complete image of a reference server.
- **Remote installation** This method builds a server from a model captured and stored on the Windows Deployment Services server.

In the dynamic datacenter, you have two staging processes. The first is aimed at the resource pool itself and addresses the generation of a new host server. Host servers can be built in one of two ways.

- You can rely on disk images or the remote installation process to generate a new host server.
- If you are using shared storage for your hardware servers and running the system disk from the shared storage, then you only need to copy this partition to create a new server image.

In each case, you need to create a reference server image and maintain it through Windows Updates. And, in order to use it to seed other server instances, you must run it through the Sysprep process. Rely on the instructions in Chapter 4 to do so. Also remember that your host servers should have at least two network interface cards, one for virtual network management and one for remote administration of the host.

The second staging process you need to address is that of virtual machines. Because of their nature, you stage virtual machines simply by copying the files that make them up. Once again, you need to create a reference server and turn it into a sysprepped image. The advantage of virtual machines is that you can and should copy the reference server files and then use this copy to generate the Sysprep.

NOTE *Keep in mind that it's not because virtual machines can be created in less than 20 minutes that you should create them at will. Make sure you continue to control server proliferation. You should always have a new machine justification policy in place.*

GS-20: Automatic Antivirus or Anti-malware Signature Reception

Activity Frequency:	Ad hoc

This is another placeholder activity. It is essential in any antivirus or anti-malware strategy. It deals with the configuration of your antivirus or endpoint protection signature update agent to recover signature updates and deliver them to all PCs and servers in your network.

This is a one-time task that cannot go unmentioned in a list of server administrative tasks. It should be supplemented with regular spot-checks on various systems to ensure the proper functioning of your antivirus signature update server.

GS-21: Scheduled Task Generation/Verification

Activity Frequency:	Ad hoc

The Task Scheduler is one of the tools administrators cannot live without because it serves to automate recurring tasks in a network. The Task Scheduler in Windows Server 2008 is located under Configuration in the Server Manager console.

1. Click Task Scheduler in Server Manager (Configuration | Task Scheduler).
2. Click Create Task in the action pane.
3. Name the task and assign its credentials.
4. Move to the Trigger tab, and select New.
5. Select the appropriate trigger. Triggers can be time or dates as well as specific events.
6. Select On An Event as the task trigger.
7. Choose either Basic or Custom as the event setting:
   a. Basic settings let you select which Event Log will be the source of the event, then which event source, and finally, which event ID to look for (see Figure 13-9).
   b. Custom settings let you create an event filter, letting you determine exactly how the task should be launched based on a series of filtered conditions.
8. Continue adding the task properties, such as conditions, actions, and settings.

Tasks are much more powerful in Vista and WS08 than ever before. You can also generate the task directly from the Event Viewer. Here, you repeat much the same process, except that the task is generated from the event itself instead of the other way around.

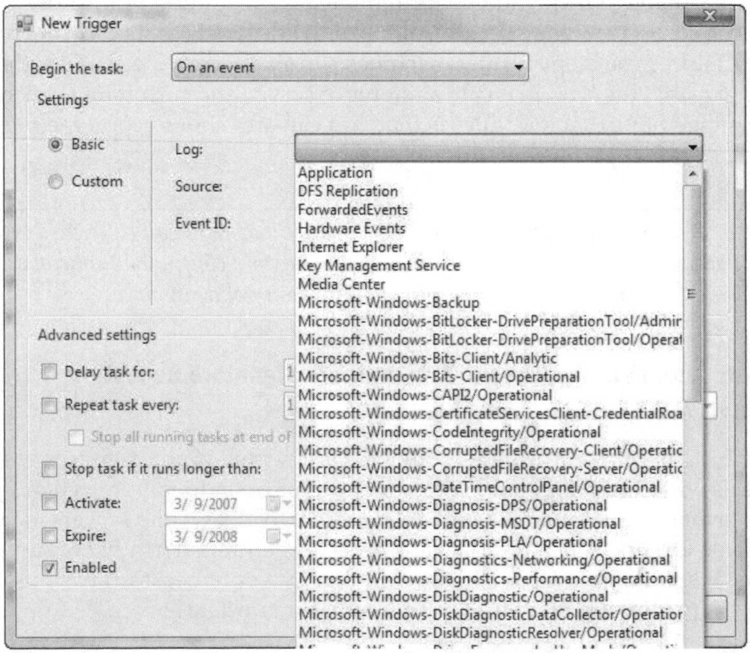

FIGURE 13-9 Using the Basic setting to attach a task to an event

When you create an automated task from the Event Viewer, use the following procedure:

1. Locate the event you want to attach the task to. You can either drill down to the event or create a filter to locate the event.
2. Either right-click the event to select Attach Task To This Event or use the action pane to click the same command. This automatically launches the Basic Task Wizard.
3. Run through the wizard's panes to generate the task.

The advantage of using this method to create the task is that it automatically fills in all of the information required to generate the trigger from the event. The disadvantage is that you can only create a basic task using this method. Of course, once the task is created, you can go to the Task Scheduler to add features and properties to the task, but this requires more steps to do so.

The last method is to use the command line to create tasks. For example, you might use:

```
schtasks /create /TN taskname /TR action /SC ONEVENT /EC System /MO
*[System/EventID=IDnumber]
```

Where *taskname* is the name you want to assign to the task, *action* is the action to perform, and *IDnumber* is the ID number of the event that will act as a trigger for the task. In this example, the source Event Log is the System Log. The task schedule is based on the occurrence of the event and is modified to identify the event ID.

You can also use the SCHTASKS command on each server to verify the status of scheduled tasks. Use the following command:

```
schtasks /query /s computername
```

Where *computername* is either the DNS name or IP address of a server.
Use SCHTASKS /? for more information.

GS-22: Security Template Creation/Modification

Activity Frequency:	**Ad hoc**

Security templates are used to assign security properties to servers. Since they are assigned as local security policies, they should contain only basic security settings, such as file, registry, and service security. Create your security templates from existing templates if you can.

NOTE *Along with GPOs and the Security Configuration Wizard, security templates and security configuration are key ways you can ensure your servers remain secure.*

Templates are used for a variety of purposes. They can be used to assign security settings to servers, or they can be used to analyze actual settings against those stored in the template. Both can be performed in either graphical or character mode.

NOTE *Security template generation procedures are outlined in Chapter 10.*

To analyze or reset a server in graphical mode:

1. Launch the Custom MMC console created in Procedure GS-17.
2. Right-click Security Configuration And Analysis, and select Open Database.
3. In the Open Database dialog box, either locate the appropriate database or type a new database name, and then click OK. The default path setting is Documents\Security\Databases.
4. Select the appropriate template from the available list, and click OK.
5. To analyze your system, right-click Security Configuration And Analysis, and select Analyze Computer Now.
6. Since every analysis or configuration operation requires a log file, a dialog box appears to ask you the location of the log file. The default path setting is Documents\Security\Logs, and the default name is the same as the database. Type the name of a new log file, use the Browse button to locate an existing file, or click OK to accept the default name. The analysis will begin.
7. Once the analysis is complete, you can see the difference in settings between the template and the computer. Simply move to a setting you wish to view and select it. Differences (if any) will be displayed in the right pane.
8. You can modify database settings to conform to the values you want to apply by moving to the appropriate value and double-clicking it. Select Define This Policy In The Database, modify the setting, and click OK. Repeat for each setting you need to modify.
9. Use the right mouse button to display the Security Configuration And Analysis context menu, and select Save to save the modifications you make to the database.
10. To configure a computer with the settings in the database, select Configure Computer Now from the same context menu. Once again, you will need to specify the location and name of the log file before the configuration can begin.

Alternatively, you can use the `SECEDIT` command to perform these tasks at the command line. Use the following command to configure a system:

```
secedit /configure /db filename.sdb /log filename.log /areas REGKEYS
FILESTORE SERVICES /quiet
```

Use the following command to analyze a system:

```
secedit /analyze /db filename.sdb /log filename.log /quiet
```

The latter can be set in a scheduled task using Procedure GS-21. Use `SECEDIT /?` for more information.

GS-23: Technical Environment Review

Activity Frequency: Ad hoc

Once in a while, you should also take the time to review your entire technical environment and see if it requires any changes. This task is usually undertaken twice a year. Use your activity logs and your troubleshooting reports to identify areas of improvement for your network and the services it delivers. You might also institute a user suggestion area. The best way to do this is to create a suggestion e-mail alias and distribute it to users.

Document each proposed change in a business case to get funding and approval for the change. Carefully document each change you actually implement.

GS-24: System and Network Documentation

Activity Frequency:	Ad hoc

You should also take the time to review your system and network documentation on an ad hoc basis. Is it up to date? Does it accurately describe your actual environment? This is not a task many of us relish as system administrators, but it is necessary nonetheless. Use appropriate tools such as Microsoft Office and Visio to perform your documentation (see Procedure GS-14).

In addition, Microsoft provides a series of tools that automatically document certain network aspects. These are the Microsoft Product Support's Reporting Tools, and they can be found by searching for their name at www.microsoft.com/download. Several tools are available to document Alliance (a special support program that includes a version for x64 PCs), Cluster, Directory Services, Network, Setup, WSUS, SQL Server, Microsoft Data Access Components (MDAC), and Exchange.

Make sure your documentation is updated on a regular basis.

TIP *You can find more information about Microsoft Reports in the Knowledge Base article 818742 at http://support.microsoft.com/kb/818742.*

GS-25: Service Level Agreement Management

Activity Frequency:	Ad hoc

Another ad hoc activity is the review of your service level agreements (SLAs). This should be done at least twice a year. SLAs refer to the agreements you enter into with your user community for the delivery of services. Services should be categorized according to priority, and different recovery times should be assigned to each priority. For example, a non-critical service can be restored in four hours or less, while a critical service should be restored within one hour.

Once again, your troubleshooting reports will be highly useful during this review. User input is also highly valuable during this review, because their needs may change as they learn to better understand the capabilities of your systems.

GS-26: Troubleshooting Priority Management

Activity Frequency:	Ad hoc

Like Procedure GS-25, troubleshooting priority management should be reviewed twice a year. This review addresses how you should prioritize your activities when several different system problems occur. It is based on past performance and actual troubleshooting experience. It relies heavily on the SLAs you enter into with your user community.

Make sure you use an approach that is based on the least amount of effort for the greatest amount of benefit. For example, if a domain controller (DC) is down at the same time as a disk fails on a file server, repair the disk first, then begin working on rebuilding the DC, because Active Directory Domain Services (ADDS) will continue to function, since you do not have only one DC per domain. This will be the most efficient way you can use your time. Use common sense to assign priorities.

GS-27: Workload Review

Activity Frequency: Ad hoc

The final review you must perform on a biannual basis is the review of your workload. You will still need to review your workload to make sure you have enough cycles to fulfill all tasks you should perform. If some tasks are not addressed at the frequency proposed in this chapter, you may require additional help. If so, carefully prepare a business case for your proposition and present it to your management. When such suggestions are well prepared and properly justified, they are rarely turned down.

Hardware Administration

All of the tasks included in hardware administration are placeholder tasks, because even though it is vital that you perform them on a regular basis, it is difficult to document exactly how you must perform these tasks because there are so many different models and approaches to hardware management in the market.

Therefore, you will need to modify each task listed here to add your own customized activities.

HW-01: Network Hardware Checkup

Activity Frequency: Weekly

Your network is usually made up of a series of switches, hubs, routers, firewalls, and so on. Their continued good health will ensure the continued proper operation of Windows Server 2008. It is, therefore, useful that you take a regular walk through the computer room to review that network hardware is running properly. This includes the following activities:

- Look over each of your network devices to make sure the proper indicator lights are turned on.
- Review machine logs and configuration settings to make sure configuration is stable and to see if intrusions are occurring.
- Verify cables and connections to make sure they are in good condition.

This task should be customized to include the tools supported by your environment.

HW-02: Server BIOS Management

Activity Frequency: Monthly

Like operating systems, Basic Input Output System (BIOS) versions continually change as manufacturers add capabilities and functionalities. Fortunately, most server manufacturers adhere to Desktop Management Task Force (www.dmtf.org) recommendations so that you no longer need to be sitting in front of a server to perform a BIOS upgrade. The tool you use will vary with the platform you are working with, but all major server manufacturers provide DMTF remote management tools. Intel even used to offer a generic DMTF remote management tool, LANDesk, that works with most Intel-based hardware. LANDesk is now available from LANDesk Software (www.landesksoftware.com). Whichever tool you use, you will often need to keep BIOS and other hardware manufacturer software up to date in order to fully qualify for ongoing support.

Once a month, you should review the availability of new BIOS editions for your hardware and check to see if you require the new BIOS in your environment. If so, download the new BIOS and use your DMTF tools to perform the upgrade on all targeted servers.

HW-03: Firmware and Server Management Software Update Management

Activity Frequency:	Monthly

In addition to BIOS software, hardware manufacturers provide both firmware and server management software. These tools support everything, from telling you the status of the components inside your server cabinets to running specific hardware components. In most cases, these tools include a large number of different components. Therefore, they tend to be upgraded on a regular basis. Once again, you'll need to keep these up to date if you want continued support from your manufacturer.

Once a month, you should review the availability of new firmware and server management software editions for your hardware and check to see if you require these new components in your environment. If so, download them and use your DMTF or server management software tools to perform the upgrade on all targeted servers.

HW-04: Device Management

Activity Frequency:	Monthly

The way Windows Server 2008 interacts with hardware is through device drivers. The interface to these device drivers is the Device Manager, a component of the Server Manager under Diagnostics and now also a component of the Custom MMC console you created in Procedure GS-17. Sometimes, drivers need to be updated or modified. In some instances, some devices may not work at all. Therefore, it is at least worthwhile to verify that there are no device errors in the Device Manager.

Device drivers are especially important on resource pool servers. To verify the status of device drivers:

1. Launch the Custom MMC console (Quick Launch area | Custom MMC).
2. Connect to the appropriate server (Action | Connect To Another Computer), and either type the server name (*servername*) or use the Browse button to locate it. Click OK when done.
3. Select the Device Manager (Computer Management | System Tools | Device Manager).
4. View the status of your devices in the details pane. All devices should have a closed tree. Any problematic device will display an open tree and a yellow question mark.
5. Right-click the problematic device to view its properties. You can also use the context menu to select Update Driver. Identify the device's manufacturer, and search for a new or updated driver. If no driver is available, deactivate the device.

Device drivers should be certified for Windows Server 2008; otherwise, you cannot guarantee their stability. By default, Windows Server will warn you if you are installing a device that is not certified.

TIP *Look to Chapter 10 for information on removable device management GPOs.*

Backup and Restore

Even though servers are designed to include redundancy for server and data protection, no organization could operate without a disaster recovery strategy that includes both a strong and regular backup strategy and a sound recovery system. The procedures outlined here are based on `WBADMIN.EXE`, the default backup tool included in Windows Server 2008. This edition of Windows Backup is much more complete than previous editions, with the addition of both the Volume Shadow Copy service and the full systems recovery option. The first lets the system take a snapshot of all data before taking the backup, resolving many issues with the backup of open files. The second lets you rebuild a server without having to reinstall its software.

TIP *Refer to Chapter 11 for more information on Windows Backup.*

But if your enterprise is serious about its data, you will most likely have a more comprehensive backup engine. The best of these is Galaxy from Commvault Systems, Inc. (www.commvault.com). This is one of the only backup tools that fully supports Active Directory Domain Services, letting you restore objects and attributes directly within the directory without having to perform an authoritative restore, an operation that is rather complex. In addition, if you have massive volumes of data, Galaxy will save you considerable time, especially for full backups, because it builds a full backup image from past incremental backups, using a unique single-instance store technology. This means that you never run out of time to do your backup because it isn't actually drawn from the systems themselves, but rather from previous backup images.

BR-01: System Disk Backup Generation

Activity Frequency:	Daily

System disk backups are critical on each server because these are the tools that protect the operating system itself. System disk data is always backed up as a whole and cannot be segregated. This is a daily task that should be automated.

TIP *You should configure backups to run in either shared storage or removable disks so that you can store them offsite.*

To schedule a system disk backup:

1. In the Server Manager console, go to Storage | Windows Server Backup.
2. Click Backup Schedule in the actions pane.
3. In the Backup Schedule Wizard, click Next and enter the information found in Table 13-2 to complete the wizard pages.

You can also perform a backup once for a special event.

Repeat the procedure to create data backups on the same schedule.

Wizard Page	Entry
Select Backup Type	There are two choices: • Full Server • Custom — if you want to exclude some volumes
Specify Backup Time	There are two choices: • Once a day and select time of day • Multiple backups every day and add the scheduled time
Specify Target Disk	You need to select the disk for the backup. You can have multiple disks. Click Show All to select the disk, and in the Available Disks window, select the disk again. A warning message will appear, notifying you that the disk will be reformatted.
Label Target Disk	Verify that the disk is labeled correctly according to the label column.

TABLE 13-2 Backup Schedule Wizard Entries

BR-02: Backup Verification

Activity Frequency: Daily

Even though backups are a lot easier to do and more reliable with WS08, you should still take the time to make sure they have been properly performed. To do so, you need to view the backup log on each file server. To check backup logs:

1. Use Procedure RA-01 to open a Remote Desktop Connection to the server you want to verify.
2. Click the Windows Server Backup tool in the Server Manager console under Storage to view the backup status, and click View Details.
3. Search for the word "Error" in the report log.

If you find errors, determine if it is a critical file and use Windows Explorer to see why the file wasn't backed up or if it needs to be recovered. Make note of the results of your investigation in your daily activity log (Procedure GS-06).

BR-03: Offsite Backup Management

Activity Frequency: Weekly

One of the key elements of a disaster recovery strategy is the protection of your backup containers. After all, if your datacenter burns down and all your backup containers burn with it, it will be rather hard for you to reconstruct your systems. Therefore, you should make sure that you store your weekly backup containers in a different site, which should be protected from disasters. This can be anything from a safety deposit box in a bank to a specialized data protection service.

This means that once a week, you should take your full weekend backup and send it offsite to a protected vault and have them return older backups to reuse the tapes. You should also consider keeping a full monthly backup offsite, as well as at least one yearly backup (this can be the monthly backup for the last month in your fiscal year).

TIP *If you implemented a replication policy for host server contents from one location to another, then all of your VSOs will be protected, because the files that make them up will be in more than one site.*

BR-04: Disaster Recovery Strategy Testing

Activity Frequency: Monthly

A disaster recovery strategy is only as good as its proven ability to recover and reconstruct your systems. Therefore, you should take the time to validate your disaster recovery strategy on a monthly basis. This means making sure that everything that makes up the disaster recovery strategy is in place and ready to support your system reconstruction at any time. For resource pools, this includes everything from having spare parts, spare servers, spare network components, offsite storage of backup disks, a sound backup disk rotation system, documented procedures for system reconstruction—especially ADDS reconstruction—and so on. This review should be based on a checklist that you use to validate each of the elements that supports system recovery. Document any changes you bring to this strategy after you complete the review.

BR-05: Restore Procedure Testing

Activity Frequency: Monthly

Backups are only as good as their ability to restore information to a system. Therefore, once a month you should perform a restore test from a random copy of your backup media to make sure it actually works. Too many organizations have been caught empty-handed when they tried to restore critical files from backup disks that were never tested, only to find out that it didn't work. To test the restore procedure, use the Server Manager console to launch the Recovery Wizard (Storage | Windows Server Backup), and enter the information from Table 13-3.

Verify the integrity of the files you restore. Destroy the files when done.

Wizard Page	Entry
Getting Started	Choose to recover data from this server or another server.
Select Date	Select the date and time for the backup you want to restore.
Select Items To Recover	Under the Available items, expand the plus sign. From the folder, click each item that you want to restore.
Select Recovery Options	There are two options for the location: • Original location • Another location: you will need to enter the full path of the location or click the Browse button. There are three options for the files and folders to restore: • Create copies so I have both versions of the file or folder • Overwrite existing files with recovered files • Don't recover any existing files and folders

TABLE 13-3 Recovery Wizard Entries

BR-06: Backup Strategy Review

Activity Frequency:	Monthly

Once a month you should also take the time to review your backup strategy. Has the volume of backups changed? Is there new information to include into your backups? Is your backup schedule appropriate? These and other questions should help you form a checklist that you can use to review your backup strategy.

Document any changes you make.

Remote Administration

Windows 2000 introduced the concept of remote server administration through Terminal Services in administration mode. This allows you to make up to two remote connections to a server without additional Terminal Services client licenses. In Windows Server 2008, this feature is called Remote Desktop Connections (RDC).

RDC is a boon to server administrators because it gives you complete access to a server's desktop without having to access the server physically. In addition, you can rely on RemoteApps to publish only the application you need to access and not the entire desktop.

NOTE *RDC is more secure because it limits access to server rooms. Administrators can work from their own desks to administer and configure servers remotely.*

RA-01: Server RDC Management

Activity Frequency:	Monthly

Once a month, you should review your remote server management practices. This review should serve to answer such questions as: Are our remote connections secure? How many administrators have remote access to servers? Do we change our administrative passwords frequently enough? Are the consoles that give remote access to servers sufficiently protected?

NOTE *Remember that Remote Desktop Connections are only required if you need to modify settings on a server. In resource pools, try to make a habit of working with a custom MMC console instead. In virtual service offerings, try to publish only the tool you need. See Chapter 9 for information about publishing applications with RemoteApps and for information on how to work with the Remote Desktop console.*

Remote Desktop Connections can only occur if the Remote Desktop setting has been enabled on the server. To enable this setting:

1. Launch Server Manager and click Configure Remote Desktop in the action pane of the Summary page.
2. In the Remote tab, select Allow Connections From Computers Running Remote Desktop With Network Level Authentication.

NOTE *If you enable RDC, you will need to deploy Remote Desktop Client 6.1 on each computer, if it is not already done.*

3. Click the Add button to list which users can connect to this computer; any members of the Administrators group can connect, even if they are not listed.
4. You do not need to do anything else if your administrators are all members of the local administrators group, because they automatically have access to the server. Alternatively, you can add remote server operators to the Remote Desktop Users built-in group (Active Directory Users and Computers | Built-in). This will give them access to the local desktop in a remote session. If they are not members of either group, you must enumerate the users one by one. Click Select Remote Users to do so.
5. Click OK in each dialog box when done.

You can also set this option remotely through Group Policy. This should be a GPO that applies to servers only. Enable the Allow Users To Connect Remotely Using Terminal Services setting (Computer Configuration | Policies | Administrative Templates | Windows Components | Terminal Services | Terminal Server | Connections). This GPO setting provides the same functionality as the check box in System Properties.

CAUTION *RDC in Administration mode allows two connections at once. The best practice is to identify immediately upon connection whether someone else is working on the server at the same time. The best way to do this is to open a Command Prompt window and type* `QUERY USER`*. If another administrator is logged on, contact this administrator to make sure you will not both be performing conflicting activities on the same server.*

RA-02: PC RDC Management

Activity Frequency:	Ad hoc

PC RDC management is the same as for servers and uses exactly the same approach (see Procedure RA-01). PCs only allow a single logon at a time. If you log on remotely to a PC while a user is already logged on, the user will be logged off automatically. If you need to provide assistance to a user, use Procedure RA-03 instead.

RA-03: User Support Through Remote Assistance

Activity Frequency:	Ad hoc

If you need to provide remote support to a user, especially while the user is still logged on, you cannot use a Remote Desktop Connection because it automatically logs off the user and logs you on. Use Remote Assistance instead.

CAUTION *Do not ask a user for their credentials so that you can log on under their security context!*

Remote Assistance works in one of two ways. It can let users request assistance from the Help desk, or it can let Help desk operators offer assistance to users. Users must explicitly accept assistance before either can proceed. Remote Assistance is controlled through two GPO settings: Solicited Remote Assistance and Offer Remote Assistance (Computer

Configuration | Policies | Administrative Templates | System | Remote Assistance). Each includes the ability to identify helpers in your organization. Solicited Remote Assistance lets you also set both the times during which users can request assistance and the request mechanism—mailto or Simple Messaging Application Programming Interface (MAPI). In addition, each lets you determine the type of assistance to offer, identifying whether support personnel can interact with the desktop or simply watch. Interaction provides the fullest support, but can represent a security risk. Both settings require a list of helpers. Helpers are user groups that are typed in the format domainname\groupname.

CAUTION *Remember that before a helper can assist a user or interact with their desktop, users must first accept the offer for Remote Assistance. Be sure to warn users never to leave their desktops unattended while someone else is interacting with it.*

CAUTION *These GPO settings do not let you select group names from ADDS; you must manually type them. Be sure to verify the information you typed before applying these GPO settings to your PCs.*

Once these settings are applied to all PCs, you can offer help in the following manner:

1. Launch Windows Remote Assistance (Start menu | All Programs | Maintenance group).
2. Click Offer To Help Someone.
3. Type the DNS name of the PC you want to connect to, and click Finish.
4. Wait for the user to accept the connection before beginning your support.

This task is set as an ad hoc task because, hopefully, you will not need to perform it on a regular basis.

You can also use a command line to do so:

```
msra /expert
```

This command will automatically launch the Offer Remote Assistance user interface. If you want to perform an offer from the command line, use:

```
msra /offerRA computername
```

File and Print Server Administration

File and print servers are sometimes the very reason organizations implement networks. Because of this, they are also often the very first servers to be put in place in a networked system. This is why they are the first specific server role examined in this book. In addition, file service management is a big part of managing resource pools.

The administration of file and print servers is divided into three categories. These include File Services, Print Services, and Cluster Services. Table 13-4 outlines the administrative activities that you must perform on an ongoing basis to ensure proper operation of the services you deliver to your user community. It also identifies the frequency of each task.

Procedure No.	Activity	Frequency	Resource Pool	Virtual Service Offerings
File Services				
FS-01	Available Free Space Verification	Daily	☑	☑
FS-02	Data Backup Management	Daily	☑	☑
FS-03	Shared Folder Management	Daily	☑	☑
FS-04	DFS Replication Service Verification	Daily	☑	☑
FS-05	Volume Shadow Copy Management	Weekly	☑	☑
FS-06	Distributed File System Management	Weekly	☑	☑
FS-07	Quota Management	Weekly		☑
FS-08	Search Service Management	Weekly		☑
FS-09	Data Disk Integrity Verification	Weekly	☑	☑
FS-10	Data Disk Defragmentation	Weekly	☑	☑
FS-11	File Access Audit Log Verification	Weekly	☑	☑
FS-12	Temporary File Cleanup	Weekly		☑
FS-13	Security Parameter Verification	Weekly	☑	☑
FS-14	Encrypted Folder Management	Weekly	☑	☑
FS-15	Data Archiving	Monthly	☑	☑
FS-16	DFS Replication Service Management	Monthly	☑	☑
FS-17	Disk and Volume Management	Ad hoc	☑	☑
Print Services				
PS-01	Print Queue Management	Daily		☑
PS-02	Printer Access Management	Weekly		☑
PS-03	Printer Driver Management	Weekly		☑
PS-04	Printer Sharing	Ad hoc		☑
PS-05	Print Spooler Drive Management	Ad hoc		☑
PS-06	Printer Location Tracking Management	Ad hoc		☑
PS-07	Massive Printer Management	Ad hoc		☑
PS-08	New Printer Model Evaluation	Ad hoc		☑
Cluster Services				
CS-01	Clusters: Cluster State Verification	Daily	☑	☑
CS-02	Clusters: Print Queue Status Verification	Daily		☑
CS-03	Clusters: Server Cluster Management	Weekly	☑	☑
CS-04	Clusters: Quorum/File Share Witness State Verification	Weekly	☑	☑

Table 13-4 File and Print Services Administration Task List

You may not need to perform all of these activities because you don't use some of the services mentioned here. You may also use a different schedule. Remember to personalize the task list to adapt it to your environment.

NOTE *Most of the activities in this section require local administrative rights or proper delegation rights to the appropriate service.*

File Service Administration

With Windows Server 2008, file service administration involves everything from formatting a new disk to integrating with Active Directory to create complex shared folder structures with the Distributed File Service. But it is mainly focused on disks and the services Windows Server 2008 can support when dealing with storage.

Four main tools can be used to manage file servers:

- Windows Explorer, because it gives access to both disks and shared folders.
- The File Server Resource Management console, because it is a single-purpose console that focuses on disks and shares.
- The `NET SHARE` command, because it is a command-line tool that can be used to script sharing operations.
- The `DISKPART` command, because it is designed to manage disks, volumes, and partitions.

FS-01: Available Free Space Verification

Activity Frequency:	Daily

Checking for free space on a server requires a view of the actual disk drives located on the server. There are several ways to do this, but the easiest is to simply open a Remote Desktop Connection (RDC) to the server whose drives you want to verify. If you haven't already done so, use Procedure RA-01 to create an RDC link to each of the servers you want to verify and then proceed as follows:

1. Launch a Remote Desktop session to the server you want to verify, and log in with your administrative credentials.
2. Use the Windows Explorer shortcut located in the Quick Launch area to click Computer.
3. Make sure you are in Tile or Detail View, and you will see the used and available space on each disk. You can also view it by clicking the disk itself and looking at the status bar at the bottom of the Windows Explorer window.
4. Note the available space for each data disk in your Available Free Space Log.
5. Close Windows Explorer when done.

Of course, if you have 500 servers, this procedure can become tedious. So you might prefer to use a more automated method. Server Manager in WS08 includes a performance monitor (Diagnostics | Reliability and Performance | Monitoring Tools | Performance Monitor). This snap-in allows you to monitor application and hardware performance, customize the data to collect in logs, define thresholds for alerts and automatic actions, generate reports, and view past performance data in different ways. To add counters click the plus sign in the details pane. It includes counters for more than 50 objects.

You can create a performance monitoring console that automatically tracks free disk space on all servers. This console will need access rights to performance counters on each server you monitor, so it is best to use the Run As Administrator command (see Procedure GS-01) to launch the Performance Monitor console (Server Manager | Diagnostics | Reliability and Performance | Monitoring Tools), and then proceed as follows:

1. Use the plus sign in the toolbar to add a counter.
2. In the Select Counters From Computer field, type the name of the server you want to view. Remember to use the Universal Naming Convention (UNC) name, for example, *ComputerName*.
3. Select LogicalDisk as the performance object and % Free Space as the counter (click the down arrow to view counters).
4. Select the system and the data disk drive(s), and click Add. Repeat for any other server you want to include. Click OK when done.
5. Now that all the servers and disks are added, use More Actions | New | Data Collector Set from the action pane.
6. Name the collector set "Free Disk Space," click Next, save it in the default location, and click Next again.
7. In the next dialog box, click Change under Run As to add appropriate credentials to this collector set. Click OK.
8. Click Save, click Close, and click Finish.
9. To run the collector, move to Server Manager | Diagnostics | Reliability and Performance | Data Collector Sets | User Defined. Right-click your collector set, and select Start.
10. Run it whenever you need to review available space on your servers.

Use this console to view free space on all file servers from now on.

Finally, you can use a simple command-line tool to verify free disk space. It works on any system and can send its output to a text file. Use the following structure:

```
freedisk /S ComputerName /D DriveName
```

Where *ComputerName* is the DNS name of the remote server and *DriveName* is either the drive or volume name you want to verify. Put this in a command file and run it as a scheduled task (see Procedure GS-21).

You can also use the File Server Resource Manager (FSRM) in either the stand-alone console (through Administrative Tools) or through Server Manager (Roles | File Services | Share and Storage Management) to run storage reports.

NOTE *In order to run storage reports on remote servers, you must ensure that the Remote Server Administration Tools | Role Administration Tools | File Services Tools | File Server Resource Manager Tools are installed on each server you want to include in the report.*

Storage management can automatically run scheduled reports on any drive, system, or data on the schedule you set. Use the following procedure:

1. Move to the Storage Reports Management node of FSRM, and select Schedule A New Report Task from the action pane.
2. On the Settings tab, click Add to include the drives you want to report on. Add each drive.
3. You can report on a variety of information:
   - Duplicate files
   - File screening audit
   - Files by file group
   - Files by owner
   - Large files
   - Least recently accessed files
   - Most recently accessed files
   - Quota usage

   Each report includes a view of the entire disk. Select the objects you want to report on and select the report format (DHTML, HTML, XML, CSV, or Text).
4. Move to the Schedule tab, and click Create Schedule.
5. Click New and then set the schedule you want. Click OK when done.
6. Click the Delivery tab, and include an e-mail address. Ideally, this will be a group address if there is more than one administrator interested in this report. By default, reports are stored in the `%SYSTEMDRIVE%\STORAGEREPORTS\SCHEDULED` folder.

CAUTION *For this server to send e-mail, it must be included in the Relay Agents list on your Simple Mail Transfer Protocol (SMTP) server.*

7. Click OK when done.

Reports are in a variety of formats; Dynamic Hypertext Markup Language (DHTML) is the default. These reports are extremely comprehensive and should be reviewed regularly.

TIP *Server Manager will only generate reports on the local server. In order to generate reports from other servers, you must use the stand-alone FSRM console because it is the only console that allows you to connect to another computer.*

FS-02: Data Backup Management

Activity Frequency:	Daily

Windows Server 2008 offers a lot more functionality in this area, especially with the Virtual Shadow Copy service. Rely on Procedure BR-01 to create the backups.

You should also take the time to make sure they have been performed properly. To do so, you need to view the backup log on each file server. Use Procedure BR-02 to review your data backup logs. If you find errors, determine if it is a critical file (data backup errors are on files in data drives only), and use Windows Explorer to see why the file wasn't backed up.

FS-03: Shared Folder Management

Activity Frequency:	Daily

Shared folder management refers to two main activities: the creation of new folders and the creation of new file shares. This may or may not be a daily activity for you; it all depends on your environment and the number of users you support. If you set it up right, this activity should be straightforward.

CAUTION *You will need to set security permissions on these folders. Remember that New Technology File System (NTFS) permissions are final permissions. This means you should concentrate on these permissions first.*

To create new folders:

1. Open a Remote Desktop Connection to the appropriate server.
2. Launch Windows Explorer (Quick Launch area | Windows Explorer), and select the D: drive (all data should be on D: drive).
3. Locate the folder level where you want to create the new folder in the left pane. Right-click in the right pane of Windows Explorer, select New, select Folder, and type the name of the folder. Choose a name that can double as a folder and a share name. Press ENTER when done. Repeat for each folder you require.
4. Apply appropriate NTFS security settings for each folder. To do so, right-click each folder name and select Properties. Move to the Security tab. Add the appropriate groups, and assign appropriate security settings to each group.

TIP *You should modify security settings on root folders because these settings are inherited whenever you create subfolders. This way, you will only need to fine-tune subfolder settings from then on.*

You can share folders and publish a share in Active Directory Domain Services. For more information on how to do this, see Chapter 8.

You can also share folders through the command line. Use the following syntax once the folder is created:

```
net share ShareName=FolderPath /grant:GroupName,full /unlimited
```

Where *ShareName* is the name of the share, *FolderPath* is the drive letter and path to the folder, and *GroupName* is the name of the group you want to assign rights to.

FS-04: DFS Replication Service Verification

Activity Frequency:	Daily

The DFS Replication service (DFSR) is at the core of both the Distributed File System and Active Directory Domain Services operations when domains are in fully functional mode for WS08. Its proper operation must be verified daily. The best way to do this is to use Server Manager.

1. Move to the DFS Replication Log (Diagnostics | Event Viewer | Applications and Services Logs | DFS Replication).
2. Identify any errors or warnings. Take appropriate action if either appears.

Make note of any corrective actions you need to take. Use Procedure GS-06 to log the different events you investigate each day.

TIP *More information on DFSR can be found at the DFS Technology Center at www.microsoft.com/windowsserver2003/technologies/storage/dfs/default.mspx.*

You can also use a command-line tool to manage DFSR: `DFRSADMIN`. Simply type the command in a command window to view its Help file.

FS-05: Volume Shadow Copy Management

Activity Frequency:	Weekly

The Volume Shadow Copy service (VSS) is a useful tool for system administrators because it provides users with the ability to restore their own files. It also provides the ability to create backups from copies or snapshots of production data, letting you back up data without affecting production environments. Refer to Chapter 6 for more information.

Shadow copies are a feature of disk volumes. To verify the status of VSS:

1. Open a Remote Desktop Connection to the appropriate server, and then open Windows Explorer (Quick Launch area | Windows Explorer).
2. Navigate to the data drive (drive D:), and right-click it to select Properties.
3. Move to the Shadow Copies tab, and click Settings.
4. In the Settings dialog box, click Details. This will display a dialog box outlining the volume shadow copies are located on, the amount of available space on the volume, and the amount of space used by VSS. Verify that enough space is available for the shadow copies, and click OK to close the dialog box.

NOTE *Shadow copies should be located on a dedicated volume. This ensures that VSS does not interfere with production service levels.*

5. Verify the maximum size allocated to VSS, and modify it if required.
6. You should also check the VSS schedule. Click Schedule, verify that everything is as it should be, and click OK when done. The default schedule is usually appropriate for most environments.
7. Close the Properties dialog box when done by clicking OK.

You can also do this from the command line:

```
vssadmin list shadows
```

This will list all of the shadow copies on the system.

```
vssadmin list shadowstorage
```

This will list the space used by shadow copies on the system.

You should make sure that VSS Restores works properly. To verify it:

1. On your own computer, launch Windows Explorer (Quick Launch area | Windows Explorer).
2. Locate a shared folder you have access to, and select a test file within this folder. Right-click it to view its previous versions.
3. On the Previous Versions tab, select the version of the file you want to restore, and click Restore. You will see a warning about overwriting newer versions. Click OK to proceed.
4. Close the Properties dialog box when done.

The file should be located in the folder you selected. While VSS does not replace backups, it offers users self-service for short-term file recoveries.

FS-06: Distributed File System Management

Activity Frequency:	Weekly

The Distributed File System (DFS) is one the most powerful file services in Windows Server 2008. It provides fully redundant file share access in either stand-alone or domain-based mode. Use the DFS Management console (Server Manager | Roles | File Services) to ensure the proper operation of this service.

1. If the DFS namespace you want to manage is not visible, use the Action menu to connect to your DFS roots (Actions pane | Add Namespaces to Display), locate the namespace you want to manage, select it, and click OK.
2. To make sure the DFS share is operating properly, right-click the DFS share name and select Check Status from the context menu.
3. All targets should show a status of online. If not, verify why the targets are not online and repair them (the server may be down).

NOTE *DFS depends heavily on the Remote Procedure Call service. Make sure this service is up and running. Also, domain-based DFS namespaces must have synchronized clocks (to support replication and location of the targets). Make sure all systems are synchronized with the PDC Emulator (this is normally the default in an Active Directory Domain Services domain).*

The DFS console can also be used to modify the DFS configuration, add new targets, add new links, configure replication, and so on.

Stand-alone DFS namespaces tend to be applied more often in server clusters. If you use server clusters and stand-alone DFS namespaces, you will have the opportunity to reuse this procedure. More on DFS is included in Chapter 8.

In addition, two command line tools can be used for DFS management: `DFSCMD` and `DFSUTIL`. Of the two, `DFSUTIL` is the most useful. Simply type the command in a command prompt to view its Help file.

FS-07: Quota Management

Activity Frequency:	Weekly

The Windows Server 2008 Quota Service is also a feature of disk drives. To verify quota status:

1. Use the Quota Management console (Server Manager | Roles | File Services | Share and Storage Management | File Server Resource Manager | Quota Management | Quotas).
2. The Quotas pane shows you existing quota entries. View all quota entries, and verify how your users are making use of shared disk space.

You'll also get warnings from the system when quotas are reached. Make sure you note which quotas or users are affected and communicate with them to ensure proper use of your shared folders.

FS-08: Search Service Management

Activity Frequency:	Weekly

The WS08 Search service will index documents in the following formats:

- Text
- Hypertext Markup Language (HTML)
- Office 95 and later
- E-mail
- Any other document for which a filter is available

For example, Adobe Corporation provides an indexing filter for documents in the PDF format. Search for "iFilter" on the Adobe Web site.

In addition, each drive must be marked for indexing and the Search service must be turned on. Drive marking is performed in the Properties dialog box for the drive under the General tab. This setting is turned on by default on all drives. Since data is located only on specific drives, you should deselect it for system drives.

To verify that the Search service is turned on, use Server Manager to view the service status (Configuration | Services). Make sure it is set to automatic startup.

To verify that the Search service is working properly, search for a document you know is on a system (Start menu | Search).

FS-09: Data Disk Integrity Verification

Activity Frequency:	Weekly

Because data is stored on drives and drives tend to be the major point of failure on any given system, it is important to verify that the volumes you use are regularly scanned for integrity.

To scan a disk for integrity, use the following command:

```
chkdsk Volume /f
```

Where *Volume* is the name of the drive or volume you want checked. This command can be set as a scheduled task (see Procedure GS-21).

You can also perform this command through the graphical interface. Use Windows Explorer to locate the disk drive you want to verify, right-click it, select Properties, move to the Tools tab, and click Check Now.

NOTE *This command can only be run in real time on non-system volumes. Since* `CHKDSK` *needs exclusive access to a volume during verification, it can only run at server startup on system volumes.*

FS-10: Data Disk Defragmentation

Activity Frequency:	Weekly

It is also important to defragment drives on a regular basis to improve performance and data access speeds.

To defragment a disk, use the following command:

```
defrag Volume /v >filename.txt
```

Where *Volume* is the name of the drive or volume you want to defragment. Using the `/V` switch enables the verbose mode, which can be piped into the file of your choice. This command can also be set as a scheduled task (see Procedure GS-21).

You can also perform this command through the graphical interface. Use Windows Explorer to locate the disk drive you want to verify, right-click it, select Properties, move to the Tools tab, and click Defragment Now.

FS-11: File Access Audit Log Verification

Activity Frequency:	Weekly

CAUTION *One of the foremost responsibilities of a file system administrator is to make sure people access only those files they are allowed to. Therefore, it is essential to enable file access auditing on data drives, especially if the data is sensitive, confidential, or secret.*

File access auditing is enabled through Group Policy and must be specifically applied to the objects you want to audit. Use the following procedure:

1. Use the Group Policy Management console (Start menu | Administrative Tools | Group Policy Management).
2. Move to the Group Policy Object container (GPMC | Forest | Domains | *Domainname* | Group Policy Objects), and locate the GPO you want to modify. This should be the Global File and Print GPO. Right-click the policy and select Edit.

3. Turn on the object access audit policy (Computer Configuration | Policies | Windows Settings | Security Settings | Local Policy | Audit Policy).
4. Next, you must identify the folders you want to audit (Computer Configuration | Policies | Windows Settings | Security Settings | File System). To do so, you must use the Add File command, locate the folder you want to audit, click the Advanced button, move to the Audit tab, click Add, locate the group you want to audit (Everyone), and identify the events you want to audit for this group. Close all dialog boxes and the Group Policy Editor when done.

TIP *This is one of the rare opportunities where the Everyone group applies because, in fact, you do not want to audit only authenticated users, but everyone who has access to the system.*

5. Use the Server Manager to view the results of the audit under Diagnostics | Event Viewer | Windows Logs | Security.

CAUTION *Auditing object access creates a lot of entries. Be careful what you choose to audit, and make sure your Security Event Log is set to an appropriate file size (Event Viewer | Windows Logs | Security | actions pane | Properties).*

FS-12: Temporary File Cleanup

Activity Frequency: Weekly

Applications need to create temporary files to ensure that users do not lose their data as they work. These temporary files are normally removed when the application closes. Unfortunately, not all applications are so well behaved. You must verify data disks for temporary or corrupt files to delete them on a regular basis.

You can do this interactively using the Disk Cleanup utility. Use the following procedure to do so:

1. To launch Disk Cleanup, go to the Start menu | Search box, and type **Disk Cleanup.**
2. Choose Files From All users on this computer, and accept the UAC prompt.
3. Disk Cleanup scans the computer for files that can be deleted. Select the files to clean up or compress, and click OK.
4. Click Yes to confirm the operation.

You can also do this by creating a global script that regularly scans drives and removes all temporary or corrupt files. This script should be run at times when few users are logged on, even though it will operate properly when users have active temporary files on the volume, because active files are locked and cannot be deleted.

The script should delete the following file types:

- *.tmp
- ~*.*

Use the following commands in your script:

```
del volume:*.tmp /s /q >filename.txt
del volume:~*.* /s /q /a:h >filename.txt
```

Where *volume:* is the name of the data drive. The `/s` and `/q` switches, respectively, mean including files located in subdirectories and don't ask for confirmation, and the `/A:H` switch ensures that you delete only temporary files because they are normally hidden from users (some users may use the tilde (~) in their filenames). Finally, piping the information into a file (*filename.txt*) gives you a complete listing of all deleted files.

FS-13: Security Parameter Verification

Activity Frequency:	Weekly

CAUTION *Security is always a concern in a networked data environment. Therefore, it is necessary to verify that security settings are appropriate on data and system drives.*

The best way to verify security settings is to use the Security Configuration Manager in analysis mode. It compares an existing security implementation to a baseline security template and outlines the differences. This means that you must keep track of all the changes you make to security settings on data drives, and you must update your baseline security template on a regular basis.

To analyze a computer and compare it to a given security policy in graphical mode, use Procedure GS-22. If you need to perform this verification on several systems, you should do so via a command line. The command to use is:

```
secedit /analyze /db filename.sdb /log filename.log
```

In addition, the `/VERBOSE` switch can be used to create a log file that is highly detailed. If no log file is specified, `SECEDIT` will automatically log all information to the scesrv.log file in the `%WINDIR%\SECURITY\LOGS` folder. To configure a computer instead of analyzing it, replace the `/ANALYZE` switch with `/CONFIGURE`.

NOTE *This command must be run locally. If you create scripts to run this command, make sure you design them to run locally on each file server.*

FS-14: Encrypted Folder Management

Activity Frequency:	Weekly

To encrypt data in shared folders, the file servers must be trusted for delegation within Active Directory Domain Services. This is a property of the server's computer account within the directory (Server Name | Properties | Delegation | Trust This Computer For Delegation To Any Service (Kerberos Only)).

In addition, folders can only contain one of two values: compression or encryption. If a folder is not available for encryption, it is because its compression value is set.

Finally, encryption settings are applied through a folder's properties (Properties | General tab | Advanced), and encrypted files and folders are displayed in green in Windows Explorer.

See Chapter 10 for more information on EFS.

TIP *For more information on EFS, see "Working with the Encrypting File System" under "Advanced PKI" at www.reso-net.com/articles.asp?m=8#c.*

FS-15: Data Archiving

Activity Frequency:	Monthly

Windows Server 2008 does not really include any special tool for archiving data, though it does include support for archival technology, such as remote offline storage. You can use WS08 Backup to perform a backup of data for archival purposes and then remove the data from the network to create additional free space, but this is not necessarily an easy task. To archive data based on creation/modification date in Windows Server 2008, you must run a Storage Report to identify all of the oldest files, then run the backup and remove them (see Procedure FS-01 for Storage Report information).

It is much simpler to create special archive shared folders and ask users to place data that can be archived into these special shares. Then, on a regular basis, back them up and delete the folder's contents.

TIP *If you need to do this on a regular basis, you should acquire a content addressable retention system. Search for them on the Internet.*

FS-16: DFS Replication Service Management

Activity Frequency:	Monthly

Procedure FS-04 specifies that you must regularly check the DFSR Event Log to make sure there are no replication errors. You also have to make sure the DFS replication rules are set properly and meet your network configuration's capabilities for replication, though this is done less often. Verify the replication topology and schedule as well.

DFSR is managed from the DFS console (Server Manager | Roles | File Services | DFS Management | Replication).

1. If you don't see your replication groups, use the Action menu to connect to them (Actions pane | Add Replication Groups To Display), locate the group you want to manage, select it, and click OK.
2. Click the replication group in the tree pane, and view its details in the details pane.
3. It if seems that there is a problem with the group, then right-click its name and choose Create Diagnostic Report.
4. Use the information in the report to repair the group and restart replication.
5. Review the replication status for each DFS replication group.

DFSR uses three different replication topologies: hub and spoke, full mesh, and custom. You can change the replication mode by right-clicking the replication group and selecting New Topology.

You can also perform these operations through the command line with the `DFSRADMIN` command. Type `DFSRADMIN` at the command prompt for more information on this powerful tool.

FS-17: Disk and Volume Management

Activity Frequency:	Ad hoc

Managing file servers also means managing disks, volumes, and partitions. The best way to do this is to use the DISKPART command-line tool. This tool includes its own command interpreter. To launch this command interpreter, open a command prompt and type DISKPART, and then press ENTER. The command interpreter starts and lists a new DISKPART prompt.

Before you can use this command interpreter, you must list, then select a disk, volume, or partition to give it focus. The object that has focus will display an asterisk. Use the following command structure within the DISKPART command interpreter:

```
list disk (or volume, or partition)
select disk number (or volume label or partition number)
```

Where *number* or *label* is the disk, volume, or partition number, or, in the case of volumes, its label (such as C, D, E, and so on).

Once an object has focus, you can use the DISKPART command environment to perform a multitude of management activities on disk objects, such as activation, deactivation, extension, creation, deletion, repair, and more.

You can also script DISKPART activities by creating a simple text-based script file and using the following command:

```
diskpart /s scriptname.txt >logfile.txt
```

By adding *logfile.txt* to the command, you can redirect the script's output to a log file you can view at a later date.

Print Service Administration

With Windows Server 2008, print service administration involves everything from installing appropriate printer drivers to managing large clusters of print servers supporting massive user communities. In fact, Microsoft has tested a two-server cluster configuration supporting over 3,000 print queues. With Vista as a client, you can expect even better performance, since Vista renders jobs locally and only sends a prepared print job to the server.

WS08 works with Version 3 print drivers—drivers that are designed to integrate more properly with the operating system to provide better fault tolerance. One of the great advantages of these print drivers is that when the printer driver fails, it does not require a server restart, but only a print spooler restart. In fact, WS08 can automatically restart the print spooler on a failure, making the failure transparent to the majority of the users connected to the printer. The only user who will notice the failure is the one whose job caused the print spooler to fail.

This is because Windows 2008 drivers are user-mode drivers as opposed to kernel-mode drivers. Kernel-mode drivers are Version 2 drivers and were used in older versions of Windows. But a faulty kernel-mode driver can crash the entire kernel, or rather, the entire server. To provide better reliability, Windows 2008 drivers were moved to user mode. In Windows Server 2008, a default Group Policy blocks the use of Version 2 drivers.

NOTE *Each printer in WS08 includes a special Troubleshooting topic under the Help menu. This provides you with a series of wizards that help debug printing problems.*

In addition, a default Group Policy blocks remote printer management on new print servers. This policy must be deactivated before you can manage print servers from the comfort of your desk. You must make sure the Group Policy affecting print servers has the following setting:

- Allow Print Spooler to Accept Client Connections = enabled (Computer Configuration | Policies | Administrative Templates | Printers)

This will allow you to manage the print server remotely, even if no printers are shared on it yet. This policy is automatically activated when you share a printer on a server.

TIP *WS08 supports printer management through a browser, but this requires the installation of Internet Information Server (IIS) on the print server. In most cases, you should choose not to install IIS on your print servers because it can make print server management more complex and WS08 supports several other remote print server management methods.*

PS-01: Print Queue Management

Activity Frequency:	Daily

Because printing is a function everyone uses on an everyday basis, you should perform a proactive print queue verification on a daily basis. To verify printer status:

1. Launch Windows Explorer (Quick Launch area | Windows Explorer).
2. Connect to the server whose printers you want to review using the server's UNC name (*servername*). You can also search for printers in Active Directory Domain Services.
3. Click each printer to view its status. Repair its status if required.
4. In this case, you may have to delete or pause jobs and then restart the print queue. All of these commands are under the File menu.

You can also use the command line to manage print queues:

```
net print \\servername\sharedprintername
```

Where *servername**sharedprintername* is the UNC name for the printer. Typing this command lists the details of the print queue. You can also use three switches: `/DELETE`, `/HOLD`, and `/RELEASE` to control print jobs. You must provide the job number to do so. For example:

```
net print \\servername\sharedprintername 10 /delete
```

PS-02: Printer Access Management

Activity Frequency:	Weekly

TIP *Printer access is controlled through access rights. As always, assigning appropriate and controlled rights is an important aspect of a system administrator's job.*

There are three basic rights that can be assigned to shared printers (Printer | Properties | Security tab):

- Print
- Manage Printers
- Manage Documents

These rights control who can do what on a printer. By default, everyone can use a printer once it is shared, but this can be changed. If, for example, you have a brand-new color printer that will be reserved for managers only, you need to change its default security settings, removing the Everyone group and assigning a Managers group Print rights. Anyone with Print rights can manage their own documents on the printer.

By default, Print Operators, Server Operators, and Administrators groups have complete control over shared printers. This means they can manage documents and stop and start printer queues. You must be a member of one of these groups to perform print management activities.

PS-03: Printer Driver Management

Activity Frequency:	Weekly

As mentioned earlier, WS08 uses Version 3 printer drivers. These may not be available for every one of your printers. If this is the case, you will need to monitor printers more closely, because Version 2 drivers can halt a server when they fail.

This is the reason why you should regularly monitor the printer manufacturer's Web site for updated printer drivers for Windows Server 2008. Then, as soon as a Version 3 printer driver is available, modify the shared printer to improve reliability. Make sure the printer driver includes Windows Server 2008 certification. This will guarantee the printer driver's compatibility with WS08.

WS08 includes a default policy that bars Version 2 drivers from being installed (Disallow Installation Of Printers Using Kernel-Mode Drivers under Computer Configuration | Policies | Administrative Templates | Printers). If you need to use kernel-mode drivers because you are using older printers, you must disable this policy setting.

CAUTION *If you deactivate this setting, make it one of your primary objectives to re-enable it as soon as possible to improve print server reliability.*

Finally, user-mode printer drivers allow users to set their own printer preferences, but these preferences are derived from the printer properties you set. Make sure you set appropriate properties. For example, if the printer is capable of double-sided printing, set it to print double-sided by default. This will make it easier for end users and save a few trees at the same time.

PS-04: Printer Sharing

Activity Frequency:	Ad hoc

Printer sharing is the main focus of print server management. Whenever you share printers in Windows Server 2008, you initiate a process that will eventually publish the printer in Active Directory Domain Services. Users will be able to search the directory for printers based on name, properties, and printer type. Make sure you enter as much detail as possible when preparing a printer for shared use.

To share a printer:

1. Right-click the printer you want to share, and select Sharing.
2. Click Share This Printer, assign a standard share name to the printer, and make sure that the list in the directory box is selected.
3. If you need to support client systems other than Windows 2000, XP, or 2008, or if you need to support both 32- and 64-bit clients, then click Additional Drivers.
4. In the Additional Drivers dialog box, select the other Windows systems you need to support, and then click OK. WS08 will ask you to provide the location of the additional drivers. Identify this location and click OK. Click OK once again to close the Additional Drivers dialog box.
5. Move to the Advanced tab, and set spooling properties. Select Start Printing After Last Page Is Spooled and Print Spooled Documents First. Other settings can remain at the default.
6. Move to the Configuration tab, and ensure the device is properly configured. Then move to the Device Settings tab, and apply default printer settings, such as duplex or double-sided printing, stapling, and paper type in each paper tray.
7. If you need to modify the security settings on the printer share, use Procedure PS-01. Click OK to close the printer Properties dialog box when done.

NOTE *With the greening of the datacenter, it no longer makes sense to print single-sided when a printer has the ability to print double-sided. Do the math: it will save you half the paper.*

PS-05: Print Spooler Drive Management

Activity Frequency: Ad hoc

Large print servers need to spool a lot of print jobs. This means a lot of disk activity. The best way to provide fast and reliable printing is to dedicate a disk drive (or partition) to print spooling. This means that you need to prepare a special drive and assign the spooling to this drive:

1. In Windows Explorer, open Printers. Select Server Properties from the File menu (or use the right mouse button anywhere in the details pane to select Server Properties from the context menu).
2. Move to the Advanced tab, and type the location for printer spooling. For example, this could be E:\Spool\Printers if E: was your dedicated spooling drive. Click OK when done.

Use Procedure FS-01 on a regular basis to make sure there is enough free space on the print spooler drive.

PS-06: Printer Location Tracking Management

Activity Frequency: **Ad hoc**

Windows Server 2008 supports Printer Location Tracking (PLT). This component is based on the Active Directory Domain Services site topology designed for your network. One of the key elements of the site topology is the subnet. Each subnet includes a name and a description. It can also include location information. Location information is stored in hierarchical form in the subnet properties under the Location tab. Each level is separated by a slash. You can use up to 256 levels in a location name, though the entire location name cannot be more than 260 characters long. Each part of the name can include up to 32 characters. For example, a printer located in the northeast corner of the first floor of the headquarters building could be identified as HQ/First Floor/Northeast Corner.

To enable Printer Location Tracking in your domain, you need the following elements:

- Subnets and subnet locations entered into Active Directory Sites and Services
- A printer location naming convention
- Location Tracking GPO enabled
- Location settings for all printers
- Location settings for all PCs and servers

To turn Printer Location Tracking on, you must enable the Pre-populate Printer Search Location text setting under Computer Configuration | Policies | Administrative Templates | Printers. This setting enables the Browse button in the Location tab for printer and computer properties within the directory. It also enables this button in the Search Printers tool. Apply this setting in a Group Policy that covers every machine in your network.

Printer location settings are set through the General tab of the Property dialog box. You can either type or click Browse to enter the location. Be as specific as you can.

NOTE *You have to perform the same operation on all computer objects in the directory. Open the Property dialog box and use the Location tab to either type or click Browse to enter the location.*

Now, whenever users use the Search tool to locate a printer, printer location will automatically be entered in the Location field, enabling your user community to find printers near them without having to know your location naming strategy. See Chapter 8 for more information on PLT.

PS-07: Massive Printer Management

Activity Frequency: **Ad hoc**

WS08 offers a series of Windows Scripting Host scripts to perform local and remote print server management. These include:

- **Prncnfg.vbs** manages printer configurations.
- **Prndrvr.vbs** manages printer drivers.
- **Prnjobs.vbs** manages print jobs.

- **Prnmngr.vbs** manages printers or printer connections.
- **Prnport.vbs** manages TCP/IP printer ports.
- **Prnqctl.vbs** manages print queues.

Each of these commands uses the following command structure:

```
cscript printcommand.vbs
```

Where *printcommand* is the name of the script you want to use. Used without switches, these commands automatically display help information. These commands are great tools for remote printer management and administration or for scripting operations that affect multiple printers at once.

CAUTION *You need to run these scripts from an elevated command prompt.*

NOTE *You can also perform massive printer modifications with the Microsoft Print Migrator. Search for Print Migrator at www.microsoft.com/download for more information. Also, see Chapter 12 for more information.*

PS-08: New Printer Model Evaluation

Activity Frequency:	**Ad hoc**

Once in a while, you will need to evaluate new printers. To enforce reliability and simplify your administration overhead, you should make sure all new printers meet the following criteria:

- Printer includes Version 3 digitally signed driver
- Printer driver has "Designed for Windows Server 2008" certification
- Printer is listed on the Microsoft Hardware Compatibility List (HCL) Web site (www.microsoft.com/hcl) or includes a certified driver
- Printer includes direct network connectivity
- Printer includes special features

NOTE *You may also decide that you do not need to acquire PostScript printers (except in special cases, such as for desktop publishing or graphics teams) because the Windows Unidriver rivals PostScript capabilities at lower cost.*

Cluster Services Management

One of Windows Server 2008's main strengths is its capability to support server clusters. WS08 can support server clusters, including between two and eight nodes, but it depends on the WS08 edition you use: the Enterprise edition supports between two- and four-node clusters, and the Datacenter edition supports between two- and eight-node clusters. Neither the Web nor Standard editions support server clustering (though they do support network load balancing clusters).

Cluster verification is important because the very nature of clusters is to provide high availability. This is only possible if the cluster is operating properly. If one node of a two-node cluster is not functioning properly, then you no longer have a redundant solution.

There are three cluster administration tools:

- Server Manager (Roles | Failover Clustering)
- The Cluster Administration console (Start menu | Administrative Tools | Cluster Administration)
- The `CLUSTER` command-line tool

The latter provides all of the functionality required for cluster administration and can also be scripted. Typing `CLUSTER /?` at the command line provides comprehensive help on this tool.

CS-01: Clusters: Cluster State Verification

Activity Frequency:	Daily

Cluster services depend upon heartbeat detection to make sure each of the nodes is up and running. If the heartbeat of a node is not detected by the cluster service, it will automatically fail-over resources to other nodes.

The first thing you should do when verifying the state of your clusters is make sure that each of the nodes is operating properly. Use the following command to do so:

```
ping nodename or nodeipaddress
```

Where *nodename* is the node's DNS name or *nodeipaddress* is the physical IP address for the public network interface card of the node.

If the nodes do not respond, there may be a problem. Verify the node status with a Remote Desktop Connection. You can easily script this procedure and pipe the entire process into a text file (using the >filename.txt switch) and simply review the results in your text file.

CS-02: Clusters: Print Queue Status Verification

Activity Frequency:	Daily

Server clusters are also useful as print servers because they provide automatic failover on printer failure. But to do so, all printers must use drivers that are updated to meet the requirements of Windows Server 2008. Use Procedure PS-03 to make sure you are using proper print drivers on the server cluster.

Cluster print queues operate the same way as normal print queues, except that they provide failover capabilities. To verify the status of the cluster print queues, use Procedure PS-01.

CS-03: Clusters: Server Cluster Management

Activity Frequency:	Weekly

As mentioned earlier, cluster management is normally performed with Server Manager, the Cluster Administrator console (Start menu | Administrative Tools | Cluster Administrator), or the cluster command-line tool. Basically, you must verify that all of the cluster's nodes are operating properly and continue to be configured properly. You use these tools to add or remove nodes, add quorum sets (shared disk storage), and configure majority node set (independent disk storage) replication.

The Cluster Administrator console is the easiest tool to use to add or remove cluster nodes, because it includes a comprehensive series of wizards to perform most of the complex clustering tasks. To perform server cluster management:

1. Launch Cluster Administrator. If you haven't already done so, use the Open Connection To Cluster dialog box to connect to a server cluster. Clusters can be managed either locally or remotely.
2. Click the cluster name, and view its status.
3. Click each cluster node, and view its status.
4. If you have a new application to add to this cluster, right-click the cluster name and select Configure Application. This starts the New Virtual Server Wizard. Provide it with appropriate answers, and select the appropriate application type.

Applications can include file shares, print spoolers, DHCP, Distributed Transaction Coordinator, Message Queuing, Volume Shadow Copies, generic applications, and so on. Each specific application type will change the wizard's behavior and ask you appropriate questions for the application type.

You should also verify the System Event Log for events that are generated by the cluster service. These events are from the ClusSvc source. Use Procedure GS-03 to check the System Log in the Event Viewer. You can sort events by type simply by clicking the Category column heading.

CS-04: Clusters: Quorum/File Share Witness State Verification

Activity Frequency:	Weekly

A quorum relies on a collection of disks that are shared between cluster members. The quorum is the shared disk that maintains cluster consistency. In WS08, quorums can be of two types: single disk units that are shared between all cluster members or a majority node set. The latter, the majority node set, includes independent disk units for each member of a cluster and can be separated on a geographic basis. The majority node set removes the single point of failure from a server cluster because it uses a file share witness to determine cluster status, but must also rely on replication to operate properly.

The cluster service maintains a Quorum Log, and it is through this log that it manages quorum operations. This log file is called `QUOLOG.LOG` and is located under the `\MSCS` folder of the quorum (`%SYSTEMROOT%\CLUSTER\QUORUMGUID\MSCS`).

CAUTION *The Quorum Log is not a regular text file. Do not attempt to modify it.*

Use Procedure CS-03 to view the quorum's state. Locate the quorum resource under Clustername | Nodename | Active Resources, right-click the quorum name, and select Properties. This will display the quorum's status under the General tab. You can also use the context menu to test failures (Initiate Failure) or to take the quorum resource offline (Take Offline).

CAUTION *Be careful with these operations. Make sure there are no users on the resource before either failure simulations or quorum resource dismounts.*

You can also use the `CLUSTER /QUORUM` command to view available quorums. As usual, you can pipe this command to a text file using the `>FILENAME.TXT` switch, and you can use this command in a script to automate the procedure.

Network Infrastructure Server Administration

Another server role that is critical to the operation of the network is the network infrastructure server. This server includes several different activities, all designed to make sure the underlying network services are functioning properly.

The administration of network infrastructure servers is divided into five categories. These include the Dynamic Host Configuration Protocol (DHCP) and/or the Windows Internet Naming Service (WINS) servers, deployment servers running Windows Deployment Services, network load balancing (NLB) servers, servers controlling either Remote Access or Virtual Private Network (VPN) connections, and Network Access Policy servers. Table 13-5 outlines the administrative activities that you must perform on an ongoing basis to ensure proper operation of the networking services you deliver, both at the resource pool level and at the user community level. It also identifies the frequency of each task.

NOTE *Remember that you should be using DNS GlobalNames Zones (GNZ) instead of WINS servers if at all possible. See Chapter 6 for more information.*

Note that this table does not include the Domain Naming Service (DNS). Though this service has traditionally been linked to network infrastructures in the past, today, it is married to Active Directory Domain Services because it forms the basis of ADDS' hierarchical structure. As such, it will be covered in Identity Server Administration.

You may not need to perform all of these activities because you don't use some of the services mentioned here. For example, large networks rarely rely on Windows Server for remote access. If so, simply ignore the task.

You may also use a different schedule. Remember to personalize the task list to adapt it to your environment.

NOTE *Most of the activities in this section require local administrative rights or proper delegation rights to the appropriate service.*

DHCP/WINS Server Administration

Both DHCP and WINS (if you use it) are services that have become quite reliable in Windows networks. This is even more so with Windows Server 2008 and is one reason why most of the tasks in this category are performed on an ad hoc basis. In regard to WINS, another reason is the fact that Windows networks are relying less and less on this service. Most networks today only include this service for legacy purposes, and with Windows

Procedure No.	Activity	Frequency	Resource Pool	Virtual Service Offerings
DHCP/WINS				
DW-01	DHCP Server State Verification	Weekly		☑
DW-02	WINS Server State Verification	Monthly		☑
DW-03	WINS Record Management	Ad hoc		☑
DW-04	DHCP Attribute Management	Ad hoc		☑
DW-05	DHCP Scope Management	Ad hoc		☑
DW-06	DHCP Reservation Management	Ad hoc		☑
DW-07	DHCP Superscope Management	Ad hoc		☑
DW-08	DHCP Multicast Scope Management	Ad hoc		☑
DW-09	DHCP Option Class Management	Ad hoc		☑
DW-10	DHCP/WDS Server Authorization	Ad hoc		☑
Deployment Servers				
DS-01	WDS Image Management	Ad hoc		☑
NLB Clusters				
NC-01	NLB Cluster State Verification	Weekly		☑
NC-02	NLB Cluster Member Management	Ad hoc		☑
Network Policy and Access				
NP-01	Remote Access Server Status Verification	Weekly	☑	☑
NP-02	Policy and Health Server Verification	Weekly	☑	☑
NP-03	Remote Access Policy Verification	Monthly	☑	☑
NP-04	VPN Connection Management	Ad hoc	☑	☑
NP-05	Policy Definition	Ad hoc	☑	☑

TABLE 13-5 Network Infrastructure Services Administration Task List

Server 2008, it can be replaced with DNS GNZs. Organizations rely less and less on this service as network applications evolve. Nevertheless, each verification task in this list is still performed on at least a monthly basis.

The tools most commonly used to manage both DHCP and WINS are:

- Server Manager, because it contains access to both services.
- The `NETSH` command-line tool manages both DHCP and WINS services. This is a shell command; that means it creates a shell environment when used and commands are entered into this shell once the focus has been set.
- The `NBTSTAT` command is also useful with WINS. It supports record management from the command line.

DW-01: DHCP Server State Verification

Activity Frequency:	Weekly

DHCP servers are designed to provide a service that forms the basis of a TCP/IP network: addressing. Each time a new client boots, it contacts the DHCP server to receive all of the information that will allow it to function on the network. Therefore, the proper operation of your DHCP servers is critical.

Once a week, you should verify the proper operation of your DHCP servers. In most networks, there will be at least two DHCP servers to provide redundancy for the service. These servers will use the same scopes, but each scope should be divided into 80/20 portions: 80 percent being hosted on one server and 20 percent on the other. This allows each DHCP server to provide backup for any given scope. Of course, if you only have 50 PCs or fewer, you'll only have a single DHCP server.

To verify the status of your DHCP servers, you need to perform three tasks:

- Check server statistics.
- Reconcile scopes.
- Check DHCP logs.

The first lets you identify how long your server has been running and how well it performs. The second is designed to avoid any errors in IP address leases. DHCP stores both detailed and summary information about a lease. Reconciling scopes allows DHCP to review both sets of information to see if there are any inconsistencies. If inconsistencies are found, they are repaired during this process. The third operation lets you see how your DHCP server behaves on a daily basis (all logs are stored in single-day format).

CAUTION *You have to be a member of the local DHCP Administrators group or the local Administrators group in order to operate and configure the DHCP server.*

To check server statistics:

1. Launch the DHCP Console (Start menu | Administrative Tools | DHCP).
2. Connect to the appropriate server (Action | Connect To Another Computer), and either type the server name (*servername*) or use the Browse button to locate it. Click OK when done.
3. Make sure you click the DHCP service and that its information is displayed in the details pane. Then right-click DHCP to select Display Statistics from the context menu.
4. This will display current statistics for the server, including uptime, discovers, offers, requests, and more. Make note of these values in your weekly DHCP log. Click Close when done.

To reconcile scopes:

1. Once again, right-click DHCP and select Reconcile All Scopes.
2. Click Verify to begin the reconciliation.

3. Click OK when DHCP indicates that all scopes are consistent.
4. Click Cancel to close the Reconcile All Scopes window.

All DHCP events are stored within the System Event Log, but DHCP also writes its own logs. These are stored under `%SYSTEMROOT%\SYSTEM32\DHCP`. These logs are enabled by default for both IPv4 and IPv6 DHCP offerings and are a property of the protocol (see Figure 13-10).

To view DHCP logs:

1. Open a Remote Desktop Connection to the DHCP server.
2. When the connection is open, launch Windows Explorer (Quick Launch area | Explorer).
3. Move to the `%SYSTEMROOT%\SYSTEM32\DHCP` folder.
4. Double-click any of the last week's logs to view them. Log files are named `DHCPSRVLOG-DAY.LOG`, where *day* is the three-character abbreviation for the day of the week. Each of the seven log files are written over every week.

NOTE *The amount of space available on the server for logging purposes will determine the amount of information DHCP will store in these log files. Make sure sufficient space is available. By default, the minimum log size is 20 megabytes (MB) and the maximum is 70 MB.*

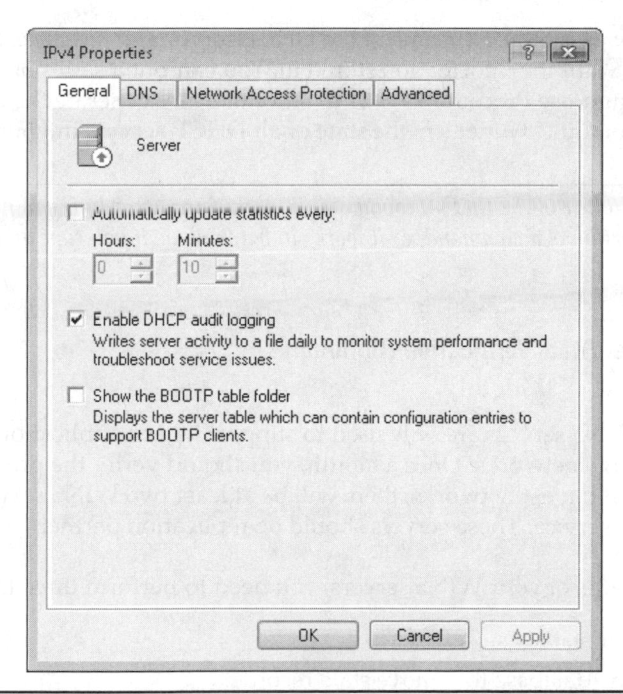

FIGURE 13-10 DHCP audit logging is enabled by default. This setting can be found in the DHCP server's properties.

The DHCP server also stores logging information in the System Event Log, but the information stored in its own log files is much more complete.

You can also use command-line tools to view information about the server. This means using the `NETSH` command within the DHCP scope. To view server information interactively, use the following commands:

```
netsh
dhcp
server ServerName
show all
```

Where *ServerName* is the DNS name of the server you want to connect to. Basically, the first command opens the `NETSH` console, the second sets the DHCP scope, the third sets focus on a specific server, and the last requests information about the server. To exit the `NETSH` console, type:

```
quit
```

TIP *To view information about `NETSH DHCP` commands, type /? at the `netsh dhcp>` command prompt.*

To automatically collect information about a DHCP server, type:

```
netsh dhcp server ServerName show all >filename.txt
```

Where *ServerName* is the DNS name of the DHCP server and *filename.txt* is the name of the output file you want the information stored in. You can put a series of these commands in a command file and use Procedure GS-21 to automatically generate the output files every week. This helps you quickly identify the state of all DHCP servers in your network.

NOTE *Note the structure of the `NETSH` command. It works interactively if you press ENTER after you type each portion of a command, or it works in batch mode if you type an entire command string at once.*

DW-02: WINS Server State Verification (Optional)

Activity Frequency: Monthly

Even though WINS servers are only used to support legacy applications, they are still required in most large networks. Once a month, you should verify the proper operation of your WINS servers. In most networks, there will be at least two WINS servers to provide redundancy for the service. These servers should be replication partners using persistent connections.

To verify the status of your WINS servers, you need to perform three tasks:

- Check server statistics.
- Scavenge the database to remove stale records.
- Check WINS logs for errors.

You may also check database consistency and check for Version ID consistency. The latter deals with how WINS manages replication. Each record is given a Version ID. The records with the highest Version ID are replicated to the server's partners.

CAUTION *You have to be a member of the local WINS Users group or the local Administrators group in order to operate and configure the WINS server.*

To check server statistics:

1. Launch the WINS console (Start menu | Administrative Tools | WINS).
2. Connect to the appropriate server through Action | Connect To Another Computer. Either type the server name (*servername*) or use the Browse button to locate it. Click OK when done.
3. Make sure you click the WINS service and that its information is displayed in the details pane. Then right-click WINS to select Display Server Statistics from the context menu.
4. This will display current statistics for the server, including uptime, discovers, offers, requests, and more. Make note of these values in your monthly WINS log. Click Close when done.

You can use the same context menu to select Scavenge Database, Check Database Consistency, and Check Version ID Consistency.

You can also use command-line tools to view information about the server. This means using the `NETSH` command within the WINS scope. To automatically collect information about a WINS server, type:

```
netsh wins server servername show statistics >filename.txt
```

Where *servername* is the DNS name of the WINS server and *filename.txt* is the name of the output file you want the information stored in. You can put a series of these commands in a command file and use Procedure GS-21 to automatically generate the output files. You can also include the `INIT SCAVENGE` command in these files to automatically initiate scavenging on your servers.

TIP *You can also collect information interactively by typing each command alone. To view information about* `NETSH WINS` *commands, type /? at the* `NETSH WINS>` *command prompt.*

WINS servers in Windows Server 2008 support dynamic database compaction. This means that each time the server database has been updated and the server is idle, it will try to recover lost space within its database. Unfortunately, this does not recover all lost space. Therefore, you should manually compact the database at least once a month to recover all lost space. To do so, you must take the WINS server offline.

Use the following series of commands to stop the service, compact the database, and restart the service:

```
sc \\servername stop wins
timeout /t 300
netsh wins server servername init compact
sc \\servername start wins
```

Here, the timeout command is required to make sure the WINS service has been stopped before the compaction begins. You can insert these commands in a command file and use Procedure GS-21 to automatically perform this operation on a monthly basis.

DW-03: WINS Record Management (Optional)

Activity Frequency: **Ad hoc**

Once in a while, the WINS record of a given machine does not appear in the database. This may be caused by a variety of reasons: the client cannot find the WINS server, the server is busy when a record arrives and cannot include it in its database, the server did not replicate a record, and so on.

This is where the `NBTSTAT` command becomes useful. It can be used to refresh NetBIOS information on individual computers. The simplest command for this is:

```
nbtstat -RR
```

This command releases information held in the WINS server and refreshes NetBIOS information locally. It must be performed on the machine whose record is to be updated.

For more information on this command, type `NBTSTAT` at the command prompt.

DW-04: DHCP Attribute Management

Activity Frequency: **Ad hoc**

Along with IP addresses, DHCP servers provide IP address attributes to their clients. These attributes are either global—that is, they are provided to all clients—or local—that is, they are provided to only those clients within a given address scope. These attributes may change from time to time; therefore, you will need to modify existing attributes or add new attributes.

In the DHCP console, these attributes are called scope options. Global scope options usually include at least the following:

- **003 Router** The address of a router.
- **006 DNS Servers** The address of at least two DNS servers.
- **015 DNS Domain Name** The domain name for the scope.
- **044 WINS/NBNS Servers** The address of at least two WINS servers (optional).
- **046 WINS/NBT Node Type** This should be set to H-node (optional). H-node resolution is best, even in wide area networks, because it greatly reduces the amount of broadcasting on each network.

TIP *DNS servers are set globally here to ensure that all clients always have a valid DNS address; though in Windows Server 2008, with the integration of Active Directory Domain Services, the DNS service is married to the Domain Controller service, placing a DNS server wherever there is a DC. You need to override the global values by local scope values because local scope options should now include the local DNS server, since DNS is now integrated with ADDS and each client must find the closest DNS server, which is usually one that is local to its network (especially in regional offices).*

To configure scope options:

1. Launch the DHCP console (Start menu | Administrative Tools | DHCP).
2. Connect to the appropriate server (Action | Connect To Another Computer), and either type the server name (*servername*) or use the Browse button to locate it. Click OK when done.
3. Move to the DHCP service (Services and Applications | DHCP).
4. To modify global options, right-click Server Options under the appropriate protocol, and choose Configure Options from the context menu.
5. Configure or modify the options you require (or as outlined earlier). Click OK when done.

This will set the global options for all scopes on this server.

To configure local scope options, expand the scope by clicking it and use the same procedure, but this time with Scope Options.

To modify either global or local scope options through the command line, use the following command:

```
netsh dhcp server servername add optiondef parameters
```

Where *servername* is the DNS name of the DHCP server and *parameters* includes the details of the modification you want to make. Use `ADD OPTIONDEF /?` for the details of the parameters setting.

DW-05: DHCP Scope Management

Activity Frequency:	Ad hoc

Once in a while, you will also need to add, remove, or modify DHCP scopes. If you use the 80/20 rule for scope redundancy (creating a scope on two servers and enabling 80 percent of the scope on one and 20 percent on the other), you will need to create each scope and exclude the appropriate range on each server. Once all scopes are created, you must join them into a superscope. Superscopes are scope groupings that allow the DHCP server to service more than one subnet. They are required whenever multinetting is used. Use the superscope to include all of the scopes in a set of server ranges. The content of superscopes should be the same on each of the servers you manage. Use Procedure DW-07 for superscope management.

To configure a DHCP scope:

1. Launch the DHCP console (Start menu | Administrative Tools | DHCP).
2. Connect to the appropriate server (Action | Connect To Another Computer), and either type the server name (*servername*) or use the Browse button to locate it. Click OK when done.
3. Right-click the protocol whose scope you want to configure under the DHCP item, and select New Scope from the context menu. DHCP will launch the New Scope Wizard. This wizard allows you to input all of the values for the scope: name, description, starting address, end address, exclusions, and even scope-specific options.
4. You will need to activate the scope once you're done. It is best to wait for activation at this stage. This lets you review all of your settings before the scope begins to service requests.
5. Remember to exclude 80 or 20 percent of the scope, depending on where you want the main portion of the scope to be hosted.

To modify scopes, right-click the scope and select Properties. To delete a scope, deactivate it first and then delete it through the context menu.

To create or delete a scope through the command line, use the following commands:

```
netsh dhcp server servername add scope parameters
netsh dhcp server servername delete scope parameters
```

Where *servername* is the DNS name of the DHCP server and *parameters* includes the details of the modification you want to make. Use `ADD SCOPE /?` or `DELETE SCOPE /?` for the details of the parameters setting.

DW-06: DHCP Reservation Management

Activity Frequency: Ad hoc

Address reservations are used to ensure that specific machines always receive the same address, but still profit from dynamic addressing. Examples of where you would use address reservations are servers, domain controllers, and client machines that run applications that may have hard-coded IP addresses.

To make sure each machine always receives the same address, you should configure your address reservations on each DHCP server that can respond to requests from machines requiring a reservation. This ensures that these clients don't receive a dynamic address by mistake.

TIP *You will require the Media Access Control (MAC) address for each of the network cards for which you want to reserve an IP address. MAC addresses can be displayed by typing* `IPCONFIG /ALL` *at the command prompt of the system for which the reservation is required.*

To configure an address reservation:

1. Launch the DHCP console (Start menu | Administrative Tools | DHCP).
2. Connect to the appropriate server (Action | Connect To Another Computer), and either type the server name (*servername*) or use the Browse button to locate it. Click OK when done.
3. Select the appropriate scope to create reservations within it. Click Reservations in the tree pane, and then right-click Reservations.
4. Choose New Reservation from the context menu.
5. Fill in the reservation details. Close the dialog box by clicking Add. Repeat as necessary.

TIP *If you use DHCP to assign static addresses to servers, you should make sure that the alternate configuration for Internet Protocol (TCP/IP) properties for each network card is set to the same values as the reservation. Use Control Panel | Network Connection to view the IP properties for each network card.*

DW-07: DHCP Superscope Management

Activity Frequency: **Ad hoc**

Superscopes are groupings of scopes that support the assignment of multiple scopes managing different subnets from the same server. Superscopes regroup all of these scopes into a single management group. One advantage of using superscopes is that you can activate the entire superscope and all its scopes in one fell swoop.

NOTE *Superscopes cannot be created until at least one scope has been created on a DHCP server.*

To create a superscope:

1. Launch the DHCP console (Start menu | Administrative Tools | DHCP).
2. Connect to the appropriate server (Action | Connect To Another Computer), and either type the server name (*servername*) or use the Browse button to locate it. Click OK when done.
3. Once at least one scope has been created, right-click DHCP and select New Superscope. This will launch the New Superscope Wizard. Click Next to proceed.
4. Name the superscope and then select the scopes that will be part of it. Close the dialog box when done.

Once a superscope is created, new scopes can be added to it in one of two ways: The scope can be created within the superscope by right-clicking the superscope name and selecting New Scope, or the scope can be created outside the superscope and added to it once created. This is done by right-clicking the scope and selecting Add To Superscope.

Scopes all need activation before they can begin to service clients. You can activate multiple scopes at once by activating a superscope. Review each scope's settings to make sure they are appropriate, and then activate the superscope. To do so, right-click the superscope name and select Activate from the context menu.

TIP *Scope activation can also act as a failsafe mechanism, because you can create spare scopes on each server before they are actually required and activate them only when they are needed.*

DW-08: DHCP Multicast Scope Management

Activity Frequency:	Ad hoc

Multicasting is different from unicasting in that a single address is used by multiple clients. The advantage of a multicast is that a single broadcast can be received by multiple clients at once, significantly reducing network traffic. Multicasting can be used when sending large files to several clients and wanting to reduce overall network traffic. Examples of multicast use are videoconferencing, large software deployments, and audio streaming.

The Windows Server 2008 DHCP server can also support the allocation of multicast scopes. When it does so, it operates using the Multicast Address Dynamic Client Allocation Protocol (MADCAP). Multicast address ranges are concentrated on Class D IP addresses. These range from 224.0.0.0 to 239.255.255.255. Addresses in this class can only be used for multicasting.

When using multicast scopes internally, you tend to work with administrative multicast scopes. The range most recommended for this scope begins with 239.192.0.0 and uses a subnet mask of 255.252.0.0 (14 bits in length). This range is known as the *IPv4 organization local scope* and is intended for use by organizations setting multicast scopes privately for internal use. Using this address, you can create up to 262,144 group addresses.

To create a multicast scope:

1. Launch the DHCP console (Start menu | Administrative Tools | DHCP).
2. Connect to the appropriate server (Action | Connect To Another Computer), and either type the server name (*servername*) or use the Browse button to locate it. Click OK when done.
3. Right-click the DHCP item, and select New Multicast Scope from the context menu. DHCP will launch the New Multicast Scope Wizard. This wizard allows you to input all of the values for the scope: scope name, description, starting address, end address, and exclusions.
4. You can also activate the scope through the wizard. Do so only if you are sure all your settings are correct.
5. Click Finish when done.

You can also create multicast scopes through the command line. Use the following command:

```
netsh dhcp server servername add mscope parameters
```

Where *servername* is the DNS name of the DHCP server and *parameters* includes the details of the modification you want to make. Use `add MSCOPE /?` for the details of the parameters setting.

DW-09: DHCP Option Class Management

Activity Frequency: Ad hoc

Windows Server 2008 supports the use of classes within DHCP. Two classes are supported: user and vendor classes. Each can be used to identify specific machines and provide them with particular settings. One example of a useful user class is a special user class for mobile clients. By identifying mobile clients, you can differentiate them from desktop clients and set their lease duration to a shorter time period than those of the PC workstations in your network. Thus, when a mobile user goes from one site to another, addresses are released when they leave the site.

User classes are quite useful when you want to designate special DHCP assignments to specific classes of machines in your network. Vendor classes are usually used when you can guarantee that users all have machines originating from the same vendor. Both classes make it possible to address client subsets through DHCP. Both must be used together to function properly.

To define user classes:

1. Launch the DHCP console (Start menu | Administrative Tools | DHCP).
2. Connect to the appropriate server (Action | Connect To Another Computer), and either type the server name (*servername*) or use the Browse button to locate it. Click OK when done.
3. Right-click DHCP and select Define User Classes.
4. Click Add in the User Class dialog box.
5. In the New Class dialog box, type the class display name and description, and then place your cursor directly below the word ASCII. Type the class name. You will note that the New Class dialog box inputs the binary values for each ASCII character as you type them. Do not modify these values! Also, class names are case-sensitive. You'll need to make note of how you spelled the class name. Click OK when done.
6. Repeat the process for each class you need to add. When all classes have been added, click Close to return to the DHCP console.
7. Next, right-click the Server Options item, and select Configure Options. Move to the Advanced tab, and select Microsoft Windows 2000 Options as the vendor class and Mobile Users as the user class.
8. Set the value for number 02, Microsoft Release DHCP Lease on Shutdown Operating System by selecting the relevant check box.
9. Next, change vendor class to DHCP Standard Options to set option 51, Lease. The value is in 0xseconds, where seconds is the number of seconds for lease duration. For example, 0x86400 means 24 hours.
10. Finally, you will need to set this user class on all mobile systems. To do so, you need to use the `IPCONFIG` command on each computer. This setting can be performed at PC staging. The command structure is as follows:

```
ipconfig /setclassid adapter_name class_id
```

For example, if your class ID is "TandTMobile," the command would be:

```
ipconfig /setclassid "Local Area Connection" TandTMobile
```

TIP *Class IDs are case-sensitive. You must type the* exact *class ID wording for it to work properly.*

User-defined class options can be assigned to either server or scope options, depending on whether they apply to systems in all scopes or only to systems in specific scopes.

TIP *User-defined classes are also useful for the assignation of domain names to systems that are located in the same physical locations but that use multiple domains. For example, if you have users in the same physical location that use different domains, such as an intranet and a development domain, you can use a user-defined class to make sure that systems register DNS values in the proper DNS domain controller. Use the user-defined class only for the smallest number of systems. This will make it easier to stage and manage the systems.*

To add a class through the command line, use the following commands:

```
netsh dhcp server servername add class parameters
```

Where *servername* is the DNS name of the DHCP server and *parameters* includes the details of the modification you want to make. Use `ADD CLASS /?` for the details of the parameters setting.

DW-10: DHCP/RIS Server Authorization

Activity Frequency:	Ad hoc

In a Windows Server 2008 network using Active Directory, servers that will affect multiple systems must be authorized. This includes DHCP services as well as Remote Installation Services (RIS). This feature is designed to make sure that rogue machines cannot send out false addresses to clients. It is also quite useful, since you can configure your server, review all settings, and correct potential errors before putting the server into service.

CAUTION *Server authorization can only be done by users with the proper credentials. You must be a domain administrator to activate a server.*

To authorize a server:

1. Launch the DHCP console (Start menu | Administrative Tools | DHCP).
2. Connect to the appropriate server (Action | Connect To Another Computer), and either type the server name (*servername*) or use the Browse button to locate it. Click OK when done.
3. Depending on the service you are authorizing, right-click DHCP and select Manage Authorized Servers from the context menu.
4. Click Authorize, type the name of the server to authorize, and click OK.
5. Click Close when done.

Your server is now ready to service clients.

Deployment Servers

Windows Server 2008 includes a core deployment technology: Windows Deployment Services (WDS). WDS can be used for both servers and workstations, but in the dynamic datacenter, it is most useful for workstations, since servers are deployed either through the replication of a virtual machine for virtual service offerings or the replication of a shared storage partition for resource pools. WDS relies on the use of a Preboot Execution Environment (PXE) network card. This means that you can start a new machine that does not include an operating system, press F12 during the boot sequence, boot from the network interface card, and select the operating system to install from the menu choices that are presented to you.

You can also use WDS to deploy operating systems to bare-metal machines through the use of Windows PE. Since WDS uses the boot sequence of a network card to contact the machine to be staged, it must supply this machine with an IP address, much in the way DHCP does. Because of this, WDS must also be authorized in Active Directory Domain Services to function.

WDS servers are mostly managed through the graphical interface (since you normally have only a few of these types of servers in any network).

DS-01: WDS Image Management

Activity Frequency:	Ad hoc

Every now and then, you will need to either modify or update WDS installation images. Modification comes when new components are added to completed images, such as service packs, hot fixes, and other program updates.

You need to use the Add Image Wizard to add or update an image:

1. Install and customize the reference system. This should include any additional software, as well as customization of elements, such as the default user profile, desktop personalization, and tool settings.
2. Capture the image using ImageX (see Chapter 4), and store it in the WDS image folder.
3. Launch the WDS console (Start menu | Administrative Tools | Windows Deployment Services).
4. Expand the tree pane to view the Install Images folder on the server you are working with.
5. Right-click the folder and select Add Install Image. This launches the Add Image Wizard.
6. Images are stored in image groups. If no image group is found, the wizard will begin by requesting that you create one. Create the image group or select the appropriate one to store this image in. Click Next.
7. Point to the image you want to upload. Images are in .wim format. Select the image and click OK. Click Next.
8. Name the image and add a description. Click Next. The system will validate the image.
9. Click Finish when done.

Use the same process to add a boot image.

You can also perform these tasks through the command line. Use the following command lines to perform the same operations:

```
wdsutil /add-image /imagefile:\\servername\sharename\imagename.wim
/imagetype:install
wdsutil /add-image /imagefile:\\servername\sharename\imagename.wim
/imagetype:boot
```

Images are validated and then loaded into the WDS store.

NOTE *Step-by-step instructions for other operations within WDS can be found at http://technet2.microsoft.com/WindowsVista/en/library/9e197135-6711-4c20-bfad-fc80fc2151301033.mspx?mfr=true.*

NLB Clusters

The Network Load Balancing (NLB) service provides high availability and scalability for IP services (both TCP and UDP) and applications by combining up to 32 servers into a single cluster. Clients access the NLB cluster by accessing a single IP address for the entire group. NLB services automatically redirect the client to a working server. They are installed by default on Windows Server 2008. NLB clusters are useful for load-balancing terminal services, streaming media, Web applications, and virtual private network servers.

Two tools are used to manage NLB clusters:

- The NLB Manager is a graphical interface that provides access to all of the NLB management commands. It is the preferred management tool.
- `NLB.EXE` is a command-line tool that is designed to manage NLB clusters. Remote Control must be enabled on the cluster for `NLB.EXE` to work.

CAUTION *It is highly recommended that you avoid activating Remote Control on NLB clusters and avoid using the `NLB.EXE` command-line tool because it exposes the cluster to potential damage from people with malicious intent. Use NLB Manager instead.*

You can also start the NLB Manager from the command line using `NLBMGR.EXE`.

NC-01: NLB Cluster State Verification

Activity Frequency:	Weekly

NLB clusters are composed of several servers responding to like requests. One of the best ways to identify the status of the NLB cluster is to enable logging and verify the logging file on a regular basis.

To enable logging:

1. Launch the NLB Manager (Start | Administrative Tools | NLB Manager).
2. Select Log Settings from the Options menu.
3. In the Log Settings dialog box, select Enable Logging and in the name of the log file. Locate the file in C:\Toolkit and name it NLBLog.txt.
4. Click OK to close the dialog box.

From now on, all NLB activity will be logged in the NLBLog file. This file is quite useful, even though all activity is displayed in the bottom pane of the NLB Manager window, because the NLB Manager only displays information about the current session, while the log file provides information about all sessions.

To review the status of the NLB cluster, locate the NLBLog file and double-click it. Review the information stored in the file. Review this file on a weekly basis.

NC-02: NLB Cluster Member Management

Activity Frequency:	Ad hoc

Once in a while, you will need to enable and disable NLB cluster members for maintenance and other purposes. Use the NLB Manager to do so:

1. Use the Remote Desktop console to connect to a member of the NLB cluster (Remote Desktop | Connection Name).
2. Launch the NLB Manager (Start | Administrative Tools | NLB Manager).
3. Select Connect To Existing from the Cluster menu.
4. In the Connect dialog box, type the name of a host, click Connect, select the cluster name, and click Finish.
5. To add a host to the cluster, right-click the cluster name and select Add Host To Cluster. Follow the instructions in the wizard to complete the operation.
6. To stop a host for maintenance purposes, right-click the host name and select Control Host | Stop. Use the same procedure with Control Host | Start to restart the host once maintenance has been performed on it.
7. Close the NLB Manager when done.

Managing your NLB hosts should be relatively straightforward.

Network Policy and Access Services

The Routing and Remote Access Service (RRAS) in Windows Server 2008 now supports several functions:

- Remote Access management and authorization
- VPN connections
- Routing within networks
- Connection sharing or Network Address Translation (NAT)

While few organizations of any size use all of the features of the RRAS service, many use both the Remote Access Service (RAS) and VPN connections, especially if they use wireless networks.

Several tools are available for managing these services. Once again, the Custom MMC console created in Procedure GS-17 will be useful for management through the graphical interface. For those who prefer to use the command line, the `NETSH` command will provide most of the functionality they require.

NP-01: Remote Access Server Status Verification

Activity Frequency:	Weekly

The first administrative activity linked to RAS is the verification of the status of your Remote Access servers. This should be done on a weekly basis.

To verify the status of a RAS server:

1. Launch the Routing and Remote Access console (Start menu | Administrative Tools | Routing and Remote Access).
2. Connect to the appropriate server (Action | Connect To Another Computer), and either type the server name (*servername*) or use the Browse button to locate it. Click OK when done.
3. Click Server Status. The status of the server, including the number of connections it currently manages, will be displayed in the right window pane.
4. Make note of the server status in your weekly report.

You should also review the RAS server activity log. This log is stored in the `%SYSTEMROOT%\SYSTEM32\LOGFILES` folder by default. To review the log:

1. Use the Remote Desktop console to connect to the RAS server you want to verify (Remote Desktop | Connection Name).
2. Launch Windows Explorer (Quick Launch area | Windows Explorer), and move to the `%SYSTEMROOT%\SYSTEM32\LOGFILES` folder.
3. Locate the current week's log file and double-click it. The log file name is `INYYMMWW.LOG`.
4. Make note of any anomalies in the file.

NOTE *Before you can view RAS log files, you must configure them. Configuration is performed under Remote Access Logging (Computer Management | Services and Applications | Routing and Remote Access | Remote Access Logging). Double-click Local File to set logging parameters. Select each of the items you want to log on the Settings tab, and set the log file format, as well as the new file frequency, on the Log File tab. Make sure the new file frequency is set to Weekly.*

NP-02: Policy and Health Service Verification

Activity Frequency:	Weekly

Windows Server 2008 provides a powerful engine for Network Access Protection (NAP). NAP relies on two key server roles to provide protection for connections to your network. These connections can be either through the wired or the wireless network and can be either internal or external.

Each week, you should verify the proper operation of your policy and health services to ensure that NAP is working properly. Service status verification can rely on Procedure GS-02, which lets you check whether a service is operational or not.

You can also rely on Server Manager to verify that NAP is working properly.

1. Use Remote Desktop to connect to the appropriate server, or use a Server Manager application that is shared through RemoteApps.
2. Launch Server Manager and go to Network Policy and Access Services (Roles | Network Policy and Access Services).
3. Review the status of your server in the summary details in the details pane.
4. Investigate and repair any untoward event.

This will help ensure your network connections are protected at all times.

NP-03: Remote Access Policy Verification

Activity Frequency:	Monthly

Windows Server 2008 manages remote access through policies. These policies are an ordered set of rules that defines whether access is granted or denied. Each policy consists of a set of conditions, a profile set to which the conditions are applied, and a set of remote access permissions. Policies are applied in the order they are listed.

WS08 allows you to centrally manage all access policies in one single location. This includes policies for connection requests, network, and health status. RAS policies are located under network policies. Policy settings are located under Server Manager | Roles | Network Policy and Access Services | NPS | Policies.

NP-04: VPN Connection Management

Activity Frequency:	Ad hoc

VPN connections are also managed through Routing and Remote Access. These include external connections from clients accessing the internal network, as well as VPN tunnels between servers, such as in the connection of branch offices to larger sites.

VPN connections running on Windows Server 2008 can use either the Point to Point Tunneling Protocol (PPTP) or the Layer 2 Tunneling Protocol (L2TP). You should aim to use the latter wherever possible. It works in conjunction with the Internet Protocol Security (IPSec) protocol to provide more secure connections than PPTP.

To create a new VPN interface:

1. Launch the Server Manager (Quick Launch area | Server Manager).
2. Move to Network Interfaces (Server Manager | Roles | Network Policy and Access Services | Routing and Remote Access | Network Interfaces), and click it once.
3. Right-click Network Interfaces and select New Demand-Dial Interface from the context menu. This launches the Demand-Dial Interface Wizard. Click Next.
4. Name the interface and click Next.
5. Select Connect Using Virtual Private Network, and click Next.
6. Select Automatic Selection, or, if you are certain you want to use L2TP, select L2TP, and click Next.
7. Enter the name of the destination address in host name format, and click Next.

8. Select Route IP Packets On This Interface and Add A User Account So A Remote Router Can Dial In, and click Next.
9. Add the static route for this interface. Use the Add button to add each part of the route, and then click Next.
10. Type the password for the dial-in connection, click Next, type the credentials for the dial-out connection, and click Next. Click Finish to create the interface.

From now on, right-click the interface and select Properties to review its settings.

NP-05: Policy Definition

Activity Frequency:	Ad hoc

Every now and then, you will need to define or review the definition of your network access policies. As mentioned in Procedure NP-03, policies are located under Server Manager | Roles | Network Policy and Access Services | NPS | Policies. This container includes three types of policies:

- Connection request policies
- Network policies
- Health policies

Each one contains policies that are used to determine if systems can connect to your network or not. Configuring policies is performed by going to this node and then right-clicking the sub-node of choice. Each policy definition process is similar, because NAP relies on a set of wizards to generate the policy. Policies are tied to the type of access you want to control. If you select Unspecified in the Type Of Network Access Server section, than the policy will apply to any type of access.

Choose your policies carefully and verify them regularly. You don't want to receive a whole series of calls from irate users who can't connect to internal resources because your policies are too strict.

Identity Server Administration

Active Directory Domain Services is the very core of the Windows Server network. It manages user identity and computer accounts; controls groups; and supports object structuring and organization through forests, domains, and organizational units. Through the power of Group Policy, it controls the behavior of the objects it contains.

The administration of identity servers is divided into two categories. These include the management of domain controllers and all the objects they contain, as well as the administration of the DNS servers. DNS servers are included here because this service is at the basis of ADDS. Without a fully functional DNS service, ADDS would be completely unreachable, since all of its own services are based on the DNS hierarchical structure and DNS records. In fact, to ensure proper ADDS operation, each domain controller should also host the DNS service.

Table 13-6 outlines the administrative activities that you must perform on an ongoing basis to ensure proper operation of the services you deliver to your user community. It also identifies the frequency of each task for both resource pools and virtual service offerings.

Procedure No.	Activity	Frequency	Resource Pool	Virtual Service Offerings
Domain Controllers				
DC-01	User Management	Daily		☑
DC-02	User Password Reset	Daily		☑
DC-03	Directory Service Log Event Verification	Daily	☑	☑
DC-04	Account Management	Daily		☑
DC-05	Security Group Management	Daily		☑
DC-06	Knowledge Consistency Checker (KCC) Service Status Management	Weekly	☑	☑
DC-07	ADDS Replication Topology Verification	Weekly	☑	☑
DC-08	Global Catalog Status Verification	Weekly	☑	☑
DC-09	Universal Administration Group Management	Weekly	☑	☑
DC-10	Account Policy Verification	Weekly		☑
DC-11	ADCS Service Verification	Weekly		☑
DC-12	ADDS Service/Admin Account Verification	Monthly	☑	☑
DC-13	Lost and Found Object Management	Monthly		☑
DC-14	Rights Delegation Management	Ad hoc		☑
DC-15	Software Installation Management	Ad hoc		☑
DC-16	GPO Management	Ad hoc	☑	☑
DC-17	Computer Object Management	Ad hoc		☑
DC-18	Distribution Group Management	Ad hoc		☑
DC-19	ADDS Forest Management	Ad hoc	☑	☑
DC-20	ADDS Information Management	Ad hoc		☑
DC-21	Schema Management	Ad hoc		☑
DC-22	Schema Access Management	Ad hoc		☑
DC-23	Schema Content Modification	Ad hoc		☑
DC-24	Schema-Modifying Software Evaluation	Ad hoc		☑

TABLE 13-6 Identity Server Administration Task List

Procedure No.	Activity	Frequency	Resource Pool	Virtual Service Offerings
Domain Controllers				
DC-25	Operations Master Role Management	Ad hoc	☑	☑
DC-26	Operations Master Role Transfer	Ad hoc	☑	☑
DC-27	Operations Master Disaster Recovery	Ad hoc	☑	☑
DC-28	Domain Controller Promotion	Ad hoc	☑	☑
DC-29	Domain Controller Disaster Recovery	Ad hoc	☑	☑
DC-30	Trust Management	Ad hoc		☑
DC-31	Forest/Domain/OU Structure Management	Ad hoc		☑
DC-32	Forest Time Service Management	Ad hoc	☑	☑
DC-33	Access Control List Management	Ad hoc		☑
DC-34	Managing Saved Queries	Ad hoc		☑
DC-35	Managing Space Within ADDS	Ad hoc	☑	☑
DC-36	Managing the LDAP Query Policy	Ad hoc		☑
DC-37	Managing the ADDS Database	Ad hoc	☑	☑
DC-38	Deleting RODCs	Ad hoc		☑
Namespace Management (DNS)				
DN-01	DNS Event Log Verification	Daily	☑	☑
DN-02	DNS Configuration Management	Monthly	☑	☑
DN-03	DNS Record Management	Ad hoc		☑
DN-04	DNS Application Partition Management	Ad hoc		☑

TABLE 13-6 Identity Server Administration Task List (*continued*)

You may not need to perform all of these activities because you don't use some of the services mentioned here. You may also use a different schedule. Remember to personalize the task list to adapt it to your environment.

NOTE *Most of the activities in this section require domain or forest (enterprise) administrative rights or proper delegation rights to the appropriate service.*

Domain Controller Administration

Domain controller administration is really Active Directory Domain Services administration. Though you will need to manage the operation of the domain controllers themselves, you also need to manage the content of the ADDS. This means using a wide variety of tools, both in graphical and command-line mode. The tools you use to manage ADDS include:

- The four Active Directory consoles: Users and Computers, Sites and Services, Domains and Trusts, and Schema.
- The Group Policy Management Console (GPMC).
- The `CSVDE` command-line tool, which is designed to perform massive user and computer account operations.
- The `DS` commands (for Directory Service), a series of commands supporting the administration of directory objects.
- The `LDIFDE` command, a powerful tool that even lets you modify ADDS schemas or database structures.
- The `NTDSUTIL` command, which is specifically designed to manage the ADDS database.
- A series of commands oriented towards Group Policy administration, such as `GPRESULT`, which identifies the result of GPO application; `gpupdate`, which updates GPOs on a system; and the `DCGPOFIX` tool, which resets GPOs to their default setting at installation.

Since the ADDS service is so critical to the proper operation of a Windows Server 2008 network, several activities are performed more frequently than with other services.

TIP *The Microsoft TechNet Script Center includes a series of Windows Scripting Host (WSH) and PowerShell sample scripts that help you perform user and group administration tasks. These scripts can be found at www.microsoft.com/technet/scriptcenter/default.mspx. Because of this, script references will not be repeated in each user- or group-related activity, unless there is one specific script that addresses the task.*

DC-01: User Management

Activity Frequency:	Daily

User management is set to a daily frequency because in larger networks, user account creation or modification is required on a regular basis. This activity is mostly initiated by request forms that come from your user base. As such, it is often performed on an ad hoc basis during the day because many administrators perform it when the request comes in. But if you want to structure your day so that you perform activities in an organized manner, you should collect all user account creation/modification requests and perform this activity only during a set period each day.

NOTE *This activity does occur in the resource pool, but not nearly at the same frequency as it does in virtual service offerings.*

To create a new user object:

1. Launch the Server Manager (Quick Launch area | Server Manager). The console automatically connects to your default domain. If you need to work with a different forest or domain controller, use Active Directory Users and Computers (Start menu | Administrative Tools | Active Directory Users and Computers) and right-click the top level of the tree node to select another forest or domain.
2. Navigate to the appropriate organizational unit (OU). This should be somewhere in the People OU structure.
3. Either right-click in the details pane to select the New | User command in the context menu or use the New User icon in the console toolbar. This activates the New Object - User Wizard.
4. This wizard displays two dialog boxes. The first deals with the account names. Here you set the user's full name, the user's display name, their logon name or their User Principal Name (UPN), and their down-level (or pre-Windows 2000) logon name. Click Next.
5. The second screen deals with the password and account restrictions. Type the password for this user, and make sure the User Must Change Password At Next Logon check box is selected. If the user is not ready to take immediate possession of the account, then you should select the Account Is Disabled option as well. Click Finish when done.

CAUTION *Be careful when you set a password to never expire. If it is for a non-user account, such as a service account—accounts that are designed to operate services—or for a generic-purpose account, you should also make sure you select the User Cannot Change Password option. This way, no one can use the account to change its password.*

You can also use much the same procedure to modify existing accounts and perform operations such as disabling accounts, renaming them, and reassigning them.

You can also automate the user creation process. The `CSVDE` command is designed to perform massive user modifications in Active Directory. Use the following command to create multiple users at once:

```
csvde -i -f filename.csv -v -k >outputfilename.txt
```

where `-i` turns on the import mode, `-f` indicates the source file for the import (*filename.csv*)—this source file must be in comma-separated value (CSV) format, `-v` puts the command in verbose mode, and `-k` tells it to ignore errors and continue to the end. You can review the *outputfilename.txt* file for the results of the operation.

NOTE *CSV files can easily be created in Microsoft Excel. They usually contain a first line indicating which values are to come. For example:* CN,Firstname,Surname,Description *should support values such as:* jdoe,Jane,Doe,Manager *or* japscott,John,Apscott,Technician *and so on. Once created, use Excel to save the file as a CSV (Comma Delimited) file.*

If you need to migrate information from one domain to another, use the `CSVDE` command to first export the information and then import the information from one domain to the other. Type `CSVDE -?` for more information.

NOTE *You can also create two other types of user objects. InetOrgPerson is a user object that has exactly the same properties as the User object. It is used to maintain compatibility with other, non-Microsoft directory services. Contact is a user object that cannot be a security principal. It is created only to include its information in the directory.*

DC-02: User Password Reset

Activity Frequency:	Daily

The most common activity administrators must perform on user accounts is the password reset. This is the reason why this is set as a daily task. Depending on the size of your network, you may not have to reset passwords daily, but chances are good you have to do it more than once a week.

CAUTION *In order to avoid replication latency, especially when you reset a password for a regional user, you should always connect to the user's closest domain controller to reset the password. This way, users don't have to wait for the change to be replicated from central DCs to regional DCs to be able to use the new password.*

To reset a user's password:

1. Begin by launching the Active Directory Users and Computers portion of Server Manager.
2. Once connected, right-click the domain name and select Find.
3. Type the user's name in the Find dialog box, and click Find Now.
4. Once you locate the proper user, right-click their name and select Reset Password.
5. In the Reset Password dialog box, type the new password, confirm it, and select User Must Change Password At Next Logon.
6. Click OK when done.
7. Notify the user of the new password.

You can also change passwords through the command line:

```
dsmod user "UserDN" -pwd a5B4c#D2eI -mustchpwd yes
```

where *UserDN* is the user's distinguished name. For example, "CN=Jane Doe, OU=People, DC=Intranet, DC=TandT, DC=Net" refers to user Jane Doe in the People OU in the Intranet. TandT.Net domain. Use quotes to encompass the entire user name.

The directory also stores a lot of information that is not necessarily available to administrators. One example is user account information. A powerful tool, `ACCTINFO.DLL`, can be found in the Account Lockout Tools (search for them at www.microsoft.com/download).

This tool must be registered on the server or workstation using the Active Directory Users and Computers console before you can use it. Run this command from an elevated command prompt:

```
regsvr32 acctinfo.dll
```

Once registered, it adds a new tab to the user object's Property page: the Additional Account Info tab (see Figure 13-11). This tab is quite useful because it provides additional information about the status of the account and also provides a button for resetting regional user passwords directly on their site DC (Set PWD on Site DC), avoiding replication delays.

CAUTION *When you register this DLL, you must stop and restart the console you are using for it to take effect. Also, this DLL seems to work only in the actual Active Directory Users and Computers console, not in Server Manager. Finally, if you created a custom console according to Procedure GS-17, then you must unload and reload the Active Directory Users and Computers snap-in for the DLL to show up.*

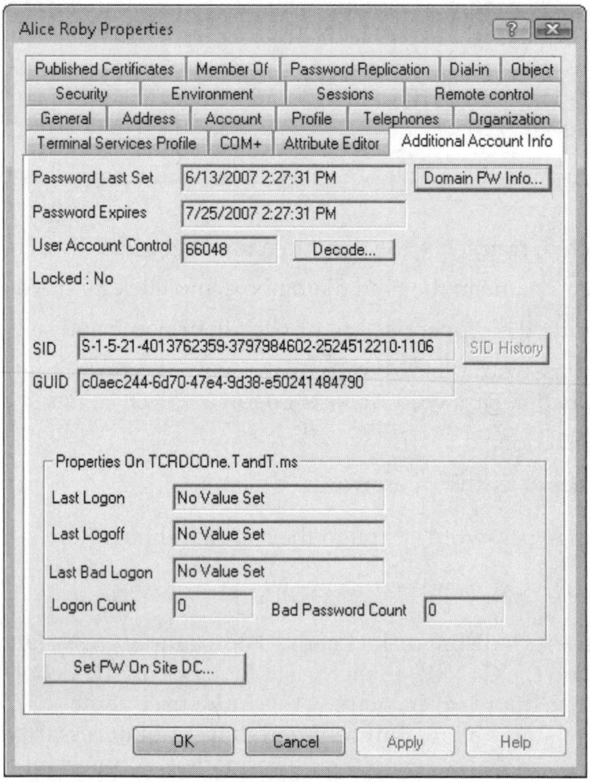

FIGURE 13-11 The Additional Account Info tab on the User Properties page

DC-03: Directory Service Log Event Verification

Activity Frequency:	Daily

The Active Directory Domain Services stores all of its information in a special Event Log, the Directory Services Log. Like all logs, this log is located under the Event Log heading in the Diagnostics | Event Viewer | Applications and Services Logs portion of Server Manager. This log lists events related to directory operation. It covers the Knowledge Consistency Checker (KCC) service, whose job is to verify and update the replication topology of your DCs; it covers directory replication; it covers the status of the ADDS database, NTDS.DIT (located in the `%SYSTEMROOT%\NTDS` folder); and much more.

Use Procedure GS-03 to view the Directory Services Log. You can export the data for reference, or you can make note of any anomalies and proceed to repair them.

Like all other logs, the Directory Services Log includes significant information about repairing problems when they occur. Log this activity in your daily activity log (Procedure GS-06).

DC-04: Account Management

Activity Frequency:	Daily

User account management activities can range from a simple modification of the data contained in the user account to massive account creation. This is why several tools are associated with these activities.

Also, since there are more than 200 attributes associated with the user account, most organizations share the data management burden among different roles. Users, for example, are responsible for updating their own information in the directory. This includes their address, their role in the organization, and other location-specific information. User representatives are often responsible for workgroup-related information in the directory: who does the user work for, in which department, and so on. Administrators are then left with user account creation, password resets, account lockout termination, and other service-related tasks. Users update their own information via the Windows Search tool or through a third-party tool; they search for their name in the directory, then modify the fields that are available to them (see Chapter 7 for information about a free tool for user updates). User representatives usually work with delegation consoles and have access to only those objects they are responsible for in the directory. Administrators use the Active Directory Users and Computers console.

Computers also have manageable accounts in Active Directory. They are contained in a special container in the directory by default: the Computers container. Like the Users container, the Computers container is not an OU. This means you need to either pre-create the accounts in appropriate OUs or move the accounts to these OUs once created.

NOTE *Microsoft offers an add-on that lets you right-click a computer account and select Remote Control. This add-on is called the Remote Control Add-on for Active Directory Users and Computers, and is located at www.microsoft.com/downloads/details.aspx?FamilyID=0A91D2E7-7594-4ABB-8239-7A7ECA6A6CB1&displaylang=en. Also, Special Operations Software offers a free add-on that lets you control Wake-on-LAN for computers through Active Directory Users and Computers at www.specopssoft.com/products/specopsgpupdate.*

Use Procedures DC-01 and DC-02 to either create new accounts or modify existing ones.

NOTE *You can also use the* `CSVDE` *command outlined in Procedure DC-01 to preload the directory with computer names. This is really helpful when you need to install new machines and you want to create all of the computer accounts in a specific OU.*

DC-05: Security Group Management

Activity Frequency:	Daily

Windows Server 2008 supports two types of groups:

- Security groups are considered security objects and can be used to assign access rights and permissions. These groups can also be used as an e-mail address. E-mails sent to the group are received by each individual user that is a member of the group.
- Distribution groups are not security-enabled. They are mostly used in conjunction with e-mail applications, such as Microsoft Exchange, or for software distribution.

NOTE *Groups within fully functional Windows Server forests can be converted from one type to another at any time. Therefore, if you find that a group no longer requires its security features, you can change it to a distribution group and remove its access rights.*

In addition to group type, Windows Server supports several different group scopes. Group scopes are determined by group location. If the group is located on a local computer, its scope will be local. This means that its members and the permissions you assign to it will affect only the computer on which the group is located. If the group is contained within a domain in a forest, it will have either a domain or a forest scope. The domain and forest modes have an impact on group functionality. In a fully functional Windows Server forest, you are able to work with the following group scopes:

- Domain Local Members can include accounts (user and computer), other domain local groups, global groups, and universal groups.
- Global Members can include accounts and other global groups from within the same domain.
- Universal Members can include accounts, global groups, and universal groups from anywhere in the forest, or even across forests, if a trust exists.

Groups, especially security groups, have specific functions. These functions are based on the AGLP rule. This rule is outlined in Chapter 7. According to this rule, users should be placed in global groups, global groups are placed in domain local or local groups, and permissions are assigned to the domain local or local groups. Universal groups are used to bridge domains and forests by placing global groups within them and placing them within domain local or local groups to grant access to resources.

The AGLP rule makes it simple to determine which group type you need to create because it contains logic. Use this logic to determine both group scope and group type when creating groups. This will greatly simplify group management.

Use Procedure DC-01 to create groups. Choose New | Group from the context menu. Follow the wizard's instructions to create the group. If you are sure of what you want to create, use the following command:

```
dsadd group "groupDN" -secgrp yes -scope scope -desc description
```

where *groupDN* is the group's distinguished name and *scope* is either "l", "g," or "u" for each of the available scopes. *Description* is the description you want to add to the group.

To manage the users in a group, first use Procedure DC-02 to locate the group, then double-click the group name. Move to the Members tab, and click Add. Type the names of the objects to add, and click Check Names. If several results are displayed, select the appropriate object(s) and click OK. Click OK to add the object. Click OK to close the Group Properties dialog box.

NOTE *You can also navigate to the container in which the objects you want to add are stored, select them, right-click them, and select Add To Group to add multiple objects at once.*

DC-06: KCC Service Status Management

Activity Frequency:	Weekly

Replication is at the core of Active Directory Domain Services. It occurs within a given site if there is more than one DC in the site, and it occurs between sites if there are DCs located in different sites. By default, intersite replication routes are managed by the KCC service. For this to occur between sites, at least one site link must be created between each site that contains a domain controller. This site link includes costing information. It will also include replication scheduling information; that is, when the DC is allowed to replicate.

NOTE *Fully functional WS08 forests and domains will rely on DFS Replication (DFSR), replicating only changes to objects. Down-level domains and forests rely on the File Replication Service (FRS), which replicates entire objects no matter which changes have occurred within them.*

The KCC uses the site link, site link schedule, and costing information to determine when to replicate, how to replicate (which route to take), and the number of servers to replicate with. Data that is replicated between sites is also compressed. DFSR compresses replication data and replicates only deltas.

CAUTION *Special values, such as password changes or account deactivations, are replicated immediately to the PDC Emulator in the domain, despite site-specific schedules. This ensures that lockouts and password changes are immediately available to the entire domain.*

To verify the frequency of your intersite replication:

1. Begin by launching the Active Directory Sites and Services portion of Server Manager.
2. Navigate to the IP Inter-site Transport (Roles | Active Directory Domain Services | Active Directory Sites and Services | Sites | Inter-site Transports | IP).
3. Right-click the site link you want to verify, and select Properties. The replication frequency is in the General tab under Replicate Every.
4. Click OK when done.

You can also use Procedure DC-03 to check for KCC-related messages in the Directory Services Event Log. To perform a KCC consistency check, use the `REPADMIN` command:

```
repadmin /kcc DCList
```

where *DCList* is the list of the DCs you want to check. You can also use the /ASYNCH switch to avoid starting a replication immediately if you have multiple DCs in your list.

NOTE *The* REPADMIN *command is also useful to display information about different aspects of replication. Use* REPADMIN /? *for more information.*

TIP *The Microsoft TechNet Script Center includes a PowerShell sample script that helps you perform service administration tasks. It can be found at www.microsoft.com/technet/scriptcenter/scripts/msh/default.mspx?mfr=true.*

DC-07: Active Directory Replication Topology Verification

Activity Frequency:	Weekly

This procedure is closely related to Procedure DC-06. For the KCC to work properly, the site topology must be properly defined. It is a good idea to verify the status of your site topology once a week at the same time as you perform the KCC service verification. This relies on the verification of the Directory Services Event Log for replication-oriented errors. Use Procedure DC-03 to do so.

There are several important factors that make intersite replication work. One of the most important is the replication latency of your network. Replication latency is calculated by multiplying the number of replication hops between the farthest ends of your wide area network by the replication frequency you have set. For example, if you have three hops (Site 1 must send it to Site 2, Site 2 to Site 3, and Site 3 to Site 4) and your replication frequency is the default 180 minutes, it will take 3 times 180 minutes, or 540 minutes, to replicate a change that was made in Site 1 to Site 4. Keep this in mind when you design your replication topology.

To verify the replication topology:

1. Begin by launching the Active Directory Sites and Services portion of Server Manager.
2. Navigate to the NTDS Settings (Roles | Active Directory Domain Services | Active Directory Sites and Services | Sites | *sitename* | Servers | *servername* | NTDS Settings) where *sitename* and *servername* are the site and server you want to verify, and click it.
3. Right-click NTDS Settings to select All Tasks | Check Replication Topology.
4. Click OK to close the Check Replication Topology dialog box.
5. Press the F5 key or select the Refresh icon in the toolbar to refresh the connections in the right pane.

You can also use the same procedure to force replication if you need to:

1. Select NTDS Settings, move to the details pane, and select the link you want to verify.
2. Right-click the link to select Replicate Now from the context menu.
3. Click OK to close the Replication Status dialog box.

There are also two command-line tools that can be used to verify replication status. To verify the replication status on a specific DC:

```
repadmin /showreps servername
```

where *servername* is the DNS name of the server you want to check. To validate DNS connections for replication:

```
dcdiag /test:replications
```

This command will list any replication errors between domain controllers. You can pipe the results of both commands to a filename to save the information. Enter any anomalies in your weekly activity log.

DC-08: Global Catalog Status Verification

Activity Frequency:	**Weekly**

The Global Catalog is crucial to the proper operation of Active Directory Domain Services. Without it, no one can find any of the objects stored in the directory. So its proper operation must be verified on a regular basis.

Global Catalogs contain two types of information: objects that have been marked as globally useful and therefore must be available everywhere and at all times, and universal group memberships. It is for this reason that at least one domain controller in each site should be designated as a Global Catalog Server (GCS). In addition, sites without a GC but with a DC should have Universal Group Membership Caching enabled. This should greatly reduce the amount of replication required between these sites.

NOTE *As outlined in Procedure DC-05, universal groups should only contain other groups, principally global groups. This way, they do not need to replicate information when global group membership is modified, because as far as the universal group is concerned, there has been no change.*

To verify that Global Catalog information is available in remote sites:

```
dsquery * -gc -s servername
```

where *servername* is the name of the remote server you want to verify. The `-GC` switch also makes sure it is a Global Catalog Server that answers the request. This command should return a list of 100 results (the default volume of the output from the `DSQUERY` command). If this query does not work, use Procedure DC-07 to force replication.

You can also automate this process by placing it in a command file along with Procedure GS-21.

To make a DC a GCS:

1. Begin by launching the Active Directory Sites and Services portion of Server Manager.
2. Navigate to the NTDS Settings (Roles | Active Directory Domain Services | Active Directory Sites and Services | Sites | *sitename* | Servers | *servername* | NTDS Settings) where *sitename* and *servername* are the site and server you want to modify, and click it.

3. Right-click NTDS Settings, and select Properties from the context menu.
4. Select the Global Catalog option on the General tab. Click OK to close the Properties dialog box.

To set Universal Group Membership Caching:

1. Begin by launching the Active Directory Sites and Services portion of Server Manager.
2. Navigate to the site you want to modify (Roles | Active Directory Domain Services | Active Directory Sites and Services | Sites | *sitename*) where *sitename* is the site you want to modify, and click it.
3. Move to the right pane, and right-click NTDS Site Settings to select Properties from the context menu.
4. Select Enable Universal Group Membership Caching, and click OK to close the dialog box.

DC-09: Universal Administration Group Management

Activity Frequency: Weekly

Windows Server 2008 includes two universal administration groups: Enterprise Administrators and Schema Administrators. These groups are granted the highest rights in an ADDS forest. By default, you should make sure the Schema Administrators group is empty. It should contain a user only when an actual schema modification is required (see Procedure DC-22). The Enterprise Administrators group should also be tightly controlled. This is why this operation is a weekly activity.

Windows Server includes a Group Policy setting that will automatically restrict the number of users in these groups. This policy is located at: Computer Configuration | Policies | Windows Settings | Security Settings | Restricted Groups.

You should add both universal administration groups to this policy. As mentioned, the Schema Administrators group should be set to be empty by default. The Enterprise Administrators group should only contain authorized administrative accounts. Use Procedure DC-16 to modify this policy.

CAUTION *To make sure this policy is applied to all, make this setting in the default domain policy of the root domain of each of the forests you manage.*

Even though you set this policy, it is possible for someone with enough administrative rights and the proper skills to circumvent it for brief time periods (GPOs are refreshed every five minutes on DCs). This is why you should regularly check the membership of these groups to make sure no one has modified them and added themselves to the groups. You can also use the ADDS change auditing procedure outlined in Chapter 10 to trap all ADDS modifications.

CAUTION *It is a good idea to create the same type of restricted group policy for the Domain Administrators group in each of the domains in your forest because this group also has elevated rights.*

DC-10: Account Policy Verification

Activity Frequency:	Weekly

The account policy is the policy that determines how accounts are managed within a given domain. This policy is usually stored within the default domain policy in order to ensure that it affects all objects in the domain. The account policy is located under Computer Configuration | Policies | Windows Settings | Security Settings. Recommended settings for this policy are listed in Table 13-7. Adapt them to your own requirements.

You need to verify this policy regularly, mostly to make sure that no one has inadvertently modified it. Use Procedure DC-16 to verify that your account policy has not been modified.

NOTE *You can combine this policy with additional fine-grained password policies. See Chapter 10 for more information.*

NOTE *All of the recommended settings for the Kerberos policy are set at the Windows Server default settings, but setting them explicitly assists your Group Policy operators in knowing what the default setting actually is.*

DC-11: ADCS Service Verification

Activity Frequency:	Weekly

Active Directory Certificate Services (ADCS) are used in a variety of instances within a Windows Server network. They support the Encrypting File System; wireless authentication; smart card authentication; virtual private network connections; and, when used with software restriction policies, they can certify your scripts and software packages, protecting you from scripted viruses. Managing the ADCS service in Windows Server can be done either through the Certificate Authority snap-in or through the `CERTUTIL` command.

Use the following command to view the status of a certificate server:

```
certutil cainfo -config camachinename\caname
```

where *camachinename* and *caname* are the computer name and certificate authority name for the targeted machine.

The `CERTUTIL` command is powerful and supports almost every operation related to certificate management in Windows Server 2008. For more information on this command, type `CERTUTIL /?` at the command prompt.

You can also use Administrative Tools | PKI View to verify the status of your ADCS servers in the network. Finally, you can also use the Certificate Manager to view the certificates associated with computer or user accounts. To do so, use Start menu | Search | CertMgr.msc.

DC-12: Active Directory Service/Admin Account Verification

Activity Frequency:	Monthly

Procedure GS-05 outlines how to create both service and administrative accounts. It also outlines how to modify their passwords on a regular basis. Both administrative and service accounts are privileged account types because they have both access rights and rights assignments that other account types do not. This is why you should take the time to verify

Setting	Recommendation	Comments
Account Policy | Password Policy		
Enforce password history	24 passwords	At the rate of one password change per month, this setting remembers two years' worth of passwords.
Maximum password age	42 days	This is approximately a month and a half.
Minimum password age	2 days	This stops users from changing their passwords too often.
Minimum password length	8 characters	This is the threshold where password crackers start taking longer to break passwords.
Password must meet complexity requirements	Enabled	This ensures that passwords must contain both alphabetic and numeric characters, both upper- and lowercase letters, as well as special symbols.
Store passwords using reversible encryption	Disabled	Enabling this setting is the same as storing plain-text passwords. It should never be enabled.
Account Policy | Account Lockout Policy		
Account lockout duration	60 minutes	This setting determines how long an account is locked after several invalid logon attempts.
Account lockout threshold	3 invalid logon attempts	After three invalid logon tries, the account is locked out.
Reset account lockout counter after	60 minutes	This must be equal to or greater than the account lockout duration.
Account Policies | Kerberos Policy		
Enforce user logon restrictions	Enabled (default)	This ensures that users have the right to access either local or network resources before granting them a Kerberos ticket.
Maximum lifetime for service ticket	600 minutes (default)	This states the duration of the session ticket that is used to initiate a connection with a server. It must be renewed when it expires.
Maximum lifetime for user ticket	10 hours (default)	This must be greater than or equal to the previous setting. It must be renewed when it expires.
Maximum lifetime for user ticket renewal	7 days (default)	This details the duration of a user's ticket-granting ticket. The user must log on again once this ticket expires.
Maximum tolerance for computer clock synchronization	5 minutes (default)	Kerberos uses timestamps to grant tickets. All computers within a domain are synchronized through the domain controllers.

TABLE 13-7 Recommended Account Policy Settings

the status of these accounts on a monthly basis. Doing so will help you ensure that there are no abuses or errors in either the use of these accounts or the way they are configured.

Use Procedure DC-16 to verify the status of rights assignments set for service accounts. Use Procedure DC-09 to make sure the group membership of all privileged accounts is tightly controlled. Enter the information in your activity log.

DC-13: Lost and Found Object Management

Activity Frequency:	Monthly

Once in a while, especially in large forests, someone will delete a container at the same time someone else is creating an object in the same container. This can be on entirely different DCs, but when replication occurs to synchronize data on the DCs, the newly created object no longer has a home. When this happens, ADDS automatically stores these objects within the LostAndFound container. This special container manages lost and found objects within the domain. Another special container, the LostAndFoundConfig container, manages lost and found objects for the forest. The latter is in the forest root domain only.

Therefore, once a month, you should verify the LostAndFound and the LostAndFoundConfig containers for objects to determine if these objects should be moved to new containers or simply deleted from the directory.

To verify the LostAndFound containers:

1. Begin by launching the Active Directory Users and Computers portion of the Server Manager.
2. Make sure the Advanced view is activated (View | Advanced Features), and click the LostAndFound container.
3. Identify any objects located within this folder. Decide if they need to be moved to other containers or if you should delete the objects.

This occurs less often in WS08 forests because of the new Lock Object feature assigned to all new objects, but you should still verify this container on a regular basis.

CAUTION *Be careful when deleting objects. Make sure you review the object's properties before doing so. Sometimes, it is best to move the object and deactivate it while you communicate with your peers to see if it is a necessary object. Remember that once deleted, SIDs are gone forever.*

DC-14: Rights Delegation Management

Activity Frequency:	Ad hoc

Active Directory management in complex environments relies on the concept of delegation. In Active Directory, it is easy to delegate management activities. Delegations can be performed at several levels: sites, organizational units, or even entire domains.

NOTE *Delegation is mostly done with organizational units. Sites and domains should rarely be delegated.*

Delegation is performed through the Delegation of Control Wizard. In addition to the delegation of control, you often have to create custom consoles to give delegated administrators access to the objects you have delegated to them. If the console is based on a particular snap-in, you will also have to make sure it is installed on the user's computer before they can use the custom console.

NOTE *You can also perform some degree of delegation through the use of Windows Server's built-in groups. Windows Server includes special groups for Account, Backup, Network Configuration, Group Policy, DNS, Print, and Server administration as well as Performance Monitoring, Certificate Publishing, and more. These groups should be used in conjunction with the ADDS Delegation of Control Wizard to delegate operations in ADDS.*

To delegate rights in Active Directory:

1. Begin by launching the Active Directory Users and Computers portion of Server Manager.
2. Locate the object you want to delegate, and right-click it to select Delegate Control from the context menu. This launches the Delegation of Control Wizard. Click Next.
3. Click the Add button to select the groups you want to delegate to. Type the name of the group, and click Check Names. Select the proper group from the results, and click OK. Click Next.
4. Select the tasks you want to delegate, and click Next. Alternatively, you can create a custom task to delegate. This will change the behavior of the wizard, and it will ask you which specific task you want to delegate on which object type.
5. Click Finish to close the wizard and complete the delegation.

To create a custom console, you need to start the console program in authoring mode in the same way as described in Procedure GS-17. Supplement it with the instructions found in Chapter 7. Test the console to ensure it operates as designed. Open it in operation mode (as opposed to authoring mode) by double-clicking its icon.

You can distribute the console by sending administrators the console file, but if the console is based on a snap-in they do not have installed, you will need to install the snap-in first. This can be done through Group Policy using software distribution. If you choose to use Group Policy for snap-in installation, you can include the console as well in the same Windows Installer executable (see Procedure DC-15). You can also use Terminal Services RemoteApps to publish the console. This method is actually much easier, since the console only needs to be maintained on central servers (see Procedure TS-06).

TIP *If you want to install only a portion of the Windows Server administrative tools on a computer instead of all of them, see Knowledge Base article number 314978 at http://support.microsoft.com/kb/314978.*

DC-15: Software Installation Management

Activity Frequency:	Ad hoc

Group Policy can be used for a wide variety of management activities, one of which is the remote delivery of software to either users or machines. It is preferable to target machines when delivering software because users can move from system to system and thus receive an installation several times.

Software can be assigned or published through GPOs. Assigned software is automatically installed on targeted machines. Published software will appear in the Add/Remove Programs item of Control Panel. Users can then choose to install it or not. Published software should only include products that are deemed optional in your network. All other software should be assigned.

In addition, all software must be packaged in Windows Installer format. This can be done with a variety of tools, the best of which are Altiris Wise Package Studio (www.wise.com) or Macrovision Installshield AdminStudio (www.installshield.com). This is one area where you don't want to try to work with free tools.

To assign a software package:

1. Begin by placing the Windows Installer setup file (`.MSI` extension) in a shared folder.
2. Launch the Group Policy Management Console.
3. Navigate to the Group Policy Objects container (Group Policy Management | Forest: *forestname* | Domains | *domainname* | Group Policy Objects).
4. Locate the GPO to edit, or create a new GPO to edit (right-click in the right pane, select New, name it, and click OK). Since software is assigned to computers, right-click the GPO and select User Settings Disabled from the GPO Status menu item.
5. Right-click the GPO to edit, and select Edit. This launches the GPO Editor.
6. Navigate to Software Installation (Computer Configuration | Policies | Software Settings), and right-click in the right pane to select New | Package from the context menu.
7. Navigate to the shared folder containing your package, and select it. Click Open.
8. Select Assigned and click OK from the Deployment dialog box.

You can right-click the newly created package to view its properties and modify additional settings. For example, you may want to add a transformation file to the package (`.MST` extension) to customize its behavior. You can also make sure it uninstalls automatically when it is no longer valid.

NOTE *You can also filter software installations with security groups. This lets you assign software installations through a single GPO while targeting different systems.*

To target a specific group with a software installation:

1. Locate the package you want to target (GPO Editor | Computer Configuration | Policies | Software Settings | Software Installations).
2. Right-click the package and select Properties.
3. Move to the Security tab.
4. Remove the Authenticated Users group and add the appropriate group (this can be a global group containing only computer accounts) with Read rights.
5. Click OK to close the Properties dialog box.

Your installation will only be installed on the targeted group because other systems will not be able to read it in the directory.

NOTE *Software installations are quickly becoming a thing of the past because they are being replaced with application virtualization. For more information on the benefits of application virtualization, see "Virtualize Your Business Desktop Environment" at www.altiris.com/upload/wp_virtualizeyourbusinessdesktopdeployment_072606.pdf. Also, see* The Definitive Guide to Vista Migration, *a free e-book from www.realtime-nexus.com/dgvm.htm.*

DC-16: GPO Management

Activity Frequency:	Ad hoc

Group Policy is one of the most powerful tools in Windows Server 2008. There are more than 2,400 GPO settings that can be applied in a Windows Server forest. These settings control everything from the appearance of a desktop to Terminal Services settings for all users. This is why you will be working with GPOs on a regular basis.

CAUTION *Be careful how many GPOs you create. Avoid using single-purpose GPOs, and use GPO filters to refine their application.*

1. Begin by launching the Group Policy Management Console (GPMC) through Start menu | Administrative Tools | Group Policy Management.
2. Navigate to the Group Policy Objects container (Computer Management | Group Policy Management | Forest: *forestname* | Domains | *domainname* | *Group Policy Objects*).
3. Locate the GPO to edit, and right-click it to select Edit from the context menu.
4. Perform the appropriate modification in the GPO Editor.
5. Add a comment to this GPO by right-clicking on the GPO name in the Editor and choosing Properties. Add comments to the Comment tab. Comments are viewed in the Details tab of the GPMC.

GPOs can be rapidly linked to any given container with the GPMC. To do so, drag-and-drop the GPO to the appropriate container.

GPOs can also be filtered. Two types of filters are available: security and Windows Management Instrumentation (WMI) filters. Security filters are simply access rights granted or denied to specific groups. WMI filters target specific results from a WMI query. For example, if all your portables are from Toshiba, you can use a WMI filter to target all Toshiba machines in your domain.

To apply filters to GPOs:

1. Begin by launching the Group Policy Management Console.
2. Navigate to the Group Policy Objects container (Computer Management | Group Policy Management | Forest: *forestname* | Domains | *domainname* | Group Policy Objects).

3. Click the GPO to filter. In the right pane, add or remove security groups to filter the GPO with security.
4. To filter the GPO with a WMI query, click the drop-down list and select the appropriate filter. Answer Yes when queried by the WMI filter dialog box. WMI filters must be created before you can apply them.

WMI filters are created by right-clicking WMI Filters and selecting New from the context menu. WMI filters are comparable to SQL queries, though they use a different language: Windows Query Language (WQL). An example of a filter for locating Toshiba laptops is:

```
Root\CimV2; Select * from Win32_ComputerSystem where manufacturer =
"Toshiba" and Model = "Satellite Pro 4200" OR Model = "Satellite Pro 4100"
```

WMI filters can be created in plain-text files and imported directly into the GPMC.

Finally, three GPO commands are really useful when working with Group Policy.

To update Group Policy on an object:

```
gpupdate
```

By default, this will update both the user and computer policies on the target system, but only changed settings. Use the `/FORCE` switch to reapply all policy settings. Use `/?` for more information.

To identify the resulting set of policies on an object:

```
gpresult /S computername /USER targetusername /Z
```

where *computername* is the name of the computer to verify results on and *targetusername* is the name of the user whose policies you want to verify. The `/Z` switch enables super verbose mode, giving you highly detailed information. You might want to pipe this command into a filename to capture all the results.

To reset either the Default Domain or the Default Domain Controller GPO to its original setting:

```
dcgpofix /ignoreschema
```

By default, this command refreshes both default policies. The `/IGNORESCHEMA` switch is most certainly required if you have added any schema modifications or any schema-modifying software to your network. If the schema is no longer in its default state and the switch is not used, the command will not work.

DC-17: Computer Object Management

Activity Frequency:	Ad hoc

All computer objects in Windows Server 2008 must have an account within the directory. This is because this account enables the directory to interact with each machine in the network. This is why machines must join an ADDS domain. This join helps put in place all of the elements that support system management within ADDS.

There are two ways to create computer objects. First, they can be created during system staging when the computer's network parameters are defined, but using this method means granting the Add Workstation To Domain right to technicians. The second method allows you to pre-create the computer accounts within the domain. The advantage of this method is that you can target the proper organizational unit for the computer account, making sure it benefits immediately from the GPO settings it requires.

To pre-create a new computer object:

1. Launch the Server Manager.
2. Navigate to the appropriate OU under the PCs OU structure.

CAUTION *The default Computers container in ADDS is not an organizational unit and therefore cannot support either delegation or the assignation of Group Policy Objects. GPOs must be assigned at the domain level to affect this container. If you want to assign GPOs to computer objects but not at the domain level, you must create a PCs OU structure.*

3. Either right-click in the right window pane to select the New | Computer command in the context menu or use the New Computer icon in the console toolbar. This activates the New Object - Computer Wizard.
4. This wizard displays two dialog boxes. The first deals with the account names. Here you set the computer's name. You also have the opportunity to identify which user group can add this computer to a domain. To do so, click Change, type the group name, click Check Names, select the right group, and click OK. Click Next.

TIP *You can create a Technicians group that can be assigned to this role. This way, you do not need to assign them any more rights than required.*

5. The second screen deals with the status of the computer in the directory. If the computer is a managed computer, then you need to click This Is A Managed Computer and type its globally unique identifier (GUID). Click Next.

NOTE *Every computer has a GUID. It can be found either in the computer's BIOS or on the computer's label along with its serial number. If you buy computers in bulk (as you should to avoid diversity as much as possible), you should get the manufacturer to provide you with a spreadsheet listing the GUIDs for each computer in the lot. You can then rely on this spreadsheet to pre-create your accounts.*

6. Click Finish to create the account.

NOTE *You should take the time to review and fill in the account's properties. It should at least be member of the appropriate groups to receive the proper software installations (see Procedure DC-15).*

You can also automate the computer account creation process. The `CSVDE` command is designed to perform massive account modifications in ADDS. Use the following command to create multiple computer accounts at once:

```
csvde -i -f filename.csv -v -k >outputfilename.txt
```

where `-i` turns on the import mode, `-f` indicates the source file for the import (*filename.csv*)—this source file must be in CSV format, `-v` puts the command in verbose mode, and `-k` tells it to ignore errors and continue to the end. You can review the *outputfilename.txt* file for the results of the operation.

TIP *If you receive spreadsheets containing machine GUIDs from your computer reseller, you can use these spreadsheets as the basis of your account creation comma-separated source file.*

DC-18: Distribution Group Management

Activity Frequency:	Ad hoc

As mentioned in Procedure DC-05, distribution groups are designed to help regroup objects that don't need or don't support access rights. An excellent example of a distribution group is a mailing list of external contacts. Users can address the group name and automatically send an e-mail to each member of the group.

CAUTION *Do not use distribution groups to duplicate security groups. Security groups have the same features as distributions groups and can also be used to target e-mail. For this reason, these groups are used much less than security groups. Since there is no need to duplicate security groups for distribution purposes, you should have much fewer distribution groups than security groups.*

Use Procedure DC-05 to create your distribution groups.

DC-19: ADDS Forest Management

Activity Frequency:	Ad hoc

Forest administrators need to manage global activities within the forest. First and foremost, the forest administrator must authorize the creation of new forests, especially permanent forests. You should aim to limit the number of permanent forests in your network. This will help you control the total cost of ownership (TCO) of your network.

CAUTION *Remember that each single instance of Active Directory Domain Services is a forest.*

Forests are created for the following reasons:

- **Different database schemas** Only one database structure can be stored within a single forest. If the schema must be different, it should be contained in a different forest. But with Active Directory Lightweight Directory Services (ADLDS), there is little need to host multiple forests for schema reasons.
- **Testing or development** If special testing is required—for example, for tools that will modify the schema of your production forest—you may need to create a testing forest. The same applies to development projects.
- **Perimeter forests** If your organization hosts an extranet or an Internet site, you may require a different forest to segregate and protect internal objects from the perimeter. Remember that you can also rely on ADLDS for this function.

CAUTION *It is a very good idea to segregate internal forests from external perimeters. This way, you do not compromise internal security if your perimeter is attacked.*

You should also limit the number of domains contained within your forest. Both domains and forests should be justified before being created. The reasons for creating a domain include:

- **Different authentication rules** Domains form the boundary for the rules used to authenticate users and computers, since they are the container into which these objects are created.
- **Different security policies for user accounts** Security policies applying to user accounts are stored within the domain. These may need to be different from one domain to another. For example, developers usually require more elevated privileges than normal users. It is a good idea to let developers work in separate domains to avoid security compromises in your production domain. You can, however, use fine-grained password policies to achieve the same goal, but in reality, you should have a separate domain because your production domain should never include generic accounts—accounts that are not assigned to a specific user—because they are difficult to track.
- **Different publication services for shared resources** All of the resources that can be shared within a domain are published through Active Directory. By default, these resources—shared printers and folders—are published only to members of the domain. You may justify a different domain to protect critical resources.

Forest administrators must authorize child domain creation before they can be staged. Use the following commands to pre-authorize a child domain in the directory:

```
ntdsutil
domain management
precreate domainDN firstdcname
quit
quit
```

where *domainDN* is the distinguished name for the child domain (for example, for the test.tandt.net domain, dc=test,dc=tandt,dc=net) and *firstdcname* is the fully qualified DNS name for the server that will be hosting the creation of the child domain. You must also delegate domain creation rights to the administrator performing the DC promotion. Use Procedure DC-14 to do so.

DC-20: ADDS Information Management

Activity Frequency:	Ad hoc

Contrary to a local computer's security account manager (SAM), Active Directory thrives on information. For example, when you publish a shared folder in the directory (see Procedure FS-03), you should take the time to identify the folder's owner in the directory. This way, if you have problems with the folder, you know who to contact. The same goes for adding user information or identifying group managers. The more information you put in the directory, the easier it will be to manage. You can use Procedures DC-01 and DC-05 to add both additional user information and group managers, but you can also use massive information management methods to add missing information.

For example, Procedure DC-01 outlines how to use the CSVDE command to add several users at once. This tool can also be used to add additional information when you create groups and other object types.

CAUTION *If you choose to add additional information, such as group managers and shared folder owners, you will have to make sure you do not delete accounts when users leave or change position. If you do so, you will have to modify ownership in each object, whereas if you simply rename existing accounts and reassign them, they will remain in all directory locations.*

DC-21: Schema Management

Activity Frequency: **Ad hoc**

The Active Directory Domain Services schema defines the structure of a forest database. By default, the Windows Server 2008 schema contains over 200 different object types and over 1,000 attributes. The ADDS schema is extensible; it allows you to add new structures to the database so that you may add content of your choice. Several tools can be used to extend the schema, but before you do so, you should ask yourself if it is really necessary.

The ADDS database is a distributed database. This means that it is spread out throughout your organization, often having domain controllers in each regional office, as well as in the central ones. Each time you change the ADDS schema, it will be replicated to all locations. Another factor that should dampen your desire to change the schema is that changes cannot be undone. Though you can deactivate new object classes or attributes added to the schema, you cannot delete them. You can, however, rename and reuse them.

With previous versions of Windows, this was a significant dilemma, but it is not so with Windows Server 2008 because it supports Active Directory Lightweight Directory Services. ADLDS is like a mini-ADDS that can run several instances on a single machine (Windows Vista or Windows Server). This means that instead of planning to modify your network operating system (NOS) ADDS, you should always consider the possibility of replacing this modification with an ADLDS instance. This will maintain your NOS ADDS in the most pristine version possible.

There will, however, be some instances when schema modification is a must. This mostly relates to NOS-related tools, such as add-ons, like Microsoft Exchange Server. Exchange, for example, more than doubles the number of objects and attributes in the NOS schema. In this case, use Procedures DC-22 and DC-23 to do modify the schema.

If you do decide to modify the schema, it should be done according to a schema modification policy. This policy includes:

- A detailed list of the members of the Enterprise Administrators universal group.
- A security and management strategy for the Schema Administrators universal group (see Procedure DC-22).
- The creation of the Schema Change Policy Holder (SCPH) role. This role is responsible for the approval or denial of all schema changes.

each of these roles, but if you have more than one domain, every domain will have one instance of each of these services. These include:

- **Relative ID (RID) Master** The master service that is responsible for the assignation of relative IDs to other domain controllers within the domain. Whenever a new object—user, computer, server, or group—is created within a domain, the domain controller that is performing the creation will assign a unique ID number. This ID number consists of a domain identification number followed by a relative identification number that is assigned at object creation. When a domain controller runs out of its pool of relative IDs, it requests an additional pool from the RID Master. The relative ID role is also the placeholder for the domain. If you need to move objects between domains in the same forest, you need to initiate the move from the RID Master.
- **Primary Domain Controller (PDC) Emulator** The master service that provides backward compatibility for Windows NT. If there are Windows NT domain controllers or Windows NT network clients within the domain, this server acts as the primary domain controller for the domain. It manages all replication to backup domain controllers (in NT, of course). If the forest operates in native mode, the PDC Emulator focuses on its two other roles: time synchronization on all DCs and computers and preferential account modification replication to other DCs. All domain controllers in the domain will set their clock according to the PDC Emulator. In addition, any account modification that is critical, such as password modification or account deactivation, will be immediately replicated to the PDC Emulator from the originating server. If a logon attempt fails on a given DC, it checks with the PDC Emulator before rejecting the attempt, because it may not have received recent password changes.
- **Infrastructure Master** The master service that manages two critical tasks. The update of references from objects in its domain to objects in other domains. This is how the forest knows to which domain an object belongs. The Infrastructure Master has a close relationship with the Global Catalog (GC). If it finds that some of its objects are out of date compared to the GC, it will request an update from the GC and send the updated information to other DCs within the domain. For this reason, the Global Catalog service should not be on a DC acting as the Infrastructure Master. The Infrastructure Master also manages the update and modification of group members within the domain. If a group includes objects from another domain and these objects are renamed or moved, the Infrastructure Master will maintain the consistency of the group and replicate it to all other domain controllers. This ensures that users maintain access rights, even though you perform maintenance operations on their accounts.

The domain-centric master roles should be separated, if possible. This depends, of course, on the size of each domain. Whatever its size, each domain should have at least two domain controllers for redundancy, load balancing, and availability.

Operations Master roles can be managed both graphically and through the command line. The three domain-centric master roles can be identified through the Active Directory Users and Computers console by right-clicking the domain name and selecting Properties.

In the domain Properties dialog box, use the appropriate tab to identify the DC holding each role. The forest-wide master roles are more independent. Use the Active Directory Domains and Trusts console to find the Domain Naming Master. Once again, right-click the domain name and select Operations Master. To find the Schema Master, use the Active Directory schema console created in Procedure DC-23.

The easiest way to find Operations Master roles is through the command line:

```
dsquery server -hasfsmo fsmoname
```

This command works for each of the five roles. The *fsmoname* for each role is as follows: `NAME` for the Domain Naming Master, `INFR` for the Infrastructure Master, `PDC` for the PDC Emulator, `RID` for the RID Master and `SCHEMA` for the Schema Master.

CAUTION *Read-only domain controllers cannot hold any FSMO role.*

DC-26: Operations Master Role Transfer

Activity Frequency:	Ad hoc

As you know, there can only be a single instance of each Operations Master role within each scope, forest, or domain. While in most cases, the forest or domain will operate for short periods of time when one or the other master is down, it is preferable to transfer the role from one DC to another if you know that one of the Operations Master DCs will be down for significant periods of time. This can happen when maintenance is scheduled on the server.

CAUTION *Transferring Operations Master roles can be dangerous to your production network if not performed properly. For example, transferring the Schema Master role improperly can damage the entire forest schema, forcing you to recover Active Directory from backups. Be sure you perform these operations carefully.*

To transfer any of the roles through the graphical interface, you basically need to use the FSMO's identification procedure, as outlined in Procedure DC-25. Here's how:

1. Launch or go to the appropriate console for the FSMO you want to transfer.
2. Right-click the domain name, select Connect To A Domain Controller, type the name of the DC you want to transfer the role to, and click OK.
3. View the FSMO Properties dialog box, and click Change.

Once again, it is easier to do so through the command line:

```
ntdsutil
roles
connection
connect to server servername
quit
transfer FSMOname
quit
quit
```

where *servername* is the DNS name for the DC you want to transfer the role to and *FSMOname* is the role you want to transfer. Type `HELP` at the `FSMO MAINTENANCE` prompt to identify FSMO names for this command, or see Procedure DC-25.

DC-27: Operations Master Disaster Recovery

Activity Frequency: **Ad hoc**

Procedure DC-26 only works when the FSMO you want to transfer is still operating. In the case of a total systems failure of an FSMO, you need to seize the FSMO role; that is, you need to tell the directory that the role must be transferred, even if it cannot contact the originating FSMO.

CAUTION *Do not seize any role if it can be transferred instead. The seizure operation does not remove the role from the originating server. The operation of two FSMOs with the same role in the same domain or forest can severely damage the directory.*

Role seizure is performed through the `NTDSUTIL` command:

```
ntdsutil
roles
connection
connect to server servername
quit
seize FSMOname
quit
quit
```

where *servername* is the DNS name for the DC you want to seize the role to and *FSMOname* is the role you want to seize. Type `help` at the `FSMO MAINTENANCE` prompt to identify FSMO names for this command, or see Procedure DC-25.

CAUTION *If you seize any role, make sure the role is completely removed from the originating server before bringing it back online in the forest or domain. If not, there can be serious damage to your ADDS.*

DC-28: Domain Controller Promotion

Activity Frequency: **Ad hoc**

Domain controllers in Windows Server 2008 are very different from older versions of Windows. In Windows Server, you can easily switch a server from DC to member server and back if you want to. All is done through the DCPromo command. This command can be accessed through a variety of methods: command line, Server Manager Add Roles command, Run command, and so on. The easiest is through Server Manager. This is launched automatically at system startup or through Start menu | Administrative Tools.

The promotion of a domain controller can be done in a number of different situations. It can be for the creation of a new forest. In this instance, you tell DCPromo that you want to install the first DC in a forest. It can be for a new tree in an existing forest. It can be for a child domain. It can also be for another DC in an existing domain or even for a read-only domain controller (RODC).

CAUTION *To use DCPromo, you either need to have Enterprise or Domain Administrator rights or have the appropriate delegated rights. Delegated rights must be provided in conjunction with Procedure DC-19 if your intent is to create a new child domain or tree in an existing forest.*

Promoting a DC is a two-step process. First, you must install the ADDS role. Then you must run the DCPromo command. See Chapter 6 for more information.

CAUTION *If you are creating a child domain in an existing forest, you must perform Procedure DN-04 before running DCPromo.*

When creating regional domain controllers, it is useful to preload the directory data during the DC promotion. This greatly reduces replication requirements, since only the differences between the actual directory and the backup from which the preload is performed are replicated.

NOTE *Before you can promote a DC using preloaded information, you must use Procedure BR-01 to create a backup from a DC in the target domain.*

To perform the DC promotion from backup files, or to access the advanced features of DC promotion, use:

```
dcpromo /adv
```

Or click the Advanced Features option in the graphical version of DCPromo.

DC-29: Domain Controller Disaster Recovery

Activity Frequency:	Ad hoc

It is rare to completely lose a DC, but it happens often enough that there is a disaster recovery procedure on DCs. There are two types of DC disaster recovery operations: non-authoritative and authoritative.

The first is the simplest. It implies that the DC that was lost did not have any unreplicated data within its directory store. When this is the case, you can simply rebuild the server, perform Procedure DC-28 to rebuild the DC (with or without backup data), and let ADDS replication do the rest. It will automatically bring the server up to date.

If there was lost data, or if there was a major data loss within the directory, and you must perform an authoritative restore, you must use the `NTDSUTIL` tool to make the restore authoritative. To perform an authoritative restore, you must begin with a normal restore. Then once the data is restored and the domain controller is still offline, you type `NTDSUTIL` to finish the job. The authoritative restore can include all or just a portion of the restored ADDS data.

1. Repair the server, if required, and start it up. During startup, press F8 to view the startup modes.
2. Select the Directory Services Restore Mode, and press ENTER.
3. This will boot into Windows. Log in with the directory restore account. Launch the backup utility and perform the restore. Once the restoration is finished, reboot the server.

4. Press F8 once again to select Directory Services Restore Mode, and press ENTER. Log in with the directory restore account. Launch the command prompt:

```
ntdsutil
authoritative restore
restore database
quit
quit
```

5. Restart the server in normal mode.

The restore database command marks all of the data in the NTDS.DIT database of this DC as authoritative. Once the server is restarted, the replication process will start and the restored information will be replicated to all other domain controllers.

If you want to restore only a portion of the directory, use the following restore command:

```
restore subtree ou=ouname,dc=dcname,dc=dcname
```

where you must supply the distinguished name of the OU you want to restore.

DC-30: Trust Management

Activity Frequency: Ad hoc

Windows Server 2008 forests automatically include transitive trusts between all of their domains. These trusts must operate properly for the forest to operate. These trusts support the operation of the forest through forest-wide replication, which includes the content of the Global Catalog, the schema, and the forest configuration.

If you are within a very large forest and there is a significant amount of interdomain operational activity, you may also consider the creation of shortcut trusts—manual trusts that are created to link two domains in a forest. The shortcut trust speeds operation because communications do not need to go through the forest hierarchy. In fact, Windows Server forests support several different types of trusts (see Table 13-8).

The first two trust types listed in Table 13-8 are created automatically when you use Procedure DC-28 to create a new child domain or tree in a forest. The others are created manually to either improve performance or enable interaction between one authentication zone and another.

CAUTION *Trust operations require high privileges. This means either Domain or Enterprise Administrators (depending on the level of trust required). You will also need privileged credentials in the target domain, especially if you are creating two-way transitive trusts.*

To create a trust:

1. Launch Active Directory Domains and Trusts (Start menu | Administrative Tools).
2. Right-click the domain you want to assign the trust to, and select Properties.
3. Move to the Trust tab in the Properties dialog box, and click New Trust. This will launch the New Trust Wizard. Click Next.
4. Type the name of the domain or forest you wish to establish the trust with. Domain names can be in NetBIOS format, but forest names must be in DNS format. Click Next.

Trust Type	Directions and Nature	Comments
Parent and Child	Two-way transitive	These are the automatic trusts that are established when a child domain is created.
Tree-root	Two-way transitive	These are the automatic trusts that are established when a new tree is created.
Forest	One- or two-way transitive	Extends the transitivity of trusts from one forest to another.
Shortcut	One- or two-way transitive	Creates a shortcut path for authentication between two domains. The domains can use this path for authentication instead of having to traverse the forest hierarchy.
Realm	One- or two-way transitive or non-transitive	Creates an authentication link between a domain and a non-Windows Kerberos realm (such as UNIX).
External	One- or two-way non-transitive	Creates an authentication link between a Windows Server domain and an NT4 domain.

Table 13-8 Windows Server Trust Types

5. Select the type of trust you wish to create (two-way, one-way: incoming or one-way: outgoing).
6. If you have administrative rights in both domains, you can select Both This Domain And The Specified Domain to create both sides of the trust at the same time. Click Next.
7. Type your administrative credentials for the target domain or forest. Click Next.
8. The wizard is ready to create the outgoing trust in the target domain or forest. Click Next. Once finished, it will ask you to configure the new trust. Click Next.
9. Select Yes, confirm the outgoing trust, and then click Next. Confirming trusts is a good idea because it tests the new trust immediately.
10. Select Yes, confirm the incoming trust, and then click Next. Review your changes and click Finish when done.

Caution *If you do not have credentials for both domains, you must run the New Trust Wizard once in each domain. In this case, you must provide the same trust password each time. It is a good idea to use very strong passwords for trust relationships. This means complex passwords that have at least 15 characters.*

Use the same procedure to create all other types of trusts. The wizard will automatically change its behavior based on the values you input in its second page.

To verify trusts:

1. Launch Active Directory Domains and Trusts.
2. Right-click the domain containing the trusts you want to verify, and select Properties.

3. Move to the Trust tab in the Properties dialog box, and select the trust you want to verify (either incoming or outgoing). Click Properties.
4. Click Validate. In the Validate Trust dialog box, determine if you want to validate the trust in both directions (if it is a two-way trust), and click OK.

CAUTION *If you verify two-way trusts in both directions, you need proper credentials in the target domain.*

To verify trusts at the command line:

```
netdom trust trustingdomainname /d:trusteddomainname /verify
```

where the domain names must be in DNS format. If the trust is a two-way trust, you will need to provide proper credentials for the target domain.

DC-31: Forest/Domain/OU Structure Management

Activity Frequency: Ad hoc

Active Directory Domain Services is a truly virtual environment. This means that there are a lot of restructuring options available in it. Your forest or domain structure does not necessarily need to be absolutely final when you put it in place. Of course, you try to plan in the most effective manner possible when you first prepare your ADDS, but you will most likely discover that as you become familiar with ADDS, you will want to improve upon your original design. Windows Server offers several tools for domain or forest restructuring:

- The Active Directory Users and Computers console fully supports drag-and-drop. Therefore it is relatively simple to restructure the contents of a single domain by dragging-and-dropping objects such as users, computers, and even organizational units from one place to another. You can even search for objects containing given characteristics and move them all at once. Be sure to use Procedure DC-16 to verify GPO links after any OU restructuring activity. Also, remember to unlock objects that have been protected from deletion before moving them.
- The `MOVETREE` command is the command-line equivalent of the Active Directory Users and Computers console. It provides more functionality because it will move objects between domains in the same forest, something the console cannot do.
- You can also use the `RENDOM` command to rename domains (found on the Microsoft Web site). This command is useful for supporting forest restructuring during corporate mergers or acquisitions or during reorganizations. You can even use this tool to rename an entire forest, one domain at a time.
- The Active Directory Migration Tool (ADMT) supports massive object moves either within forests or between forests, even NT domains (found on the Microsoft Web site). This powerful tool gives you greater flexibility during large reorganizations. See Chapter 12 for more information.

NOTE *The last two tools are fairly complex and require significant testing before you proceed. Be sure to become thoroughly familiar with these tools before using them in a production environment. For example, if you use the rename domain tool improperly, your domain could become corrupt, forcing you to recover it from backups.*

The MOVETREE command lets you move objects and track the movements by piping the information into archivable record files. In addition, it includes a /CHECK switch, which will only test the move. Included with the /VERBOSE switch, this will give you a lot of information about the potential move before you actually perform it. Also, by default, the /START switch will automatically verify a move and perform the move only if the verification operation completes without errors. For example, to test a move of the HR OU into the Admin OU from Server1 to Server2 in the TandT.net domain and pipe the results into a file, type:

```
movetree /check /s server1.tandt.net /d server2.tandt.net /sdn
OU=HR,DC=tandt,DC=net /ddn OU=HR,OU=Admin,DC=tandt,DC=net /verbose >filename.txt
```

Use MOVETREE /? for more information.

NOTE *Remember that organizational units are used for four reasons: to delegate object administration, to assign Group Policies to objects, to regroup or categorize objects, and to hide objects. The latter is performed through the assignation or denial of read permissions to the OU. Use Procedure DC-34 to assign appropriate permissions to OUs.*

DC-32: Forest Time Service Management

Activity Frequency: Ad hoc

Active Directory includes a time synchronization hierarchy. This hierarchy is based on the PDC Emulator within each domain of the forest. The forest root domain PDC Emulator is normally synchronized with an external time source, and each child domain PDC emulator synchronizes with the PDC Emulator from the forest root domain. Each computer or server in each domain synchronizes with its own PDC Emulator.

Time synchronization in Windows Server is managed in two ways: The first is through the W32TM command. This command lets you control time on individual computers. The second is through the domain hierarchy. If you wish to use alternate time sources, Windows Server includes several GPOs that let you control time globally within domains.

By default, Windows Server 2008 networks are configured to use TIME.WINDOWS.COM as the Simple Network Time Protocol (SNTP) time source. If your network cannot reach this time source, your server will generate W32Time errors, such as error number 12.

If you wish to set a different time source server for the forest root PDC Emulator, use the W32TM command-line tool. For example, the command to use to set an Eastern Time Zone clock with three source time servers would be:

```
w32tm /config /manualpeerlist:"ntp2.usno.navy.mil, tick.usno.navy.mil,
tock.usno.navy.mil" /update
```

This will set the forest root PDC Emulator to synchronize time with one of the three computer systems listed, and it will immediately update the time service. Remember that to do this you will have to open UDP port 123 in your firewall to allow SNTP traffic. Other time sources are available. Use your favorite Internet search tool to locate them.

To verify that the command was successful, type:

```
net time /querysntp
```

This should return the three new time sources as the result.

NOTE *A list of public time servers is available at http://support.ntp.org/bin/view/Servers/WebHome. You must type in the address with upper and lowercase characters for it to work.*

There is really no need to configure GPOs for time synchronization, because every computer joined to a domain automatically obtains its time settings from the PDC Emulator.

DC-33: Access Control List Management

Activity Frequency:	Ad hoc

One of the four reasons you use organizational units is to hide objects in the directory. Since users have the ability to query the directory, it is a good idea to hide sensitive objects, such as service or administrative accounts.

CAUTION *This should be taken as a security best practice. The first part of hacking is having the information on hand. If you hide the information by applying access control lists to OUs, you will have a more secure network.*

NOTE *Before performing this task, use Procedure DC-05 to create a security group called Denied Users, and assign all users from whom you want to hide information to this group. Make sure you do not include your administrative accounts in this group; otherwise, you will also be denied access to the hidden information. Do not assign the Domain Users group to this group because it will include your account. Also, you might add this group to Template User Accounts so that it is assigned by default to each new user account.*

To secure the contents of an OU:

1. Launch Server Manager and move to Active Directory Users and Computers (Roles | Active Directory Domain Services | Active Directory Users and Computers).
2. Expand the domain name and either move to or create the OU you want to modify. To create an OU, right-click the parent object (domain or parent OU), and select New | Organizational Unit.
3. Right-click the OU and select Properties from the context menu.
4. Move to the Security tab. Click Add. Type **Denied Users,** and click OK.
5. Assign the Deny Read permission to the Denied Users group. Click OK to close the dialog box.

From now on, all the objects you place in this OU will be hidden from all the users that are members of the Denied Users group.

CAUTION *Be very careful with this operation because in ADDS, denies always override allow permissions, so even though you (as an administrator) have full rights to this object, all you have to do is be a member of the Denied Users group to lose access to the objects in the OU.*

DC-34: Managing Saved Queries

Activity Frequency: Ad hoc

Active Directory Domain Services allows you to create and save queries you use on a regular basis. This means that if you're looking for a series of objects whose selection is complex, you can create the query once, save it, and then reuse it on a regular basis.

All saved queries are stored within the Saved Queries folder within the directory. This folder is located directly below Active Directory Users and Computers in its console.

To create a saved query:

1. Launch Server Manager and move to Active Directory Users and Computers (Roles | Active Directory Domain Services | Active Directory Users and Computers).
2. Right-click Saved Queries and select New | Query.
3. Type the name of the query (for example, Disabled Accounts) and a description for it. To define the query, click Define Query.
4. In the Define Query dialog box, select the criterion for your query. For example, if you are looking for all disabled accounts, select Disabled Accounts in the Common Queries category. Click OK.
5. Click OK again to save the query.

From now on, all you need to do to locate all the disabled accounts in your directory is double-click the Disabled Accounts query.

DC-35: Managing Space Within ADDS

Activity Frequency: Ad hoc

Windows Server 2008 supports the assignation of NT Directory Service (NTDS) quotas—quotas that are assigned to security principals within Active Directory. These quotas control the number of objects a security principal can create within any given ADDS partition.

CAUTION *Assigning NTDS quotas is good practice, because it ensures that no one user or computer account can create enough objects in ADDS to create a denial of service situation by creating so many objects that the DC will run out of storage space. This situation could also affect network bandwidth as the attacked DC tries to replicate all new data to its peers.*

Quotas affect every object in the directory. For example, if you set general quotas to 1,000, then that means that no single ADDS object can own more than 1,000 other objects. This includes both active objects and tombstone objects—objects that have been removed from the directory but not yet deleted (because the removal has not been replicated to all partners yet). You can also set a weight on tombstone data. This means that instead of allowing a tombstone object to have the same weight as an active object, you could tell the directory that they take up less space than active objects.

Finally, you can also create groups and assign them different quotas than the general quota. For example, if you want to give print servers the right to own more than 1,000 print queues, you would create a group, include all the print servers in it, and grant it a higher quota. By default, the directory does not contain any quotas.

Quotas can be assigned to every directory partition—configuration, domain, and application—but not the schema partition. The latter cannot hold quotas. For more information on application partitions, see Procedure DN-04.

NOTE *A quota value of -1 signifies an unlimited quota.*

To set general quotas:

```
dsadd quota partitionname -acct accountname -qlimit value
```

where *partitionname* is the distinguished name of the partition to which you want to add a quota, *accountname* is the distinguished name of the account (this can be a user, group, computer, or InetOrgPerson object), and *value* is the amount of the quota you are adding.

To obtain the names of the partitions in your directory, type:

```
dsquery partition
```

To view a quota limit or verify the results of your previous command, type:

```
dsget quota domainroot -qlimit ">=499"
```

This will list all of the accounts that have a limit greater than or equal to 499.

You should set quotas on all partitions (except the schema, of course). In most organizations, a quota limit of 500 will be appropriate. Remember that you can always create exception quotas.

Quotas should be set for two groups: Domain Users and Domain Computers. This way, you address most of the valid accounts in your domains.

CAUTION *Quotas are set at the domain level. Be sure to assign quotas in each domain in your forest.*

For example, to set a quota of 500 for the Domain Users group on the TandT.net domain partition, type:

```
dsadd quota dc=TandT,dc=net -acct "cn=Domain Users,cn=users,dc=TandT,
dc=net" -qlimit 500
```

NOTE *The Domain Users distinguished name is in quotes because there is a space in the group's name.*

DC-36: Managing the LDAP Query Policy

Activity Frequency:	Ad hoc

By default, Active Directory Domain Services do not contain an assigned LDAP query policy. This policy controls how LDAP queries will be treated by the directory. At least one policy should be assigned to each domain in your forest.

CAUTION *Assigning an LDAP query policy is good practice, because it protects the directory from denial of service attacks based on LDAP queries. While this is good practice for internal-facing directories, it is an absolute must for any Active Directory that is located in a perimeter or demilitarized network zone.*

Don't worry if you feel you don't know enough about LDAP to define a query policy; ADDS includes a default query policy that can be used to protect your directory. To assign the default query policy to your directory:

1. Launch Server Manager and move to Active Directory Sites and Services (Roles | Active Directory Domain Services | Active Directory Sites and Services).
2. Click the name of a domain controller (Computer Management | Active Directory Sites and Services | Sites | *sitename* | Servers | *DCname*) where *sitename* and *DCname* are the names of the site where the DC is located and the name of the DC you want to view.
3. Right-click NTDS Settings in the details pane, and select Properties.
4. On the General tab, select Default Query Policy from the Query Policy drop-down list.
5. Click OK.

This operation is only required on one DC in the domain.

To modify or create your own query policy, use the `NTDSUTIL` command in the `LDAP POLICIES` context. Use the WS08 Help system to find out more information about this command.

DC-37: Managing the ADDS Database

Activity Frequency:	Ad hoc

Active Directory Domain Services automatically compacts the NTDS.DIT database on a regular basis, but this compaction does not clear unused space from the database—it only reorganizes data to make it more accessible. Once in a while, you will want to compact the database to clear unused space and reduce its size. The command used to do so is the `NTDSUTIL` command.

CAUTION *Compacting the database must be done offline. This means you must stop the ADDS service before performing this operation. This service can only be stopped if the DC you are stopping is able to contact another DC in the network—one more good reason for having at least two DCs in any domain. You can also use the* `NET STOP NTDS` *command to do so.*

1. Once the ADDS service has been stopped, launch an elevated command console and type:

```
ntdsutil
files
compact to temporaryfoldername
quit
quit
```

where *temporaryfoldername* is the name of the destination folder where the compacted database will be stored temporarily. Make sure the operation completes properly.

NOTE *In very large directories, this operation may take quite some time.*

2. Next, delete all of the log files:

```
cd\windows\ntds
Del *.log
```

3. Now make a backup of NTDS.DIT:

```
copy NTDS.DIT backupfolder
```

   where *backupfolder* is the name of the destination folder where the backed up database will be stored. Make sure the backup is fully secured.

4. Copy the compacted database back to the original folder:

```
copy temporaryfoldername\ntds.dit
```

   where *temporaryfoldername* is the name of the destination folder where the compacted database was temporarily stored. Overwrite the original NTDS.DIT file.

5. Now check the integrity of the new compacted file:

```
ntdsutil
files
integrity
quit
quit
```

Once the integrity check is complete, restart the ADDS service. Repeat on every other DC in your forest.

You can script this entire operation using the command line if you want to automate it. You should, however, perform the operation interactively, because if something goes wrong and you are not aware of it, your DC will no longer be functional.

DC-38: Deleting RODCs

Activity Frequency:	Ad hoc

Read-only domain controllers are used to provide authentication services in remote offices where you cannot guarantee the security of the server. Once in a while (hopefully never), you may lose an RODC. In this event, you need to delete the RODC from your directory so that it will also automatically reset the passwords for each user account that was stored in the compromised RODC. This way, malicious attackers will not be able to use these passwords to log into your network.

To delete the RODC and reset passwords:

1. Use Server Manager to go to Active Directory Users and Computers (Roles | Active Directory Domain Services | Active Directory Users and Computers).
2. Move to the Domain Controllers OU.

CAUTION *All DCs should be left within the Domain Controllers OU because they are affected by special Group Policies that secure this vital server role.*

3. Locate the missing RODC, select it, and press DELETE.
4. In the Delete Domain Controller dialog box, select Reset All Passwords For User Accounts That Were Cached On This Read-only Domain Controller as well as Export The List Of Accounts That Were Cached On This Read-Only Domain Controller To This File, and enter the name of the file to export the list to. Click OK to perform the deletion.
5. Use the exported list to inform the affected users that their password has been reset and that they will need to contact the Help desk before they can log in.

Hopefully, you will never need to perform this operation. But in case you do, it will continue to secure access to your directory.

Namespace Server Management (DNS)

The Domain Naming Service (DNS) is at the very core of the operation of Active Directory Domain Services. It supports the logon process, and it provides the hierarchical structure of the ADDS database. As a best practice, you should always marry the domain controller function with the DNS service.

Like all services, the Windows Server DNS includes several tools for management and administration. The first is the DNS console, which is added automatically to the Computer Management console on servers where the service is installed. This DNS console can also be access through the Server Manager interface. In addition, Windows Server includes the `DNSCMD` command-line tool. Finally, the `NSLOOKUP` and `IPCONFIG` commands are useful for DNS updates and problem troubleshooting.

DN-01: DNS Event Log Verification

Activity Frequency:	Daily

DNS automatically records its event information in the DNS Server Log of the Event Viewer. It is recommended that you verify this log daily to ensure the proper operation of your DNS. To verify the DNS Event Log:

1. Launch Server Manager and go to Diagnostics | Event Viewer | Applications and Services | DNS Server.
2. Review the log content for the last day. Take appropriate action if you identify warnings or errors.

You can also enable a temporary trace log directly within DNS. To do so, right-click the DNS server name (Computer Management | Services and Applications | DNS | *servername*), move to the Debug Logging tab, and enable the Log Packets For Debugging option. You may type the log filename if you wish, but by default, the log file is named `DNS.LOG` and is located in the `%SYSTEMROOT%\SYSTEM32\DNS` folder. Don't forget to turn off extra logging when you're done because it puts an additional strain on the DNS server.

DN-02: DNS Configuration Management

Activity Frequency:	Monthly

Most organizations will use two DNS infrastructures: an internal infrastructure based on Windows Server and integrated to the production Active Directory Domain Services and an external infrastructure that may or may not be based on Windows technologies.

The latter depends on when you created your Internet zones and the technological choices you made at the time.

Once thing is certain (or should be): Your internal DNS structure will run on Windows Server because you are using ADDS. Because Windows Server supports automatic addition and removal of DNS records (in conjunction with the DHCP service), all your DNS servers should be set to enable automatic scavenging of stale records (Server Manager | Roles | DNS Server | DNS | *servername* | Properties | Advanced tab). This automatically keeps your DNS database clean.

You can perform this activity manually by right-clicking the server name in the DNS console and selecting Scavenge Stale Resource Records. It is also a good idea to select Update Server Data Files (from the same context menu) on a regular basis. You can also initiate scavenging from the command line:

```
dnscmd servername /startscavenging
```

where *servername* is the name of the server you want to initiate scavenging on.

DN-03: DNS Record Management

Activity Frequency:	Ad hoc

Even though DNS is dynamic in Windows Server, you will find that you need to add and remove records manually once in a while. To add a DNS record:

1. Launch Server Manager.
2. Move to DNS (Roles | DNS Server | DNS). Click the appropriate forward or reverse lookup zone to load it into the console.
3. Right-click the zone and select New *recordtype*, where *recordtype* is the type of record you want to create.
4. Fill in the appropriate information for the record, and click OK to create it.

You can also manage records from the command-line:

```
dnscmd servername /recordadd zone nodename recordtype recorddata
```

where *servername* is the server you want to perform the operation on, *zone* and *nodename* is where you want to locate the record in DNS, *recordtype* is the type of record you want to add, and *recorddata* is the information you want to add. You can also use the `DNSCMD` command to enumerate all records on a server:

```
dnscmd servername /enumrecords zone @ >filename.txt
```

Using the `@` symbol automatically enumerates all records in the zone root. You pipe this command into a file to capture all output.

DN-04: DNS Application Partition Management

Activity Frequency:	Ad hoc

Active Directory Domain Services stores DNS information in application partitions. These partitions allow you to create a specific replication scope within the directory. For example, by default, forest-wide DNS information is contained in a forest-wide partition and domain-centric DNS information is contained only within the actual domain. DNS application partitions are created automatically as you install DNS through DCPromo (Procedure DC-28), but you can also create them manually through the context menu of the DNS server in the DNS console.

You can also use the `DNSCMD` command to create additional partitions:

```
dnscmd /CreateBuiltinDirectoryPartitions option
```

where *option* refers to the partition scope and can be either `/DOMAIN`, `/FOREST`, or `/ALLDOMAINS`. To enumerate existing partitions:

```
dnscmd /EnumDirectoryPartitions
```

TIP *When creating a multidomain forest, you use "dummy" delegations to force the DCPromo Wizard to install DNS and create the domain application partition in the domain itself. DCPromo now takes care of this operation automatically as it promotes the first DC in a child domain.*

Application and Collaboration Server Administration

So far, you've covered a number of different administrative tasks treating both member servers and domain controllers. The final tasks discussed here are focused on sharing applications to support both generic and mission-critical functionalities within your network. Because of this, several server roles are covered in the same chapter. Each plays a part in the application sharing process.

Application servers include servers that either run Web-based applications using the .NET Framework or they run more conventional applications whose functionalities are sometimes provided remotely through Windows Terminal Services. Application servers also include Windows SharePoint Services.

In addition, as an administrator, you'll need to monitor the proper operation of all servers, especially to identify if the resources that have been provided for each service meet the demand. Table 13-9 outlines the administrative activities required to ensure proper operation of the application services you deliver to your user community. It also includes activities related to performance management. As always, the frequency of each task is also covered in this table, as well as its applicability to resource pools and virtual service offerings.

Remember to personalize the task list to adapt it to your environment.

NOTE *Most of the activities in this section require local administrative rights or proper delegation rights to the appropriate service.*

Administration of Dedicated Web Servers

Windows Server 2008 includes the dedicated Web server through its Web edition. This edition is a trimmed-down version of the Standard edition and has limited functionality at certain levels. For example, it cannot support the domain controller role.

Procedure No.	Activity	Frequency	Resource Pool	Virtual Service Offerings
Dedicated Web Servers				
WS-01	Application Event Log Verification	Daily	☑	☑
WS-02	IIS Server Status Verification	Weekly		☑
WS-03	IIS Server Usage Statistic Generation	Monthly		☑
WS-04	Web Server Log Verification	Monthly		☑
WS-05	IIS Security Patch Verification	Ad hoc		☑
WS-06	Web Server Configuration Management	Ad hoc		☑
Applications Servers				
AS-01	Shared Application State Verification	Weekly		☑
AS-02	COM+ Application Administration	Weekly		☑
AS-03	Database Server Administration	Weekly		☑
AS-04	Server Application Client Access	Ad hoc		☑
Terminal Servers				
TS-01	Terminal Services Connection Management	Weekly	☑	☑
TS-02	Terminal Services Printer Management	Ad hoc		☑
TS-03	Terminal Services Licensing Administration	Ad hoc		☑
TS-04	Terminal Services User Access Administration	Ad hoc		☑
TS-05	Terminal Service RemoteApp Management	Ad hoc	☑	☑
Windows SharePoint Services				
SP-01	Windows SharePoint Services Verification	Daily		☑
SP-02	WSS Backup Generation	Daily		☑
SP-03	Diagnostic Logging	Monthly		☑
SP-04	Usage Analysis	Monthly		☑
SP-05	Security Credentials Verification	Ad hoc		☑
Performance and Monitoring				
PM-01	Router and Firewall Log Verification	Daily	☑	☑
PM-02	General Disk Space Monitoring	Weekly	☑	☑
PM-03	System Resource Management	Weekly	☑	☑
PM-04	Network Traffic Monitoring	Weekly	☑	☑
PM-05	Server Capacity Management	Monthly	☑	☑
PM-06	System Diagnostics	Ad hoc	☑	☑

Table 13-9 Application Services Administration Task List

Though not all of your Web servers will be dedicated, the actions you perform to administer Web servers are the same, whether they are dedicated or not. You should, however, consider running dedicated Web servers because of security reasons: The smaller the service footprint on a server, the better you can protect it.

The activities covered here will focus mostly on the use of the Internet Information Services (IIS) Manager console and the APPCMD command-line tool.

WS-01: Application Event Log Verification

Activity Frequency: Daily

IIS sends its errors to the Windows Application Event Log. These errors include anything from the launch of Web sites to errors when client requests fail. To view this log, you use the same steps as Procedure GS-03:

1. Launch Server Manager.
2. Move to the Application Event Log (Diagnostic | Event Viewer | Windows Logs | Application).
3. This log stores all events related to applications. You might want to filter or sort events to view only IIS events. The best way to do so is to click the Source button in the header of the details pane. This automatically sorts all errors according to source. Locate IIS events by searching for application service provider (ASP) events.
4. Identify any errors or warnings. Take appropriate action if either appears.

By default, IIS only logs a subset of ASP errors into the event log. Other logs are generated by IIS itself and are stored in %SYSTEMDRIVE%\INETPUB\LOGS\LOGFILES.

WS-02: IIS Server Status Verification

Activity Frequency: Weekly

You should also regularly verify the status of your Web servers and the Web sites they host. This task is set to a weekly frequency, but depending on the criticality of your Web server (external presence, company access point, 24/7 operation), you may decide to do it on a daily basis.

There are two ways to do this. The first involves the Internet Information Services (IIS) Manager console. To verify the status of Web servers:

1. Launch the IIS Manager (Start menu | Administrative Tools | IIS Manager).
2. Verify that each Web site is running by right-clicking it and viewing the status of its service. You can also right-click the site and select Browse from the context menu. The IIS Manager will display the site in the details pane.
3. Close or minimize IIS Manager when done.

You can also verify the status of each server and Web site through the command line. This is the second way to verify server status. Use the following command:

```
appcmd list site
```

You must connect to the server first in order to run this command.

WS08: IIS Server Usage Statistic Generation

Activity Frequency:	Monthly

One of the activities that you should do on a regular (monthly) basis is the gathering of Web server usage statistics. These statistics will help you identify if your servers have the capacity to respond to all requests over time. They will also be useful for the evaluation of peak and off-peak Web site usage.

The best way to view Web server statistics is to use performance counters. You can create a performance monitoring console that automatically tracks Web site usage on all servers. This console will need access rights to performance counters on each server you monitor, so it is best to use the Run As Administrator command to launch Server Manager and then proceed as follows:

1. Use Procedure FS-01 to create a new data collector set.
2. Add counters for the Web Service as the performance object, and add the following counters using All Instances:
   - Anonymous Users/sec.
   - Current Anonymous Users
   - NonAnonymous Users/sec.
   - Current NonAnonymous Users
   - Connection Attemps/sec.
3. Repeat the procedure with Web Service Cache and File Cache Hits as the performance objects.

NOTE *You must monitor both the Web Service and the Web Service Cache if you want to see the total number of users visiting your sites.*

4. Repeat for each Web server.
5. Set the schedule to run monthly.

This will automatically log all Web usage activity.

WS-04: Web Server Log Verification

Activity Frequency:	Monthly

Besides logging events to the Event Log, IIS logs all events automatically in its own journal. It includes detailed information about each Web site.

Log files are stored under the `%SYSTEMDRIVE%\INETPUB\LOGS\LOGFILES` folder. To view the content of your log files, move to this folder and double-click any file.

CAUTION *It is a good idea to review IIS log files on a regular basis for potential attacks. Look for repeating patterns in the way users visit your site. If your site has authentication enabled, look for repeated attempts to log in from unknown sources.*

NOTE *You should use Procedure FS-02 to make regular backups of your IIS log files. You should also clear the log files after you back them up to clear up disk space on the IIS server.*

WS-05: IIS Security Patch Verification

Activity Frequency:	Ad hoc

IIS has long been a hacker's favorite. This is why you need to pay special attention to security patches for this service.

NOTE *This task is set as ad hoc because you never know when there will be a need to perform it. At minimum, you should perform it on a monthly basis.*

Use Procedure GS-14 to verify security updates from both the Microsoft Web site and other sites such as the SANS Institute. For Microsoft information, go to the Microsoft Security Bulletin site at www.microsoft.com/technet/security/current.aspx. Select IIS 7.0 under Product/Technology, and click Go.

Download, test, and install any applicable patches. If you haven't already done so, you should use Procedure GS-13 to sign up for security bulletin notification.

TIP *You can also subscribe to the Microsoft Hot Fix and Security Bulletin Really Simple Syndication (RSS) feed at www.microsoft.com/technet/security/bulletin/secrss.aspx.*

WS-06: Web Server Configuration Management

Activity Frequency:	Ad hoc

IIS includes the ability to share configurations between servers. This is performed through the Shared Configuration feature. Basically, you set each IIS server to share a central configuration. This way, you need only make a change in one location and have it apply to multiple servers. If you're running a Web farm using the Network Load Balancing service, you can easily generate a single configuration for the front-end Web servers and then share it with all of the others.

Make sure your Web server configuration is finalized, and then proceed as follows to share the configuration:

1. Configurations are stored within the `%SYSTEMROOT%\SYSTEM32\INETSRV\CONFIG` folder. Share this folder on the source server.
2. Map a network drive to the shared folder, with appropriate credentials on the servers with which you want to share the configuration. Use a service account (see Procedure GS-05) to map this drive so that it will always work.
3. Launch IIS Manager (Administrative Tools | IIS Manager). On the home page, double-click Shared Configuration under the Management section.
4. Select Enable Shared Configuration, type the path to the shared file using the mapped drive (you can also use a UNC path), type the service account username and password, and click Apply in the action pane. Your servers will all share the same configuration.

5. Return to the source server, go to Shared Configuration, and click Export Configuration in the action pane. Type the encryption password, and click OK. This will back up your source configuration to protect it.

To create a backup of the configuration using the command line:

```
appcmd add backup BackupName
```

where *BackupName* is the name of the backup. This will further protect the source configuration.

Administration of Application Servers

Conventional application servers run applications in shared mode. In comparison to Web servers, the application server is much more of a file server sharing an application folder. Applications are loaded into the server's memory, and users make use of the server's capacity to run the shared application.

Because of the nature of conventional application servers, many of the operations used to administer them resemble the operations used to manage file servers.

Application servers also run both COM+ and .NET Framework applications. In addition, they can host databases and relational database systems. Finally, you need to manage the resources on application servers to ensure they provide adequate performance.

AS-01: Shared Application State Verification

Activity Frequency: Weekly

You should regularly verify the state of the shared applications you run. There are several ways to do so, but the one you choose depends on the type of application you're running. Take, for example, a shared version of Microsoft Office. The shared version is configured by performing an administrative installation of Office on a server in a file share. Then you perform a minimal installation on users' computers. Users run the application by launching it on their desktops. The application mostly runs on the server using the server's processing capacity to perform the operations users need.

But because Office runs in this manner, it is difficult to verify if the application is running properly. You could always go to a computer that has the client components installed and simply launch the application. This will tell you if it is performing properly. But you can also use the connectivity tools in Windows Server to view connections to the application's shared folder. This will tell you the number of users currently running the application and the files they currently have opened, letting you devise which applications are currently open.

To verify connections and open files:

1. Launch Computer Management and move to the Sessions node (Computer Management | System Tools | Shared Folders | Sessions). View the number of open sessions in the details pane.
2. Next, move to Open Files (Computer Management | System Tools | Shared Folders | Open Files). View the files that are currently in use in the details pane.
3. If you need to close the share or an open file, you can right-click the share or file in the details pane and select Close Session or Close Open File from the context menu in each respective item.

NOTE *You should send a message to users if you are going to close either a session or a file. Use the* `NET SEND` *command to do so. Type* `NET SEND /?` *for more information.*

You can also view open sessions and open files through the command line:

```
net session servername
net file
```

where *servername* is the NetBIOS name of the server in *servername* format.

NOTE *Like Server Manager, the* `NET FILE` *command cannot be executed remotely. You must be on the server itself to use this command.*

AS-02: COM+ Application Administration

Activity Frequency:	Weekly

COM+ application administration is greatly facilitated in Windows Server 2008. This version of Windows offers several powerful management features for the operation of COM+ applications:

- **Applications as NT services** All COM+ applications can be configured as NT Services making applications load at boot time or on demand as required.
- **Low-memory activation gates** Windows Server can check memory allocations before it starts a process, allowing it to shut down an application if it will exhaust memory resources. This allows other applications running on the server to continue operation while only the faulty application fails.
- **Web services** Any COM+ object can be treated as a Web service, and any Web service can be treated as a COM+ object, greatly extending the remoting capabilities of your applications.
- **Application partitions** In terms of application support, these partitions allow you to host several instances of the same or different versions of COM+ objects on the same server. If, for example, you have 500 customers running a hosted application, you can create 500 partitions, one for each customer, segregating their operational environment from all of the others.
- **Application recycling** Some applications have a tendency to have degraded performance over time due to memory leaks and other programmatic issues. Windows Server can recycle a process by gracefully shutting it down and restarting it on a regular basis. This can be done either administratively or through the COM+ software development kit. Administratively, it is applied through the Component Services console by right-clicking a COM+ component, selecting Properties, and modifying the elements on the Pooling & Recycling tab. By default all COM+ applications use recycling.

Verifying the state of COM+ applications focuses on using the Component Services snap-in to verify if COM+ components are running or not. You can also use the new COM+ features of Windows Server to add resilience to your COM+ applications.

CAUTION *Be wary of modifying security settings on COM+ components. One wrong move, and the application will not work anymore and you'll have a very hard time trying to find the problem.*

To run an application as a service:

1. Launch the Computer Management console.
2. Move to Computers in Component Services (Computer Management | Component Services | Computers).
3. Connect to the appropriate server, if required (Action | New | Computer), and either type the server name (*servername*) or use the Browse button to locate it. Click OK when done.
4. Locate the COM+ component you want to run as a service, and right-click it to select Properties from the context menu.
5. Move to the Activation tab, and click Run As NT Service. Windows Server will warn you that it may reset some settings. Click OK, click Next, and click Set Up New Service.
6. In the Service Setup dialog box, choose the startup type, set the error handling level, and identify dependencies. Click Create to set up the service.
7. Click OK to close the Properties dialog box.

To enable and manage application partitions in Active Directory, first enable partitions on the server:

1. Launch the Computer Management console.
2. Move to Computers in Component Services (Computer Management | Component Services | Computers).
3. Connect to the appropriate server, if required (Action | New | Computer), and either type the server name (*servername*) or use the Browse button to locate it. Click OK when done.
4. Locate the server for which you want to enable partitions, and right-click it to select Properties from the context menu.
5. Move to the Options tab, and select Enable Partitions. You can also select Check Local Store When Choosing Partition For User, but do so only if you want the server to locally store partitions as well as within ADDS. Click OK.
6. Next, move to the Active Directory Users and Computers. Enable Advanced Features (View | Advanced Features).
7. Create partitions in the ComPartitions container (Active Directory Users and Computers | System | ComPartitions), and create partition sets or groups of partitions under ComPartitionSets. Partition sets are used to assign partition access to users and groups.
8. Once partitions are created in ADDS, return to Component Services in Computer Management, locate the computer you want to include in the partition, and right-click COM+ Partitions to select New | Partition. This launches the New Partition Wizard.

9. Click Next. Determine the partition type. It can be a previously exported partition, or it can be an empty partition. If your development team has prepared the partition previously, select the first option; otherwise, select Create An Empty Partition. Click Browse Directory to find the partition you created in ADDS, select the partition, and click Add. Click Next and then click Finish.
10. Finally, you can protect the partition against deletion by right-clicking it and selecting Properties. Click Disable Deletion in the Advanced tab. Click OK when done.

Application partition users should be assigned in ADDS so that they are available domain-wide.

AS-03: Database Server Administration

Activity Frequency:	Weekly

Windows Server 2008 is the ideal database server because it has the ability to manage processes intelligently. SQL Server 2005 and 2008 have been optimized to run on this platform, but Windows Server will also support other databases that run on Windows. WS08 includes the Windows Internal Database, which is a runtime version of SQL Server 2005 Express. Few management activities apply to this internal database, since it is mostly a runtime database. It is still important to mention here that one of your system administration tasks for application servers involves database administration. At the very least, it means you need to verify the status of the server, its memory availability, and the proper operation of its disks.

Use Procedure GS-02 to verify the status of your database services. Use Procedure FS-01 or PM-02 to verify the status of the disks running the database system. And use Procedure PM-05 to verify the status of random access memory (RAM) on your database servers.

AS-04: Server Application Client Access

Activity Frequency:	Ad hoc

Granting access to conventional applications is performed in much the same way as granting access to file shares. In fact, since the application resides on a file share and that file share access is managed through groups (usually global groups), granting or denying access to an application can be as simple as inserting or removing a user account from the appropriate group. Use Procedure FS-03 to grant group access to new shared applications, and use Procedure DC-05 to add or remove users from the appropriate security group.

But some shared applications require the delivery of a portion of code on the desktop to be able to run. This is the case for Microsoft Office, for example. Use Procedure DC-15 to deliver it to the right desktops.

Administration of Terminal Services

One of the greatest features of Windows Server 2008 is Terminal Services (TS). This service enables you to publish applications to remote computers, giving them full access to programs running in a Windows Server environment. The greatest advantage is in deployment. Since the application operates on the TS server, it is the only place it needs to be installed, updated, and maintained. Unlike conventional shared applications, no client component is required other than the Remote Desktop Connection (RDC) agent. Besides the RDC client, you only need to deploy a shortcut to users, and this shortcut doesn't change, even though you may upgrade or otherwise modify the application.

NOTE *If clients are running Windows Vista, they already have the RDC client.*

Terminal Services supports sound redirection to client PCs; thus, if you operate a multimedia application on the server, users will hear the information just as if the application were running on their own workstation. In addition, the Windows Server version of Terminal Services supports higher-quality graphics, including true color and the highest level of resolution supported by client hardware, as well as monitor spanning, when user systems have multiple monitors. Resolution and color must be set on both the client and the server to operate. Finally, TS is now integrated with Group Policy, allowing you to control Terminal Services features centrally.

Thin-client models are becoming more and more popular, especially with the proliferation of wireless Pocket PCs and the Tablet PC. Both make server application hosting more and more attractive.

CAUTION *Not all applications are "Terminal Services–aware." Be sure to verify the support an application has for Terminal Services before acquiring it.*

The tools you use to work with Terminal Services include:

- Server Manager, to add the role and configure Terminal Services.
- The Group Policy Management console, to centrally control TS GPOs.
- Terminal Services Manager, to configure TS connections.
- Command-line tools, for session and user management.

TS-01: Terminal Services Connection Management

Activity Frequency: Weekly

You should verify TS connections at least on a weekly basis. The best tool to do so is the Terminal Services Manager. Unfortunately, this console cannot be added to the Global MMC.

NOTE *To obtain full functionality from the Terminal Services Manager console, you must first connect to a TS server remotely and then launch the console on the server. This places you within the TS environment and gives you access to such features as remote control and connection creations.*

To verify TS connections:

1. Open an RDC connection to the appropriate server.
2. On the TS server, launch the Terminal Services Manager (Start menu | Administrative Tools | Terminal Services Manager).

NOTE *It is a good idea to place this tool in the Quick Launch area for every TS server.*

3. Click the server name in the left pane to view current connections. Click the domain name in the left pane to view connections on other servers in your domain.
4. Review the status of each connection.

You can use the TS Manager to perform administrative activities. For example, if you want to view a session in progress or assist a user, you right-click the user's connection and select Remote Control. This will launch a window, letting you view the user's actions on the server.

You can also review connections through the command line. To identify all TS servers in your domain:

```
query termserver
```

This command lists all Terminal Services servers in your domain. If more than a single page is displayed, it pauses at each new page.

To view the connections on a TS server:

```
query session /server:servername /counter
```

where *servername* is the DNS name of the server. Using the /COUNTER switch also displays the information about the current TS counters, including the number of sessions created and terminated. You can also pipe the results of this query into a text file and schedule the task using Procedure GS-21 on a weekly basis. This allows you to verify connection status simply by reviewing the results in the text file.

TS-02: Terminal Services Printer Management

Activity Frequency:	Ad hoc

Through the configuration of Group Policies for Terminal Services, printers may be automatically created when users connect to a Terminal Services session. When users disconnect from a session, even if sometimes they do not always use the proper method, these printers are automatically deleted from the Terminal Services server. But special conditions must be met for these printers to be created.

Mostly, your GPO must define client printing settings. Terminal Services printing settings are found in Computer Configuration | Policies | Administrative Templates | Windows Components | Terminal Services | Client/Server Data Redirection. By default, Terminal Services allows printer redirection and LPT port redirection, and automatically sets the client's default printer as the default printer for the TS session. If you want to specify these settings explicitly, use Procedure DC-16 to apply these settings to a GPO that affects all TS users.

TS-03: Terminal Services Licensing Administration

Activity Frequency:	Ad hoc

Unlicensed TS servers will only allow clients to operate for 120 days, after which all sessions will end and the Terminal Services server will no longer respond to client requests. In order to license servers, you must install a Terminal Services License Server. This server must be activated by Microsoft before it can begin to issue licenses to your enterprise. Activation is automatic if your server is connected to the Internet.

Once the server is activated, you can add new Client License Key (CLK) packs as your TS client population grows. These packs must be purchased from Microsoft before they can be added to your network.

To add a new CLK pack:

1. Launch the Terminal Services Licensing console (Start menu | Administrative Tools | Terminal Services Licensing).
2. Right-click the server name and select Install Licenses from the context menu. This starts the Terminal Services CAL Installation Wizard.
3. Enter the appropriate licensing information in Program and Client License Information, and then click Next.
4. The wizard then connects to the Microsoft Clearing House and installs the license key packs. Click Finish when done.

TS-04: Terminal Services User Access Administration

Activity Frequency:	Ad hoc

By default, Terminal Services servers issue licenses to any computer that requests one. You must enable the License Server Security Group GPO setting (Computer Configuration | Policies | Administrative Templates | Windows Components | Terminal Services | Licensing) to restrict TS sessions to authorized groups of computers or users only. Use Procedure DC-16 to do so, and make sure this policy is applied to all TS servers.

Once this is done, you will need to create global groups for users (or computers) that are allowed to use Terminal Services and place these groups within the local Terminal Services Computers group that is created by the policy. Then you can use Procedure DC-05 to add or remove users from the global group and thus enable or disable their access to your TS servers.

TS-05: Terminal Service RemoteApp Management

Activity Frequency:	Ad hoc

Terminal Services applications should be installed in multiuser mode. This is a requirement for all applications that are shared through Terminal Services.

To install a new application on a Terminal Services server, type the following command in an elevated command prompt:

```
change user /install
```

This sets the Terminal Services server in installation mode. Perform the application installation. Then type the following command:

```
change user /execute
```

This resets the Terminal Services server in execution mode.

NOTE *The Terminal Services application operation model is slightly different from the standard Windows model because of the multiuser environment. You should always check for* compatibility scripts *for the applications you install. These scripts modify standard installations to make them TS-compatible. They should be run after the application installation. Scripts are found in the* `%SYSTEMROOT%\APPLICATION COMPATIBILITY SCRIPTS\INSTALL` *folder.*

1. Once the application is installed, move to Server Manager and navigate to Roles | Terminal Services | TS RemoteApp Manager.
2. Click Add RemoteApps in the action pane. This launches the RemoteApp Wizard. Click Next.
3. Select the program to add to the RemoteApps list. This list displays all known installed applications. You can view its properties before moving on to the next page. The Properties page lets you control command-line arguments as well as icons and whether or not the application will be available in TS Web Access. Click OK when done.
4. You can also add all of the applications at once in this page if you want to. Click Next.
5. Review your options and click Finish when ready. Use the Previous button to correct any settings that don't look right.

Refer to Chapter 9 for instructions on how to deploy the RemoteApp you just made available.

Windows SharePoint Services Administration

Windows SharePoint Services (WSS) provides a powerful model for team collaboration through the integration of several Web technologies, including blogs, team sites, My Sites, and much more. WSS is built upon IIS 7, but includes its own tools for system administration:

- The SharePoint 3.0 Central Administration Web site
- The `STSADM` command

Both provide support for the administrative tasks you need to perform. SharePoint, in fact, is well organized for administration, since the Central Administration Web site includes a special Operations page listing activities operators must perform (see Figure 13-12). Many are one-time operations for configuration of the server, while others are ongoing operations. Ongoing operations are covered here. One-time configuration operations were covered in Chapter 9.

TIP *More information on WSS can be found at the WSS TechCenter at http://technet2.microsoft.com/windowsserver/WSS/en/library/dec1c405-b54b-4c1b-976f-3fa6d814cda51033.mspx?mfr=true.*

SP-01: Windows SharePoint Services Verification

Activity Frequency:	Daily

Since WSS is built upon IIS version 7, it relies on the same interface for logging events. You can, therefore, rely on Procedure AS-01 to verify the WSS Event Log. Of course, you can also use Server Manager | Roles | Windows SharePoint Services to get a quick overview of the status of your WSS services. If any untoward events have occurred, they will be displayed in the Summary view this node includes.

But for complete event overview, you should actually go to the Event Log (Server Manager | Diagnostics | Event Viewer). Verify these logs on a daily basis.

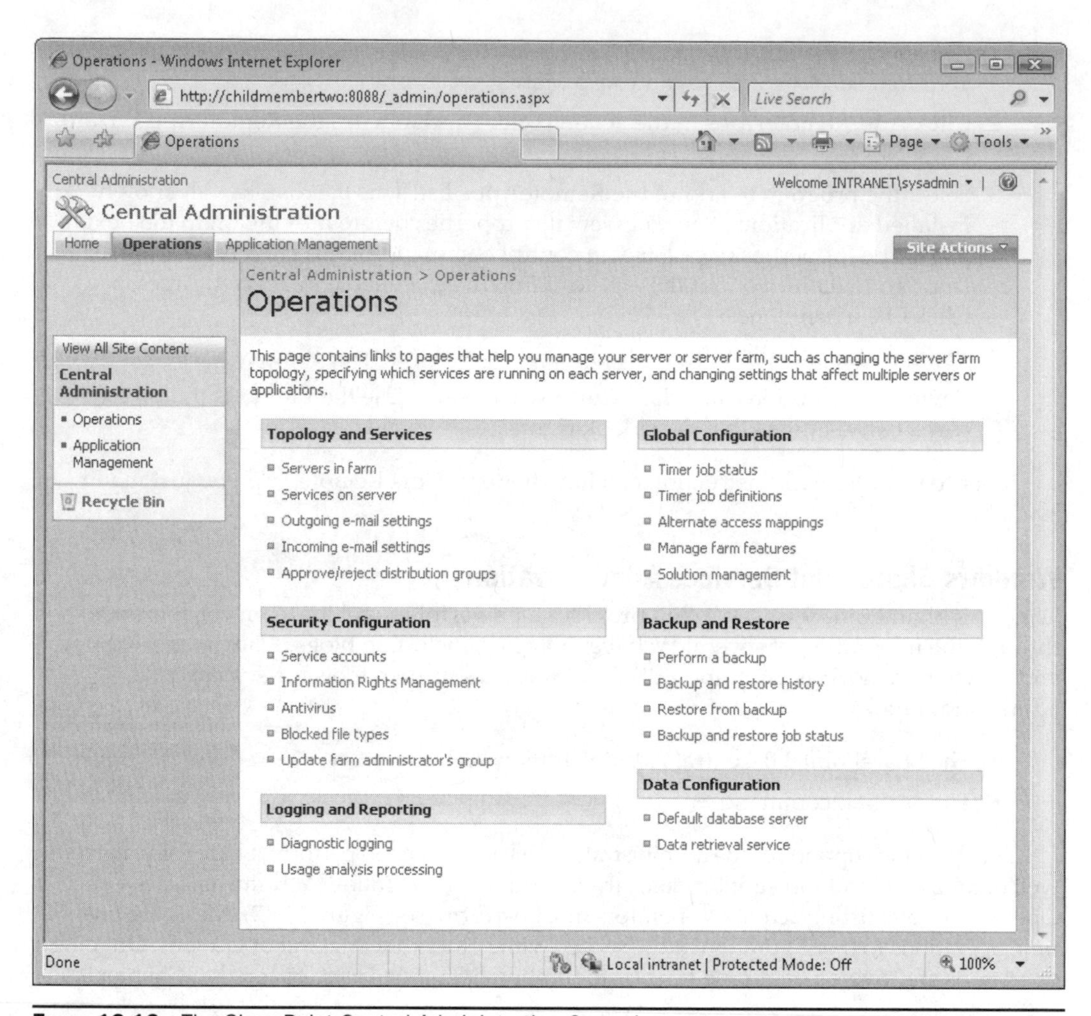

FIGURE 13-12 The SharePoint Central Administration Operations page

SP-02: Windows SharePoint Services Backup Generation

Activity Frequency:	Daily

SharePoint Services do not rely on Windows Server Backup to perform backups, though, of course, when you create a complete backup of the server, you will also generate a complete backup of WSS data. But restoring WSS from this complete backup is difficult. This is why you should use the WSS Backup tool to perform these backups.

Backups and restores are managed from the Central Administration Web site:

1. Launch SharePoint Central Administration (Start menu | Administrative Tools).
2. Click the Operations tab. This moves you to the Operations page.
3. Click Perform A Backup under the Backup and Restore section. This displays the Backup page.

4. Select the component to back up. If this is your first backup, select all the components. Clicking the Farm component will automatically select all of the components.
5. Click Continue To Backup Operations.
6. Enter the path to the backup folder. Ideally, this will be a network location in UNC format.
7. Click OK to begin the backup.

The backup begins and displays progress information. This information is updated every 30 seconds. A log of the backup is also written to the destination folder. The log file name is SPBACKUP.LOG.

To perform the same operation through the command line, use:

```
stsadm -o backup -directory \\servername\sharename -backupmethod full
```

Where *servername* and *sharename* are the UNC path for the backup folder. This backs up the entire farm. Use Procedure GS-21 to create a scheduled task that performs this backup on a daily basis.

NOTE *The STSADM command is found in the SharePoint bin folder, which is located under %PROGRAMFILES%\COMMON FILES\MICROSOFT SHARED\WEB SERVER EXTENSIONS\12\BIN on an x86 server and in %DRIVE%\PROGRAM FILES (X86)\COMMON FILES\MICROSOFT SHARED\WEB SERVER EXTENSIONS\12\BIN on an x64 server. Since this path is not included in your server variable for automated paths, this is an excellent opportunity to use the Elevated Command Prompt Here feature discussed in Procedure GS-01.*

Use a similar procedure to restore the data in the event of a loss. Test your backups regularly to ensure they work properly.

SP-03: Diagnostic Logging

Activity Frequency: Monthly

When verifying whether your WSS infrastructure is working properly, you need to view its diagnostics reports. Trace logs are automatically generated by WSS. The settings for these logs are set on the Diagnostics Logging page (Central Administration | Operations | Logging and Reporting | Diagnostics Logging | Trace Log section). By default, these logs are stored under %PROGRAMFILES%\COMMON FILES\MICROSOFT SHARED\WEB SERVER EXTENSIONS\12\LOGS for x86 servers and under %DRIVE%\PROGRAM FILES (X86)\COMMON FILES\MICROSOFT SHARED\WEB SERVER EXTENSIONS\12\LOGS for x64 servers.

Review the content of these logs once a month. Look for unusual events, and take appropriate action if you discover them.

SP-04: Usage Analysis

Activity Frequency: Monthly

WSS is a powerful collaboration tool, and unlike file services, you can find out just how popular it is in your organization by performing usage analysis and generating usage reports. First, you must turn on usage analysis processing.

1. Go to the Operations page in Central Administration, and click Usage Analysis Processing under the Logging and Reporting section. First, enable logging. Then identify the location to store logging files, and finally, identify the number of log files to create. Creating multiple files will keep each file smaller.
2. Next, turn on the processing settings. Select Enable Usage Analysis Processing, and then identify the times of day to process usage. Ideally, you will use peak times, but you must temper this with service responsiveness, because processing takes up resources from the WSS server. This is the reason why this is done on a monthly basis.
3. Review the log files once they have been generated.

SP-05: Security Credentials Verification

Activity Frequency:	Ad hoc

Every now and then, you must change your service account passwords. In SharePoint, these passwords are stored within the SharePoint configuration. Because of this, changing the password for the service accounts that run SharePoint cannot only be done within ADDS. It must also be done in SharePoint.

NOTE *This task is set as ad hoc because it really depends on the schedule you set for service account password changes. However, it should be done regularly—for example, every two months—and, of course, it must be done at any time you believe that the passwords could be compromised.*

Affected passwords potentially include the following services:

- SQL Server (MSSQLSERVER) service
- SQL Server Agent (MSSQLSERVER) service
- SQL Server Full Text Search (MSSQLSERVER) service [optional]
- SharePoint Central Administration Web Site application pool
- Windows SharePoint Services Timer service
- Windows SharePoint Services Search service
- The default access account
- Application pool identity for all Web applications used by Windows SharePoint Services 3.0

Use the following strategy to change the passwords:

1. First, change all passwords in ADDS. Use Procedure GS-05 to do so.
2. Next, go to the Services node in Server Manager (Configuration | Services), locate the following services, right-click them, select Properties, go to the Log On tab, and type and confirm the new password. Stop and restart the service to ensure that the new password is correct.
   - SQL Server (MSSQLSERVER) service
   - SQL Server Agent (MSSQLSERVER) service
   - SQL Server Full Text Search (MSSQLSERVER) service [optional]

3. Next, change the passwords for the Central Administration Web Site application pool and SharePoint Services Timer service by using the STSADM tool. Navigate to the appropriate location (see Procedure SP-02), and open an elevated command prompt:

   ```
   stsadm -o updatefarmcredentials -userlogin domain\username password
   newpassword
   iisreset /noforce
   ```

   Where *domain\username* is the username in down-level format and *newpassword* is the changed password. When done, reset the IIS service.

4. Now change the password for the SharePoint Services Search service, as well as the default access account. In Central Administration, go to the Operations page. Click Services On Server under the Topology and Services section. Click Windows SharePoint Search Services. Type the applicable new passwords in each Password box on this page, and click OK. Using Central Administration ensures that the operation you performed in step 3 worked, but you can also change these passwords through the command line:

   ```
   stsadm -o spsearch -farmserviceaccount domain\username
   -farmservicepassword newpassword
   stsadm -o spsearch -farmcontentaccessaccount domain\username
   -farmcontentaccesspassword newpassword
   ```

5. Now set the password for the Web application pools. Return to the Operations page, and click Service Accounts under the Security Configuration section. Click Web Application Pool, select the Windows SharePoint Services Web Application from the Web Service drop-down list, and select SharePoint – 80 from the Application Pool drop-down list. Type the new password and click OK. Verify that WSS is working properly when done.

TIP *More information on this procedure is outlined at http://technet2.microsoft.com/windowsserver/WSS/en/library/dec1c405-b54b-4c1b-976f-3fa6d814cda51033.mspx?mfr=true.*

Performance and Monitoring Administration

The last activity category that administrators must plan for in their busy schedule is performance and monitoring, which means evaluating if the technologies you have in place perform well, if their capacity is adequate to the task, and if they require fine-tuning or additional components. It also includes the verification and monitoring of critical systems to ensure that they are operating properly. Several tools can be used for this activity. Three are especially useful:

- The Performance console, which includes the Reliability Monitor
- The Network Monitor
- The Windows System Resource Manager

These tools provide powerful performance management.

PM-01: Router and Firewall Log Verification

Activity Frequency: Daily

Monitoring activities include the verification of log files from all sources. Routers and firewalls are not necessarily based on Windows Server 2008, though this operating system can perform both tasks. In fact, the routing capabilities of Windows Server rival those that complex routers such as Cisco or Nortel can provide. Windows Server routers even support Open Shortest Path First (OSPF) routing.

NOTE *Many networks do not rely on Windows Server for either routing or firewall protection. Rather, they rely on specialized hardware to perform these tasks. If this is the case in your network, you should still verify both logs on a weekly basis.*

Both the firewall and the routing features of Windows Server support activity logging. The routing feature mostly uses the System Event Log for activity logging. You can use Procedure GS-03 to check the appropriate logs on a weekly basis.

If you do not rely on WS08 for routing or firewall protection, then verify the logs for the systems you do rely on. When you verify either the routing or the firewall logs, look for unusual patterns in the log entries. This will help you identify suspect behavior.

PM-02: General Disk Space Monitoring

Activity Frequency: Weekly

In Procedure FS-01, you verify free disk space for data disks on file servers. It is also good practice to perform the same verification on all of the disks of your servers. You can use the same procedure to perform this verification. System disks especially tend to stock temporary files and, therefore, have the possibility of running out of space.

In addition, resource pools have a tendency to use up a lot of space because virtual service offerings often use dynamic disks—disks that will automatically expand in size as information is stored within them. As a good practice, you should ensure that all data disks for resource pools include more space than the maximum size of all VSO disks that are stored on them. But nevertheless, you should perform disk space verifications on an ongoing basis. You should check this console on a weekly basis.

NOTE *If more automated solutions are needed, Microsoft System Center Operations Manager (SCOM) can be used to provide proactive alerting on disk space issues. More information is available on the Microsoft Web site.*

PM-03: System Resource Management

Activity Frequency: Weekly

The Enterprise and Datacenter editions of Windows Server 2008 include an additional tool for system resource management. It is the Windows System Resource Manager (WSRM). This tool is a feature and can be added through Add Features in Server Manager.

WSRM can be used in two manners. First, it can be used to profile applications. This means that it helps you identify how many resources an application requires on a regular basis. When operating in this mode, WSRM only logs events in the application event log when the application exceeds its allowed limits. This helps you fine-tune application requirements.

The second mode offered by the WSRM is the manage mode. In this mode, WSRM uses its allocation policies to control how many resources applications can use on a server. If applications exceed their resource allocations, WSRM can even stop the application from executing.

WSRM also supports Alerts and Event Monitoring. This is a powerful tool that is designed to help you control CPU, disk, and memory usage on large multiprocessing servers.

By default, the WSRM includes two management policies: the default policy, which simply reports on application use, and the Equal per User policy which allocates resources equally based on the number of users connected to an application.

Operating the WSRM is similar to operating the Performance console—you determine what to manage by adding and removing counters for specific objects. Finally, the WSRM supports application auditing, letting you know how and when applications are used on your servers.

Use the WSRM to first evaluate how your applications are being used; then apply management policies. Make sure you thoroughly test your policies before applying then in your production environment. You can use Procedure DC-05 to create special security groups that can be used as pilots for your new management policies. This way, you will be able to get a feel for the WSRM before you fully implement it in your network. When you're ready, you can use the Calendar to determine when which policy should be applied.

NOTE *If you are managing several servers with WSRM, you may need to dedicate resources to it, since it is resource-intensive. You might consider placing it on a dedicated management server if this is the case.*

PM-04: Network Traffic Monitoring

Activity Frequency: Weekly

Windows Server 2008 can also run the Network Monitor, a tool that allows you to capture network packets and view the content of the traffic on your networks. This tool is not available by default.

TIP *Network Monitor must be downloaded from www.microsoft.com/downloads/details.aspx?FamilyID=18b1d59d-f4d8-4213-8d17-2f6dde7d7aac&DisplayLang=en.*

This tool is best installed on a workstation, since it can monitor traffic remotely. Once the Network Monitor is installed, it can be accessed through Start menu | All Programs | Microsoft Network Monitor 3.1 then click Microsoft Network Monitor 3.1. Since you intend to use this tool on a weekly basis, you should place it in your Quick Launch area.

CAUTION *Network Monitor can be installed on either servers or workstations. It is preferable to install this tool on a workstation to secure and limit its use.*

To view traffic on your network:

1. Launch the Network Monitor and provide appropriate credentials for its use.
2. Choose the network interface to monitor. By default, Network Monitor selects the local network interface.

3. Click the Start button on the toolbar to begin capturing packets.
4. Click Stop And View Traffic when you have captured enough data.
5. In the View Traffic pane, examine the data provided by the traffic on your network. Close the View Traffic pane to return to the Network Monitor. Save the capture so that you can perform future comparisons. Close the Network Monitor when done.

Look for unusual patterns to identify unauthorized behavior on your network. This task should be done weekly, but you may decide to perform it at different times to get a more complete picture of the traffic patterns on your network.

PM-05: Server Capacity Management

Activity Frequency: Monthly

Server capacity management should be reviewed on a monthly basis. The best tool for viewing server capacity is the Performance console. It allows you to capture data on how your servers perform on a regular basis.

NOTE *You should also use this procedure every time you stage a new server to create an original baseline for it. This way, you can compare results to the original baseline and determine how the workload is changing, as well as what you need to modify on the server to maintain performance levels.*

You can use Procedure FS-01 to create a special server-capacity monitoring console that will track the following elements for each server in your network:

- Free disk space (% free physical disk space and % free logical disk space)
- Disk usage time (% physical disk time and % logical disk time)
- Disk reads and writes (physical disk reads per second and physical disk writes per second)
- Disk queuing (average disk queue length)—*active by default*
- Memory usage (available memory bytes)
- Memory paging (memory pages per second)—*active by default*
- Paging file activity (% paging file usage)
- Processor usage (% processor time)—*active by default*
- Interrupts (processor interrupts per second)
- Multiple processor usage (system processor queue length)
- Server service (total server bytes per second)
- Server work items (server work item shortages)
- Server work queues (server work queue length)
- Server paged pool (server pool paged peak)

Use the Explain button to learn what each setting refers to. Monitor these settings over time to identify how your servers perform. Once you are confident that you know how your servers should perform, set or adjust your service level agreements based on this performance. Then, if you see long-term performance deviations (compared to the original baseline), you can increase server capacity through its growth mechanisms.

PM-06: System Diagnostics

Activity Frequency: Ad hoc

Once in a while, you will need to perform system diagnostics on a server to help identify recurring problems. So far, you've used several procedures to help examine items like the Event Logs and review how servers perform on an ongoing basis. But when you do identify problems, you sometimes need to get more information about the troublesome system. One good tool for this job is the System Information console (Start menu | All Programs | Accessories | System Tools | System Information).

This console provides information about the hardware resources, components, software environment, and Internet settings on any server in your network. To view information from another server, click View | Remote Computer and type the name of the server you want to view.

You can also view system history through the Windows Reliability Monitor (Server Manager | Diagnostics | Reliability and Performance | Monitoring Tools | Reliability Monitor), letting you identify changes to your systems over time (see Figure 13-13).

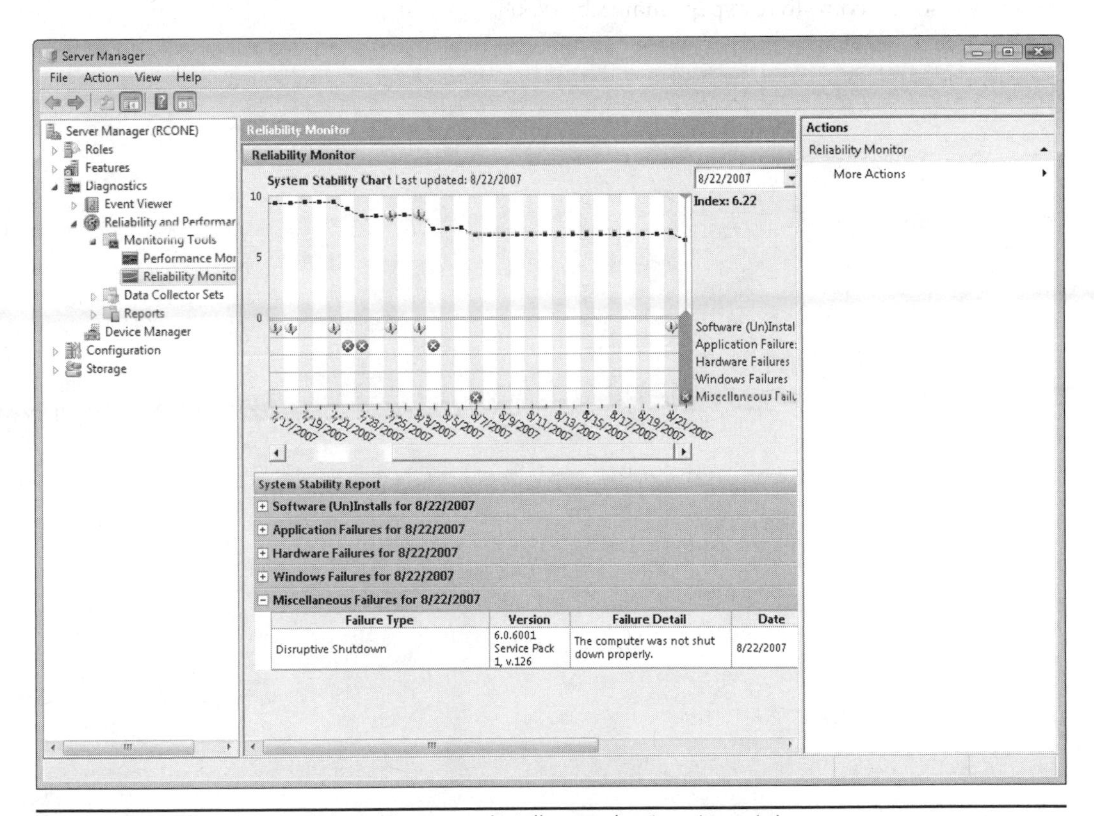

FIGURE 13-13 The System Information console tells you about system status.

The Reliability Monitor tracks every change to your system and lets you find out what might have happened to make your system unresponsive. Verify it whenever an issue affecting performance arises on a server.

Final Notes

This chapter provides over 150 different tasks that administrators should perform on a regular basis to properly manage their Windows Server networks. Its goal is to help simplify the workload administrators everywhere must undertake to ensure their network properly delivers services to their user communities and to ensure that their resource pools support these virtual service offerings properly.

Rely on the schedule outlined here. Several hundreds of administrators have followed the course this list is based on and have learned that while overtime may not be a thing of the past, at least it is no longer a constant.

If you find that some tasks have not been covered, or if you find new and innovative ways to perform the tasks listed here, feel free to share them with us. We, in turn, will place them on the companion Web site to help further enhance the administration experience for Windows Server networks.

You can contact us at Infos@Reso-Net.com. Don't forget to visit the companion Web site at www.reso-net.com/livre.asp?p=main&b=WS08.

Index

B

C

D

G

M

N

P

W

X

Z

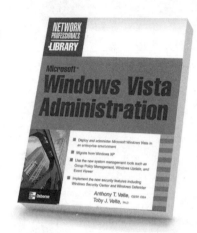

Stop Hackers in Their Tracks

Hacking Exposed Wireless
Johnny Cache & Vincent Liu

Hacking Exposed: Web Applications, Second Edition
Joel Scambray, Mike Shema & Caleb Sima

Hacking Exposed Windows, Third Edition
Joel Scambray & Stuart McClure

Hacking Exposed Web 2.0
Rich Cannings, Himanshu Dwived & Zane Lackey

Gray Hat Hacking, Second Edition
Shon Harris, Allen Harper, Chris Eagle & Jonathan Ness

Hacking Exposed VoIP
David Endler & Mark Collier

Hacking Exposed Linux, Third Edition
ISECOM

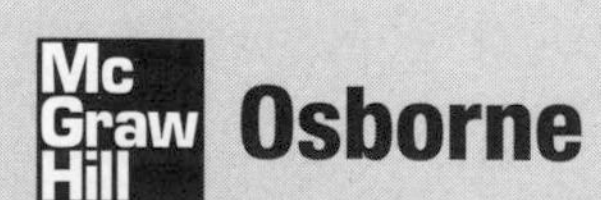

MHPROFESSIONAL.COM